READINGS I

Groupware and Computer-Supported Cooperative Work

READINGS IN

Groupware and Computer-Supported Cooperative Work

ASSISTING

HUMAN-HUMAN

COLLABORATION

WRITTEN AND EDITED

BY RONALD M. BAECKER

Sponsoring Editor: *Michael B. Morgan*
Production Manager: *Yonie Overton*
Production Editor: *Carol Leyba*
Editorial Coordinator: *Douglas Sery*
Editorial Assistance: *Martha Ghent and Fran Taylor*
Cover Designer: *Ross Carron, Carron Design*
Pasteup/Additional Composition: *Metro Typography & Design*
Printer: *Edwards Brothers, Inc.*

Morgan Kaufmann Publishers, Inc.
Editorial Office:
2929 Campus Drive, Suite 260
San Mateo, CA 94403

96 95 94 93   4 3 2 1

Library of Congress Cataloging-in-Publication Data
is available for this book

ISBN 1-55860-241-0

Brief Contents

Detailed Contents

Part III. Asynchronous Groupware   397

Part IV. Synchronous Groupware   581

Part V. Summary and Conclusions   849

This book is an organized collection of readings from the research literature of groupware and computer-supported cooperative work, introduced and set in context by brief introductory essays.

We define *computer-supported* cooperative work (CSCW) as computer-assisted coordinated activity such as communication and problem solving carried out by a group of collaborating individuals. Groupware is the multi-user software supporting CSCW systems or, in the words of Malone (cited in Coleman and Shapiro, 1992), "information technology used to help people work together more effectively." CSCW may also be viewed as an emerging scientific discipline that guides the thoughtful and appropriate design and development of groupware (Greenberg, 1991a).

Groupware represents a paradigm shift for computer science, one in which *human-human* rather than human-machine communications and problem solving are emphasized. Although our focus in terms of groupware is on computer-supported cooperative *work*, we shall also hint at the role of groupware in such activities as education and play.

The paradigm shift has resulted from a number of converging phenomena:

- The technological opportunities afforded by pervasive computer networking, which has led to widespread use of electronic mail and computer conferencing

- The desire to extend personal computing technology to support small group interaction and computing, sometimes known as *workgroup computing*

- The development by management information systems researchers of technology to support decision making by groups of executives and managers

- The merging of computing and telecommunications, and the search for new communications applications that usefully consume significant bandwidth

- The increasing interest in telecommuting

- The seductive fascination of videoconferencing

- The continual introduction of new standards and supporting technologies, such as ISDN (the Integrated Standard Digital Network).

Some of these phenomena can be quantified (Coleman, 1992a). Rosall (1992) of International Data Corporation (IDC) predicts that LANs will support 36 million users worldwide by 1995. She also predicts that the worldwide public e-mail user base is expected to grow from 4.9 million in 1991 to 38 million by 1996. From a 1991 survey of the corporate use of messaging technologies by 100 Fortune 500 companies, she reports that 98% currently use e-mail, 84% use voice mail, 65% use LAN-based messaging, 52% use LAN, host fax servers, and gateways, and 42% use Electronic Data Interchange. Rosall stresses the high priority that corporations place on the integration of these various media with one another and with online information systems. Cross (1992) estimates that there are 25 million people currently working at home at least part-time and that this number will grow to 45 million by 1995. The size of the teleconferencing industry in 1991 was $1.4 billion (Saffo, 1992).

Groupware is thus one of the fastest growing areas in the computer and telecommunications industry (see Coleman, 1992a; Kirkpatrick, 1992; Wilke, 1992). Coleman (1992b) claims to have identified "over 400 groupware products and almost as many vendors" and reports (1992c) that WorkGroup Technologies projects a $2 billion groupware market by 1995. More conservative estimates for 1995 include $900 million cited by Higgs (1992) of InfoCorp/Gartner Group, $600 million attributed to IDC by Petre (1992), and $500 million reckoned by Saffo (1992) of Institute for the Future.

Despite the size and projected growth of these markets, there is no single source where one can obtain an up-to-date and comprehensive introduction to the rapidly expanding research literature of groupware and computer-supported cooperative work. This book is intended to be that single source.

Directed at researchers, managers, and computer professionals developing or purchasing groupware technologies, this volume can also be used in university research programs and graduate and advanced undergraduate courses focused on CSCW or more generally on human-computer interaction. The book is a by-product of my efforts in organizing and teaching a graduate seminar on groupware and CSCW for the past three years at the University of Toronto.

How This Book Was Written

During the past three years as I sought to organize in my own mind the vast and multidisciplinary research literature of groupware, I had occasion to review many of the key papers in the field. From mid-1991 through mid-1992 I read, reviewed, or skimmed over 1000 papers and book chapters in over 100 different books and journals from a variety of disciplines. I also sent requests to over 60 leading researchers in the field for copies of all their publications on topics related to CSCW or groupware. From this raw material, and based on a method of organizing the literature that I had developed and refined over the three years, roughly 75 papers and book excerpts were selected for inclusion.

Papers were selected on the basis of the following criteria:

- Excellence in terms of technical innovation or behavioral insights or ideally along both these dimensions

- Clarity of expression and presentation

- Breadth of coverage of the field

- Utility as a source for further readings

- Historical significance and influence on the field (although this criterion often came in conflict with the previous one, since historical significance often suggests early papers, whereas utility often suggests more recent works)

I also have attempted in the choice of some papers and in the crafting of the original supporting text to indicate how the research of the past decade has influenced the groupware marketplace that is now emerging, and to intersperse among the pure research papers a few whose concerns are application practice and experience.

Two Ways to Use This Book

One should not be daunted by the size of this book. True, you may start at the beginning with the foundation chapters and proceed through the text from front to back. However, those who are impatient to begin reading immediately about groupware technologies and their impacts can look at Part I and then proceed quickly to Parts III or IV. Browsing and nonlinear reading are encouraged; to facilitate this, we include numerous forward and backward pointers in the introductory chapter essays. To ease the use of individual chapters, we begin them where possible with introductory, tutorial, or survey papers.

With Gratitude to Those Who Helped Me

Many people assisted directly or indirectly in compiling, writing, and editing this volume. I am grateful to Mark Abel, Clarence (Skip) Ellis, Jonathan Grudin, Beverly Harrison, Christian Heath, Rich Helms, Hiroshi Ishii, Jim Larson, Paul Luff, Marilyn Mantei, and Lee Sproull for suggestions and comments on draft versions of the manuscript.

Professor Saul Greenberg of the University of Calgary and his fall 1991 CSCW class tested an early draft of the text and provided insightful feedback and a number of suggestions that greatly improved the final version. Saul's assistance was particularly valuable in helping me improve the organization of the book.

My own graduate seminar in Groupware and Computer-supported Cooperative Work, held in the winter of 1991–92, resulted in additional improvements in the book's structure and contents. I am sincerely thankful for the constructive participation of the auditors, including Wendy Cukier, George Fitzmaurice, Marc Griffiths, and William Hunt, and especially of the two registered students who reviewed each candidate paper—Caroline Haythornthwaite and Mike Sheasby. Caroline's insights in reviewing additional papers and in commenting on an almost final manuscript are greatly appreciated.

My own understanding of the field has grown in pace with the progress of our research on the CAVE-

CAT (Computer Audio Video Enhanced Collaboration and Telepresence) project at the University of Toronto. I have benefited from interactions with various members of our research team over the past three years, including Garry Beirne, Bill Buxton, Mark Chignell, Andrew Clement, Chris DiGiano, Beverly Harrison, William Hunt, Jin Li, Gifford Louie, Iva Lu, Scott MacKenzie, Marilyn Mantei, Kelly Mawby, Tom Milligan, Gale Moore, Dimitrios Nastos, Russell Owen, Ilona Posner, Blaine Price, Abigail Sellen, Mike Sheasby, Ian Small, Tracy Narine, and Barry Wellman. Barbara Whitmer and Maria Casas have consistently provided excellent administrative and clerical support. I am also indebted to Ilona Posner for her careful and skillful preparation of the index, and to Alex Mitchell for additional help with the bibliography and proofreading.

Research support to our laboratory from the Natural Science and Engineering Research Council of Canada, the Information Technology Research Centre of Ontario, the Institute for Robotics and Intelligent Systems of Canada, Apple Computer's Advanced Technology Group and Human Interface Group, the IBM Canada Laboratory Centre for Advanced Studies, Digital Equipment Corporation, and Alias Research is gratefully acknowledged.

Mike Morgan at Morgan Kaufmann Publishers contributed his usual keen publishing insight to the planning and execution of the volume. My thanks also for assistance to Doug Sery and Carol Leyba at Morgan Kaufmann.

Acknowledgements

Abel, M. (1990). Experiences in Exploratory Distributed Organization. From *Intellectual Teamwork: Social and Technological Foundations of Cooperative Work* (pp. 489-510), edited by J. Galegher, R. Kraut, C. Egido, 1990, Hillsdale, NJ: Lawrence Erlbaum. © 1990 by Lawrence Erlbaum Associates. Reprinted by permission.

Bannon, L., and Schmidt, K. (1991). CSCW: Four Characters in Search of a Context. In J. M. Bowers and D.D. Benford (Eds.), *Studies in Computer Supported Cooperative Work: Theory, Practice, and Design*. Proceedings of the First European Conference on Computer Supported Cooperative Work, pp. 3-16. Held in 1989. North-Holland.

Borenstein, N., and Thyberg, C.A. (1991). Power, Ease of Use and Cooperative Work in a Practical Multimedia Message System. *International Journal of Man-Machine Studies*, 34(2), pp. 229-259. Reprinted by permission of Harcourt Brace Jovanovich Limited.

Brittan, D. (1992). Being There: The Promise of Multimedia Communications. *MIT Technology Review*, May/June 1992, pp. 42-50. Reprinted with permission from *Technology Review*, copyright 1992.

Bullen, C.V., and Bennett, J.L. (1991). Groupware in Practice: An Interpretation of Work Experiences. In C. Dunlop and R. Kling (Eds.), *Computerization and Controversy: Value Conflicts and Social Choices*, pp. 257-287. ©1991 by Academic Press, Inc.

Buxton, W. (1992). Telepresence: Integrating Shared Task and Person Spaces. From *Proceedings of Graphic Interface 92*, pp. 123-129. Morgan Kaufmann Publishers.

Cerf, V. G. (1991). Networks. *Scientific American* 265 (3), September 1991, pp. 72-81. Reprinted with permission. Copyright ©1991 Scientific American, Inc. All rights reserved.

Clark, H.H., and Brennan, S.E. (1991). Grounding in Communication. From *Perspectives on Socially Shared Cognition* (pp. 127-149), edited by L.B. Resnick, R.M. Levine, and S.D. Teasley. Copyright 1991 by the American Psychological Association. Reprinted by permission.

Clement, A. (1990). Cooperative Support for Computer Work: A Social Perspective on the Empowering of End Users. In F. Halasz (Ed.), *CSCW 90: Proceedings of the Conference on Computer-Supported Cooperative Work*, Los Angeles, Oct. 7-10, 1990, pp. 223-236. Copyright 1990, Association for Computing Machinery, Inc. Reprinted by permission.

Conklin, E.J. (1992). Capturing Organizational Memory. In D. Coleman (Ed.), *Groupware '92*, pp. 133-137. Morgan Kaufmann Publishers.

Conklin, J. (1987). Hypertext: An Introduction and Survey. © 1987 IEEE. Reprinted, with permission, from *IEEE Computer*, 20(9), pp. 17-20; 32-41, September 1987.

Crowley, T., Milazzo, P., Baker, E., Forsdick, H., and Tomlinson, R. (1990). MMConf: An Infrastructure for Building Shared Multimedia Applications. In F. Halasz (Ed.), *CSCW 90: Proceedings of the Conference on Computer-Supported Cooperative Work*, Los Angeles, Oct. 7-10, 1990, pp. 329-342. Copyright 1990, Association for Computing Machinery, Inc. Reprinted by permission.

Dewan, P., and Choudhary, R. (1991). Primitives for Programming Multi-User Interfaces. *Proceedings of UIST '91*, pp. 41-48. Copyright 1991, Association for Computing Machinery, Inc. Reprinted by permission.

Dourish, P., and Bly, S. (1992). Portholes: Supporting Awareness in a Distributed Work Group. In *Proceedings of CHI '92*, pp. 541-547. Copyright 1992, Association for Computing Machinery, Inc. Reprinted by permission.

Ellis, C., Gibbs, S., and Rein, G., (1991). Groupware: Some Issues and Experiences. *Communications of the ACM*, 34(1), pp. 38-58. Copyright 1991, Association for Computing Machinery, Inc. Reprinted by permission.

Elrod, S., et al. (1992). Liveboard: A Large Interactive Display Supporting Group Meetings, Presentations, and Remote Collaboration. In *Proceedings of CHI '92*, pp. 599-607. Copyright 1992, Association for Computing Machinery, Inc. Reprinted by permission.

Eveland, J.D., and Bikson, T.K. (1988). Work Group Structures and Computer Support: A Field Experiment. *ACM Transactions on Office Information Systems*, 6(4), pp. 354-379. Copyright 1988, Association for Computing Machinery, Inc. Reprinted by permission.

Fafchamps, D. (1991). Ethnographic Workflow Analysis: Specifications for Design. In *Human Aspects of Computing: Design and Use of Interactive Systems and Work with Terminals*, pp. 709-715. Elsevier.

Finholt, T., and Sproull, L.S. (1990). Electronic Groups at Work. *Organization Science*, 1(1), pp. 41-64.

Flor, N.V. and Hutchins, E.L. (1991). Analyzing Distributed Cognition in Software Teams: A Case Study of Team Programming During Perfective Software Maintenance. In J. Joenemann-Belliveau, T.G. Moher, and S.P. Robertson (Eds.), *Empirical Studies of Programmers: Fourth Workshop*, pp. 36-64, Ablex. Reprinted with the permission of Ablex Publishing Corporation.

Flores, F., et al. (1988). Computer Systems and the Design of Organizational Interaction. *ACM Transactions on Office Information Systems*, 6(2), pp. 153-172. Copyright 1988, Association for Computing Machinery, Inc. Reprinted by permission.

Fox, E.A. (1991). Advances in Interactive Digital Multimedia Systems. © 1991 IEEE. Reprinted, with permission, from *IEEE Computer*, 24(10), pp. 9-21, October 1991.

Gaver, B. (1991). Sound Support for Collaboration. In L. Bannon, M. Robinson, M., and K. Schmidt (Eds.), *ECSCW '91, Proceedings of the Second European Conference on Computer Supported Cooperative Work*, pp. 293-308. © 1991, Kluwer Academic Publishers. Reprinted with permission of Kluwer Academic Publishers.

Goldberg, Y., et al. (1992). Active Mail: A Framework for Integrated Group Applications. In D. Coleman (Ed.), *Groupware '92*, pp. 222-224. Morgan Kaufmann Publishers.

Greenberg, S., Roseman, M., Webster, D., and Bohnet, R. (1992). Issues and Experiences Designing and Implementing Two Group Drawing Tools. ©1992 IEEE. Reprinted, with permission, from *Proceedings of the 25th Annual Hawaii International Conference on the System Sciences*, Hawaii, January 1992, Vol. 4, pp. 139-150.

Greif, I. (1992). Designing Group-enabled Applications: A Spreadsheet Application. In D. Coleman (Ed.), *Groupware '92*, pp. 515-525. Morgan Kaufmann Publishers.

Grudin, J. Groupware and Cooperative Work. In Brenda Laurel, *The Art of Human Computer Interface Design*, ©1990, by Apple Computer, Inc. Reprinted with permission of Addison-Wesley Publishing Company.

Harrison, S., and Minneman, S. (1990). The Media Space: A Research Project into the Use of Video as a Design Medium. In *Proceedings of the Conference on Participatory Design*, Seattle, WA, March 31-April 1, 1990, pp. 43; 48; 51-58. This paper was presented at the PDC '90 Conference of Computer Professionals for Social Responsibility, P.O. Box 717, Palo Alto, CA 94302.

Heath, C., and Luff, P. (1991). Disembodied Contact: Communication through Video in a Multi-Media Office Environment. In *Proceedings of CHI '91*, pp. 99-103. Copyright 1991, Association for Computing Machinery, Inc. Reprinted by permission.

Hill, R.D. (1992). Languages for the Construction of Multi-User Multi-Media Synchronous (MUMMS) Applications. In B.A. Myers (Ed.), *Languages for Developing User Interfaces*, pp. 125-143. © 1992, Boston: Jones & Bartlett Publishers. Reprinted by permission.

Hollan, J., and Stornetta, S. (1992). Beyond Being There. In *Proceedings of CHI '92*, pp. 119-125. Copyright 1992, Association for Computing Machinery, Inc. Reprinted by permission.

Ishii, H., and Ohkubo, M. (1990). Design of Team Workstation: A Realtime Shared Workspace Fusing Desktops and Computer Screens. In S. Gibbs and A.A. Verrijn-Stuart (Eds.), *Multi-User Interfaces and Applications*, pp. 131-142. North-Holland.

Ishii, H., and Kobayashi, M. (1992). Clearboard: A Seamless Medium for Shared Drawing and Conversation with Eye Contact. In *Proceedings of CHI '92*, pp. 525-532. Copyright 1992, Association for Computing Machinery, Inc. Reprinted by permission.

Jay, A. (1976). How to Run a Meeting. *Harvard Business Review*, 54(2), March-April 1976, pp. 43-57. Reprinted by permission of *Harvard Business Review*. © 1976 by the President and Fellows of Harvard College; all rights reserved.

Kraut, R.E., Fish, R.S., Root, R.W., and Chalfonte, B.L. (1990). Informal Communication in Organizations: Form, Function, and Technology. In S. Oskamp and S. Spacapan (Eds.), *People's Reactions to Technology in Factories, Offices, and Aerospace*, The Claremont Symposium on Applied Social Psychology, pp. 145-199. ©1990, Sage Publications. Reprinted by permission of Sage Publications, Inc.

Krueger, M. (1991). *Artificial Reality II*, pp. 34-41. ©1991, Addison-Wesley Publishing Co. Inc. Reprinted by permission of the publisher.

Kyng, M. (1991). Designing for Cooperation—Cooperating in Design. *Communications of the ACM*, 34(12), pp. 65-73. Copyright 1991, Association for Computing Machinery, Inc. Reprinted by permission.

Lai, K.-Y., Malone, T.W., and Yu, K.-C. (1988). Object Lens: A 'Spreadsheet' for Cooperative Work. *ACM Transactions on Office Information Systems*, 6(4), pp. 332-353. Copyright 1988, Association for Computing Machinery, Inc. Reprinted by permission.

Landow, G. (1990). Hypertext and Collaborative Work: The Example of Intermedia. From *Intellectual Teamwork: Social and Technological Foundations of Cooperative Work* (pp. 407-415, 423-428), edited by J. Galegher, R. Kraut, and C. Egido, 1990, Hillsdale, NJ: Lawrence Erlbaum. ©1990, Lawrence Erlbaum Associates. Reprinted by permission.

Lange, Beth (1992). Electronic Group Calendaring: Experiences and Expectations. In D. Coleman (Ed.), *Groupware '92*, pp. 428-432. Morgan Kaufmann Publishers.

Lauwers, J.C., and Lantz, K.A. (1990). Collaboration Awareness in Support of Collaboration Transparency: Requirements for the Next Generation of Shared Window Systems. In *Proceedings of CHI '90*, pp. 303-311. Copyright 1990, Association for Computing Machinery, Inc. Reprinted by permission.

Lauwers, J.C., Joseph, T.A., Lantz, K.A., and Romanow, A.L. (1990). Replicated Architectures for Shared Window Systems: A Critique. In *Proceedings of the Conference on Office Information Systems*, Cambridge, MA, April 1990, pp. 249-260. Copyright 1990, Association for Computing Machinery, Inc. Reprinted by permission.

Malone, T.W., and Crowston, K. (1990). What is Coordination Theory and How Can It Help Design Cooperative Work Systems. In F. Halasz (Ed.), *CSCW 90: Proceedings of the Conference on Computer-Supported Cooperative Work*, Los Angeles, Oct. 7-10, 1990, pp. 357-370. Copyright 1990, Association for Computing Machinery, Inc. Reprinted by permission.

Malone. T.W., Grant, K.R., Lai, K.-Y., Rao, R., and Rosenblitt, D.A. (1989). The Information Lens: An Intelligent System for Information Sharing and Coordination. From *Technological Support for Work Group Collaboration* (pp. 65-88), edited by M. H. Olson, 1989, Hillsdale, NJ: Lawrence Erlbaum. ©1989 Lawrence Erlbaum Associates. Reprinted by permission.

Mantei, M. (1989). Observations of Executives Using a Computerized Supported Meeting Environment. *International Journal of Decision Support Systems*, 5, June 1989, pp. 153-166. Elsevier.

Mantei, M., Baecker, R., Sellen, A., Buxton, W., Milligan, T., and Wellman, B. (1991). Experiences in the Use of a Media Space. In *Proceedings of CHI '91*, New Orleans, LA, pp. 203-208. Copyright 1991, Association for Computing Machinery, Inc. Reprinted by permission.

McGrath, J.E. *Groups: Interaction and Performance.* © 1984, pp. 12-17, 29-37, 60-66. Reprinted by permission of Prentice Hall, Englewood Cliffs, New Jersey.

McGrath, J.E. (1991). Time, Interaction, and Performance. *Small Group Research*, 22(2), May 1991, pp. 147-174. ©1991, Sage Publications Inc. Reprinted by permission of Sage Publications, Inc.

Mintzberg, H. (1984). A Typology of Organizational Structure. In Miller/Friesen (Eds.), *ORGANIZATIONS: A Quantum View*, pp. 68-86. ©1984. Reprinted by permission of Prentice Hall, Englewood Cliffs, New Jersey.

Nardi, B.A. and Miller, J.R. (1991). Twinkling Lights and Nested Loops: Distributed Problem Solving and Spreadsheet Development. *International Journal of Man-Machine Studies*, 34(2), pp. 161-184. Reprinted by permission of Harcourt Brace Jovanovich Limited.

Neuwirth, C.M., Kaufer, D.S., Chandhok, R., and Morris, J.H. (1990). Issues in the Design of Computer Support for Co-authoring and Commenting. In F. Halasz (Ed.), *CSCW 90: Proceedings of the Conference on Computer-Supported Cooperative Work*, Los Angeles, Oct. 7-10, 1990, pp. 183-195. Copyright 1990, Association for Computing Machinery, Inc. Reprinted by permission.

Nunamaker, J.F., Vogel, D.R., Heminger, A., Martz, B., Grohowski, R., and McGoff, C. (1989). Experiences at IBM with Group Support Systems: A Field Study. *Decision Support Systems*, 5(2), June 1989, pp. 183-196. North Holland.

Nunamaker, J.F., Dennis, A.R., Valacich, J.S., Vogel, D.R., and George, J.F., (1991). Electronic Meeting Systems to Support Group Work, *Communications of the ACM*, 34(7), July 1991, pp. 40-61. Copyright 1991, Association for Computing Machinery, Inc. Reprinted by permission.

Pinsonneault, A., and Kraemer, K.L. (1989). The Impact of Technological Cupport on Groups: An Assessment of the Empirical Research, *Decision Support Systems*, 5(2), June 1989, pp. 197-216. North Holland.

Posner, I., and Baecker, R. (1991). How People Write Together. ©1992 IEEE. Reprinted, with permission, from *Proceedings of the Twenty-Fifth International Conference on the System Sciences*, Hawaii, January 1992, pp. xx.

Post, B. (1991). Building the Business Case for Group Support Technology. © 1992 IEEE. Reprinted, with permission, from *Proceedings of the Twenty-Fifth International Conference on the System Sciences*, Hawaii, January 1992, Vol. 4, pp. 34-45.

Robinson, Mike (1991). Computer Supported Cooperative Work: Cases and Concepts. This article is originally published in *Proceedings of Groupware '91*, pp. 59-75, published by the Software Engineering Research Center (SERC), P.O. Box 424, 3500 AK Utrecht, The Netherlands.

Rodden, T., and Blair, G. (1991). CSCW and Distributed Systems: The Problem of Control. In L. Bannon, M. Robinson, and K. Schmidt (Eds.), *ECSCW '91, Proceedings of the Second European Conference on Computer Supported Cooperative Work*, pp. 49-64. © 1991, Kluwer Academic Publishers. Reprinted by permission of Kluwer Academic Publishers.

Scardamalia, M., and Bereiter, C. (1991). High Levels of Agency for Children in Knowledge Building: A Challenge for the Design of New Knowledge Media. From *The Journal of the Learning Sciences*, 1(1), pp. 42-45, 58-66. © 1991, Lawrence Erlbaum Associates. Reprinted by permission.

Schatz, Bruce R. (1991-92). Building an Electronic Community System. *Journal of Management Information Systems*, 8(3), Winter 1991-1992, pp. 87-107. Reprinted by permission of H.E. Sharpe, Inc.

Short, J., Williams, E., and Christie, D. (1976). *The Social Psychology of Telecommunications*, pp. 43-60, 77-89. © 1976, John Wiley & Sons. Reproduced by permission of John Wiley and Sons Limited.

Sproull, Robert (1991). A Lesson in Electronic Mail. In L. Sproull, L. and S. Kiesler, *Connections: New Ways of Working in the Networked Organization*, pp. 177-184. © 1991, The MIT Press. Reprinted with permission.

Sproull, L., and S. Kiesler (1991). *Connections: New Ways of Working in the Networked Organization*, pp. 79-101. © 1991, The MIT Press. Reprinted with permission.

Stefik, M., Bobrow, D.G., Foster, G., Lanning, S., and Tatar, D. (1987). WYSIWIS Revised: Early Experiences with Multiuser Interfaces. *ACM Transactions on Office Information Systems*, 5(2), pp. 147-167. Copyright 1987, Association for Computing Machinery, Inc. Reprinted by permission.

Suchman, L., and Trigg, R. (1991). Understanding Practice: Video as a Medium for Reflection and Design. From *Design at Work: Cooperative Design of Computer Systems* (pp. 65-89), edited by J. Greenbaum and M. Kyng, 1991, Hillsdale, NJ: Lawrence Erlbaum. ©1991 by Lawrence Erlbaum Associates. Reprinted by permission.

Tang, J.C. (1991). Findings from Observational Studies of Collaborative Work. *International Journal of Man-Machine Studies*, 34(2), pp. 143-160. Reprinted by permission of Harcourt Brace Jovanovich Limited.

Tatar, D.G., Foster, G., and Bobrow, D.G. (1991). Design for Conversation: Lessons from Cognoter. *International Journal of Man-Machine Studies*, 34(2), pp. 185-209. Reprinted by permission of Harcourt Brace Jovanovich Limited.

Turoff, M. (1991). Computer-Mediated Communication Requirements for Group Support. *Journal of Organizational Computing*, 1, pp. 85; 94-113. Reprinted with the permission of Ablex Publishing Corporation.

Viller, S. (1991). The Group Facilitators: A CSCW Perspective. In L. Bannon, M. Robinson, and K. Schmidt, *ECSCW '91, Proceedings of the Second European Conference on Computer Supported Cooperative Work*, pp. 81-95. © 1991, Kluwer Academic Publishers. Reprinted by permission of Kluwer Academic Publishers.

Yakemovic, K.C. Burgess., and Conklin, E.J. (1990). Report on a Development Project Use of an Issue-Based Information System. In F. Halasz (Ed.), *CSCW 90: Proceedings of the Conference on Computer-Supported Cooperative Work*, Los Angeles, Oct. 7-10, 1990, pp. 105-118. Copyright 1990, Association for Computing Machinery, Inc. Reprinted by permission.

PART I
Introduction

Computer-supported cooperative work (Greif, 1988; Galegher, Kraut, and Egido, 1990; Greenberg, 1991a) is computer-assisted coordinated activity such as problem solving and communication carried out by a group of collaborating individuals. The multi-user software supporting CSCW systems is known as *groupware*, although the latter term is sometimes broadened to incorporate the styles and practices in group process and dynamics that are essential for any collaborative activity to succeed, whether or not it is supported by computer. CSCW may also be viewed as the emerging scientific discipline that guides the thoughtful and appropriate design and development of groupware (Greenberg, 1991a).

There is much controversy over the definition and nature of groupware and CSCW. Malone (cited in Coleman and Shapiro, 1992) defines groupware quite cleanly as "information technology used to help people work together more effectively." Winograd (cited in Coleman and Shapiro, 1992) defines it as "a state of mind." Peter and Trudy Johnson-Lenz, who used the term publicly in a 1980 lecture to mean "intentional group processes plus software to support them" (Johnson-Lenzes, 1980, 1981, 1982) now describe it as "computer-mediated culture" (Johnson-Lenzes, 1992). Grudin (1991a) notes how different investigators define groupware in different ways, some including network file servers, some including database software, some including electronic mail, and some including none of these. Although Dyson (1992) notes that "'groupware' is about as useful a term as 'singleware,'" she goes on to state (p. 10):

> More than a way of coding or building applications, groupware is a way to define, structure, and link applications, data and the people who use them.

Lynch, Snyder, and Vogel (1990, p. 160) point out:

Groupware is distinguished from normal software by the basic assumption it makes: groupware makes the user aware that he is part of a group, while most other software seeks to hide and protect users from each other. . . .Groupware. . .is software that accentuates the multiple user environment, coordinating and orchestrating things so that users can 'see' each other, yet do not conflict with each other.

Although currently viewed by some as a product category or a market, it seems likely that by the year 2000 many or most software tools will be *group-aware*, and that it may therefore no longer be useful to speak of groupware other than as a state of mind or as computer-mediated culture.

One can also debate at length about the nature of CSCW. Greenberg (1991a) notes that *computer-supported cooperative work* may make use of technologies *other than the computer*, may *disrupt* activities of individuals while assisting those of the group, may support *competition* as well as cooperation, and may assist *casual and social interactions* as well as those more typically thought of as work. A thoughtful discussion of the term CSCW appears in Bannon and Schmidt (1991; included in Chapter 1 of this volume).

Yet examples of CSCW are now commonplace. The most successful CSCW technology to date has been *electronic mail* (Sproull and Kiesler, 1991a; excerpts included in Chapter 7 of this volume). A structured form of electronic mail in which messages are organized by topic and dialogues are often mediated by a convenor is known as *computer conferencing* (Hiltz and Turoff, 1978; Hiltz, 1984). Since CSCW is based on the convergence of telecommunications and computation, it can incorporate *teleconferencing*, the act of conferring at a distance with the aid of technologies such as audio and video links. The result is often known as *desktop videoconferencing*. The computer can also be used to facilitate joint problem solving rather than communication *per se*, as, for example, in systems for *collaborative writing or drawing*. If the problem solving is instead directed at issue organization and decision support, the CSCW system is then usually known as a *group decision support system*.

Groupware and CSCW systems thus represent a paradigm shift for computer science, one which emphasizes *human-human* rather than human-machine coordination, communications, and problem solving. CSCW systems can integrate voice and video communication with *shared digital workspaces* and can support work that occurs both synchronously and asynchronously. Thus groupware technology enables an expansion of both the concept of a *meeting* and that of *collaborative work*, allowing participants to transcend the requirements of being in the same place and working together at the same time.

Many current approaches to groupware are applicable only to relatively small groups of individuals who could participate collaboratively in a meeting, joint design or authoring effort, or planning exercise. Yet technologies such as electronic mail and conferencing systems may facilitate the synergistic functioning of very large numbers of individuals, even entire organizations. This volume introduces the research literature dealing with software designed both for groups and for organizations, although greater emphasis is placed on software for groups.

A Guide to This Book

We begin our study of CSCW in Chapter 1: Introduction to Computer-supported Cooperative Work with overview papers that survey groupware technologies and their design, development, and use. Chapter 2: The Adoption, Deployment, and Use of Groupware looks more closely at issues that affect how groupware is introduced and whether or not this can be done successfully. These chapters set the stage for all that follows and introduce themes that will recur throughout the volume.

Computer scientists developing groupware have begun to realize that technical brilliance is not enough. Many groupware applications created to date have failed (Grudin, 1989; Markus and Connolly, 1990; Grudin, 1991, submitted for publication), despite using what may appear to be elegant technology. Even more so than with conventional single-user systems, groupware can only be successful insofar as it is responsive to the social and organizational

context in which it is embedded.

Understanding this context can be aided by insights from a variety of disciplines. The *psychology and sociology of groups* (Berne, 1963; McGrath, 1984, excerpts included in Chapter 3 of this volume; Eddy, 1985; Hackman, 1990; Cole and Nast-Cole, 1992) can help us understand group processes and interactions. The *sociology of organizations* (Mintzberg, 1984; Schein, 1985; Scott, 1987; March, 1988; Pugh and Hickson, 1989; Pugh, 1990) informs us about organizational structure and process and about how technology is introduced into and used in organizations. *Anthropology* and *sociology* contribute the use of *ethnomethodology* and *conversation analysis* (Garfinkel, 1967; Atkinson and Heritage, 1984; Suchman, 1987; see also Chapter 4). The *psychology of media* (Short, Williams, and Christie, 1976) teaches us about the behavioral impacts of media and telecommunications (see also McLuhan, 1964, 1988). *Linguistics* is a source of insight into conversations and dialogue structure (Winograd and Flores, 1986). Book excerpts and papers presenting relevant results from these disciplines appear in Part II: Behavioral Foundations and Enabling Technologies; in Chapter 3: Human Behavior in Groups and Organizations; and in Chapter 4: Groupware Design and Evaluation Methodologies.

One of the key concepts that emerges from the modern ethnographic studies of work process is that human problem-solving behavior is often better understood as an intelligent adaptation to a particular situation depending upon an individual's capability, a task, and an environment than as the routine enactment of preconstructed plans and techniques (see, for example, Suchman, 1983, 1987). One implication of this realization is that we should be wary of too great a reliance upon generic behavioral science theory, and should augment it and enrich it with specific case studies of real cooperative work practice. A number of such studies are presented in Chapter 5: Case Studies of Cooperative Work.

Yet knowledge of behavioral science, whether generic or specific, does not by itself guarantee successful innovation in CSCW. Groupware development is complex and requires expertise in many areas of computer science. *Human-computer* interaction contributes insights into user interface design. *Networking and communications* teach us about distributed systems. *Operating systems* and *database systems* provide useful models of concurrency control. *Windowing systems and environments* lend us implementation tools. *Audio and video technology* is required for multi-media aspects of CSCW. Finally, *artificial intelligence* informs us about the construction of intelligent agents. A number of key ideas from these disciplines are presented in the readings of Chapter 6: Enabling Technologies and Theories.

Most taxonomies of CSCW technologies distinguish them in terms of their abilities to bridge time and to bridge space. All systems are classified as occurring in one of the four quadrants of a 2x2 matrix such as that depicted below.

Because of its simplicity, we shall adopt the above approach in this volume. Yet it is admittedly somewhat problematic. Many systems already provide capabilities from several quadrants. Groupware technologies of the future need to span all quadrants (see Chapter 14), which is usually described as "any time, any place" groupware. Different approaches to building a taxonomy of groupware are described in Grudin (1991, submitted for publication) (see the Notes section of Chapter 2), and Dyson (1992), who classifies groupware in terms of managing the work *process* or the work *content*, and in terms of centering the control with the users, with a centralized agent, or with the work itself.

Electronic mail and computer conferencing systems *transcend the limitations of time* and *space*, allowing *asynchronous* communications and problem solving among groups of physically dispersed individuals. Part III: Asynchronous Groupware begins with papers on electronic mail and conferencing (Chapter 7: Electronic Mail and Computer Con-

ferencing). There follows a chapter on systems that take advantage of message structure, that possess some "intelligence," and that deal with work transactions or *workflows* (Chapter 8: Structured Messages, Agents, and Workflows). The third chapter of Part III covers cooperative *hypertext* systems that incorporate a growing corpus of interrelated documents and messages and that often thereby create an *organizational memory* (Chapter 9: Cooperative Hypertext and Organizational Memory). The papers deal with both technical issues of design and implementation as well as issues of effectiveness and social impact.

A second major kind of collaboration technology is that of *synchronous* groupware, software which assists a group of individuals in working together *at the same time* to carry out a task such as communicating, making a decision, planning a new initiative, structuring a proposal, writing a paper, or sketching a design. Part IV: Synchronous Groupware includes papers that deal with examples of such technology and their use.

There can be a fine line between "synchronous" and "asynchronous" systems. Some attempts at synchronous implementations have actually foundered because of delays in updating and synchronizing screens (see, for example, Tatar, Foster, and Bobrow, 1991, included in Chapter 10 of this volume). Some asynchronous implementations (see, for example, Greif, 1992, included in Chapter 10 of this volume) encourage the transmission of state and the synchro-

Time and space-based views of CSCW technologies	One group site	Multiple individual or group sites
Synchronous communications	Desktop conferencing systems	
	Electronic meeting and decision rooms	Media spaces
Asynchronous communications		E-mail and conferencing
		Structured messaging, agents, and workflows
		Cooperative hypertext and organizational memory

nization of work being carried out independently at different workstations. Despite the fuzziness of the line, the goal of achieving a *shared digital workspace*, of allowing collaborators at different workstations to examine and edit a shared view of a document, typically leads to a style of interface and to a set of implementation problems that distinguish the synchronous systems from asynchronous ones.

Chapter 10: Desktop Conferencing describes systems that typically provide capabilities for synchronous collaborative writing, editing, drawing, and design. These systems are sometimes used in a single group site, and sometimes from multiple sites. In either case, creating and modifying real-time consistent views of a shared digital workspace is difficult to achieve. The system and language capabilities required to do so are described in Chapter 11: System and Language Support for Desktop Conferencing.

Another way to look at synchronous groupware is in terms of where the collaborators are located. Decision support systems usually involve individuals *working together* in an *electronic meeting room* (Mantei, 1989, included in Chapter 12 of this volume), mostly working synchronously, but sometimes working independently for a while until a facilitator reconvenes group attention and discussion. Alternatively, a number of efforts are directed at groupware for synchronous problem solving by teams of *physically dispersed* individuals. Many of the resulting systems incorporate video and audio links as well as shared digital workspaces, and are now commonly referred to as *media spaces* (Stults, 1986, 1988; Buxton and Moran, 1990; Ishii, 1990a; Mantei et al., 1991, included in Chapter 13 of this volume). Media spaces of this kind therefore support what Buxton (1992, included in Chapter 13 of this volume) calls a shared *interpersonal space* as well as a shared *task space*. Chapter 12: Electronic Meeting and Decision Rooms and Chapter 13: Media Spaces present a number of readings that discuss the technical and behavioral challenges and opportunities that arise with these two kinds of groupware.

Groupware is an exciting new frontier for computer science and for computer technology. Part V: Summary and Conclusions and Chapter 14: The Future of Groupware for CSCW attempt to integrate the diverse themes of this book and to suggest what problems need to be solved in order for groupware to achieve greater success in the future.

Notes and Guide to Further Reading

As with so many aspects of modern computing, Doug Engelbart (1963, 1982) had one of the earliest visions of CSCW—the enhancing of human intellect through technologically-mediated and -facilitated formal collaboration. In the mid-1960s his Augmented Knowledge Workshop (Engelbart and English, 1968; Engelbart, 1984) demonstrated the use of hypertext and hierarchically structured documents which were accessible through shared workspaces and discussable over audio and video links.

The early 70s saw the beginnings of electronic mail (see Licklider and Vezza, 1978, for a comprehensive and insightful early review of the technical characteristics and the political, social, and economic impacts of information networks) and computer conferencing (for a review of early history and significant developments see Turoff, 1971, 1991; Kupperman and Wilcox, 1972; Kupperman, Wilcox, and Smith, 1975).

There also began at this time audio, audiographic, and video teleconferencing (Kelleher and Cross, 1985) technologies that failed to live up to early enthusiasms because they were grounded in part on naive goals of significant travel reductions (Grudin, 1989; Egido, 1990). The use of media technology to enhance informal collaboration was forecast by Gordon Thompson (1975) of Bell Northern Research through his concept of *electronic sidewalks*. Other pioneering work in Canada was that of Herb Bown and Doug O'Brien at the Communications Research Centre of the Department of Communications with their concept of a *common visual space* (Sawchuk et al., 1978).

The term *groupware* was coined by Peter and Trudy Johnson-Lenz (1982, p. 47) as follows:

> "GROUPWARE=
> intentional GROUP processes and procedures to achieve specific purposes +
> softWARE tools designed to support and facilitate the group's work."

Their early and insightful paper included discussions of structured communication forms such as messaging, conferencing, filtered exchanges, relational structures, voting, and decision support tools. The term "groupware" became fashionable after it was discovered by the media in the late 80s (Richman, 1987). The phrase "computer-supported cooperative work" was coined by Irene Greif and Paul Cashman in 1984 in the call for an invitation-only workshop on CSCW held in Cambridge, Massachusetts (Bannon and Schmidt, 1991, included in Chapter 1 of this volume; Grudin, 1992, personal communication).

As has been the case so often with experimental computer science of the past two decades, the Xerox Palo Alto Research Centre (PARC) was instrumental in sparking the field both with its Colab meeting room (Stefik, Foster, Bobrow, Kahn, Lanning, and Suchman, 1987) and with the Palo Alto-Portland media link (Abel, 1990, included in Chapter 13 of this volume). Another major contributing thread was the group decision support system that arose out of the management information systems (MIS) community (Dennis, George, Jessup, Nunamaker, and Vogel, 1988; Kraemer and King, 1988).

The 1980s saw a rapid expansion in the development and use of collaborative technologies, including the development of such novel forms as group decision support systems and media spaces. Earliest contributors to these areas are acknowledged in the sections of this book that deal with such applications.

Books on CSCW and groupware

Three excellent recent collections of *original* papers on groupware and CSCW are Galegher, Kraut, and Egido (Eds.) (1990), Greenberg (Ed.) (1991a), and Bostrom, Watson, and Kinney (Eds.) (1992). Each of these collections consists of about 15 papers. The Greenberg book also contains an excellent annotated bibliography of papers published through the early part of 1991.

A set of important early papers on CSCW is the classic *reprint* collection edited by Greif (Ed.) (1988). Marca and Bock (Eds.) (1992) is a recent *reprint* collection of papers on groupware intended for use by software engineers. Each of these collections consists of approximately 30 papers. There is almost no overlap in included papers between the Greif book and this volume. Nine of the papers that appear in Marca and Bock also appear in this volume. The two books were conceived and designed independently.

Johansen (1988) provides a marketplace-oriented introduction to groupware and to its applications to enhance the functioning of business teams. Two more recent books in a similar vein are Opper and Fersko-Weiss (1990) and Schrage (1990). Hiltz and Turoff (1978), Kerr and Hiltz (1982), and Hiltz (1984) review over a decade worth of early research on computer conferencing systems at the New Jersey Institute of Technology. Two other references on electronic meetings and on new communication media are Johansen, Vallee, and Spangler (1979) and Rice and Associates (1984). Sproull and Kiesler (1991a) is a recent comprehensive and insightful treatment of the uses and impacts of electronic mail and computer conferencing.

Other relevant books

Bikson and Eveland (1986) and Kraut (Ed.) (1987) are useful introductions to new office technology and its impacts. Teleconferencing and its impacts are reviewed by Johansen (1984), Olgren and Parker (Eds.) (1983), and Parker and Olgren (Eds.) (1984). Winograd and Flores (1986) and Vaske and Grantham (1990) provide useful background to relevant cognitive science, psychology, sociology, and anthropology.

Conference proceedings dealing primarily with CSCW

The emergence in the late 80s of regular conferences on CSCW research and development helped spur the growth of the field as a scientific discipline. Currently, these alternate between North America and Europe. The proceedings of the North American conferences, which began in 1986, are Greif (1986), Suchman (1988), Halasz (1990), and Turner and Kraut (1992), which documents the conference held in Toronto from 31 October through 4 November 1992. The proceedings of the European conferences are Bowers and Benford (1991), which consists of papers from a conference held in 1989, and Bannon, Robinson, and Schmidt (1991). Three other notable conferences are recorded in Olson (1989), Gibbs and Verrijn-Stuart (1990), and Hendriks (1991).

The first major commercial groupware conference and exposition is documented in Coleman (1992a).

Journals dealing primarily with CSCW

The *Journal of Organizational Computing*, published by Ablex, began in 1991. Even more recent is *Computer-supported Cooperative Work*, published by Kluwer beginning late in 1992.

Books dealing with HCI

The success of groupware will depend in great part on the quality of the interface provided to the users. Books providing advanced treatment of issues in user interface design and human-computer interaction include the forthcoming Baecker, Buxton, and Grudin (1993), the first edition of this volume—Baecker and Buxton (1987), Norman and Draper (1986), Suchman (1987), Laurel (1990), and Shneiderman (1992).

Conference proceedings dealing peripherally with CSCW

Many papers dealing with computer-supported cooperative work are presented at the annual ACM-sponsored conference entitled Human Factors of Computing Systems, also known as the CHI or the SIGCHI conference. Other conferences with significant CSCW content include the ACM Conference on Office Information Systems and the IEEE-sponsored Hawaii International Conference on the System Sciences.

Journals dealing peripherally with CSCW

Notable CSCW papers may also be found in the journals *Communications of the ACM*, *ACM Transactions on Office Information Systems*, *Human-Computer Interaction*, and in the soon-to-be-established *ACM Transactions on Computer-Human Interaction*. The December 1991 issue of *Communications of the ACM* is devoted to CSCW (Grudin, Ed., 1991c).

Groupware video tapes

Increasingly, developers of groupware are documenting their work with video tapes demonstrating and discussing their systems. Video tapes are cited (for example, Mantei, 1990v) and included in the Reference section. Many of these videos have been reviewed and are published in the *ACM SIGGRAPH Video Review*. These tapes can be purchased from:

SIGGRAPH Video Review Order Department
c/o First Priority
P.O. Box 576
Itasca IL USA 60143-0576
Phone (within USA):   1-800-523-5503
Phone (outside USA):   +1-708-250-0807
Fax: +1-708-250-0038

Introduction to Computer-supported Cooperative Work

"Groupware: Some Issues and Experiences" by Ellis, Gibbs, and Rein (1991) reviews CSCW technology in depth, and introduces critical issues of implementation. The authors provide a definition of groupware which stresses the notions of *common task* and *shared environment*. After surveying a number of groupware technologies, they describe the perspectives on groupware provided by the fields of distributed systems, communications, human-computer interaction, artificial intelligence, and social theory. Real-time groupware is then illustrated by presenting the design and usage of a synchronous group outline viewing editor. Finally, the authors discuss a number of design issues including some dealing with group interfaces, group processes, concurrency control, and other system issues.

A number of classic "first generation" CSCW applications are reviewed and critiqued by Robinson (1991a) in "Computer-supported Cooperative Work: Cases and Concepts." These include software for group authoring, calendar management, conversation management, work team support, group decision support, and spontaneous interaction. Of particular interest is the "Wage Bargainer" system developed in 1987 by the Open University, for it illustrates how conventional single-user software, in this case, a spreadsheet, can be used as groupware. Robinson then goes on to propose a number of "CSCW specific" concepts, namely, *articulation work*, *situated action*, *mutual influence*, *shared information space*, *shared material*, *double level language*, and *equality*.

In "CSCW: Four Characters in Search of a Context," Bannon and Schmidt (1991) present a thoughtful discussion of the phrase "computer-supported cooperative work," and an analysis of three specific requirements of CSCW: *supporting articulation work*, *sharing an information space*, and *designing effective socio-technical systems*. They suggest that the "computer support of cooperative work should aim at supporting self-organization of cooperative ensembles as opposed to disrupting cooperative work by computerizing formal procedures." Their discussion of sharing an information space is in terms of a number of important social and behavioral issues and provides a useful complement to the discussion of concurrency control presented by Ellis, Gibbs, and Rein (1991). The authors close with an enumeration of "the multitude of forms of social interaction that play a part in shaping work organizations in any real world work setting" and that therefore must be considered in the development of any effective CSCW application.

In the final paper, "Being There: The Promise of Multimedia Communications," Brittan (1992) reviews a number of current research activities in the field of desktop video/multimedia conferencing. Included are projects investigating *virtual meeting rooms*, *open shared workspaces*, *video-based drawing tools*, and *virtual hallways*, many of which we shall revisit in Chapter 13 of this volume. The paper concludes with several cautionary notes: a mention of the massive amounts of required bandwidth, a question about the utility and effectiveness of the video channel, and a concern for the serious issues of privacy raised by ubiquitous video in the workplace. We shall return to the latter issue in Chapter 14.

Notes and Guide to Further Reading

An early and influential survey of the technology and uses of computer-supported cooperative work is *Groupware: Computer Support for Business Teams* by Robert Johansen (1988; see also Johansen, 1991a,b), one of the chief "evangelists" of the groupware field. Johansen (1988, Ch. 2, p. 41) defines and illustrates 17 different approaches to computer-supported teams, listed below in the order of his prediction of increasing difficulty in implementation:

- Face-to-face meeting facilitation

- Group decision support systems

- Computer extensions of telephony

- Presentation support software

- Project management software

- Calendar management for groups

- Group authoring software

- Computer-supported face-to-face meetings

- PC screen sharing software

- Computer conferencing systems

- Text-filtering software

- Computer-assisted audio-video teleconferences

- Conversational structuring

- Group memory management

- Computer-supported spontaneous interaction

- Comprehensive work team support

- Nonhuman participants in team meetings.

He then classifies them in terms of whether they provide face-to-face meeting support, support between meetings, or electronic meeting support, in terms of their geographic and time dispersion (see Introduction to Part I), and in terms of the primary advantage being to small or large groups. Although one can argue with the wisdom of hindsight about some of his categorizations, the breadth of his vision and the methods with which he structures these diverse approaches by comparing and contrasting them are still valuable.

The time-space categorization of groupware used by Johansen and also used in this book was originally stimulated by an early and influential paper by DeSanctis and Gallupe (1987). A more recent review of CSCW in the context of its role in organizations is Applegate (1981; see also Applegate, Ellis, Holsapple, Radermacher, and Whinston, 1991). Other useful analyses of CSCW are Baecker (1991) and Mantei (1992).

Further information about double-level languages may be found in Robinson (1991c), and about the wage bargainer system in Robinson (1991b). Throughout this book we shall present contributions that describe rather dazzling groupware technology. Yet Ray Panko (1990) has reminded us that very simple existing software can often be made to function as what he calls *humble groupware*. The wage bargainer system is a case of humble groupware. A spreadsheet and a couple of stand-alone PCs were used in an organization to facilitate a very difficult group communications and bargaining process. The lesson is that we should neither be dazzled by the technology nor by the promise of technology per se, for of equal or greater importance is the social and organizational context in which any technology is used.

GROUPWARE

Groupware reflects a change in emphasis from using the computer to solve problems to using the computer to facilitate human interaction. This article describes categories and examples of groupware and discusses some underlying research and development issues. GROVE, a novel group editor, is explained in some detail as a salient groupware example.

SOME ISSUES AND EXPERIENCES

C.A. Ellis,
S.J. Gibbs, and
G.L. Rein

Illustration: Eva K. Sutton, Untitled.

Society acquires much of its character from the ways in which people interact. Although the computer in the home or office is now commonplace, our interaction with one another is more or less the same now as it was a decade ago. As the technologies of computers and other forms of electronic communication continue to converge, however, people will continue to interact in new and different ways.

One probable outcome of this technological marriage is the electronic workplace—an organization-wide system that integrates information processing and communication activities. The study of such systems is part of a new multidisciplinary field: *Computer-Supported Cooperative Work* (CSCW) [29]. Drawing on the expertise and collaboration of many specialists, including social scientists and computer scientists, CSCW looks at how groups work and seeks to discover how technology (especially computers) can help them work.

Commercial CSCW products, such as *The Coordinator*™ [24] and other PC-based software [67], are often referred to as examples of *groupware*. This term is frequently used almost synonymously with CSCW technology (see [8] or [44] for general descriptions of, and strong motivation for groupware). Others define groupware as software for small or narrowly focused groups, not organization-wide support [30]. We propose a somewhat broader view, suggesting that groupware be viewed as the class of applications, for small groups and for organizations, arising from the merging of computers and large information bases and communications technology. These applications may or may not specifically support cooperation.

This article explores groupware in this larger sense and delineates classes of design issues facing groupware developers. It is divided into five main sections. First, the **Overview** defines groupware in terms of a group's common task and its need for a shared environment. Since our definition of groupware covers a range of systems, the second section provides a **Taxonomy of Groupware Systems.** The third describes the widely ranging **Perspectives** of those who build these systems. The fourth section, **Concepts and Example,** introduces some common groupware concepts, and applies these to GROVE, one example of a groupware system. The fifth section contains a discussion of some Design Issues facing groupware designers and developers. Our emphasis in this section is upon system-level issues within real-time groupware. In our conclusion to this article we both issue a note of caution concerning the difficulty of developing successful groupware due to social and organizational effects, and indicate that there is much interesting work remaining to be done in this field.

Overview

Most software systems only support the interaction between a user and the system. Whether preparing a document, querying a database, or even playing a video game, the user interacts solely with the computer. Even systems designed for multiuser applications, such as office information systems, provide minimal support for user-to-user interaction. This type of support is clearly needed, since a significant portion of a person's activities occur in a group, rather than an individual, context. As we begin to focus on how to support this group interaction, we must attend to three key areas: communication, collaboration, and coordination.

The Importance of Communication, Collaboration, and Coordination

Computer-based or computer-mediated communication, such as electronic mail, is not fully integrated with other forms of communication. The primarily asynchronous, text-based world of electronic mail and bulletin boards exists separately from the synchronous world of telephone and face-to-face conversations. While applications such as voice mail or talk programs blur this distinction somewhat, there are still gaps between the asynchronous and the synchronous worlds. One cannot transfer a document between two arbitrary phone numbers, for example, and it is uncommon to originate a telephone conversation from a workstation. Integrating telecommunications and computer processing technologies will help bridge these gaps.

Similar to communication, collaboration is a cornerstone of group activity. Effective collaboration demands that people share information. Unfortunately, current information systems—database systems in particular—go to great lengths to insulate users from each other. As an example, consider two designers working with a CAD database. Seldom are they able to simultaneously modify different parts of the same object and be aware of each other's changes; rather, they must check the object in and out and tell each other what they have done. Many tasks require an even finer granularity of sharing. What is needed are shared environments that unobtrusively offer up-to-date group context and explicit notification of each user's actions when appropriate.

The effectiveness of communication and collaboration can be enhanced if a group's activities are coordinated. Without coordination, for example, a team of programmers or writers will often engage in conflicting or repetitive actions. Coordination can be viewed as an activity in itself, as a necessary overhead when several parties are performing a task [62]. While current database applications contribute somewhat to the coordination of groups—by providing multiple access to shared objects—most software tools offer only a single-user perspective and thus do little to assist this important function.

A Definition of Groupware

The goal of groupware is to assist groups in communicating, in collaborating, and in coordinating their activities. Specifically, we define groupware as:

> computer-based systems that support groups of people engaged in a common task (or goal) and that provide an interface to a shared environment.

The notions of a *common task* and a *shared environment* are crucial to this definition. This excludes multiuser systems, such as time-sharing systems, whose users may not share a common task. Note also that the definition does not specify that the users be active simultaneously. Groupware that specifically supports simultaneous activity is called *real-time groupware;* otherwise, it is *non-real-time groupware.* The emphasis of this article is real-time groupware and system-level issues.

The term groupware was first defined by Johnson-Lenz [46] to refer to a computer-based system plus the social group processes. In his book on groupware [44], Johansen restricts his definition to the computer-based system. Our definition follows the line of reasoning of Johansen since this article is primarily concerned with system-level issues. All of the authors mentioned agree with us that the system and the group are intimately interacting entities. Successful technological augmentation of a task or process depends upon a delicate balance between good social processes and procedures with appropriately structured technology.

The Groupware Spectrum

There is no rigid dividing line between systems that are considered groupware and those that are not. Since systems support common tasks and shared environments to varying degrees, it is appropriate to think of a groupware spectrum with different systems at different points on the spectrum. Of course, this spectrum is multidimensional; two dimensions are illustrated in Figure 1. Following are two examples of systems described according to our definition's common task dimension:

1. A conventional timesharing system supports many users concurrently performing their separate and independent tasks. Since they are not working in a tightly coupled mode on a common task, this system is usually low on the groupware spectrum.
2. In contrast, consider a software review system that electronically allows a group of designers to evaluate a software module during a real-time interaction. This system assists people who are focusing on the same specific task at the same time, and who are closely interacting. It is high on the groupware spectrum.

Other systems, such as those described in the following examples, can be placed on the groupware spectrum according to how they fit the shared environment part of our definition. In other words, to what extent do they provide information about the participants, the current state of the project, and the social atmosphere?

1. The typical electronic mail system transmits messages, but it provides few environmental cues. Therefore it is rather low on the groupware spectrum.

2. In contrast, the "electronic classroom" system [74] uses multiple windows to post information about the subject being taught, and about the environment. Emulating a traditional classroom, this system allows an instructor to present an on-line lecture to students at remote personal workstations. In addition to the blackboard controlled by the teacher, windows display the attendance list, students' questions and comments, and the classroom status. Many commands facilitate lecture delivery and class interaction. This system is high on the groupware spectrum.

Over time, systems can migrate to higher points on the groupware spectrum. For example, Engelbart's pioneering work on augmenting the intellect in the 1960s demonstrated multiuser systems with groupware capabilities similar to some of today's research prototypes. Engelbart's On-Line System [NLS] [21], an early hypertext system, contained advanced features such as filters for selectively viewing information, and support for online conferencing. Today's improved technology and enhanced user interfaces have boosted this type of system higher on the groupware spectrum. Additionally, the technological infrastructure required for groupware's wide use—an infrastructure missing in the 1960s—is now emerging.

Taxonomy of Groupware Systems

This section presents two taxonomies useful for viewing the variety of groupware. The first taxonomy is based upon notions of time and space; the second on application-level functionality.

Time Space Taxonomy

Groupware can be conceived to help a face-to-face group, or a group that is distributed over many locations. Furthermore a groupware system can be conceived to enhance communication and collaboration within a real-time interaction, or an asynchronous, non-real-time interaction. These time and space considerations suggest the four categories of groupware represented by the 2x2 matrix shown in Figure 2. Meeting room technology would be within the upper left cell; a real-time document editor within the lower left cell; a physical bulletin board within the upper right cell; and an electronic mail system within the lower right cell.

A comprehensive groupware system might best serve the needs of all of the quadrants. For example, it would be quite helpful to have the same base functionality, and user interface look and feel (a) while I am using a computer to edit a document in real-time with a group (same time/same place or same time/different place) and (b) while I am alone editing in my office or home (different time). Of course, there are other dimensions, such as group size, that can be added to this simple 2x2 matrix. Further details of this taxonomy are presented by Johansen [45].

Application-Level Taxonomy

The second taxonomy presented in

FIGURE 1. Two Dimensions of the Groupware Spectrum.

FIGURE 2. Groupware Time Space Matrix.

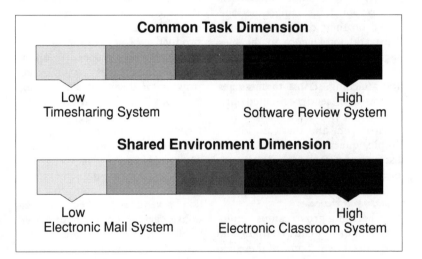

Common Task Dimension

Low
Timesharing System

High
Software Review System

Shared Environment Dimension

Low
Electronic Mail System

High
Electronic Classroom System

	Same Time	Different Times
Same Place	face-to-face interaction	asynchronous interaction
Different Places	synchronous distributed interaction	asynchronous distributed interaction

this section is based on application-level functionality and is not meant to be comprehensive; furthermore, many of the defined categories overlap. This taxonomy is intended primarily to give a general idea of the breadth of the groupware domain.

Message Systems

The most familiar example of groupware is the computer-based message system, which supports the asynchronous exchange of textual messages between groups of users. Examples include electronic mail and computer conferencing or bulletin board systems. The proliferation of such systems has led to the "information overload" phenomenon [37]. Some recent message systems help manage information overload by easing the user's processing burden. "Intelligence" is sometimes added to the message delivery system; for example, the Information Lens [63] lets users specify rules that automatically file or reroute incoming messages based on their content. Other systems add intelligence to the messages themselves; the Imail system [38], for example, has a language for attaching scripts to messages. Scripts are sender-specified programs that execute in the receiver's environment and that can, for example, query the receiver, report back to the sender, or cause the message to be rerouted.

Multiuser Editors

Members of a group can use multiuser editors to jointly compose and edit a document. Some of these editors, such as ForComment™ [67], are for asynchronous use, and conveniently separate the text supplied by the author from the comments of various reviewers. Real-time group editors allow a group of people to edit the same object at the same time. The object being edited is usually divided into logical segments; for example, a document could be split into sections or a program into procedures or modules. Typically, a multiuser editor allows

concurrent read access to any segment, but only to one writer per segment. The editor transparently manages locking and synchronization, and users edit the shared object as they would a private object. Examples include the Collaborative Editing System (CES) [28], Shared Book [58], and Quilt [22, 57].

Some multiuser editors provide explicit notification of other users' actions. For example, Mercury [47], an editor intended for programming teams, informs users when their code needs to be changed because of program modifications made by others. The DistEdit system [49] tries to provide a toolkit for building and supporting multiple group editors.

Group Decision Support Systems and Electronic Meeting Rooms

Group Decision Support Systems (GDSSs) provide computer-based facilities for the exploration of unstructured problems in a group setting (see [51] or [16] for recent surveys). The goal is to improve the productivity of decision-making meetings, either by speeding up the decision-making process or by improving the quality of the resulting decisions [51]. There are GDSS aids for decision structuring, such as alternative ranking and voting tools, and for idea generation [2] or issue analysis [11].

Many GDSSs are implemented as electronic meeting rooms that contain several networked workstations, large computer-controlled public displays, and audio/video equipment (examples are discussed in [2, 12, 16, 64, 77 and 78]). Some of these facilities require a specially trained operator; others assume operational competence among the group members.

A well-known example is the PlexCenter Planning and Decision Support Laboratory at the University of Arizona [2]. The facility provides a large U-shaped conference table with eight personal workstations; a workstation in each of four break-out rooms; a video disk; and

a large-screen projection system that can display screens of individual workstations or a compilation of screens. The conference table workstations are recessed to enhance the participants' line of sight and to encourage interaction. They communicate over a local area network and run software tools for electronic brainstorming, stakeholder identification and analysis, and issue analysis.

Recent work at the University of Arizona has concentrated on the support of larger groups. The current large group facility has 24 workstations designed to support up to 48 people. The support of large groups presents unique challenges and opportunities.

Computer Conferencing

The computer serves as a communications medium in a variety of ways. In particular, it has provided three new approaches in the way people carry out conferences: real-time computer conferencing, computer teleconferencing, and desktop conferencing.

Real-Time Computer Conferencing

Real-time computer conferencing allows a group of users, who are either gathered in an electronic meeting room or physically dispersed, to interact synchronously through their workstations or terminals. When a group is physically dispersed, an audio link, such as a conference call, is often established.

There are two basic approaches to implementing real-time computer conferencing software [73]. The first embeds an unmodified single-user application in a *conferencing environment* that multiplexes the application's output to each participant's display [42]. Input comes from one user at a time, and a *floor passing* protocol (determining who has the floor) exchanges input control among users [56]. Examples include *terminal linking* (a service found in some time-sharing systems) and *replicated windows* (typically implemented by a window server that drives a set of displays in tandem). The second approach is to design the application specifically to account for the presence of multiple users. Some examples are Real Time Calendar [RTCAL] [73], a meeting scheduling system, and Cognoter [78], a real-time group note-taking system.

Each approach has its advantages and disadvantages. While the first allows existing applications to be used, each user has an identical view of the application—there is no per-user context. The second approach offers the possibility of a richer interface, but the application must be built from the ground up or with considerable additional effort.

Computer Teleconferencing

Telecommunication support for group interaction is referred to as teleconferencing [43]. The most familiar examples of teleconferencing are conference calls and video conferencing. Teleconferencing tends to be awkward, requiring special rooms and sometimes trained operators. Newer systems provide workstation-based interfaces to a conference and make the process more accessible. Xerox, for example, established an audio/video link for use by a project team split between Portland and Palo Alto [26]. Most video interactions occurred between large Commons areas at each site, but project members could also access video channels through their office workstations. A similar system, CRUISER [72], lets users electronically roam the hallways by browsing video channels.

Desktop Conferencing

Teleconferencing is not only relatively inaccessible, but it also has the disadvantage of not letting participants share text and graphics (see [18] for a discussion of the failure of video conferencing). Real-time computer conferencing does not offer video capabilities. A third type of computer-supported conferencing combines the advantages of teleconferencing and real-time

conferencing while mitigating their drawbacks. Dubbed *desktop conferencing,* this method still uses the workstation as the conference interface, but it also runs applications shared by the participants. Modern desktop conferencing systems support multiple video windows per workstation. This allows display of dynamic views of information, and dynamic video images of participants [80].

An example of desktop conferencing is the MMConf system [14]. MMConf provides a shared display of a multimedia document, as well as communications channels for voice and shared pointers. Another example is the Rapport multimedia conferencing system [1]. Rapport is designed for workstations connected by a multimedia network (a network capable of transmitting data, voice, and video). The system supports various forms of interaction, from simple telephone-like conversations to multiparty shared-display interaction.

Intelligent Agents

Not all the participants in an electronic meeting are people. Multiplayer computer games, for example, might automatically generate participants if the number of people is too low for a challenging game. Such nonhuman participants are a special case of intelligent agents (a similar concept is "surrogates" [44]). In general, intelligent agents are responsible for a specific set of tasks, and the user interface makes their actions resemble those of other users.

As a specific example, we have developed a groupware toolkit that includes an agent named Liza [25]. One of the tools in the toolkit displays the pictures and locations of all session participants. When Liza joins a session, a picture of an intelligent-looking android is also displayed, indicating to the group that Liza is *participating.* Liza's participation means that a set of rules owned by Liza become active; these rules monitor session activity and result

in Liza suggesting changes of content or form.

Coordination Systems

The coordination problem is the "integration and harmonious adjustment of individual work efforts toward the accomplishment of a larger goal" [76]. Coordination systems address this problem in a variety of ways. Typically these systems allow individuals to view their actions, as well as the relevant actions of others, within the context of the overall goal. Systems may also trigger users' actions by informing users of the states of their actions and their wait conditions, or by generating automatic reminders and alerts. Coordination systems can be categorized by one of the four types of models they embrace: form, procedure, conversation, or communication-structure oriented.

Form-oriented models typically focus on the routing of documents (forms) in organizational procedures. These systems address coordination by explicitly modeling organizational activity as fixed processes [59, 83]. In some of the more recent systems there is an effort to make process support more flexible. For example, in Electronic Circulation Folders [ECF] [48] exception handling is addressed through migration specifications that describe all the possible task migration routes in terms of the steps to be carried out in processing organizational documents.

Procedure-oriented models view organizational procedures as programmable processes; hence the phrase "process programming" [3, 68, 69]. This approach was first applied to coordination problems in the software process domain and takes the view that software process descriptions should be thought of and implemented as software. The development of process programs is itself a rigorous process consisting of specification, design, implementation, and testing/verification phases [69].

Conversation-oriented models are based on the observation that people coordinate their activities via their conversation [15, 24, 65, 81]. The underlying theoretical basis for many systems embracing the conversation model is speech act theory [75]. For example, The Coordinator [24] is based on a set of speech acts (i.e., requests, promises, etc.) and contains a model of legal conversational moves (e.g., a request has to be issued before a promise can be made). As users make conversational moves, typically through electronic mail, the system tracks their requests and commitments.

Communication structure-oriented models describe organizational activities in terms of role relationships [10, 39, 77]. For example, in the ITT approach [39, 40], a person's electronic work environment is composed of a set of centers, where each center represents a function for which the person is responsible. Within centers are roles that perform the work and objects that form the work materials for carrying out the function of that center. Centers and roles have connections to other centers and roles, and the behavior of the connections is governed by the role scripts of the interacting roles.

Summary

As mentioned, overlap exists in these categories. As the demand for integrated systems increases, we see more merging of these functionalities. Intelligent message systems can and have been used for coordination. Desktop conferencing systems can and have been used for group editing. Nevertheless, many systems can be categorized according to their primary emphasis and intent. This, in turn, may depend upon the perspectives of the system designers.

Perspectives

As the preceding section's taxonomy suggests, groupware relies on the approaches and contributions of many disciplines. In particular, there are at least five key disciplines or perspectives for successful groupware: distributed systems, communications, human-computer interaction, artificial intelligence (AI), and social theory. It is important to note that the relationship between groupware and these five domains of study is a mutually beneficial one. Not only does each discipline advance our understanding of the theory and practice of groupware, but groupware presents challenging topics of research for all five domains—topics that without groupware might never be explored.

Of equal importance is the notion that a given groupware system usually combines the perspectives of two or more of these disciplines. We can see the desktop conferencing paradigm, for example, as having been derived in either of two ways:

1. by starting with communications technology and enhancing this with further computing power and display devices at the phone receiver, or
2. by starting with the personal workstation (distributed systems perspective) and integrating communications capabilities.

Distributed Systems Perspective

Because their users are often distributed in time and/or space, many multiuser systems are naturally considered to be *distributed* systems. The distributed systems perspective explores and emphasizes this decentralization of data and control. Essentially, this type of system infers global system properties and maintains consistency of the global state by observing and manipulating local parameters.

The investigation of efficient algorithms for distributed operating systems and distributed databases is a major research area in distributed systems theory. Some of these research results are applicable to groupware systems. For example, implementing electronic mail systems evokes complex distributed-systems issues related to robustness: recipients should be able to receive messages even when the mail server is unavailable. One solution is to replicate message storage on multiple server machines [6]. Discovering and implementing the required algorithms—algorithms that will keep these servers consistent and maintain a distributed name lookup facility—is a challenging task.

Communications Perspective

This perspective emphasizes the exchange of information between remote agents. Primary concerns include increasing connectivity and bandwidth, and protocols for the exchange of many types of information—text, graphics, voice and video.

One of the commonly posed challenges of groupware to communications technology is how to make distributed interactions as effective as face-to-face interactions. Perhaps the correct view of this challenge is that a remote interaction, supported by appropriate technology, presents an alternative medium. While this will not replace face-to-face communication, it may actually be preferable in some situations for some groups because certain difficulties, inconveniences, and breakdowns can be eliminated or minimized. For example, distributed interactions allow participants to access other relevant information, either via the computer or in a book on the shelf, without interrupting the interaction flow. This is analogous to findings on the use of telephone, electronic mail, and other technologies. While none of these replace face-to-face interaction, each has a niche where it is a unique and useful mode of communication. The challenge, then, is to apply appropriate technological combinations to the classes of interactions that will benefit the most from the new medium.

Human-Computer Interaction Perspective

This perspective emphasizes the importance of the user interface in computer systems. Human-computer interaction is itself a multidisciplinary field, relying on the diverse skills of graphics and industrial designers, computer graphics experts (who study display technologies, input devices, and interaction techniques), and cognitive scientists (who study human cognitive, perceptual, and motor skills).

Until recently, most user interface research has focused on single-user systems. Groupware challenges researchers to broaden this perspective, to address the issues of human-computer interaction within the context of multiuser or *group* interfaces. Since these interfaces are sensitive to such factors as group dynamics and organizational structure—factors not normally considered relevant to user interface design—it is vital that social scientists and end users play a role in the development of group interfaces.

Artificial Intelligence Perspective

With an emphasis on theories of intelligent behavior, this perspective seeks to develop techniques and technologies for imbuing machines with human-like attributes. The artificial intelligence (AI) approach is usually heuristic or augmentative, allowing information to accrue through user-machine interaction rather than being initially complete and structured.

This approach blends well with groupware's requirements. For example, groupware designed for use by different groups must be flexible and accommodate a variety of team behaviors and tasks: research suggests that two different teams performing the same task use group technology in very different ways [71]. Similarly, the same team performing two separate tasks uses the technology differently for each task.

AI may, in the long run, provide one of the most significant contributions to groupware. This technology could transform machines from passive agents that process and present information to active agents that enhance interactions. The challenge is to ensure that the system's activity enhances interaction in a way that is procedurally and socially desirable to the participants.

Social Theory Perspective

This perspective emphasizes social theory, or sociology, in the design of groupware systems. Systems designed from this perspective embody the principles and explanations derived from sociological research. The developers of Quilt [22], for example, conducted systematic research on the social aspects of writing, and from this research they derived the requirements for their collaborative editing environment. As a result, Quilt assigns document access rights according to interactions between users' social roles, the nature of the information, and the stage of the writing project.

Systems such as this ask people to develop a new or different awareness, one that can be difficult to maintain until it is internalized. For example, Quilt users must be aware when their working styles—which are often based on informal agreements—change, so that the system can be reconfigured to provide appropriate access controls. With The Coordinator [24], users need to learn about the language implications of requests and promises, because the system makes these speech acts explicit by automatically recording them in a group calendar. Both examples suggest the need for coaching. Perhaps the systems themselves could coach users, both by encouraging and teaching users the theories on which the systems are based.

Real-Time Groupware Concepts and Example

The vocabulary and ideas embodied in groupware are still evolving. In this section, we list some important terms useful for explanation and comparison of groupware systems, followed by an illustrative real-time groupware system. Our emphasis throughout the remainder of this paper is on real-time groupware. Functionality, design issues, and usage experience of GROVE, a real-time group text editor allowing simultaneous editing of private, shared, and public views of a document will also be explained.

- *shared context.* A shared context is a set of objects where the objects and the actions performed on the objects are visible to a set of users. Examples include document objects within coauthoring systems and class notes within electronic classrooms. This notion of shared context is a subset of the larger, more elusive concept of a *shared environment* discussed earlier.
- *group window.* A group window is a collection of windows whose instances appear on different dis-

The artificial intelligence (AI) approach is usually heuristic or augmentative, allowing information to accrue through user-machine interaction rather than being initially complete and structured.

play surfaces. The instances are connected. For example, drawing a circle in one instance makes a circle appear in the other instances, or scrolling one instance makes the others scroll.

- *telepointer*. A telepointer is a cursor that appears on more than one display and that can be moved by different users. When it is moved on one display, it moves on all displays.
- *view*. A view is a visual, or multimedia representation of some portion of a shared context. Different views may contain the same information but differ in their presentation (for instance, an array of numbers can be presented as a table or as a graph), or they can use the same presentation but refer to different portions of the shared context.
- *synchronous and asynchronous interaction*. In synchronous interactions, such as spoken conversations, people interact in real time. Asynchronous interactions are those in which people interact over an extended period of time such as in postal correspondence. Most groupware systems support only one of these interaction modes.
- *session*. A session is a period of synchronous interaction supported by a groupware system. Examples include formal meetings and informal work group discussions.
- *role*. A role is a set of privileges and responsibilities attributed to a person, or sometimes to a system module. Roles can be formally or informally attributed. For example, the person who happens to like to talk and visit with many people may informally take on the role of information gatekeeper. The head of a group may officially have the role of manager [37].

GROVE: A Groupware Example

The *GR*oup *O*utline *V*iewing *E*ditor (GROVE), [20], is an example of real-time groupware that illustrates some of the concepts just introduced. GROVE, implemented at MCC, is a simple text editor designed for use by a group of people simultaneously editing an outline during a work session.

Within a GROVE *session*, each user has his or her own workstation and bitmap display. Thus each user can see and manipulate one or more *views* of the text being worked on in multiple overlapping windows on his or her screen. GROVE separates the concept of a view from the concept of a viewer. A *view* is a subset of the items in an outline determined by read access privileges. A *viewer* is a group window for seeing a contiguous subset of a view. GROVE views and viewers are categorized as private, shared, and public. A *private view* contains items which only a particular user can read, a *shared view* contains items readable by an enumerated set of users, and a *public view* contains items readable by all users.

Figure 3 shows a GROVE group window—group windows provide the shared viewers for synchronous interactions among users.

In addition to displaying views, group windows indicate who is able to use the window and who is actually participating in the session at any given time. This information is provided by displaying images of the people who are members of the view (or simply printing their names if their images are not available) along the bottom border of the window. Thus as users enter or leave the session, their pictures appear and disappear in all appropriate group windows. The window in Figure 3 appears on the workstations of the three users shown along the bottom border, and each user knows that the others have joined the session. Users can modify the underlying outline by performing standard editing operations (insert, delete, cut, paste, and so on) in a group window. When this is done, all three of the users immediately see the modification. Outline items which are grey (like the last item, in Figure 3) rather than black on a particular user's screen cannot be modified by that user. Users can also open and close parts of the outline (by mousing on the small buttons on the left-hand side) or change the read and write permissions of outline items.

Participants can enter and leave a GROVE session at any time. When users enter (or reenter) a session, they receive an up-to-date document unless they choose to retrieve a previously stored version. The current context, is maintained even though changes may have occurred during their absence from the session. A session terminates when there are no remaining participants.

Design Issues and Rationale

GROVE was built as an experimental prototype to explore systems implementation issues, and to gain usage experience. We chose to build this system from scratch rather than beginning with the code of an existing editor because we wanted to understand, control, and modularize the code in particular ways. We were especially concerned with the user interface, and wanted to carefully architect the system's features and its look and feel. In keeping with the experimental nature of this tool, we chose to minimize the functionality and coding time spent on the standard editing features, and to concentrate on its groupware features. These features include the private, shared, and public group window support; the shared context present in the user interface; and the replicated architecture to allow fine-grained (keystroke level) concurrent editing and notification.

The architecture uses a local editor and replicated document at each user's workstation, and a centralized coordinator that serializes the operations of the various editors. This forced us to immediately face problems of response times, concurrent actions, and data inconsistencies. These are problems that plague real-time groupware systems in general. We have investigated this further, and using some concepts from the distributed systems literature, have devised an algorithm for distributed concurrency control. This eliminates the need for centralized coordination as will be shown in the later section on concurrency control.

GROVE proposes an alternative style of interaction. It is designed to encourage and assist in tightly coupled interaction as opposed to the majority of systems for editing documents or doing multiuser computing. The default in GROVE is a mode where everyone can see and edit everything, and there is absolutely *no locking* while editing. New users ask "Isn't it chaotic to all edit in the same document, even the same paragraph, at the same time?" and "Why would a group ever want to edit in the same line of text at the same time?" Indeed, this editor is at the opposite extreme from most CASE systems which force a group of software engineers to lock modules and work in a very isolated and serial manner. The answer to the above questions are related to groups learning to work in new and original ways. Part of the answer is that after a learning period, it is not chaotic, but rather surprisingly useful, because social protocol mediates. The above questions imply that we can learn a lot by observing teams using this editor for *real work*. In the next subsection, we report on our observation and reflection on some of this usage.

Usage Experience

Groupware developers need to be conscious of the potential effects of technology on people, their work and interactions. A sensitivity to this dimension can make the difference between a groupware system which is accepted and used regularly within an organization, and one that is rejected [32]. Issues of user friendliness, flexibility, and technological control must be considered during design and implementation. Much can be learned from ongoing observation and empirical study of groupware systems.

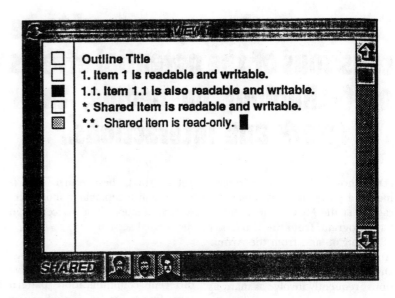

FIGURE 3. A GROVE Group Window.

GROVE has been used by several groups for a variety of design activities, from planning joint papers and presentations to brainstorming. In general, sessions can be divided into three types:

1. **face-to-face sessions** in the electronic meeting room at our lab where there are three Sun workstations and an electronic blackboard,
2. **distributed sessions** where the participants work from machines in their offices and use a conference call on speaker phones for voice communication, and
3. **mixed-mode sessions** where some of the participants are face-to-face and others are distributed.

Table 1 lists the session type, group size, and task for fifteen GROVE sessions. The early sessions were mostly face-to-face sessions where we (the GROVE creators) used the tool and fine-tuned it. More recent sessions have primarily been distributed or mixed-mode sessions

Session Type	**Number of Users**	**Task**
distributed	3	Identify issues in a project description.
face-to-face	3	Refine list of issues in project description.
face-to-face	3	Outline a technical report.
distributed	3	Plan a managerial presentation.
face-to-face	3	Continue planning a managerial presentation.
face-to-face	2	Plan a tutorial.
face-to-face	3	Discuss project plans.
face-to-face	3	Discuss software enhancements for a system.
face-to-face	3	Continue to discuss project plans.
face-to-face	3	Continue to discuss project plans.
mixed-mode	5	Identify similarities/differences of two projects.
distributed	3	Remote session test.
distributed	5	Brainstorm on two related topics.
distributed	5	Outline a paper.
mixed-mode	6	Outline a paper.

TABLE 1. *Summary of GROVE Sessions*

Groupware developers need to be conscious of the potential effects of technology on people, their work and interactions.

across thousands of miles, and have included participants at remote locations at the MCC Human Interface Program, from the University of Michigan, and from the Arthur Andersen Consulting Company. Distributed and mixed-mode sessions frequently involve as many as five or six people.

From the user's perspective, distributed editing sessions are distinctly different experiences from face-to-face editing sessions. Here are some pro and con observations regarding distributed sessions:

Increases information access. Participants in distributed sessions who reside in their offices have access to their local books and files. This sometimes allows easy access to important information that would not otherwise be available during the session. People have commented positively on the convenience, comfort, and familiarity associated with remaining in their offices.

Encourages parallel work within the group. People often divide into subgroups to work on different parts of the task by using a social protocol and shared views. Then their work is merged with the rest of the group's work by changing the access rights on the shared items to public items. This is also done in face-to-face sessions, but not as frequently as in distributed sessions (perhaps because there are more participants in a typical distributed session).

It is easy for distributed members to drop out for a while, do something else (such as work on some code in another window or

get a drink), then return. This is not socially acceptable in most face-to-face situations, but is accepted in distributed sessions.

Makes discussion more difficult. Distributed sessions have a noticeably different communication pattern from face-to-face sessions. Because our phones are not full-duplex, only one person's voice is transmitted at a time. Consequently, people tend to take turns and are unusually polite—if they are impolite or uncooperative, remarks get cut off and the discussion is incomprehensible.

Makes group focus more difficult, requiring more concentration. People have commented that in general, face-to-face sessions feel shorter, seem to accomplish more in less time, and are frequently more exhilarating. In contrast, distributed and mixed-mode sessions seem to require more concentration and are more tiring. Since discussion is more difficult when some of the group members are distributed, people appear to work harder (i.e., they make a conscious effort) to get and give feedback.

Cuts down on social interaction. Distributed sessions tend to be more serious. Since there is less interchange about nontask-related topics, people tend to focus on the task immediately. The effect is a possible efficiency gain from time saved and a possible loss from social needs.

Most of the face-to-face sessions seem to have more intense, richer interactions, but we think the reasons are deeper than simply the

ability to look directly at other participants. Group members rarely look directly at each other during face-to-face sessions, but being in the same room seems to increase the awareness of other members' activities to the point where highly cooperative work can be done. Most of the GROVE cooperative usage techniques have emerged in the face-to-face sessions, then have been used again in the distributed sessions because they were successful in the face-to-face environment.

In addition to comparing distributed with face-to-face sessions, it is interesting to compare group editing (in the synchronous or real-time sense) with single-user editing. Our observations regarding group editing are:

Can be confusing, unfocused, and chaotic. Many things can be going on at once. Several people may be busy in different parts of the outline. At times someone starts wordsmithing a public item while another is still working on it. Since GROVE does not provide a telepointer or other explicit turn-taking mechanisms, actions on the public view (such as scrolling or opening and closing items) are generally disruptive unless accompanied by some verbal explanation. Without verbal explanations, such as "Let's scroll to the next page" or "I'm opening line 2," one wonders "Who is doing this?" and "Why is this being changed?"

Collisions are surprisingly infrequent. Awareness of others' activities is frequently at a subconscious level. As one user expressed it, "During the brainstorming phase, I remember feeling that I was totally occupied with entering my own thoughts as fast as I could. I didn't feel at the time that I was paying much attention to what others were doing—but I know I was . . . First of all, there was very little duplication (most of the items were fresh material), so I must have been reading others' contributions without being aware of it. Secondly, there were very few collisions with people working in the same item at the same time—I was aware of where others were working and steered clear of their space."

Can be efficient. Group editing provides many opportunities for parallel work. The most interesting cooperation patterns also involve an agreed-upon social protocol for using the tool. For example, GROVE does not have an easy way to move a subtree: one group's protocol was that one person should create new empty items where he or she wanted to move the existing lines, then each person took responsibility for cutting and pasting certain agreed-upon lines to new locations in the outline. The group accomplished the subtree move in less time than if one person had done it alone.

Can help prevent information loss, leading to a tangible group product. All the groups observed have produced significant outlines at the end of their GROVE sessions. These outlines are *group compositions that emerge out of the contributions of individuals.* The mechanism for generating the outline is a fascinating process which can consist of any of the following actions:

- **independent entry**—a user enters information while paying little attention to what is already there or what is being discussed,
- **reflective entry**—a user comments on, appends to, or modifies what has already been entered (perhaps by other users),
- **consensus entry**—as the result of discussion the group decides on an appropriate entry or modification,
- **partitioned entry**—the group assigns particular members to refine or reorganize particular parts of the outline, and
- **recorded entry**—a user paraphrases what is being discussed verbally.

This variety of contribution styles has two effects. First, there is little

information loss (as compared with having a single person enter information), and consequently all groups have a significant, tangible product at the end of their sessions. The production of tangible output leads to interactions with high satisfaction/productivity ratings. Second, different groups tend to use the tool in different ways, perhaps adapting it to how they already work or experimenting with new formats.

Can make learning a natural aspect of tool use. Since people are using the same tool at the same time for a shared purpose, when one has a question, friendly help is right at hand. The shared context makes the exchange between requester and provider efficient and relevant.

An unexpected finding is that GROVE users say they now find using single-user tools frustrating. Once one has experienced the flexibility and support provided by a groupware tool, one wants groupware features in all tools. For example, one group had a distributed session in which they used a document-processing system to review slides for a joint talk. This system was basically a single-user tool, despite its shared desktop feature. People could not edit slides on the spot and effect a shared view of the slide. They were constantly saving and closing-and-reopening document files. There was no support for multiple writers—whoever saved last was what the system remembered. Although this system had powerful graphics and formatting capabilities, it was not adequate for the task at hand and users missed GROVE's collaborative editing features.

Design Issues

Groupware systems of the future will probably incorporate contributions from most, if not all, of the five disciplines of study previously outlined. Furthermore, the groupware designer will increasingly be called on to grapple with several important issues that bear directly

on a system's success. Researchers are currently exploring methods and techniques for resolving these issues, but many key research problems remain to be solved. This section focuses on groupware research, describing the problems that continue to face groupware designers and developers. The emphasis of this section is on real-time groupware designed for use by small- to medium-sized groups. We focus on this form of groupware since we feel it is here that technical challenges faced by groupware designers are most apparent.

Group Interfaces

Group interfaces differ from single-user interfaces in that they depict group activity and are controlled by multiple users rather than a single user. One example of a group interface is the GROVE group window illustrated in Figure 3. Other examples include interfaces to real-time computer conferencing systems and to multiplayer games.

Group interfaces introduce design problems not presented by single-user interfaces. A basic problem is how to manage complexity: multiple users can produce a higher level of activity and a greater degree of concurrency than single users, and the interface must support this complex behavior.

Other important questions are: What single-user interface techniques and concepts are useful for constructing group interfaces? Where do they fail, pointing to the need for new concepts? For example, is something like a scrollbar useful when it can be manipulated by more than one person, or is it simply too distracting?

WYSIWIS Issues

One approach to constructing group interfaces is known as WYSIWIS [78]. This acronym stands for "What You See Is What I See" and denotes interfaces in which the shared context is guaranteed to appear the same to all participants. The advantages of WYSIWIS are a strong sense of shared context (e.g., people can refer to something by position) and simple implementation. Its major disadvantage is that it can be inflexible.

Experience has shown that users often want independent control over such details as window placement and size, and may require customized information within the window. The contents of the GROVE window in Figure 3, for example, vary among users in that color indicates user-specific write permissions (i.e., black text is read/write, gray text is read-only). This is an example of *relaxed* as opposed to *strict* WYSIWIS. Stefik et al. [78] have suggested that WYSIWIS can be relaxed along four key dimensions: display space (the display objects to which WYSIWIS is applied), time of display (when displays are synchronized), subgroup population (the set of participants involved or affected), and congruence of view (the visual congruence of displayed information).

Group Focus and Distraction Issues
A good group interface should depict overall group activity and at the same time not be overly distracting. For example, when one user creates or scrolls a group window, opens or closes a group window, or modifies an object another person is viewing/working on, other users can be distracted.

This points up a fundamental difference between single-user and multiuser interfaces. With single-user interfaces, users usually have the mental context to interpret any display changes that result from their actions. As a result, the sudden disappearance of text at the touch of a button is acceptable; in fact, much effort goes toward increasing the system's responsiveness. By contrast, with group interfaces, users are generally not as aware of others' contexts and can less easily interpret sudden display changes resulting from others' actions.

What is needed are ways to provide contextual clues to the group's activity. A simple solution is for participants to audibly announce their intentions prior to taking action—suitable in some situations but often burdensome. A promising alternative is to use real-time animation to depict smoothly changing group activity. For example, text could materialize gradually or change in color as it is entered. This approach, however, introduces a new set of problems. First, animation is computationally expensive and requires specialized workstation hardware. Second, it is difficult to find visual metaphors that are suitable for animating operations, although work on artificial realities and responsive environments [54, 55] seems promising. Finally, any solution to this problem must take into account the dual needs for speed and continuity: the system's real-time responsiveness to the user making changes must not be sacrificed for the smooth, continuous notification to other users.

Issues Related to Group Dynamics
Group interfaces must match a group's usage patterns. Single-user text editors often rely on simple interfaces; characters appear and disappear as they are inserted and deleted. Multiuser text editors, must contend with a diversity of usage patterns as we observed with GROVE. The text was generated as independent, reflective, consensus, partitioned, and recorded entries and, therefore required much richer interfaces.

An experimental *cloudburst*

FIGURE 4. Portion of an Editing Window Using the Cloudburst Model.

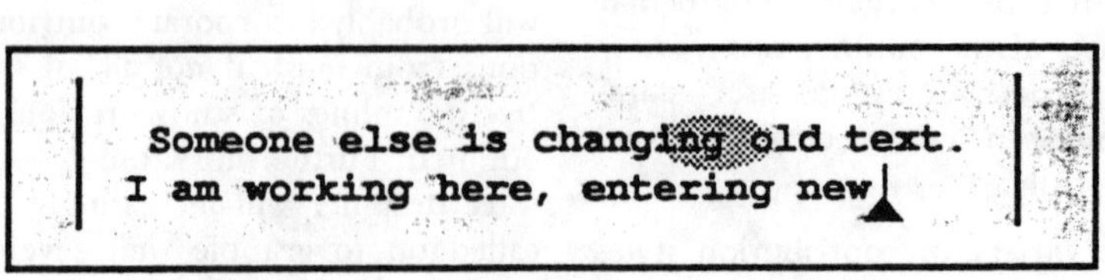

model of multiuser text editing illustrates some needed group interface techniques. This model applies two techniques and is illustrated in Figure 4.

First, the text is aged so that recently entered text appears in bright blue and then gradually changes to black. Second, while textual modifications (insertions and deletions) are immediately visible to the person who initiates them, they are indicated on other users' displays by the appearance of clouds over the original text. The position and size of a cloud indicates the approximate location and extent of the modification. When a user has stopped typing for some time, the clouds on his or her display disappear and the new text is displayed, first in blue and gradually changing to black. The rationale for this interface is that an active user is only marginally interested in others' changes, which should therefore be indicated subtly and not disruptively. By the same token, when the changes are merged, everyone should be made aware of their contents.

Issues Related to Screen Space Management
Screen space is a limited resource in single-user applications, but it is even more of a problem with group interfaces in which each user can create windows that appear on other users' screens. Techniques for managing window proliferation are needed.

One approach is to aggregate windows into functional sets, or *rooms*, each of which corresponds to a particular task [9, 61]. Participants can move from room to room or be *teleported* by other users. When a room is entered, the windows associated with that room are opened.

> **Someone else is changing old text. I am working here, entering new**

A second approach is to let one of the users bear some of the burden of maintaining window order. The LIZA system [25] provides a monitor tool, for example, which allows one user to open and close windows used by participants. This approach is particularly useful with inexperienced users.

Issues Related to Group Interface Toolkits

Single-user interface technology has matured significantly during the past decade. The advances can be attributed in part to the work on user interface management systems (see [60] for a summary) and in part to the proliferation of window systems and their interface toolkits.

Many of these single-user interface concepts can be generalized to multiuser interfaces. Group windows are one example, telepointers another. Several questions remain open, because there is little experience with these generalized techniques. Should there be group windows for subgroups? Should there be multiple telepointers for the multiple subgroups? What are the intuitive ways to share telepointers? Experience with showing all users' cursors on every screen suggests that groupware developers must be careful not to clutter the screen or overload the participants [78]. The point is that group interface toolkits must not simply be extensions of existing toolkits; rather, they must introduce new constructs that better accommodate shared usage.

Group Processes

Some well-defined tasks, such as code walk-throughs, require the participation of a set of users and are called *group processes*. Group processes offer increased synergy and parallelism, but the required coordination overhead can burden the group and dampen its effectiveness. Groupware technology seeks to enhance the benefits while minimizing the overhead.

Group Protocols

Protocols are mutually agreed upon ways of interacting. These protocols may be built into the hardware and software, called *technological protocols*, or left to the control of the participants, called *social protocols*. Examples of technological protocols are the floor control mechanisms in several conferencing systems [1, 27, 56]. These systems can only process one user's input requests at a time, imposing on participants a group process of turn-taking.

Alternatively, control of the group process can be left to the group's social etiquettes which are mutually understood and agreed upon, but not enforced by the groupware system. Social protocols include formal rules or policies, such as *Robert's Rules of Order*, and less formal practices, such as polite turn-taking or hand-raising. In GROVE, social protocols control the use of public windows. For example, anyone can scroll a public window at will, but a group quickly learns that this is disruptive unless accompanied by a verbal explanation along the lines of "Let's scroll to the next page."

Each approach to group processes has advantages and disadvantages. Leaving the processes to social protocols encourages collaboration: the group must develop its own protocols, and consequently the groupware itself is more adaptive. Social protocols (in particular, ad hoc protocols), however, can be unfair, distracting, or inefficient. In contrast, embedding a group process in software as a technological protocol ensures that the process is followed, provides more structure to the group's activity, and assists less experienced users. Technological protocols can be overly restrictive: a group's idiosyncratic working style may not be supported, and the system can constrain a group that needs to use different processes for different activities.

Group Operations

At times, it is appropriate and insightful to view the work of multiple people as a single operation. We call the resultant operations *group operations*. There are many cases of groups accomplishing a task with more speed and accuracy than would be possible by a single individual. Examples include basketball teams, and fire-fighting teams. In other cases the complex procedures carried out by a group are easier to understand if they are not divided into specific tasks performed by specific individuals.

Group operations occur in both synchronous and asynchronous situations. Office procedures present an asynchronous situation and have been studied extensively in the context of the office information systems [5, 13, 83]. Problems associated with supporting these procedures include the following: organizational knowledge, exceptions, coordination and unstructured activity. Knowledge of an organization's structure, history and goals, is useful when following office procedures [5], yet this knowledge is volatile and difficult to specify. Exceptions are frequent since offices are *open systems* [33]; in particular, they contain incomplete and partial information about their day-to-day activities, making it impossible to identify all the situations encountered by an office procedure. Office procedures consist of many parallel asynchronous tasks related by temporal constraints. There is a need for coordination—a mechanism for informing users of required tasks and reminding them of commitments. Finally, since office procedures are not entirely routine, unstructured activities, such as planning and problem solving, can occur at various points within an office procedure [70].

Synchronous group operations are one of the characteristics distinguishing groupware from other systems. The problems described above for asynchronous group operations also apply in the synchronous realm. This can be illustrated by considering a hypothetical vote tool intended for small groups. Suppose the tool functions as follows:

When a user activates the tool, a window containing a type-in area and "Start Vote" and "Stop Vote" buttons appears on that person's display. After this user enters the issue to be voted on and selects "Start Vote," a group window appears on all session participants' displays. The group window contains four buttons for voting ("Yes," "No," "Undecided," and "Uncast"), and a bar chart showing the tallies of the participants' votes.

The following paragraphs refer to this tool in discussions of the issues involved in supporting synchronous group operations.

Organizational and Social Factors. It is easy to build a tool with the above functionality; the difficulty lies in designing it to be useful in a number of different situations. The tool allows participants to change their votes, displays partial results, lets anyone pose an issue for voting, and provides anonymity (unless the users can see each others' actions). How closely this functionality matches a given group's needs depends on both organizational factors (e.g., whether it is a group of peers or a stratified, and perhaps less democratic, group) and social factors (e.g., how open or trusting the group is). In general, specializing a tool to meet a group's particular needs requires *group* knowledge (e.g., user and group profiles) as well as *organizational knowledge.*

Exceptions and Coordination. The voting tool example also points out the need for exception handling and coordination in synchronous group operations. Typical exceptions occur when a noncooperative user fails to complete his or her role in the operation, or when the group composition changes (a person unexpectedly leaves or enters during a vote). Coordination is necessary since group operations impose obligations on the participants and response times vary. A simple solution is to let the group resolve such

difficulties using alternative communication channels, such as audio. The system should at least help detect problems, however, (e.g., by monitoring the progress of vote) and allow dynamic reconfiguration of the operation's parameters (e.g., changing role assignments or group size).

Integration of Activity Support. Asynchronous and synchronous operations are complementary subparts of larger tasks or activities. For example, system design projects include both high-level asynchronous tasks, such as requirements analysis, and synchronous activity, such as face-to-face meetings. A meeting proceeds in a largely unstructured way, but it can contain islands of structured synchronous operations—such as voting or brainstorming. This calls for integrating support for structured/ unstructured activity on the one hand and for synchronous/asynchronous activity on the other. For instance, our voting tool should store vote results so that the group can use the results in the context of other tools and activities. In other words, the designer of group process support tools should look beyond the group and account for factors such as the group's goals and its place in the larger context of the organization or society.

Concurrency Control

Groupware systems need concurrency control to resolve conflicts between participants' simultaneous operations. With a group editor such as GROVE, for example, one person might delete a sentence while a second person inserts a word into the sentence. Groupware presents a unique set of concurrency problems, and many of the approaches to handling concurrency in database applications— such as explicit locking or transaction processing—are not only inappropriate for groupware but can actually hinder tightly coupled teamwork.

The following lists some of the

concurrency-related issues facing groupware designers.

- **Responsiveness**—Interactions like group brainstorming and decision making are sometimes best carried out synchronously. Real-time systems supporting these activities must not hinder the group's cadence. To ensure this, two properties are required: a short *response time*, or the time it takes for a user's own interface to reflect his or her actions; and a short *notification time*, which is the time required for these actions to be propagated to everyone's interfaces.

- **Group Interface**—Group interfaces are based on techniques such as WYSIWIS and group windows, which require identical or near identical displays. If the concurrency control scheme is such that one user's actions are not immediately seen by others, then the effect on the group's dynamics must be considered and the scheme allowed only if it is not disruptive. A session's cohesiveness is lost, for instance, when each participant is viewing a slightly different or out-of-date version.

- **Wide-Area Distribution**—A primary benefit of groupware is that it allows people to work together, in real time, even when separated by great physical distances. With current communications technology, transmission times and rates for wide-area networks tend to be slower than for local area networks; the possible impact on response time must therefore be considered. In addition, communications failures are more likely, pointing out the need for resilient concurrency control algorithms.

- **Data Replication**—Because a real-time groupware system requires short response time, its data state may be replicated at each user's site. Many potentially expensive operations can be performed locally. Consider, for instance, a joint editing session between a user in Los Angeles and one in New York. Typically, each user would be working in a shared context with group windows. If the object being edited is not replicated, then even scrolling or repairing window damage could require communication between the two sites—leading to a potentially catastrophic degradation in response time.

- **Robustness**—Robustness refers to the recovery from unusual circumstances, such as component failures or unpredictable user actions. Recovery from a site crash or a communications link breakdown—typical instances of component failure—is a familiar concern in distributed systems and a major one in groupware. Groupware must also be concerned with recovery from user actions. For example, adding a new user to a set of users issuing database transactions is not normally problematic—but adding a participant to a groupware session can result in a major system reconfiguration. The system's concurrency control algorithm must adapt to such a reconfiguration, recovering easily from such unexpected user actions as abrupt session entries or departures.

We will now describe several concurrency control methods. Of particular interest are techniques useful to real-time groupware, because real-time systems exaggerate the concurrency problems we have just outlined. The discussion begins with traditional distributed systems techniques and ends with the newer groupware approaches, which strive for greater freedom and sharing.

Simple Locking
One solution to concurrency is simply to lock data before it is written. Deadlock can be prevented by the usual techniques, such as two-phase locking, or by methods more suited to interactive environments. For example, the system might visually indicate locked resources [58], de-

creasing the likelihood of requests for these resources.

Locking presents three problems. First, the overhead of requesting and obtaining the lock, including wait time if the data is already locked, causes a degradation in response time. Second, there is the question of granularity: for example, with text editing it is not clear what should be locked when a user moves the cursor to the middle of a line and inserts a character. Should the enclosing paragraph or sentence be locked, or just the word or character? Participants are less constrained as the locking granularity increases, but fine-grained locking adds system overhead. The third problem involves the timing of lock requests and releases. Should the lock in a text editor be requested when the cursor is moved, or when the key is struck? The system should not burden users with these decisions, but it is difficult to embed automatic locking in editor commands. If locks are released when the cursor is moved, then a user might copy text in one location, only to be prevented from pasting it back into the previous location. The system, in short, hinders the free flow of group activity.

More flexible locking mechanisms have been investigated and reported in the literature. Tickle locks [28] allow the lock to be released to another requester after an idle period; soft locks [17] allow locks to be broken by explicit override commands. Numerous other schemes notify users when locks are obtained or conflicting requests submitted.

Transaction Mechanisms
Transaction mechanisms have allowed for successful concurrency control in non-real-time groupware systems, such as CES [28] and Quilt [22, 57]. For real-time groupware, these mechanisms present several problems. Distributed concurrency control algorithms, based on transaction processing, are difficult to implement, incurring a cost in user

response time. Transactions implemented by using locks lead to the problems described above. Other methods, such as timestamps, may cause the system to abort a user's actions. (Only user-requested aborts should be shown by the user interface.) Generally, long transactions are not well-suited to interactive use, because changes made during a transaction are not visible to other users until the transaction commits. Short (e.g., per-keystroke) transactions are too expensive.

These problems point to a basic philosophical difference between database and groupware systems. The former strive to give each user the illusion of being the system's only user, while groupware systems strive to make each user's actions visible to others. Shielding a user from seeing the intermediate states of others' transactions is in direct opposition to the goals of groupware. There has been some work on opening up transactions [4], but the emphasis of this work has been on coordinating nested transactions and not on allowing for interactive data sharing.

Turn-Taking Protocols
Turn-taking protocols, such as floor control, can be viewed as a concurrency control mechanism. The main problem with this approach is that it is limited to those situations in which a single active user fits the dynamics of the session. It is particularly ill-suited for sessions with high parallelism, inhibiting the free and natural flow of information. Additionally, leaving floor control to a social protocol can result in conflicting operations: users often err in following the protocol, or they simply refuse to follow it, and consequently, several people act as though they have the floor.

Centralized Controller
Another concurrency control solution is to introduce a centralized controller process. Assume that data is replicated over all user workstations. The controller re-

ceives user requests for operations and broadcasts these requests to all users. Since the same operations are performed in the same order for all users, all copies of the data remain the same.

This solution introduces the usual problems associated with centralized components (e.g., a single point of failure, a bottleneck). Several other problems also arise. Since operations are performed when they come back from the controller rather than at the time they are requested, responsiveness is lost. The interface of a user issuing a request should be locked until the request has been processed; otherwise, a subsequent request referring to a particular data state might be performed when the data is in a different state.

Dependency-Detection
The dependency-detection model [79] is another approach to concurrency control in multiuser systems. Dependency detection uses operation timestamps to detect conflicting operations, which are then resolved manually. The great advantage of this method is that no synchronization is necessary: nonconflicting operations are performed immediately upon receipt, and response is very good. Mechanisms involving the user are generally valuable in groupware applications, however, any method that requires user intervention to assure data integrity is vulnerable to user error.

Reversible Execution
Reversible execution [73] is yet another approach to concurrency control in groupware systems. Operations are executed immediately, but information is retained so that the operations can be undone later if necessary. Many promising concurrency control mechanisms fall within this category. Such mechanisms define a global time ordering for the operations. When two or more interfering operations have been executed concurrently, one (or more) of these operations is

undone and reexecuted in the correct order.

Similar to dependency-detection, this method is very responsive. The need to globally order operations is a disadvantage, however, as is the unpleasant possibility that an operation will appear on the user's screen and then, needing to be undone, disappear.

Operation Transformations
A final approach to groupware concurrency control is operation transformation. Used in GROVE, this technique can be viewed as a dependency-detection solution with automatic, rather than manual, conflict resolution.

Operation transformation allows for high responsiveness. Each user has his or her own copy of the GROVE editor, and when an operation is requested (a key is typed, for example), this copy locally performs the operation immediately. It then broadcasts the operation, along with a *state vector* indicating how many operations it has recently processed from other workstations. Each editor-copy has its own state vector, with which it compares incoming state vectors. If the received and local state vectors are equal, the broadcast operation is executed as requested; otherwise it is *transformed* before execution. The specific transformation is dependent on operation type (for example, an insert or a delete) and on a log of operations already performed [19].

Other System Issues
As this article has shown, groupware encompasses a wide range of systems—from relatively straightforward electronic mail systems to state-of-the-art, real-time, multiuser tools. Regardless of a system's place on the groupware spectrum, groupware designers face a common set of implementation issues. Some of these issues are described in this section.

Communication Protocols
Effective communication is vital to successful groupware. Unfortu-

nately, current communications technology is not as fully capable of supporting groupware as one might hope.

First, fully integrated data communications and digitized audio/video is not universally available. Groupware developers need protocols that account for the differing requirements of the various media. With audio or video, for example, the occasional loss of data is not disastrous, but a short transmission time is crucial. Additionally, the telephone and the workstation need to be integrated at the system level. Existing prototypes, such as the Etherphone™ [82], are promising, but there is no single network and addressing scheme with an inclusive protocol suite that is accepted as a standard.

A second problem is inadequate support for multiparty communication [73]. Real-time computer conferences often require that messages be sent to a specific set of addresses; such restricted broadcasts are called *multicasts*. Current protocols, whether virtual circuit or datagram based, are better suited for communication between two parties than for general multicasts.

Finally, standardization of data exchange formats is essential if groupware systems are to be useful across organizational boundaries. The office document architecture [41] and other information exchange protocols are steps in this direction.

Access Control
Access control determines who can access what and in what manner. Effective access control is important for groupware systems, which tend to focus activity and to increase the likelihood of user-to-user interference. Theoretical and applied research on protection structures, such as capability lists, has dealt only with non-real-time multiuser systems where users are not tightly coupled [23]. These results need to be thought about in the context of groupware's requirements.

Groupware's access control re-

Effective access control is important for groupware systems, which tend to focus activity and to increase the likelihood of user-to-user interference.

quirements have been described in other literature [27]. For example, if a group task is viewed in terms of its participants' roles, access constraints are usefully specified in terms of roles rather than individuals. Access permissions are not static, but can be granted and revoked. A system can simplify the process of obtaining appropriate access rights by supporting negotiation between parties.

Groupware's requirements can lead to complex access models, a complexity that must be managed. Since access information changes frequently, there must be *lightweight* access control mechanisms that allow end-users to easily specify changes. User interfaces should smoothly mesh the access model with the user's conceptual model of the system. Changing an object's access permissions should, for example, be as easy as dragging the object from one container to another.

Notification

In a single-user environment, it is important to notify the user when constraints are being violated, or when automatic operations provoke triggers or alerters. Notification is even more vital in a multiuser environment, because users must know when other users make changes that affect their work. This points out the need for a *notification mechanism*—a way of alerting and modifying one user's interface in response to actions performed by someone at another interface.

In synchronous interactions, *real-time notification* is critical; in fact, notification and response

times should be comparable. There are different granularities of notification; at the finest level, any user action—keystrokes, mouse motion—results in notification. For example, GROVE is based on keystroke-level notification: as one user types a character, this text becomes visible to the other users. Coarser levels of notification occur as user actions are chunked into larger aggregates. A text-editing system, for instance, could notify once a line or paragraph is completed. Factors such as performance, group size, and task are involved in choosing an appropriate level and style of notification. In general, however, we suggest that a fine-grained level of notification is useful for groups working in a tightly coupled manner, such as when reviewing a document or jointly operating a spreadsheet. As the focus shifts from group tasks to individual tasks—leading toward more asynchronous interaction—coarser notification becomes more appropriate.

Concluding Remarks

We have shown how the conceptual underpinning of groupware—the merging of computer and communications technology—applies to a broad range of systems. We have explored the technical problems associated with designing and building these systems, showing how groupware casts a new light on some traditional computer science issues. Information sharing in the groupware context leads, for example, to unexplored problems in distributed systems and user interface design that emphasize group inter-

action.

Although the prospects of groupware appear bright, we must take into account a history of expensive and repetitive failure [30]. Applications such as video conferencing and on-line calendars have largely been disappointments. These failures are not simply the result of poor technology, but can also be traced to designers' naive assumptions about the use of the technology [7].

Thus, an important area not covered in this article is the social and organizational aspects of groupware design—introduction, usage, and evolution. It should be noted that frequently a tool's effect on a group is not easily predicted or well understood [46]. As mentioned earlier, the system and the group are intimately interacting entities. A substantial literature explores the impact of computer technology on organizations and individuals [34,52,53,66]. Ultimately, groupware should be evaluated along many dimensions in terms of its utility to groups, organizations and societies.

Groupware research and development should proceed as an *inter*disciplinary endeavor. We use the word interdisciplinary as opposed to multidisciplinary to stress that the contributions and approaches of the many disciplines, and of end users, must be *integrated*, and not simply considered. It is our belief that in groupware design, it is very difficult to separate technical issues from social concerns—and that the methods and theories of the social sciences will prove critical to groupware's success.

Acknowledgments.

The authors would like to thank Les Belady, Pete Cook and Bill Curtis for encouraging and supporting groupware research at MCC. Michael Begeman, Kim Fairchild, John Fehr, Mike Graf, Bill Janssen and Tom Smith provided many contributions to MCC's early groupware projects. For their many thought-provoking conversations,

we thank Jeff Conklin, Ira Forman, Jonathan Grudin, Nancy Penning
ton, Steve Poltrock and Baldev Singh. We are indebted to Peter Marks, Glenn Bruns, Nancy Gore, as well as numerous colleagues at other institutions, and anonymous referees for their constructive reviews of early drafts of this article. Finally we would like to express our appreciation to those people who provided us with excellent technical support at MCC. ▄

References

1. Ahuja, S.R., Ensor, J.R., and Horn, D.N. The Rapport multimedia conferencing system. In *Proceedings of the Conference on Office Information Systems* (Palo Alto, Calif., Mar. 23–25). ACM, New York, 1988, pp. 1–8.

2. Applegate, L.M., Konsynski, B.R., and Nunamaker, J.F. A group decision support system for idea generation and issue analysis in organization planning. In *Proceedings of the First Conference on Computer-Supported Cooperative Work* (Austin, Tex., Dec. 3–5). ACM, New York, 1986, pp. 16–34.

3. Balzer, R., Process programming: passing into a new phase. In *Proceedings of the Fourth International Software Process Workshop* (Devon, UK, May 11–13). *Softw. Eng. Not.,* ACM SIGSOFT *14,* 4 (June 1989), 43–45.

4. Bancilhon, F., Kim, W., and Korth, H. A model of CAD transactions. In *Proceedings of the Eleventh International Conference on Very Large Data Bases* (Stockholm, Sweden, Aug. 21–23). Very Large Data Base Endowment, Saratoga, Calif., 1985, pp. 25–33.

5. Barber, G. Supporting organizational problem solving with a work station. *ACM Trans. Off. Inf. Syst. 1,* 1 (Jan 1983), 45–67.

6. Birrel, A.D., Levin, R., Needham, R.M., and Schroeder, M.D. Grapevine: An exercise in distributed computing. *Commun. ACM 25,* 4 (Apr. 1982), 260–274.

7. Bodker, S., Knudsen, J.L., Kyng, M., Ehn, P., and Madsen, K.H. Computer support for cooperative design. In *Proceedings of Conference on Computer-Supported Cooperative Work* (Portland, Oreg., Sept. 26–28). ACM, New York, 1988, pp. 377–394.

8. *Byte.* December, 1988.

9. Card, S., Henderson, D.A. The use of multiple virtual workspaces to reduce space contention in a graphical user interface. *ACM Trans. Graphics.* ACM, New York, 1987.

10. Cashman, P.M., Stroll, D. Developing the management systems of the 1990s: The role of collaborative work. In *Technological Support for Work Group Collaboration.* M.H. Olson, Ed., Lawrence Erlbaum Associates, Publishers, Hillsdale, N.J., 1989, 129–146.

11. Conklin, J., and Begeman, M. gIBIS: A hypertext tool for exploratory policy discussion. In *Proceedings of Second Conference on Computer-Supported Cooperative Work* (Portland, Oreg., Sept. 26–28). ACM, New York, 1988, pp. 140–152.

12. Cook, P., Ellis, C., Graf, M., Rein, G., and Smith, T. Project Nick: Meetings augmentation and analysis. *ACM Trans. Off. Inf. Syst. 5,* 2 (Apr. 1987), 132–146.

13. Croft, B.W., and Lefkowitz, L.S. Task support in an office system. *ACM Trans. Off. Inf. Syst. 2,* 3 (July 1984), 197–212.

14. Crowley, T. et.al. MMConf: An infrastructure for building shared multimedia applications. In *Proceedings of the Third Conference on Computer-Supported Cooperative Work* (Los Angeles, Calif., Oct. 8–10). ACM, New York, 1990.

15. DeCindio, F., DeMichelis, G., Simone, C., Vassallo, R., Zanaboni, A.M. CHAOS as coordination technology. In *Proceedings of the First Conference on Computer-Supported Cooperative Work* (Austin, Tex, Dec. 3–5), 1986, pp. 325–342.

16. Dennis, A.R., Joey, F.G., Jessup, L.M., Nunamaker, J.F., and Vogel, D.R. Information Technology to Support Electronic Meetings. *MIS Quarterly 12,* 4 (December 1988), pp. 591–619.

17. Ege, A., and Ellis, C.A. Design and implementation of GORDION, an object base management system. In *Proceedings of the International Conference on Data Engineering* (Los Angles, Calif., Feb. 3–5). IEEE, Washington, D.C., 1987, pp. 226–234.

18. Egido, C. Video conferencing as a technology to support group work: A review of its failures. In *Proceedings of the Second Conference on Computer-Supported Cooperative Work* (Portland, Oreg., Sept. 23–25). ACM, New York, 1988, pp. 13–24.

19. Ellis, C.A., and Gibbs, S.J. Concurrency control in groupware systems. In *Proceedings of the ACM SIGMOD '89 Conference on the Management of Data* (Seattle Wash., May 2–4 1989) ACM, New York.

20. Ellis, C.A., Gibbs, S.J., and Rein, G.L. Design and use of a group editor. In *Engineering for Human-Computer Interaction.* G. Cockton, Ed., North-Holland, Amsterdam, 1990, 13–25.

21. Engelbart, D.C., and English, W.K. A research center for augmenting human intellect. In *Proceedings of the Fall Joint Computer Conference* (San Francisco, Calif., Dec. 9–11). AFIPS, Reston, Va., 1968, pp. 395–410.

22. Fish, R., Kraut, R., Leland, M., and Cohen, M. Quilt: A collaborative tool for cooperative writing. In *Proceedings of the Conference on Office Information Systems* (Palo Alto, Calif. Mar. 23–25). ACM, New York, 1988, pp. 30–37.

23. Fites, P.E., Kratz, P.J., and Brebner, A.F. *Control and Security of Computer Information Systems,* Computer Science Press, Rockville, Md, 1989.

24. Flores, F., Graves, M., Hartfield, B., and Winograd, T. Computer systems and the design of organizational interaction. *ACM Trans. Off. Inf. Syst. 6,* 2 (Apr. 1988), 153–172.

25. Gibbs, S.J. LIZA: An extensible groupware toolkit. In *Proceedings of the ACM SIGCHI Conference on Human Factors in Computing Systems* (Austin, Tex., April 30–May 4). ACM, New York, 1989.

26. Goodman, G.O., and Abel, M.J. Collaboration research in SCL. In *Proceedings of the First Conference on Computer-Supported Cooperative Work* (Austin, Tex. Dec. 3–5). ACM, New York, 1986, pp. 246–251.

27. Greif, I., and Sarin, S. Data sharing in group work. In *Proceedings of the First Conference on Computer-Supported Cooperative Work* (Austin, Tex., Dec. 3–5). ACM, New York, 1986, pp. 175–183.

28. Greif, I., Seliger, R., and Weihl, W. Atomic data abstractions in a distributed collaborative editing system. In *Proceedings of the 13th Annual Symposium on Principles of Programming Languages.* (St. Petersburg, Fla., Jan. 13–15). ACM, New York, 1986, pp. 160–172.

29. Greif, I., Ed., *Computer-Supported Cooperative Work: A Book of Readings.* Morgan Kaufmann, San Mateo, Calif., 1988.

30. Grudin, J. Why CSCW applications fail: Problems in the design and evaluation of organizational interfaces. In *Proceedings of the Second Conference on Computer-Supported Cooperative Work* (Portland, Oreg., Sept. 26–28). ACM, New York, 1988, pp. 85–93.

31. Grudin, J., Poltrock, S. Computer-supported cooperative work and groupware. Tutorial presented at the *ACM SIGCHI Conference on Human Factors in Computing Systems.* (Seattle, Wash., Apr. 2). ACM, New York, 1990.

32. Harper, R.R., Hughes, J.A., Shapiro, D.Z. Working in harmony: An examination of computer technology in air traffic control. In *Proceedings of the First European Conference on Computer-Supported Cooperative Work.* (Gatwick, London, UK, Sept. 13–15). 1989.

33. Hewitt, C. Offices are open systems. *ACM Trans. Off. Inf. Syst. 4*, 3 (July 1986), 271–287.

34. Hiltz, S.R. *Online Communities: A Case Study of the Office of the Future.* Ablex Press, 1984.

35. Hiltz, S.R., Turoff, M. *The Network Nation: Human Communication via Computer.* Addison Wesley, 1978.

36. Hiltz, S.R., and Turoff, M. The evolution of user behavior in a computerized conferencing system. *Commun. ACM 24*, 11 (Nov. 1981), 739–751.

37. Hiltz, S.R., and Turoff, M. Structuring computer-mediated communication systems to avoid information overload. *Commun. ACM 28*, 7 (July 1985), 680–689.

38. Hogg, J. Intelligent message systems. In *Office Automation*, D. Tsichritzis, Ed. Springer-Verlag, New York, 1985, pp. 113–133.

39. Holt A.W. Diplans: A new language for the study and implementation of coordination. *ACM Trans. Off. Inf. Syst. 6*, 2 (April 1988), 109–125.

40. Holt, A.W., Ramsey, H.R., and Grimes, J.D. Coordination system technology as the basis for a programming environment. *Electrical Commun. 57*, 4 (1983), 307–314.

41. Horak, W. Office document architecture and interchange formats: Current status of international standardization. *IEEE Comput. 18*, 10 (Oct. 1985), 50–60.

42. Ishii, H. Design of Team WorkStation: A realtime shared workspace fusing desktops and computer screens. In *Proceedings of the IFIP WG 8.4 Conference on multi-User Interfaces and Applications* (Heraklion, Greece, Sept. 24–26). IFIP, 1990.

43. Johansen, R. *Teleconferencing and Beyond: Communications in the Office of the Future.* McGraw-Hill, N. Y., 1984.

44. Johansen, R. *Groupware: Computer Support for Business Teams.* The Free Press, N. Y., 1988.

45. Johansen, R. *Leading Business Teams.* Addison-Wesley, Reading, Mass. (to be published 1991).

46. Johnson-Lentz, P. and Johnson-Lentz, T. Groupware: The process and impacts of design choices. In *Computer-Mediated Communication Systems: Status and Evaluation*, E.B. Kerr, and S.R. Hiltz, Academic Press, New York, N. Y., 1982.

47. Kaiser, G.E., Kaplan, S.M., and Micallef, J. Multiuser, distributed language-based environments. *IEEE Softw. 4*, 6 (Nov. 1987), 58–67.

48. Karbe, B. Ramsperger, N. Weiss, P. Support of cooperative work by electronic circulation folders. In *Proceedings of the Conference on Office Information Systems* (Cambridge, Mass., April 25–27). ACM, New York, 1990, pp. 109–117.

49. Knister, M.J., Prakash, A. DistEdit: A distributed toolkit for supporting multiple group editors. In *Proceedings of the Third Conference on Computer-Supported Cooperative Work* (Los Angeles, Calif., Oct. 8–10). ACM, New York, 1990.

50. Koszarek, J.L. et.al. A multi-user document review tool. In *Proceedings of the IFIP WG 8.4 Conference on Multi-User Interfaces and Applications* (Heraklion, Greece, Sept. 24–26). IFIP, 1990.

51. Kraemer, K.L., and King, J.L. Computer-based systems for cooperative work and group decision making. *ACM Comput. Surv. 20*, 2 (June 1988), 115–146.

52. Kraut, R.E. Social issues and white-collar technology: an overview. *Technology and the Transformation of White-Collar Work*, Erlbaum Associates, Hillsdale, Calif., 1987, 1–21.

53. Kraut, R., Egido, C., and Galegher, J. Patterns of contact and communication in scientific research collaboration. In *Proceedings of the Second Conference on Computer-Supported Cooperative Work* (Portland, Oreg, Sept. 26–28). ACM, New York, 1988, pp. 1–12.

54. Krueger, M.W. *Artificial Reality.* Addison-Wesley, Reading, Mass., 1983.

55. Krueger, M.W., Gionfriddo, T., and Hinrichsen, K. VIDEOPLACE: An artificial reality. In *Proceedings of the CHI '85 Conference on Human Factors in Computing Systems* (San Francisco, Calif., April 14–18). ACM, New York, 1985, pp. 35–40.

56. Lantz, K. An experiment in integrated multimedia conferencing. In *Proceedings of the First Conference on Computer-Supported Cooperative Work* (Austin, Tex., Dec. 3–5) ACM, New York, 1986, pp. 267–275.

57. Leland, M.D.P., Fish, R.S., and Kraut, R.E. Collaborative document production using Quilt. In *Proceedings of the Conference on Computer-Supported Cooperative Work* (Portland, Oreg., Sept. 26–28). ACM, New York, 1988, pp. 206–215.

58. Lewis, B.T., and Hodges, J.D. Shared Books: Collaborative publication management for an office information system. In *Proceedings of the Conference on Office Information Systems* (Palo Alto, Calif., Mar. 23–25). ACM, New York, 1988, pp. 197–204.

59. Lochovsky, F.H., Hogg, J.S., Weiser, S.P., Mendelzon, A.O. OTM: Specifying office tasks. In *Proceedings of the Conference on Office Information Systems* (Palo Alto, Calif., March 23–25). ACM, New York, 1988, pp. 46–53.

60. Löwgren, J. History, state and future of user interface management systems. *SIGCHI Bulletin 20*, 1 (July 1988), 32–44.

61. Madsen, C.M. Approaching group communication by means of an office building metaphor. In *Proceedings of the First European Conference on Computer-Supported Cooperative Work* (Gatwick, London, UK, September 13–15). 1989.

62. Malone, T., and Crowston, K. What is coordination theory and how can it help design cooperative work systems? In *Proceedings of the Third Conference on Computer-Supported Cooperative Work* (Los Angeles, Calif., Oct. 8–10). ACM, New York, 1990, pp. 357–370.

63. Malone, T., Grant, K., Turbak, F., Brobst, S., and Cohen, M. Intelligent information-sharing systems,

Commun. ACM 30, 5 (May 1987), 390–402.

64. Mantei, M. Capturing the capture lab concepts: A case study in the design of computer supported meeting environments. In *Proceedings of the Second Conference on Computer-Supported Cooperative Work* (Portland, Oreg., Sept. 26–28). ACM, New York, 1988, pp. 257–270.

65. von Martial, F. A conversation model for resolving conflicts among distributed office activities. In *Proceedings of the ACM Conference on Office Information Systems* (Cambridge, Mass., Apr. 25–27). ACM, New York, 1990, pp. 99–108

66. Olson, M.H., and Lucas, H.C. Jr., The impact of office automation on the organization: Some implications for research and practice. *Commun. ACM 25*, 11 (Nov. 1982), 838–847.

67. Opper, S. A groupware toolbox. *Byte* (December, 1988).

68. Osterweil, L. Software processes are software too. In *Proceedings of the 3d International Software Process Workshop* (Breckenridge, Colo., Nov. 17–19). Computer Society Press of the IEEE, Washington, D.C., 1986, pp. 79–80.

69. Osterweil, L. Automated support for the enactment of rigorously described software processes. In *Proceedings of the Fourth International Software Process Workshop* (Devon, UK, May 11–13, 1988). *Soft. Eng. Not,* ACM SIGSOFT *14*, 4 (June 1989), 122–125.

70. Panko, R.R. 38 offices: Analyzing needs in individual offices. *ACM Trans. Off. Inf. Syst. 2*, 3 (July 1984), 226–234.

71. Rein, G., and Ellis, C. The Nick experiment reinterpreted: implications for developers and evaluators of groupware. *Office: Tech. and People 5*, 1 (January 1990), 47–75.

72. Root, R.W. Design of a multi-media vehicle for social browsing. In *Proceedings of the Second Conference on Computer-Supported Cooperative Work* (Portland, Oreg., Sept. 26–28). ACM, New York, 1988, pp. 25–38.

73. Sarin, S., and Greif, I. Computer-based real-time conferencing systems. *IEEE Comput. 18*, 10 (Oct. 1985), 33–45.

74. Scigliano, J.A., Centini, B.A., and Joslyn, D.L. A Real-time Unix-based Electronic Classroom. In *Proceedings of the IEEE Southeastcon '87* (Tampa, Fla., April 5–8). IEEE, New York, 1987.

75. Searle, J.R. *Speech Acts: An Essay in the Philosophy of Language.* Cambridge University Press, 1969.

76. Singh, B. Invited talk on coordination systems at the *Organizational Computing Conference* (November 13–14, 1989, Austin, Texas).

77. Sluizer, S., and Cashman P.M. XCP: An experimental tool for managing cooperative activity. In *Proceedings of the 1985 ACM Computer Science Conference.* ACM, New York, 1985, pp. 251–258.

78. Stefik, M., Bobrow, D.G., Foster, G., Lanning, S., and Tartar, D. WYSIWIS revised: Early experiences with multiuser interfaces. *ACM Trans. Off. Inf. Syst. 5*, 2 (Apr. 1987), 147–186.

79. Stefik, M., Foster, G., Bobrow, D.G., Kahn, K., Lanning, S., and Suchman, L. Beyond the chalkboard: Computer support for collaboration and problem solving in meetings. *Commun. ACM 30*, 1 (Jan. 1987), 32–47.

80. Watabe, K., et.al. A distributed multiparty desktop conferencing system and its architecture. In *Proceedings of the IEEE Phoenix Conference on Computers and Communications* (Phoenix, Ariz., Mar.). IEEE, New York, 1990, pp. 386–393.

81. Woo, C.C. SACT: a tool for automating semi-structured organizational communication. In *Proceedings of the Conference on Office Information Systems* (Cambridge, Mass., Apr. 25–27). ACM, New York, 1990, pp. 89–98.

82. Zelleger, P.T., Terry, D.B., and Swinehart, D.C. An overview of the Etherphone system and its applications. In *Proceedings of the Second IEEE Conference on Computer Workstations* (Santa Clara, Calif., Mar. 7–10). IEEE, Washington, D.C., 1988, pp. 160–168.

83. Zisman, M.D. Representation, specification, and automation of office procedures. Ph.D. dissertation, Wharton School, Univ. of Pennsylvania, Philadelphia, Pa., 1977.

Categories and Subject Descriptors: D.2.2 [**Software Engineering**]: Tools and Techniques—*user interfaces;* H.1.2 [**Models and Principles**]: User/Machine Systems—*human information processing;* H.4.3 [**Information Systems Applications**]: Communications Applications; K.4.0 [**Computers and Society**]: General

General Terms: Design, Human Factors

Additional Key Words and Phrases: Computer-Supported Cooperative Work, coordination, multiuser interfaces, organizational interfaces

About the Authors:
CLARENCE ELLIS is a senior member of the technical staff in the Software Technology Program at the Microelectronics and Computer Technology Corporation (MCC) and adjunct professor at the University of Texas. His research efforts have recently been in the areas of collaboration and coordination systems, office information systems, and distributed systems.

SIMON GIBBS is an assistant professor at the Centre Universitaire d'Informatique, University of Geneva, Switzerland. He is currently working on software information systems and multimedia programming. Author's Present Address: Centre Universitaire d'Informatique, University of Geneva, 12 Rue du Lac, Geneva 1207, Switzerland. simon@cuisun.unige.ch

GAIL REIN is a member of technical staff in the Software Technology Program at Microelectronics and Computer Technology Corporation (MCC). Her research interests are in multiuser interfaces, visual languages, distributed systems, group work dynamics, and technology transfer.

Authors' Present Address: Clarence Ellis and Gail Rein are with MCC, 3500 Balcones Center Drive, Austin, TX, 78759-6509. ellis@mcc.com, rein@mcc.com

Computer Supported Co-operative Work: Cases and Concepts

M. Robinson
Sageforce Ltd.
61 Kings Road
Kingston-on-Thames
Surrey KT2 5JA, England

Abstract

CSCW is a new field of research in Europe, the USA, and Japan. Its original thrust was to develop software with groups of users to increase their competence in working together. It grew from some failures of, and problems inherited from Office Automation and Management Information Systems; from some sociological intuitions about ways people might work together; and from new interfacing and networking technologies. The content of the field is illustrated by some "first generation" CSCW applications: group authoring; calendar management and meeting scheduling; action co-ordination in organisations; nursing; wage bargaining; informal conversation; and large meetings. These applications had a mixed reception. Some CSCW specific concepts emerged that started to account for this experience, and to influence future CSCW design. These were: articulation work; situated action; unanticipated use; mutual influence; shared information space; shared material; double level language; equality; and "flipover". The implementation of these concepts forms a preliminary agenda for CSCW.

Contents

This article is originally published in the *Proceedings of Groupware'91*, published by the Software Engineering Research Centre – SERC, P.O. Box 424, 3500 AK Utrecht, the Netherlands.

1   Introduction

CSCW is a new field of research and development, involving increasing numbers of institutions in Europe, the USA, and Japan. It grew from fairly unsystematic attempts by various developers to generate software that would increase the competence of people working together. This in turn was partly a response to: failures of and problems inherited from Office Automation and Management Information Systems (See, for instance, [Sco78, FGHW88, Lyy89, Sch91]); some sociological intuitions about ways people might work together; and a search for uses of new interfacing, networking, and multi-media technologies.

The applications that emerged had a mixed reception. Some of them are reviewed in the first part of this chapter. A series of conferences and meetings between 1984 and 1991 considered them—and the nature of the common enterprise that was christened CSCW. Simultaneously, in papers and books, some "CSCW specific concepts" emerged. A selection of these will be summarised in the second part of this chapter.

In one sense these "CSCW specific concepts" are based on, and help account for past work in the field. In another, they form a preliminary agenda for research, design, and implementation of CSCW applications. The unique quality, and some of the excitement of CSCW is well summarised in the following quotation:

> ".... CSCW is neither solely a tool or technology business, nor just a new way to study computer impact on the work place. Instead, in CSCW, equal emphasis is put on *the distinctive qualities of co-operative work processes, and on questions of design: how to mould computer technology to fit into and support these work processes.* Due to the prominent role placed on the process of design, the issue in CSCW is not just how the work process is currently organised, but also how it *could* be organised."   [Lyy89]

2   Some CSCW Applications

The full range of current CSCW applications is best understood from the published proceedings of the last four conferences [GS88, BB91, ACM90, BRS91], and the books of readings by Greif [Gre88] and Galegher et al., [GKE90]. Seven examples will be given here to illustrate the range of technology, and the negative as well as positive aspects of the learning process that is CSCW.[1]

2.1   GROVE (Group Authoring Software)

The GROVE system was developed at MCC, Texas, in 1988 [EGR91]. The need was for several researchers to write a joint paper under considerable time-pressures. This came together with an objective to explore "distributed meetings", where the participants are not in the same place at the same time.

GROVE is basically an "outliner" similar to those found in many word processors. The main difference was that it had a real-time group editor. Participants would connect to it and each other with computer and a voice links. The various co-authors remained in their own offices. The voice link was a loudspeaker phone. Everyone had their hands free, but could talk with anyone else in the group. Each had a personal workstation, running the outliner. Each could select any part of the outline to work on or develop. Thus one author could be developing the framework for say, a definition of shared databases in Section 3 of the paper; another could be working on "graphics" in Section 5; another on whether the Introduction would be too long if examples were included; and so on. All authors could see what the others were doing, and what progress was being made, by "paging up and down" the document.

Each workstation had a private and public window onto the underlying document. There was also the possibility of shared screens between group members. Entry was anonymous, although the verbal channel allowed people to ask who was doing what.

---

[1] With the exception of CRUISER, the applications considered in this section (GROVE, Electronic Meeting Scheduling, The CO-ORDINATOR™, The Florence Project, the "Wage Bargainer"; the Arizona Decision Room) are largely based on text taken from "Double Level Languages & Co-operative Working" [Rob91].

It is interesting to note that some of the usual software design problems were not solved in advance of trying out GROVE. For instance, there was no built-in "access contention" resolution method. This meant there was nothing to prevent any two authors attacking the same bit of text simultaneously:

> "It was a shock to find someone else wordsmithing a sentence I was in the middle of writing."

The automatic renumbering (when someone added or deleted a line) was also experienced as "abrupt".

> "You are working on a screen when there is a flash of renumbering as someone has changed something higher up. Or you suddenly see words jump around as a consequence of what someone else is doing. You don't actually see it coming as you would in a normal meeting...."

Despite this lack of polish, by September 1988, 11 out of the 12 groups that used GROVE loved it. There were many anecdotes and an enthusiasm to use it again. GROVE stands out as a CSCW application because of the spontaneous enthusiasm expressed by its users, and because of its fundamental simplicity.

2.2   Calendar Management

In an excellent review titled "Why CSCW Applications Fail", Grudin [Gru88] points out that many systems, applications, and features that support co-operative work share two characteristics: high cost and low success. He looks at the track record of electronic calendars to show how the dubious track record of many applications can be traced to a common dynamic—a "disparity between those who will benefit and those who must do the work." The point is clearly made, and is worth quoting at length.

> "Where electronic calendars are in use on a large or networked system, an automatic meeting scheduling feature is often provided [Ehr87a, Ehr87b]. The concept that underlies automatic meeting scheduling is simple: the person scheduling the meeting specifies a distribution list and the system checks the calendar for each person, finding a time convenient for all. The system then notifies all involved of the tentative schedule.

> For automatic meeting scheduling to work efficiently, everyone involved must maintain a personal calendar and be willing to let the computer schedule their free time more often than not. Data reported by Ehrlich (ibid) suggest that neither of these requirements are generally satisfied.

> Electronic calendars are *not* electronic versions of paper calendars. They serve communication functions, primarily for managers and executives with personal secretaries who maintain the calendars. An electronic calendar may be used simultaneously by the secretary for scheduling, the manager for reviewing, and other group members for locating or planning. Ehrlich describes the successful use of the electronic calendar in detail; a key point is that "the secretary's role is critical"; those who do not have a secretary are much less likely to maintain an electronic calendar. Another relevant finding is that for managers, "free time is never really free". Unauthorised scheduling of a manager's apparently open time "can be sufficient motivation for total rejection of the system by the manager."

> Thus, electronic calendars are voluntarily maintained primarily by managers and executives (or their secretaries). This has dire consequences for automatic meeting scheduling. If a manager wants to meet with non-management subordinates, few of the latter are likely to maintain electronic calendars. The scheduling program will find all times open, schedule a meeting, and conflicts will ensue. "In order to take full advantage of an electronic calendar, all members of a group must commit to using this medium,"

[Ehr87b]. If managers or executives keeping online calendars wish to meet among themselves, automatic scheduling could work. But as noted above, free time is often not truly free for such managers; it would be wise to consult with their secretaries anyway. Thus automatic meeting scheduling may rarely be used in this situation either.

The simple meeting scheduling feature previews the pattern that emerges from the major applications discussed later. Who would benefit from automatic meeting scheduling? The person who calls the meeting: in general, the manager would benefit. But who would have to do *additional* work to make the application succeed? The subordinates, who would have to maintain electronic calendars that they would not otherwise use. ....."

When an organisation introduces a comprehensive *system* it may be possible to dismiss or redeploy those that refuse to use it. When a CSCW *application* is introduced, these drastic options are not available. Applications in which some people benefit at the expense of extra work for others are unlikely to be successful.

The Electronic Calendar looks like a good idea. It meets many of the frustrations that are often voiced about scheduling meetings. It comes unstuck in most cases because it does not take the practical work processes of *all* staff members into account.

2.3   The CO-ORDINATOR™

This is probably the best known CSCW E-Mail application. Its function is "conversation management"—particularly it "reminds you when some action is asked or committed" [Act89]. It is based on the major ideas of Speech Act Theory [Aus62, Sea79, Flo82].

> "... language cannot be understood as the transmission of information.
>
> Language is a form of human social action, directed towards the creation of what Maturana calls 'mutual orientation'. This orientation is not grounded in a correspondence between language and the world, but exists as a consensual domain—as interlinked patterns of activity. The shift from language as description to language as action is the basis for speech act theory, which emphasises the *act* of language rather than its representational role."   [WF86, page 76]

From this it follows that the most valuable role for the computer is to *mediate* communication between people—as opposed to participating or replacing people—a common perception in Artificial Intelligence projects. This idea is the deeper one that conversation (not description) is the fundamental organisational unit.

> "We ask 'Who makes requests and promises to whom, and how are those conversations carried to completion?'"   (ibid p. 168)

and

> "We are not proposing that a computer can 'understand' speech acts by analysing natural language utterances. It is impossible to formulate a precise correspondence between combinations of words and the structure of the commitments listened to in a conversation. What we propose is to make the user aware of this structure and to provide tools for working with it explicitly."   (ibid p. 159)

The CO-ORDINATOR™ was designed as a computer-based Electronic Mail system to facilitate exchange, clarification, and negotiation of commitment in organisations. There is little doubt that the CO-ORDINATOR™ was also intended to facilitate "co-operative working"; as a way of deepening realistic democracy and respect for people in organisations. Flores had been the Minister, in the Chilean Allende government, concerned with Project Cybersyn [Bee75, Bee81]. This is directly recognised as a predecessor of the CO-ORDINATOR™. Further, there is a recognition of skill (or the need for "reskilling" [Coo80]) that seems to place the project outside the Taylorist paradigm.

"Anyone in a position to direct actions that affect the economic, political, or physical conditions of others is in some sense a manager. In all but the most routinized jobs, a worker functions in some ways as a manager, requesting and initiating actions that affect the work of others."   (ibid p. 143)

While one report [JOW86] suggests user acceptance, many others do not, and take a highly critical position of the performance and nature of the CO-ORDINATOR™ [BBBG88, GC88]. Bowers and Churcher [BC88] raise important linguistic problems about "conversations for action", but the nub of the objections seems to be that the CO-ORDINATOR™ is experienced as excluding negotiation. This has led to the observation that it works in stable, hierarchical, authoritarian organisations, but not elsewhere. Those who defend the co-ordinator do little to dispel this impression.

"Kent Hancock of EDS reported a more favourable experience with the CO-ORDINA-TOR™. EDS has a reputation as a company with strict rules and strong discipline. 'In our management structure we try to think of each other as equals all the way up and down the management chain' said Hancock. His verdict on the CO-ORDINATOR™: 'It is a good communication tool and it gets the job done by forcing compliance'." [Dur88]

With friends like this, the CO-ORDINATOR™ hardly needs its enemies to whisper about the "world's first fascist computer system". How has this unfortunate reversal of the original intentions come about? How did the adoption of radical speech act theory lead to this level of discontent?

Grantham & Carasik [GC88] provide some interesting evidence. The CO-ORDINATOR™ was introduced, for a six month trial, to 15 "technical professionals" at Pacific Bell who used frequent phone and E-mail communication with each other.

"The basic finding was that the use of the software prompted expression of emotional, or affective states in almost all subjects. In most cases, these expressions were not solicited but occurred freely. The most cogent observation was simply the stoppage of use by a majority of subjects. In this sense their actions spoke louder than their words. When questioned, they stated that the format of their interaction pattern encouraged by the software was "unnatural", "uncomfortable", and "made no sense" to them.

Subjects reported feeling overly restricted in "how they can talk to one another" in the speech act paradigm. Although, most admitted not understanding what the underlying language paradigm was; they felt that an intellectual understanding would not ally their felt emotional states. ....

..... it was revealed that a large part of the communication occurring during the trial period was designed to formulate new rules of group behaviour. ....

Subjects openly expressed the need and desire for a communications medium which would augment their search for common understanding. Open ended, free flowing, almost serendipitous conversations were the norm for this group of individuals."

and

"It is our conclusion therefore, that the CO-ORDINATOR™ failed to be incorporated into a normal workflow pattern because it, and its underlying paradigms of work, failed to acknowledge the experienced phenomenon of work. The CO-ORDINATOR™ makes explicit and textual a dimension of human communication which is otherwise contained in the overall context of interaction. It further makes the unsupported assumption that participants in the system will willingly share the designers' view that one *should* be extremely explicit about the nature of one's utterances.

This assumption violates the phenomenology of work which embeds a process of nego-tiating the agreement of meaning among workgroup members. Pask's [Pas80] conver-sation theory gets to this point when he makes the distinction between communication and conversation. Communication is a process of transmission of information between, and among group members. Conversation is distinct, in that it implies a process of concept sharing and development of agreement of the interpretation of meaning events.

In this sense the CO-ORDINATOR™ supports a process of communication, but does not necessarily support the process of conversation, or the negotiation of meaning interpretation among group members."

While it is too early to bring in a verdict on a system still under development, and on the basis of relatively few cases, it appears that the CO-ORDINATOR™ violates some basic CSCW concepts considered later.

2.4   Work Team Support—The Florence Project

Four researchers from the University of Oslo set out to:

> "... explore whether—and how—computer systems can be used in nurses' daily work rather than focusing on more administrative work tasks, carried out by head nurses and the like."   [BB88]

The system was developed around a need identified by the nurses themselves:

> "I wish we (ie.. the nurses) could talk about computer systems which support co-operation with others—it would be beneficial to our work if the nurses stopped being the information network in hospitals."   (ibid)

Another need was explicated in more detail on the cardiological ward, which often treated emergency heart attacks:

> "The patients stay in the ward for a rather short time, approximately 3 days. According to the nurses this means the patients are replaced so often that it is hard to get to know them. On the other hand, its impossible to increase the stay since this would require extra personal. Because the patients stay for a short time, and are emergency cases, it is difficult to organise the work according to primary nursing. This means the nurses have to give a rather detailed report every day."   (ibid)

The nurses information function was complex. It involved at least passing all relevant information to the next shift, co-ordinating information with other nurses to have an overview of the state of the ward, arranging for different medical doctors to meet (or conveying information to them individually), and relaying the doctors' daily programmes for each patient back to the ward.

All these meetings cut into the time available for patient care. The CSCW supported competence would be a way of "packaging variety" [ZR89] so that everyone got the necessary information without all the meetings. The equality that was not recognised in the Electronic Calendar is found here:

> "Due to the project being a research project, the nurses were free to not use the system. As researchers and outsiders we could not force the nurses to use the system. The only possible reason for using it was the nurses' own motivation based on their own positive evaluation of the system."   (ibid)

There was a sensitivity to the nurses own way of talking and acting:

> "We seldom talk about co-operation in our daily work, we just do it. One example of this "wordless" connection is the concept "overview". The nurses use "lack of overview" to explain the rejection of different suggestions for changes. Overview seems to relate to the nurses' "inner picture" of the ward. This inner picture has to be in common (to some extent) to the nurses in a ward, and it seems to be the basis for their co-operation. The nurses are not able to explicate what gives overview, but they are quick to tell if something is not useful for getting an overview."   (ibid)

There was a sensitivity to the existing "system", which utilised "scraps of paper"

"At the beginning of each shift, there is a meeting where one nurse from the preceding shift gives the new comers a status report. Each of them writes down the most important information on their own scraps (of paper). During the shift the nurses use the scraps to look up information, and to write down important observations and happenings. The sheets are "use-once-paper", ie. the sheets are out of date the next shift." (ibid)

and the computerised system was based on it.

"The information in the Work Sheets is presented in a way that gives the nurses overview of the patients in the ward. It is this overview that is the basis for the decisions made by the nurses during a shift."

"... the Work Sheets contain only the parts of the patient information which the nurses have in common. Compared to the nurses' scraps, the Work Sheet does not add structure to the information. And the process of using the information is not standardised. Like the scraps, the Work Sheet will support the non-formalised professional decision making."   (ibid)

The formalised Work Sheets "fix" information that the nursing group has decided to be relevant, enabling their "non-formalised professional" evaluations and decision making to happen around them. The importance of the structure of the Work Sheets is highlighted by the fact that

"... one of the kernel groups has refused to use the computer system. But they produce Work Sheets nevertheless. They know how to get "empty" Work Sheets, and then they fill in the information by hand."   (ibid)

2.5   A Group Decision Support System—The "Wage Bargainer"

The "Wage Bargainer" was developed in 1987 by the Open University as part of the WISDOM Project to explore collective uses of new technology [Rob89, Rob90]. The context was a "real co-operative" (enterprise owned and controlled by its workers). The problem was two hundred people in a dozen or so workgroups, with a wage structure that had "evolved" over 19 years. During this time, the organisation had increased in size sixfold, and many new specialisms and functions had developed. The wage structure had become so complicated that it was almost incomprehensible. Anomalies abounded, as did the discontent that they gave rise to.

Since the organisation was a co-operative, there was no external owner, or separate management to bargain with. No single group could *impose* a new structure. In practice, and in some way, the workers had to bargain with each other. This situation had been evaded in previous years by acceptance of National Agreements reached by various appropriate unions. The glaring anomalies now meant some other way had to be found.

The Open University team provided a spreadsheet. Each group had its "own" screen. This showed their salary and salary range, in figures and as "points" on the wage scale; overtime rates, and overtime actually paid; number of workers in the group; extra costs of insurance contributions; etc. Each group screen was driven by an underlying table of wage scales and actual salaries. Each screen also showed the consequences of the current situation, and of any changes, to the co-operative as a whole.

Each group could change any of the factors that directly affected it (wage scale range, increments, overtime rate, number of workers, etc.). Although *any* group could make *any* change, what the co-op *could* pay was determined by the relation of all the "claims" taken together to its total (budgeted) income. Each group had to evaluate its claim in the light of other claims. Negotiations were reflected in the "groups screens" but took place directly. Negotiation was not a part of the computer system.

The "Wage Bargainer" was well received. A great deal of experimentation took place, as well as some fantasy realisation. One group claimed parity with Civil Service Grades, and awarded themselves an appropriate increase that ate up the surplus for the whole organisation. There was also considerable interest in what others were actually paid. Although this information had previously been available in theory, in practice it had been too difficult to get. Finally it was agreed that the reality of the budget income was such that a 3% across-the-board increase was the minimum everyone would accept, and the most that could be paid. The anomalies remain, but the problem the anomalies were causing was resolved.

The "Wage Bargainer" was a simple and obvious application that was received with enthusiasm as a useful tool. It enabled the co-operative to achieve a satisfactory resolution of the wage question. Most people did not get as much as they would have liked—but they understood why, and accepted it. The final result could not have been deduced (or algorithmically derived) from the original claims. The mutual adaptations, the ability to take new positions, allowed by iteration and discussion were a necessary part of the process.

It was recognised that individual viewpoints always have a context. Contexts—especially when the context is people in co-operating groups—are mobile. Meanings are not *and cannot be* divorced from context. "Freezing" viewpoints is the best way of rendering them meaningless. CSCW applications cannot rely on participants having fixed positions—or on frozen representations of fixed positions. Rather they should support a process of mutual influence.

2.6   Computer Supported Spontaneous Interaction—CRUISER

At first sight, CRUISER [Roo88] appears to be a typical hi-tech, high cost system suited only to luxurious offices in the US. Computer support for gossip appears to be a decadent luxury! Or does it?

First, what is informal interaction?

> "... the fact that people move around the workplace in the course of their daily activities. They go to lunch, get coffee, visit colleagues, make copies, and so on. During the course of these excursions they are likely to bump into other people on similar errands, or to pass by people working in their offices."   (ibid)

And why is this of any significance?

> "[All84] states that social interactions and resulting personal relationships are critical to the success and effectiveness of the organization: they foster the development of mutual understanding, define the channels though which information flows into and throughout the organization, and increase the effectiveness of communications among technical employees. Workplace social relationships are also known to be important elements of job satisfaction and sources of social support [Loc76]

> .... Kraut, Galegher and Egido [KGE88] have observed that collaborations actually operate on two "inextricably intertwined" levels of activity—personal relationships and research tasks. They argue that the major facilitator of processes at both levels is good communication, ie. frequent, low-cost face-to-face interaction, especially the brief unplanned encounters where important bits of technical and personal information can be exchanged "on the fly". They conclude the simple effects of physical proximity and frequency of interaction probably directly affect the success of collaborations....." (ibid)

This raises the question of how to most effectively support work between colleagues and collaborators when they are necessarily separated by large offices or different workplaces. CRUISER attempts to tackle this problem. It takes its name from "cruising"—the teenage practice of the '50's of piling into someone's car to visit coffee bars in search of social encounters.

Technically, the design assumes the availability of desktop full-motion video communications; high quality full duplex audio; a switched multimedia network under the control of a local computer; and integration of video images and computer-generated graphics. Root [Roo88] says of it:

> "CRUISER is designed round the concept of virtual personal communities which can exist only in a virtual world, a place in which proximity is rendered irrelevant by providing instant access to anyone anywhere. CRUISER derives much of its power from two ideas: first that users can have a variety of mechanisms for browsing the virtual world in search of social encounters. and second, that the virtual world is independent

of the physical world, and can be organised and populated according to the needs of the user".

In practice, CRUISER provides a 2D map of the office building (which may or may not be veridical). The user can wander the corridors, look into other peoples offices, visit the common area or the printer, and so on. Communication is by microphones and video cameras placed in every office and common area.

CRUISER is taking on a real problem of project and team work support. It recognises a subtlety that is often missed—the importance of informal communication. It has some sensitive features, by analogy with workplace practice, to allow several levels of privacy. But there remains a very serious question. Who would want a video camera watching them, and a microphone listening to them in their office? There is a very long history of resistance to any form of monitoring (eg. the tachograph). Is it even desirable that "resistance to change" should be overcome? Bannon et al. [BBD88] raise the spectre of the "Panopticon"—Bentham's prison where the warder sees into every cell—as a very real potential for abuse of CSCW. Computer support has to be sensitive, not just to people's working practices, but to their culture and their politics. It is unlikely that CRUISER will clear this hurdle. Technical excellence is not the prime hallmark of a CSCW application.

2.7   The Arizona Groups Decision Support System (GDSS)

The problem addressed here is the large meeting. Small meetings are familiar to most people. They are rich and flexible. While it is true that fruitful meetings depend on skills that can be taught and learned [OU86], this learning takes place on a strong base of existing experience.

Large meetings are a different problem. They

> "... are time consuming and expensive. They are often seen as boring or irrelevant. They may be ill-attended or unrepresentative. They may be dominated by a few people. They may go round in circles without reaching a decision. Decisions may have more to do with how much time there is left than with the issue in hand. Complex issues may be oversimplified, or presented in a lop-sided way. Important alternatives may be suppressed in setting the agenda. And so on."   [Rob89]

The ability to have a real say in a large meeting concerned with a complex issue would be a new competence. This possibility has been explored at the Management Information Systems Department of the University of Arizona.

The research has concentrated on the development of a Group Decision Support System (GDSS) which is embodied in a Meeting Environment, sometimes also called a "Decision Room".

> "A large U-shaped table is equipped with up to 16 networked micro-computers that are recessed into the table to facilitate interaction among participants. A microcomputer attached to a large screen projection system is also on the network, which permits display of work done at individual workstations, or of aggregated information from the total group. Break-out rooms are equipped with microcomputers that are networked to the microcomputers at the main conference table. The output from these small group sessions can be displayed on the large screen projector for small group presentations and can be updated and integrated with planning session results."   [VNAK]

The system supports a variety of software, including Electronic Brainstorming, Assumption Surfacing, Issue Analysis, Stakeholder Identification and Analysis, etc. These are intended to support a wide variety of group tasks, demands, and styles in a flexible way.

Unusually, the work at Arizona has concentrated on supporting large groups of more than 8 people. The current Environment will support up to 32 people. A new facility is under construction that will support 64 people in one meeting. Some results to date are:

> "Efficiency considerations of Group Decision Support Systems become increasingly apparent as group size increases. It is difficult to demonstrate that GDSS promotes efficiency for small groups (eg. of size 3 to 5). For larger groups (eg. of size 8 and up)

the GDSS enhances group efficiency by facilitating input from all group members in a relatively simultaneous fashion. Members need not "wait their turn" to contribute to the question or problem before the group. ...

Group effectiveness when using decision support systems is enhanced as group size increased. For groups of six to eight or more, the effectiveness of GDSS becomes particularly apparent in facilitating and co-ordination of large numbers of issues associated with a complex question. Small groups, by contrast, often find that while the GDSS is interesting, it is difficult to suggest that any striking measure of increased effectiveness has been attained.

Member satisfaction with the group process is better when the groups are larger. For larger groups, the reduction of equivocality on issues associated with complex problems or questions that exceed the capabilities of individual members or small groups to address is more readily apparent. Larger groups appreciate the structuring inherent with the GDSS to keep the group from becoming "bogged down" or subject to domination by member personalities. Small groups are more frustrated by GDSS constraints, and are less likely to conclude that GDSS is more effective or efficient than an unstructured face-to-face meeting for the relatively less complex questions typically addressed by small groups."

(ibid)

In summary, we can say that systems designed for, or used in support of small groups have had patchy results [RE88]. Usually they were attempting to "improve" an activity people could do reasonably well unaided. In such circumstances, people can afford to be "picky", and the software provided has to be very good indeed.

There is a clear organisational need in industry, in national and local government [GLC85, Coc88], for large meetings to deal with complex or controversial projects [BU88]. Without the involvement of relatively large numbers of people, much necessary expertise and even crucial viewpoints are left out of the decision making process. Unfortunately, to date, large meetings have usually been found to be impracticable and/or ineffective.

The evidence suggests that computer support for things people couldn't do without it (like large meetings) is likely to be appreciated if it works at all. This is re-enforced by the Arizona experience. Although the overall project is ambitious and sophisticated, some of the tools are less so. The microcomputers involved, for instance, are IBM PC's—which are certainly not the most user-friendly machines available. Response times in some applications would be unacceptable in other contexts—for instance, the mean time spent waiting for the screen[2] during Electronic Brainstorming was half a minute! [NAK87] Yet the Meeting Environment provides a way of doing what could not be done without it , and this is appreciated by the users. Again we see that the design concept may be more important than the technical excellence of a CSCW product.

3   Some "CSCW Specific" Concepts

In one sense, CSCW is a new attempt at old problems. In addition to the problems of Office Automation and Management Information Systems mentioned earlier, it is worth mentioning the failures of planning (see [Suc87]) and of participatory democracy in the workplace. (see [BBS79, Rob83, Sal79, RW86])

The central problem lies in the nature of the reality that has to be dealt with. This is best illustrated in a comment by Sheil [She83].

"I had approached those offices convinced (with the confidence of not having realised that there might be an alternative) that office procedures were, at least in principle, clearly defined methods of processing information. Programs, in other words. Things that could be transcribed, analysed, maybe even reprogrammed for a different "machine". But, above all, *I assumed that they existed, independently of my enquiries*. And that is fantasy."

(ibid Emphasis added)

---

[2][Mar89] reports that the original version of Electronic Brainstorming took one minute to send and recover files, but that the current version has a response time of under 12 seconds even with groups of 24.

This section will outline ten concepts that seem to be basic to CSCW. They are not mutually exclusive, and there are many overlaps. They are not a checklist, or taxonomy, against which applications can be measured—although it is interesting to notice their absence or presence in particular applications, and to consider how this relates to their usefulness or otherwise. These "CSCW specific concepts" are based on, and help account for past work in the field. They also form a preliminary agenda for research, design, and implementation of second generation CSCW applications.

"Articulation Work"

> "No representation of the world is either complete or permanent. Rather, any description is a snapshot of historical processes in which differing viewpoints, local contingencies, and multiple interests have been temporarily reconciled.
>
> ..... even apparently simple pieces of information such as entries on fixed forms are the result of many negotiations and struggles. These may include ad hoc decisions by clerks, responses to patron complaints, the organisations policy decisions, the rules of regulatory bodies, and the limits of the local database management systems. In order to create adequate representations, then, office workers must somehow reconcile multiple viewpoints with inconsistent and evolving knowledge bases. Since no centralized authority can possibly anticipate all the contingencies that might arise locally, *office workers always have some discretion* in deciding how this reconciliation is to be accomplished. ....
>
> *Without an understanding of articulation, the gap between requirements and the actual work process in the office will remain inaccessible to analysis. ...... When the articulation of the work is deleted in representations of that work, the resulting task descriptions can only be uneasily superimposed on the flow of work.*
>
> It will always be the case that in any local situation actors "fiddle" or shift requirements in order to get their work done in the face of local contingencies. We argue here that *such articulation* is not extraneous to requirements analysis, but *central to it.*" [GS86]

The calendar management problems that we considered earlier seem to exclude the possibility of articulation work. Entries on fixed forms are kept, if at all, by many people for many diverse reasons. These disparate entries are then unproblematically aggregated to produce a meeting date and time. This procedure seems to ignore Gerson and Star's observation that "even apparently simple pieces of information such as entries on fixed forms are the result of many negotiations and struggles". The experience with automatic meeting scheduling seems to confirm their remark "When the articulation of the work is deleted in representations of that work, the resulting task descriptions can only be uneasily superimposed on the flow of work." The challenge for CSCW is to find ways of supporting work that are negotiable, and do not marginalise the articulation work that lies at the centre of "orderliness" in the office.

"Situated Action"

> "There are few physical activities that are a necessary part of performing the action of turning on a light. Depending on the context, vastly different patterns of behavior can be classified as the same action. For example, turning on a light usually involves flipping a light switch, but in some circumstances it may involve tightening the light bulb (in the basement) or hitting the wall (in an old house). Although we have knowledge about how the action can be performed, this does not define what the action is. The key defining characteristic of turning on the light seems to be that the agent is performing some activity which will cause the light, which was off when the action started, to become on when the action ends. An important side effect of this definition is that we could recognize an observed pattern of activity as "turning on the light" even if we had never seen or thought about that pattern previously."   ([All84] cited in [Suc87])

On which Suchman [Suc87] comments:

"Allen's point is twofold. First, the "same" action as a matter of intended effect can be achieved in any number of ways, where the ways are contingent on circumstance rather than on definitional properties of the action. And secondly, while an action can be accounted for post hoc with reference to its intended effect, an action's course cannot be predicted from knowledge of the actor's intent, nor can the course be inferred from the observation of the outcome."   (p. 34)

She makes a similar observation earlier

".... the problem of meaningful action turns on the observation that behavior is inherently subject to indefinitely many ascriptions of meaning or intent, while meaning and intent are expressible through an indefinite number of possible behaviors."   (p. 3)

And remarks that this is useful and desirable state of affairs.

"It is precisely because our plans are inherently vague—because we can state our intentions without having to describe the actual course that our actions will take—that an intentional vocabulary is so useful for our everyday affairs."   (p. 38)

In effect, Suchman has advanced an impossibility theorem; a conclusive and straightforward argument that there can be no a priori or algorithmic connection between any particular plan and any specific action. This insight underpins the "failure of planning" and has important implications for the design of CSCW applications: they should beware of trying to anticipate too much about any work situation.

The idea of situated action is remarkably similar to the idea of articulation work, yet there is a difference of emphasis which is valuable for an understanding of CSCW. Gerson and Star stress the distinction and yet the connectedness of representation with action. Suchman, on the other hand, stresses the autonomy of plan and action. This is illustrated by the Florence Project. There obviously is an overall plan for dealing with cardiac patients. But this has nothing to do with the nurses' "overview" of the ward—the crucial aspect "discovered" by CSCW analysis. The "overview" is an aid to understanding constantly changing context. It is the best way of situating action—realising the agenda set out in the plan—within this flux of context.

"Mutual Influence"

"Participants should be able to retract, restate, change, or take a totally different position in the light of views and feelings expressed by others."   [Rob91]

A central problem of co-operative working is that people usually do not know the thoughts, intentions, and feelings of, or "facts" available to others with respect to a particular issue. These are discovered in the course of conversations and discussions in formal meetings and informal encounters.

A bad CSCW application can hinder this process in a variety of ways. It can attempt to substitute for meetings, while excluding the emotive and meta-linguistic nuances. It can block informal conversation. The latter is cited by Egido [Egi88] as a major reason for the confinement of videoconferencing to small market niches. Bad systems can also "freeze" viewpoints. A frozen viewpoint is then an "object" that has to be reconnected to other "objects" in some way—whereas in a real conversation, utterances are often integral parts of other utterances. They take their meaning from their immediate context. They are temporary placemarkers in a fluid whole.

A central property of conversation and discussion is that people change their minds (preferences, choices, viewpoints) in the light of the whole discussion, including their own previous expressions. CSCW applications should reflect this. Apart from the problems of inequality noted by Grudin with Electronic Meeting Scheduling, such applications also violate the desideratum of mutual influence. Choices about free time and its meaning (if people can be persuaded to make them) are frozen. The choices are algorithmically put together again as a "conclusion" to the question "when should we meet?". An iterative procedure—assisting rather than automating meeting scheduling—might be an improvement. "Tuesday at 10 looks good for most people. Are you still available?"

"The ability to retract, restate, change, or express different views in the light of the whole conversation means that participants must have access, in some way, to the whole conversation. Nevertheless, applications that support this are not required to be intelligent, or even particularly sophisticated." [Rob91]

The idea of mutual influence has much in common with both situated action and articulation work. This time the stress is on the social context of actions, plans, and representations; on the process of articulation and negotiation, rather than the plans or actions that flow from it. The Open University "Wage Bargainer", considered earlier, was an explicit and reasonably successful attempt to explore the potential of computer support in the exercise of mutual influence.

"Shared Information Space"

"The computer ... as a medium that could be used dynamically ... to help people to share their view of the world with others through joint manipulation of each person's personal models of the situation.

The emphasis on the need to share models ... is echoed in the work of Thompson [Tho84]. He has put forward the concept of an increase in the shared information space of the communicating parties as the key feature of radical innovations in communications technology. In his view, the move from speech, to writing, to print effected three significant changes in the surrounding culture—a change in the ease with which stored human experience can be accessed, an increase in the size of the common information space shared by the communicants, and an increase in the ease with which new ideas can be propagated throughout society. As these features are difficult to measure directly, he proposes a "test of significance" for each as follows:

1. Must affect the way in which people index information;

2. Must increase the range of strategies open to the communicants for the interrupt act;

3. Must increase the probability of transmitting or receiving an interesting but unexpected message.

If we turn out attention to computer communication, we find that most of the available facilities do not provide a very rich information space—especially if the focus is on "real time" facilities." [Ban89]

Shared information space is one of the few ideas unconditionally endorsed by Bannon, who is often rightly more sensitive to the implicit dangers than the potential benefits of CSCW applications. In this context, shared information space is obviously necessary as the context in which articulation work, situated action, and mutual influence fit together. But it provides further and deeper cues. It indicates that the shared information space must include the subjectivities of the participants. More than this, the space is "co-constructed" [FIT] and constantly re-constructed by the participants, even if it appears to have "objective" status.

Finally, shared information space shows how the technological elements and the social matrix may fit symbiotically together. The computer may provide an infrastructure for action. In the best cases, this can be thought of as a backdrop against with the traffic of conversation [Atk79] can realize new potentials and innovative structures by building on human action whose significance had previously been unseen and taken for granted—such as the "interrupt act". Currently we are able to "interrupt"—question and clarify—only in face to face situations. The most revolutionary property of the "shared information space" currently in the process of being born may be the ability to "interrupt"—which is really the ability to participate—in a much larger social space.

Projects such as CRUISER illustrate both the potential and the dangers of such a march into the unknown. In addition to the technology, major new forms of politeness, a much amplified sense of respect for other human beings, will be necessary. Fortunately, the precepts of CSCW—as counterposed to those of "Scientific Management" [Tay47]—give us a reasonable start in this endeavour.

"Shared Material"

> "Two ways of co-ordinating co-operative work can be identified. One is by explicit communication about how the work is to be performed. Another is less explicit, mediated by the **shared material** used in the work **process**. A simple example is the way two people carry a table. A part of the co-ordination may take place as explicit communication, for example in a discussion of how to get a table through a door. When the table is carried, however, the two people can follow each others actions because the actions get mediated through the shared material. This co-ordination is not necessarily explicit. Also it has been learned. There is a big difference between two persons first attempt at carrying something together, and the way people with experience do it. The learning is both on the part of the individual, and on the part of the team. ..... The pattern of co-operation is not fixed, it is often defined by the actors." [Sør89]

Pål Sørgaard's notion of "shared material" is orthogonal to the ideas considered so far, but vital for their realisation. Situated action, mutual influence, etc. all need to be grounded in shared material—else the actions may pass each other meaninglessly like ships in the night. Participants need to share a "world" as well as a "space". But the idea of shared material goes further. In the same paper, Sørgaard proposes that it has a programmatic function. Effective computer support for work processes should support dialogue and joint manipulation of shared objects, because, to anticipate the next section, dialogue is always dialogue about something. GROVE, The "Wage Bargainer", the Florence Project, and the Arizona GDSS all provide shared and manipulable material. Sørgaard himself proposed a railway booking system, where the booking clerks have access to iconic, shared, and manipulable models of the trains and their current seating arrangements. He also proposed that object oriented programming provides a crucial tool in the production of such shared materials.

"Double Level Language"

> "In general, it can be said that any non-trivial collective activity requires effective communication that allows both ambiguity and clarity. These ideas of ambiguity and clarity can be developed as the "cultural" and "formal" aspects of language as used by participants in projects and organisations. "Computer support" is valuable insofar as it facilitates the separation and interaction between the "formal" and the "cultural". Applications and restrictions that support one level at the expense of the other tend to fail.
>
> The "formal" level is essential as it provides a common reference point for participants. A sort of "external world" that can be pointed at, and whose behaviour is rule governed and predictable.
>
> The "cultural" level is a different type of "world". It is an interweaving of subjectivities in which the possible and the counterfactual [Els78] are as significant as the "given"...... interpretation and viewpoint take the place of rules and predictability......
>
> The formal level is meaningless without interpretation, and the cultural level is vacuous without being grounded.[3]" [Rob91]

---

[3] This distinction has been pursued in a more formal way by Lofgren [Lof89].

> "*The linguistic complementarity.* Every language that can naturally be considered a language contains descriptions and interpretations that are complementary within the language. That is, as long as we stay within a language L, we cannot completely describe L only in terms of its own sentences. Both description and interpretation processes (both sentences and interpretation processes; both models and description processes) are needed in interaction for a full account of L. However, there may be a metalanguage, with a higher describability than that of L, allowing a complete description of L. In that case, we say that the complementarity is *transcendable*. If no such metalanguage can exist, the complementarity is *nontranscendable*."

The distinction between "formal" and "cultural" levels of language is considered nontranscendable. One implication of importance is that it is not possible to change (or improve!) both levels simultaneously.

Seymour Papert once said that "learning to learn is always learning to learn about something". The idea of "double level language" is similar to this. Conversation (even conversation about conversation) is always conversation about something.

The living conversation, with changes of perspective, mood, intention, and interpretation, with its constant search for the right words[4], is the "cultural" level. Papert's "something" is the "formal" level as captured in the conversation. If we *move* tables, as in Sørgaard's example, we are moving things with particular physical and aesthetic properties and relations. If we *talk* about tables, then we experience the object (the "something") of our conversation as having formal properties and relations[5]. We may conceptualise this experience as "having a model" or "knowing the logic of ..." or as simply "understanding". We may conceptualise it as the *talking*, and the *something* the talking is about.

Many conversations come unstuck because this distinction cannot be established (perhaps for reasons of time-pressure, or numbers of people involved) or cannot be maintained (perhaps for reasons of complexity or conflict). Laing [Lai76] and Bateson [Bat73] have both explored the pathologies that follow from such breakdowns. The enormous potential value of "computer support" in CSCW is that it may allow the distinction to be maintained with larger numbers of people for more complex problems. Issues that were intractable in "unsupported" dialogue may become amenable to mutual learning. Management of complexity may start to supplant "chop" solutions[6].

The two levels of language are brought together in a "shared information space". The models at the formal level are what we index. The conversation or dialogue at the cultural level is where we need to be able to interrupt unpredictably, and where interesting and unexpected messages happen. Unsatisfying, unco-operative work happens where one or the other level of language is excluded from the shared information space.

The "formal level", in the examples, is the Outliner in GROVE; the Meeting Scheduler layout; the Message Structure in the CO-ORDINATOR™; the Work Sheets in the Florence Project; the spreadsheet in the "Wage Bargainer"; and Electronic Brainstorming (or other menu items) in the Arizona Meeting Environment.

The "cultural level" is absent with the Meeting Scheduler and CO-ORDINATOR™, and this resulted in observable problems. The "cultural level" takes the form of direct talking in the "Wage Bargainer", Florence, and the Meeting Environment; and takes place over the phone in GROVE. Members of the groups could talk to each other about the situation *and the representation of the situation* they were dealing with. They were not barred from interpretation, ambiguity, "feints", questions, comment, conditional suggestions, and all the other things that are possible in conversations.

The elimination of either the cultural or the formal level of language would have resulted in unusable systems. With GROVE, the group needed to know (or to be able to ask) why someone was making changes—not just that they were making changes. Here the "cultural level" was necessary to interpret the "formal level". With the "Wage Bargainer", it was important to know how committed other groups were to their claims—not just that they had made them. Conversely, it would have been difficult and confusing to know about the motive and commitment to a claim without knowing exactly what was being proposed—which was the situation before the introduction of the "Wage Bargainer". Here the "formal level" was necessary to ground the "cultural level". It was important that precision and ambiguity were separated out, and that they could interact, each helping to define, and providing a reference point for the other.

Equality

In the section on "Calendar Management", Grudin's analysis of the problems of automatic meeting scheduling was examined. It seems to point the way for another, different basic concept for CSCW. Grudin [Gru88] repeats the problem in two bullet points:

---

[4] T.S. Elliot's Four Quartets catch this elusive idea best in poetry. He speaks of words bending and breaking under the stain of communication—of finally only having the right words for the things we no longer wish to say.

[5] If it does not, we are not talking about tables, we are defining them.

[6] For instance, the "guillotine", the majority vote, the dictate—the general Arthurian approach of cutting the Gordian Knot.

- "The application fails because it requires that some people do additional work, while those people are not the ones who perceive a direct benefit from the use of the application.

- The design process fails because our intuitions are poor for multi-user applications—decision makers see the potential benefits for people similar to themselves, but don't see the implications of the fact that extra work will be required of others."

Grudin suggests that this is not an insurmountable problem.

> "Computer support for the activities of individuals in their group and organisational contexts will unquestionably change the way people live in significant ways. It is difficult to imagine anything more important of fascinating than trying to understand and guide that change. ....
>
> We need to have a better understanding of how groups and organisations function and evolve than is reflected in most of the systems that have been developed. At the same time, we also need to know more about individual differences in responding to technology if we are to develop systems that can support entire groups. One approach may be the contextual research of John Whiteside and his colleagues [WBH87]. Another is that used at Aarhus University in Denmark: "The Aarhus people start out with a problem situation defined by workers, and work beside them a long time in order to develop a new system that is "owned" by the workers ...... This is different from traditional systems development, as you can imagine, and you can't simply package a set of techniques to do the job ... see Ehn and Kyng [EK87]" (Liam Bannon, personal communication)"   [Gru88]

Equality, in the complex sense of sensitivity to feelings, intuitions, and perspectives which are not necessarily articulated, and not usually considered part of the work process at all, is a necessary condition for "understanding and guiding that change". Understanding the distribution of benefit and work in different contexts is an important first step in this area—as is the transformation suggested by Bannon of the concept of "ownership".

4   A Last Note

There is an implicit difficulty with most of the concepts considered to far. Distinctions have been made between "representation of work" and "articulation of work"; between "plan" and "situated action"; between "shared space" and "shared material"; between "formal" and "cultural" levels of language; and between "who will do the work" and "who will benefit from it". This was inevitable. Conversations have fixed points and flowing movements. Contexts, assumptions, and much else has to be "taken-for-granted" in order to concentrate on some particular aspect, action, topic, or objective (as in this chapter). Any dialogue makes distinctions, and the distinctions depend on an uncountable number of assumptions.

This is essentially Suchman's [Suc87] point about a "continually receding horizon of understandings". Citing an experiment by Garfinkel [Gar72], she says that his aim

> "was to press the common sense notion that background knowledge is a body of things, thought but unsaid, that stands behind behaviour and makes it intelligible. His request was that the students provide a complete description of what was communicated, in one particular conversation, as a matter of participants' shared knowledge. Students were asked to report a simple conversation by writing on the left hand side of a piece of paper what was said, and on the right hand side what it was that they and their partners actually understood was being talked about.
>
> ...... they gave up with the complaint that the task was impossible.

The students' dilemma was not simply that they were being asked to write "everything" that was said, where that consisted of some bounded, albeit vast, content. It was rather that the task of enumerating what was talked about itself extended what was talked about, providing a continually receding horizon of understandings to be accounted for. The assignment, it turned out, was not to describe some existing content, but to generate it." (ibid p. 46)

And again,

"Actual attempt to include the background assumptions of a statement as part of its semantic content, however, run up against the fact that there is no fixed set of assumptions that underlie a given statement. As a consequence, the elaboration of background assumptions is fundamentally *ad hoc* and arbitrary, and each elaboration of assumptions in principle introduces further assumptions to be elaborated, *ad infinitum*." (ibid p. 60)

To rephrase: conversations and distinctions rely on assumptions that are not only uncountable—they may not exist until they are generated. To paraphrase Bateson, this chapter has talked about CSCW distinctions as if they were somethings, and somethings that could be counted. But of course thats all nonsense. Distinctions cannot be counted any more than the bats in a psychiatrists inkblot—because there are none.

What are the implications for CSCW?

- Firstly, reflectively, it must never take itself too seriously.

- Second, empirically, it must anticipate the collapse of distinctions as a conversation refocuses.

- Third, methodologically, it will be unpredictable when and if context or assumption will become salient, and what impact it will have on the distinctions in the conversation. de Zeeuw & Robinson [ZR89] have pointed to the *"flipover"* phenomenon in the context of "double level language". The "formal" level may become the interpretation, and the previous interpretation its object, suddenly fixed, formalised. This has of course long been recognised as a component of innovation. Its salience here is its ubiquity in the most ordinary of everyday exchanges. Similar remarks can be made about the "flipover" possibilities of "representation/articulation", "plan/situated action", "benefit/work", and so on. Which is which depends on local circumstances, local actors, and local "closures". "Flipover" is also why the subject matter of CSCW is not amenable to the formalism of prediction (and hence classical experimental method). The possibility of prediction assumes a causality that is not present in local closures: in re-interpretation and situated action.

- Fourth, for design, the implication is that "flipover" can be anticipated, but not predicted. It is the essence of human, as opposed to machine, activity systems. The question is whether design will support or try to block the possibility of "flipover". Both the CO-ORDINATOR™ and Meeting Schedulers assume that the processes embodied in their formalisms will be concluded, should be concluded, and will be the same processes at the end as they were at the beginning. GROVE and the "Wage Bargainer" make no such assumptions about use, and consequently integrate smoothly into human activities. They allow for "conversational repair"; for *re-establishing* the distinction between the talking and the somethings we are talking about. From the point of view of a systems designer, this will look like "unanticipated use"—artifacts may be used in conversational ways and conversations may at times be regarded as artifacts. From a full CSCW point of view, this is "redesign in use", and should be allowed and supported by the application. In conclusion, it may be said that *CSCW applications should support the process of making distinctions, not the distinctions themselves.*

References

[ACM90] ACM. *Proceedings of the Conference on Computer Supported Cooperative Work (CSCW'90) (Los Angeles, California)*, October 1990.

[Act89] Action Technologies. *The CO-ORDINATOR II*, 1989.

[All84]   T.J. Allen. *Managing the Flow of Technology*. MIT Press, Cambridge, 1984.

[Atk79]   R. Atkin. A kinematics for decision making. In G. Pask and M. Robinson, editors, *Current Scientific Approaches to Decision Making in Complex Systems*, London, 1979. ARI European Research Office.

[Aus62]   J.L. Austin. *How to Do Things with Words*. Harvard University Press Cambridge MA, Cambridge, 1962.

[Ban89]   L. Bannon. Shared information spaces: Cooperative user support networks. In *Proceedings of the Conference "Mutual Uses of Science and Cybernetics" (Amsterdam, The Netherlands, March 27-April 1)*. University of Amsterdam, 1989.

[Bat73]   G. Bateson. *Steps to an Ecology of Mind*. Paladin, London, 1973.

[BB88]   G. Bjerknes and T. Bratteteig. The memoirs of two survivors: or the evaluation of a computer system for co-operative work. In *Proceedings of the Conference on Computer-Supported Cooperative Work (Portland, Oregon, September 26-28)*, New York, 1988. ACM.

[BB91]   J.M. Bowers and S.D. Benford, editors. *Studies in Computer Supported Co-operative Work: Theory, Practice, and Design*, Amsterdam and New York, 1991. North Holland.

[BBBG88]   T.K. Bikson, J.H. Bair, R. Barry, and C.E. Grantham. Communication, co-ordination, and group performance. In *Proceedings of the Conference on Computer-Supported Cooperative Work (Portland, Oregon, September 26-28)*, New York, 1988. ACM. Panel Discussion.

[BBD88]   L. Bannon, N. Bjørn-Andersen, and B. Due-Thomsen. Computer support for cooperative work: a appraisal and critique. In Bullinger et al, editor, *EURINFO'88: Information systems for organizational effectiveness*, Amsterdam, 1988. North-Holland.

[BBS79]   T. Baumgartner, T.R. Burns, and D. Sekulic. *Self Management, Market, and Political Institutions in Conflict*. Work and Power Sage, London, 1979.

[BC88]   J. Bowers and J. Churcher. Local and global structuring of computer mediated communication: Developing linguistic perspectives on CSCW in COSMOS. In *Proceedings of the Conference on Computer-Supported Cooperative Work (Portland, Oregon, September 26-28)*, New York, 1988. ACM.

[Bee75]   S. Beer. Fanfare for effective freedom: Cybernetic praxis in government. In *Platform for Change*, Chichester, United Kingdom, 1975. J. Wiley and Sons.

[Bee81]   S. Beer. *Brain of the Firm*. J. Wiley and Sons, Chichester, United Kingdom, second edition, 1981.

[BRS91]   L. Bannon, M. Robinson, and K. Schmidt, editors. *Proceedings of the Second European Conference on Computer Supported Cooperative Work*, Dordrecht, The Netherlands, 1991. Kluwer Academic Publishers.

[BU88]   T. R. Burns and R. Ueberhorst. *Creative Democracy: Systematic Conflict Resolution and Policymaking in World of High Science and Technology*. Praeger, New York. 1988.

[Coc88]   A. Cochrane, editor. *Developing Local Economic Strategies*. Open University Press, Milton Keynes, 1988.

[Coo80]   M. Cooley, editor. *Architect or Bee?* Hand & Brain, Slough, United Kingdom, 1980.

[Dur88]   T. Durham. Organisational dinosaurs take on a human face. *Computing*, November 1988.

[Egi88]   C. Egido. Videoconferencing as a techology to support group work: a review of its failure. In *Proceedings of the Conference on Computer-Supported Cooperative Work (Portland, Oregon, September 26-28)*, New York, 1988. ACM.

[EGR91]   C. Ellis, S. Gibbs, and G. Rein. Groupware: some issues and experiences. *Communications of the ACM*, 34(1):38–58, January 1991.

[Ehr87a]   S.F. Ehrlich. Social and psychological factors influencing the design of office communication systems. In *Proceedings of CHI'87 and GI'87: Human Factors in Computing Systems (Toronto, Canada, April 5-9)*, 1987.

[Ehr87b]   S.F. Ehrlich. Strategies for encouraging successful adoption of office communication systems. *ACM Transactions on Office Information Systems*, 5:340–357, 1987.

[EK87]   P. Ehn and M. Kyng. The collective resource approach to systems design. In G. Bjerknes, P. Ehn, and M. Kyng, editors, *Computers and Democracy—a Scandinavian Challenge*, Aldershot, United Kingdom, 1987. Gower.

[Els78]   J. Elster. *Logic and Society: Contradictions and Possible Worlds*. J. Wiley and Sons, Chichester, United Kingdom, 1978.

[FGHW88]   F. Flores, M. Graves, B. Hartfield, and T. Winograd. Computer systems and the design of organizational interaction. *ACM Transactions on Office Information Systems*, 6(2):153–172, April 1988.

[FIT]   O. Forsgren, K. Ivanov, and N. Torbjorn. A co-constructive view of the information society: The case of the NUDU project in Unea, Sweden. Draft Photocopy.

[Flo82]   F.C. Flores. *Management and communication in the office of the future*. Hermenet Inc., San Francisco, 1982.

[Gar72]   H. Garfinkel. Remarks on ethnomethodology. In J. Mckinney and E. Tiryakian, editors, *Directions in Sociolinguistics: the Ethnology of Communication*, New York, 1972. Holt, Rinehart & Winston.

[GC88]   C.E. Grantham and R.P. Carasik. *The Phenomenology of Computer Supported Co-operative Work*. Interpersonal Software, Berkeley, California, 1988.

[GKE90]   J. Galegher, R. Kraut, and C. Egido. *Intellectual Teamwork: Social and Technological Foundations of Cooperative Work*. Lawrence Ehrlbaum, London and New Jersey, 1990.

[GLC85]   The London industrial strategy. Technical report, GLC (Greater London Council), London, 1985.

[Gre88]   I. Greif, editor. *Computer-Supported Cooperative Work: A Book of Readings*. Morgan Kaufmann, San Mateo, California, 1988.

[Gru88]   J. Grudin. Why CSCW applications fail: Problems in the design and evaluation of organizational interfaces. In *Proceedings of the Conference on Computer-Supported Cooperative Work (Portland, Oregon, September 26-28)*, New York, 1988. ACM.

[GS86]   E. Gerson and S. Star. Analysing due process in the workplace. *ACM Transactions on Office Information Systems*, 4(3), 1986.

[GS88]   I. Greif and L. Suchman, editors. *CSCW '88: Proceedings of the Conference on Computer Supported Co-operative Work (Portland, Oregon, September 26-29)*, 1988.

[JOW86]   B. Johnson, M. Olson, and G. Weaver. Using a computer-based tool to support collaboration: A field experiment, 1986.

[KGE88]   R. Kraut, J. Galegher, and C. Egido. Patterns of communication and contact in scientific research collaboration. In *Proceedings of the Conference on Technology and Co-operative Work (Tucson, Arizona, February 25-27)*, Hillsdale, New Jersey, 1988. Erlbaum.

[Lai76]   R.D. Laing. *Do You Love Me?* Pantheon, New York, 1976.

[Loc76]   E. Locke. The nature and cause of job satisfaction. In M. Dunnette, editor, *Handbook of Industrial and Organisational Psychology*, Chicago, 1976. Rand McNally College Publishing Co.

[Lof89]   L. Lofgren. Cybernetics, science, and complementarity. In *Proceedings of the Conference "Mutual Uses of Science and Cybernetics" (Amsterdam, The Netherlands, March 27-April 1)*. University of Amsterdam, 1989.

[Lyy89]   K. Lyytinen. Computer Supported Co-operative Work (CSCW)—Issues and challenges. Technical report, Department of Computer Science, University of Jyväskylä, Finland, 1989.

[Mar89]   B. Martz. Personal communication, 1989.

[NAK87]   J.F. Nunamaker, L.M. Applegate, and B.R Konsynski. Facilitating group creativity: Experience with a Group Decision Support System. *Journal of Management Information Systems*, 3(4), 1987.

[OU86]   Open University. *Co-operative Working*, Milton Keynes, 1986. Centre for Continuing Education, Open University Press.

[Pas80]   G. Pask. The limits of togetherness. In S.H. Lavington, editor, *Proceedings of Information Processing'80*, Amsterdam, 1980. North Holland.

[RE88]   G.L. Rein and C.A. Ellis. The Nick Summer experiment: A field study of the usage of meeting support technology by software design teams. MCC Technical Report STP-018-88, MCC, Software Technology Program, Austin, Texas, 1988.

[Rob83]   M. Robinson, editor. *Size is a historic problem in all communities*, London, September 1983. Kingston & Richmond Co-operative Development Agency. Proceedings of the Inaugural Meeting of theLarge Co-operatives Network.

[Rob89]   M. Robinson. Mass conversation: An examination of computer techniques for many to many communication. In *Proceedings of the Conference "Problems of Impossible Worlds"*. Systeemgroep Nederland, 1989.

[Rob90]   M. Robinson. Pay bargaining in workers' co-operatives. In F. Geyer and J. van der Zouwen, editors, *Self Referencing in Social Systems*, USA, 1990. Intersystems Publications.

[Rob91]   M. Robinson. Double level languages and co-operative working. *AI & Society*, 5:34–60, 1991.

[Roo88]   R.W. Root. Design of a multi-media vehicle for social browsing. In *Proceedings of the Conference on Computer-Supported Cooperative Work (Portland, Oregon, September 26-28)*, New York, 1988. ACM.

[RW86]   J. Rothschild and J. Whitt. *The Co-operative Workplace: Potentials and dilemmas of organizational democracy and participation*. Cambridge University Press, Cambridge, 1986.

[Sal79]   G. Salaman. *Work Organisations: Resistance and Control*. Longman, London, 1979.

[Sch91]   K. Schmidt. Riding a tiger, or computer supported cooperative work. In *Proceedings of the Second European Conference on Computer Supported Cooperative Work*, Dordrecht, The Netherlands, 1991. Kluwer Academic Publishers.

[Sco78]   M.S. Scott Morton. *Decision Support Systems*. Addison Wesley, Reading, Massachusetts, 1978.

[Sea79]   J.R. Searle. *Expression & Meaning: Studies in the Theory of Speech Acts*. Cambridge University Press, Cambridge, 1979.

[She83]   B. Sheil. Coping with complexity. *Office Technology and People*, 1, 1983.

[Sør89]   P. Sørgaard. Object oriented programming and computerised shared material. Technical report, Computer Science Department, Aarhus University, Denmark, 1989.

[Suc87]   L.A. Suchman. *Plans and Situated Actions: the problem of human machine communication*. Cambridge University Press, New York, 1987.

[Tay47]   F. Taylor. *Scientific Management*. Harper & Row, 1947.

[Tho84]   G. Thompson. Three characterizations of communications revolutions. In S. Winkler, editor, *Computer Communication: Impacts and Implications*, New York, 1984. International Conference on Computer Communication.

[VNAK]   D. Vogel, J. Nunamaker, L. Applegate, and B. Konsynski. Group decision support systems: Determinants of success. Forthcoming.

[WBH87]   J. Whiteside, J. Bennett, and K. Holtzblatt. Usability engineering: our experience and evolution. In M. Helander, editor, *Handbook of Human Computer Interaction*, Amsterdam, 1987. North Holland.

[WF86]   T. Winograd and F. Flores. *Understanding Computers and Cognition*. Addison Wesley, Reading, Massachusetts, 1986.

[ZR89]   G. de Zeeuw and M. Robinson. "Support, survival, & culture": An introduction to the OOC research program. Technical report, University of Amsterdam, Amsterdam, 1989.

CSCW: Four Characters in Search of a Context*

Liam J. Bannon
Department of Computer Science
Aarhus University
DK-8000 Aarhus C, Denmark
bannon@daimi.dk

Kjeld Schmidt
Cognitive Systems Group
Risø National Laboratory
DK-4000 Roskilde, Denmark
kschmidt@risoe.dk

Abstract: The title of this paper was chosen to highlight the fact that the label CSCW, although widely adopted as the acronym for the field of Computer Supported Cooperative Work, has been applied to computer applications of very different ilk. It is not at all clear what are the unique identifying elements of this research area. This paper provides a framework for approaching the issue of cooperative work and its possible computer support. The core issues are identified and prospects for the field are outlined.

1. What is CSCW?

In a recent seminar, Irene Greif (1988b), one of the originators of the term 'Computer-Supported Cooperative Work' (together with Paul Cashman), commented that they coined the phrase partly as a shorthand way of referring to a set of concerns about supporting multiple individuals working together with computer systems. The meaning of the individual words in the term were not especially highlighted. With the subsequent abbreviation of the term Computer Supported Cooperative Work to that of CSCW, attention to the individual words was expected to be even further reduced, as the field would come to be represented simply by the acronym. This has not occurred. This may be in part due to the fact that the boundaries of the field are difficult to circumscribe and that a core definition of the field does not exist, – other than the very descriptive one of CSCW being a field which covers anything to do with computer support for activities in which more than one person is involved.

If we take this extremely broad categorization of the field, it is hard to see how anything of the form of a coherent research area can emerge from such a loose description. However, as noted by Bannon et al. (1988), having CSCW simply as an "umbrella term" could be advantageous:

"What at first sight might appear to be a weakness of the field, having such a diversity of backgrounds and perspectives, is seen by us as a potential strength, if utilized properly. We believe that for the moment the name CSCW simply serves as a useful forum for a variety of researchers with different backgrounds and techniques to discuss their work, and allows for the cross-fertilization of ideas, for the fostering of multi-disciplinary perspectives on the field that is essential if we are to produce applications that really are useful"

Granted that this interdisciplinary commingling has already occurred, the time may now be ripe for a more incisive probe of what the conceptual underpinnings of the field might be. Already at the 1988 CSCW Conference one could sense a certain tension among the participants, which we believe was generated by the lack of a shared perspective on the field.

1.1. The Crux of CSCW

According to the British sociologist of science, Richard Whitley, a research area is defined by a *problem situation*: "A research area can be said to exist when scientists concur on the nature of the uncertainty common to a set of problem situations" (Whitley, 1974).

Applying this criterion to our topic, we may ask what are the problem situations addressed by researchers working under the CSCW label? Are the problem situations in fact related? Do scientists in the area actually concur on the uncertainty common to this set of problem situations? Are they exploring the same basic issues? This is questionable when one notes that studies formerly appearing under the rubric of Office Information Systems or Computer Mediated Communication now appear under the CSCW banner.

Indeed, unpacking the individual characters in the term, the "CW" or "Cooperative Work" aspect has itself come under some scrutiny. What does it mean? Collaborative work, collective work, group work, cooperative work: do the distinctions matter for our purposes? Well, to the extent that we are supposedly trying to support "it" with computers, it probably would be a good idea to know what we are talking about, as certainly at present the label seems to be applied to just about anything, like face-to-face meeting facilitation, desk-top presentation, project management, multi-user applications, text-filtering software, electronic mail, computer conferencing, hypertext, etc.

Even if we have some shared notion of what "cooperative work" is, what is the role of "CS", of "Computer Support" for this activity? Today, performing cooperative work through the medium of the computer can be an extremely trying and exasperating experience. It has been said that what we have to be concerned about in thinking of computer technology with respect to cooperative work is not the "support" notion, but first of all ensuring that the computer does not *disrupt* the collaborative activity that is already going on!

CSCW cannot be defined in term of the *techniques* being applied. CSCW is a research area aimed at the design of application systems, and like any other application area CSCW, in its

What's in a name? And does it really matter, after all? In some sense, in the great scheme of things, names don't matter that much in many situations. As long as we all know what is designated by the name, the name itself is of minor importance. However, we should occasionally examine the assumptions that may be implicit in the name. For instance, in the song "A boy named Sue", the name did matter! Likewise, the name 'Artificial Intelligence' (– "the Very Idea!" as the philosopher John Haugeland notes in the title of one of his books), implies a certain view on the nature of "intelligence", so also with the term "Expert Systems". In the same vein, the name 'Office Automation' promised to automate office work, a project since desertvedly denounced as ludicrous and ultimately abandoned as unattainable. Do we have similar problems with the name Computer Supported Cooperative Work?

* With apologies to Luigi Pirandello, author of the play "Six Characters in Search of an Author".

search for applicable techniques, potentially draws upon the whole field of computer science. What unites CSCW is *the support requirements of cooperative work*. Accordingly, a technology-driven approach to CSCW will inevitably dilute the field. To some extent, the current lack of unity of the CSCW field bears witness to that.

CSCW should be conceived as an endeavor to understand the nature and characteristics of cooperative work with the objective of designing adequate computer-based technologies. That is, CSCW is a research area addressing questions like the following: What are the specific characteristics of cooperative work as opposed to work performed by individuals in seclusion? What are the reasons for the emergence of cooperative work patterns? How can computer-based technology be applied to enhance cooperative work relations? How can computers be applied to alleviate the logistic problems of cooperative work? How should designers approach the complex and delicate problems of designing systems that will shape social relationships? And so forth. The focus is to *understand*, so as to *better support*, cooperative work itself.

1.2. The Target Area of CSCW: Cooperative Work

'Cooperative work', the term picked by Greif and Cashman to designate the application area to be addressed by the new field, happens to be a term with a long history in the social sciences. It was used as early as the first half of the 19th century by economists (e.g., Ure, 1835; Wakefield, 1849) and was picked up and defined formally by Marx (1867) as "multiple individuals working together in a planned way in the same production process or in different but connected production processes." In this century, the term has been used extensively in the German tradition of sociology of work (e.g., Popitz et al., 1957; Bahrdt, 1958; Dahrendorf, 1959; Kern and Schumann, 1970; Mickler et al., 1976; as well as by other authors (e.g., Miller and Form, 1964; Thompson, 1967).

There are many forms of cooperative work, and distinctions between such terms as cooperative work, collaborative work, collective work, and group work, are not well established in the CSCW community. Without wishing to impose a formal taxonomy on a set of terms that have loosely defined everyday connotations, we believe that analyzing the meaning of cooperative work is necessary due to the wildly disparate uses of the term in the field at present. For instance, for Ehn (1988) *all work* is essentially cooperative, in that it depends upon others for its successful performance. Taking this stance would seem to imply that there is no additional clarification achieved by adding the term 'cooperative' to that of 'work'. At another extreme, Sørgaard (1987) has a very specific set of criteria for what would count as cooperative work, for instance, that it is non-hierarchical, relatively autonomous, etc. From yet another perspective, e.g. that of Howard (1987), the term 'cooperative work' is inappropriate because of the ideology inherent in the term, a 'too sweet' label for the realities of everyday work situations. He prefers an allegedly more open term, 'collective work', which he sees as being induced in a variety of ways through the use of computers in general. Kling (1988) concurs, arguing however for the more open, if not exactly neutral, term 'coordinated work'.

Replacing the term 'cooperative work' with that of 'group work' or defining the former by the latter does not help much. Greif, in an introduction to the field (1988a), claims that CSCW is an "identifiable research field focused on the role of the computer in group work". The term 'group' is quite blurred and is often used to designate any kind of social interaction. For instance, in his book on *Groupware*, Johansen (1988) mentions "teams, projects, meetings, committees, task forces" etc. as examples of "groups" and even includes interaction among workers, supervisors and management in manufacturing operations, "often across both distances and work shifts", under the same notion.

Generally, however, a group is defined as a relatively closed and fixed ensemble[1] of people sharing the same 'goal' and engaged in incessant and direct communication. The notion of a shared goal is murky and dubious, however. The cooperative process of decision making in a group is a very differentiated process involving the interaction of multiple goals of different scope and nature as well as different heuristics, conceptual frameworks, etc. We will revert to this point later in this paper. For now, the informal definition suggested by Bahrdt (1984) will do: we will use the term 'group' if its members perceive themselves as a "we". This usage is in accord with daily usage of the word 'group'. Even with this, more relaxed, definition of 'group', however, the notion of group work does not encompass the rich and complex reality of cooperative work. As pointed out by Popitz and associates in their classic study (1957), the group is not the specific unit of cooperation in modern industrial plants. The workers operating a rolling mill in a steel plant, for example, cooperate by monitoring and adjusting the state of the machine system. They are often not constituted as a "group" and they often interact without communicating in the sense of symbolic interaction. Likewise, in various domains, for instance administrative work, engineering design, and scientific research, actors often cooperate at "arm's length", without direct communication and without necessarily knowing each other or knowing of each other, via a more or less *shared information space*, that is, a 'space' comprising data, personal beliefs, shared concepts, professional heuristics etc.

So, the concepts of "group" and "group work" designate specific types of cooperative relations characterized by shared responsibilities. In some cases, groups are formed spontaneously in response to the requirements of the situation. In a hospital, for instance, a group ("task force") is formed on an *ad hoc* basis to deal with an emergency situation. In other cases, groups have a quasi-permanent character like, for instance, project teams. While such situations do belong to the problem situations addressed by CSCW, we certainly do not want to restrict the scope of CSCW to those cases where the responsibility of performing a task has been allocated to or assumed by a relatively closed and fixed collective.

Cooperative work is constituted by *work processes that are related as to content*, that is, processes pertaining to the production of a particular product or service.[2] In contrast to the spontaneous linking of interrelated production processes via an anonymous market, cooperative work relationships are characterized by being planned or rather premeditated.

Cooperative work comprises *indirect* as well as *direct* and *distributed* as well as *collective* modes of interaction. Work conducted *collectively*, by a group, is merely one specific mode of cooperative work. Cooperative work may also be conducted in a *distributed* manner, i.e., by an ensemble of semi-autonomous workers changing their behavior as circumstances change and planning their own strategies. Furthermore, cooperative work may be conducted *indirectly*, i.e., mediated by the changing state of the transformation process, or *directly*, i.e. by means of interpersonal communication.

---

1 The term "ensemble" has been used by Sartre (1960) to designate an, as yet, unstructured aggregation of people; we use it as a neutral and general designation of the set of people engaged in a cooperative undertaking that does not imply any specific organizational form.

2 Thus, the boundaries of cooperative work networks are defined by actual cooperative behavior and are not necessarily congruent with the boundaries of formal organizations. A cooperative work process may cross corporate boundaries and may involve partners in different companies at different sites, each of the partners producing but a component of the finished product. On the other hand, a corporation may have multiple cooperative work processes with no mutual interaction.

The concept of cooperative work does not imply a particular degree of participation or self-determination on the part of the workers, nor a particularly democratic management style. Actually, the concept has historically been developed and used in analyses of the harsh realities of industrial life (e.g., Ure, 1835; Marx, 1867; Popitz et al., 1957). Nor are we saying, "Thou shalt cooperate!"; cooperative work is not better, or worse, than individual work. It is merely technically necessary or economically beneficial in certain work environments.

Work having multifarious facets, it is no wonder that multiple, more or less synonymous terms abound: collective work, collaborative work, coordination, articulation work etc. We do not have to abstain from using any of these terms. They all have different connotations and designate different types or facets of cooperative work. The term 'collective work', for instance, designates cooperative work where the cooperating ensemble is sharing the responsibility for accomplishing the task. The emphasis of the concept is the fusion of the members of the ensemble into a whole, a 'collective'. That is, the term is conceptually close to 'group' and particular 'collaborative work', on the other hand, gives special stress to a particular 'team' work. The term 'collaborative work', on the other hand, gives special stress to a particular expression of interaction or organization such as comradely feelings, equality of status, formation of a distinct group identity etc. Hence, unlike research areas like Artificial Intelligence and Office Automation, the name of our field is quite pertinent.

In sum, the term "cooperative work" is the general and neutral designation of multiple persons working together to produce a product or service. It does not imply specific forms of interaction or organization such as comradely feelings, equality of status, formation of a distinct group identity etc. Hence, unlike research areas like Artificial Intelligence and Office Automation, the name of our field is quite pertinent.

2.   Perceptions of the CSCW field

Within the field of CSCW, loosely construed, one can find a number of different perspectives adopted by researchers. Howard (1988) coined the term "strict constructionists" to describe those in the field focused on the development of computer systems to support group work, and he noted their tendency to use themselves as objects of analysis in the provision of support tools. These people, mainly implementers, are interested in building widgets, and they see the area of CSCW as a possible leverage point for creating novel applications. Most of these people equate the CSCW field with Groupware. What is Groupware? In a relatively straightforward fashion, it can be defined simply as software that supports groups. There are a number of problems with accepting this terminological sleight of hand. First of all, the Groupware label explicitly limits the attention of CSCW to 'groups', with all the ensuing problems discussed above.

People working on Groupware have a focused goal, namely to design new widgets that might support teams or groups. On the down side, however, often the focus is only on supporting the design group itself, 'widgets for the boys', so to speak. Generalizing from one's own research setting to settings in the "real world" can be fraught with problems, as many researchers have learned to their cost. The Groupware community does this because it is unashamedly technology-oriented. It does not need to understand the application area. It focuses on solving the technical problems of providing multiple-user facilities for any application program (database, word processor, calendar, etc.) and can be viewed as an extension of the user interface to cater for multiple users (Greif, 1988b). Thus, perhaps Greif (1988b) is correct in viewing Groupware as a passing fad, or phase, in that all software in the future will be Groupware to the extent that it will support cooperative work patterns, e.g., word processors facilitating joint authoring, just as state-of-the-art software is now 'user friendly'.

To summarize, we reject the equation of Groupware with CSCW because of its technological focus and its narrowness in the face of the multiplicity of social forms of cooperative work manifest in the world.

Howard (1988) has labelled the remainder of the field, the larger part, as "loose constructionists", a heterogeneous collection of people, some of whom are drawn to the area due to their dissatisfaction with current uses of technology to support work processes, others because they see in this area a chance for groups who traditionally have not had a voice in the design of computer systems to have one. Some wish to make the design of computing systems more democratic, so that the resulting systems will actually support cooperative working, rather than hinder it, where the word 'cooperative' here has a positive value associated with it, connected with workplace democracy. Part of the rationale here is that for truly 'cooperative' work, in their sense, one should design systems in a cooperative manner, and ways of achieving this need to be investigated, tried out, and propagated. So a focus is on alternatives to traditional systems and systems design, alternative ways of doing design, of involving users, etc. (see, e.g., Ehn and Kyng, 1987; Kyng, 1988; Bødker et al., 1988). Howard believes that many in this group focus ultimately too much on the *design* of technology, in a sense believing if we get the technology right, then cooperative working will follow. He believes that the problem is not so much that computer systems do not support cooperative work, or that computers disrupt it, but rather that they induce or compel a "collectivization" of work in ways that we do not fully understand, and it is this process that needs to be understood and should serve as the basis for a scientific discipline of CSCW.

Yet another group, not explicitly identified in Howard's analysis, though some would fit in his second category, are those social scientists interested in studying the use of novel CSCW applications and also showing how their kinds of analyses of group processes (with or without mediating technologies) might affect the future design of CSCW systems. Some of this work has the air of "what social science can do for you" about it, without much idea of exactly how these insights might be useful in the design of useful CSCW systems, though others are more directly attempting to apply their insights in design teams.

3.   Core Issues for CSCW

Whereas Groupware addresses the technical problems of enhancing the human-computer interface by providing multiple-user facilities for, in principle, any application program, CSCW needs to address the following specific requirements of cooperative work:

- articulating cooperative work;
- sharing an information space;
- adapting the technology to the organization, and *vice versa*.

In our opinion, meeting these requirements constitute the core issues of the CSCW field.

3.1.   Supporting Articulation Work

Any cooperative effort involves a number of secondary tasks of mediating and controlling the association of individuals. First, tasks are to be allocated to different members of the cooperating ensemble: which worker is to do what, where, when? Second, by assigning a task to a worker, that worker is rendered accountable for accomplishing that task according to certain criteria: when, where, how, how soon, what level of quality, etc. Finally, in the terminology suggested by Strauss (1985), cooperative work requires 'articulation work': The numerous tasks, clusters of tasks, and segments of the trajectory of tasks need to be meshed. Likewise, the efforts of individuals and ensembles need to be meshed. In the words of Gerson and Star (1986), articulation consists of all the tasks needed "to coordinate a particular task, including scheduling subtasks, recovering from errors, and assembling resources."

In work environments characterized by task uncertainty, due to, e.g., an unstable or contradictory environment, task allocation and articulation cannot be planned in advance. In these work environments task allocation and articulation is negotiated and renegotiated more or less continuously. This has been demonstrated very convincingly in the domain of office work.

The commonly accepted view of what constitutes an office still relies heavily on the traditional bureaucratic model: people who perform a number of tasks according to a set of well-specified 'procedures', that have been developed by management as efficient and effective means to certain ends. In this model, many assumptions are made about the rational basis for action, and the common goals of the employees within the organization. The traditional formal organization chart is presumed to show the actual lines of authority and the "correct" pattern of information flow and communication. Despite many studies, dating as far back as the First World War, by industrial sociologists and others pointing to the existence of informal networks of communication (the "grapevine") and of informal groups that affect organizational activity by controlling information and coordinating work output, the early computer systems developed to "automate the office" were built by designers who implicitly assumed much of the traditional office model. Designers were "automating a fiction" as Beau Sheil (1983) so aptly put it.

Such systems have now been admitted as failures (Lyytinen & Hirschheim, 1987). Researchers and practitioners are beginning to appreciate the inherent complexity of supposedly 'routine' tasks and the difficulty of capturing the tacit knowledge and "day-to-day" informal practices of office workers. More recent studies, performed by anthropologists and sociologists, have emphasized the rich nature of many allegedly 'routine' activities in the office and the complex pattern of decision-making and negotiation engaged in by co-workers, even at relatively 'low' positions within the organization (Wynn, 1979; Suchman, 1983; Gerson and Star, 1986). Suchman (1983) gives a concise account of this discrepancy between the office procedures that supposedly govern office work and the practical action carried out by office workers. She notes: "the procedural structure of organizational activities is the product of the orderly work of the office, rather than the reflection of some enduring structure that stands behind that work." It is not that office procedures are irrelevant, it is just that these procedures are constituted by a number of activities, often requiring negotiation with co-workers, the result of which can be interpreted as performance according to procedures.

The 'informal' interactions that take place in the office thus not only serve important psychological functions in terms of acting as a human support network for people, for example, providing companionship and emotional support, but are crucial to the actual conduct of the work process itself. Evidence for this is apparent when workers "work-to-rule", i.e., perform exactly as specified by the office procedures, no more and no less. The result is usually that the office grinds to a halt very quickly!

So, what does this imply for the design of office support systems? Building computer systems where work is seen as simply being concerned with "information flow", and neglecting the articulation work needed to make the "flow" possible, can lead to serious problems. Computer-support of cooperative work should aim at supporting self-organization of cooperative ensembles as opposed to disrupting cooperative work by computerizing formal procedures.

In the same vein, Robinson in his paper on "double-level languages" (1989) states that a CSCW application should support at least two interacting "levels of language". In addition to that, the naked functionality of the CSCW application, the system should have facilities that allow users to freely negotiate task allocation and articulation. That is, the system should provide multiple alternative channels of interaction. As an example of a system providing a simple, yet effective, alternative channel for cooperative task articulation, Robinson cites the GROVE system developed by MCC (Austin, Texas) in 1988. Basically, GROVE is a multi-user outline processor, allowing multiple users to cooperate on drafting a common text. In addition to the interactions visible through the ongoing online textual modifications, the users could talk to each other about what was going on, and why, by means of a voice link. In the terminology suggested by Robinson, the voice link provided "the second level of language". Robinson's insightful remarks are worth quoting here:

"It can be said that any non-trivial collective activity requires effective communication that allows both ambiguity and clarity. These ideas of ambiguity and clarity can be developed as the 'formal' and 'cultural' aspects of language as used by participants in projects and organizations. 'Computer support' is valuable insofar as it facilitates the separation and interaction between the 'formal' and the 'cultural'. Applications and restrictions that support one level at the expense of the other tend to fail. The formal level is essential as it provides a common reference point for participants. A sort of 'external world' that can be pointed at, and whose behavior is rule-governed and predictable. The cultural level is a different type of world. It is an inter-weaving of subjectivities in which the possible and the counterfactual are as significant as the 'given'. The formal level is meaningless without interpretation, and the cultural level is vacuous without being grounded."

We can utilize this distinction when we analyze other CSCW applications. Take, for example, the Co-ordinator mail system developed by Flores and Winograd (Winograd, 1986). In his analysis of this system, Robinson (1989) notes how some reviewers have criticized the system because it forces people to be explicit about their commitments in their messages. But, he comments, and we concur:

"There is no objection to making 'explicit and textual' a dimension of communication. Indeed, in general, such separations of 'formal' and 'cultural' levels are seen as creative and desirable. The Co-ordinator falls down, not because it has a formalised ('textual') dimension, but because it has excluded, marginalised, and even illegitimised the 'cultural' dimension of conversation. Unless these two levels interact, fruitful co-operation will not happen."

Or, take the early CSCW project management support tool XCP (Sluizer and Cashman, 1984). In the words of its designers,

"XCP is an experimental coordinator tool which assists an organization in implementing and maintaining its procedures. Its goal is to reduce the costs of communicating, coordinating and deciding by carrying out formal plans of cooperative activity in partnership with its users. It tracks, prods, and manages the relational complexity as captured in the formal plan, so that human resources are available for more productive tasks. [...] An important effect is that XCP encourages an organization to clearly define formal procedural obligations and relationships."

It would appear that XCP assumes that what people do in many work settings is to follow procedures. No wonder the authors note the difficulty involved in developing and "debugging" the formal protocol. The generalization of such an approach to a wide range of office situations seems unrealistic. It too appears to exclude the "cultural" dimension of task articulation.

3.2. Sharing an Information Space

How to support a shared information space is one of the core problems for the CSCW field. This issue predates computer technology; it is fundamental to cooperative work, although the problems are aggravated by the increased scope and intensity of cooperative work relations facilitated by computer systems. As observed above, cooperative work may be conducted in a distributed and indirect way, and because of that, computer systems meant to support cooperative work must support retrieval of information filed by other workers, perhaps unknown, in another work context, perhaps also unknown. In addition to that, even work conducted collectively and directly may require the interaction of people with multiple goals of different scope and nature as well as different heuristics, conceptual frameworks, etc. This gives rise to a series of problems, quite apart from the technical problems of concurrency control etc. in multi-user applications (cf., e.g., Greif and Sarin, 1987; Stefik et al. 1987). We give a brief account of some of these problems below.

First, people prefer different problem solving strategies or heuristics. Accordingly, decisions bear the stamp of the strategy applied in reaching the decision. They are the result of biased reasoning. In cooperative decision making, then, which we regard as the norm in even supposedly 'routine' office work, people discount for the biases of their colleagues. This point was brought home very eloquently by Cyert and March in their classic study (1963):

"For the bulk of our subjects in both experiments, the idea that estimates communicated from other individuals should be taken at face value (or that their own estimates would be so taken) was not really viewed as reasonable. For every bias, there was a bias discount."

Thus cooperative decision making involves a continuous process of assessing the validity of the information produced by colleagues. In cooperative work settings involving discretionary decision making, the exercise of mutual critique of the decisions arrived at by colleagues is mandatory for all participants. In order to be able to assess information generated by discretionary decision making, each participant must be able to access the identity of the originator of a given unit of information. That is, a shared information space must be *transparent*. Problems of information-ownership and the responsibility for its upkeep and dissemination to others, have been neglected in much of the information systems literature, though the work of Nurminen and his colleagues on Human-Scale Information Systems partly addresses this important issue (see Hellman, 1989, for some information on this framework).

Second, decisions are always generated within a specific conceptual framework, as answers to specific questions. Thus knowledge of the perspective applied by the person in reaching a decision and producing information is indispensable to colleagues supposed to act intelligently on information conveyed to them. Accordingly, in addition to the task-related information being conveyed (the message itself, so to speak), a shared information space must provide contextual knowledge of the conceptual frame of reference of the originator. Thus, a computer-based system supporting cooperative work involving decision making should enhance the ability of cooperating workers to interrelate their partial and parochial domain knowledge and facilitate the expression and communication of alternative perspectives on a given problem. This requires a representation of the problem domain as a whole as well as a representation, in some form, of the mappings between perspectives on that problem domain. Again, we are not very far along in understanding how to build in such properties into our systems, despite the converging evidence that these kinds of supports are required by people. To summarize, then, data-bases for cooperative decision making must be transparent in terms of the identity of the originator of information and the strategies and perspectives applied in producing the information.

Yet a third problem, albeit one that has had some public discussion, has been the presupposition among many designers of information systems that information is something innocent and neutral. This view implied that to design an information system for a company one needed only to consider the data flows and files existing in that company. Consequently, a common data base containing all the relevant data from different parts of the organization, providing managers with a unified data model of the organization, was believed to be attainable. In the words of Ciborra (1985), hard reality has condemned this idea to the reign of utopia. In fact, the conventional notion of organizations as being monolithic entities is quite naive. Organizations are not perfectly collaborative systems. Rather, the perspective on organizations that views them as a mixture of collaboration and conflict, overt and covert, appears to be more illuminating and have greater explanatory potential than the traditional 'rationalistic' account. We view organizations as a coalition of individuals motivated by individual interests and aspirations and pursuing individual goals (Cyert and March, 1963). Accordingly, in organizational

settings information is used daily for misrepresentation purposes. Most of the information generated and processed in organizations is subject to misrepresentation because it has been generated, gathered and communicated in a context of goal incongruence and discord of interests and motives.

On the one hand, the requirement of transparency is amplified by this divergence. That is, knowledge of the identity of the originator and the situational context motivating the production and dissemination of the information is required so as to enable any user of the information to interpret the likely motives of the originator. On the other hand, however, the requirement of transparency is moderated by the divergence of interests and motives. A certain degree of opaqueness is required for discretionary decision making to be conducted in an environment charged with colliding interests. Hence, *transparency must be bounded*. The idea of a comprehensive, fully transparent database is not realistic. A worker engaged in cooperative decision making must be able to control the dissemination of information pertaining to his or her work: what is to be revealed, when, to whom, in which form?

These realities of organizational life must be investigated seriously if CSCW is to be turned from a fascinating laboratory research activity into an activity producing useful real world systems. By flatly ignoring the diversity and discord of the 'goals' of the participants involved, the differentiation of strategies, and the incongruence of the conceptual frames of reference within a cooperating ensemble, the proponents of the prevailing 'group work' oriented approach to CSCW evade the problems of a shared information space. Instead, they tend to focus on the technical problems of multi-user systems, that is, they also can be viewed as ultimately accepting a technology-oriented approach to the problem, with its concomitant limitations.

3.3. Designing Socio-technical Systems

The issue of changes in organizational life caused by technological developments has a long history. By changing the allocation of functions between humans and their implements, changes in technology induce changes in the work organization. Roberts' "self-acting mule" (1830), for instance, performed the functions of directly controlling the spinning operations. Because of that, the skilled spinners could be removed from cotton manufacturing and be replaced by semi-skilled operators. The "self-acting mule" induced the transition to the work organization of the modern factory.

Because of its flexibility, the computer is an agent of organizational change *par excellence* and, hence, designing computer-based systems for cooperative work settings is like writing in water. By careful analysis and design, the information system may be designed to match the current social structure of the labor processes. But this change of technology, in turn, induces a change of the social structure of the labor processes. This has been the bitter experience of a plethora of office automation projects and installations, designed to match the traditional allocation of tasks in the office. The Office Automation experience has unequivocally demonstrated that the potentials in terms of productivity, flexibility, product quality, etc. of information technology in the office cannot be realized without a corresponding change in the allocation of tasks among staff. (Hammer, 1984; Skousen, 1986; Hedberg et al., 1987; Schmidt, 1987).

To an extent, any software application project involves the design not just of a technical subsystem, but it also embodies - implicitly if not explicitly - assumptions about how this system will be used within organizations. The system is an organizational change agent. That is, knowingly or unknowingly, the designer does not merely design a computer system. What is being designed is a work organization. Some researchers and designers acknowledge this. For instance, Winograd (1986) notes:

"Every time a computer-based system is built and introduced into a work setting, the work is redesigned - either consciously or unconsciously. We cannot choose to have no impact, just as we cannot chose to be outside of a perspective. We can make conscious choices as to which ones to follow and what consequences we anticipate."

When we are addressing the task of designing computer-based systems to support cooperative work, however, we need to understand and control far better the interaction between technique and work organization than has heretofore been the case (see also Bødker et al., 1988). The old problems of fitting technology into the workplace have become acute for CSCW.

First, when we move from narrow domains and start to discuss computer support for the coordination and control of a large portion of everyday workplace activities, the assumptions about the use situation surface as more and more important variables. An adequate understanding of what is really going on in the workplace (see sections 3.1 and 3.2) becomes crucial to acceptance and use of these systems.

Second, if we are to design really usable systems to support cooperative work we need to develop a theoretical framework that will help us understand the complex interactions between the technical subsystem, the work organization, and the requirements of the task environment. To design CSCW systems designers must analyze the target organizations in order to come up with answers to such questions as: What are the reasons for this particular task allocation? Can it be attributed to customary privileges or prejudices? Is it imposed by labor market agreements? Is it required by law? Or is it required by the customer, e.g., to ensure specific quality requirements? Can it be attributed to the technical resources at hand in the given case. Can it be attributed to the available facilities for information retrieval or communication, for instance? And so forth. In short, can and should the current task allocation be changed by design?

Thus, we believe that designers of CSCW applications must be able to distinguish analytically the multitude of forms of social interaction that play a part in shaping work organizations in any real world work setting, for example:

- The forms of interaction in the labor process itself as determined by the natural and technical resources available.
- The organizational setting of the interaction.
- The customary privileges and prejudices of task allocation.
- Institutional forms of expressing and regulating conflicts of interest, etc.
- The forms of social control in the work place.
- The forms of allocation of power and authority.
- The impact of the function of the enterprise in the socio-economic system at large.
- The impact of the structure and state of the labor market.

And so forth.

The required theoretical framework that would help analysts and designers to deal with these issues, however, is not imminent (see Schmidt, 1988, for an initial assault on the problem). As pointed out by Howard (1988) the CSCW field is in short supply of detailed studies on the effects of current generation CSCW systems on the nature of work processes. Thus, we need to perform more detailed empirical studies, as well as design incremental modifications to existing systems and observe their effects.

4. Conclusion

In his plenary address to CSCW '88, the psychologist Don Norman gave a number of examples of the primitive level of present-day interfaces to computer systems. This was in the context of the individual computer user. Without wishing to be defeatist, Norman then amusingly noted the lack of knowledge that existed currently with respect to group processes and cooperative cognition, and cautioned against excessive optimism in designing successful computer systems to support cooperative working. His admonishments are worth noting. At the same time, applications are being developed for cooperative work settings and products are being shipped. Without a resolution to, or, at least, an attempt to come to grips with, the kinds of problems inherent in designing for CSCW applications identified in this paper, the likelihood for success is minimal. The challenge to designers in the field is large, as we still have not done enough to evaluate the impact of our early systems in this area. Thus there is ample work for both the implementers and the social scientists concerned with these issues!

5. References

Hans Paul Bahrdt (1958): *Industriebürokratie. Versuch einer Soziologie des Industrialisierten Bürobetriebes und seiner Angestellten*, Ferdinand Enke Verlag, Stuttgart.

Hans Paul Bahrdt (1984): *Schlüsselbegriffe der Soziologie*, Verlag C.H. Beck, München.

Liam Bannon, N. Bjørn-Andersen, and B. Due-Thomsen (1988): "Computer Support for Cooperative Work: An appraisal and critique," in H. J. Bullinger et al. (eds.): *EURINFO '88. Information Systems for Organizational Effectiveness*, North-Holland, Amsterdam, 1988.

Susanne Bødker, P. Ehn, J. Knudsen, M. Kyng, and K. Madsen (1988): "Computer Support for Cooperative Design", *CSCW '88. Proceedings of the Conference on Computer-Supported Cooperative Work, September 26-28, 1988, Portland, Oregon*, ACM, New York, NY, 1988, pp. 377-394.

Claudio U. Ciborra (1985): "Reframing the Role of Computers in Organizations: The Transaction Costs Approach," *Proceedings of Sixth International Conference on Information Systems, Indianapolis, December 16-18, 1985*.

Richard M. Cyert and James G. March (1963): *A Behavioral Theory of the Firm*, Prentice-Hall, Englewood Cliffs, N.J.

Ralf Dahrendorf (1959): *Sozialstruktur des Betriebes*, Gabler, Wiesbaden.

Pelle Ehn (1988): Remarks in panel discussion on "CSCW: What does it mean?", *CSCW '88. Proceedings of the Conference on Computer-Supported Cooperative Work, September 26-28, 1988, Portland, Oregon*, ACM, New York, NY, 1988.

Elihu M. Gerson and Susan Leigh Star (1986): "Analyzing Due Process in the Workplace," *ACM Transactions on Office Information Systems*, vol. 4, no. 3, July 1986, pp. 257-270.

Irene Greif and Sunil Sarin (1987): "Data Sharing in Group Work", *ACM TRansactions on Office Information Systems*, vol. 5, no. 2, April 1987, pp. 187-211.

Irene Greif (ed.) (1988a): *Computer-Supported Cooperative Work: A Book of Readings*, Morgan Kaufman, San Mateo, California.

Irene Greif (1988b): Remarks in panel discussion on "CSCW: What does it mean?", *CSCW '88. Proceedings of the Conference on Computer-Supported Cooperative Work, September 26-28, 1988, Portland, Oregon*, ACM, New York, NY, 1988.

Jonathan Grudin (1988): "Why CSCW Applications Fail: Problems in the Design and Evaluation of Organizational Interfaces", *CSCW '88. Proceedings of the Conference on Computer-Supported Cooperative Work, September 26-28, 1988, Portland, Oregon*, ACM, New York, NY, 1988, pp. 85-93.

Michael Hammer (1984): "The OA Mirage," *Datamation*, vol. 30, no. 2, February 1984, pp. 36-46.

Bo Hedberg et al. (1987): *Kejsarens nya kontor. Fallstudier om datoranvändning*, Liber, Malmö, Sweden.

Lucy Suchman (1983): "Office procedures as practical action", *ACM Transactions on Office Information Systems*, vol. 1, 1983, pp. 320-328.

Sørgaard, P. (1987) "A cooperative work perspective on use and development of computer artifacts", paper presented at 10th Information Systems Research Seminar in Scandinavia (IRIS) Conference, Vaskivesi, Finland, 1987. [DAIMI PB-234, Computer Science Dept., Aarhus University, DK-8000 Denmark].

James D. Thompson (1967): *Organizations in action. Social science bases of administrative theory*, Mc Graw-Hill, New York, etc.

Andrew Ure (1835): *The Philosophy of Manufactures*, London.

Edward Wakefield (1849): *A view of the art of colonization...*. London.

Richard Whitley (1974): "Cognitive and social institutionalization of scientific specialties and research areas," in Whitley (ed.): *Social Processes of Scientific Development*, Routledge and Kegan Paul, London, 1974, pp. 69-95.

Terry Winograd (1986): "A language/action perspective on the design of cooperative work", *CSCW '86. Proceedings. Conference on Computer-Supported Cooperative Work. December 3-5, 1986. Austin, Texas*, ACM, 1986, pp. 203-220.

Eleanor Wynn (1979): *Office conversation as an information medium*, Unpublished Ph.D. dissertation, University of California, Berkeley, CA, 1979.

Ritta Hellman (1989): "The Human-Scale IS Approach - An Operationalization", in H. Klein and K. Kumar (eds.): *Systems Development for Human Progress*, North-Holland, Amsterdam, 1989, pp. 225-240.

Robert Howard (1987): "Systems Design and Social Responsibility: The Political Implications of 'Computer-Supported Cooperative Work': A Commentary", *Office: Technology and People*, vol. 3, no. 2, 1987.

Robert Howard (1988): Remarks in panel discussion on "CSCW: What does it mean?", *CSCW '88. Proceedings of the Conference on Computer-Supported Cooperative Work, September 26-28, 1988. Portland, Oregon*, ACM, New York, NY, 1988.

Robert Johansen (1988): *Groupware. Computer Support for Business Teams*, The Free Press, New York and London, 1988.

Horst Kern and Michael Schumann (1970): *Industriearbeit und Arbeiterbewusstsein. Eine empirische Untersuchung über den Einfluß der aktuellen technischen Entwicklung auf die industrielle Arbeit und das Arbeiterbewußtsein*, vol. I-II, Frankfurt am Main.

Rob Kling (1988): Remarks in panel discussion on "CSCW: What does it mean?", *CSCW '88. Proceedings of the Conference on Computer-Supported Cooperative Work, September 26-28, 1988. Portland, Oregon*, ACM, New York, NY, 1988.

Morten Kyng (1988): "Designing for a Dollar a Day", *CSCW '88. Proceedings of the Conference on Computer-Supported Cooperative Work, September 26-28, 1988, Portland, Oregon*, ACM, New York, NY, 1988, pp. 178-188.

K. Lyytinen and Rudy Hirschheim (1987): "Information System Failures: A Survey and Classification of Empirical Literature", *Oxford Surveys in Information Technology*, vol. 4, 1987, pp. 257-309.

Karl Marx (1867): *Das Kapital. Kritik der politischen Ökonomie*, vol. 1; MEGA, vol. II/5.

Otfried Mickler et al. (1976): *Technik, Arbeitsorganisation und Arbeit. Eine empirische Untersuchung in der automatischen Produktion*, Aspekte Verlag, Frankfurt am Main.

Delbert C. Miller and William H. Form (1964): *Industrial Sociology. The Sociology of Work Organizations*, 2nd ed., Harper & Row, New York etc.

Heinrich Popitz, H. P. Bahrdt, E. A. Jüres, and H. Kesting (1957): *Technik und Industriearbeit. Soziologische Untersuchungen in der Hüttenindustrie*, J. C. B. Mohr, Tübingen.

Mike Robinson (1989): "Double Level Languages and Co-operative Working", *Support, Society and Culture. Mutual uses of Cybernetics and Science. Proceedings. Conference. March 27-April 1, 1989, Amsterdam*, pp. 79-114.

Jean-Paul Sartre (1960): *Critique de la raison dialectique*, vol. I, Gallimard, Paris.

Kjeld Schmidt (1987): *Kontorautomation - realitet eller reklame?*, Kommuneinformation, Copenhagen.

Kjeld Schmidt (1988): "Cooperative Work: A Conceptual Framework", Position paper for workshop on "New Technology, Distributed Decision Making and Responsibility," Bad Homburg, May 1988. [Revised edition in Rasmussen, Leplat, and Brehmer (eds.): *Modelling Distributed Decision Making*, Wiley (forthcoming)].

Beau Sheil (1983): "Coping with Complexity", *Office: Technology and People*, vol. 1, 1983.

Thomas Skousen (1986): *Kontorautomatisering og medarbejderindflydelse. 3 succeshistorier fra erhvervsliv og offentlig sektor*, Samfundslitteratur, Copenhagen.

S. Sluizer and P. Cashman (1984): "XCP. An Experimental Tool for Supporting Office Procedures", *Proceedings. First International Conference on Office Automation*, IEEE-CS Press, December 1984, pp. 73-80.

Mark Stefik, G. Foster, D. Bobrow, K. Kahn, S. Lanning, L. Suchman (1987): "Beyond the Chalkboard: Computer support for collaboration and problem solving in meetings", *Communications of the ACM*, vol. 30, no. 1, pp. 32-47, January 1987.

Anselm Strauss (1985): "Work and the Division of Labor," *The Sociological Quarterly*, vol. 26, no. 1, 1985, pp. 1-19.

Being There

THE PROMISE OF MULTIMEDIA COMMUNICATIONS

BY DAVID BRITTAN

WHEN Chris Turner's grandmother bought her first TV set, back in 1954, she would nervously cover up the screen whenever it wasn't on. The Orwellian powers she ascribed to the new medium were, of course, well beyond the technology of the day. But Turner has worked hard to change all that, and will tell you that life in a world of two-way video isn't half bad.

When he arrives at his job each morning at Olivetti Research Laboratory in Cambridge, England, Turner clips on an electronic badge that links him to the lab's experimental video and audio communication system, known as Pandora. The badge emits infrared signals that allow his fellow research engineers to find him whenever they want to chat. Once paged, Turner can sit down at the nearest computer terminal and begin a conversation with up to five other people, whose faces show up in different windows on the screen.

Thanks to Pandora's "video news server," Turner can also click an icon on his screen to catch recorded BBC news and weather reports. He can even send video mail. "I might send a message to Ian downstairs—'Are we going out for a beer this lunchtime?'—that he's going to read when he gets back to his workstation in 15 minutes."

Why do you need to see a video image of someone just to be asked out for a beer? "Well, you don't," Turner admits,

Experiments in combining voice and data

with video could bring richer communication to desktops—

and redefine "the office."

With Cruiser—a computer-
controlled video and audio
communication system—
Bellcore researchers are
studying ways to bring
people face to face with
distant co-workers.

"but don't you think it's rather criminal that you can't?" In his view, the advent of two-way video on computer workstations is a matter of manifest destiny. He insists that as desktop computers grow more adept at combining different media—graphics and audio as well as text—"people are going to ask 'Where's the video?' They'll see that what we do with computers now is akin to selling people cars and only giving them two wheels."

Turner's frustration with the limits of existing media is shared by everyone who works in the burgeoning field of multimedia communications. The Information Age has allowed companies that used to be housed in one location to fan out across the globe. Scientists are almost as likely to collaborate with colleagues on the next continent as across campus. And industrial projects are often so large that those engaged in them couldn't possibly work in close proximity. Yet the technologies that have allowed this migration also saddle users with limitations that were never a problem when intellectual teamwork meant working side by side.

The telephone permits fairly natural conversation, but both sender and receiver must be available at the same time. Electronic mail doesn't provide the immediate feedback people take for granted in ordinary discourse. And even sophisticated products that are labeled multimedia don't let you see the person you're talking to. For example, BBN/Slate, a multimedia system from Bolt Beranek and Newman, enables co-workers to collaborate on documents consisting of text, graphics, and audio. And users of Wang's Freestyle system can annotate an electronic document with speech and handwriting and pass it along to a co-worker, who then sees and hears the comments in the order in which they were made. But without video, important visual cues such as facial expressions, hand gestures, and body language are lost. The illusion of face-to-face contact, after all, requires a face.

Several companies do offer video conferencing systems, some integrated with fax machines and able to display spreadsheets and other text. But most of these systems are bulky and expensive. They also require special rooms, so consultations must be scheduled in advance. In fact, the only technology that lets widely separated people meet, show work in progress, and col-

Chris Turner displays the electronic badge that enables fellow Olivetti engineers to track him down for video chats over Pandora. Future versions of the experimental video system will be in color.

laborate as effectively as if they shared an office is still the airplane.

By bringing two-way video to desktop computers, multimedia researchers hope to recapture some of the flexibility and human warmth that electronic communication has lacked. In this quest they are benefiting from recent technical advances. For instance, compression technology—which reduces the amount of data needed to send video by transmitting only the new information needed for each successive video frame—is enabling higher-quality images to travel over less expensive lines. And the price of video equipment is falling, even as cameras and processors grow in sophistication and shrink in size.

Still, it could be several years before video/multimedia tools land on people's desks, according to Stephen Reynolds, an analyst at Link Resources in New York, which has just completed a major study of the field. Reynolds predicts that the first successful products will be designed for a single user—software such as spreadsheets and databases annotated with voice and perhaps animated graphics. The next generation of these products will allow sharing over networks. "Video," he says, "will come along a little bit behind that stuff."

If desktop video/multimedia systems aren't exactly busting out of the lab, it's not because people aren't excited about them. "We looked at the consumer market, as well as the business and education markets, and found plenty of interest," says Reynolds. What appears to be holding up commercialization is uncertainty about which features people will find most valuable. For example, will they want systems designed for structured conferences where annotations are done using a keyboard or mouse? Or will they gravitate toward more informal setups, where participants drop in for video chats and scrawl notes on sheets of paper? To compound the problem, nobody knows what sorts of networks will be available to carry the rich new media anytime soon, or how readily users will invest in systems that require so much bandwidth.

As developers wrestle with these uncertainties, they are testing a variety of approaches, trying out assumptions about people's work habits, and refining the technology accordingly. Each project treats video differently. Yet each could play a role in shaping the way we'll work and communicate a few years hence.

DAVID BRITTAN is an associate editor of Technology Review.

Building Rapport

Researchers at AT&T Bell Laboratories in Holmdel, N.J., are pursuing what might be called an egalitarian approach to multimedia communications. "We're trying to develop a model that can access any computer, any set of people," says Sudhir Ahuja, who heads the team developing the labs' experimental Rapport system. The idea is to present "one uniform interface" for e-mail, voice, video, and computer communications and allow people to work with their favorite word processor, CAD system, or financial planning program on virtually any kind of project.

The metaphor Ahuja uses is a "virtual meeting room." To start a Rapport conference, users simply "enter" the meeting room on their screen and call up other people to invite them to join in. What participants see, at least if they're using the full-blown version of Rapport, are video images of the conferees in separate windows on a Sun workstation. The documents they are discussing are displayed in another window. Although only one person at a time can manipulate the software, everyone can see the results. To "raise a hand" or point to various sections of a document, users manipulate a mouse that controls an arrow with their name on it. If someone new wants to join the conference, a "beeper" service alerts the participants.

"In Rapport," says Ahuja, "you can make these virtual meeting rooms hang around for days—go to lunch, come back and continue the meeting, then leave again." Similarly, he says, Rapport lets people switch freely from one conference to another.

The system also has a "store-and-forward" function that can allow meetings to be saved and passed on to other people. An engineering team, for example, might brainstorm on a design, then forward a portion of the discussion across the country to people in marketing, who could add their comments and return the meeting file to the engineers.

In the Rapport approach, live video may actually turn out to be secondary to other modes of discourse. While Ahuja finds prerecorded video useful—Rapport users can show videotape presentations to other participants—he is not convinced that talking heads are the cornerstone of a successful meeting. "What we have found is that video is very good at the start of the conversation, to get a feel for the person," says Ahuja. "But even in a regular meeting, you don't look at the person all the time—you look at the blackboard, you write, you look for information. You make eye contact occasionally, just to test whether the person is paying attention. So it isn't video that dominates a conversation but rather information-sharing." In fact, says Ahuja, the Bell Labs researchers often run Rapport using just voice and data.

Ahuja is now studying ways of tailoring the system to

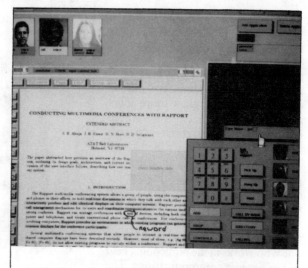

Bell Labs' Rapport system lets co-workers jointly edit computer files as they discuss them. Participants may communicate through voice and data only, as they are doing here, or add full-motion video.

different needs: executives may want to run Rapport using only notebook computers, while product designers may need powerful workstations, he says.

A Show of Hands

For Hiroshi Ishii, at the Human Interface Laboratories of Japan's NTT, what's missing in systems like Rapport is the familiar desktop, where, even in the late twentieth century, the human hand still makes useful marks on paper. His TeamWorkStation is designed to bridge gaps between the desktop, the personal computer, and telecommunications. The metaphor behind Team-WorkStation is the "open shared workspace": members of a work group ought to be able to bring a wide variety of tools, both old and new, to a cooperative work session and use them simultaneously.

It was this principle that led Ishii to choose video as the basic medium of his research project. At the heart of each workstation is a Macintosh computer with two screens, one for individual work and the other for shared work. A speaker phone and two miniature video cameras—one for faces and one, mounted on a flexible desk lamp, to capture the desktop and the user's hand gestures—provide the audiovisual link.

Two to four people work together, viewing each other in a window of the shared screen. In another window they share computer files, which they grab from their individual screens by dragging a mouse, or books and papers, which they convey by pointing a camera at the desktop. If one person draws a diagram on a piece of paper that shows up on the shared screen, someone else can add to the drawing by sketching on his or her own pad. The participants see a synthesis of the old and the

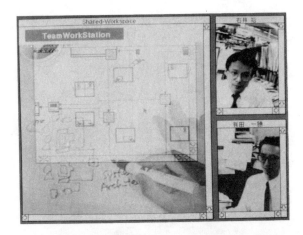

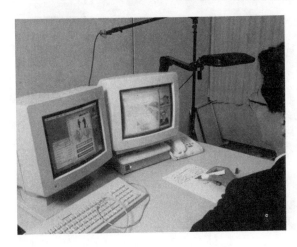

Top:
With NTT's TeamWorkStation, users can
transfer work from their individual screen (left)
to a "shared workspace" (right) for collaboration.
Tiny cameras mounted on the black boom
and on the lamp send images of the user's
face and desktop to the shared screen.
Bottom:
The system can then superimpose the image
of a hand pointing and making corrections onto
that of a document lying on a
co-worker's desktop.

new, with a translucent image of the hand as it modifies the diagram. They can also point and gesture by placing their hands under the camera.

A disadvantage of this "overlay" approach is that the end product of the collaboration exists only in bits and pieces on different desktops. When people share software, changes are easily incorporated into a document. But when the medium of collaboration is video, users have to go through extra steps, such as making a hard copy with a video printer or storing the document with a video digitizer.

Ishii maintains, however, that not all co-workers need to manipulate the end product. He points to research suggesting that when two people collaborate, one tends to perform a task while the other monitors progress and makes suggestions. In trials at NTT, he reports, "we seldom felt the necessity of editing other people's diagrams directly. If a diagram had to be changed, the originator would usually change it." A major reason for this role division, according to Ishii, is that the second person respects the originator's "ownership" of a document.

Even though, like Rapport, TeamWorkStation allows people to work together on the same software, Ishii has found that people prefer the video overlay mode. Having used TeamWorkStation to redesign the system itself, Ishii and his co-workers concluded that pointing and drawing with hands was both faster and more expressive than using a mouse. So Rapport and TeamWorkStation appear to be on different tracks, one leading to a system where video creeps in only as needed, and the other leading to a system where video is the vehicle.

The Camera Never Blinks

Xerox Palo Alto Research Center (PARC), from which Ishii got many of his ideas, has ventured even further down that second track. A project called Media Space—intended specifically for collaboration in design work—eschews the shared computer applications possible on Rapport and TeamWorkStation in favor of video alone.

"We see design less as a technical activity and more as a social activity," says PARC researcher Scott Minneman. To the developers of Media Space, computers are too rigid and compartmentalized to allow the social component of design to flourish. "While computer-aided design is very much about precision," says Minneman, "video allows people to negotiate and make ambiguous statements: 'We need this to run longer' or 'That piece needs to be heftier or feel different.'"

Media Space—a project that has been replicated at Rank Xerox EuroPARC in Cambridge, England, and at the University of Toronto—links 25 or 30 offices through workstations outfitted with video cameras and monitors. Although the cameras are always on, they face in whatever direction the users elect to point them.

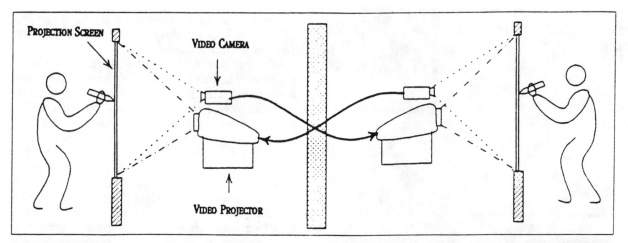

Half a dozen people can view one another at once. According to Minneman, Media Space has been used successfully for collaborative work within his building as well as between researchers at Palo Alto and another Xerox lab in Portland, Ore.

In the experiment with Portland, monitors were placed not only on workers' desks but in the common rooms of the two sites. If someone in one common room wanted to speak to a colleague in the other common room, he or she would simply yell that person's name. "It's a very casual communications medium," says Minneman. That's also true of the office-to-office connections, he says. "In a lot of teleconferencing systems, the configuration is fixed. But in Media Space, the configuration is totally up to the user. So if you realize that what you want the person to be seeing is a piece of paper on your desk, you simply pull your camera over and aim it at your desk."

PARC researchers have tested Media Space in a number of non-Xerox settings. A 1987 office design project brought together three architects who had never met. Connected only by video images of one another and of their hand-drawn sketches, the architects spent two days hashing out their philosophical differences, drawing and redrawing, and finally producing a workable design. When it was all over, they unanimously reported that the work had gone faster than if they had collaborated in person. One architect found it helpful to see the others' drawings right side up—something that's often difficult when designers are sitting around a table. Perhaps more important was a tendency to remain focused on the work—to "cut out a certain amount of debris that's usually in the face-to-face world," as one designer put it.

But such studies pointed up the need for a shared space in which to draw collaboratively, as in Team-WorkStation's overlay mode. The PARC researchers have responded by building a number of video-based drawing tools while trying to avoid what Minneman sees as a common flaw of interactive systems: the drawing surface is separate from the screen. In PARC's prototypes, he says, "you actually work on the surface where

Above: Pay no attention to that man behind the curtain: he's actually sketching on a remote VideoWhiteboard, a TV projection screen developed at Xerox Palo Alto Research Center for collaborative drawing. Xerox researchers believe that such simple video tools preserve the social element of design better than computer-based drawing programs.
Top: How it's done.

the effects of your actions are appearing. In our experience there's a big advantage to how familiar and comfortable and recognizable that is."

The tools are disarmingly simple. Users of Video-Draw sketch directly on an upward-facing monitor with an erasable marker, and an overhead camera sends the sketch to someone else's monitor. When the other person adds to the drawing, his or her marks—and the hand making them—appear on the original screen.

VideoWhiteboard, another drawing tool, is a high-tech version of shadow puppet theater. Designers at different locations jointly draw on a wall-sized "whiteboard"—a translucent rear-projection TV screen. A camera behind the screen sees silhouettes of whatever marks the person's pen makes, and these are then projected onto a colleague's whiteboard. Because the camera also picks up the shadow of the person drawing, the

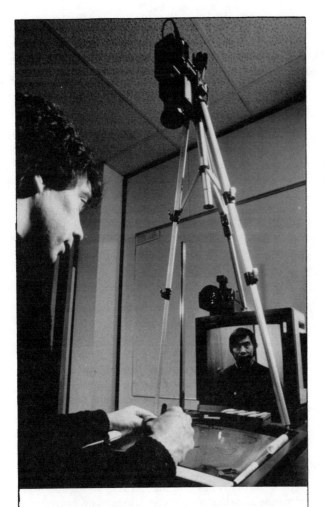

Xerox PARC's VideoDraw allows designers to sketch together while viewing each other over the Media Space system. Drawing directly on a monitor reproduces the familiar experience of putting pen to paper.

face-to-face design sessions knows how to quickly modify a drawing, he says. "People just scribble things out, or change the line weight by making several strokes over the line they care about. People automatically use these same mechanisms with VideoDraw and VideoWhiteboard."

In fact, after experimenting with shared computerized design tools, the PARC researchers are coming to the same conclusion as NTT's Hiroshi Ishii: users prefer more fluid, manual techniques. Experience with Video-Com, an experimental drawing system that combines images of the drafters' hands with the ability to edit and resize marks and print them out or save them as computer files, bears this out. "In most situations where we've put this into real use," says Minneman, "we find people spending all their time in the more casual realm." Minneman acknowledges, though, that such findings are inconclusive. "We're suspicious—and I suspect Hiroshi is—that this just means we're not doing it quite right yet."

Chance Encounters

It may be hard to imagine a multimedia approach more casual than PARC's, but Robert Fish and his colleagues at Bellcore in Morristown, N.J.—the research arm of the seven "Baby Bells"—have reduced informal communication to a science. Through a computer-controlled video and audio system called Cruiser, the Bellcore researchers hope to allow far-flung workers to simulate chance hallway encounters or drop-in visits to colleagues' offices. Trial runs of Cruiser are now being set up at a number of universities.

Besides allowing users to make video calls to their colleagues, Cruiser has some special features to promote spontaneous conversations. For example, users can ask the system to set up calls to other people at random, displaying their faces on each party's screen. If neither party wants to visit, the call is disconnected after three seconds. Another feature lets users take one-second glances into different offices to see who's available to talk. (Users can activate a "private" command that blocks incoming video calls.)

Cruiser's developers have seen several types of behavior that are not possible with other media. For example, people often make quick calls in the "glance" mode—especially first thing in the morning and right after lunch—just to get a sense of who is around and might be reachable later. Sometimes, too, callers who find that another party is out will simply keep the video connection open to catch the person when he or she returns. And then there's the "virtual shared office," where pairs of people collaborating on a project stay in video contact for hours at a time, going about their own work but occasionally having a conversation.

With its seeming potential for promoting idle

colleague gets the impression that the drawer is standing on the other side of the screen. The effect is so convincing that in one case a woman who was having trouble hearing what the other person was saying instinctively put her ear closer to the screen—and her colleague spoke louder.

"We've found that people learn to use these systems incredibly quickly," says Minneman, "because there's really nothing to learn—no menus, no mouse, no special tools."

Like TeamWorkstation, VideoDraw and Video-Whiteboeard don't let you rotate, resize, or move figures the way sophisticated drafting programs do. But Minneman contends that this is not necessarily a drawback. Anyone who has used pencil and paper in

chitchat, one can't help wondering if Cruiser is really a virtual shared water cooler. Yet 90 percent of the calls people make on it are work-related—or so people report in Bellcore trials. Of course, says Fish, "conversations whose contents are work-related also serve a social function, in the sense that people use them to maintain familiarity with each other and each other's work."

One troublesome finding is that calls are mostly short—three minutes or less. People tend to use the system for greeting, scheduling, giving status reports, and asking quick questions, but not for complex problem solving or decision making. All too often, Fish reports, users start a conversation on Cruiser, then pick up their papers and take them to a colleague's office for consultation—something that collaborators at remote sites won't have the luxury of doing.

Having arrived at the same crossroads as PARC researchers when they decided to build a "shared drawing space," Bellcore researchers are outfitting Cruiser with document-sharing tools such as a computer drawing system. But wait—what about the awesome power of video to convey familiar hand drawings? Fish maintains that video's resolution is too low for transmitting detailed documents. Systems like Xerox's VideoDraw are OK for making initial design sketches, he says, because they use markers that make thick lines. "But if I want you to see something I've already done, I have to have the ability to integrate documents that already exist." Indeed, NTT's Ishii admits that he and his colleagues send detailed documents via e-mail or fax instead of over TeamWorkStation's video links.

Another refinement is meant to allow Cruiser users to approach other people more naturally. Normally when one sees a co-worker 20 feet down the hall, one begins looking for clues as to whether that person is available to talk; the co-worker may avoid eye contact, for example, or seem to be in a rush. "But when somebody made a Cruiser call," says Fish, "they would connect to you and there would be this full-fidelity, full-resolution image—head to shoulders—sitting two feet away from you, which was pretty darned difficult to ignore." In other words, Cruiser bypassed the familiar negotiation process. Today users see a postage stamp–size still image of a caller. If they want to visit, they click on the face, and only then does it become a full-size moving image.

As Fish and other multimedia developers have discovered, there is no underestimating the challenges of getting technology and psychology to mesh. Even a simple concept like VideoWindow, a huge eight-foot by three-foot TV screen that provides an informal connection between two sites, has been full of surprises. In trials at Bellcore, VideoWindow has been placed in two common rooms on different floors. The idea is to present the illusion of a window, with microphones and speakers

Bellcore designed VideoWindow as an informal link between separate groups of employees. But the system's life-size images could be used in business conferences, distributed classrooms, and medical consultation.

placed to give the impression that sound is emanating from whoever is talking.

But even a window is a barrier of sorts. Although the researchers witnessed "greetings, extended social conversation, work coordination, and the discussion of new research ideas across the VideoWindow system," users were only 40 percent as likely to strike up a conversation as people meeting face to face. One reason may be that people normally assume that if they can see and hear someone else, the person can also see and hear them. With VideoWindow, it's possible to be out of camera and microphone range yet still able to detect somebody on screen. What's more, conversations often break down because people are unable to speak privately, a possibility that's usually taken for granted even in a crowded room. It's also hard for users to make eye contact: because the camera is in a fixed location and people are moving, co-workers seldom know whether someone on the other side is looking at them. Finally, it's easier to ignore people appearing in the VideoWindow than colleagues in the same room. Although some of these problems sound like a challenge for Miss Manners, Fish and his colleagues have concluded that a few can be solved by "rethinking how video cameras and monitors are designed and placed in personal communications systems."

Is It 1984 Yet?

With all the work that remains to be done on multimedia communications, developers hesitate to predict when their projects might assume marketable form. Ahuja, at Bell Labs, gives a tentative figure of "a couple of years" for a commercial version of Rapport. Others merely note that their technology has been patented, is being closely watched by vendors, and might be available for licensing. "In fact," says Xerox PARC's Minneman, "a lot of the phone companies are really interested in VideoDraw and VideoWhiteboard because they see these systems as ways of selling massive amounts of bandwidth."

Meanwhile, developers are checking out possible obstacles to market acceptance. First, there's the Orwell thing. "To many people, the presence of a video camera in a room is rather too close to Big Brother for comfort," notes an Olivetti research report. "Anyone proposing to exploit video technology will have to take this attitude into account." The report goes on to recommend that users be granted full control over where a camera points and whether it is on.

But can measures such as turning off the camera or pressing a "do not disturb" button shield workers from the eye of an intrusive boss? Only if people feel free to use them, warns Gary Marx, an MIT professor of urban studies and planning who specializes in privacy issues. Some companies now pressure employees to keep their home fax machines and computers on round the clock, he says. Likewise, people who turn off their video cameras might come to be seen as bad corporate citizens. The only real insurance against such monitoring, says Marx, is a corporate climate that gives employees a legitimate choice.

Of course, certain folks are just plain camera-shy. When Olivetti Research Lab demonstrates Pandora for visitors, "some people hate it," notes Turner. "They say 'Oh my God, a camera' as they cringe and run out of the room. But are these the same people who refused to leave messages on answering machines 10 years ago?" Turner maintains that users will grow less skittish as the technology becomes more familiar.

Then there's the "massive amounts of bandwidth" that Minneman was referring to. Bandwidth—the data-carrying capacity a network needs to transmit video and other media—could pose the biggest barrier to making multimedia communications routine. Ahuja says Rapport can be used for "minimal conferences" (voice and data only) over two ordinary phone lines. But video is a glutton for bandwidth. The Ethernet data network so common in the office world has an effective bandwidth of about 6 megabits per second. While the transmission speed of compressed video falls well within this capacity—on the order of 56 kilobits to 1.5 megabits per second—office networks would quickly become saturated if more than a few video calls and other data transmissions were going on at once. Only the newer and more expensive "broadband" office networks, with capacities in the hundreds of megabits per second, will do—and these are still a rarity.

Not unrelated is the question of whether the benefits of setting aside a lot of extra bandwidth for video will justify the costs. Although most developers say they have a gut feeling that multimedia systems will greatly enhance productivity, not everyone is convinced that those gains will come from the bandwidth-hogging video dimension.

After conducting numerous studies of the way people use experimental multimedia, Robert Kraut, Bellcore's director of interpersonal communications research, concludes that video has special attractions but not special benefits. "We find that people use video a lot—often instead of the telephone. But there's a huge amount of redundancy between the information you can pick up from voice and what you get over the video channel." In fact, he says, faces are much better at deception: people are more apt to "put up a good front, looking confident when they really don't know what they're doing." Considering these drawbacks, says Kraut, "my guess is that people won't pay huge amounts more for video channels than they now pay for telephones."

An even bigger question is how to connect a local multimedia network with networks in other parts of the country and the world. An answer designers frequently proffer is ISDN—the "integrated services digital network" that firms and phone companies are beginning to install for just such purposes. But ISDN is now available only in certain areas, and no one knows how long it will take to expand the system nationally and worldwide.

The spread of multimedia communications tools could hasten such expansion. And in the meantime, says Reynolds, of Link Resources, private companies that offer fiber-optic and satellite links might provide a good alternative to public networks. But because nationwide broadband connections are not yet at hand, he says, "the first successful multimedia networking will probably be done within a company at one site."

What will the world be like when multimedia networks do become ubiquitous? Many observers foresee big changes in the white-collar workplace. Not only will many kinds of business meetings be unnecessary, Reynolds predicts, but so will some commutes. As employees respond to family commitments by turning up the pressure on companies to establish work-at-home policies, he says, multimedia networks will allow corporate sites to shrink: "If you have 15 employees, you might only need room for 10 in the office at any one time."

But powerful as the new tools may be, no one expects them to eliminate the need for human contact. Although in theory desktop multimedia systems could spawn the "virtual company," where everybody works at home, says Ahuja, experience with Rapport has taught him that "there is no substitute for meeting face to face and establishing *real* rapport." ∎

CHAPTER 2
The Adoption, Deployment, and Use of Groupware

This chapter includes as readings three papers that shed additional light on the pragmatics of groupware and on how it can best be introduced and applied.

"Groupware in Practice: An Interpretation of Work Experiences" by Bullen and Bennett (1991) reports the findings of interviews with 223 people who were using "groupware" systems in 25 enterprises of various size and character. The information technology tools studied included facilities for construction/editing, electronic exchange of text, name and address files, and electronic calendars. They suggest, from a design perspective, that electronic message communication has proved to be the primary tool to date, that message linking is a key improvement provided by electronic communications, that both the functionality and how it is offered are important, and that tools must be integrated to be maximally useful. They also assert, from an organizational perspective, that people report the most value from tools paralleling non-electronic activities, that people will not use the technology if the benefits to be gained do not clearly outweigh the resources that must be invested, that groupware implementation is simultaneously a social and technical intervention (Kling and Iacono, 1989), that process redesign may be required to realize productivity improvements, and that creating productive teams is a challenge. They stress the importance of four organizational factors: champions, expectations, training, and evolution.

Many of the points made by Bullen and Bennett are illustrated in the case study by Post (1992). The study reports on the work of a consulting organization within the Boeing Company in building a business case with a quantifiable cost-benefit ratio for the intro-

duction of group decision support technology (see Chapter 12). The work included an investigation of technical feasibility, planning and staffing, definition of business case parameters to be used in a cost-benefit evaluation, design and pre-testing of the evaluation methodology, construction of a test facility, software acquisition, facilitator training, use in 64 measured group support technology sessions, and evaluation.

In "Groupware and Cooperative Work: Problems and Prospects," Grudin (1990) identifies five factors contributing to the failure of groupware. Failure can occur if the people who have to do additional work are not the people who perceive direct benefit from use of an application, if the technology threatens existing political structures or certain key individuals, or if it does not allow for the wide range of exception handling and improvisation that characterizes much group activity. Failure can also occur because the complexity of the applications makes it very difficult to learn and generalize from our past experiences, and because our intuitions are especially poor for multi-user applications. Grudin closes the paper by suggesting that electronic mail is successful because it avoids most of these problems, and by describing some implications of his theories for organizational change.

Notes and Guide to Further Reading

A shorter version of the Bullen and Bennett (1991) paper is Bullen and Bennett (1990). The group decision support technology used in the study by Post is described in more detail in Chapter 12 of this volume, as are other studies of the adoption, use, and effectiveness of such technology.

Grudin (1989, 1991a, b) has written extensively on the nature of computer-supported cooperative work and on the development, adoption, deployment, and use of groupware. Grudin (1991a) suggests that the development of groupware is a result of the convergence of an internal contract development context producing applications on mainframes with a product development context producing applications on microcomputers. Grudin (1991, submitted for publication) proposes a new formulation of the time-place groupware taxonomy, in which time is characterized as *same, different,* and *extended,* and place is characterized as *same, different,* or *distributed.* He also adds to his list of five problems to produce a list of eight challenges for groupware developers. The three new challenges are the need to achieve "critical mass"; the need to provide "unobtrusive" features to support group work, since they may be used relatively infrequently; and the need to introduce groupware into the workplace in a very careful and skillful manner.

Several others have investigated issues involved in the adoption of groupware. Ehrlich (1987a, b) focuses on adoption strategies required for office communication systems such as electronic mail, voice mail, and electronic calendars. Francik, Rudman, Cooper, and Levine (1991) is a recent review of adoption strategies for groupware technologies based on experiences with a multimedia communications system. Sanderson (1992) discusses the implementation of a videoconference system. Orlikowski (1992) examines cognitive and structural issues in the adoption of a system for organizational memory (see Chapter 9). The need for new interactive media to achieve "critical mass" is stressed and explored in depth in Markus (1990). The fact that payoffs to users who adopt groupware depend upon the behavior of others is explained in Markus and Connelly (1990). Ishii (1990b) and Aizu (1991) challenge us to be aware of differences between cultures that should affect how groupware technologies are designed and will influence how they are used.

Groupware is of course only one of many information technologies whose introduction depends critically upon the social and political context in which it is to be used and which in turn modifies the work environment after it is in use. Rob Kling and his co-workers have over the years written most thoughtfully on these issues. Kling (1980) develops social analyses of computing in terms of theories of *systems rationalism* and *segmented institutionalism.* Kling and Scacchi (1982) contrasts the *discrete-entity* and the *web* models of computing and the impacts of computing. Two other relevant papers are Kling and Iacono (1984), which discusses the role of computing for social control, and Klein (1986). A thought-provoking collection of essays and papers on the value conflicts, social choices, and social impacts of computing is Dunlop and Kling (1991).

Groupware in Practice: An Interpretation of Work Experiences

Christine V. Bullen • John L. Bennett

Introduction

The fact that personal computer (PC) availability in the work place is growing at an astounding rate is being heralded from many corners:

We're going from 11 million to 34 million PCs by 1994. PCs now make up about half the electronic keyboards in use but will account for 70% of the total in 1994. (Dalton, 1988)

About 7 million PCs and 300,000 multiuser systems were installed in the United States by early 1985; and these numbers are still growing at about 15% annually. By 1985, there were terminals or microcomputers for at least 10 million people, or 20% of the United States' white collar work force. (Kling and Iacono, 1989)

The usual assumption, that the use of personal computers contributes to increased worker productivity, is turning into an open question: Loveman reports that at a national economy level, researchers have failed to establish a significant relationship between information technology investments and increased productivity (Loveman, 1988).

What aspects of PC use *could* contribute to measurable increased productivity? How do we get beyond the extravagant claims often associated with PCs to discover the reality of their value? Are changes in the organizational workplace or in the design of systems needed to bring the potential into actual realization? We believe that understanding how PCs are being used now can be important for understanding the value that PCs could potentially bring to the office environment.

Computerization and Controversy. Copyright © 1991 by Academic Press, Inc. All rights of reproduction in any form reserved
ISBN 0-12-224356-0.

One area where personal computers are being brought into use is to support work of business teams.

> Business teams are becoming a way of life in many organizations. . . . Business teams are seen by many as a wave of the future. (Bullen and Johansen, 1988)

> Traditional departments will serve as guardians of standards, as centers for training, and the assignment of specialists; they won't be where the work gets done. That will happen largely in task-focused teams. (Drucker 1988; see also Reich, 1987)

Our particular focus is on looking at people who work in teams and are networked through personal computer workstations. We seek to understand the value that the technology brings to the office environment. We believe the quality of the results of using information technology to support group work has the potential to far exceed what is achieved today through the use of PCs by relatively isolated individuals within organizations.

If indeed teamwork is an important form of office work now—and will be more so in the future—then investigating how teams of people work and studying the use of personal computer workstations in a team environment should be valuable for understanding how information technology is used and how this is affecting productivity in today's organizations. The MIT Commission on Industrial Productivity found the following:

> The third recurring weakness of the U.S. production system that emerged from our industry studies is a widespread failure of cooperation within and among companies. . . . Most thriving firms in the U.S. . . . have learned to integrate technology in their . . . strategies and to link [their strategies] to organizational changes that promote teamwork, training and continuous learning (Berger et al., 1989).

The presence of PCs networked together in communication paths provides the physical infrastructure. But is a new kind of software needed to provide tools for team processes? A term that has become popular during the last few years is *groupware*, software that is intended to be used in support of interpersonal work within an organization:

> *Groupware* is a generic term for specialized computer aids that are designed for the use of collaborative work groups. Typically, these groups are small, project-oriented teams that have important tasks and tight deadlines. . . . Sometimes, groupware is used by permanent groups or departments. . . . Group interactions may be formal or informal, spontaneous or planned, structured or unstructured" (Johansen, 1988; see also Engelbart, 1963, 1968; Hiltz and Turoff, 1978; Stevens, 1981; Hiltz and Kerr, 1981; Kerr and Hiltz, 1982; Rice 1984).

Our questions about the use of PCs, the role of PCs when teams are linked through communications networks, the underlying issue of productivity, and the role of specialized software for use on PCs and workstations all served as background as we began this research project. We used a case study methodology to investigate the current status of group work in organizations and to observe how computer-based tools were being employed in the facilitation of group work. Our purposes in this research are to develop insight on factors that should be influencing software design and to report experiences that can help guide managers who put group support systems into practice.

Research Design

An interview framework (see Appendix I) served as a focus for data gathering. While the outline provided for initial distinctions we knew would be of interest, we let other distinctions emerge from our interviews. This work illustrates a research methodology often used by anthropologists and titled in a variety of ways, including *exploratory observation* (Malone, 1983) and *contextual inquiry* (Bennett *et al.*, 1990). This type of study is not intended to be a controlled experiment or a large sample survey. The technique focuses on interacting with people in their own contexts as they do actual work. The goal of data gathering is to obtain insights through observation, interviews, and interaction. The challenge of this methodology is that it relies on the skill of the observer to report and interpret accurately, while allowing unexpected phenomena to emerge from the examples studied. This approach often results in uncovering research questions that can be investigated through controlled experiments or additional contextual inquiry. Our conclusions present such opportunities for further research.

We spoke with 223 people in 25 organizations, represented at 31 sites (see Table 1 for details on companies, number of interviews, and groupware systems available in each). Each interview lasted a minimum of one hour, with the longest interview lasting two hours. In almost every case, the interviews were carried out in the individual's office or work area.

The 25 organizations represented a wide range of industries and size of companies. We chose organizations in which groupware systems were available, and those systems helped to define the set of groupware systems that we studied. Organization names are coded, as our agreement with those interviewed guaranteed confidentiality. We consulted with each organization to choose groups for our interviews that met the following criteria:

- cohesive business teams, facing challenging environmental conditions that would emphasize the importance of coordination for achieving their goals and objectives; and

- teams that had some form of information technology available to support the work of the group.

The size of our work groups ranged from 7 to 35 people. Those interviewed included individuals at all levels of management within the target work group and, where appropriate, support personnel (administrative assistants and secretaries). In most organizations, the managers to whom the work group reported were also included as part of the case study to help establish some of the contextual information.

We did not choose our groups for study on the basis of a statistically random sample. We contacted potential research sites on the basis of referrals and our own knowledge of their use of technology. However, the resulting sample is drawn from a wide variety of industries, and it includes a wide range of organizational sizes and geographic dispersion. Although these characteristics do not guarantee that the results can be generalized, they do suggest that we are not seeing isolated and unusual instances of groupware tool use.

Conducting a study of work groups raises some interesting questions about how to

Table 1. Companies Studied with Revenues,* Number of People Interviewed, and Groupware Systems Available

Company	Revenues in Billions	Number of People Interviewed	Groupware Systems
BigChem	$30.00	8	PROFS, Higgins, The Coordinator (V.I)
SoapCo	17.00	30	Other, Metaphor, ForComment
InsurCo	12.00	5	PROFS, Higgins
OilCo	11.00	5	PROFS
ExploreCo	10.00	3	Other
ConstrucCo	10.00	3	PROFS, Other
FoodCo	9.60	3	PROFS, The Coordinator (V.I), Higgins
TerminalCo	9.40	10	All-In-1
RBOC	8.00	10	PROFS, Higgins
HealthCo	8.00	20	All-In-1
BankCo	6.80	5	All-In-1
MedCons	6.00	3	PROFS, ForComment
LawCo	5.00	3	Higgins
ServBuro	4.40	13	The Coordinator (V.I)
SnackCo	2.00	35	The Coordinator (V.I), Other
BeerCo	1.40	6	Metaphor
SmallCons	1.40	10	Other
CableCo	1.00	15	The Coordinator (V.I)
SmallChem	1.00	5	The Coordinator (V.I)
PubServBuro	0.90	3	PROFS, Other
TransDist	0.18	10	The Coordinator (V.I)
SmallRes	**	3	Other
IndCons	**	2	The Coordinator (V.I)
StateBuro	n/a	3	PROFS, ForComment
BigU	n/a	10	PROFS, ForComment, Other

PROFS available in many places; studied in 2.
*Revenues approximate, 1988.
**Revenues less than $1 million.

typical weekly topics: external issues like marketing and client management, internal issues like getting the work done, administrative issues like corporate planning and training. The work group includes everyone from the president and founder to the support staff.

At SoapCo, the work group is a flexible concept such that at times it involves an organizational entity at one location (e.g., the Boston marketing group), and at other times it consists of the worldwide instances of the organizational entity (e.g., all marketing groups), and under still other circumstances, the work group is a subset of entities (e.g., Boston, Chicago, and San Francisco marketing groups). Within each group, levels of management range from corporate vice president to support staff. The overriding functional responsibility focuses the work of each group on one primary area.

In the world of electronic communications, the composition of work groups is showing important changes from those observed in the past. Because of flexibility provided by communication technology of all kinds, it is becoming more difficult to identify a formal organizational unit as a work group. That is, some people co-located in an office area do not necessarily work together as a group, and people geographically separated may form a team focused on achieving a common work result. Through the power of electronic media, these groups are dynamic and fluid; this is true for both formal and information organizational units.

The traditional concept of an 'organization' is no longer useful to managers or students of organizations. It is dominated by models of structure and physical identity at a time when telecommunications has eroded the boundaries between firms and changed the nature of coordination across geographic location (Keen, 1988).

Given our research interest in the factors important for software specifically designed for use by teams, we had to develop a working definition of what constitutes *groupware*. Early notions of groupware reflected a clear connection between the software tool and the group processes. However, current manifestations of groupware tools appear to focus on the technical qualities of functionality and may, in effect, ignore the dynamics of group use.

We have employed a broad definition in our research in order to accommodate the evolving nature of this field. In time, *groupware* will probably be narrowed to include only those tools specifically designed to support group work. However, at present, it is useful to include all tools being used to support group work, even if the tools represent user adaptation of an existing technology (e.g., group agreement to share files and calendars on a system designed to keep such functionality private). Therefore, our working definition of groupware is computer-based tools that can be used by work groups to facilitate the exchange and sharing of information.

A number of systems, with a large variety of functionality, fall under this groupware umbrella. Figure 1 illustrates a framework for organizing these systems using the dimensions of time and place to create four domains that describe circumstances of interpersonal work (Bullen and Johansen, 1988):

- same time, same place
- same time, different place
- different time, same place

define inclusion in a work group. What are its bounds? Work groups have been defined as "identifiable and bounded subsystems of a whole organization [with a] recognized purpose, which unifies the people and activities" (Trist, 1981); "collaborating groups of information workers" (Bikson *et al.*, 1989); and "multiple individuals acting as a bounded whole in order to get something done" (Rousseau, 1983).

We found a variety of organizational forms constituting work groups and organizational conditions in which the work groups functioned. For example, at CableCo the work group coincides with the organizational department, although it is spread geographically across the continental United States. Four levels of management are included: corporate functional vice president, regional directors, geographic managers, and support staff. As a growing firm, this functional area is dealing with business pressure to support corporate client growth, a rapidly expanding customer group, hiring and training of new staff, and planning and managing new initiatives in international markets.

At SmallCons, the work group consists of the entire firm. As a very small organization, the work group handles a full range of organizational tasks. The following represent

• different time, different place

	SAME TIME	DIFFERENT TIMES
SAME PLACE	Meeting Facilitation Group DSS Room	Presentation Project Management Team Room
DIFFERENT PLACES	Conference Calls Video Conf Screen Sharing Spontaneous Mtgs	Email Computer Conf Collab Write Conversational Struc

Figure 1. Categorizing systems with respect to time and place.

Although each of these domains is important and the four are interdependent, for this study we decided to investigate those computer systems that can be used to facilitate work in the different time, different place domain. (The other domains are being extensively studied by a number of organizations, including the University of Arizona, the University of Michigan, IBM, GM, DEC, MCC, and others.)

Information Technology Tools Studied

In the course of the case studies, we focused on the use of eight different information technology systems at various times and various locations. The choice of the specific systems was influenced by their presence at the organizations that agreed to participate. Within the various systems a number of functions can be considered as tools that can be used for support of groups. In order to describe these systems broadly, we make the following generalizations. All of the systems studied provide the following functionality:

Construction/editing facilities. All systems provide at least a rudimentary text creation and editing facility. Some include elaborate editors and provide function to import graphics. One special-purpose system (ForComment) focuses on joint authorship and editing as an aspect of group work.

Electronic exchange of text. This includes electronic mail and/or conferencing, gateways to other systems (both internal and external, e.g., facsimile transfer), and document transfer. As a result of the text being captured in a computer-readable form, the content can be reused, edited, re-sent, etc. Capabilities with respect to exchange of graphics, images, and spreadsheet data differ in different tool environments. Some of the tools provide ways to manage the exchange of text through folders or through automatically linking related messages.

Directory. This functionality at a minimum provides a name and electronic address file to support data exchange by users of the system. Some of the tools provide a traditional "little black book" functionality, where extensive data on mailing addresses, multiple telephone numbers, and notes about individuals (e.g., secretary's name) can be stored.

Time marking and time keeping. All the tools except one (ForComment) provide a facility for recording events scheduled for a particular date. The capability ranges from this basic task to recording, for example, repetitive events, reminders, and "to do" lists, and linking these data to other system functions.

General tools. Some of the systems provide tools for the support of work in financial and budgeting areas, and because of the ways in which the tools can be used, support some project tracking capability.

Integration across the functionality provided is an interesting concept in groupware research for two specific reasons:

1. We found people hindered in the use of tools because of problems associated with the degree of integration.

2. This term is used imprecisely by both vendors and users as a measure of quality in describing groupware systems. Therefore it showed up often in our interviews and we feel there is value in defining integration and exploring its application to these systems.

The concept of *integration of function* needed for support of group work is a relative term. One aspect of integration can be measured by examining the process required for each user to move freely between functions, and by looking for the presence of system-dictated steps (e.g., log off from one function, log on to another function). Another aspect is the extent to which the software enables the user to move data from one function to another without requiring special transformations. Thus, integration, as we use the term, refers to the *flow of control* during work by an individual or by team members, and to the *flow of data* during the process of individual interaction with the software or during interaction among team members.

Integration within and across the functional categories listed above differed significantly among the various tools. As a result some of the systems resembled a group of functions rather than a cohesive package. Brief descriptions of the individual systems appear in Appendix II. Table 2 shows a list of the systems and gives the general categories of functionality provided in each. We do not provide here specific information on the details of operation for each tool. The range of capability is wide in terms of search mechanisms, ordering rules, etc.

Observations, Key Issues, and Conclusions

In this section we summarize the results of our study. It is important to understand that, because of the complexity of intervening factors, the observations we report here do not have simple explanations. Research by Iacono and Kling (1988) and Markus and Forman (1989) supports the notion that we need to take multiple perspectives in performing research in organizations. We have found the framework suggested by Iacono and Kling (shown in Table 3) to be particularly useful to us as we sorted out factors influencing the adoption of technology. From a tool perspective, technical solutions are offered as if the innovative benefits of the function would overshadow any historical, political, and social factors that might be present in the environment. Instead, Iacono and Kling find that the environments into which computer-based tools are introduced should be viewed as institutions. As institutions, the environments exhibit many barriers to adoption that have little or nothing to do with the technical merits of the innovative tools. Consideration of historical, political, and social factors can forewarn those developing tools and those introducing them into the environment where computer-based support is provided.

We conceptualize these patterns as the social organization of computing. We define 'social organization of computing' as the choices about computing (both social and technical) which become embedded in work environments and which are experienced by the users as part of the social practices in their everyday work world (Iacono and Kling, 1988).

Other researchers have stressed the importance of understanding the balance between a technology perspective and an organizational one. Bikson *et al.* (1989) comment

group members are interdependent not only on one another but also on the technology, and technical and organizational issues are closely interrelated. The more advanced the information-handling tools provided to the group, the more critical it becomes to give equivalent and concurrent attention to the social processes through which these tools are deployed, and to seek a mutual adaptation rather than maximization of either the social or technical system in isolation (p. 89). (See also Mumford and Ward, 1968.)

In making our observations and drawing conclusions we were struck by the importance of understanding the complex interplay of factors that influenced the specific organizations we studied. However, in order to simplify the presentation of our conclusions we have sorted them into two categories:

From a design perspective. In this category we discuss those conclusions that designers ought to consider when conceptualizing functionality for groupware systems. Our conclusions suggest that while designers must be concerned about the technical solutions, they need to go beyond the "tool perspective" to include an appreciation for organizational factors that may influence the use of groupware systems.

From an organizational perspective. In this category we discuss those conclusions that management ought to consider when planning for and implementing groupware systems. These conclusions suggest ways in which managers could anticipate organizational factors that might influence the groupware implementation process and subsequent use. However, managers must also be careful to not fall into a pure "institutional perspective" to the exclusion of concern about the quality of the technical solutions.

As with any categorization, this dichotomy of conclusions is an oversimplification that we make for analysis purposes. These groupings clearly overlap, and we believe designers will find useful information in the second grouping, and managers will benefit from the conclusions in the first category.

As interviewers, observers, and interpreters of these work experiences, we have been conscious of these perspectives. In the following discussion of key issues and conclusions we support the ideas using observations and quotations from our field work. Some of the

Table 2. Tools Studied

	Construction/Editing Facilities	Electronic Exchange of Text	Directory	Time Marking/Time Keeping	General Tools
All-In-1	Yes	Yes	Yes	Yes	Some
ForComment	Yes	Specialized	Specialized	No	No
Higgins	Yes	Yes	Yes	Yes	Yes
In-House System 1	Yes	Yes	Specialized	No	Some
In-House System 2	Yes	Yes	No	No	No
Metaphor	Yes	Yes	Specialized	Some	Specialized
PROFS	Yes	Yes	Yes	Yes	Some
The Coordinator (V.I)	Yes	Yes	Specialized	Yes	Some

researchable questions that emerged are suggested in each section. However, others can be formed from the work reported here.

From a Design Perspective

Electronic Message Communication is the Primary Tool

The functionality for sending and receiving electronic messages, available in all of the products we studied, was by far the function most heavily used and universally stated as valuable.

"I love this tool. I can reach people and they can reach me anytime, anyplace and discuss anything." (Senior Manager, SnackCo)

The desire to have support for communication within a work group was usually the primary motivation for acquiring the tool. People quickly learned the electronic messaging functions, and this contrasted with their failure to use many of the other functions available in these systems. The simple presence of function in a groupware tool does not in any way mean that it will be used. In each system we studied, several of the available functions were ignored by the using groups. However the electronic messaging capability, regardless of its user interface design, ease or difficulty, or level of sophistication, was used extensively. In several instances interface features were either ignored or adapted by the people to accomplish a simplified process of communicating electronically.

For example, the interface provided by The Coordinator (Version I) contains language related to the underlying theory of speech acts (Searle, 1969). This terminology is intended to lead the users to think about what they are doing and then to characterize particular communications as one of several choices, e.g., a request or promise, etc. While the software provides a choice for simple e-mail (called "free form"), we found people consistently sending each other "requests" regardless of the content of the message. Not surprisingly, "request" is the first menu choice and where the cursor falls by default. Many people we interviewed reported that they ignored the choices and just "hit enter" to send a message. However, they had high praise for the tool:

"The Coordinator gets the information out! . . . The Coordinator opens communication lines." (Senior Manager, CableCo)

"The Coordinator's major advantage: instant communication with a large audience." (Senior Manager, SnackCo)

In another example, the user interface for Higgins electronic mail walks the user through a series of steps to answer questions about how to assign key words, follow-up dates, etc. A person using Higgins to help manage information or for sharing messages in the groupware sense would answer these questions. However, the users we observed skipped through this menu leaving blanks in most categories. People reported that they understood the value of the categories, and knew that they "should" be filling the blanks, but that they were in a hurry and just wanted to get the message sent.

One possible response to this observation is that the message-flow needs of work groups are so great that they overshadow the other system-based activities. This

Table 3.   Iacono and Kling Framework

	Tool Perspective	Institution Perspective
Historical *past decisions that may limit future actions*	Assume freedom from past; focus on future technology perfection; less attention to present; assume individuals free to move in new direction. Groups less a factor.	Interests served in past are present in current situation; those commitments constrain future choices; individuals assume current activities will persist; interdependence of groups.
Political *control over access to resources*	Local control and self-interest assumed paramount; potential conflicts rarely recognized; assume power of technology will overcome political barriers.	Shared control and shared interest groups recognized; specialization limits possible changes; organizational structure (social-structure) may hinder adaptation and survival.
Social *staff skills, patterns of control and discipline*	Local and simple negotiating context without constraints from other sources.	Complex and overlapping negotiating contexts within and among groups.

immediately suggests that we need a definition for this kind of communication, which, on the basis of what we observed, could be termed sending and receiving messages. Any of a number of the tools provided as part of a groupware system can be also thought of as entering into "communication" in the sense that they can be used to support transfer of information in some way, for example:

- calendar entries
- expense reports
- reports of project status
- telephone directory
- spreadsheets
- budget reports
- tickler files/to do lists.

It is interesting to note that these particular functions tend to be separated from electronic messaging in the information technology tools themselves. We do not support this distinction as correct. However, as we observed and interviewed people, we found that they acted as if this separation of functionality was real for them, and they generally spoke in terms of "e-mail and the other things the system can do."

This raises the interesting point of how to distinguish between what people say they do (or want to do) with information technology tools versus what people think they should or should not do because they have been influenced by the tools at hand. We cannot answer this question definitively. We can, however, say that given the choices existing in information technology tools today, the people we studied used what we are calling "message functions" almost exclusively.

Our interviewees frequently stated that they chose groupware systems because of the mix of functionality offered. Given that, an important question is: Why do they *not* use most of the functions?

For example, users say they want groupware tools that provide calendaring functions. Yet in the majority of organizations we studied the calendar tools were not being used. People gave a variety of reasons; the net result is the fact that although the desired function was present, this did not in and of itself mean that it was used.

"We thought having the calendaring function available on PROFS would be useful in organizing meetings, but no one has taken the time to learn about it." (Manager, InsurCo)

"One of the reasons we chose Higgins was because of the wide range of functionality it provides. However, most people just use the e-mail." (Support Staff, RBOC)

If developers commit resources to provide function, it is important to understand what is seen by users as a barrier between "offered" (by the system) and "used" (by the people). Other factors, as we shall report, were important in determining whether a function was used.

Our field observations show that the tool people use the most is electronic messaging. The message flow needs of work groups appear to be so great that messaging overshadows other system-based functions. If we can assume that these busy people would use just those system portions essential for their work, we may conclude that electronic

messaging support is what is most needed. In the following sections, however, we discuss other factors that increase the complexity of forming this conclusion. A researchable question here revolves around gaining a better understanding of the value to the user of the electronic messaging function as compared to the value of other functionality. Another research topic raised by this conclusion is understanding the barriers to effective use of the functionality other than electronic messaging.

Message Linking is a Key Improvement Provided by Electronic Communications

One aspect of electronic message communication that stood out in our interviews was the ability to link messages concerned with one subject area or with a distribution list. This functionality is provided in two of the tools (Higgins and The Coordinator) and it is also inherent in the concept of computer conferencing, which is available in All-in-1 (VAX Notes) and in In-House System I.

Computer conferencing organizes all electronic messages according to topic areas. Therefore, when a message is composed and sent, it is addressed to a topic. The concept of a *topic* is not limited in any way, and can in fact represent a project, general discussion, software release, distribution list, individual, etc.

People reported in our interviews that they gained much value by being able to "look in one place for all discussion pertaining to project XYZ." In contrast to this observation, users of e-mail systems like PROFS and All-in-1 (without VAX Notes), complained about the difficulties of tracking down related messages and managing their mail folders (i.e., files for grouping messages by categories).

Message linking provides four primary values:

- collection of notes in one place
- chronological record
- ability for latecomers to view an entire record of interaction
- knowledge of the "right" place to put new messages.

In The Coordinator (Version I) this functionality is embodied in a concept basic to the underlying theory: the "conversation" is the primary unit of interaction. Because of this, each time someone replies to a message, the reply is automatically linked to all previous messages in the stream and becomes part of the "conversation."

"I use the traceback function a lot to find out how we arrived at a particular point in the conversation." (Senior Manager, SnackCo)

"If I receive an answer to my request that is not linked, I get annoyed because it messes up the ability to follow back through the conversation." (Manager, CableCo)

Users found this feature of The Coordinator one of the most valuable aspects of the tool.

Our interviews showed clearly that people value the ability to group and link messages that are related by subject. This "computer conferencing" capability has been available for more than 15 years in electronic communication systems (Johansen, 1988). However, general understanding of how it works and general availability to users has been limited. It remains interesting to us that this functionality should be singled out by many users as a key benefit of groupware.

Historically, knowledge workers have always sought ways to organize the volume of information they manage. The first major innovation to affect this process was the vertical file system (the file cabinet, in 1892), which facilitated the grouping of correspondence by subject:

[Vertical files] had several advantages over [other forms of filing]. Most importantly, the folders allowed related papers to be grouped together and easily removed from the files for use. . . . The new equipment alone was not enough to make storage and retrieval efficient. In a textbook on filing published by the Library Bureau, vertical filing of correspondence was defined as including the *organization* of papers in the files, as well as the filing apparatus itself: "The definition of vertical filing as applied to correspondence is—the bringing together, in one place, all correspondence to, from or about an individual, firm, place or subject, filed on edge, usually in folders and behind guides, making for speed, accuracy and accessibility." (Yates, 1989)

In effect, nothing has changed: groupware message linking or conferencing allows people to carry out this task for electronic correspondence!

The need represented in our interviews (i.e., comments on the value of message linking) is one that should be carefully investigated by both designers and implementers of groupware. People use message linking to manage communications and documents, keep records, and develop "group memory." This conclusion may be telling us a great deal more than is at first obvious: rather than looking at "fancy," innovative functions for groupware systems, designers should be focusing on how to better solve the basic need of office workers, i.e., managing large volumes of information. There may well be ways other than those we see today for designers to address these needs and better serve the groupware user.

What Functionality is Included and How It Is Offered are Important Factors

It became very clear through our interviews that people did not use some of the functionality in groupware systems because of the design of the tool. There are two characteristics of design quality that we observed.

What functionality is included. One of the best examples of functionality requested by "the marketplace" but not used effectively is the calendaring function. The explanations we were given in our interviews focused on one fact: electronic calendars in their current form cannot replace traditional paper ones. The topic of electronic calendars would justify a separate paper, but we can summarize some of the key problems.

1. Traditional calendars are not simply places where you record times for events to take place on dates, though electronic calendars are usually limited to such a simple function. Traditional calendars have notes on them, contain telephone numbers, are often color coded, and have other papers attached (such as yellow sticky notes or paper-clipped memos, letters, etc.). The nonhomogeneity of traditional calendars is actually an asset for finding important information (there are parallels here with Malone's (1983) findings on desk organization).

"I honestly tried to use the calendar in Higgins, but I found it frustrating to not

have my familiar book with all its messy notes, colors, and papers clips." (Senior Manager, RBOC)

2. Electronic calendars are not portable, and paper copies of the information contained in the computer are inadequate substitutes. Notes made on the paper copies often do not get keyed back into the computer-based version.

"I need a portable calendar for traveling. My secretary makes me a copy of the computer one for trips, but it is ugly and hard to read. Then I have to make notes on it and do not put them in the computer, and everything gets out of sync for a while." (Manager, HealthCo)

3. The group calendaring value of electronic calendaring is lost unless everyone cooperates. People do not have an incentive to maintain their calendars in such a way that they support group use. In addition, people object to the notion that others (not their secretaries) may schedule their time.

"We tried to use it to schedule meetings and found that several guys weren't keeping their calendars up to date. So almost as many phone calls get made and it takes just as long." (Secretary, ConstrucCo)

4. The process of setting up meetings is not always a mechanical one. There are times when negotiation is required to secure the presence of all desired parties.

"When we set up meetings we have to go through lots of negotiation since the board is made up of members from many locations. Dates for regular meetings get established well in advance and put on everyone's calendar. But setting up special meetings requires lots of personal contact." (Administrative Assistant, TransDist)

5. Very often those who take time to input the information never gain the value of group calendaring because others (usually secretaries) do the group scheduling. Therefore people see a basic economic imbalance of input effort to output value (see also Grudin, 1988).

"It seems I do all the work and Harry's secretary gets all the benefits!" (Manager, BigU)

The calendar function has potential for supporting important group activities (keeping track of time commitments), but the current combination of software and hardware is seen by users as "not up to our needs."

How the functionality is offered. The second aspect of functionality relates to the way it is offered to users. Aside from the functional limitations mentioned above, calendaring was not used in several of the systems because people found the process of use awkward (e.g., no easy way to indicate recurring events). In other examples, people reported that they could not use a tool effectively because they could not remember how to access a particular function and could find no effective help on-line or in the written manuals.

Aspects of the user interface design were also important factors in the reaction people had to The Coordinator (Version I)(see also Bair and Gale, 1988). Although people in fact used the package, and stated that the product was valuable to them:

"It's great for communication breakdowns since you can backtrack the conversations and find out what went wrong." (Manager, SnackCo)

they also commented on the terminology of the interface:

"I am not enchanted with the verbiage." (Manager, ServBuro)

Two other products, ForComment and Higgins, were consistently praised for their interfaces, even though some other aspects of their designs were criticized.

"ForComment is a joy to use; it's so easy to understand the menu items without a manual or checking 'Help'." (Senior Manager, SoapCo)

"Higgins menus are self-evident, and the use of color is really nice." (Manager, RBOC)

It has long been recognized that user interface design is a critical element in the successful use of a software product (Martin, 1973). Therefore it is not surprising that it continues to be an important element in the case of groupware tools. However, it may be that because people in a work group use these tools, additional factors must be considered in interface design. For example, in a single-user product, like the spreadsheet, designers must be concerned about how each user interprets menus and takes action. In addition, must address the issue of how what that user does is interpreted by many others, individually and as a group. Additionally, the individual is acting as a representative of the group that may influence how the tool is used and interpreted.

It is important to note that an intergroup transaction is not the same as an interpersonal one, although both take place between individuals. A group member involved in intergroup transactions acts as a representative of the group in accordance with the group's expectations. The member is not acting solely on an individual agenda (in Ancona, 1987).

For example, one person may choose to use an all-lower-case character style to indicate "informality" in notes. This style may be detrimental in communication if other users interpret this as not having enough concern to compose a note properly. The judgment of this user's behavior can then be made not only against that individual, but against the group as being, for example, unprofessional. Such issues introduce many more layers of complexity into the interface design process, and they emerge from a social analysis of our interview data rather than an analysis that looks purely at the technological merits of a design.

In conclusion, it is clear from our interviews that the quality of design, both in terms of functionality provided and access to that functionality, is an important factor in how and whether people use groupware tools. The researchable questions suggested by this conclusion focus on gaining a better understanding of 1) interface design in software that serves a team of users, and 2) the actual tasks carried out by individuals acting as members of groups.

Isolated Tools Hinder Productive Use of Groupware Systems

The tools are considered isolated with respect to the flow of user control during work and with respect to the flow of data among tools (as discussed earlier). In some cases the

process of accessing the function of a second tool when using one tool (i.e., flow of control) requires an awkward sequence of user actions. Other cases require the transfer of data from one tool to another (i.e., flow of data). (See also Nielsen et al., 1986.)

Transfer of user control. In several of the organizations we studied, it was necessary for the people to go through a series of steps in order to move from the groupware tool they were using for their business group/team to other tools they were required to use for tasks relating to the firm as a whole. For example, some groups used a personal computer e-mail system like those available on Higgins or The Coordinator within their departments, but they had to change to a mainframe-based tool like PROFS or All-In-1 for e-mail access to other parts of their companies. This was universally considered to be an aggravation and a waste of time, regardless of the ease or difficulty associated with the switch.

"I want to log on to The Coordinator and Excell at the same time because I need to bounce back and forth from moment to moment." (Manager, SmallChem)

"Because Forecasting uses Metaphor to analyze sales data from last year, pricing people are using HP3000's, and I have my analysis programs on a Compaq 386, I have a heck of a time moving between functions I need to access when we set up a promotional campaign." (Manager, BeerCo)

"It's such a pain. I actually have to crawl behind my desk and change plugs. Is this modern technology?!!!" (Analyst, SnackCo)

Transfer of data. Tools that were not completely integrated required that the result from one task be consciously moved into the environment of another tool in order to perform additional tasks. Most users were annoyed by this step, irrespective of its ease or difficulty. From the examples given above to illustrate flow of control problems, it is clear that transfer of data is also a problem at some of the sites.

"I know it is hard to believe, but we actually have to print the output from the HP3000 programs and key the data in to the Compaq 386 because we haven't found a more cost-effective way to move the data across directly." (Analyst, BeerCo)

The ForComment system, highly praised in most respects, was singled out here with respect to data transfer. In order to use ForComment, the person must import text created elsewhere. Although this is a straightforward step, users consistently commented that they would prefer that the functionality provided by ForComment be available as part of the word processor they used to create the text.

"I love ForComment, but I wish it were part of our word processing package. I am always afraid something will get lost in the transfer, so I take the time to check the whole document." (Manager, BigU)

With respect to both flow of control and flow of data, the interviews showed very clearly that a lack of integration from either integration perspective was a barrier to the use of some groupware tools. In addition Ancona's (1987) research on boundary management (i.e., the management of the group's relations with environments and individuals external to the group) raises an interesting point with respect to flow of control. She found that teams equally matched on group process characteristics could be differentiated based on their boundary management capability. This implies that boundary management is a key aspect of team performance and, therefore, productivity. If teams are using groupware systems that interfere with their ability to perform boundary management (e.g., the team e-mail system is not easily connected to the organizational e-mail system), their productivity may be adversely affected. From this we conclude that productive use of groupware is reduced when the tools are isolated.

From an Organizational Perspective

People Report Most Value from Tools That Parallel Their Non-electronic Activities

Those we interviewed reported that use of e-mail, for example, was "easy" because it was analogous to, but better than, what they did without groupware tools. People saw computer messaging as an improvement over "the old way" because it was faster, traceable, geography- and time-independent, and accessible from almost any location (e.g., at home, while traveling). Therefore it was easy for people to see the benefits to them in learning how to communicate electronically.

Other functions provided by the systems either differed significantly from what people saw as needed (e.g., electronic calendars) or presented capabilities that they were not currently employing. In the latter category, functions such as project tracking, reminders, directories, and expense tracking all represent tasks that the people interviewed were not doing. Therefore, to use the electronic version of these tools would require them to expend resources for activities they did not normally carry out or carried out only infrequently.

We therefore conclude that the designers, developers, and installers of groupware tools are presented with an interesting challenge: How are people going to make a transition to the new practices that some of the functionality enables? Part of the answer lies in designing functionality that is easy to learn and to remember after long periods of non-use. However, another part of the answer is found in the organizational considerations related to examining current work processes.

Benefits Gained Need to Balance or Outweigh the Invested Resource

The benefits from some of the functionality (other than that provided for messaging) were neither clear nor balanced in our interviewees' minds. In fact users often perceived extra effort on their part for no corresponding gain. For example, people currently do not have an incentive to maintain an electronic calendar to support group use. They see the work involved as redundant (since most also wanted to have a portable calendar on paper in any case). Though they agreed that their managers and groups would benefit, the value to them personally was too far removed to motivate their behavior. They likened their maintaining calendars and project information to "keypunching" activities. Yet the group value of electronic calendaring is realized only when everyone cooperates.

Messaging functions, however, had a beneficial impact on them directly. They experienced the satisfaction of "getting the message out," "putting the ball in the other guy's court," assigning tasks to group members, etc. On the receiving side, they had a record

of what they were expected to do and, through being on copy lists, had a sense of being in touch with what was going on in the group. They had no need to conceptualize anything beyond a personal benefit.

Other functions as mentioned previously (e.g., project tracking, reminders, etc.) actually required additional effort on the part of the users to learn to do things in a different way, independent of the technology. Although the people we interviewed often said things like "I should do expense tracking," "I know it would be more efficient if I kept an electronic directory," "I could really benefit from the reminder function," invariably they were unwilling to adapt their behavior and invest the personal resources necessary to employ this kind of functionality. They had not identified benefits to using the technology that equalled or exceeded their resource investment.

Grudin explores "the disparity between who does the work and who gets the benefit" and raises some serious questions about whether groupware applications will ever succeed:

Not all groupware introduces such a disparity—with electronic mail, for example, everyone generally shares the benefits and burdens equally. But electronic mail may turn out to be more the exception that proves the rule unless greater care is taken to distribute the benefit in other applications (Grudin, 1989).

Therefore, we can conclude that unless there is a balance between the effort required on the part of the user and the benefit delivered to that user, a person is not likely to employ the functionality present in a tool. Other forms of motivation (e.g., management directives, group agreement, education) can be important in influencing the perception of balance. Research to investigate motivation and change management as part of the implementation of groupware technology could be beneficial in understanding the dynamics here.

Groupware Implementation Is Simultaneously a Social and Technical Intervention

Our research observations support Kling and Iacono (1989): "computerization is simultaneously a social and technical intervention." One of the most important aspects of this complex intervention is that it is a "strategic intervention" (Kling and Iacono, 1989, p. 342). Whether the strategy of technology introduction is made explicit or kept implicit, it exists and can have a significant impact on the organization.

In our research we saw the effects of strategies on the individuals we interviewed. For example, when a groupware system was introduced as a way to streamline procedures by merely training new users in the mechanics of the tools, we saw people using a minimum of the functionality present in the systems. That is, people used what they were taught to use without any innovative thinking on their parts about either 1) how to employ other functionality present in the groupware systems, or 2) how to use what they had learned creatively to have an impact on the way they carried out their work. When instruction went beyond mechanical steps, however, to include, for example, a presentation on the concepts of groupware, or material on how to relate the groupware functionality to accomplishing their work tasks, then people made use of, and applied creative thinking to using, the functionality present in the tool.

When a groupware system was introduced as a new technology to experiment with, the people did not take it seriously and did not look for ways to augment their productivity. When decision makers held high expectations for productivity enhancement through groupware, yet gave no attention to examining the work process, people reported that they felt under pressure to perform better while learning a new tool and without a clear understanding of how the tool would make a difference. In many of these cases, the introduction of the groupware system had a negative effect on productivity.

Organizational factors in the following four general categories showed up as consistently important as we interviewed people in the 25 organizations.

Champions. Management support for the introduction of groupware tools varied significantly in our sample. In some organizations, support for the tool emanated from the top levels of the firm:

"When the president wanted us to use this e-mail package without even looking at any others, we thought it was strange, but had enough faith in [him] to try it." (Senior Manager, CableCo)

At others, like SnackCo, the management support was at the departmental level:

"We thought this tool was weird, but if WW asked us to try it, we knew it was worth doing." (Manager)

In some instances, the support came lower in the organization in the form of middle management individuals who felt they could engineer successful pilots and demonstrate the value of the tools to upper management:

"Through my own coaching and interpersonal skills I have been able to teach people and win them over to the value of using The Coordinator. Now management is paying attention." (Manager, ServBuro)

Though these instances of managerial support represent very different levels of power within each organization, they demonstrate the importance in general of a committed leader in the introduction of a new technology. Management literature for decades has discussed the value of leadership and champions for the successful implementation of an innovation. In the area of groupware tools, this common wisdom continues to be valid. However, as the previous observations have shown, and the next observations will suggest, managerial support by itself cannot guarantee successful implementation by itself.

Expectations. We observed two different work groups in one organization in which the same software had been introduced. In one of these groups (Group A) the tool was originally described as a new technology that the group members should familiarize themselves with and see what they could use it for. In the other group (Group B) the tool was described as an important new technology that was going to be used to improve communication throughout the organization. Five years later, when we conducted our interviews, the original attitudes were present in these two groups and were influencing the use of the software. As a result, in Group A the tool had never been taken seriously and was still considered "an experiment" and informal. In Group B the tool was described by people as "critical to their jobs."

It is clear from our studies and those of others "that the kinds of expectations with which an organization approaches new information technology do much to define the consequences that will be observed" (Carroll and Perin, 1988). Therefore the way in which new groupware tools are introduced into the work group will influence the ways in which they are used.

Training. Those interviewed generally described the training that they had received in the use of their software as directed toward building procedural or mechanical skills —basic instruction in what keys to push to accomplish specific tasks. This was true for all the tools we studied. However, in the case of The Coordinator, we did interview some users who had received training that included an introduction to the theory underlying this product. A subset of this group reported that the ideas were too sophisticated for them and their colleagues to assimilate:

"The linguistic concept went over most people's heads." (Manager, SnackCo)

"The training left me cold, but we pursued the value on our own." (Senior Manager, CableCo)

However, some reported that knowledge of the theory helped them to use the tool and to implement the communication practices that the tool supports:

"Knowledge of speech-act theory has really helped me use The Coordinator to be more effective in my daily communication." (Manager, ServBuro)

"The workshops were inspirational and make using The Coordinator vocabulary much easier." (Manager, SnackCo)

Given the previous observations that people are not using the functionality provided by these tools, the fact that they have received only basic, mechanical training would tend to indicate that the training is not adequate.

"Training was not very good, but we figured it out." (Manager, MedCons)

Evolution. After an initial introduction into the use of a groupware tool, the users we interviewed tended to "practice" only those procedures that they needed to accomplish their most urgent business tasks. As a result, much of what they were initially trained to do but did not continue to do regularly was forgotten.

"Two weeks after the training program I could barely remember how to get to my file directory." (Senior Manager, LawCo)

In the use of any system, people will encounter special case needs for functions from time to time in their work. Those interviewed did not regularly look up procedures in a manual when these situations arose. When online help was available, most who used it were unable to find what they needed. Instead, the typical form of help sought was to ask a colleague or subordinate.

"I refuse to read manuals and documentation; they aren't even written in English!" (Manager, BigChem)

"The only copy of the manual I could find was two years old and inappropriate to the version I am using." (Manager, SoapCo)

"On-line 'Help' is a bust. It never covers the exact problem I'm having and is written with lots of jargon." (Senior Manager, FoodCo)

"I always ask Joe for help. He can tell me in two seconds where I've gone wrong." (Support Staff, BigU)

"Sue explains my mistakes in the context of our work. That makes it easier for me to remember for next time." (Senior Manager, TerminalCo)

Some of the organizations provided a person or group to serve as the designated support source to which the users would turn for help. These organizations appeared to understand the evolutionary nature of a person's use of software, and they supported that evolution through a formal organizational entity. Other sites we studied assumed that once the initial training had taken place, no formal corporate role of an ongoing nature was needed. In these cases, de facto support grew up in the form of individuals in work groups who became "local gurus."

"Dick has become the guy we all go to for help. He's part of our department and understands our questions best." (Manager, TerminalCo)

"The Infocenter has been wonderful in supporting the use of this tool. They are always available and polite in telling you where you made your mistakes." (Senior Manager, OilCo)

We observed what might be called a "plateau of competence" in using a tool. Without a timely and user-appropriate incentive to move beyond self-standardized use, people tend to settle into standard operations (Rosson, 1985). We observed close group interaction serving as a constructive stimulus for individuals. In SnackCo a central person sent out a newsletter of hints and ideas that was found useful by some. However, the presence of new ideas was countered by pressure to "get the job done," so many people found little time to try new things. This suggests that such stimuli must be in the form of easily tried procedures with immediately visible value so that they fit into the practices carried out during a busy day.

In each of the categories—champions, expectations, training, evolution—we saw a need for sensitivity to organizational issues. In addition the degree and timing of organizational intervention must be planned. The risk of failure increases when the multiple organizational factors are not considered. In the case of groupware technology, there is very little experience in understanding these factors, which may be particularly complex because of the "group" aspects of the application.

Process Redesign May Be Required to Realize Productivity Improvement

We have just suggested that organizations should consider the perspectives of people at all levels when introducing technology. It is also interesting to consider the extent to which organizations need to alter their basic processes in order to achieve higher levels of coordination and productivity.

This process redesign may occur on a variety of levels. For example, traditional process redesign looks at formal processes that have been established in an organization in order to achieve its business goals and objectives. These processes are reevaluated for a variety of reasons, including changes in products or services, changes in the structure of industry, and the impacts of new technology on basic functions (e.g., manufacturing or distribution channels).

However, process redesign can be employed on a local level in an organization. For example, the process of work coordination in a department or the process of conducting meetings may be areas in which productivity gains could be achieved through rethinking and redesigning the traditional forms (e.g., Whiteside and Wixon, 1988). In our field work we observed instances of management expecting substantial productivity improvement to result from the simple act of putting a groupware system into place. In these instances our interviews did not uncover any significant change in how people approached their jobs. Some felt that the new technology created more work for them and therefore made them less productive.

Whenever we observed the implementation of groupware technology without a concurrent examination of how work procedures and coordination might change or evolve, we saw that these systems had very little impact on the perceived productivity of the groups. These observations lead us to the conclusion that in some cases when groupware systems are implemented, not enough attention is being placed on examining the basic processes of work and how technology may enhance these processes. Therefore, process redesign may be required to achieve productive benefits in using groupware technology.

Creating Productive Teams Is a Challenge

Managers in some of the organizations we studied had explicit goals of changing the way work was carried out, moving their groups to new planes of performance, creating "paradigm shifts":

"I am intrigued by the linguistic theory underlying The Coordinator and would like to see everyone undergo a paradigm shift and significantly change the way they interact." (Senior Manager, SnackCo)

Does the current generation of groupware systems facilitate this process? What is truly needed to create productive teams? In *TeamWork* (Larson and LaFasto, 1989), the authors present eight characteristics of high-performing teams, which they draw out of interviews with publicly acclaimed high-performing teams, including sports, science and technology, and industry. Most of these appear to reflect generally understood notions of good teamwork, and they are described at a somewhat abstract level, e.g., "clear elevating goal," "competent team members," "collaborative climate."

They also raise many questions in terms of *how* these characteristics are operationalized. In the context of our research, how can technology be applied to facilitate the creation of the key elements necessary to create productive teams?

The partnership of organizational process and technology is very clear. Management must carry out specific tasks to bring forth productive team characteristics. High-performing teams can be created without any technology. However, in the fast-paced, geographically dispersed environment of today's corporation, groupware technology could enhance the individual's ability to carry out the appropriate tasks.

Examining people's attitudes appears to be an important step in understanding barriers to productive teamwork. In our interviews we noted that when people saw the immediate value to themselves of using a function (e.g., messaging) they quickly adapted to its use. However when it was in the interests of the "higher good"—that is, the team, department, or organization would benefit—the incentive for the individual was missing. In these situations it took other motivators to cause people to use these tools. Some of the motivators included

- a charismatic leader
- orders from higher management
- workshops on organizational issues
- obtaining group agreement and individual permission.

In other words, the technology alone, regardless of its potential value, attractiveness, or ease of use, could not inspire people to use it. In addition, introducing new technology into a poorly operating work group is unlikely to improve its performance. In fact researchers have found that new technology may very well degrade performance because its introduction brings more complexity and a threat to the people on the team (Henderson and Cooprider, 1988).

The well-known concept of *unfreezing* in organizational change theory (Lewin, 1952) seems applicable here. The potential users of groupware systems need to *open up* or *unfreeze* to the possible value of learning to use the technology. Unfreezing is not a simple matter of mechanical training, but rather an organizational process that includes training, education, and rethinking the goals of the team and then considering how work results will be accomplished from the new perspective.

One of the lessons that comes out of *TeamWork* is that much of the success of teams depends on communication among team members on key issues. One of groupware's greatest values, according to our research, is the support it provides for electronic messaging. Our conclusion here is that if a groupware system can facilitate team interaction and information exchange, it has the potential to move group work into the realm of high-performance teams.

Summary

Is groupware to new to study conclusively? We have learned from innovation research (Rogers, 1983) that it takes time for new ideas to be assimilated by people. Although the technology for electronic mail and conferencing has been available for 15 years (Engelbart, 1964, Johansen, 1988), the concept of technology to support work groups has been discussed for only about four years. (Engelbart in the early 1960s developed pioneering technology especially designed to support high-performance teams, but this work was

not well known outside the computer science community.) We may therefore be observing the use of these new tools when they are in their infancy and before people have learned to think about them as essential tools for effective office work.

Nonetheless, experiences gained from studying people as they learn to use new tools can benefit the designers of the next tool generation, thereby helping to accelerate the process of acceptance and use of these tools. We also believe that managers can learn to be sensitive to the complex balance that exists between the organization and the technology.

Our observations were consistent across a wide range of organizations. Work groups at the largest organization we studied, BigChem with $30 billion in revenues, experienced the same challenges in organizing work and using information technology as did those at the smallest organizations. Work groups at companies recognized as being "forward thinking," "networked," and participatory in management style did not differ in their problems or their attempted solutions from work groups in companies characterized as "conservative," hierarchical, and traditional in management style.

For example, CableCo ($1 billion in revenues) is a very young, quickly growing, highly successful company with a participatory management style. The work group consisted of nine people who had concerns related to effective communication and management of tasks in an accelerating, fast-paced environment that spanned several time zones. At SoapCo ($17 billion in revenues) one work group consisted of 15 people who expressed exactly the same concerns and were attempting to use information technology in the same way to support their work group. SoapCo is a very old company with a long tradition of hierarchical, conservative management, and with longstanding procedures for accomplishing tasks. *A priori*, we might have assumed the differing environments in these two organizations would have dictated different approaches to solving the coordination problems. We found this to be true neither here nor at other research sites. Apparently today's business environment of global, 24-hour marketplaces with the concurrent acceleration of information and coordination needs brings the same challenges in managing work groups to diverse organizations.

We have discussed major questions and conclusions about work groups and their use of information technology. We see an important interplay of factors in our major conclusions. For example, people seem to need training beyond the simple mechanical instruction that usually accompanies groupware tools. Because groupware is a relatively new technology, this may change in the future as the tools are more widely known and used. Their inherent value may become more obvious to people and they will adapt to their use more easily.

However, the organizational inhibitors that we observed cannot be dismissed. Recognizing the long-lasting constraints of history and the power of politics in the organization at the same time as considering the new possibilities for technology support may result in new insights. These contrast with insights suggested when using traditional requirements analysis, often focused on individual users to the exclusion of organizational factors. Understanding the interplay of

1. economic balances (i.e., input resources versus output value) inherent in the use of a tool,

2. the differential impacts on organizational roles (e.g., managerial impacts as compared with support staff impacts), and

3. the organizational readiness (i.e., management attention through planned change or intervention)

may lead management toward different technological paths than those discovered through simple analysis.

We have stated earlier that managing the volume of information has been traditionally, and still is, the major task facing knowledge workers. As we have interviewed, observed teams, and better understood the tasks they are undertaking, we have come to the conclusion that a groupware system like The Coordinator could have an effect on knowledge work by compressing it. That is, use of The Coordinator as its designers intended could reduce the volume and complexity of information so that managing the content and meaning of interaction would dominate managing volume.

Revolutionizing work may be an effective role for groupware systems in organizations. Most of today's groupware systems are not designed to do this. Instead they attempt to provide electronic support for the tasks people are believed to carry out in performing knowledge work in groups. If indeed the concept of work groups and business teams is the organizational concept of the future, it becomes critical to understand better the interaction of individuals in these groups and how information technology can support or even enhance the work of groups.

Acknowledgments

The authors acknowledge the many individuals who agreed to be interviewed, and who interacted with us in the course of this research. Without their cooperation and genuine interest in the topic, it would have been very difficult to learn about the experience of groupware use in organizations. We thank David L. Anderson who assisted us in the fieldwork and provided support for the ideas presented here. We also acknowledge the following for their valuable roles in reviewing drafts: John Henderson, J. Debra Hofman, Bob Johansen, Wendy Kellogg, Bob Mack, Tom Malone, Wanda Orlikowski, Judith A. Quillard, John Richards, and JoAnne Yates.

Appendix I

Case Study Interview Outline

General background information on the organization, the work group, and the individual being interviewed;

Detailed information on the work group or project:

- Members
- Description
- Mode of operation

meeting frequency
forms of communication (face-to-face, phone, electronic, video)
levels of stress
leadership
boundary management (relationship to world outside project);

Description of how tasks are accomplished;

Determination of information technology (IT) tools that are used to facilitate task accomplishment with detailed description of use;

Determination of general sense of satisfaction with existing mode of operation;

Suggestions for change;

Probing of interviewee's sense of the future:

- Types of group work that will take place;
- Changes anticipated for organization as a whole;
- Needs for different IT tools.

Appendix II

All-In-1™

All-In-1 is more accurately described as a family of tools or even an office tool environment. This system resides on a centralized computer, with PCs often serving as a means of access (both local and remote). It does not provide flow of data integration but does provide flow of control within its environment. The basic tool offers a variety of functions ranging from electronic mail to a spreadsheet package. An organization can customize All-In-1 by adding other commercial products under the general All-In-1 "umbrella." For example the popular word-processing software, Word Perfect, can be installed to operate under All-In-1. The extent to which the functionality provided under All-In-1 can be used as groupware depends on which functions are used and on what agreement the people in the organizational unit reach on how the functions will be used.

The logical groupware use of this tool involves employing the electronic mail function and VAX Notes (computer conferencing) for communication and the exchange of documents. A calendar function can be used for scheduling group meetings.

The basic All-In-1 functions described above are in use at three organizations in our study.

ForComment™

ForComment is a single-purpose system. It assists users in group authoring or editing of documents. This system is available in single PC and local area network configurations. ForComment "imports" text produced in most of the popular word processing environments or ASCII and allows multiple authors or reviewers to rewrite and/or comment on the document. Control over the final version of the document always remains with one individual, the designated primary author. Proposed rewrites and comments are noted through a symbol in the margin, and the actual text of the revision is displayed in a second window on the viewer's screen. Each entry is identified by reviewers' initials, color coding, and date of entry. The software automatically merges entries from multiple reviewers so that the primary author reviews a single, aggregated version. In this respect ForComment provides flow of data integration.

ForComment is used by four organizations in our sample. Each organization uses it unmodified as provided by the vendor.

Higgins™

Higgins is a personal computer system based on a local area network that provides a variety of functionality including electronic mail, personal information organization, project tracking, and project expense tracking. The electronic mail function links messages and their associated replies, allowing users to trace the history of communications leading to a current message. All of the functions are integrated on Higgins both with respect to flow of control and to flow of data. For example, a user can employ key words to find all entries dealing with specific categories. Therefore the name "project xyz" can be used to find electronic mail, "to do" entries, expense reports, calendar entries, etc., that relate to that project by its code name. In this way Higgins can be used both as a personal organization tool and as a groupware tool.

Higgins is used in five of the organizations in our sample, in each case in a stand alone local area network (LAN) mode as provided by the vendor.

In-House System I

One large organization in our sample developed its own global electronic mail, conferencing, and document exchange system. This system resides on a mainframe computer and is accessed by PCs acting as workstations (both locally and remote). Both integration in terms of flow of data and flow of control exist to varying degrees in this system. Development of increased integration in both areas is a current priority. This system has been in worldwide use by a very large number of people at this organization for more than 10 years.

In-House System II

One small organization in our sample developed its own relatively basic electronic messaging tool. This system resides on a centralized computer and is accessed by both local and remote PCs. The system is used primarily in the United States (although one European node is in place) and has been in use for approximately eight years.

Metaphor™

Metaphor provides high-end specialized, networked workstations and software to support professionals, managers, and executives in constructing complex queries against multiple databases. Users build queries by specifying data elements graphically and then by linking sequences of operations on that data. These queries can be saved in "capsules" for later use or for use by others. Data results can be passed to others on the specialized local area network in the form of spreadsheets, reports, and graphs. The graphic user interface is intended for easy and effective use by business professionals (such as marketing analysts) who need to review and aggregate data extracted from large databases. Flow of control and flow of data integration exist within the Metaphor environment.

Metaphor is in use at two sites in our sample. In one of those sites it is being used as a stand-alone system; in the other it is designed with a gateway into the corporate data network.

PROFS™

PROFS is a general purpose office system tool. This system resides on a centralized computer with PCs often serving as a means for access (both local and remote). PROFS includes functionality for electronic mail, calendaring, reminders, and folders for mail management. Other than the electronic mail component, the extent to which PROFS can be used as groupware depends upon the agreements people in an organization reach for allowing access to calendars and folders. Flow of control integration exists to a limited degree within the PROFS environment.

PROFS was studied at two of our sites.

The Coordinator System™ (Version I)

The Coordinator System (TCS) is a groupware system that was designed to support people in effective action during the course of their work in an organization. The system is generally available in two hardware configurations: either on a PC/local area network or via dial-up mode supported by the vendor. TCS differs from most of the other products we examined in that the software implementation is based on an underlying theory of human interaction. The theory suggests that the basic unit of interaction is a conversation, and that people use language (speech acts) to make requests, promise results, decline requests, declare commitments completed, etc. The software makes these distinctions visible and thereby is designed to encourage people to conduct their interactions in a way presumed (under the theory) to be more effective.

The Coordinator Version I is available in seven of the organizations in our sample. Technical details of the implementations differ (e.g., remote mail, local area network), but these differences do not play an important role in what the users see, or how they tend to employ the tool. The fact that Version I is the tool we studied is, however, important because the user interface of Version I differs significantly from that of Version II. Version II became available in 1989, and it is currently being marketed and used in a number of organizations.

The degree to which flow of control integration exists in a TCS implementation depends upon the nature of the implementation and bridges that have been established to other systems. Flow of data integration exists in some of the tools.

References

Ancona, Deborah Gladstein (1987). "Groups in Organizations," in Clyde Hendrick (ed.), *Group Processes and Intergroup Relations*. Sage Publications, Newbury Park, Cal., pp. 207–230.

Bair, James H., and Stephen Gale (1988). "An Investigation of the Coordinator as an Example of Computer Supported Cooperative Work." Extended Abstract, submitted to the Second Conference on Computer-Supported Cooperative Work, Portland, Oregon, September.

Bennett, J.L., K. Holtzblatt, S. Jones, and D. Wixon (1970). "Usability Engineering: Using Contextual Inquiry," tutorial at CHI '90, Empowering People (Seattle, WA, April 1–5), ACM, New York.

Berger, Suzanne, Michael Dertouzos, Richard K. Lester, Robert M. Solow, and Lester C. Thurow (1989). "Toward a New Industrial America," *Scientific American*. 260(6), pp. 39–47.

Bikson, Tora K., J.D. Eveland, and Barbara Gutek (1989). "Flexible Interactive Technologies for Multi-Person Tasks: Current Problems and Future Prospects," in Margrethe H. Olson (ed.), *Technological Support for Work Group Collaboration*. Lawrence Erlbaum Associates, Inc., Hillsdale, New Jersey, pp. 89–112.

Blomberg, Jeanette (1988). "The Variable Impact of Computer Technologies on the Organization of Work Activities," in Irene Greif (ed.), *Computer-Supported Cooperative Work: A Book of Readings*. Morgan Kaufmann Publishers, Inc., San Mateo, Cal.

Bullen, Christine V., and Robert R. Johansen (1988). "Groupware: A Key to Managing Business Teams?" CISR Work Paper # 169, Center for Information Systems Research, MIT, Cambridge, Mass.

Carroll, John S., and Constance Perin (1988). "How Expectations About Microcomputers Influence Their Organizational Consequences," Management in the 1990s Working Paper 80-044, Sloan School of Management, MIT, Cambridge, Mass.

Dalton, Richard (1988). *Open Systems*. (March). p. 7.

Drucker, Peter (1988). "The New Organization," *Harvard Business Review*. January–February.

Engelbart, Douglas C. (1963). "A Conceptual Framework for the Augmentation of Man's Intellect," in P. Howerton (ed.), *Vistas in Information Handling*. Spartan Books, Washington, D.C., pp. 1–29.

Engelbart, Douglas C., and William K. English (1988). "A Research Center for Augmenting Human Intellect," originally published in 1968 and reprinted in Irene Greif (ed.), *Computer-Supported Cooperative Work: A Book of Readings*. Morgan Kaufmann Publishers, Inc., San Mateo, Cal.

Grudin, Jonathan (1988). "Why CSCW Applications Fail: Problems in the Design and Evaluation of Organizational Interfaces," *Proceedings of the Conference on Computer-Supported Cooperative Work*, September 26–28, Portland, Oregon, pp. 85–93.

Grudin, Jonathan (1989). "Why Groupware Applications Fail: Problems in Design and Evaluation," *Office: Technology and People*. 4(3), pp. 245–264.

Henderson, J.C., and J. Cooprider (1988). "Dimensions of I/S Planning and Design Technology," Working Paper # 181, MIT Center for Information Systems Research, Cambridge, Mass.

Hiltz, S.R., and E.B. Kerr (1981). "Studies of Computer-Mediated Communication Systems: A Synthesis of the Findings," Final Report to the National Science Foundation.

Hiltz, S.R. and M. Turoff (1978). *The Network Nation: Human Communication via Computer*. Addison-Wesley Publishing Company, Inc., Reading, Mass.

Iacono, Suzanne, and Rob Kling (1988). "Computer Systems as Institutions: Social Dimensions of Computing in Organizations," *Proceedings of the Ninth International Conference on Information Systems*, 11/30–12/3, Minneapolis, Minn., pp. 101–110.

Johansen, Robert (1988). *Groupware: Computer Support for Business Teams*. The Free Press, New York.

Keen, Peter, G.W. (1988). "The 'Metabusiness' Evolution: Challenging the Status Quo," *ICIT Advance* (October), Washington, D.C.

Kerr, Elaine B., and Starr Roxanne Hiltz (1982). *Computer-Mediated Communication Systems: Status and Evaluation*. Academic Press, New York.

Kling, Rob, and Suzanne Iacono (1989). "Desktop Computerization & the Organization of Work," in Tom Forester *Computers in the Human Context*. MIT Press, Cambridge, Mass.

Larson, Carl E., and Frank M.J. LaFasto (1989). *TeamWork*. Sage Publications, Newbury Park, Cal.

Lewin, Kurt (1952). "Group Decision and Social Change," in G.E. Swanson, T.N. Newcome, and E.L. Hartley (eds.), *Readings in Social Psychology* (revised edition). Holt, New York.

Loveman, Gary W. (1988). "An Assessment of the Productivity Impact of Information Technologies," MIT Management in the 1990s Working Paper 88-504, Massachusetts Institute of Technology, Cambridge, Mass.

Malone, Thomas W. (1983). "How Do People Organize Their Desks? Implications for the Design of Office Information Systems," *ACM Transactions on Office Information Systems*. 1(1)(January). pp. 99–112.

Markus, M. Lynne, and Janis Forman (1989). "A Social Analysis of Group Technology Use," UCLA Information Systems Research Program Working Paper # 2-90. July.

Martin, James (1973). *Design of Man-Computer Dialogues*. Prentice-Hall, Englewood Cliffs, New Jersey.

Mumford, E., and T.B. Ward (1968). *Computers: Planning for People*. Batsford, London.

Neilsen, J., R. Mack, K. Bergendorff, and N. Grischkowsky (1986). "Integrated Software Usage in the Professional Work Environment: Evidence from Questionnaires and Interviews," in *Proceedings of CHI '86 Human Factors in Computing Systems* (Boston, April 13–17). ACM, New York, pp. 162–167.

Reich, Robert B. (1987). "Entrepreneurship Reconsidered: The Team as Hero," *Harvard Business Review*. May–June, pp. 77–83.

Rice, Ronald, and Associates (1984). *The New Media*. Sage, Beverly Hills, Cal.

Rogers, Everett (1983). *The Diffusion of Innovation*. Free Press, New York.

Rosson, Mary Beth (1985). "The Role of Experience in Editing," *Proceedings of INTERACT84*. Elsevier North-Holland, Amsterdam.

Rousseau, D.M. (1983). "Technology in Organizations: A Constructive Review and Analytic Framework," in Seashore, S.E. E.E. Lawler, P.H. Mirvis, and C. Caman (eds.), *Assessing Organizational Changes: A Guide to Methods, Measures and Practices*. Wiley & Sons, New York.

Searle, John R. (1969). *Speech Acts*. Cambridge University Press, Cambridge, England.

Stevens, Chandler Harrison (1981). "Many-to-Many Communications," Working Paper # 72, MIT Center for Information Systems Research, Cambridge, Mass.

Trist, E.L. (1981). "The Sociotechnical Perspective," in Van de Ven, A.H., and W.F. Joyce (eds.), *Perspectives on Organization, Design and Behavior*. John Wiley & Sons, New York.

Whiteside, John, and Dennis Wixon (1988). "Contextualism as a World View for the Reformation of Meetings," in *Proceedings of the Conference on Computer-Supported Cooperative Work*. Association for Computing Machinery, New York.

Yates, JoAnne (1989). *Control Through Communication: The Rise of System in American Management*. Johns Hopkins University Press, Baltimore, Md.

Building the Business Case for Group Support Technology

Brad Quinn Post

Professional Services Organization
The Boeing Company

Abstract

As groupwork gains recognition, emerging group support technologies raise questions about the merits of these systems relative to group performance and return on investment. Business case variables of efficiency, quality, effectiveness, customer satisfaction and decision-making are useful in measuring the potential contribution that group support technologies offer.

This paper presents findings from a recent field study that used business case concepts as its design approach. The paper explores the infrastructure development requirements for building a business case study. Such a framework is useful to business decision-makers and researchers interested in the deployment of these technologies in complex business environments.

1: Business Case Framework

This paper presents findings from a 1991 field study conducted at a major American corporation concerning the business benefits of group support technology. Both quasi-experimental and qualitative study design elements were used to provide an objective basis for developing a business case evaluation.

The purpose of the study was to produce answers to typical business case questions such as: "What are the measurable benefits of the technology?" "How does the technology improve group work quality?" "What is the return on investment?" "Does the support technology enhance or detract from current business team practices?" These and other similar business issues were addressed in the design and execution of this technology evaluation effort.

The professionally operated business demands objective and balanced analysis, as well as dispassionate recommendations. The business case framework is a straight-forward conceptualization and analysis of the concerns that should be considered when attempting to make sound business technology investments, such as group support technologies.

This paper reviews the results of a study involving synchronous group support technology, distinguished by specific business case variables that are important to understanding the effects of collaborative solutions on group performance. The study addresses a research question that has been given little attention: How well does group support technology fare as a business case or proposition in a complex organization? Business case variables include costs, benefits and qualitative considerations valued by the organization.

This research question makes sense and needs consideration because the business enterprise is the ultimate target customer for the Group Decision Support Systems (GDSS) field. Important also is the fact that the field of GDSS is immature and requires extensive empirical exploration (Johansen 1988; Van-Gundy 1987; DeSanctis and Gallupe 1987; Nunamaker et al. 1989(a) 1989(b); Vogel et al. 1989; Vogel and Nunamaker 1990). Despite its following, this field of inquiry is scattered (Kraemer and King 1988) and will benefit from further conceptualization of its aims. A fundamental purpose of GDSS should be to add value to the organization in at least two ways: heightened group performance from the perspectives of efficiency and effectiveness and second, improved group work quality and process (Pinsonneault and Kraemer 1990). The relevance of business case concepts is given some attention by Tanniru and Jain (1989), who found that most group decisions have to be eventually translated into financial terms before they are meaningful to management.

2: Group Work and Business

Doing business today means accomplishing group work. The modern organization depends on the participation, and increasingly on the consensus, of its principals, employees and interested others--all of whom are potential stakeholders in the innumerable business processes and decisions that create success.

While often overlooked, the significance of groups in business has long been accepted--at least in academic quarters. The well-known Hawthorne studies, which began at Western Electric in 1929, led engineers and scientists to ascribe much of the variance they observed in worker productivity to group behavior variables. Prior to these important findings, group work was not given much attention in critical circles of research. (Barnard 1938).

2.1: Emergence of business teams

The salience of business teams in today's business environment is due to many factors, some of which are not well understood. In his authoritative work about business team technology, Robert Johansen (1988) points to a series of driving forces which underlie the pivotal position that groups now play:

- Deregulation
- The downsizing of middle manage-ment
- Increased reliance on contract work
- Mergers and acquisitions
- Globalization

Groups now form the bedrock of most business operations and, as such, have emerged as a critical unit of analysis in the ongoing effort to increase the quality of our products and services. Just under-standing business group behavior alone cannot produce the results we seek for our organiza-tion, our customers and the community in which we work.

2.2: Group process model

Effectively harnessing business teams is a question of dynamic social psychology, management science and technology. The myriad factors shaping the activity and variability of each group effort cannot be readily tamed as in an economist's *ceteris paribus* function equation. Instead, the productivity, quality and effectiveness of any given business team is a function of a complex model not presently well explained by research or practice (McGrath 1984).

For business, the daunting challenge of developing effective patterns of teamwork can best be viewed in terms of group process characteristics. Initial efforts to describe these processes using business entity models suggest that further work in this area will be valuable in understanding group performance (McGoff et al

1990). By designing processes that minimize variance in team performance, we will be in better position to con-duct business using team resources. Technological leverage applied to teams make these efforts all the more critical.

The Technology Supported Group Process Enter-prise Model that was employed in this research, shown in Figure 1, presents the extended set of entities and relationships that framed this study. The model helped established a structured basis for contrasting technolo-gy supported group work and traditional group work in process-oriented terms. This modeling also provided a

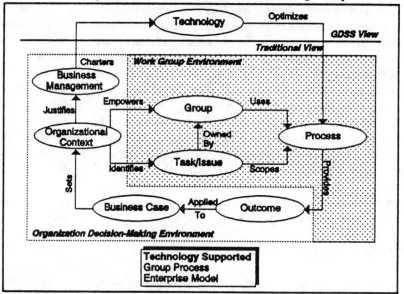

Figure 1

useful heuristic for defining our quasi-experimental comparisons, thus helping overcome some of the thorny control and approach problems long prevalent in this field (Lewis and Keleman 1988; Kraemer and King 1988).

3: Group Support Technology

For nearly three decades, the use of computer-based tools in support of group work has been a vision of futurists, commercial developers, research institutions and major corporations.

The GDSS focal area grew out of exploratory interest in group work (Gray et al 1981; Huber 1982) and the concurrent drive to expand the longstanding field of Decision Support Systems (DSS). These emergent group support technologies were timely be-cause of the concomitant rise of the business team (Johansen 1988) in corporate enterprise. Despite their increasing visibility, these technologies are not appro-priate for every organizational setting. Organizational boundaries, differing cultural and management structures can limit GDSS utilization (Kydd and Jones 1989). At the same time, a recent study of 135 randomly selected organizations indicates that GDSS tools are gradually being incorporated into many explicit information system strategies (Beauclair and Straub 1990).

GDSS and "groupware" tools perform functions such as electronic brainstorming, issue organization and analysis, as well as alternative evaluation, voting and policy formation functions. Tasks supported are far-ranging, but research has demonstrated their impact on mission development, planning and strategy, issue documentation and evaluation, assumption surfacing, stakeholder identification, policy formulation, nominal group work, system requirements, group negotiation and idea development (Diehl and Stroebe 1987; Campbell 1990; Vogel and Nunamaker 1990). While there are more than a few technologies available, many share closely related features and appear to be based on similar metaphors (Nunamaker 1989; Boose et al 1992). The scope of these technologies suggest a robust marketplace, however, the evidence is that widespread acceptance is slow in building (Kraemer and King 1988), and that empirical research is needed to better understand their application, limitations and business value.

GDSS specialists argue that meaningful group support technology research should be clearly tied to both group performance and satisfaction variables, because the purpose of these systems is to promote the overall efficiency and quality of group work.

4: Creating an Evaluation Infrastructure

Planning for this technology evaluation and business case study began with a technical feasibility review of leading GDSS products that supported the Company's team collaboration functions. With more than 160,000 employees globally, the Company has a rich, diverse infrastructure making its teamwork composition difficult to map in any straight-forward categorization. Indeed, it is the vitality and magnitude of the Company's group resources and processes that make it attractive from a GDSS research perspective.

Since the Company should be characterized as heterogenous from the standpoint of its team environments, it presents a challenge to the typical field study configuration, where limited access organizationally, functionally, and geographically, might lead to biases or gaps in the selection of groups for study. The organization sponsoring and managing this study is a unique operation, providing management consulting, systems integration and group facilitation services inside the Company. This consulting organization has a history spanning more than twenty years and provides technical and managerial support throughout the Company on a world-wide basis. Among the many offerings delivered by this organization, and of particular importance to this study, are these key products and services:

- Group Facilitation and Consultation,
- Process Improvement,
- Decision Support,
- Consensus,
- Management Counsel,
- Planning and
- Technology Deployment.

4.1: TeamFocus

At the time the study began, this consulting organization was considering the efficacy of acquiring and deploying group support technology in support of its client requirements. As a first phase of the effort, a technical feasibility assessment was conducted. This involved the formation of a small group of specialists who reviewed current research and product literature. They also consulted with Company researchers outside this organization who had kept abreast of GDSS issues and technologies and participated in product demonstrations. Based on this review, they prepared a statement of work to produce a technical feasibility report. This statement of work focused on the narrow objective of reviewing a leading group support technology which would become available commercially within a short timeframe. This technology was TeamFocus, produced jointly by IBM, the University of Arizona and the Ventana Corporation. The product offering included utilities and eight tools: electronic brainstorming, idea organization, issue analysis, policy formation, alternative evaluation, voting, a data dictionary and group questionnaire. The product featured anonymous participation (Connolly et al 1990) and full session documentation. The questionnaire tool provided for evaluation data collection.

4.2: Technical feasibility review

The technical feasibility review included an evaluation tour of some five IBM TeamFocus facilities in the Washington D.C. area by two members of the feasibility team—a technical consultant and a management consultant. The technical consultant was primarily concerned with functionality, performance, architecture, documentation, platform, state of software maturity and maintenance-support criteria. The management consultant areas of interest were product definition from a user standpoint, product lifecycle and stability, embedded or methodological neutrality, tool set capabilities, applications currently deployed, early-on commercial experience, as well as service capability and program management.

Based on this field tour and follow-on calls to others familiar with this product offering, a technical feasibility report was prepared and presented to the sponsoring organization's management team. The report presented a series of findings as well as recommendations to proceed with a full-scale evaluation of the technology to determine its business case efficacy for possible use within the Company. The scope of the recommended actions included the following key action items:

1. Formation of an evaluation team.
2. Development of a detailed evaluation study plan.
3. Order of magnitude business case estimate.
4. Definition of business case metrics and evaluation methods.
5. Customer acquisition strategy for evaluation.
6. Capital and operating budget for evaluation.
7. Approvals for rapid acquisition of software, hardware and a technology test facility.
8. Design evaluation across significant group practice areas.

Total elapsed time from the chartering of this feasibility review to the presentation of the report's findings and recommendations was 15 days. The recommended schedule for the evaluation was to develop the study infrastructure and complete the entire evaluation cycle, including the presentation of a business case report at its conclusion, within nine months. This proposal was accepted by the organization's management team and the study was initiated the next day.

4.3: Planning and staffing

An evaluation team was formed by the newly assigned program manager. Members of the team were selected to fill what were initially six positions, but which soon became ten different part-time job assignments. Over a three month period, five facilitators joined the team. Two customer contact positions were assigned to the effort, as was a technical manager, and an evaluator. The facilitators chosen all had group session facilitation experience including involvement with the organization's high visibility product offerings called Consensus and Preferred Process.

The customer contact assignees each had extensive professional experience as consultants and as sales

force principals associated with both information services and management services. These individuals had specific knowledge of a wide range of internal customer accounts throughout the Company. The technical manager was chosen because of the extensive scope of his skill and relevant experience with the development of technology applications, including local area networks, and hardware and software testing. Similarly, the evaluator was asked to support the team because of his reputation for his structured approach to program planning. The program manager was chosen by the organization's management team because of his early-on involvement in the feasibility review, interest and organizational skills.

Early-on tasks of the evaluation program team centered on the development of a plan, the negotiation of a software agreement with the vendor, the acquisition of hardware, facility furnishings, reconstruction of an existing conference room, development of a customer strategy, creation of marketing materials and the design of business case metrics for the evaluation. Concurrently, the first two facilitators assigned to the team began an extensive training schedule which began with a structured five day course provided by IBM. The training focused on technical briefings and session mock-ups given by instructors highly experienced with TeamFocus software and facilitation methodology. This preliminary education was followed by a deliberately slow-paced series of varied, short practice sessions at the sponsoring organization's newly built evaluation facility.

The evaluation program plan rested on the definition of a business criteria for the research, specific objectives to be met and application areas to be tested. The metrics important to the business case were closely aligned with these objectives. The agreed upon business objectives for the evaluation were to evaluate TeamFocus technology and associated group support methodology to:
- Determine business benefits and costs,
- Assess integration issues with existing services,
- Define customer impacts and
- Develop insight about group support technology.

4.4: Business case parameters

High level business case issues were also established from the outset of the study. The business case was built to answer these pivotal questions:
[FLOWTIME]
To what extent does the group support technology help customers make faster decisions?
[QUALITY]

Does the technology significantly enhance the customer decision process with quantification, traceability and increased exchange of participant knowledge?
[ROI]
What is the documented return on investment?
[VALUE]
How does group support technology add value to the customer's business?
[COST-BENEFIT]
Does the technology make the organization a more efficient provider of consulting services?

These business case questions drove the development of indices employed in this study. As part of the staging for the evaluation, a preliminary productivity analysis was prepared. On the basis of this preliminary exercise final approval was given for funding the business study. The analysis assumed that the evaluation facility would have a 70% utilization rate. The analysis projected a conservative productivity gain for all session participants using the facility averaging 25%. Using authoritative operating and capital budget research, standard six-year lifecycle costs were predicted to be $384,000, with $117,000 of these costs occurring in the first year. With an average operating savings of $175,000 due to productivity, the five-year cash savings was calculated to be $164,000 (present value). The ROI calculation derived from these values was 42.6%—well above the Company requirement of 25% or better.

4.5: The test facility

The facility was built on a "shoestring" basis to conserve resources. Its configuration included surplus XT workstations, an AT class facilitator workstation and a 386 fileserver. Portable color projection equipment was purchased along with state-of-the art screen-graber technology that allowed screen capture and VGA display of computer screen data. Existing light and furniture was adapted to requirements. The overall result was a low-cost, practical GDSS facility readied in less than a month's time.

4.6: Design and pre-testing

In parallel with these infrastructure developments was the definition of an evaluation methodology, data architecture and comprehensive business case metrics. These efforts initially focused on the latter issue, evaluation indices, and soon thereafter on the procedures for measurement, data collection, analysis and reporting. To help ensure both sound measurement protocols and criteria, experts outside the team were consulted. The metrics were crafted on a preliminary basis, then alpha tested using team members during mock-up sessions conducted primarily as practice for the newly trained facilitators. The results of these alpha sessions led to the improvement and formalization of the measurements as well as the multi-stage data collection process.

Beta tests were then conducted with outside customers who were considered by the team to be "friendlies." Despite this informal labelling, these groups were generally representative of customer segments currently being served by the sponsoring organization. In addition, they were considered to be "experienced" customers who would be open to early involvement with the evaluation program. Like the alpha phase, this phase was conducted to extend team exposure to session work with "live" customers, with emphasis placed on testing the evaluation methodology, facilitation techniques, software behavior and process mechanics. The beta sessions were useful and led to the final configuration of both the evaluation and general facilitation methods that were initially deployed during the first leg of the evaluation program.

For the purposes of this study, a total of 45 variables were defined. Among them were 13 measurements of calendar time, labor and cost. This set of indices was critical to the business case in terms of quantifying costs and benefits. Additionally, the team constructed a set of scaled questionnaire measures that were directed to participants on-line at the end of the sessions. These measures focused on customer satisfaction, utility, perceptions of quality, ergonomic and economic questions.

The on-line questionnaire also contained nominal measures (yes-no values) assessing participant decision-making, understanding of session objectives, adherence to the session purpose and role awareness by the participant. Coupled with the on-line measurements, essay questionnaires were distributed for completion by group session participants after reflection. These essay questions focused on issues regarding user acceptance of the technology as well as the session process, criticisms of both the technology and process, suggestions for improvement and an open opportunity to express opinions concerning the strengths of the technology and the session, if any.

As shown in Figure 2, the evaluation methodology approved by the team for implementation involved several measurement points. The first of these occurred at the time of the pre-session interviews with customers, where group session requirements were operationalized. This information was documented with session planning worksheets which were also used in the capture of detailed estimates of traditional customer group process metrics such as working day flowtime and labor factors. This traditional group process estimation information was carefully defined in terms of the normal customer requirements for conducting a group process to achieve a specific result. The pre-session planning worksheet establishes the group session information baseline in terms of these key elements:

- Customer identification and category
- Purpose of the session
- Session objectives
- Deliverables (such as a specific decision, plan, recommendation, list of priorities, definition of work statement, solution to problem and the like)
- Value of session to customer business
- Roles of session participants
- Customer's current group process
- Satisfaction with current group practices

- Customer traditional process estimates for same session/same result
- Session agenda and software tool pathway
- Precise brainstorming questions
- Description of in-depth focus areas

As these evaluation components were fielded, a database application was designed, tested, and fielded for daily use by the evaluator and other team members. The database included the design of data entry screens and reports that ensured efficient and accurate data storage and retrieval operations. An early decision was made by the team to share all session results and business case evaluation data with session customers within three days following each group process event with TeamFocus. Session data was captured, stored and a data report was produced in graphical and business analytical form.

Following a quality check of each rapidly produced group session report, the facilitator responsible for the session delivered to the customer the data report along

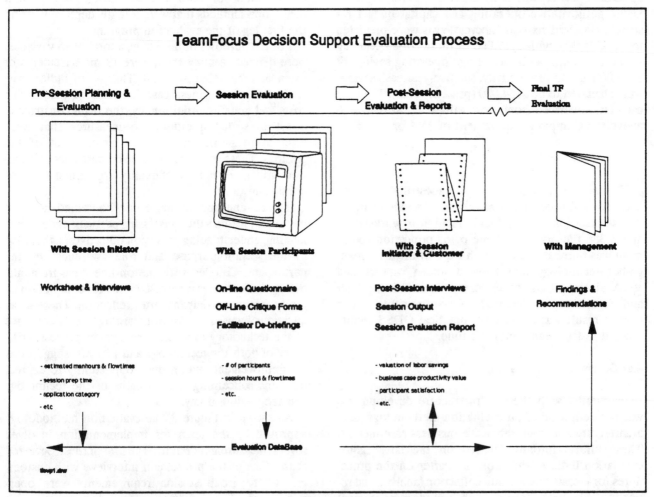

Figure 2

with session documentation in a specially bound book. This approach was designed into the evaluation to ensure that all customers were an integral part of the evaluation milieu and therefore could provide the team with a richer set of feedback. The customer was part of the quality consciousness of the method, a concept based on the Japanese business model of customer involvement called Quality Function Deployment (Zultner 1990; Gause and Weinberg 1989; Akao 1989).

4.7: Group session start-up and process control

The first leg of the formal business case evaluation carefully staged technology support to customer groups who were solicited to help the team launch the program. Each of these initial groups had legitimate group process requirements and each was accommodated on the basis of full-cycle pre-session planning, documentation, session facilitation, post-session evaluation and facilitator follow-up. Lessons learned during this early stage were significant and were discussed at length on a *post-mortem* basis the day after each session. These deliberations included detailed review of the pre-session and in-session process mechanics with in-depth attention given to modeling our approaches to enhance future session efficiency and effectiveness. Since each group session was unique, the precise pathway for software tool utilization had to be optimized by the facilitator and customer during the planning and execution stages of each session.

From the outset of the study, serious attention was paid to the software itself, its performance capabilities and shortfalls, as well as captured bugs and agreed-upon work-arounds. Bug report forms were completed for each problem encountered by facilitators and other team members. These reports became the data trail for related communications with the vendor over the course of the evaluation. Similarly, hardware and lanware issues were also reviewed, with the technical manager taking the lead in determining the best courses of action. The combined software and hardware technical issues required a series of system adjustments, equipment and component replacements and repairs as well as the proverbial acts of "ghost-busting" less finite problems.

Stabilizing the evaluation process and environment was the critical priority during the first weeks of the evaluation program. A key step in this effort was the development of the TeamFocus Customer Lifecycle Procedures. These standards were the result of the team's efforts to define a cradle-to-grave process for conducting group sessions. While procedural approaches are not customary in group process circles, the

function of the Lifecycle Procedures was to minimize variance across the many endogenous and exogenous factors affecting an objective evaluation. The Customer Lifecycle Procedures were spread across five distinct phases of activity:

Phase 1—Customer Acquisition
Phase 2—Session Planning
Phase 3—Session Activities
Phase 4—Evaluation Administration
Phase 5—Post-Session Follow-up

This structure helped establish a firm basis for rapid deployment as a business service offering, should the technology evaluation and business case warrant that decision downstream. Throughout the stabilization of the effort, the team was determined to provide a professionally delivered product to all customers during the evaluation so that the "real-world" business benefits of the technology could be clearly recognized.

4.8: Customer acquisition

To ensure the validity and success of the evaluation it was critical that there were sufficient customers, with substantive group tasks and issues, that were representative of the Company's life blood. This meant that the evaluation serve a relatively large number of clients. A minimum of 62 session clients was established as a study requirement for statistical reasons. A population roughly similar to Company organizational and functional sectors, including both upper, middle and lower management strata, as well as staff groups was targeted. These requirements necessitated a relatively focused customer solicitation approach. Educational and marketing aides proved useful in the customer acquisition effort. Since the sponsoring organization and all team members had extensive customer relationships previously established, developing initial leads was not a significant problem. However, it is clear to the team that other GDSS operations, those without similar relationships with customers, may well find the hurdle of finding customers a major challenge.

Several team members took responsibility for developing a customer lead list and contacting them systematically. Daily and weekly reviews were held to assess each qualified lead and how best to involve them as participants within a short period of time. The scheduling of group sessions was problematic from the outset of the program for several reasons:

- Customers wanted relatively immediate session service, despite the team process requirements that called for two weeks lead time, and

- Customers exhibited typical group management behavior by rescheduling or canceling planned TeamFocus sessions late enough so that other sessions could not be substituted.

These problems challenged the conduct of the evaluation and threatened the team's ability to cost-effectively develop a representative customer set. The first response was to express irritation that time was wasted in pre-planning sessions which were too often rescheduled. It was decided that these customers were acting normally since the typical group process includes meeting changes. Thereafter, the customer coordination efforts, indeed the entire lifecycle approach to working with customers cradle to grave, was amended in several ways:

1. Initial customer communication was enhanced with messages about the importance of a firm, committed schedule.
2. The difficulty of rescheduling a session with less than two weeks notice was emphasized.
3. The facilitator was assigned to the session immediately after the initial qualifying contact.
4. The facilitator established a "contract" with the customer as well as a direct communication tie, functioning as a risk assessment-abatement loop.
5. The pace and coverage of the customer contact effort was intensified to ensure that a ready stream of customers, which later became a backlog, was pre-planned and available for load-leveling of the schedule.

4.9: Facilitator training

The relevance of the facilitator in GDSS settings is dramatic (Phillips and Phillips 1990). Training and developing new facilitators, beyond the original two that started with the evaluation team on Day One, required special effort. Vendor training provided to each facilitator as they joined the team was not sufficient. New facilitators would return from their initial training eager to begin work leading sessions, but were ill equipped to do so. This was true despite their prior group facilitation and consultation experience and demonstrated ability. There were several deficiency patterns tied to this problem.

First, the training provided by the vendor, while certainly useful and necessary, did not emphasize sufficient hands-on practice time with the software. The training lasted five days, but because there were too few participants in the early vendor seminars, facilitator-trainees did not experience full size group dynamics. Also, the vendor training was not "real" enough as it relied too often on insignificant test problems and issues—nothing like the complex and dense issues areas which our facilitators faced in the actual evaluation sessions. Second, the vendor training program did not give the facilitators adequate exposure to varied GDSS techniques.

A series of changes in the training approach were undertaken:

- The vendor was consulted and a large number of improvements were negotiated.
- Seasoned "lead" facilitators were given direct responsibility for giving each new facilitator a graduated series of apprenticeship lessons and experiences.
- New facilitators were asked to conduct mock sessions and lead them using volunteers from within the sponsoring organization.
- New facilitators were given extra attention by the program manager and customer coordinator so that their concerns were understood and met.
- A conscious effort was made to expose new facilitators to as much of the program evaluation infrastructure as practical (metrics, procedures, management issues, budgets, program schedules, events, vendor communications and the like).

These and other less important changes reduced training and apprenticeship duration from 3.75 months to 2 months. It is envisioned that the learning curve for most facilitators will extend up to two years as they develop all the software and GDSS facilitation skills necessary to be effective with virtually any group that comes forward.

5: Evaluation Results

The data shown here represents some 64 measured group support technology sessions that employed TeamFocus tools and procedures adopted for use in the study. The results suggest that a business case approach to technology evaluation can produce stark findings as well as reinforce existing research. A summary of these evaluation data is shown in Figure 3. There were 654 persons attending the evaluated group sessions. Mean group size was 10.2 persons. The average session length was 4.7 hours. Mean pre-session preparation time was 16.7 hours, with the customer spending 7.8 hours and the evaluation group spending 8.9 hours of that time. Post session labor averaged 4.5 hours, with most of this time spent by the evaluation group completing the documentation and meeting with the customer for each session. Savings data shown in the figure are discussed in Section 5:2.

The distribution of the sessions by major category included in this study is shown in Figure 4. These categories are particularly relevant to the organization sponsoring this evaluation, as they are representative of major work categories considered relevant to this study. The Preferred Process activity area, which is similar to information systems planning, amounted to 11% of the sessions evaluated. The data indicates that one-quarter of the sessions involved planning work. The Consensus activity (11%) is a structured development and problem-solving service provided by this particular organization. Only 2 sessions are categorized as management sessions, despite the fact that most of the evaluation events had management participation. The management strategy category was only applied to those sessions composed entirely of managers, whose activity centered on matters of management. Two other areas of significant activity were requirements definition (28%) and survey work (22%). The first of these was a high volume activity for the Company geared to information systems development. The second is a human resources function associated with the Company's employee surveys. These distribution data indicate a relatively strong conformity with the average workload distribution of the sponsoring organization.

5.1: Measuring the business case

The study captured business case (effectiveness and efficiency) data through direct accounting and closely controlled estimation procedures. Direct charging of all labor hours was established for each session. This labor track captured all time spent from the first pre-session planning event held with a customer, through preparation and staging, actual session activity and all post-session work attributable to the particular customer. Time accounting included both the evaluation staff and the session participants. Estimation data were gathered through structured interview and pre-session questionnaire documentation concerning both the flowtime and the labor that would be expended using the customer's traditional group process approach.

These estimates were operationalized in terms of the specific deliverables and session objectives established during the pre-session planning work. Customers were asked to carefully consider the deliverables defined for their particular group session and to calculate the group time in work days and hours for the team mem-

bers involved if they used their traditional group processes. To ensure extra care, the group manager was instructed to provide conservative estimates. These estimates were also revisited by the customer at the conclusion of the session to provide an estimation validity check.

5.2: Efficiency

Perhaps the most dramatic results of these group support technology session evaluations are shown in Figure 3. These numbers tell much of the business case story. The total flowtime in calendar days saved during the nine month evaluation equaled 1,773 or 91%. The mean labor savings per session was $6,754 and totalled $432,260 for the Company. These financial results are compelling, especially when the number of sessions is taken into consideration. Further, since this is a new technology, having all of the inherent "start-up" business burdens, it is significant that this evaluation generated labor savings for the Company during the first stage of an evaluation effort. These data, along with flowtime and other efficiency data points create an optimistic business case picture.

Presented in Figure 5, is a general depiction of a business case for the technology evaluation. This business case information provides an objective basis for making decisions about the wisdom of deploying group support technology as part of this organization's consulting practice. These calculations show average operating benefits will be $1,057,000, thus providing average operating savings of $591,000, based on a 5-year lifecycle investment of $348,000. The return on

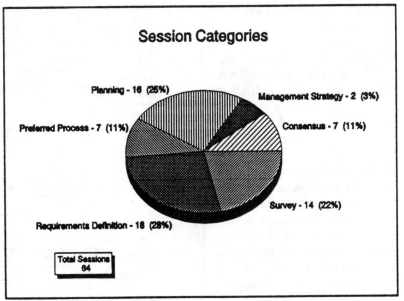

Figure 4

Evaluation Data Summary

Session Activity

- 64 Sessions
- 654 Participants - Mean of 10.2 per Session
- Mean Session Length of 4.7 Hours
- Mean Preparation Time (Hours)
  - Customer - 7.8
  - PSO - 8.9
  - Total - 16.7
- Mean Post-Session Time - 4.5 Hours
- Current Booking Lead Time - 29 Days

Savings to Company

- $432,260 Total Labor Dollars Saved
- $6,754 Mean Labor Dollars Saved per Session
- $1,446 Mean Labor Dollars Saved per Session Hour
- 11,678 Total Labor Hours Saved (71%)
- 1,773 Total Days of Flowtime Saved (91%)

Figure 3

investment will equal 170%. These business case findings help Company management make well-founded technology investment decisions.

5.3: Effectiveness

All of the 654 persons participating in group session evaluations completed an on-line questionnaire. These surveys were aimed a measuring the effectiveness of the group support technology and delivery methodology. Scaled questions were designed to elicit participant judgments about each element of this portion of the business case study.

The results of this group participant survey are shown in Figure 6. As these data indicate, participants rated the technology and delivery methods with relative enthusiasm. All of the means were significantly above the mid-point of each of the satisfaction and agreement scales used. Standard deviations indicate fairly homogenous response distributions. Clearly, the highest positive response was the respondents' willingness to participate in another session (4.37). Significant to the sponsoring organi-

zation, was the high value placed on the group session facilitator (4.24).

Participants reported a high degree of comfort with the software tools (4.14) and the computer keyboard (4.06). These last two variables were considered "tripwires" in the study because of concerns on the part of some managers over potential "fear of computing" participant responses to the group technology.

Overall, the session participants rated the effectiveness of the technology and methodology high in terms of enhanced quality (3.91), more insightful information (3.90) and improved channels of communication (3.82). These data point to a strong showing for the technology and its positive impact on the Company's current group business practices.

5.4: Quality and customer satisfaction

An additional follow-up questionnaire was systematically administered to the managers of all completed group sessions. These questionnaires were mailed to the group leaders several weeks following their sessions. An overall rate of return of 74% was achieved. The data from this source are shown in Figure 7.

Participant Questionnaire Responses

Question	Mean	Std Dev
Improved Channels of Communications	3.82	0.49
Helped Set Clear Objectives	3.63	0.62
Provide Insightful Information	3.90	0.46
Produced More Complete Decision-Making	3.69	0.56
Higher Quality or More Valuable Session Results	3.91	0.51
Improved Teamwork and Morale	3.62	0.54
Increased Commitment to Results of Session	3.54	0.61
Enabled Greater Efficiency and ROI	4.02	0.46

Scaling: 1 - No Benefit to 5 - Great Benefit   Participants 654

Question	Mean	Std Dev
Session Well Suited to Group's Objectives	4.04	0.49
Comfortable Using the GDSS Tools	4.14	0.39
Personal Responsibility for Group's Decisions	3.70	0.55
Other Meeting Would not Have Produced Same Ideas	3.52	0.52
Results Achieved in Much Less Time	4.04	0.51
Willing to Participate in Another TeamFocus Session	4.37	0.46
My Group Could Use Team Focus on A Regular Basis	3.55	0.56
Comfortable Using the Keyboard	4.06	0.40
Facilitator Beneficial to Session	4.24	0.45

Scaling: 1 - Strongly Disagree to 5 - Strongly Agree   Participants 654

Figure 6

Business Case Productivity Analysis ($000)		
Average Operating Benefits Labor (@ 80% utilization)	1,057	71% Productivity Gain
Average Operating Expenses	466	
Average Operating Savings	591	
Investment	348	5-Year Lifecycle w/Labor
ROI	170%	

Figure 5

This instrument utilized scaled questions that sought respondent data concerning quality, utilization and customer satisfaction variables. The response means

Follow-up Questionnaire Responses

Question	Mean	Std Dev
A decision by consensus was reached in session	4.77	1.38
Organization has made use of session output/product	4.83	1.37
TeamFocus improved dicision-making and information gathering	5.04	1.07
Required results were obtained from session	4.88	1.08
TeamFocus allowed organization to shorten schedule or reduce resource usage	5.04	1.23
Facilitator and services added value to the TeamFocus session	5.54	0.78
Would use TeamFocus again	5.38	1.08

Scaling: 1 - Strongly disagree to 6 - Strongly agree   Respondees = 24

Figure 7

show a high level of satisfaction and utility associated with the results of these technology supported group sessions. Of particular interest is that these customers indicated that session products were used by their organizations (4.83), that session objectives and requirements were met (4.88) and that the services provided before, during and after these sessions added value (5.54). Taken together, the results of these post-sessions surveys make it clear that groups and their parent organizations reap significant benefits from using this technology and the attendant delivery services.

6: Conclusions

The results of this study demonstrate the value of business metrics in the design of GDSS research, as well as in the development and deployment of the programs using these technologies. These variables have *a priori* significance to decision-makers throughout the world, whether they operate in large commercial settings, applied research environments or small entrepreneurial organizations.

Group Decision Support Systems can only be valuable to the extent that they are deployed and integrated with organizational infrastructure elements which are at once both dynamic and complex. The opportunity available to the GDSS industry is in creating value for organizations by providing an effective means of performing group work.

This study raises other concerns that future research efforts should address, such as understanding the costs of information and the costs of decisions in group settings and the relative consequences of group support technologies.

References

Akao, Yoji, "Recent Aspects of QFD on Service Industry in Japan," International Conference on Quality Control 1989 Proceedings. International Academy for Quality.

Allport, F., "The Influence of the Group upon Association and Thought," Journal of Experimental Psychology", 3, 1920, pp. 159-182.

Barnard, Chester (1938), "The Executive Function," The Functions of the Executive, Harvard University Press, pp. 215-34.

Beauclair, Renee A. and Straub, Detmar, W., "Utilizing GDSS Technology: Final Report on a Recent Empirical Study," Information & Management, 18, 5, 1990, pp. 213-220.

Boose, J., Bradshaw, J., Koszarek, J. and Shema, D., "Better Group Decisions: Using Knowledge Based Acquisition Techniques to Build Richer Decision Models," submitted to Hawaii International Conference on Systems Sciences, 1992.

Campbell, Terry L., "Technology Update: Group Decision Support Systems, Journal of Accountancy, 170, 1990, pp.47-50.

Connolly, Terry, L.M. Jessup and J.S. Valacich, "Effects of Anonymity and Evaluative Tone on Idea Generation in Computer-Mediated Groups," Management Science, 36, 6 (1990), pp.689-703.

DeSanctis, Gerardine and Gallupe,R.B., "A foundation for the Study of Group Decision Support Systems," Management Science, 33, 5, 1987, pp.589-609.

Diehl, M. and W. Stroebe, "Productivity Loss in Brainstorming Groups: Toward the Solution of a Riddle," J. Social Personality and Social Psychology, 53, 3 (1987), 497-509.

Gause, Donald C. and Gerald Weinberg, Exploring Requirements: Quality Before Design. Dorsett House, 1989.

Gray, P., Aronofsky, J.S., Berry, N., Helmer, O.Kane, G.R. and Perkins, T.E., "The SMU Decision Room Project," Proceedings of the Conference on Decision Support Systems, Execucom Systems Corporation, 1981, pp. 122-129.

Huber, "Decision support systems: Their present nature and future applications," Decision Making: An Interdisciplinary Inquiry, G.R. Ungson and D. N. Braunstein, Eds., Kent, 1982, pp. 249-262.

Johansen, Robert, Groupware: Computer Support for Business Teams, The Free Press, 1988.

Kraemer, Kenneth L. and King, John Leslie, "Computer-based Systems for Cooperative Work and Group Decision Making," ACM Computing Surveys, Vol. 20, No. 2, June, 1988, pp. 116-145.

Kydd, Christine T. and Jones, Louise H., "Corporate Productivity and Shared Information Technology," Information & Management, 17, 5, 1989, pp. 277-282.

Lewis, L. Floyd and Keleman, Ken, S., "Issues in Group Decision Support System (GDSS) Design," Journal of Information Science, 14, 6, 1988, pp. 347-354.

McGoff, C., Hunt, A., Vogel, D. and Nunamaker, J., "IBM's Experience with GroupSystems," Interfaces 20:6 November-December 1990, pp. 39-52.

McGrath, J.E., Groups: Interaction and Performance, Prentice-Hall, 1984.

Nunamaker, Jay et al., "Experiences at IBM with Group Support Systems: A Field Study," Decision Support Systems, 5, 1989(a), pp.183-196.

Nunamaker, J., Vogel, D. and Konsynski, B., "Interaction of Task and Technology to Support Large Groups," Decision Support Systems, 5, 1989(b), pp.139-152.

Phillips, Lawrence D. and Phillips, Maryann C., "Facilitated Work Groups: Theory and Practice," London School of Economics & Political Science, 1990.

Pinsonneault, Alan and Kraemer, Kenneth L., "The Effects of Electronic Meetings on Group Processes and Outcomes: An Assess-

ment of the Empirical Research," European Journal of Operational Research, 46, 2, 1990, pp. 143-161.

Tanniru, Mohan R., and Jain, Hermant, "Knowledge Based GDSS to Support Reciprocally Interdependent Decisions," Decision Support Systems, 5, 3, 1989, pp. 287-301.

VanGundy, Arthur B., "Idea Collection Methods: Blending Old and New Technology," Journal of Data Collection, 27, 1, 1987, pp.14-19.

Vogel, Douglas R., et al, "Electronic Meeting System Experience at IBM," Journal of Management Information Systems, Winter, Vol.6, 3, 1989-90, pp.25-43.

Vogel, Douglas and Nunamaker, Jay, "Group Decision Support System Impact: Multi-Methodological Exploration," Information & Management, 18, 1990, pp.15-18.

Zultner, Richard E., "Software Quality Deployment: Applying QFD to Software," Transactions from the 2nd Symposium on QFD, American Society for Quality Control, 1990.

Groupware and Cooperative Work:
Problems and Prospects

Jonathan Grudin
Human Interface Laboratory MCC

COMPUTER APPLICATIONS THAT SUPPORT GROUPS are commonly known as *groupware*. Although electronic mail and bulletin boards are still the only widely known examples, considerable effort has gone into developing other groupware applications. As networks spread, we will see more voice applications, coauthoring tools, intelligent databases, group decision support systems, and other applications designed with the understanding that most work is carried out in a social context. However, progress may be slower than expected and may eventually lead us in unanticipated directions. In the first half of this chapter I describe problems that have led to expensive, repeated failures of groupware development efforts; in the second half, a groupware success story demonstrates the importance of focusing our analysis on the work setting and provides a basis for speculating about the future.

Problems in the Development of Groupware

Why is groupware more difficult than single-user applications to design and evaluate? First of all, because individuals interact with the groupware product, it has all of the usual interface design problems. What's worse, group members with different backgrounds, experiences, and preferences may all have to use the same groupware application. For example, different individuals may choose to use different word processors—or some may choose to write by hand—but two coauthors must agree to use the same coauthoring tool!

Another complication for groupware design is that within a group, individuals take on different roles. Thus, consider the differences within these pairs who might work together: author/editor, sender/recipient, speaker/listener, and supervisor/subordinate. Note that the same person can shift in role, being author at one moment and then, perhaps when reading a collaborator's contribution, editor. The software must support not only several people working together on a task, but also their different and potentially shifting roles.

A further complication is that once we enter the realm of group dynamics, various social, motivational, political, and economic factors come into the picture. These usually play little or no role in the design of single-user applications such as word processors or spreadsheets, but are central in the design of a system to support meeting management, for example.

Another obstacle is the difficulty of studying groups—group processes are often variable and context-sensitive, and usually unfold over a much longer time frame than individual activities. Days or weeks may be needed to observe the pattern of use of a group calendar or even an electronic mail system, with the further complication that the activity occurs in different locations. Organizational change that results from introducing the technology may take even longer to observe. And finally, after one *has* observed a group in action, it is hard to generalize to other groups—each group is different, and a group's experiences with an application are highly influenced by the conditions under which it is introduced.

In a recent paper [Grudin, 1989b], I examined several groupware applications that have failed to live up to their promise. In each case, my analysis was based on personal involvement in the design, evaluation, or use of the application as well as on the published literature. Five factors contributing to groupware failure were identified:

• Groupware applications often fail because they require that some people do additional work, and those people are *not* the ones who perceive a direct benefit from the use of the application.

• Groupware may lead to activity that violates social taboos, threatens existing political structures, or otherwise demotivates users who are crucial to its success.

• Groupware may fail if it does not allow for the wide range of exception handling and improvisation that characterizes much group activity.

• We fail to learn from experience because these complex applications introduce almost insurmountable obstacles to meaningful, generalizable analysis and evaluation.

• The groupware development process fails because our intuitions are especially poor for multiuser applications.

THE DISPARITY BETWEEN WHO DOES THE WORK AND WHO GETS THE BENEFIT

Given the different preferences, experience, roles, and tasks of members of a group, a new groupware application will never afford every member precisely the same benefit. When it is introduced, some people will have to adjust more than others. One can hope that the differences are not great—but often they are. There should be a collective benefit from using the application; ideally, everyone will also benefit individually, even if some benefit more than others. However, this ideal is rarely found; most groupware requires *additional* work for some users, who enter or process information that the application requires or produces.

Consider, for example, the automatic meeting scheduling feature that accompanies many electronic calendar systems. The underlying concept is simple: the person scheduling the meeting specifies a distribution list and the system checks each person's calendar, finding a time convenient for all. The immediate beneficiary is the manager or secretary who initiates a typical meeting, but for the feature to work efficiently, *everyone* in the group must maintain a personal calendar and be willing to let the computer schedule their free time. Ehrlich [1987a, 1987b] reports that electronic calendars are typically used as communication devices by managers. They are often not maintained by individual contributors. Thus, successful use of automatic meeting scheduling requires additional work for those group members who would not otherwise maintain electronic calendars. As a result, this groupware feature is rarely used.

Similarly, consider voice products, such as voice annotation to documents. The advantages of digitized voice over handwritten or typed input are almost all advantages for the speaker: speech is faster to produce, conveys emotion and nuance easily, and may be available without access to a computer terminal. The disadvantages to digitized voice, however, are overwhelmingly problems for the listener. It is harder to understand than typed or written material, slower to take in, not easily scanned or reviewed, more likely to contain errors, and more difficult to manipulate—for example, proposed edits to a document will have to be typed in by the listener anyway. This disparity may contribute to the repeated failure of voice products to meet sales projections [Aucella, 1987]. When is it acceptable for speakers to thus burden listeners? Possibly when users are speakers and listeners in equal measure, or where there is no alternative, as when use of hands or a keyboard is not possible. A disparity may also be accepted when the speaker is of higher status than the listener, as with dictation machines,

monitor. Thus "sabotaged," the work management system was of little use and was eventually quietly withdrawn.

Another active groupware development area that has failed to meet expectations is meeting management or group decision support systems [Kraemer and King, 1988]. The appeal of improving the efficiency of meetings is clear, but the decision-making process is often complex and subtle, with participants holding partially hidden agendas, relying on knowledge of the personalities of the others involved, and showing sensitivity to social customs and motivational concerns. Because such factors are never represented explicitly in a support system, the computer participates at a great disadvantage. In one case, a group considered using an issue-based information system in which arguments, counter-arguments, and decisions are entered by participants, creating a record of the decision-making process that can be used for subsequent review and exploration of alternatives. The plan to use the system was abandoned when it was recognized that the manager wanted the group to project a strong impression of consensus; the explicit record of opposing positions that the system would immortalize was politically unacceptable.

Exception Handling in Workgroups

Software may be designed to support group activities or procedures as they are "supposed to" happen, but descriptions of "typical" procedures can be misleading. Suchman [1983] argues persuasively that a wide range of error, exception handling, and improvisation are characteristic of human activity. Group activity may be particularly variable—strict adherence to a standard procedure may often be more the exception than the rule. But given the overall difficulty of developing software to support group activity, the desire to build the design around specific work procedures may be especially strong.

The problems that can result are illustrated in a case study by Rowe [1985; 1987]. Computerized stock control and sales order processing systems were introduced at a chocolate factory that is part of a large food company. Severe problems arose when the computer services division of the food company installed the systems in the chocolate factory:

(People in) computer services refer to a "production mentality" where (chocolate factory) staff respond to problems as and when they arise, are eager to keep production operating and are loathe to indulge in long-term planning and adopt specific procedures. Most important, they expect others to adjust to them, and resist the discipline the computer imposes . . . . Moreover, not only did management fail to impose set procedures, but further ad hoc arrangements were positively encouraged by the sales department, as in the case of one customer who was assured that they could amend their Friday order up to 1:00 p.m. on a Monday. No doubt it believed it was working in

where an executive's time is deemed valuable enough to warrant the arduous transcription effort.

As a third example, consider a project management application on a distributed system, covering the scheduling and chronicling of activities, the creation and evaluation of plans and schedules, the management of product versions and changes, and the monitoring of resources and responsibilities. Such applications are being developed [Sathi et al., 1986]. Clearly, the primary beneficiary is the project leader or manager; equally evident is that successful use will require other group members to enter considerable information that is typically not kept on-line. This may be resisted. For example, one ten-year project culminated in a "computer-assisted management system" installed on an aircraft carrier, "its primary purpose to help the Commanding Officer and his department heads administer the ship" [McCracken and Akscyn, 1984]. One factor contributing to its eventual replacement by a system that lacked management features was the difficulty of getting everyone to use it [Kling, 1987].

Social, Political, and Motivational Factors

Groupware may be resisted if it interferes with the subtle and complex social dynamics that are common to groups. The computer is happiest in the world of explicit, concrete information. Central to group activity, however, are social, motivational, political, and economic factors that are rarely explicit or stable. Often unconsciously, our actions are guided by social conventions and by our knowledge of the personalities of people around us. It will be difficult to make such conventions, knowledge, and personal agendas available to the computer—a secretary's implicit knowledge of a manager's priorities may be difficult to impart to an on-line calendar. For example, secretaries know that managers' unscheduled time is rarely really free; unauthorized scheduling of a manager's apparently open time can lead to total rejection of automatic meeting scheduling [Ehrlich, 1987a]. Even trying to make social knowledge explicit may be a problem—we often tactfully keep our motivations and agendas (and our opinions of other people) to ourselves. Yet unless such information is made explicit, groupware will be insensitive to it.

With one work management system, any employee who identified and reported a priority problem began getting system-generated requests for progress reports to be forwarded to the Chief Executive Officer—a blatant example of a design that ignores the sensitivity of certain communications. So employees stopped reporting problems. The vigilant system noted that employees had stopped using it and alerted the administrator. The employees dealt with the resulting complaints by writing programs that periodically opened files and changed dates, which satisfied the watchful, automatic

determining acceptance, such as user training, management buy-in, and vendor follow-through. Given these interacting influences, evaluation may require a full implementation. Even then, establishing which underlying factors brought it about.

Finally, the difficulty of evaluation is increased dramatically by the complexity of an application that provides features and interfaces that vary according to users' jobs, backgrounds, and preferences. A single-user application may be adopted if it appeals to a reasonable fraction of the members of a group. Groupware often will have to appeal to all group members.

The Breakdown of Intuitive Decision-making

Thousands of developer-years and hundreds of millions of dollars have been committed to various application areas that could be termed groupware, despite little or no return [Grudin, 1989b]. Often, the same mistakes are made over and over. How does this happen?

Decision-makers in a position to commit resources to development projects rely heavily on intuition. The experience and track record of a development manager considering a groupware application is generally based on single-user applications. Intuition is likely to be a far more reliable guide to single-user applications than to multiuser applications. A manager with good intuition may quickly get a feel for the user's experience with a word processor or spreadsheet, for example, but fail to appreciate the intricate requirements of a groupware application that requires participation by a range of user types.

Not surprisingly, decision-makers are often drawn to applications that selectively benefit one subset of the user population: managers. Consider the active groupware development areas: group decision support systems primarily benefit decision-makers; project management applications primarily benefit project managers; automatic meeting schedulers benefit those who convene meetings; digitized voice products appeal to those who rely on speech (remember the dictation machine). Similarly, managers may see themselves as prospective casual users of features such as a natural language interface and may support their development, without recognizing either their limited utility for heavy users or their development cost [Grudin, 1989b].

This bias is understandable—each of us has ideas about what will help us do our job. But managers tend to underestimate the down side, the unwelcome extra work required of other users to maintain such an application, a burden that often leads to neglect or resistance. For example, a group decision support system or work management application may require many people to learn the system and then enter data, may record information that participants would prefer not to have widely disseminated,

the best interests of the company, but its actions created considerable problems for those trying to operate the computer.

In some areas, the manual system continued to be used out of necessity. At one point, the general manager "became convinced that someone was sabotaging the system."

Here Suchman's observation is critical: if more human activity is ad hoc problem solving than we realize, if descriptions of "standard process" are often post hoc rationalizations, the workers' behavior that seemed pathological to the computer services division may well have been an optimal response to the work environment. For example, catering to the needs of specific customers is often considered good, when it can be done.

The general manager recommended that the system be withdrawn, but "he was overruled by group head office, who were not prepared to lose face over the installation." By hiring new personnel and taking other expensive measures, the management made the system work. This points out another problem facing groupware. The system described by Rowe was a large, expensive system: upper management was prepared to do a lot to make it succeed. But a typical groupware application or feature, such as meeting scheduling or voice annotation or even meeting support, will rarely have the same degree of visibility and backing—and thus would fail under similar circumstances.

The Underestimated Difficulty of Evaluating Groupware

Task analysis, design, and evaluation are never easy, but they are far more difficult for multiuser applications than for single-user applications. An individual's success with a particular spreadsheet or word processor is unlikely to be affected by differing backgrounds or by the personalities of other group members, so single users can be tested in a lab on the perceptual, cognitive, and motor variables that have been the focus for single-user applications. But it is difficult to create a lab situation that accurately reflects the social, motivational, economic, and political dynamics that are quite likely to affect the use of groupware.

Thus, evaluation of groupware requires a different approach, based on the methodologies of social psychology and anthropology. These skills are absent in most development environments, where human factors engineers and cognitive psychologists are only starting to be accepted. These methods are more time-consuming. Much of a person's use of a spreadsheet might be observed in a single hour, for example, but group interactions typically unfold over days or weeks. Furthermore, the methods are less precise. Evaluating groupware "in the field" is remarkably complex because of the number of people to observe at each site, the wide variability of group composition, and the range of environmental factors that play roles in

and may block other means to influence decision-making, such as private lobbying. Also, as described above, managers may fail to appreciate the difficulty of developing and evaluating good groupware. Finally, they may not recognize that because systems and applications are getting cheaper and thus less visible to management, users will less often be forced to do additional work to ensure an application's success. For example, an expensive voice messaging system failed initially at one site, but succeeded when top management insisted on its use and removed the alternatives; however, no such push is likely for a much less visible voice annotation feature.

Of course, managers are not alone in having poor intuition for multiuser applications. As researchers, designers, implementers, users, evaluators, or managers, our computer experience is generally based on single-user applications. This history determined the skills we acquired, the intuitions we developed, and the way we view our work. For example, human factors engineers are trained to apply techniques based on perceptual, cognitive, and motor psychology to study phenomena of brief duration, but are unfamiliar with the techniques of social psychology or anthropology needed to study group dynamics over time.

In particular, we are not trained to think deeply about the disparity between the benefit obtained by and the work required of different user categories, beyond distinctions among novice, casual, and heavy users. We may rely on feedback from a few "typical users," often the target audience, the principal beneficiaries of the application. For groupware, this leads us to focus on managers. For example, the greatest user interface challenge for an intelligent project management application will be to minimize the information entry effort required of each worker. But instead, attention is directed toward information display, toward the user interface for the principle beneficiary, the manager. "Managers must know what information is needed, where to locate it, and how to interpret and use it. Equally important is that they be able to do so without great effort" [Sathi et al., 1986]. This may appeal to the manager sponsoring the project, but *exclusive* focus on improving the system for its principal beneficiary is not wise.

The converse may also occur: a decision-maker may not recognize the value of an application that primarily benefits nonmanagers, even when it would provide a collective benefit to the organization. This is particularly true for applications that might create additional work for the manager. The second half of this paper addresses this point in the context of electronic mail, a groupware success story.

Computer Supported Cooperative Work: A Shift in Perspective

Computer support, even of individuals, is already changing the way groups and organizations function. But the problems described above suggest that the technology-driven approach to progress that works relatively well with single-user applications is failing with multiuser targets. We need to understand more about how groups and organizations function and evolve, as well as more about individual differences. This has long been pointed out by visionaries such as Douglas Engelbart, but it is easier to recognize the problem than to truly escape the technology orientation that is reflected in the term *groupware* itself. Research and development methodologies that truly focus on users' work and workplaces are only starting to appear [for example, see Bjerknes et al., 1987; Bodker et al., 1988; Whiteside et al., 1988].

The term *computer supported cooperative work*, adopted by a number of researchers and developers, explicitly identifies "work" as the central concern. Even with that emphasis, many members manifest a technology-driven focus. [See Greif, 1988, for an overview; Grudin, 1989a, reviews a recent collection of research papers.] Successful proponents of a work-centered approach include a number of Scandinavian researchers who stress the importance of "workplace democracy"—engaging the users or workers meaningfully in the design process, a slow mutual education process that results in users becoming true members of the design team [Bjerknes et al., 1987; Bodker et al., 1988].

This time-consuming, labor-intensive approach may not be equally appropriate for all development projects. It is still evolving but has already taken the tremendously important step of bringing computer scientists into meaningful contact with labor unions, historians, and economic theorists. Advances in computer support for group activity will require sensitivity to issues such as the balance of work and benefit, social conventions within organizations, and political and motivational concerns—issues that have long interested unions, economists, management or organizational design specialists, and others. The knowledge and approaches of these fields must now be joined with computer science.

Electronic Mail: Viewing a Groupware Success from an Organizational Perspective

The potential for electronic mail to augment group activity was foreseen thirty years ago; today, a variety of related computer-mediated communication forms establish it as the clearest groupware success story. How has electronic mail, broadly defined to include distributed communications such as electronic bulletin boards, avoided the pitfalls into which most groupware stumbles? Is electronic mail a potential model for groupware? In the remainder of this chapter, I analyze electronic mail in the organizational context, describe the effect this medium is beginning to have on the structure of work, and speculate on emerging changes in industry and academia. How does electronic mail fare with the five obstacles to groupware described above?

- Who does the work and who benefits? Insofar as the sender/recipient distinction is concerned, electronic mail provides an equitable balance. The person with a message to communicate does a little more work to type it, while the receiver can read it easily and whenever convenient; thus, the primary beneficiary typically does a little more work.

- Compatibility with social practices: The essentially conversational format of electronic mail allows us to apply existing social conventions. However, there are differences, which lead to clearly identified problems such as "flaming" and "junk e-mail," and to more subtle but crucial problems described below.

- Exception-handling: the asynchronous, informal nature of most electronic mail makes it flexible, although mail applications have been developed that impose more structure—and that may suffer accordingly [see the discussion of The Coordinator in Grudin, 1989a].

- Difficulty of evaluation: As with all groupware, the overall costs and benefits of electronic mail are difficult to assess.

- Poor intuitions for groupware: Our intuitions concerning electronic mail may be improving as its use spreads.

To summarize, electronic mail avoids most of the problems that hamper other groupware. Its use within organizations is spreading, although not with explosive speed. Its progress has been anomalous: less through the normal product development and marketing processes than by spreading from academic and public sources. Understanding why this is true may be the key to understanding the future of groupware and the impact of infor-mation technology on organizations.

The key user distinction for electronic mail in most organizations is not that of sender and receiver, it is that of manager and subordinate. In fact, this is likely to be the key distinction for any groupware application, not because the technology itself recognizes the supervisor-subordinate distinction, but because that distinction is so critical in the workplace itself. The reception of technology in an organization is determined by the distinctions found in the workplace; to understand this, we must free ourselves from a bias to focus on the distinctions designed into the technology.

In hierarchic organizations, the types of work done by managers and by workers are quite different—as are the rewards. In the United States in particular, we tend to downplay these differences. We often aim for collab-oration between labor and management. But some tension exists in orga-nizations large enough to support and profit from electronic mail, and even where tension isn't evident, the roles of manager and subordinate differ.

Unlike the other groupware applications discussed, electronic mail does not selectively benefit managers or decision-makers. In fact, the contrary is probably true. The asynchronous nature of electronic mail may bother managers whose time is tightly budgeted: "Mostly, a lot of times, I won't respond. I'll print the message and stick it in their file and wait until their weekly meeting," one manager noted in an interview. The ability for anyone to disseminate information rapidly can create new and not always welcome challenges for managers, whose jobs often involve filtering and routing information. In a classic bureaucracy, lateral communication is mini-mized—information flows up and down through the hierarchy. Managers are aware of everything entering or leaving their groups. The resulting inflexibility can lead to inefficiency; rigid bureaucracies, from the Soviet Union to the U.S. Navy, abound with tales of undercover exchange systems devised to cope with this inefficiency. Electronic mail, like the telephone on each worker's desk, supports more efficient lateral communication—but it is threatening to the bureaucratic organization and creates difficulties for managers who rely on the hierarchical organizational model.

For example, one managerial responsibility is to absorb information from higher levels and tailor its presentation to subordinates to maximize their understanding or obtain a desired response. If a manager receives such information electronically, it is easier to forward it without such tailoring. In fact, editing may be counterproductive, because other elec-tronic versions of the message may exist and may be forwarded laterally into the group, immediately revealing any tampering. This places the man-ager in a no-win situation. Similarly, the ability of anyone to send a message instantly to everyone in an organization creates a volatility that manage-ment must cope with.

In a powerful essay based on field studies, Constance Perin [1988] makes a convincing case that "these electronic social formations represent new sources of industrial conflict . . . they are seen as subverting legitimated organizational structures." While noting the collective value of electronic communication to large organizations, Perin describes how it comes into conflict with traditional organizational practice. For example, "the very 'invisibility' of electronic social fields, which may be cultivated bureaucrat-ically because they are believed to enhance productivity, also delegitimates them and becomes the source of managerial negativism and suspicion." A case study by Fanning and Raphael [1986], cited by Perin, concludes that electronic mail "is simply not a management tool, if by management we mean those above the level of project leader . . . . a medium which allows widely separated people to aggregate their needs is, in fact, quite frighten-ing. Some managers correctly foresee that such a system can be most upsetting to the current established order, and do not participate in it as a result."

Where does this leave electronic mail and the groupware that builds on it? Although Perin describes cases of individual managers discouraging or terminating its use, many large organizations have assumed an overall benefit and have successfully introduced electronic mail. Many students and professionals are growing accustomed to it. Thus, the forces Perin describes are likely to play themselves out over time, eroding management control and changing the nature of organizations. Some organizations were designed according to notions of efficiency and control that are quickly becoming outmoded; finding new organizational forms, and minimizing the cost of shifting to them, are challenges for the near future.

Implications for Organizational Change

In summary, by enhancing communication, worker-centered groupware will tend to undermine the authority structure of those hierarchic organizations with relatively incomplete standardization of work processes. Furthermore, the resulting decentralization of control will *further reduce* the prospects for success of groupware that selectively benefits management—which includes most groupware being developed today. Management that has lost some of its ability to control events may find it more difficult to mandate the use of applications that benefit management at the expense of other workers. Thus, successful groupware products may be those whose use clearly benefits subordinates; one example is a group decision support system that is used as part of a *process* that is designed to ensure benefits to all participants, in particular to those usually disadvantaged in meetings [e.g, McGoff, cited in Grudin, 1989a]. In particular, there is promise for groupware that builds on electronic mail, such as the Object Lens system [Lai and Malone, 1988], whose users can fill in message templates and other forms to filter or share information in varied, flexible ways.

The changes in organizations and societies that are eventually traced to technological innovation have rarely been predicted; the effects of groupware will surely follow that pattern. However, we can look for signs of specific changes that may occur. The two examples below suggest how the success of electronic mail may lead to the reorganization of work processes and the birth of new organizational forms.

FROM HACKER CONSULTING TO PURE ADHOCRACY

In *Hackers*, Steven Levy [1984] describes the birth and death in the 1960s and 1970s of the "hacker ethic," central to which was the view that "all information should be free"—including the engineering designs, product plans, and software that were at one time freely exchanged in computer laboratories and clubs. The book charts the erosion of this ethic as one after another of these forms of information became commercially important.

Although different kinds of information are now involved, today's electronic bulletin boards and mail networks support extensive consulting activity. For many users, access is free or inexpensive. By 1985, the capability for using such networks to guide research, development, and even marketing had been noted [Perlman, 1985]. The flow of information through them is reminiscent of the hacker ethic—one can pose a question and get free advice, some of it of high quality.

The commercial potential increases as networks rapidly expand and interconnect. Following the precedents described by Levy, network "hacking" may yield to commercial exploitation—to network-based consulting organizations that go well beyond existing on-line newsletters, extending the electronic market concept [Malone et al., 1987]. A central service may screen consultants, route requests for services, possibly oversee contracts, and monitor problems. An exchange could lead to an individual contract or to the assembly of a team for specific work, drawn from available and qualified individuals on the net. A project might rely on electronic mediation or might bring participants together for a limited time. An early example is Photosource International, a business run from a farmhouse. Photosource International brings together professional photographers and their customers, primarily publishers of newspapers, magazines, and books. Initially a paper newsletter, it now uses networks to reach about 40 percent of its customers. Photo buyers submit descriptions of photos or assignments to one of three distribution lists, based on price range. In addition to providing the forum, Photosource International uses feedback from photo sellers to rate photo buyer performance and requests evidence of professional history from sellers who wish to appear on the highest-level distribution list. Ultimately, specialized network-based services of this type may consolidate, enabling multidisciplinary teams to be assembled electronically.

This generalization of a consulting company is an extreme form of "adhocracy," an organizational structure that "is able to fuse experts drawn from different specialties into smoothly functioning project teams," [Mintzberg, 1984]. Adhocracies include present-day consulting, advertising, and film companies. They are highly decentralized organizations of professionals deployed in small teams in response to changing conditions in dynamic, complex environments. The adhocracy is the organizational type that least adheres to traditional management principles, relying on constant contact to coordinate among teams. Electronic mail should increase the efficiency of an adhocracy, rather than threatening it as it threatens the hierarchic, bureaucratic organization.

THE IVORY TOWER GETS A SILICON FINISH

A good place to look for portents of change is the research university, where some departments have pioneered the use of electronic mail. There

mendously. One drawback is that interdisciplinary cross-fertilization may be reduced as this capability for specialization is utilized and extended. Another likely consequence is a dramatically increased polarization of research and teaching functions, with advanced instruction itself occurring more through electronic exchange and with a new approach to basic instruction that has yet to evolve.

Acknowledgments

My understanding of the significance of electronic mail was greatly abetted by Constance Perin and my need to keep working on it was patiently pointed out by Liam Bannon. Don Norman, Jim Hollan, Steve Poltrock, Will Hill, and Wayne Wilner commented usefully on an early draft.

References

Aucella, A. F. "Voice: Technology Searching for Communication Needs." in *Proc. CHI+GI '87 Human Factors in Computing Systems*, Toronto, April 5-9, 1987, pp. 41-44.

Bjerknes, G., P. Ehn, and M. Kyng, eds. *Computers and Democracy - A Scandinavian Challenge*. Aldershot, UK: Gower, 1987.

Bodker, S., P. Ehn, J. Knudsen, M. Kyng, and K. Madsen. "Computer Support for Cooperative Design." In *Proc. CSCW '88 Conference on Computer-Supported Cooperative Work*, Portland, OR, September 26-28, 1988.

Ehrlich, S. F. "Social and Psychological Factors Influencing the Design of Office Communication Systems." In *Proc. CHI+GI '87 Human Factors in Computing Systems*, Toronto, April 5-9, 1987, pp. 323-39.

Ehrlich, S. F. (1987). "Strategies for Encouraging Successful Adoption of Office Communication Systems." ACM Transactions on Office Information Systems. Vol. 5: 340-57.

Fanning, T., and B. Raphael. "Computer Teleconferencing: Experience at Hewlett Packard." In *Proc. CSCW '86 Conference on Computer-Supported Cooperative Work*, Austin, TX, December 3-5, 1986.

Greif, I., ed. *Computer-supported Cooperative Work: A Book of Readings*. San Mateo, CA: Morgan Kaufmann, 1988.

Grudin, J. CSCW '88: Report on the conference and review of the proceedings. *SIGCHI Bulletin*, Vol. 20 (1989):80-84.

Grudin, J. "Why Groupware Applications Fail: Problems in Design and Evaluation." *Office: Technology and People*, Vol. 4, no. 3 (1989): 245-264.

are suggestions that a significant transformation in research and higher education is underway. The forces at work have parallels in other technologies, so first consider some better-understood influences of several advances that preceded the computer.

Technologies—transportation, print, film, telephone, radio, television—have eroded traditional social and cultural barriers, as captured in McLuhan's concept of the global village. For example, as a college freshman twenty years ago, I shared a dormitory with students from many regions of the United States. We discovered a large common experience that transcended geography and even social class; specific television programming was the most easily recognized factor, with wide-scale product distribution and other influences also evident. This revolution continues as the technological infrastructure spreads over the globe. The Vietnam War was brought into the American home two decades ago; China's recent embrace of travel and electronic media shaped the 1989 student strike.

However, a counteracting tendency works against homogenization. Telephones allow corporate headquarters to be geographically removed from manufacturing plants, automobiles allow social restratification into urban-suburban groupings, and with cable and the relaxation of government monopolies in television, greater choice again allows people to regroup or diverge. Electronic mail and bulletin boards provide almost unlimited specialization according to personal interests, thus contributing to this reorganization.

Campuses have been to some extent communities apart, "ivory towers" focused on research and learning, distanced from local influences. As a result, to produce peers with whom to discuss ideas and collaborate, research faculty have had to take the time to explain the foundation of their own work to students and colleagues, including those with different specialties or from different departments. Building a common understanding, a mutual set of interests, was an effortful bur necessary part of being a community of scholars. No longer is this true. A researcher with access to electronic mail (plus more journals, more conferences, FAX, and lower telephone costs) can contact a large number of researchers at other institutions who already have very closely matched interests. One can easily obtain high-quality feedback on ideas without investing the time to educate students or colleagues.

Geographic proximity is still an important factor in full-fledged scientific collaboration [Kraut et al., 1988], but electronic mail and broader bandwidth groupware successors may change that. Two-party exchanges between colleagues with an established common purpose and active electronic group discussions are widespread, especially in computer science departments. The resulting efficiency of communication, which is likely to spread quickly through the academic world, can accelerate research progress tre-

Kling, R. "The Social Dimensions of Computerization." Plenary address given at CHI+GI '87 Human Factors in Computing Systems, Toronto, April 5-9, 1987.

Kraemer, K., and J. King. "Computer-based Systems for Cooperative Work and Group Decision-making." *ACM Computing Surveys*, Vol. 20 (1988):115-46.

Kraut, R. E., C. Egido, and J. Galegher. "Patterns of Contact and Communication in Scientific Research Collaboration." In *Proc. CSCW '88 Conference on Computer-Supported Cooperative Work*, Portland, OR, September 26-28, 1988.

Lai, K. Y., and T. W. Malone. "Object Lens: A 'Spreadsheet' for Cooperative Work." In *Proc. CSCW '88 Conference on Computer-Supported Cooperative Work*, Portland, OR, September 26-28, 1988.

Levy, S. *Hackers*. Garden City, NY: Anchor Press/Doubleday, 1985.

Malone, T. W., J. Yates, and R. I. Benjamin. "Electronic Markets and Electronic Hierarchies." *Communications of the ACM*, Vol. 30, No. 6 (1987): 484-97.

McCracken, D. L., and R. M. Akscyn. "Experience with the ZOG Human-Computer Interface System." *Int. J. Man-Machine Studies*, Vol. 21 (1984):293-310.

Mintzberg, H. "A Typology of Organizational Structure." In *Organizations: A Quantum View*, D. Miller and P. H. Friesen, eds. Englewood Cliffs, NJ: Prentice Hall, 1984.

Perin, C. "Electronic Social Fields in Bureaucracies." American Anthropological Association, Organized Session, "Egalitarian Ideologies and Class Contradictions in American Society." Washington, DC, November 15, 1989.

Perlman, G. "USENET: Doing Research on the Network." *UNIX/World* (December, 1985):75-81.

Rowe, C. J. (1985). "Identifying Causes of Failure: A Case Study in Computerized Stock Control." *Behaviour and Information Technology*, Vol. 4:63-72

Rowe, C. J. "Introducing a Sales Order Processing System: The Importance of Human, Organizational and Ergonomic Factors." *Behaviour and Information Technology*, Vol. 6 (1987):455-65.

Sathi, A., T. E. Morton, and S. F. Roth. "Callisto: An Intelligent Project Management System." *AI Magazine* (Winter, 1986):34-52. Reprinted in Greif, I., ed. *Computer-supported Cooperative Work: A Book of Readings*. San Mateo, CA: Morgan Kaufmann, 1988, pp. 269-309.

Suchman, L. "Office Procedures as Practical Action: Models of Work and System Design." *ACM Transactions on Office Information Systems*, Vol. 1 (1983):320-28.

Whiteside, J., J. Bennett, and K. Holtzblatt. "Usability Engineering: Our Experience and Evolution." In *Handbook of Human-Computer Interaction*, M. Helander, ed. Amsterdam: North-Holland, 1988.

PART II
Behavioral Foundations and Enabling Technologies

Our goal in Part II is to help bridge the gaps in background and language among the many different kinds of people who are involved with the development and use of groupware for computer-supported cooperative work.

Effective groupware can facilitate group processes such as discussing and negotiating, planning and problem solving, and writing and designing. Thus any thoughtful development of groupware must proceed from an informed view of the nature of small group dynamics. Although the relevant background could occupy the space of many volumes, we attempt in Part II to highlight the key issues from the behavioral and social sciences that are important for understanding the nature of group work and the impact of technology on group process. We shall also provide pointers for further study.

We begin in Chapter 3 with an introduction to small group process and dynamics. Three papers deal with theories of group process, two deal with meeting management and with the role of facilitation in CSCW, and two review media impacts on group interactions. The final paper broadens the focus from the group to the organization, and gives a feeling for the variety of forms and structures that are found in organizations.

Chapter 4 examines approaches to the design and evaluation of groupware. We introduce *participatory design* as a collaborative method for the design of collaborative software, and the use of *ethnomethodology* and *conversation analysis* to help understand and characterize group processes and groupware usage.

One implication of the ethnomethodological approach is that the insights developed in Chapter 3 needed to be grounded, tested, and augmented in the specific contexts of real applications and real work practice. Thus Chapter 5 presents a number of case studies of cooperative work, not necessarily involving any computers or any special collaborative technology. These cluster into two categories: papers dealing with relatively formal and structured collaborative activities such as writing, design, spreadsheet development, and programming; and papers dealing with relatively informal and loosely structured collaborative activities such as scientific research and office work. The paper on cooperative programming introduces *distributed cognition* as a theory that helps us understand the behavior of teams of people engaged in complex cognitive tasks.

Yet the design of effective groupware requires not only deep behavioral understanding, but also sophisticated technological innovation. In Chapter 6 we shift our focus to the technical foundations that support such innovation. Although many areas of modern computer science and many kinds of technology are involved, we concentrate on some of the more important aspects of networking and communications technology, software for communication and coordination, and theories that inform the appropriate design of such technologies.

We begin with a brief introduction to computer networks, the foundation technology for both communications and data sharing using computers. Next is a survey of *digital multimedia* technology. A third paper reviews *non-speech audio* as an interface technology for CSCW. There follows a brief introduction to *hypertext*, a fundamental building block of much asynchronous groupware, and a paper on *coordination theory*. We conclude with a paper on *distributed systems* and *concurrency control*, technologies that are required for realizing shared digital workspaces across a variety of computer networks.

PART II

Behavioral Foundations and Enabling Technologies

CHAPTER 3
Human Behavior in Groups and Organizations

A comprehensive and analytical presentation of the research results on group process is the landmark text *Groups: Interaction and Performance* by McGrath (1984). McGrath (1984, pp. 6-7) first enumerates types of social aggregations as follows:

- Artificial aggregations: Statistical group, or social category

- Unorganized aggregates: Audience, crowd, public

- Units with patterned relationships: Culture, subculture, kinship group

- Structured social units: Society, community, family

- Deliberately designed social unit: Organization, suborganization, crew (or work team)

- Less deliberately designed social unit: Association, friendship group

He then defines groups as "those social aggregates that involve mutual awareness and potential mutual interaction," by which he includes "families (kin groups and other residential groups); work crews and other organized task performance teams; and friendship (or social) groups."

We include three excerpts from McGrath's text in this volume: two in this chapter and one in the following chapter. The excerpt from the "Groups and Human Behavior" chapter (McGrath, 1984, pp. 12–17) presents a conceptual framework for the study of groups that highlights the relationship between group dynamics and the elements that influence it:

- The properties of individuals

- The relationships among individuals as members of the group, in other words, the group's structure

- The properties of the environment in which the group functions

- The task or situation to be carried out by the group

- The "behavior setting," which he defines as the fit between the group's structure and the task.

More recently, McGrath (1990, 1991) has developed a new theory of groups dealing with Time, Interaction, and Performance (TIP). We include his 1991 paper by that name. He begins by criticizing much of the existing work on the behavior of groups by noting that it is rooted in empirical evidence which has been gathered on ad hoc, laboratory groups of limited mission and under limited conditions. He provides some pointers to recent literature that better takes account of the physical, temporal, and social contexts in which real groups operate. He then analyzes group behavior in terms of three functions—*production, member support,* and *group well-being,* and four modes—*inception, problem solving, conflict resolution,* and *execution.* He observes the importance of temporal aspects of behavior in groups such as scheduling, synchronization, and allocation of temporal resources. He closes by discussing aspects of the group interaction process such as tasks and acts.

"How to Run a Meeting" by Antony Jay (1976) discusses the art of running a meeting. His presentation covers the functions of a meeting, such as defining a group and strengthening a group's commitment to the decisions it makes, and the various objectives of a meeting, such as deciding what to do and how to do it. He stresses the need for meeting preparation, describes the role of the chairman, and discusses methods for conducting a meeting effectively.

The quality of meetings depends critically upon the chairman as well as the participants, the meeting space (see paper by Mantei in Chapter 12 of this volume), and the meeting technology. Many groups recommend the use of a trained meeting facilitator to lead and moderate both traditional as well as computerized meetings. "The Group Facilitator: A CSCW Perspective" by Viller (1991) describes the role of the facilitator and some actions for dealing with group process problems. These are typically termed *interventions.* Viller then discusses methods for facilitation in computer conferences (Chapter 7) and in computer-based face-to-face meetings (Chapter 12), and suggests how the computer can be programmed to aid the process of facilitation.

Psychologists of media impacts have over the years helped to illuminate group processes and the ways in which they are influenced by the communication context in which they take place. We include two excerpts from Short, Williams, and Christie's classic *The Social Psychology of Telecommunications.* The first excerpt, a chapter entitled "Visual Communication and Social Interaction" (Short, Williams, and Christie, 1976, pp. 43–60) reviews what is known about the functions of non-verbal cues and the visual channel in the social interaction of a pair or small group of individuals. Six functions are postulated for non-verbal cues: *mutual attention and responsiveness, channel control, feedback, illustrations, emblems,* and *interpersonal attitudes.* The provision of feedback on interpersonal attitudes is then elaborated in terms of the roles of proximity and orientation, physical appearance, non-verbal signals from the body and face, eye gaze, and mutual gaze or eye contact, as well as the relationship between verbal and visual communication. The authors conclude as follows (p. 60):

> Thus, the tasks which would be expected to be the most sensitive to variation in the medium of communication are tasks in which the expression of emotion (and perception of this emotion) is an important part of the interaction, tasks with a great need for timing and coordination of the speaker's activity with the response of the other, and, finally, tasks on which there is the greatest need to manipulate others.

The second excerpt from McGrath (1984, pp. 60–66), taken from a chapter entitled "A Typology of Tasks," focuses on the nature of *tasks.* McGrath proposes a novel taxonomy of group tasks, one that we have found to generate useful insights while envisioning and categorizing various kinds of groupware. The author begins by suggesting that there are four general processes involved in tasks: *to generate* (alternatives), *to choose* (alternatives), *to negotiate,* and *to execute.* He arrives at his *group task circumflex* by dividing:

- "To generate" into generating plans and generating ideas

- "To choose" into solving problems with correct answers and deciding issues with no right answer

- "To negotiate" into resolving conflicts of viewpoint and resolving conflicts of interest

- "To execute" into resolving conflicts of power and executing performance tasks.

The second excerpt from Short, Williams, and Christie (1976, pp. 77–89), entitled "Communication Modes and Task Performance," explores the relationships between communication modes and group performance on tasks such as bargaining (resolving conflicts of interest) and problem solving (consisting of both kinds of McGrath's choice tasks). Examples are given to illustrate how the removal or attenuation of cues normally present in face-to-face communication affects group behavior. We are reminded that we must always be sensitive to the changes in our work styles and interaction dynamics that will inevitably result from any use of new communications media, for example, computer conferencing or desktop videoconferencing.

A number of forms of so-called "groupware," for example, computer conferencing and organizational memory technologies, could more appropriately be classified as "orgware" ("organizationware"). We therefore close this chapter by broadening the focus from the group to the organization. In "A Typology of Organizational Structure," Mintzberg (1984) gives a feeling for the great variety of forms and structures that are found in organizations. The author identifies five basic parts of the organization: the *operating core*, the *strategic apex*, the *middle line*, *technostructure*, and *support staff*. (He adds *ideology* in a later version, published as Mintzberg, 1989.) He describes a number of coordinating mechanisms: direct supervision, standardization of work processes, standardization of outputs, standardization of skills, and mutual adjustment. (He adds "standardization of norms" in Mintzberg, 1989.) These coordinating mechanisms come into play in different ways as a result of various options in the structural design of organizations, such as job specialization, training, planning and control, and decentralization; and as a result of a number of contextual factors, such as age and size of the organization. The body of the paper describes five different kinds of organizations which are distinguished in terms of their key coordinating mechanism, which part of the organization is key, and the type of decentralization: *simple structure* (called an *entrepreneurial organization* in Mintzberg, 1989), *machine bureaucracy*, *professional bureaucracy*, *divisionalized form*, and *adhocracy* (called an *innovative organization* in Mintzberg, 1989). Mintzberg (1989) also adds two new kinds, the *missionary organization* and the *political organization*.

Notes and Guide to Further Reading

The entire text of *Groups: Interaction and Performance* by McGrath (1984) is highly recommended. A vastly expanded version of Mintzberg's typology of organizations appears as many chapters in a recent book (Mintzberg, 1989). Malone and Rockart (1991) discuss the impact of computers and networks on the management of organizations. March (1991) focuses on how decisions happen in organizations. Perin (1991) contrasts *structure* and *process* views of organizations. Hewett (1986) and Gerson and Star (1986) present perspectives on organizational information systems in terms of *due process*. Dubs and Hayne (1992) discuss the concept of facilitation of group meetings in a distributed environment.

Other texts on group and organization structure, process, and behavior are listed in the Notes section of Part I.

The entire text of Short, Williams, and Christie's *The Social Psychology of Telecommunications* (1976) is also recommended, especially the important discussion of *social presence* theory which appears in Chapter 5. Williams (1977) is a summary of early research results comparing face-to-face to mediated communication. Daft and Lengel (1986) discusses information processing by organizations in terms of uncertainty, equivocality, and *media richness*. An approach to studying communication and media in terms of *genres of organizational communication* is presented in Yates and Orlikowski (1991). Recent studies of media impacts on group process are listed in the Notes section of Chapter 13.

GROUPS AND HUMAN BEHAVIOR

(Excerpt)

from

Groups: Interaction and Performance

Joseph E. McGrath

. . .

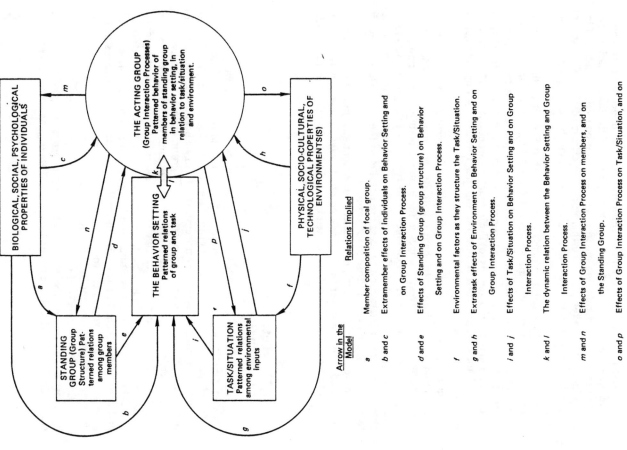

Arrow in the Model	Relations Implied
a	Member composition of focal group.
b and c	Extramember effects of individuals on Behavior Setting and on Group Interaction Process.
d and e	Effects of Standing Group (group structure) on Behavior Setting and on Group Interaction Process.
f	Environmental factors as they structure the Task/Situation.
g and h	Extratask effects of Environment on Behavior Setting and on Group Interaction Process.
i and j	Effects of Task/Situation on Behavior Setting and on Group Interaction Process.
k and l	The dynamic relation between the Behavior Setting and Group Interaction Process.
m and n	Effects of Group Interaction Process on members, and on the Standing Group.
o and p	Effects of Group Interaction Process on Task/Situation, and on the Environment.

FIGURE 1-1 A Conceptual Framework for the Study of Groups

A CONCEPTUAL FRAMEWORK FOR THE STUDY OF GROUPS

There are many different perspectives from which one can view a group, and many ambiguities already noted in defining groups and their membership. For such a complex and ambiguous set of concepts, it is often useful to adopt a frame of reference, a map, that models or lays out systematically the various parts of the topic as a research problem. This section offers such a conceptual model for the study of groups (see Figure 1-1).

The point of such a model is to lay out the underlying logic of the problem in a way that can serve as a guiding framework for exploring the problem in its various aspects. For a complex problem, you cannot study everything at once, you cannot think about everything at the same time. This kind of model lets us take the total problem apart, so we can think about and examine evidence about a manageable chunk of it, and then be able to fit the parts back together again. Furthermore, such a framework tells us what batches of things to look at—what sets of variables are likely to be important—and at the same time offers a logic for deciding what sets of relations among these variables are likely to be important to consider.

Note that this is intended to be a model of the problem (i.e., studying groups systematically), rather than a theory or model of groups. Such models are sometimes called "metatheories." They reflect a way of looking at the problem that encompasses a whole family of possible substantive theories. But they do not specify any one particular theory. Here, we are talking about *classes* of properties or variables, and the logical relations between those classes. But there is no specification of specific sets of relations between specific sets of variables—as there would be in a substantive theory.

Main Classes of Variables

The central feature, the "essence," of a group lies in the interaction of its members—the *behaving together*, in some recognized relation to one another, of two or more people who also have some past and/or future relation to each other. So *group interaction process* is the centerpiece of the model.

Certain things go into that group process. For one thing, there are participants, or group members. They come to a group interaction with all their "properties" (traits, characteristics, beliefs, habits, etc.). A member may be strong, or extroverted, or wise, or old, or female, or bellicose, or clumsy, or many other things. *Some* of these properties of members may affect group interaction. So, if one wants to understand and perhaps predict aspects of group interaction process, one must take these group member properties into account.

These participants make up the group being considered, and one can think about the pattern of relations among group members, *prior to* any group interaction process, as another batch of potentially important properties or variables. Do group members like each other? Do they have differential influence on each other (for example, does one person exercise more leadership or dominance than the others)? How many members are there and how long have they belonged to this group? Group members are related to each other in many ways; a lot of those relations affect how they behave in relation to one another when they interact. These patterns of relations among members—aspects of *group structure*—also must be taken into account if one wants to understand and predict group interaction process.

Group interaction takes place somewhere, in some *environment*. It may involve a group of workers doing their jobs in an assembly plant; a set of executives holding a conference in a company meeting room; a County Planning Board having its monthly meeting; a family eating dinner on a Wednesday evening in April; a football team getting a dressing room talk between halves of a game; a group of kids playing with some old tires in a dump; two couples at a night-club; an airplane crew flying from Texas to Toronto; a Broadway company rehearsing in a theater. In all of those cases, the group interaction is taking place in an environment that includes both physical and social aspects. Many of these can make a difference in how members behave, hence can alter group interaction process.

Group interaction not only takes place somewhere, it involves the group *doing something*. One very important aspect of all of those settings just enumerated is the "task." Any group interaction (actually, any intact portion of such an interaction) can be characterized in terms of the task(s) that the group (or its members) is trying to carry out: giving (and receiving) a lecture or a sermon or a play; processing steel; assembling an auto; choosing a new vice president; deciding on a zoning variance; preparing a budget justification; arbitrating a grievance; enjoying dinner; having a good time at the nightclub, on the backpacking trip, or in the dump. The task, as you can see from those examples, involves informally assumed goals (e.g., having a good time) as well as assigned jobs (e.g., assembling an auto). What the group is doing, or trying to do, as well as where this is taking place, affects group interaction process in many ways. So, the task situation represents another class of "factors" one must take into account if one wishes to understand and predict group interaction process.

These major classes of inputs—properties of group members; properties of the standing group (group structure); properties of the task/situation; and properties of the surrounding environment—set the conditions under which group interaction takes place. Furthermore, the effects of these four sets of properties, singly and in combination, are forces that shape the group interaction process.

The group interaction process itself is both the result of these shaping forces and the source of some additional forces. While group interaction is greatly affected by those sets of input variables—properties of members, of the group, of the task, and of the environment—it is also patterned, in part, by forces internal to (or indigenous to) the interaction process itself. The latter part of this chapter delves further into the internal forces of group interaction process.

Furthermore, the interaction process and its results represent sources (forces) that potentially lead to changes in those very input conditions: changes in the members themselves; changes in the group structure, or the patterns of relations among members; and changes in the relation of the group to its tasks and to its environment. So, these sets of outputs (or outcomes, or consequences) of group interaction process are parallel to the input classes and, in fact, represent changes in those input variables.

These classes of factors, or "panels," of potentially important variables, are related to one another in relatively complex ways. These panels, and the relations among them, are diagrammed in Figure 1-1. The parts of that model are discussed next.

A Model of Effects by and on Groups

The conceptual framework for study of groups starts with two givens: individual people, who are the members of the group in question (what will be referred to, at times, as the focal group, for clarity of reference); and the environment in which those people are embedded. So we begin with two panels of potentially relevant properties: properties of the group members as individuals; and properties of the physical, socio-cultural and technological environment(s). The former panel includes biographical and demographic characteristics (age, gender, etc.); personality dispositions; beliefs, attitudes and values; moods, feelings, states of mind; and drives, needs, motives, goals and expectations. The latter, environmental, panel includes conditions of the general physical environment (noise, heat, lighting, etc.) and of the social environment (inter-group conflict, loyalty, alienation, etc.).

Both of these panels of variables are huge, perhaps even infinite. So it is necessary to be very selective in terms of what properties are to be included in a study. Such selectivity is one of the functions of theory, as noted earlier. That is, theory functions as a guide to the investigator in selecting variables for study that are thought to be germane to the problem.

When people become interrelated, as when they are members of a group, they develop patterned relationships among themselves—patterned in terms of status, of power, of affection, and of many other aspects. These patterned relationships among group members constitute a group structure. There are many such patterns, such group structures—as many as there are variables or properties on which members can be connected to one another. These include, *at least*: structures defined in terms of composition of members; structure defined in terms of division of labor on tasks; communication structures; power structures and interpersonal relations structures. In the model, the *collection* of all these structures is called the *standing group* (to distinguish it from the *acting group*).

Environmental properties, too, are patterned; and one particular portion is of special importance in the present discussion. That important part is the set of environmental demands/constraints/opportunities that combine to form a particular task and situation. Environmental properties "play into" more than one task/situation, of course, and even more than one at the same time, just as group members "belong to" more than one group, and even more than one at the same time. So, for clarity, we probably should designate our referent as the focal task/situation, recognizing that the environment abounds with "tasks."

We can consider the juxtaposition of the standing group and the task as the Behavior Setting. The term, behavior setting, is borrowed from the work of Roger Barker and his colleagues (Barker, 1965; Barker & Wright, 1955). But the reader should be warned that I am changing the use of that term in one important respect. When Barker talks of the behavior setting, he is dealing with individuals behaving in environments, or individuals behaving in task/situations; but Barker does not use concepts of group, group structure, or group process at all. Barker sees individuals, and their behavior, as related to one another primarily through the demands of the situation.

In the model, the behavior setting represents a pattern—a fit—between the group as a structured entity (the standing group) and the task/situation as a structured set of requirements/demands/opportunities/possibilities/constraints. Notice, too, that the framework has both properties of individuals and properties of the environment "playing into" the behavior setting directly, as well as indirectly through the group and the task. This is equivalent to saying that, while a particular concert (behavior setting and group interaction process) is to be viewed as *mainly* a juxtaposition of a particular orchestra (standing group) with a particular set of musical compositions (task/situation), properties of the orchestra members (M) and of the concert hall, the city, and perhaps the time of year (E), can also have effects on the results.

All of these form the "inputs" for what I am calling group interaction process (GIP), or the *acting group*. GIP refers to the *processes* that take place when group members actually interact, in behavior settings that carry task structures and environmental effects. Such activity can be described in terms of many processes, including (at least) general structural properties such as level

and rate of interaction, distribution of participation, extent of member involvement, and so forth, all of which might be labeled *morphological properties*; the flow of influence; the flow of information or communications; the flow of work; and the flow of interpersonal affect. The *acting group* is the term used in this book for the collection of all of these interactive processes. In a sense, the behavior setting refers to the time-place-thing-person complex that serves as the site for the behavior of the acting group. The acting group and the behavior setting are the "action" and "state" sides of the same coin. In Barker's terms, the behavior setting is "circumjacent to" the group interaction process. This is represented in Figure 1-1 by showing the behavior-setting-to-group-interaction-process relation, and the reciprocal relation, as a double arrow, K and L. Individuals are often changed (for example, their attitudes are influenced) as a result of being members of an acting group. Group interaction can change the structure of the standing group; for example, it can change the pattern of attraction among members. Group interaction sometimes results in effects on the environment; and it quite often results in a shift in the relation of the focal group to its task/situation. Such changes are usually dealt with in terms of task performance effectiveness or task productivity.

The group interaction process feeds back into, and has effects on, all the panels of input variables out of which it has sprung. Individuals are often changed (for example, their attitudes are influenced) as a result of being

All of these effects (the eleven input arrows, *a* to *k*, and the five feedback arrows, *l* to *p*, in Figure 1-1) are important in principle, and are worthy of study. But many of them have been more thoroughly studied than others, and some of them are of more theoretical or practical significance than others. So the organization of later parts of this book will reflect selective treatment of some of these classes of relations more thoroughly than others. One basis for the selection of particular sets of relations for special attention is my particular conception of the interaction process and what it entails. That conceptualization will be presented next.

REFERENCES

BARKER, R. G. Explorations in ecological psychology. *American Psychologist*, 1965, *20*, 1-14.

BARKER, R. G., & Wright, H. F. *Midwest and its children: The psychological ecology of an American town*. New York: Harper & Row, 1955.

This article presents a theory of groups. The theory takes a more molar perspective on groups than has often been the case in group research. It gives special emphasis to temporal processes in group interaction and task performance. The three main sections of the article present the theory as a series of propositions about the nature of groups, temporal processes in group behavior, and temporal aspects of interaction, respectively. The final section presents brief comments on some implications and potential applications of the theory.

TIME, INTERACTION, AND PERFORMANCE (TIP)
A Theory of Groups

JOSEPH E. McGRATH
University of Illinois

This article contains a theory about groups and how they do what they do. It gives special attention to temporal processes in group interaction and performance (hence the acronym, TIP). It is an attempt to conceptualize groups and group activity at a level of molarity and complexity that reflects, to some degree, the nature of groups in everyday life.

For over half a century, social psychologists have studied groups. Although research interest in groups has waxed and waned, that research effort has accumulated an impressive volume of empir-ical work (not all of which is yet thoroughly integrated). That work has also included a number of efforts to formulate both limited and general theories. Useful integrations of portions of past empirical research on groups are given in Bales and Cohen (1979); Davis, Bray, and Holt (1977); Hackman and Morris (1972); Hare (1973, 1976); Kelley and Thibaut (1954, 1978); Levine and Moreland (1990); McGrath (1978, 1984); McGrath and Altman (1966); Moreland and Levine (1982, 1984, 1988); Steiner (1972); Thibaut and Kelley (1959); and Zander (1979a, 1979b), among others. Both the empirical evidence resulting from that work and the theoretical formulations based on it have added much to our appreciation of how groups form, develop, and carry out their activities.

Yet there are some serious limitations to much of that earlier work, especially regarding the degree to which it reflects the structures and processes of naturally occurring groups as we meet them in our everyday lives. In part, those limits reflect features of the methodological and conceptual paradigms that have dominated the group research field, along with most of social psychology, within that same period of time: an analytic paradigm that presumes directional causal relations among isolated factors with little regard for physical, temporal, or social context. Much of the empirical foundation of group theory derives from study of a limited range of types of ad hoc groups under controlled experimental conditions. Most of that work involves very small groups (two to four members) with constant membership arbitrarily assigned by an experimenter that exist only for a limited time without past or future as a group, isolated rather than embedded in any larger social units (organizations, communities). These groups are studied while performing single and relatively simple tasks assigned to them by the experimenter (i.e., not tasks indigenous to those groups) under "context-stripped" conditions.

Such limiting features of the groups on which empirical evidence has been gathered systematically constrain the scope of the theories built on that evidence. The theories do not purport to be about ad hoc, laboratory groups and under limited conditions. To the contrary, most group theories purport to be about

AUTHOR'S NOTE: *Research reported in this article was supported, in part, by National Science Foundation grants BNS 85-06805, BNS 87-05151, and IRI 89-05640 (J. E. McGrath, principal investigator). I wish to acknowledge contributions to these research programs by Janice R. Kelly, Purdue University; Gail Clark Futoran, Texas Tech University; David A. Harrison, Texas University at Arlington; Scott W. VanderStoep, University of Michigan; Deborah Gruenfeld, University of Illinois; Anne Gilles, University of Illinois; Dennis Stewart, University of Miami of Ohio; Nancy L. Rotchford, BankAmerica, San Francisco; Andrea B. Hollingshead, University of Illinois. Correspondence regarding this article should be sent to Joseph E. McGrath, Psychology Department, University of Illinois, 603 E. Daniel St., Champaign, IL 61820.*

SMALL GROUP RESEARCH, Vol. 22 No. 2, May 1991 147-174
© 1991 Sage Publications, Inc.

Werner, Haggard, Altman, & Oxley, 1988); Gersick's work on time-linked transitions in work groups (Gersick, 1988, 1989); extensive work by Moreland and Levine on group development and socialization of members into the group (e.g., Levine & Moreland, 1985, 1990; Moreland & Levine, 1982, 1984, 1988); and the work of Poole and colleagues on adaptive structuration theory (e.g., Poole & DeSanctis, 1989; Poole & Roth, 1988a, 1988b). The theory presented here has been influenced considerably by work within that new, temporally oriented tradition and is an attempt to make a contribution to it.

The theory of time, interaction, and performance (TIP theory) presented here is based on a substantial body of work we have done in recent years within a continuing program of research on temporal factors in individual, group, and organizational contexts. The material in this article draws heavily on a number of earlier publications from our research program dealing with groups, time, and related topics (Futoran, Kelly, & McGrath, 1989; Kelly, 1988; Kelly & McGrath, 1988; Kelly, Futoran, & McGrath, 1990; McGrath, 1987; McGrath & Beehr, 1990; McGrath & Kelly, 1986, 1990; McGrath, Kelly, & Machatka, 1984; McGrath & Rotchford, 1983). This article attempts to integrate ideas from those separate presentations into a single systematic theoretical statement, taking into account other research and theory, especially work in that new, temporally oriented tradition.

The conceptual formulation presented here is about the nature of groups and of their interaction and performance. It emphasizes temporal patterning of interaction and performance in such groups. It is expressed as a series of propositions that present assumptions underlying the model; empirical generalizations adduced from several substantial research literatures (on groups, on time, and on communication) and from earlier work in our research program; and hypotheses that are, in principle, testable. The three main sections of the article present propositions about the nature of groups, about temporal patterning in groups, and about the interaction process in groups, respectively. The brief final section comments on some implications and potential applications of the theory.

groups in general and, by implication, about naturally occurring groups. But the groups we meet in those theories, like the groups used in most studies, differ markedly from the kinds of groups we meet in everyday affairs. The groups that inhabit our theories and experiments are of relatively constant membership. Their activity entails going about some experimenter- or supervisor-assigned, singular, simple, well-practiced task—and nothing else. Those groups never have to decide which tasks to do or to do next. They never have to do without essential materials, personnel, or other resources. They never have to reckon with disputes, with "freeloaders," and so on—unless, of course, those are the specific issues of concern for the theorist-experimenter.

Many of the groups we meet in everyday living are not like that at all. They have pasts together, and they expect to have futures. Yet they have variable membership from one occasion to another. They seldom exist in isolation; they are embedded within larger social aggregates—communities, organizations, neighborhoods, kin networks, and departments. Sometimes they do specific tasks, but along with that they usually are engaged in goal-directed activities having to do with interests of specific members and of the group itself, as well as pursuing "production" goals. Even their pursuit of production goals is often not composed of repetitive, unrelated tasks, as in successive "trials" of an experiment but, rather, of complex sequences of interdependent tasks that compose a larger "project." And they often have more than one such project going at the same time. These and other activities, indigenous to many everyday groups, are largely neglected in past group theories based on studies of limited, context-stripped groups.

In recent years, a somewhat different paradigm for small group research has begun to take shape. Work in this tradition treats groups dynamically and attempts to take full account of the physical, temporal, and social context within which those groups are embedded. Unlike most earlier work on small groups, it gives particular attention to temporal issues. Notable contributions to that new tradition include the work of Altman and colleagues from a transactional perspective (e.g., Altman, Vinsel, & Brown, 1981;

PROPOSITIONS ABOUT THE NATURE OF GROUPS

Proposition 1: Groups are assumed to be complex, intact social systems that engage in multiple, interdependent functions, on multiple, concurrent projects, while partially nested within, and loosely coupled to, surrounding systems.

Multiple functions. Groups are multifunctioned. They make contributions to systems at each of three levels:

1. to the systems in which they are embedded (e.g., an organization),
2. to their component parts, that is, their members, and
3. to the group itself, as an intact and continuing social structure.

Those are, respectively, the group's *production function,* its *member-support function,* and its *group well-being function.* (These parallel the criteria for group effectiveness specified in Hackman, 1985.) These three functions, though analytically distinguishable, are inseparably intertwined in concrete systems.

Purposeful activity. Groups engage in purposeful activity at three partially nested levels: *projects, tasks,* and *steps.* A project is a mission, a set of activities in the service of a goal or goals (Little, 1983). A task is a sequence of activities instrumental to completion of a particular project. A step is an activity that is a proper part of a task. These levels of activity are also levels of purpose: Steps and tasks have instrumental value insofar as they contribute to projects. Completed projects have intrinsic value for the group's three contribution functions.

Ordinarily, at any one time, a group will be engaged in activities associated with multiple concurrent projects and having to do with all three contribution functions. A group thus requires some means for coordination of multiple functions on multiple concurrent projects that overlap in time, place, and members.

Partial nesting. Groups, their members, and the organizations within which they are embedded usually are partially nested systems. Individuals are partially nested within the groups of which they are members. Partial nesting means that a given individual is ordinarily not a member of one and only one group but, rather, is a member of multiple groups at any one time. Thus group members are not "proper parts" but rather "participating parts" of any given group to which they belong. Groups also often are partially nested within the embedding system of which they are a part (an organization, a community, etc.)

Loose coupling. Most work groups can be regarded as loosely coupled systems at two levels. Individual group members are loosely coupled to one another, and the behavior of the group as a unit is loosely coupled to the larger social units within which that group is embedded. *Coupling,* here, refers to the strength, directness, and complexity of causal relations among parts of a system (see, e.g., Weick, 1976, 1982).

A caveat. Much of the work of natural groups gets done by individuals or subgroups, acting when the "main" group is not in session: One member of a research team has an insight that solves a key problem for the whole team, two group members go into town in early morning to pick up supplies needed for the group's work that day, and so on. Thus even the observation of "all" group meetings and the recording of "all" group actions and communications still cannot capture the totality of the flow of work in that group, much less the totality of group life beyond direct task performance. Direct empirical evidence about work in naturally occurring groups (or in groups created for purposes of research) is ultimately limited to data derived from events and actions that take place while group members are acting in concert. That limit is implicit throughout this article.

Proposition 2: All group action involves one or another of four modes of group activity:
Mode I: inception and acceptance of a project (goal choice),
Mode II: solution of technical issues (means choice),

FUNCTIONS

	Production	Well-being	Member Support
Mode I **Inception**	Production Demand/ Opportunity	Interaction Demand/ Opportunity	Inclusion Demand/ Opportunity
Mode II **Problem** **Solving**	Technical Problem Solving	Role Network Definition	Position/ Status Attainments
Mode III **Conflict** **Resolution**	Policy Conflict Resolution	Power/ Payoff Distribution	Contribution/ Payoff Relationships
Mode IV **Execution**	Performance	Interaction	Participation

(Left margin label: M O D E S)

Figure 1: Modes and Functions

Mode III: resolution of conflict, that is, of political issues (policy choice), and

Mode IV: execution of the performance requirements of the project (goal attainment).

These modes of activity apply to all projects, and they transcend the various group functions. There is a distinctive but parallel set of modes for activities related to the production function, the member-support function, and the well-being function (see Figure 1).

Modes are potential, not required, forms of activity. Modes I and IV (inception and execution) are involved in all group tasks and projects; Modes II (technical problem solving) and III (conflict resolution) may or may not be involved in any given group activity. Furthermore, groups are always acting, in one or another of these four modes, with respect to each of the three functions, but they are not necessarily engaged in the same mode for all functions, nor are they necessarily engaged in the same mode for a given function on different projects that may be concurrent.

There is much similarity between several of these modes and the quadrants of the task performance space or task circumplex postulated in McGrath (1984). Noting the similarities may make this article easier to follow for readers who are familiar with that other work, but it is important to note the differences as well. Quadrants II, III, and IV of that task circumplex, whose key functions are choose, negotiate, and execute, respectively, are closely aligned with Modes II, III, and IV here. Quadrant I of the circumplex, for which the key function is to generate (ideas and plans), however, is not at all isomorphic with Mode I (project inception). Moreover, the task circumplex dealt only with the group's production function. Furthermore, the quadrants of the task circumplex were conceptualized as more or less mutually exclusive alternatives to one another at the task level, whereas the modes of activity presented here are regarded as potential components of activity at the project level — some or all of which may be involved in carrying out the tasks of any given project.

Modes of the production function. The four modes of the production function reflect the relation between the group as a functional unit and the environmental circumstances within which that group is operating. They are akin to what are often referred to as problem-solving or task-performance phases (see McGrath, 1984; Poole & Roth, 1988a, 1988b).

Mode I of the production function has to do with project inception—choosing among sets of production or achievement opportunities (and demands). Groups acquire a project in one or another of three ways: A member may propose it; an outside agent (e.g., boss or experimenter) may assign it; or the group may undertake a given project simply by engaging in the ordinary activity of that group. Mode I involves a choice of goals and a consequent selection (often implicitly) of an initial performance strategy.

A number of studies have shown that groups tend to select an initial work strategy early, often with seemingly little deliberation, and typically continue following that initial strategy until forced to change by inadequate task performance (Hackman, Brousseau, & Wiess, 1977; Gersick, 1988, 1989). Thus inputs to the group early in a project, regarding strategy and process, are likely to have especially high impact.

Mode II of the production function is a technical problem-solving mode—attempts to determine the most appropriate means (techniques, procedures, or algorithms) by which to carry out the project. Mode II involves a choice of means.

This is the mode to which group research has given the most attention. It is the focus of attention in studies of problem solving, decision making, and the like (for reviews, see Hackman & Morris, 1972; Kelley & Thibaut, 1954; McGrath, 1984; Steiner, 1972). In those studies, the other three modes of the production function are generally rendered moot: Project inception is not problematic because groups are assigned the task. The execution mode for these kinds of problems is trivial once the means has been determined. Conflicts of priorities are treated as error, as are time and attention

devoted by the group to the nonproduction functions—often labeled pejoratively as "process losses" (Steiner, 1972).

Mode III of the production function is a political preference-resolving mode—attempts to resolve potentially conflicting preferences, values, or interests within the group. Mode III involves a choice of policies. This mode has been given some study in group research, notably in work on negotiations and on such matters as jury deliberations (e.g., Davis et al., 1977; Vidmar & McGrath, 1970).

Mode IV of the production function is the execution mode—carrying out, in real time and space, the behaviors necessary and sufficient to attain the goals of a project in which the group is engaged. Mode IV involves goal attainment. It can be assessed in terms of some combination of quantity, quality, and speed of production of some end product(s).

Modes of the well-being function. The four modes of the group well-being function describe activities that have to do with development and maintenance of the group as a system; hence they reflect relations among group members.

Mode I (inception) for the group well-being function involves choices among sets of interaction opportunities (and demands). Mode II (technical problem solving) for the well-being function involves role-net definition. The group decides technical staffing questions: who will do what, when, and with whom. This mode involves choices of interpersonal means. Mode III (conflict resolution) for the well-being function involves power and payoff allocation. The group resolves political issues regarding who controls the distribution of work and rewards. This mode involves the resolution of political issues of interpersonal status, power, and payoff. Mode IV (execution) for the well-being function involves interaction. The group carries out concrete interpersonal activities involved in the performance process of a given project.

Modes of the member-support function. The four modes of the member-support function describe activities that have to do with

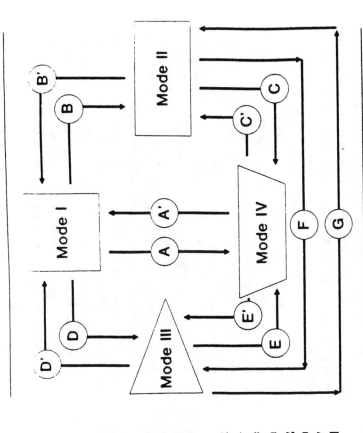

Figure 2: Four Modes and Alternative Paths

the ways in which the individual is embedded within the group; hence they reflect relations between individual members and the group.

Mode I (inception) for the member-support function involves choices about inclusion and participation opportunities (and demands). The individual may choose inclusion in the group, with whatever rewards that entails, in return for his or her participation, loyalty, and commitment to the group. Sometimes, of course, member inclusion in a given group for a given project is not entirely voluntary. In those cases, that member's participation, loyalty, and commitment is also potentially problematic.

Mode II (technical problem solving) for the member-support function involves position and status attainment. This mode includes both the self-selection side and the group-assignment side of the practices and policies by which individual members attain positions or roles in the group. These range enormously among groups. They tend to be entirely informal and even implicit in friendship and other informal groups. In many formal groups, they are highly routinized and explicit procedures or highly ritualized rites of passage.

Mode III (conflict resolution) for the member-support function involves negotiation (and renegotiation) of the individual's expected contributions to and payoff from the group's purposeful activities. Mode IV (execution) for the member-support function involves members' concrete participation in the group's activities.

Proposition 3: The four modes of activity are not a fixed sequence of phases but, rather, are a set of alternative kinds of activity in which the group and its members may engage.

Although all projects begin with Mode I and end with Mode IV, any given project may or may not entail Modes II or III for any of the three functions. There are alternative time-activity paths, from Mode I to Mode IV, for completion of the production, well-being, and support functions (see Figure 2).

The direct path—from Mode I inception (opportunity for production, interaction, or participation) to Mode IV execution (actual production, interaction, or participation)—is the default path for all functions on most group projects (link A in Figure 2). TIP theory assumes that a group will use the default path if it can, and in any case will use the least complex path that its purposes, resources, and circumstances will allow.

This view contrasts with most theories that invoke "problem-solving phase sequences." Most phase-sequence theories invoke what Poole and Roth (1988a, 1988b) call a "unitary phase sequence," namely, that there is one "most rational" or "most efficient" sequence. The theory presented here does not posit such a

given group may use different paths for different functions on each of multiple concurrent projects. A given project may require a complex path involving three or all four modes, or an even more complicated path, for at least one function but only require the direct two-mode default path (link A) for one or both of the other functions.

In the past, group researchers have been too quick to label such complex patterns as "process losses" (Steiner, 1972). That concept, or its cousins, has been used, pejoratively, to imply that any group activity that did not seem to fit the researcher's preconceived picture of what a direct, "efficient" performance of the task ought to look like was somehow evidence of a deficiency in that group. Such labeling implies the assumption that the group had (or should have had) only the experimenter- or manager-assigned task on its agenda. It also carries the implication that there must be some flaw in the group's structure, behavior, or character that needs "fixing" — typically by importing the researcher's favorite techniques (such as NGT, Delphi, and the like) that purportedly will "improve" group performance.

TIP theory holds that such complexity of paths, modes, and functions is by no means evidence of process losses. Rather, it more likely is evidence of one or more of three other circumstances: (a) that the group is giving attention to the well-being and member-support functions, as well as to the production function; (b) that the group is attempting to resolve technical or political problems within the production function, of which the researcher may be unaware; or (c) that the group might be engaged in some project other than (or in addition to) the one the experimenter is tracking. TIP theory assumes that when a group engages in any path more complex than the default path, it does so for good and sufficient reasons — reasons to which the researcher may or may not be privy. TIP theory thus takes the perspective of the group rather than the viewpoint of the researcher (or of the supervisor). In these circumstances, the proper question to ask is not how do we get the group not to do these "extraneous" things, but rather what conditions led the group to need or want to use a more complex time-activity path. In TIP

most rational or most efficient phase sequence but, rather, posits a default sequence that is a "satisfying" or "least effort" path. TIP theory asserts that the default path will prevail unless conditions warrant some more complex path (see below).

For example, a group will use a three-mode path (Modes I, II, and IV, links B-C in Figure 2) for its production, well-being, or member-support functions, respectively, when it needs to identify or construct a logically correct or preferred means for solution of the technical issues involved in its project or projects or needs to deal with role-net definition or redefinition or needs to deal with issues related to members' position and status attainment. These needs might arise, for example, if the group had a project involving new tasks or if it had new members or if conditions in the embedding system had changed substantially.

A group will use a different three-mode path (Modes I, III, and IV, links D-E in Figure 2) for its production, well-being, or member-support functions when it needs to resolve a set of conflicting interests or values related to performance on the project or needs to deal with issues of power allocation or payoff distribution in the group. These needs also might arise with the coming of new tasks, new members, or new operating conditions.

Sometimes even more complex paths are required for completion of the production, well-being, or member-support functions. For example, sometimes groups attempt direct execution (i.e., Modes I-IV) but encounter technical or political problems and are forced to engage in Mode II or III before execution. Sometimes they find that technical problems are really political problems (or embed them) and, therefore, have to go from Mode II to Mode III. Sometimes they find that political problems, when resolved, create new technical problems; hence they may have to go from Mode II to Mode III and back again to Mode II. Such complex cases might follow paths such as links A-C-C, or links A-E'-E, or links A-A'-D-G-C, in Figure 2).

Interaction of functions, modes, and projects. Group activity always entails an interplay of functions, modes, and projects. A

theory, such complex paths suggest long-run effectiveness on the part of the group, even if at a small cost in short-run performance rate on the task to which the researcher is attending (see Poole & Roth, 1988a, 1988b, for an alternative perspective on these phase-sequence issues).

KEY POINTS THUS FAR

The first three propositions of the theory are largely definitional and scene setting. They represent groups and their activities in a molar and complex way. Groups are simultaneously performing a number of functions with respect to a number of projects. There are multiple alternative time-activity paths by which groups can do what they are doing. Use of more complex paths indicates presence of conditions calling for those complex activities rather than indicating some culpability or inadequacy of the group.

PROPOSITIONS ABOUT TEMPORAL ASPECTS OF BEHAVIOR IN GROUPS

Proposition 4: Behavior in work groups shows many forms of complex temporal patterning, including
1. temporal aspects of the flow of work in groups, which raise issues of scheduling, synchronization, and time allocation (see Proposition 5),
2. problems of efficiently matching periods of time with bundles of activities (see Proposition 6), and
3. entrainment processes leading to patterns of synchronization, both of group members' behavior with one another, and of group behavior with "external" events (see Proposition 7; for more detail, see McGrath & Kelly, 1986, 1990).

Proposition 5: All collective action entails (at least) three generic temporal problems that both organizations and individuals must reckon with.

The three generic temporal problems (see McGrath & Kelly, 1986; McGrath et al., 1984; McGrath & Rotchford, 1983) are

1. temporal ambiguity (when particular events will occur and recur and how long they will last),
2. conflicting temporal interests and requirements, and
3. scarcity of temporal resources.

Characteristic organizational responses to these temporal problems are, respectively,

1. scheduling of activities,
2. synchronization of activities by different segments of the organization, and
3. allocation of temporal (and other) resources to projects.

Parallel individual responses are

1. making temporal commitments,
2. negotiating norms for behavior sequencing, and
3. regulating flow of task and interpersonal interaction.

There is always some degree of lack of fit between organization and individual responses to these temporal issues. Such lack of fit gives rise to residual temporal problems that have to do with

1. establishing and enforcing deadlines,
2. establishing norms to get smooth dynamic teamwork, and
3. regulating flow of task and interpersonal interaction to resolve inefficient or inequitable demand-capability matches.

These residual problems—deadlines, dynamic coordination, and regulating flow of interaction—often get played out in group contexts. They become ubiquitous issues for all three functions of groups doing multiple concurrent projects in real time.

Proposition 6: A temporally efficient flow of work in groups requires complex matching of bundles of activities to particular periods of time.

Time as experienced violates two Newtonian assumptions: (a) that time is infinitely divisible and (b) that units of time are homogeneous and interchangeable (McGrath & Kelly, 1986, 1990). Units of time, as experienced, are epochal or "lumpy," not smooth and homogeneous. Periods of time that are equal in Newtonian terms are not necessarily interchangeable as to what activities can be done in them. Therefore, the fit between a particular bundle of activities and a particular period of time is particular, not arbitrary. Neither bundles of activity nor periods of time can be divided (or combined) without limit and without cost (see below).

Some periods of time are more versatile than others regarding what range of activities can be done in them. For example, the range of activities that can be done efficiently in nighttime hours is far less than the range for daytime; and, in our culture, the range of activities that can be done efficiently on Sunday is different from the range of activities of a weekday.

Conversely, some bundles of activities are more flexible than others regarding at what times they can be done efficiently. For example, the range of times at which banking or grocery shopping can be done is greatly restricted in some communities, less so in others. Activity bundles also vary in terms of how "modular" they are; that is, how efficiently they can be aggregated or subdivided to fit within a time period of a particular size and temporal location. There are both upper and lower bounds on such "modularity." For example, it is not efficient to do laundry one sock at a time, but it is also not efficient to aggregate it over an entire month. Similarly, some material can be read effectively in short periods of a few minutes each, whereas other material requires substantial blocks of time for effective reading.

Proposition 7: One major form of temporal patterning is social entrainment.

Entrainment refers to synchronization (temporal coordination) of phase and periodicity of two or more processes. *Social entrainment* refers to entrainment of processes that are behavioral not physiological (see Kelly, 1988; Kelly, Futoran, & McGrath, 1990; Kelly & McGrath, 1985; McGrath & Kelly, 1986, 1990; McGrath et al., 1984).

Entrainment operates at various system levels: within individuals, between individuals, and between groups and their embedding systems. Entrainment can be internal or external to a given social unit. That is, it refers both to mutual synchronization of two or more endogenous rhythms and to entrainment of an internal rhythm (or bundle of rhythms) to an external signal or cycle that serves as a pacer. Entrainment is a form of loose coupling (see Proposition 1). Synchronization is induced, not compelled, by the entraining process.

Features of social entrainment. Social entrainment (or synchronization) operates for a wide range of individual, group, and organizational processes. Patterns of entrainment vary with group, task, and situational conditions. They also vary for group performance under different time-pressure conditions. Such variations in patterns of entrainment arise partly through differences in perceptions and expectations that accompany different task conditions (e.g., experiences of different forms of difficulty; see Kelly et al., 1990). Entrainment processes operate for patterns of communication and interaction, as well as for rate and quality of task performance (Kelly & McGrath, 1985).

Interdependence of modes, functions, and entrainment processes. Modes, functions, and entrainment processes operate interdependently. Groups often need different paths for different functions on a given project and often are engaged in multiple concurrent projects. Time pressure often leads groups to focus only on the direct path (link A) of the production function. This may reduce the quality of production, and interpersonal issues may suffer from lack of attention. Groups with ample time tend to use all of the available time. This enables them (but does not compel them) to engage in activities that can enhance the quality of production and to give appropriate amounts of attention to well-being and member-support functions (Kelly, 1988; Kelly et al., 1990; Kelly & McGrath, 1985; McGrath & Kelly, 1986, 1990; McGrath et al., 1984). Such social entrainment processes apparently hold for "natural" groups created to carry out specific single projects within a predetermined "life span" (Gersick, 1988, 1989), as well as for laboratory groups doing experimenter-assigned tasks.

PROPOSITIONS ABOUT GROUP INTERACTION PROCESS

Proposition 8: In TIP theory, *group interaction process* refers to the flow of work in groups at a micro level.

The unit of interaction is a single act or input of a group member. Each act can be referenced to three axes: type of act, source of act, and time of act. The first axis has to do with identifying how each act relates to the group's ongoing activity. The second axis has to do with identifying the source (and target) of each act. The third axis has to do with specifying when the act took place—the time when each act began and ended, hence its serial position, its duration, and its temporal location. These axes, together, identify interruptions and overlaps in speakers and periods of silence (a conjoint nonaction by all members), as well as various types of one-speaker-at-a-time acts (see Futoran et al., 1989).

Proposition 9: In TIP theory, it is assumed that at any point in interaction, a group has a current purpose or objective that can be regarded as its focal task.

The *focal task of a group* refers to what the group is explicitly trying to accomplish at that time. In TIP theory, functions are characterized at the project level with tasks and steps subsumed under them; but interaction acts are characterized at the level of a focal task. A focal task may relate to the well-being, support, or production functions. Such a focal task, therefore, can have "socio-emotional" rather than "instrumental" content.

Proposition 10: Each act can be regarded as either germane to the group's current "focal task" or not germane to it.

Acts that are germane to the focal task. An act can be germane to the focal task in one of four ways: a task proposal, such as a proposed answer to a task problem or the execution of a task step; a process proposal, a contribution to the group's management, such as suggesting a shift in activities, strategies, or goals; a task evaluation, of one's own or another's prior task contribution or contributions; or a process evaluation, of one's own or another's prior process contribution or contributions. Each of these four types of acts can be divided into subtypes (e.g., evaluations can be positive or negative, and they can involve suggestions for modification or outright rejection).

Acts that are not germane to the focal task. Acts that are not germane to a group's focal task can occur in any of several forms: acts that have personal or interpersonal content that is pertinent to the group or to some of its members but not to the focal task; acts that have content related to the group's ongoing project or projects but that digress from the group's focal task (e.g., irrelevant anecdotes about content related to the group's project); acts that have content related to situational or environmental conditions (e.g., complaints about an overheated workplace).

Proposition 11: Acts have situated, rather than generic, meanings in relation to the modes, functions, and paths of group activity.

process (e.g., "I don't think this approach is getting anyplace. We are just going around in circles on this") could serve Modes II or III of the production function or any of the modes of the well-being or support functions. Acts have situated meanings, not generic ones, and although we may isolate individual acts for analytic purposes, their meanings for the group derive from the context within which they are embedded. To gain understanding of the meaning of a specific act, hence its relation to the modes and functions, one needs to consider what has gone before and what follows it. Therefore, how acts are aggregated is crucial to any analysis of group interaction process.

Proposition 12: Various aspects of the flow of work in groups are reflected in different forms of aggregation of acts.

Although such an approach is not essential to TIP theory, the discussion in Propositions 8-11 presupposes that the flow of work in groups can best be examined by first "parsing" the flow of interaction into specific events and acts and then aggregating acts over types, over members, or over periods of time. Such aggregations can be done in a number of forms, each of which deals with different aspects of the temporal relations between acts:

1. Work-flow analyses can be done in terms of comparisons of distributions of (absolute or relative) frequencies of different types of acts, by different (types of) members, during different periods of time (or by two or all three of these facets simultaneously).

2. Work-flow analyses also can be done in terms of comparisons of durations (or proportions of time) for different types of act, for different members, and for different periods of time (or for two or all three of these facets).

3. Work-flow analyses can examine sequences of two, three, or more acts in terms of sequences of act types (e.g., what kinds of acts follow a negative evaluation?); sequences of related content (e.g., do some tasks produce longer chains of content-related acts than others?); sequences of speakers (e.g., how often does member C follow member A?); and combinations of these.

Acts are related to the modes, functions, and paths of group process, but those relations are complex, and there is not a single isomorphic mapping between a given type of act and a given mode-function-path.

Germane acts. The four types of act that are germane to the focal task are related to the modes of activity and to paths through those modes for all three functions. Task proposals are often Mode IV activities, and sometimes Mode II activities, of the production function. Process proposals may involve Mode I (project acquisition, goal acceptance) activities or may involve an effort to shift the group to an alternative path with regard to its production function. Evaluations of task contributions may reflect a concern for quality in Mode IV, execution. But evaluations, especially negative evaluations, also may reflect Mode III activities of any of the three functions or Mode II activities of the well-being and support functions. Evaluations of process proposals may reflect Mode I, II, or III activity of the production function or any mode of the well-being and support functions.

Nongermane acts. Nongermane acts also reflect various modes of activity and functions. Interpersonal acts may indicate effort to attend to some modes of the well-being function. Personal acts may mark a concern with the member-support function, especially Modes II and III. Task digressions may be attempts to elaborate on task contributions—hence may reflect efforts toward Mode II or Mode IV of the production function. Such task digressions may also reflect an effort to redirect the group from its attempt at direct task execution (link A). Situational reactions may be surrogates for negative process evaluations or otherwise reflect efforts to redirect the group.

Acts have situated meanings. In TIP theory, the meaning of an act depends in part on its context. Therefore, it is not appropriate to attempt a one-to-one mapping between act type and mode-function combinations. For example, an act coded as an evaluation of

The preceding discussion of the situated meaning of individual acts points to alternative possibilities for analysis of interaction process. Instead of using an act-by-act categorization of ongoing process, group interaction can be studied by constructing what might be regarded as "qualitative aggregations" of acts.

An example of such an approach is the technique developed by Gersick (1988, 1989). She condensed transcripts of group work into contiguous, content-related segments and characterized the activity within each of those relatively short segments. She then coded the segments with respect to occurrence of acts of particular interest (e.g., timing acts, contributions to the product), which she aggregated quantitatively. But at the same time, she also used the descriptions of segments to develop a "story" of group process over extended periods of time for multiple meetings of the group. This permitted her to display "meeting maps" indicating who made what kinds of inputs at what points in the group's meetings, hence to more nearly grasp the situated meanings of those acts. A qualitative-aggregation approach such as Gersick's has the advantage of taking fully into account the context-dependent or situated meanings of acts, but it has the disadvantage of losing much detailed information at the more micro level of specific acts.

Each of these four different ways of combining information over specific actions — frequencies or proportions, durations or relative durations, sequences, and more molar or more qualitative aggregations — offers different but useful information about the temporal patterning of work in groups. There is no reason for TIP theory (or any given empirical study) to prefer one of these to the exclusion of the others. Judicious use of all of them would seem best suited to help us gain further understanding of the operation and impact of temporal processes on groups.

SOME IMPLICATIONS OF TIP THEORY

This condensed presentation of TIP theory contains a number of implications for the nature of groups and of their operation and at the same time raises a number of issues about work in groups that have received only limited attention in past research. Three sets of such implications are noted below as examples.

Impact of changes in group, task, and circumstances. Several propositions of the theory imply that major shifts in the pattern of group activity (i.e., in the mode-function sequences by which groups carry out their work) will follow from (a) changes in group membership, (b) changes in the type and difficulty level of the projects and tasks the group is undertaking, and (c) changes in operating conditions (such as time limits, connections to other units, and the like) under which the group is working. There is really very little empirical evidence to draw on to support or refute those implications, because remarkably little research has been done on the effects of even such major changes as loss, addition, or substitution of new members or the impact of changing a group's basic mission or tasks, even though such changes are ubiquitous in natural groups. (The marked preference for studying groups as static entities, with constant membership, tasks, and operating conditions, is another consequence of our discipline's strong reliance on the static-analytic methodological and conceptual paradigm that was noted at the beginning of this article.) TIP theory highlights the need for systematic empirical study of the impact of such changes on work groups and their actions.

Situated versus generic meaning of acts. One of the most interesting sets of implications of TIP theory arises from its recognition that a given act or act sequence takes its meaning partly from the context in which it occurs. Most systems for observing and coding interaction process (including the TEMPO system developed earlier in our research program) are built on the implicit assumption that a given act has the same meaning (in terms of the coding system being used) no matter who performs it and no matter when it occurs in the group's activity. A proposed solution is a proposed solution, and a negative evaluation is a negative evaluation, regardless of its source, target, timing, or context. But when TIP theory attempts to map types of acts to mode-function sequences, it becomes clear that a given type of act may involve different meanings (i.e., different modes and functions), depending on the circumstances under which it occurs. For example, a proposed solution after the group has already reached a final decision is hardly to be considered equivalent to a proposed solution made early in the group's work. Similarly, a negative evaluation early in the group's work is more likely to function as an attempt to improve quality of a given task performance than is a negative evaluation at the end of the group's session.

Such issues have been little studied in group research, in part because they have been assumed away by the underlying paradigm. Here, again, there is a clear need for empirical research not to determine whether meanings in interaction are situated or generic (doubtless both are true in part) but, rather, to determine the sets of conditions under which acts take their meaning from the circumstances within which they are performed.

Consequences of modifications in group communication systems. TIP theory also has implications for the likely effects of the introduction of technological enhancements (e.g., computers) within the group's communication system — a more and more frequent fact of life in natural work groups. An earlier version of TIP theory was applied for a preliminary analysis of effects of such enhancements (McGrath, 1990), suggesting that such enhancements are likely to have both desirable and undesirable effects. Poole and colleagues have carried out a similar analysis working from adaptive structuration theory (Poole & DeSanctis, 1989). But those treatments leave many questions still unanswered and many issues unaddressed. In the light of the increasingly varied uses of computer-mediated communications to aid group work, further research along these lines is another critical need. Such research can both make use of TIP theory to guide its inquiries and provide feedback to the theory regarding empirical support of its propositions.

REFERENCES

Altman, I., Vinsel, A. M., & Brown, B. B. (1981). Dialectic conceptions in social psychology: An application to social penetration and privacy regulation. In L. Berkowitz (Ed.), *Advances in experimental social psychology* (Vol. 14). New York: Academic Press.

Bales, R. F., & Cohen, S. P. (1979). *SYMLOG: A system for the multi-level observation of groups.* New York: Free Press.

Davis, J. H., Bray, R. M., & Holt, R. W. (1977). The empirical study of social decision processes in juries: A critical review. In J. Tapp & F. Levine (Eds.), *Law, justice and the individual in society: Psychological and legal issues.* New York: Holt, Rinehart & Winston.

Futoran, G. C., Kelly, J. R., & McGrath, J. E. (1989). TEMPO: A time-based system for analysis of group interaction process. *Basic and Applied Social Psychology, 10,* 211-232.

Gersick, C.J.G. (1988). Time and transition in work teams: Toward a new model of group development. *Academy of Management Journal, 31,* 9-41.

Gersick, C.J.G. (1989). Marking time: Predictable transitions in task groups. *Academy of Management Journal, 32,* 274-309.

Hackman, J. R. (1985). Doing research that makes a difference. In E. E. Lawler, A. M. Mohrman, S. A. Mohrman, G. E. Ledford, T. G. Cummings, & Associates (Eds.), *Doing research that is useful for theory and practice.* San Francisco: Jossey-Bass.

Hackman, J. R., Brousseau, K. R., & Weiss, J. A. (1977). The interaction of task design and group performance strategies in determining group effectiveness. *Organizational Behavior and Human Performance, 16,* 350-365.

Hackman, J. R., & Morris, C. G. (1972). Group tasks, group interaction process, and group performance effectiveness: A review and proposed integration. In L. Berkowitz (Ed.), *Advances in experimental social psychology* (Vol. 8). New York: Academic Press.

Hare, A. P. (1973). Theories of group development and categories for interaction analysis. *Small Group Behavior, 4,* 259-304.

Hare, A. P. (1976). *Handbook of small group research* (2nd ed.). New York: Free Press.

Kelley, H. H., & Thibaut, J. W. (1954). Experimental studies of group problem solving. In L. Lindzey (Ed.), *Handbook of social psychology.* Reading, MA: Addison-Wesley.

Kelley, H. H., & Thibaut, J. W. (1978). *Interpersonal relations: A theory of interdependence.* New York: Wiley.

Kelly, J. R. (1988). Entrainment in individual and group behavior. In J. E. McGrath (Ed.), *The social psychology of time: New perspectives* (pp. 89-110). Newbury Park, CA: Sage.

Kelly, J. R., Futoran, G. C., & McGrath, J. E. (1990). Capacity and capability: Seven studies of entrainment of task performance rates. *Small Group Research, 21,* 283-314.

Kelly, J. R., & McGrath, J. E. (1985). Effects of time limits and task types on task performance and interaction of four-person groups. *Journal of Personality and Social Psychology, 49,* 395-407.

Kelly, J. R., & McGrath, J. E. (1988). *On time and method.* Newbury Park, CA: Sage.

Levine, J. M., & Moreland, R. L. (1985). Innovation and socialization in small groups. In S. Moscovici, G. Mugny, & E. Van Abermaet (Eds.), *Perspectives on minority influence* (pp. 143-169). Cambridge: Cambridge University Press.

Levine, J. M., & Moreland, R. L. (1990). Progress in small group research. *Annual Review of Psychology, 41,* 585-634.

Little, B. R. (1983). Personal projects: A rationale and method for investigation. *Environment & Behavior, 15*, 273-309.

McGrath, J. E. (1978). Small group research. *American Behavioral Scientist, 21*, 651-674.

McGrath, J. E. (1984). *Groups: Interaction and performance.* Englewood Cliffs, NJ: Prentice-Hall.

McGrath, J. E. (1987). *Toward a time-based theory of functional groups.* Technical Report 87-1. Champaign: Psychology Department, University of Illinois.

McGrath, J. E. (1990). Time matters in groups. In J. Galegher, R. E. Kraut, & C. Egido (Eds.), *Intellectual teamwork: Social and technical bases of collaborative work* (pp. 23-61). Hillsdale, NJ: Erlbaum.

McGrath, J. E., & Altman, I. (1966). *Small group research: A synthesis and critique of the field.* New York: Holt, Rinehart & Winston.

McGrath, J. E., & Beehr, T. A. (1990). Time and the stress process: Some temporal issues in the conceptualization and measurement of stress. *Stress Medicine, 6*, 93-104.

McGrath, J. E., & Kelly, J. R. (1986). *Time and human interaction: Toward a social psychology of time.* New York: Guilford.

McGrath, J. E., & Kelly, J. R. (1990). *Temporal context and temporal patterning in social psychology: A preliminary statement of a social psychological theory of time.* Manuscript submitted for publication.

McGrath, J. E., Kelly, J. R., & Machatka, D. E. (1984). The social psychology of time: Entrainment of behavior in social and organizational settings. In S. Oskamp (Ed.), *Applied social psychology annual* (Vol. 5, pp. 21-44). Beverly Hills, CA: Sage.

McGrath, J. E., & Rotchford, N. L. (1983). Time and behavior in organizations. In L. Cummings & B. Staw (Eds.), *Research in Organizational Behavior* (Vol. 5, pp. 57-101). Greenwich, CT: JAI.

Moreland, R. L., & Levine, J. M. (1982). Socialization in small groups: Temporal changes in individual-group relations. In L. Berkowitz (Ed.), *Advances in experimental social psychology* (Vol. 15, pp. 137-192). New York: Academic Press.

Moreland, R. L., & Levine, J. M. (1984). Role transitions in small groups. In V. Allen & E. Van de Vliert (Eds.), *Role transitions: Explorations and explanations* (pp. 181-195). New York: Plenum.

Moreland, R. L., & Levine, J. M. (1988). Group dynamics over time: Development and socialization in small groups. In J. E. McGrath (Ed.), *The social psychology of time: New perspectives* (pp. 151-181). Newbury Park, CA: Sage.

Poole, M. S., & DeSanctis, G. (1989). Understanding the use of group decision support systems: The theory of adaptive structuration. In C. Steinfield & J. Fulk (Eds.), *Theoretical approaches to information technologies in organizations.* Beverly Hills, CA: Sage.

Poole, M. S., & Roth, J. (1988a). Decision development in small groups: IV. A typology of group decision paths. *Human Communication Research, 15*, 323-356.

Poole, M. S., & Roth, J. (1988b). Decision development in small groups: V. Test of a contingency model. *Human Communication Research, 15*, 549-589.

Steiner, I. D. (1972). *Group process and productivity.* New York: Academic Press.

Thibaut, J. W., & Kelley, H. H. (1959). *The social psychology of groups.* New York: Wiley.

Vidmar, N., & McGrath, J. E. (1970). Forces affecting success in negotiation groups. *Behavioral Science, 15*, 154-163.

Weick, K. E. (1976). Educational organizations as loosely coupled systems. *Administrative Sciences Quarterly, 21*, 1-19.

Weick, K. E. (1982). Managing organizational change among loosely coupled elements. In P. S. Goodman & Associates (Eds.), *Change in organizations: New perspectives on theory, research and practice* (pp. 375-408). San Francisco: Jossey-Bass.

Werner, C. M., Haggard, L. M., Altman, I., & Oxley, D. (1988). Temporal qualities of rituals and celebrations: A comparison of Christmas Street and Zuni Shalako. In J. E. McGrath (Ed.), *The social psychology of time: New perspectives* (pp. 203-232). Newbury Park, CA: Sage.

Zander, A. F. (1979a). The psychology of small group processes. *Annual Review of Psychology, 30*, 417-471.

Zander, A. F. (1979b). The study of group behavior during four decades. *Journal of Applied Behavioral Science, 15*, 272-282.

Joseph E. McGrath is a professor of psychology at the University of Illinois, Urbana-Champaign. He received his Ph.D. in social psychology from the University of Michigan in 1955. His research interests include small group processes, social psychological factors in stress, research methodology, and the social psychology of time.

How to
run
a meeting

Antony Jay

*At critical points things
may go wrong,
but here are ways of putting
them right*

Why is it that any single meeting may be a waste of time, an irritant, or a barrier to the achievement of an organization's objectives? The answer lies in the fact, as the author says, that "all sorts of human crosscurrents can sweep the discussion off course, and errors of psychology and technique on the chairman's part can defeat its purposes." This article offers guidelines on how to right things that go wrong in meetings. The discussion covers the functions of a meeting, the distinctions in size and type of meetings, ways to define the objectives, making preparations, the chairman's role, and ways to conduct a meeting that will achieve its objectives.

Mr. Jay is chairman of Video Arts Ltd., a London-based producer of training films for industry. Currently, the company is producing a film (featuring John Cleese of Monty Python) on the subject of meetings, and this article springs from the research Mr. Jay did for that project. He has also written many TV documentaries, such as *Royal Family*, and authored several books, including *Management & Machiavelli* (Holt, Rinehart & Winston, 1968).

Drawings by Robert Osborn.

Harvard Business Review, 54(2), March-April 1976, pp. 43-57.
Reprinted by permission of *Harvard Business Review*. © 1976 by the President and Fellows of Harvard College; all rights reserved.

Why have a meeting anyway? Why indeed? A great many important matters are quite satisfactorily conducted by a single individual who consults nobody. A great many more are resolved by a letter, a memo, a phone call, or a simple conversation between two people. Sometimes five minutes spent with six people separately is more effective and productive than a half-hour meeting with them all together.

Certainly a great many meetings waste a great deal of everyone's time and seem to be held for historical rather than practical reasons; many long-established committees are little more than memorials to dead problems. It would probably save no end of managerial time if every committee had to discuss its own dissolution once a year, and put up a case if it felt it should continue for another twelve months. If this requirement did nothing else, it would at least refocus the minds of the committee members on their purposes and objectives.

But having said that, and granting that "referring the matter to a committee" can be a device for diluting authority, diffusing responsibility, and delaying decisions, I cannot deny that meetings fulfill a deep human need. Man is a social species. In every organization and every human culture of which we have record, people come together in small groups at regular and frequent intervals, and in larger "tribal" gatherings from time to time. If there are no meetings in the places where they work, people's attachment to the organizations they work for will be small, and they will meet in regular formal or

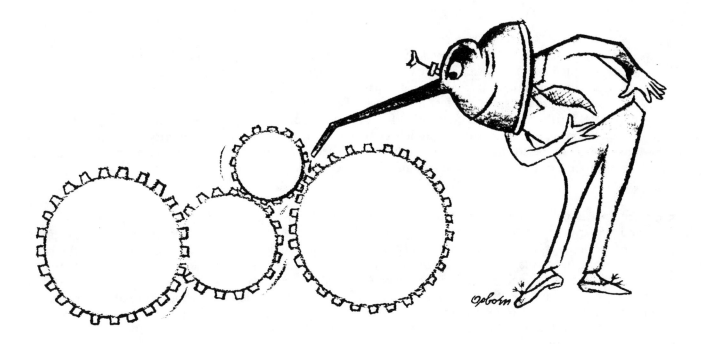

informal gatherings in associations, societies, teams, clubs, or pubs when work is over.

This need for meetings is clearly something more positive than just a legacy from our primitive hunting past. From time to time, some technomaniac or other comes up with a vision of the executive who never leaves his home, who controls his whole operation from an all-electronic, multichannel, microwave, fiber-optic video display dream console in his living room. But any manager who has ever had to make an organization work greets this vision with a smile that soon stretches into a yawn.

There is a world of science fiction, and a world of human reality; and those who live in the world of human reality know that it is held together by face-to-face meetings. A meeting still performs functions that will never be taken over by telephones, teleprinters, Xerox copiers, tape recorders, television monitors, or any other technological instruments of the information revolution.

Functions of a meeting

At this point, it may help us understand the meaning of meetings if we look at the six main functions

that meetings will always perform better than any of the more recent communication devices:

1

In the simplest and most basic way, a meeting defines the team, the group, or the unit. Those present belong to it; those absent do not. Everyone is able to look around and perceive the whole group and sense the collective identity of which he or she forms a part. We all know who we are—whether we are on the board of Universal International, in the overseas sales department of Flexitube, Inc., a member of the school management committee, on the East Hampton football team, or in Section No. 2 of Platoon 4, Company B.

2

A meeting is the place where the group revises, updates, and adds to what it knows *as a group*. Every group creates its own pool of shared knowledge, experience, judgment, and folklore. But the pool consists only of what the individuals have experienced or discussed as a group—i.e., those things which every individual knows that all the others know, too. This pool not only helps all members to do their jobs more intelligently, but it also greatly increases the speed and efficiency of all communications among them. The group knows that all special nuances and wider implications in a brief statement will be immediately clear to its members. An enormous amount of material can be left unsaid that would have to be made explicit to an outsider.

But this pool needs constant refreshing and replenishing, and occasionally the removal of impurities. So the simple business of exchanging information and ideas that members have acquired separately or in smaller groups since the last meeting is an important contribution to the strength of the group. By questioning and commenting on new contributions, the group performs an important "digestive" process that extracts what's valuable and discards the rest.

Some ethologists call this capacity to share knowledge and experience among a group "the social mind," conceiving it as a single mind dispersed among a number of skulls. They recognize that this "social mind" has a special creative power, too. A group of people meeting together can often produce better ideas, plans, and decisions than can a single individual, or a number of individuals, each working alone. The meeting can of course also produce worse outputs or none at all, if it is a bad meeting.

However, when the combined experience, knowledge, judgment, authority, and imagination of a half dozen people are brought to bear on issues, a great many plans and decisions are improved and sometimes transformed. The original idea that one person might have come up with singly is tested, amplified, refined, and shaped by argument and discussion (which often acts on people as some sort of chemical stimulant to better performance), until it satisfies far more requirements and overcomes many more objections than it could in its original form.

3

A meeting helps every individual understand both the collective aim of the group and the way in which his own and everyone else's work can contribute to the group's success.

4

A meeting creates in all present a commitment to the decisions it makes and the objectives it pursues. Once something has been decided, even if you originally argued against it, your membership in the group entails an obligation to accept the decision. The alternative is to leave the group, but in practice this is very rarely a dilemma of significance. Real opposition to decisions within organizations usually consists of one part disagreement with the decision to nine parts resentment at not being consulted before the decision. For most people on most issues, it is enough to know that their views were heard and considered. They may regret that they were not followed, but they accept the outcome.

And just as the decision of any team is binding on all the members, so the decisions of a meeting of people higher up in an organization carry a greater authority than any decision by a single executive. It is much harder to challenge a decision of the board than of the chief executive acting on his own. The decision-making authority of a meeting is of special importance for long-term policies and procedures.

5

In the world of management, a meeting is very often the only occasion where the team or group actually exists and works as a group, and the only time when the supervisor, manager, or executive is actually perceived as the leader of the team, rather than as the official to whom individuals report. In some jobs the leader does guide his team through his personal presence—not just the leader of a pit gang or construction team, but also the chef in the hotel kitchen and the maître d'hôtel in the restaurant, or the supervisor in a department store. But in large administrative headquarters, the daily or weekly meeting is often the only time when the leader is ever perceived to be guiding a team rather than doing a job.

6

A meeting is a status arena. It is no good to pretend that people are not or should not be concerned with their status relative to the other members in a group. It is just another part of human nature that we have to live with. It is a not insignificant fact that the word *order* means (a) hierarchy or pecking order; (b) an instruction or command; and (c) stability and the way things ought to be, as in "put your affairs in order," or "law and order." All three definitions are aspects of the same idea, which is indivisible.

Since a meeting is so often the only time when members get the chance to find out their relative standing, the "arena" function is inevitable. When a group is new, has a new leader, or is composed of people like department heads who are in competition for promotion and who do not work in a single team outside the meeting, "arena behavior" is likely to figure more largely, even to the point of dominating the proceedings. However, it will hardly signify with a long-established group that meets regularly.

Despite the fact that a meeting can perform all of the foregoing main functions, there is no guarantee that it will do so in any given situation. It is all too possible that any single meeting may be a waste of

time, an irritant, or a barrier to the achievement of the organization's objectives.

What sort of meeting?

While my purpose in this article is to show the critical points at which most meetings go wrong, and to indicate ways of putting them right, I must first draw some important distinctions in the size and type of meetings that we are dealing with.

Meetings can be graded by *size* into three broad categories: (1) the assembly—100 or more people who are expected to do little more than listen to the main speaker or speakers; (2) the council—40 or 50 people who are basically there to listen to the main speaker or speakers but who can come in with questions or comments and who may be asked to contribute something on their own account; and (3) the committee—up to 10 (or at the most 12) people, all of whom more or less speak on an equal footing under the guidance and control of a chairman.

We are concerned in this article only with the "committee" meeting, though it may be described as a committee, a subcommittee, a study group, a project team, a working party, a board, or by any of dozens of other titles. It is by far the most common meeting all over the world, and can perhaps be traced back to the primitive hunting band through which our species evolved. Beyond doubt it constitutes the bulk of the 11 million meetings that—so it has been calculated—take place every day in the United States.

Apart from the distinction of size, there are certain considerations regarding the *type* of meeting that profoundly affect its nature. For instance:

Frequency—A daily meeting is different from a weekly one, and a weekly meeting from a monthly one. Irregular, ad hoc, quarterly, and annual meetings are different again. On the whole, the frequency of meetings defines—or perhaps even determines—the degree of unity of the group.

Composition—Do the members work together on the same project, such as the nursing and ancillary staff on the same ward of a hospital? Do they work on different but parallel tasks, like a meeting of the company's plant managers or regional sales managers? Or are they a diverse group—strangers to each other, perhaps—united only by the meeting itself and by a common interest in realizing its objectives?

Motivation—Do the members have a common objective in their work, like a football team? Or do they to some extent have a competitive working relationship, like managers of subsidiary companies at a meeting with the chief executive, or the heads of research, production, and marketing discussing finance allocation for the coming year? Or does the desire for success through the meeting itself unify them, like a neighborhood action group or a new product design committee?

Decision process—How does the meeting group ultimately reach its decisions? By a general consensus, "the feeling of the meeting"? By a majority vote? Or are the decisions left entirely to the chairman himself, after he has listened to the facts, opinions, and discussions?

Kinds of meetings

The experienced meeting-goer will recognize that, although there seem to be five quite different methods of analyzing a meeting, in practice there is a tendency for certain kinds of meetings to sort themselves out into one of three categories. Consider:

The *daily meeting*, where people work together on the same project with a common objective and reach decisions informally by general agreement.

The *weekly* or *monthly meeting*, where members work on different but parallel projects and where there is a certain competitive element and a greater likelihood that the chairman will make the final decision himself.

The *irregular, occasional,* or *"special project" meeting,* composed of people whose normal work does not bring them into contact and whose work has little or no relationship to the others'. They are united only by the project the meeting exists to promote and motivated by the desire that the project should succeed. Though actual voting is uncommon, every member effectively has a veto.

Of these three kinds of meeting, it is the first—the workface type—that is probably the most common. It is also, oddly enough, the one most likely

to be successful. Operational imperatives usually ensure that it is brief, and the participants' experience of working side by side ensures that communication is good.

The other two types are a different matter. In these meetings all sorts of human crosscurrents can sweep the discussion off course, and errors of psychology and technique on the chairman's part can defeat its purposes. Moreover, these meetings are likely to bring together the more senior people and to produce decisions that profoundly affect the efficiency, prosperity, and even survival of the whole organization. It is, therefore, toward these higher-level meetings that the lessons of this article are primarily directed.

Before the meeting

The most important question you should ask is: "What is this meeting intended to achieve?" You can ask it in different ways—"What would be the likely consequences of not holding it?" "When it is over, how shall I judge whether it was a success or a failure?"—but unless you have a very clear requirement from the meeting, there is a grave danger that it will be a waste of everyone's time.

Defining the objective

You have already looked at the six main functions that all meetings perform, but if you are trying to use a meeting to achieve definite objectives, there are in practice only certain types of objectives it can really achieve. Every item on the agenda can be placed in one of the following four categories, or divided up into sections that fall into one or more of them:

1

Informative-digestive—Obviously, it is a waste of time for the meeting to give out purely factual information that would be better circulated in a document. But if the information should be heard from a particular person, or if it needs some clarification and comment to make sense of it, or if it has deep implications for the members of the meeting, then it is perfectly proper to introduce an item onto the agenda that requires no conclusion, decision, or

action from the meeting; it is enough, simply, that the meeting should receive and discuss a report.

The "informative-digestive" function includes progress reports—to keep the group up to date on the current status of projects it is responsible for or that affect its deliberations—and review of completed projects in order to come to a collective judgment and to see what can be learned from them for the next time.

2

Constructive-originative—This "What shall we do?" function embraces all items that require something new to be devised, such as a new policy, a new strategy, a new sales target, a new product, a new marketing plan, a new procedure, and so forth. This sort of discussion asks people to contribute their knowledge, experience, judgment, and ideas. Obviously, the plan will probably be inadequate unless all relevant parties are present and pitching in.

3

Executive responsibilities—This is the "How shall we do it?" function, which comes after it has been decided what the members are going to do; at this point, executive responsibilities for the different components of the task have to be distributed around the table. Whereas in the second function the con-

tributors' importance is their knowledge and ideas, here their contribution is the responsibility for implementing the plan. The fact that they and their subordinates are affected by it makes their contribution especially significant.

It is of course possible to allocate these executive responsibilities without a meeting, by separate individual briefings, but several considerations often make a meeting desirable:

First, it enables the members as a group to find the best way of achieving the objectives.

Second, it enables each member to understand and influence the way in which his own job fits in with the jobs of the others and with the collective task.

Third, if the meeting is discussing the implementation of a decision taken at a higher level, securing the group's consent may be of prime importance. If so, the fact that the group has the opportunity to formulate the detailed action plan itself may be the decisive factor in securing its agreement, because in that case the final decision belongs, as it were, to the group. Everyone is committed to what the group decides and is collectively responsible for the final shape of the project, as well as individually answerable for his own part in it. Ideally, this sort of agenda item starts with a policy, and ends with an action plan.

4

Legislative framework: Above and around all considerations of "What to do" and "How to do it," there is a framework—a departmental or divisional organization—and a system of rules, routines, and procedures within and through which all the activity takes place. Changing this framework and introducing a new organization or new procedures can be deeply disturbing to committee members and a threat to their status and long-term security. Yet leaving it unchanged can stop the organization from adapting to a changing world. At whatever level this change happens, it must have the support of all the perceived leaders whose groups are affected by it.

The key leaders for this legislative function must collectively make or confirm the decision; if there is any important dissent, it is very dangerous to close the discussion and make the decision by decree. The group leaders cannot expect quick decisions if they are seeking to change the organization framework and routines that people have grown up with. Thus they must be prepared to leave these items unresolved for further discussion and consultation. As Francis Bacon put it—and it has never been put better—"Counsels to which time hath not been called, time will not ratify."

Making preparations

The four different functions just discussed may of course be performed by a single meeting, as the group proceeds through the agenda. Consequently, it may be a useful exercise for the chairman to go through the agenda, writing beside each item which function it is intended to fulfill. This exercise helps clarify what is expected from the discussion and helps focus on which people to bring in and what questions to ask them.

People

The value and success of a committe meeting are seriously threatened if too many people are present. Between 4 and 7 is generally ideal, 10 is tolerable, and 12 is the outside limit. So the chairman should do everything he can to keep numbers down, consistent with the need to invite everyone with an important contribution to make.

The leader may have to leave out people who expect to come or who have always come. For this job he may need tact; but since people generally preserve a fiction that they are overworked already and dislike serving on committees, it is not usually hard to secure their consent to stay away.

If the leader sees no way of getting the meeting down to a manageable size, he can try the following devices: (a) analyze the agenda to see whether everyone has to be present for every item (he may be able to structure the agenda so that some people can leave at half time and others can arrive); (b) ask himself whether he doesn't really need two separate, smaller meetings rather than one big one; and (c) determine whether one or two groups can be asked to thrash some of the topics out in advance so that only one of them needs to come in with its proposals.

Remember, too, that a few words with a member on the day before a meeting can increase the value of the meeting itself, either by ensuring that an important point is raised that comes better from the floor than from the chair or by preventing a time-wasting discussion of a subject that need not be touched on at all.

Papers

The agenda is by far the most important piece of paper. Properly drawn up, it has a power of speeding and clarifying a meeting that very few people understand or harness. The main fault is to make it unnecessarily brief and vague. For example, the phrase "development budget" tells nobody very much, whereas the longer explanation "To discuss the proposal for reduction of the 1976–1977 development budget now that the introduction of our new product has been postponed" helps all committee members to form some views or even just to look up facts and figures in advance.

Thus the leader should not be afraid of a long agenda, provided that the length is the result of his analyzing and defining each item more closely, rather than of his adding more items than the meeting can reasonably consider in the time allowed. He should try to include, very briefly, some indication of the reason for each topic to be discussed. If one item is of special interest to the group, it is often a good idea to single it out for special mention in a covering note.

The leader should also bear in mind the useful device of heading each item "For information," "For discussion," or "For decision" so that those at the meeting know where they are trying to get to.

And finally, the chairman should not circulate the agenda too far in advance, since the less organized members will forget it or lose it. Two or three days is about right—unless the supporting papers are voluminous.

Other 'paper' considerations: The order of items on the agenda is important. Some aspects are obvious—the items that need urgent decision have to come before those that can wait till next time. Equally, the leader does not discuss the budget for the reequipment program before discussing whether to put the reequipment off until next year. But some aspects are not so obvious. Consider:

☐

The early part of a meeting tends to be more lively and creative than the end of it, so if an item needs mental energy, bright ideas, and clear heads, it may be better to put it high up on the list. Equally, if there is one item of great interest and concern to everyone, it may be a good idea to hold it back for a while and get some other useful work done first. Then the star item can be introduced to carry the meeting over the attention lag that sets in after the first 15 to 20 minutes of the meeting.

☐

Some items unite the meeting in a common front while others divide the members one from another. The leader may want to start with unity before entering into division, or he may prefer the other way around. The point is to be aware of the choice and to make it consciously, because it is apt to make a difference to the whole atmosphere of the meeting. It is almost always a good idea to find a unifying item with which to end the meeting.

☐

A common fault is to dwell too long on trivial but urgent items, to the exclusion of subjects of fundamental importance whose significance is long-term rather than immediate. This can be remedied by putting on the agenda the time at which discussion of the important long-term issue will begin—and by sticking to it.

☐

Very few business meetings achieve anything of value after two hours, and an hour and a half is enough time to allocate for most purposes.

☐

It is often a good idea to put the finishing time of a meeting on the agenda as well as the starting time.

☐

If meetings have a tendency to go on too long, the chairman should arrange to start them one hour before lunch or one hour before the end of work. Generally, items that ought to be kept brief can be introduced ten minutes from a fixed end point.

☐

The practice of circulating background or proposal papers along with the minutes is, in principle, a good one. It not only saves time, but it also helps in formulating useful questions and considerations in advance. But the whole idea is sabotaged once the papers get too long; they should be brief or provide a short summary. If they are circulated, obviously the chairman has to read them, or at least must not be caught not having read them.

(One chairman, more noted for his cunning than his conscientiousness, is said to have spent 30 seconds before each meeting going through all the papers he had not read with a thick red pen, marking lines and question marks in the margins at random, and making sure these were accidentally made visible to the meeting while the subject was being discussed.)

☐

If papers are produced at the meeting for discussion, they should obviously be brief and simple, since everyone has to read them. It is a supreme folly to bring a group of people together to read six pages of closely printed sheets to themselves. The exception is certain kinds of financial and statistical papers whose function is to support and illustrate verbal points as reference documents rather than to be swallowed whole: these are often better tabled at the meeting.

☐

All items should be thought of and thought about in advance if they are to be usefully discussed. Listing "Any other business" on the agenda is an invitation to waste time. This does not absolutely preclude the chairman's announcing an extra agenda item at a meeting if something really urgent and unforeseen crops up or is suggested to him by a member, provided it is fairly simple and straightforward. Nor does it preclude his leaving time for general unstructured discussion after the close of the meeting.

☐

The chairman, in going through the agenda items in advance, can usefully insert his own brief notes of points he wants to be sure are not omitted from the discussion. A brief marginal scribble of "How much notice?" or "Standby arrangements?" or whatever is all that is necessary.

The chairman's job

Let's say that you have just been appointed chairman of the committee. You tell everyone that it is a bore or a chore. You also tell them that you have been appointed "for my sins." But the point is that you tell them. There is no getting away from it: some sort of honor or glory attaches to the chairman's role. Almost everyone is in some way pleased and proud to be made chairman of something. And that is three quarters of the trouble.

Master or servant?

Their appointment as committee chairman takes people in different ways. Some seize the opportunity to impose their will on a group that they see themselves licensed to dominate. Their chairmanship is a harangue, interspersed with demands for group agreement.

Others are more like scoutmasters, for whom the collective activity of the group is satisfaction enough, with no need for achievement. Their chairmanship is more like the endless stoking and fueling of a campfire that is not cooking anything.

And there are the insecure or lazy chairmen who look to the meeting for reassurance and support in their ineffectiveness and inactivity, so that they can spread the responsibility for their indecisiveness among the whole group. They seize on every expression of disagreement or doubt as a justification for avoiding decision or action.

But even the large majority who do not go to those extremes still feel a certain pleasurable tumescence of the ego when they take their place at the head of the table for the first time. The feeling is no sin: the sin is to indulge it or to assume that the pleasure is shared by the other members of the meeting.

It is the chairman's self-indulgence that is the greatest single barrier to the success of a meeting. His first duty, then, is to be aware of the temptation and

of the dangers of yielding to it. The clearest of the danger signals is hearing himself talking a lot during a discussion.

One of the best chairmen I have ever served under makes it a rule to restrict her interventions to a single sentence, or at most two. She forbids herself ever to contribute a paragraph to a meeting she is chairing. It is a harsh rule, but you would be hard put to find a regular attender of her meetings (or anyone else's) who thought it was a bad one.

There is, in fact, only one legitimate source of pleasure in chairmanship, and that is pleasure in the achievements of the meeting—and to be legitimate, it must be shared by all those present. Meetings are *necessary* for all sorts of basic and primitive human reasons, but they are *useful* only if they are seen by all present to be getting somewhere—and somewhere they know they could not have gotten to individually.

If the chairman is to make sure that the meeting achieves valuable objectives, he will be more effective seeing himself as the servant of the group rather than as its master. His role then becomes that of assisting the group toward the best conclusion or decision in the most efficient manner possible: to interpret and clarify; to move the discussion forward; and to bring it to a resolution that everyone understands and accepts as being the will of the meeting, even if the individuals do not necessarily agree with it.

His true source of authority with the members is the strength of his perceived commitment to their combined objective and his skill and efficiency in helping and guiding them to its achievement. Control and discipline then become not the act of imposing his will on the group but of imposing the group's will on any individual who is in danger of diverting or delaying the progress of the discussion and so from realizing the objective.

Once the members realize that the leader is impelled by his commitment to their common objective, it does not take great force of personality for him to control the meeting. Indeed, a sense of urgency and a clear desire to reach the best conclusion as quickly as possible are a much more effective disciplinary instrument than a big gavel. The effective chairman can then hold the discussion to the point by indicating that there is no time to pursue a particular idea now, that there is no time for long speeches, that the group has to get through

this item and on to the next one, rather than by resorting to pulling rank.

There are many polite ways the chairman can indicate a slight impatience even when someone else is speaking—by leaning forward, fixing his eyes on the speaker, tensing his muscles, raising his eyebrows, or nodding briefly to show the point is taken. And when replying or commenting, the chairman can indicate by the speed, brevity, and finality of his intonation that "we have to move on." Conversely, he can reward the sort of contribution he is seeking by the opposite expressions and intonations, showing that there is plenty of time for that sort of idea, and encouraging the speaker to develop the point.

After a few meetings, all present readily understand this nonverbal language of chairmanship. It is the chairman's chief instrument of educating the group into the general type of "meeting behavior" that he is looking for. He is still the servant of the group, but like a hired mountain guide, he is the one who knows the destination, the route, the weather signs, and the time the journey will take. So if he suggests that the members walk a bit faster, they take his advice.

This role of servant rather than master is often obscured in large organizations by the fact that the chairman is frequently the line manager of the members: this does not, however, change the reality of the role of chairman. The point is easier to see in, say, a neighborhood action group. The question in that case is, simply, "Through which person's chairmanship do we collectively have the best chance of getting the children's playground built?"

However, one special problem is posed by this definition of the chairman's role, and it has an extremely interesting answer. The question is: How can the chairman combine his role with the role of a member advocating one side of an argument?

The answer comes from some interesting studies by researchers who sat in on hundreds of meetings to find out how they work. Their consensus finding is that most of the effective discussions have, in fact, two leaders: one they call a "team," or "social," leader; the other a "task," or "project," leader.

Regardless of whether leadership is in fact a single or a dual function, for our purposes it is enough to say that the chairman's best role is that of social leader. If he wants a particular point to be strongly advocated, he ensures that it is someone else who leads off the task discussion, and he holds back until much later in the argument. He might indeed change or modify his view through hearing the discussion, but even if he does not it is much easier for him to show support for someone else's point later in the discussion, after listening to the arguments. Then, he can summarize in favor of the one he prefers.

The task advocate might regularly be the chairman's second-in-command, or a different person might advocate for different items on the agenda. On some subjects, the chairman might well be the task advocate himself, especially if they do not involve conflict within the group. The important point is that the chairman has to keep his "social leadership" even if it means sacrificing his "task leadership." However, if the designated task advocate persists in championing a cause through two or three meetings, he risks building up quite a head of antagonism to him among the other members. Even so, this antagonism harms the group less by being directed at the "task leader" than at the "social leader."

Structure of discussion

It may seem that there is no right way or wrong way to structure a committee meeting discussion.

A subject is raised, people say what they think, and finally a decision is reached, or the discussion is terminated. There is some truth in this. Moreover, it would be a mistake to try and tie every discussion of every item down to a single immutable format.

Nevertheless, there is a logical order to a group discussion, and while there can be reasons for not following it, there is no justification for not being aware of it. In practice, very few discussions are inhibited, and many are expedited, by a conscious adherence to the following stages, which follow exactly the same pattern as a visit to the doctor:

"*What seems to be the trouble?*" The reason for an item being on a meeting agenda is usually like the symptom we go to the doctor with: "I keep getting this pain in my back" is analogous to "Sales have risen in Germany but fallen in France." In both cases it is clear that something is wrong and that something ought to be done to put it right. But until the visit to the doctor, or the meeting of the European marketing committee, that is about all we really know.

"*How long has this been going on?*" The doctor will start with a case history of all the relevant background facts, and so will the committee discussion. A solid basis of shared and agreed-on facts is the best foundation to build any decision on, and a set of pertinent questions will help establish it. For example, when did French sales start to fall off? Have German sales risen exceptionally? Has France had delivery problems, or less sales effort, or weaker advertising? Have we lost market share, or are our competitors' sales falling too? If the answers to all these questions, and more, are not established at the start, a lot of discussion may be wasted later.

"*Would you just lie down on the couch?*" The doctor will then conduct a physical examination to find out how the patient is now. The committee, too, will want to know how things stand at this moment. Is action being taken? Do long-term orders show the same trend? What are the latest figures? What is the current stock position? How much money is left in the advertising budget?

"*You seem to have slipped a disc.*" When the facts are established, you can move toward a dignosis. A doctor may seem to do this quickly, but that is the result of experience and practice. He is, in fact, rapidly eliminating all the impossible or far-fetched explanations until he leaves himself with a short list. The committee, too, will hazard and eliminate a

variety of diagnoses until it homes in on the most probable—for example, the company's recent energetic and highly successful advertising campaign in Germany plus new packaging by the market leader in France.

"Take this round to the druggist." Again, the doctor is likely to take a shortcut that a committee meeting may be wise to avoid. The doctor comes out with a single prescription, and the committee, too, may agree quickly on a single course of action.

But if the course is not so clear, it is better to take this step in two stages: (a) construct a series of options—do not, at first, reject any suggestions outright but try to select and combine the promising elements from all of them until a number of thought-out, coherent, and sensible suggestions are on the table; and (b) only when you have generated these options do you start to choose among them. Then you can discuss and decide whether to pick the course based on repackaging and point-of-sale promotion, or the one based on advertising and a price cut, or the one that bides its time and saves the money for heavier new-product promotion next year.

If the item is at all complex or especially significant, it is important for the chairman not only to have

the proposed course of the discussion in his own head, but also to announce it so that everyone knows. A good idea is to write the headings on an easel pad with a felt pen. This saves much of the time wasting and confusion that result when people raise items in the wrong place because they were not privy to the chairman's secret that the right place was coming up later on in the discussion.

Conducting the meeting

Just as the driver of a car has two tasks, to follow his route and to manage his vehicle, so the chairman's job can be divided into two corresponding tasks, dealing with the subject and dealing with the people.

Dealing with the subject

The essence of this task is to follow the structure of discussion as just described in the previous section. This, in turn, entails listening carefully and keeping the meeting pointed toward the objective.

At the start of the discussion of any item, the chairman should make it clear where the meeting should try to get to by the end. Are the members hoping to make a clear decision or firm recommendation? Is it a preliminary deliberation to give the members something to go away with and think about? Are they looking for a variety of different lines to be pursued outside the meeting? Do they have to approve the proposal, or merely note it?

The chairman may give them a choice: "If we can agree on a course of action, that's fine. If not, we'll have to set up a working party to report and recommend before next month's meeting."

The chairman should make sure that all the members understand the issue and why they are discussing it. Often it will be obvious, or else they may have been through it before. If not, then he or someone he has briefed before the meeting should give a short introduction, with some indication of the reason the item is on the agenda; the story so far; the present position; what needs to be established, resolved, or proposed; and some indication of lines of inquiry or courses of action that have been suggested or explored, as well as arguments on both sides of the issue.

If the discussion is at all likely to be long or complex, the chairman should propose to the meeting a structure for it with headings (written up if necessary), as I stated at the end of the section on "Structure of discussion." He should listen carefully in case people jump too far ahead (e.g., start proposing a course of action before the meeting has agreed on the cause of the trouble), or go back over old ground, or start repeating points that have been made earlier. He has to head discussion off sterile or irrelevant areas very quickly (e.g., the rights and wrongs of past decisions that it is too late to change, or distant prospects that are too remote to affect present actions).

It is the chairman's responsibility to prevent misunderstanding and confusion. If he does not follow an argument or understand a reference, he should seek clarification from the speaker. If he thinks two people are using the same word with different meanings, he should intervene (e.g., one member using *promotion* to mean point-of-sale advertising only, and another also including media publicity).

He may also have to clarify by asking people for facts or experience that perhaps influence their view but are not known to others in the meeting. And he should be on the lookout for points where an interim summary would be helpful. This device frequently takes only a few seconds, and acts like a life belt to some of the members who are getting out of their depth.

Sometimes a meeting will have to discuss a draft document. If there are faults in it, the members should agree on what the faults are and the chairman should delegate someone to produce a new draft later. The group should never try to redraft around the table.

Perhaps one of the most common faults of chairmanship is the failure to terminate the discussion early enough. Sometimes chairmen do not realize that the meeting has effectively reached an agreement, and consequently they let the discussion go on for another few minutes, getting nowhere at all. Even more often, they are not quick enough to close a discussion *before* agreement has been reached.

A discussion should be closed once it has become clear that (a) more facts are required before further progress can be made, (b) discussion has revealed that the meeting needs the views of people not present, (c) members need more time to think about the subject and perhaps discuss it with colleagues, (d) events are changing and likely to alter or clarify the basis of the decision quite soon, (e) there is not going to be enough time at this meeting to go over the subject properly, or (f) it is becoming clear that two or three of the members can settle this outside the meeting without taking up the time of the rest. The fact that the decision is difficult, likely to be disputed, or going to be unwelcome to somebody, however, is not a reason for postponement.

At the end of the discussion of each agenda item, the chairman should give a brief and clear summary of what has been agreed on. This can act as the dictation of the actual minutes. It serves not merely to put the item on record, but also to help people realize that something worthwhile has been achieved. It also answers the question "Where did all that get us?" If the summary involves action by a member of the meeting, he should be asked to confirm his acceptance of the undertaking.

Dealing with the people

There is only one way to ensure that a meeting starts on time, and that is to start it on time. Latecomers who find that the meeting has begun without them soon learn the lesson. The alternative is that the prompt and punctual members will soon realize that a meeting never starts until ten minutes after the advertised time, and they will also learn the lesson.

Punctuality at future meetings can be wonderfully reinforced by the practice of listing late arrivals (and early departures) in the minutes. Its ostensible and perfectly proper purpose is to call the latecomer's attention to the fact that he was absent when a decision was reached. Its side effect, however, is to tell everyone on the circulation list that he was late, and people do not want that sort of information about themselves published too frequently.

There is a growing volume of work on the significance of seating positions and their effect on group behavior and relationships. Not all the findings are generally agreed on. What does seem true is that:

☐
Having members sit face to face across a table facilitates opposition, conflict, and disagreement, though of course it does not turn allies into enemies. But

it does suggest that the chairman should think about whom he seats opposite himself.

☐

Sitting side by side makes disagreements and confrontation harder. This in turn suggests that the chairman can exploit the friendship-value of the seats next to him.

☐

There is a "dead man's corner" on the chairman's right, especially if a number of people are seated in line along from him (it does not apply if he is alone at the head of the table).

☐

As a general rule, proximity to the chairman is a sign of honor and favor. This is most marked when he is at the head of a long, narrow table. The greater the distance, the lower the rank—just as the lower-status positions were "below the salt" at medieval refectories.

Control the garrulous

In most meetings someone takes a long time to say very little. As chairman, your sense of urgency should help indicate to him the need for brevity. You can also suggest that if he is going to take a long time it might be better for him to write a paper. If it is urgent to stop him in full flight, there is a useful device of picking on a phrase (it really doesn't matter what phrase) as he utters it as an excuse for cutting in and offering it to someone else: "Inevitable decline—that's very interesting. George, do you agree that the decline is inevitable?"

Draw out the silent

In any properly run meeting, as simple arithmetic will show, most of the people will be silent most of the time. Silence can indicate general agreement, or no important contribution to make, or the need to wait and hear more before saying anything, or too good a lunch, and none of these need worry you. But there are two kinds of silence you must break:

1

The silence of diffidence. Someone may have a valuable contribution to make but be sufficiently nervous about its possible reception to keep it to himself. It is important that when you draw out such a contribution, you should express interest and pleasure (though not necessarily agreement) to encourage further contributions of that sort.

2

The silence of hostility. This is not hostility to ideas, but to you as the chairman, to the meeting, and to the process by which decisions are being reached.

This sort of total detachment from the whole proceedings is usually the symptom of some feeling of affront. If you probe it, you will usually find that there is something bursting to come out, and that it is better out than in.

Protect the weak

Junior members of the meeting may provoke the disagreement of their seniors, which is perfectly reasonable. But if the disagreement escalates to the point of suggesting that they have no right to contribute, the meeting is weakened. So you may have to take pains to commend their contribution for its usefulness, as a pre-emptive measure. You can reinforce this action by taking a written note of a point they make (always a plus for a member of a meeting) and by referring to it again later in the discussion (a double-plus).

Encourage the clash of ideas

But, at the same time, discourage the clash of personalities. A good meeting is not a series of dialogues between individual members and the chairman. Instead, it is a crossflow of discussion and debate, with the chairman occasionally guiding, mediating, probing, stimulating, and summarizing, but mostly letting the others thrash ideas out. However, the meeting must be a contention of *ideas*, not people.

If two people are starting to get heated, widen the discussion by asking a question of a neutral member of the meeting, preferably a question that requires a purely factual answer.

Watch out for the suggestion-squashing reflex

Students of meetings have reduced everything that can be said into questions, answers, positive reactions, and negative reactions. Questions can only seek, and answers only supply, three types of response: information, opinion, and suggestion.

In almost every modern organization, it is the suggestions that contain the seeds of future success. Although very few suggestions will ever lead to anything, almost all of them need to be given every chance. The trouble is that suggestions are much easier to ridicule than facts or opinions. If people feel that making a suggestion will provoke the negative reaction of being laughed at or squashed, they will soon stop. And if there is any status-jostling going on at the meeting, it is all too easy to use the occasion of someone's making a suggestion as the opportunity to take him down a peg. It is all too easy and a formula to ensure sterile meetings.

The answer is for you to take special notice and show special warmth when anyone makes a suggestion, and to discourage as sharply as you can the squashing-reflex. This can often be achieved by requiring the squasher to produce a better suggestion on the spot. Few suggestions can stand up to squashing in their pristine state: your reflex must be to pick out the best part of one and get the other committee members to help build it into something that might work.

Come to the most senior people last

Obviously, this cannot be a rule, but once someone of high authority has pronounced on a topic, the less senior members are likely to be inhibited. If you work up the pecking order instead of down it, you are apt to get a wider spread of views and ideas. But the juniors who start it off should only be asked for contributions within their personal experience and competence. ("Peter, you were at the Frankfurt Exhibition—what reactions did you pick up there?")

Close on a note of achievement

Even if the final item is left unresolved, you can refer to an earlier item that was well resolved as you close the meeting and thank the group.

If the meeting is not a regular one, fix the time and place of the next one before dispersing. A little time spent with appointment diaries at the end, especially if it is a gathering of five or more members, can save hours of secretarial telephoning later.

Following the meeting

Your secretary may take the minutes (or better still, one of the members), but the minutes are your responsibility. They can be very brief, but they should include these facts:

☐
The time and date of the meeting, where it was held, and who chaired it.
☐
Names of all present and apologies for absence.
☐
All agenda items (and other items) discussed and all decisions reached. If action was agreed on, record (and underline) the name of the person responsible for the assignment.
☐
The time at which the meeting ended (important, because it may be significant later to know whether the discussion lasted 15 minutes or 6 hours).
☐
The date, time, and place of the next committee meeting.

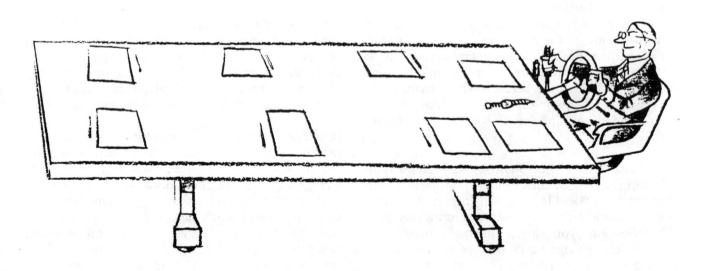

Proceedings of the Second European Conference on Computer-Supported Cooperative Work
Bannon, L., Robinson, M. & Schmidt, K. (Editors)
September 25-27, 1991, Amsterdam, The Netherlands

The Group Facilitator: A CSCW Perspective

Stephen Viller
Department of Computation, UMIST, United Kingdom.

What unites CSCW research is the need to help people work together (Greif, 1988) or, to be more precise, "...the support requirements of cooperative work." (Bannon & Schmidt, 1989). An important contribution to the understanding of these requirements, therefore, are the results from research into group working, its structure, and dynamics. A well recognised concept in group work is the role of the group facilitator; someone who's responsibility it is to assist the group in achieving its objectives. This recognition, however, is not yet reflected by work published under the CSCW banner. This paper aims to take a first step at addressing this omission.

1 Introduction

CSCW is a subject that draws on research in numerous disciplines, such as computer science, psychology, sociology, and artificial intelligence. What distinguishes it from these other areas is that whilst group work may be considered a special interest for them, the provision of computer-support for groups of people working together is central to CSCW (Greif, 1988). Group work itself is a much longer established discipline which can be traced back to the beginnings of sociology and social psychology at the turn of the century (McGrath, 1984). Over this period, a number of concepts have become established in the wealth of research that has been undertaken. For example, the group's task - its reason for existence - can be divided into its content (what is to be achieved) and process (how it is to be achieved). Furthermore, the group process may be divided into task behaviours - aimed at achieving the group's task; and maintenance (or socio-emotional) behaviours - aimed at maintaining the group as a cohesive unit. These two types of behaviour are antagonistic, and group members must engage in both types as they progress towards fulfilment of the task (Smith, Beck, Cooper, Cox, Ottaway & Talbot, 1982). It is in smoothing out the problems in group process that the skills of a facilitator become important. Someone who understands group processes and can therefore assist a group to understand its problems, and find solutions for them, is a valuable asset to any group.

When group interaction takes place via computers, then CSCW is the relevant discipline for its study. The role of the facilitator, however, has been largely neglected by CSCW research, despite the importance of such a role in improving the effectiveness of group work. The need for the facilitator's role to be discussed in the context of CSCW systems is the motivation behind this paper.

In what follows, a description of the facilitator's role is given, and the effects of computer communication via computer on this role are considered. Four 'CSCW scenarios' are identified, and the facilitator's role is examined in two of them. Finally, the extent to which the role should be supported and/or automated is discussed.

2 The Role of the Facilitator

Research and practice in group work use a multitude of terms for the person who has the facilitating role within a group. In social work and psychotherapy for example, the group may have a *worker* (Douglas, 1970), or *therapist* (Whitaker, 1985). Another major application of group work is in the management sciences, where groups have much clearer defined tasks in terms of furthering the aims of the organisation concerned. These groups are typically made up of members who already exist within some other organisational structure and therefore have an established relationship between one another. These groups will usually have a *leader* (Smith et al., 1982), who will also quite often be the most senior member of the group in terms of the organisational structure.

A feature common to these group situations is the notion of someone who's role is to assist the process of group working, generically referred to as a facilitator. The term facilitator itself denotes a set of skills and behaviours that may be applied by a group-worker, teacher, manager, therapist, coordinator, and so on. The application of these skills may be different in the various contexts. Nevertheless, "facilitator" is a readily identifiable, common 'core' of skills and behaviours that may be used by any of the above.

The Shorter Oxford English Dictionary defines facilitate as ''To render easier; to promote, help forward''. The role of a group facilitator, therefore, is concerned with assisting the other group members in performing their collective task as a group.

2.1 The 'Central Person'

Early work on the role of the group facilitator introduced the concept of the *central person* (Redl, 1942). This person is so named because s/he evokes a common emotional response in the other group members, and the group formative processes take place through her/him. Redl defined this person as someone who provides an object of identification, an object of drives, and an ego support for the other members of the group. Douglas (1970) states that this role definition is not very useful in itself because of the static nature in which it treats groups. Heap (1968) noted, however, that the static description of the central person applies very well to the initial stages of a group's development, and can therefore be modified to take into account the dynamics of group work.

At the initial stages in a group's lifecycle, the relationship towards the facilitator may be all that is common to the other group members, and thus the facilitator becomes the group's central person. A facilitator, with their knowledge of group process, can utilise this position to improve group cohesion, and for the setting of group norms. As a group develops, individuals will identify themselves more as group members, and the common relationship of everyone towards the central person will become less important (Douglas, 1970). During these middle stages of the group's lifecycle, the central person's role is much more that of enabler, sitting back from the group and only intervening when necessary. Finally, as the group nears its end, the role of the central person becomes more important again, as s/he assists the other members through the process of winding-up the group. The precise role played by the facilitator at this stage will depend upon the circumstances in which the group is breaking up; for example, whether or not the group has fully achieved its purpose (Douglas, 1970).

2.2 Membership Status

Opinions differ on the facilitator's status within a group. Some of this difference can be explained by the 'bias' of the source. For example, if the facilitator is to perform some leadership function for the group - as in management situations - then s/he will be in a position of power over the other group members. Conversely, if s/he is someone who is brought in from outside of the group as a professional facilitator, then her/his function will be more of an assistant to the group, helping the other group members to achieve their objectives without having any stake in the outcome. This second example describes the facilitator's role in its generic sense, the key factor being that the facilitator is concerned with enabling the *process* of the group achieving its aims, whilst having no stake in the *content* of these aims. Three different views of this relationship between facilitator and group are presented in figure 1, which is adapted from Douglas (1970). The first viewpoint is the status of the facilitator when a group is first set up, the second illustrates the status of the facilitator in its generic sense, whilst the third represents

	'Multi-Headed Beast' syndrome
SYMPTOMS	Digressions; interruptions; multiple topics; no listening; no integration of ideas.
POSSIBLE CAUSES	No agreement on agenda: no process design; mixing problem-solving strategies.
POSSIBLE INTERVENTIONS	• Suggest round robin to clarify task • List perceptions of task • Seek synthesis (rephrase, find continuities, categories) • Formulate/reformulate agenda
	'Feuding Factions' syndrome
SYMPTOMS	Repetitious arguments; open attacks, anger.
POSSIBLE CAUSES	Hidden agendas/power struggles; fear of change.
POSSIBLE INTERVENTIONS	• Stop action: "we're having difficulty agreeing on a solution..." • Allow individual to privately list criteria • List criteria independently of alternatives • Measure alternatives against criteria.
	'Dominant Species' syndrome
SYMPTOMS	'Plops'; 'unequal air-time'; passive/aggressive body language; withdrawal
POSSIBLE CAUSES	Dominance: not heard, frustrated Withdrawn: afraid, frustrated, insulated

POSSIBLE INTERVENTIONS	**Direct:** question/poll under-participators; thank/limit over-participators
	Interpretative: At end of meeting, share perceptions on levels of participation • self rating
	  • round robin on views
	  • solicit norms on participation

	'Recycling' syndrome
SYMPTOMS	'Broken record' behaviour; irritation with lack of progress; failure to gain consensus.
POSSIBLE CAUSES	Ideas not being recorded: confusion about problem-solving process.
POSSIBLE INTERVENTIONS	• Introduce/reintroduce problem-solving steps • identify which issues belong to which steps • identify 'where we are, where we've been, where we're going'.
	'Sleeping Meeting' syndrome
SYMPTOMS	Long silences; absence of energy/ideas; withdrawal.
POSSIBLE CAUSES	Fear of volatile issue: hostility; depression, fatigue.

POSSIBLE INTERVENTIONS	• Describe observation - 'blocked condition of meeting'
	• Suggest mood-check
	• Then: - take a break
	   - address underlying problem
	   - decide on action plan to rectify
	• and/or - return to task, allotting time to address the problem at end of meeting.

Table I: Generic Meeting Problem Syndromes

when a member of the group performs the role of the facilitator (as in management situations).

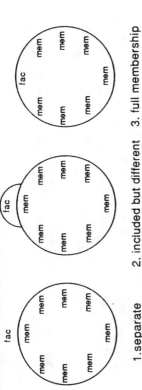

1.separate   2. included but different   3. full membership

mem: group member   fac: facilitator

Figure 1: Membership status of facilitator

2.3 Intervention strategies

The role of the facilitator described so far is open to criticism for its relatively static nature. A group working environment is by no means static, with participation by, and relationships between, the various members changing throughout a group's life. Whilst the dynamic aspect of group work is one of its advantages, problems can develop, and when they occur the facilitator's role takes on greater importance. It is necessary for any facilitator to be able to recognise when a problem is developing, and to also have the skill and knowledge of how to enable the group to deal with it. Any action that a facilitator takes to 'correct' group process problems is known as an *intervention*. Five *Generic Problem Syndromes* (along with their symptoms, possible causes, and possible interventions) have been identified by Westley & Waters (1988) - presented in table I - along with two intervention methods: *Interpretation*; and *Direct Action*.

2.3.1 Interpretation Method

This type of intervention involves the facilitator shifting the focus of the group away from task-content to process in two steps. First of all, after a process problem has been diagnosed, the facilitator articulates the observed cues to the group in as neutral a manner as possible. Descriptive language is used, whilst avoiding over-generalising and being evaluative. Subsequently, the group is directed to focus on the process problem that has been identified. If the facilitator has a clear picture of the problem, then a diagnosis can be proposed to the group. Alternatively, s/he can invite the group to discuss the problem as a result of her/his reporting it. The following discussion in the group should aim at solving the identified problem. For this, it is essential that the facilitator is capable of suggesting a *design* for the solution - how the group can solve its problem and return to the content of its task - otherwise a breakdown in the group is inevitable.

2.3.2 Direct Action Method

As opposed to the above method, where the flow of the meeting is suspended to deal with a process problem. This method directly manipulates the processes of the group, for example: preventing interruptions until the current speaker finishes; or encouraging a hesitant participant by giving positive feedback to their contribution. This type of intervention is not suited to all situations, or to all individual facilitation styles. It would be unsuitable, for example, if the problem is part of an underlying trend that would be better dealt with explicitly through the use of an interpretative intervention.

The choice of intervention method made by the facilitator will depend upon both the nature of the problem, and on the facilitator's personality and experience of group working. The interpretative method is more likely to be successful for a facilitator who is not very experienced or who is not sure how to solve a particular problem. Either method may be resisted by the other group-members, although the interpretative method is less likely to be seen as manipulative.

3 Face-to-Face versus Computer-mediated Communication

Having introduced the facilitator's role in its traditional sense, this section will give a brief comparison of face-to-face and computer-mediated communication, prior to investigating 'electronic' facilitators, and their role in CSCW.

Face-to-face communication can be broken down into audio and visual channels, with each being decomposed further, as shown in figure 2 (Hiltz & Turoff, 1978). This model of face-to-face communication illustrates the richness of the medium, thus allowing a facilitator many ways of monitoring, and intervening in the group process, in a face-to-face meeting.

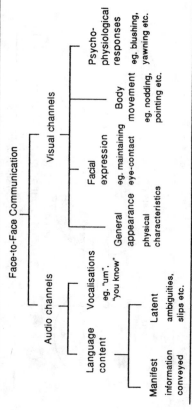

Figure 2: Face-to-face Communication Model

Communicating via computers replaces the above channels with (usually) a single visual channel conveying the language content. This can have a number of effects on the quality of communication, and obviously has implications for the facilitator's role in the group. Some of the differences are outlined below.

3.1 Extra Visual Channel

The written form of computer mediated communication provides an additional visual channel for participants to utilise. The use of indentation, numbering, capital letters, and spacing enables individuals to structure their communication, thus aiding comprehension by the message's recipients.

3.2 Expression

The visual channels convey information about the speaker and hearer's feelings as well as enabling the use of gestures to reinforce what is being said. Without this information, participants can only treat messages on 'face value', being without access to any signals that may indicate deliberate misinformation, for example, on the part of the 'speaker' (eg. lack of eye contact).

3.3 Precision

Not only are individuals able to structure their messages, they can take as long as they wish to do so, taking time to ensure that what they write is expressed correctly. This leads to more organised communication than is usually observed in a face-to-face situation.

3.4 Participation

Without the information about people's general appearance etc. being conveyed, individuals from the groups in society that are traditionally discriminated against (eg. women, disabled people, or people of different ethnic origin), stand more chance of being treated according to what they say rather than what they look like.[1]

3.5 Turn-Taking

In face-to-face communication, the cues governing turn-taking in conversation are usually conveyed as vocalisations, through body language, and by facial

---

1   This could only now be said to apply to the more primitive mailing systems that provide very little information about the sender. It also assumes that the sender does not, intentionally or unintentionally, reveal the information. eg. in their message style.

Facilitating (moderating) computer conferencing systems is seen as a means of reducing communication problems that are due to the lack of the face-to-face communication channels. Whilst it is acknowledged that a conference can be successful in the absence of a facilitator, this is the exception to the rule (Brochet, 1985). Feenberg (1986) outlines seven functions that characterise the role of the facilitator in computer conferences, these are: Setting the contexts, setting the norms, setting the agenda, recognition, prompting, weaving[2], and meta-commenting.

If the last four of the above items are shared by other members of the group, the conference is likely to be more successful, in fact, Feenberg (1986) states that they are listed as functions of the moderator more to ensure that they are carried out, rather than being exclusive to the facilitating role.

Brochet (1985) gives a different classification in terms of what stage the conference is at. The stages given are:

• Successful beginnings;
• Nurturing the introductory stages;
• Maintaining the mature conference; and
• Wrapping up the conference.

Successful beginnings is concerned with the setting up of the conference - deciding on the topic, setting an agenda, inviting potential participants, etc. Also included at this stage are activities such as organising training on the system to be used; introductory 'parties', where participants may meet face-to-face; and maybe also organising an initial face-to-face meeting to get the conference started. Kerr (1986) also encourages the setting-up of a face-to-face training session to assist group cohesion.

The introductory stages require nurturing on three levels: firstly, the facilitator must ensure that both system hardware and software are available and serviceable; secondly, the facilitator needs to set ground-rules and norms regarding, for example, defining success for the group, group decision-making process(es) used, and copyright issues; finally, the facilitator is responsible for stimulating discussion and identifying new topics.

During the 'mature' stages of the conference, the facilitator plays a number of roles to maintain participation and cohesion amongst the members of the conference. Brochet (1985) gives these roles as: organiser; goal-setter; discriminator[3]; host; explainer; and entertainer. The facilitator must ensure that discussion does not stray off the agreed topic of the conference, if necessary highlighting the need for a separate conference to be set up for the discussion of matters arising from the present topic.

---

[2] This function in particular illustrates an effect of the communication medium on the facilitator's role. Here, the phenomena of multiple turns in messages (Bowers & Churcher, 1988) necessitates the 'weaving' together of threads of one conversation across many messages.

[3] As in discriminating between useful and useless ideas, and in helping to make complex matters simple.

---

expression (Levinson, 1983). Therefore, the removal of the audio and visual channels in computer-mediated communication interferes with the normal turn-taking mechanisms. This affects synchronous, rather than asynchronous communication, with messages in the latter mode potentially taking up more than one turn in a conversation (Bowers & Churcher, 1988).

4 The Facilitator in CSCW

A broadly accepted framework for the study of CSCW systems classifies the type of work according to its temporal and geographical distribution (eg. (Cook, Ellis, Graf, Rein & Smith, 1987), (Ellis, Gibbs & Rein, 1991)). In this two-dimensional space, four types of cooperative working can be identified (see figure 3). These working types correspond to four different meeting types, or scenarios, in which the cooperative work is supported by computers. The remainder of this section will concentrate on two of these scenarios, and the implications on the role of a group facilitator in each one is discussed.

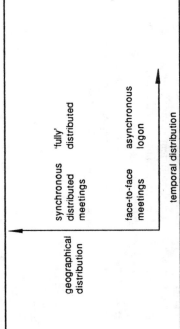

Figure 3: CSCW Scenarios

4.1 'Fully' Distributed

This is the longest established type of computer-mediated communication, and (probably because of this) the only scenario for which specific research on the facilitator's role was found (known usually in this context as the *moderator* (Brochet, 1985), (Feenberg, 1986), (Kerr, 1986)). Computer Conferencing systems, or Bulletin Board systems, have been in use since the late 1960's, and numerous examples exist in both academic and industrial contexts (Quarterman & Hoskins, 1986), encompassing early systems, such as EIES (Hiltz & Turoff, 1978) through to recent Computer-Based Messaging Systems, such as COSMOS (Young, 1988).

It is helpful to announce the 'wrapping-up' of a conference well in advance, as this type of announcement can quite often lead to a flurry of last-minute contributions. The facilitator should close the conference down in two stages: firstly making it into a 'read-only' conference, allowing participants to copy any information they wish to keep; then finally 'purging' the conference from the system.

In this scenario, the facilitator must assist the group as in a face-to-face meeting, whilst working via a modified communication medium as described in section 3. Important cues used by the facilitator in face-to-face settings are now missing, and the asynchronous nature of this scenario requires her/him to work with the group over days or weeks rather than minutes or hours. Support for the facilitator in this scenario, therefore, must compensate for these aspects of the communication medium that make her/his job harder. Without specific support, for example, the facilitator will not know how much the different members are participating, other than through the number and length of messages transmitted. The system, however, is able to monitor such things as login frequency, messages that have not been read by individuals, activity on text editors etc. This information can be provided to the facilitator in such a way as to supplement her/his 'picture' of the group's performance, and to enable her/him to facilitate more effectively.

4.2 Computer-Supported Meetings

Participants in this type of meeting are able to use all of the usual face-to-face channels, in addition to the extra visual channel provided by computer-mediated communication. It is unlikely, however, that both types of communication will be used simultaneously to their full; experiences indicating that participants will switch between the two (see, eg. Foster & Stefik (1986)). The facilitator, therefore, will also need to switch to whichever means of communication the other group members are using at the time.

This type of cooperative working is the focus for a growing number of research projects and systems, with more established examples being Colab at Xerox PARC (Foster & Stefik, 1986), (Stefik, Bobrow, Foster, Lanning & Tatar, 1987), and Project Nick at MCC (Cook et al., 1987). Of the two projects, Colab appears to 'hard-wire' the role of the facilitator by incorporating it into the processes of its tools. For example, the Cognoter tool (Foster & Stefik, 1986) structures a group's efforts in collaboratively organising their thoughts for the purpose of making a presentation. With this tool, the process is supported in three stages: brainstorming; ordering; and evaluation, with the participants guided through the process by the tool. Whilst noting the danger of the tool being too prescriptive, they also recognise that a 'funneling' environment would assist group-members to achieve their goals in a more efficient manner. In other words, the tool implements some aspects of the facilitator's role and 'imposes' this facilitation through the structuring of the process.

Project Nick (Cook et al., 1987), however, supports a human facilitator with the provision of the following features: there is a means for the facilitator to record the group-process activities using minimal keystrokes/mouse movements; in addition to this, there is an allowance for other group-members to communicate comments about the group-process to the facilitator. The facilitator is thus able to keep a record of, for example, how much time is spent participating in the group process by the various individual members, and therefore monitor over or under participation, as well as keep an overall record of the time taken for different agenda items etc. Furthermore, explicit comments on members' feelings about the group process (eg. boredom, need to push on, etc.) can be received by the facilitator to enhance the information that s/he has collected through her/his participation in the group session. This information can be used to facilitate the group in a more effective manner and will supplement the facilitator's impressions of the group process obtained through observing the members' interactions, as in face-to-face communication.

In this scenario, therefore, the facilitator has a larger choice of communication channels to use for monitoring the group process. At the same time, s/he has the same increased choice of channel to use when making interventions. For example, eye contact can be utilised to prevent an interruption with less distraction for the other group members. Similarly, there is less need to prevent sub-groups or side-discussions from forming since these also can take place, to a large extent, without distraction for the other members of the group.[4] Means to monitor such communication, that is potentially detrimental to the group's working together as a unit, should be provided for the facilitator. The extent to which such monitoring could take place - should facilitators be allowed to 'tap' private conversations, or should they only be provided information regarding who is talking to whom, and how often? - is an area for debate, dependant upon how much 'power' is desirable for a facilitator to have over other group members.

5 Allocation of Tasks

When allocating tasks for a computer system between the computer and its user(s), the extent to which the tasks are automated can be looked at as a continuum between no support (a completely human system) through to full support (a completely automated system). These two extremes, however, will not be considered here. Considering the importance of the facilitator's role, to provide computer support for a group without specifically supporting the facilitator is to make the task of facilitating the group harder, and less effective. Furthermore, group facilitation is an essentially human task, which if carried out by computer

---

4   There are obviously limits to this as a sub-group or side-discussion could take over the discussion for the whole group, with those not involved unaware except for their knowledge of keyboards being used without any resultant messages appearing on their screens.

alone will not be fulfilled sufficiently. This section will consider, therefore, how computer support can augment the role of the facilitator in terms of her/his individual tasks, and group tasks.

5.1 Support for Individual Tasks

The individual tasks referred to here are the tasks that a facilitator carries out when working with a group, that are private to the facilitator. Over and above the tools that each member of the group will possess to support their tasks (for example, word processing facilities, 'notebook', graphics generation, database access etc.), there are tasks specific to a facilitator that must also be supported. These facilitator support tools should be aimed at supporting the tasks that are seen as the facilitator's responsibility, and will include: time-keeping aids; monitoring of the group in terms of degree of participation of each member; creation and maintenance of an agenda; and support for administrative tasks.

These support tools are therefore aimed at the level of collecting and structuring information about the group to enable the facilitator to make 'better informed' decisions and to facilitate more effectively. For example, an agenda creation and maintenance tool could be combined with a time-keeping aid in order to set points in the agenda that should be reached by a certain time (in order to coordinate with another group working on a related task perhaps). These times should be agreed upon by the whole group during its initial stages and the tool can then keep the facilitator informed as to how well the group is running to schedule. The emphasis here, then, is that any such tool is providing information, not directives, and how the group is conducted is still down to the judgement of the individual facilitator. In a similar vein, providing a monitoring tool will enable a facilitator to have a clear picture of which group-members are monopolising the discussion, or conversely, which members are under-participating. Once again, the tool should be aimed at providing the facilitator with structured information that can be acted upon, or not, as decided by the individual facilitator.

5.2 Support for Group Tasks

In contrast with the above, this allocation of tasks sees the computer taking a more 'active' role in group facilitation. In essence, this is an extension of the above allocation, with the computer automating part of the facilitator's role, rather than just supporting it. Obviously, it would be easy to propose that the tools required in such a system would simply continue with the information as structured by the tools mentioned above, and act upon it according to some heuristics. Whilst this sounds fine in theory, decisions would have to be made in practice as to whether group members will find computer-made interventions desirable. Similarly, the parts of the facilitator role that are automated should not require other members of

the group to modify the way in which they interact with each other, as this would almost certainly be resisted (Grudin, 1988).

Another aspect of the facilitator's role that could be automated is the support of decision-making procedures. Kraemer & King (1986), review a number of group-support technologies and includes three methods of automating the group decision-making process. These *structured group process* methods are: social judgement analysis, delphi technique; and nominal group technique.

In reviewing the above, McGrath (1984) notes that when compared with interactive groups (as opposed to structured), all the methods perform better than the average, but significantly worse than the 'best individual' performance (they actually perform at about the same level as second best individual). It can be seen, therefore, that whilst they can all potentially be automated, they are by no means perfect.

One further area that has potential for automation is the monitoring of over and under participation of the group-members. This monitoring would take different forms dependent upon the scenario in which it is used. Essentially, this would go one step further than the supported individual task of reporting the amount of participation to the facilitator by the system. Rather than structuring the information to enable the facilitator to make better informed interventions, the system itself would make the interventions, perhaps by informing participants of the proportion of group participation they 'are responsible for', if they exceed or fall below certain limits. As mentioned above, the way in which system interventions are made will have to be decided upon carefully to avoid putting off people from becoming members of the group.

6 Conclusion

The omission, to a large extent, of any consideration for the role of the facilitator in CSCW systems was the impetus for the work presented in this paper. The facilitator is a well established and important role in 'traditional' group work, existing to enable the other members of a group to achieve the group's objectives by assisting them in negotiating any problems that may occur.

Communicating via computer has a number of effects on the interaction between members of a group, and therefore on the actions undertaken by the facilitator when performing her/his duties. These effects differ depending upon the 'scenario' in which the interaction takes place, but are primarily due to the removal of the face-to-face channels of communication, the addition of a new computer-mediated channel, and interaction between usage of the two types of channel.

To provide support for a group without also supporting the group's facilitator is an omission which inevitably will be detrimental to the effectiveness of the group. Therefore, support for the facilitator's role must be considered when designing CSCW systems. How the role could, or should, be supported is a matter for further research. The extent to which the role is supported, or automated, in particular CSCW systems will depend on the application concerned. Consideration must be given, however, to the effect that this support will have on the facilitator, and especially on the other members of the group.

Acknowledgements

I would like to thank Martin Lea (Department of Psychology, University of Manchester) and Linda Macaulay (Department of Computation, UMIST) for their encouragement and assistance throughout the production of this paper. This paper is the result of work funded by a SERC Advanced Course Studentship at the University of Manchester Department of Psychology.

References

Bannon, L.J. & Schmidt, K. (1989): "CSCW: four characters in search of a context", in J.Bowers & S.Benford (ed.): *EC-CSCW'89: Proceedings of the First European Conference on Computer Supported Cooperative Work*, Computer Sciences Company, Gatwick, UK, pp. 358-372.

Bowers, J. & Churcher, J. (1988): "Local and global structuring of computer mediated communication: developing linguistic perspectives on CSCW in COSMOS", in I.Greif (ed.): *CSCW'88 Proceedings of the Conference on Computer-Supported Cooperative Work*, ACM, Portland, Oregon, pp. 125-139.

Brochet, M.G. (1985): "Effective moderation of computer conferences: notes and suggestions", in M.Brochet (ed.): *17th Ontario Universities Computing Conference Proceedings*, pp. 123-130.

Cook, P., Ellis, C., Graf, M., Rein, G. & Smith, T. (1987): "Project Nick: meetings augmentation and analysis", *ACM Transactions on Office Information Systems*, vol. 5, no. 2, pp. 132-146.

Douglas, T. (1970): *A Decade of Small Group Theory, 1960-1970*, Bookstall Publications, London.

Ellis, C.A., Gibbs, S.J. & Rein, G.L. (1991): "Groupware: some issues and experiences", *Communications of the ACM*, vol. 34. no. 1, pp. 38-58.

Feenberg, A. (1986): "Network design: an operating manual for computer conferencing", *IEEE Transactions on Professional Communications*, vol. PC29, no. 1, pp. 2-7.

Foster, G. & Stefik, M. (1986): "Cognoter, theory and practice of a Colab-orative tool", in D.Petersen (ed.): *CSCW'86- Proceedings of the Conference on Computer-Supported Cooperative Work*, ACM, Austin, Texas, pp. 7-15.

Greif, I. (1988): "Overview", in I.Greif (ed.): *Computer Supported Cooperative Work: A Book of Readings*, Morgan Kaufmann Publishers Inc., San Mateo, CA. pp. 5-12.

Grudin, J. (1988): "Why CSCW applications fail: problems in the design and evaluation of organisational interfaces", in I.Greif (ed.): *CSCW'88 Proceedings of the Conference on Computer-Supported Cooperative Work*, ACM, Portland, Oregon, pp. 85-93.

Heap, K. (1968): *The Social Group Worker as Central Person*, Case Conference, Cited in Douglas (1970).

Hiltz, S.R. & Turoff, M. (1978): *The Network Nation. Human Communication via Computer*, Addison-Wesley, Reading, MA.

Kerr, E.B. (1986): "Electronic leadership: a guide to moderating online conferences", *IEEE Transactions on Professional Communications*, vol. PC29, no. 1, pp. 12-18.

Kraemer, K. & King, J.L. (1986): "Computer-based systems for cooperative work and group decision making: status of use and problems in development", in D.Petersen (ed.): *CSCW'86- Proceedings of the Conference on Computer-Supported Cooperative Work*, ACM, Austin, Texas, pp. 353-375.

Levinson, S.C. (1983): *Pragmatics*, Cambridge University Press, Cambridge.

McGrath, J.E. (1984): *Groups: Interaction and Performance*, Prentice-Hall, Englewood Cliffs.

Quarterman, J.S. & Hoskins, J.C. (1986): "Notable computer networks", *Communications of the ACM*, vol. 29, no. 10, pp. 932-971.

Redl, F. (1942): "Types of group formation, group emotion and leadership.", *Psychiatry*, vol. V, no. 4.

Smith, M., Beck, J., Cooper, C.L., Cox, C., Ottaway, D. & Talbot, R. (1982): *Introducing Organisational Behaviour*, Macmillan, Houndmills.

Stefik, M.. Bobrow, D.G., Foster, G., Lanning, S. & Tatar, D. (1987): "WYSIWIS revised: early experiences with multiuser interfaces", *ACM Transactions on Office Information Systems*, vol. 5, no. 2, pp. 147-167.

Westley, F. & Waters, J.A. (1988): "Group facilitation skills for managers", *Management Education and Development*, vol. 19, no. 2, pp. 134-143.

Whitaker, D.S. (1985): *Using Groups to Help People*, Tavistock/Routledge, London.

Young, R.E. (1988) (ed.): *Interim Report on the Cosmos Project*, Cosmos Coordinators Office, Queen Mary College, London.

Reprinted from *The Social Psychology of Telecommunications*, pp. 43-60. © 1976, John Wiley & Sons. Reproduced by permission of John Wiley and Sons Limited.

Visual Communication and Social Interaction

John Short, Ederyn Williams, and Bruce Christie

THE ROLE OF 'MEDIUM' IN THE COMMUNICATION PROCESS

As we saw at the beginning of Chapter 3 the word 'communication' has been used at different times with a wide variety of meanings; however, for our immediate purposes we shall use one of the more familiar social psychological definitions, that proposed by Cherry (1957): 'the physical signals whereby one individual can influence the behaviour of another'. It is readily apparent that constraints on these physical signals could affect the influence each individual has on the other. We use the term 'medium of communication' to describe the system of constraints on the physical signals available in any particular situation. Psychologists and others have long given extensive consideration to the ways in which one individual can influence the behaviour of another and the expression 'the medium is the message' has virtually achieved the status of a cliché. Surprisingly, however, in relation to the total effort expended on the investigation of social interaction, 'medium',—this apparently fundamental complex of variables—has received remarkably little attention.

Investigators have probed such points as whether or not one should counter the arguments available to the other side or simply give a partisan one-sided message. But scarcely anyone has looked into the question of whether or not one is more persuasive if physically present. The conditions conducive to effective problem solving have been extensively investigated but although the question of whether problems are solved more effectively when people are brought together in groups than when they merely act as individuals is a familiar issue, little effort has been expended on the means by which they are brought together. Do they need to be physically present to produce any sort of 'group cohesion'? Is audio contact sufficient to produce synergistic effects, or is visual feedback as to the reactions of others essential to effective group interaction? Again medium of communication is an almost forgotten variable.

The new media discussed in Chapter 1 are primarily directed at remedying what is the most obvious defect of the simple telephone—the fact that one cannot see the other person or group. Thus in discussing the effectiveness of these visual media, the fundamental question is—what is lacking in telephone communication that is present in face-to-face communication? If it is simply the lack of the visual channel, what sort of visual channel need be provided? In short, what is the function of the visual channel?

GENERAL FUNCTIONS OF NON-VERBAL SIGNALS AND THE EFFECTS OF MEDIUM

In normal face-to-face interaction, the participants exchange in addition to the verbal material, a range of non-verbal cues such as facial expression, direction of gaze, posture, dress and physical distance. Birdwhistell (1970) distinguishes two types of function for these cues. The first is directly concerned with the passage of information from one individual to another, the second is concerned with the 'integrational aspects' of the communication process. Integrational activity includes all behaviour that 'keeps the system in operation, regulates the interaction process, cross-references particular messages to comprehensibility in a particular context and relates the particular context to the larger contexts of which the interaction is but a special situation' (Birdwhistell, 1970).

Of the six functions for non-verbal cues during face-to-face interaction listed by Argyle (1969) three could be classified as integrational and three as informational. Starting with the three integrational functions, Argyle's six functions are as follows.

(1) *Mutual attention and responsiveness.* During the conversation there must be continuous evidence that the other is attending and responding. This is done chiefly by eye-gaze, head nods and gestures. However, mutual attention can also be signalled by brief utterances such as 'yes', 'ah ha', 'ummm' and so on. These are used in ordinary conversation and should function perfectly to take over the load borne by non-verbal signals. The fact that most people are practised in telephone conversation makes this replacement still more likely.

(2) *Channel control.* Head nods and eye movements are used in determining who shall speak and for how long. Interactors do not appear to be aware of making or receiving these signals. This function is likely to be more seriously affected by the removal of the visual cues. Argyle, Lalljee and Cook (1968) found that during two-person conversations there were more pauses and interruptions when the visual cues were reduced. Cook and Lalljee (1972) compared the conversation of subjects communicating face-to-face and those communicating over a microphone–loudspeaker system. They found that there were fewer interruptions, utterances differed in length and there were more requests for repeats in the no-vision condition. The explanation suggested for the unexpected result of more interruptions in the visible condition was that the subjects were more confident in their placing of interruptions. Jaffe and Feldstein (1970) found less

simultaneous speech in the no-vision condition together with shorter pauses both between and within speeches. Kasl and Mahl (1965) found more filled pauses in a no-vision condition. There is thus abundant, although sometimes conflicting, evidence of changes in conversational behaviour with the removal of the visual channel.

There is some evidence that such disturbances in conversational behaviour can be reflected in changes in more directly outcome-related measures. For instance, Miller and Hewgill (1964) found that when non-fluencies such as pauses were varied, ratings of the speaker on competence and power (although not trustworthiness) were lowered (similarly Sharp and McClung, 1966).

(3) *Feedback.* In order to plan his utterances, the speaker needs to know how the other is reacting to what has gone before. Non-verbal signals may sensitively track agreement or disagreement and other moment-to-moment changes in affect. In this respect, it is an important property of non-verbal signalling that it can go on simultaneously with verbal communication without interrupting it. If the visual channel is removed, the speaker must wait for a verbal reply from the listener before he has any feedback on his remarks. This could be sufficiently serious to lead to changes in the conversational topic: people might avoid topics (e.g. personal matters) where, lacking feedback, embarrassment or misunderstanding seems too probable. Speakers normally adapt the on-going message to the responses of the recipient (whether he is happy, comprehending, surprised, annoyed, etc.). The removal of this feedback could impair the efficiency of the adaptation of the message to the listener, and thus lower the speaker's persuasive impact. Consequently, one would expect that tasks on which the present behaviour of one individual is maximally contingent on the moment-to-moment affective reactions of the other, would be maximally sensitive to variation in the medium.

(4) *Illustrations.* Speech is accompanied by gestures of the hands which may be used to illustrate an object or action, to point to objects or directions, or for emphasis. The informational redundancy introduced by gesture will improve the clarity of the message (confirmed experimentally by Popelka and Berger, 1971). For articulate subjects this illustrative function is likely to be readily replaceable by words if the video channel is removed. But to the extent that this replacement does not occur, some of the impact of the message may be dissipated. 'The heart is stirred more slowly by the ear than by the eye', wrote Horace in his *Art of Poetry.*

(5) *Emblems.* This term is used to refer to gestures being used instead of a word, for instance a head-shake for 'No'. Except in special circumstances (such as the deaf) this category can be considered as less important than the others. It is in any case, by definition, replaceable by words in the absence of the visual channel.

(6) *Interpersonal attitudes.* Non-verbal cues may be used by the listener as a vital source of information about the speaker's attitude to him and the speaker's intentions of, say, threat. Proximity, gesture, facial expression and eye-gaze—all the cues discussed earlier—may be used as sources of this affective information. Non-verbal cues can indicate changes in a relationship, for example the change from a relaxed to a more formal posture. Information is also conveyed about the speaker's affective reaction (pride, uncertainty, embarrassment or whatever) to what may be verbally a completely emotion-free statement. Thus, Argyle also includes under this heading the information about how the communicator sees himself and would like to be treated. For instance, Rosenfeld (1966) showed that subjects seeking approval smiled more and used more head nods.

Function (3) ('feedback') is to a large extent just a particularly important special instance of the interpersonal attitudes function. The former is primarily concerned with moment-to-moment changes (the perception of which is particularly liable to be affected by medium) and the latter with more long-term changes in affect. These two functions are together by far the most important functions of the visual signalling lacking in audio-only communication.

While there has been very little discussion of the functions of the visual channel as a whole, there has been a considerable amount of research into the functions of the individual cues. Wiener and Mehrabian (1968) point out that each channel is likely to be differentially used according to its effectiveness for sending different types of information. Thus although certain common functions may be discerned, it would be wrong to expect each channel to carry the same kind of messages. Space does not permit a comprehensive review of the literature for each individual channel, but the following sections summarize some of the key literature to illustrate the principal role of the visual channel—the provision of feedback on interpersonal attitudes.

PROXIMITY AND ORIENTATION

Physical separation is perhaps the factor which is most obviously varied when communication is by a telecommunications link rather than face-to-face. There is now a considerable volume of work on the importance of the distance at which people choose to converse, Hall (1963) suggests a four-point classification of degrees of proximity: up to 1½ ft 'intimate', 1½ to 4 ft 'personal', 4 to 12 ft 'social' and more than 12 ft 'public'. Each distance is thought appropriate for the activity after which it is named. Different non-verbal cues are thought to be relevant at different ranges; for example, pupil size may be relevant at the intimate distance (Hess, 1965) but at the public distance even eye-contact (mutual gaze) can no longer be discriminated sufficiently accurately to be useful. The distinction between these four degrees of proximity has never been demonstrated other than theoretically.

A variety of independent variables have been shown to affect the preferred distance for conversation. The simplest of these is culture: Arabs tend to sit closer than Americans (Watson and Graves, 1966) and British subjects in Cook's (1971) experiments showed positional preferences different from those of Sommer's (1965) American subjects. Personality factors are also relevant: extroverts tend to approach the experimenter more closely than do introverts (Patterson and Holmes, 1966). Argyle and Dean (1965) asked subjects to stand at a comfortable distance from (a) a life-size photograph, (b) the first author with his eyes shut and (c) the first author with his eyes open. Subjects stood closer when the author had his eyes shut than when open, and closer to the photograph than to the real person.

Although the material in the previous paragraph adds up to fairly convincing evidence that the distance people select for their conversation is not random, and a particular distance is preferred, precisely what is signalled by proximity is not clear. There have been attempts to demonstrate that distance can directly determine people's perceptions of one another: Porter, Argyle and Salter (1970) varied the distance between a confederate and the subject (3, 4 or 8 ft). However, proximity did not account for a significant proportion of the variance on any of the 21 rating scales. It could be argued that the variations in distance used in this study were not substantial. On the other hand, Scherer and Schiff (1973) found that perceived 'intimacy' increased as distance decreased (6, 4½ or 3 ft). Patterson and Sechrest (1970), using an interview situation with a stooge seated at different distances, found a significant negative relationship between distance (2, 4, 6 or 8 ft) and ratings of 'friendly', 'aggressive', 'dominant' and 'extroverted'. At the closer distance, this relationship was reversed, perhaps because of compensatory behaviour. Such compensation also appeared in an experiment by Argyle and Dean (1965) who found that visual interaction was reduced at close distances. To summarize: although there is substantial evidence that distance may be an indicative cue (relevant information for an outside observer), the evidence that it is of communicative worth (relevant for the participants) is uncertain.

Nevertheless, despite this uncertain evidence of communicative use, and doubts about what is signalled by proximity, proximity is important because there is evidence that it can affect the outcome of quite complex tasks. Albert and Dabbs (1970) investigated the variation of attitude change with distance of the communicator (1½, 4½ or 14 ft). Attitude change on the topic of the message was found to decrease linearly as distance decreased, being in fact contrary to the advocated direction at the closest distance. Selective attention to the message was found to be greatest at the middle distance (the conventionally appropriate distance) while, at either the excessively close or the excessively far distance, attention was apparently shifted to the physical appearance of the speaker. Ratings of the speaker on

scales such as 'warm', 'sensitive', 'friendly', were not affected by distance. These results suggest that there may be an optimal distance (which probably varies with task) and that departures in either direction can impair performance. Sensenig, Reed and Miller (1972) had pairs of subjects play the Prisoner's Dilemma game (a simple game requiring a succession of choices between a cooperative and competitive strategy) seated either physically close or separated by a substantial distance (3 ft and 20 ft respectively). With greater distance, there were significantly fewer cooperative choices, smaller earnings and greater differences in outcome between the two players. In the 'far' condition, cooperative choices were practically non-existent in the later trials.

People select a particular orientation for their conversation just as they select a particular distance. For a competitive task people tend to sit opposite one another, while for a cooperative task the side-by-side position is preferred (Sommer 1965). McBride, King and James (1965) found that physiological arousal as measured by the galvanic skin response increases as a person gets closer to another and that this increase is greater for an approach from the front than for an approach from the side. Orientation may be important to the design of video systems: video systems impose an orientation (opposite one another) on the participants in a way in which neither an audio system nor face-to-face do (a very unnatural picture would result if the camera were not mounted in the vicinity of the monitor, i.e. opposite the subject). Evidence as to the effects of orientation is as yet too scant to make any hard predictions.

The influence of physical proximity on a telecommunicated interaction will be somewhat different from the influence on a face-to-face interaction. Behaviour concerned with approach and avoidance is simply not possible in a telephone interaction. One reason why proximity is important in face-to-face interaction is the effect it has on the salience of other non-verbal signals. In telephone conversation this ceases to be relevant and in conversation over a video link the analogous factor of image size is unlikely to be under the conscious control of the participants, being principally determined by the design of the camera and studio.

There is still, however, the possibility of effects of medium determined by the apparent (or psychological) proximity. The psychological proximity of a telephone contact is open to conjecture. It is probably affected by knowledge of actual physical location, system quality, task content, acquaintance with the other and many other factors. It does seem most probable that a telephone contact is apparently further away than any face-to-face contact, if only by analogy with the usual physical distance of a telephone contact (though McLuhan, 1964, argues the reverse). There is thus the important possibility that proximity, although unreal as a cue in any physical sense, may distort the interaction by imposing a constant distant level of apparent proximity on the interaction.

Some evidence to support such a hypothesis was produced in an experiment by Stapley (1972) in which subjects were asked to match the apparent sizes of a live face and a television picture. It was consistently found that the television picture had to produce a much larger retinal image to have the same apparent proximity.

It seems likely, then, that differences in apparent physical proximity produced by different media relate not only to the size of the retinal image of the other given by the system, but also to the 'social presence' engendered by the medium. The concept of 'social presence' will be more thoroughly discussed in Chapter 5, and we shall thus leave this line of thought until that chapter.

PHYSICAL APPEARANCE

In everyday life, physical appearance constitutes a very important source of information for individuals who do not know one another. In fact, initial judgements (apart from what is known in advance) must be made entirely on the basis of physical appearance. Thus, Thornton (1944) found that confederates wearing glasses were rated as more intelligent and industrious than those not wearing glasses. The effects, however, are only short-lived, for Argyle and McHenry (1971) demonstrated that they wore off rapidly with further acquaintance. There is evidence too that the outcome of interactions may be affected by variations in physical attractiveness (Singer, 1964) or by style of dress.

Thus, at least in interactions with strangers, physical appearance is one important cue which is not available in the absence of the visual channel. The effects of medium can be expected to vary with the level of acquaintance; that is to say, the video channel would be expected to be more useful for interactions with strangers than for interactions with familiar persons.

DYNAMIC NON-VERBAL SIGNALS FROM THE TRUNK AND ARMS

The dynamic non-verbal signals used in conversation can usefully be subdivided into those emitted from the regions of the body below the neck and those from above the neck (Ekman, 1965). We will consider first the information that can be derived from the lower region—the arms and trunk.

The simplest dynamic source of information is posture: standing, sitting, slouching, etc. Everyday experience, for instance in the interview situation, confirms that posture can be used as a source of information about personality and mood: is the other confident or relaxed, respectful or aggressive?

There is some laboratory work on the nature of the inferences made from posture. For example, James (1932), unfortunately only using still photographs of a masked male model, found four dimensions of posture on which subjects were able to agree on an interpretation; position of the head and trunk were found to be the most important indicators, with hand and arm position allowing for discrimination within the categories. Mehrabian (1968) also teased out some specific cues: forward lean of the trunk was found to convey a positive attitude towards the other, higher rates of gesticulation, smaller reclining angles, more head nodding and lower rate of self-manipulation were associated with greater perceived and intended persuasiveness. It could be argued that experiments such as this only demonstrate the existence of cultural stereotypes as to the meaning of various postures, but the existence of such stereotypes is difficult to explain if they do not, at least under some circumstances, form a basis of judgement.

As well as the everyday experience and laboratory evidence mentioned so far, there is also some observational evidence that subjects do respond to the cues emitted by the other. Scheflen (1965), for instance, showed that the posture of one person in a therapy group is related to that of the others with implications for his relationship to the others: for example, a posture consonant with others in the group may indicate sympathetic agreement.

Posture can only be changed at a relatively slow rate. The information capacity of this channel is therefore relatively low compared to that of the verbal channel. It is most appropriate for information relevant to long-term aspects of the conversation, acting as a background for the interpretation of other channels; mood changes only slowly through the interaction, and personality, also signalled by posture, does not change. Posture is, of course, a cue that is not available in the absence of the visual channel. If a picture of the other person is provided (perhaps by a television system) posture may or may not be available as a cue depending on the type of picture: if the picture is just of the head, as with many videophone devices, almost all the information from posture will be lost. If a more complete picture is provided, the postural cues will be retained, but at some trade-off against the smaller signals (such as eye movements) which are less visible with a more remote picture.

FACIAL SIGNALS

It is everyday experience that information is derived from people's facial expressions: are they surprised, interested, happy, sad, angry and so on? Indeed there are few nameable emotions which the very large literature has not investigated in relation to facial expression. Such work assumes that there are discrete emotional states such as 'joy', 'fear', 'anger' and indeed even more complex emotions such as 'pity',

The variety of possible facial movements (Birdwhistell, 1968, lists 33 discrete movements or 'kinemes' associated with the face) taken with the rapidity of transition between these kinemes, probably accounts for the fact that, at least in our culture, the face is the most expressive part of the body. It is also the part of the body that is most visible and most attended to during interaction and thus usually the area that is most consciously controlled.

In line with Wiener and Mehrabian's (1968) remark that different channels can be expected to carry different types of information according to their suitability, there has been some theorizing about the different types of information communicated by facial and bodily cues. Ekman (1965) found the head to be more informative about the nature of the emotion (whether the person is angry, sad, etc.) while the body is more informative about the intensity of the emotion. If correct, this hypothesis would explain why research on the interpretation of non-verbal cues, has concentrated largely on the facial cues rather than the bodily cues. From arguments based on the relative sending capacities of the different channels, the extent to which they are under conscious control and the sender's awareness of the channel attended to, Ekman and Friesen (1969) suggest that the body and feet would be the most useful cues in the identification of lying. They may provide information at variance with the carefully controlled verbal and facial signals. Experiments provided partial support for this hypothesis. Deception situations may thus be a special case in which the body cues are particularly important. In such a situation, a video picture showing the whole person (as opposed to just the head) would be particularly useful. In other situations, the head is the most crucial region and accordingly a larger picture of the head would be more useful.

There is a limited amount of experimental material to support Ekman's (1965) hypothesis that the face is used in the recognition of emotion and the body in the judgement of intensity. Shapiro, Foster and Powell (1968) found that in judging genuineness, empathy and warmth in therapists, subjects responded more to facial than body cues; with body cues alone performance was negligible. Dittman (1962) found that high degrees of emotional arousal were accompanied by body movements which could not, however, be interpreted as meaning anything specific.

Whatever the relative importance of facial and bodily cues, there can be no doubt that both can constitute an important source of information about the mood and personality of the other—a source of information removed with the absence of a visual channel.

DIRECTION OF EYE-GAZE

Poets and novelists from Shakespeare to Sartre have long been aware

and that there are standard facial expressions for each. A review by Vine (1970) summarizes several serious inadequacies of these studies: for example, most have relied on still photographs of actors working without any context, to give very exaggerated poses.

However, more recent work by Ekman (1971), using still photographs and unobtrusive filming of facial expressions has shown that there is pan-cultural consistency in both the encoding (i.e. production) and decoding (i.e. interpretation) of facial expressions of emotion. This suggests that the earlier work cannot be easily dismissed as demonstrating merely cultural stereotypes as to the interpretation of posed facial expressions. Rather, it seems that facial expressions are consistent across many cultures, and may even be innately determined, as implied by Darwin (1872).

Another body of work on facial expressions (e.g. Osgood, 1966, Frijda, 1968) has attempted to factor analyse the responses to facial emotions. This is somewhat superior to the other approach, in that it does not rely so heavily on the arbitrary selection by the experimenter of the emotions investigated. However, such work has shed more light on the classification of emotions than on the part played by various non-verbal signals in the recognition of emotions.

There have been attempts to describe all the possible facial and bodily movements after the manner of structural linguistics (Birdwhistell, 1952). Birdwhistell introduced the term 'kinesics' for the description of such visible movements. Speech is typically accompanied by kinesic stress markers in synchrony with the vocal emphasis. For instance, an upward and lateral movement of the head together with elevation of the eyebrows typically appears in conjunction with a rise in pitch at the end of a sentence to indicate an interrogative. This is an example of the way in which non-verbal signals can interact with signals in both verbal and non-verbal channels to elaborate or modify the total message. However, this structuralist approach is concerned with the description of the cues rather than their function and is thus not itself directly productive in attempts to assess the effects of the removal of the cues.

An important limitation of most studies of facial expression is that they have ignored context effects. Contextual effects are known to be important even in the identification of one's own emotion (Schacter and Singer, 1962). They must be much more important in the identification of the emotion of others, for when internal cues are not available identification must depend on the external cues available. Context effects might be expected to be particularly important in situations where there are rapid moment-to-moment changes in the mood of the participants. This could be expected to interact with the other difficulties caused by the absence of the visual channel, thus rendering such tasks particularly sensitive to the absence of the non-verbal cues.

of the importance of gaze in human relationships (Champness, 1970). In the last ten years, psychologists have also turned their attention to this channel. The comparative ease of obtaining objective measures of this gaze may account for the great increase and considerable success of this type of work.

An extensive review by Kendon (1967) describes three functions of gaze. Firstly, 'monitoring', looks at the other can serve to provide feedback at points where this is required: for example, in deciding whether to continue speaking to clarify a point, whether to change the subject, or whether to yield the floor to the other. Gaze also fulfils a 'regulatory' function being related to floor apportionment (when each person speaks in a conversation). A speaker looks away as he starts to speak and terminates his speech with a sustained gaze. A speaker wishing to hold the floor at a pause point, looks away. Inappropriate eye movements are related to non-fluencies and interruptions: if a speaker fails to look up on completion of an utterance, reply is delayed in 71% instead of the ordinary 29% of instances. Finally, there is the 'expressive' function. Kendon's data were collected from recordings of two-person conversations during the course of which it was noted that subjects tended to look away at points of high emotion. Another example of the expressive function is the sustained gaze associated with interruptions and short questions when the speaker 'bears down' on the other.

Eye-gaze can also be a stable measure of individual differences (Exline and Winter, 1965, Exline, 1971). Strongman and Champness (1968) used frequency of looking away from eye contact as a measure of dominance. Consistent dominance hierarchies were found in groups of subjects who met one another in all possible pairs. Absence of this visual channel, apart from disturbing the regulation of the interaction and the integration of one person's behaviour with the other's, removes what is both an important expressive tool and a vital source of information about the other.

MUTUAL GAZE AND ARGYLE'S INTIMACY EQUILIBRIUM

Argyle (1969) suggests that one function of looking is to establish a relationship: for example, a person will look more if he wants to establish a closer relationship. Eye-contact (mutual gaze) is thought to be particularly significant. Argyle and Dean (1965) postulate an optimum level of 'intimacy'. 'Intimacy' is a function of eye-contact, proximity, conversation topic and so on; changes in one will produce compensating changes in the others. The hypothesis was produced in response to the observation that eye-contact is generally sought after, but too much creates discomfort; for instance, eye-contact is reduced when people are placed very close together (Argyle and Dean, 1965, Goldberg *et al.* 1969).

A number of observations were linked by Argyle with the equilibrium of intimacy hypothesis. Exline and Winter (1965) found that a person looks more at someone he likes. Exline (1963) found that people high on affiliative motivation look more in non-competitive than in competitive situations. When the conversation topic is more intimate there is less looking (Exline, Gray and Schuette, 1965). Indications of the predicted compensatory changes in non-verbal expressions of intimacy have also been found (Patterson, 1973). However, the ambiguity as to the direction of causality reduces the predictive power of the theory.

Consider an example to illustrate this. If an audio medium increases the apparent distance and reduces eye-contact, would one predict an increase in the friendliness of the conversation (to restore the optimum level of 'intimacy') or a decrease in the friendliness of the conversation (to be consistent with the level of 'intimacy' suggested by the non-verbal signals)?

Eye-contact has been shown to have communicative as well as indicative worth. Ellsworth and Carlsmith (1968) found that with positive verbal content, frequent eye-contact produces more positive evaluations of a confederate, while, with negative verbal content, frequent eye-contact produces more negative evaluations. The converse result (negative verbal content, frequent eye-contact, more positive evaluations) has also appeared (Scheritz and Helmreich, 1973). Results appear to be dependent on the sex of the dyads and the level of personal involvement in the interaction. Kleck and Nuessle (1968), using silent films of a confederate in conversation with a subject, in which the confederate had either high or low amounts of eye-contact (80% or 15% of the time), found that subjects rated the high eye-contact confederate as friendlier, warmer and so on. Stass and Willis (1967) showed that subjects were more likely to choose as partners for an experiment those with high eye-contact during an introduction than those with low eye-contact. Finally, Nichols and Champness (1971) showed that the galvanic skin responses (palmar sweating) of subjects were greater during periods of eye-contact with another than in periods of unreciprocated gaze; heart rates, too, give indication of greater emotional arousal under condition of eye-contact (Kleinke and Pohlen, 1971).

Many of the above experiments used confederates with a very artificial pattern of looking. One experiment relevant to the intimacy equilibrium theory that did not, was conducted by Champness (unpublished). In any interaction, a chance eye-contact (based on the assumption that subjects do not interact and eye-contact arises by chance) can be obtained:

$$\text{Expected eye-contact} = \frac{\text{A's looking time} \times \text{B's looking time}}{\text{Total time}}$$

Subjects discussed issues on which they were known either to agree or disagree. The discrepancies between the actual eye-contact and the 'expected eye-contact' were examined. There was an interesting effect such that when subjects disagreed there was less eye-contact than expected by chance, while when they agreed there was more than expected by chance.

Eye-contact is thus an important cue that is not available in most video telephone conversation. The visual channel available in most video systems does not restore eye-contact as a cue; it makes things even worse. The camera cannot be placed exactly in line with the picture of the eyes, so if person A thinks he is looking person B in the eye, he will appear to B to be looking elsewhere (shiftily sideways if the camera is mounted on the side, modestly downwards if the camera is mounted above the monitor). The regulatory function of eye-contact may thus be worse than removed, its operation may be reversed. For example, when thinking he is looking away during an utterance, A may look at the camera; on such occasions B may experience eye-contact and take it as his turn to speak. This effect could be sufficient to account for the disturbances in interrupting behaviour found by Champness (1971) when a video condition was compared with an audio and a face-to-face condition. Some experience and training in the use of video systems may be required before such problems are overcome.

Removal of the visual channel prevents the integrative functions of eye-gaze cues. Replacement of the ordinary visual channel by a picture of the other might distort these functions. The same holds for the expressive functions: reducing apparent eye-contact might affect evaluations of the other, vary the intimacy of the conversation and alter the apparent level of conflict. Thus, as was the case with proximity, altering a non-verbal cue (in the video condition) may have very definite negative implications which may be qualitatively and not just quantitatively different from the effects obtained by removing the cue altogether (as in telephone conversation).

In an experiment by Shapiro (1968) trained raters were asked to rate segments of therapy presented via one of three modes (audio only, video only, or audio + video channels). In general, the two partial modes were equal in their agreement with the combined mode, suggesting that the visual cues were as powerful as the auditory cues. Further, as the judges were trained on audio-only material, the procedure was probably biassed against the video mode.

Rowley and Keller (1962) using a procedure involving the operant conditioning of a class of verbal behaviour and employing as reinforcers either the verbalization 'good' or a head nod, found that the verbal reinforcer was significantly more effective. One wonders what would have been the result had the head nod been more vigorous and accompanied by a smile. Another experiment was conducted by Argyle *et al.* (1970). Subjects rated a video recording of a confederate who read three passages in various tones of voice with corresponding facial expression such that the non-verbal information sometimes conflicted with the verbal content of the messages. The results showed that, in this context, the non-verbal cues had more impact than the verbal cues.

Such experiments tackling the relative importance of verbal and non-verbal behaviour are up against an almost insuperable problem in having to choose what non-verbal behaviour and what verbal behaviour are to be compared in efficacy. Furthermore, designs in which the isolated channels are compared are unsatisfactory because it is not clear to what extent the information normally conveyed in one channel can, if necessary, be conveyed by the other; the two types of information can interact. Finally, there is the point that even a source manyfold less important than another source can still have some importance. The only safe conclusion is that the relative importance of the various channels varies according to the particular people, situation and subject matter involved, and attempts to compare them in this way are of dubious value.

Thus, although at first sight relevant, these comparative studies provide only more evidence for the already well-substantiated conclusion that non-verbal behaviours are important sources of information in some circumstances.

COMPARISONS OF VERBAL AND VISUAL COMMUNICATION

Much of the information available in the visual channels is also available in the audio channel from such cues as tone of voice, choice of words, pausing behaviour, and so on. If there is complete duplication of the information (redundancy in the information theory sense of the word) no effects of removing the visual channel would be expected. At the other extreme, if there is no duplication of information between the two channels, the effects of removing the visual channel would depend on the relative importance of the visual and auditory cues. Reality is likely to lie between the two extremes. The relative importance of the two sources of information is thus a matter of some interest. There have been a few investigations of relevance.

Are qualitative comparisons of verbal and non-verbal behaviour any more fruitful in the attempt to assess the implications of the removal of the visual channel? Ruesch (1966) gives a full list of the similarities and differences. The most significant of the differences is the relative sophistication of the verbal system. Most individuals would find it difficult to transmit non-verbally high-level cognitive information such as the possible effects of alteration in the bank rate on inflation. Verbal communication is manifestly coded (language) but non-verbal communication is coded to a much smaller extent. Some meanings are culturally determined and there are special sign languages for the deaf, but most non-verbal signalling is more universal (laughter, shoulder-shrugs and startle reactions for instance, see Ekman, 1971). The information in the non-verbal signals is more of an affective than a cognitive nature.

This is not to deny that affective information is also transmitted via verbal channels, but it does mean that where the affective information is of critical importance, the absence of the visual signals may be particularly damaging to effective communication. Tasks in which two people combine to solve arithmetic problems would, from this point of view, not be expected to be affected by the removal of the visual channel.

What sorts of information are carried specifically by the visual non-verbal channels? One obvious category is that which the visual communicator does not want to express verbally. For example, in an ordinary business context there is something of a taboo on direct expression of attitudes towards others; boredom, similarly, is more likely to be expressed non-verbally than verbally.

A second category of information carried particularly by the visual non-verbal channels is 'unconscious communication'. A series of studies on experimenter bias have shown that non-verbal cues may have considerable effect, even unintentionally. Rosenthal (1967) lists smiles, head-nods and other facial movements among the cues with which the experimenter may unwittingly influence the subject. In mixed-sex interactions, sex-related differences were found in the relative reliance on the visual and auditory channels for such signals, suggesting the possibility of sex differences in reaction to the removal of the visual channel.

MULTICHANNEL COMMUNICATION

A key issue in the interpretation of the literature on the functions of the individual non-verbal signals is the relationship between the various individual channels.

Birdwhistell (1970) pointed out that while communication is 'a continuous process made up of isolable discrete units, these units are multifunctional, they have distinguishable contrast meaning at one level, and cross referencing function at another. *None of these units has meaning in and of itself*.' In attempting to assess the functions of the visual channel, it is therefore dangerous to confine attention at any one time to individual cues such as posture, eye-gaze, proximity and the like. The channels do interact (see for example Argyle and Dean, 1965). In particular one must beware of moving from the observation that a particular channel is 'redundant' (in the strict information theory sense of 'conveying no new information') to the position that it is without function and could be removed without distorting the communication process and outcome. Studies of media must look at relevant combinations of channels. Important overall properties of

communication may be missed if attention is restricted to individual channels.

The addition of the visual channel to the audio-only system represented by the telephone, permits the use of a variety of new signs transmitted in the visual channel. This information must be combined with that from the audio channel. Understanding the communication is thus a bisensory perception task. It is not appropriate to go deeply into the literature on bisensory perception because the experiments and the theory (which draws heavily on signal detection theory) have largely been concerned with the detection of simple physical stimuli (Loveless et al., 1970, for review). Any extrapolation of the results to complex stimuli extended in time such as occur in freely interactive conversations would probably be unwarranted. However, there is one distinction that is relevant in the present context; this is the distinction between the case in which the two channels are both relevant and that in which only one channel is relevant.

The latter case is usually referred to as 'accessory stimulation'. An important practical example of this is noise. There is no simple relationship between noise level and performance; it seems that noise can function either to distract or to alert the subject, depending on the task (Hockey, 1969). The tasks relevant in the present context are not vigilance tasks; the distraction function is therefore more likely. Irrelevant information (perhaps provided by the video channel) could under some circumstances be a positive hindrance.

When the information in both channels is relevant, the addition of the second channel will have the effect of improving the chances of detection of difficult stimuli (provided that the human system is not already loaded to its maximum channel capacity). For example, insincerity might be more easily detected by observation of tone of voice coupled with gaze aversion, than by either separately. Similarly there is experimental evidence to support the widely held view that audio-visual channels are better than either separately for educational instruction purposes (Hsia, 1968).

Referring strictly to the informational aspects of communication, the addition of the visual channel to the 'audio-only' system will improve performance on signals for which it is relevant and, in so far as it is a distraction, impair performance on activities for which it is not relevant. The possible distraction effect may depend on task complexity. The impairment associated with the addition of irrelevant information (Shaw, 1958) is more likely to be serious if the task is complex and the participants therefore susceptible to 'stimulus overload' (Milgram, 1970).

Another important issue concerning the interaction between channels is the possibility of substitution between signals. The foregoing overview has noted a number of examples of apparent compensatory behaviours between channels such as eye-gaze and physical proximity. Shulman and Stone (1970) noted that people used voice volume to adapt to difference in proximity. Much of the information conveyed by the visual non-verbal signals can also be conveyed verbally. Indeed there are a number of auditory non-verbal signals (such as tone of voice pausing behaviour, and paralinguistic material such as 'um', 'ah', 'er' and so on) conveying information very similar to that conveyed by the visual non-verbal signals, whose operation is not likely to be significantly affected by the variations in the medium of communication with which we are concerned. The extent of the likely substitution between signals is very uncertain. This being the case, one can not even say with certainty that communication outcomes will be affected by the removal of the visual channel; one can only point to the type of tasks most likely to be affected and the effects to be expected.

expect the transmission of cognitive information to be relatively unaffected.

Thus, the tasks which would be expected to be most sensitive to variation in the medium of communication are tasks in which the expression of emotion (and perception of this emotion) is an important part of the interaction, tasks with a great need for timing and coordination of the speaker's activity with the responses of the other, and finally, tasks on which there is the greatest need to manipulate others. On tasks on which there is no need to manipulate others, the performance of the pair will approximate more nearly the sum of the performances of the individuals, and as such is less likely to be disturbed by variations in the link between them.

VISUAL COMMUNICATION—OVERVIEW

Cherry (1957) defined communication as an exchange of 'signs' (physical signals by which one organism affects the state of the other in a two-organism system). This definition is conveniently operational and in some senses general, for it allows that the signal be emitted either intentionally or unintentionally and be received either consciously or unconsciously. The constant problem is to know whether the signals emitted by one party are used by the other. A distinction is thus commonly made between cues which signal a certain state in the sender ('indicative cues') and cues to which the other responds in some way or another ('communicative' cues). The foregoing summary provides abundant evidence for the indicative worth of visual signals, but the evidence is in many cases somewhat incomplete when it comes to the communicative worth. Lack of evidence of use is, of course, not to be interpreted as evidence of non-use. Whilst for some types of visual information it may be an assumption to say that they are used, it is every bit as much an assumption to say that the information is derived from the auditory channel only. We must recognize that the communication stream is a total stream and it is dangerous to isolate items of information in individual channels from the total message. Information that may be duplicated, set in context or amplified, in another channel may still be important.

In most cases, the functions of the non-verbal cues have been in some way related to forming, building or maintaining the relationship between the interactants. The absence of the visual channel reduces the possibilities for expression of socio-emotional material and decreases the information available about the other's self-image, attitudes, moods and reactions. So, regarding the medium as an information transmission system, the removal of the visual channel is likely to produce a serious disturbance of the affective interaction; one would

REFERENCES

(Mimeographed Communications Studies Group papers are available from Post Office Telecommunications (TMk3.3.1.) Room 120, 2-12 Gresham Street, London EC2V 7Ag.)

Albert, S. A, and Dabbs, J. M. (1970). 'Physical distance and persuasion', *J. Pers. Soc. Psychol.*, 15, 265-70.

Argyle, M., and Dean, J. (1965). 'Eye contact, distance and affiliation', *Sociometry*, 28, 289-304.

Argyle, M., Lalljee, M., and Cook, M. (1968). 'The effects of visibility on interaction in the dyad', *Human Relations*, 21, 3-17.

Argyle, M. (1969). *Social Interaction.* Methuen, London.

Argyle, M., Salter, V., Nicholson, H., Williams, M., and Burgess, P. (1970). 'The communication of inferior and superior attitudes by verbal and nonverbal signals', *Brit. J. Soc. Clin. Psychol.*, 9, 222-31.

Argyle, M., and McHenty, R. (1971). 'Do spectacles really affect judgements of intelligence?', *Brit. J. Soc. Slin. Psychol.*, 10, 27-9.

Birdwhistell, R. L. (1952). *Introduction to Kinesics.* University of Louisville Press, Louisville.

Birdwhistell, R. L. (1968). 'Body behaviour and communication', in Sills, D. (Ed.) *International Encyclopedia of Social Science*, Vol. 3. McMillan, New York.

Birdwhistell, R. L. (1970). *Kinesics and Context.* University of Philadelphia Press, Philadelphia.

Champness, B. G. (1970). 'Mutual glance and the significance of the look', *Advancement of Science*, March, 309-12.

Champness, D. H. (1971). *Bargaining at Bell Laboratories.* Unpublished Communications Studies Group paper no. E/71270/CH.

Cherry, C. (1957). *On Human Communication.* MIT Press, Cambridge, Mass.

Cook, M. (1971). *Nonverbal Signalling in Social Interaction.* Unpublished Ph.D. thesis, Oxford University.

Cook, M., and Lalljee, M. (1972). 'Verbal substitutes for verbal signals in interaction', *Semiotica*, 6, 212-21.

Darwin, C. (1972). *The Expression of the Emotions in Man and Animals.* John Murray, London.

Dittman, A. T. (1962). 'The relationship between body movements and moods in interviews', *J. Consulting. Psychol.*, 26, 480.

Ekman, P. (1965). 'Communication through nonverbal behaviour: A source of information about an interpersonal relationship', in Tomkins, S. S., and Izard, C. E. (Eds) *Affect, Cognition and Personality.* Tavistock, London.

Ekman, P., and Friesen, W. V. (1969). 'Nonverbal leakage and clues to deception', *Psychiatry*, 32, 88-105.

Ekman, P. (1971). 'Universals and cultural differences in facial expressions of emotion', in Cole, J. K. (Ed.) *Nebraska Symposium on Motivation.* University of Nebraska Press, Lincoln.

Ellsworth, P. C., and Carlsmith, J. M., (1968). 'Effects of eye contact and verbval content on affective response to a dyadic interaction', *J. Pers Soc Psychol.*, 10, 15-20.

Exline, R. V. (1963). 'Explorations in the process of person perception: Visual interaction in relation to competition, sex and need for affiliation', *J. Pers. Soc. Psychol.*, 31, 1-20.

Exline, R. V., Gray, D., and Schuette, D. (1965). 'Visual behaviour in a dyad as affected by interview content and sex on respondent', *J. Pers. Soc Psychol.*, 1, 201-9.

Exline, R. V., and Winder, L. C. (1965). 'Affective relations and mutual glances in dyads', in Tomkins, S. S., and Izard, C. E. (Eds.) *Affect, Cognition and Personality.* Springer, New York.

Frijda, N. H. (1968). 'Recognition of emotion', in Berkowitz, L. (Ed.) *Advances in Experimental Social Psychology.* Academic Press, New York.

Goldberg, G. N., Kiesler, C. A., and Collins, B. E. (1969). 'Visual behaviour and face-to-face distance interaction', *Sociometry*, 32, 43-53.

Hall, E. T. (1963). 'A system for the notation of proxemic bahaviour', *Amer. Anthropologist*, 65, 1003-26.

Hess, E. H. (1965). 'Attitude and pupil size'. *Scientific American*, 22, 46-55.

Hockey, R. (1969). 'Noise and efficiency: the visual task', *New Scientist*, May, 244-6.

Hsia, H. J. (1968). 'Output, error, equivocation and recalled information in auditory, visual and audio-visual processing with constraint and noise', *J. Communication.*

Jaffe, J. and Feldstein, S. (1970). *Rhythms of Dialogue.* Academic Press, New York.

James, W. T. (1932). 'A study of the expression of bodily posture', *J. Genet. Psychol.*, 7, 405-37.

Kasl, S. V., and Mahl, G. F. (1965). 'The relations of disturbances and hesitations in spontaneous speech to anxiety', *J. Pers Soc Psychol.*, 1, 425-33.

Kendon, A. (1967). 'Some functions of gaze direction in social interaction', *Acta Psychologica*, 26, 1-47.

Kleck, R. E., and Nuessle, W. (1968). 'Congruence between the indicative and communicative functions of eye contact in interpersonal relations', *Brit. J. Soc. Clin. Psychol.*, 7, 241-6.

Kleinke, C. L., and Pohlen. {/ D/ (1971). 'Affective and emotional responses as a function of other person's gaze and cooperativeness in a two-person game', *J. Pers. Soc. Psychol.*, 17, 308-13.

Rosenfeld, H. M. (1966). 'Instrumental affiliative functions of facial and gestural expressions', *J. Pers. Soc. Psychol.*, 4, 65-72.

Rosenthal, R. (1967). 'Covert communication in the psychological experiment', *Psychol. Bull.*, 67, 356-67.

Rowley, V., and Keller, E. D. (1962). 'Changes in children's verbal behaviour as a function of social approval and manifest anxiety', *J. Abn. Soc. Psychol.*, 65, 53-7.

Ruesch, J. (1966). 'Nonverbal language and therapy', *Psychiatry*, 18, 323-30.

Sharp, M., and McClung, T. (1966). 'Effects of organization on the speaker's ethos'. *Speech. Monog.*, 33, 182-3.

Schacter, S., and Singer, J. E. (1962). 'Cognitive, social and physiological determinants of emotional state', *Psychol. Rev.*, 69, 379-99.

Scheflen, A. E. (1965). *Stream and Structure of Communication Behaviour*. Eastern Pennsylvania Psychiatric Association, Commonwealth of Pennsylvania.

Scherer, S. E., and Schiff, M. R. (1973). 'Perceived intimacy, physical distance and eye contact', *Perceptual and Motor Skills*, 36, 835-41.

Scheritz and Helmreich, R. (1973). 'Interactive effects of eye contact and verbal content on interpersonal attraction in dyads', *J. Pers. Soc. Psychol.*, 25, 6-14.

Sensenig, J., Reed, T. E., and Miller, J. S. (1972). 'Cooperation in the Prisoner's Dilemma as a function of interpersonal distance', *Psychon. Sci.*, 26, 105-6.

Shapiro, J. F. (1968). 'Relationships between visual and auditory cues of therapeutic effectiveness', *J. Clin. Psychol.*, 24, 233-6.

Shapiro, J. G., Foster, C. P., and Powwel, T. (1968). 'Facial and bodily cues of genuineness, empathy and warmth', *J. Clin. Psychol.*, 24, 233-6.

Shaw, M. E. (1958). 'Some effects of irrelevant information on problem solving by small groups', *J. Soc. Psychol.*, 47, 33-7.

Loveless, N. E., Brebner, J., and Hamilton, P. (1970). 'Bisensory presentation of information', *Psychol. Bull.*, 73, 161-99.

McBride, G., King, M. G., and James, J. W. (1965). 'Social proximity effects on galvanic skin responsiveness in adult humans', *J. Psychol.*, 61, 153-7.

McLuhan, M. (1964). *Understanding Media*. Routledge and Kegan Paul, London.

Mehrabian, A. (1968). 'Inference of attitudes from the posture, orientation and distance of a communicator', *J. Consult. Clin. Psychol.*, 32, 296-308.

Milgram, S. (1970). 'The experience of living in cities', *Science*, 13, 1461-8.

Miller, G. R., and Hewgill, M. A. (1964). 'The effects of variations in nonfluency on audience ratings of source credibility', *Quart. J. Speech*, 50, 36-44.

Nicholls, K. A., and Champness, B. G. (1971). 'Eye gaze and the GSR', *J. Exp. Soc. Psychol.*, 7, 623-6.

Osgood, Co E. (1966). 'Dimensionality of the semantic space for communication via facial expression', *Scand . J. Psychol.*, 7, 1-30.

Patterson, M. L. and Holmes, D. S. (1966). *Social interaction correlates of the MPI extraversion-introversion*. Paper read at the annual meeting of the American Psychological Association, New York.

Patterson, M. L. and Sechrest, L. B. (1970). 'Interpersonal distance and impression formation', *J. Pers.*, 38, 161-6.

Patterson, M. L. (1973). 'Compensation in nonverbal immediacy behaviour: A review', *Sociometry*, 36, 237-52.

Popelka, G. R., and Berger, K. W. (1971). 'Gestures and visual speech reception', *Amer. Annals of the Deaf*, 434-6.

Porter, E., Argyle, M., and Salter, V. (1970). 'What is signalled by proximity?', *Perceptual and Motor Skills*, 30, 39-42.

Shulman, A. D., and Stone, M. (1970). Expectation Confirmation-Disconfirmation as a Determinant of Interpersonal Behaviour: A study of Loudness of Voice. Presented at the Southwestern Psychological Association meeting, St. Louis.

Singer, J. E. (1964). 'The use of manipulative strategies: Machiavellianism and attractiveness', *Sociometry*, 27, 128-150.

Sommer, S. (1965). 'Further studies in small group ecology', *Sociometry*, 28, 337-48.

Stapley, B. (1972). *Visual Enhancement of Telephone Conversations*. Unpublished Ph.D. thesis. Imperial College, University of London.

Stass, J. W., and Willis, F. N. (1967). 'Eye contact, pupil dilation and personal preference', *Psychon. Sci.*, 7, 375-6.

Strongman, K. T., and Champness, B. G. (1968). 'Dominance hierarchies and conflict in eye contact', *Acta Psychologica*, 28, 376-86.

Vine, I. (1970). 'Communication by facial visual signals', in Crook, J. K. (Ed.), *Social Behaviour in Animals and Man*. Academic Press, London.

Watson, O. M., and Graves, T. D. (1966). 'Quantitative research in proxemic behaviour', *Amer. Anthropologist*, 68, 971-85.

Wiener, M. and Mehrabian, A. (1968). *Language within Language: Immediacy, A Channel in Verbal Communication*, Appleton-Century-Crofts, New York.

A TYPOLOGY OF TASKS

(Excerpt)

from

Groups: Interaction and Performance

Joseph E. McGrath

. . .

A CIRCUMPLEX MODEL OF GROUP TASK TYPES

The past work of Shaw, Carter, Hackman, Steiner, Shiflett, Taylor, Lorge, Davis, Laughlin, and their colleagues, has provided important bases for a task classification. I want to extract main ideas from several of these, elaborate on some of those ideas, and fit them together into a conceptually related set of distinctions about tasks. Ideally, the categories of such a classification schema should be (a) mutually exclusive (that is, a task fits in one and only one category); (b) collectively exhaustive (that is, all tasks fit in some category); and (c) logically related to one another. They also should be (d) useful, in that they

should point up differences between and relations among the items (tasks) that would not otherwise have been noticed. The framework offered here should be judged against those standards—especially the last one, usefulness. That framework is diagrammed in Figure 5–1, and listed in Table 5–1.

Begin by considering Hackman's three types of task: production (actually, *generating ideas or images*); discussion (dealing with issues); and problem-solving (actually, *generating plans for action*). These can be regarded as labels for the particular performance processes that are engaged by the task. In other words, they indicate what the group (or individual) is to *do*. I would like to propose that there are four general processes: to Generate (alternatives); to Choose (alternatives); to Negotiate; and to Execute.

FIGURE 5–1   The Group Task Circumplex

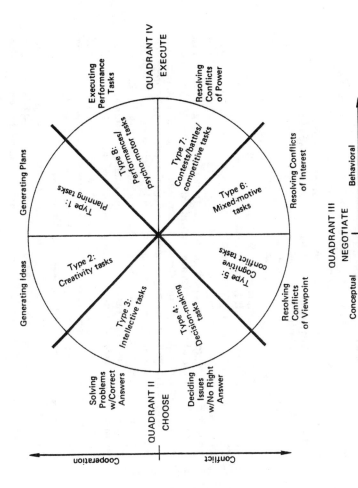

© 1984, pp. 60–66. Reprinted by permission of Prentice Hall, Englewood Cliffs, New Jersey.

TABLE 5-1　Quadrants, Task Types, and Key Concepts of the Task Circumplex

QUADRANT I:　GENERATE

Type 1. *Planning Tasks:* Generating plans. E.g.: Hackman's "problem-solving" task type. Key notion: Action-oriented Plan.

Type 2. *Creativity Tasks:* Generating ideas. E.g.: Hackman's "production" tasks; "brainstorming" tasks. Key notion: Creativity.

QUADRANT II:　CHOOSE

Type 3. *Intellective Tasks:* Solving problems with a correct answer. E.g.: Laughlin's intellective tasks, with correct and compelling answers; logic problems and other problem-solving tasks with correct but not compelling answers; tasks for which expert consensus defines answers. Key notion: Correct answer.

Type 4. *Decision-Making Tasks:* Dealing with tasks for which the preferred or agreed upon answer is the correct one. E.g.: tasks used in risky shift, choice shift, and polarization studies; juries. Key notion: Preferred answer.

QUADRANT III:　NEGOTIATE

Type 5. *Cognitive Conflict Tasks:* Resolving conflicts of viewpoint (not of interests). E.g.: cognitive conflict tasks used in social judgment theory work; some jury tasks. Key notion: Resolving policy conflicts.

Type 6. *Mixed-Motive Tasks:* Resolving conflicts of motive-interest. E.g.: negotiations and bargaining tasks; mixed-motive dilemma tasks; coalition formation/reward allocation tasks. Key notion: Resolving pay-off conflicts.

QUADRANT IV:　EXECUTE

Type 7. *Contests/Battles:* Resolving conflicts of power; competing for victory. E.g.: wars, all winner-take-all conflicts, competitive sports. Key notion: Winning.

Type 8. *Performances:* Psychomotor tasks performed against objective or absolute standards of excellence, e.g., many physical tasks; some sports events. Key notion: Excelling.

While Hackman's production and his problem-solving categories both refer to the Generate process as used here—generate creative ideas, on the one hand, and generate plans for action on the other—his work suggests another process: an implementation or action-oriented process. Hackman's work, however, was limited to tasks of a paper and pencil variety that could and did yield written products (words, numbers and perhaps pictorial displays). But much of the work of the world involves *performance of physical tasks* that require manipulations, motor behaviors and complex psychomotor activities. So an Execute (or Implement, or Perform) process is certainly needed in any task classification that aspires to completeness. Within this Execute process, at least two subsets of tasks are involved: (a) tasks for which the focal group is engaged in competition (combat) with an opposing (or enemy) group, with results of that contest (win/lose) determining the pay-offs; and (b) tasks for which the focal group is not in contest with an opponent, but rather is striving in relation to "nature," and for which pay-offs are determined by the group's performance in relation to some objective or external or absolute performance standards.

When all these distinctions are taken together, the results can be presented in a circular array that, in some usages, is called a circumplex. This Task Circumplex, presented in Figure 5-1, contains a number of distinctions and relations between types of tasks. First of all, the four quadrants are the four performance processes already discussed (a variation of the Hackman trio, plus Negotiation). Each of the processes is divided into two subtypes, using some of the distinctions noted here. Quadrant I, Generate, is divided into Generating Plans and Generating Ideas. The former is similar to Hackman's problem-solving type; it is related to the adjacent performance category in having an emphasis on action-orientation. The latter, Generating Ideas, is similar to Hackman's production type. It is the locus for "creativity" tasks; it is related to the adjacent intellectual problem category in having an emphasis on cognitive matters.

Quadrant II, Choose, is also divided into two types: (3) Intellective tasks and (4) Decision-Making tasks. The terms and the distinctions are borrowed from Laughlin (1980). The former refers to tasks for which there is a demonstrable right answer, and the group task is to invent/select/compute that correct answer. The latter refers to tasks for which there is not a demonstrably correct answer, and for which the group's task is to select, by some consensus, a *preferred* alternative. For intellective tasks, at least three subsets can be identified, based on differing criteria of correctness. The first subset includes those tasks for which the demonstrably correct answer is also intuitively compelling once it is put forth (i.e., the Eureka tasks). Probably, such intuitively compelling right answers are based on very widely held cultural norms and beliefs. A second subset of intellective tasks includes those for which there is a demonstrably correct answer—in terms of the "facts," logic and criteria of some more or less technical area—but it is relatively difficult to demonstrate that logic in a way that is intuitively compelling to members of the task performing group. The third subset of intellective tasks includes those for which the "correct" answer is based on a *consensus of experts*. Such tasks have been used, for example, in studies developing models of the "accuracy" of judgments of freely interacting groups as compared, for example, to individuals, or to statisticized

Consider Laughlin's distinction between intellective tasks, for which there is a demonstrably correct answer, with the group's task being to find and choose that correct answer, and discussion tasks, for which the right answer *is* the group's consensus, and the group's task is to attain consensus. These represent two different aspects of the Choose process. Davis, Laughlin, & Komorita (1976) also distinguish between groups engaged in cooperative interaction and those engaged in competitive or mixed-motive interaction. When the group's task is to resolve conflicts, the process involved is not so much to Choose as it is to Negotiate. Some of these conflicts among group members are conflicts of viewpoint. Brehmer (1976) calls them cognitive conflicts. Some of the conflicts among members are conflicts of interests or motive; these are the kind Davis, Laughlin and Komorita had in mind in their competitive interaction category.

groups, or to groups whose interaction has been experimentally constrained. (See, for example, Eils & John, 1980; Einhorn, Hogarth, & Klempfer, 1977; Rohrbaugh, 1979.) These three subtasks represent a progression from correctness defined solely in cognitive idea terms toward correctness defined in consensus terms.

A similar but less clearly distinctive set of subtypes can be distinguished within the Decision-Making category. Whereas the correct answers of intellective tasks are based either on cultural norms, logic and broadly known facts, or on expert consensus, the "correct" answers for decision-making tasks are based on peer consensus about what is morally right or what is to be preferred. For some of these, answers draw on cultural values, presumably broadly shared in the population from which group members are drawn. Others may involve social comparison and other social influence processes operating among the particular individuals who are the group's members. Still others may involve consensus attained by sharing relevant information. Thus, decision-making tasks, like intellective tasks, have internal differentiations that shift, by degrees, from being very similar to the category adjacent to one of its "borders" (i.e., intellective tasks) to being similar to the task type adjacent to its other border (i.e., cognitive conflict tasks).

Quadrant III, Negotiate, is more or less an extension of Quadrant II, Choose, under conditions where there is intra-unit conflict. The key word here is not *solve*, but *resolve*. It, too, has two types: Resolving Conflicts of Viewpoint and Resolving Conflicts of Interest. The first refers to cases where members of the group do not just have different *preferences*, but have *systematically different preference structures*. They may interpret information differently, may give different weights to different dimensions, and/or may relate dimensions to preferences via different functional forms. Davis (1980) suggests that such differences of viewpoint may occur for subpopulations who are potential jurors, at least for certain types of cases. Hammond, Brehmer, and colleagues (e.g., Hammond, Stewart, Brehmer, & Steinmann, 1975; Brehmer, 1976) in their development of Social Judgment Theory, have induced such "judgment policy" differences experimentally and have studied their effects on group decisions. They insist that such cognitive conflicts are far more pervasive than we have recognized, because conflict is almost always construed as conflict of interest or of motive.

Such conflicts of interest form the other task types of the Negotiate quadrant. We can distinguish several subtypes, including: (a) tasks involving conflicts of both viewpoints and interests or pay-offs, and involving multiple dimensions of dissent, perhaps exemplified by labor/management negotiations; (b) tasks requiring resolution along a single, quantified dimension, such as those studied under the label of bargaining; (c) tasks in which the two (or more) parties' joint choices determine pay-offs to each, such as the prisoner's dilemma game, the N-person prisoner's dilemma, and studies of other social dilemmas; and (d) tasks in which opposing members try to establish subsets (coalitions) that can control allocation of payoffs. These subtasks range from those with an emphasis on resolution (compromise, agreement) to those with an emphasis on power. Again, these subtypes shade from one border of the category to the other.

Quadrant IV deals with overt, physical behavior, with the execution of manual and psychomotor tasks. Such tasks are very heavily represented in the workaday world and, against that baserate, are quite underrepresented in research on groups. Again, there are two types: *Contests* and *Performances*. *Contests* are tasks for which the unit of focus, the group, is in competition with an opponent, an enemy, and performance results will be interpreted in terms of a winner and a loser, with pay-offs in those terms as well. These range from "battles," where the focus is on conquest of an opponent and winner-take-all distribution of pay-offs, to "competitions," where there is a lot of emphasis on standards of performance excellence over and above the reckoning of winners and losers. The former are power based conflicts of interest that are adjacent to the *Negotiation* task type, especially the winning-coalition subtype. The latter approach *Performances*, the other adjacent task category.

Performances are those overt task executions that do not involve competition against an enemy, but rather involve striving to meet standards of excellence (or, sometimes, standards of "sufficiency"), with pay-offs tied to such standards rather than to "victory" over an opponent. These ordinarily involve complex sets of activities requiring coordination between members and over time. Much of the work of the world—lifting, connecting, extruding, digging, pushing—falls in this category, but not much of the study of small groups. These tasks can be subclassified in a myriad of ways, including type of material being worked upon, type of activity involved, intended product of the activity, and many others. Perhaps one useful subclassification is the distinction between *continuous process* and *batch process* tasks. A related distinction is between those in which the internal timing of activities is and is not crucial. Consideration of time dependent tasks brings us back to the planning tasks of Quadrant I, for which sequence and schedule are crucial parts.

Thus, not only are the four quadrants (the four performance processes) distinguished from but related to one another, each of the eight task types is related to its neighboring types on each side. Furthermore, the subtypes within each task type can be ordered, more or less, in a progression that moves, by small transition steps, from one boundary of the category to the other.

The task circumplex is a two-dimensional representation, and it is possible to describe the two dimensions of that space. If the circumplex is placed so that Quadrant I spans "12 o'clock" (with task type 1 to the right, and task type 2 to the left, of that point), the horizontal dimension reflects a contrast between behavioral or action tasks to the right (types 1, 8, 7, and 6) and conceptual or intellectual tasks to the left (types 2, 3, 4, and 5). The vertical dimension reflects a contrast between cooperation or facilitative compliance at the top (types 3, 2, 1, and 8) and conflict or contrient interdependence at the bottom (types 4, 5, 6, and 7). These two dimensions—intellectual versus behavioral, and cooperation versus conflict—are relatively familiar distinctions about groups and group tasks. Another very familiar set of concepts, the trio of cognitive, affective (or evaluative) and conative, can also be located within this circumplex space. Each of these three components of tasks reaches a maximum at a different point around the circle. The cognitive component of tasks peaks in the vicinity of task types 1 and 2. The affective or evaluative component of tasks peaks near task type 5. The conative or behavioral component of tasks peaks near task type 8.

Thus, the task circumplex seems to represent a reasonable attempt to classify group tasks. Collectively, the eight types can accommodate virtually all tasks used in group research, and many that might have been used but have not been used in that work. The crucial test, of course, is whether or not this taxonomy of tasks can be used to summarize, compare and clarify the research on group task performance, and whether that leads to new insights about the task performance process.

References

BREHMER, B. Social judgement theory and the analysis of interpersonal conflict. *Psychological Bulletin*, 1976, 83, 985-1003.

DAVIS, J. H. Group decision and procedural justice. In M. Fishbein (Ed.), *Progress in social psychology* (Vol. 1). Hillsdale, NJ: Erlbaum, 1980.

DAVIS, J. H., LAUGHLIN, P. R., & KOMORITA, S. S. The social psychology of small groups: Cooperative and mixed-motive interaction. *Annual Review of Psychology*, 1976, 27, 501-541.

EILS, L. C., III., & JOHN, R. S. A criterion validation of multiattribute utility analysis and of group communication strategy. *Organizational Behavior and Human Performance*, 1980, 25, 268-88.

EINHORN, H. J., HOGARTH, R. M., & KLEMPFER, E. Quality of group judgement. *Psychological Bulletin*, 1977, 84, 158-172.

HAMMOND, K. R., STEWART, T. R., BREHMER, B., & STEINMANN, D. O. Social judgement theory. In M. F. Kaplan & S. Schwartz (Eds.), *Human judgement and decision processes*. New York: Academic Press, 1975.

LAUGHLIN, P. R. Social combination processes of cooperative, problem-solving groups as verbal intellective tasks. In M. Fishbein (Ed.), *Progress in social psychology* (Vol. 1). Hillsdale, NJ: Erlbaum, 1980.

Communication Modes and Task Performance

John Short, Ederyn Williams, and Bruce Christie

There have been many studies which have explored the effects on performance of various types of task of varying the link between the participants. To what extent do these experiments bear out our general hypotheses about the functions of the visual channel? What sort of tasks have been found experimentally to be sensitive to the medium of communication and what is the nature of the sensitivity?

A large percentage of the literature of social psychology could be construed as relevant but we can discuss only those in which medium has in some sense been manipulated. Unfortunately, medium of communication has seldom previously been the variable of central concern and most of these studies therefore have, for our present purpose, one or more serious limitations. Variations in the medium have frequently been very crude (e.g. communication versus no communication); interaction is often constrained by extraordinary means (e.g. no partner to communicate with); the tasks have usually been very artificial and clearly distinct from normal work tasks, and finally investigators have often been more concerned with the process than the outcome, so that outcome measures have not been obtained. Nonetheless much of the material is instructive.

THE EFFECTS OF THE PRESENCE OF OTHERS

Before considering the more subtle effects of medium on complex interactions, it is appropriate to consider the simplest way in which an individual can impact on another: the mere presence of others has been shown to affect performance on a variety of tasks. Two isolated individuals unaware of one another's existence and with no communication can naturally have no influence on one another, but as soon as contact occurs, performance is affected. The effects of the presence of others can be either facilitative (for example, on signal detection, Bergum and Lehr, 1963, and chain association, Allport, 1920) or detrimental (on tasks such as nonsense syllable learning, Pessin, 1933). These seemingly conflicting results can be reconciled by assuming that the presence of others increases the individual's arousal (Zajonc, 1965). It is reasonably well accepted that experiments on learning have shown that high drive (or arousal) enhances the emission of dominant (well-learned) responses. If, for a given task, the dominant

Reprinted from *The Social Psychology of Telecommunications*, pp. 77–89. © 1976, John Wiley & Sons. Reproduced by permission of John Wiley and Sons Limited.

responses are largely correct this will improve performance, but if, as is more likely to be the case in a learning task, the dominant response is incorrect, the presence of other people will impair performance. In a similar vein, Allport (1920) concluded that complex intellectual processes were impaired in the presence of others, while response production was facilitated. Thus he found that subjects writing refutations of arguments produced longer but worse passages in the presence of an audience. In support of the hypothesis of an increase in motivation, it was found that it was the slower individuals who were most affected by the audience.

There is now a variety of evidence taken to support Zajonc's hypothesis. Although much of this is based on experiments using animals, experiments using human subjects have given similar results. For example, Zajonc and Sales (1966) demonstrated that on a task in which the subjects tried to identify what were, in reality, meaningless sets of lines, the likelihood of practised responses was increased relative to that of the less practised ones in the presence of an audience. Increased arousal may not be the whole story, for there is some evidence that the presence of others can arouse social motives which inhibit task performance. For example, on word-association tasks, the presence of an audience can make subjects more cautious and lead to longer response latencies (Wapner and Alper, 1952). This would also explain the more usual and less individual associations found by Allport (1920) with a similar task.

The word 'presence' need not be taken too literally. The effects of audience are also obtainable with the knowledge that others are working on the same problem in another room (Dashiell, 1935). Wapner and Alper (1952) found that an invisible audience known to be watching through a one-way mirror was even more inhibiting of response than a visible audience. The latter result is potentially important, because the telephone likewise represents a system in which one's performance is being monitored while one has relatively little feedback as to the reactions of the other party.

Medium of communication could be said to vary the presence of the other, as in our Social Presence hypothesis. What effect then would be expected on task performance? The evidence for Zajonc's hypothesis is as yet sufficiently limited that one hesitates to draw any firm conclusions. The chief obstacle to inference is the definition of the response; which responses are relevant and which are dominant? In animal experiments with a single performance measure, this poses relatively little problem, but consider a concrete example to illustrate the difficulties of applying the theory—a debate between two individuals who initially disagree and must come to some agreement. What is the dominant response? Perhaps it is each person expressing his own point of view; in this case conflict would be exacerbated face-to-face. Perhaps it is each compromising to reach agreement (that is the object of the interaction); in this case agreement would be easier in the face-to-face condition. Perhaps the dominant response is something else altogether, such as the community consensus view on the issue under dispute. Finally, there is the added complication that the dominant response might differ for the two individuals. In the absence of any simple behavioural measure directly related to individual motivation, the value of any prediction is dubious.

This work suggests that just the physical absence of the other (as in telecommunication) would be expected to affect task performance, but, owing to ambiguities of response definition, specific effects on performance in complex interactive tasks are not easy to deduce from the previous work on mere presence.

CONFORMITY AND ANONYMITY

There is another body of work in which the effects of the presence of others has been examined: the literature on conformity. The paradigmatic experiment in the conformity literature involves the subject in giving judgements of simple stimuli while confronted with judgements, purporting to come from other members of a group, which are at variance with his own initial position. In such a situation, subjects tend to shift their stated views towards the view suggested by the others. The conformity effect is particularly marked with difficult problems where there is no objectively correct, clearly defined, answer (Blake and Mouton, 1961). The problems used in the attitude-change literature and the sort of problems encountered in everyday business both usually answer this description.

The relevance of this work stems largely from an independent variable which has been examined in relation to this phenomenon: anonymity. It is a well-substantiated finding that anonymity decreases the magnitude of the conforming response. 'Anonymity' should not be taken too literally, for although sometimes meaning 'not having to give one's name' before responding (e.g. Mouton, Blake and Olmstead, 1956) it can also mean physical separation (e.g. Deutsch and Gerard, 1955). In this more general sense, 'anonymity' could be varied by medium of communication. Although the two experiments just mentioned used simple physical stimuli (metronome clicks and line lengths respectively), the same effect of anonymity is found with judgements of more complex stimuli such as the artistic merit of a painting (Argyle, 1957) or the action that should be taken to deal with a juvenile delinquent (Raven, 1959).

On the assumption that removing the visual channel increases the anonymity of the situation, one would therefore expect less conforming when communication was over an audio link. It is perhaps unwise to put too much weight on this conclusion, for the following reasons:

(a) There are situations in which anonymity can increase conformity. For example, Gerard (1964) reanalysing the Deutsch and Gerard (1955) data found that among those individuals who were initially unconforming, those tested subsequently in the anonymous condition showed more yielding. The presence of the visual channel, might be felt to increase commitment to one's initial discrepant position. Thus, removing the visual channel, while making it easier to remain independent when independence was felt to be appropriate, might make it easier to yield when yielding could be interpreted as loss of face or otherwise inappropriate.

(b) Deutsch and Gerard (1955) drew a distinction between informational and normative social influence: the former in which subjects conform as a result of the information provided by the group, and the latter in which they conform because of the sanctions conferred by the group for non-conformity. Normative influence is dependent on the degree of interdependence among group members and the attractiveness of the group to the individual. Anonymity manipulates the normative influence. However, informational influence might also be affected by medium; this latter effect could work in the opposite direction (more conforming in the audio condition). It is thus difficult to predict what effects, if any, should be expected.

(c) Finally, all the above studies were non-interactive in the sense that free verbal interaction was not permitted (Argyle allowed note-passing but the others permitted only knowledge of the judgement of others). Extrapolation to interactive situations may be unjustified.

STUDIES OF MEDIA DIFFERENCES IN THE MECHANICS OF INTERACTION

Some studies have been concerned with the mechanisms of interaction rather than the outcome of the task (for instance, Cook and Lalljee, 1972, found little effect on a number of simple measures such as number of questions and pauses, when the visual channel was not available).

Two such experiments, however, are relevant. In one, Argyle, Lalljee and Cook (1968) conducted a series of experiments in which the visibility of one member of a dyad was systematically varied with the use of masks and dark glasses. Interaction was found to be disturbed in various ways as the visual cues were removed (the person with visual feedback tended to dominate the encounter, there were more interruptions and greater reported difficulty of interaction). However, a later experiment in which visibility was reduced symmetrically, although finding some effects on pauses and interruptions found little

reported difficulty of interaction. It appears that the asymmetry was the basis for the previous effects. The other relevant experiment, by Moscovici and Plon (1966), showed that compared to subjects who sat face-to-face (whether visible or screened from one another) subjects who sat back-to-back or side-by-side spoke in a style that was more formal, like the written form. Here again, the effects of medium seem to derive from the unfamiliarity (of the two latter orientations) rather than the physical constraints imposed by the removal of the visual channel.

These two studies are noteworthy because they suggest that some effects of medium may be due more to strangeness than to the objective constraints of the system. The usefulness of a strange system such as a closed-circuit television might therefore be expected to increase with experience.

A more recent study (Wilson and Williams, 1975) compared telephone and face-to-face conversations from the 'Watergate' transcripts. There were three initial hypotheses:

(a) That there are verbal substitutes in telephone conversations for visual cues (following Cook and Lalljee, 1972).
(b) That the uncertainty engendered by lack of non-verbal feedback on the telephone influences verbal processes.
(c) That telephone conversations are, or are felt to be, less pleasant than face-to-face ones (following the Social Presence hypothesis, that suggests that telephone communication is intrinsically less sociable, more impersonal, and that, unless the task requires such psychological 'distance', the mismatch is felt to be unpleasant).

A number of measures were extracted from the transcripts (e.g. length of conversation, number of agreements and disagreements, number of questions, length of utterances), and the various significant differences found were felt by the authors to support the 'lack of feedback' and 'telephone unpleasant' hypotheses, though there was less evidence for the 'verbal substitutes for visual cues' hypothesis.

STUDIES OF INFORMATION TRANSMISSION

Let us consider now what could be viewed as the simplest true type of communication: information transmission. This is a necessary element of all meaningful interaction including problem solving. How is this fundamental type of communication affected by the medium used?

This question was first examined by Champness and Reid (1970), who explored the accuracy with which their subjects (students) were able to transmit the contents of a business letter over three media of communication (face-to-face, telephone and 'face-to-face' with a separating opaque screen). No effects of medium of communication were found on any of the experimental measures, which included time to complete the task and several measures of accuracy, nor did the subjects perceive any difference in accuracy.

This experiment represents an example of what appears to be a whole class of person-to-person interactions which for all practical purposes may be relatively insensitive to the effects of communications media. Tasks in which only one individual is active and where the feedback function is consequently of little importance have generally been found not to be affected by the medium used. This result is obtained over and over again in a variety of experimental contexts.

Davies (1971) conducted experiments to compare face-to-face and teletype as media for the communication of factual information. The only effect of medium was that the teletype was found to be the most effective mode (provided that time was adequate); a result consonant with the rest of the literature on the comparative effectiveness of the written and spoken word. Reanalysis of Davies' data shows that there was a tendency towards better recall of the arguments in the two audio-only conditions than in the two conditions where the visual channel was available. However, the effect was not statistically significant and there was no effect on confidence in accuracy of recall. Nor was there any effect on the response strategy selected on the basis of the material presented or on opinion change in response to the communication.

While these two experiments may seem insufficient for generalization, it seems that the initial hypothesis, that since information transmission does not require a close interpersonal relationship to be successful, then we will find no effect of medium of communication for such tasks, is likely to be confirmed.

EFFECTS OF COMMUNICATION IN BARGAINING GAMES

McClintock, Nuttin and McNeel (1970) examined the effect of visual presence on behaviour in a two-person bargaining game. The task involved both persons making simultaneous choices from two alternatives, so as to give one of four possible combined choices, each of which was associated with a particular payoff for each individual. Auditory communication was not permitted. The visual presence of the other did not affect choices in the game.

A number of experiments have investigated the effect of a variable referred to as 'communication' on cooperation in two-person games. There is general confidence that increasing communication increases cooperation (Swensson, 1967, Daniels, 1967, Voissem and Sistrunk, 1971). However, the evidence for this has not been altogether consistent (see Terhune, 1968, for a review). The reason for the inconsistency is probably the variation in the tasks used and the wide

range of definitions of what constitutes communication: for example, Loomis (1959), Daniels (1967), and Voissem and Sistrunk (1971) allowed the passage of standardized notes, Terhune (1968) allowed subjects to compose their own messages, and Deutsch (1958) allowed free speech.

Although this work does at first sight suggest some very definite effects of medium, any general inference is unjustified. Firstly, investigations of communication have typically been confined to the presence or absence of communication (e.g. Deutsch and Krauss, 1962) rather than to variations in the type of communication. This, in turn, has meant that the tasks are of such a nature that they can be conducted without any verbal communication. Neither the variations in communication nor the type of tasks used have been appropriate to the present purpose. Secondly, increased communication will not necessarily increase cooperation; Krauss and Deutsch (1966) point out that subjects must use the opportunity to engage in communication relevant to cooperation (this was not found to be the case in their own 1962 experiment). The effect is therefore very task dependent. If it is mainly threats which comprise the communications, then bargaining efficiency and cooperation are more likely to be impaired than improved (Froman and Cohen, 1969).

Finally, the tasks used in these studies have always been simple games in which it has not been possible to interpret unambiguously what is meant by cooperation; for instance, cooperation is frequently confounded with efficient bargaining (as in the Prisoners' dilemma game). Whilst it may be true that this is reasonable because the two are usually confounded, it is nonetheless an obstacle to inference when either (or both) could be affected by medium.

COMMUNICATION MODALITY AND ATTITUDE CHANGE

There is some early work on the question of modality in the literature on attitude change. This is mainly directed at the relative impact of the written and the spoken word. The weight of this evidence is that the spoken word has more persuasive impact (Cantril and Allport, 1935, Elliot, 1937). There have been some contradictory observations (e.g. Wall and Boyd, 1971, found more attitude change in response to a written than in response to a live presentation).

Despite observations that the impact of the spoken word is as great or greater, comprehension is generally found to be greater with the written word (Toussaint, 1960). Two possible explanations suggest themselves. The first is that there is more yielding to the spoken message; McGuire (1969) summarizes: "There must be some felt difference in the receiver's relation to the source depending on whether he is listening or reading the message. Perhaps he feels more anxiety or greater pressure from self interest or good taste to conform when the more personalised modality is used'. Another possibility would be that many people read by subvocal or internalized speech and in so doing impose their own intonation on the material. This would have implications for meaning in that the force of the material could be dissipated or misdirected. These two possibilities are not mutually exclusive and both would predict an increase in impact with the addition of the visual channel to the audio-only channel. The visual signals could either reduce the ambiguity of the message and so sharpen the argument, or increase the awareness of the other and so add force to the message.

A third possibility, however, is that the difference between the written and live presentations arises because the written mode allows the possibility of rereading or checking difficult or important passages. In view of this possible effect, it is probably unwise to argue from the comparison of these two media to other media comparisons.

Evidence on the relative effectiveness of live and taped speeches is slight. McGuire (1969) cites a study by Wilke (1934) as showing that a speech heard directly produced more opinion change and less hostility than one heard over a loudspeaker. Also cited are attempts to communicate hypnotic suggestion via a tape recorder (Estabrook, 1930); however, it is not known whether any attempts were made to evaluate the effectiveness of this procedure. Frandsen (1963) had subjects attend to high or low threat appeals presented live, by television or by tape. He hypothesized that the degree to which the speaker's threats were personalized would interact with his 'closeness' to the audience. There was no significant effect of medium on the dependent measures (shift in opinion and recall of argument). In both cases, there were trends such that in the face-to-face condition there tended to be more opinion change and more recalled than in the taped condition. The results must therefore be considered inconclusive.

However, Croft *et al.* (1969) in a similar experiment did find a significant difference between the media used. Students watched a live presentation or a videotape of the same person giving a short, antiathletics talk. Post-experimental measures showed significantly greater attitude change amongst those who had received the face-to-face presentation, although the 'videotape' group also changed their attitudes to a significant degree.

Finally, Wall and Boyd (1971) presented subjects with a live, a written and a videotaped message. It was found that the written produced more attitude change than either of the other two (which did not differ). An audio-only condition was not included in this experiment.

In summary, this evidence, all from non-interactive situations where a source communicated with a recipient but not vice versa, suggests that there may be more opinion change in face-to-face situations than with audio-only communication, though written communication may

be the most effective of all. However, it would be unwise to generalize from this data to conclude that the same result will occur in a more interactive attitude change situation, where each party is simultaneously (or nearly so) trying to persuade the other. Results from such situations will be described in Chapter 7.

PROBLEM SOLVING

More important for our present purposes than the foregoing are the experiments which did require genuine two-way interaction between the participants; a number of studies of cooperative problem solving meet this criterion.

First in this category is that of Champness and Davies (1971). Participants in this experiment were required to discuss a problem and agree on the best possible solution; the 'problem' was what to do about an old, loyal worker who is holding up a serial production process in a motor-component factory. Pairs of subjects discussed the problem either face-to-face or by telephone, having in both cases twelve minutes to reach agreement. None of the outcome measures (including nature of the solution, satisfaction with the solution or agreement between individuals) was affected by the medium used. However, an important result of the experiment was that despite the fact that the outcome was not affected, other measures indicated that medium did affect what went on before the final solution was agreed.

At the level of the mechanics of the interaction it was noted that whilst in the face-to-face condition there was a highly significant correlation ($p < 0.001$) between the speech lengths of the two members of each pair, there was no such correlation in the telephone condition. This indicates a more satisfactory matching of their behaviour in the presence of the visual channel. A more startling finding was obtained from the analysis of the content of the conversation when it was found that a significantly ($p < 0.02$) higher proportion of the solutions discussed in the face-to-face condition than in the telephone condition were concerned directly with the problem worker. In assessing the effects of medium of communication on problem solving it may thus be necessary to distinguish between different levels. At the level of the processes leading up to the final solution, effects can be observed. However, as we shall see, at the level of the outcome a whole series of experiments have failed to find effects of medium (at least within the range of media studied).

For example, later experiments by Davies (1971a and 1971b) used a task which was almost antithetical to the problem used above. Whereas the task in the Champness and Davies experiment was 'open-ended', the new task was a closed deductive type of task which permitted precise scoring of the quality of the final solutions. Neither experiment found any indications of any effect of medium (telephone or face-to-face) on the quality of the final solution. It seems improbable that this absence of effect was due simply to the crudity of the measuring instrument, for the scoring procedure did readily distinguish between individuals who had had varying times for individual thought about the problem prior to the discussion with their partner. Although there were thus no effects of medium on the outcome, effects were again observed in the processes leading up to the solution. The principal finding in this respect was that subjects took significantly longer in the face-to-face condition (this fact accounted too for subsidiary findings such as the observation that more suggestions were discussed in the face-to-face conversations than in the telephone conversations). Since the face-to-face discussions were longer but failed to produce better solutions, one is tempted to argue that the telephone conversations were more efficient. It is a recurring finding in interviews with users of new audio conference systems that the interactions are shorter than they would have been had the meeting been conducted face-to-face (there is further discussion of this finding in Chapter 9). In some cases (as for instance Davies' experiments) the time difference may arise from the discomfort of holding a telephone handset for long periods of time; but with systems where the audio quality is excellent and there are loudspeakers rather than handsets, this argument cannot apply and there may be real grounds for believing that the face-to-face interactions are in some way more enjoyable. Such effects may occur in problem-solving situations but it is obvious that unless they affect aspects of the interaction relevant to the final solution, no effect on the outcome will be observed.

Other researchers have manipulated medium of communication primarily out of an interest in man's abilities to interact with computers (Chapanis, 1971, Chapanis, Ochsman, Parrish and Weeks, 1972). The experiments arising from this source all follow the basic paradigm of one subject seeking information from another in order to solve a problem. Chapanis et al. (1972) describe two problems that have been used: in the 'equipment-assembly problem' the 'seeker' had to assemble a lightweight trash-can toter, having been given the parts and tools but not the instructions (which were with his partner). In a second problem, the 'seeker' had to find the nearest doctor to a designated address in Washington.

A wide range of communication media (from face-to-face to written communication) were investigated. The problems used had only one correct solution and all subjects eventually reach the solution; it is therefore not possible to examine the quality of the solutions. The most revealing measure is the time taken to reach the solutions. This did not differ significantly between the 'communication-rich' mode (full face-to-face) and audio-only communication. Predictably, the written media were considerably slower than the others, but a more striking finding was also obtained: the subjects in the audio-only mode

exchanged ten times more messages than the subjects in the handwriting mode, and the subjects in the communication-rich mode exchanged more messages than the subjects in the voice-only mode. It seems that the face-to-face medium actually encourages conversation, with the result that the less-rich media are more efficient (per message though not per minute, in this case).

A similar experiment by Woodside, Cavers and Buck (1971) also used simple cooperative problems in which the information was split between two participants. One task was a crossword puzzle, the other a simple resource-allocation task (one side given the properties of the resources and the other side the specifications). No effects of medium (face-to-face, telephone or telephone with a graphics sending facility) were found.

The cooperative tasks we have been considering in this section would not seem to require a close personal relationship between the two subjects. We would therefore not expect the Social Presence of the medium to be important for the satisfactory completion of the task. A cold, impersonal medium should be as satisfactory as a warm, personal one. It is noteworthy that generally we do not find media effects at the level of task outcome, but only at the more subtle level of the person-to-person interaction that precedes task completion. How much of this interaction is directly related to the task, and how much is social, we do not know, but we would hypothesize that many of the media effects observed at this level reflect a greater emphasis on social, as opposed to directly task-oriented interaction over the warmer more sociable media such as face-to-face.

MISCELLANEOUS MEDIA COMPARISONS

Various other experiments have compared the effects of different media of communication on tasks that do not fit neatly into our previous categories. One of the most important is that of Milgram (1965). He used a similar paradigm to his earlier experiments, in which a naive subject, under the instructions of an 'experimenter', was persuaded to give seemingly very painful shocks to another person (in actuality, the other person was a confederate, and did not receive any shocks, but as far as the subject knew these shocks were getting through and, at the higher levels, were causing severe pain). In this experiment, both the immediacy (and the Social Presence) of the 'victim' and of the experimenter were varied, to see the effect on the willingness of the subject to give shocks. To compare with the base condition, where the 'victim' was invisible and inaudible (except for pounding on the intervening wall), Milgram used a 'voice-feedback' condition, where the 'victim' could be heard but not seen, a 'proximity' situation where the victim was face-to-face with the subject, and finally a 'touch proximity' situation where the subject actually had to hold the victim's hand down on the shock plate. Each of these increases in immediacy produced a corresponding decrease in obedience: in the 'remote' condition, 34% of subjects defied the experimenter; in the audio-only condition, 37% defied him; in the face-to-face condition, 60% defied him; and lastly, in the 'touch proximity' situation, 70% defied the experimenter.

The other variation was in the proximity of the experimenter. Here there were just two conditions: the experimenter was physically present (face-to-face), or he was at the other end of a telephone link. It was found that three times as many subjects were obedient in the face-to-face condition as in the telephone condition, a statistically significant difference. Clearly the experimenter was less able to obtain obedience when he was not physically present, and this was further emphasized by the observation that some of the 'obedient' subjects in the telephone condition in fact cheated by giving lower voltage shocks than required, and lying to the distant experimenter about their actions.

A later experiment (Penner and Hawkins, 1971) using a situation in which a fast reaction time allegedly delivered an electric shock to a victim, found that performance was not affected by whether the 'harmer' and 'harmed' were in visual contact. Identification of the victim by name however did reduce aggression. Anonymity again appears to be affecting task behaviour.

Two experiments have investigated the effects of the presence of the visual channel using the Kogan and Wallach choice-dilemma problems. The typical finding using this instrument is the so-called 'risky shift' (that after a group discussion, individuals make riskier decisions than they did before the discussion): Lamm (1967) had non-participating subjects listen to the group discussion, a second group could see as well as hear the discussion. The viewers showed more risky shift than the listeners but the difference was not statistically significant. Kogan and Wallach (1967) separated the members of the groups such that during the discussion they could not see one another. The results were similar to those from face-to-face groups run on previous occasions. There is some doubt that affective processes are involved at all in the production of the risky shift (Vinokur, 1971), as the crucial factor may be merely the exchange of information relevant to the task. It would then be consistent with the affective nature of non-verbal communication, that there was no effect of removing the visual channel.

A number of studies in an educational context have compared the effectiveness of instructional television with ordinary face-to-face teaching. Generally such studies fail to find any difference (Allen, 1971). Audio-only presentations also appear to have been satisfactory in the context of language laboratories. However, in view of the number of possible confounding factors and the difficulties of assessing effectiveness, any conclusion on the basis of these studies as to whether or not there is any difference between the face-to-face and televised presentations is probably unjustified.

OVERVIEW OF AREAS OF SENSITIVITY TO MEDIUM

The experimental evidence thus far bears out our general hypothesis derived from the literature on non-verbal communication as to the tasks which would be insensitive to medium of communication (tasks with little need for rapid feedback about the other person's reactions). While some of the experiments have found minor effects of medium, these scattered positive results do not critically test any coherent general theory either about which tasks will be sensitive or about how they will be affected. The next two chapters provide more stringent tests of the theories in the areas of greatest expected sensitivity.

REFERENCES

(Mimeographed Communications Studies Group papers are available from Post Office Telecommunications (TMk3.3.1.) Room 120, 2-12 Gresham Street, London EC2V 7Ag.)

Allen, W. H. (1971). 'Instructional media research: Past, present and future', Audio-Visual Communications Review, 19, 5-17.

Allport, F. H. (1920). 'The influence of the group upon association and thought', J. Exp. Psychol, 3, 159-82.

Argyle, M. (1957). 'Social pressure in public and private situations', J. Abn. Soc. Psychol., 54, 172-5.

Argyle, M., Lalljee, M., and Cook, M. (1968). 'The effects of visibility on interaction in the dyad', Human Relations, 21, 3-17.

Bergum, B. O., and Lehr, D. J. (1963). 'Effects of authoritarianism on vigilance performance', J. Applied Psychol., 47, 75-7.

Blake, R. R., and Mouton, J. S. (1961). 'Competition, communication and conformity', in Berg, I. A. and Bass, B. M. (Eds.), Conformity and Deviation. Harper, New York.

Cantril, H., and Allport, G. W. (1935). The Psychology of Radio. Harper, New York.

Champness, B. G., and Reid, A. A. L. (1970). The Efficiency of Information Transmission: A Preliminary Comparison Between Face-to-face Meetings and the Telephone. Unpublished Communications Studies Group paper.

Champness, B. G., and Davies, M. F. (1971). The Maier pilot experiment. Unpublished Communications Studies Group paper no. E72011/CH.

Chapanis, A. (1971). 'Prelude to 001: explorations in human communication', Amer. Psychologist, 26, 949-61.

Chapanis, A., Ochsman, R., Parrish, R., and Weeks, G. (1972). 'Studies in interactive communication: I. The effects of four communication modes on the behaviour of teams during cooperative problem solving', Hum. Fac, 14, 487-509.

McGuire, W. J. (1969). 'The nature of attitudes and attitude change', in Lindzey, G., and Aronson, E. (Eds.) *The Handbook of Social Psychology*, Vol. 3. Addison Wesley, Reading, Mass.

Milgram, S. (1965). 'Some conditions of obedience to authority', *Human relations*, 18, 57-75.

Moscovici, S., and Plon, M. (1966). 'Les situations colloques: observations theoretiques et experimentales', *Bulletin de Psychologie*, 247, 702-22.

Mouton, J. S., Blake, R. R., and Olmstead, J. A. (1956). 'The relationship between frequency of yielding and the disclosure of personal identity', *J. Pers.*, 24, 339-47.

Penner, L. A. and Hawkins, H. L. (1971). 'The effects of visual contact and aggressor identification on interpersonal aggression', *Psychon. Sci.*, 24, 261-3.

Pessin, J. (1933). 'The comparative effects of social and mechanical stimulation on memorising', *Amer. J. Psychol.*, 45, 263-70.

Raven, B. H. (1959). 'Social influence on opinions and the communication of related content', *J. Abn. Soc. Psychol.*, 58, 119-28.

Swensson, R. G. (1967). 'Cooperation in the prisoner's dilemma game: I. The effects of asymmetrical payoff information and explicit communication', *Behavl. Sci.*, 12, 314-22.

Terhune, K. W. (1968). 'Motives, situation and interpersonal conflict within the Prisoner's Dilemma', *J. Pers. Soc. Psychol.*, 8, monograph part 2.

Toussaint, J. H. (1960). 'A classified summary of listening 1950-59', *J. Communication*, 10, 125-34.

Vinokur, A. (1971). 'Review and theoretical analysis of the effects of group processes upon individual and group decisions involving risk', *Psychol. Bull.*, 76, 231-50.

Voissem, N. H., and Sistrunk, F. (1971). 'Communication schedule and cooperative game behaviour', *J. Pers. Soc. Psychol.*, 19, 160-7.

Wall, V. D., and Boyd, J. A. (1971). 'Channel variation and attitude change', *J. Communication*, 21, 363-7.

Wapner, S., and Alper, T. G. (1952). 'The effect of an audience on behaviour in a choice situation', *J. Abn. Soc. Psuchol.*, 47, 222-9.

Wilke, W. H. (1934). 'An experimental analysis of speech: the radio and the printed page as a psychological device', *Arch. Psychol. (NY)*, 169.

Wilson, C., and Williams, E. (1975). *Watergate Words: A Naturalistic Study of Media and Communication*. Unpublished Communications Studies Group paper.

Woodside, C., M. Cavers, J. K., and Buck, I. K. (1971). *Evaluation of a Video Addition to the Telephone for Engineering Conversations*. Unpublished company data.

Zajonc, R. B. (1965). 'Social facilitation', *Science*, 149, 269-74.

Zajonc, R. B., and Sales, S. M. (1966). 'Social facilitation of dominant and subordinate responses', *J. Exp. Soc. Psychol.*, 2, 160-8.

Cook, M., and Lalljee, M. (1972). 'Verbal substitutes for verbal signals in interaction', *Semiotica*, 6, 212-21.

Croft, R. G., Stimpson, D. V., Ross, W. L., Bray, R. M., and Breglio, V. J. (1969). 'Comparison of attitude changes elicited by live and videotape classroom presentations', *Audio-Visual Communications Review*, 17, 215-21.

Daniels, V. (1967). 'Communication, incentive and structural variables in interpersonal exchange and negotiation', *J. Exp. Soc. Psychol.*, 3, 47-74.

Dashiell, J. F. (1935). 'Experimental studies of the influence of social situations on the behaviour of individual human adults', in Murchison, C. (Ed.) *Handbook of Social Psychology*. Clark University Press, Worcester, Mass.

Davies, M. A. (1971). *Communication Effectiveness as a Function of Mode*. Unpublished M.A. thesis, University of Waterloo.

Davies, M. F. (1971a). *Cooperative Problem Solving: An Exploratory Study*. Unpublished Communications Studies Group paper no. E71159/DV.

Davies, M. F. (1971b). *Cooperative Problem Solving: A Follow-up Study*. Unpublished Communications Studies Group paper no. E71252/DV.

Deutsch, M., and Gerard, H. B. (1955). 'A study of normative and informational social influence upon individual judgement', *J. Abn. Soc. Psychol.*, 51, 629-36.

Deutsch, M. (1958). 'Trust and suspicion', *J. Conflict Resolution*, 2, 265-79.

Deutsch, M., and Krauss, R. M. (1962). 'Studies of interpersonal bargaining', *J. Conflict Resolution*, 4, 52-76.

Elliot, F. R. (1937). 'Eye versus ear moulding opinion', *Public Opinion Quarterly*, 1, 83-7.

Estabrook, G. G. (1930). 'A standardized hypnotic technique dictated to a victrola record', *Amer. J. Psychol.*, 42, 115-6.

Frandsen, K. D. (1963). 'Effects of threat appeals and media of transmission', *Speech Monographs*, 30, 101-4.

Froman, L. A., and Cohen, M. D. (1969). 'Threats and bargaining efficiency', *Behav. Sci.*, 14, 147-53.

Gerard, H. B. (1964). 'Conformity and commitment to the group', *J. Abn. Soc. Psychol.*, 68, 209-11.

Kogan, N., and Wallach, M. A. (1967). 'Effects of physical separation of group members upon risk taking', *Human Relations*, 20, 41-8.

Krauss, R. M., and Deutsch, M. (1966). 'Communication in interpersonal bargaining', *J. Pers. Soc. Psychol.*, 4, 572-7.

Lamm, H. (1967). 'Will an observer advise higher risk taking after hearing a discussion of the decision problem', *J. Pers. Soc. Psychol.*, 6, 467-71.

Loomis, J. L. (1959). 'Communication, the development of trust and cooperative behaviour', *Human relations*, 12, 305-15.

McClintock, C. G., Nuttin, J. M., and McNeel, S. P. (1970). 'Sociometric choice, visual presence, and game playing behaviour', *Behavl. Sci.*, 15, 124-31.

A Typology of Organizational Structure

Henry Mintzberg

The "one best way" approach has dominated our thinking about organizational structure since the turn of the century. There is a right way and a wrong way to design an organization. This approach is best captured in Colonel Urwick's famous principle of the 1930s that "no supervisor can supervise directly the work of more than five, or at the most, six subordinates whose work interlocks" (Urwick, 1956: 41). But "one best way" thinking continues to the present day, for example in the activities of consultants who believe that every organization needs MBO, or LRP, or OD.

A variety of failures, however, has made it clear that organizations differ, that long-range planning systems or organizational development programs are good for some but not others. Just as it would be foolish to restrict a foreman to a span of control of six assembly-line workers whose work interlocks, so too is there little sense in forcing formal planning on a firm that must remain highly flexible in an unpredictable market (as many firms discovered during the early days of the energy crisis).

And so recent management theory has moved away from the "one best way" approach, toward an "it all depends" approach, formally known as "contingency theory." Structure should reflect the organization's situa-

tion—for example, its age, size, type of production system, the extent to which its environment is complex and dynamic. To cite some of the more established relationships, larger organizations need more formalized structures—more rules, more planning, tighter job descriptions; so do those in stable environments and those in mass production. Organizations in more complex environments need higher degrees of decentralization; those diversified in many markets need divisionalized instead of functional structures.

This chapter argues that the "it all depends" approach does not go far enough, that structures are rightfully designed on the basis of a third approach, which might be called the "getting it all together" or, as described in Chapter 1, the "configuration" approach. Spans of control, types of formalization and decentralization, planning systems, and matrix structures should not be picked and chosen independently, the way a shopper picks vegetables at the market or a diner a meal at a buffet table. Rather, these and other parameters of organizational design should logically configure into internally consistent groupings. Like most phenomena—atoms, ants, and stars—characteristics of organizations appear to fall into natural clusters, or configurations.

We can, in fact, go a step farther and include in these configurations not only the design parameters but also the so-called contingency factors. In other words, the organization's type of environment, its production system, even its age and its size, can in some sense be "chosen" to achieve consistency with the elements of its structure. The important implication of this conclusion, in sharp contrast to that of contingency theory, is that organizations can select their situations in accordance with their structural designs just as much as they can select their designs in accordance with their situations. Diversified firms may divisionalize, but there is also evidence that divisionalized firms have a propensity to further diversify.[1] Stable environments may encourage the formalization (bureaucratization) of structure, but bureaucracies also have a habit of trying to stabilize their environments. And in contrast, entrepreneurial firms, which operate in dynamic environments, need to maintain flexible structures. But such firms also seek out and try to remain in dynamic environments in which they can outmaneuver the bureaucracies. In other words, no one factor—structural or situational—determines the others; rather, all are often logically formed into tightly knit configurations.

When the enormous amount of research that has been done on organizational structuring is looked at in the light of this conclusion, much of its confusion falls away, and a convergence is evident around five configura-

---

This chapter, authored by Henry Mintzberg, is drawn from two articles, "Configurations of Organizational Structure," in H. Meltzer and :V. R. Nord, *Making Organizations Humane and Productive* (New York: John Wiley, 1981) and "Structure in 5's: A Synthesis of the Research on Organization Design," *Management Science* (1980) 322–41, which themselves are based on *The Structuring of Organizations: A Synthesis of the Research* (Englewood Cliffs, N.J.: Prentice-Hall, Inc., 1979).

[1]See R. P. Rumelt, *Strategy, Structure and Economic Performance* (Division Research, Graduate School of Business Administration, Harvard University, 1974, pp. 76–77); and L. E. Fouraker and J. M. Stopford, "Organizational Structure and Multinational Strategy," *Administrative Science Quarterly*, 1968: 47–64.

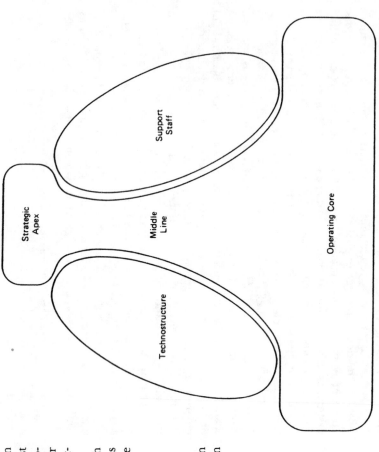

FIGURE 3-1 The Five Basic Parts of the Organization. From Henry Mintzberg, *The Structuring of Organizations* (Englewood Cliffs, N.J.: Prentice-Hall, Inc., 1979).

tions, which are distinct in their structural designs, in the situations in which they are found, and even in the periods of history in which they first developed. They are labeled Simple Structure, Machine Bureaucracy, Professional Bureaucracy, Divisionalized Form, and Adhocracy. This chapter describes them and seeks to show their relevance in the design and functioning of organizations.

To understand the five configurations, we must first understand each of the elements that make them up. After reviewing the various elements briefly, we shall show how all of them cluster together to form our five configurations.

THE ELEMENTS OF THE FIVE CONFIGURATIONS

Organizational structure becomes a problem when more than one person must coordinate different tasks to get a single job done. That coordination can be effected in five basic ways:

Direct supervision. One person gives direct orders to others and so coordinates their work, as when an entrepreneur tells different machine operators to make specific parts of an assembly.

Standardization of work processes. One person designs the general work procedures of others to ensure that these are all coordinated, as when a methods engineer specifies how an assembler should bolt a fender onto an automobile.

Standardization of outputs. One person specifies the general outputs of the work of another, as when headquarters tells a division manager to generate sales growth of 10% in a given quarter so that the firm can meet its overall growth goal.

Standardization of skills. A person is trained in a certain way so that he or she coordinates automatically with others, as when a surgeon and an anesthesiologist perform together in the operating room without having to utter a single word.

Mutual adjustment. Two or more people communicate informally among themselves to coordinate their work, as when a team of experts meet together in a space agency to design a new rocket component.

Different parts of the organization play different roles in the accomplishment of work and of these forms of coordination. Our framework introduces five basic parts of the organization, shown in Figure 3-1 and listed below:

The *operating core* is where the basic work of producing the organization's products and services gets done, where the workers assemble automobiles and the surgeons remove appendixes.

The *strategic apex* is the home of top management, where the organization is managed from a general perspective.

The *middle line* comprises all those managers who stand in a direct line relationship between the strategic apex and the operating core; among their other tasks, the managers of the middle line (as well as those of the strategic apex) carry out whatever direct supervision is necessary.

The *technostructure* includes the staff analysts who design the systems by which work processes and outputs are standardized in the organization. And the *support staff* comprises all those specialists who provide support to the organization outside of its operating workflow—in the typical manufacturing firm, everything from the cafeteria staff and the mailroom to the public relations department and the legal counsel.

The division of the labor of the organization into different tasks and the achievement of the various kinds of coordination among these tasks are accomplished through the use of a set of "design parameters," which are described in Table 3-1.

These parameters include (1) for the design of specific positions: the extent to which their tasks are specialized and their procedures formalized (by job descriptions, rules, and the like), and the extent to which the positions require formal training and indoctrination; (2) for the design of the hierarchy: the bases on which units are grouped (notably by function performed or market served) and the size of each of the units (that is, the span of control of its managers); (3) for the fleshing out of the hierarchy through lateral relationships: the use of action planning and performance control systems and of "liaison devices" such as task forces, integrating managers, and matrix structure; and (4) for the design of the decision-making system: the extent to which power is delegated down the chain of authority (called vertical decentralization) and out from that chain of authority to nonmanagers—operators, analysts, and support staffers (called horizontal decentralization).

TABLE 3-1: The Design Parameters

Job specialization refers to the number of tasks in a given job and the worker's control over these tasks. A job is *horizontally* specialized to the extent that it encompasses few, narrowly defined tasks, *vertically* specialized to the extent that the worker lacks control of the tasks performed. *Unskilled* jobs are typically highly specialized in both dimensions: skilled or *professional* jobs are typically specialized horizontally but not vertically. "Job enrichment" refers to the enlargement of jobs in both the vertical and horizontal dimensions.

Behavior formalization refers to the standardization of work processes by the imposition of operating instructions, job descriptions, rules, regulations, and the like. Structures that rely on standardization for coordination are generally referred to as *bureaucratic*, those that do not as *organic*.

Training and indoctrination refers to the use of formal instructional programs to establish and standardize in people the requisite skills, knowledge, and norms to do particular jobs in organizations. Training is a key design parameter in all work we call professional. Training and formalization are basically substitutes for achieving the standardization (in effect, the bureaucratization) of behavior. In one, the standards are internalized in formal training as skills or norms; in other, they are imposed on the job as rules.

Unit grouping refers to the choice of the bases by which positions are grouped together into units, and these units into higher-order units. Grouping encourages coordination by putting different jobs under common supervision, by requiring them to share common resources and achieve common measures of performance, and by facilitating mutual adjustment among them. The various bases for grouping—by work process, product, client, area, etc.—can be reduced to two fundamental ones—by the *function* performed or the *market* served.

Unit size refers to the number of positions (or units) contained in a single unit. The equivalent term *span of control* is not used here because sometimes units

continued

TABLE 3-1: Continued

are kept small despite an absence of close supervisory control. For example, when experts coordinate extensively by mutual adjustment, as in an engineering team in a space agency, they will form into small teams. In this case, unit size is small and span of control is low despite a relative absence of direct supervision. In contrast, when work is highly standardized (because of either formalization or training), unit size can be very large because there is little need for direct supervision. One foreman can supervise dozens of assemblers because they work according to very tight instructions.

Planning and control systems are used to standardize outputs. They may be divided into two types: *action planning* systems, which specify the results of specific actions before they are taken (for example, that holes should be drilled with diameters of three centimeters); and *performance control* systems, which specify the results of whole ranges of actions after the fact (for example, that sales of a division should grow by 10% in a given year).

Liaison devices are a whole set of mechanisms used to encourage mutual adjustment within and between units. They range from *liaison positions* (such as the purchasing engineer who stands between purchasing and engineering), through *task forces* and *standing committees* that bring together members of many departments, and *integrating managers* (such as brand managers), finally to fully developed *matrix structures*.

Vertical decentralization describes the extent to which decision-making power is delegated to managers down the middle line; *horizontal decentralization* describes the extent to which nonmanagers (that is, people in the operating core, technostructure, and support staff) control decision processes. Moreover, decentralization may be *selective*—concerning only specific kinds of decisions—or *parallel*—concerning many kinds of decision altogether. Five types of decentralization may be described: (1) vertical and horizontal centralization, where all power rests at the strategic apex; (2) limited horizontal decentralization (selective), where the strategic apex shares some power with the technostructure that standardizes everybody else's work; (3) limited vertical decentralization (parallel), where managers of market-based units are delegated the power to control most of the decisions concerning their line units; (4) vertical and horizontal decentralization, where most of the power rests in the operating core, at the bottom of the structure; and (5) selective vertical and horizontal decentralization, where the power over different decisions is dispersed widely in the organization, among managers, staff experts, and operators who work in groups at various levels in the hierarchy.

A number of contingency or situational factors influence the choice of these design parameters, and vice versa. These include the age and size of the organization; its technical system of production; various characteristics of its environment, such as stability and complexity; and its power system, for example, whether or not it is tightly controlled from the outside. Some of their influences on the design parameters are summarized in Table 3-2.

3-1) five types of decentralization. In fact, the five configurations bring all of these fives together. Specifically:

The natural tendency of a *strategic apex* concerned with tight control is to coordinate by *direct supervision*; when that is what the organization needs, *vertical and horizontal centralization* results, and the organization tends to use what we call the *Simple Structure*.

The *technostructure* encourages coordination by *standardization* (especially of *work process*, the tightest form), since it designs the systems of standards; when that is what the organization needs, it accepts *limited horizontal decentralization* to the technostructure, and a configuration called *Machine Bureaucracy* results.

The workers of the *operating core* prefer autonomy above all, which they come closest to achieving when coordination of their work is effected mainly by the *standardization of skills*; organizations that must rely on this form of coordination accept *vertical and horizontal decentralization* to their highly skilled operators and use the *Professional Bureaucracy* configuration.

The managers of the *middle line* try to balkanize the structure, to encourage *limited vertical decentralization* to their level so that their units can operate as semiautonomous entities, controlled from above only by performance control systems based on *standardization of outputs*; when this is what the organization needs, the *Divisionalized Form* results.

And when the *support staff* (and sometimes the operators as well) favor collaboration—the working together in groups whose tasks are coordinated by *mutual adjustment*—and this is what the organization needs, *selective vertical and horizontal decentralization* results, and the structure takes on the form of what we call the *Adhocracy*.

Let us now take a closer look at each of these five structural configurations, whose characteristics are summarized in Table 3-3.

The Simple Structure

As shown in Figure 3-2, the Simple Structure is characterized, above all, by what it is *not*—elaborated. Typically, it has little or no technostructure, few support staffers, a loose division of labor, minimal differentiation among its units, and a small middle line hierarchy. Little of its behavior is formalized, and it makes minimal use of planning, training, or the liaison devices. It is, above all, organic. Its coordination is effected largely by direct supervision. Specifically, power over all important decisions tends to be centralized in the hands of the chief executive officer. Thus, the strategic apex emerges as the key part of the structure; indeed, the structure often consists of little more than a one-person strategic apex and an organic operating core. Grouping into units—if it exists at all—more often than not is on a loose functional basis. Likewise, decision making is informal, with the centralization of power allowing for rapid response.

TABLE 3-2:   The Contingency Factors

Age and Size have both been shown in the research to have important effects on structure. In particular, the older and/or larger an organization, the more formalized its behavior. Moreover, it has been found that the larger the organization, the larger the size of its average unit and the more elaborate its structure; that is, the more specialized its tasks, the more differentiated its units, and the more developed its administrative component of middle line and technostructure. Finally, Stinchcombe (1965) has shown that the structure of an organization often reflects the age of founding of its industry.

Technical System has been found to affect certain design parameters significantly. For one thing, the more regulating the technical system—in other words, the more it controls the work of the operators—the more formalized is their work and the more bureaucratic is the structure of the operating core. And the more sophisticated the technical system—that is, the more difficult it is to understand—the more elaborate the administrative structure; specifically, the larger and more professional the support staff, the greater the selective decentralization (of technical decisions to that staff), and the greater the use of liaison devices (to coordinate the work of the staff). Finally, Woodward (1965) has shown how the automation of the work of the operating core tends to transform a bureaucratic administrative structure into an organic one.

Environment is another major contingency factor discussed in the literature. Dynamic environments have been identified with organic structures, and complex environments with decentralized ones. However, laboratory evidence suggests that hostile environments might lead organizations to centralize their structures temporarily. And disparities in the environment appear to encourage selective decentralization to differentiated work constellations. Finally, there is a good deal of evidence that diversification of the organization's markets encourages the use of market basis for grouping at high levels, assuming favorable economies of scale.

Power factors have also been shown to have selective effects on structure. Most important, external control of organizations appears to increase formalization and centralization. The need for power of the various members can influence the distribution of decision-making authority, especially in the case of a chief executive whose strong need for power tends to increase centralization. And fashion has been shown to have an influence on structure, sometimes driving organizations to favor inappropriate but fashionable structures.

Note: For references supporting these relationships, see Mintzberg (1979).

CONFIGURING THE ELEMENTS

Up to this point, we have introduced a host of bits and pieces about the structuring of organizations: lots of trees, but still no forests. But a number of forests begin to emerge as we stand back from the specifics and try to perceive the whole picture.

The number 5 appeared frequently in our discussion. There were five coordinating mechanisms, five parts of the organization, and (in Table

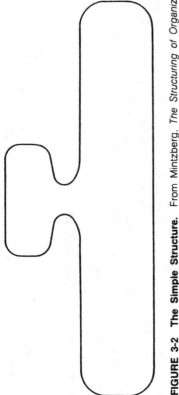

FIGURE 3-2 The Simple Structure. From Mintzberg. *The Structuring of Organizations.*

Above all, the environment of the Simple Structure tends to be at the same time simple and dynamic. A simple environment can be comprehended by a single individual, and so allows decision making to be controlled by that individual. And a dynamic environment requires organic structure. Because the future state of the environment cannot be predicted, the organization cannot effect coordination by standardization. Another condition common to Simple Structure is a technical system that is neither sophisticated nor regulating. A sophisticated system would require an elaborate support structure, to which power over technical decisions would have to be delegated, whereas a regulating one would call for bureaucratization of the operating core. Young organizations and small organizations also tend to use the Simple Structure, because they have not yet had the time, or yet reached the scale of operations, required for bureaucratization. Finally, extreme hostility in their environments forces most organizations to use the Simple Structure, no matter how they are normally organized. To deal with crises, organizations tend to centralize at the top temporarily, and to suspend their standard operating procedures.

The classic case of the Simple Structure is, of course, the entrepreneurial firm. The firm is aggressive and often innovative, continually searching for risky environments where the bureaucracies hesitate to operate. But it is also careful to remain in a market niche that its entrepreneur can fully comprehend. Entrepreneurial firms are usually small, so that they can remain organic and their entrepreneurs can retain tight control. Also, they are often young, in part because the attrition rate among entrepreneurial firms is so high, and in part because those that survive tend to make the transition to bureaucracy as they age. Inside the structure, all revolves around the entrepreneur. Its goals are his or her goals, its strategy his or her vision of its place in the world. Most entrepreneurs loathe bureaucratic procedures as impositions on their flexibility. Their unpredictable maneuvering keeps their structures lean, flexible, organic. Khandwalla (1977) found this structural form in his research on Ca-

TABLE 3-3: Dimensions of the Five Structural Configurations

	SIMPLE STRUCTURE	MACHINE BUREAUCRACY	PROFESSIONAL BUREAUCRACY	DIVISIONALIZED FORM	ADHOCRACY
KEY COORDINATING MECHANISM	DIRECT SUPERVISION	STANDARDIZATION OF WORK	STANDARDIZATION OF SKILLS	STANDARDIZATION OF OUTPUTS	MUTUAL ADJUSTMENT
KEY PART OF ORGANIZATION	STRATEGIC APEX	TECHNOSTRUCTURE	OPERATING CORE	MIDDLE LINE	SUPPORT STAFF (WITH OPERATING CORE IN OP. AD.)
Design Parameters					
Specialization of Jobs	Little specialization	*Much horizontal and vertical specialization*	*Much horizontal specialization*	Some horizontal and vertical specialization (between divisions and HQ)	*Much horizontal specialization*
Training and Indoctrination	Little training and indoctrination	Little training and indoctrination	*Much training and indoctrination*	Some training and indoctrination (of division managers)	Much training
Formalization of Behavior: Bureaucratic/Organic	Little formalization *Organic*	*Much formalization* Bureaucratic	Little formalization Bureaucratic	Much formalization (within divisions) Bureaucratic	Little formalization Organic
Grouping	Usually functional	*Usually functional*	Functional and market	*Market*	*Functional and market*
Unit Size	Wide	Wide at bottom, narrow elsewhere	Wide at bottom, narrow elsewhere	Wide (at top)	*Narrow throughout*
Planning and Control Systems	Little planning and control	Action planning	Little planning and control	*Much performance control*	Limited action planning (esp. in adm. ad.)
Liaison Devices	Few liaison devices	Few liaison devices	Liaison devices in administration	Few liaison devices	*Many liaison devices throughout*
Decentralization	*Centralization*	*Limited horizontal decentralization*	*Horizontal and vertical decentralization*	*Limited vertical decentralization*	*Selective decentralization*
Contingency Factors					
Age and Size	Typically young and small	Typically old and large	Varies	Typically old and very large	Typically young (Op. Ad.)
Technical System	Simple, not regulating	Regulating but not automated, not very complex	Not regulating or complex	Divisible, otherwise typically like machine bureaucracy	Very complex, often automated (in Adm. Ad.); not regulating or complex (in Op. Ad.)
Environment	Simple and dynamic; sometimes hostile	Simple and stable	Complex and stable	Relatively simple and stable; diversified markets (especially products and services)	Complex and dynamic; sometimes disparate (in Adm. Ad.)
Power	Chief-executive control; often owner-managed; not fashionable	Technocratic and external control; not fashionable	Professional-operator control; fashionable	Middle-line control; fashionable (especially in industry)	Expert control; very fashionable

ᵃItalic type designates key design parameter.

nadian companies. Pugh et al. (1969) also allude to this form in what they call "implicitly structured organizations," and Woodward (1965) describes such a structure among the smaller unit production and single-purpose process firms.

The Machine Bureaucracy

A second clear configuration of the design parameters has held up consistently in the research: highly specialized, routine operating tasks, very formalized procedures and large-sized units in the operating core, reliance on the functional basis for grouping tasks throughout the structure, little use made of training and of the liaison devices, relatively centralized power for decision making with some use of action planning systems, and an elaborate administrative structure with a sharp distinction between line and staff. This is the structure Woodward (1965) found in the mass-production firms, Burns and Stalker (1961) in the textile industry, Crozier (1964) in the tobacco monopoly, Lawrence and Lorsch (1967) in the container firm; it is the structure the Aston group (Pugh et al., 1969) referred to as "workflow bureaucracy."

Despite its sharp distinction between line and staff, because the Machine Bureaucracy depends above all on standardization of work processes for coordination, the technostructure, which houses the many analysts who do the standardizing, emerges as the key part of the structure. Consequently, these analysts develop some informal power, with the result that the organization can be described as having limited horizontal decentralization. The analysts gain their power largely at the expense of the operators, whose work they formalize to a high degree, and of the first-line managers, who would otherwise supervise the operators directly. But the emphasis on standardization extends well above the operating core, and with it follows the analysts' influence. Rules and regulations—an obsession with control—permeate the entire structure; formal communication is favored at all levels; decision making tends to follow the formal chain of authority. Only at the strategic apex are the different functional responsibilities brought together; therefore, only at that level can the major decisions be made, hence the centralization of the structure in the vertical dimension.

The Machine Bureaucracy is typically associated with environments that are both simple and stable. The work of complex environments cannot be rationalized into simple operating tasks, and that of dynamic environments cannot be predicted, made repetitive, and so standardized. Thus the Machine Bureaucracy responds to a simple, stable environment, and in turn seeks to ensure that its environment remains both simple and stable. In fact, this helps to explain the large size of the support staff in the Machine Bureaucracy, as shown in Figure 3-3. To ensure stability, the Machine Bureaucracy prefers to make rather than buy—to supply its own support services wherever possible so that it can closely control them. In

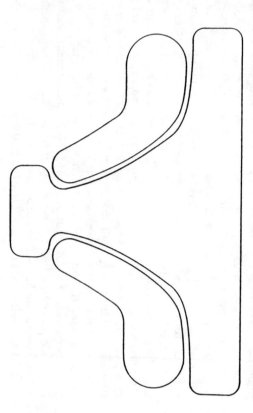

FIGURE 3-3 The Machine Bureaucracy. From Mintzberg, *The Structuring of Organizations.*

addition, the Machine Bureaucracy is typically found in the mature organization, large enough to have the scale of operations that allows for repetition and standardization, and old enough to have been able to settle on the standards it wishes to use. Machine Bureaucracies also tend to be identified with regulating technical systems, since these routinize work and so enable that work to be standardized. But they are not typically found with sophisticated or automated technical systems because, as noted earlier, one disperses power to the support staff and the other calls for organic structure in administration, thereby driving the organization to a different configuration. Finally, the Machine Bureaucracy is often associated with external control. The greater the external control of an organization, the more its structure tends to be centralized and formalized, the two prime design parameters of the Machine Bureaucracy.

Typical examples of organizations drawn to the Machine Bureaucracy configuration are mass-production firms; service firms with simple, repetitive work, such as insurance and telephone companies; government agencies with similar work, such as post offices and tax collection departments; and organizations that have special needs for safety, such as airlines and fire departments.

The Professional Bureaucracy

Organizations can be bureaucratic without being centralized: that is, their behavior can be standardized by a coordinating mechanism that allows for decentralization, a reliance on the standardization of skills, a reliance on which gives rise to the configuration called

Professional Bureaucracy, found typically in school systems, social-work agencies, accounting firms, and craft manufacturing firms. The organization hires highly trained specialists—called professionals—in its operating core, and then gives them considerable autonomy in their work. In other words, professionals work relatively free not only of the administrative hierarchy but also of their own colleagues. Much of the necessary coordination is achieved by design—by the standard skills that predetermine behavior. And this autonomy in the operating core means that the operating units are typically very large, as shown in Figure 3-4, and that the structure is decentralized in both the vertical and horizontal dimensions. In other words, much of the formal and informal power of the Professional Bureaucracy rests in its operating core, clearly its key part. Not only do the professionals control their own work, but they also tend to maintain collective control of the administrative apparatus of the organization. Managers of the middle line, in order to have power in the Professional Bureaucracy, must be professionals themselves, and must maintain the support of the professional operators. Moreover, they typically share the administrative tasks with the operating professionals. At the administrative level, however, in contrast with the operating level, tasks require a good deal of mutual adjustment, achieved in large part through standing committees, task forces, and other liaison devices.

The technostructure is minimal in this configuration, because the complex work of the operating professionals cannot easily be formalized, nor can its outputs be standardized by action planning and performance control systems. The support staff is, however, highly elaborated, as shown in Figure 3-4, largely to carry out the simpler, more routine work and to back up the high-priced professionals. As a result, the support staff tend to be split in a machine-bureaucratic pocket off to one side of the Professional Bureaucracy. For the support staff of these organizations, there is no democracy, only the oligarchy of the professionals. Finally, a curious feature

of this configuration is that it uses the functional and market bases for grouping concurrently in its operating core. That is, clients are categorized and served in terms of functional specialties—chemistry students by the chemistry department in the university, cardiac patients by the cardiac department in the hospital.[2]

The Professional Bureaucracy typically appears in conjunction with an environment that is both complex and stable. Complexity demands the use of skills and knowledge that can be learned only in extensive training programs, and stability ensures that these skills settle down to become the standard operating procedures of the organization. Age and size are not important factors in this configuration: The organization tends to use the same standard skills no matter how small or young it is, because its professionals bring these skills with them when they first join the organization. So unlike the Machine Bureaucracy, which must design its own standards, in the Professional Bureaucracy little time and no scale of operations are required to establish standards. The technical system is of importance in this configuration only for what it is not—neither regulating, nor sophisticated, nor automated. Any one of these characteristics would destroy individual operator autonomy in favor of administrative or peer-group influence, and so drive the organization to a different configuration. Finally, fashion is a factor, simply because it has proven to the advantage of all kinds of operator groups to have their work defined as professional; this enables them to demand influence and autonomy in the organization. For this reason, Professional Bureaucracy is a highly fashionable structure today.

The Divisionalized Form

The Divisionalized Form is not so much a complete structure as the superimposition of one structure on others. This structure can be described as market-based, with a central headquarters overseeing a set of divisions, each charged with serving its own markets. In this way there need be little interdependence between the divisions (beyond that which Thompson [1967] refers to as the "pooled" type), and little in the way of close coordination. Each division is thus given a good deal of autonomy. The result is the limited, parallel form of vertical decentralization.[3] with the middle line emerging as the key part of the organization. Moreover,

[2] It is interesting to note that in Simon's (1957: 30) criticism in *Administrative Behavior* of the ambiguities in the classical distinction between grouping by process and by purpose, all his examples are drawn from professional work.

[3] "Limited" means that the equating of divisionalization with "decentralization," as is done in so much of the literature, is simply not correct. In fact, as Perrow (1974: 38) points out, the most famous example of divisionalization—that of General Motors in the 1920s—was clearly one of the relative *centralization* of the structure.

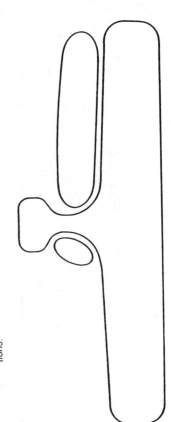

FIGURE 3-4   The Professional Bureaucracy.   From Mintzberg, *The Structuring of Organizations.*

market diversity; specifically, that of products and services. (Diversity only in region or client leads, as Channon [1976] has shown, to an incomplete form of divisionalization, with certain "critical" functions concentrated at headquarters, as in the case of purchasing in a regionally diversified retailing chain.) But by the same token, it has also been found that divisionalization encourages further diversification (Rumelt, 1974: 76–77; Fouraker and Stopford, 1968), headquarters being encouraged to do so by the ease with which it can add divisions and by the pressures from the corps of aggressive general managers trained in the middle lines of such structures. Otherwise, as befits a structure that houses Machine Bureaucracies, the Divisionalized Form shares many of their conditions—an environment that is neither very complex nor very dynamic, and an organization that is typically large and mature. In effect, the Divisionalized Form is the common structural response to an integrated Machine Bureaucracy that has diversified its product or service lines horizontally (that is, in conglomerate fashion).

The Divisionalized Form is very fashionable in industry. It is found in pure or partial form among the vast majority of America's largest corporations, the notable exceptions being those with giant economies of scale in their traditional businesses (Wrigley, 1970; Rumelt, 1974). It is also found outside the sphere of business (in the form of multiveriries, conglomerate unions, and government itself), but often in impure form owing to the difficulty of developing relevant performance measures.

The Adhocracy

Sophisticated innovation requires a fifth and very different structural configuration, one that is able to fuse experts drawn from different specialties into smoothly functioning project teams. Adhocracy is such a configuration, consisting of organic structure with little formalization of behavior; extensive horizontal job specialization based on formal training; a tendency to group the professional specialists in functional units for housekeeping purposes but to deploy them in small, market-based teams to do their project work. It relies on the liaison devices to encourage mutual adjustment—the key coordinating mechanism—within and between these teams, and decentralizes power selectively to these teams, which are located at various places in the organization and involve various mixtures of line managers and staff and operating experts. Of all the configurations, Adhocracy shows the least reverence for the classical principles of management. It gives quasi-formal authority to staff personnel, thereby blurring the line–staff distinction, and it relies extensively on matrix structure, combining functional and market bases for grouping concurrently and thereby dispensing with the principle of unity of command.

Adhocracies may be divided into two main types. In the *Operating*

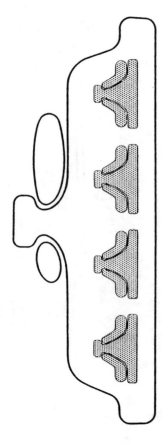

FIGURE 3-5   The Divisionalized Form.   From Mintzberg, *The Structuring of Organizations.*

without the need for close coordination, a large number of divisions can report to the one central headquarters. The main concern of that headquarters then becomes to find a mechanism to coordinate the goals of the divisions with its own, without sacrificing divisional autonomy. And that it does by standardizing the outputs of the divisions—specifically, by relying on performance control systems to impose performance standards on the divisions and then monitor their results. Hence, Figure 3-5 shows a small headquarters technostructure, which is charged with designing and operating the performance control system. Also shown is a small headquarters support staff. Included here are those units that serve all the divisions (such as legal counsel), with other support units dispersed to the divisions to serve their particular needs (such as industrial relations).

Finally, there arises the question of what structure is found in the divisions themselves. Although in principle the Divisionalized Form is supposed to work with any kind of structure in the divisions, in fact there is reason to believe, as illustrated in Figure 3-5, that the divisions are driven to use the Machine Bureaucracy. The Divisionalized Form requires the establishment for each division of clearly defined performance standards, the existence of which depend on two major assumptions. First, each division must be treated as a single integrated system with a single, consistent set of goals. In other words, although the divisions may be loosely coupled within each other, the assumption is that each is tightly coupled within. Second, goals must be operational ones—in other words, lend themselves to quantitative measures of performance control. And these two assumptions hold only in one configuration, the one that is both bureaucratic (that is, operates in a stable enough environment to be able to establish performance standards) and integrated; in other words, in Machine Bureaucracy. Moreover, as noted earlier, external control drives organizations toward Machine Bureaucracy. Here the headquarters constitutes external control of the divisions.

One factor above all encourages the use of the Divisionalized Form—

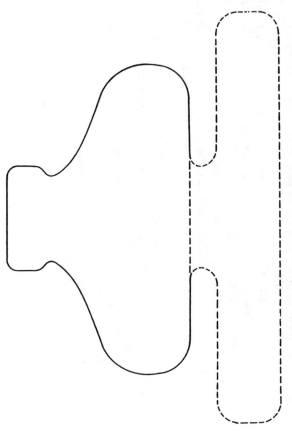

FIGURE 3-6 The Adhocracy. From Mintzberg. *The Structuring of Organizations.*

Adhocracy, the innovation is carried out directly on behalf of the clients, as in the case of consulting firms, advertising agencies, and film companies. In effect, there corresponds to every Professional Bureaucracy an Operating Adhocracy that does similar work but with a broader orientation. For every consulting firm that seeks to pigeonhole each client problem into the most relevant standard skill within its given repertoire, there is another that treats that problem as a unique challenge requiring a creative solution. The former, because of its standardization, can allow its professional operators to work on their own; the latter, in order to achieve innovation, must group its professionals in multidisciplinary teams so as to encourage mutual adjustment. In the Operating Adhocracy, the administrative and operating work tend to blend into a single effort. In other words, ad hoc project work does not allow a sharp differentiation of the planning and design of the work from its actual execution.

In the *Administrative Adhocracy*, the project work serves the organization itself, as in the case of chemical firms and space agencies. And here the administrative and operating components are sharply differentiated; in fact, the operating core is typically truncated from the rest of the organization—set up as a separate structure, contracted out, or automated—so that the administrative component is free to function as an Adhocracy.

Figure 3-6 shows both types of Adhocracies, with the blurring of the line–staff distinction in both cases and the truncation of the operating core (indicated by dotted lines), or else, in the case of the Operating Adhocracy, its inclusion in the mass of activities in the administrative center. The figure also shows a partial blurring of the strategic apex with the rest of the structure. This is because in project work, strategy is not imposed from above. Rather, it emerges from the stream of ad hoc decisions made for all the projects. Hence, everyone who is involved in the project work—and in the Adhocracy that can mean everyone in the organization—is involved in strategy making. The key role of the support staff should be underlined here, especially in the Administrative Adhocracy, which houses many of its experts in that staff.

Adhocracy is clearly positioned in environments that are both dynamic and complex. These are the ones that demand sophisticated innovation, the kind of innovation that calls for organic structure with a good deal of decentralization. Disparate forces in the environment, by encouraging selective decentralization to differentiated work constellations, as noted earlier, also encourage use of Adhocracy, notably the administrative kind. Age—or at least youth—is another condition associated with Adhocracy, because time encourages an organization to bureaucratize—for example, by settling on the set of skills it performs best and so converting itself from an Operating Adhocracy into a Professional Bureaucracy. Moreover, because Operating Adhocracies in particular are such vulnerable structures—they can never be sure where their next project will come from—they tend

to be very young on average. Many of them either die early or else shift to bureaucratic configurations to escape the uncertainty.

Adhocracies of the administrative kind are also associated with technical systems that are sophisticated and automated. Sophistication requires that power over decisions concerning the technical system be given to specialists in the support staff, thereby creating selective decentralization to a work constellation that makes heavy use of the liaison devices. And automation in the operating core transforms a bureaucratic administrative structure into an organic one, because it frees the organization of the need to control operators by technocratic standards. The standards are built right into the machines. In effect, the support staff, being charged with the selection and engineering of the automated equipment, takes over the function of designing the work of the operating core. The result is the Adhocracy configuration.

Finally, fashion is an important factor, because every characteristic of Adhocracy is very much in vogue today—emphasis on expertise, organic and matrix structure, teams and task forces, decentralization without power concentration, sophisticated and automated technical systems, youth, and complex, dynamic environments. In fact, perhaps the best support for Stinchcombe's claim, cited earlier, that structure reflects the age of founding of the industry, comes from the observation that although Adhocracy seems to be used in few industries that were fully developed before World War II, it is found extensively in almost every one that developed

References

BURNS, T., and G. STALKER *The Management of Innovation*. London: Tavistock, 1961.

CHANDLER, M. K., and J. B. SAYLES *Managing Large Systems*. New York: Harper & Row, 1971.

CHANNON, D. "Corporate Evolution in the Service Industries: 1950-1974," in L. Hannah, ed., *Corporate Strategy and Management Organization*. London: McMillan, 1976.

CROZIER, M. *The Bureaucratic Phenomenon*. Chicago: University of Chicago Press, 1964.

FOURAKER, L. E., and J. M. STOPFORD "Organizational Structure and Multinational Strategy," *Administrative Science Quarterly*, 13 (1968) 47-64.

GALBRAITH, J. *Designing Complex Organizations*. Reading, Mass.: Addison-Wesley, 1973.

KHANDWALLA, P. *The Design of Organizations*. New York: Harcourt Brace Jovanovich, 1977.

LAWRENCE, P. R., and J. W. LORSCH *Organization and Environment*. Boston: Harvard University Press, 1967.

MINTZBERG, H. "Strategy Making in Three Modes," *California Management Review*, 16 (1973), 44-58.

PERROW, C. "Is Business Really Changing?" *Organizational Dynamics*, Summer 1974, 31-44.

PUGH, D. S., D. J. HICKSON, and C. R. HININGS "An Empirical Taxonomy of Structures of Work Organizations," *Administrative Science Quarterly*, 14 (1969), 115-26.

RUMELT, R. P. *Strategy, Structure, and Economic Performance*. Cambridge, Mass.: Division of Research, Graduate School of Business Administration, Harvard University, 1974.

SIMON, H. A. *Administrative Behavior*. New York: Free Press, 1957

STINCHCOMBE, A. L. "Social Structure and Organizations," in J. G. March, ed., *Handbook of Organizations*, Chap. 4. Chicago: Rand McNally, 1965.

THOMPSON, J. *Organizations in Action*. New York: McGraw-Hill, 1967.

URWICK, L. F. "The Manager's Span of Control," *Harvard Business Review*, May-June 1956, pp. 39-47.

WOODWARD, J. *Industrial Organization: Theory and Practice*. London: Oxford University Press, 1965.

WRIGLEY, L. "Diversification and Divisional Autonomy." D.B.A. Thesis, Harvard Business School, 1970.

since that time. Thus, it is described by Lawrence and Lorsch (1967) in plastics companies, by Chandler and Sayles (1971) in NASA, by Woodward (1965) in modern process production, and by Galbraith (1973) in the Boeing Company. Adhocracy seems clearly to be the structure of *our* age.

BEYOND THE FIVE CONFIGURATIONS

Our five configurations have been referred to in this chapter as ideal or pure types. The question then arises as to where—or whether—they can be found. It is clear that each configuration is a simplification, understanding the true complexity of all but the simplest organizational structures. In that sense, every sentence in our description of the configurations has been an overstatement (including this one!). And yet our reading of the research literature suggests that in many cases, the need to favor one of the five coordinating mechanisms introduced earlier draws the organization toward one of the configurations. It is presumably its search for harmony in structure and situation that causes an organization to favor one of the pure types.

Other structures, of course, emerge differently. Some appear to be in transition from one pure type to another, in response to a changed situation. Others exhibit structures that can be described as hybrids of the configurations, perhaps because different forces pull them toward different pure types. The symphony orchestra, for example, seems to use a combination of Simple Structure and Professional Bureaucracy: It hires highly trained musicians and relies largely on their standardized skills to produce its music, yet it also requires a strong, sometimes autocratic, leader to weld them into a tightly coordinated unit. Other hybrids seem to be dysfunctional, as in the case of the organization that no sooner gives its middle managers autonomy subject to performance control, as in the Divisionalized Form, than it takes it away by direct supervision, as in the Simple Structure. School systems, police forces, and the like are often forced to centralize power inappropriately because of the external controls imposed upon them. Would-be Professional Bureaucracies become Machine Bureaucracies, to the regret of operator and client alike.

The point to be emphasized is not that the five configurations represent some final typology; but that together as a set they represent a conceptual framework that can be used to help us comprehend organizational behavior: how structures emerge, how and why they change over time, and why certain pathologies plague organizational design.

## CHAPTER 4

Groupware Design and Evaluation Methodologies

The field of CSCW is, in a sense, an extension of the field of *human-computer interaction*, the study of the processes and technologies of interaction between human and computer (Baecker and Buxton, 1987; Baecker, Buxton, and Grudin, 1993). Three of the major achievements of human-computer interaction and user interface design during the past decade have been:

- The concept of *iterative design*, in which systems are developed and improved through successive stages of design, implementation, and usability testing (Gould and Lewis, 1985; Gould, 1988)

- The concept of *user-centered design*, in which systems are developed and improved through user involvement and input at every stage of the design cycle (Gould and Lewis, 1985; Norman and Draper, 1986; Gould, 1988; Olson and Olson, 1991)

- The concept of *multidisciplinary design*, in which systems and interfaces are developed and improved through the coordinated work of experts from a variety of disciplines, including, for example, computer science, psychology, and graphic design (Kim, 1990).

Because of the complexities and subtleties when groups interact, design and evaluation processes for groupware technologies need to be more sophisticated than those for single-user software. The first reading in this chapter highlights an approach to design pioneered in Scandinavia, which variously is called *the collective resource approach*, *participatory design*, or *cooperative design* (Bjerknes, Ehn, and Kyng, 1987; Greenbaum and Kyng, 1991). This approach goes beyond what is typically known as user-centered design in two major ways:

- Users must be involved in design from the outset, not merely as clients, consultants, or subjects, but as equal participants and co-designers.

- Both the process and end result of designing and implementing computer technology are intensely political; recognizing this early on and dealing with it openly gives us the best chance of satisfactorily resolving the real political conflicts that arise out of computerization.

"Designing for Cooperation—Cooperating in Design" by Kyng (1991) reviews and illustrates the collective resource approach and shows how it can lead to cooperative design. Stress is placed on building cooperation throughout the design process, even through the choice of language; for example, the term *mutual learning* is adopted in place of the conventional phrase *analysis*. A variety of methods and tools for cooperative design are then presented.

We now turn our attention to the evaluation of groupware and its impacts. An excerpt from "Methods for the Study of Groups," a chapter in McGrath (1984, pp. 29–37), reviews issues in the choice of a research strategy to study group behavior. McGrath stresses the three goals of *generalizability, precision,* and *realism* in the gathering of research evidence. It is impossible to maximize all three in a single study, so tradeoffs among these goals must be considered when one chooses a research method. Methods are categorized in terms of a taxonomy of research strategies, including *laboratory experiments, field studies,* and *sample surveys.* The excerpt concludes with a discussion of what one compares and what one learns when conducting a study of group behavior.

McGrath's methods are drawn primarily from psychology and sociology. Anthropologists have during the last decade joined the research community that observes and tries to understand human behavior in its use of information technology. One of the major strengths they have brought to this endeavor is the viewpoint of *interaction analysis.* Detailed recordings and analyses are made of human verbal and non-verbal behavior and of the "conversations" that occur in both individual and group usage of and interaction with technology. "Understanding Practice: Video as a Medium for Reflection and Design" by Suchman and Trigg (1991) provides a brief introduction to the use of interaction analysis in the development of computer technology. Interaction analysis is described in terms of *ethnography* and *ethnomethodology* (see Notes below). Stress is placed on the role of artifacts in facilitating coordination of the activities of co-workers. Methods of interaction analysis using video data collection and *protocol analysis* are described in some detail, as is a computer environment for video analysis.

A design methodology influenced by ethnography that assumes lesser user involvement than does participatory design is presented by Fafchamps (1991) in "Ethnographic Workflow Analysis: Specifications for Design." With the goal of providing designers with "timely design specifications that are faithful to the users' actual work practices," she proposes five methods of ethnographic data collection: collection of *thinking aloud* protocols, guided tours of work spaces, structured observation of work, collection of written artifacts, and focused interviews. Systematic data analysis is aimed at identifying breakdowns in carrying out tasks, typical actions, routine sequences of actions, comments on work objects and

procedures, and descriptions of the work environment or infrastructure.

Much of group behavior, whether aided or not by technology, is mediated by conversation. "Grounding in Communication" by Clark and Brennan (1991) illustrates *conversation analysis,* which has become a vital tool for understanding the impacts of groupware. The paper deals with the role and nature of *common ground* in cooperative work. The authors define common ground as "mutual knowledge, mutual beliefs, and mutual assumptions." They describe how *grounding* contributes to conversation, and propose *the principle of least collaborative effort,* suggesting that, in conversation, participants try to minimize their collaborative effort, the work that they both do in carrying out the conversation. They later turn their attention to how grounding changes with the medium of conversation, and list eight constraints that a medium may impose on communication between two people: *copresence, visibility, audibility, cotemporality, simultaneity, sequentiality, reviewability,* and *revisability.* Common communication media are then described in terms of these constraints.

Notes and Guide to Further Reading

Ehn (1979), Bjerknes, Ehn, and Kyng (Eds.) (1987), Greenbaum and Kyng (Eds.) (1991), Schuler and Namioko (Eds.) (1992), Schuler and Namioko (Eds.) (1992), and Muller, Kuhn, and Meskill (Eds.) (1992) review participatory design and cooperative design. Schuler and Namioko (Eds.) (1992) is a collection of papers based on a conference documented in Schuler and Namioko (Eds.) (1990), with many of the contributions substantially enhanced and other new chapters added. Bødker and Grønbaek (1991a, b) provide good illustrations of cooperative prototyping activities. Muller (1991, 1992) presents an interesting approach to participatory design using "low-tech objects" such as magic markers and post-its and "high(er)-tech recording" using video. Kuutti and Arvonen (1992) suggest that *activity theory* is useful for identifying and evaluating potential CSCW applications.

Bannon (1991) suggests the human-computer interaction field needs to move from the study of "human factors" in the laboratory to the study of "human actors" in real live work contexts. Aiding us in this effort can be interaction analysis, a painstaking and delicate craft rooted in a number of disciplines from sociology and anthropology, namely ethnography, ethnomethodology, and conversation analysis. One introduction to ethnography is Hammersley and Atkinson (1989), who define it as follows (p. 2):

> ... for us ethnography (or participant observation, a cognate term) is simply one social research method, albeit a somewhat unusual one, drawing as it does on a wide range of sources of information. The ethnographer participates, overtly or covertly, in people's daily lives for an extended period of time, watching what happens, listening to what is said, asking questions, in fact collecting whatever data are available to throw light on the issues with which he or she is concerned.

Good sources on ethnomethodology are Garfinkel (1967, 1986) and Heritage (1984). Garfinkel (1967, p. vii) describes it as follows:

> Ethnomethodological studies analyze everyday activities as members' [sociologists'] methods for making those same activities visibly-rational-and-reportable-for-all-practical-purposes, i.e., "accountable," as organizations of commonplace everyday activities.

An essential tool of ethnomethodology is conversation analysis (Atkinson and Heritage, Eds., 1984; Roger and Bull, Eds., 1989; Luff, Gilbert, and Frohlich, Eds., 1990; Hirst, 1991). Roger and Bull (1989, p. 3) describe the relationship between conversation analysis and ethnomethodology as follows:

> Conversation analysis has developed over the past 15 years within the framework of ethnomethodology. The term "ethnomethodology was coined by Garfinkel. ... What is proposed is that any competent member of society (including the professional social scientist) is equipped with a methodology for analysing social phenomena; the term "ethnomethodology" thus refers to the study of the ways in which everyday common-sense activities are analysed by participants, and of the ways in which these analyses are incorporated into courses of action. The most promi-

nent development within ethnomethodology is undoubtedly that which has become to be known as conversation analysis, which examines the procedures used in the production of ordinary conversation.

A classic example of interaction analysis is the work of Suchman (1987). Other more recent examples include Linde (1988), Hutchins (1990), Heath and Luff (1991a), Suchman (1991), and Flor and Hutchins (1991, included in Chapter 5 of this volume). Luff, Heath, and Greatbatch (1992) explore the use of paper and screen-based documentation in both synchronous and asynchronous collaborative activity. Hughes, Randall, and Shapiro (1992) and Bentley, Rodden, Sawyer, Sommerville, Hughes, Randall, and Shapiro (1992) apply ethnography to the study of air traffic control and to systems design for air traffic control. Reder and Schwab (1988) apply conversation analysis to study *channel choice* and *channel switching* in communication among individuals who can communicate using a number of different media. Whittaker, Brennan, and Clark (1991) apply conversation analysis to the study of communication using a shared electronic whiteboard with and without the addition of a speech channel. McCarthy, Miles, and Monk (1991) apply conversation analysis to compare communication with and without a shared workspace.

Another outstanding example of an interactive system for the analysis of video records of group interaction and behavior is presented by Losada and Markovitch (1990) in "GroupAnalyzer: A System for Dynamic Analysis of Group Interaction." The GroupAnalyzer system facilitates the real-time coding of individuals' behavior in a meeting using the SYMLOG formalism of Bales (1950; see also Bales and Cohen, 1979). Data captured during the coding phase can later be analyzed using a set of analysis and display modules which present static and dynamic (animated) graph and time-series descriptions of the data. Harrison and Baecker (1992) is a systematic review of design criteria for video analysis systems, a survey of existing technology, and a presentation of a novel system for video annotation and analysis. Van der Velden (1992v) is a video presentation on a new system for video analysis. Ericsson and Simon (1980) is a deep exploration of the nature and validity of verbal reports as data.

DESIGNING FOR COOPERATION:
COOPERATING IN DESIGN

This article will discuss how to design computer applications that enhance the quality of work and products, and will relate the discussion to current themes in the field of Computer-Supported Cooperative Work (CSCW). Cooperation is a key element of computer use and work practice, yet here a specific "CSCW approach is not taken." Instead the focus is cooperation as an important aspect of work that should be integrated into most computer support efforts. In order to develop successful computer support, however, other aspects such as power, conflict and control must also be considered.

In the Scandinavian projects that form the background of this article, we focused on moderate to large-scale systems where this approach—paying close attention to "collaborative" aspects—was almost a necessity. As the stand-alone PC and the dedicated word-processor disappear, this broad view will receive growing recognition, and several of the lessons are applicable to many CSCW issues.

In the next section I discuss examples of collaborative aspects of work that were ignored by traditional computer support and consider to what extent these examples represent general organizational trends that may also constitute hindrances to the introduction of groupware.

We started with the view that work is fundamentally social. Most activity, and certainly its meaning, arises in a context of cooperation. This led us to focus on the use situation as the basis for design.

Crucial aspects of work are often poorly understood in traditional system development, leading to severe difficulties when a system is introduced. We argue that several such difficulties are magnified when the system being developed falls in the CSCW category, and that alternative approaches to computer systems design are needed.

The approach that my colleagues and I advocate falls under the category that in the United States is becoming known as Participatory Design [30].

We emphasize an <u>active</u> <u>cooperation</u> between users and professional designers. This does not happen by itself. Just as good computer support <u>fits</u> the work and skills of the users, good design processes and design support must fit both users and designers. So far the needs of designers and managers[1] have dominated, and we are only beginning to develop tools and techniques that support active user participation in design. The development of such cooperative design is the topic of the rest of the article.

Morten Kyng

A first step is to obtain user involvement in the design process—to create space for users to act. This can include developing new group-based, end-user controlled forms of work as part of the design process. Next, there is a need to get past the role of evaluators only, to encourage users to participate fully in the design process.

To emphasize the cooperation between designers and users in early project activities, we adopt the term "mutual learning" to replace the widely used term "analysis" [5, 20, 32]. Mutual learning implies that designers learn about the application area and users learn about new technical possibilities. Furthermore, mutual learning encompasses the development and learning of new ways of cooperating that may be required of users and designers.[2]

Cooperative design is an outcome of our research on the design of computer applications that enhance the quality of work and products. In its simplest form it is a way for users and designers to apply their knowledge and experience in designing computer systems. Taken further, it can bridge the gap between tradition and innovation—between existing concepts and objects in the application area and the emerging future with new computer support and changed ways of working. Cooperative design, however, is also an instance of cooperative work, and computer support for cooperative design is an instance of computer support for cooperative work. We will look at computer support for cooperative design in this light.

[1]Managerial interest in external control of the development process has had strong impact on methods, techniques, and tools [7, 8, 9, 13]. In this article, however, I focus on the needs of those involved in the design process itself, particularly with respect to cooperation.

[2]Here and elsewhere in the article, we assume that cooperative design implies that a project group of system designers and end-users/practitioners are doing the design work together. The concepts (end-)users and designers are used only reluctantly, since the users in question are in fact designing.

The Collective Resource Approach: Fighting Decreased Cooperation

The approach on which the work in this article is based was developed in Scandinavia over the last two decades; the history is reviewed in Ehn and Kyng [9]. It started with a dissatisfaction with the way in which computers were introduced and how they changed work processes in Scandinavian companies in the 1970s—particularly in the case of production control. Although conditions improved for some employees, a common trend for many workers was:

- less need for experience and skill,
- less control over and understanding of the production process,
- increased division of labor, and
- less planning as part of the job. [8, p. 214]

Interpreted in CSCW terms, this quite literally reduced cooperation on the shop floor. What typically happened was that the basis for decisions about production control issues changed from manual, paper-based handling of information, to computer-based information processing. The manual system involved the foremen and many of the workers, whereas the new computer-based system was only accessible to those whom management and systems designers wanted to be players in the planning process. In many industrial settings the workers were not considered potential players, but only information providers, as illustrated in the following examples.

Two-way Terminals

In the 1970s the dominant view on production planning in a typical machine shop was that detailed planning could and should be done in advance by a few engineers. They made production flow plans, which were then used to produce detailed specifications for each machine operator, who in turn kept the engineers informed about the progress at his or her machine by entering machine-, operator- and job/batch-data through a simple and robust terminal. These simple terminals generally only provided for entering a limited set of messages. They could not be used to receive the production data used in planning.

From the engineers' perspective, this was no problem, since they did not see a need for the workers to participate in the planning process. For many workers and, as it came to be recognized slowly over the next fifteen years, for many of the employers too, there was a problem. The exclusion of the workers from the planning loop reduced both the job content (leading to decreased motivation, increased absenteeism, and so forth) and the overall efficiency, particularly in dynamic environments exhibiting factors that were not reflected in the computer-supported planning. Based on this experience, what might have been the first general CSCW demand was formulated and adopted by many Scandinavian trade union locals:

Demand for "Two-way terminals, or cross contact"
- Production control systems must allow workers to acquire production information that they deem relevant to their work.
- Terminal-based systems must allow workers to exchange information that they deem relevant.

This demand could not be met by the American and German systems then in widespread use, due to hardware limitations, namely, systems with terminals that only allowed for data entry. Even as new systems emerged, based on "two-way terminals," their modus operandi was not "CSCW for all," but rather "CSCW for the few and detailed control of the many." And the reason was mainly that this was the way that managers wanted it to be.

One question such examples raise for collaborative computing is whether to focus on *pure* CSCW, which in this case means the development of a system for the few production planners/engineers, or whether to consider demands such as those raised by the workers in our example. As pointed out by Bob Howard in his talk delivered to the first biennial Conference on Computer-Supported Cooperative Work, the "Mom-and-apple-pie" connotations of the word cooperative tends to obscure the fact that work involves a fair degree of conflict [19, pp. 175–176]. As indicated earlier, ignoring conflict could lead to systems for the few, or systems which fail during introduction due to the designers' inadequate understanding of organizational realities.

Two Passwords—Or an Interlude on Conflict and Cooperation

Before we discuss problems in understanding such organizational realities, let us move to a simple example that illustates how explicit recognition of conflicting interest may result in what could be considered as CSCW on a low level.

In many industrial companies a cornerstone of the planning process is a detailed table listing the estimated time for each basic operation at each type of machine. Obviously, the numbers in these tables are of great importance to the workers, since they represent the amount of work they are expected to do in a given period of time. In evaluating a new computer system, a local union noticed that all that was needed to make changes to the local table in a particular shop was the password of one foreman. The union had the system modified so that work rate changes required the passwords of both a foreman and a shop steward; i.e., the system now forced foremen and shop stewards to cooperate on such changes.

Stated more generally, once conflict is recognized, the procedures set up to handle it, such as negotiation, often have clear cooperative aspects.

The Use Situation

In cases such as these, workplace politics or conflicts of interests be-

tween different groups are, of course, important. The critical factor, however, is often found to be an inadequate understanding of the organizational realities of the use situation. In this section we look at examples that illustrate how lack of understanding of the existing use situation directly creates new

Courtesy of Merete Bartholdy/idea by Niels Henrik Frey

problems with the introduction of computer support. Once again the examples concern cooperative aspects of work, but not "typical CSCW applications." It can argued however, that with typical CSCW applications the exemplifed problems will be more and not less apparent.

Snow—A Cold, White Substance or a Word for Flexibility in Payment?

At a Danish shipyard, where I worked as a consultant for the local union in the late 1970s, a new computerized wage system created unforeseen problems. In one shop the

manager and his foremen had developed their own use of the wage system. First they decided how much they wanted to pay people, and then they found some way to get the system to do it, even if it meant entering that they were paying people to shovel snow in the middle of the summer. Since this shop was one of the most profitable, this practice was accepted. The new computer system included a lot of checking, however, and produced an alert when it detected snow-shoveling between May and October. Thus, this locally developed use of the wage system came to an end, because it violated a low-level rule implemented in the computer system.

Stated more generally, the new system made local variations visible and public in such a way that the central levels of the organization could no longer ignore deviations from formal but low-level standards, even though these deviations contributed to high-level goals.

Catch the Initial Keystroke

Perhaps a graver example is found in the newspaper industry, where we can see how the external view of managers and system designers does not recognize the ways that practice evolves and changes the content of concepts in use. It concerns proofreading and illustrates how a serious decrease in quality can result from the introduction of a computer system designed with an erroneous (and partly ideological) understanding of key aspects of a complex work process.

A decade ago a major trend in the newspaper industry was to integrate the systems used by the journalists with those for typesetting. "Catch the initial keystroke" was the slogan, and the major goal was to save money by producing the plates for printing directly from the manuscript produced by the journalists, eliminating the need for typesetting. This process also eliminated the traditional step of proofreading, but in theory this was no problem. In theory, proofreading just

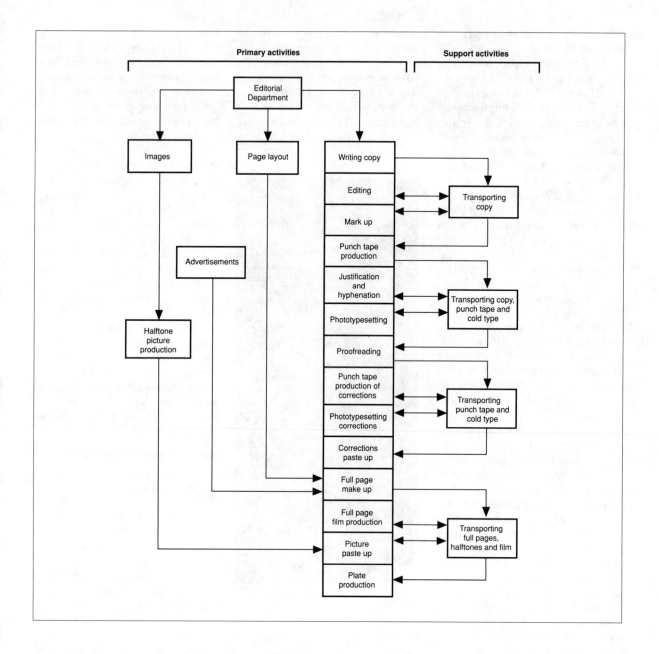

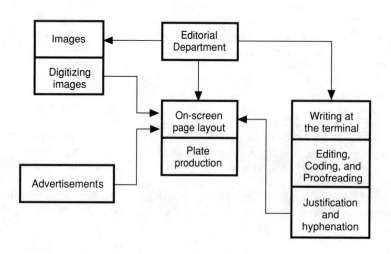

consisted of checking the typeset article to verify that it matched the manuscript. The reality of proofreading, however, was different. A skilled proofreader corrected spelling and punctuation, checked that the policy of the newspaper with respect to the mentioning of names was handled correctly, and to some extent changed awkward use of language. Thus the elimination of proofreading led to a noticeable decline in quality. Also affected were the assistant editors. They now had to spend time checking punctuation and so forth, and consequently had less time for higher-level editorial concerns [see 21].

Users and Design

Problems of "fitting" computer support to work have probably been around since end users came into existence as a group distinct from programmers/designers. For at least two decades user involvement has been proposed as a solution by several authors writing from a variety of perspectives. In a panel paper for the ACM conference on Computer and Human Interaction (CHI '91) Michael Muller identified three convergent arguments in favor of "broad and diverse participation in design":

- combination of diverse sources of expertise,
- ownership and commitment by all of the people who will eventually work on or with the product,
- participation in decision-making by the people who will be affected by the design decisions [26, p. 391].

Although no serious theoretical critique has been raised against user involvement per se, and although most people agree to the

idea once introduced to it, user involvement has gained acceptance slowly. It is outside the scope of this article to focus on the general issue of users and design. I will, however, briefly point to some relevant literature from both the U.S. and Europe, although I obviously have to leave out numerous important contributions. The book *Towards Creative Systems Design* by Henry Lucas [23] presented one of the first accounts of the view that users should design their own systems. A more moderate as well as more influential view is presented in papers by Gould et al. [11, 12] who argue in favor of:

(1) early—continual—focus on users and tasks,
(2) early—continual—user–testing, and
(3) iterative design.

In Europe the issues have been presented in the books *System Design For, With and By the Users* [2], and *Computers and Democracy—A Scandinavian Challenge* [1]. Some of the most recent contributions include the article "Interactive systems: Bridging the gaps Between Developers and Users" by Grudin [15], and the books *Design at Work: Cooperative Design of Computer Systems* [13] and *Participatory Design* [30].

Looking at Design as Work Involving Cooperation and Conflict

Taking one step back we notice that design itself may be viewed as work with strong cooperative aspects, but also characterized by conflict and domination. In other words, when talking about participatory or cooperative design we run the risk of being misled by the "Mom-and-apple-pie" connotations, just as with other instances of CSCW. In the Scandinavian projects that form the basis of the work described here, our approach has been to develop design practices that cover a broad spectrum of activities: from independent end-user activities through "negotiations" to "cooperative design" involving end-users and designers [9]. All of these activ-

ities are crucial to successful design—although their relative importance varies greatly from project to project. In the rest of this article, however, the focus is on the cooperative aspects of design. The examples highlight end-user/designer cooperation.

Cooperative Design

It is not possible to follow a simple recipe to avoid the pitfalls illustrated in the preceding sections and design software that will support cooperation and skill development among users. One of the primary reasons is that much of the crucial knowledge of the application area, sometimes referred to as "tacit knowledge," is neither accessible to an outside observer nor by our system description methods [3, 6, 7, 13, 28, 31].

To bring tacit knowledge to bear in design, it is necessary to create situations in which users encounter the computer support being developed in a concrete way, "triggering" the knowledge and allowing them to apply it in their evaluation of the emerging design. We call this way of working "cooperative design" [14] to emphasize the importance of bringing together the competence of designers and users. The key idea is to move the focus from discussions of system descriptions to cooperative action, using mock-ups and prototypes to simulate prospective work situations.

The Design Process

In the design process, two sets of players must act creatively: end users and professional system designers. This requires that both groups understand major aspects of the process, the techniques and the tools applied, and that both groups learn from the process. Historically, the designers' perspectives have dominated completely, as illustrated by the following examples from the Utopia project [9]. In this project, a group of professional system designers and skilled graphical workers cooperated over several years to develop computer support

FIGURE 1
System description of manual

FIGURE 2
System descriptions of computer-based production of newspapers

that enhances the quality of work and products in the graphics industry.

The first example that illustrates the domination of the designer's perspective concerns the initial work of a design team, usually called *analysis*. Here the professional designers analyze or learn about the user organization and the application area. When the group of professional system designers and graphical workers carried this out in the Utopia project, it was clear that only half of the group learned very much—the skilled graphical workers already knew most of what the professional system designers learned during the initial analysis. To balance this, we supplemented the designer-oriented analysis by teaching the participating users about technological possibilities and trends, about different, but in some way related, applications (e.g., from advertising, movie production and cartography), and about cooperative design. Today, when we design systems, we speak less of analysis than of "mutual learning."

Another example of system designer bias in design work is the use of the concept *information system*. During our first cooperative design projects we realized that most users do not think about the applications they use as information systems. They think in terms of concrete products such as WordPerfect and Linotron 606—not in terms of types of applications and peripherals such as word processors, or laser photo-typesetters. In the early stages of a cooperative design process, the participants develop a partially shared understanding, a common language. An important element is the joint creation of useful design concepts related to the application domain. Part of the development is to move the understanding of the users from concrete instances to more general concepts. It is to introduce supplementary concepts such as desktop laser printer, and to create an understanding of trends with respect to

price, size, resolution and quality. Such concepts must be grounded in the application domain, however, if they are to support users in tapping their professional skills. The traditional computer science view reflects the opposite grounding, converting everyday objects such as addresses or telephone numbers to abstract datatypes, while treating truncated *real numbers* as basic objects.

Working With Familiar Objects

When representations of our design visions are being built, both users and designers should be able to understand the objects that make the visions concrete—the users mainly from an application or use perspective, the designers mainly from a development or construction and modification perspective. The more the users understand the possibilities for modification and change, however, the more effectively they can apply their competence in the application domain to the design process, by moving from evaluating to creating.

In the Utopia project, much of the design work relied on mock-ups built of paper, plywood, matchboxes, and so forth, to exploit the users' familiarity with these materials [22]. To illustrate the point, consider the process of changing the layout of a tablet menu. In the early stages of the Utopia project this consisted of drawing the new layout on a piece of paper and pasting this on a plywood "tablet." The simple and familiar nature of these steps made this kind of modification accessible to all of the participants. Bødker and Grønbæk [4] and Grønbæk [16] explored possibilities for "cooperative prototyping" using commercially available prototyping environments. In setting up teams of designers and users who cooperate by using prototypes, we find that only limited prototype manipulation is currently accessible to users. Using direct manipulation, however, as in Apple HyperCard, for example, a number of changes can be done "on-line" by the de-

signers in such a way that the participating users can follow what is happening.

Inspired by Nygaard's notion of "profession-oriented languages" [27], we are currently exploring the potential for specialized, application-specific design environments that contain large numbers of application domain objects. These objects are specializations in the object-oriented sense, providing the full power of the underlying general object-oriented programming environment together with more general presentation-objects. Thus developers can specialize objects further or revert to more general versions.

Two elements in the success of such an approach are developing a hierarchy of layers that gradually move from the concepts of the application domain to those of the computer; and developing tools for modifying objects and moving between the layers that are based on the competence of the users [18].

From Prototype to Production— What is the Difference?

The ideas for computer support for cooperative design that we have outlined have not yet been tried out in any real design projects. We do, however, have some indication of expected difficulties. One of these relates to the status or nature of an object in contrasting early prototypes and production versions. The design objects, (i.e. the prototype objects), are no longer made of materials familiar to the users, and furthermore, prototype objects are now made from the same type of material as the objects of the future production version. Thus users often have difficulty understanding the limitations of a prototype. For example, if a prototype uses outlines rather than full pictures for positioning, users might be unsure of what is intended for the final design. In our experience, the first step toward a shared understanding of the objects is social, not technical [see 10, 22]. Recurring discussions of the status of objects, particularly in relation to the visions of the emerging production system, are important in keeping a design team on a common track.

Supporting Users in Transferring Old Distinctions to New Objects

The problem of distinguishing prototype-aspects from production-version-aspects is only one of several examples of problems relating to the handling of distinctions in

FIGURE 3
Manual production of newspapers

computer-supported cooperative design. There are a number of more general difficulties in transferring knowledge and experience from the handling of noncomputer-based artifacts to computer-based objects. Some elements that are essential to our understanding and handling of most physical objects are almost absent in the world of the computer.

The first of these elements relates to the identity of an object. The psychologist Jens Mammen [25] argues that it is a fundamental human capability to create relations to individual objects that extend beyond any set of specific features of the objects. For example, when one recognizes the phone in one's office, it is not primarily by attributes such as color, but by knowing about the enduring nature of phones and the social conventions that govern when people move

them around. Applying this view to computer support, including support for design, implies that the elements or objects that provide support for a work process should be at least potentially distinguishable as individual entities, exist over time, and be recognizable as previously encountered objects due both to their familiar properties and to "rules" that govern their existence. This is only rarely the case.

A basic principle underlying the predominant view of computers in both system engineering and computer science is that a copy of a set of bits is just as good as the original set—just as a particular arithmetic operation adding 3 and 7 will give the same result as another adding of 3 and 7. In several respects this quality is highly valued, a simple example being the ability to avoid loss of signal quality when using digital techniques as opposed to analog. In many cases, however, the identity of an object in a computer system is crucial. From our own application domain of system design, the problem of version control is well-known. Our field is abundant with examples—including disasters—of the consequences of mistaking one version of a system for another. Generally we resort to ad hoc conventions for making such distinctions, usually at the level of naming conventions for files on a word processor.

Closely related to the distinction

between original and copy is the notion of location. Most individual objects of our everyday life, which we identify and handle so routinely, are characterized by a unique place in time and space. In group settings, this allows us to organize work so that changes in location trigger the right actions. In the development of computer support for geographically distributed groups, supporting a *location concept*, perhaps by supporting access to temporal information and some form of addresses in the network, seems

FIGURE 4
A mock-up from the UTOPIA project of computer-based newspaper production

particularly desirable. In this way the analogy with other jointly used objects can be a basis for developing new cooperation practices.

As a routine CSCW example consider the use of an electronic calendar. If a manager is travelling with a laptop that contains a copy of his or her calendar, there is usually no support for considering this version to be the original and the one residing on the departmental minicomputer to be a copy. This can unnecessarily complicate the cooperation between the manager and the secretary in scheduling meetings and so forth. A positive example is found in one of our early prototypes of computer support for cooperative design. The prototype supported the use of scanned material, voice, and objects from other applications. As a result, the "author" of a hand-drawn object or a "voice-object" was easily distinguishable, as was that changes had been made.

Moving Between Two Worlds

In any real development project, there are always limits to mutual learning. The developers do not become skilled practitioners in the application area and the users do not become technical experts. One of the challenges of cooperative design is to support creative collaboration, despite the fundamental differences among the participants. Another major challenge relates to the ability to move between the worlds of the users and the designers. Making design tools more accessible to users may come at the expense of the connection to the implementation tools as illustrated by the following examples. In the extreme case the two types of tools operate on different materials. This is quite obvious when we design using paper and plywood. Even with most database application generators and Computer-Aided Software Engineering (CASE) tools, the connection is weak between the application area objects such as forms, reports and diagrams on the one hand and the programs of the final implementation on the other.

With database application generators such as OMNIS 5, it is possible to create a simple, initial prototype with screen layouts and record formats in a reasonably straightforward manner using a direct manipulation interface builder. This first prototype can eventually be refined to a more sophisticated production version using tools that require programming skills. Once you begin to refine your prototype with the more advanced programming tools, however, you often lose the possibility of working on it with the simpler direct manipulation tools, even when what you want to do is clearly within the conceptual domain of these tools.

Within the world of CASE tools there is a related issue known as *reverse engineering*. With a CASE tool the initial overall design, with object hierarchies and communication links, for example, can be constructed using a graphical representation. This representation is then used to generate a program skeleton, which in turn can be used as a basis for programming a prototype and eventually a production version. Such a graphical representation is often a good supplement to the prototype itself in discussions of changes to the design. Nonetheless, if changes made by the users and designers involve the structure of the initial design, it is usually not possible to port them back to the graphical representation. In practice the result is that the graphical representations slowly degenerate and become useless, thereby adding to the users' difficulties in understanding the system being designed.

Interpreted in the framework of our initial discussion of computer support, we can say that until now these CASE tools have been designed with an inadequate understanding of the use situation—in this case, design that requires automatic updates of the graphical representations.

A key criterion for our current development of computer support for cooperative design is that no design tool should make the material representing the system being designed inaccessible to the other design tools. Thus the people using these tools are able to switch freely between them as required by the design process. Formulated in terms of the understanding of these people this implies an ability to access—at all times—those aspects of an emerging design that are considered *meaningful*. We have realized this interoperability through the use of common representations in terms of abstract syntax trees [24], text, Petri Nets and hypermedia links. Thus CASE-like tools work on the common representations through a graphical interface with boxes and connecting lines [29]. And "user interface objects" are designed using a "direct manipulation interface" [17]. Since each tool understands the common representations, new CASE diagrams and user interface objects can automatically be generated at any time to reflect the current structure of the system.

This approach has the potential of taking an important step from implementation tools toward user accessible tools. There is probably a long way to go, however, before end users wield computer-based design tools and materials as easily as they do pens, scissors and cardboard boxes.

Acknowledgments
Thanks to Jonathan Grudin for proposing the writing of this article and for continual support during the process. Ellen Francik, Joan Greenbaum, Jonathan Grudin, Hiroshi Ishii, Naomi Miyake, Carrie Rudman, and Randall Trigg provided valuable comments on earlier drafts, and the suggestions of Francik and Rudman helped me to reorganize the article. **C**

References
1. Bjerknes, G., Ehn, P. and Kyng, M., Eds. *Computers and Democracy—A Scandinavian Challenge.* Avebury, Aldershot, UK 1987.
2. Briefs, U., Ciborra, C. and Schneider, L., Eds. *System Design for, With and by the Users.* North-Holland, Amsterdam 1983.
3. Bødker, S. *Through the Interface—A Human Activity Approach to User Interface Design.* Lawrence Erlbaum Assoc., Hillsdale, N.J. 1991.
4. Bødker, S. and Grønbaek, K. Design in action: From Prototyping by Demonstration to Cooperative Prototyping. In *Design at Work: Cooperative Design of Computer Systems,* J. Greenbaum and M. Kyng Eds., Lawrence Erlbaum Assoc., N.J., 1991.
5. DeMarco, T. *Structured Analysis and System Specification.* Yourdon Press/Prentice Hall, N.Y. 1978.
6. Dreyfus, H.L. and Dreyfus, S.D. Mind Over Machine—*The Power of Human Intuition and Expertise in the Era of the Computer.* Basil Blackwell, Glasgow, 1986.

7. Ehn, P. *Work-Oriented Design of Computer Artifacts*. Lawrence Erlbaum Assoc. and Falköping, Sweden: Arbetslivscentrum, 1989.

8. Ehn, P. and Kyng, M. A tool perspective on design of interactive computer support for skilled workers. In *Proceedings from the Seventh Scandinavian Research Seminar on Systemeering*, Part I M. Sääksjärvi, Ed. Helsinki, Finland: Helsinki School of Economics, 1984, pp 211–242.

9. Ehn, P. and Kyng, M. The collective resource approach to system design. In *Computers and Democracy—a Scandinavian Challenge*, G. Bjerknes, P. Ehn, and M. Kyng Eds., Aldershot, UK: Avebury, 1987, 17–57.

10. Ehn, P. and Kyng, M. Cardboard Computers: Mocking-it-up or hands-on the future. In *Design at Work: Cooperative Design of Computer Systems* J. Greenbaum and M. Kyng Eds. Hillsdale, N.J., Lawrence Erlbaum Associates, 1991, 169–195.

11. Gould, J.D., Boies, S.J., Levy, S., Richards, J.T. and Schoonard, J. The 1984 Olympic Message System: A test of behavioral principles of system design. *Commun. ACM 30*, 9 (1987), 758–769.

12. Gould, J.D. and Lewis, C. Designing for usability: Key principles and what designers think. *Commun. ACM 28*, 3 (1985), 300–311.

13. Greenbaum, J. and Kyng, M. Situated design. In J. Greenbaum and M. Kyng Eds.: *Design at Work: Cooperative Design of Computer Systems*, Lawrence Erlbaum Associates, Hillsdale, N.J., 1991, 1–24

14. Greenbaum, J. and Kyng, M. Eds. *Design at Work: Cooperative Design of Computer Systems*. Lawrence Erlbaum Associates, Hillsdale, N.J., 1991.

15. Grudin, J. Interactive systems: Bridging the gaps between developers and users. *IEEE Comput.* (Apr. 1991), 59–69.

16. Grøbæk, K. Prototyping and active user involvement in system development: Towards a cooperative prototyping approach. Ph.D. dissertation. Aarhus: The Computer Science Dept., Aarhus University, Denmark 1991.

17. Grønbæk, K., Hviid, A. and Trigg, R. ApplBuilder—an object-oriented application generator supporting rapid prototyping. Aarhus: The Computer Science Dept., Aarhus University, 1991. To be published in Jean-Claude Ed., *Proceedings of the Fourth International Conference on Software Engineering and its Applications* (Toulouse, Dec. 9–13, 1991)

18. Henderson, A. and Kyng, M. There's no place like home: Continuing design in use. In *Design at Work: Cooperative Design of Computer Systems* J. Greenbaum and M. Kyng Eds., Lawrence Erlbaum Associates, Hillsdale, N.J., 1991.

19. Howard, R. System design and social responsibility. the political implications of computer-supported cooperative work. *Off: Tech. and People 3* (1987), Oxford 175–187.

20. Jackson, M. *System Development*. Prentice-Hall, Englewood Cliffs, N.J., 1983.

21. Kammersgaard, J. and Kyng, M. Edb og arbejdets organisering på dagbladet Information, UTOPIA Rep. 17. Aarhus: The Computer Science Dept., Aarhus University. (In Danish. Edp and the organization of work at the newspaper *Information*), 1984.

22. Kyng, M. Designing for a dollar a day. *Off: Tech. and People 4* (1988), Oxford 157–170.

23. Lucas, H. *Towards Creative Systems Design*. Columbia University Press, N.Y., 1974.

24. Madsen, O.L. and Nørgaard, C. An object-oriented metaprogramming system. *Hawaii International Conference on System Sciences 21* (1988), Washington, D.C. 406–415.

25. Mammen, J. *Den Menneskelige sans*. København: Dansk psykologisk Forlag. (In Danish. The Human Faculty), 1983.

26. Muller, M. Participatory design in Britain and North America: Responding to the "Scandinavian Challenge." In *Reaching Through Technology, CHI '91 Conference Proceedings* S.P. Robertson, G.M. Olson and J.S. Olson Eds.: (New Orleans, La. Apr. 28–May 2, 1991 ACM, N.Y., (1991), 389–392.

27. Nygaard, K. Profession oriented languages. Presented as Keynote Speech at Medical Informatics Europe 84. Entitled User Oriented Languages in Roger et al, Eds. In *Proceedings* (Brussels, 1984).

28. Polanyi, M. *The Tacit Dimension*. Anchor Books, Doubleday and Company, N.Y., 1967.

29. Sandvad, E. *Object-Oriented Development—Integrating Analysis, Design and Implementation*. Daimi PB-302. Aarhus: The Computer Science Dept, Aarhus University, Denmark 1990.

30. Schuler, D. and Namioka, A., Eds. *Participatory Design*. Lawrence Erlbaum Associates, Hillsdale, N.J., To be published in 1992.

31. Winograd, T. and Flores, F. *Understanding Computers and Cognition—A New Foundation for Design*. Ablex, Norwood, N.J., 1986.

32. Yourdon, E. *Modern Structured Analysis*. Yourdon Press/Prentice Hall, N.Y., 1989.

CR Categories and Subject Descriptors: D.2.2 [**Software Engineering**]: Tools and Techniques; H.1.2 [**Models and Principles**]: User/Machine Systems—*human information processing;* H.5.3 [**Information Interfaces and Presentation**]: Group and Organization Interfaces—*evaluation/methodology; organizational design; theory and models;* K.4.3 [**Computers and Society**]: Organizational Impacts; K.6.1 [**Management of Computing and Information Systems**]: Project and People Management—*systems analysis and design; systems development;* K.6.3 [**Management of Computing and Information Systems**]: Software Management—*software development*

General Terms: Design

Additional Key Words and Phrases: Computer-supported cooperative work, cooperative design, groupwork, multiuser systems, participatory design

About the Author:

MORTEN KYNG is an associate professor at the Computer Science Department, Aarhus University, Denmark. He teaches system development and does research on tools and techniques for the cooperative design of computer systems. **Author's Present Address:** Computer Science Department, Aarhus University, Bld. 540, Ny Munkegade; DK-8000 Aarhus C; Denmark. email: mkyng@daimi.aau.dk

This work has been supported by The Information program of the Danish research Councils, grant no. 5.26. 18.19/5.21.08.05.

METHODS FOR THE STUDY OF GROUPS
(Excerpt)

from
Groups: Interaction and Performance

Joseph E. McGrath

. . .

OVERVIEW: METHODS AS OPPORTUNITIES AND LIMITATIONS

When we learn something in science, that knowledge is based on use of some combination of empirical and theoretical methods. The meaning of that knowledge and the confidence we can have in it are both contingent on the methods by which it was obtained. All methods used to gather and analyze evidence offer both opportunities not available with other methods and limitations inherent in the use of those particular methods.

In the group research area, the use of questionnaires or other forms of self-report provides a good example of this dual nature of methods. On the one hand, self-report measures (questionnaires, interviews, rating scales, and the like) are a direct way, and sometimes the only apparent way, to get evidence about certain kinds of variables that are worthy of study: attitudes, feelings, retrospective recall of experiences early in life, and the like. On the other hand, such self-report measures have some serious flaws. For example, respondents

may try to appear competent, to be consistent, to answer in socially desirable ways, to please the researcher. These flaws limit and potentially distort the information gained from such measures. Alternative data collection approaches, such as observation of overt behavior, may avoid some of these particular weaknesses but will suffer other ones. In any case they may be difficult or impossible to adapt to measure particular kinds of variables. For example, how do you observe a feeling?

Such is the dilemma of empirical science: *all methods have inherent flaws—though each has certain advantages.* These flaws cannot be avoided. But what the researcher can do is to bring more than one approach, more than one method, to bear on each aspect of a problem. If only one method is used, there is no way to separate out the part that is the "true" measure of the concept in question from the part that reflects mainly the method itself. Multiple methods, carefully picked so that they each have different weaknesses, can add strength to one another by offsetting each other's weaknesses, and can add strength to the resulting evidence if they show consistent outcomes across divergent methods.

The same problems, and the same prescription for dealing with them, apply at the level of research strategy as well as at the level of methods of data collection. Laboratory experiments, for example, have some great strengths. They can permit precise measurement of effects, deliberate manipulation of presumed causes, and strong inferences about cause-effect relations. But they also have some serious flaws. They often greatly narrow the scope of the problem; they study it in artificial settings; and researchers using laboratory experiments are likely to make the matter worse by using obtrusive and artificial procedures and measures. There are several alternatives to laboratory experiments, including field studies and sample surveys. (There are at least five other strategies; see the next section of this chapter). Each of these other strategies offers different strengths, some of them offsetting the weaknesses of the laboratory; but each also has different inherent weaknesses, some of these being the very strengths of the laboratory method. *No one strategy, used alone, is very useful; each of them is far too flawed.* But again, the researcher needs to take advantage of multiple approaches—not so much within a single study, which usually must use a single strategy as a practical matter, but over several studies of the same problem. The approaches need to be chosen so that the weaknesses of each can be offset by the strengths of another strategy. If we obtain *consistent outcomes across studies using different strategies,* we can be more confident that those outcomes have to do with the phenomena we are studying, not just with our methods.

Incidentally, one can view the kind of interplay between theory and data suggested in chapter 2 as a specific form of use of multiple strategies. Some of the possible alternative strategies are theoretical, not empirical. (See next section of this chapter.) When we yoke a formal theory with a laboratory experiment, or with a sample survey, we are applying two alternative strategies with different strengths and weaknesses, and the *consistency* between them is the core of the resulting evidence.

The central notions in all this discussion, concerning methods at both the strategy and measure levels, are (a) that *methods enable but also limit evidence,*

(b) that *all methods are flawed, but all are valuable;* (c) that the *different flaws of various methods can be offset by* (simultaneous or successive) *use of multiple methods;* and (d) that such *multiple methods should be chosen to have patterned diversity,* so that *strengths of some offset weaknesses of others.* Given these principles, it follows that one ought not ask whether any given study is flawless and therefore to be believed ("is it valid?"). Rather, one should ask whether the evidence from that study is *consistent with* other evidence on the same problem, from other strategies, done by other methods. If two sets of evidence based on different methods *are consistent,* both of those studies gain in credibility. If the two sets are *not consistent,* that raises doubts about the credibility of *both* sets—equal or unequal doubts, depending on what else is known about the problem from still other studies, what methods are involved and what is known about their usefulness and limitations, and so forth. Conversely, if all of the studies of a given problem are based on the *same methods,* then the body of information thus gained is very much contingent on and limited by the flaws of those methods; and that information must be regarded with some degree of skepticism until it can be shown to hold for a broader array of methods. The fundamental principle is that *empirical knowledge,* in group research as elsewhere in science, *requires consistency or convergence of evidence across studies or sets of data that are based on different strategies and methods for acquiring that evidence.* These issues are discussed further, and a more detailed listing and description of strategies and methods is given, in the following parts of this chapter.

of related variables (B) necessarily intrude upon the situation and reduce its "naturalness," or realism (that is, reduce C). Conversely, the things you can do to keep high realism of context (C) will reduce the generality of the populations to which your results can be applied (A) or the precision of the information you generate (B), or both.

The nature of this strategic dilemma is made clearer in Figure 3–1, which shows a set of eight alternative research strategies or settings in relation to one another. That figure shows where among the strategies each of three desired features—generalizability over populations (A), precision in control and measurement of behavior (B), and realism of context (C)—is at its maximum. It also shows, though, that strategies that maximize one of these are far from the maximum point for the other two. The spatial relations in Figure 3–1 emphasize the dilemma just discussed: the very things that help increase one of the desired features—A, B, and C—also reduce the other two. *It is not possible to maximize, simultaneously, all three.* Any one research strategy is limited in what it can do; and research done by any one strategy is flawed—although different strategies have different flaws.

The strategies listed in Figure 3–1 are in four pairs. Some are familiar ones. Field studies refer to efforts to make direct observations of "natural,"

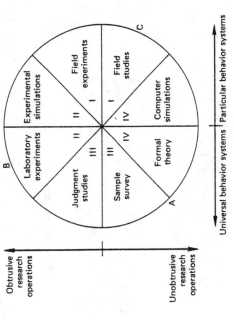

FIGURE 3-1   Research Strategies

I.   Settings in natural systems.
II.   Contrived and created settings.
III. No observation of behavior required.
IV.   Behavior not setting dependent.
A.   Point of maximum concern with generality over actors.
B.   Point of maximum concern with precision measurement of behavior.
C.   Point of maximum concern with system character of context.

STRATEGIC LEVEL ISSUES: CHOOSING A SETTING FOR A STUDY

Research evidence, in social and behavioral sciences, always involves *somebody doing something, in some situation.* When we get such evidence, we can, therefore, "reference" it on three aspects or facets: Whose behavior is it about (which Actors)? What behaviors is it about (which Behaviors)? What situations is it about (which Contexts)?

When you gather a batch of research evidence, you are always trying to maximize three things:

1. The *generalizability of the evidence over populations of actors* (A).
2. The *precision of measurement of the behaviors* (and precision of control over extraneous facets or variables that are not being studied) (B).
3. The *realism of the situation or context* (in relation to the contexts to which you want your evidence to refer) (C).

While you always want to maximize A, B, and C simultaneously, *you cannot.* This is one fundamental dilemma of research methods. The very things you can do to increase one of these reduces one or both of the other two. For example, the things you do to increase precision of measurement of behavior and control ongoing systems (in the present context that means existing groups), while intruding on and disturbing those systems as little as possible. Laboratory experiments are attempts to create the "essence" of some general class of systems (for the present case, groups) in a context in which the researcher can control all (or at least very many) of the extraneous features of the situation, in order to be able to maximize the essential features with precision. Field experiments are field studies with one major intervention, the deliberate manipulation of some feature whose effects are to be studied. An experimental simulation is a laboratory study in which an effort is made to create a system that is like some class of naturally occurring systems (such as what are called mock juries later in this book), but which are artificial in that they are created by the researcher for study, and people perform in them for research purposes rather than for purposes stemming from their own lives.

Sample surveys are efforts to get information from a broad (and well devised) sample of actors, usually in the form of verbal responses to a relatively small set of questions. Judgment studies are efforts to get responses (usually from a very small and somewhat casually selected sample of "judges") about a systematically patterned and precisely calibrated set of stimuli. Surveys gain much generalizability over populations (A), but give up a lot in precision of measurement (B) to do so. Judgment studies have less generalizability over actors (A), but retain considerable precision of measurement (B). Both surveys and judgment studies try to deemphasize context—actually, to uncouple the behavior (judgment) from the context in which it is done. Thus, both are very low on realism of context (C).

The fourth pair of strategies are theoretical, not empirical. The term formal theory is used here to mean general theory. Such theories are high on generalizability over populations (A) because they attempt to be general; they are not very high on realism of context (C) because by being general they do not deal very concretely with any one context; and they are very low on precision of measurement of behavior (B), because, since they are theoretical rather than empirical, they in fact involve no behaviors. The strategy called computer simulation refers to attempts to model a specific real life system or class of systems. Such effects are also theoretical rather than empirical; hence they are low on B because they do not involve behavior. In comparison to formal theories, computer simulations are higher in C, because they are system-specific; but they thereby lose in A, because they are limited to populations indigenous to that class of systems.

To sum up: Field studies gain realism (C) at the price of low generalizability (A) and lack of precision (B). Laboratory experiments maximize precision of measurement and control of variables (B), at the price of lack of realism (C) and low generalizability (A). Surveys have high generalizability (A) but get it by giving up much realism (C) and much precision (B). Formal theories get much realism (C) and much precision (B). The other four strategies are combinations located in between those four just discussed; they have the intermediate gains and losses implied by their positions in the "strategy circle" of Figure 3-1.

Doing research is *not* to be regarded as trying to find the right strategy. There is no right one. Indeed, they are all "wrong," in the sense that each is inherently limited, flawed. But they are all potentially useful. In considering any set of evidence, one should take into account what strategies were used in obtaining various parts of it, hence the strengths and limitations of that evidence at the strategic level.

DESIGN LEVEL ISSUES: WHAT WILL YOU COMPARE AND WHAT WILL YOU LEARN?

Any study needs a plan for what data will be gathered, how that data will be aggregated and partitioned, and what comparisons will be made within it. Such a study plan is often called a *research design*. As is evident from the preceding discussion, choice of one or another of the various strategies will limit the kinds of designs you can use. But there are also some general features of study designs, and it is those features that are to be discussed here.

Correlation versus Comparison

All research questions can be boiled down to variations of a few basic question forms. One is the *baserate* question: How often (at what rate, or what proportion of the time) does X occur? That is a purely descriptive matter, but is often a very crucial underpinning of other information. A second general form of question is the *relational* question: Are X and Y related? Do they occur together? That question has two major forms. In the correlational form, it is: Is there systematic *covariation* in the value (or amount or degree) of X and the value of Y? For example, does age covary with happiness? A high correlation between X and Y means that when X occurs at a high value, Y is also likely to occur at a high value; and when X is at a low value, Y is also likely to be at a low value. In the example from above, this would mean that older people were, by and large, happier than younger ones. The correlation between X and Y could equally well be high and *negative*, if high values of X went with low values of Y and vice versa. If that were the case for the example, then younger people would be, by and large, happier. There is little or no correlation between X and Y if knowing X doesn't help predict the value of Y. In the example, that would mean that older and younger people both vary in happiness, with some of each having high levels and some of each having less.

Given the example chosen here, of age and happiness, it certainly might occur to the reader that the highest level of happiness might occur, systematically, at some time other than in extreme old age or extreme youth. For example, happiness might increase up to age fifty, then decline. That would describe a nonlinear correlation (and, technically, a nonmonotonic one). There are statistical tools to test for such nonlinearity, although social scientists far too often do not use them when the evidence to be examined might well require them. But as the shape of the relation becomes more complicated—for example, if happiness decreased from young child to adolescent, then increased to age fifty, then decreased, but flattened out after sixty-five—our statistical tools become more cumbersome to use and many of them become less adequate to the task of assessing such complex forms of relation.

Much research in the social and behavioral sciences makes use of correlations, linear and nonlinear, that involve two, three, or more variables. Such a correlational approach requires being able to measure the presence or values of X, and of Y, for a series of "cases" that vary on X and on Y. It can tell you whether X and Y go together; but it *cannot* help you decide whether X is a cause of Y, or vice versa, or neither.

Another form of the relational question is the *comparison* or *difference* question. The difference question involves asking, essentially, whether Y is present (or at a high value) under conditions where X is present (or at a high value), and absent (or low) when X is absent (or low). For example: Do groups perform tasks better (Y) when members like each other (X) than when they do not (X' or "not-X")? You could approach this question in either of two ways. You could go around collecting measures of "liking" until you had found a bunch of groups high on it and another bunch of groups low on it (and perhaps a bunch at intermediate levels), and then compare their average performance scores. That would be, in effect, just a messy version of the correlational approach. The other approach would be to set up some other groups whose members do not like each other and set up some other groups with members who do like each other; then to give both sets of groups some common tasks to perform; and then to see if the average task performance (Y) of the "high liking" groups (X) is higher than the average task performance of the "low liking" groups (X'). For the comparison to be most useful, you would need to make sure that the two sets of groups were the same, or comparable, on all the other factors that might affect task performance—such as difficulty of the task, availability of task materials, quality of working conditions, task-related abilities, experience and training of members, and the like. You might render the groups comparable on some of these factors by *controlling* them at a single *constant* value for all groups of both sets. For example, you probably would want to have all groups in both conditions do exactly the same tasks. For some other variables, such as intelligence or abilities of members, that you could not hold at a constant value for all cases, you might want to *match* the groups, on the average, between the two conditions. You might even want to *manipulate* a second or third variable in addition to group liking—perhaps group size, for example. But you can only manipulate, match, and control a limited number of variables in any one study. You have to do something else about all the rest of the rather large set of potentially relevant factors.

That something else is called *randomization*, or random assignment of cases to conditions. Randomization means use of a random assignment procedure to allocate cases (groups) to conditions (high liking versus low liking, or, if you were also manipulating a second variable such as size, high-liking-large-groups versus high-liking-small-groups versus low-liking-large-groups versus low-liking-small-groups), so that any given case is equally likely to be in any of the conditions.

To do what has been called a "true experiment" (see Campbell & Stanley, 1966), you *must* have randomization of cases to conditions. If you do, then you

strengthen the credibility of your information about high X going with high Y (and low X with low Y); and, since *you* caused X to be high in one set of groups and low in the other, it is at least plausible that X is a cause of Y. If instead of doing such a true experiment, you had just let things vary, measured X and Y, and correlated them, then X might have caused Y, or Y might have caused X, or both X and Y might have been caused by something else that you didn't pay attention to.

You can see that true experiments are potentially powerful techniques for *learning about causal relations among variables*. But, as in all aspects of research methodology, you buy this high power at a high price in two ways: (a) a reduction in the *scope* of your study, insofar as you hold variables constant, and insofar as you make your experimental variables (the X's) occur only at a couple of levels (high or low liking, or three-person versus six-person groups, for example) so that the results of that study will be thereby limited in generalizability; and (b) a reduction in realism of context, inasmuch as your activities (rather than "nature") have created the groups, designed the tasks, and elicited behavior that served your purposes, not the group members' purposes. It has been said that such an experiment lets you learn a lot about very little, whereas a correlational study may let you learn very little about a lot.

Forms of Validity

A study needs to have high validity in regard to four different types of validity questions (see Cook & Campbell, 1979). One, to which we have been attending in the preceding description of the "true experiment," is called *internal validity*. That has to do with the degree to which results let you infer about causal relations. A second form of validity has been called *statistical conclusion validity*. That refers to the confidence with which you can say that there is a *real difference* (in Y scores) between X cases and X' cases. Internal validity deals with a logical question, how to rule out alternative explanations (such as, that Y caused X or that both X and Y stemmed from unmeasured factor Z). But statistical conclusion validity is a statistical question, usually posed in some variation of the following form: How likely is it that the difference in average Y values, between the X batch of cases and the X' batch of cases, could have occurred by *chance*? If the probability of such a chance occurrence is less than 1 in 100 (written $p < .01$), or sometimes if it is less than 1 in 20 ($p < .05$), the researcher may conclude that results cannot be attributed only to chance. Usually, such results are said to be "significant" at the .01 or the .05 level.

When results are significant, the researcher may conclude that the hypothesis that only chance was operating *does not* account for the results; but he or she *may not* logically conclude that the hypothesis of interest ("X causes Y") *does* account for them. It is only if the researcher can eliminate most other plausible rival hypotheses (e.g., that Y causes X; that Y is caused by factor Z that also differed between groups, etc.), by the logic of his or her study design, that he or she can continue to entertain the X-causes-Y hypothesis as a plausible—but by no means certain—explanation for the results.

A study also needs to have clearly defined theoretical concepts and conceptual relations, and clearly specified mappings (or translations) of those concepts into empirical operations. This is called *construct validity*. Finally, the researcher needs to have some basis for estimating how the obtained results would hold up if the hypothesis were tested on other populations of actors, using other measures of the same variables, in other situations and on other occasions in this same situation. Such estimates of generalizability refer to what is called *external validity*.

It will probably be apparent that the devices used to increase internal validity and statistical conclusion validity—the techniques used to gain precision—will threaten the external validity of that particular set of data. But the relation is not a symmetrical one. One should *not* leap to the conclusion that the converse is true. Things that aid external validity (e.g., large and varied samples) may either hinder or help internal validity or have no effect on it. Moreover, it is certainly *not* the case that things that *decrease* internal validity (e.g., not using randomization, or not using experimental manipulation) will somehow increase external validity. If you don't know what you found out in your study (i.e., if your study is low in internal validity or in statistical conclusion validity or in construct validity) then you cannot really determine whether or not, or how broadly, you can generalize it (i.e., what external validity it has)—but it doesn't matter anyhow. If you do know what you found out (i.e., if your study has high internal, statistical and construct validity), then it is important to try to determine how robust and general (i.e., how externally valid) those findings are likely to be.

There is much more to be said about study design, about difference versus correlation studies, about forms of validity, and about ways of dealing with plausible hypotheses that are alternatives to the hypothesis being tested—far more than can be said here. (For further reading on these questions, see Campbell & Stanley, 1966; Cook & Campbell, 1979; Runkel & McGrath, 1972). But perhaps what has been said serves to make several important points:

1. Results depend on methods.
2. All methods have limitations, hence any one set of results is limited, flawed.
3. It is not possible to maximize all desirable features of method in any one study; trade-offs and dilemmas are involved.
4. Each study—each set of results—must be interpreted in relation to other sets of evidence bearing on the same questions.

Some of these same points were made in regard to strategic issues, and some will apply, again, in the discussion of issues at the operational level that now follows.

References

CAMPBELL, D. T., & STANLEY, J. L. *Experimental and quasi-experimental designs for research.* Chicago, IL: Rand-McNally, 1966.

COOK, T. D., & CAMPBELL, D. T. *Quasi-experimental design: Design and analysis issues for field settings.* Chicago: Rand-McNally, 1979.

RUNKEL, P. J., & McGRATH, J. E., *Research on human behavior: A systematic guide to method.* New York: Holt, Rinehart & Winston, 1972.

Reprinted from *Design at Work: Cooperative Design of Computer Systems* (pp. 65-89), edited by J. Greenbaum and M. Kyng, 1991, Hillsdale, NJ: Lawrence Erlbaum. ©1991 by Lawrence Erlbaum Associates. Reprinted by permission.

Understanding Practice: Video as a Medium for Reflection and Design

Lucy A. Suchman and Randall H. Trigg

Work as Situated Activity

In exploring the design of new technologies at work, we begin with the view that work is a form of situated activity. By this we mean that work activities in every case take place at particular times, in particular places, and in relation to specific social and technological circumstances. From this perspective, the organization of work is a complex, ongoing interaction of people with each other and with the technologies that are available to them.

Because of the intimate relation between work and technology, the development of the artifacts with which people work and the development of their work practices go hand in hand. Available technologies afford certain resources and constraints on how the work gets done, and peoples' ways of working give the technologies their shape and significance. Our research goal has been to understand that work/technology relation both more generally, developing theoretical constructs that can deepen our understanding across work settings, and more specifically, in terms of the detail of just how the relationship develops in and through the work's course in a particular setting.

Routine Trouble in an Airline Operations Room

We are currently engaged in a project to study the relation between facilities design and everyday work practice. Our goal in the Workplace Project is to understand design effectiveness from both designers' and users' points of view, through an intensive field study of a complex work setting. After extended deliberations, we decided to locate our three-year study at a local airport. The airport is particularly interesting from our perspective in that during the course of our study a new terminal will open. This will provide us the opportunity to look at the process of design, use and redesign in a kind of accelerated time frame, as people move their operations from facilities whose design has been developed, modified, and adapted to over time, into new facilities based on projections of use which we assume will be more and less accurate. Our first task, therefore, has been to look as closely as we can at the organization of work operations in the existing terminal.

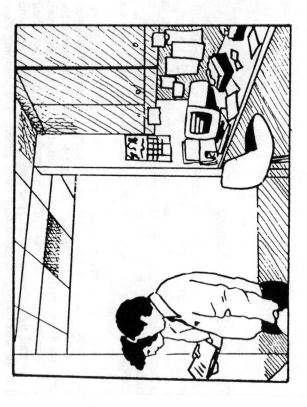

Figure 1a. The "Ops Room."

During one evening of fieldwork at an airline operations room, we observed the management of some "routine trouble" through the deployment of a variety of artifacts and communications technolo-

gies. Before exploring the details of the incident, some background on airport operations and the particular work of this room is in order.

Figure 1b. The "Ops Room."

The operations room is a communications center that coordinates the ground operations of a single airline (see Figures 1a and 1b). In this "Ops Room," staff consists of five airline employees. Each has specific responsibilities relevant to getting planes into and out of gates and to transferring baggage and passengers between planes. Their efforts are especially concerned during what are called "complexes." These are periods lasting approximately an hour, when all of the gates belonging to the airline fill with incoming planes, transfers are made between the gates, and then all of the planes depart. There are eight complexes in a normal workday. On the evening in question, the Ops Room was managing a multiple airplane "swap," which, among other maneuvers, involves one airplane arriving at gate 18 during complex 7 and departing from gate 14 during complex 8, an hour or two later.

The information necessary to coordinate the work of a complex is present both online (in an airline-wide computer system) and on paper documents called "complex sheets" (see Figure 2). These sheets contain matrices mapping incoming to outgoing planes, and include cells for each transfer of people and baggage required during the time the complex is on the ground. The dynamic nature of the complex is captured on the sheet by ordering the rows and columns of the matrix chronologically. Thus an Ops Room member checking off completed transfers should generally be moving diagonally downward and to the right across the cells of the matrix. Delayed flights display themselves as groups of cells left behind in this process.

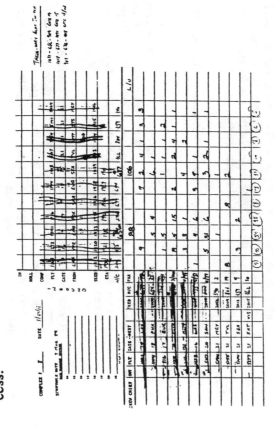

Figure 2. The complex sheet.

The dynamics of the complex in question, however, present problems for these established procedures. The major problem is that the aircraft swap takes place across two successive complexes, and thus stretches the complex sheet design in various ways.

In the interaction transcribed below, we focus on the activities of two Ops Room employees: BP (Baggage Planner) and PP (Passenger Planner). For our purposes, it's enough to say that BP coordinates and communicates with crew chiefs on the ramp, while PP plays a similar role with respect to ticket and gate agents inside the terminal. In the first sequence of the interaction, BP approaches PP with a question about tonight's plane swap (Figure 1a). PP pro-

vides an explanation and volunteers that perhaps he should have noted the complex sheet differently (Figure 1b):[1]

5:49:34 pm

BP: ((BP sitting at her workstation looks over her shoulder.))
Dave? (2.0) ((Gets up with clipboard and complex sheet and walks over to stand beside PP)) I'm sorry to keep bugging you I just want to make sure I figure this out.

PP: Okay. <inaudible>

BP: Nine-oh-nine inbound:

PP: Takes out ten-eighteen=

BP: =Ten-eighteen, but you've got gate eighteen?

PP: Uh, okay, here's the problem.

BP: Isn't that supposed to be

PP: He comes into eighteen, but then eh, we're going to move him off of eighteen to fourteen so this ((reference to complex sheet)) is right.

BP: Okay, that's right. Okay, that's r: 's the one they're

PP: This here plane is going to be moved after that seven o'clock departures, uh, complex seven goes out.

BP: Okay, right.

PP: So, I should have put eighteen slash fourteen and then eighteen. Okay, I got it.

BP: Right, okay, yes I saw fourteen and then eighteen. Okay, I got it. ((Goes back to her desk and sits down.))

The complication here is that flight 909 comes in to gate 18 during complex 7, the aircraft is moved to gate 14, and it then departs, during complex 8, as flight 1018. The complex sheet, however, shows only that Flight 909 comes in to gate 18, leaving it unclear as to how flight 1018 could then leave from gate 14. The difficulty arises from the fact that the complex sheet a) is not designed to show the movement of aircraft and b) is designed to cover only one complex at a time. The solution devised by PP, refined in this exchange with BP, is to annotate the sheet to show the plane "swap" across the two complexes.

1 Our transcription conventions are derived from those of Jefferson (1984). (A condensed glossary of Jefferson's transcription symbols can be found in Heritage (1984), pp. 312-314). In the transcripts, equal signs (=) indicate "latching," i.e. the beginning of one utterance following directly on the end of the prior with no gap. Numbers in parentheses indicate elapsed time in seconds. Thus (2.0) indicates a pause of two seconds. Colons indicate prolongation of the immediately preceding sound.

can then ask how well those purposes are served by its current design. We have found that the complex sheet acts as

1. A *reproducible representation* of the intended motion of people and baggage over the course of some complex. Note that we're not saying it's a set of instructions; its users generally know exactly what to do, they just need access to the projected particulars of a given complex;

2. A *template* which is filled in, in various ways, depending on features of the particular complex and on needs of the user. In fact this templating happens at several levels. First, the matrix format (layout, number of rows and columns, etc.) is a template onto which the projected incoming and outgoing flight numbers and arrival/departure times are notated. This happens every morning, so that when they arrive for work, the staff in the Ops Room has sheets for each of the day's complexes. The complex sheets at that point have labelled rows and columns, but empty cells. Two members of the Ops Room staff (BP and PP) fill in the cells with projected baggage/people transfers. This must be done close to the time of the complex, and is done differently for the two intended user groups, that is, ramp crew and gate agents. Next, the sheet is copied and distributed to the crews assigned to the upcoming complex. The activity at each stage then, is to (a) receive a document partially completed, (b) add information to the document by accessing resources only now available, and (c) copy the document and distribute it to others, or to a file;

3. A *medium* for notating the events of the complex as they happen, in such a way that irregular or problematic sub-events stand out. Once filled in and distributed, the sheet again becomes a template on which BP and PP add highlighting marks during the complex itself. The pattern of cell highlighting (moving diagonally down and to the right) makes missed or delayed transfers apparent as unhighlighted cells left behind the advancing front;

4. An enduring *physical record* for future reference of what happened during this complex. Once the complex is completed, BP and PP file their highlighted versions of the sheets;

5. A *transparent artifact* that stands in for situations out on the ramp and provides a shared object for communication between people during the course of the complex. In the case at hand, we see BP and PP first communicating in person over the sheet and then PP and the gate crew chiefs communicating, this time on the radio, but again with reference to the sheet. In this respect the complex sheet serves implicitly as the kind of "context support system" proposed by the Knowledge and Work Project at

Almost immediately following this interchange, PP decides to check the online information to make sure that it correctly (and readably) reflects the state of the world:

(3.0)

PP: Think I put that in the oh-ess-oh-star ((a program on the airline computer system)). I better double check that. ((Sits down at computer and begins typing.))

Having clarified the online record, PP makes two announcements over the radio, each designed to help the gate agents make sense of the situation. The first encourages them to check their computers for the latest information. The second proposes the same modification to their copies of the complex sheet that was arrived at earlier with BP.

6:00:23 pm

PP: ((Leaning over to speak into radio)) Once again, just a reminder to everybody, make sure you check complex seven and eight in the oh-ess-oh-star. There's a lot of information in there. It might be a little bit, uh, hard to understand on that ten-eighteen outbound, that airplane is gonna come in on gate eighteen and be moved to fourteen. So if there's any question on the gate for ten-eighteen outbound, that departure will be gate fourteen.

(2.0)

Radio: ((Female voice)) Thank you David I was about to call you about that.

(2.0)

PP: ((into the radio)) Yeah, Crystal and for everybody else nine-oh-nine inbound is the aircraft that makes up that ten-eighteen and when he comes in, he parks at eighteen but, due to the problem tonight with all these changes we'll have to move that aircraft over to fourteen, after the seven o'clock departure.

(10)

PP: ((again into the radio)) On that complex seven cut sheet uh, if it would make it any easier, where it says that three-way aircraft switch up there in the corner (.5) the third flight number listed, nine-oh-nine in, ten-eighteen out, says gate eighteen, put a slash behind that put fourteen behind it.

Using the Complex Sheet

Now suppose that we are interested in exploring new technologies for this workplace. And suppose further that the complex sheet is being considered for replacement or augmentation. Careful reflection on the activities of using complex sheets might first make clear the multiple purposes for which the complex sheet is used, so we

Turku, Finland (Hellman, 1989). It makes available to practitioners the cooperative structure of their work.

Suppose now that we're interested in the ways the complex sheet technology breaks down (or at least is stretched), given the multiple purposes it is meant to serve. One problem that has been mentioned to us by Ops Room staff involves changes that must be made to the sheet after it has been copied and distributed to ramp and gate crews. Because updating outstanding copies is difficult and because the cost of missing one sheet can be high (we were told a story about baggage transferred to the wrong plane for precisely this reason), the Ops Room waits until the last possible moment before the complex to copy the sheets, and makes subsequent changes only with difficulty.

A second problem is illustrated in this incident as well. In this case the complex sheet must be changed to represent a state of affairs unanticipated in its original design. That is, the sheet for one complex must be notated with information about another complex. In this case, PP has done just that and copies have been distributed. BP has trouble interpreting the added notation, however, and inquires further of PP. Together BP and PP arrive at a change to the notation that better communicates PP's intentions. PP then decides to communicate the change to gate crew personnel, in case they encounter a similar problem.

Designing for Practice

One might look at this situation and conclude that the basic complex sheet format should be modified to support notations referring to subsequent complexes. But for every form, procedure, or routine in a workplace, new situations inevitably occur that stretch the form in unanticipated ways. Similarly, one might argue for replacing the complex sheet with a computer-based representation, so that changes instantly propagate to the versions on the various crews' computers. However, computerized forms have their own problems; for example, the loss of ease with which the document can now be transported.

Incidents like these convince us that, given the inevitable tradeoffs, effective design involves a co-evolution of artifacts with practice. Where artifacts can be designed by their users, this development goes on over the course of their use. To some extent, however, an initial design must be based on a projection, in one time and place, of work to be done, often by other people than the designer, in another time and place. Moreover, artifacts are frequently (either intentionally or unintentionally) somewhat intractable in their design, allowing little in the way of modification or redesign over the course

of their use. In such cases, either the work practice adapts to the demands of the artifact, or the artifact is not used.

Whatever the relation between design and use in time, space, and participants, some amount of projection is a central aspect of design. This suggests to us the importance, in the design of tools, of realistic scenarios of their use. Designers interested in augmenting or replacing current artifacts like complex sheets do well to understand how they work, as well as what their limits are. In addition, those interested in supporting the design of modifiable artifacts do well to understand the everyday processes of modification exemplified in the complex sheet case described above.

Design realism can be achieved, we believe, through new methods for understanding the organization of work practice in detail. Such understandings provide a basis for involving practitioners directly in the process of reflection and design through, for example, collaborative production and review of videotapes and rapid prototyping. In the remainder of this chapter we focus on the methods we use for understanding work practice: using video records as a tool for reflection.

A Perspective on Work Practice and Design

In every setting where we look at technologies in use, we start with the assumption that work practice is fundamentally social. Basically, this is so in that any activity, whether characterized by conflict or by cooperation, relies on a foundation of meaningful, mutually intelligible interaction. Moreover it is the community, rather than the individual, that defines what a given domain of work is and what it means to accomplish it successfully. Finally, every occasion of work, however individualistic it may appear, involves some others, either in the form of co-workers or of recipients.

This basic sociality recommends that wherever we go we look for the human interactions that make up the work and define what counts as competent practice. Whether in a place like an airport, where work is closely coordinated among multiple participants, or in the case of a single user of a stand-alone machine, getting the work done requires some form of collaborative interaction. Even if the relevant others are absent, as in the case of the single user of the machine, we can still learn much from viewing the machine's use as an interaction with the machine itself, and with the communicative artifacts that its designer left behind. As we explain in detail below, this sociality is what makes analyses of human interaction so relevant to technology design.

Design and Use

A general requirement for the development of new technology is successful translation between the conception of the technology held by its designers and the reality of those for whom it is ostensibly designed. This ranges from international development efforts to introduce new technologies to traditional work ways, through industrial efforts to introduce information systems into modern offices (see Suchman & Jordan, 1988). Where technologies are designed at a distance from the situation of their use, as most are, there is an inevitable gap between scenarios of use and users' actual circumstances.

While design scenarios always simplify the projected situation of use, they can be based in more and less adequate understandings of users' practice (see Blomberg & Henderson, 1990). Over the past decade, we have been working to develop methods through which we can come to appreciate the subtleties of work practice in specific settings and to relate those understandings to design.[2] Our research strategy has been to undertake studies of technology and practice in a range of settings; for example, in a U.S. accounting office, rural Mayan communities in Mexico, Western hospitals, computer research laboratories, at photocopy machines, over various remote communications links, and so forth. Through these studies we have begun to apply perspectives from sociology and anthropology to problems in technology design and use. What we see consistently is that the closeness of designers to those who use an artifact (including the possibility that designer and user are one and the same) directly determines the artifact's appropriateness to its situation of use.

The Politics of Artifacts

Anthropologists of technology like Winner (1980), Latour (1986), and Akrich (1987) have pointed to the intrinsically political nature of technical artifacts. "Artifacts have politics," in Winner's phrase, not only in the sense that they embody the ideologies and agendas of their designers, but in the less obvious, more pervasive sense that they "constitute active elements in the organization of the relationships of people to each other and with their environment" (Akrich, 1987, p. 1). Artifacts take their significance from the social world, in other words, at the same time that they mediate our interactions with that world. Winner (1980) offers the example of overpasses in the neighborhood of Jones Beach on Long Island, New York. By

restricting the height of overpasses to be less than that required by public transit buses, the designer Robert Moses effectively restricted access to the beach to those who could afford a private automobile. More specifically, "one consequence was to limit access of racial minorities and low-income groups to Jones Beach, Moses' widely acclaimed public park" (p. 23).

Ethnography and Interaction Analysis

Informed by these perspectives, our work makes use of two related methods for research: ethnography and interaction analysis. Ethnography, the traditional method of social and cultural anthropology, involves the careful study of activities and relations between them in a complex social setting. Such studies require extended participant observation of the internal life of a setting, in order to understand what participants themselves take to be relevant aspects of their activity. Importantly, this may include things that are so familiar to them as to be unremarkable (and therefore missing from their accounts of how they work), although being evident in what they can actually be seen to do.

Interaction analysis is concerned with detailed investigation of the interaction of people with each other and with the material environment.[3] Our use of interaction analysis is inspired by prior work in anthropology and sociology, particularly ethnomethodology and conversation analysis (see for example Atkinson & Heritage, 1984; Garfinkel, 1986; Goodwin, 1981; Goodwin & Heritage, 1990; Heritage, 1984; Sacks, Schegloff, & Jefferson, 1974). In work settings, where our studies have been centered, our analyses focus on the joint definition and accomplishment of the work at hand, through the organization of interaction and the use of supporting technologies and artifacts.

Situations of Use

Our goal in doing studies of work is to identify routine practices, problems, and possibilities for development within a given activity or setting. In the case of the airport operations room, we learned about the difficulties of propagating changes to complex sheets by recording an instance of everyday trouble, as well as by hearing Ops Room members' stories about misdirected baggage. The ideal site for investigations of technology in use, in our view, are these "naturally occurring" occasions of work activity, in the settings in

---

2 The "we" here refers to a group of researchers at Xerox Palo Alto Research Center, Palo Alto, CA.

3 For more details on both interaction analysis and its application to design see Jordan, Henderson, and Tatar (in prep.).

which such activities ordinarily take place. That is, in settings designed by the participants themselves, over time, rather than contrived by the researcher for purposes of the analysis. The first task for such studies is to come to understand peoples' current work practices, using the technologies that are available to them.

A variation on this approach is to investigate the organization of work practice and the use of technologies in situations that we, as researchers, construct. Within those situations, we invite the participants to use whatever tools they choose, and to organize their work in whatever ways they choose. So, for example, we might be interested in understanding how people use shared drawing spaces such as whiteboards or poster paper to do joint design work (Tang, 1989). We ask people who use whiteboards in the course of their everyday practice to come and do some of their own work, but at a time and place that we propose, and with video cameras set up to record their interaction. A further variation occurs when we have an early prototype of a new tool, and invite people to come in to use the prototype, again to do their work but in a time and place that we propose (see for example, Minneman & Bly, 1990).

A situation constructed for purposes of investigation, in contrast to a study carried out wherever the activities of interest are under way, is itself a kind of prototyping. That is, rather than experimental "control," we are really after a way of prototyping either our methods for looking at the details of work practice, or a tool, ideally based on prior study in actual work settings, that we are not quite ready to put out into the world. Like all prototyping, such studies should be done as rapidly as possible, with as strong a feedback mechanism as we can design. And as soon as we can, we should get ourselves out into the world again.

What We Record

In recording within actual work settings, our strategy is to find multiple solutions to the problem of capturing the complex activities that work involves.

Setting-oriented records are made using a stationary camera, positioned to cover as much as possible of the activity in a given physical space. The use of the complex sheet described earlier was recorded with camera and microphone positioned to include all four seated operations room workers in the field of view, and to pick up as much of their talk as possible.

Person-oriented records, in contrast, attempt to understand the work from a particular person's point of view. Depending on the nature of their work, this may require recording equipment that travels with the person being recorded. For example, in order to

understand the use of the complex sheet by ramp crew members in more detail, we would need to accompany them as they move around the planes and in the terminal.

An object-oriented record would track a particular technology or artifact. We might trace a complex sheet from the time it is first generated (as an empty matrix) through its markup and highlighting by operations room members, to its filing and possible eventual recovery by auditors. Instrumenting the computers used by operations room personnel to provide machine audit trails yields a different sort of object-oriented record.

Finally, task-oriented records may require multiple recordings of distributed individuals working toward a common goal. A prime example of a task-oriented record would be if during the aircraft swap described above we could have had access not only to activity inside the operations room itself, but also at the two relevant gates and out on the ramp.

How We Work as Researchers

The first analysis we undertake after recording an extended sequence of activity is a rough content log of the entire videotape. Such a log describes observed events and indexes them chronologically by clock time. This rough summary of what happened can expedite the process of searching for particular remembered instances. In addition, the log identifies issues raised in the course of viewing the tape again. Such issue-based logging might include, for example, marking an event as being of inherent interest and possibly representative of a new theme or category (e.g., extending a complex sheet across two complexes); labelling an event as being representative of a given theme or category (e.g., modifiability of artifacts); or generating proposals for further fieldwork (e.g., studying the use of the complex sheet on the ramp).

Frequently, a sequence of recorded activity is picked out as being of particular interest and deserving of more systematic analysis. A first step toward such analysis is a careful transcription (see Jefferson, 1984). Though transcribing talk is almost always central to any interactional study, detailed sequential analyses can also focus on non-vocal dimensions of interaction such as the participants' gaze, gestures, and body positions (see Goodwin, 1981; Heath, 1986; Kendon, 1985). Furthermore, in our work, we have found it valuable to analyze activity in terms of peoples' interactions with various artifacts or technologies. This requires detailed transcriptions of the actions of people using machines, concatenated with machine records to show the interactional organization between person and machine, and the interrelation of that human-machine interaction with the talk and activity of other people (see, for example, Suchman, 1987, chap. 6).

The task of interaction analysis is to uncover the regularity and efficacy of peoples' relations with each other and their use of the resources that their environment affords. To see this regularity requires a productive interaction between an emerging theory and a rich body of specific instances. As we accumulate studies of interaction in specific settings we begin to develop a set of both general observations (e.g., the interorganization of talk and nonvocal activity) and specific analyses (e.g., the specialized concerns and practices of people in this particular domain and/or this particular setting). As an analysis begins to develop over a body of videotapes, it becomes necessary to construct "collections"; that is, instances of interaction that one wants to see as a class. In setting such instances side by side, the commonalities and distinctive features among them are made more visible:

For example, on one videotape of an American hospital birth it was noted that at the beginning of a particular uterine contraction the eyes of all those present—nurse, husband, medical student—went to the electronic fetal monitor by the woman's bedside. A behavioral pattern was proposed that when a monitor is present, birth attendants' eyes will move to that equipment when a contraction begins. The pattern was checked against other contractions in this particular labor, on tapes of other American hospital births where monitors were present, as well as against monitored contractions in European hospitals. It was found that the pattern held overwhelmingly. In the few cases where it did not, evidence for some competing local activity was available to explain the discrepancy, e.g., the woman was very distraught or the doctor was just at that time doing an examination and therefore had his or her eyes on her. When examining videotapes of births where monitors were not used, it was found that crossculturally in the absence of monitoring equipment, the focus of attention almost always shifts to the woman when a contraction begins. A generalization was then proposed which states that in the presence of high-technology equipment the attentional focus of medical personnel as well as of non-staff attendants shifts from the patient to the machinery. (Jordan, Henderson, & Tatar, in prep.)

Having a videotape in hand in no way eliminates the need for thoughtful interpretation of the meaning of the events it records. However, video-based interaction analysis affords a powerful corrective to our tendency to see in a scene what we expect to see:

For example, in certain circumstances we expect a couple who are in close physical proximity and who are smiling at each other to

also touch each other. Observers frequently report that they have seen such touches even though on replay it is clear that none occurred. Errors of this sort are invisible on a paper-and-pencil record, but a tape segment can be played over and over again, and questions of what is on the tape versus what observers think they saw can be resolved by recourse to the tape as the final authority. This jolting experience of periodically having one's confidence in what one (thinks one) saw shaken, instills a healthy skepticism about the validity of observations that were made without the possibility to check the record more than once. (Jordan, Henderson, & Tatar, in prep.)

The work of interaction analysis is time consuming and labor intensive for the researcher. It requires the painstaking work of viewing, transcribing and searching videotapes for sequences relevant to a developing analysis. However, a compelling case for the value of this labor is made in Jordan, Henderson, & Tatar (in prep.):

Even for a trained observer, it is simply impossible to note the overlapping activities of several persons with any accuracy or any hope of catching adequate detail. Consider an excerpt from field-notes, a paper-and-pencil snapshot of a birth: "midwife bathing baby, mother in hammock; father out to dispose of placenta; grandmother rummaging in cardboard box" (Jordan, 1983). The videotape provides an incomparably richer record. The kind of talk (or silence) going on at the time, the procedural details of the bath, the mother's eyes on the infant, the grandmother's rummaging for oil and baby wraps, the looks, the body orientations, all of that is lost and probably not recoverable from memory. It is also not recoverable from the memory of participants by interviewing after the fact. Similarly, the details of manipulative procedures such as the arranging of flight-status strips on the work panel of air traffic controllers (Anderson, forthcoming) or the details of moving a cursor while text editing, are impossible to capture in words, both because of the density of behavioral details and because we lack a ready descriptive vocabulary for bodily behavior which could be captured in notes.

This work is not easily delegated. Particularly where conceptual categories are under construction, it is difficult to instruct another as to where to look. More importantly, it is precisely in the repeated, careful working through of the primary materials that theoretical insights arise. In this way, analysis is something like iterative design. Articulations of themes and categories arise from familiarity with the materials and are constantly reevaluated against those materials. This in turn renews and extends one's familiarity. Furthermore, the identification of new themes and categories can lead one to return to the field or workplace to gather new materials.

Tools for Activity Analysis

As we have seen, the work of video-based interaction analysis involves a continual interweaving of multiple activities: viewing and re-viewing video records both individually and in groups, generating activity or "content" logs for each record, conducting detailed sequential analyses of selected portions of the records, integrating multiple records (often in different media) of the same activity, identifying conceptual categories and gathering "collections" of instances, and finally, juxtaposing multiple analytic perspectives on the same activity.

Assume for a moment that we have obtained a set of video records of activity in a workplace, including practitioners' work with a particular technology of interest. What tools, in particular what computer-based resources, are available to help manage and manipulate them? The sort of video analysis discussed here suggests possibilities for computer support: the need to generate useful abstractions while retaining their relation to unique instances and the need to capture multiple perspectives on the same piece of recorded activity.

Figure 3 shows part of an ongoing analysis of the operations room activity discussed earlier. The image is taken from the screen of a computer-based "activity representation" tool that we are in the process of developing.[4] Our tool is an example of a hypermedia system in that it represents information in linked, browsable networks.[5] Nodes in the network could include verbal transcripts, records of participants' gaze or other non-vocal activity captured in some graphical notation, brief comments or annotations, or indeed, a videotape itself.

Three "windows" appear in Figure 3: a text window displaying a portion of the verbal transcript, a graphics window depicting our understanding of the three-way aircraft switch, and a three-paned "worksheet" window used to control and annotate the video record. The worksheet's "Content log" pane serves as a canvas on which bits of text and graphics are positioned, ordered chronologically according to the time of the events they depict.

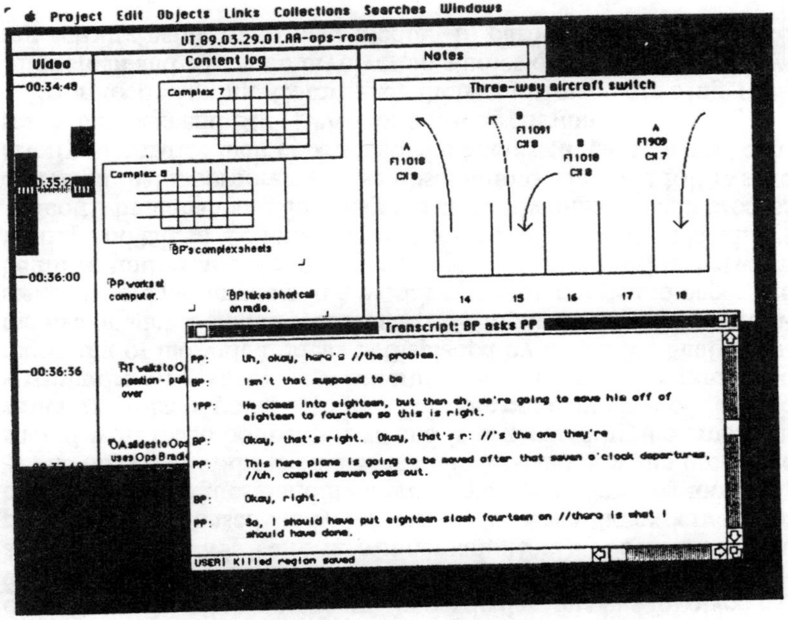

Figure 3. A computer-based environment for video analysis.

The "Video" pane includes ruler-like markings indicating relative time from the start of the tape. The small scroll bar appearing just under "00:35:24" indicates the current position of the videotape. When the videotape is playing this scroll bar moves down the pane. The three filled rectangles in the video pane mark the locations of *active links*. As the scroll bar moves past these link markers, the linked materials are automatically displayed in separate windows. The larger rectangle is linked to the graphics displayed in the "Three-way aircraft switch" window while the two smaller rectangles link to positions within the transcript.

The tool enables us to maintain and interrelate multiple perspectives on a work activity. Perspectives can differ on the basis of the dimension of activity picked out (e.g., talk, gaze, gesture, use of technology), or the viewer (e.g., different researchers, designers, and practitioners). In doing cooperative design we need to share materials: If video provides the catalyst for multidisciplinary collaborative work, then tools with which to study, represent, and discuss video records provide the ongoing support.

---

4 The tool described here was designed and prototyped in collaboration with Jeremy Roschelle and Roy Pea of the Institute for Research on Learning, with support from Apple Computer.
5 For an introduction to hypermedia and a survey of the major systems, see Conklin (1987).

Who Participates

Most video-based analysis of activity makes use of a preconceived coding scheme, carried along largely unchanged from one study to the next. Our approach, in contrast, is to craft and refine our conceptual framework through the ongoing work of analysis. A basic strategy is to use multiple perspectives, drawing on designers, people informed about interaction analysis, and those able to unravel the intricacies of practice in a given domain. Although our use of these methods to date has been primarily in the context of traditional research, we believe they can be developed in the service of cooperative design. In our current working group, researchers bring tapes and transcripts from their respective projects to a weekly two-hour meeting.[6] The group offers a forum in which researchers can identify the possibilities that a particular tape affords. The entire working session is audiotaped, so that with those proposals and insights in hand, individual researchers or project groups can direct their more intensive work outside the lab to a particular line of analysis. Lines of analysis developed outside the lab in turn can be brought back to the larger group for reactions and new insights.

In a typical session, someone provides a brief introduction to the setting of the recorded activity and the project's interests in coming to understand that activity better. The group then works from a running videotape that is stopped whenever anyone observes something of interest. Group members propose interpretations for what is going on, attempting to provide some grounding or evidence in the materials at hand. Such proposals usually require repeated reviewings of the tape, until alternative formulations are laid out or the group agrees on one interpretation. Often an observation leads to further questions to be asked out in the field, at which point the questions are noted and viewing continues.

As well as being the focus of discussion for researchers and designers, video records can afford a basis for conversation with work practitioners. In a process developed most extensively by Frankel (1983) in working with student physicians, participants in a recorded interaction review the tape along with researchers. They are invited to stop the tape at any point and offer comments on what they see. Their comments are audiotaped, and then flagged at the place on the videotape that occasioned them.

This gives some idea of how participants structure the event, i.e. where they see significant segments as beginning and ending; it also gives information on troubles that may be invisible to the analyst, on resources and methods used by participants to solve their problems, and on many other issues of importance to participants. Frankel, for example, asked patients and physicians who had been videotaped during medical consultations to stop the tape when they saw something of interest. There was a substantial overlap in *where* they stopped the tape, but the explanations they gave for *why* they stopped the tape were widely divergent between patients and physicians, indicating substantially different views of what their interactions were about. Elicitation based on video tapes has the advantage of staying much closer to the actual events than if one were to ask questions in a situation removed from the activity of interest to the researcher. (Jordan, Henderson, & Tatar, in prep.)

With these experiences as background, we hope to engage practitioners themselves in the process of analysis in order to collaborate on both work and system development.

Applying Video Analysis to System Design

Together with colleagues at Xerox Palo Alto Research Center (PARC), we have been exploring the technological as well as the social-interactional resources of collaborative work practice, focusing on the use of available artifacts. In particular, this has involved extensive studies of the use of shared drawing surfaces (see, for example, Tang, 1989; Tang & Minneman, 1990). To illustrate the power of video-based study for design, we trace the experience of two of our colleagues building a prototype shared drawing tool.

The objective of these studies is to understand how the use of the shared workspace both supports and is organized by the emergent structure of the ongoing activity. The conventional view of a shared writing/drawing space as a medium for the communication and recording of individual ideas is displaced by a detailed analysis of the use of such a shared workspace. By looking closely at each instance where participants in a working session put pen to paper, we begin to understand the complex sequential relationship between writing and talk in the joint accomplishment of the work at hand.

Scott Minneman and Sara Bly are currently engaged in a process of design that incorporates these observations. In what follows we briefly summarize their experience; the interested reader should consult Minneman and Bly (1990) for a full discussion.

Prior to designing Commune, their multi-user drawing tool, Minneman and Bly were involved in studies of collaborative drawing activity using traditional media. In particular, Bly conducted

---

6 We do this regularly through the Interaction Analysis Laboratory, a joint activity of Xerox PARC and the Institue for Research on Learning in Palo Alto, and through the Design Interaction Analysis Laboratory at Xerox PARC.

studies of a pair of user interface designers working in three communicative environments: face-to-face, in offices joined by a slow-scan video link, and over the telephone. This research revealed the work required to maintain coordination and co-presence as interactional and representational resources became less accessible and more difficult to share. In the Office Design Project (Weber & Minneman, 1987; Stults, 1988), three architects collaborated for two days on the design of an office space, communicating only via audio and video links. As Minneman and Bly (1990) put it:

> The results of these examples of using Media Spaces for everyday drawing activities indicated that better tools were needed to support individuals and groups collaborating remotely. It was also believed that such tools might easily generalize to support collaborative design work in other environments. The need for finding a solution to shared drawing support was apparent: the next step was to understand how and why drawing surfaces were already being used. (p. 2)

One resource for gaining such understandings is a workgroup at PARC consisting of anthropologists, computer scientists and designers called the Designer Interaction Analysis Lab (DIAL) (described in Tatar, 1989). This group meets regularly to apply the methods of interaction analysis to concrete problems in system design. The group views videotapes of people working with traditional as well as prototype technologies, noting the subtleties of established work practices with familiar artifacts, as well as the problems and adaptations encountered by practitioners using new technologies.

One major finding from [DIAL-related] studies has been the importance of the *process* of the collaboration in contrast to the actual artifacts or markings on the shared work surface. Process includes the use of gestures, the ability to interact in the same space, the use of references, the lack of distraction caused by the drawing action, and the feeling of close interaction. Observing the use of drawing surfaces has pointed out the potential value of providing not only shared marks in a tool for distributed use but also support for the interactive process. (Minneman & Bly, 1990, p. 3)

The studies left several questions unanswered, however, suggesting "that the capabilities of a shared drawing tool might best be *evolved* through use, rather than through analysis and design alone" (p. 3). This led to a minimalist design for the Commune shared drawing tool, modeling the user interface after a single shared sheet of paper with marking pens. The first prototype could thus be developed in short order and made available to casual "walk-up" users almost immediately thereafter. Videotapes were made of these encounters as well as of one extended working session by two user interface designers. Initial study of this data indicates the "ease with which almost all users began using the system..." (p. 5).

As Minneman and Bly (1990) point out, such careful use-based prototyping isn't always the most natural path for designers:

> Despite the initial success of our development cycle for Commune, there is considerable temptation to revert to design evolution based solely on intuitions and the technological possibilities offered by the prototyping platform. (p. 6)

Our purpose in applying video analysis to design is to resist such temptation by developing methods that encourage the move from analysis to development to further analysis. The goal is to tie both intuitions and technological possibilities to detailed understandings of real work practice.

Reflection and Design

During meetings in the course of assembling this book, Pelle Ehn provided what we found to be a helpful formulation of the relations among the book's authors. Some of us are reflective practitioners, he said, referring to the book by Donald Schön (1983). And others of us are practicing reflectors. What we share is the goal of bringing the two together. Theorizing or reflecting and engaging in some form of practice are essential to every kind of human endeavor, be it research, design, or any other form of work practice. To develop simultaneously our ways of working together and our technological systems will require a joint enterprise that recognizes, encourages, and develops both the quality of our work practice and our powers of reflection, with respect for both and without privilege to either.

In Figure 4, this joint enterprise is depicted in the form of a triangle linking three perspectives: research, design, and practice. We deliberately have not said researchers, designers, and practitioners, because our goal is to view these not only as a division of labor between participants in the system development process, but as places from which to look. Depending on where one stands, at which corner of the triangle, one adopts a different perspective.

As a consequence of personal preference, experience, and training, we are likely to distribute ourselves differently across these perspectives. We believe that the most satisfactory organization may take the form of collaborations wherein some of us take on primary responsibility for one of these perspectives, and others of us for other perspectives. However, we want to think of these, not as

Examples of such pairwise collaborations can be found throughout research and industry wherever people concern themselves with work practice and technology. What we now hope to foster are collaborations among all three perspectives simultaneously, that is, activity occurring in the center of the triangle. Consider the case of the videotaped working session excerpted at the start of this paper. In a joint session of practitioners, researchers and designers looking at the recording, the various groups might have overlapping but not identical goals. All might share the goal of understanding better what happened in the interaction, though the participants might be reflecting on their work together, the researchers investigating the interactional organization of the work, and the designers searching for ideas for new prototypes. We hope that such cross-perspectival cooperations become the norm in the future, particularly in cases that today involve only one of the parties. We believe that the video medium can catalyze such collaborations to the greater understanding and imagination of all concerned.

Acknowledgments

We are grateful to Liam Bannon, Susanne Bødker, Bengt Brattgård, Bo Dahlbom, Pelle Ehn, Joan Greenbaum, Austin Henderson, Berit Holmqvist, Jana Kana-Essig, Morten Kyng, Jens Kaasbøl, and Jesper Strandgaard Pedersen, for comments on earlier drafts of this paper.

References

Akrich, M. (1987). How can technical objects be described? Paper presented at the Second Workshop on Social and Historical Studies of Technology, Twente University, The Netherlands.

Anderson, R. J., Hughes, J. A., Schapiro, D. Z., & Sharrock, W. W. with Harper, R. & Gibbons, S. (forthcoming). Flying planes can be dangerous: A framework for analysing the work of air traffic control. Submitted to *Human-Computer Interaction*. Hillsdale, NJ: Lawrence Erlbaum Associates.

Atkinson, J. M. & Heritage, J. C. (1984). *Structures of social action: Studies in conversation analysis*. Cambridge, UK: Cambridge University Press.

Blomberg, J. & Henderson, A. (1990). Reflections on participatory design: Lessons from the Trillium experience. *Proceedings*

absolute, fixed positions but as relative to each other. And we want all to have facility at moving between perspectives.

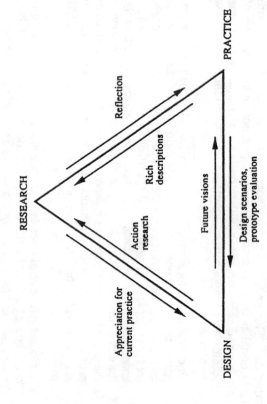

Figure 4. Video as a medium for conversation and learning.

In Figure 4, the arrows appearing along the edges of the triangle indicate the kind of contributions that one perspective can make to another:

- Using the perspective of research, practitioners reflect on their current practice;
- Using the perspective of design, practitioners envision future work practices and new technologies;
- Using the perspective of practice, researchers gain the insights that only confrontations with reality can provide;
- Using the perspective of design, researchers bring an action-oriented involvement to their traditional analytic work practice;
- Using the perspective of practice, designers working with users better understand the implications of prototypes and scenarios for new designs;
- Using the perspective of research, designers gain new insights from observing current practice so as to respect the present when designing for the future.

CHI'90 Human Factors in Computing Systems (Seattle, April 1-5). ACM, New York, 353-360.

Conklin, J. (1987). Hypertext: A survey and introduction. *IEEE Computer, 20* (9), 17-41.

Frankel, R. (1983). The laying on of hands: Aspects of the organization of gaze, touch and talk in a medical encounter. In S. Fisher & A. Todd (Eds.), *The social organization of doctor-patient communication* (pp. 10-33). Washington, DC: Center for Applied Linguistics.

Garfinkel, H. (Ed.). (1986). *Ethnomethodological studies of work.* London: Routledge & Kegan Paul.

Goodwin, C. (1981). *Conversational organization: Interaction between speakers and hearers.* New York: Academic Press.

Goodwin, C. & Heritage, J. (1990). Conversation Analysis. Prepared for *Annual Review of Anthropology*, 1990.

Heath, C. (1986). *Body movement and speech in medical interaction.* Cambridge, UK: Cambridge University Press.

Hellman, R. (1989). Emancipation of and by computer-supported cooperative work. In *Scandinavian Journal of Information Systems, 1,* 143-161.

Heritage, J. C. (1984). *Garfinkel and ethnomethodology.* Cambridge, UK: Polity Press.

Jefferson, G. (1984). Caricature versus detail: On capturing the particulars of pronunciation in transcripts of conversational data. *Tilburg Papers on Language and Literature No. 31,* University of Tilburg, Netherlands.

Jordan, B. (1983). *Birth in four cultures* (3rd ed.). Montreal: Eden Press.

Jordan, B. (1987). High Technology: The Case of Obstetrics. *World Health Forum 8*(3), 312-319. Geneva: World Health Organization.

Jordan, B., Henderson, A., & Tatar, D. (In preparation). *Interaction analysis: Foundations and practice.* Palo Alto: Xerox Palo Alto Research Center.

Kendon, A. (1985). Behavioural foundations for the process of frame attunement in face-to-face interaction. In G. Ginsburt, M. Brenner, & M. von Cranach (Eds.), *Discovery Strategies in the Psychology of Action.* London, UK: Academic Press, 229-253.

Latour, B. (1986). *How to write* The Prince *for machines as well as for machinations.* Working paper, Seminar on Technology and Social Change, Edinburgh.

Minneman, S. & Bly, S. (1990). Experiences in the development of a multi-user drawing tool. *Proceedings of the Third Guelph Symposium on Computer-mediated Communication.* Ontario: University of Guelph.

Sacks, H., Schegloff, E. A., & Jefferson, G. (1974). A simplest systematics for the organization of turn-taking for conversation. *Language, 50,* 696-735.

Schön, D. (1983). *The reflective practitioner.* New York: Basic Books.

Stults, R. (1988). Experimental uses of video to support design. Palo Alto, CA: Xerox Palo Alto Research Center.

Suchman, L. (1987). *Plans and situated actions.* Cambridge, UK: Cambridge University Press.

Suchman, L. & Jordan, B. (1989). Computerization and women's knowledge. In K. Tijdens, M. Jennings, I. Wagner, & M. Weggelaar (Eds.), *Women, work and computerization: Forming new alliances* (pp. 153-160). Amsterdam: North-Holland.

Tang, J. C. (1989). *Listing, drawing and gesturing in design: A study of the use of shared workspaces by design teams.* Technical report SSL-89-3 (Ph.D. Dissertation, Stanford University). Palo Alto, CA: Xerox Palo Alto Research Center.

Tang, J. C. & Minneman, S. (1990). VideoDraw: A video interface for collaborative drawing. *Proceedings CHI'90 Human Factors in Computing Systems, Seattle, April 1-5* (pp. 313-320). New York: ACM.

Tatar, D. (1989). A preliminary report on using video to shape the design of a new technology. *SIGCHI Bulletin, 21,* 2, 108-111.

Weber, K. & Minneman, S. (1987). *The office design video project* [Videotape]. Palo Alto, CA: Xerox Palo Alto Research Center.

Winner, L. (1980). Do artifacts have politics? *Daedalus, 109,* 121-136.

ETHNOGRAPHIC WORKFLOW ANALYSIS:

SPECIFICATIONS FOR DESIGN

Danielle Fafchamps

Hewlett-Packard Laboratories, 1501 Page Mill Road,
P.O. Box 10490, Palo Alto, CA 94303-0969, USA
fafchamps@hplabs.hpl.hp.com

ABSTRACT

Ethnographic workflow analysis is a design methodology developed to study information-related behavior in the work place. Designers in the Physician Workstation Project used this methodology to study the work practice of physicians. This paper describes a minimal conceptual framework and techniques for data collection and analysis, presents ethnographic data collected in the teaching and private clinics of two health care institutions, and illustrates the translation of ethnographic data into functional specifications for the design of the physician workstation interface.

Key words: clinical applications, design methodologies, ethnography, observational studies, physician workstations.

1. INTRODUCTION

Design methodologies have been proposed to bring the users' perspective into the design process: user-centered strategies [Norman & Draper, 1986], rapid prototyping [Bødker & Grønbæk, 1990], contextual design [Wixon & Holtzblatt, 1990] and participatory design [Kyng, et al., 1990; Namioka & Schuler, 1990]. These methodologies promote a democratic synergy between designers and users, and assume users' active participation throughout the design cycle. Users' involvement in design is best achieved when users have a personal stake in the product being developed, when management is supportive, and when the users' organization contributes to the costs, both financial and logistics. Designers of "off-the-shelf" products find it difficult to engage users in system design when their management does not perceive an immediate benefit for the organization. We encountered this difficulty. We are working on the design of a physician workstation [Tang et al, 1991] and our target users have a hectic work pace with very little time for activities that are not work-related. We devised a design methodology that brings the users' voices into the design, but does not disrupt the flow of their day-to-day activities. This paper describes ethnographic workflow analysis, the design methodology we use to capture and model information-related behavior in professional environments. Concrete examples from the Physician Workstation Project illustrate the translation of ethnographic data into design specifications.

Reprinted from *Human Aspects of Computing: Design and Use of Interactive Systems and Work with Terminals*, pp. 709-715. Elsevier.

2. ETHNOGRAPHIC WORKFLOW ANALYSIS

Ethnography [Bauman & Sherzer, 1975; Clifford, 1983] has been advocated to provide descriptions of users' practices for design purpose [Suchman, 1985]. However, the use of ethnography in industrial R&D faces three challenges. First, ethnography belongs to a research tradition that has evolved concepts and themes relevant for describing cultural and social patterns (e.g., kinship, systems of production, political organizations), not for the modelling of work patterns. Second, anthropological research requires that ethnographers spend about a year in the field. In industrial settings, ethnographers must deliver reliable data in a much shorter time. Third, the typical product of an ethnography is a description, but engineers should not have to make the design inferences from the ethnographic descriptions. It is the role of ethnographers to articulate their results into concrete design specifications.

Ethnographic workflow analysis provides designers with timely design specifications that are faithful to the users' actual work practices. The methodology is useful for modelling information-related work practices and for deriving specifications for the design of information systems to support these practices. The methodology includes a minimal conceptual framework and techniques for data collection and analysis.

2.1 A MINIMAL CONCEPTUAL FRAMEWORK

The minimal conceptual framework focusses and constrains the scope of data collection and analysis for the investigation of information-related work practices. The framework has four main concepts inspired from the theory of activity [Wertsch, 1981]: professional environment, context of work, event, and pattern (fig. 1).

- PROFESSIONAL ENVIRONMENT refers to a community of people who share a professional goal. For example, a clinical practice and a pediatric intensive care unit are professional environments where patient care is the common goal of various

professionals (physicians, physicians-assistants, nurses, technicians, and administrative personnel).

- CONTEXTS OF WORK are structured work practices that may be labelled, e.g., patient visits, or may not be labelled, e.g., in teaching practice, one physician will check all labs results daily and annotate them as normal or abnormal. Contexts of work span a continuum from highly routinized to less routinized.

- EVENTS are the building blocks of contexts of work, e.g., patient data queries during the patient visit.

- PATTERNS. Work practices are characterized in terms of patterns. A pattern is the minimal unit of analysis.

These four concepts are relevant for the study of information-related behavior, but they are not tightly coupled to a theory, a domain, or to engineering. There are advantages in having a "neutral" terminology. First, because they are not bound to a theoretical framework, these concepts facilitate the creative exploration of work practices. Theory has not provided designers with guidelines, and it has been argued that designers should instead focus on what users do in the course of their work [Carroll, 1990]. Second, the concepts are domain independent, hence, they facilitate comparisons of information-related work practices across professional domains. Third, the concepts are not tied to engineering. They do not presuppose technological solutions, yet, they are understandable to designers unfamiliar with social science research.

2.2 DATA COLLECTION

Participant observation is typically presented as the main technique of ethnographic data collection. However, this technique is difficult to define [Ellen, 1984]. We identified five techniques for data collection that are researcher-independent and meet our goal for the study of information-related work practices:

- THINKING ALOUD: professionals describe what they are doing as they are doing it.

- GUIDED TOUR: individuals are asked to give a guided tour of their work space, both private (e.g., their office) and shared.

- STRUCTURED OBSERVATIONS are used to record meetings, face-to-face and phone interactions.

- WRITTEN ARTIFACTS, formal and informal (e.g., reports, stick-on notes) are collected and the professionals' descriptions of these artifacts are recorded.

- FOCUSED INTERVIEWS are useful to explore specific aspects of work that cannot be satisfactorily captured through other techniques.

Initially, we asked "What if" questions to purposefully stimulate the professionals' vision of technological solutions for their practice. We obtained little or no answer and eventually we eliminated these questions from our data collection—unless the professionals themselves initiated the discussion.

In the context of the design of the physician workstation, we used these techniques during the seven weeks of data collection in the teaching and private clinics of two large American institutions. All data were tape-recorded and transcribed and the ethnographer's notes were incorporated into the final transcripts of the recorded data.

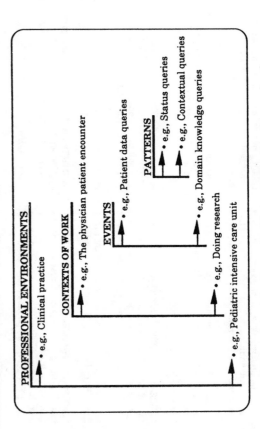

PROFESSIONAL ENVIRONMENTS
- e.g., Clinical practice

CONTEXTS OF WORK
- e.g., The physician patient encounter

EVENTS
- e.g., Patient data queries

PATTERNS
- e.g., Status queries
- e.g., Contextual queries
- e.g., Domain knowledge queries
- e.g., Doing research
- e.g., Pediatric intensive care unit

Figure 1. A minimal conceptual framework for the ethnography of information-related work practices.

2.3 DATA ANALYSIS

We use themes analysis and coding techniques to identify patterns in the data. In the tradition of linguistic and anthropological research, themes analysis is based on the tracing of recurrent topics of verbal interaction, and of recurrent patterns of behavior [Werner & Schoepfle, 1987]. For example, we used themes analysis to characterize the queries that physicians want answered about patient data prior to, or during, the patient encounter. In addition to the inductive analysis of emergent themes, we systematically analysed the data according to the following broad themes:

- BREAKDOWNS. An actual or foreseen problematic situation. E.g.,
  Physician: Now, what I want to do is look back and see to make sure every piece of paper that comes through here cannot be found in the chart unless I put my initial on it. If I don't do that, things fall through the cracks, okay?

- SERIES OF ACTIONS. This category includes routines or processes. E.g.,
  Physician [after dictating notes on a patient]: I have referred [the patient] to the plastic surgeon and I will make out the consultation sheet. She will take it out there and give it to [the receptionist] who will call up and make an appointment with [the plastic surgeon).

- ACTIONS. An action is one of a kind information-related behavior. E.g.,
  Physician: 'I [always] dictate phone calls.'

- COMMENTS ON OBJECTS, PROCEDURES, ENTITIES, OTHERS AND SELF. This category includes the professionals' comments (positive, negative, or wishes) on objects (e.g., a document, a database), procedures, entities (e.g., another department), others (e.g., health care professionals, patients) and on self.
  E.g., Physician: The phones are what kill you in terms of getting through the clinic.

- DESCRIPTIONS include statements on the information infrastructure of the clinic (e.g., 'here, we use a chemotherapy flowchart'), information facts (e.g., 'we receive about 100 phone calls a day') as well as baseline job descriptions (e.g., 'I teach [...] do research, [...] see patients in clinic, [...] and I am Chief of the Clinic').

Our experience demonstrates that, for the purpose of system design, these themes are useful to focus the analysis on information access, management, and sharing. The ethnographic data are first organized into these broad themes, then patterns are identified within each theme. For example, we characterize the information-related breakdowns that different types of professionals encounter in a given work context, or we identify what procedures are perceived as problematic, or not problematic, from the multiple perspectives of professionals who work together.

Finally, modelling of the users' work practices is not the prerogative of the ethnographer alone. Target users, typically as paid consultants, are involved in the translation of the ethnographic data into design specifications.

3. DESIGN SPECIFICATIONS

We described elsewhere the contribution of the ethnographic workflow analysis to the definition of the problems that a physician workstation should address [Tang and Fafchamps, 1991]. Here, we present the translation of ethnographic data into functional specifications for the design of the physician workstation interface during the patient encounter. We illustrate this process with ethnographic evidence from the physicians' query patterns typical of this context of work, and we describe two displays that were built from the ethnographic data—the Patient Status display and the Patient Details display. The layout of the displays is not yet definite, and specific ergonomic issues are not considered here.

3.1. THE PATIENT STATUS DISPLAY

Analysis of transcripts of physicians' interviews, of the focused observations and of the physicians' "thinking aloud" showed recurring queries:

- What is the reason for the visit?
- What are the active problems?
- What is the status of health maintenance routines?
- What drugs or treatments are current?
- What labs results are current?
- Who else is seeing this patient?

These queries are typical of the preparatory stage of all patient encounters recorded in the ethnographic data. We observed the same patterns both in teaching and in private clinics. Using queries abstracted from the ethnographic data, a set of functional specifications were developed for a *Patient Status* display. The system brings the Patient Status display (fig. 1) in response to the physician's first request for a patient's information in the specific context of a patient visit.

Figure 1. The Patient Status display

The Patient Status display presents summary information to readily establish a patient context for the physician. From the left, the top portion of the display shows: demographic information, the reason for today's appointment (hypertension and new onset chest pain), vital signs and allergies. The lower portion of the display presents: the active problems, active medications, and current labs. In the middle of the display is an alert the knowledge server generated based on embedded domain knowledge. Here, the alert message indicates that a cholesterol result (part of the fasting metabolic panel listed under New Labs) has been posted since the patient's last visit. The knowledge server interpreted the result as borderline high for this specific patient. The system also generated a reminder that the patient is on hydrochlorothiazide, a medication that can exacerbate an elevated cholesterol. Queries about who else is seeing the patient and about the health maintenance routines are answered in the right portion of the display which includes: recent (i.e., since last appointment) clinics or hospital admissions and the physicians involved, future appointments, and an up-to-date health maintenance record. Data for the Patient Status display are integrated from multiples data bases within an institution. The application programs view patient data through a single abstract data model in the object-oriented database. This Patient Status display cues the physician for the relevant patient data. Detailed information about specific cues are accessible in the *Patient Details* display.

3.2 THE PATIENT DETAILS DISPLAY

We used themes analyses to characterize what detailed questions physicians wanted answered about patient data. We collated questions that had a similar topic (e.g., labs and procedures, medications and treatment, and diagnosis) and served a similar purpose. Sample queries are presented below:

- what are the trends in [name of test]?
- how long has the patient been on [name of drug/treatment]?
- what are the past medications for this patient?
- why was [name of drug/treatment] prescribed?
- how much [name of drug/treatment] has the patient taken/received, over [period of time]?
- how did [patient parameters] change when patient was taking [name of drug, name of treatment]?
- what diagnostic studies were done in the past?
- how long has the patient had the [name of symtom, name of disease]?
- how do [patient parameters] evolved over [period of time]?
- was the patient ever diagnosed with [name of disease, name of symptom]?
- which problems are active/passive?

These queries are contextual because they require that the answers include relevant contextual details. We used these queries to design the Patient Details display. From the Patient Status display, the physician who wants more information about a patient selects the "Show Details" button (middle of display in fig. 1) and the system presents the Patient Details display (fig. 2).

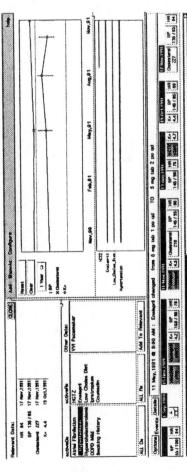

Figure 2. The Patient Details display

The Patient Details display presents the physician with more patient-specific information. Figure 2 assumes that the physician selected (highlight shown in fig. 1) hypertension as the problem focus for viewing the patient data. The system displays information relevant to this problem focus: parameters to monitor the disease (e.g., blood pressure and heart rate), medications (e.g., enalapril and hydrochlorothiazide), and labs (e.g., potassium, creatinine). The system shows relevant start dates, changes in dosages,

and trends of disease parameters, as well as the potential complications of therapy (e.g., change in potassium level).

4. SUMMARY

Designers of "off-the-shelf" systems cannot always rely on the active collaboration of users throughout the design cycle. We proposed a methodology that brings the users' voice into the design, but does not require that users interrupt their activities to participate to the design process. Ethnographic workflow analysis is useful to model the information-related behavior of users and to prescribe functional specifications for system design. We illustrated the relevance of the methodology to system design with concrete examples from the design of a clinical information system.

ACKNOWLEDGEMENTS

We thank our colleagues Robin Jeffries, Nancy Kendzierski and Paul Tang for thoughtful comments on an earlier version of this paper.

REFERENCES

Bauman, R. and J. Sherzer. *The ethnography of speaking.* Annual Review of Anthropology, 43, 95:119, 1975.

Bødker, S. and K. Grønbæk. *Cooperative prototyping studies: Users and designers envision a dental case record system.* J. Bowers and S. Benford (Eds.) Studies in computer supported cooperative work: Theory, practice and design. New-York, North-Holland, 315:332, 1991.

Carroll, J. *Infinite detail and emulation in an ontologically minimized HCI.* Human factors in computing systems. CHI'90 Conference Proceedings, Seattle, Washington, April 1-5, 321:327, 1990.

Clifford, J. *On ethnographic authority.* Representations, 1, 118:146, Spring 1983.

Ellen, R.F. (ED). *Ethnographic research.* New York: Academic Press, Harcourt Brace Jovanovich Pub., 1984.

Kyng, M., Møller, K., and J. Greenbaum. *Design at work: Cooperative design of computer systems.* Hillsdale, NJ: Lawrence Erlbaum Ass., 1990.

Namioka, A., and D. Schuler (Eds.) *PDC'90.* Proceedings of the Participatory Design Conference. Seattle, Washington, March 31-April 1, 1990.

Norman, D., and S. Draper. (Eds.). *User centered system design: New perspective on human-computer interactions.* Hillsdale, NJ: Lawrence Erlbaum Ass, 1986.

Suchman, L. *Technology in use.* Human factors in computing systems, CHI'85 Conference Proceedings, San Francisco, California, April 14-18, 89:91, 1985.

Tang, P.C., Annevelink, J., Fafchamps, D., Stanton, W. and C.Y. Young. *Physician workstations: Integrated information management for clinicians.* Submitted for publication.

Tang, P.C. and D. Fafchamps. *The medical record: Clinical tool or impediment?* Submitted for publication.

Werner, O. and M. Schoepfle. *Ethnographic analysis and data management.* (Vol 2). Beverly Hills: Sage Publications, 1987.

Wertsch, J.(Eds.). *The concept of activity in Soviet psychology.* Armonk, NY: Sharpe, 1981.

Wixon, D. and K. Holtzblatt. *Contextual design: an emergent view of system design.* CHI'90 Conference Proceedings, Seattle, Washington, April 1-5, 329:336, 1990.

GROUNDING IN COMMUNICATION

HERBERT H. CLARK AND SUSAN E. BRENNAN

GROUNDING

It takes two people working together to play a duet, shake hands, play chess, waltz, teach, or make love. To succeed, the two of them have to coordinate both the content and process of what they are doing. Alan and Barbara, on the piano, must come to play the same Mozart duet. This is coordination of content. They must also synchronize their entrances and exits, coordinate how loudly to play forte and pianissimo, and otherwise adjust to each other's tempo and dynamics. This is coordination of process. They cannot even begin to coordinate on content without assuming a vast amount of shared information or common ground—that is, mutual knowledge, mutual beliefs, and mutual assumptions (Clark & Carlson, 1982; Clark & Marshall, 1981; Lewis, 1969; Schelling, 1960). And to coordinate on process, they need to update their common ground moment by moment. All collective actions are built on common ground and its accumulation.

We thank many colleagues for discussion of the issues we take up here. The research was supported in part by National Science Foundation Grant BNS 83-20284 and a National Science Foundation Graduate Fellowship.

Correspondence concerning this chapter should be addressed to Herbert H. Clark, Department of Psychology, Jordan Hall, Building 420, Stanford University, Stanford, CA 94305-2130, or Susan E. Brennan, Department of Psychology, State University of New York at Stony Brook, Stony Brook NY 11794-2500.

Communication, of course, is a collective activity of the first order. When Alan speaks to Barbara, he must do more than merely plan and issue utterances, and she must do more than just listen and understand. They have to coordinate on content (Grice, 1975, 1978). When Alan refers to "my dogs," the two of them must reach the mutual belief that he is referring to his feet. They must also coordinate on process. Speech is evanescent, and so Alan must try to speak only when he thinks Barbara is attending to, hearing, and trying to understand what he is saying, and she must guide him by giving him evidence that she is doing just this. Accomplishing this, once again, requires the two of them to keep track of their common ground and its moment-by-moment changes.

In communication, common ground cannot be properly updated without a process we shall call *grounding* (see Clark & Schaefer, 1987, 1989; Clark & Wilkes-Gibbs, 1986; Isaacs & Clark, 1987). In conversation, for example, the participants try to establish that what has been said has been understood. In our terminology, they try to ground what has been said—that is, make it part of their common ground. But how they do this changes a great deal from one situation to the next. Grounding takes one shape in face-to-face conversation but another in personal letters. It takes one shape in casual gossip but another in calls to directory assistance.

Grounding is so basic to communication—indeed, to all collective actions—that it is important to understand how it works. In this chapter we take up two main factors that shape it. One is *purpose*—what the two people are trying to accomplish in their communication. The other is the *medium of communication*—the techniques available in the medium for accomplishing that purpose, and what it costs to use them. We begin by briefly describing grounding as it appears in casual face-to-face conversation. We then consider how it gets shaped by other purposes and in other media.

Grounding in Conversation

What does it take to contribute to conversation? Suppose Alan utters to Barbara, "Do you and your husband have a car?" In the standard view of speech acts (e.g., Bach & Harnish, 1979; Searle, 1969), what Alan has done is *ask* Barbara whether she and her husband have a car, and, in this way, he has carried the conversation forward. But this isn't quite right. Consider this actual exchange:[1]

Alan: Now, - um, do you and your husband have a j- car
Barbara: - have a car?
Alan: Yeah
Barbara: No -

Even though Alan has uttered "Do you and your husband have a car?", he hasn't managed to ask Barbara whether she and her husband have a car. We know this because Barbara indicates, with "- have a car?", that she hasn't understood him.[2] Only after Alan has answered her query (with "yeah") and she is willing to answer the original question ("no -") do the two of them apparently believe he has succeeded. So asking a question requires more than uttering an interrogative sentence. It must also be established that the respondent has understood what the questioner meant.

Of course, understanding can never be perfect. We assume that the criterion people try to reach in conversation is as follows (Clark & Schaefer, 1989; Clark & Wilkes-Gibbs, 1986): The contributor and his or her partners mutually believe that the partners have understood what the contributor meant to a criterion sufficient for current purposes. This is called the *grounding criterion*. Technically, then, grounding is the collective process by which the participants try to reach this mutual belief. To see some of the forms grounding takes in conversation, let us consider the process of contributing to conversation. Here we will follow a model proposed by Clark and Schaefer (1989) that was founded on a long tradition of work on turns and repairs by Sacks, Schegloff, Jefferson, and others (e.g., Sacks, Schegloff, & Jefferson, 1974; Schegloff, Jefferson, & Sacks, 1977; Schegloff, 1982).

Contributing to Conversation

Most contributions to conversation begin with the potential contributor presenting an utterance to his or her partner. In our example, Alan presents Barbara with the utterance, "Now, - um do you and your husband have a j- car." Why does he present it? Because he wants Barbara to hear it, register it, and understand what he means by it. But he cannot know whether he has succeeded unless she provides evidence of her understanding. In our example, indeed, she provides evidence that she has *not* understood him yet. It is only after the exchange, "- have a car?" and "yeah," that she gives positive evidence of understanding by initiating the answer "no." So contributing to conversation generally divides into two phases:

[1] All examples, except those marked otherwise, come from the so-called London-Lund corpus (Svartvik & Quirk, 1980). We retain the following symbols from the London-Lund notation: "." for a brief pause (of one light syllable); "-" for a unit pause (of one stress unit or foot), ".." for the end of a tone unit, which we mark only if it comes mid-turn; "(laughs)" for contextual comments; "((words))" or double parentheses for incomprehensible words; and "**yes*" or asterisks for paired instances of simultaneous talk.

[2] Actually, the word *ask* is ambiguous between "utter an interrogative sentence" and "succeed in getting the addressee to recognize that you want certain information." Note that you can say, "Ken asked Julia 'Are you coming' but failed to ask her whether she was coming because she couldn't hear him." We will use *ask* in the second sense.

Presentation phase: A presents utterance *u* for B to consider. He does so on the assumption that, if B gives evidence *e* or stronger, he can believe that she understands what he means by *u*.

Acceptance phase: B accepts utterance *u* by giving evidence *e* that she believes she understands what A means by *u*. She does so on the assumption that, once A registers that evidence. he will also believe that she understands.

It takes both phases for a contribution to be complete.

The presentation phase can become very complicated. One way is by self-repairs. In our example, Alan doesn't present the pristine utterance, "Do you and your husband have a car," but rather the messier, "now, - um do you and your husband have a j- car." He expects Barbara to see, for example, that "j-" isn't part of the sentence he is ultimately committed to. Establishing what he is and is not ultimately committed to is no easy task. Another complication is embedding. The presentation itself can contain distinct contributions each with its own presentation and acceptance phases (we will see examples of embedding later in this chapter).

Grounding becomes most evident in the acceptance phase. By the end of A's presentation of some utterance *u*, the partner B may believe she is in one of these states for all or part of *u*:

State 0: B didn't notice that A uttered any *u*.
State 1: B noticed that A uttered some *u* (but wasn't in state 2).
State 2: B correctly heard *u* (but wasn't in state 3).
State 3: B understood what A meant by *u*.

In our example, Barbara apparently thinks she is in state 3 for the first part of Alan's presentation but in state 2 for the final phrase. Because she wants to be in state 3 for the entire presentation, she needs to clear up her understanding of the final phrase. This is what leads her to initiate the *side sequence* (Jefferson, 1972) or *insertion sequence* (Schegloff, 1972) with "- have a car?" All of this is part of the acceptance phase, and so Alan's contribution divides up this way:

Presentation phase:
    Alan: Now, - um do you and your husband have a j-car
Acceptance phase:
    Barbara: - have a car?
    Alan: Yeah

Actually, the acceptance phase only gets completed when Barbara initiates the answer "no" and Alan accepts it as the evidence he needs. Barbara's "- have a car?" is the presentation phase of a contribution that is wholly contained within the acceptance phase of the main contribution. It is accepted when Alan

says "yeah," which is itself a presentation with its own acceptance (see Clark & Schaefer, 1987). So contributions often emerge in hierarchies. They may contain contributions embedded within both their presentation and their acceptance phases.

There is an essential difference, therefore, between merely uttering some words—a presentation—and doing what one intends to do by uttering them—a contribution. When you say to a friend, "I want you to meet Mr. Jones," it isn't guaranteed that you have succeeded in introducing him to Mr. Jones. His hearing aid may have been off. He may have misheard you. Or he may have misunderstood you, as Chico did Groucho in this exchange:

Groucho: Ravelli, I want you to meet Mr. Jones.
Chico: Awright, where should I meet him?

Even without Chico around, grounding is essential.

Evidence in Grounding

Once we utter something in a conversation, one might suppose, all we need to look for is *negative evidence*—evidence that we have been misheard or misunderstood. If we find some, we repair the problem, but if we don't, we assume, by default, that we have been understood. This is, indeed, what is explicitly or tacitly assumed in many accounts of language use (e.g., Grosz & Sidner, 1986; Litman & Allen, 1987; Stalnaker, 1978). When Barbara says "- have a car?" she is giving Alan negative evidence and a clue to what she has misunderstood. But if negative evidence is all we looked for, we would often accept information we had little justification for accepting. In fact, people ordinarily reach for a higher criterion. As the contribution model says, people ultimately seek *positive evidence* of understanding. Let us look at the three most common forms of positive evidence and see how they work.

First, *acknowledgments* are the most obvious form of positive evidence. By acknowledgments we mean much of what has been called *back-channel responses*. These include continuers such as *uh huh*, *yeah*, and the British *m* (Schegloff, 1982), as in the following example:

B: Um well I ha((dn't)) done any English at *all.*
A: *((1 syll))*
B: You know, since O-level.
A: Yea .
B: And I went to some second year seminars. where there are only about half a dozen people.
A: *m*
B: *and* they discussed what ((a)) word was,
A: **m**
B: **and -** what's a sentence, that's *ev*en more difficult.

A: *yeah* yeah -
(and so on)

Continuers are used by partners, according to Schegloff, to signal that they are passing up the opportunity to initiate a repair on the turn so far and, by implication, that they think they have understood the turn so far. Acknowledgments also include assessments, such as gosh, really, and good God (see Goodwin, 1986), and gestures such as head nods that have much the same force as continuers (see Goodwin, 1981). Acknowledgments are generally produced without the speaker taking a turn at talk.

A second, common form of positive evidence is the initiation of the relevant next turn. Consider this exchange:

A: Did you know mother had been drinking -
B: I don't think, mother had been drinking at all .

Suppose A is trying to ask B a question. If B understands it, she can be expected to answer it in her next turn. Questions and answers form what are called adjacency pairs, and once the first part of an adjacency pair is on the floor, the second part is conditionally relevant as the next turn (Schegloff & Sacks, 1973). So A looks for B to provide not just any utterance, but an answer to his question. If B's utterance is appropriate as an answer, as in our example, it is also evidence that she has understood A's question. If it is not appropriate, it is evidence that she has not understood A's question, as caricatured here:

Miss Dimple: Where can I get a hold of you?
Chico: I don't know, lady. You see, I'm very ticklish.
Miss Dimple: I mean, where do you live?
Chico: I live with my brother.

Chico's answer gives Miss Dimple evidence that he has misunderstood her question, and that leads to the correction in her following turn (for an authentic, spontaneous example, see Clark & Schaefer, 1989). So B may initiate the next turn as positive evidence of her understanding, but A will not take it that way unless it shows her understanding to be correct.

What makes a next turn appropriate or relevant? That isn't difficult to decide for the second part of an adjacency pair—the answer to a question, the response to a request, or the acceptance of an invitation. It also isn't difficult to decide for most other next turns. Conversation generally divides into coherent sections that have identifiable entries, bodies, and exits (see, e.g., Schegloff & Sacks, 1973). These sections are devoted to one or another social process, such as making plans or exchanging information. Most turns are designed to carry that process forward and give evidence about the speaker's understanding of the previous step in the process. As Sacks et al. (1974, p. 728) noted, "Regularly, then, a turn's talk will display its speaker's understanding of a prior turn's talk, or whatever other

talk it marks itself as directed to.'' Initiating the relevant next turn is ordinarily an excellent piece of positive evidence.

Requiring positive evidence of understanding seems to lead to an infinite regress. The problem is this: When B says "uh huh" or "you're there all day" in response to A's presentation, she herself is making a presentation. Now her presentation, being more words, requires positive evidence of understanding from A, which requires him to give more words. But his words constitute another presentation that she must accept with more words, and so on ad infinitum. If every presentation were accepted with positive evidence in the form of words, the process would spin out to infinity. Empirically, it is easy to show that people do not take an infinite number of words to contribute to a conversation. How, then, do they do it?

There is no infinite regress in the contribution model because some forms of evidence, such as the relevant next turn and continued attention (our next form of evidence), do not have separate presentations. A relevant next turn provides positive evidence of understanding of the presentation phase it follows, but it does so by initiating the next contribution without a break. So although the acceptance process can spin out for many turns, it usually ends with the partner initiating a relevant next turn. Take the following example, in which A is presenting a book identification number:

A: F .six two
B: F six two
A: Yes
B: Thanks very much

The first presentation is accepted with a repetition, the repetition with an acknowledgment, and the acknowledgment with a thanks, which is the next contribution at the level of original contribution.

The third and most basic form of positive evidence is continued attention. In conversation people monitor what their partners are doing moment by moment—in particular, what they are attending to. If Alan presented an utterance while Barbara wasn't paying attention, he could hardly assume that she was understanding him. She must show that she is paying attention, and one way is through eye gaze. Suppose she is looking away from Alan. As Goodwin (1981) has shown, Alan can try to capture her gaze—and also, presumably, her attention—by starting an utterance. Just as she begins turning to him, he will start the utterance over again. Or he can start an utterance, pause until she starts turning, and then go on with the utterance. Speakers have many ways of getting a partner's attention.

Positive evidence of understanding comes with attention that is unbroken or undisturbed. Alan has reason to believe Barbara is following him as long as she continues to attend to him in the expected way. Whenever she turns to listen to someone else, looks puzzled, or hangs up the telephone, Alan has reason to believe that he has lost her. She is no longer hearing or understanding to criterion. Ordinarily, that will push him into taking corrective action.

Least Collaborative Effort

People apparently don't like to work any harder than they have to, and in language use this truism has been embodied in several principles of least effort. The traditional version exhorts the speaker: Don't expend any more effort than you need to get your addressees to understand you with as little effort. Grice (1975) expressed this idea in terms of two maxims: *Quantity*—Make your contribution as informative as is required for the current purpose of the exchange, but do not make your contribution more informative than is required—and *Manner*—Be brief (avoid unnecessary prolixity). According to both versions, speakers are supposed to create what we will call *proper utterances*, ones they believe will be readily and fully understood by their addressees.

The principle of least effort, however, assumes flawless presentations and trouble-free acceptances. It does not allow for grounding and, therefore, cannot do justice to what really happens in conversations. Here are just three problems with this principle (Clark & Wilkes-Gibbs, 1986).

1. *Time pressure.* Speakers appear to limit the time and effort they allow for planning and issuing each utterance, and that often leads them to issue improper utterances. They may utter a sentence or phrase, discover it to be inadequate, and then amend it, as in "Number 7's the goofy guy that's falling over—with his leg kicked up." They may start a phrase, think better of it, and start a different phrase, as in "We must ha- we're big enough to stand on our own feet now." They may create patently improper parts of utterances, such as *what's his name* in "If he puts it into the diplomatic bag, as um - what's his name, Micky Cohn did, . then it's not so bad." They may invite their interlocutors to complete their utterances, as in this exchange (Wilkes-Gibbs, 1986):

> A: That tree has, uh, uh
> B: Tentworms.
> A: Yeah.
> B: Yeah.

If all these speakers had taken the time and effort needed, they could have produced proper utterances—flawless performances. They didn't. The principle of least effort says that they should have.

2. *Errors.* Speakers often issue improper utterances because they make errors and have to repair them, as in Alan's "now, - um do you and your husband have a j- car?" If Alan had taken more time and effort, he could have avoided errors and dysfluencies. Why didn't he?

3. *Ignorance.* Speakers sometimes realize they just don't know enough about their interlocutor to design a proper utterance, so they are forced to issue an improper utterance instead. Take the person who was trying to identify an abstract figure that resembled an ice skater (Clark & Wilkes-Gibbs, 1986), who said, "Um, the next one's the person ice skating that has two arms?" Why the question intonation, or what Sacks and Schegloff (1979) have called a *try marker?* With it the speaker was indicating that he was not sure that his definite description "the person ice skating that has two arms" was adequate to pick out the right figure. He was asking his partner whether it was adequate and, if it was not, inviting an alternative description. Here, no matter how hard the speaker tried, he might not have managed a proper utterance. So why did he do what he did?

The principle of least effort, it has been argued, must therefore be replaced with the following principle (Clark & Wilkes-Gibbs, 1986):

The principle of least collaborative effort: In conversation, the participants try to minimize their collaborative effort—the work that both do from the initiation of each contribution to its mutual acceptance.

Such a principle helps account for many phenomena. Consider repairs. As Schegloff et al. (1977) noted, speakers have two strong preferences about repairs: (a) They prefer to repair their own utterances rather than let their interlocutors do it, and (b) they prefer to initiate their own repairs rather than let their interlocutors prompt them to do it. Although these two preferences have many causes, the upshot is that they minimize collaborative effort. As for preference 1, it generally takes less effort for the speaker than for an interlocutor to make a repair. An interlocutor will usually need extra turns, and he or she has to get the speaker to accept the repair anyway. As for preference 2, it usually takes less effort for the speaker than for an interlocutor to initiate a repair. The interlocutor will generally create extra turns in doing so, whereas the speaker will not. Every extra turn adds to collaborative effort.

Also, speakers often realize that it will take more collaborative effort to design a proper utterance than to design an improper utterance and enlist their addressees' help. Speakers, for example, can present a provisional utterance and add try markers to ask for confirmation. They can present a difficult utterance in installments and check for understanding after each installment (as we will describe later). They can invite addressees to complete an utterance they are having trouble with. And they have many other collaborative techniques at their disposal. The principle of least collaborative effort is essential for a full account of face-to-face conversation.

GROUNDING CHANGES WITH PURPOSE

People in conversation generally try to establish collective purposes (Grice, 1975). If they are planning a party, that may be their overall collective purpose. In each section of the conversation, their purpose might be to complete pieces of that plan, and in each subsection it would be even more specific. Other times their overall purpose might be to get acquainted, swap gossip, or instruct and learn. Grounding should change with these purposes. If addressees are to understand what the speaker meant "to a criterion sufficient for current purposes," then the criterion should change as their collective purposes change. So, too, should the techniques they exploit. Techniques should change, for example, with the content of the conversation—with what needs to be understood. Indeed, specialized techniques have evolved for grounding different types of content. We will illustrate with two types of content—references and verbatim content.

Grounding References

Many conversations focus on objects and their identities; when they do, it becomes crucial to identify the objects quickly and securely. Conversations like these arise, for example, when an expert is teaching a novice how to build things, and the two of them refer again and again to pieces of the construction. They arise in court when lawyers and witnesses try to establish the identities of persons, places, and things. They also arise in tasks in which people have to arrange figures, post cards, blocks, color chips, or other such objects. In psychology, an entire industry has been built on this type of task patterned after Krauss and Weinheimer's (1964, 1966, 1967) original referential communication task. Yet conversations like these are common enough in real life.

The purpose of interest here is to establish *referential identity*—that is, the mutual belief that the addressees have correctly identified a referent. There are several common techniques for establishing this.

1. *Alternative descriptions.* When speakers refer to objects, they typically use one or more referring expressions—a definite or indefinite description, proper noun, demonstrative, or pronoun. One way their partners can demonstrate that they have identified the referent or can check on its identity is by presenting an alternative description, as in this interchange:

A: Well, that young gentleman from - ((the park)) .
B: Joe Joe Wright you mean? - - *(- - laughs)*
A: *yes, (laughs) yes*
B: ((God)). I thought it was old Joe Wright who(('d)) walked in at first

A describes a referent as "that young gentleman from the park"; B gives evidence of having identified the man by offering an alternative description; he adds the question intonation to get confirmation of that description; and A accepts that description. This technique is common whenever referential identity is at stake (e.g., Clark & Wilkes-Gibbs, 1986; Isaacs & Clark, 1987).

2. *Indicative gestures.* When a speaker refers to a nearby object, the partners can give positive evidence that they have identified it by pointing, looking, or touching. In this example, S had been handed a photograph of a flower patch (Clark, Schreuder, & Buttrick, 1983):

B: How would you describe the color of this flower?
S: You mean this one [pointing]?
B: Yes.
S: It's off yellow.

S confirmed the referent of B's "this flower" by pointing.

3. *Referential installments.* It is often important to establish the identity of a referent before saying something about it. The reason is simple. Until the referent has been properly identified, the rest of the utterance will be difficult, if not impossible, to understand. The speaker can secure the reference by treating it as an installment of the utterance to be confirmed separately. Take this exchange between an expert and a novice assembling a pump (Cohen, 1984):

S: Take the spout—the little one that looks like the end of an oil can—
J: Okay.
S: and put that on the opening in the other large tube. With the round top.

In the first line, S presents "the spout—the little one that looks like the end of an oil can" and then pauses for evidence that J has identified the referent. He goes on only when that installment has been grounded.

In English, there is a specialized construction for just this purpose called *left-dislocation.* It is traditionally illustrated with invented examples such as *Your dog he just bit me.* This example begins with a "left dislocated" noun phrase, *your dog,* followed by a full sentence with a pronoun, *he,* referring to the same object. In genuine conversation, left-dislocation rarely looks like this. A more typical example is this second exchange from S and J:

S: Okay now, the small blue cap we talked about before?
J: Yeah.
S: Put that over the hole on the side of that tube—
J: Yeah.
S: —that is nearest to the top, or nearest to the red handle.

As Geluykens (1988) has shown, 29% of the left dislocated noun phrases in the London-Lund corpus (Svartvik & Quirk, 1980) are followed by an intervening move from the interlocutor (either a continuer or something more extensive), as in our example. Another 52% are followed by a pause during which the partner could have nodded acceptance. Left-dislocation may have evolved for just this specialized purpose—grounding references separately.

4. *Trial references.* Speakers can also initiate the grounding process for a reference in mid-utterance. When speakers find themselves about to present a name or description that they are not sure is entirely correct or comprehensible, they can present it with a *try marker* followed by a slight pause, and get their partners to confirm or correct it before completing the presentation. Consider this example:

A: So I wrote off to . Bill. . uh who ((had)) presumably disappeared by this time, certainly, a man called Annegra?
B: Yeah, Allegra.
A: Allegra, uh replied. . uh and I . put . two other people [continues].

A apparently wants to assert, "A man called Annegra replied, and I . . . ." But being uncertain about the name *Annegra*, he presents it with a try marker. B confirms, with "yeah," that she knows who he is referring to, but then corrects the name to *Allegra*. A accepts the correction by re-presenting *Allegra* and continuing. The entire correction is made swiftly and efficiently.

There are other techniques adapted for this purpose, but the four we have mentioned give an idea of their range and specialization.

Grounding Verbatim Content

Sometimes it is important to register the verbatim content of what is said. When a friend tells you a telephone number, you do more than listen for the gist of it. You try to get it verbatim so that you can copy it down or rehearse it until you dial the number. The same goes for names, addresses, book titles, credit card numbers, bank accounts, dollar amounts, and library call numbers. These are specialized situations, and specialized grounding techniques have evolved for them. Here are a few:

1. *Verbatim displays.* When customers call directory enquiries for a telephone number, they often confirm the number they are given with a verbatim display, as in this British example (Clark & Schaefer, 1987):

O: It's Cambridge 12345
C: 12345
O: That's right.
C: Thank you very much.

C confirms the number that O has presented him by repeating it verbatim, "12345." In the British calls studied by Clark and Schaefer (1987), customers responded to the operators' number presentations with verbatim displays over 70% of the time. Operators, in turn, often responded to the customers' presentations of names, towns, and street addresses with verbatim displays.

2. *Installments.* When speakers present a lot of information to be registered verbatim, they generally cut it up into bite-sized chunks, or installments, and receive verbatim displays on each installment, as in this example:

A: Ah, what ((are you)) now, *where*
C: *yes* forty-nine Skipton Place
A: Forty-one
C: Nine . nine
A: Forty-nine, Skipton Place,
C: W one .
A: Skipton Place, . W one, ((so)) Mr D Challam
C: Yes
A: Forty-nine Skipton Place, W one,
C: Yes
A: Right oh.

C divides his address into repeatable chunks, and A gives a verbatim display for each. Speakers seem able to divide most types of information into such chunks. They do it spontaneously, for example, for recipes presented over the telephone (Goldberg, 1975).

Dividing a presentation into repeatable installments is based on the tacit recognition that people have limited immediate memory spans. Even the telephone company recognizes this and divides telephone numbers into conventional installments of three or four digits in size. In the calls to directory enquiries studied by Clark and Schaefer (1987), British operators always divided numbers of seven or more digits into their conventional groupings.

3. *Spelling.* For many words, getting the verbatim content right means getting the spelling right. So contributors often spell out critical words, as in the following:

A: The name is Iain, . I A I N .
C: m
A: Lathom-Meadows, that's L A T . . H O M . . hyphen, - Meadows,
C: Yes .

Or they have other tricks for getting the spelling right, as illustrated here:

B: And my name. is James Persian-Omo, that's Persian like the carpet
C: Yes
B: Hyphen. . Omo like the detergent, O M O
C: Yeah.

Other times, it is the partners who do the spelling as they confirm a name.

On occasion, two partners in conversation will set different criteria, one stricter than the other. Imagine a father instructing a 5-year-old son on how to play a game or work a machine. The son may think he understands an instruction while the father still has serious doubts. The father may go on testing for understanding long after the son thinks he needs to.

To summarize, specialized techniques have evolved for grounding special pieces of conversation. When it is critical that a reference be well established, people will use techniques that are custom designed for that purpose. When it is the verbatim content that is crucial, they will use other techniques. In this way, grounding changes with the current purpose.

GROUNDING CHANGES WITH THE MEDIUM

By the principle of least collaborative effort, people should try to ground with as little combined effort as needed. But what takes effort changes dramatically with the communication medium. The techniques available in one medium may not be available in another, and even when a technique is available, it may cost more in one medium than in the other. Our prediction is straightforward: People should ground with those techniques available in a medium that lead to the least collaborative effort.

Consider the acknowledgment *okay*. In face-to-face or telephone conversations, it can be timed precisely so that it constitutes evidence of understanding and not an interruption. In keyboard teleconferencing—when people communicate over keyboards and screens—it is difficult to time an acknowledgment precisely, and trying to do so may interrupt the other typist. So the cost of an acknowledgment is higher in this medium.

Media come in a great variety, and new ones are being introduced every year. Think of the telegraph, videotape, picturephone, express mail, fax machines, electronic bulletin boards, and little yellow post-it notes. Here we will consider a sample of two-way personal media: face-to-face conversation, the telephone, video teleconferencing, keyboard teleconferencing, answering machines, electronic mail (email), and personal letters. For now we will put aside such one-way, broadcastable media as books, newspapers, television, and radio. Some personal media have been compared experimentally (see, for example, Ochsman & Chapanis, 1974), but most of these studies identify and describe differences without a theoretical framework for explaining them. We propose to set them in a framework that will account for many of their differences.

Constraints on Grounding

Personal media vary on many dimensions that affect grounding. Here are eight constraints that a medium may impose on communication between two people, A and B.

1. *Copresence: A and B share the same physical environment.* In face-to-face conversation, the participants are usually in the same surroundings and can readily see and hear what each other is doing and looking at. In other media there is no such possibility.

2. *Visibility: A and B are visible to each other.* In face-to-face conversation, the participants can see each other, and in other media they cannot. They may also be able to see each other, as in video teleconferencing, without being able to see what each other is doing or looking at.

3. *Audibility: A and B communicate by speaking.* Face to face, on the telephone, and with some kinds of teleconferencing, participants can hear each other and take note of timing and intonation. In other media they cannot. An answering machine preserves intonation, but only some aspects of utterance timing.

4. *Cotemporality: B receives at roughly the same time as A produces.* In most conversations, an utterance is produced just about when it is received and understood, without delay. In media such as letters and electronic mail, this is not the case.

5. *Simultaneity: A and B can send and receive at once and simultaneously.* Sometimes messages can be conveyed and received by both parties at once, as when a hearer smiles during a speaker's utterance. Simultaneous utterances are also allowed, for example, in the keyboard teleconferencing program called *talk*, where what both parties type appears letter by letter in two distinct halves of the screen. Other media are cotemporal but not simultaneous, such as the kind of keyboard teleconferencing that transmits characters only after the typist hits a carriage return.

6. *Sequentiality: A's and B's turns cannot get out of sequence.* In face-to-face conversation, turns ordinarily form a sequence that does not include intervening turns from different conversations with other people. With email, answering machines, and letters, a message and its reply may be separated by any number of irrelevant messages or activities; interruptions do not have the same force.

7. *Reviewability: B can review A's messages.* Speech fades quickly, but in media such as email, letters, and recorded messages, an utterance stays behind as an artifact that can be reviewed later by either of the partners—or even by a third party. In keyboard teleconferencing, the last few utterances stay visible on the screen for awhile.

8. *Revisability: A can revise messages for B.* Some media, such as letters and email, allow a participant to revise an utterance privately before sending it to a partner. In face-to-face and telephone conversations, most self-repairs must be done publicly. Some kinds of keyboard teleconferencing fall in between; what a person types appears on the partner's screen only after every carriage return, rather than letter by letter.

Table 1
SEVEN MEDIA AND THEIR ASSOCIATED CONSTRAINTS

Medium	Constraints
Face-to-face	Copresence, visibility, audibility, cotemporality, simultaneity, sequentiality
Telephone	Audibility, cotemporality, simultaneity, sequentiality
Video teleconference	Visibility, audibility, cotemporality, simultaneity, sequentiality
Terminal teleconference	Cotemporality, sequentiality, reviewability
Answering machines	Audibility, reviewability
Electronic mail	Reviewability, revisability
Letters	Reviewability, revisability

There are other differences across media, but these are among the most important for grounding. Table 1 characterizes seven personal media by these constraints.

Costs of Grounding

When a medium lacks one of these characteristics, it generally forces people to use alternative grounding techniques. It does so because the costs of the various techniques of grounding change. We will describe eleven costs that change. The first two, formulation and production costs, are paid by the speaker. The next two, reception and understanding costs, are paid by the addressee. The rest are paid by both. We emphasize that these costs are not independent of each other.

Formulation costs

It costs time and effort to formulate and reformulate utterances. It costs more to plan complicated than simple utterances, more to retrieve uncommon than common words, and more to create descriptions for unfamiliar than familiar objects. It costs more to formulate perfect than imperfect utterances. As we will see, these costs are often traded off for others, depending on the medium.

Production costs

The act of producing an utterance itself has a cost that varies from medium to medium. It takes little effort (for most of us) to speak or gesture, more effort to type on a computer keyboard or typewriter, and the most effort (for many of us, anyway) to write by hand. Speaking is swift, typing is slower, and handwriting is slowest. These costs are traded off for other costs as well. People are willing to use more words talking than in typewriting to accomplish a goal, and the faster people are at typing, the more words they are willing to use.

Reception costs

Listening is generally easy, and reading harder, although it may be easier to read than to listen to complicated instructions or abstract arguments. It also costs to have to wait while the speaker produces a turn. This wait takes its toll in keyboard conversations when addressees must suffer as they watch an utterance appear letter by letter with painstaking backspacing to repair misspellings.

Understanding costs

It is also more costly for people to understand certain words, constructions, and concepts than others, regardless of the medium. The costs can be compounded when contextual clues are missing. Email, for example, is neither cotemporal nor sequential. That makes understanding harder because the addressee has to imagine appropriate contexts for both the sender and the message, and to remember what the message is in response to, even when the "subject" field of the message is filled in.

Start-up costs

This is the cost of starting up a new discourse. It is the cost of getting B initially to notice that A has uttered something and to accept that he or she has been addressed. Start-up costs are minimal face to face, where A need only get B's attention and speak. They are a bit higher when A must get to a telephone, look up a number, dial it, and determine that the answerer is B. They are often higher yet in email. First, A has to get access to the right software and hardware, find the right email address, and start the message. Second, the message may not reach the addressee if the channel is unreliable or the address has typos in it. Third, depending on the system, the sender may or may not be notified of its delivery. And finally, once the message is delivered, there is no guarantee that the addressee will read it right away. There are similar start-up costs in writing letters.

Delay costs

These are the costs of delaying an utterance in order to plan, revise, and execute it more carefully. In face-to-face conversation, as in all cotemporal and simultaneous media, these costs are high because of the way delays, even brief delays, are interpreted. When speakers leave too long a gap before starting a turn, they may be misheard as dropping out of the conversation or as implying other more damaging things. And when they leave too long a pause in the middle of a turn, they may be misheard as having finished their turn. With the pressure to minimize both midturn pauses and preturn gaps, speakers are often forced to utter words they may have to revise or to let their addressees help them out. Even when it is clear that a delay is due to the speaker's production difficulty, it costs the addressees to wait. In media without cotemporality—such as email and personal letters— delays that would be crippling in conversation are not even noticeable, and so their costs are nil. But in cotemporal media, the cost of a delay can be high: When the drugged Juliet failed to respond, Romeo did himself in.

Delay costs often trade off with formulation costs. In writing letters, we can take our time planning and revising each sentence. Computerized text editing has made this even easier. But in face-to-face and telephone conversations, where delay costs are high, we have to formulate utterances quickly. That forces us to use simpler constructions and to be satisfied with less than perfect utterances. The other media lie between these two extremes.

Asynchrony costs

In conversation, people time their utterances with great precision (Jefferson, 1973). They can begin an utterance precisely at the completion of the prior speaker's turn. They can time acknowledgments to mark what it is they are acknowledging. They can interrupt a particular word to show agreement or disagreement on some aspect of it. In media without copresence, visibility, audibility, or simultaneity, timing is much less precise, and without cotemporality, it is altogether impossible. So grounding techniques that rely on precision of timing should go up in cost when production and reception are asynchronous.

Speaker change costs

In conversation the general rule is, "Two people can speak at the same time only for short periods or about limited content." The rule is usually simplified to "One speaker at a time" (see Sacks et al., 1974), and it tends to hold for other media as well. But the cost of changing speakers varies with the medium. In face-to-face conversation it is low. The participants find it easy to arrange for one speaker to stop and another to start. There are regular rules for turn taking in which the points of possible change in speakers are frequent, easily marked, and readily recognized, and the changes can be instantaneous. Also, the costs of simultaneous speech, at least for short intervals and limited content, are minor. The participants usually continue to understand without disruption.

The cost of changing speakers is higher in media with fewer cues for changes in turns. Costs are quite high, for example, in keyboard teleconferencing, where the points of speaker change are not as easily marked or readily recognized. These points may need to be marked by a convention such as the use of "o" (for "over"), a device that is also used by airplane pilots and citizens' band radio operators, when only one party can be heard at a time. Speaker change costs are greater still in letters, answering machines, and email, where it may take much

Display costs

In face-to-face conversation, it is easy to point to, nod at, or present an object for our interlocutors. It is also easy to gaze at our interlocutors to show them we are attending, to monitor their facial expressions, or to pick them out as addressees. In media without copresence, gestures cost a lot, are severely limited, or are out of the question. In video teleconferencing, we can use only a limited range of gestures, and we cannot always look at someone as a way of designating "you." Showing pictures is possible with media such as video, fax machines, and letters.

Fault costs

There are costs associated with producing an utterance fault, that is, any mistake or missaying. Some faults lead to failures in understanding, and failures in one utterance are likely to undermine the next one. The costs of these faults increase with the gravity of the failures. Other faults make the speaker look foolish, illiterate, or impolite, so they also have their costs. The cost of most faults trades off with what it costs to repair them (our next category) or to prevent them in the first place. To avoid paying fault costs, speakers may elect to pay more in formulation costs. But it depends on the medium. In conversation, a hearer may expect faults from a speaker because the production of speech is so spontaneous. In email, faults are not as easily justified, because the sender has already had a chance to revise them, and because the damage done is not as easily repaired.

Repair costs

Some repairs take little time or effort; others take a lot, and still others are impossible to make. Because faults tend to snowball, speakers should want to repair them as quickly as possible. In audible conversation, as we noted earlier, speakers prefer to initiate and make their own repairs, and there is evidence that they interrupt themselves and make these repairs just as soon as they detect a fault (Levelt, 1983). These preferences tend to minimize the cost of a repair. Self-corrections take fewer words and turns than do repairs by others, and so do repairs initiated by oneself rather than by others. These preferences also help minimize the cost of faults: They tend to remove a fault from the floor as quickly as possible. In media that are not cotemporal, repairs initiated or made by others become very costly indeed, so speakers will try hard to avoid relying on others to repair misunderstandings. It is less costly for them to revise what they say before sending it. Another way to minimize repair costs may be to change to a different medium to make the repair.

Cost Tradeoffs

People manage to communicate effectively by all the media we have mentioned, but that does not mean that they do so in the same way in each medium. The way people proceed reflects the costs they incur. Recall the intermediate states 0 to 3 mentioned earlier for face-to-face conversation: (0) A and B failing to establish any connection yet, (1) A getting B's attention, (2) B perceiving A's utterance correctly, and (3) B understanding what A meant. There are costs to getting to each state, and in some media the states are quite distinct. In media that are not cotemporal, there is the additional problem that A does not have immediate evidence as to which of these states B is in with respect to A's utterance. In a medium such as email, B's lack of response can be highly ambiguous. Did she not get the message, did she get it and not read it, did she read it and choose not to respond, did she not understand it, or what? A does not know whether B is in state 0, 1, 2, or 3.

Once we assume that people need to ground what they say and that they trade off on the costs of grounding, we can account for some of the differences in language use across media. Consider a study reported by Cohen (1984) in which tutors instructed students on assembling a pump. Their communication was either by telephone or by keyboard. Over the telephone, tutors would first get students to identify an object, and only when they had confirmed its identification did they ask students to do something to do with it.

S: Uh, now there's a little plastic blue cap.
J: Yep.
S: Put that on the top hole in the cylinder you just worked with.

In contrast, in keyboard conversations, tutors would identify an object and instruct students what to do with it all in a single turn.

K: Next, take the blue cap that has the pink thing on it and screw it to the blue piece you just screwed on.

That is, there were many more separate requests for identification over the telephone than in keyboard conversations. According to Cohen, "Speakers attempt to achieve more detailed goals in giving instructions than do users of keyboards" (Cohen, 1984, p. 97).

But why? The principle of least effort suggests a reason: The two media have different profiles of grounding costs. Over the telephone, it doesn't cost much to produce an utterance or change speakers. On a keyboard, it costs much more. So to minimize these costs, tutors and students on a keyboard might seek and provide evidence after larger constituents; that is, they should try to do more within each turn than they would over the telephone. This prediction would account

for the difference Cohen describes between the two media. In addition, repairs are more costly over the keyboard; if tutors and students are aware of this, they might formulate their utterances more carefully. But because delay costs can be just as high over the keyboard as on the telephone, and speaker change costs are higher, there are likely to be more misunderstandings over a keyboard, and repairs will take more collaborative effort. The differences among these and other media can be explained by the techniques participants choose for grounding. They balance the perceived costs for formulation, production, reception, understanding, start-up, delay, timing, speaker change, display, faults, and repair.

Medium and Purpose Interact

Grounding techniques depend on both purpose and medium, and these sometimes interact. Face-to-face conversations appear to be preferred for reprimanding, whereas telephone conversations or letters may be preferred for refusing an unreasonable request (Furnham, 1982). In a study of working groups, face-to-face conversation was preferred for negotiating and reaching consensus, whereas email was preferred for coordinating schedules, assigning tasks, and making progress reports (Finholt, Sproull, & Kiesler, 1990).

These preferences can be explained in terms of the costs associated with each medium relative to the participants' purposes. Sometimes the participants want a reviewable record of a conversation—as for schedules, task assignments, and progress reports; and other times they do not. Sometimes speakers want to get a hearer's full attention, and sometimes they want to avoid interrupting. Sometimes people want their reactions to be seen, as in negotiating and reaching consensus, and sometimes they do not. Which medium is best for which purpose, then, depends on the form grounding takes in a medium and whether that serves the participants' purposes.

Finally, as more participants join the conversation and the medium must support the work of a whole group, costs and tradeoffs shift. Start-up costs may be greater. Reception costs will increase if a hearer must put effort into identifying who is speaking or writing. Fault costs and repair costs will be higher when a group is involved. Any medium that supports cooperative work can be evaluated in terms of the techniques it allows for grounding.

CONCLUSION

Grounding is essential to communication. Once we have formulated a message, we must do more than just send it off. We need to assure ourselves that it has been understood as we intended it to be. Otherwise, we have little assurance that the discourse we are taking part in will proceed in an orderly way. For whatever we say, our goal is to reach the grounding criterion: that we and our addressees mutually believe that they have understood what we meant well enough for current purposes. This is the process we have called *grounding*.

The techniques we use for grounding change both with purpose and with medium. Special techniques have evolved, for example, for grounding references to objects and for grounding the verbatim content of what is said. Grounding techniques also change with the medium. In the framework we have offered, media differ in the costs they impose on such actions as delaying speech, starting up a turn, changing speakers, making errors, and repairing errors. In grounding what we say, we try to minimize effort for us and our partners. Ordinarily, this means paying as few of these costs as possible.

The lesson is that communication is a collective activity. It requires the coordinated action of all the participants. Grounding is crucial for keeping that coordination on track.

References

Bach, K., & Harnish, R. M. (1979). *Linguistic communication and speech acts.* Cambridge, MA: MIT Press.

Clark, H. H., & Carlson, T. (1982). Hearers and speech acts. *Language, 58*(2), 332–373.

Clark, H. H., & Marshall, C. R. (1981). Definite reference and mutual knowledge. In A. K. Joshi, B. L. Webber, & I. A. Sag (Eds.), *Elements of discourse understanding* (pp. 10–63). Cambridge, England: Cambridge University Press.

Clark, H. H., & Schaefer, E. F. (1987). Collaborating on contributions to conversations. *Language and Cognitive Processes, 2*(1), 19–41.

Clark, H. H., & Schaefer, E. F. (1989). Contributing to discourse. *Cognitive Science, 13,* 259–294.

Clark, H. H., Schreuder, R., & Buttrick, S. (1983). Common ground and the understanding of demonstrative reference. *Journal of Verbal Learning and Verbal Behavior, 22,* 1–39.

Clark, H. H., & Wilkes-Gibbs, D. (1986). Referring as a collaborative process. *Cognition, 22,* 1–39.

Cohen, P. R. (1984). The pragmatics of referring and the modality of communication. *Computational Linguistics, 10*(2), 97–146.

Finholt, T., Sproull, L., & Kiesler, S. (1990). Communication and performance in ad hoc task groups. In J. Galegher, R. Kraut, & C. Egido (Eds.), *Intellectual teamwork: Social and technological foundations of cooperative work* (pp. 291–326). Hillsdale, NJ: Erlbaum.

Furnham, A. (1982). The message, the context, and the medium. *Language and Communication, 2,* 33–47.

Geluykens, R. (1988). The interactional nature of referent-introduction. *Papers from the 24th Regional Meeting, Chicago Linguistic Society,* 141–154.

Goldberg, C. (1975). A system for the transfer of instructions in natural settings. *Semiotica, 14,* 269–296.

Goodwin, C. (1981). *Conversational organization: Interaction between speakers and hearers.* New York: Academic Press.

Goodwin, C. (1986). Between and within: Alternative sequential treatments of continuers and assessments. *Human Studies, 9,* 205–217.

Grice, H. P. (1975). Logic and conversation. In P. Cole & J. L. Morgan (Eds.), *Syntax and semantics, Volume 3: Speech acts* (pp. 225–242). New York: Seminar Press.

Grice, H. P. (1978). Some further notes on logic and conversation. In P. Cole (Ed.), *Syntax and semantics, volume 9: Pragmatics* (pp. 113–128). New York: Academic Press.

Grosz, B. J., & Sidner, C. L. (1986). Attention, intentions, and the structure of discourse. *Computational Linguistics, 12,* 175–204.

Isaacs, E. A., & Clark, H. H. (1987). References in conversation between experts and novices. *Journal of Experimental Psychology, 116,* 26–37.

Jefferson, G. (1972). Side sequences. In D. Sudnow (Ed.), *Studies in social interaction* (pp. 294–338). New York: Free Press.

Jefferson, G. (1973). A case of precision timing in ordinary conversation: Overlapped tag-positioned address terms in closing sequences. *Semiotica, 9,* 47–96.

Krauss, R. M., & Weinheimer, S. (1964). Changes in reference phases as a function of frequency of usage in social interaction: A preliminary study. *Psychonomic Study, 1,* 113–114.

Krauss, R. M., & Weinheimer, S. (1966). Concurrent feedback, confirmation, and the encoding of referents in verbal communication. *Journal of Personality and Social Psychology, 4,* 343–346.

Krauss, R. M., & Weinheimer, S. (1967). Effect of referent similarity and communication mode on verbal encoding. *Journal of Verbal Learning and Verbal Behavior, 6,* 359–363.

Levelt, W. J. M. (1983). Monitoring and self-repair in speech. *Cognition, 14,* 41–104.

Lewis, D. K. (1969). *Convention: A philosophical study.* Cambridge, MA: Harvard University Press.

Litman, D. J., & Allen, J. F. (1987). A plan recognition model for subdialogues in conversation. *Cognitive Science, 11,* 163–200.

Ochsman, R. B., & Chapanis, A. (1974). The effects of 10 communication modes on the behavior of teams during cooperative problem-solving. *International Journal of Man–Machine Studies, 6,* 579–619.

Sacks, H., & Schegloff, E. A. (1979). Two preferences in the organization of reference to persons in conversation and their interaction. In G. Psathas (Ed.), *Everyday language: Studies in ethnomethodology* (pp. 15–21). New York: Irvington.

Sacks, H., Schegloff, E. A., & Jefferson, G. (1974). A simplest systematics for the organization of turn-taking in conversation. *Language, 50,* 696–735.

Schegloff, E. A. (1972). Notes on a conversational practice: Formulating place. In D. Sudnow (Ed.), *Studies in social interaction* (pp. 75–119). New York: Free Press.

Schegloff, E. A. (1982). Discourse as an interactional achievement: Some uses of "uh huh" and other things that come between sentences. In D. Tannen (Ed.), *Analyzing discourse: Text and talk. Georgetown University Roundtable on Languages and Linguistics 1981* (pp. 71–93). Washington, DC: Georgetown University Press.

Schegloff, E. A., Jefferson, G., & Sacks, H. (1977). The preference for self-correction in the organization of repair in conversation. *Language, 53,* 361–382.

Schegloff, E. A., & Sacks, H. (1973). Opening up closings. *Semiotica, 8,* 289–327.

Schelling, T. C. (1960). *The strategy of conflict.* Oxford: Oxford University Press.

Searle, J. R. (1969). *Speech acts.* Cambridge, England: Cambridge University Press.

Stalnaker, R. C. (1978). Assertion. In P. Cole (Ed.), *Syntax and semantics, Volume 9: Pragmatics* (pp. 315–332). New York: Academic Press.

Svartvik, J., & Quirk, R. (Eds.). (1980). *A corpus of English conversation.* Lund, Sweden: Gleerup.

Wilkes-Gibbs, D. (1986). *Collaborative processes of language use in conversation.* Unpublished doctoral dissertation, Stanford University, Stanford, CA.

CHAPTER 5
Case Studies of Cooperative Work

We begin with four case studies of more or less formal, relatively structured, cooperative activities.

The first reading in this chapter, "How People Write Together" by Posner and Baecker (1992), illustrates the use of interview techniques to reveal the highly textured, multifaceted nature of collaborative activity. The authors develop a taxonomy of collaborative writing that includes a number of participant *roles*, writing *activities*, writing *strategies*, and document *control methods*. The study also reveals the extent to which real collaboration flows smoothly between phases of brainstorming, planning, writing, and editing, and between synchronous and asynchronous activities, findings that provide helpful guidance in the design of collaborative writing technologies.

"Findings from Observational Studies of Collaborative Work" by Tang (1991) uses in-depth behavioral observations and video analysis of collaborative drawing to shed light on the nature of the design process. Tang develops a framework for analyzing drawing space activity in terms of *actions* (how the activity was produced) and *functions* (what the activity accomplished). Actions are *to list*, *to draw*, and *to gesture*; functions are *to store information*, *to express ideas*, and *to mediate interaction*. The study emphasizes that gesture is vital to effective collaborative interaction, that the *process* of creating and using drawings conveys significant information not contained in the resulting drawings, that the drawing space is an important resource for mediating the collaboration, and that the spatial orientation of the collaborators and their drawing space helps structure their activity.

In contrast to these studies of collaborative writing and design, the work of Nardi and Miller (1991), reported on in "Twinkling Lights and Nested Loops: Distributed Problem-Solving and Spreadsheet Development," began as an investigation of spreadsheet use that was thought to be an individual activity. To their surprise, the authors found in an ethnographic study that collaborative development of spreadsheets is the rule, not the exception, and that spreadsheets effectively support the sharing of both programming and domain expertise. They suggest that this is facilitated because the spreadsheet can be viewed as consisting of two distinct programming layers, thus enabling an effective distribution of computational tasks across users with different levels of programming skill, and because the spreadsheet's strong visual format for structuring and presenting data supports the sharing of domain knowledge among co-workers.

One of the weaknesses of many existing approaches to the study of group process is that they fail to account for and describe the complex cognitive processes that occur in group problem- solving activity. *Distributed cognition* is a new branch of *cognitive science* (Gardner, 1985; Collins and Smith, 1987; Stillings, Feinstein, Garfield, Rissland, Rosenbaum, Weisler, and Baker-Ward, 1987; Posner, 1989) devoted to "the study of the representations of knowledge both inside the heads of individuals and in the world, the propagation of knowledge between different individuals and artifacts, and the transformations which external structures undergo when operated on by individuals and artifacts" (Flor and Hutchins, 1991). This paper illustrates the emerging theory of distributed cognition by analyzing video protocols of the work of two experienced programmers adding a command to a medium-size program. The example is used to suggest seven system-level properties of distributed cognition: the reuse of system knowledge, the sharing of goals and plans, the creation of efficient communication, the ability to search through larger spaces of alternatives, the joint production of ambiguous plan segments, a shared memory for old plans, and the division of labor and specification of functional roles.

With the next two readings, we shift our focus to activities that are more informal and have less structure, and that typically involve larger networks of people.

For many years, Bob Kraut and co-workers have carried out an elegant series of studies stressing the importance of informal, unplanned communication in scientific research. We therefore include as our next reading their paper entitled "Informal Communication in Organizations: Form, Function, and Technology" (Kraut, Fish, Root, and Chalfonte, 1990). They begin by contrasting formal and informal communication along a number of dimensions. This is followed by a description of the surface characteristics of informal conversations, including frequency and initiation, location, and duration. They then discuss the content and uses of informal communication, including its perceived value for production and social functions, its effect on person perception, its role in sustaining the momentum in collaboration, and its effect on the frequency of collaborations in scientific research. From all of this, they suggest that we need to pay more attention to the development of means and technology to support informal communication, and then they

describe two prototype systems of this kind, VideoWindow and Cruiser. This anticipates, in a sense, the fuller treatments of media space technology to enhance collaboration that appear in Chapter 13.

A final illustration of the role and nature of informal collaboration is the work of Clement (1990) represented in "Cooperative Support for Computer Work: A Social Perspective on the Empowering of End Users." As with Nardi and Miller, this paper and the earlier Clement and Parsons (1990) deal with a context that appears to be traditional single-user computing, for example, office work on desktop computers by secretarial and administrative staff within university settings. The perhaps not so surprising result is that primary determinants of individual productivity are timely access to appropriate expertise and the ability of the users to cooperate among themselves. Both Kraut's and Clement's findings suggest that support for cooperative work and informal communication needs to be included in all modern computer systems.

Notes and Guide to Further Reading

Ede and Lunsford (1990), Sharples (in press), Beck (in press), Posner (1991), and Posner and Baecker (1992, submitted for publication) are good sources on the processes of collaborative writing.

Tang (1989, 1990) provides more detail on the processes of collaborative drawing. Of particular interest is Lakin (1988, 1990), who views manipulating text-graphics for working groups as a performing art similar to dance, and who develops visual languages for cooperation in this performing medium.

Nardi and Miller (1990) provide additional insights on the use of spreadsheets. Greif (1992, included in Chapter 10 of this volume) discusses the *group-enabling* of spreadsheets.

Brown and Newman (1985) argue the need to move from a focus on *cognitive ergonomics* to *social ergonomics*. Resnick, Levine, and Teasley (1991) is a recent volume exploring issues in distributed cognition. Mackay (1990) discusses patterns of sharing of customizable software. Berlin and Jeffries (1992) report observations of learning behavior that occur in consulting sessions between apprentice and expert programmers.

Kraut, Egido, and Galegher (1988, 1990) and Kraut, Galegher, and Egido (1988) further stress and illuminate the importance of informal, unplanned communication in scientific research.

Other relevant studies of collaborative work include Linde (1988), Ancona and Caldwell (1990), Cicourel (1990), Hutchins (1990), Reder and Schwab (1990), Heath and Luff (1991a), Suchman (1991), and Schwab, Hart-Landsberg, Reder, and Abel (1992). Grønbaek, Kyng, and Mogensen (1992) and Rogers (1992) examine the nature of cooperative work in engineering practices.

How People Write Together

Ilona R. Posner and Ronald M. Baecker
Dynamic Graphics Project, Computer Systems Research Institute
University of Toronto, Canada M5S 1A1
+1-416-978-6619, FAX: +1-416-978-5184
Internet: ilona@dgp.toronto.edu

Abstract

Builders of groupware writing technologies need a better understanding of collaborative writing if their systems are to adequately address user needs. This paper presents a taxonomy of joint writing based on an analysis of interviews with authors who have written documents together. The taxonomy describes joint writing in terms of four components: roles *played in the collaboration,* activities *performed in the writing process,* document control methods *used, and* writing strategies *employed. The paper concludes by outlining a set of design requirements for collaborative writing that are suggested by the interviews and the taxonomy, and by evaluating six existing systems with respect to these requirements.*

Introduction

A survey of 700 professionals, who spend much of their time writing, found that 87% of them write cooperatively (Ede and Lunsford, 1990). Much work in business and academia is performed by groups of people (Bair, 1985). Not surprisingly, the development of joint authoring systems has become a major focus in Computer Supported Cooperative Work. Most systems make assumptions about how joint documents are created (see the system comparison in Table 3). For example, some systems support synchronous writing, while others assume asynchronous document creation; some support outlining of ideas, others the writing of text, and still others annotations to existing text; some systems support several authors, while others assume a single author with several commenters. This paper examines the extent to which these approaches reflect the actual processes followed in joint writing.

Significant efforts have gone into studying the way individuals write (Flower, Schriver, Carey, Haas, and Hayes, 1989; Freedman, Dyson, Flower, and Chafe, 1987; Bereiter and Scardamalia, 1982). The interest in joint writing research arose in the late 1980's, manifesting itself in surveys conducted on professional writers (Ede and Lunsford, 1990; Allen, Atkinson, Morgan, Moore, and Snow, 1987). These surveys showed that a vast majority of written work is performed jointly. At the same time, research by Kraut, Galegher, and Egido (1986) and Kraut, Egido, and Galegher (1988) identified proximity as a key ingredient for successful scientific collaboration. Both Eveland and Bikson (1988) and Galegher and Kraut (1990) found that computer technology affected the communication between participants and the final jointly written product.

Although this existing work has uncovered ubiquity and consequence data on collaborative writing, it does not inform us about the joint writing process sufficiently to guide the design of collaborative writing technology. Our research, therefore, differs from past research in its focus on the joint writing process, a close examination of how the document text is created and controlled in the context of the events that lead to the completion of each project.

We used interviews to obtain a formulation of joint writing processes that take place (Posner, 1991; Posner and Baecker, submitted for review). This paper first describes some general observation about joint writing based on the interviews, and then presents in detail the emerging taxonomy of the joint writing process.

Interviews

To uncover the actual collaborative writing process we conducted interviews with individuals about their participation in several collaborative writing projects. The interviewees varied in their occupations, background interests, and levels of writing skill. The collaborative projects varied in the number of participants, previous joint work, status relationships in the collaborating group, and tasks performed.

Candidates were found through an informal referral process. We conducted a total of 10 tape recorded interviews, each approximately one hour in length, based on the questions listed in the Appendix. During these interviews 22 joint writing projects were discussed. Each person interviewed discussed at least two joint writing projects, thus demonstrating how the same individual worked on different projects, in different groups, and, in some cases, on both successful and unsuccessful ventures.

The individuals interviewed worked in medicine, computer science, psychology, journalism, and freelance writing. The joint writing projects included course assignments, journal articles, a TV script, and a best-selling book. Projects lasted from several days to several years. Groups consisted both of peers and student-supervisor teams. Some collaborations were formed voluntarily from a desire to work together, while other collaborations resulted from work demands.

Further details about the interviews appear in Posner (1991).

This article is revised from the original which appeared in *Proceedings of the Twenty-Fifth International Conference on the System Sciences*, Hawaii, January 1992. ©1992 IEEE. Reprinted, with permission.

General Results

Participants in joint projects bring with them *expectations about joint writing*. These attitudes uncovered in the interviews range from "I don't like it! I don't write with others if I can help it!" 1[], to "I quite like it... It's fun working with other people, you're not lonely! ... It's a lot more fun than working alone!" 10[]. (The numbers that follow quotations refer to the interview number [project number]. The square brackets are empty if reference is made in general and not to a specific project.)

Coauthors also bring expectations about the effects of group work on the *quality of the written document*. Most authors believed that a group generated document is superior to one generated alone:

> "Working with others improves the final product ... ideas are more refined - bad ones are removed or reworked." 3[6]

Despite this positive attitude, a journalist had a different view:

> "[Journalism is] a tough business to try to be accurate. You do your best to try and check things. You're often on deadline. It is often difficult to check and also we're very fallible individuals. With two people, you double the chances of making mistakes! ..." 6[12]

The interviews showed that *authorship conventions* vary widely between fields and even among groups within fields. In some cases name order in the author list indicated relative contributions to the paper:

> "Authorship indicates who did most work on the project, who contributed most ideas. ... It didn't matter who did the writing as long as the ideas got out." 4[]

In other fields the order of authorship is predetermined; for example in medicine "the supervisor goes last as a rule" 5[]. In journalism, the division of credit is less definite:

> "You only get a byline if you contribute a significant percentage of the story ... Top line goes to who ever did more work. Sometimes it is alphabetical, and sometimes it's random ... It's more like the luck of the draw." 6[]

In psychology we discovered a disparity. In one psychology department the supervisor automatically receives first authorship on all joint papers, while in another such assumptions do not exist:

> "Order of authors establishes a hierarchy. ... First author does most of the writing and presents the paper at conferences." 3[]

Another popular authorship convention is to alternate first authorship on different papers; this was seen mainly among well established groups of collaborators.

Some interviewees noted the effects of *group size and composition* on the outcome of the joint writing project:

> "Should have a maximum of one collaborator. ... It is good to have someone to bounce ideas off. Ideally this person should have special expertise." 1[2]

> "Good to have a supervisor to help focus on the concepts. ... I would have been happier on my own or with one other person." 5[10]

> "With just two people working on the project it is harder to confront problems without endangering the work ... It's good to have more than two, an odd number of people to settle disputes." 8[16]

The *status of group members*, either similar or different, can lead to problems in working groups. We recorded reports of differences in status impairing the work progress:

> "When working with a supervisor, you might take the supervisor's view and accept it, then later realize this is not necessarily true. Where as with a peer, you can work out the issues right away, which may save time." 3[5]

Equal status groups run into different but equally serious problems, including struggles for leadership and the problems of confronting members who are not contributing their expected share of work:

> "One writer on a team has the dominant push ... I think that there will always be one that's slightly dominant." 10[]

> "Hard to deal with different levels of commitment to the project. You feel like the other guy is slacking off but it is very difficult to bring this up with just the two of you ..." 8[16]

Among other factors that can cause problems on group projects are different *individual working styles*:

> "Different working styles were an issue. One of us liked to have things done in advance, while the other liked to leave things till the very last moment. ... A good compatible work team makes all the difference." 8[16]

In another group, where participants had different working styles, one of the members avoided this problem by carefully managing to suppress several individual preferences for the good of the group progress:

> "I very consciously tried to stay out of the way, not to nit pick." 7[14]

The factor that was most often mentioned as important to the success of a group was *trust among the participants*. When individuals are willing to contribute a significant amount of their time and energy to a project, they need to be certain that their efforts will be appreciated and rewarded. One project failed because of this:

> "Trust was a problem. ... People worried about getting enough credit. ... People killed it not the ideas." 4[9]

Groups that succeed despite lack of trust, result in difficult experiences for the participants:

> "There are people who don't have integrity and they can be dangerous, if you're on a project with them ... sharing a byline. ... It was a nightmarish experience ... I could not trust that the stuff appearing under my name was the type of stuff that I'd want my name associated with." 6[12]

Technology and distance can contribute to this lack of trust and, thus, need to be carefully managed to facilitate group projects.

Criticism is another sensitive issue that can lead to interpersonal problems which can be detrimental to the success of a group project. Relative status of group members can influence the ease of criticizing someone's work. Interviewees discussed several conflicts that arose as a result of criticism by members of equal status:

"It is difficult to critique and be criticized by fellow students ... each ego bound. The supervisor would have more leeway to criticize." 5[10]

"It was a bit of a strain ... your skin can't be too thin when you are a writer ... He had little experience as a writer ... He was very protective of his ideas ... He would always raise his voice. ... We had a producer who would arbitrate and he'd bow to her." 10[22]

The interviews also revealed the *use of technology* by collaborating groups. All groups used word processors to produce their documents. The vast majority had face-to-face meetings, with only one exception. Attitudes towards face-to-face meetings varied, especially in valuing their effectiveness for getting work done:

"Most productive work came out of face-to-face discussions. ... Best ideas come when you are outside of a meeting, talking about something totally unrelated." 3[6]

"Embellishments, new ideas, new ways of looking at things are discovered alone ... brought to the meetings. ... About 5 minutes of work gets done in an hour of collaboration [face-to-face meeting]." 4[8]

Many interviewees discussed frustrations with *technology,* including the drawbacks of *writing tools.* The use of conventional editors in a joint writing project posed problems:

"I would get email saying change page 4 line 2, but in my version page 4 is completely different ... [incorporating the changes by comparing different paper versions] was very awkward, time consuming, and error prone." 3[6]

Use of different machines by collaborators introduced other difficulties:

"We had to transfer the electronic file from one machine to another which was very complicated ... Then I had to change the format of the new sections ... by hand. ... It was all very time consuming." 2[4]

Communication tools were seen as obstacles to smooth group interaction. The communication medium used to transmit a message may influence the structure of that message or the way that message is received (Sproull and Kiesler, 1986). One group ran into this problem when participants received both electronic and verbal messages:

"There is a very big difference between getting an electronic message and a verbal one. ... The result is confusion. ... Technology gets in the way. It always gets in the way. Very few situations where technology makes things better." 4[9]

Many groups that spent some time working at a distance faced problems with communication bandwidth:

"Communication bandwidth problems ... long delays waiting for documents to arrive ... logistically very difficult. Proximity would have saved time." 7[14]

Interviewees seemed to agree that proximity was the solution to many of these problems, which is suggested by the work of Kraut et al. (1988). Proximity was sought even if the collaborators had to travel a great distance at significant financial and personal cost:

"If this work required a more collaborative contribution, I would have been tempted to just fly there instead of trying to cope with it over a distance." 3[5]

One of our research emphases is the support of remote collaboration through the use of video and audio connections. We proposed this possibility in the interviews and received encouraging feedback:

"You can really develop a fairly good relationship with somebody over the phone, without ever talking to them [face to face] ... Generally, the people that I really want to keep up with I'll go to lunch with ... A video connection would be almost like meeting them in a way." 6[]

"I love the phone! ... I have many telephone relationships. ... We spend a lot of time on the phone when neither of us wants to write. We do cryptics on the phone. ... But to have a picture! To have actually not only a voice but a face, it would be wonderful! I think a video screen would be great, especially when working overseas." 10[]

However, not everyone was enthusiastic about this prospect:

"[Generally, I don't actively seek out people] but when it comes to collaboration I like to have the people in the same room. ... I find that technology gets in the way." 4[]

Writing Process and Taxonomy

One of the most complex aspects of group writing is the writing process itself. Initially it seems that each project and each group employs a unique process that is not repeated by any other group. Yet through a closer examination of the interview results we have been able to develop a taxonomy which helps us see the similarities and patterns amidst this diversity.

The results are summarized in Table 1a, with the help of a supporting legend presented in Table 1b. Further details appear in Posner (1991). Of particular value was the production of a set of *writing process diagrams,* which are explained and illustrated in Posner (1991) and in Posner and Baecker (submitted for review).

The taxonomy is composed of four different categories: *roles, activities, document control methods,* and *writing strategies.* Each of these provides a different perspective for examining the joint writing process. Roles looks at the process from the individual's point of view, analyzing the part played by each individual on the writing team. Activities categorize the actions performed while working on the project. Document control methods describe how the writing process is managed and coordinated. Finally, writing strategies focus on the text creation process.

Among the previous research, the work that most closely resembles our findings is Ede and Lunsford (1990). They also see writing divided into several related activities, including brainstorming, notetaking, organizational planning, writing, revising, and editing. They discovered that groups have different ways of assigning responsibility for the product, including having one person responsible, sharing the responsibility, and having a superior responsible. They recognized several organizational patterns used in group writing. Two patterns, for example, are "One member plans and writes draft. Group or team revises." and "Team or group plans and outlines. One member writes the entire draft. Team or group revises." There are many such patterns possible. The writing strategies and document control methods of our taxonomy allow a finer-grained and more complete description of these patterns and can therefore be used to define more precisely the collaborative writing process.

Roles

The interviews demonstrated the existence of different roles within groups. The way that roles are assigned to individuals varied between groups. Some of the roles were decided by organizational hierarchies, while others resulted from time constraints on the group members.

The consultant role was found in fourteen groups. In supervisor-student groups the supervisor often played the consultant role, while the student wrote the text [1,6,9,10]. Similar role assignment was seen in the producer-writer group [22]. In other groups, all members started out with the intention of contributing by writing but later the group member with the least time to dedicate to the project, usually the busiest member, fell into the consultant role [4,5,7,11,14].

Roles of some group members were sometimes imposed by the available technology. If all group members did not have access to similar software, the writing work was given to the individuals with the technology and the remaining members worked as consultants or reviewers [13,16,17,21].

The editor role had varying respect. Among journalists, for example, it is well accepted that, "Editor gets the final say" 6[]. In mature groups, editors' comments were well received. In these situations editors made small corrections without notifying the writer, while bigger changes were explicitly discussed [5,6,17,19,20]. In newly formed groups where the participants had equal status, the editor's role was more difficult:

Table 1a: Writing Process Details

Interview results encompassing the four categories: roles, activities, document control methods, and writing strategies.

Project Number	1	2	3	4	5	6	7	8	9	10	11	12	13	14	15	16	17	18	19	20	21	22
Interview Number	1	1	2	2	3	3	4	4	4	5	5	6	6	7	7	8	8	9	9	10	10	10
Roles																						
Writer	y	y	y	y	y	y	y	y	y	y	y	y	y	y	y	y	y	y	y	y	y	y
Consultant	y	.	.	y	y	y	y	.	y	y	y	.	y	y	.	y	y	.	.	.	y	y
Editor	.	y	.	.	y	y	.	.	y	y	.	y	y	.	.	y	y	.	.	.	.	y
Reviewer	.	.	.	y	.	y	.	.	.	.	.	y	y	.	.	.	y	.	y	.	.	.
Equal work [y]	n	.	.	n	n	n	n	.	na	.	na	.	n	n	.	.	.	.	.	.	.	.
Activities																						
Group Size N=	2	3	2	3	2	3	3	2	5	4	3	2	4	3	2	2	3	2	3	2	3	3
# brainstorm [N]	.	.	.	2	1	.	2	.	2	.	2	.	2	2	.	.	.	.	2	.	.	2
# research [N]	.	.	.	2	1	2	1	.	.	3	1	.	3	2	.	.	.	.	2	.	2	2
# initial plan [N]	.	.	1	2	1	.	2	.	.	.	2	.	2	2	.	.	.	.	2	.	.	2
# write [N]	1	.	.	2	.	2	1	.	3	.	2	.	3	2	.	.	.	.	2	.	.	2
# write most! [N]	1	.	.	2	1	1	1	.	3	.	1	.	1	2	.	1	1	.	2	.	2	2
Control change[n]	.	.	y	y	y	y	.	y	y	y	.	y	y	y	y	y	y	y	y	y	.	y
# edit doc. [N]	1	.	.	2	.	2	1	.	3	.	1	.	2	2	.	.	.	.	.	.	.	2
# final edit [N]	1	.	.	1	1	.	1	.	na	1	na	1	1	1	.	1	1	.	1	.	.	2
# review [N]	.	.	.	.	.	.	.	1	.	.	.	.	.	2	.	.	.	.	.	.	.	.
Document control	# represents priority of ranking																					
Centralized	1	.	.	1	1	1	1	.	.	1	1	.	1	1	.	1	1	.	.	.	2	.
Relay	.	.	2	.	.	2	.	2	.	2	.	.	.	.	1	.	.	2	2	1	.	2
Independent	.	1	.	2	.	.	.	1	2	2	1	2	2	2	2	.	.	2	1	1		
Shared	.	1	.	.	.	.	1	2	.	2	.	.	.	.	1	1	.	.	.			
Writing strategy	# represents approximate order of occurrence																					
Single writer	12	.	2		12	1	12	.	.	3	2	3	2	2	.	34	14	1	.	.	.	.
Scribe	.	.	.	.	.	.	.	.	.	.	.	.	.	.	2	2	.	.	1	1	12	
Separate writ.	.	1	2	1	.	2	.	13	12	1	1	1	1	1	12	1	3	3	2	3	2	3
Joint writing	.	2	1	.	.	.	.	2	.	2	.	.	3	.	.	2	13	24	.	.		
Consulted	2	.	2	2	1	2	.	1	13	12	3	2	2	.	4	4	.	.	.	2	23	
Project Number	1	2	3	4	5	6	7	8	9	10	11	12	13	14	15	16	17	18	19	20	21	22

Table 1b: Legend Explaining the Categories in Table 1a

Roles	The types of roles played by individuals on the writing projects.
Writer	Responsible for transforming abstract ideas into coherent and organized text.
Consultant	Works very closely with writers but does not take part in writing of text.
Editor	Makes changes to documents that were written by someone else.
Reviewer	Gives comments about document, which are accepted or ignored by the writer.
Equal work	This indicates whether all the team members contributed equal efforts to the project. "y," the default response means yes, the effort was equal, while "n" means it was not, and "na" means that the information was not available.
Activities	This describes the writing process used by the group or activities performed by individual members. The default value in this section of the table, indicated by a period ".", is "N," the "Group Size". The numbers indicate how many individuals, other than N, participated in certain activities.
# brainstorm	Number of people that took part in brainstorming at the start of the project.
# initial plan	Number of people that participated in initial planning of the document.
# write	Number of those that contributed to creating the document text.
# write most!	Number of those that wrote significant parts of the document.
Control changes	indicates transfers of document control between individuals during writing.
# edit doc.	Number of people who made changes to the electronic document.
# final edit	Number who took part in editing the final version of the document.
Document Control Methods	This section examines control methods used on each project. The numbers appearing in this section are used to rank the priority of each control method. For example, on Project 3 the primary control method used was "shared" while the secondary strategy was "relay."
Centralized	One individual controls the document throughout the project.
Relay	One person at a time is in control, but control passes between team members.
Independent	Each team member works on a separate part of the document and maintains control of this part throughout the writing process.
Shared	Simultaneous and equal access and writing privileges are available to several team members at once.
Writing Strategies	This section describes the means or steps by which the text was created. Throughout projects, different writing strategies are used; their order of occurrence is indicated in the table. For example, the first project used the "single writer" strategy at first and then the "single writer(consulted)" strategy. The entries in this section should be read as all single digit numbers, "1" and "2", not "12."
Single writer	One person writes the document based on discussions with other group members.
Scribe	This is used in a group meeting where one individual takes the role of writing down the group's thoughts.
Separate writers	This is used by individuals who break up the document into parts with each one writing and being responsible for a different part.
Joint writing	This is used by a group that writes the document together, deciding on the exact wording and sentence structure used in the text.
Consulted	This category is to be read in conjunction with the entry in the writing strategy sections. For example, on project 9 the initial writing strategy is separate writers (consulted), where individuals are working separately on the segments of the text but their work is closely guided by a consultant; afterwards, the consultations cease and the separate writers strategy is used.

*"Most writers are very sensitive about their work ...
I remember how it used to hurt any criticism ...
You have to realize that you're writing something
for people to change." 10[22]*

Different roles exist on joint writing projects. The interviews indicate that their occurrence and distribution depend on discipline expectations, group composition, time constraints, and available technology.

Activities

The interviews supported our belief that the roles people play and the activities that they perform are closely related. However, several activities can be performed by one individual in a single role.

The activities which are synonymous with certain role names are performed by individuals playing those roles; for example, writers write, editors edit, reviewers review. We also observed that brainstorming and planning of the document are performed by writers together with their consultants. If a group needed to conduct research, this activity was assigned in a way that minimized the cost to the group; that is, the least busy member or the member of lowest status did the research on behalf of the group. The review of the final manuscript was conducted by all group members. The only exceptions to this were in groups where the participants were geographically dispersed, time was extremely limited, and transmission of the manuscripts and the comments was difficult.

Writing Strategies and Document Control Methods

In the joint writing process the writing strategies and document control methods are very closely related. The writing strategy is the *process view*, which describes how the text is created, by whom, and when. The document control method is the *object view*, which describes how the document is managed, by whom, and when. Because these two topics are interrelated, we will address the interview results using the writing strategies and deal with the document control issues in the context of each writing strategy.

Single Writer Strategy

The single writer strategy is the case of one team member writing the document, while the others assist.

This strategy was very popular. Thirteen of the twenty-two groups used the single writer strategy at some point in the project [1,4-7,10-14,16-18]. For example, Project 1 consisted of a student working with his supervisor on a paper for a journal. The student wrote the document while the supervisor consulted, staying closely involved throughout the project.

On six projects, using single writer strategies, we observed a hierarchical difference among participants [1,5-7,10,11]. In four of these projects a lower status member played the writer role, while the higher status individual consulted [1,5,6,10].

The single writer role was also assigned to the individual most familiar with the required format or the structure of the final document. Four projects [6,7,16,17] used this assignment strategy, where the standard formats included write-ups of experiments and a paper submitted to a particular conference.

Some groups made a conscious decision to use the single writer strategy [6,10,13,17] in order to have a uniformly written document, with one individual's style of writing present in the text:

> *"When I write it has to be under my control or I cannot write effectively ... If two people write separate sections, the sections sound completely different." 3[6]*

On two of these projects [10,13], the single writer strategy was used following other strategies. The final version of the document was produced by one individual;

this, the journalist claimed, was the standard approach used in his field. Both of these groups had writing assistance from others in form of text, much of which was changed by the final writer to reflect that individual's writing style.

Not all groups selected this strategy voluntarily. In seven cases, the available technology guided the selection of the single writer strategy. Two groups [1,16] did not have access to compatible technology and had no way of transmitting information between their computers. This limitation was a large factor in the implementation of the single writer strategy. The single strategy also occurred when group members were geographically dispersed [4,5,7,13,14]. In each case a single writer composed the document while other participants assisted the writer.

The use of the single writer strategy usually implies the use of the centralized document control method. In eleven of the above thirteen groups the writer maintained control of the document. In two cases [12,18], there was a single writer, but the control was shared because group members had access to networked computers and thus equal access to the joint document. In such situations social protocols often guide the accessibility to the document. For example, the amount of involvement with a document is related to the access to the document: the writer has full access, a co-writer and consultant may have read and comment access, a reviewer may have read only access, while outsiders may not have any access.

Scribe Strategy

The scribe writing strategy is used when individuals are working together and one of them writes down the group's thoughts and decisions, while the others are engaged in a general discussion of the ideas to be expressed in the document (Austin, Liker, and McLeod, 1990).

In the interviews, five projects [16,17,20-22] used the scribe strategy. One interviewee described this writing approach as "driving on the keyboard." The interviewee explained:

> *"I did most of the writing when we were working together. Once I made him write, or what I call 'drive' on the keyboard, then he realized how hard it is to transform ideas into words." 10[22]*

All the uses of the scribe strategy that we encountered occurred early in the project life during the brainstorming and planning activities. This strategy is usually adopted out of necessity to record the meeting information. The scribe has a very difficult job, participating in the meeting, and at the same time, transforming the group discussion into a document. As a result, the product of the scribe's effort is used as an extension of the group memory and results in guidelines for the team rather than a document draft.

The application of the scribe strategy is often technology driven. If different technology had been available to these groups, the joint writing strategy could have been an option.

The document control used in conjunction with the scribe strategy was divided between centralized and relay control methods.   Three projects [16,17,21] used centralized control with the scribe writing strategy,

"When I was at the keyboard typing I was really in control ... my words were used and my style." 10[21]

In the other two groups [20,22], the writer or scribe position was interchanged between the participants. First one would work as a scribe, then the other implying a relay control method; Mantei (1989) refers to this as the "alternating scribe" method and notes that this method occurs frequently when the technology supports it.

Separate Writers Strategy

If the document is divided into parts and different individuals write the various parts, then the separate writers strategy is being used.

The separate strategy is very popular in joint projects.   Only three of the twenty-two projects did not use the separate strategy at least once [1,5,7].

By partitioning the document, the group can work in parallel, thereby speeding up the writing process. Time pressure was responsible for the use of the separate writers approach on twelve projects [8-12,16-22].

Many projects demand expertise in different areas and subgroups are often formed to represent complementary skill sets.   In the interviews we observed eleven such cases [2-4,6,11-16,21].

Some interviewees had different reasons for preferring the separate writers strategy.   One individual felt it easiest to work in a group when the responsibility was divided among group members [14].   A freelance writer admitted that separate writing entails fewer distractions:

"We tended to sit around and chat and do cryptic crosswords together.   This way [by working apart] we'd separate and we knew that we had to do the work.   You'd have to do the work and bring it in for others to see." 10[21]

The journalist explained that the separate writers strategy often followed by the single writer strategy is most popular in his field:

"It's very rare when two people write together. Usually one writes one part another writes another part.   Then, they send it to a third person who puts it together or one of them puts it all together." 6[13]

In three instances the separate writers approach was influenced by the available technology [2,10,21].   One interviewee discussed such an experience:

"We all had different computers ... We just wrote differently [separately], met talked about each others ideas, took the suggestions, rewrote, and compiled it all. ... We didn't have the time to have a secretary retype it all. ... The producers objected to the lack

of consistency in style ... they said, 'One of you is more prose, one of you is funny, and one of you is more mythological'." 10[21]

This quotation demonstrates the major problem with the separate writers strategy.   Following the separate work there still remains the need to unite the resulting segments in order to create a uniform style.

When using the separate writers strategy, there are several possible document control options.   The most common combination is with independent control, used in fifteen groups [2-4,9-17,20-22].   In this combination, the individuals writing continuously control their segments of the document.   As we saw in the above quotation, the result of this approach can be a segmented and disjoint document.

A combination that appears to be more effective is the relay control method.   For example, in the case of a supervisor-student team that wrote a paper together.   The interviewee explained:

"I don't usually write things so closely intertwined. ... What struck me is how seamlessly we could exchange the documents back and forth between us. It worked very well ... We were thinking along parallel lines.   I didn't really expect this.   It just worked out very well." 7[15]

In another case, we have an example of how separate writing can be used effectively when the writers understand one another.   A pair of researchers who worked together for many years, spent much time developing ideas, debating alternatives, and trying to prove their theories.   When the time came to write the details were clear:

"When one got down to writing, there was no question about what had to get down on paper." 4[8]

While actually writing they follow a tightly interwoven process:

"We ping ponged the paper back and forth. ... We'd get mad at each other.   Work things out ... it was a very pleasant experience until the very end ... The actual collaboration was very fluid, very pleasant." 4[8]

Four other groups also combined separate writers strategy and relay document control methods [3,6,18,19].

In five other groups separate writers was used, but the documents were available to several group members simultaneously, implying a shared control method [3,8,9,18,19].   In work on a best-seller book [19], the interviewee explained their work process:

"It wasn't like we took ownership of any one chapter.   We knew what we wanted to do, so we just did it. ... Whoever started something would usually continue it until it was at a point where it can be edited easier.   But there were places where I would start it and he'd continue it and vice versa; you'd get some block and you don't know how to do it..." 9[19]

Here, we see the subtlety of the difference between relay and shared control methods: shared means both have access, whereas, relay means only one at a time has access. In the case of the joint book, project [19], where both coauthors had access to the latest version of the document, but only used it one at a time, we see shared control.

Joint Writing Strategy

Joint writing is a strategy in which several group members compose the text together, and even minute components of the text are decided by a group effort.

In the interviews, nine groups worked on some parts of their documents jointly [2,3,8,10,12,15,18-20]. We observed that joint writing can have different effects on group cohesion. Some groups enjoyed the joint writing experience while others found it frustrating and harmful to group unity. The maturity of the group influenced the success of the joint writing session; an experienced group was able to work together more smoothly than a new group. All old groups that utilized this strategy had a pleasant experience [3,8,15,19]. Two new groups found this strategy beneficial [18,20], but three others found it frustrating [2,10,12].

We examined at what point in the project life the joint strategy was used and discovered that the groups who attempted joint writing late in the project were the same new groups that described this approach as ineffective [2,10,12]. In each of these cases, the joint writing attempts resulted in conflicts between group members and disrupted the group cohesion. One interviewee described these conflicts:

> "Everyone gave comments on everyone else's work ... We argued about every sentence. The final decision went whoever yelled loudest!" 1[2]

The interviews suggested that, early on in a project, groups can write jointly to produce an outline of their ideas, at which point opinions are still forming. Later in a project's life the individuals' ideas are better defined and more difficult to integrate.

Another important aspect leading to the success of the joint writing strategy is the document control method that is used with it. Groups 8, 18, and 19 used a shared control method. Each team of two writers used a shared work space consisting of a white board and two markers. Four groups combined joint writing with relay document control [3,15,19,20]; the control passed between the participants while both decided on the changes that should be made. The final and the least successful combination of joint writing occurred with independent document control [2,10,12]. In each case we saw group members of equal status trying to decide on changes to be made to parts of the document that were written and controlled by one individual. The suggestions and changes that were brought up during these interactions were badly received by the writers and owners of the segments. These observed difficulties resulted from a combination of factors including the newness of the group, the equal status of the members,

the lateness of the attempt at joint writing, and the individual control methods.

Consulted Strategies

The consulted approach is not a complete strategy in itself but a combination of the other writing strategies. A strategy represented as single(consulted), for example, implies that there was a single writer who worked very closely with a consultant throughout the project, as opposed to the single strategy where the document reflects the work of one person with minimal assistance from others.

In the interviews we observed fifteen projects using consulted strategies: single(consulted) [1,4-7,10-14,16,17], separate(consulted) [9-11,21,22], and scribe(consulted) [22]. We did not encounter an example of the theoretically possible joint(consulted) strategy, where a group is divided into subgroups with one subgroup writing while the other participants consult.

Several groups used more than one type of consulted strategy. For example, on project 22 the team members were two writers and a producer with the product being a series of scripts for television. The two writers started out working together using the simple scribe writing strategy, with the senior writer working as scribe. They decided to switch roles and the junior writer became scribe but had difficulty with this role. The senior writer felt obliged to assist:

> "Once I made him write, or what I call 'drive' on the keyboard, then he realized how hard it is to transform ideas into words. ... Even when he was writing I was helping him with how to phrase things." 10[22]

This is an example of the unusual scribe(consulted) combination strategy. Later in this project the separate(consulted) writing strategy was adopted, with the producer serving as a consultant and an arbiter to guide the progress and settle disputes.

Implications for System Design

The interviews and the taxonomy demonstrate that approaches to joint writing vary considerably (see Table 2). Further details on the taxonomy, as well as findings from a laboratory study of collaborative writing (carried out through a variety of communications media) that corroborate the results from the interviews, appear in Posner (1991) and Posner and Baecker (submitted for review).

These results also suggest a set of design requirements that collaborative writing systems should support. All of these requirements need not necessarily be supported in software technology; some can be incorporated into the larger social system in which the technology is used. The requirements are now listed followed by a description of how existing groupware writing tools satisfy the requirements.

Table 2: Interview Results Summary
Summary of the percentages of the 22 projects studied in which a particular strategy or method occurs.
Since multiple strategies and methods often occur in a project, percentages do not add to 100%.

Writing strategies		Document control methods	
Separate writers	86%	Independent	64%
Single writer	59	Centralized	55
Joint writing	41	Relay	36
Scribe	23	Shared	27
Consulted	68%	Document control changes	77%
Single writer	55		
Separate writers	23	Work equally divided	59%
Scribe	05		
Joint writing	00		

Design Requirements

Collaborative writing projects often depend on several individuals contributing to the writing; feedback is most effective when directed to the author of a segment:

Requirement 1: Preserve collaborator identities.

Group writing differs significantly from individual writing by the amount of communication among the participants. Communication includes messages dealing with the document text, project scheduling, and social interactions; systems should facilitate these communications:

Requirement 2: Support communication among collaborators — document annotations, synchronous interactions, and asynchronous messages.

Roles

Roles that individuals play on projects define their contributions and commitments to the project. Misunderstanding of commitments can lead to conflicts within a group:

Requirement 3: Make collaborator roles explicit.

Activities

Activities occur in different sequences and combinations on collaborative writing projects:

Requirement 4: Support the six primary writing activities: brainstorming, researching, planning, writing, editing, reviewing.

It is unrealistic to expect that one tool will be sufficient to support all the different activities. To compensate for this shortcoming systems must provide smooth transitions between the different activities:

Requirement 5: Support transitions between activities.

Varieties of information are required throughout the writing process. Systems can facilitate the organization and the access to information:

Requirement 6: Provide access to relevant information.

Planning is crucial in collaborative writing. Effective plans can reduce redundancy, misunderstandings, and even the work load for the group:

Requirement 7: Make plans explicit — process and outline plans.

With several individuals working on a document, it is important to be able to quickly discover what changes were made, who made them, and when they were made:

Requirement 8: Provide version control mechanisms — change indicators.

Document Control Methods

Participants on a project may want to access the document at the same time or in sequence; systems should allow flexible access:

Requirement 9: Support concurrent and sequential document access.

Different types of document access may improve the writing process. If consultants can read the document and provide comments early in the writing, the overall project time may be reduced:

Requirement 10: Support several document access methods: write, comment, read.

Many collaborative documents are subdivided. Each segment can have different individuals working in different roles, on different activities, and using different document control methods and writing strategies. Systems should allow flexibility for several document segments but maintain connections for the entire document:

Requirement 11: Support separate document segments.

Writing Strategies

Writing strategies used on collaborative projects fall into two categories, using either one writer or several writers:

Requirement 12: Support one and several writers .

Writing can be done by several individuals working either at the same time or at different times:

Requirement 13: Support synchronous and asynchronous writing.

Design Requirements and Existing Systems

We shall now briefly describe six existing systems that support collaborative writing, and see how well they conform to the proposed requirements for collaborative systems (see Table 3).

Aspects, by Group Technologies (1990), is a collaborative conferencing system that runs on networked computers and provides writing, drawing, and painting tools. **ForComment** (Edwards, Levine, and Kurland, 1986) supports asynchronous annotations by several people, with each collaborator accessing a different layer for creating annotations using text, voice, or hand drawings. **GROVE** (Ellis, Gibbs, and Rein, 1989) is an outlining tool designed for users at remote sites working on networked computers. **PREP** (Neuwirth, Kaufer, Chandhok, and Morris, 1990) is a writing tool that provides asynchronous access to documents and can be thought of as a "spreadsheet for documents," because it provides a column based interface where text is presented in columns of visually linked chunks. **Quilt** (Fish, Kraut, Leland, and Cohen, 1987; Leland, Fish, and Kraut, 1988) is a multi-user hypermedia communications and coordination tool which combines computer conferencing with multi-media email. **ShrEdit** (Killey, 1990) is intended for simultaneous writing by several users working on networked computers in a conference room. **SASSE** (Mawby, 1991; Nastos, 1992), a shared editor based on our research, supports synchronous and asynchronous writing over local and wide area networks, and uses color to distinguish contributions from individual writers.

Although most of these systems satisfy a number of our requirements, it is clear that progress can still be made (Mawby, 1991; Nastos, 1992).

Table 3:   How Existing Collaborative Writing Systems Satisfy the Design Requirements

Requirement	Aspects	ForCom.	GROVE	PREP	Quilt	SASSE	ShrEdit
1. Preserve identities	++	++	++	+	++	++	++
2. Enhance communication							
Annotations	.	++	++	++	++	++	++
Asynchronous	.	++	.	.	++	++	+
Synchronous	++	.	.	+	.	++	++
3. Make roles explicit	++	.	++	.	++	+	.
4. Variety of activities							
brainstorming	++	.	+	+	+	++	++
researching	.	.	.	.	.	.	.
planning (outline)	+	.	++	++	+	++	+
writing	++	.	.	++	+	++	++
editing	++	.	.	++	+	++	++
reviewing	.	++	.	++	++	++	+
5. Transitions between activities	+	.	.	++	++	++	+
6. Access to relevant information	+	?	?	+	++	.	+
7. Make plans explicit							
Process plans	.	.	.	+	.	.	.
Outline plans	.	.	++	++	+	++	.
8. Version control mechanisms	++	.	.	+	.	++	.
9. Document access							
Synchronous	++	.	++	.	.	++	++
Sequential	++	++	++	++	++	++	++
10. Several access methods							
Write	++	.	++	++	++	++	++
Comment	.	++	.	++	++	++	+
Read only	++	.	++	++	++	+	.
11. Separate document segments	++	.	?	+	++	.	.
12. Number of writers							
One writer	++	++	?	++	++	++	++
Several writers	++	.	++	++	++	++	++
13. Writing approach							
Synchronous	++	.	++	.	.	++	++
Asynchronous	++	++	++	++	++	++	++
	Aspects	ForCom.	GROVE	PREP	Quilt	SASSE	ShrEdit

Notation:

++	system provides support
+	system can handle but does not specifically support
.	system does not support
?	not clear if support is provided

Conclusions

This study has demonstrated the rich variety of methods that groups use to write collaboratively. Technology therefore needs to be flexible and permissive, allowing groups to change strategies and processes at any time during the project with minimal distraction. Smooth transitions should be supported between using technology and conventional methods of writing, between individual work and group work, between planning, outlining, writing, and annotating the document, and between synchronous and asynchronous work by group members (Baecker, 1991). Technology that strictly enforces limited approaches and that is not sufficiently flexible will constrain the group writing process and likely lead to frustration and eventually lack of use of the prescriptive technology.

Acknowledgements

We gratefully acknowledge the support to our laboratory from the Natural Sciences and Engineering Research Council of Canada, the Information Technology Research Centre of Ontario, the Institute for Robotics and Intelligent Systems of Canada, Apple Computer's Human Interface Group and Advanced Technology Group, Xerox PARC and EuroPARC, Digital Equipment Corporation, the IBM Canada Lab Centre for Advanced Studies, and Alias Research. We are indebted to Marilyn Mantei for assistance with this work and for valuable comments on a draft of this paper. We'd like to thank Gary Olson, Lola McGuffin, Robert Fish, David Kaufer, Ravinder Chandhok, and Dimitri Nastos for help with the table comparing collaborative writing systems.

References

Allen, N.J., Atkinson, D., Morgan, M., Moore, T., and Snow, C. (1987). What Experienced Collaborators Say about Collaborative Writing. *Iowa State Journal of Business and Technical Communication*. Sept. 1987. 70-90.

Austin, L., Liker, J. and McLeod (1990). Determinants and Patterns of Control over Technology in a Computerized Meeting Room. *Proceedings of CSCW '90*. 39-51.

Baecker, R. (1991). New Paradigms for Computing in the Nineties. *Proceedings of Graphics Interface '91*, Morgan Kaufmann Publishers, 224-229.

Bair, J.H. (1985). The Need for Collaboration Tools in Offices. *Proceedings of AFIPS'85*, Office Automation Conference. Atlanta, GA., February, 1985. 59-68.

Bereiter, C. and Scardamalia, M. (1982). From Conversation to Composition. In R. Glasner (ed), *Advances in Instructional Psychology*, Vol. 2. Laurence Erlbaum Assoc.

Ede, L. and Lunsford, A. (1990). *Singular Texts/Plural Authors: Perspectives on Collaborative Writing.* Southern Illinois University Press.

Edwards, M.U., Levine, J.A., and Kurland, D.M. (1986). *ForComment.* Broderbund.

Ellis, C., Gibbs, S.J., and Rein, G. (1989). Design and Use of a Group Editor. MCC Technical Report, Number STP-263-88, June 1989.

Eveland, J.D. and Bikson, T.K. (1988). Work Group Structures and Computer Support: A Field Experiment. *Proceedings of CSCW'88..* 324-343.

Fish, R.S., Kraut, R.E., Leland, M.D.P., and Cohen, M. (1987). Quilt: a Collaborative Tool for Cooperative Writing. *Proceedings of COIS'88.* 30-37.

Flower, L., Schriver, K.A., Carey, L., Haas, C., and Hayes, J.R. (1989). Planning in Writing: The Cognition of a Constructive Process. Center for the Study of Writing Technical Report, No. 34. Carnegie Mellon University, July 1989.

Freedman, S.W., Dyson, A.H., Flower, L., and Chafe, W. (1987). Research in Writing: Past, Present, and Future. Technical Report by Center for the Study of Writing, No. 1. Carnegie Mellon University, August 1987.

Galegher, J. and Kraut, R.E. (1990). Computer-Mediated Communication for Intellectual Teamwork: A Field Experiment in Group Writing. *Proceedings of CSCW'90.* 65-78.

Group Technologies, Inc. (1990). *Aspects: The First Simultaneous Conference Software for the Macintosh.* Group Technologies, Inc. Arlington, VA.

Killey, L. (1990). *ShrEdit 1.0: A Shared Editor for Apple Macintosh. User's Guide and Technical Description.* Cognitive Science and Machine Intelligence Laboratory, University of Michigan, Ann Arbor, MI. June 1990. (unpublished).

Kraut, R.E., Egido, C., and Galegher, J. (1988). Patterns of Contact in Communication in Scientific Research Collaboration. *Proceedings of CSCW'88.* 1-12.

Kraut, R.E., Galegher, J., and Egido, C. (1986). Relationships and Tasks in Scientific Research Collaborations. Appears in I. Greif (ed), *Computer-Supported Cooperative Work: A Book of Readings.* Morgan Kaufman Publ. 1988.

Leland, M.D.P., Fish, R.S., and Kraut, R.E. (1988). Collaborative Document Production Using Quilt. *Proceedings of CSCW'88.* 206-215.

Mantei, M.M. (1989). A Study of Executives Using a Computer Supported Meeting Environment. *International Journal of Decision Support Systems*, June 1989.

Mawby, K. (1991). *Designing Collaborative Writing Tools*. M.Sc. Thesis, University of Toronto.

Nastos, D. (in preparation). *A Structured Environment for Collaborative Writing*. M.Sc. Thesis, University of Toronto.

Neuwirth, C.M., Kaufer, D.S., Chandhok, R., and Morris, J.H. (1990). Issues in the Design of Computer Support for Co-authoring and Commenting. *Proceedings of CSCW'90*. 183-195.

Posner, I.R. (1991). *A Study of Joint Writing*. M.Sc. Thesis, University of Toronto.

Posner, I.R. and Baecker, R.M. (submitted for review). A Study of Collaborative Writing.

Sproull, L. and Kiesler, S. (1986). Reducing Social Context Cues: Electronic Mail in Organizational Communication. Appears in I. Greif (ed), *Computer-Supported Cooperative Work: A Book of Readings*. Morgan Kaufman Publ. 1988.

Appendix: Interview Questions (slightly abridged)

The following questions were asked in each interview, not necessarily in this order, but as they arose naturally in the context of the conversation.

I am studying how people write together. I would like to talk to you about the most recent (one especially memorable) joint authoring project you participated in. Statement re confidentiality...

Background
• When did this take place? How long did the entire project take?
• What type of document were you working on? How long was the final document?
• Who were the participants? Were these people peers/subordinates/superiors? How were they chosen? Personalities...? Special skills...? (known previously, not, ...) How important was it for everyone to work together?
• What were you doing at that point in your life? (type of job, educational training, ...)
• Describe in detail one day that you were working together on the project (the time of year, weather, location, purpose of meeting, productiveness of meeting, outcome of the meeting, ...)

Process
• Did the writing proceed in stages or steps? What were the stages (planning/writing/revising/...)? What happened at each stage of the writing process?
• How did you share the work? Who did what? Was the work evenly divided? How was this decided on? Which stages of the writing (planning, drafting, revising, ...) involved groups of people and which were done by individuals?
• Was the process planned at the start or decided on over time? Was the plan followed?
• Was the process explicit? (Decide to do A,B,C then do A,B,C.) Or did individuals just do things?
• Was the process used similar to your usual writing style when writing alone or when writing with others?
• Would you say the process used was a success? Why or why not?

Control
• Sometimes one or more persons take charge of the document. Did this type of thing happen during your writing? Who was this person? How was he/she chosen?
• How did you find the errors? How did you fix the errors? Did everyone take part in reviewing the document and suggesting changes? How were the changes done? (permissions...)
• How was the final document compiled? Was anyone in charge of this stage?
• Afterwords, how was credit divided? Was this discussed early on during the writing? (How many authors? Who's first?)

Problems
• How did the relationships work out? What other types of problems did you encounter during the writing?
• How did you handle/settle your disagreements?

Technology
• What is your educational/technical background?
• What type of technology was used in the project? (Computers/typewriters/telephone/fax) At what stages of the project was technology used?
• What did you like/dislike about available technology? Did it ever get in the way? What would have made it easier to use?
• What type of technology would have facilitated the writing process?
• What else would you like to be able to do with the technology?

Is there anything else? Have I covered everything?
• Would you say that this project was a success?
• Would you choose these people to work with again?
• What is your attitude towards joint writing? (positive/negative)

Int. J. Man–Machine Studies (1991) **34**, 143–160

Findings from observational studies of collaborative work

JOHN C. TANG

System Sciences Laboratory, Xerox Palo Alto Research Center, 3333 Coyote Hill Road, Palo Alto, CA 94304, USA

(Received April 1990 and accepted in revised form August 1990)

The work activity of small groups of three to four people was videotaped and analysed in order to understand collaborative work and to guide the development of tools to support it. The analysis focused on the group's shared drawing activity—their listing, drawing, gesturing and talking around a shared drawing surface. This analysis identified specific features of collaborative work activity that raise design implications for collaborative technology: (1) collaborators use hand gestures to uniquely communicate significant information; (2) the process of creating and using drawings conveys much information not contained in the resulting drawings; (3) the drawing space is an important resource for the group in mediating their collaboration; (4) there is a fluent mix of activity in the drawing space; and (5) the spatial orientation among the collaborators and the drawing space has a role in structuring their activity. These observations are illustrated with examples from the video data, and the design implications they raise are discussed.

1. Introduction

Building computer tools to support collaborative work requires re-examining the design assumptions that have hitherto been used in building tools for individual use. The needs of a group using a tool collaboratively, are different from those of an individual user, and these differences should be reflected in the design of the technology. The research reported in this paper is premised on the need to observe and understand what people actually do when engaged in an activity in order to guide the design, development and introduction of tools to support that activity. Figure 1 represents how this approach is applied to observing, understanding and supporting collaborative work. This paper reports on findings from studies that observed collaborative work, leading to a better understanding of that activity and raising implications for the design of tools to support it.

This research focuses on studying the collaborative drawing space activity of small teams—the writing, freehand drawing and gesturing activities that occur when three or four people work around whiteboards or large sheets of paper. Much human collaboration involves a shared drawing surface (e.g. paper sheets, chalkboards, computer screens, cocktail napkins), and recent research has been exploring computer support for collaborative drawing activity (Lakin, 1986; Stefik, Foster, Bobrow, Kahn, Lanning & Suchman, 1987). However, collaborative drawing tools should not be based only on what features computer technology offers or how computers have been applied to support individual activity. Rather, the design of collaborative technology needs to be guided by an understanding of how collaborative

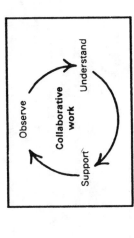

FIGURE 1. Research approach. Actual collaborative work activity is observed in order to understand it and identify opportunities to support it.†

work is accomplished. By understanding what resources the collaborators use and what hindrances they encounter in their work, tools can be designed to augment resources while removing obstacles in collaborative activity.

In this research, video-based interaction analysis methods (Goodwin, 1981; Heath, 1986) are applied to study collaborative drawing activity. This approach involves analysing videotaped samples of collaborative activity to understand how collaboration is accomplished through interactions among the participants and the artifacts in their environment. It emphasizes studying people working on a realistic task in a natural working environment, since that context has a major influence on the work activity. By comparing and contrasting among the many interactions that occur in the data, specific resources that collaborators use and hindrances that they encounter can be identified.

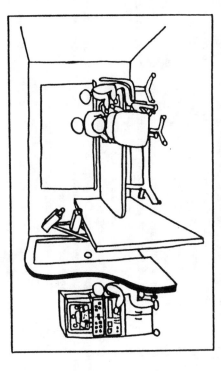

FIGURE 2. Configuration for videotaping collaborative work. Three or four collaborators work around a table on a pad of paper sheets. Their activity is monitored by the experimenter next door and recorded on videotape.

† I would like to acknowledge Scott Minneman (Unpublished data) for initially composing this representation for the relationship of observing, understanding and intervening in an activity.

Eight short sessions (approximately 1–1/2 h) of three to four person teams working on a conceptual design task were videotaped for analysis. Figure 2 shows the typical configuration for videotaping the collaborative activity. Four different design tasks were used in the sessions; all of them emphasized the human-machine interface design for an interactive, computer-controlled system (see sample problem statement in Appendix A). These tasks elicited a substantial amount of group interaction and collaborative drawing activity. For six of the sessions, the groups worked around a conference table sharing a pad of large paper sheets; two groups used a wall-mounted whiteboard. The meetings observed were the first sessions that the participants worked together on the task as a group, thus capturing the earlier, more conceptual stages of the design process. Tang (1989) describes the observational methodology in more detail.

In this paper, an analysis of collaborative drawing space activity is presented. Evidence from the video data is used to illustrate the resources and hindrances in shared drawing activity identified by this analysis. Finally, the design implications for tools to support collaborative work are identified and discussed.

2. Analysis of collaborative drawing space activity

The analysis focused on how the collaborators accomplished their work through their activity in the drawing space. Initial analysis of the data led to a framework (Figure 3) for organizing the study of drawing-space activity. This framework lays out categories of what actions occurred in the drawing space and what functions those actions accomplished. Although this framework is a rather simplified characterization of actual collaborative drawing activity, it has proven to be a useful tool for analysing the activity. Attempting to classify the observed activity into the categories of the framework helped identify resources and hindrances in collaborative drawing activity, as described in Section 3. This section presents the framework, illustrates it with examples from the videotape data, and describes how it was used to identify trends in the data.

2.1. FRAMEWORK FOR STUDYING DRAWING SPACE ACTIVITY

The framework in Figure 3 lays out relationships between *actions* that occur in the drawing space, and *functions* that are accomplished through those actions.

The *actions* describe the means for producing the activities:
(1) *List*: actions producing non-spatially located text (alpha-numeric notes);
(2) *Draw*: actions producing graphic artifacts, including textual captions;
(3) *Gesture*: purposeful hand movements which communicate information (e.g. enacting simulations, pointing to objects in the drawing space).

The analysis focused on the list, draw and gesture actions of the group; clearly, their talk was also a substantial part of their activity. While conversation analysis focuses mainly on interaction through conversation (Levinson, 1983), and some research studies drawing activity irrespective of the talk (Lakin, 1986), the research presented here studies collaborative drawing activity in the context of the group's talk. Although their talk was not analysed by classifying it according to various categories, it was used to help interpret and analyse their drawing space activity. By recording the activity on videotape, the context of the complete activity of the session (including the verbal dialog) is available for analysis.

The *functions* in Figure 3 describe the purpose that the activity accomplishes:
(1) *Store information*: preserving information in some form for later reference, typically after attaining group agreement;
(2) *Express ideas*: interactively creating representations of ideas in some tangible form, to enable the group to perceive, react to and build on them;
(3) *Mediate interaction*: facilitating the collaboration of the group (e.g. moderating the turn-taking, directing the group's attention).

While this set of actions and functions does not completely describe all of the activities that occur in the drawing space, it was used as a framework for structuring the analysis.

2.2. ILLUSTRATING THE FRAMEWORK

The categories of the framework are illustrated with examples from a scene in the videotape data, represented in Figure 4. This figure shows a section of transcript of the verbal dialog, annotated with brief descriptions of every drawing space activity that occurred during the section. In order to denote episodes of drawing space activity, an icon is placed in the text of the transcript at approximately the point in the talk where an action begins. That icon is linked to a note describing the drawing space action. The region of the drawing space where the participants are making their marks and sketches is shown on the right side of the figure. The "S" numbers identify which participant is speaking or acting. The line numbers along the left margin will be used throughout this paper to indicate locations in the transcript section. This representation was developed in the NoteCards hypertext environment (Halasz, Moran & Trigg, 1987).

This particular group's design task was to integrate the remote control units of several different entertainment appliances (e.g. television, stereo, videocassette recorder) into one multi-function remote control (see problem statement in Appendix A). This design session took place in 1987, before commercial versions of such a device were common. In this section of the session, the group is discussing new actions for operating the controls on a multi-function remote control.

To summarize what happens in this section, S2 elicits proposals for how to move icons around on a display screen, drawing a news desk icon as an example. S3 gesturally enacts an idea, sliding his finger over the icon to move it around, and

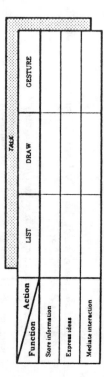

Action	TASK		
Function	LIST	DRAW	GESTURE
Store information			
Express ideas			
Mediate interaction			

FIGURE 3. Framework for analysing drawing space activity. A framework for categorizing drawing space activity according to *actions* (how the activity was produced) and *functions* (what the activity accomplished).

FIGURE 5. A gesture example. S3, on the far right, enacts the "slide and tap" idea by sliding his finger across a sketch of a display screen. (Split screen image combines a view of the whole group on top with a closeup of the drawing space on the bottom.)

consider the many other meaningful gestures and body motions beyond hand gestures that occur in collaborative activity.

The hand gesture marked in line 8 of the transcript is shown in Figure 5. This example illustrates how gesture is used to enact or simulate the slide and tap idea. S3 slides his finger over the sketch of the news desk, acting out how he would move the news desk icon across the display screen. Other examples of gesture include pointing at a sketch or signaling towards another group member.

Several of the observed actions displayed characteristics of more than one category (e.g. an activity that involved both listing and drawing). These actions were classified according to what action they primarily constituted. For example, the action noted in line 21 where S2 draws an arrow and writes "slide + tap" is categorized as a draw action, even though the resulting artifact is largely text. It is classified as a draw action because the text is spatially located and integrated with other graphic marks to the extent that the text provides graphic, as well as semantic, information.

2.2.2 Functions: storing information, expressing ideas and mediating interaction
Using the drawing space to store information involves preserving or recording the information to facilitate later reference. This function typically involves chunking the information in some persistent form, such as a textual label or a sketch. There is also some evidence that gestures can help store information, which will be discussed later. An example of using the drawing space to store information is shown on line 16 of the transcript in Figure 4. When S2 perceives that an idea is being proposed, he writes down a label ("slide or tap") at the top of the page.

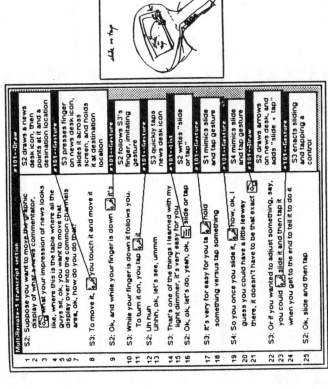

FIGURE 4. Annotated transcript section from a design session. A section of transcript from a design session, annotated with notes describing the episodes of listing, drawing and gesturing that occurred. The marks made in the drawing space during this section are shown at the right.

tapping the icon to activate it. After imitating the gesture, S2 documents this idea as "slide or tap". Meanwhile, the other participants imitate the gesture while S3 continues to elaborate on the idea.

2.2.1. Actions: listing, drawing and gesturing
Listing and drawing are the actions most commonly associated with drawing space activity. List actions result in alpha-numeric text where its spatial location is not of major significance. A simple example of a list action is shown in line 16 of the transcript section in Figure 4, where S2 writes the phrase "slide or tap" at the top of the page. Draw actions result in graphic marks, typically a sketch. A typical draw action is illustrated in line 3 of the transcript, where S2 draws a graphical representation for an icon of a news desk.

Hand gesture actions are more difficult to classify. They are defined as purposeful or intentional hand movements that communicate information. However, for practical reasons, many of the incidental gestures that naturally accompany human dialog (e.g. twiddling a pen, scratching a chin) are not included. The intent is to include hand gestures as a significant drawing-space action without accounting for every hand motion made in the design session. More research is also needed to

Using the drawing space to express ideas is a more interactive use of the drawing space intended for later reference, expressing ideas interactively elicits a response or reaction in the present time. For example, in lines 1–7 of the transcript, S2 draws a sketch of a news desk icon as he asks about how to move icons around on the display screen. Other collaborators enact gestures over it (lines 8 and 19) and S2 adds to the sketch (line 21), demonstrating that it is a working drawing rather than a documentary one. Expressing ideas involves using the drawing space as a working scratchpad to represent and interactively construct ideas with others, or to refine one's own thinking.

The drawing space is also used to mediate the interaction of the group, typically by using it to help negotiate the conversational turn-taking or direct the group's focus of attention. As part of the gesture that is marked in line 11 of the transcript, S3's hand moves deliberately toward the sketch, effectively commanding a turn in preparation for his acting out part of the slide and tap idea. Other forms of focusing attention include pointing to a location, or shifting attention from the group drawing to a personal doodle (demonstrating apparent loss of interest in the conversation).

2.3. USING THE FRAMEWORK IN THE ANALYSIS

In order to explore the utility of the framework, portions of the videotaped data were catalogued according to its action and function categories. For one entire one hour and a half design session and a 10 minute section of a second design session (where the group specified a design for one of their ideas), a log of every instance of drawing space activity was made. Each instance was categorized as to what action (listing, drawing, gesturing) and function (store information, express ideas, mediate interaction) it primarily accomplished. This exercise not only led to a deeper familiarity with the data, but also helped focus the analysis on trends that became apparent in the data. For example, it was observed that over one third of the instances of drawing space activity were categorized as a gesture action, suggesting that hand gestures are a prominent part of drawing space activity. Appendix B includes more details about categorizing and counting drawing space activities.

In attempting to catalogue the observed drawing space activity according to the framework it quickly became apparent that the activity is not accurately described by such clean and distinct categories. Rather, actual activity is composed of a fluent mix of listing, drawing and gesturing, and these actions often accomplish more than one function. Although the framework is a simplified characterization of how the activity actually occurs, it has proven to be a useful perspective from which to study collaborative drawing activity.

3. Resources and hindrances in collaborative drawing activity

The analysis of the videotapes led to identifying specific resources used and hindrances encountered by the participants in collaborative drawing activity. The analysis also suggested a grouping for the categories of the framework that illustrates the resources and hindrances identified. As shown in Figure 6, the framework can be grouped into four areas: conventional view, gestural expression, expressing ideas, and mediating interaction. This grouping highlights three aspects

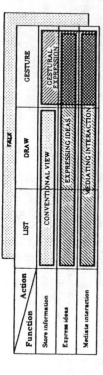

FIGURE 6. Beyond the conventional view of drawing space activity. This organization of the framework illustrates three other aspects of drawing space activity beyond storing information through listing and drawing.

of drawing space activity that go beyond the activities that are conventionally considered to be useful in the drawing space.

The "conventional view" of drawing space activity is characterized by its use to record information in text and graphics to document the work that occurred during a session. In the categories of the framework, this activity translates into storing information through listing text and drawing graphics, as indicated in Figure 6. This view is concerned primarily with the resulting text and graphics, and is typically the extent of drawing activity supported by conventional computer tools (e.g. Computer Aided Design tools, graphic editors, fax machines).

However, the video data illustrate that there are other important aspects of drawing space activity. Hand gestures form a substantial proportion of drawing space activity. These gestures accomplish significant work in the collaborative process, and are not incidental to the activity. Furthermore, the drawing space is frequently used to express ideas, not just document them. The drawing space is also a key resource for mediating group interaction. In order to effectively support collaborative drawing, the design of support tools should account for these additional aspects of drawing space activity.

This organization of the framework helped identify several observations on collaborative drawing activity:

- hand gestures are a significant resource for communicating information;
- the process of creating and using drawings conveys important information not found in the resulting drawings;
- the drawing space is a key resource for mediating the group's interaction;
- collaborators fluently intermix among drawing space actions and functions;
- the spatial orientation among the collaborators and the drawing space structures drawing space activity.

Specific resources and hindrances associated with these observations are discussed in this section.

3.1. THE ROLE OF HAND GESTURES

The prevalence of hand gestures in collaborative drawing activity is obvious. Yet a deeper understanding of what gestures accomplish is needed, especially in considering how to design tools to support them. The use of gesture in face-to-face communication is widely discussed and debated in the literature (McNeill, 1985; Kendon, 1986; Feyereisen, 1987). The research presented here focuses on hand gestures in relation to drawing activity and artifacts in the drawing space.

As highlighted in the framework in Figure 6, hand gestures can be used to accomplish any of the three drawing space functions. Although gestures do not leave behind any persistent record in the drawing space, some evidence suggests they can be used to help store information. In the sessions observed, the participants did not experience any problems in remembering hand gestures later in the session or even in later meetings. One aid for remembering gestures is for other collaborators to imitate a hand gesture. In the transcript represented in Figure 4, S3 demonstrates the "slide and tap" gesture in line 8 and that gesture is imitated by three other collaborators (lines 9, 17 and 19). Gestures can also be documented with a label or a sketch, as in line 21 where S2 draws an arrow next to "slide + tap". Through these techniques, the groups observed managed to preserve the information communicated through their gestures.

Hand gestures are commonly used to express ideas, the second function depicted in the framework. The transcript section shows several examples of gestures (lines 8, 9, 11, 23) that express ideas by enacting a simulation of them. Gestures are particularly well-suited to demonstrating a sequence of actions, such as how a person would interact with a proposed machine. Although enacting simulations is a common use of gesture, most current collaboration technology does not support this use of gesture. Hand gestures are also used to mediate the group's interaction. Pointing to locations often directs the group's attention to a common location, and subtle cues from hand gestures (e.g. waving a hand to take a turn of talk) can help the group negotiate the use of a shared drawing space. These mediating gestures are usually unremarkable and typically do not add new information by themselves. Yet, they play an instrumental role in organizing the group's interaction.

In all of these uses of gesture, it would be difficult to accomplish the same effect in any other way. In this sense, hand gestures are a crucial resource for uniquely accomplishing work in collaborative drawing activity. Further analysis of gestural activity identified specific resources or problems associated with gestures.

An important resource in the use of hand gestures is that they are often enacted in relation to objects in the drawing space, such as an existing sketch. The gestures enacting the "slide and tap" idea (lines 8, 9, 11 and 23 in the transcript) are all done in relation to a sketch on the paper sheet. The sketch provides the context needed for interpreting the actions demonstrated by the gestures. Hand gestures are also conducted in relation to the location of the other people in the group, such as pointing to another participant. These observations indicate that it is important to not only see *gestures*, but to see them *in relation to* the sketches and other objects in the drawing space. The spatial relationship between hand gestures and their referents is a resource used in interpreting collaborative drawing activity.

This resource of gesturing in relation to the drawing space is altered in computer-augmented meeting rooms (Cook, Ellis, Graf, Rein & Smith, 1986; Stefik *et al.*, 1987; Mantei, 1988), where each participant has a personal workstation and these workstations are networked together to allow the group to share images. One aspect of gesturing in relation to sketches can be accomplished using a "telepointer" (Stefik, Brobow, Foster, Lanning & Tatar, 1986), a large cursor that appears on a shared window that any participant can use to point at particular objects in the window. However, telepointing only supports the use of hand gestures to refer to objects in the drawing space. Computer-augmented meeting rooms are unable to support some of the other uses of gesture, such as enacting ideas over a sketch in the drawing space. Participants tend to enact such gestures over their personal workstation screen in front of them, yet the other participants often cannot see these gestures in relation to the referent sketch on the screen.

Another resource in the use of hand gestures is their timing with the accompanying verbal dialog. Hand gestures that express ideas are usually directly accompanied by a verbal explanation of the idea. This direct relationship contrasts with the observation that drawing or listing can be timed to come before, during, after, or without accompanying talk. Since gestures are closely associated with speech, any technology that conveys gestures should avoid disrupting their relationship in time with the accompanying talk.

One problem observed with hand gestures is that sometimes they are not perceived by other group members whose attention is focused elsewhere. Being able to view gestures clearly is often difficult, especially in meetings with many participants. Meetings in computer-augmented rooms that are cluttered with computer equipment, or meetings involving participants in physically remote locations pose greater challenges in sharing gestures. Most current collaborative technology does not adequately convey gestures so that all of the participants can share in viewing them.

3.2. THE IMPORTANCE OF THE PROCESS OF CREATING AND USING DRAWINGS

One of the distinctions that the framework helps reveal is the difference between using the drawing space to store information and using it to express ideas. This contrast between documentary and expressive drawing space activities highlights the relationship between the resulting *artifacts* marked on the drawing space and the *process* of making those artifacts. Typically the goal of storing information is to produce an *artifact* that records information for later recall. The *process* of creating that artifact can be troublesome, since the rest of the group must either wait during that process or can continue working, leaving the documenter behind. However, when expressing ideas, the goal is to enlist the collaboration of the group to develop ideas. Having the group experience and participate in the *process* of creating expressive artifacts is an integral part of expressing ideas.

The importance of experiencing the process of creating and using drawings, especially when expressing ideas, is indicated by the fact that the resulting drawings often do not make sense by themselves. They can only be interpreted in the context of the accompanying dialog or interaction of the participants. This observation is especially apparent with hand gestures, which do not leave behind any persistent artifact, yet do communicate significant information. As can be seen in Figure 4, the resulting marks made in the drawing space do not make much sense without the accompanying dialog and group interaction. It is through the process of seeing how those marks are created and referred to, along with the accompanying verbal explanation, that the group can come to an understanding of what the marks mean. Sharing in the process of creating and using drawings is an important resource that the group uses in order to interpret many of the drawings and gestures produced.

A key resource in the process of creating and using drawings is the timing of activities among the participants. In contrast to storing information, which is often accomplished by a solitary participant, expressing ideas or mediating interaction sometimes involves several people working together in the drawing space. This collaborative process of building on and interactively developing representations in the drawing space often involves fine-grained interactions in time among the participants. Timing a gesture or a drawing with a verbal explanation of it, or timing an activity to coordinate with the activity of other participants, were observed to be important uses of timing. It is in part this familiar sense of timing that enables the group to coordinate the highly engaged, collaborative activity observed in the video data. Timing is a particular concern with computer technology, which can introduce processing and transmission delays that cause the objects appearing on a shared computer screen to fall out of synchrony from the accompanying verbal explanation.

3.3. THE USE OF THE DRAWING SPACE IN MEDIATING INTERACTION

An integral part of collaborative activity is how the group mediates their interaction—how the collaborators take turns talking or how they negotiate sharing a common drawing space. In face-to-face interaction, one key resource that a group uses to help mediate their interaction is a close physical proximity among the collaborators. This proximity allows a peripheral awareness of the other participants and their actions. Many intricate and coordinated hand motions were observed, such as avoiding collisions with other hands or working closely together on a sketch. These coordinated actions demonstrate an awareness of the other participants, enabled by being in close proximity with them.

Often, more than one person at a time was observed to be active in the drawing space, indicating the need for concurrent access to the drawing space. Figure 7 shows how the gestures of S3 and S2 (indicated in lines 8 and 9 in the transcript)

overlap in time. Sometimes participants even wanted to work in the same area of the drawing space at the same time. Since this was physically impossible, one person would have to wait for the other to vacate the drawing area before being able to mark on the paper. Just as overlapping talk occurs as part of smooth turn taking in conversation (Goodwin & Goodwin, 1987), concurrent activity in the drawing space can be a resource for helping the group smoothly negotiate using it.

By having concurrent access to the drawing space, the collaborators can work in parallel, easing bottlenecks such as the time it takes to store information. It is also a resource for reducing the competition for conversational turn taking, since other people can work in the shared drawing space while one person is talking and holding the audio floor. However, this increased parallelism can be a problem because it makes it harder to keep a shared focus as a group. Thus, concurrent access to the drawing space can at times be a problem as well as a resource.

Another resource available in face-to-face interaction is being able to associate the marks being made with the person who is making them. This resource helps the collaborators interpret the resulting marks and mediate their interaction. Knowing who created the marks often provides additional context for making sense of them. Also, actions in the drawing space are often used to bid for a turn in the conversation. Other group members must be able to associate such actions with the person initiating them in order to yield a turn to him or her. In current computer-augmented meeting rooms, it can be difficult to establish the relationship between the marks appearing on a shared computer screen and who is making them.

3.4. THE FLUENT INTERMIXING AMONG DRAWING SPACE ACTIONS AND FUNCTIONS

One resource observed in collaborative drawing activity does not explicitly appear in the framework in Figure 6, but is a direct result from using the framework to study the activity. As mentioned previously, attempting to categorize drawing space activity according to the framework revealed that the activity does not fit exclusively into separate categories. For example, when S2 draws an arrow and writes "slide + tap" (noted in line 21 of the transcript) it is classified primarily as drawing, even though the action also includes writing text. Likewise, drawing and gesturing mix together when S2 draws a picture of the news desk icon and then points at it (line 3). Rapid alternation between writing and drawing was also observed by Bly (1988) in her studies of a pair of collaborators in various workspace environments. The data show that collaborators naturally and fluently intermix listing with drawing and drawing with gesturing. However, most computer tools (e.g. MacPaint), separate text and graphics into different nodes.

Similarly, some of the activity accomplished more than one function. For example, when S3 enacts tapping the icon to activate it (line 11 in the transcript), his gesture also appears to help him take a turn in the conversation. This observation of accomplishing multiple purposes in human interaction is commonly noted in studies of human activity, especially conversation analysis (Goodwin, 1981). Being able to perform more than one function or action at a time is a resource that the collaborators use to smoothly accomplish their work. Personal computer tools that rigidly separate the activity into the various categories, such as graphic editors that

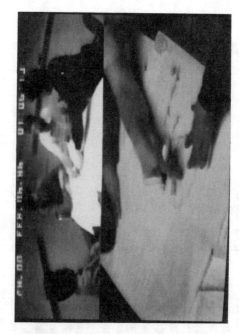

FIGURE 7. Multiple people active in the drawing space. S3 (far right) and S2 (middle) enact gestures at the same time in the drawing space.

separate text and graphics into different modes, often become a hindrance to the user. Such categorization would be even more problematic in collaborative tools.

Tools to support collaborative drawing activity should not rigidly separate the activity into the actions or functions of the framework. Although these categories are descriptive and useful for analysis, they are not prescriptive suggestions for governing the behavior in the drawing space. Collaborators do not shape their drawing activity according to the actions and functions of the framework, and neither should tools to support shared drawing activity.

3.5. THE ROLE OF SPATIAL ORIENTATION TO THE DRAWING SPACE

Spatial orientation with respect to the drawing space was observed to be both a problem and a resource for the collaborators. It is a problem because people seated around a shared drawing space do not see things at the same orientation (see Figure 7). Instead, objects will appear upside-down or at odd angles to various group members. This situation can make it difficult for the group to share a common physical view of the drawing space and to draw in proper orientation relative to existing sketches. This difficulty is especially noticeable when a group member tries to add text to a drawing that is not oriented to be in front of him or her.

However, orientation was also used as a resource in the group's drawing space activity. Sometimes sketches are drawn in relation to existing drawings or facing a particular group member, so as to establish a context and audience for that sketch. Conversely, marks drawn intentionally small and close to oneself effectively place them within a personal boundary not intended for others to perceive. These observations indicate the utility of providing a common view of the drawing space without losing the ways that orientation is meaningfully used.

4. Design implications

Several design implications are suggested by the resources and hindrances observed in collaborative work. The design of tools to support collaborative drawing activity should consider:

- conveying gestures, maintaining their relationship to the drawing space;
- conveying the process of creating and using drawings, with minimal time delay;
- providing concurrent access to the drawing space;
- allowing intermixing among drawing space actions and functions; and
- enabling all participants to share a common view of the drawing space.

Tools should support gestural expression, since gestures constitute a substantial part of drawing space activity and they communicate much information that can not be readily expressed otherwise. Collaborators should be able to see each others' gestures, and see them in relation to the drawing space and the other participants. Conveying gestures is especially relevant in computer-augmented meeting rooms (where the computer equipment can obstruct a clear view of all the participants) and in remote collaboration (where the participants can not directly see each other). Since gestures are often timed with the accompanying speech, audio must be shared among all participants without introducing any delays in timing.

Collaborators need to see not only the resulting marks, but also the process of creating and using those marks. It is through the interactive process of creating and using marks that the collaborators can come to interpret the marks and smoothly negotiate sharing the drawing space. This process must be conveyed among the collaborators with minimal time delay, to enable coordination with the accompanying talk and other activity. The processing and transmission delays that are inherent in current computer systems can disturb the use of timing as a resource to coordinate group work.

Tools should also provide all group members with concurrent access to the drawing space. Concurrent access should be allowed to the point of being able to work in the same drawing area at the same time. The data show examples where this amount of concurrent access might have been useful. Prototype tools that offer this capability should be constructed and observed in use to determine if the benefits of this capability outweigh the problems that are introduced.

The collaborators should be allowed to fluently intermix among the action and function categories of the framework. Conventional computer tools tend to separate actions into different modes (e.g. text from graphics). However, the naturally occurring activity observed does not exhibit such segregation. Especially in collaborative work, with multiple participants engaged in multiple activities, it is important not to introduce any hindrances in moving fluently from one activity to another.

The tools should also enable all collaborators to have a common view of the shared drawing space, allowing them to see the text and graphics created in the shared space in an upright and proper orientation. Sharing a common view allows each participant to easily perceive and add onto marks made by the other collaborators. Collaborators should still be able to use spatial orientation in the drawing space as a resource, to direct work toward a particular audience or denote space for private work. Providing a common view of the shared space while still allowing these uses of spatial orientation needs to be explored.

Some of these design implications have been embodied in two prototype shared drawing tools: Commune (Minneman & Bly, 1990) and VideoDraw (Tang & Minneman, 1990). Elements of these design implications are also exhibited in other tools that can be applied to shared drawing: VIDEOPLACE (Krueger, 1982), SharedARK (Smith, O'Shea, O'Malley, Scanlon & Taylor, 1989), Freestyle (Francik & Akagi, 1989), and TeamWorkStation (Ishii, 1990). More research is needed to study the use of these and other tools in realistic collaborative situations. Analysing the use of these tools will both suggest specific design improvements for the tools and lead to new perspectives on understanding collaborative work.

5. Discussion

Studying collaborative work activity has led to several observations on how collaborators use a shared drawing space:

- hand gestures, and their relationship to the drawing space, convey significant information;
- the process of creating and using drawings conveys important information not found in the resulting drawings;
- proximity and concurrent access to the drawing space are key resources for mediating the group's interaction;

- collaborators fluently intermix among drawing space actions and functions;
- collaborators need to share a common view of the drawing space, but also use spatial orientation to distinguish regions in the drawing space.

These observations indicate that collaborators rely not only on sharing a view of the drawings and surrounding activity, but also need a sense of awareness of the other participants for effective collaboration. The role of hand gestures, the importance of the process of creating and using drawings, and the use of the drawing space to help mediate interaction are only a few elements that contribute to a shared awareness among the collaborators. Continued research to understand what other resources the collaborators use to maintain this awareness is needed in order to build collaborative tools that enable this sense of awareness. This understanding is especially important in considering tools for remote collaboration or computer supported collaboration, where many of the cues available in face-to-face interaction are absent.

Many of these observations involve resources that the participants use to communicate and to mediate their collaboration. Gestures, the process of making drawings, concurrent access to the drawing space, fluent intermixing of drawing space actions, and the ability to associate the marks with who is making them, all contribute to maintaining effective communication and collaboration. Collaborative drawing tools should support or enhance these resources used to coordinate communication and interaction. Yet, with the current elementary understanding of the collaborative process, tools should not attempt to impose a structure to manage this coordination on behalf of the participants. For example, due to design tradeoffs made in some computer-augmented meeting rooms, such as Capture Lab (Mantei, 1988), only one person at a time can be active in the shared computer screen. However, in the actual collaborative drawing activity studied here, concurrent activity in the shared drawing space was observed to be a resource used by the group to help negotiate their collaboration. This resource would be compromised if access to the shared space is restricted to only one person at a time.

People are generally skilled at coordinating their communication and interaction with each other, and how they accomplish this is not well understood. Consequently, tools to support collaboration should not impose a structure that attempts to manage the interaction of the collaborators for them. Instead, tools should facilitate the participants' own abilities to coordinate their communication and collaboration.

Observing collaborative work has led to a better understanding of that activity and to the design of new tools to support it. In turn, observing how these tools are used not only further refines the design of those tools but also leads to new perspectives in understanding collaborative work. By repeatedly cycling through this process of observing, understanding and supporting collaborative activity (see Figure 1), tools that effectively support the work practice of collaborators can be developed.

I thank Larry Leifer for advising and encouraging me through the graduate research on which this work is based. Lucy Suchman provided consistent guidance and support, and introduced me to a new perspective on studying human activity. My thanks to Sara Bly, Austin Henderson, Scott Minneman and Deborah Tatar for their insights and discussions that they shared in this research. I acknowledge Xerox PARC for funding this research, and the members of the Interaction Analysis Lab there for their help in analysing the videotapes. The Center for Design Research at Stanford University and the System Sciences Laboratory at Xerox PARC provided environments that fostered this research.

References

BLY, S. A. (1988). A use of drawing surfaces in different collaborative settings. In Proceedings of the Conference on Computer-Supported Cooperative Work, Portland, Oregon. pp. 250–256.

COOK, P., ELLIS, C., GRAF, M., REIN, G. & SMITH, T. (1986). Project Nick: meetings augmentation and analysis. In Proceedings of the Conference on Computer-Supported Cooperative Work. Austin, Texas, pp. 132–146.

FEYEREISEN, P. (1987). Gestures and speech, interactions and separations: a reply to McNeill (1985). Psychological Review, 94, 493–498.

FRANCIK, E. & AKAGI, K. (1989). Designing a computer pencil and tablet for handwriting. In Proceedings of the Human Factors Society 33rd Annual Meeting Denver, Colorado, pp. 445–449.

GOODWIN, C. (1981). Conversational Organization: Interaction Between Speakers and Hearers. New York: Academic Press.

GOODWIN, C. & GOODWIN, M. J. (1987). Concurrent operations on talk: notes on the interactive organization of assessments. IPRA Papers in Pragmatics, 1, 1–54.

HALASZ, F. G., MORAN, T. P. & TRIGG, R. H. (1987). NoteCards in a nutshell. In Proceedings of the Conference on Computer-Human Interaction and Graphics Interface, Toronto, pp. 45–52.

HEATH, C. (1986). Body Movement and Speech in Medical Interaction. Cambridge, UK: Cambridge University Press.

ISHII, H. (1990). TeamWorkStation: towards a seamless shared workspace. In Proceedings of the Conference on Computer-Supported Cooperative Work, Los Angeles, California, pp. 13–26.

KENDON, A. (1986). Current issues in the study of gesture. In J. L. NESPOULOUS, P. PERRON & A. R. LECOURS, Eds. The Biological Foundations of Gestures: Motor and Semiotic Aspects, pp. 23–47. Hillsdale, NJ: Lawrence Erlbaum Associates.

KRUEGER, M. W. (1982). Artificial Reality. Reading, MA: Addison-Wesley.

LAKIN, F. (1986). A performing medium for working group graphics. In Proceedings of the Conference on Computer-Supported Cooperative Work. Austin, Texas, pp. 255–266. Reprinted (1988) in I. GREIF, Ed. Computer-Supported Cooperative Work: A Book of Readings, pp. 367–396. San Mateo, CA: Morgan Kaufmann.

LEVINSON, S. C. (1983). Conversational structure. In Pragmatics, pp. 284–370. Cambridge, UK: Cambridge University Press.

MANTEI, M. (1988). Capturing the capture lab concepts: a case study in the design of computer supported meeting environments. In Proceedings of the Conference on Computer-Supported Cooperative Work. Portland, Oregon. pp. 257–270.

McNEILL, D. (1985). So you think gestures are nonverbal? Psychological Review, 92, 350–371.

MINNEMAN, S. L. & BLY, S. A. (1990). Experiences in the development of a multi-user drawing tool. In Proceedings of the Third Guelph Symposium on Computer Mediated Communication, Guelph, Ontario, pp. 154–167.

SMITH, R. B., O'SHEA, T., O'MALLEY, C., SCANLON, E. & TAYLOR, J. (1989). Preliminary experiments with a distributed, multi-media, problem solving environment. In Proceedings of the First European Conference on Computer Supported Cooperative Work: EC-CSCW '89, London, pp. 19–34.

STEFIK, M., BOBROW, D. G., FOSTER, G., LANNING, S. & TATAR, D. (1986). WYSIWIS revised: early experiences with multiuser interfaces. In Proceedings of the Conference on Computer-Supported Cooperative Work. Austin, Texas, pp. 276–290. Reprinted (1987). ACM Transactions on Office Information Systems, 5, 147–167.

STEFIK, M., FOSTER, G., BOBROW, D. G., KAHN, K., LANNING, S. & SUCHMAN, L. (1987). Beyond the chalkboard: computer support for collaboration and problem solving in meetings. *Communications of the ACM. 30*, pp. 32–47. Reprinted (1988) in I. Greif, Ed. *Computer-Supported Cooperative Work: A Book of Readings*, pp. 335–366. San Mateo, CA: Morgan Kaufmann.

TANG, J. C. (1989). *Listing, Drawing and Gesturing in Design: A Study of the Use of Shared Workspaces by Design Teams*, Xerox PARC Technical Report SSL-89-3. Ph.d. thesis, Stanford University.

TANG, J. C. & MINNEMAN, S. L. (1990). VideoDraw: a video interface for collaborative drawing. In *Proceedings of the Conference on Computer–Human Interaction*, Seattle, WA. pp. 313–320.

Appendix A

Assignment statement for the design session:

You have been hired as designers and human factors experts to make recommendations on the future (two to five year) directions in user-interface design for hand-held remote controllers for home use. In particular, this manufacturer is interested in integrated, multi-purpose remote controllers that might use a video display for feedback; the display could either be integral with the device or superimposed on television.

Become familiar with the controls and features of the following three sets of devices.
(1) Televisions, Radios, Tape Recorders.
(2) Analog and Digital Clocks.
(3) VCR's, Compact Disk Players, Receivers, Tape Decks, Phonographs and Graphic Equalizers.

Prepare at least two typical scenarios that, between them, exercise at least three different devices (from all devices above).

Model—Prepare a 3-D mock-up of the physical parts of your design.
Story-board—Prepare a story-board that illustrates at least the two scenarios.
Instructions—Prepare an instruction manual or card that, along with the device makes all of its functions self explanatory.

Appendix B

This appendix presents more details about how the drawing space activity was categorized into the actions and functions of the framework and counted. This exercise of categorizing and counting helped identify some trends in the data that focused the analysis. However, categorizing and counting human activity is an inherently subjective process, and the numbers presented in this appendix should be regarded as indicators, not precise measurements.

The drawing activity was first categorized into discrete units of listing, drawing or gesturing. A unit of activity is described as an act of listing, drawing or gesturing accomplished by one participant to express a thought, idea or piece of information to some level of completion. A unit is not defined strictly by mechanical parameters (e.g. pen touches paper, a duration of time). Rather, the activity was categorized according to semantic units (e.g. documenting a phrase, sketching a remote control shape, enacting a control gesture). Several guidelines were used to help determine the boundaries of units of activity:

- It is specific to a participant (i.e. another participant performing a similar activity is logged as a separate unit);
- it may occur in different spurts over a short period of time (e.g. completing a drawing may be interrupted by pausing to talk but still be counted as one unit);
- it is often indicated by cues from the accompanying talk or mechanical behavior (e.g. shifts in the discussion topic, long pauses, laying down the pen).

Incidental activities that naturally accompany talk (e.g. hand waving, graphic marks that have no apparent intent) are not logged as units of activity.

Each workspace activity was categorized according to what action (listing, drawing, gesturing) and function (storing information, expressing ideas, mediating interaction) it primarily accomplished. Many of the observed workspace activities displayed characteristics of more than one category (e.g. an activity that involved both drawing and gesturing, or that both expressed an idea and directed attention). In some cases, these activities were classified into more than one category, to represent their dual nature. Some insights gained from using this framework emerged from the difficulty in classifying drawing space activities into the categories of the framework and accounting for all of the observed activities.

Figure 8 shows the distribution of drawing space activity units according to the categories in the framework. These statistics were collected from a design session that lasted one hour and a half. The data indicate that a substantial proportion (35%) of the activity involved using gestures. Besides using the drawing space to store information, it was used extensively to express ideas and mediate interaction. Hence, the research focused on the use of hand gestures and the process of creating and using drawings in collaborative activity. Tang (1989) reports on more details from this analysis of units of drawing space activities.

Action / Function	LIST	DRAW	GESTURE	Total
Store information	40	19	1	60 (27%)
Express ideas	2	63	33	98 (43%)
Mediate interaction	0	21	46	67 (30%)
Total	42 (19%)	103 (46%)	80 (35%)	225

FIGURE 8. Distribution of drawing space activities in the framework. Drawing space activities from a 1-1/2 hour design session classified according to the actions and functions of the framework.

Int. J. Man–Machine Studies (1991) **34**, 161–184

Twinkling lights and nested loops: distributed problem solving and spreadsheet development

Bonnie A. Nardi and James R. Miller

Hewlett-Packard Laboratories, Human-Computer Interaction Department, 1501 Page Mill Road, Palo Alto, CA 94304 USA

(Received April 1990 and accepted in revised form August 1990)

In contrast to the common view of spreadsheets as "single-user" programs, we have found that spreadsheets offer surprisingly strong support for cooperative development of a wide variety of applications. Ethnographic interviews with spreadsheet users showed that nearly all of the spreadsheets used in the work environments studied were the result of collaborative work by people with different levels of programming and domain expertise. We describe how spreadsheet users cooperate in developing, debugging and using spreadsheets. We examine the properties of spreadsheet software that enable cooperation, arguing that: (1) the division of the spreadsheet into two distinct programming layers permits effective distribution of computational tasks across users with different levels of programming skill; and (2) the spreadsheet's strong visual format for structuring and presenting data supports sharing of domain knowledge among co-workers.

1. Introduction

People organize themselves and their work so that problems can be solved collectively (Vygotsky, 1979; Bosk, 1980; Lave, 1988; Newman, 1989; Seifert & Hutchins, 1989). We are interested in the artifacts that support and encourage this collective problem solving. A spreadsheet is a "cognitive artifact" (Norman, unpublished manuscript; Chandrasekaran, 1981; Holland & Valsiner, 1988; Norman & Hutchins, 1988) that can be understood and shared by a group of people, providing a point of cognitive contact that mediates cooperative work. In this paper we examine the shared development of spreadsheet applications. We report the results of our ethnographic study of spreadsheet use in which we found that users with different levels of programming skill and domain knowledge collaborate informally to produce spreadsheet applications. In the first part of the paper we present a descriptive, empirical report of collaborative work practices, documenting the kinds of cooperation found among spreadsheet users, and the ways in which problem solving is distributed across users with different skills and interests. In the second part of the paper we describe and analyse the characteristics of spreadsheet software that support cooperative work.

In contrast to studies of computer-supported cooperative work (CSCW) that focus on software systems specifically designed to support cooperative work within an organization (Grudin, 1988), we address how a certain class of traditional personal computer applications—spreadsheets—function as *de facto* cooperative work environments. We describe how spreadsheet users work together, even though spreadsheets lack "designed-in" technological support for cooperative work.

We use the term "cooperative work" in the general sense of "multiple persons working together to produce a product or service" (Bannon & Schmidt, 1989). In this paper we want to draw attention to a form of cooperative computing already well established in office environments. As we will describe, spreadsheets emerge as the product of several people working together, through not in formally designated teams, task forces, or committees. On the contrary, spreadsheet work flows across different users in fluid, informal ways, and cooperation among spreadsheet users has a spontaneous, self-directed character.

Our research highlights two forms of cooperative work that are central to computer-based work and that have received little attention in the CSCW community: the sharing of programming expertise and the sharing of domain knowledge. Because of the CSCW emphasis on computer systems that enhance interpersonal communication (e.g. e-mail, remote conferencing, shared white-boards), the importance of collaboration in programming itself has been over-looked. The current interest in "empowering users" through participatory design methods (Bjerknes, Ehn & Kyng, 1987) and end user programming systems (Panko, 1988) will, we believe, begin to draw attention to collaborative programming practices of the kind we describe in this paper. The sharing of domain knowledge has been only implicitly recognized in CSCW research; studies tend to focus on communication techniques themselves, rather than on what is being communicated. In this paper we discuss the implications of the particular visual representation of the spreadsheet for communicating analyses based on numeric data.

Since 1986 about five million spreadsheet programs have been sold to personal computer users (Alsop, 1989). Spreadsheets deserve our interest as the only widely used end user programming environment; text editing and drawing packages are used by many, but involve no programming. With spreadsheets, even unsophisticated users can write programs in the form of formulas that establish numerical relations between data values. Users who show no particular interest in computers *per se* voluntarily write their own spreadsheet programs, motivated by interests beyond or completely unrelated to job requirements—a claim that cannot be made for any other kind of software that we know of. In large part this is because the spreadsheet's "twinkling lights"†—the automatically updating cell values—prove irresistible. Spreadsheet users experience a real sense of computational power as their modifications to data values and formulas appear instantly and visibly in the spreadsheet.

Despite the prevalence of spreadsheets in the personal computing world, spreadsheets have not been widely studied. Kay (1984), Hutchins, Hollan and Norman (1986), and Lewis and Olson (1987) enumerated some of the benefits of spreadsheets which include a concrete, visible representation of data values, immediate feedback to the user, and the ability to apply formulas to blocks of cells. There are some experimental studies of spreadsheet use that focused on small aspects of the user interface; for example, Olson and Nilsen (1987) contrasted the methods by which subjects entered formulas in two different spreadsheet products. (See also Brown & Gould, 1987; Napier, Lane, Batsell & Guadango, 1989.) In

---

† We are indebted to Ralph Kimball of Application Design Incorporated of Los Gatos, California for this turn of phrase.

0020-7373/91/020161 + 24$03.00/0

another type of study, Doyle (1990) reported his experiences of teaching students to use Lotus 1-2-3,† though most of his observations could apply to any kind of software (e.g. inconsistencies in file naming conventions). Other researchers have used spreadsheets as a model for various kinds of programming environments (Van Emden, Ohki & Takeuchi, 1985; Lewis & Olson, 1987; Piersol, 1986; Spenke & Beilken, 1989).

Our study began with the traditional "single-user application" perspective. We were (and still are) interested in spreadsheets as computational devices, and wanted to learn more about how spreadsheets users take the basic structure of a spreadsheet and mould it into an application that addresses some specific need. In particular, we were interested in the success *non-programmers* have had in building spreadsheet applications. We saw no reason to dispute Grudin's (1988) comments that spreadsheets are "single-user applications" in which "an individual's success... is not likely to be affected by the backgrounds of other group members", and that "motivational and political factors" are unimportant for spreadsheet users. However, as the study progressed, we were struck by two things:

- **Spreadsheet co-development is the rule, not the exception.** In the office environments we studied, most spreadsheets come about through the efforts of more than one person. The feeling of co-development is very strong; people regularly spoke of how "we" built a spreadsheet, and were very aware of the cooperative nature of the development process.
- **Spreadsheets support the sharing of both programming and domain expertise.** Because of our focus on end-user programming, we soon noticed that one reason spreadsheet users are so productive is that they successfully enlist the help of other, more knowledgeable users in constructing their spreadsheets. In the same way, experienced co-workers share domain knowledge with less experienced colleagues, using the spreadsheet as a medium of communication.

We do not mean to suggest that spreadsheets are never developed by individual users working completely independently. But presupposing that spreadsheets are "single-user" applications, blinds us to seeing the cooperative use of spreadsheets of which we found much evidence in our study. We will describe how spreadsheet users:

(1) share programming expertise through exchanges of code;
(2) transfer domain knowledge via spreadsheet templates and the direct editing of spreadsheets;
(3) debug spreadsheets cooperatively;
(4) use spreadsheets for cooperative work in meetings and other group settings; and
(5) train each other in new spreadsheet techniques.

We will elaborate these activities via ethnographic examples from the research.

2. Methods and informants

The ideas presented in this paper are based on our ethnographic research including extensive interviewing of spreadsheet users, and analysis of some of their spread-

† Lotus and 1-2-3 are registered trademarks of Lotus Development Corporation.

sheets which we collected during the course of interviewing. We have chosen to study a small number of people in some depth to learn how they construct, debug and use spreadsheets. We are interested in the kinds of problems for which people use spreadsheets and how they themselves structure the problem solving process—topics that by their very nature cannot be studied under the controlled conditions of the laboratory. We have also examined and worked with several different spreadsheet products including VisiCalc (the original personal computer spreadsheet), Lotus 1-2-3 and Microsoft Excel.†

For the field research we interviewed and tape recorded conversations with spreadsheet users in their offices and homes.‡ Our informants were found through an informal process of referral. We told them that we were interested in software for users with little formal programming education and that we wanted to talk to people actively using spreadsheets. The interviews were conversational in style, intended to capture users' experiences in their own words. A fixed set of open-ended questions was asked of each user (see the appendix for the list of questions), though the questions were asked as they arose naturally in the context of the conversation, not necessarily in the order in which they appear in the appendix. During the interview sessions we viewed users' spreadsheets on-line, and sometimes in paper form, and discussed the uses and construction of the spreadsheets. The material in this paper is based on about 350 pages of transcribed interviews with 11 users, though we focus on a smaller subset here to provide ethnographic detail.

Informants in the study were college-educated people employed in diverse companies, from small start-ups to large corporations of several thousand employees. Informants had varying degrees of computer experience ranging from someone who had only recently learned to use a computer to professional programmers. Most were non-programmers with three to five years experience with spreadsheets. Informant names used here are fictitious. Five sets of spreadsheet users illustrate the cooperative nature of spreadsheet development:

† Microsoft and Excel are registered trademarks of Microsoft Corporation.
‡ The interviews were conducted by the first author. We use the plural "we" here for expository ease.
§ All those in our study use either Lotus 1-2-3 or Microsoft Excel.

- *Betty and Buzz* run a start-up company with eight employees. Betty is the chief financial officer of the company and Buzz a developer of the product the company produces. Betty does not have a technical background though she has acquired substantial computer knowledge on her own, largely through using spreadsheets. Buzz is a professional programmer. They use spreadsheets for their customer lists, prospective customer lists, product sales, evaluation units, tradeshow activity and accounts receivable.
- *Ray* manages a finance department for a large corporation and has a large staff. He has an engineering degree and an MBA, and some limited programming experience. He uses spreadsheets to plan budget allocations across several different departments, to track departmental expenses and headcounts, and to forecast future budgetary needs.
- *Louis*, in his seventies, is semi-retired and works as an engineering consultant about two hours a day for a large manufacturing corporation. He has been working with Lotus 1-2-3§ for about a year, and has no other computer experience of any kind (he uses Lotus as his word processor). Louis's main application is analysing test data from his engineering simulations of radar designs. He learned Lotus with the help of his son Peter, an architectural engineer.

- *Laura and Jeremy* work for a medium size high tech equipment manufacturer. Laura is an accountant, the controller of the company. She directs a staff of eight, all of whom use spreadsheets. Laura is knowledgeable about spreadsheets but has no programming experience. Jeremy, Laura's manager, is the chief financial officer of the company. He is skilled at spreadsheet macro and template development.

- *Jennifer* is an accountant in a rapidly growing telecommunications company. She works closely with the chief financial officer of the company. Jennifer has been working with spreadsheets for about five years. She took a course in BASIC in college but has no other computer science education.

Segments from the interviews will be presented at some length as we feel it is most convincing to let users speak for themselves. The segments are verbatim transcriptions.

3. Cooperative development of spreadsheets

3.1. BRIDGING DIFFERENCES IN PROGRAMMING EXPERTISE

Spreadsheets support cooperative work among people with different levels of programming skill. We have found it useful to break the continuum of skill level into three groups: non-programmers, local developers and programmers. Non-programmers have little or no formal training or experience in programming. Local developers have substantial experience with some applications, and often much more willingness to read manuals. Programmers have a thorough grasp of at least one general programming language and a broad, general understanding of computing. Local developers typically serve as consultants for non-programmers in their work environments. Local developers may in turn seek assistance from programmers.

It is also important to note that the three kinds of users vary along another related dimension: *interest in computing.* In some cases non-programmers may be budding hackers, but many are simply neutral towards computers, regarding them as a means to an end rather than objects of intrinsic interest. A key to understanding non-programmers' interaction with computers is to recognize that they are not simply under-skilled programmers who need assistance learning the complexities of programming. Rather, they are not programmers at all. They are business professionals or scientists or other kinds of domain specialists whose jobs involve computational tasks. In contrast, local developers show a direct interest in computing, though their skills may be limited in comparison to programmers as a result of other demands on their time.

Betty and Buzz's work on spreadsheets for their company's finances offers a good example of cooperation among spreadsheet users with different levels of programming skill. As individuals, Betty and Buzz are quite different. Betty has a strong focus on her work as chief financial officer, and claims few programming skills. She has limited knowledge of the more sophisticated capabilities of the spreadsheet product she uses, knows little about the features of competing spreadsheets, and relies on Buzz and other more experienced users for assistance with difficult programming tasks, training, and consulting. In contrast, Buzz has a clear technical focus and strong programming skills. He is well-informed about the capabilities of the spreadsheet product in use in the company and of other competing products, and provides Betty with the technical expertise she needs.

From this perspective, then, Betty and Buzz seem to be the stereotypical end-user/developer pair, and it is easy to imagine their development of a spreadsheet to be equally stereotypical: Betty specifies what the spreadsheet should do based on her knowledge of the domain, and Buzz implements it. *This is not the case.* Their cooperative spreadsheet development departs from this scenario in two important ways:

(1) Betty constructs her basic spreadsheets *without assistance from Buzz.* She programs the parameters, data values and formulas into her models. In addition, Betty is completely responsible for the design and implementation of the user interface. She makes effective use of color, shading, fonts, outlines, and blank cells to structure and highlight the information in her spreadsheets.

(2) When Buzz helps Betty with a complex part of the spreadsheet such as graphing or a complex formula, his work is expressed in terms of Betty's original work. He adds small, more advanced pieces of code to Betty's basic spreadsheet, Betty is the main developer and he plays an adjunct role as consultant.

This is an important shift in the responsibility of system design and implementation. Non-programmers can be responsible for most of the development of a spreadsheet, implementing large applications that they would not undertake if they had to use conventional programming techniques. Non-programmers may never learn to program recursive functions and nested loops, but they can be extremely productive with spreadsheets. Because less experienced spreadsheet users become engaged and involved with their spreadsheets, they are motivated to reach out to more experienced users when they find themselves approaching the limits of their understanding of, or interest in, more sophisticated programming techniques.

Non-programming spreadsheet users benefit from the knowledge of local developers and programmers in two ways:

(1) Local developers and programmers *contribute code* to the spreadsheets of less experienced users. Their contributions may include: macros; the development of sophisticated graphs and charts; custom presentation formats, such as a new format for displaying cell values; formulas with advanced spreadsheet functions such as date-time operations; and complex formulas, such as a formula with many levels of nested conditionals.

(2) Experienced users *teach less experienced users* about advanced spreadsheet features. This teaching occurs informally, not in training classes. Often a user will see a feature in someone else's spreadsheet that they would like to have, and he or she simply asks how to use it.

As shown in the way Betty and Buzz divide up spreadsheet tasks, the problem solving needed to produce a spreadsheet is distributed across a person who knows the domain well and can build most of the model, and more sophisticated users whose advanced knowledge is used to enhance the spreadsheet model, or to help the less experienced user improve spreadsheet skills. Compare this division of labor with traditional computing which requires the services of a data processing department, or expert system development in which knowledge engineers are necessary. In these cases, the domain specialist has no role as a developer, and domain knowledge must first be filtered through a systems analyst, programmer, or knowledge engineer before it is formulated into a program.

Our interview with Ray offers another example of co-development. Ray is a local developer who makes use of programmers for some aspects of spreadsheet development. As with Betty and Buzz, the chief difference between the spreadsheet environment and traditional programming is that more experienced users develop only specific pieces of the spreadsheet program, working directly off the basic work done by the original user. For example, Ray recently commissioned a set of Lotus macros for custom menus to guide data input for the spreadsheets used by his staff. He prefers to concentrate on using spreadsheets for forecasting future trends and allocating money among the departments he serves—his real work. Ray is not interested in becoming an expert macro writer, even though he has taken an advanced Lotus 1-2-3 class where macros were covered. In the following exchange we are looking at the custom menus:

Interviewer: ... [these menus] look like they'd be pretty useful. And who developed those for you?
Ray: A programmer down in Customer Support.
Interviewer: Okay, not somebody in your group. You just sent out the work, and ...
Ray: Yeah, well, essentially, you know, I came at it conceptually, this is what I'd like to see, and they developed it. So [the programmer] made [the menus] interactive, set up the customized use.

Ray has reached the limits of his interest in programming advanced spreadsheet features himself. But he is not limited to spreadsheets without these features; he distributes the work to someone who has more interest in such things. This task distribution is similar to traditional software development in that a user provides a specification to a developer for implementation. The difference, however, is that here the user has constructed the program into which the contributed code fits. In some sense, the roles of user and "chief programmer" (Brooks, 1975) have been merged.

Spreadsheets also support cooperation between users with different programming expertise via tutoring and consulting exchanges. For example, Louis has learned almost everything he knows about Lotus 1-2-3 from his son Peter. He avoids the manual, finding it easier to be tutored by Peter. Louis's spreadsheet use, highlights an important feature of the cooperative development of spreadsheets: because the initial effort to build something really useful is relatively small, less experienced users, having had the reward of actually developing a real application, are motivated to continue to learn more, at least up to a point. Louis is starting to have Peter teach him about controlling the presentation format; for the first several months of use he concentrated only on creating basic models of parameters, data values and formulas. In general, users like Louis successfully engage other, more experienced users in the development of their spreadsheet models. They make use of more experienced users—i.e. more experienced problem-solving resources—in a very productive manner, building on their existing knowledge in a self-paced way, as they feel ready to advance.

Distributing tasks across different users and sharing programming expertise are characteristic of many programming environments—programming in Pascal or Lisp or C would almost certainly involve such collaboration. However, with spreadsheets the collaboration is specified quite differently: the end user, usually relegated to "naive user" status in traditional software development, comes center stage, appearing in the role of main developer. Spreadsheets have been successful because

they give real computational power to non-programmers. Accountants and biologists and engineers who may never have taken a computer science course build useful, often complex spreadsheet applications (Arganbright, 1986). Spreadsheet users are not "naive users" or "novices"; they command knowledge of both their domain of interest and the programming techniques necessary to analyse problems in their domain. With spreadsheets, problem solving is distributed such that end users do not rely on programmers as the indispensable implementers of a set of specifications; instead end users are *assisted by* programmers who supply them with small pieces of complex code, or with training in advance features, as they build their own applications.

4. Bridging differences in domain expertise

An important aspect of cooperative work is the sharing of domain knowledge. Because spreadsheet users build their own applications, spreadsheets allow the direct transfer of domain expertise between co-workers, obviating the need to include a programmer or other outside specialist in the development cycle. Domain knowledge flows from manager to staff since managers tend to be more experienced than those they supervise, and also from staff to manager, as staff members often have specialized local knowledge needed by managers. This direct transfer of domain expertise provides efficient knowledge sharing and helps co-workers learn from one another. Instead of transferring domain expertise to a programmer or systems analyst or knowledge engineer who may never need it again, less experienced workers directly benefit from the knowledge of co-workers.

Spreadsheets mediate collaborative work by providing a physical medium in which users share domain knowledge. Spreadsheet users distribute domain expertise by directly editing each other's spreadsheets, and by sharing templates. For example, Laura works very closely with Jeremy, her manager, in developing spreadsheets. Jeremy happens to be a skilled spreadsheet user who provides macros and tutoring that Laura and her staff use. However, the more interesting distinction to be drawn here is centered around Jeremy's greater experience with their company, its manufacturing and marketing procedures, and its managerial and budgeting practices. Spreadsheets provide a foundation for thinking about different aspects of the budgeting process and for controlling budgeting activity. In the annual "Budget Estimates" spreadsheet that Laura is responsible for, many critical data values are based on assumptions about product sales, costs of production, headcounts, and other variables that must be estimated accurately for the spreadsheet to produce valid results. Through a series of direct edits to the spreadsheet, Laura and Jeremy fine-tune the structure and data values in "Budget Estimates". Laura describes this process:

Interviewer: Now when you say you and your boss work on this thing [the spreadsheet] together, what does that mean? Does he take piece A and you take piece B—how do you divide up [the work]?
Laura: How did we divide it up? It wasn't quite like that. I think more ... not so much that we divided things up and said, "OK, you do this page and you do this section of the spreadsheet and I'll do that section," it was more ... I did the majority of the input and first round of looking at things for reasonableness. Reasonableness means, "What does the bottom line look like?" When you look at the 12 months in the year, do you have some

funny swings that you could smooth out? Because you want it to be a little bit smoother. So what can you do for that? Or, if you do have some funny spikes or troughs, can you explain them? For example, there's one really big trade show that everybody in the industry goes to....So our sales that month are typically low and our expenses are high. This trade show is very, very expensive...

Interviewer: So there's a spike in your [expenses and a trough in sales]...

Laura: Yeah. So as long as you can *explain* it, then that's OK. So what my boss did was, I would do the first round of things and then I would give him the floppy or the print-outs and I'd say, "Well this looks funny to me. I don't know, is that OK, is it normal? Should we try to do something about it?" And so what he did was he took the spreadsheets and then he would just make minor adjustments.

Interviewer: Now was he adjusting formulas or data or...?

Laura: Data.

Interviewer:...So it was a process of fine tuning the basic model that you had developed. And then you of course had to get his changes back, and look at them and understand them.

Laura: Yes. And one thing he did do, was, he added another section to the model, just another higher level of analysis where he compared it to our estimate for this year. He basically just created another page in the model—he added that on.

In preparing a budget that involves guesswork about critical variables, Laura is able to benefit from her manager's experience. They communicate via the spreadsheet as he literally takes her spreadsheet and makes changes directly to the model. She has laid the groundwork, provided the first line of defense in the "reasonableness" checking; Jeremy then adjusts values to conform to his more experienced view of what a good estimate looks like. Jeremy also made a major structural change to the spreadsheet, adding another level of analysis that he felt would provide a useful comparison. The spreadsheet was cooperatively constructed, though not in a simple division of tasks; instead the model emerged in successive approximations as Laura and Jeremy passed it back and forth for incremental refinement.

Spreadsheet users often exchange templates as a way of distributing domain expertise. Jeremy, for example, prepares budget templates used by Laura and her staff. They contain formulas and a basic structure for data that he works out in the because of his greater knowledge of the business. Laura and her staff fill in the templates according to their individual areas. Laura and her staff are doing more than "data entry"; as in the "Budget Estimates" spreadsheet, estimates requiring an understanding of many factors often make up a significant aspect of a spreadsheet, and deriving these estimates demands thought. Users such as Laura may also specialize a template if their particular area requires additional information, such as another budget line item. The use of templates takes advantage of domain expertise at local levels, such as that of Laura and her staff, and higher levels, such as Jeremy's.

Ray's work with spreadsheets provides another example of how users share spreadsheet templates. Ray prepared "targeting templates" for his staff in order to standardize the process of targeting expenses. Because of his wider perspective looking across several departments, Ray is in the best position to develop a standard. The templates also contain the custom menus that facilitate data input. Each staff member builds the spreadsheet for his or her area on top of the template, insuring that minimum requirements for data collection and analysis are met, and

insuring that the best possible information at the local level goes into the spreadsheets. Ray links them together. In these spreadsheets, problem solving is distributed over users who vary in both level of programming skill and domain knowledge: Ray, a local developer with domain expertise, provided the basic template; a programmer created the menus constructed of macros; and Ray's staff members, domain experts in their departments, supply data values for their respective areas.

5. Cooperative use

Many spreadsheets are destined from the start for the boardroom or the boss's desk or the auditor's file. In our study, spreadsheet users were very much aware of the importance of presenting their spreadsheets to others—Laura stated, "I usually think in terms of my stuff [her spreadsheets] as being used by somebody else"—and users constructed spreadsheets with effective presentation in mind.

Spreadsheets are a common sight at meetings and in informal exchanges between co-workers—usually in paper copy or slide format. The use of paper copies and slides of spreadsheets is another means by which co-workers share domain knowledge. Some workers work with spreadsheets exclusively in hardcopy form and are not users of the software—for example executives who analyse and modify paper copies of spreadsheet models prepared by their staff members, and who present spreadsheets on slides and handouts at meetings.

In the following exchange we are discussing a budgeting spreadsheet Jennifer created for her company's chief financial officer. She condensed 43 pages of data from a mainframe application (prepared by the MIS department) into one summary page. We begin by looking at the MIS data:

Jennifer: These are the budget numbers. And then it shows the detail of what was purchased against those budget numbers, and when and how much month-to-date and year-to-date against those. And it shows the actual [amount] spent and variance from the budget.

Interviewer: And this really does have a lot of detail—it's down to the fabric on the chairs.

Jennifer: Uh huh, ha!...everybody wants to know what we spent our money on, and, "How much do we have left?"

Interviewer: Now what do you do with this information?

Jennifer:...we have a presentation for the Board of Directors and the CFO [Chief Financial Officer] makes, but I prepare all this information for him. I compile this. I condense it onto a spreadsheet....So I summarize the larger items, say, you know, the H-P 3000 [a Hewlett-Packard computer recently purchased by her company] for example. That's one of the big items that I pull out....The Board of Directors does not want to see [a lot of] detail—they just want something very summarized....So now it's down from 43 pages to one page. So mine shows the year-to-date budget....but it's all summarized into large dollar value items within each functional area.
...

Interviewer: Now what happens...when they go into the meeting and the CFO presents it? Does he explain it to the Board of Directors, or just put it up on a slide, or, what do they do with this?

Jennifer:...he hands out a copy to everybody, and then he puts it up on a slide, and he goes through each of the areas where they are going to be over [-budget]. And he was also presenting this so he could get approval for next quarter's budget....he was showing them the....Q3 [Third Quarter] forecast column, and saying, "Okay, that is how much we will need to approve it." And, "Where are we going from here?" Also, "What are we anticipating?"

The spreadsheet artifact is used by the CFO to organize and stimulate discussion in the Board of Directors meeting. The structures and cell values of the spreadsheet are meaningful to the board members; for example, the CFO points to the "Q3 forecast column" and individual data values such as the number showing "how much we need to approve (the Q3 budget)." Larger issues, e.g. "Where are we going from here?" are also introduced in the context of viewing the spreadsheet in the meeting.

Later in the interview Jennifer describes how the summary spreadsheet was created. The creation of this spreadsheet is an example of cooperative development; we include it here to show how development and use flow together as users collaborate in creating a spreadsheet whose ultimate purpose is a presentation to others. The final spreadsheet presented to the Board was the result of quite a multi-media production: Jennifer created the original spreadsheet in Excel, gave a paper copy to the CFO for his input, made pencil annotations on another paper copy because the CFO's changes came back via voice mail, and finally updated the on-line spreadsheet:

Interviewer: ... What are your little pencil scribbles on here [a paper copy of the one-page spreadsheet]?
Jennifer: Oh, this is what I gave to the CFO at first, just comparing Q2 year-to-date budget to Q2 year-to-date actuals. And he said, "Well, for the board meeting I want [some other things]". Every time you do this he wants it differently. So I can't anticipate it. I just give him what I think [he wants] and then he says, "Ah, no, well, I want to have projected Q3 and projected Q4, and then total projected, and then have the whole year's plan on there". So that is what I was scribbling on here.
Interviewer: Was this in a meeting with him where he was telling you?
Jennifer: Actually he sent me a voice mail message. So that is why I take notes and go back and listen to the message again and say, "Now did I write this down right?"

Laura also described the use of spreadsheets in meetings. Her comments show that the spreadsheet organizes discussion, as we have seen in the preceding example. She notes the clarifications required to reveal assumptions underlying the spreadsheet models. Making such clarifications is often a part of meetings where spreadsheets are presented. Some spreadsheet users, including Laura, attach memos which list their assumptions (e.g. a budget allocation is based on department revenue not headcount). In the following discussion Laura describes a meeting she attended where executives are poring over spreadsheets and memos:

Laura: ...So he [the president of the company] is sitting there and he's looking at [the spreadsheets and memos], and you're just kind of sitting there [she mimics slumping over in boredom, waiting for the president to ask a question] and he refers back and forth to various pages, whether he's looking at the budget [a spreadsheet] or whether he's looking at the last year's actuals [a spreadsheet] or he's looking at a list of assumptions.
Interviewer: So he looks at all of them?
Laura: That's right Yeah...And occasionally he asks a question and you say, "Oh, okay, that's this here. [She points to an imaginary spot of importance on the spreadsheet.] And you know here's this and this. And *this* was the [she waves her hand indicating a phrase like "such-and-such"] and *that* was because of [another gesture], or, "Oh, I didn't think about that!"

Laura explains how spreadsheets are used in distributed locations:

Laura: ...And also another thing that's really classic, I mean I've experienced this before [at other jobs], is you do about as much as you can...and then he [the executive] gets on the airplane to go to England [or wherever] and he's on a plane for 10 or 12 hours and he looks at [the spreadsheets] again. And he's totally uninterrupted. ...And he probably has more space up there than he does in his office! And then...they'll get where they are [going] and either phone call or fax.
Interviewer: To ask you a question?
Laura: Yeah. To get an explanation, or more detail, or "What did you say here? What did you assume there?"

...

Laura: [Last year my boss and I spent a lot of time on a large spreadsheet that had to be faxed.]...We had to make some modifications in the spreadsheet...to add more types of expenses, or break things out into more detail. And we sat there together sort of hunched around the screen. We had to fax about 40 [pages of print-out]. No, it was more than that. We faxed a hundred pages to England one night...because they had to have it. They needed to have it prior to the meetings.
Interviewer: Wow.
Laura: So they would have an opportunity to digest it and come up with their list of questions.

As the descriptions show, though the spreadsheet provides a great deal of useful data, and is meaningful to the executives and others who use them, it does not fully expose all the assumptions in a model. However, the necessary verbal explanations are quickly produced (as in the faxed spreadsheet followed up by phone calls) because the spreadsheet developers are also the domain experts—there is no need to involve programmers or MIS personnel. While spreadsheets could benefit by better facilities for exposing assumptions, the spreadsheet artifact works as well as it does because users themselves control the process of putting information into spreadsheet models. Problem solving is handled locally, without requiring the intervention of personnel from other work groups—especially valuable, as Laura described, in fighting last minute fires.

A rather emblematic example of the cooperative use of spreadsheets is provided by Louis's meticulous black binder of spreadsheet print-outs that he carries between home (where his computer is) and office (where he has meetings). Although Louis's current spreadsheets contain none of the advanced presentation features provided by spreadsheet products (because he is just learning them), the simple print-outs are a regular feature of Louis's meetings with his colleagues as they discuss new designs for radar. It is a major benefit for Louis, an unsophisticated spreadsheet user, that the development environment and the presentation environment are the same in spreadsheets; once Louis has programmed his model, he has also created an effective presentation for group discussions, with no additional work.

Though users developing spreadsheets sometimes viewed each other's spreadsheets on-line, we found no extended examples of cooperative use of on-line spreadsheets, e.g. for the duration of a meeting. Hardcopies were virtually always used, and seemed to work well since the contents of the spreadsheets were being studied not manipulated. Productive uses of on-line spreadsheets are easily imagined, e.g. organizing a meeting around trying out different what-if scenarios and projecting the spreadsheet views overhead.

6. Cooperative debugging

In an experiment, Brown and Gould (1987) found that almost half of all spreadsheets constructed by experienced spreadsheet users contained errors. Most errors were in the formulas. Formula errors were most commonly caused by inserting erroneous cell references into formulas (pointing to the wrong cell or typing the wrong cell reference); incorrectly copying a formula so that the new formula got erroneous cell references; and putting the wrong item in a column. It is difficult to know how representative these specific types of errors are because the data consisted of only 11 formula errors, out of a total of 17 errors across the nine subjects in the study (each subject committed at least one error in at least one of the three spreadsheets they constructed for the study). It does seem likely that formula errors are more common than data entry errors since much more can go wrong in a formula.

While Brown and Gould's finding seems generally valid, if it were taken out of context—that is, out of the context of the experimenter's laboratory—it could be misinterpreted to suggest that spreadsheets in actual use are full of errors. In our study we found that users devote considerable effort to debugging their spreadsheet models—they are very self-conscious about the probability of error and routinely track down errors before they can do any real harm. Spreadsheet users specifically look for those errors that could have serious consequences. For example, a spreadsheet model with a value for department headcount that is off by one would probably have some budgetary or political implications, whereas being off by one in a forecast of annual budget dollars would not.

Debugging is a task that is distributed across the group—in particular, managers monitor their staffs' spreadsheets. Cooperation is valuable in error correction tasks (in many settings) as errors that become, through over-familiarity, invisible to their authors, are readily apparent when subject to the fresh scrutiny of new viewers.

In the following exchange we are discussing sources of error in the spreadsheets prepared by Ray's staff. Ray checks these spreadsheets himself. He uses "reasonableness checks" (inspecting values to see that they fall within reasonable ranges); footing and cross-footing;† spot checking values with a calculator; and examining formulas, recording the results of the formula checking with pencil and paper:

Interviewer: [Are the staff errors] usually in the data entry of the formulas, or does it vary?
Ray: It's mostly in the formulas. Because I think everybody is careful about making sure they have tie numbers‡ so that you can get the data in. I'm not saying it doesn't happen in data entry, but I think usually it's the formulas that are suspect. Either it's a question of the right kind of formula, or it's a situation where they weren't really careful in terms of ... what comes first, and link it to what, and that sort of thing, they've got to be careful in that.
Interviewer: [It sounds like] you guys are pretty careful about checking things.
Ray: Yeah, we're pretty careful. Where I think it can get a little difficult is when you have a really large spreadsheet—it's a big model or something—and sometimes it's difficult to check, you know, a pretty extensive spreadsheet.
Interviewer: You mean because of the volume of data, or volume of formulas? What is it about the size that makes it harder?
Ray: You got a tremendous amount of formulas in there that are pointing all kinds of different directions, and you know, it's a pretty big pass to kind of walk back through the whole thing. So you have to be very careful.

† Making sure that the sum of row totals matches the sum of column totals.
‡ A tie number is a known quantity; it provides a sort of anchor within the spreadsheet. If a tie number is incorrect, dependent values are sure to be wrong (unless, by rare chance, incorrect values cancel each other out).

Here Ray noted the difficulty of tracing relations through large spreadsheets ("formulas that are pointing all kinds of different directions"). He finds that while his analysts are generally careful, there is room for error, so he does some checking.

Other informants described similar procedures for catching errors. Laura, for example, described how she verifies cell references in formulas by writing them down and tracing them to their origin in the spreadsheet. Like Ray, she noted that a major source of errors in spreadsheets is complex formulas in large spreadsheets.

Norman (1987) and Seifert and Hutchins (1989) argue that error in the real world is inevitable. Seifert and Hutchins (1989) studied cooperative error correction on board large ships, finding that virtually all navigational errors were "detected and corrected within the navigation team." The errors in spreadsheets could be at least a little less "inevitable" with improvements to spreadsheet software such as views showing cell relations more clearly (perhaps through the use of color, highlighting and filtering), and mechanisms to constrain cell values to allow range and bounds checking. Even with improvements, however, there would still be need for vigilance to eliminate errors, which are, as Norman, Seifert and Hutchins point out, inevitable in the real world. For spreadsheet debugging, as for tasks in other rather different domains (such as navigating large ships), a key part of the error correction solution lies in distributing the work across a group.

7. How spreadsheets support cooperative work practices

We have documented in some detail how spreadsheet users develop, debug and use spreadsheets cooperatively. We now examine the spreadsheet itself, focusing on the support for cooperative work implicit in its design. Though spreadsheets were not deliberately designed to support cooperative work, they nevertheless have two key characteristics that enable collaboration:

(1) Spreadsheet functionality is divided into two distinct programming layers—a *fundamental layer* and an *advanced layer*—that provide a basis for cooperative programming. By cleanly separating basic development tasks from more advanced functionality, the spreadsheet permits a distribution of tasks in which end users accomplish the basic implementation of a spreadsheet model, and those with more sophisticated programming knowledge provide smaller, more advanced contributions in the form of code and training. The notion of "layers" is intended to capture the different aspects of spreadsheet functionality as they relate to the user's tasks of *learning and using spreadsheets*.†

(2) The visual clarity of the spreadsheet *table* exposes the structure and intent of users' models, encouraging the sharing of domain knowledge across users with different levels and kinds of domain knowledge.

7.1. THE SPREADSHEET'S PROGRAMMING LAYERS

How do spreadsheets both meet the needs of the non-programmer and allow for the development of sophisticated applications? The answer lies in the articulation of the two programming layers: the fundamental layer, sufficient for constructing basic

† The layers do not map onto any aspect of the implementation of a spreadsheet product, or a manufacturer's description of a product.

programs, is completely self-contained and independent from the advanced layer of more sophisticated features.

The fundamental layer allows users to build basic spreadsheet models that solve real problems in their domain of interest. Users who know nothing about the advanced layer can create spreadsheets. In our study, Louis was such a user; his work was accomplished entirely within the fundamental layer, and he was just beginning to explore the advanced layer. Once users have grasped the fundamental layer, they learn the advanced layer. The advanced layer is composed of a variety of individual features that can be learned and used separately. Progress in learning advanced spreadsheet features may be very fast or very slow, depending on the user.

Because the features of the fundamental and advanced layers are independent and separately manipulated, the end user can proceed with the main programming of a spreadsheet, leaving more advanced development to local developers or programmers, or learning advanced features when they are needed. We have seen how Ray drew the line at writing macros for data entry, assigning the task to a programmer.

We now look in more detail at the fundamental and advanced layers.

7.1.1. The fundamental layer

To solve a problem with a spreadsheet, the user requires facilities for *computation, presentation* and *modeling*. The fundamental layer meets these needs. It is composed of two parts: the *formula language*† which enables computation; and the spreadsheet *table* which provides both a means of structuring data into a model, and a presentation format.

The formula language allows users to compute values in their models by expressing relations among cell values. Each cell value may be a constant or a derived value. A formula is associated with the individual cell whose value it computes. The formula language offers a basic set of arithmetic, financial, statistical and logical functions. To use the formula language, the user must master only two concepts: cells as variables, and functions as relations between variables. The simple algebraic syntax of the formula language is easy to write and understand.

In our study we found that most users normally use fewer than 10 functions in their formulas. Users employ those functions pertinent to their domain (e.g. financial analysis) and do not have need for other functions. Spreadsheet users are productive with a small number of functions because the functions provide *high-level, task-specific operations that do not have to be built up from lower level primitives*. For example, a common spreadsheet operation is to sum the values of a range of cells within a column. The user writes a simple formula that specifies the sum operation and the cells that contain the values to be summed. The cell range is specified compactly by its first and last cell; e.g. SUM(C1:C8) sums cells 1–8 in Column C. In a general programming language, computing this sum would require at least writing a loop iterating through elements of an array, and creating variable names for the loop counter and summation variable. Spreadsheet functions obviate the need to create variable names (cells are named by their position in the grid), and

† We refer to "the formula language" because most spreadsheet products have nearly identical languages which differ only in small syntactic details.

the need to create intermediate variables to hold results—non task-related actions that many users find confusing and tiresome (Lewis & Olson, 1987).

Once the user has created some variables and established their relations in formulas, the spreadsheet takes care of the rest. It is responsible for automatically updating dependent values as independent values change. There is no programming effort necessary on the part of the user to make this happen. The spreadsheet user's task is to write a series of small formulas, each associated with an individual cell, rather than the more difficult task of specifying the full control loop of a program as a set of procedures.

The spreadsheet table solves the presentation problems of the basic spreadsheet application. The cells of the table are used to present data values, labels and annotations. In the process of developing the spreadsheet, i.e. entering the data, labels and annotations into the table, the user is at the same time creating the user interface, at no additional development cost. Even a very simple table with no use of color or shading or variable fonts for cell entries is an effective visual format for data presentation (Jarvenpaa & Dickson, 1988; Cameron, 1989; Hoadley, 1990, Nardi & Miller, 1990.

Spreadsheet users must be able to represent the structure of the problem they are trying to solve. The spreadsheet table is a structuring device: the main parameters of a problem are organized into the rows and columns of the spreadsheet, and constants and calculated values are placed in cells. Rows and columns are used to represent the main parameters of a problem. Users know that related things go in rows and columns, and spreadsheet applications take advantage of the simple but powerful semantics provided by the row/column convention. Each cell represents and displays one variable. For calculated values, the spreadsheet associates a visual object, the cell itself, with a small program, the formula. Program code is this distributed over a visual grid, providing a system of compact, comprehensible, easily located program modules (Nardi & Miller, 1990).

What distinguishes the fundamental layer of spreadsheets from the operations a beginner user might learn in a general programming language? First, the high-level facilities for computation, modeling and presentation that we have described shield users from the necessity of working with lower level programming primitives. Users can concentrate more fully on understanding and solving their problems, with much less cognitive overhead devoted to the distraction of coping with the mechanics of the software itself.

Second, because the spreadsheet has so much "built-in" functionality (automatic update, the table as a presentation device), and a high-level language (the formula language), it takes only a few hours for non-programmers to learn to build simple spreadsheet models that solve a real problem in their domain of interest. After a small investment of time, the beginning spreadsheet user has a functioning program of real use (not a toy program or completed exercise), and also an effective visual representation of the application. The spreadsheet user's first efforts yield a complete application, rather than the partial solution that would result from writing the same application in a general programming language. The fast, early success spreadsheet users' experience motivates them to continue to use the software (Nardi & Miller, 1990; Warner, 1990; also Brock, personal communication; Flystra, personal communication).

learn them when they wish to. Very slow progress in learning features of the advanced layer does not impede the user's ability to do constructive work. Spreadsheets provide a self-paced course of study because the features of the advanced layer are inessential for basic application development and independent of other functionality.

Over time, the distribution of problem solving tasks of an individual user changes; users take on new development tasks as they acquire knowledge of additional spreadsheet functionality. For example, Jeremy described how he "discovered" macro programming. Jeremy is an executive—the chief financial officer of his company—and has never taken a computer science class. He received his MBA from Harvard Business School just prior to the time when quantitative methods (including mandatory instruction in the use of spreadsheets) were introduced into the curriculum. In the following discussion Jeremy explains how he learned about macros from reading the Lotus 1-2-3 manual and talking to programmers. We are examining one of his macros that selects files for printing and sets up printing parameters. The macro utilizes a counter, branching, and binary variables that can have 0 or 1 as values. We have been looking at each line of the macro in detail:

Jeremy: . . . And then [the macro] compares [this variable] with the counter over here.
Interviewer: So this is real programming, basically.
Jeremy: Yes, right! And unfortunately that's what I had to do for me to be able to do this. It is exactly—a program. . . . I found that out later. I didn't realize [that I was programming]. I thought I was being very clever—I was inventing something new!
Interviewer: How did you find out later? Talking to other programmers?
Jeremy: Yeah, well, exactly. I was talking to our programmer, he came over and I showed him, "Look what I've done!" And he looked at me and he says, "Well, any time you want to be a rookie programmer on my staff, you just passed, you just made the grade".
Interviewer: But you were actually able to figure out how to do this by looking at examples in the manual?
Jeremy: That's right. Yeah, because I just mapped out: What is it that I want to do? . . . What I would like to do is to have a series of instructions and have the macro search for those instructions, and based on certain yes/no conditions either perform the operation or go to the next step. That's really all I'm after. And so I kept on looking for [branching mechanisms], and once I found them in the book I found so many different places where I could use them.

There is a gradual tendency for end users to include more complex features in their spreadsheets and to utilize local developers and programmers less. It should be remembered however, that this process may be very gradual, and would not happen at all for many users if they did not have an easy route of entry through the fundamental layer. In contrast, many students resist the frustration and tedium of learning general programming languages and do not become adept at programming in them.

In our study, spreadsheet users most commonly learnt new spreadsheet functionality in collaboration with other users. The non-programmers were extremely resistant to reading manuals (in contrast to local developers like Jeremy who kept searching the manual till he found what he wanted). Non-programmers commented that the manuals often did not explain everything they needed to know to actually use the feature they were trying to learn about. Since this meant that they would

7.1.2. The advanced layer

The advanced layer of the spreadsheet provides functionality that is unnecessary for constructing a basic spreadsheet model. We call its features "advanced" because basic work proceeds without them, not because they are necessarily difficult to learn.

The features of the advanced layer are inessential for basic work, but very useful. They are: conditional and iterative control constructs; macros; advanced functions such as database, date-time, and error trapping functions; graphs and charts; and a user interface toolkit. Each part may be learned and used completely independently of any other part. Some of the advanced capabilities are very easy to learn, such as how to change column width (the first thing Louis was learning), and others are more difficult, such as the use of macros (well-understood by Buzz and Jeremy, used in simple form by Jennifer, understood but avoided by Ray, and not known by Louis, Betty and Laura).

Users learn selected parts of the advanced layer as they need them, and as they feel ready to. Some users in our study could build a spreadsheet and significantly modify the user interface after a day-long training class, and others did nothing but build basic spreadsheets using only the formula language and modeling capabilities of the spreadsheet for several months before learning anything else. Most users do not know all the aspects of the advanced layer.†

The control constructs in the advanced layer of the spreadsheet are simple but useful. They allow users to write IF-THEN-ELSE statements within an individual formula, and to iterate functions over a cell range (a rectangular group of contiguous cells).

The user interface toolkit gives users control over column width, row height, fonts, shading, outlining, color and formatting of cell values (though not all spreadsheet products provide all of these capabilities). Spreadsheets allow users to split the screen so that non-contiguous portions of a spreadsheet may be viewed at once. The graphing and charting capabilities provide graphic views of the individual data values in the cells of the spreadsheet table. Macros allow users to reuse sequences of keystokes. "Advanced" macros provide more general facilities for data and file manipulation, screen control and controlling interaction with the user during macro execution (e.g. in Lotus 1-2-3, the macro command "GETLABEL" displays a prompt in a control panel, waits for the response to the prompt, and enters the response as a label in a cell). The advanced macros are much like traditional programming functions, but they are stored, loaded, edited and manipulated like other spreadsheet macros.

As we have noted, advanced spreadsheet features often find their way into the spreadsheets of non-programmers as code written by more skilled users. Many users reach the limits of their interest in learning advanced features, at least certain ones such as macros, and do not learn to use them. But spreadsheets also provide a growth path for those interested in continuing to learn. Because the individual features of the advanced layer are independent of one another, users can selectively

† We had the fun of stumping Buzz, during an interview, with our knowledge of the IRR—internal rate of return—function in Excel.

have to ask someone to supply the missing information anyway, it seemed easier to ask at the outset.†

Several users in the study, even after learning many aspects of the advanced layer, still relied on more experienced users to show them how to do new things.

7.2. THE SPREADSHEET TABLE

The strong visual representation of an application embedded in the spreadsheet table allows users to directly share domain knowledge through templates and direct edits to the spreadsheets of others, and to collectively use spreadsheets in meetings and other exchanges. Users are able to understand and interpret each other's models with relative ease because the tabular format of the spreadsheet presents such a clear depiction of the parameters and data values in spreadsheet applications.

Spreadsheets have done well at data display by borrowing a commonly used display format—that of the table. Cameron (1989) pointed out that tables have been in use for 5000 years. Inventory tables, multiplication tables and tables of reciprocal values have been found by archaeologists excavating Middle Eastern cultures. Modern times brought us VisiCalc, in tabular format. VisiCalc was modeled directly on the tabular grid of accountants' columnar paper which contains numbered rows and columns. Today's spreadsheets, while much enhanced in functionality, have not changed the basic VisiCalc format in the smallest detail. A tabular grid in which rows are labeled with numbers and columns are labeled with letters characterizes all commercially available spreadsheets.

Tables excel at showing a large amount of data in a small space and in helping users to identify individual data values (Jarvenpaa & Dickson, 1989)—precisely what is needed for spreadsheet applications because they contain many numeric values, each of which may be important to understanding an application. The perceptual reasons that tables so effectively display discrete data items are not well understood. Cleveland suggests that the notion of "clustering"—the ability to hold a collection of objects in short-term memory and carry out further visual and mental processing—applies to many visual forms (Cleveland, Unpublished data), and it seems relevant to tables. The arrangement of data items in rows and columns appears to permit efficient clustering as users can remember the values in a row or column and then perform other cognitive tasks that involve the values.

The semantics of rows, columns and cells are agreed upon and well understood by spreadsheet users. Because tables are so commonly used to display data of many kinds, most spreadsheet users are already familiar with them. Jarvenpaa and Dickson (1988) noted that many people must be taught to correctly interpret

† Manuals may be confusing at a more fundamental level. Louis gave up completely on manual reading (getting his son Peter to tutor him instead) when he could not figure out the sense in which the word "default" was being used in his Lotus 1-2-3 documentation. (Louis had a rather old copy of the manual, and the newer Lotus 1-2-3 manuals may be less confusing.) The meaning did not jibe with what he understood "default" to mean, nor with the dictionary definition, which, puzzling over the manual, he looked up. During our interview he showed us the definition. Webster's Ninth New Collegiate Dictionary defines default as "failure to do something required by duty or law"; also failure to appear in court, to pay a debt, meet a contract, or agreement, or failure to compete in or finish an appointed contest. Louis' confusion is understandable.

plotted line graphs, but most people are already practised at understanding tables. Users readily comprehend that in a spreadsheet, rows and columns are used to represent the main parameters of a model, and each cell represents and displays one variable. In looking at the spreadsheets of co-workers, the conventions of rows, columns and cells permit users to interpret the intentions of the developer.

Spreadsheets fare less well at clearly exposing the formulas underlying the cell values in the table. As we described in our discussion of debugging, checking a formula from a co-worker's spreadsheet (or from one's own spreadsheet for that matter) involves an awkward pencil and paper procedure of tracking down and verifying cell references in the formulas.† In our study we found that users do follow the pencil and paper procedures to ensure that formulas are correct, but many users cited the necessity of doing this as their main complaint about spreadsheets.

8. Implications for computer supported cooperative work

Our research focused on a single cognitive artifact—the spreadsheet. In the course of examining its structure, following it into meetings, finding out how people use it to solve certain kinds of problems, we learned two things of broad interest to CSCW research:

(1) As users gain more control over computational resources through the use of end user programming systems, cooperative work practices should be anticipated and taken advantage of by designers of such systems. Users will inevitably vary in their skill level, and computational tasks can be distributed over users with different skills through the sharing of code and training.

(2) One of the most fundamental reasons to engage in any kind of cooperative work is to share domain knowledge. Software systems that provide a strong visual format which exposes the structure and data of users' problem-solving models will support and encourage the exchange of domain knowledge.

End user software systems must provide basic development capabilities for non-programmers—what has made spreadsheets so successful is putting computational power into the hands of domain experts. In this distribution of computing tasks, development is shifted away from programmers; they supply limited but technically advanced assistance to developer/domain experts.

The layered design of spreadsheet software seems a good model for other software systems—the ability to build complete, if simple, models with basic, easily learned functionality is the key to getting users off to a quick, rewarding start. The spreadsheet provides for distributed programming by separating the basic functionality of the fundamental layer from the useful but unnecessary features of the advanced layer. End user programming systems should take advantage of the fact that local developers and programmers can reinforce and extend the programs of non-programmers through cooperative work practices—users need not be limited by their lack of programming sophistication.

Non-programmers attain rapid proficiency with the functionality of the fundamental layer because its operations are high-level and task-specific. This implies

† Some spreadsheet products provide views of the table in which the formulas are shown instead of cell values. This has its uses, but is not sufficient for formula verification because the cell values are no longer visible, and long formulas are truncated.

that end user programming systems must develop rather domain specific languages and interaction techniques whose operations will make sense to some particular set of users. The requirement that user programming languages be task-specific, contrasts sharply with the commonly advocated proposal to empower end users by helping them acquire competence in using general programming languages (Lewis & Olson, 1987; Maulsby & Witten, 1989; Neal, 1989). In general, we feel that users should be supported at their level of interest, which for many is to perform specific computational tasks within their own specialized domain, not to become computer programmers.

Just as spreadsheets distribute problem solving tasks *across* users differently than traditional computing, there is a different temporal distribution of tasks taken on by an individual user. Some users go on, over time, to learn and use new spreadsheet features (often very slowly)—in contrast to those who completely give up on general programming languages. Once users have successfully developed their own applications, they can begin to add new software techniques to their repertoire as they are ready. Through collaborations with more experienced users, spreadsheet users progress into the advanced layer. It is precisely because users have been supported by a high-level, task-specific software system that allowed them to get their work done and to experience a sense of accomplishment that they can then make progress, if they choose, in learning more general techniques. When spreadsheet users learn macros or the use of conditional and iterative facilities or formatting tricks, they venture into the realm of general programming. Such learning may occur in glacial time from the perspective of an experienced programmer, but perhaps that is appropriate for users whose primary accomplishments lie outside the field of programming.

Spreadsheets succeed because they combine an expressive high level programming language with a powerful visual format to organize and display data. Because the spreadsheet table so clearly exposes the structure and content of spreadsheet applications, co-workers easily and directly exchange domain knowledge. The shared semantics of the table facilitate knowledge transfer between co-workers; the very structure of the rows, columns and cells of the table transmits a great deal of information.

The lesson to be learned from the tabular structure of the spreadsheet is that simple, familiar visual notations form a good backbone for many kinds of scientific, engineering and business applications. Visual notations are based on human visual abilities such as detecting linear patterns or enclosure, that people perform almost effortlessly. Many diagrammatic visual notations such as tables, graphs, plots, panels and maps have been refined over hundreds if not thousands of years (Tufte, 1983; Cameron, 1989). They are capable of showing a large quantity of data in a small space, and of representing semantic information about relations among data. Like the spreadsheet table, these visual notations are simple but expressive, compact but rich in information.

We expect to see computer-based versions of tables, graphs, plots, panels and maps evolve into more sophisticated visual/semantic mechanisms, utilizing knowledge-based representations and interactive editing and browsing techniques such as filtering and fish-eye views (Furnas, 1986; Ciccarelli & Nardi, 1988). Today, visual notations are commonly used for display purposes, but it is less common for

users to be able to manipulate their components—to be able to ask about the values behind a point on a plot, for example, or to expand a region on a map to show more detail. It is even less common for these displays and their components to possess any semantic information about their relationships to other displays or components—for example, constraints between specific values, or the mapping from one notation to another.

Visual notations with well-defined semantics for expressing relations will provide useful reusable computational structures. Filling a middle ground between the expressivity of general programming languages and the particular semantics of specific applications, they represent a fairly generic set of semantic relations, applicable across a wide variety of domains. New visual notations are possible and useful as Harel (1988) has shown with his work on statecharts. Statecharts formally describe a collection of sets and the relationships between them. Although Harel's work is quite new, Bear, Coleman and Hayes (1989) have already created an interesting extension to statecharts called object charts, for use in designing object-oriented software systems. Heydon, Maimone, Tygard, Wing and Zaremski (1989) used statecharts to model a language for specifying operation system security configurations.

As we have tried to show in our discussion of cooperative work practices among spreadsheet users, spreadsheets support an informal but effective interchange of programming expertise and domain knowledge. Spreadsheets achieve the distribution of cognitive tasks across different kinds of users in a highly congenial way; sojourners of the twinkling lights mix it up with crafters of nested loops—and all with software for which no explicit design attention was given to "cooperative use".

Many thanks to Lucy Berlin, Susan Brennan, Dave Duis, Danielle Fafchamps, Martin Griss, Jeff Johnson, Nancy Kendzierski, Robin Jeffries, Jasmina Pavlin and Craig Zarmer for helpful discussions and comments on earlier drafts of this paper. Thanks also to our informants, who showed great generosity in taking the time to talk to us, and provided careful explanations of their work with spreadsheets.

References

ALSOP, S. (1989). Q & A: Quindlen and Alsop: Spreadsheet users seem satisfied with what they already have. *InfoWorld*, September 11, 102–103.

ARGANBRIGHT, D. (1986). Mathematical modeling with spreadsheets. *Abacus*, 3, 18–31.

BANNON, L. & SCHMIDT, K. (1989). CSCW: Four characters in search of a context. *Proceedings of the First European Conference on Computer Supported Cooperative Work EC-CSCW'89*, September 13–15, Gatwick, London, pp. 358–372.

BEAR, S., COLEMAN, D. & HAYES, F. (1989). *Introducing Objectcharts, or How to Use Statecharts in Object-oriented Design*, HPL-Report-ISC-TM-89-167. Bristol. England: Hewlett-Packard Laboratories.

BJERKNES, G., EHN, P. & KYNG, M. (1987). *Computers and Democracy: A Scandinavian Challenge*. Brookfield, Vermont: Gower Publishing Company.

BOSK, C. (1980). Occupational rituals in patient management. *New England Journal of Medicine*, 303, 71–76.

BROOKS, F. (1975). *The Mythical Man Month: Essays on Software Engineering*. Reading, MA: Addison-Wesley.

BROWN, P. & GOULD, J. D. (1987). How people create spreadsheets. *ACM Transactions on Office Information Systems*, 5, 258–272.

CHANDRASEKARAN, B. (1981). Natural and social system metaphors for distributed problem solving: Introduction to the issue. *IEEE Transactions on Systems, Man and Cybernetics,* **SMC-11,** 1–5.

CAMERON (1989). *A Cognitive Model for Tabular Editing,* OSO-CISRC Research Report, Ohio State University.

CICCARELLI, E. & NARDI, B. (1988). Browsing schematics: Query-filtered graphs with context nodes. In *Proceedings of the Second Annual Workshop on Space Operations, Automation and Robotics (SOAR'88),* July 20–23, Dayton, Ohio, pp. 193–204.

DOYLE, J. R. (1990). Naive users and the Lotus interface: A field study. *Behavior and Information Technology,* **9,** 81–89.

FURNAS, G. (1986). Generalized fisheye views. *Proceedings of CHI'86, Conference on Human Factors in Computing Systems,* April 13–17, Boston, pp. 16–23.

GRUDIN, J. (1988). Why CSCW applications fail: Problems in the design and evaluation of organizational interfaces. In *CSCW'88: Proceedings of the Conference on Computer Supported Cooperative Work.* September 26–28, 1988, Portland, Oregon, pp. 85–93.

HAREL, D. (1988). On visual formalisms. *Communications of the ACM,* **31,** 514–520.

HEYDON, A., MAIMONE, M., TYGAR, J., WING, J. & ZAREMSKI, A. (1989). Constraining pictures with pictures. In *Proceedings of IFIPS'89,* August, San Francisco, pp. 157–162.

HOADLEY, E. (1990). Investigating the effects of color. *Communications of the ACM,* **33,** 120–125.

HOLLAND, D. & VALSINER, J. (1988). Cognition, symbols and Vygotsky's developmental psychology. *Ethos,* **16,** 247–272.

HUTCHINS, E., HOLLAN, J. & NORMAN, D. (1986). Direct manipulation interfaces. In D. Norman & S. Draper, Eds. *User Centered System Design.* pp. 87–124. Hillsdale, NJ.: Erlbaum Publishers.

JARVENPANA & DICKSON (1988). Graphics and managerial decision making: Research based guidelines. *Communications of the ACM,* **31,** 764–744.

KAY, A. (1984). Computer software. *Scientific American,* **5,** 53–59.

LAVE, J. (1988). *Cognition in Practice: Mind, Mathematics and Culture in Everyday Life.* Cambridge: Cambridge University Press.

LEWIS, G. & OLSON, G. (1987). Can principles of cognition lower the barriers to programming? *Empirical Studies of Programmers: Second Workshop.* pp. 248–263. Norwood, NJ: Ablex Publishing.

MAULSBY, D. & WITTEN, I. (1989). Inducing programs in a direct-manipulation environment. In *Proceedings of CHI'89, Conference on Human Factors in Computing Systems.* April 30–May 4, 1989. Austin, Texas. pp. 57–62.

NAPIER, H., LANE, D., BATSEL, R. & GUADANGO, N. (1989). Impact of a restricted natural language interface on ease of learning and productivity. *Communications of the ACM,* **32,** 1190–1198.

NARDI, B. & MILLER, J. R. (1990). The spreadsheet interface: A basis for end user programming. In *Proceedings of Interact '90,* 27–31 August, Cambridge, UK, pp. 977–983.

NEAL, L. (1989). A system for example-based programming. In *Proceedings of CHI'89, Conference on Human Factors in Computing Systems,* April 30–May 4, Austin, Texas.

NEWMAN, D. (1989). Apprenticeship or tutorial: Models for interaction with an intelligent instructional system. *Proceedings of the Eleventh Annual Conference of the Cognitive Science Society,* August 16–19, Ann Arbor, Michigan.

NORMAN, D. (1987). *The Psychology of Everyday Things.* New York: Basic Books.

NORMAN, D. & HUTCHINS, E. (1988). *Computation via Direct Manipulation.* Final Report to Office of Naval Research, Contract No. N00014-85-C-0133. University of California, San Diego.

OLSON, J. & NILSEN, E. (1987). Analysis of the cognition involved in spreadsheet software interaction. *Human–Computer Interaction.* 3, 309–349.

PANKO, R. (1988). *End User Computing; Management, Applications, and Technology.* New York: John Wiley and Sons.

PIERSOL, K. (1986). Object-oriented spreadsheets: The analytic spreadsheet package. In *Proceedings of OOPSLA'86,* September, pp. 385–390.

SEIFERT, C. & HUTCHINS, E. (1989). Learning from error. In *Proceedings of the Eleventh Annual Conference of the Cognitive Science Society,* August 16–19, Ann Arbor, Michigan, pp. 42–49.

SPENKE, M. & BEILKEN, C. (1989). A spreadsheet interface for logic programming. In *Proceedings of CHI'89 Conference on Human Factors in Computing Systems,* April 30–May 4, Austin, Texas, pp. 75–83.

TUFTE, E. (1983). *The Visual Display of Quantitative Information.* Cheshire, CT: Graphics Press.

VAN EMDEN, M., OHKI, M. & TAKEUCHI, A. (1985). *Spreadsheets with Incremental Queries as a User Interface for Logic Programming,* ICOT Technical Report TR-144.

VYGOTSKY, L. S. (1979). *Thought and Language.* Cambridge, MA: MIT Press.

WARNER, J. (1990). Visual data analysis into the '90s. *Pixel,* **1,** 40–44.

Appendix: Spreadsheet study questions

(1) What do you do here (i.e. what are the tasks of your job)?

(2) What do you do with spreadsheets? (This question involved looking at actual spreadsheets on-line and/or in paper copy. We looked at spreadsheet structure, the use of annotations and labels, formula complexity, how spreadsheets are used during meetings, etc. as part of this question.)

(3) Who else uses this spreadsheet (i.e. of those we talk about in Question 2)?

(4) How did you create this spreadsheet (i.e. of those we talk about in Question 2)? Or alternatively, who created it and who else uses it?

(5) How accurate is your spreadsheet? How do you know?

(6) How do you find errors?

(7) How do you fix errors?

(8) Are there any problems you tried to solve with spreadsheets where the spreadsheet approach didn't work? If so, what are they and what were the problems?

(9) What is your educational background?

(10) What do you like about spreadsheets?

(11) What do you dislike about spreadsheets?

(12) What would make spreadsheets easier to use?

(13) What else would you like spreadsheets to do?

Analyzing Distributed Cognition in Software Teams: A Case Study of Team Programming During Perfective Software Maintenance

Nick V. Flor
Edwin L. Hutchins

Distributed Cognition Lab
Department of Cognitive Science
University of California, San Diego
La Jolla, CA 92093-0515
nflor@ucsd.edu
ehutchins@ucsd.edu

Abstract

This paper introduces a new approach – *Distributed Cognition* – to viewing collaborative activities and analyzes a pair of programmers performing a perfective software maintenance task in accordance with this approach. Distributed Cognition takes as its unit of analysis a complex cognitive system: collections of individuals and artifacts that participate in the performance of a task. The external structures exchanged by the agents of complex cognitive systems comprise its "mental" state and unlike individual cognition, where mental states are inaccessible, these states are observable and available for direct analysis. Through an analysis of these structures, their trajectories through the system, and their transformations, it will be demonstrated that complex cognitive systems engaged in software development tasks possess cognitive properties distinct from those of individual programmers. These properties are important for the system's successful completion of the task, yet they are ignored in studies of individual programmers. Studies of system level cognitive properties, when combined with existing research on the cognitive properties of individual programmers, should lead to a more comprehensive understanding of the process of software development. Before this integration can be made, however, these system level properties must be uncovered. The following research is a step in this direction.

1. Introduction

Most of the experimental research on programmers is concerned with their individual cognition. The emphasis is in detailing how programming knowledge is represented in the heads of programmers – both experts and novices – and of how this knowledge subsequently effects the development and comprehension of computer programs (c.f. Koenemann & Robertson, 1991; Omerod, 1991; Guerin and Matthews, 1990; Rist, 1989; Soloway et al, 1988). Software development, however, can be a highly social activity involving frequent interactions between programmers and with their development tools in the performance of a task; this is especially true for large software projects in industry and academia. In these circumstances, the development and comprehension of computer programs is a function of how well the system performs as a whole. Individual skill is just one important variable. There are other system level variables that are just as important including project team structure (Mantei, 1981), how well programmers communicate with each other and with other groups within their organization (Krasner, Curtis, Iscoe, 1987), and how effective programmers are at using their development tools. These variables are simply not considered in most studies of individual programmers. Unfortunately, under the current experimental paradigm, taking system level properties into account involves providing and controlling for a large number of variables. But even controlling for one variable, individual differences, in single programmer studies has been shown to be extremely difficult (Curtis, 1988). Viewed in this light, the study of system level properties seems too complex, yet they are just too important to be ignored.

This paper attempts to solve this problem by proposing a new approach for studying programmers. The process of programming is viewed as involving a complex cognitive system with properties that are distinct from the cognitive properties of individual programmers. Through an analysis of the real-time, interactive distribution of information between programmers performing a collaborative programming task, some of these properties will be uncovered.

The paper is organized into four main sections. The first briefly describes the theory of distributed cognition. The details of the experiment will then be summarized. This is followed by a detailed analysis of the activities of a pair of programmers performing a perfective software maintenance task. From this analysis some of the system level cognitive properties that are important for successful task completion, and are not emphasized in studies of individual programmers, will be discussed.

2. Distributed Cognition and Complex Cognitive Systems

Distributed cognition is a new branch of cognitive science devoted to the study of: the representation of knowledge both inside the heads of individuals and in the world (Norman, in press); the propagation of knowledge between different individuals and artifacts (Hutchins and Klausen, in press; Hutchins, 1990); and the transformations which external structures undergo when operated on by individuals and artifacts (Flor, 1991). By studying cognitive phenomena in this fashion it is hoped that an understanding of how intelligence is manifested at the systems level, as opposed to the individual cognitive level, will be obtained.

Reprinted from J. Joenemann-Belliveau, T.G. Moher, and S.P. Robertson (Eds.), *Empirical Studies of Programmers: Fourth Workshop*, pp. 36-64, Ablex. Reprinted with the permission of Ablex Publishing Corporation.

2.1. The Importance of Good External Representations

A fundamental tenet of distributed cognition is that behavior results from the interaction between external and internal representational structures (Zhang, 1990). How effective an individual is at solving a problem depends as much on good external representations as it does good internal ones. Take, for example, the game "15". In this game, two players alternate selecting three numbers from 1-9 (without replacement); the winner is the player whose numbers first sum to 15. Based purely on these rules, a good strategy for picking numbers is hard to find. Viewed under a different representation, however, the problem becomes trivial. The numbers can be represented in a 3x3 magic square for the number 15 (a magic square is a matrix whose row, column and diagonal sums are equal), and the selection strategy is similar to that used in the game tic-tac-toe! (see figure 1).

8	1	6
3	5	7
4	9	2

Figure 1: The game of "15" viewed as tic-tac-toe.
(Adapted from Norman (1988). *The Psychology of Everyday Things*)

The power of good external representations are twofold: (1) they organize information so that it is in the right place at the right time; and (2) they encode information in a form that is more explicit and thus easier to use (Kirsh, 1990). In the above example, the information is organized in a manner that makes explicit which numbers are available for selection at each step of the game. Furthermore, by representing the game as an isomorph of tic-tac-toe, the player's next choice is apparent with little problem solving effort.

The term *external structured representational media*, external SRMs or ESRMs for short, is used in place of *task relevant information* to refer to structures in the environment that contain task relevant information. Task relevant information is a more precise term reserved for those cases when an external SRM is being used to further the progress of a task. A reference manual on a shelf, for example, is an external SRM. When it is being read to help solve a problem, it is both an external SRM and task relevant information.

The role of external structures influencing software development and some of their cognitive implications for individual programmers has been noted by Guindon (1990a, 1990b).

2.2. Complex Cognitive Systems and External Structures as the System's Mental State

Equally important to solving a problem are the other actors and artifacts in the environment. Complex problems often require collaboration between a number of different individuals and artifacts for their successful solution. Together these agents comprise a *complex cognitive system* and effective interactions are necessary to successfully complete a task. These interactions serve the purpose of exchanging task relevant information and are also used to create the external structures required for the task's completion (see figure 2).

Figure 2. An Example of A Complex Cognitive System.

The constituents are the 3 engineers and the writing artifacts. External structured representational media (ESRMs) include spoken items and written items. Internal structured representational media are represented as structure charts in bubbles. Behavior is a function of both internal and external structures.

Clearly, the system performs the task and not any single individual. From a distributed cognition perspective, the system is an intelligent entity but, unlike individuals whose internal representations are not available for direct analysis, *the representations used by complex cognitive systems are in the external environment and available for inspection* (c.f. Thordsen and Klein, 1989). Examples of these representations include spoken words, writings, and operations on tools – all of which are perceivable and can be captured on recordable media, e.g. video tapes, for later analysis. These external representations can be viewed as the complex cognitive system's "mental" state. By characterizing this mental state and combining this knowledge with a knowledge of internal representations gleaned from cognitive psychology, a more complete understanding of the system will emerge.

In industry, software development typically involves the coordination of activities between many different complex cognitive systems both within the same organization, e.g. marketing, quality assurance, and management groups (Curtis, Krasner, Iscoe, 1988); and with complex cognitive systems at other organizations. This paper focuses on a complex cognitive system consisting of two programmers collaborating on a perfective software maintenance task.

2.3. A Method For Analyzing Distributed Cognition in Complex Cognitive Systems

A distributed cognition analysis of a complex cognitive system emphasizes the description of the goal required external structures created by the agents in the system, and the identification of other external structures used in support of these goal relevant structures. In terms of software development, goal required external structures are source code fragments written by the programmers. Examples of other external structures which support the creation of source code include verbal/written communication and reference manuals.

While this method can be classified as an observational one, it differs from those traditionally employed in the social sciences – which describe systems based on regularities in observation – because the descriptions are based on the assumption that the complex cognitive system is a computational system, i.e. the system's primary goal is to transform external structures until they are in a form representing its goal state. This is illustrated graphically below in figure 3:

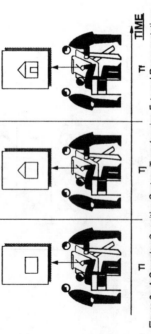

Figure 3: A Complex Cognitive System Transforming External Representations.
Tt, Tj, and Tf represent different time slices. The goal of this particular system is to create a drawing of a house. Goal required structures are marks on the paper. Verbal communication results in the exchange of other external structures that are causal to the creation of the goal structure.

This assumption places relevance on the description of external structures, the trajectories of these structures, and the transformations they undergo when operated on by the system's agents. In sum, the method involves first charting the progress of goal required external structures. The distribution of other external structures prior to the output of a goal required structure, are then examined. These descriptions can subsequently be used to constrain the types of task relevant internal structures possessed by the system agents; to help ascertain how the system can

be improved through the addition or modification of actors and artifacts; or to characterize system properties.

3.   Analyzing Distributed Cognition During Perfective Software Maintenance

Perfective software maintenance – the stage of software development devoted to the addition of new functionality to an existing software package (Lientz and Swanson, 1980) – provides an interesting domain in which to study distributed cognition. The group of programmers that must maintain the software are typically not the same group of programmers that designed and implemented it. Because of this, most maintenance tasks are highly underspecified and require effective interactions between the maintenance team and their development tools for their successful completion.

Complicating matters further is the fact that the programs to be maintained are often of sufficient size and complexity that it becomes prohibitively expensive to fully understand all their details and the consequences of any change to them. Maintenance programmers must therefore rely on good strategies for comprehending and making changes to local sections of source code.

The goal of the following study was to characterize some of the system variables important for the successful performance of the task, by analyzing the real-time, interactive distribution of information in a software maintenance complex cognitive system (figure 4, below).

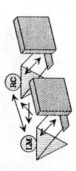

Figure 4.   The Complex Cognitive System in the Experiment
The arrows represent possible SRM trajectories.   The subjects were in visual range of each others computer displays (indicated by the crossed arrows).   The documentation artifacts are not shown.

3.1.   The Task

The task was to add a command to a program called *Gold*. *Gold* was a real-time, multi-player, graphic adventure game written in the C programming language.   The specific task was to add a *whisper* command to the game.   Whisper took as input a player and a message string and only sent that message string to the player specified.   It was similar in operation to the talk command, which was already implemented, except that the talk command sent a message to all players in the game.

Conceptually, the program could be divided into two distinct modules: a client module and a server module. The average number of lines per module was approximately 1500 and this was spread out over 40 subroutines in 7 source files. Ten new logical routines were needed to successfully complete the whisper command, six in the client module and four in the server module (refer to Appendix A, Part A). Although the modifications needed to implement this change appear too slight from a development standpoint to need multiple subjects, we believe that from a maintenance perspective the task is complex enough to warrant several programmers.

The program used two constructs that most programmers are not familiar with: internet domain sockets for interprocess communication, and screen curses for displaying character graphics. The sockets gave the program the interesting side-effect of not being entirely linked through function calls[1], potentially hindering understandability for programmers employing a systematic strategy (Littman, Pinto, Letovsky, and Soloway, 1986) for program comprehension.

3.2. Subjects

Two professional programmers, subjects LM (female) and RC (male), from a local high-tech firm were run as subjects. Both LM and RC had been employed by the same company for 3 years and had bachelor's degrees in computer science. They had served together on a project for approximately 3 months.

Two programmer teams were selected for theoretical reasons – the unit of analysis in systems of distributed cognition involves a number of individuals and artifacts. Also, as noted by Miyake (1986), the need to coordinate action among the two programmers provides a natural context for the verbal expression of many task relevant internal states.

3.3. Apparatus

Each programmer had at their disposal a computer terminal, and an 8 page document describing the task and which also included some documentation concerning the program to be maintained. The operating system used was UNIX, which the subjects had extensive experience using both on the job and as undergraduates.

Two video cameras were used to record external interactions between subjects and their artifacts. These video signals fed into a video-multiplexer which combined their inputs into a split-screen display. One half of the display was devoted to the computer screens and the other had a broad field of vision to capture the subjects' interactions with each other and their artifacts. The script program was run on both subjects' terminals to capture both keystrokes entered and all output displayed to their screens. This display was subsequently recorded onto videotape.

The audio track of the video tape was copied onto audio tape and a written transcription was made. The computer output was filtered to remove everything but the commands entered and the times they were entered. Interactions with the documentation were also transcribed. It is primarily these three artifacts that were used to perform the analysis. In the analysis, the original videotape and computer script data were only referred to in order to resolve ambiguous situations.

3.4. Analysis

A detailed analysis of the entire task is beyond the scope of this paper. The interested reader is asked to refer to Flor (1991) for a more extensive and formal treatment. Instead, an analysis of the development of a portion of the ten required changes is given. This change represents the programmers first attempt at writing logical routine #1, the user input routine (see Appendix A). The relevant state of the file edited before and after their changes is described in Appendix B. Their verbal transcript during this change is represented in its entirety in Appendix C. In the analysis that follows, numbers in parentheses refer to line numbers in this transcript.

The analysis begins at a point after which the subjects have decided to add a user input routine to the file command.c. They both bring up this file on their respective computers and then have the following exchange:

LINE #	SUBJ.	TRANSCRIPT
1	LM	well how come you're changing shouldn't only one of us change?
2	RC	no, I'm not changing it. I'm just looking at it.
3	LM	okay I'll change then.
4	RC	okay you change then.
5	RC	I got a good idea, why don't you change it and I'll just look at it.
6	LM	[laughs] Why don't I just change it and you just tell me

In this exchange they establish divisions of labor, choosing a collaborative strategy in which RC is the *teller*, whose functional role is to figure out what changes need to be made, and where LM is the *changer*, whose role is to implement the changes RC decides on (6). An examination of the video tape after this exchange shows RC turning to face LM's screen.

Taken literally, this collaborative system can be graphically represented as follows (see figure 5).

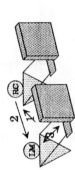

Figure 5. The Teller/Changer Collaborative System

The arrows represent SRM trajectories and the numbers on the arrows denote the sequence of events. i.e., (1) RC gets information from LM's terminal; (2) RC then determines what changes need to be made and tells LM to do them; (3) LM implements RC's commands on her computer.

---

[1] More specifically, the client module sends output to the server module via an operating system call. This causes the operating system to send an interrupt to the server's i/o handler, whose function name is different from the operating system call's function name. Programmers, therefore, that start out in the client module and try to understand code by following subroutine calls are never led to the server module.

It will become clear after the analysis, however, that these roles are not followed exclusively. The division of labor establishes trajectories for the propagation of representational state across external SRMs.

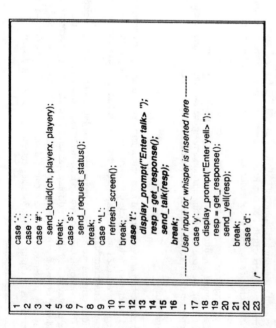

Figure 6. A Portion of the Source Code Prior to the Change
The user input code for the talk command, lines 12-16, is shown in bold type.

The format for the remainder of the analysis is as follows: source code fragments (goal required external structures) are presented first followed by transcripts of the verbal communication (external support structures) which preceded the change. A detailed analysis of these structures will then be performed. The goal required external structures are shown inside two pictures of computer screens. The left screen indicates the state of the code prior to the change, and the right screen shows the state of the code after the change. The verbal transcripts are contained in tables. The transcripts are excerpts from the main transcript in Appendix C, but with the addition of LM's keystrokes (denoted by the term KEY in the subject field of the

transcript[2]). The state of the screen prior to the change is duplicated, from Appendix B part A, in figure 6.

3.4.1. Change #1

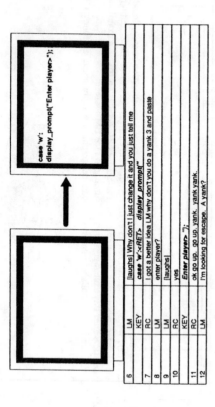

#		
6	LM	[laughs] Why don't I just change it and you just tell me
	KEY	case 'w':<RET> display_prompt("
7	RC	I got a better idea LM why don't you do a yank 3 and paste
8	LM	enter player?
9	LM	[laughs]
10	RC	yes
	KEY	Enter player> ");
11	RC	ok go up. go up. yank. yank yank.
12	LM	I'm looking for escape. A yank?

This passage provides the first examples of several system level properties: the reuse of system knowledge, the coordination of plans between agents, and the joint problem solving of ambiguous plan segments. These will be discussed in turn.

The Reuse of System Knowledge. Both LM and RC have the same goal – to copy the user input code for the talk command (refer to Figure 6, lines 12-16) and modify it to fit the requirements of the whisper command. From a system perspective, the complex cognitive system is reusing its internal structures – albeit external structures from the programmers' perspective – to facilitate the problem solution. It is interesting to note that this process can be viewed as analogous to what a cognitive psychologist would term schema retrieval and accommodation in the case of an individual mind.

The Negotiation and Coordination of Plans. Although LM and RC share the same goal, they differ in the particular plan with which to accomplish this goal. LM's plan is to manually copy the talk code, whereas RC has the less labor intensive plan of using the editor to copy and paste the talk code. Since their plans differ, they must somehow negotiate which plan to use and to

---

[2]The KEY field contains both data and vi editor commands. The editor commands used are defined as follows: 'h', 'l', 'k', and 'j' move the cursor left, right, up, and down, respectively; 'i' puts the editor in insert mode; <ESC> puts the editor in edit mode; 'x' deletes one character; 'yy' copies a line of data into a buffer; 'p' pastes data from a buffer; and 'dw' deletes one word.

coordinate its execution. In the transcript, RC tries to get LM to initiate his plan (7), but she has already started her plan (see *KEY* strokes after line 6). Visually noting this, he waits for a convenient point to interrupt and insert his plan again (11). The process of coordinating plans is similar to turn-taking in conversation (Sack, Schegloff, Jefferson, 1974). From this perspective, the completion of the typing of a programming statement can be viewed as a cue for other programmers to insert their plans.

The Joint Problem Solving of Ambiguous Plan Segments. LM executes much of her plan without interacting with RC (refer to *KEY* strokes after line 6). This is evidence of an assumption of shared goals between both programmers. Because goals, and more importantly the results of these goals, are shared, there is no need on LM's part to coordinate or negotiate her actions. Most of what she types is plan independent, i.e. both plans would have resulted in the same structures being output. When she does get to a point where the code could have several implementations, i.e. the prompt string for display_prompt (), she proposes a solution and offers it for discussion (8). This act allows RC to participate in the problem solving process if he so desires. He agrees to this (10), and in doing so demonstrates not only his approval of her solution, but also his understanding of her plan.

3.4.2. Change #2

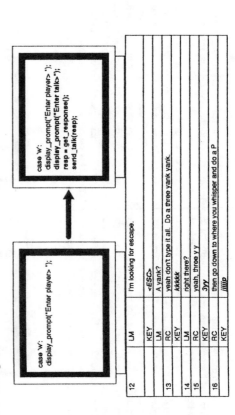

the participants to understand what otherwise would be highly ambiguous statements. Change #2 demonstrates that this property holds not just for participants in discourse but also for participants in collaborative programming.

LM acknowledges her acceptance of RC's plan with a question (12). RC then tells LM to perform a copy operation (13). In his command there are two highly underspecified statements: "don't type *it all*", and "*do a three yank yank.*" Without LM sharing a knowledge of RC's plans, she would not be able to understand these statements. Take the latter statement, for example. RC does not specify the location to copy from, the exact keystrokes needed to copy a block, or even that a copy operation is what he desires. Despite this, LM is able to correctly place the cursor to the start of the block of code to be copied before querying RC about its correctness (14). After she has positioned the cursor, he is more specific about the keystrokes needed to copy the block (15). In (16), however, he underspecifies *where* to paste the code block while specifying the exact keystroke needed to paste the block, but she is still able to find the correct location for the block paste.

This is not to argue, however, that RC should be more explicit in his commands. Expounding details like the exact location to copy and paste a block of code could involve the time consuming exchange of a large amount of unnecessary external structures.

Although the subjects do not state it explicitly, both RC and LM's actions demonstrate two important items: (i) she knows what his plans are; (ii) he knows that she knows what his plans are. It is this intersubjectively shared knowledge (D'Andrade, 1987) that allows RC to underspecify his statements. Because of (i) he does not *have to* specify the operations explicitly. Because of (ii), he *does not* specify his actions precisely. The sharing of plans and goals supports the use of very condensed or underspecified descriptions.

3.4.3. Change #3

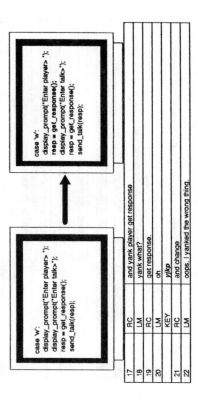

Shared goals and plans result in a number of interesting system properties. Foremost among these is efficient system communication. Clark and Schaeffer (1989) refer to the shared set of assumptions and knowledge between participants in discourse as common ground, and it allows

23	KEY	ul
	RC	do a yy
	KEY	yrtktp

Transcript for Change #3 (cont.)

Making too many assumptions about shared goals and plans can also lead to miscommunication. When this happens an uneven distribution of knowledge exists and the system must respond to this before continuing on. This occurs during change #3.

RC makes a highly underspecified statement (17). The intent of this statement is for LM to "copy a get_response() statement and place it underneath the display_prompt() that queries for the player name." The statement RC does make (17) can be viewed as a code he has invented that refers to this intent, but is not shared by LM. This causes her to question his command (18). RCs response is more underspecified, both in terms of where to copy from and where to paste to, but this time she is able to grasp his intent (20). By accident, she copies and pastes the wrong portion of code. RC, upon seeing LM paste the code, starts to introduce his next command (21). This is an example of RC missing the cue that signals his plan's turn. LM interrupts with an acknowledgement of her error (22). This causes RC to forego his current command and adopt the subgoal of helping LM (23).

3.4.4. Change #4

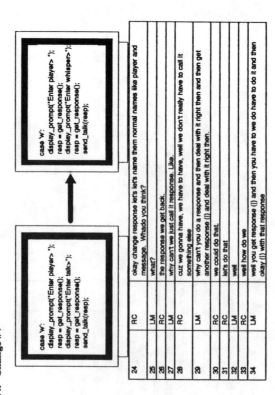

```
case w:
display_prompt("Enter player> ");
resp = get_response();
display_prompt("Enter talk> ");
resp = get_response();
send_talk(resp);
```

```
case w:
display_prompt("Enter player> ");
resp = get_response();
display_prompt("Enter whisper> ");
resp = get_response();
send_talk(resp);
```

24	RC	okay change response lets lets name them normal names like player and message. Whado you think?
25	LM	what?
26	RC	the response we get back.
27	LM	why can't we just call it response. Like.
28	RC	cuz we gonna have, we have to have, well we don't really have to call it something else
29	LM	why can't you do a response and then deal with it right then and then get another response (I) and deal with it right then.
30	RC	we could do that.
31	RC	lets do that
32	LM	well
33	RC	well how do we
34	LM	well (I) get response (I) and then you have to we do have to do it and then okay (I) with that response

35	RC	I guess we could
36	RC	We gotta figure out what to do with the string that identifies the player right?
37	LM	so we'll call it
38	RC	I don't know identify player.
39	LM	identify player. Okay. ID player
40	RC	Maybe something exists like that like that. Let's find out how (I) find out what player. mm hmm
41	LM	Oh, okay right. I'm getting ahead of the game here.
...		...
66	LM	okay then we have to do something to ID the player.
67	RC	okay.
68	RC	okay wait wait wait wait wait wait (mumble?)
69	LM	oh okay what
70	RC	let's just do, let's just start real simple
71	LM	what does this
72	RC	leave it what it leave instead of saving enter talk change that to enter whisper dw\whisper><ESC>
	KEY	(positions cursor to beginning of talk)

Transcript for Change #4 (cont.)

The actual change that gets performed is slight, but the events leading up to it are extremely interesting. They provide an example of shared plans being violated, resulting in overt plan negotiation and the emergence of an important property of complex cognitive systems – the exploration of alternative strategies.

RC starts off by instructing LM to modify the resp variables to have names like player and message (24), but he ends his command with a question. This has the effect of opening up for negotiation the rest of the strategy for naming variables.

RCs variable naming plan conflicts with LM's expectations of how this plan should be executed (27) and she takes this opportunity to offer a counter plan (29). The counter plan involves performing the operations that need the particular response directly below the appropriate get_response() call. RC agrees with this course of action (31) and they establish the more precise subgoal of determining what to do with the response that identifies the player (36). He makes the suggestion that there may already exist code that identifies a player (40). At this point they employ two different strategies, using different external SRMs, to searching for code that identifies players. RC gets on his computer to search for an identify player routine. LM picks up the user documentation and scans the command summary page to see if any other user commands could possibly need an identify player routine. After much searching (42)-(76) (not shown, refer to Appendix C) RC dismisses this subgoal (68)-(70), and opts to perform a "simpler" one (70). Without explaining what this means, he instructs LM to modify the display_prompt() string to be in accordance with the requirements of the whisper command (72). His verbal instructions to her are again underspecified, but a review of the video transcript reveals that RC points to the section of code on LM's screen that he wants changed.

This violation of shared expectations leads to the emergence of an important property of complex cognitive systems: they are systems that explore a larger number of alternatives than a single programmer might. Individually, either programmer might have stayed with their original plan. Together, they must convince the other that their plan is the more viable one. This discussion leads to a higher likelihood of the correct plan being chosen, but it does not come without a cost. There is communicational overhead associated with exploring alternatives, e.g., there were about 50 conversational turns that were executed before they arrived at their final course of action.

3.4.5. Change #5

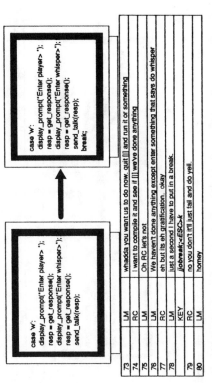

```
case 'w':
    display_prompt("Enter player> ");
    resp = get_response();
    display_prompt("Enter whisper>");
    resp = get_response();
    send_talk(resp);
```

73	LM	whadda you want us to do now. quit [	] and run it or something
74	RC	I want to compile it and see if [	] we've done anything
75	LM	Oh RC let's not
76	LM	We haven't done anything except enter something that says do whisper
77	RC	eh but its eh gratification. okay
78	LM	just a second I have to put in a break.
	KEY	//jobreak;<ESC>-k
79	RC	no you don't it'll just fail and do yell.
80	LM	homey

This exchange provides more examples of shared expectations of plans being violated and new courses of action being negotiated. The conflicting plans are particularly interesting because they point out the difference between agents following an externally suggested course of action and an internally suggested one.

LM, unclear about the RC's simpler strategy (see change #4), asks for clarification (73). In doing so, she seems to propose her desired course of action. When RC clarifies his intentions (74), LM argues against them (75)-(76). This suggests that the course of action she proposed in (73), i.e., "quit and run it or something", was in fact her guess about his intentions. RC agrees with her argument (77). LM then adds the break statement without prompting from RC, and an examination of the videotape shows that after adding the break statement she leaves the cursor at the beginning of the `send_talk()` routine. LM's change is likely to be a result of RCs plan to quit out of the editor and compile the program.

RCs simpler plan also points out an interesting action strategy. Recall that his plan involves quitting out of the edit session, compiling the program, and possibly running the program. This has the interesting side-effect of allowing the compiler to catch their errors, thus determining their next course of action. If there are no compiler errors, then running the program and

observing errant behaviors will suggest new courses of action. These are instances of situated action (Suchman, 1987), where the course of action and the organization of the world in which the action is taken, mutually constrain each other. By letting the compiler or program – parts of the programmers' external environment – dictate their next action, the programmers are spared the potentially time-consuming task of deciding what to do next. This is to be contrasted with change #4, where LM allows her internal model of how responses should be handled, dictate their course of action.

3.4.6. Change #6

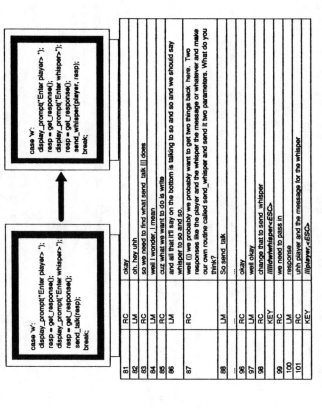

```
case 'w':
    display_prompt("Enter player> ");
    resp = get_response();
    display_prompt("Enter whisper>");
    resp = get_response();
    send_whisper(player, resp);
    break;
```

81	RC	okay
82	LM	oh, hey uhh
83	RC	so we need to find what send [|] does
84	LM	well I wonder, I mean
85	RC	cuz what we want to do is write
86	LM	and all that it'll say on the bottom is talking to so and so and we should say whisper to so and so.
87	RC	well (I) we probably want to get two things back here. Two responses like the player and the whisper the message or whatever and make our own routine called send_whisper and send it two parameters. What do you think?
88	LM	So send talk
...		
96	RC	okay
97	LM	well okay
98	RC	change that to send whisper
	KEY	//llldwhwhisper<ESC>
99	RC	we need to pass in
100	LM	response
101	RC	uhh player and the message for the whisper
	KEY	//lplayer,<ESC>

It has already been demonstrated that actors in a complex cognitive system make assumptions about the goals and plans of other actors, and that these assumptions are updated during the course of interaction. It is also the case, however, that actors make assumptions about the knowledge and behavior of system artifacts. In particular, the collaborating programmers make and share assumptions about what subroutines in the source code do.

Since his simpler plan of quitting out of the editor and compiling the program was rejected, RC proposes the new plan of determining what the subroutine send_talk() does (83). This is also an example of situated action – RC uses the emerging and unforeseen structure of the source code, an external SRM in his environment, as a resource in determining what his next course of action should be. Note, however, that there are two other routines that could have been chosen for further examination: get_response() or display_prompt(). The fact that there is no discussion about examining these routines in more detail is evidence that both programmers share similar assumptions about their operations and that they do not believe them to be problematic.

After RC proposes his new plan, LM states what she believes send_talk() will display on the players' screens (86). RC then suggests creating a send_whisper() command and passing it the player name and the whisper message as parameters (87). He ends this suggestion with a question asking her what she thinks of the plan. This has the effect of opening up the plan for negotiation. After LM's eventual agreement (97), RC instructs her to change the routine name send_talk() to send_whisper() (98). He then tells her to modify the parameters to be appropriate for the whisper command (99)-(101). In doing so, we see another interesting consequence of shared knowledge, the joint production of verbalizations. He starts a sentence (99), and she finishes it (100).

3.4.7. Change #7

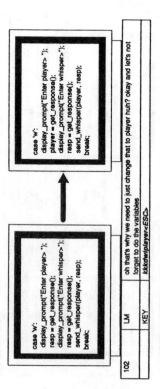

```
case w':
  display_prompt("Enter player> ");
  resp = get_response();
  display_prompt("Enter whisper> ");
  resp = get_response();
  send_whisper(player, resp);
  break;
```

```
case w':
  display_prompt("Enter player> ");
  player = get_response();
  display_prompt("Enter whisper> ");
  resp = get_response();
  send_whisper(player, resp);
  break;
```

102	
LM	oh that's why we need to just change that to player huh? okay and lets not forget to do the variables
KEY	kkktowlplayer>~ESC>

Because of the nature of ill-structured tasks, there is often insufficient information for selecting the right plan. Thus there is the potential for an incorrect or less efficient course of action to be adopted. Fortunately, refuted plans do not disappear. The process of negotiating plans distributes them between the actors. If at a later time, it is discovered that the current course of action is wrong, that plan may later be independently adopted by an actor who is not necessarily its originator. This occurs during change #7.

LM, upon changing the parameters for the send_whisper() routine notices that player has not been assigned. She therefore modifies the get_response() routine to be consistent with this change. Prior to doing so LM announces her intentions (102), making explicit reference to RC's earlier variable change strategy (24).

Her actions demonstrate not only a shared understanding of RC's plans, but more importantly a memory of his past plans. A knowledge of past plans is potentially useful in situations where the programmers are exploring several different alternatives and need to backtrack to an earlier plan.

4. Discussion

A cursory examination of just the source code before and after the above changes have been made, suggests that the programmers performed the seemingly trivial strategy of copying the user input code for the talk command and modifying it to fit the requirements of the corresponding code for the whisper command (refer to Appendix A, parts A and B). A detailed analysis, however, reveals a complex set of activities in support of this strategy. During these activities many interesting system properties emerged. Seven of these system level properties will be summarized below. Numbers in parentheses again refer to the verbal transcript in Appendix C.

4.1. Property 1: The Reuse of System Knowledge

The most prominent aspect of the system was its reuse of existing subroutines. From the programmers' perspective this involved the use of external structures, rather than internal ones, to solve the problem. From a systems perspective, however, these external structures are internal ones. And just as individuals reuse internal structures to help them solve problems, so too does this more abstract system reuse its internal structures.

More specifically cognitive science tells us that individuals organize their knowledge in terms of functionally relevant units, or schemas (Schank and Abelson, 1977; Rumelhart and Ortony, 1977; Minsky, 1975). When faced with a problem, the relevant schemas are retrieved and accommodated to meet the demands of this problem. The programmers' use of the *copy and modify* strategy can be viewed as a system level analog to the use of schemas at the individual level. Existing subroutines (schemas) are copied (retrieved) and modified (accommodated) to fit the requirements of the new command. External structured representations can therefore be viewed as the complex cognitive systems declarative "memory". Because these representations are publicly accessible multiple individuals can help each other cooperatively. This results in changes being negotiated explicitly and being subject to critical and possibly more extensive evaluation than any individual alone would perform. These negotiation processes can be viewed as meta-rules for revising public schemata.

While there is a large literature on software reuse, it is primarily concerned with designing software to be more reusable and making reusable software components more accessible, rather than with how programmers reuse code fragments.

4.2. Property 2: The Sharing of Goals and Plans

Collaborating programmers attempt to maintain a shared set of goals and plans during interactions. Goals specify what needs to be done, and plans specify the means by which the goals are achieved. For example, in the present analysis, the programmers' goal was to copy the user input routine for the talk command and to modify it to fit the requirements of the whisper command. One plan they partially executed to achieve this goal was to copy and then modify the talk routines by hand (LM's, lines 6-12). The plan they eventually adopted was to use the editor's copy and paste functions to copy the talk command and afterwards perform the modifications by hand (RC's, lines 11-16). The sharing of goals and plans leads to several different system properties: efficient communication, searches through larger spaces of alternatives, and shared memory for "old" alternative plans.

This phenomenon has also been observed, albeit at longer time-frames, by Curtis et al. (1988), where they describe how software development teams attempt to maintain common representational formats and shared system models.

4.3. Property 3: Efficient Communication

Programmers successful in sharing goals and plans, create an environment in which efficient communication can occur. Conversational details do not have to be fully specified, thus minimizing the amount of talk required to encode that which must be communicated. The current state of the problem combined with the programmers' shared goals and plans are sufficient to determine the intent of most utterances.

Underspecified commands occur throughout the analysis. A good example of this is in lines (13)-(16) where RC underspecifies the locations for LM to copy from and paste to.

4.4. Property 4: Searching Through Larger Spaces of Alternatives

A system with multiple actors possesses greater potential for the generation of more diverse plans for at least three reasons: (1) the actors bring different prior experiences to the task; (2) they may have different access to task relevant information; (3) they stand in different relationships to the problem by virtue of their functional roles.

An important consequence of the attempt to share goals and plans is that when they are in conflict, the programmers must overtly negotiate a shared course of action. In doing so, they explore a larger number of alternatives than a single programmer alone might do. This reduces the chances of selecting a bad plan. The analysis contains three good examples of this. In lines 6-12, the choice of plans is between copy and edit (RC's) or typing it in by hand (LM's). Either

LM or RC's plan would have resulted in the same goal, but RC's plan was the quicker of the two and they eventually adopted it. In lines 24-72, the choice is between identifying the player in the current routine (LM's), or postponing it for a later routine (RC's). RC's plan was the correct one but they explored LM's for a while. Finally, in lines 73-81, the choice is between quitting out and compiling (RC's) or to keep editing (LM's). In this case LM's plan was both the correct one and the one they pursued.

4.5. Property 5: Joint Productions of Ambiguous Plan Segments

A consequence of intersubjectively shared knowledge of system goals and plans is that agents in complex cognitive systems will allow other agents in the system to participate in the production of ambiguous plans. This is exemplified in change #1, lines 8-10, where LM queries RC for the content of the response string. From a system perspective allowing agents to jointly produce ambiguous structures is desirable because it potentially results in greater common ground, thus facilitating communication and problem solving during development.

It should be noted that the data suggests a tradeoff between common ground and the exploration of alternatives. If agents possess too much common ground, they may communicate more efficiently but there may be less of a tendency to explore alternative courses of action. Conversely, if the amount of common ground is small the agents may spend too much time negotiating alternative plans, e.g. change #4.

4.6. Property 6: Shared Memory for Old Plans

A memory for old alternative plans is useful in situations where the subjects are exploring a course of action, decide on it being unproductive, and have to backtrack to one of possibly many, older alternative plans. A single programmer alone may forget one of these alternative plans. Backtracking to an older plan occurs in line 66, when LM reminds RC of their old plan to identify a player; and in line 102, where LM verbalizes her realization of the intent of the plan RC originally presented in line 24.

4.7. Property 7: Divisions of Labor and Collaborative Interaction Systems

Programmers in complex cognitive systems negotiate divisions of labor. These divisions of labor specify who does what task in the system. If they work jointly on a task, they also specify functional roles. Together the divisions of labor and specifications of functional roles designate a collaborative interaction system. The particular system adopted by LM and RC was the "Teller/Changer" collaborative system (refer to figure 5, and line 6 in the verbal transcript). The literal interpretation of this system is that RC's function is to examine LM's computer screen, formulate a solution, and tell LM what to do. LM's function is to type whatever RC tells her. The analysis, however, shows that these functional roles are only followed very loosely, e.g., LM initiates changes 1 and 7 without prompting from RC.

It is more correct to say that when they establish functional roles, they are ensuring that trajectories exist for the propagation of representational state across external SRMs. The trajectories in this example are: (1) from LM's screen to RC eyes; (2) between LM and RC; and trivially, (3) between LM and her computer.

This collaborative system has a number of interesting cognitive implications. Not having to worry about low level interactions with the keyboard and terminal potentially allows RC to work at a more conceptual level. LM becomes his user interface, but she is a smart interface able to accept radically underspecified commands.

5. Summary

We have offered a system level approach to the study of cognition during software development. Successful software development is viewed as a consequence not of any single programmer's cognition, but of an interaction of programmers and development artifacts in a system of distributed cognition. These systems have cognitive properties distinct from those of individuals agents. The activities of a pair of programmers performing a perfective software maintenance task were analyzed in detail to illustrate some of these properties.

This type of analysis has been largely ignored in studies of programmers and a complete understanding of the software development process will not emerge until many more of these types of analyses have been conducted and combined with the growing literature on individual programmers. This paper takes the initial step of showing how system level properties can be studied and identifies some of the system variables that affect task performance. Future research must be conducted, however, to ascertain the relative effects of these variables on software development, and to integrate this information with data from individual programmer studies.

6. Acknowledgements

Research support was provided by grant NCC 2-591 to Donald Norman and Edwin Hutchins from the Ames Research Center of the National Aeronautics & Space Administration in the Aviation Safety/Automation Program. Everett Palmer served as technical monitor. Additional support was provided by a special San Diego Research Fellowship awarded to the first author from the University of California in San Diego.

Special thanks to the Distributed Cognition Lab for providing insightful discussion on this topic, and to Randall Camp and Laura Mansfield for volunteering their time and effort.

7. References

Clark, H., and Schaefer, E. (1989). Contributing to Discourse. *Cognitive Science.* 13:259-294.

Curtis, B. (1988). The impact of individual differences in programmers. In G. C. van der Veer, T. R. G. Green, J.-M. Hoc, & D. M. Murray (Eds.), *Working with computers: Theory versus outcome,* 279-294. London: Academic Press.

Curtis, B., Krasner, H., and Iscoe, N. (1988). A Field Study of the Software Design Process for Large Systems. *Communications of the ACM,* 31(11): 1268-1287.

D'Andrade (1987). A Folk Model of the Mind. In D. Holland and N. Quinn (Eds.), *Cultural Models in Language and Thought,* Cambridge: Cambridge University Press.

Flor, N. (1991). Modeling Distributed Cognition in Complex Cognitive Systems. *Masters Project; UCSD Technical Report.* San Diego: University of California, Department of Cognitive Science.

Guerin, B. and Matthews, A. (1990). The Effects of Semantic Complexity on Expert and Novice Computer Program Recall and Comprehension. *Journal of General Psychology,* 117(4): 379-389.

Guindon, R. (1990a). Designing the Design Process: Exploiting Opportunistic Thoughts. *Human-Computer Interaction,* 5: 305-344.

Guindon, R. (1990b). Knowledge Exploited by Experts During Software System Design. *International Journal of Man-Machine Studies,* 33: 279-304.

Hutchins, E. and Klausen, T. (in press). Distributed Cognition in an Airline Cockpit. In D. Middleton, and Y. Engestrom, (Eds.). *Communication and Cognition at Work,* CA: Sage Publications.

Hutchins, E. (1990). The Technology of Team Navigation. In J. Galegher, R. Kraut, and C. Egido, (Eds.) *Intellectual Teamwork. Social and Technological Foundations of Cooperative Work.* NJ: LEA.

Kirsh, D. (1990). When is Information Explicitly Represented? In P. Hanson (Ed.), *Information, Language, and Cognition.* University of British Columbia Press.

Koenemann, J., and Robertson, S. P. (1991). Expert Problem Solving Strategies for Program Comprehension. *CHI '91 Proceedings.*

Krasner, H., Curtis, B., and Iscoe, N. (1987). Communication Breakdowns and Boundary Spanning Activities on Large Programming Projects. *Empirical Studies of Programmers: Second Workshop.* Norwood, NJ: Ablex Publishing.

Lientz, B. P., and Swanson, E. B. (1980). *Software Maintenance Management. A Study of the Maintenance of Computer Application Software in 487 Data Processing Organizations.* Reading, MA: Addison-Wesley.

Litman, D. C., Pinto, J., Letovsky, S., and Soloway, E. (1986). Mental Models and Software Maintenance. *In* E. Soloway and S. Iyengar (Eds.), *Empirical Studies of Programmers.* Norwood, NJ: Ablex.

Mantei, M. (1981). The Effect of Programming Team Structure on Programming Tasks. *Communications of the ACM,* 24(3): 106-113.

Minsky, M. (1975). A Framework for Representing Knowledge. In P.H. Winston (Ed.), *The Psychology of Computer Vision.* NY: McGraw-Hill.

Miyake, Naomi. (1986). Constructive Interaction and the Iterative Process of Understanding. *Cognitive Science,* 10:515-177.

Norman, D. (in press). Cognitive Artifacts. In J.M. Carroll (Ed.), *Designing Interaction: Psychology at the human-computer interface.* NY: Cambridge University Press.

Norman, D. (1988). *The Psychology of Everyday Things.* NY: Basic Books.

Omerod, T. (1991). Human Cognition and Programming. In J-M. Hoc, T.R.G. Green, R. Samurcay and D.J. Gilmore (Eds) *The Psychology of Programming,* San Diego: Academic Press.

Rist, R. (1989). Schema Creation in Programming. *Cognitive Science,* 13(3): 389-414.

Rumelhart, D. and Ortony, A. (1977). The Representation of Knowledge in Memory. In R.C Anderson, R.J. Spiro, and W.E. Mantague (Eds.). *Schooling and the Acquisition of Knowledge.* NJ: Erlbaum.

Sacks, H., Schegloff, E., and Jefferson, G. (1974). A Simplest Systematics for the Organization of Turn-Taking for Conversation. *Language,* 50(4): 695-735.

Schank, R., and Abelson, R. (1977). *Scripts, Plans, Goals, and Understanding.* NJ: Erlbaum.

Soloway, E., Adelson, B., and Ehrlich, K. (1988). Knowledge and Processes in the Comprehension of Computer Programs. In M. Chi, R. Glaser, and M. Farr, (Eds.), *The Nature of Expertise,* NJ: LEA.

Suchman, L. (1987). *Plans and Situated Action.* MA: Cambridge University Press.

Thordsen, M. L., and Klein, G. A. (1989). Cognitive Processes of the Team Mind. *1989 Proceedings of the IEEE International Conference on Systems, Man, and Cybernetics.*

Zhang, J. (1990). The Interaction of Internal and External Information in a Problem Solving Task. *UCSD Technical Report #9005.* San Diego: University of California, Department of Cognitive Science.

APPENDIX A:
The Ten Logical Routines, Their Implementation and The Developmental Course of These Routines

#	LOGICAL ROUTINES	IMPLEMENTATION
1	Get user input	added case statement to the routine cmd_parser() in client/command.c
2	Format user input	created the routine
3	Send user input to server	send whisper() in client/io_handler.c
4	Parse incoming server command	added a case statement to the routine cmd_parser() in server/command.c
5	Execute server command	created the server routines:
6	Format server command	do whisper() in io_handler.c &
7	Send server command to client	write player() in command.c
8	Parse incoming client command	case statement in execute event() in command.c
9	Execute client command	display whisper() in display.c
10	Display results	

Part A. The 10 logical routines and their actual implementation by the subjects.

change #	time	command_input	send_whisper	cmd_parser	do_whisper	write_player	execute_event	display_whisper
1	0:45:34	1/2 (LM)						
2	0:52:02		1/2 (RC)					
3	1:02:28				1/6 (RC)			
4	1:02:43			1/1 (LM)				1/1 (RC)
5	1:11:20							
6	1:11:27						1/1 (LM)	
7	1:21:08	2/2 (RC)						
8	1:25:13				2/6 (RC)			
9	1:43:16		2/2 (RC)					
10	1:43:38					1/10 (LM)		
11	1:46:34					2/10 (LM)		
12	1:52:36				3/6 (LM)	3/10(RC)		
13	1:59:06					4/10(RC)		
14	2:00:07							
15	2:00:19				4/6 (LM)	5/10 (LM)		
16	2:06:35							
17	2:10:15				5/6 (LM)	6/10 (LM)		
18	2:13:46					7/10(RC)		
19	2:26:44					8/10(RC)		
20	2:27:29					9/10(RC)		
21	2:33:42							
22	2:39:00				6/6 (LM)	10/10 (LM)		
23	2:39:51							

Part B. The Development of The Physical Routines

Times indicate when the change was completed. Changes are represented as fractions of the total number of changes made to that routine and the initials of the subject that modified the routine are in parentheses. For example, the 7/10(RC) under the column write_player indicates that RC is making the seventh out of ten changes to the subroutine write_player().

APPENDIX B: Computer Transcript of Change 1

```
 1    case ':':
 2    case '::':
 3    case '#':
 4        send_build(ch, playerx, playery);
 5        break;
 6    case 's':
 7        send_request_status();
 8        break;
 9    case "/L":
10        refresh_screen();
11        break;
12    case 't':
13        display_prompt("Enter talk> ");
14        resp = get_response();
15        send_talk(resp);
16        break;
17    case 'y':
18        display_prompt("Enter yell> ");
19        resp = get_response();
20        send_yell(resp);
21        break;
22    case 'd':
23
```

Part A. A section of the source code prior to the addition of the user input code for the whisper command. The numbers to the left are line numbers added for reference purposes and do not actually occur in the source code.

```
    case ':':
    case '::':
    case '#':
        send_build(ch, playerx, playery);
        break;
    case 's':
        send_request_status();
        break;
    case "/L":
        refresh_screen();
        break;
    case 't':
        display_prompt("Enter talk> ");
        resp = get_response();
        send_talk(resp);
        break;
    case 'w':
        display_prompt("Enter player> ");
        player = get_response();
        display_prompt("Enter whisper> ");
        resp = get_response();
        send_whisper(player,resp);
        break;
```

Part B. The completed source code.

APPENDIX C: Verbal Transcript During Intermediate Computation 1

CHNG #	LINE #	SUBJ.	TRANSCRIPT
	1	LM	well how come you're changing shouldn't only one of us change?
	2	RC	no, I'm not changing it. I'm just looking at it.
	3	LM	okay I'll change then.
	4	RC	okay you change then.
Div. Lab.	5	RC	I got a good idea, why don't you change it and I'll just look at it.
	6	LM	[laughs] Why don't I just change it and you just tell me
	7	RC	I got a better idea LM why don't you do a yank 3 and paste
	8	LM	enter player?
	9	LM	[laughs]
	10	RC	yes
1	11	RC	ok go up. go up. yank. yank. yank yank.
	12	LM	I'm looking for escape. A yank?
	13	RC	yeah don't type it all. Do a three yank yank.
	14	LM	right there?
	15	RC	yeah, three y y
2	16	RC	then go down to where you whisper and do a P
	17	RC	and yank player get response
	18	LM	yank what?
	19	RC	get response.
	20	LM	oh
	21	RC	and change
	22	RC	oops. I yanked the wrong thing.
3	23	RC	do a yy
	24	RC	okay change response lets lets name them normal names like player and message. Whado you think?
	25	LM	what?
	26	RC	the response we get back.
	27	LM	cuz we can just call it response. Like.
	28	RC	why can't we just call it response. Like, well we have to have, well we don't really have to call it something else
	29	LM	why can't you do a response and then deal with it right then and then get another response (I) and deal with it right then.
	30	RC	we could do that.
	31	RC	lets do that
	32	LM	well
	33	RC	well how do we
	34	LM	well you get response (I) and then you have to we we do have to do it and then okay (I) with that response
	35	RC	I guess we could
	36	RC	We gotta figure out what to do with the string that identifies the player right?
	37	LM	so we'll call it
	38	RC	I don't know identify player.
	39	LM	identify player. Okay. ID player
	40	RC	Maybe something exists like that like that. Lets find out how (I) find out what player. mm hmm
	41	LM	Oh, okay right. I'm getting ahead of the game here.
	42	LM	dag gum it the escape button is just in the wrong place. I like to do this (??) oo
	43	RC	I quit
	44	BOTH	[laugh]
	45	LM	[ahem] Wait are we both vi-ing the same file
	46	RC	Yeah, so don't change anything.
	47	LM	Yeah we are..
	48	LM	What are these other things do? Nothing else um...
	49	LM	Nothing else identifies a player
	50	RC	no?
	51	LM	We can send destroy to player X
	52	LM	Destroy doesn't work.
	53	LM	Whats send destroy? I mean do? Send Destroy
	54	LM	D
	55	RC	its commented out
	56	RC	its commented out!! [laughs]
	57	LM	Lets uncomment it
	58	LM	okay you do it, you're making the changes.
	59	RC	Okay where is it? [laughs]
	60	LM	uh just go down just a little bit below the top, it's not very far down.
	61	RC	Lets not change the direction.
	62	LM	Lets not change the (I) destroy thing cuz that could just really screw things up.
	63	LM	okay
	64	RC	could confuse things. makes sense
	65	LM	okay then we have to do something to ID the player.
	66	LM	okay.
	67	RC	okay wait wait wait wait wait [mumble?]
	68	RC	oh okay what
	69	LM	lets just do, lets just start real simple
	70	RC	what does this
	71	LM	leave it what it leave instead of saying enter talk change that to enter whisper
4	72	RC	whadda you want us to do now. quit [|] and run it or something
	73	RC	I want to compile it and see if [|] we've done anything
	74	RC	Oh RC lets not
	75	LM	We haven't done anything except enter something that says do whisper
	76	LM	eh but its eh gratification. okay
	77	RC	just a second I have to put in a break.
	78	RC	no you don't it'll just fall and do yell.
	79	LM	homey
5	80	LM	okay
	81	RC	oh, hey uhh
	82	LM	so we need to find what send_talk [|] does
	83	RC	well I wonder, I mean
	84	LM	cuz what we want to do is write
	85	LM	and all that it'll say on the bottom is talking to so and so and we should say whisper to so and so.
	86	LM	well (I) we probably we probably want to get two things back. Two responses like the player and the whisper the message or whatever and make our own routine called send_whisper and send it two parameters. What do you think?
	87	RC	So send_talk
	88	LM	its cold in here.
	89	LM	It is!
	90	RC	It's hurting my hands.
	91	LM	You can probably sue.
	92	RC	[laughs]
	93	LM	oh wait did you sign that already. Oh he doesn't have it, rip it up.
	94	RC	whoooshheeet!
	95	LM	it's like my arm is going numb. I think I'm gonna sue Nick Flor [laughs]
	96	RC	okay
	97	LM	well okay

CHNG	LINE #	SUBJ.	
	98	RC	change that to send_whisper
	99	RC	we need to pass in
	100	LM	response
6	101	RC	uhh player and the message for the whisper
7	102	LM	oh that's why we need to just change that to player huh? okay and let's not forget to do the variables

The code for the user interface routine comprised seven changes. **CHNG** provides a rough indication of where the various changes occurred. **LINE #** provides an index for the transcript. **SUBJ.** indicates which subject is speaking.

The sequence of characters (|) or [|], indicates that the next conversational turn was said in parallel at the point where the sequence appears.

Reprinted from S. Oskamp and S. Spacapan (Eds.), *People's Reactions to Technology in Factories, Offices, and Aerospace*, The Claremont Symposium on Applied Social Psychology, pp. 145-199. ©1990, Sage Publications. Reprinted by permission of Sage Publications, Inc.

Informal Communication in Organizations: Form, Function, and Technology

ROBERT E. KRAUT
ROBERT S. FISH
ROBERT W. ROOT
BARBARA L. CHALFONTE

Most of the work that people do in organizations requires some degree of active cooperation and communication with others. This is true of routine clerical work and it is equally true of creative work, such as scientific research or engineering development. Indeed, in some scientific fields, over 65% of publications are jointly authored (Over, 1982), and most research projects, regardless of authorship, require support staffs of clerks, research assistants, or technicians.

Individual members of groups need to communicate with one another to accomplish their production and social functions; within organizations, groups need to communicate with other groups. The communication used is both formal and informal. Our goal as authors of this chapter is to understand the communication processes underlying group work in order to improve the communication technologies that groups have available to them. Our assumption is that by understanding how groups and organizations work and by comparing their communication needs to current communication technologies, we will be able to identify gaps in the array of communication tools that are available to people in organizations. We are especially interested in communication tools to support distributed groups. For instance, what would it take to have a nationwide task force meet and write a report as easily as if it were housed in a single building?

When we look around our places of work, we notice that informal communication seems to be a dominant activity. People read at their desks but are interrupted by phone calls. They leave to attend a department meeting but stop on the way to discuss a matter with a colleague. To answer questions about office procedure, they phone the person at the next desk rather than consult the appropriate manual. The conversations seem fluid and undesigned and yet, clearly, work is being accomplished. In looking at the contrast between formal and informal communication, it occurred to us that the more spontaneous and informal the communication, the less well it was supported by communication technology. We realized that we had well-established procedures for scheduling meetings and writing reports but little technology to support bumping into a colleague in the hall. Thus our interest was drawn toward understanding more about the nature and value of informal and spontaneous communicative activity and whether technology could be fruitfully employed to aid it.

While our attempts to understand informal communication have taken a number of empirical approaches, our interest in enabling technologies has been focused on the uses of audio-video communications media. The history of video as a communication technology has been a mixed one, showing great successes as a method of broadcasting entertainment, a mixed record as a method of disseminating educational information, and a dismal record as a mechanism for interpersonal communication. The lack of market success for such items as video telephones and video conferencing systems seems to contradict our intuitions about the value of visual contact in interpersonal communication. However, because these technologies had been primarily geared toward relatively *formal* communication occasions, we began to explore whether video's employment in systems for *informal* communication might be more successful. In particular, we thought that because video simultaneously reminds a person of a need to talk to someone and

provides a communication channel through which to carry on the conversation, it might become the technology to support spontaneous, informal communication.

The remainder of this chapter elaborates our thesis that informal communication is an important mechanism to help achieve both the production goals and the social goals of groups. The chapter starts by more fully describing what we mean by informal communication, conceptually and through example, and then details some features common to episodes of informal communication. Next, the chapter examines some of the ways in which informal communication supplements more formal communication processes to aid both the production and social components of group work. While the examples and data in this chapter come from studies of informal communication in research and development (R&D) environments, we do not think the insights gained are limited to these environments. Finally, the chapter describes two experimental telecommunication systems aimed at supporting informal communication at a distance.

The Nature of Informal Communication

Theorists have long recognized that organizations have available to them communication methods varying in formality, that they tend to deploy these different methods for tasks varying in uncertainty, and that matching the informality of the methods with the uncertainty of the task leads to better organizational outcomes. At both the organizational and small-group level, the coordination of activity is the production-oriented task that has been examined in most detail. Coordination is the activity of directing individuals' efforts toward achieving common and explicitly recognized goals (Blau & Scott, 1962). As Van de Ven, Delbecq, and Koenig (1976) describe it, "coordination means integrating or linking together different parts of an organization to accomplish a collective set of tasks" (p. 322). Explicit coordination is necessary in part because individuals within an organization have only partially overlapping goals. Thus, one of the aims of coordination is to ensure that the disparate individuals come to share the same goals. But even if this aim were achieved and their goals were identical, the input-output dependencies among individuals require that their efforts be sequenced and interrelated efficiently.

The coordination mechanisms used by organizations differ in their degree of formality—that is, in their degree of prespecification, conventionality, and rule boundedness. At the formal end of the dimension, coordination is accomplished by adherence to common rules, regulations, and standard operating procedures; through preestablished plans, schedules, and forecasts; and through memos, management information reports, and other standardized communications. These formal coordination mechanisms have in common communication that is specified in advance, unidirectional, and relatively impoverished.

Informal communication is a loosely defined concept and is often treated as the residual category in organizational theory. According to this perspective, informal communication is that which remains when rules and hierarchies are eliminated as ways of coordinating activities. More positively, informal communication is communication that is spontaneous, interactive, and rich. Coordination by feedback (March & Simon, 1958), through organismic communication networks (Tushman & Nadler, 1978), or by clan mechanisms (Ouchi, 1980) are alternate ways of describing coordination by informal communication. The essence of these informal communication systems is their lack of prespecification. Information is not prepackaged and then shipped intact to a recipient; courses of action are not precomputed and then executed without modification. Rather, information is often exchanged interactively, through meetings and conversations, and courses of action are worked out in the context of the circumstances into which the actions must fit.

Figure 5.1 illustrates several of the variables that we think distinguish formal from informal communication. At the heart of what we term informal communication is its spontaneous and unplanned nature. Conversations take place at the time, with the participants, and about the topics at hand. None of these characteristics—timing, participants, or agenda—is scheduled in advance. Moreover, during its course, the communication changes to take into account the participants' current interests and understandings. In this sense, informal communication is truly interactive, with all participants in the communication being able to respond to what they perceive to be the current state of affairs, including the communication up until that point and their perception of the other participants' reactions to it. Through this feedback mechanism, informal communication can be more effective than formal chan-

nels because participants in the conversations elaborate or modify what they have to say in order to deal with someone else's objections or misunderstandings (e.g., Kraut, Lewis, & Swezey, 1982).

Our distinction between formal and informal communication parallels Daft and Lengel's (1984) distinction between impoverished and rich communication channels, although we add the criterion of spontaneity to their criteria of bandwidth and underactivity. According to Daft and Lengel (1986), rich communication channels are ones that "can overcome different frames of reference or clarify ambiguous issues to change understanding in a timely manner" (p. 560). In order of decreasing richness, they consider face-to-face communication, telephone, personal documents (such as letters), impersonal documents, and numeric documents. (See also Stohl & Redding, 1987, for further discussion of the formal-informal distinction, regarding communication.)

There are both structural and functional characteristics of communication occasions that cause the communication to be more or less formal. Among structural characteristics, the nature of the relationship among the participants influences its formality. For example, conversations among strangers or those with highly unequal status will be more formal than conversations among close friends or peers. The frequency of communication also influences its formality. If communication partners have the ability to communicate with each other many times a day, they need not stand on ceremony in their communication; the communication then moves from a formal to an informal style (Brown & Fraser, 1979). The nature of the communication setting also influences the formality of communication within it. A discussion in a

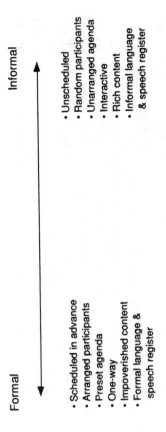

Formal   Informal

- Scheduled in advance   · Unscheduled
- Arranged participants   · Random participants
- Preset agenda   · Unarranged agenda
- One-way   · Interactive
- Impoverished content   · Rich content
- Formal language & speech register   · Informal language & speech register

Figure 5.1. The Formality Dimension of Communication

board room is likely to be more formal than one in the corporate fitness center. Finally, the communication channel itself may partially determine the formality of a communication event. By their nature, for example, telephone and face-to-face discussions are more interactive and rich than are computer mail systems and, as a consequence, they are more informal. Subdividing media more finely, computer-generated information systems reports and human-generated memoranda are more formal than are scheduled meetings and electronic bulletin boards, which in turn are more formal than telephone calls or hallway chats.

In terms of functional characteristics, formal and informal communication systems seem best suited to different types of activities. Formal communication tends to be used for coordinating relatively routine transactions within groups and organizations. For example, in a large corporation, one might go through a procurement process simply by following the steps specified in the corporate purchasing guide. The material specification, purchase requisition forms, bidding procedures, criteria for selecting one vendor over another, and stages in the approval process would all be specified in advance. In the extreme, the rule book could so totally describe the conditions under which certain actions should occur and the precise ways of executing them that a factory's computerized, just-in-time procurement system could place orders with suppliers without human intervention.

However, these formal coordination mechanisms often fail in the face of novel or unplanned events. Novelty, unexpectedness, and uncertainty are frequent in organizations and are often components of what appear to be routine procedures (e.g., Suchman & Wynn, 1984). Under these circumstances, informal communication seems needed for coordination in the face of uncertainty and equivocality (Daft & Lengel, 1986). Thus, while a group might purchase a new desk by delegating the responsibility to one member and then following the purchasing rules, they would not think of hiring a division manager simply by following the procedures laid out in the personnel guide. Instead they would have plenty of informal communication with one another about the type of person they wanted as a leader and with the candidates to assess their qualities. Informal communication is needed in this case because, compared to buying furniture, personnel procurement is a rare event, with considerable consequences, and it is also highly uncertain, given the difficulty of predicting the characteristics of people.

Research findings lend support to these hypotheses. For example, when work groups are engaged in more complex tasks — that is, tasks that are varied, lack routine procedures, and require group members to think through solutions — such groups are far more likely to communicate directly with other group members and to have more scheduled and unscheduled meetings to coordinate their activities (Van de Ven et al., 1976). Daft and Lengel (1984) have shown that organizational members prefer rich and interactive media, such as face-to-face meetings, when they have value conflicts and other disagreements to work out. And Argote (1982) has shown that when groups with greater task uncertainty do engage in meetings and unscheduled communication to coordinate their activity, they are more successful in performing their work than if they rely on standard procedures.

In sum, we have argued that informal communication supports organizational and group coordination, especially under conditions of uncertainty. Coordination is an example of a production function of groups. When people work in groups within organizations, they must achieve three goals to be successful: production, group maintenance, and member support (Hackman, 1987; McGrath, 1984, in press). They must actually accomplish productive work — write the reports, make the decisions, construct the software, allocate the budgets, defend clients, or do whatever the particular group is assigned to do. In addition, groups must achieve two social goals. First, they must sustain themselves over time, and most groups have life spans of multiple projects. To sustain themselves, groups have to recruit and socialize members, keep them happy enough so that they want to maintain membership, garner external resources, and do the sundry other activities that ensure the group's continuing survival. The second social goal that the group must attempt to achieve is to support the needs of individual group members so that they feel satisfied with their work, relationships, and membership in the group. By most criteria, a team whose members are unhappy with their work and hostile toward one another would be deemed a failure, even if they accomplished their tasks. In scientific research teams, for example, scientists must feel that they are making useful contributions and that their contributions are being recognized; such teams often break up if this recognition is not forthcoming (Kraut, Galegher, & Egido, 1988).

There is reason to think that informal communication is particularly useful in supporting the social functions of groups. This is because

these issues, as suggested by the recent controversy concerning the value of research on room-temperature nuclear fusion. In terms of social relations, the uncertainties are in establishing trust in potential research collaborators and in defining an equitable division of labor and credit for jointly planned work (see Kraut, Galegher, & Egido, 1988, for a more complete discussion of these dilemmas in scientific research). For these two reasons—the importance of collaboration and the essentially uncertain nature of the research enterprise—we believed that informal communication would play an extremely important role in research and development; as a result, the R&D domain would provide an interesting lens through which to view the dynamics and functions of informal communication.

In this section we describe three examples of informal communication. The episodes come from samples of videotaped interactions we collected from hallways, copy centers, entryways, and other commons areas in one building of a large R&D laboratory. These episodes were collected by turning on an unattended videotape camera at random times for hour-long intervals. The camera was large, plainly visible, and identified with a sign stating that recording for research purposes was occurring. During most of the 12 hours that were recorded, there was no social interaction at the recording sites because either no one was present or only one person was. When two people were present, most social interactions were minimal. A typical scenario would be for two people to walk past each other in the hall, acknowledging each others' existence by a stereotyped pattern of glances toward and away from each other (Goffman, 1963) or with a brief "hello" in passing.

Given this context, the excerpts presented below are by no means random selections from episodes in which at least two people were videotaped. Rather, they were selected because they illuminate both the dynamics and functions of informal communication. Thus, they provide a useful counterpoint to the more schematic and quantitative descriptions of informal communication presented in later sections.

Episode 1: The Call

The first episode illustrates the beginning of what we have called an opportunistic, work-related conversation. Andrew is returning to his

---

organizations are less explicit in regulating social relationships than in regulating other aspects of work procedures. For example, corporate personnel guides frequently describe the bureaucratic procedures for annual performance appraisals, but they neither attempt to nor could they regulate the ad hoc personal judgments that supervisors make of the people reporting to them. A vast literature in social psychology suggests that relatively unstructured and informal communication is at the basis of the social processes, such as person perception and liking, which underlie group maintenance and member support (e.g., Festinger, Schacter, & Back, 1950; Zajonc, 1968). To give one example, Gabarro (1987) describes the development of mutual expectations and trust that sustains the work relationships among managers; when a CEO no longer trusts the judgments of his or her subordinates, the subordinate is frequently transferred, demoted, or fired. "[Mutual expectations] . . . typically worked out over time during a succession of routine interactions, such as ad hoc encounters, meetings, progress reviews, and discussions of task-based problems" (p. 184). These are the mechanisms of informal communication.

The Dynamics of Informal Communication in R&D

Moving from abstract discussion of communication styles, groups, and organizations in general, this section, as well as subsequent ones, will discuss several examples of informal communication and examine its functions in the context of the research and development process among scientists and engineers. We focus on informal communication in research and development for two reasons. First, as we have seen previously, most research is collaborative, requiring coordination and communication. Second, the central feature of this domain is dealing with uncertainty in both production and social relations. In terms of production, the object of research in both science and engineering is to create novelty. In embarking on a research project, scientists and engineers must make the equivocal judgments of whether their goal is a valuable one and whether their methods are appropriate and will meet with success. Even when the project is completed, they are still left with amount of information about the world in which they live. They learn or are reminded of who the local inhabitants are and the goings-on in their offices give some indication of their characteristics, interests, and current activities. While much of this information is not immediately relevant to the tasks at hand, these observations of the workplace provide some of the background knowledge through which people make sense of the subsequent information they acquire. For example, they provide a basis for the mutual knowledge that people need to understand one another (Clark & Marshall, 1981; Krauss & Fussel, in press) and the firm-specific knowledge that employees acquire in the first years of working for the company.

In this episode Abel, a researcher, is walking down the hallway, glancing into offices as he goes. He sees another researcher, Baker, whom he knows, notices that Baker has spotted him, and says hello while passing by. The next scene occurs seven seconds later when, even though Abel has already passed Baker's office, two phenomena cause him to reverse his steps and stop to have a brief discussion with Baker. First, the mere sight of Baker served as a stimulus that jogged Abel's memory that he had something to say to him. Second, the "hello" served as a channel checking routine, indicating that Baker's attention was free and that he was available for conversation. This confluence of topic and availability, which Baker's visual presence provided, was the minimum precondition for a conversation to occur.

In the third scene, another researcher, Charlie, walks down the hall, also glancing in offices as he goes. He observes Abel and Baker in conversation, and turns his head farther to see them as he is walking. Although he does not slow down, his actions indicate that this is an interesting event for him. This observation provides Charlie with background information that may be useful in the future. By catching a glimpse of the participants in ongoing conversation, Charlie may be able to make inferences about the relationship between the participants or the topic of the conversation. In this way he learns about social relationships, alliances, crises, and collaborations in the laboratory. In the final seen, Abel finishes his discussion with Baker and continues on to his original destination. During this 35-second sequence, Abel and Baker, who had not planned to speak, got a little bit of work done and provided some information to Charlie, which he can use to better understand his work environment.

office when he sees Bob backing out of a meeting in an office at the end of the hallway. Bob is unaware of Andrew's presence. Andrew calls in to Bob, timing his call by observing when Bob has concluded his participation in the meeting. Bob turns around, recognizes Andrew, and acknowledges his presence with a smile. He starts walking toward Andrew, who remains stationary until Bob reaches him. In the final scene of the episode, Andrew and Bob are walking off together down the hallway, discussing the difficulties they have had contacting a mutual colleague.

Both Bob and Andrew abandoned their original goals (concluding a meeting or returning to an office, respectively). As a result of serendipitously seeing each other in the hallway, they were able to pass information about the status of a project and to solve a problem that was hindering the project's progress. Andrew told Bob that he had not been able to contact a colleague, and Bob suggested a way of doing so. This is a common mechanism through which small collaborative teams do project management (see Kraut, Galegher, & Egido, 1988, for a description of communication in scientific research teams). For small groups, this informal project management serves the production function of coordination and problem solving efficiently, assuming team members run into each other enough. It has the additional benefit of keeping group members informed of and involved with many of the minor decisions and crises that occur in any project. Thus it serves the social functions of groups, by keeping group members committed to the projects of which they are a part.

Episode 2: Stop Short

Like the previous episode, Episode 2 shows the chance initiation of a work-related conversation. In addition, it also demonstrates how people pick up background information about their work environment by merely navigating its hallways. A typical sequence observed as people walk down the halls is for them to peer into open offices and public spaces as they go to the printer, copy machine, bathroom, or other destination. They usually do not slow down, but simply turn their heads as they pass open doorways. This process of browsing the social environment while on other business provides people with a substantial

methods that organizations use to get their work done, transmit organizational culture and firm-specific knowledge, and maintain the loyalty and goodwill of their members.

The episodes reviewed here share several noteworthy features. First, all were unplanned and unanticipated. The participants all engaged in more or less useful conversations, but they did not know such conversations would take place even seconds before they occurred.

Second, the visual channel was a prerequisite for these interactions to occur. In each example, the visual channel was instrumental in identifying a partner for conversation, in identifying the precise moment when the potential partner was available, and in establishing a topic for the conversations. In each case, the initiator of the conversation first saw and recognized a potential partner whom he already knew. As Kendon and Ferber (1973) describe it, sighting is a necessary preinteraction phase of a greeting. Recognizing someone to talk to is not simply a passive process of following one's mother's advice to refrain from talking to strangers. Rather, seeing someone often brings with it a social obligation to acknowledge that person's presence with a greeting. In the candy machine example, Barry seemed to be responding to this social obligation as he went out of his way to greet Chester.

In addition, the visual channel was used to identify an opportunity for conversation. By looking at a potential target of conversation, the initiator can often interpret the target's locus of attention and infer whether and when he or she is available for conversation. In the call example, the initiator could see when the target had disengaged from his previous conversation and was available to be hailed. Potential conversationalists often use the visual channel to synchronize their behaviors (see Kendon & Ferber, 1973) to make sure there is a clear channel between them. For example, in the call episode, after Andrew hailed Bob, he did not engage in conversation until Bob had turned around, engaged in eye contact, and acknowledged his presence with a smile.

Seeing someone also serves as a potent stimulus to evoke topics of conversation. In the call episode, the sight of Bob appeared to remind Andrew of project information of which Bob should be aware. In the stop short episode, seeing Baker and saying hello to him clearly reminded Abel of a topic of conversation, and he reversed his tracks to follow it up. In the candy machine example, Barry's sighting of Chester appeared to remind him of Chester's wedding and Barry's

Episode 3: At the Candy Machine

Episode 3 is more blatantly social than the previous episodes. In the first scene, Ann and Barry are having an informal, social discussion in front of some vending machines as they take a break from work. Barry sees a coworker, Chester, walking by on his way to the elevator and hails him. Chester stops, and Barry, with Ann in tow, approaches him. Ann, who did not know Chester, is introduced, and the three have a discussion regarding Chester's wedding. Barry asks, "When's the big day?" He recognizes that Ann does not know Chester and explains that Chester is to be married. Chester replies that his wedding was last weekend, and both Ann and Barry congratulate Chester.

Three functions are served in this brief episode. First, Barry is maintaining social bonds with two coworkers, Chester and Ann. These minor social pleasantries are undoubtedly useful in developing and maintaining social networks in organizations. They form the basis of many mutual obligations and work exchanges in organizations. For example, if Barry needs information, it should be easier for him to call upon either Ann or Chester for help than it would be if they had never engaged in these social pleasantries. Second, Barry acted as a social catalyst by introducing Ann and Chester and providing information to each about the other. Ann should now have an easier time talking to and dealing with Chester than she would have if the introduction had never been made. Finally, during the discussion of Chester's wedding, Barry inadvertently reveals to Ann information about the closeness of Barry and Chester's relationship: They are coworkers who know each other, but not well, and who marginally keep up with each other's affairs through work place gossip. Ann can store these facts as potentially interesting background information that helps her understand her work environment.

Shared Features of the Episodes

None of these brief episodes of informal communication was especially significant in its own right. If any one of them had failed to occur, no careers would have been ruined or projects stymied. Yet episodes like these occur hundreds of times a day in both small and large departments. We believe that in the aggregate, they are fundamental

social obligation to inquire about it. Thus the visual channel is often instrumental in establishing topics of conversation.

A third characteristic illustrated by the examples is that both production and social work often get done in these informal conversations. Though one might characterize a conversation as having a main purpose, the production and social goals frequently co-occur; whether a conversation is work-related or social is a matter of degree. Sometimes a conversation is directly related to production. In the call episode, the participants coordinated their activity, informed each other about the status of their project, and solved a minor problem that was impeding progress. Yet it is clear from the smiles and positive effect displayed in this episode that the participants were enjoying each other's company as well. Other times, a conversation is basically social, as in the candy machine example, where members of an organization were able to establish and reaffirm their bonds to each other. But even here, it appears that coworkers were forging bonds that would underlie later work activity. Many times, informal conversations do not directly support the work at hand. However, even these often provide background information that might be useful for completing a work assignment or acquiring more general organizational competence (Granovetter, 1973).

Surface Characteristics of Informal Conversations

The following two sections describe some features and functions of informal communication more systematically and quantitatively. Casual observation suggests that brief encounters of the sort described above are extremely common in organizations. We concentrate (although not exclusively) on these brief and unplanned encounters because they are so common. Like an ethnologist, we start with the assumption that if a behavior pattern occurs frequently enough, it is likely to be important for a species or group. As social observers, we have a responsibility to describe these behavior patterns and to understand the functions that they might serve.

Some features of these conversations are easily observable. These surface characteristics, as we will call them, comprise information about informal communication that can be obtained through simple methods. In this section we present descriptive data about the surface characteristics of informal communication—specifically, how frequently informal conversations occur, how long they last, where they are initiated, where they are likely to take place, and how long they last.

If we use the frequency with which informal communication occurs as a measure of importance, then numerous studies have shown that informal communication is vitally important in organizations. Since at least the time of Mintzberg's (1973) study, organizational researchers have observed that informal communication is the dominant activity of managers. Sproull (1984) reviewed the evidence from seven studies of managerial communication in which managers ranged from mid-level rank (e.g., factory heads and school principals) to the most senior (e.g., CEOs of moderate-sized corporations and college presidents). Data collection included both direct observations of the managers by researchers who shadowed them during their workday and managers' self-reports of communication in daily diaries. Across the seven studies, verbal interaction accounted for about 75% of the managers' workdays. About 50% of this verbal interaction consisted of unscheduled face-to-face meetings with an additional 12% consisting of unscheduled telephone calls. Together these figures indicate that almost 50% of the typical manager's time is consumed by the unscheduled conversation that we consider informal communication. In general, informal communication appears to be a frequent and therefore important activity through which managers find out information, communicate opinions, and make decisions.

This characteristic of managers is also true of researchers in R&D environments. We make this statement based on data we collected in a study of conversations occurring in buildings of an industrial research laboratory and a state university. The aim of the study was to examine the characteristics of a sample of face-to-face interactions among members of these two organizations. We identified conversations occurring in a sample of locations in buildings within the organizations at randomly determined times. When a conversation was identified by a researcher, participants in the conversation were asked to complete a brief questionnaire describing it.

To sample conversations, a researcher first identified blocks of seating locations in a building, such as offices located along a corridor or desks within a large, group office.[1] The researcher went to these blocks at random times and made a single pass through the area (i.e., each individual was observed only once). The researcher interrupted every face-to-face conversation observed during the sampling period, explaining, "We are trying to understand what functions conversations serve in organizations," and asked all people involved in the conversation to complete a brief questionnaire at the end of the conversation. The questionnaire requested a description of the conversation (e.g., how it came about, where it occurred, its length, and its topic), the usefulness of the conversations for various functions (e.g., maintaining a working relationship, coordinating work, keeping up with workplace information), and the relationship between the participants (e.g., their organizational ties, project status, and frequency of other communication).

The researchers identified 522 sites (occupied desks or offices) where conversations could have occurred and observed 695 individuals. At the time of observations, 121 (23%) of these sites actually contained a conversation representing 267 individuals (38%). We had at least one usable response from 117 of the 121 conversations (97% response rate). In terms of individuals, the response rate was 83%.

Frequency and Initiation of Informal Conversations

At any moment in the R&D organizations we observed, 38% of the people present were engaged in face-to-face conversation. As one index of the informality of conversation, we asked respondents to indicate how these conversations came to be. This was operationalized as the degree to which the conversation was scheduled or spontaneous. Unlike previous researchers (e.g., Van de Ven et al., 1976), we distinguished among degrees of spontaneity, assuming that the more spontaneous the conversation, the more informal it was likely to be on many dimensions. All participants were asked to categorize the degree of preplanning that characterized the conversation in which they had just been involved. The four categories were: (a) a conversation that was previously scheduled (we term this *scheduled*), (b) one in which the initiator set out specifically to visit another party (*intended*), (c) one in which the initiator had planned to talk with other participants at some time and took advantage of a chance encounter to have the conversation (*opportunistic*), or (d) a spontaneous interaction in which the initiator had not planned to talk with other participants (*spontaneous*). Each respondent characterized the meeting individually. Because each par-

ticipant was likely to have a different view of how the conversation began, we organized the data by conversation and assigned an initiation value to the conversational unit. This value was defined as the most preplanned (least spontaneous) of any respondent's classification (ordered scheduled < intended < opportunistic < spontaneous on the spontaneity dimension). Thus, if the initiator of a conversation categorized it as intended and the other party classified it as spontaneous, we categorized the conversation as a whole as intended. This scheme provided a conservative estimate of spontaneity and also handled rating differences based on the role of the participants in the conversation.

The distribution of 117 conversations that we identified was as follows: 12%, scheduled; 36%, intended; 21%, opportunistic; and 31%, spontaneous. If we assume that only scheduled meetings are truly formal, then by this definition 88% of the conversations we sampled were informal. This is a conservative estimate because many scheduled meetings, particularly in an R&D environment, contain elements characteristic of informal communication. For example, a research planning meeting is typically highly interactive. This type of scheduled meeting is in sharp contrast with the elaborately choreographed activity at an annual shareholders meeting or a product-rollout meeting.

The 36% of conversations that were classified as intended by at least one of the parties are functionally equivalent to ambulatory phone calls, in that one person has intentionally gone in search of another in order to have a conversation. From the perspective of the intended object of this search, however, the conversation may appear entirely spontaneous because he or she had not anticipated its occurrence. The remainder of the conversations, about 50% of the total, happened by chance, with no preplanning on the part of any participant in the conversation. These conversations would not have occurred had the participants not wandered past each other's offices on the way to the copier machine, chanced upon each other in the hallway, or otherwise bumped into each other as they moved around in their physical environment. About 40% of chance encounters (21% of the total) were opportunistic; that is, they were triggered by the sight of a person with whom one party had previously formed an unacted-upon intention to talk. In the remaining 31% of the cases, no party to the conversation had anticipated its occurrence, and it was only the opportunity for conversation presented by the physical proximity of the participants that led to the spontaneous initiation of conversation.

Initiation of conversation seems to be a joint function of the salience or importance of the conversational topic and the ease of the conversational execution. In the case of both scheduled and intended conversations, the topic is important enough for somebody to initiate action that will lead to a discussion of that topic; groups schedule a meeting or individuals leave their offices in search of a suitable conversational partner. Opportunistic conversations are more complex. In some cases, there may be no topic that is important enough to warrant immediate action, and a conversation is simply deferred. Often, however, a manager or researcher in the course of making a decision feels the need to consult with a colleague, but other events or thoughts intrude (see Mintzberg, 1973; Reder & Schwab, 1988; Sproull, 1984, for evidence on the short attention spans of managers and researchers), and both the decision and the need to consult are placed on hold. In either case, when the decision-maker later comes across the colleagues in the hallway, two phenomena occur. Upon seeing the colleague, simple associative mechanisms remind the decision-maker of the original need for consultation and increase the temporary salience of the suspended decision, perhaps even reinstating the original decision-making context. Second, being in the colleague's presence simultaneously lowers the cost of communication. The decision-maker can see whether the colleague is available and has a clear channel through which the conversation can start (see Kendon & Ferber, 1973, on the initiation of interaction).

Spontaneous interactions are even more interesting. In these cases, there is no previous topic or need for consultation. Instead, the mere opportunity for conversation created by the presence of a suitable partner and availability of a clear channel serve to generate a conversation. Observations that we will review later in this chapter suggest that conversations, especially spontaneous ones, typically occur among people who already know each other from other contexts. At any occasion, they may have nothing in particular to say to each other, but norms of politeness require that they acknowledge each other's presence and perhaps exchange greetings. These passing social encounters occasionally evolve into substantive conversations. The topics for these conversations may be based on other activities in the environment or some other experience of joint interest that is remembered or generated during the course of the conversation (the candy machine conversation described previously is a typical case).

Location of Informal Conversations

Conversations that differ in their degree of spontaneity also differ on other characteristics. First, most conversations involve people who are housed close to each other. In our survey, each participant reported the location of the sampled conversation in relation to the location of his or her office. The choices given were: (1) the participant's office, (2) next door, (3) the same corridor, (4) the same floor, (5) the same wing/section of building, (6) a different wing/section of building, (7) the same campus/site, (8) a different campus/site. Each conversation was coded to reflect the farthest distance that any participant in the conversation had to travel in order to participate in that conversation.

Workplace conversations are, in general, quite local events, usually involving people who are in close physical proximity. As Figure 5.2 shows, 52% of all conversations involved people located within the same corridor, and 87% of them took place among people who shared the same floor in a building.

Our data are thus consistent with other observations showing the exponential decay of conversations with physical distance. Indeed, Zipf's (1949) principle of least effort predicts that the closest colleagues will have the most conversations. Whether it is because random motion causes people to have greater interaction by chance with those to whom they are closest (because people intentionally try to limit their contact efforts to those who are closest), or because organizations co-locate people who have the most need for communication, studies have shown time and again that physical proximity is strongly associated with frequency of interaction (see Allen, 1977; Festinger, Schacter, & Back, 1950; Kraut, Egido, & Galegher, in press; Zipf, 1949). Floor boundaries are an especially important functional barrier for all types of face-to-face communication.

These distance effects, however, are more powerful for more spontaneous conversations. In general, the data show that the more spontaneous the conversation, the greater the likelihood that participants' offices were located close to each other ($r[111] = .23$, $p < .02$). For example, fully 40% of the spontaneous conversations occurred among inhabitants of the same office. Of the spontaneous and opportunistic conversations, 91% occurred among people on the same floor, while only 82% of the combined intended and scheduled meetings did so.

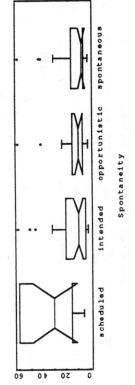

Figure 5.3. Duration of Conversations, Shown by Box Plots

NOTE: The waist of each box plot represents the median, and the notch around the waist represents one standard error on either side of the median. The box itself contains the middle half of the data, while the whiskers extending from the box reach to the most extreme nonoutlier. Outliers are plotted individually.

estimates was used as the duration for a given conversation. To reduce outliers in the data, conversations that lasted longer than 60 minutes were assigned a length of 60 minutes. In general, the more spontaneous the conversation, the briefer it tended to be (r[115] = .26, p < .02). In particular, Figure 5.3 shows that scheduled meetings were substantially longer than other types of conversations which, in turn, did not differ from one another. The median length of a scheduled meeting was about 30 minutes, while intended, opportunistic, and spontaneous meetings tended to last less than one third of this time—each with a median of less than 10 minutes.

Summary

Some of the characteristics of informal conversations are readily apparent from observations of conversations in progress. Informal communication tends to be frequent, accounting for over 85% of the interactions in our sample of conversations in R&D environments. While some of the informal interactions we sampled (about 35% of all conversations) were intended in that one of the participants sought out another, about 50% of the conversations were unplanned in that participants did not know they were going to speak to each other until they physically happened across each other. This result is consistent with the

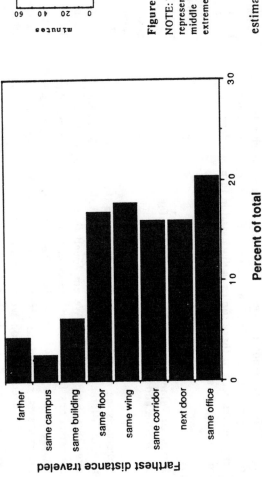

Figure 5.2. The Location of Conversations (*N* = 113)

It is probably for this reason that the more spontaneous conversations were composed of people who frequently communicate with each other. We asked participants to indicate how frequently they had spoken to their conversational partner in the preceding five workdays; we scored the mean of their responses per conversation. In general, most of these face-to-face conversations were but one of a series. The mean frequency of communication was 12.5 times in the preceding five days (*s.d.* = 14.6), but the more spontaneous (and therefore informal) conversations tended to occur among those who talked together most frequently (r[112] = .18, p < .06).

Duration of Informal Conversations

Differences in spontaneity and therefore in the degree of informality of a conversation were also associated with differences in conversation duration. Each participant in our survey estimated the length of the conversation in which they were involved; the mean of all participants'

principle that informal communication, like most other sorts of communication, is distance sensitive. In other words, it happens most often with people who are in physical proximity. Finally, informal conversations tend to be shorter than more formal communications. This tendency may be indicative of the types of uses to which informal communications are put in the workplace, a topic we take up more fully in the next section.

The Content and Uses of Informal Conversation

Having looked at some of the surface characteristics of informal conversations, we now turn our attention toward understanding the uses to which such conversations are put. This includes understanding something about the content of conversations that we consider informal as well as the role that conversations of this sort play in the functions of the workplace. Four studies are represented below that investigate the functions for which people perceive informal communication to be useful, the effects informal communication has on familiarity with and liking for one's coworkers, the effects on collaboration when informal communication is not allowed, and, finally, the relationship between informal communication and the success or failure of research collaborations. As each of these topics is discussed in turn, we describe the methods of the studies that provide the relevant data.

Perceived Value of Informal Communication for Production and Social Functions

Perhaps the most direct way of determining the value of conversations of different sorts is to ask participants to evaluate this immediately after they have occurred. We employed this strategy for 57 of the conversations from the study described above in which researchers sampled ongoing conversations in an R&D environment. Using 5-point Likert scales, respondents rated the outcomes of their conversations. Scores for a conversation were based on the mean judgment of all participants in that conversation. Adopting a variant of McGrath's (in press) model for group functions, we measured the degree to which conversations supported the production and social functions of group work, including both member support and group maintenance. The production function was measured by a 5-item scale with such questions as, "How useful was this conversation in getting your work done?" "How productive was this conversation?" and "How useful was this conversation for coordinating your work?" The social function of the conversation was measured by a 3-item Likert scale with the following questions: "How enjoyable was this conversation?" "How much did you learn about each other through this conversation?" and "How useful was this conversation for maintaining a working relationship?" The production measure was quite reliable (Cronbach's alpha = .89); the social functions measure was less so (Cronbach's alpha = .46). While we expected that the theoretical distinction between production and social functions of a conversation would be sharply reflected in the rating responses, results of a factor analysis indicated otherwise. In particular, the question about maintaining a working relationship loaded on both the production and the social factors. As a result, the two scales were moderately correlated ($r = .26$), lending support to the idea that both social and production functions are intertwined in real work groups. If one is going satisfactorily, the other is apt to do so as well.

A repeated-measures analysis of variance on these data revealed that, overall, the more spontaneous a conversation, the less valuable it was perceived as being ($F [1,55] = 3.9, p = .05$). However, this conclusion must be tempered by the interaction revealed by Figure 5.4, which shows that the effect for spontaneity exists only for the production dependent variable ($F[1,55] = 3.5, p < .07$). Figure 5.4, top panel, shows that both scheduled meetings and intended meetings were perceived as more valuable for getting work done than were opportunistic meetings or spontaneous meetings ($t(52) = 2.6; p = .01$). The relationship between preplanning and perceived value for production was partially a function of the length of the meetings, as the data above have demonstrated. Planned meetings were longer and, as a result, allowed more time for planning, discussion, and decision making. However, the relationship between preplanned and perceived value for production remained even when the duration of the meeting was held constant through multiple regression (standardized beta = .37, $df = 1,54, p < .01$). On the other hand, as shown in Figure 5.4, bottom panel, the value of conversations for social functions was unrelated to their spontaneity (standardized

consultation and decision-making opportunities. When they are working on a problem and need information or advice, they go down the hall and solicit it during a brief chat, rather than scheduling the time, agenda, and participants in advance.

In terms of social functions, all types of conversations provided some opportunity to enjoy the company of coworkers, to learn more about them, and to build bonds with them. Again, though, because scheduled meetings occur relatively infrequently and consume greater amounts of time, they fulfill the social functions inefficiently. Here, the brief and informal intended, opportunistic, and spontaneous conversations have an edge because they represent the vast majority of conversations in organizations.

The Effects of Informal Communication on Person Perception

Much research in both industry and academia is developed through voluntary collaboration. A fundamental requirement for these collaborations to occur is for researchers seeking partners to identify others with appropriate research interests and personal characteristics (see Hagstrom, 1965; Kraut, Galegher, & Egido, 1988, for a fuller discussion of the initiation of research collaborations). All else being equal, researchers want to work with people who are competent enough to do their share of the work and take only their share of the credit, and likable in their personal characteristics. Here we test the hypothesis that informal communication is the mechanism that researchers use to size up the pool of potential collaborators before becoming committed to working with any one of them.

We have seen that communication, especially unscheduled communication, increases as the distance between conversational participants decreases, and that participants in conversations report that unscheduled communication is especially useful for supporting the social functions of groups. Our hypothesis is that increases in informal communication will also have an effect on one's perception of coworkers; in particular, the more one communicates with someone, the more one is familiar with their work, is accurate in judging them, and likes them personally. These questions were examined in a survey of 51 scientists

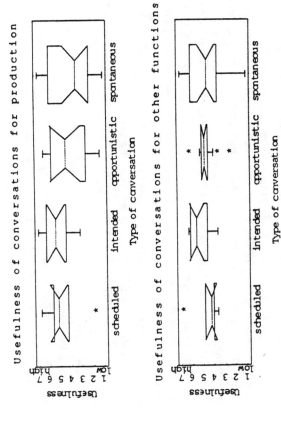

Figure 5.4. Value of Conversations for Production and for Social Functions
NOTE: For explanation of box plots, refer to Figure 5.3.

beta = .008, $df = 1,54$, $p > .50$). Brief hallway encounters were as valuable as hour-long, scheduled meetings in terms of getting to know coworkers and maintaining working relationships with them.

If one simultaneously considers the value of different types of conversations, the frequency with which they occur, and their duration, it is clear that much important work in R&D organizations occurs in unscheduled meetings. Both our own data and the earlier literature show that much of the detailed planning associated with a product gets done in relatively long, arranged meetings in which participants wrestle with their research ideas and set research directions (Kraut, Galegher, & Egido, 1988). Yet many smaller decisions and much of the coordination during the execution of the project itself get done in briefer and more spontaneous encounters. In terms of production, intended meetings are as valuable as scheduled ones for getting tasks accomplished; yet on a per basis. In terms of production, intended meetings are as valuable as scheduled ones for getting tasks accomplished; yet they occur four times as frequently as scheduled meetings, yet on a per meeting basis take only one third as much time to accomplish. Scientists, engineers, and managers use these meetings as "just-in-time"

and engineers within a single building in a research and development laboratory. The major purpose of the survey was to examine the relationship of informal communications among these researchers to measures of person perception and attitudes toward each other. For the purposes of this study, we treated physical proximity as a surrogate for frequent, informal interaction.

Individuals partaking in this study completed questionnaires in which they rated their familiarity with other participants and with the work of those participants. In addition, for those persons in the study with whom they were sufficiently familiar, they rated the degree to which those individuals and the degree to which they found their work to be interesting, important, and well executed. In the analyses that follow, results are reported as mean Pearson correlations between proximity and other measures of interest. Because each participant had a spatial relationship to and judged 50 other participants, we can compute a Pearson correlation between proximity and the person perception measures for each participant. Analyses are based on the means of these individual correlations, corrected by the Fisher formula.

Indices of Proximity

Participants in the survey were located on two floors of a single research building. We developed two proximity measures for each respondent. Like Allen (1977), Festinger, Schacter, and Back (1950), and Monge and Kirste (1980), we treated proximity as more than the linear distance between offices. Rather, functional proximity is the opportunity to engage in interaction and is moderated by architectural and organizational features as well as linear distance. We assumed that locations on different corridors, sections of the buildings, or floors were separated by more than physical distance. The first index of proximity (within-floor proximity) for each pair of participants was the shortest-path distance² between office locations (adjusting these distances if the shortest path crossed hallways or wings of the building) × -1. Approximately half the targets of person perception had offices located on the same floor as a rater, and half had offices on an adjacent floor. We assumed that for each respondent, targets on the same floor were functionally closer than targets on an adjacent floor. Thus, the second proximity index (between-floor proximity) was coded 1 if a target was on the same floor and 0 if the target was on a different floor.

Familiarity

Using 7-point Likert scales, respondents rated how familiar they were with 50 other members of the organization and their work. In addition, if they were sufficiently familiar with these organizational members and their work, respondents had the opportunity to rate how much they liked each of these members and respected their technical work. We treated willingness to make the ratings as a sign of familiarity and failure to do so as a sign of lack of familiarity. The correlations among these four measures ranged from .70 to .84. We therefore constructed a single measure of familiarity from these measures by standardizing and averaging them (Cronbach alpha = .87).

Participants were much more likely to be familiar with colleagues on the same floor than with colleagues on an adjacent floor (the mean Pearson correlation between the familiarity scale and between-floor proximity = .41, $t[50]$ = 19.6; $p < .0001$). For example, respondents thought that they knew enough about their colleagues' technical work to judge it for 42% of their colleagues whose offices were on the same floor as theirs, but made this judgment for only 17% of their colleagues on an adjacent floor. For researchers with offices on the same floor, the closer their offices, the better they knew each other; however, this proximity effect within floors was smaller than the between-floor effect (the mean Pearson correlation between the familiarity scale and within-floor proximity = .11, $t[43]$ = 3.8; $p < .001$). On the other hand, among colleagues on different floors, further increases in distance had no relationship to judgments of familiarity. Essentially, when two people were already a floor apart, increasing the distance by a hallway or more had very little effect on their perceived familiarity.

Liking

Just as proximity was associated with familiarity, it was also associated with one's liking for colleagues and respect for their work. Among those whom respondents knew well enough to judge, participants reported liking colleagues on the same floor far more than their colleagues on a different floor (the mean Pearson correlation between liking and between-floor proximity = .40, $t[50]$ = 118.1; $p < .0001$). Respondents tended to like their colleagues on their own floor more the closer their offices were to those of the respondents (the mean Pearson correlation between liking and within-floor proximity = .08, $t[46]$ = 1.87; $p < .07$).

The results for respondents' respect for other people's work showed a similar pattern. They had greater respect for the technical work produced by people on their own floor than for work produced on a different floor (the mean Pearson correlation between the respect for work and between-floor proximity = .31, $t[50] = 13.2; p < .001$). Moreover, for others with offices on their own floor, respondents tended to have more respect for the work of people closer to them than for people farther away (the mean Pearson correlation between the respect for work and within-floor proximity = .09, $t[44] = 1.68; p < .10$).

Summary

We have shown that physical proximity, which we have treated as a proxy for frequent and informal communication, is associated with several measures of person perception. As the opportunity for informal communication with colleagues increases, so does one's familiarity with them and their work, as well as liking for them and their work. While these findings are not new (see Allen, 1977; Bossard, 1932; Maisonneuve, Palmade, & Fourment, 1952; Segal, 1974) and our use of physical proximity means they are not definitive, either (e.g., Berscheid & Walster, 1969; Pelz & Andrews, 1966; Tajfel, 1970; Zajonc, 1968), they are interesting because they suggest the power that informal communication and the physical proximity that supports it can have on important social psychological processes in organizations.

Informal Communication and Momentum in Collaboration

Another method of gaining some insight into the uses of informal communication in the workplace is to investigate situations in which informal communication channels are limited or eliminated. We explored this possibility by conducting an experiment comparing two small work groups, one of which could use both formal and informal means to communicate while the other was limited to relatively formal mechanisms. The first of the groups was successful and the second was not. We suspect that their difference in success was caused by their differences in informal communication, although a case study cannot prove this suspicion.

The experiment compared two collaborations, a "remote" collaboration that was constrained to use relatively formal communications

channels, and a "standard" collaboration that used both formal and informal channels (Fish, 1988). Both collaborations involved researchers interested in investigating new concepts for a telecommunications system. The remote collaboration consisted of two people, a Ph.D. in electrical engineering and a Ph.D. in psychology; the standard collaboration consisted of three people, two Ph.D.s in psychology and one in computer science. All members of both teams had successfully collaborated in the past, completing projects of a similar nature and difficulty, but they had never collaborated together. Going into the experiment, each collaboration was judged as having a reasonable chance of success.

In addition to the preexisting differences in group size and personnel, the imposed constraint on which the collaborations differed was the communication mechanisms available to carry on their work. Two members of the standard collaboration had adjacent offices, and the third was on an adjacent floor of the same building. They had no constraints on their communication and communicated via scheduled project meetings, impromptu discussions in the hall, electronic mail, and telephone. In contrast, for the purposes of the experiment, the remote group agreed to have no face-to-face meetings in which they discussed their project. They refrained from both scheduled face-to-face meetings and impromptu discussions. Although their offices were on the same corridor and they continued to see each other casually and to have informal discussions, they refrained from discussing their joint project during these get-togethers. This restraint had the practical consequence of shifting their communication to more formal channels, such as scheduled video teleconferences or noninteractive electronic mail.

The video teleconference available to the remote collaboration consisted of a full motion, two-way, video/audio connection between their offices, supported by a shared electronic blackboard. These technologies required that a member of the collaboration had to schedule a meeting and then set up a connection with the other member to interact with him. Thus, like a genuinely remote collaboration, the opportunity for unplanned interaction was lowered although, with some effort, collaborators had at their disposal the means for high-quality interaction.

In order to understand how these collaborations proceeded, it is helpful to examine the data on two levels, process and outcome. The first level involves communication episodes, where we can compare the nature and quality of particular interactions; the second is a global level, where we can compare the outcomes of the collaborations as measured by their joint output, such as papers, programs, or artifacts. The data collected for this study consisted of records noting the date, length, and content of meetings between collaborators; video tapes and transcripts of most meetings for both the remote and standard groups; and the papers, programs, and artifacts produced by the collaborators.

Process

The first dimension for comparison is the quality of the meetings each collaboration held. One might expect substantial differences here because the remote collaboration could only hold meetings using its video/audio/data linkup, while the standard collaboration could hold meetings face-to-face. Using the transcripts from the meetings, the quality of the meetings was compared to criteria extracted from handbooks for running meetings (Doyle & Straus, 1985; Gordon, 1985). These criteria basically judge a meeting on whether the participants know why they are there and what they want from the meeting, whether during the course of the meeting some work is done toward meeting these objectives, and whether the participants are able to arrive at some common understanding of the meeting's outcome. To assess the quality of meetings by these criteria, one coder judged samples from the beginning, middle, and end of the transcriptions of each meeting and noted whether (a) participants explicitly mentioned their purposes for the meeting, (b) the content of their conversation was relevant to these purposes, (c) they summarized the meeting's accomplishments, and (d) they planned what they wanted to accomplish by their next meeting. By these criteria, and contrary to our expectations, all of the meetings—of both the remote and the standard groups—were of uniformly high quality. In particular, the remote, electronic meetings seemed as successful by these criteria as the face-to-face meetings of the standard group. This observation is consistent with the prior literature showing only minor differences between face-to-face and video-mediated meetings (e.g., Williams, 1977).

Qualitatively, the remote meetings seemed concentrated and intensely focused on work. Most of the collaborators' time was spent talking. In about 10% of the time during only two meetings, they supplemented their discussions with drawing on the video terminals to illustrate user interface concepts. This was similar to the behavior among the standard collaborators who used a whiteboard about 10% of the time during two meetings to illustrate user behavior and to outline their paper. Primarily, participants in the remote collaboration attended to and talked to each other on the video screens. Indeed, even though the video images in this teleconferencing system were not very large or of very high quality, and they did not support eye contact, they seemed to compel a polite attentiveness that was similar to the behavior found in the face-to-face meetings of the standard collaboration.

The remote and face-to-face meetings did differ in two major respects and one minor one. First, scheduled meetings in the standard collaboration were almost twice as long as the scheduled meetings in the remote group and appeared less efficient (mean length = 1 hour, 18 minutes for the standard collaboration versus 38 minutes for the remote collaboration; $t[25] = 4.12$; $p < .001$).

Second, meetings in the standard collaboration were more social and less task-focused than were the remote collaboration meetings; that is, they were filled with episodes of talk not directly related to the work at hand. Thus they were less efficient from a production point of view, but probably more effective at creating group solidarity. Anecdotes, workplace gossip, humor, and polite chit-chat all occurred relatively frequently. We examined 342 thirty-second segments of conversation from the standard and remote collaboration and coded whether they contained any social, non-task-oriented conversation. About 20% of the sampling units (38/188) in the standard collaboration were social, while only 5% of the sampling units (8/154) in the remote collaboration were social; $t(340) = 3.0$, $p < .05$.

Third, participants in the remote collaboration spent substantial time talking about the technology for their communication and work, while this was rarely an issue in the standard collaboration. The remote collaboration discussed tools for collaboration in about 14% of the sampling units, while the standard collaboration mentioned tools in only 2% of the sampling units. This difference in attention to technology may reflect the greater difficulty that members of the remote collaboration had in using their communication tools, or it may simply be an artifact of the novelty introduced by the experiment.

Outcomes

Even though the remote collaboration had "good" task-oriented meetings when examined one at a time, they had great difficulty in

settled on the direction of its work quickly and then was able to produce a steady stream of outputs, while the remote collaboration continually redefined and reallocated its work roles. While the remote collaborators always came out of a meeting highly motivated and sure that they would fulfill their promised work assignments, they were never able to deliver any significant work outputs in the long run, and the collaboration eventually petered out.

Other Communication Modes

The collaborators had other mechanisms for communication besides scheduled meetings. The standard collaboration had impromptu meetings that it engaged in frequently; it held pairwise conversations several times per week. These impromptu meetings were either spontaneous, where a chance encounter evolved into project talk, or intended, where one collaborator sought out another to discuss a specific problem. Sometimes one collaborator would run into another in the hall, and after exchanging a few comments, they would realize that a meeting involving all team members was in order; the third partner would then be fetched to see if a near-term meeting was possible.

In addition, both groups used electronic mail. By the criteria of Figure 5.1, electronic mail falls between scheduled meetings and impromptu hallway meetings on the formality dimension. It is more spontaneous than a scheduled meeting, but less interactive. Because the remote group was prevented from using informal face-to-face conversation to motivate its work, it might very well have taken advantage of electronic mail to carry some of the coordination burden. However, excluding the exchange of document drafts, participants in the standard collaboration exchanged 190 electronic mail messages among themselves that contained about 22,000 words, while participants in the remote collaboration exchanged only 51 messages, containing about 8,000 words. On average, these numbers represent about 6.8 messages per person per month (about 1,250 words) for the standard group and 1.8 messages per person per month (about 170 words) for the remote group. On the basis of these data, collaborators in the standard group had both a higher rate of communication and longer messages than members of the remote group. Here we find some evidence that both the content of the interaction, as measured by the length of the messages, and the coordination process, as measured by the frequency of the messages, was compromised in the remote collaboration.

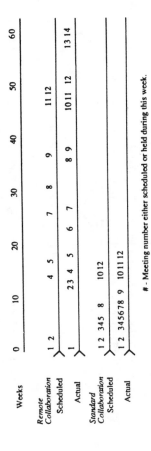

Figure 5.5. Timing of Collaborative Meetings
NOTE: For a few meetings, the initially scheduled date was not recorded in either the meeting transcript or the electronic mail.

communication when considered more globally. In particular, the remote collaborators communicated too infrequently to get their work done. Figure 5.5 shows the timing of meetings for the two collaborations over the course of their first dozen meetings. Each actual meeting and scheduled meeting is numbered chronologically. The remote group took more than twice as long as the standard group (a year versus 20 weeks) to accomplish their first dozen meetings.

Figure 5.5 also compares when meetings actually occurred with their initially scheduled dates. As can be seen, not only did the remote collaboration meet infrequently, but they were also less likely to meet close to the date they had originally scheduled to do so. For example, they had planned their second meeting to occur within two weeks of their first meeting, but it didn't actually take place until almost three months later. Thus, while the quality of each of the remote collaboration's meetings was high, their lower frequency meant that less work was accomplished in a given period of time.

If we examine meeting transcripts for the degree to which collaborators used the meetings to motivate their partners and coordinate their work, again we find few differences between the remote and standard collaborations. On this episodic level, the participants of both collaborations used their meetings to find out what their collaborators had accomplished and to motivate their partners. However, if we look at the global outcome of this effort, we find that the standard collaboration

Interpretation

These results suggest that the suppression of informal communication opportunities between members of the remote collaboration had a negative—perhaps even fatal—effect on the work of these collaborators. Because the opportunities for informal interaction did not exist, the participants had to rely on more formal, scheduled meetings to get the work done. However, because scheduling meetings takes time and effort, a lower overall frequency of meetings took place, which in turn resulted in less work being done by the collaborators, particularly in solving the problem of refining their work plan. Thus the collaborators were not as timely in giving each other feedback on the directions their joint work should go, and therefore they took longer to construct and select among the alternatives that guided the course of their work. This problem never became clear to the participants in the remote collaboration because each meeting, in and of itself, seemed productive and useful, and the participants did not have other, more informal contacts that they could use to supplement these meetings.

In contrast, the participants in the standard collaboration used their high frequency of meetings, both formal and informal, to construct and select among alternatives quickly. The frequency of contact increased the utility of each meeting because questions that were posed could be answered quickly before too much intervening time dulled the memory regarding the point of interest. The informal contact served to reinforce decisions once they were jointly made and created meetings spontaneously if an issue had to be addressed. The velocity of the cycle of interchange among the collaborators was increased in this way, and this process served to hasten the pace of the entire collaboration.

This case study illustrates, to some degree, how formal and informal communication are used within the context of a working relationship to complement and supplement each other in driving a piece of work toward completion. Each serves a role in maintaining the social underpinnings of the relationship, and each provides some elements necessary for coordination of the production aspects of joint work.

Informal Communication and the Success of Collaborations

On the basis of a single case study, the previous section argued that more informal communication can lead to more successful collabora-

tion. This section looks at a similar question using archival data to assess the patterns of authorship among working scientists and engineers. We attempted to determine whether physical proximity, which we view as a proxy for informal communications, was associated with successful collaboration. If a research team works together and publishes a joint paper, at some level it has solved the problems of group work, including identifying suitable partners, planning and executing work, and maintaining personal relationships.

We generated a data set based on the population of working scientists and engineers in an industrial research laboratory. The research laboratory consisted of approximately 500 Ph.D. and M.S.-level researchers in the physical, engineering, computer, and behavioral sciences. The organizational structure had three levels (laboratories, with approximately 125 members each; departments, with approximately 30 members each; and groups, with approximately 7 members each). The company was split between two campuses, located approximately 40 miles apart. Each building consisted of several floors with several wings per floor. We focused our analysis on a sample of 164 collaborating researchers, all those who had published at least two internal research reports in the preceding 30 months—at least one of these reports had to have a coauthor, and the other was either a solo-authored report or had a coauthor not included in the first report. For each of the 13,366 unique pairs of researchers ($164 \times 163 \div 2$) in the sample, we obtained data on four measures: collaboration, physical proximity, organizational proximity, and research similarity.

Collaboration

Data on whether each possible pair published at least one internal research report together were obtained from a company-maintained data base of internal publications (scored 0 for no publication and 1 for a joint-authored report). Of the 164 scientists and engineers in the sample, 126 had published at least one joint article with another member in the sample.

Physical Proximity

Using the organizational phone book—which listed office addresses with codes for building, floor, and corridor—we computed a measure of physical proximity. Offices were coded 4 if they were on the same corridor of the same building, 3 if they were on same floor of the same building, but a different corridor, 2 if they were on different floors of the same building, and 1 if they were in different buildings.

Organizational Proximity

Proximity on the organizational chart was coded 4 if the pair were in th same group, 3 if they were in the same department, 2 if they were in the same laboratory, and 1 if they were in different laboratories.

Research Similarity

For each pair, we estimated the similarity of their publications on which they did not share authorship. The research similarity index is based on information retrieval techniques developed to identify semantic similarity in large text sources (Deerwester, Dumais, Furnas, & Landauer, in press). Basically, one derives the concepts in large samples of texts by computing a singular value decomposition of a text-by-word matrix, akin to factor analysis. The texts we used were abstracts of each author's noncollaborative articles. The centroid of the words in each author's abstracts was used to represent his or her work in a 30-dimensional space. The similarity of a pair of abstracts is the closeness of the concepts they contain in this semantic space. Although this is a continuous measure, for some measures we treated it categorically, differentiating the top quartile from the rest (see Kraut, Galegher, & Egido, in press, for a more complete description of the methodology).

A logit analysis of the bibliographic data showed that research similarity, organizational proximity, and physical proximity all independently increased the odds of collaboration. Holding constant both research similarity and organizational proximity, the coefficient for physical proximity = .613 (standard error = .143, $t = 4.26$; $p < .001$). Table 5.1 shows the relationship between proximity and collaboration in a contingency table. It demonstrates that increases in physical proximity were associated with increases in successful collaboration both for researchers in the same department and those in different departments, and both for researchers with similar and dissimilar research interests.

All the phenomena we identified above probably contribute to this association of physical proximity and successful collaboration. Researchers who have offices close to one another have many more

These four measures were then examined in a number of ways. We found, for example, that researchers were most likely to achieve successful collaborations with those who were physically close to them—83% of the collaborations occurred among researchers with offices on the same floor, even though these represented only 26% of the potential collaborators. This finding is consistent with our earlier hypothesis that proximity leads to informal communication, and informal communication aids successful collaboration. However, the interpretation of this relationship is not this straightforward. The influence of physical proximity occurs partly because this organization, like many others, physically co-locates those who have needs for sustained and frequent communication; researchers in the same organization and those with research interests in common are far more likely to have offices on the same corridor than are arbitrary pairs of researchers.

Table 5.1
Association of Proximity and Collaboration

| | Research Similarity | | | | Organizational Proximity | | | |
| | Lowest 3/4 | | Highest 1/4 | | Different Departments | | Same Departments | |
Location	Potential Collaborators	Actually Collaborating %	Potential Collaborators	Actually Collaborating %	Potential Collaborators	Actually Collaborating %	Potential Collaborators	Actually Collaborating %
Same corridor	260	.77	333	14.41	399	6.02	194	13.40
Same floor	1755	.45	1122	4.19	2416	.70	469	8.10
Different floor, same building	3463	.06	1012	1.17	4447	.29	42	2.38
Different building	4534	.01	858	.69	5387	.13	12	0.00
Total	10023	.13	3343	3.38	12649	.48	717	9.07

opportunities for conversations. As a result, they are likely to know and like one another and to know of and respect one another's work. The frequent, low-cost contact made possible by physical proximity creates many opportunities for potential collaborators to become acquainted, to identify common interests, to assess interpersonal compatibility, and to do preliminary planning before they become committed to working together. In a typical collaborative relationship, neither partner starts out specifically seeking a collaborator to help carry out an already well-defined project. Rather, research projects frequently emerge from the preexisting interests and expertise of the participants in the course of casual discussion. These initial discussions became more intense and focused after researchers became committed to working together. These observations suggest that informal communication is important because it allows researchers to know about their neighbors and to develop common interests.

Once a project is started, frequent, informal communication serves as a coordination and project-management tool that helps keep the project moving forward. The coordination required of researchers becomes substantially more difficult to perform when they are not located in the same place or, as we discovered in the preceding section, when they have other constraints on their informal communication.

Summary

The preceding sections have shown that informal communication is frequent in R&D organizations, that it aids organizational members in learning about one another and their work, that it supports both production work and the social relations that underlie the work, and that it provides a critical mechanism that collaborators rely on to start joint work, maintain it, and drive it to conclusion.

Proximity leads to increased frequency of communication in general, and of informal communication specifically. Proximate colleagues have more opportunity for intended, opportunistic, and spontaneous conversations. Increased informal communication between colleagues leads to greater familiarity as well as increased respect for colleagues and their work. One would expect that the familiarity and mutual respect fostered by informal communication would be a prerequisite or at least a powerful facilitator for successful working relationships and

collaborations. Colleagues need to be familiar with one another in order to seek information from and dispense information to the appropriate parties. They must be familiar with one another and share a similar perspective, context, and working culture for successful collaboration. Colleagues who collaborate must also like one another and the work that each does in order to maintain the working group and continue successful collaboration over time.

Technology for Informal Communication

In many circumstances, the ideal of close physical proximity for a working group cannot be realized. The realities of organizations may preclude individuals who are supposed to be working together from having their offices near one another. Communities of scientists, in particular, are often distributed across the nation or world. University departments often hire for breadth and may have only a single researcher covering a subspecialty. Graduate students in the job market, junior faculty denied tenure, and other faculty lured to a new institution by prestige or money frequently move far away from their advisors, colleagues, or collaborators. These factors mean that in the world of science, colleagues who would make the most suitable collaborators are often hundreds of miles away. In addition, in industry, many projects, such as software development, are so large that physical proximity for the entire staff becomes a topological impossibility. For this reason, we became interested in creating artificial proximity through the use of technology.

In the previous sections, we have seen some of the characteristics of physical proximity that make it especially suitable for informal communication. Here we review some of these characteristics and draw implications for features that artificial proximity must provide.

A Concentration of Suitable Partners

Any system that wishes to support informal interaction must provide access to a suitable population of others. In the physical world, concentration is accomplished by putting people who need to communicate close together. For example, as Table 5.1 showed, researchers in the same subunit and those who share research interests tend to be located in the same area in a building.

In the telecommunications domain, everyone who is connected to a common network is in some sense equally accessible, absent the constraints of distance-sensitive charges and unfamiliar addresses. Thus, as long as a sufficient proportion of the relevant population is connected, a population of suitable partners is also available (see Markus, 1987). Yet, because everyone is equally accessible—friends and strangers, similar and dissimilar people—the availability of suitable partners may be too diffuse to create an effective community for informal interaction. Dialing a phone number at random or posting a message to a nationwide electronic bulletin board is unlikely to put the initiator in touch with an appropriate research partner. The requirement for a telecommunications system to support informal interaction is to concentrate suitable partners.

Co-presence

For informal interaction to occur, people need an environmental mechanism that brings them together in the same place at the same time. In the physical world, this mechanism can be a lunchroom, coffee lounge, or other space where people convene, or it can involve the complexity of movement around a workplace. In the R&D laboratories we studied, people were constantly moving around. At any time, almost 50% of the staff were out of their offices, and the episodes presented previously show that unplanned interactions occur frequently during these travels. Yet much information technology, such as electronic libraries and data bases, reduces the need for physical movement to get work done, thereby reducing the opportunities for casual interaction (e.g., Kraut, Dumais, & Koch, 1989). Similarly, separating people (into branch locations, for example) reduces the likelihood that they will occupy a common physical space and thereby reduces the likelihood of informal interactions as well.

The essence of telecommunications—literally communication from afar—is co-presence without physical proximity. While most telecommunications assume intentional action to initiate communication with a particular other, it is possible to devise other idioms for nonintentional telecommunications. Electronic bulletin boards, in which readers come across the postings of other bulletin-board users, are one such example.

Low Personal Costs

The cost of communication, in terms of the amount of effort needed to initiate and conduct a conversation, is very low in the casual encounters we described previously. Often the contact is a side effect of other activities and, as such, involves no extra cost. To provide this low-cost communication when people are dispersed, we need to make getting in touch with others as easy as bumping into them in the hallway. The behavioral costs of accessing a communications system and getting in touch with the desired other party are an important determinant of that system's usefulness. If the costs of using a communication source are too high (e.g., Cullan, 1983), as is the case with many of the "traditional" teleconferencing systems (Egido, in press), the user will be either unable or unwilling to use that system for the brief, frequent, spontaneous conversations that are characteristic of informal communication.

Visual Channel

The visual channel plays an important role in informal communication. As discussed previously, seeing someone provides a means for recognizing the presence of another person, determining who he or she is, and assessing that person's availability for interaction. It also serves as a stimulus for picking a topic of conversation—reminding one person about something he or she wanted to discuss with another. Finally, the visual channel combined with the audio channel provides a medium by which the conversation is actually accomplished. A technology for informal interaction must support both audio and video communication if we are to successfully stimulate chance encounters.

These characteristics of physical proximity suggest some boundary conditions on potential telecommunication technologies to support informal communication. We use them to form the initial requirements for technologies to support informal interactions. Two prototype telecommunication systems that take different approaches to solving these problems are described below—the VideoWindow System and Cruiser.

The VideoWindow Teleconferencing System

Imagine sitting in your workplace lounge drinking coffee with some colleagues. Now imagine that you and your colleagues are still in the

audio provides sound localization so that the speaker's voice appears to originate from the location of the speaker's image. The system is left on 24 hours a day. To use it, a person need only walk into the room, glance at the window, and say "hello" to a person at the other end. At first glance, the VideoWindow System offers a very powerful sense of shared space and presence at a very low behavioral cost to the user.

In order to look more closely at the effects of the VideoWindow System on informal communication, we conducted a 3-month trial in our laboratory. Two commons areas on different floors of a building were connected using the VideoWindow System. Over the course of the experiment, participants were questioned about their use of the system; their knowledge of other participants, both local and remote; and their feelings about the technology. Video records were kept of face-to-face interactions in the lounge areas and of interactions that took place over the VideoWindow System.

We observed a total of 628 instances in which people were present at both ends of the VideoWindow System (364 cases of exactly 2 people, 264 cases of more than 2 people). Each instance represented an opportunity for people to strike up a conversation across the Video-Window System link. These opportunities were actually converted into verbal interaction (either a greeting or a conversation) on 153 occasions. This conversation rate of 24% represents 11% of the 2-person opportunities and 32% of the 3-or-more-person opportunities actually being used for interaction.

The videotapes of these interactions across the VideoWindow System suggest that in some cases the system was a relatively transparent medium. Many interactions that took place via the window seemed indistinguishable from similar face-to-face interactions. People often spoke and acted in a fashion that, at least superficially, seemed altered in only minor ways by the technology. They spoke a little louder and often embedded a discussion of the VideoWindow System itself in their discussion. Most of the 153 interactions we recorded would not have occurred had the system not been in place.

Yet the conversion ratio across the VideoWindow was substantially lower than the conversion ratio for face-to-face opportunities. For this comparison, we examined 81 cases in which two people were together on a single side of the VideoWindow—that is, in the same room—and thus had an opportunity to converse face-to-face. Disregarding the 29 cases in which the face-to-face people were already talking prior to entering the VideoWindow room, we found that 31% of the face-to-face

Figure 5.6. Illustration of the VideoWindow System in Use

same room, but are separated by a large sheet of glass that does not interfere with your ability to carry on a clear, two-way conversation. Finally, imagine that you have split the room into two parts and moved one part 50 miles down the road, without impairing the quality of your interaction with your friends. That scenario illustrates the goal of the VideoWindow project: to extend a shared space over considerable distance without impairing the quality of the interaction among users or requiring any special actions to establish a conversation.

The VideoWindow System (Bellcore, 1989) connects two public lounge areas with high-bandwidth video channels and full-duplex four-channel audio. Figure 5.6 illustrates the VideoWindow System in use. The video images are projected onto a 3-foot-high by 8-foot-wide "picture window," roughly twice the width of usual projection TV. This allows nearly the entire lounge area to be visible, with people appearing to be about the same size as if sitting across the room. The four-channel

opportunities were converted into interaction. This is almost three times the conversion rate for pairs across the VideoWindow.

This version of the VideoWindow System had some properties that worked against the initiation and maintenance of informal interactions. Some of the missed opportunities to converse across the VideoWindow System were due to design flaws in the user interface. About 18% of missed opportunities could be attributed directly to problems with camera and microphone placement. For example, people often tried to strike up a conversation by moving closer to the window. This caused their head to move out of the picture so that they could not be recognized, and put them out of microphone range so they could not be heard. This type of flaw could be fixed with feedback that let a communicator know whether he or she could be seen at the other side of the system. Other problems may be more endemic to the underlying technology. Eye contact is an example. Humans can shift their gaze to meet another's eyes wherever that person may be, but conventional cameras have a fixed point of view. This leads to anomalies in apparent eye contact that do not occur when people are face-to-face. Another problem is that it is easy for people to stand out of camera range where they can see the image in the window but not be seen by people at the other end. (Note the man at the left edge of Figure 5.6, who can see others in the system, but cannot be seen by them.) This contrasts with face-to-face interaction, where covert observation rarely occurs and frequently requires active concealment on the observer's part. Solving these sorts of problems requires rethinking how video cameras and monitors are designed and placed in personal communications systems.

Once a conversation was initiated, communication over the Video-Window System sometimes broke down. One problem was that the system made it difficult to establish private conversations in otherwise public areas. In fact, the ability to make a conversation private was one of the most frequently requested improvements mentioned by users in our sample. When people in a conventional meeting room wish to exchange private information, they simply move closer together and lower their voices. This capability is not supported by the Video-Window System or any teleconferencing systems designed to link public areas together with hands-free audio. Teleconferencing technology is designed to allow several people to converse clearly at the same time. The case of private conversations illustrates a more general point: Technology-mediated systems do not currently have the communica-tion flexibility and ability to manipulate media characteristics that we take for granted in face-to-face conversations.

Another class of problems stems from the social and environmental context in which the VideoWindow System is situated. A VideoWindow System installation requires that users go to the room in which it is installed in order to use it. This imposes a moderate behavioral cost on users to access the technology unless they are already using the public space. The centralized nature of the VideoWindow System also results in a sampling problem: Potential encounters are limited to the set of people who occupy the system's extended space at the same time. On average, people are more likely to be someplace other than in the VideoWindow System room. In addition, the probability of being acquainted with persons at the other end may be low, given the low degree of familiarity with people at remote locations. As we have seen, even within a single building, a person is less than half as likely to know someone on an adjacent floor as someone on his or her own floor.

Although the VideoWindow System can support informal interaction at a distance and may be useful in some contexts, its implementation requires careful attention to social detail. One could imagine connecting the cafeterias of two research organizations whose members already know one another and who have reason to work together. In other circumstances (where the VideoWindow System connects strangers, and where people occupy the system locations infrequently), the probability of encountering a suitable partner and striking up a conversation is low. So, even though VideoWindow System may extend the boundaries of one's physical space and increase the absolute number of people with whom one can interact, it does not necessarily extend the effective work space or social environment in which most people work and in which most informal conversations take place.

However, even when all these problems are accounted for, the VideoWindow System was not as effective as we had expected due to factors we still do not understand. One problem may be that the mechanisms that the human perceptual system uses to judge the distance and size of objects do not operate correctly in this technology. In addition, it may be that even with life-sized images, the psychological distance to someone at the other end of a VideoWindow System link is greater than that in a comparable face-to-face situation. People had to work hard in the face-to-face situation to ignore someone who was physically in the same room. When they wanted to avoid conversation, people went to great lengths to avoid eye contact. In contrast, ignoring another person on the opposite side of the VideoWindow System was much easier, and looking at them didn't seem to create the obligation to engage in conversation. In spite of its value, then, the VideoWindow System currently does not provide the same degree of social intimacy as does face-to-face interaction.

The implications of this experiment are clear. First, we must pay close attention to the human factors of system design. Simply connecting two locations is not enough—we must also ensure that the technology can be used easily and without errors. Problems must be engineered out of the system. This is especially important with audio/video systems, because while these technologies appear to be like face-to-face communication, the subtleties of camera framing and audio placement lead to important differences that users can't be expected to understand. To solve these problems, we must learn more about how the characteristics of basic video technology affect the usability of telecommunication systems and about the difficulties caused by fixed camera positions and audio that is insensitive to user behavior. Second, we must reduce the behavioral cost to the user of gaining access to the technology in the first place. One solution to this problem is to bring the system to the user. Finally, we must address the person-sampling problem; the user must be able to get in touch with the right people regardless of location.

Cruiser

The Cruiser system (Fish, 1989; Root, 1988) is a switched telecommunication system (like the telephone) that allows a user to have an audio and video connection to any other user in the Cruiser network. It was designed to support informal communication at a distance among colleagues, while solving several of the problems identified during the VideoWindow System experiment. In particular, it lowers the behavioral cost of communication by placing audio and video equipment on the user's desktop. In addition, Cruiser provides innovative mechanisms for initiating connections between users to encourage frequent, informal, and unplanned communication among members of a distributed community. These mechanisms provide access to a large but select group of conversational partners independent of location.

Cruiser and Informal Communication

Users of this network can treat it merely as a video telephone and call any other user directly. However, Cruiser was explicitly designed to support serendipitous interactions, and a measure of its success is the extent to which it leads to fruitful or enjoyable conversations that were unintended. One mechanism for these chance encounters is the "cruise." Here, Cruiser tries to simulate the experience of walking through a hallway and stopping to chat with whomever one encounters along the way. The virtual hallway is the set of offices and other locations connected to the system. The set of locations the user actually visits is called a path; this can be one or several stops along the cruise. A single command causes Cruiser to switch to each location on the user's path in turn, pausing to give the user a brief audio and video "peek" into each office along the way. Both parties can see each other and can determine whether they wish to have a conversation and if their partner is available. If the user spots someone to chat with, another command interrupts the cruise and connects the two locations until the user decides to move on again. If the user does not wish to converse, the connection times out after a few seconds.

The path can be explicitly set by users who type a list of other users to visit. More interestingly, the path can be determined by the Cruiser system itself, by selecting from a pool of potential conversational partners. Users, a system administrator, or intelligent software can create a separate pool for each user and assign to each person in the pool a weight indicating the relative probability of that person being visited on a cruise. For example, users may list people whom they would like to see more frequently. The system administrator may add other people to this list based on such criteria as similarity of background or current work projects. In an R&D organization, for example, one might have researchers in small specialty areas "running into" one another and keeping in touch over the Cruiser system. Finally, the pool of potential partners might be updated by computer programs that monitor the environment, add to the pool, and change probabilities depending on current conditions. For example, if a member of a research organization publishes a new research report in a user's area of expertise, software might increase the weight that partner has in the user's pool. Similarly, a computer program could change the weight of individuals in a user's pool depending on the history of that user's other communication activities (i.e., telephone calls or electronic mail). For example, Cruiser might increase the opportunity for chance encounters with people one is already going out of one's way to reach.

Cruises can be explicitly initiated by typing the "cruise" command. The motivation may be work-related (e.g., "I need an answer to a question. Who is around to help me?") or social (e.g., "I'm bored. Who is free for a chat?"). In addition, cruises and opportunities to converse with other users may happen as side effects of other noncommunication-oriented activities. Just as a person might stop to converse with someone while walking down the hall to pick up a computer output, the Cruiser software itself might initiate a cruise when a user types the "print" command on a computer terminal. Linking a cruise to the reading of electronic mail or bulletin boards is especially appropriate because by executing these computer commands a user is implicitly saying, "I am interrupting my ongoing activities to be put into contact with social information."

Cruiser connections may also be initiated when two users are participating in the same event. Cruiser can connect offices with public conference rooms so that a user might attend a lecture through Cruiser. Just as conversations often break out among the audience at a lecture, such is also the case with Cruiser—one can scan and be connected to other people using Cruiser to attend the lecture. Combining special video hardware (called picture-in-picture devices) with audio switching allows such conversations to take place without disrupting the lecture.

Issues in the Trade-Off of Access and Control

We hypothesize that these technologies can be used to overcome some of the barriers to informal interaction that physical dispersion introduces. Although we have conducted a behavioral experiment with the VideoWindow System and discovered some of its limitations, at the time this book went to press, we still have little experience with the use of Cruiser.

The capabilities that VideoWindow and Cruiser provide come at a price. In particular, the value of informal communication is often asymmetrical. While we want easy access to other people, we want to control access to ourselves. Examining conventional conversations in the workplace, we see that a convenient, intentional communication for

one person is an interruption for the person who is being addressed. We are discovering in building our technology prototypes that important design issues consist of resolving the trade-off between achieving access to others and protecting their time and privacy.

One of the things that makes some work settings a social environment is the relatively free access coworkers have to one another. People often gather in hallways, cafeterias, and other common areas where they are free to converse. Offices are often open to coworkers, providing accessible communication channels for both signaling and interaction. It is considered appropriate behavior to glance into an open office while walking down the hallway, and it is usually acceptable to drop in and have a chat on the spur of the moment. While these characteristics of offices are undoubtedly culturally variable (Hall, 1966) and depend on the relative status of coworkers and current trends in both architecture and job design, they are common in the relatively open and relaxed research and development environments we observed. For these mechanisms to work, people need to make themselves available. The bulk of this chapter has tried to demonstrate that people do indeed make themselves available and that, as a result, informal interaction is one of the primary communication tools of the workplace.

For telecommunication systems to support informal interaction, people need to make themselves available in this medium as well. With the VideoWindow System, public spaces must be continually connected to support drop-in conversations. Cruiser requires that users leave a camera and microphone constantly on in their offices. As a result, both of these technologies raise questions of privacy and control that pose fundamental problems for the design of telecommunication systems for informal interaction.

At the heart of the matter is the trade-off between easy access for informal communication and the ability to control one's communication environment. Users have two major concerns. First, they are worried that their privacy will be violated; others will see them and learn information about them without the user's ability to control what is imparted or without their knowledge. Users are concerned about giving off both visual and verbal information (Sundstrom, 1987). Surprisingly, most potential users of Cruiser and other video communication prototypes with similar goals (Abel, in press) believe that audio information is more revealing than video. Compounding this general concern about privacy is the worry that those with power might abuse the system by snooping surreptitiously. The second major concern of users is about uncontrolled intrusions; telecommunication provides an additional channel through which visitors can intrude into the user's work space. For all the value of informal communication, it has the drawback of consuming a scarce resource: time. Telecommunication systems like Cruiser enlarge the pool of people who can steal time from priority tasks. People of high status in organizations have developed both social and technological mechanisms, such as secretaries, appointment calendars, and answering machines, to prevent interruption. In a sense, Cruiser subverts these mechanisms. Potential users of Cruiser do not want to be open to a large number of people who intrude upon their space and take up their time.

In the physical environment of the office, these matters are partially regulated through social conventions that dictate who can interrupt whom, when to knock, and so on. In a public space, a conversation may be made private by the participants lowering their voices or moving to a private space. Office occupants may exert direct and explicit control over their local environment, for example, by closing the door to the office and refusing to answer their phone. These simple acts create barriers to the flow of information in or out of the office and signal to potential visitors about the occupant's availability for interruption.

These considerations have led us to design a number of features for providing users with control over their privacy and access. First is the use of reciprocal views, or the "see and be seen" strategy. When a person visits another office using Cruiser, two things happen: The visitor can see and hear what is happening in the other office, and the occupant of the visited office also sees and hears what is happening in the visitor's office. This feature ensures that occupants are not spied upon or observed without their knowledge. Next, in order to give users the ability to look into an office to ascertain the occupant's presence or simply glance in while passing by, we have adopted the notion of a limited duration "peek" (Goodman & Abel, 1987), still following the principle of reciprocal viewing. This feature provides sufficient time to see if the occupant is available but limits the duration of an intrusion. Third, we have heard from many people that one advantage of the real office is that they can hear someone walking past the doorway. We simulate this in Cruiser by providing an audible signal when someone peeks into a user's office.

Finally, we can provide a number of controls to give occupants the functional equivalent of a door between them and Cruiser's virtual hallway. Occupants have the option of setting a busy flag on the audio

and/or the video signals emanating from their offices. When a busy flag is set, visitors will receive a notice on their workstation that a channel is not available. If, for example, the video is open but the audio is busy, a visitor will still get the short visual peek into the office but will not be able to hear anything. If an interaction ensues, the occupant may, of course, allow audio communications at any time. These privacy flags may either be set explicitly with a workstation command or implicitly by sensors attached to the physical door or telephone so that the busy flag is set when the office door is shut or the telephone is in use.

A more sophisticated possibility is based on the existence of a hierarchy within the workplace that gives certain people greater privileges to interrupt than others. In general, those with higher status and those with important business (secretaries, for example) have greater freedom to interrupt than peers or lower status individuals. The system already knows who is visiting whom. The addition of organizational and status information can let it exercise a modicum of "intelligence" in deciding when a visitor might interrupt a conversation or override a privacy flag. Balancing the interruption privileges of high-status visitors against the privacy concerns of other individuals requires sophisticated filters and careful design in order to prevent abuses and maintain user confidence in the technology. If a rich simulation of office etiquette makes the technology more effective, however, then more advanced software techniques from the artificial intelligence domain could be utilized.

Many of these features—selective media blocking, reciprocal views, visual status cues, and user-specific filters—will be incorporated into Cruiser and evaluated in field trials, but, again, there is a design trade-off: At what point do the protection schemes increase the cost of communication to the point where drop-in interactions will simply not occur, thereby defeating the goals of the system? One intent of our experimental trials is to reveal whether these manipulations are either necessary or sufficient for users' acceptance of the system.

Conclusions

The intricate choreography necessary to do work in organizations requires effective coordination. Throughout this chapter, we have argued that informal communication, generally mediated by physical proximity, is crucial for this coordination to occur. Informal encounters are useful means of getting people to know and like one another, of creating a common context and perspective, and of supporting planning and coordination in group work. Indeed, without them, collaboration is less likely to start and less productive if it does occur. Physical proximity helps by allowing appropriate people to encounter one another frequently, by supporting visual channels to induce and assess readiness for communication, and by supporting highly interactive conversation.

What happens when groups get too large or spread out to allow physical proximity to support informal communication? Telecommunication and computer technology may be able to take the place of proximity. In this light, we presented the VideoWindow System and Cruiser. The VideoWindow System is based on the concept of extending a large shared space and providing informal communication access via video and audio. The system is available 24 hours a day, and workers merely enter the room, "bump" into someone on the other end, and converse. Cruiser is based on the metaphor of walking along a hallway and stopping to talk with whomever is encountered along the way. Cruiser provides informal communication access by putting the audio and video equipment on the user's desktop and by using a switched audio-video network to connect offices and other locations together, leading to a large number of potential connections.

We have discovered that designing telecommunication systems to support informal interaction at a distance requires the resolution of many trade-offs. System designers must understand and be sensitive to the needs and concerns of system users. They must be alert to the subtleties of etiquette and the protocols that govern social interactions, be concerned with the possibility of unwanted intrusions or surveillance, and balance the need for casual access against the desire for control of one's personal space. A system must provide access and openness as well as restrictions and privacy. There is a need for mechanisms that support subtle communication protocols and are sensitive to the social context in which communication systems are embedded. We need to explore these issues with real prototypes and users, and we need to develop appropriate design and evaluation methodologies for innovative system design and effective evaluation. It remains to be seen whether we will be able to solve these problems in the VideoWindow and Cruiser systems.

Notes

1. Sunita Ashar and Jonathon Shulman served as able research assistants in this data collection.

2. Steven Rohall wrote the program to compute the distances.

References

Abel, M. J. (in press). Experiences in an exploratory distributed organization. In J. Galegher & R. Kraut (Eds.), *Intellectual teamwork: The social and technological bases of cooperative work*. Hillsdale, NJ: Erlbaum.

Allen, T. (1977). *Managing the flow of technology*. Cambridge, MA: MIT Press.

Argote, L. (1982). Input uncertainty and organizational coordination in hospital emergency units. *Administrative Science Quarterly, 27*, 420-434.

Bellcore, or Bell Communications Research. (1989). *The VideoWindow Teleconferencing Service model* (Special Report SR-ARH-001424). Morristown, NJ: Author.

Berscheid, E., & Walster, E. H. (1969). *Interpersonal attraction*. Reading, MA: Addison-Wesley.

Blau, P. M., & Scott, W. R. (1962). *Formal organizations*. San Francisco: Scott, Foresman.

Bossard, J. (1932). Residential propinquity as a factor in marriage selection. *American Journal of Sociology, 38*, 219-224.

Brown, P., & Fraser, C. (1979). Speech as a marker of situation. In K. Schere & H. Giles (Eds.), *Social markers in speech* (pp. 33-62). New York: Cambridge University Press.

Clark, H., & Marshall, C. R. (1981). Definite reference and mutual knowledge. In A. K. Joshi, B. L. Webber, & I. A. Sag (Eds.), *Elements of discourse understanding* (pp. 10-63). Cambridge: Cambridge University Press.

Cullan, M. J. (1983). Environmental scanning: The effects of task complexity and source accessibility on information gathering behavior. *Decision Science, 14*, 194-206.

Daft, R. L., & Lengel, R. H. (1984). Information richness: A new approach to managerial behavior and organizational design. In B. Staw & L. L. Cummings (Eds.), *Research in organizational behavior* (Vol. 6, pp. 191-233). Greenwich, CT: JAI Press.

Daft, R. L., & Lengel, R. H. (1986). Organizational information requirements, media richness, and structural design. *Management Science, 32*, 554-571.

Deerwester, S., Dumais, S., Furnas, G., & Landauer, T. (in press). Indexing by latent semantic analysis. *Journal of the American Society for Information Systems*.

Doyle, M., & Straus, D. (1985). *How to make meetings work*. New York: Jove.

Egido, C. (in press). Teleconferencing as a technology to support cooperative work: Its possibilities and limitations. In J. Galegher & R. Kraut (Eds.), *Intellectual teamwork: The social and technological bases of cooperative work*. Hillsdale, NJ: Erlbaum.

Festinger, L., Schacter, S., & Back, K. (1950). *Social pressures in informal groups: A study of human factors in housing*. Stanford, CA: Stanford University Press.

Fish, R. S. (1988, February). *Comparison of remote and standard collaborations*. Paper presented at the Workshop on Computer-Supported Cooperative Work, Tucson, AZ.

Over, R. (1982). Collaborative research and publication in psychology. *American Psychologist, 37*, 996-1001.

Pelz, D. C., & Andrews, F. M. (1966). *Scientists in organizations*. New York: John Wiley.

Reder, S., & Schwab, R. (1988). The communicative economy of the workgroup: Multi-channel genres of communication. In *Proceedings of the 1988 conference on computer-supported cooperative work* (pp. 354-368). New York: ACM Press.

Root, R. W. (1988). Design of a multimedia vehicle for social browsing. In *Proceedings of the 1988 conference on computer-supported cooperative work* (pp. 25-38). New York: ACM Press.

Segal, N. W. (1974). Alphabet and attraction: An unobtrusive measure of the effect of propinquity in a field setting. *Journal of Personality and Social Psychology, 30*, 654-657.

Sproull, K. (1984). The nature of managerial attention. In L. Sproull & P. Larkey (Eds.), *Advances in information processing in organizations* (pp. 9-27). Greenwich, CT: JAI Press.

Stohl, C., & Redding, W. C. (1987). Messages and message exchange processes. In J. Jablin, L. Putnam, K. Roberts, & L. Porter (Eds.), *Handbook of organizational communication* (pp. 451-502). Newbury Park, CA: Sage.

Suchman, L., & Wynn, E. (1984). Procedures and problems in the office. *Office: Technology and People, 2*, 113-154.

Sundstrom, E. (1987). Privacy in the office. In J. D. Wineman (Ed.), *Behavioral issues in office design* (pp. 177-201). New York: Van Nostrand Reinhold.

Tajfel, H. (1970). Experiments in intergroup discrimination. *Scientific American, 223*, 96-102.

Tushman, M. L., & Nadler, D. (1978). Information processing as an integrating concept in organizational design. *Academy of Management Review, 3*, 613-624.

Van de Ven, A. H., Delbecq, A. L., & Koenig, R., Jr. (1976). Determinants of coordination modes within organizations. *American Sociological Review, 41*, 322-338.

Williams, E. (1977). Experimental comparisons of face-to-face and mediated communications: A review. *Psychological Bulletin, 84*, 963-976.

Zajonc, R. B. (1968). Attitudinal effects of mere exposure. *Journal of Personality and Social Psychology, 9*, 1-27.

Zipf, G. K. (1949). *Human behavior and the principle of least effort*. Cambridge, MA: Addison-Wesley.

Fish, R. S. (1989). Cruiser: A multimedia system for social browsing. *SIGGRAPH Video Review* (Video Cassette), Issue 45, Item 6.

Gabarro, J. J. (1987). The development of working relationships. In J. W. Lorsch (Ed.), *Handbook of organizational behavior* (pp. 172-189). Englewood Cliffs, NJ: Prentice-Hall.

Goffman, E. (1963). *Behavior in public places*. New York: Free Press.

Goodman, G. O., & Abel, M. J. (1987). Communication and collaboration: Facilitating cooperative work through communication. *Office: Technology and People, 3*, 129-146.

Gordon, M. (1985). *How to plan and conduct a successful meeting*. New York: Sterling.

Granovetter, M. (1973). The strength of weak ties. *American Journal of Sociology, 68*, 1360-1380.

Hackman, J. R. (1987). The design of work teams. In J. W. Lorsch (Ed.), *Handbook of organizational behavior* (pp. 315-342). Englewood Cliffs, NJ: Prentice-Hall.

Hagstrom, W. O. (1965). *The scientific community*. Carbondale: Southern Illinois University Press.

Hall, E. T. (1966). *The hidden dimension*. Garden City, NY: Doubleday.

Kendon, A., & Ferber, A. (1973). A description of some human greetings. In R. Michael & J. Crook (Eds.), *Comparative ecology and behavior of primates* (pp. 591-668). London: Academic Press.

Krauss, R. M., & Fussel, S. (in press). Mutual knowledge and communicative effectiveness. In J. Galegher & R. Kraut (Eds.), *Intellectual teamwork: The social and technological bases of cooperative work*. Hillsdale, NJ: Erlbaum.

Kraut, R. E, Dumais, S., & Koch, S. (1989). Computerization, productivity and quality of work-life. *Communications of the ACM, 32*, 220-238.

Kraut, R. E., Egido, C., & Galegher, J. (in press). Patterns of contact and communication in scientific research collaboration. In J. Galegher & R. Kraut (Eds.), *Intellectual teamwork: The social and technological bases of cooperative work*. Hillsdale, NJ: Erlbaum.

Kraut, R. E., Galegher, J., & Egido, C. (1988). Relationships and tasks in scientific collaboration. *Human-Computer Interaction, 3*, 31-58.

Kraut, R. E., Galegher, J., & Egido, C. (1989). *Informal communication in scientific work*. Unpublished manuscript, Bell Communications Research, Morristown, NJ.

Kraut, R. E., Lewis, S. H., & Swezey, L. W. (1982). Listener responsiveness and the coordination of conversation. *Journal of Personality and Social Psychology, 43*, 718-731.

Maisonneuve, J. A., Palmade, G., & Fourment, C. (1952). Selective choices and propinquity. *Sociometry, 15*, 135-140.

March, J. G., & Simon, H. A. (1958). *Organization*. New York: John Wiley.

Markus, L. (1987). Toward a "critical mass" theory of interactive media: Universal access, interdependence and diffusion. *Communication Research, 14*, 491-511.

McGrath, J. E. (1984). *Groups: Interaction and performance*. Englewood Cliffs, NJ: Prentice-Hall.

McGrath, J. E. (in press). Time matters in groups. In J. Galegher & R. Kraut (Eds.), *Intellectual teamwork: The social and technological bases of cooperative work*. Hillsdale, NJ: Erlbaum.

Mintzberg, H. (1973). *The nature of managerial work*. New York: Harper & Row.

Monge, P. R., & Kirste, K. (1980). Measuring proximity in human organizations. *Social Psychology Quarterly, 43*, 110-115.

Ouchi, W. G. (1980). Markets, bureaucracies, and clans. *Administrative Science Quarterly, 25*, 129-141.

Cooperative Support for Computer Work: A Social Perspective on the Empowering of End Users

Andrew Clement

Faculty of Library and Information Science
University of Toronto
140 St. George Street
Toronto, Canada M5S 1A1

INTRODUCTION

The image of computers being used to empower people is a potent and appealing one. For the many working people whose autonomy is routinely challenged by the constraints of large organizations or the vagaries of the market, the spread of sophisticated desktop computers holds the promise of gaining in personal control. While testimonials to the efficacy of desktop computers and announcements of their increased capabilities are regular fare in the media and casual conversation, the easy equation of personal computing power with personal power is an attractive simplification that needs closer scrutiny.

An essential ingredient of this equation is mastery over the technology itself. Despite the popular promotion of desktop computers as being "personal", "easy to use", and even "friendly", the reality for many users is quite different. That the technology is in fact complex, often difficult to apply and requires considerable organizational resources is demonstrated by the growing demand for training and technical support. (George, et al; 1989; Panko, 1988) A surprising amount of learning and adaptation effort turns out to be required. Particularly disadvantaged in this respect are secretaries and other workers at the bottom of the office hierarchy. Though numerically a significant group who play a vital support role in organizations, they generally lack the clout to have their needs better addressed.

The highly social nature of work must also be taken into account. People generally do not work alone but in conjunction with others. Power is therefore not simply a personal matter but depends on organizational relationships. The realization of this fundamentally collective nature of work is one of the key concepts of computer supported cooperative work (CSCW) which distinguishes it from other areas of computing and makes CSCW particularly relevant to fulfilling the promise of computing as a means for empowerment.

This paper explores the question of empowerment through computerization by looking at common problems of computer use in the context of office group work. In particular it examines the difficulties that secretaries confront when attempting to master desktop computing and the cooperative solutions they have developed to overcome them. The data used in this analysis is derived from two research projects conducted at a large Canadian university. Based on the findings, the paper outlines proposals for the design and implementation of CSCW applications intended to enhance the power of clerks and secretaries, office workers who are relatively resource weak. We begin our discussion by examining the notion of power in the context of human computer interaction within work organizations.

THE NEED FOR EMPOWERMENT

As the organizational sociologist, Rosabeth Moss Kanter, has observed, "power" is a "loaded" term (1977, p. 166.). While everyone appears to want more of it, they often mean quite different things. Kanter defines power simply as the "ability to get things done" (p. 166), and regards it as "synonymous with autonomy and freedom of action" (p. 197). This definition is useful in helping us see that power is not just a question of dominance but one of effectiveness. Organizations that have large numbers of relatively powerless members are not only depriving the employees as individuals but also diminishing the contributions they can make to the overall enterprise. When empowerment does not involve the subordination of others, it is something to be encouraged and promoted, especially among those who are least powerful. Computerization of office work presents a particularly valuable opportunity to pursue this goal.

Kanter also notes that "the powerful are those with access to the tools for action" (p. 166). While she makes no specific reference to computers, their relevance in this context is obvious. Many organizational actions involve the performance of information processing tasks that are amenable to computerization and thus expanding the capabilities of computers and extending their availability to a wider group of people can clearly be regarded as a process of empowerment. However, the shortcomings of this interpretation become apparent when we examine the terms "access" and "tool" more closely and especially when we enlarge our notion of action beyond the narrow technical one of the performance of well specified tasks.

Contrary to popular usage, a computer is not intrinsically a tool, if by that term we mean a device that is largely under the control of its user. (Kling, 1987) Being a tool implies that the user should at least have discretion about whether or not to use it for any particular task and understand its operation sufficiently to achieve desired results. Desktop computers in organizations often do not meet these criteria - using the machine frequently becomes the only authorized way for those low in the organization's hierarchy to perform assigned tasks and difficulties in usage are widespread. (Clement & Parsons, 1990; Gasser, 1986, Kling & Scacchi, 1982) This also reflects on the notion of access, which obviously means more than physical availability, since the capabilities of the system may be effectively out of reach through ignorance of operation, awkwardness of interface, narrowness of application, etc. In extreme cases, users even experience increased powerlessness when forced to use a rigid, constraining, inscrutable and unreliable computer system - and hence from the users perspective, the very antithesis of the ideal tool.

Transforming a given computing facility into an effective tool for action and realizing some of its empowering potential, typically involves users in a prolonged process of learning and adaptation. They must not only do this on their, but also as part of their work groups and the organization. (Johnson and Rice, 1987) This is because the implications for computer use in general cannot be divorced from the wider social worlds within which computing is inevitably embedded. (see Kling, 1980; Kling and Scacchi, 1982) It is here that a CSCW perspective has much to offer. By starting with collectivities of workers as the analytic vantage point, it encourages us to see the possibilities and implications of computer use within the context of organizational structures and processes.

Work organizations are not exclusively rational enterprises in which a consensus can be assumed about what tasks should be done and by whom. They are primarily social systems driven not only by clearly articulated common goals but, as well, by a host of varied and often conflicting personal aspirations. Indeed, as sociologist Charles Perrow (1979) has noted, organizations don't have goals so much as uses. This means that taking action by computer is not simply the manipulation of abstract information flows but involves influencing the behavior of others. From this social perspective, personal power is not a property of the individual user but depends fundamentally upon the structure of social relationships in which he or she participates. Empowerment cannot be accomplished without both drawing upon, and at the same time changing, existing social relationships. If this is not to be achieved at the expense of others, then it must build on and strengthen relationships in ways that are mutually enhancing - i.e. through cooperative work[1].

Ben Shneiderman (1987) argues that designers of human-computer interaction need to "fight" for users. The basic design principle he identifies as necessary for this to work is to recognize the diversity of users (1987, p. 52) and typically this means taking into account such factors as differences in users' experience. Thus, if our aim is to help empower people in their interactions with computers, this principle requires us to understand the prior distribution of power among users and develop strategies attuned to specific user constituencies. Most of the literature on end user computing (EUC) focuses explicitly or implicitly on managerial, professional or technical personnel (e.g. Nelson, 1989), while secretarial and clerical workers have received much less attention. Ray Panko notes, for example, that secretaries have tended to be excluded from access to the dominant means for assisting users, namely Information Centers (1988, p. 16). This has occurred in spite of their large numbers and the critical support role they play in efficient organizational operation. The reasons for this oversight are complex and deeply rooted in historical patterns, but can largely be accounted for by the fact that as women performing low status service jobs involving tacit knowledge, secretaries have not been able to press their needs with regard to computing as effectively as others[2]. This lack of power and the consequent lack of resources can be seen as an example of "reinforcement politics", whereby those already with greater influence are better able to guide computerization to serve their interests (Danziger et al, 1982).

The desire for greater influence can be seen as threatening to established patterns of power. However, as we will illustrate later, the demand by secretaries can be for greater support to enable them to improve work performance with computers. Furthermore, as Kanter and others have suggested, the exaggerated centralization of power that is endemic in contemporary organizations is dysfunctional and influence should be more widely distributed. The preferential empowering of secretaries and other "resource weak" groups low in the organizational hierarchy, should thus in general be seen as a positive development that is beneficial to the organization as a whole.

EMPOWERMENT THROUGH COOPERATION

In seeking ways to assist resource weak computer users gain in power, it is helpful to examine the strategies they have adopted in the past to compensate for their relative lack of influence. Approaches that build upon existing sources of strength are much more likely to succeed than those ignore them. Two studies conducted with office support groups shed light on this question and reveal the importance of informal mechanisms of cooperation. The research developed in response to the difficulties that office staff experienced in using personal computers, primarily for word processing.

The widespread introduction of desktop computers for office support work at York University began in 1984 when administrators in the Faculty of Arts installed over one hundred PC-compatible computers. The secretaries were not consulted about this beforehand, and in many cases the equipment arrived in the academic department office without warning to the staff. The initial training was minimal and, according the Dean responsible, was intended as much to desensitize secretaries fears as it was to instruct them in the use of the technology. Complaints by staff prompted managers to provide some temporary additional training and support. Secretaries also took their complaints to the Technology Committee of the staff union. This lead to collaboration between the chair of the committee and the author, a computer scientist on the faculty. Together they initiated an action-oriented research project entitled Self-Managed Office Automation (SMOAP). The aim was to help the office staff assess their needs and demonstrate that, with appropriate resources under their control, they could support their own use of computers.

A subsequent research study, entitled Office Automation Knowledge Requirements (OAKR) was designed to investigate in greater detail what office workers needed to know about computer use and how they acquired the knowledge. It was conducted in the Secretariat of the university, a high-level, Type II (i.e. non-procedural, Panko and Sprague, 1982) secretarial office serving the central governing bodies of the university (i.e., the Senate, Board of Governors, and their subcommittees). The work group consisted of five women and two men and had a reputation for being an early and effective adopter of desktop computing. It was one of the first administrative groups on campus to install a local area network (LAN) to which all members had access through PC's on their desks. The study examined the ways in which the work group cooperated to make the technology work for them.

Informal collaborative networks

Early in the SMOAP project we conducted a survey of the entire secretarial support staff in the Faculties of Arts and Fine Arts. More than 90% responded to the mailed questionnaire, all of whom were women (N=96). The results were quite consistent with those of a smaller, but more detailed study of secretaries conducted at Carnegie Mellon University (Hartman, 1987). Generally they viewed their computers very favorably in terms of potential usefulness, but were frustrated by the way in which the technology had been implemented. They reported learning much more by studying on their own and discussing with co-workers than from formal courses or other external sources of expertise. They dealt with the usage problems primarily through mutual support within the work groups rather than by referring to written manuals or to outside specialists. A comment by one secretary summarized well the overall reaction:

> *I certainly feel that there was a great lack of consultation with the staff in the introduction of computers, and it is only due to the efforts of the staff themselves that this has had any success at all. I feel strongly that training has been inadequate in the extreme and that computers are not being used as they should be. With proper training there is so much that could be done. The staff neither have the time nor the facilities to expand on their knowledge.* (Clement, 1989, p.38)

The later OAKR study probed more deeply the problems that staff encountered and the patterns of cooperation they developed in response. The members of the Secretariat faced persistent difficulties in using the computer system despite their training and years of experience. As one of the administrative secretaries commented:

This office .. is shameful. .. We have the latest software and all this technology and no one knows how to use it [properly].

In the course of using word processing packages, transmitting messages via electronic mail, filing electronic documents, and the like, staff experienced recurrent difficulties. During open ended interviewing within the work group, each member was asked to identify who helps whom in attempting to resolve such difficulties. Figure 1 (Clement and Parsons, 1990) shows the network of co-operation that these inquiries revealed. The arrows depict the direction of information flow indicated by response to the question "Who do you go to for help?". In addition, each person was also asked to maintain a diary for a two week period to record incidents in which their normal work was interrupted by some lack in their knowledge about the computer systems. The four diaries that were completed report a total of 40 distinct incidents. Of these, 25 involved conferring with someone else when such interruptions arose. The results are shown in Figure 2. Note that incidents shown as loops on a single person were resolved without consulting another person and that 11 arrows represent multiple consultations. Both these diagrams reveal a consistent pattern of collaborative support, which, interestingly, corresponds neither to the pattern of work flow through the Secretariat nor to the authority structure (shown as dashed lines in Figure 1). Like the SMOAP respondents, the Secretariat staff found the assistance they obtained from each other was, in general, more satisfactory than that obtained from outside the group. In effect these users developed an effective, informal network of support based on local expertise that considerably enhanced their mastery over a complex and changing technology.

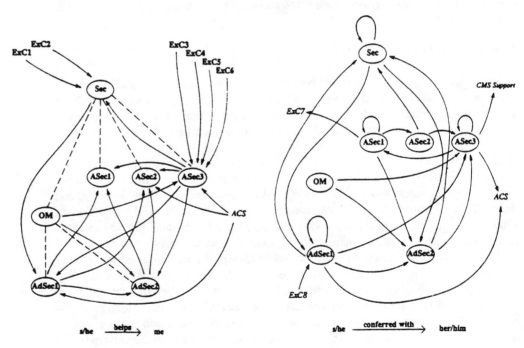

Figure 1. Who helps me with computer problems?

Figure 2. Who conferred with whom?

LEGEND:

Sec: Secretary
AdSec: Administrative Secretary
ExC: External Contact

ASec: Assistant Secretary
OM: Office Manager
ACS: Academic Computing Services

Industrial sociologists have known for decades that group cooperation is a vital ingredient in production work (e.g. Homans, 1950). Studies of computer users have repeatedly revealed the importance of collaboration based on spontaneously emerging local experts (see Bannon, 1986; Lee, 1986; Nelson and Cheney, 1987; and Scharer, 1983) Recent research (George et al, 1989) suggests that even when substantial training is available, this local assistance will remain essential. Thus, given the characteristics of desktop technologies and the "situated" nature of the office work to which it is applied (Suchman, 1987), these findings on the need for collaboration are not surprising. What is surprising, however, is that there has been so little further exploration of these informal support networks and that the results that are available have not been applied in any systematic way to the implementation of desktop computing. Even those who develop computer supported cooperative work (CSCW) applications and thus recognize that people work in groups, concentrate almost exclusively on supporting well defined tasks or general communications while ignoring the informal facilitation of the basic meta-task of simply learning to use and adapt the technology[3]. This represents an important component of "articulation" work, which Bannon and Schmidt (1989) argue is a core issue in the CSCW field.

These attempts by users to empower themselves through local, informal support networks generally do not represent a challenge to managers. Users may become frustrated over their difficulties with using computers, but seldom is there sufficient motivation or opportunity for an overt dispute to develop. However, as we shall see with the SMOAP project and its aftermath, demands by users for empowerment that are not met adequately by intra-group cooperation can lead to more overt, and contentious, collective action.

A self-management alternative

The main focus of SMOAP was a microcomputer resource center established by the staff union with the support of the university administration. Twenty-five support staff, all women, from six academic department offices, used the center for instruction, problem solving assistance and access to a small library of software and print materials. The focal activity was a weekly meeting in which the representatives from each department discussed the problems they faced with computer use. Detailed minutes from each meeting were distributed to all participants and served as a principal data source for the research. Our approach was inspired chiefly by the socio-technical systems (Mumford and Henshall, 1979; Mumford, 1983) and Scandinavian (Bjerknes et al., 1987; Briefs et al., 1983; Howard, 1985) schools of systems design. Our original intention was to assist secretaries master desktop computing through the collective analysis and redesign of computer related work tasks; however, according to wishes they expressed in the early goal setting meetings, we shifted our emphasis to providing more basic software training. While their immediate goal was to increase software competency (particularly with word processing), they also discussed concerns over heavy workloads, upgraded job descriptions, developing new computer uses, ergonomic issues and getting greater recognition from management for their contribution to the operation of the university.

A formal questionnaire evaluation conducted upon termination of the five month project showed that the response by the participants was overwhelmingly favorable. They felt that they had learned a great deal about computerization and about the benefits of working together more closely. They expressed a general desire to establish a similar facility on a permanent basis. The following comments reflect the commonly expressed sentiment for greater control over their interaction with computers and the importance of collective action (Clement & Zelechow, 1987):

> *[It's a] relief to know that there is a place - on campus - to find out the how, what, where and when - you can deal with problems arising from understaffing and computerization. There are problems and this is a positive and realistic approach to dealing with these.*

> *[The project] has made me think less about "MY JOB" and more about "OUR JOBS" - collectively. - has given me the incentive to work more closely with the others in my dept.*

> *It has given me hope!*

> *Apart from technical knowledge I got from the project, my participation has enabled me to see more deeply into the problem of office automation, and how it has affected most of us as secretaries. I discover I'm not alone in my "struggles" and it's necessary for us to come together to make the machine work for us, not vice-versa.*

> *I now feel there is concrete hope for staff demands. re: ergonomics, staff input in decision making, staff independence over access to training and procedure making. Through my own initiative to learn and develop new skills, I have created new systems and procedures for carrying out my responsibilities.*

> *I have a greater sense of being able to control my work now - rather than my work controlling me.*

These remarks take on added significance in light of subsequent events. Several months after the project ended and the resource center closed, the support staff union went on strike. One of the three main issues that kept the 1,100 members out for over two weeks, was the demand for staff-run microcomputer training. This demand was ultimately met, and in early 1988 a training programme was established[4]. It is modeled on the SMOAP project and is headed by the former project coordinator. The Microcomputer Training Programme now has a regular budget funded by the administration, a former secretary as Trainer/Administrator and trains over 300 staff per year in using software popular for wordprocessing, spreadsheets and hard disk management. It is jointly managed by a committee with equal representation by the support staff union and the administration. The union selects the full-time Coordinator, who is responsible for day to day operation, and has effective veto over decisions. Even though the shape of the Programme continues to be negotiated between the parties, it already presents a distinctively worker-centred alternative, in both focus and management, to the standard Information Centre approach to the support of desktop computing (Panko, 1988).

Although there was no direct involvement of the SMOAP researchers in organizing the strike or mobilizing support for it, the union president who lead the strike felt the experience of the project played an important role. She identified three ways in which the project was influential: it gave a specific focus for union demands regarding training; it enabled the bargaining committee to articulate the necessary resources in contract language; and it gave the proposal credibility in the eyes of management. (Interview, May 1989) It was a concrete example the union leadership was proud of and could use to persuade both the membership and the employer that the concept of a staff-run programme was a viable one.

The SMOAP project and the Training Programme clearly represent successful attempts by the office staff themselves to gain additional support needed for working with computers. This required forms of cooperation that go well beyond the local collaboration we discussed earlier. During the project, support staff from different departments who in general did not otherwise work directly together or know each other discovered common difficulties and identified common remedies. This process was carried out on a much larger scale during bargaining with their employer when they developed strong collective pressure for the establishment of their own microcomputer training facility. The significance of the project comes not so much from the specific techniques used in the meetings or other activities but more from the fact that it adopted a worker-centred approach the staff could respond to. The project helped make legitimate and more visible the widely felt concerns the staff had about how they had been treated over computerization and offered a feasible solution. In terms of Lukes' (1974) conception of power, it enabled the staff to change the political agenda by translating their numerous but isolated frustrations into an item they could bargain over and win.

It is important to recognize that in both of these research projects, the principal concerns of the staff involved was to do better the tasks that were expected of them. What was remarkable was that despite the inadequate support, so many staff became active collectively in seeking the required skills. In this light, the more contentious aspects of the workers reactions should not be seen as dysfunctional, but instead as a healthy response to prevailing difficulties. They are better viewed as symptomatic of the deeper structural adjustments that all organizations must undergo when carrying out rapid and widespread computerization.

Certainly if desktop computing was easier to master or the administration had devoted greater attention to its adoption, staff would likely not have responded as strongly as they did. However, we should not expect that the technologists who design desktop computing, and the managers who implement it, will necessarily be willing or able to do so in the best interests of all parties. Rather, we should expect that inter-group and broad collective cooperation by support staff to exert greater control over desktop computerization will continue to be vital to their empowerment.

IMPLICATIONS FOR DESIGN AND IMPLEMENTATION

These examples of cooperation can provide some guidance to those who would design and implement desktop computing in the service of support staff. This research underscores the well recognized need for improving the human-computer interface (see Norman and Draper, 1986; Shneiderman, 1987) so that many of the frustrations and inefficiencies that staff experienced can be reduced. More importantly, there needs to be greater facilitation of the different ways that users cooperate to master computing technology.

While designers have recently given attention to the technical support of cooperative work through "groupware", both for specific application domains and for general purpose communications (e.g. electronic mail), there has been comparatively little work done to help users collaborate informally in learning to use the technology or in repairing interactional breakdowns when they occur. An unobtrusive way which could assist novices is to implement analog of "beaten tracks" through a system's menu choices. Just as the cumulative effect of people walking across terrain provides clues as to the route to follow, so indications (e.g. though relative intensity) of menu selections that are most frequently selected in the immediate workplace would help newcomers avoid pitfalls. A tempting extension of this is to provide facilities so that when a user experiences difficulties she could request the system to suggest other workers who are likely to be able to assist. Potential collaborators would become known to the system through a combination of the automatic recording of usage patterns and voluntary self-identification. In essence the system would then act as a kind of "dating service" for matching learners with spontaneously emerging local experts. Useful tips and comments that emerge from the resulting collaboration could then be stored at the relevant nodes to create a user-grown form of Answer Garden (see Ackerman and Malone, 1990). The systematic recording of usage patterns could also be valuable for identifying common problems and sharing innovations. However, each of these possibilities carry a potential danger in that the records generated could be used by superiors for monitoring work performance, with the possible threat of disciplinary action. Even between peers, there will be reluctance to impose on others or to reveal ignorance. Great care should be taken so that users can maintain their anonymity until they choose otherwise, so that exploratory behavior would not be inhibited by fear of sanction. The great degree of mutual trust that would be required for this to work well is better regarded as a prerequisite to implementation rather than a hoped for outcome.

The more general type of cooperation involved in discussing common problems and mobilizing support for particular remedies could be facilitated through standard means such as electronic mail, computer conferencing and bulletin boards. A guiding principle should be one of open communication, but again, in some cases, it may be necessary to protect individual and group privacy. This can be seen in the example of an electronic mail system described by Zuboff. A flourishing discussion among women in a large company about strategies for "professional improvement" quickly died out when it became known that more senior managers started collecting transcripts and asking questions (1988, pp. 382-383). There needs to be the electronic equivalent of private meeting spaces where support staff can get together as peers to share experiences and formulate individual or collective responses. They could incorporate the principle of reciprocity, whereby all participants to a discussion, whether silent or contributing, are mutually identifiable (see Kraut et al, forthcoming). At the same time, the anonymity that is valuable in such group processes as idea generation and voting could be selectively preserved. The technical arrangements for this would be obvious extensions of standard measures for security, but would need to be reviewed by auditors selected and trusted by users.

The empowerment that can come from the technical facilitation of cooperation is likely to be modest. Our research suggests that the implementation strategy is much more important than any particular characteristics of the technology. For instance, it could have helped reduce staff frustration if instead of IBM PC based technology, management had introduced Apple Macintosh computers with their better support for human computer interaction. However, much of the difficulty of mapping current office work onto computers and adjusting work patterns would have remained. A major source of difficulties that the secretaries faced was the implicit adoption by implementors of the "super typewriter" metaphor, in which the computer is seen as a "personal", easy to use, more efficient substitute for a secretary's conventional typewriter. This goes a long way in explaining why almost all resources were devoted to the purchase of hardware and software and very little to training and support. It also contributed to the feelings of frustration and inadequacy the secretaries felt when it turned out to be much more difficult to learn than they had been lead to believe[5]. Viewing secretaries largely as typers of documents allows their skills and learning needs to be regarded as peripheral in importance. In these circumstances, the development of local collaborative networks and broader forms of cooperation are belated reactions to a difficult situation. Though necessary, this response is costly in terms of personal frustration and organizational efficiency.

Instead, what is needed is to see desktop computing, especially in office group settings, as a complex and far-reaching intervention into a social system. Secretaries, among others, play a central, if under-rated, role in its successful adoption. In the spirit of Grudin's (1990) advice to enlarge our notion of "user interface", we should welcome users organizing themselves into support networks and agents of political action. To help realize this potential requires more than just inviting participation and providing the technical means for cooperation. Designers and implementors can also contribute by adopting attitudes and methods that encourage the self-identified interests of end users to surface as legitimate demands for active consideration. In particular, the implementation metaphor of desktop computing consisting of a collection of intrinsically empowering "products" that need only to be accepted by users must be subordinated to a social "process" oriented approach driven by the evolving needs of users (Floyd, 1987). A growing body of research into participation in system development by resource-weak groups, particularly women, is available to guide this effort. (Benston, 1989; Bjerknes et al, 1987; Bjorn-Andersen, 1986; Clement et al, 1989; Docherty et al, 1987; Ehn, 1988; Green et al, 1989; Kyng, 1988; Olerup et al, 1985; Tijdens et al, 1989)

SUMMARY AND CONCLUSIONS

This research supports Shneiderman's assertion that "the computer revolution will be judged not by the complexity or power of technology but by the service to human needs" (1987, p. 434). The secretaries in our studies were empowered in their interaction with desktop computers not simply by the capabilities of the technology, but in significant ways by their ability to cooperate among themselves. They developed local collaborative networks and collectively drove the establishment of their own computer training programme. In the process, they enhanced their power in a broader organizational sense - illustrating interpersonal and political dimensions of cooperative work that has been relatively invisible in CSCW studies to date. Those seeking to empower users through their interaction with computers should recognize and facilitate these forms of cooperative support for computer work.

---

[1]As Bannon and Schmidt (1989) note, the term "cooperative work" has a long history and a range of meanings. They prefer to use it in the general and neutral sense of "multiple persons working together to produce a product or service." (p. 362) This is quite appropriate for defining the field of CSCW. We use the term here in a more socially normative sense - to designate voluntary coordination of effort for mutual benefit.

[2]Much can be said here about the social construction of skill and authoritative knowledge, the sources and consequences of pay/employment inequity, chronic underevaluation, invisibility, etc. pertaining to the historic and complex dynamics of "women's work" generally and secretarial subordination in particular. See Acker, 1989; Cockburn, 1983, 1985; Suchman and Jordan, 1988; Olerup et al, 1985.

[3]For a notable exception to this, see Kraut et al. (forthcoming).

[4]The other two staff demands were for ergonomic computer furniture and to negotiate a "pay equity" wage adjustment plan. The staff "won" a committment of $250,000 for the new furniture, but settled the strike without contract language on pay equity.

[5]Presenting a microcomputer running wordprocessing software as a form of typewriter is obviously useful in training novices to the technology. (Mack et al, 1983) However, the limitations to the metaphor become apparent if it then blinds one to the complexities that users inevitably face.

ACKNOWLEDGEMENTS

This research relied heavily upon the active collaboration I enjoyed with Ann Zelechow (SMOAP) and Darrell Parsons (OAKR). Nor would it have been possible without the participation of more than 100 secretaries at York University. Several administrators also cooperated generously. Funding was provided by Labour Canada and NSERC. Jonathan Grudin and John Bowers gave helpful comments on an earlier draft of the paper.

REFERENCES

Acker, J., *Doing Comparable Worth: Gender, Class and Pay Equity*, Temple University, 1989.

Ackerman, M. S., and Malone, T. W., "Answer Garden: A tool for growing organizational memory", *Proceedings of the 5th Conference on Office Information Systems*, Cambridge, MA., April 25 - 27, 1990, pp. 31-37.

Bannon, L., "Helping Users Help Each Other", in Norman and Draper (eds.), *User Centered System Design*, 1986.

Bannon, L. and Schmidt, K., "CSCW: Four Characters in Search of a Context", *Proceedings of the First European Conference on Computer Supported Cooperative Work*, London, Sept. 12-15, 1989.

Benston, M., "Feminism and Systems Design: Questions of Control", in Tomm, (ed.), *The Effect of Feminist Approaches on Research Methodologies*, Calgary, University of Calgary, 1989.

Bjerknes, G., Ehn, P. and Kyng, M., (eds.), *Computers and Democracy - A Scandinavian Challenge*, Avebury, 1987.

Bjorn-Andersen, N., "Implementation of Office Systems", in *Office Systems*, A. Verrijn-Stuart and R. Hirschheim, (eds.), Elsevier, 1986, pp. 177-191.

Briefs, U., Ciborra, C. and Schneider L., (eds.), *Systems Design For, With and By the Users*, North-Holland, 1983.

Clement, A., and Parsons, D., "Work Group Knowledge Requirements for Desktop Computing", *Proceedings of the 23rd Hawaii International Conference on System Science*, Kailua-Kona, Hawaii, January 2-5, 1990, pp. 84-93.

Clement, A., Parsons, D., and Zelechow, A., "Toward Worker-Centred Support for Desktop Computing", IFIP Working Conference on *Information System, Work and Organization Design*, Berlin, GDR, July 10-13, 1989.

Clement, A., and Zelechow, A., "Self-Managed Office Automation Project", Final project report, Technology Impact Research Fund, Labour Canada, Ottawa, 1987.

Clement, A., "A Canadian Case Study Report: Towards Self-Managed Automation in Small Offices", *Information Technology for Development*, Oxford University Press, 1989, Vol. 4, #2, pp. 185-233.

Cockburn, C., *Brothers: Male Dominance and Technological Change*, Pluto Press, 1983.

Cockburn, C., *Machinery of Dominance*, Pluto Press, 1985.

Danziger, J., Dutton, W., Kling, R., and Kraemer, K., *Computers and Politics: High Technology in American Local Government*, Columbia University Press, 1982.

Docherty, P., et al, *Systems Design for Human Development and Productivity: Participation and Beyond*, Elsevier, 1987.

Ehn, P., *Work-Oriented Design of Computer Artifacts*, Arbetslivscentrum, 1988.

Floyd, C., "Outline of a Paradigm Change in Software Engineering", in Bjerknes, Ehn and Kyng (eds.), *Computers and Democracy*, 1987.

Gasser, L., "The Integration of Computing and Routine Work", *ACM Transactions on Office Information Systems* 4(3), 1986, pp. 205-225.

George, J., Kling, R., and Iacono, S., "The Role of Training and Support in Desktop Computing", PPRO, UC Irvine, 1989.

Green, E., Owen, J., Pain, D. and Stone, I., "Human-Centred Systems ... Women-Centred Systems?': Gender Divisions and Office Computer Systems Design", paper presented to the BSA Annual Conference 'Sociology in Action', Plymouth Polytechnic, March 20-23, 1989.

Grudin, J., "interface", *Third Conference on Computer Supported Cooperative Work*, Los Angeles, October 10-14, 1990 (this volume).

Hartman, K., "Secretaries and Computers", in *Computing and Change on Campus*, Kiesler, S. and Sproull, L. (eds.), Cambridge University Press, 1987, pp. 114-130.

Homans, G., *The Human Group*, Harcourt, Brace & World, 1950.

Howard, R., "UTOPIA: Where Workers Craft New Technology", *Technology Review*, April, 1985, pp. 43-49.

Johnson, B., and Rice, R., *Managing Organizational Innovation: The evolution from word processing to office information systems*, Columbia University Press, 1987.

Kanter, R. M., *Men and Women of the Corporation*, Basic Books, 1977.

Kling, R., "Social Analysis of Computing: Theoretical orientations in recent empirical research", *Computing Surveys* 12 (1), 1980, pp. 61-110.

Kling, R., "Computerization as an Ongoing Social and Political Process", in Bjerknes *et al.* (eds.) *Computers and Democracy*, 1987, pp. 117-136.

Kling, R., and Scacchi, W., "The Web of Computing: Computer technology as social organization", in *Advances in Computers*, Vol. 21, 1982, pp. 1-90.

Kraut, R. E., Fish, R. S., Root, R. W. and Chalfonte, B. L., "Informal Communication in Organizations: Form, Function and Technology", to appear in S.

Oskamp and S. Spacapan (eds.) *Human Reactions to Technology: Clarement Symposium on Applied Social Psychology*, Sage (forthcoming).

Kyng, M., "Designing for a dollar a day", *Proceedings of the Second Conference on Computer Supported Cooperative Work*, Portland, pp. 178-188, Sept. 25-27, 1988.

Lee, D.M., "Usage Patterns and Sources of Assistance for Personal Computer Users", *MIS Quarterly*, Dec., pp. 313-325, 1986

Lukes, S., *Power: A Radical View*, Macmillan, 1974.

Mack, R.L., Lewis, C.H. and Carroll, J.M., "Learning to Use Word Processors: Problems and Prospects", *ACM Transactions on Office Information Systems* 1(3), 1983, pp. 254-271.

Mumford, E., *Designing Secretaries: The participative design of a word processing system*, Manchester Business School, 1983.

Mumford, E., and Henshall, D., *A Participative Approach to Computer Systems Design*, John Wiley, 1979.

Nelson, R.R. and Cheney, P.H., "Training End Users: An Exploratory Study", *MIS Quarterly*, Dec. 1987, pp. 546-559.

Nelson, R. R., (ed.) *End-User Computing: Concepts, Issues and Applications*, Wiley, 1989.

Norman, D., and Draper, S., *User Centered System Design: New Perspectives of Human-Computer Interaction*, Lawrence Erlbaum Associates, Hillsdale, NJ, 1986.

Olerup, A., Schneider, L., and Monod, E. *Women, Work and Computerization: Opportunities and Disadvantages*, North-Holland, 1985.

Panko, R., and Sprague, R., "Toward a New Framework for Office Support", *Proceedings of the 1982 Conference on Information Systems*, Philadelphia, Association for Computing Machinery, June, 1982.

Panko, R., *End User Computing: Management, Applications and Technology*, Wiley, 1988.

Perrow, C., *Complex Organizations: A Critical Essay*, 2nd. ed., Scott, Foresman, 1979.

Scharer, L.L., "User Training: Less is More", *Datamation*, July, pp. 175-182, 1983.

Shneiderman, B., *Designing the User Interface: Strategies for Effective Human-Computer Interaction*, Addison-Wesley, 1987.

Suchman, L., *Plans and Situated Actions: The problem of human-machine communication*, Cambridge University Press, 1987.

Suchman, L., and Jordan, B., "Computerization and Women's Knowledge", in *Women, Work and Computerization*, Tijdens, K. et al, (eds.) North Holland, 1989, pp. pp. 153-160.

Tijdens, K., Jennings, M., Wagner, I. and Weggelaar, M., *Women, Work and Computerization: Forming New Alliances*, North-Holland, 1989.

Zuboff, S., *In the Age of the Smart Machine: The Future of Work and Power*, Basic Books, 1988.

CHAPTER 6
Enabling Technologies and Theories

Most groupware relies upon the linking together of individual workstations over either *local area networks* or *wide area networks*. "Networks" by Vinton Cerf (1991) reviews the *circuit switching* and *packet switching* approaches to network design, discusses a variety of technologies for network implementation, and introduces the *Integrated Services Digital Network (ISDN)*, an internationally standardized digital network that holds great significance for the unified transmission of digital, voice, and ultimately video data. The author then explains the *Open Systems Interconnection Reference Model* that underlies the implementation of most modern networks, and mentions the important issue of network security.

Since some groupware uses video and audio technology for linking individuals located at remote sites, we need to be cognizant of important aspects of video technology, including the topic of bandwidth compression to allow video to be transmitted at lower cost. "Advances in Interactive Digital Multimedia Systems" by Edward Fox (1991c) discusses these topics, beginning with a survey of digital storage media such as CD-ROM. *Video bandwidth compression* methods are motivated by the need to optimize the storage of and playback of video from CD-ROM, but the techniques apply equally to the transmission of video. The paper concludes with a discussion of standards for *digital multimedia*.

The groupware of the 90s, as the personal computer "singleware" of the 80s, will be enabled by the increasing accessibility of computers afforded by advances in human-computer interface technology (see Notes below). Bill Gaver has developed a strategy of enhancing the richness and communicativeness of interfaces by representing interface events by *auditory icons* consisting of "everyday sounds." "Sound Support for Collaboration" (Gaver, 1991) shows how *non-speech audio* can assist in cooperative work at various levels of engagement, ranging from *general awareness* to *serendipitous communication* to *focused collaboration*. He illustrates the concept with descriptions of the use of non-speech audio in two systems, the Arkola bottling plant simulation (Gaver, Smith, and O'Shea, 1991) and the Environmental Audio Reminders project (Gaver, Moran, MacLean, Lövstrand, Dourish, Carter, and Buxton, 1992). Auditory feedback in the Arkola simulation helps maintain a common awareness despite the division of labor in the work, and allows participants to have areas of primary responsibility but still join together to solve problems. Auditory cues in the EAR system enable a relatively unconscious awareness of ongoing events.

The use of modern interface technology to enhance collaboration provides an interesting contrast to the theories discussed in Short, Williams, and Christie (1976, excerpted in Chapter 3 of this volume). They discuss the impacts on communication and collaboration caused by the removal of cues normally present in face-to-face communication. Gaver's work illustrates the possibilities of enriching media spaces (see Chapter 13 of this volume) by reintroducing cues or even by adding cues not present in normal face-to-face communication.

Another foundation technology for groupware is *hypertext*. Jeff Conklin (1987) provides an introduction to this technology in "Hypertext: An Introduction and Survey," from which we include some excerpts (pp. 17–20, 32–41). Conklin begins by sketching what hypertext is not, then lists some characteristics of typical systems, and itemizes four broad application areas for which hypertext systems have been developed. The latter parts of his paper describe the essence of hypertext in terms of nodes and links as the basic building blocks, and suggest some advantages and disadvantages of hypertext.

It is clear that one significant aspect of group process is that of *coordination*. The reading by Malone and Crowston (1990) first defines coordination theory very broadly as a "body of principles . . . about how actors can work together harmoniously." They then cite a variety of existing approaches to coordination theory that are rooted in computer science, linguistics (see, for example, the reading by Flores, Graves, Hartfield, and Winograd, 1988, included in Chapter 8 of this volume), organization theory (see, for example, the reading by Mintzberg included in Chapter 3 of this volume, and also Malone, 1985), philosophy and rhetoric, and management and economics. After developing a narrow definition of coordination as "the act of managing interdependencies between activities performed to achieve a goal," they sketch a framework for a theory of coordination.

Effective groupware implementation requires the solution of a difficult technical problem, that of *concurrency control*. Groupware systems are *distributed systems*, in which multiple processes compute concurrently on multiple distributed databases. These databases must remain consistent, and the results of the interrelated computations must not depend on the transmission delays between individual processes, despite the varieties of networking technologies that may be used. "CSCW and Distributed Systems: The Problem of Control" by Tom Rodden and Gordon Blair (1991) characterizes CSCW systems along two dimensions: their form of cooperation and their geographical nature. The importance of *control* is stressed. Methods of supporting control for CSCW are presented in terms of various forms of *transparency* in distributed systems.

Notes and Guide to Further Reading

A classic text on networking and communications is Tanenbaum (1988). Other useful texts are Bartee (Ed.) (1986), Dordick (1986), Stallings (Ed.) (1990), and Stallings (Ed.) (1992a). The *X.500 Directory Service* is described in Prinz and Pennelli (1991). One measure of the growth of wide-area networking and communications can be seen in the growth of the pioneering Internet, an international network of educational, corporate, and government computers. The following table, adapted from Lottor (1992), charts the growth of Internet hosts over the past 10 years.

Date	Hosts
8/81	213
8/83	562
10/85	1,961
12/87	28,174
10/89	159,000
10/91	617,000

Lederberg and Uncapher (1989; see also Rosenberg, 1991) is a report on an invitational workshop that produced recommendations for a research agenda designed to lead to a "National Collaboratory," a U.S.-based initiative to employ networking, communications, and computer technology on an even wider scale to facilitate collaboration at a distance and the more productive use of scarce and expensive national assets.

The need to integrate computer, audio, and video communications, and the resulting coming together of computers and telecommunications, has led to the development of the Integrated Services Digital Network (ISDN), a technology which promises to provide a unified solution to the transmission of voice, computer, and ultimately video data (through *broadband ISDN*). ISDN and broadband ISDN are covered in depth in Böcker (1988), Bartee (Ed.) (1989), and Stallings (Ed.) (1992b).

Recent advances in video and multimedia technology are covered in depth in special issues of the *Communications of the ACM* (Fox, Ed., 1989, 1991a), *IEEE Computer* (Fox, Ed., 1991b), and *IEEE Com-*

puter Graphics and Applications (Grimes and Potel, Eds., 1991).

The modern *graphical user interface (GUI)* was pioneered by Xerox (Johnson, Roberts, Verplank, Smith, Irby, Beard, and Mackey, 1989) and first successfully commercialized by Apple with its Macintosh computer. The complexities of modern GUIs have led to the creation of an increasing variety of interface development tools. A recent survey paper by Myers (1992) is the best single introduction to interface development tools. The *look-and-feel* of key GUIs as well as the graphic design principles that underlie their construction is well described in Marcus (1992). Baecker, Buxton, and Grudin (1993) is a comprehensive review of modern interface technology, user interface design, and human-computer interaction (see also the Notes section of Chapter 4). The origins of the use of non-speech audio at the interface may be found in Gaver (1986, 1989; see also Buxton, 1989).

One aspect of linking together workstations on either a local area or wide area network is spanning the physical and logical distance between workstations. Another key aspect is management of the real estate on individual screens. *Windowing systems and environments* receive and interpret input from user devices and control and allocate screen real estate, thus often enabling the use of a workstation for multiple interleaved concurrent activities. Introductions to windowing environments may be found in Hopgood (1986), Gosling, Rosenthal, and Arden (1989), and Steinhart, Callow, LaVallee, and Greco (1989). The important *X window manager* is described in Scheifler and Gettys (1986), Scheifler, Gettys, and Newman (1988), and Jones (1989).

Bush (1945) proposed the *Memex*, a kind of hypertext system, in a paper published in the *Atlantic Monthly* in 1945. The earliest work on hypertext was that of Engelbart and his collaborators (see the Notes section of the Introduction). The term "hypertext" was coined by Ted Nelson in 1965 (Neilsen, 1990). An important review paper discussing key issues is that by Halasz (1988). Shneiderman and Kearsley (1989) and Neilsen (1990) are books on hypertext.

Coordination theory is discussed in greater detail in a longer report by Malone and Crowston (1991). Other related theories and references are cited near the end of the Notes section of Chapter 11.

An excellent introduction to distributed systems may be found in Couloris and Dollimore (1988). A good place to begin is the introductory chapter in this book, followed by Chapter 7 on "Shared Files." In that chapter, the authors describe a variety of algorithms designed to guarantee consistency in shared files despite failures of individual computers or processes and despite the differences in the order and timing with which individual transactions are carried out. Mullender (1989) is another good book on distributed systems. A very theoretical introduction to concurrency control is Papadimitriou (1986). Concurrency control in groupware systems is discussed in Ellis, Gibbs, and Rein (1991, included in Chapter 1 of this volume), and in Ellis and Gibbs (1989). Database replication in an environment in which servers are "rarely connected" is described in Kawell, Beckhardt, Halvorsen, Ozzie, and Greif (1988).

Networks

*As the diversity of computer applications increases,
the burgeoning flow of megabit traffic between machines
will be accommodated by wider and smoother highways*

by Vinton G. Cerf

A web of glass spans the globe. Through it, brief sparks of light incessantly fly, linking machines chip to chip and people face to face. Ours is the age of information, in which machines have joined humans in the exchange and creation of knowledge.

As the diversity and sophistication of computational machinery have increased, so have the demands on the networks transporting the information and knowledge generated. Pathways must carry scientific and technological data and also provide links for everything from entertainment to complex computational modeling. Systems must be able to sustain communication rates that range from a few characters per second to billions of characters per second, a span that encompasses keyboard character strokes, high-resolution X-ray diffraction imagery and full-motion supercomputer weather simulations. Moreover, multifunction programs may need to talk to other multifunction programs; for example, a user running a word-processing program, a spreadsheet and a desktop graphics program may want to set up a collaborative link with a colleague running similar programs at a distant site.

What is needed to support the burgeoning flow of megabit traffic? What structures are already in place, and what must be built? How should the existing infrastructure—the set of products, services and functions underlying all aspects of networking—be modified? How can users make appropriate choices about the quality of service (speed, accuracy and security, for example)? And how will the system execute these decisions? Such questions fuel current research and development in computer networking. They are made even more challenging by the communications support that multiple applications may need: one can imagine that an unknown arbitrary number of programs running in an arbitrary number of computers may need to communicate with one another at arbitrary times. To meet these requirements, the networking technology must find a way to facilitate the exchange of information among many different computers concurrently. Indeed, the shift from the need to support simple, remote interactive access to a computer to the more difficult task of supporting machine-to-machine interaction has profoundly influenced the development of computer networking technology.

One prerequisite to any successful form of communication is the choice of a common language. In computer networking, it is essential that the communicating programs share conventions for representing the information in digital form and procedures for coordinating communication paths. Like their human counterparts, communicating computers must agree on ground rules for interaction. In personal terms, we might agree to use the postal service to exchange postcards and to use English as our common language.

A computer communications protocol consists of a set of conventions that determine how digital information will be exchanged between programs. The conventions can become quite complex, and so they are often organized in a hierarchy with the most basic agreements at the lowest levels and the more sophisticated and special-purpose agreements toward the top.

Once a language and a set of conventions have been chosen, the next question is how to minimize the number of interfaces ("spigots") required to link a computer to the network. The most effective way is multiplexing: each computer feeds information into a single high-capacity link to the network, to which the other computers are in turn connected [see illustration on next page]. Information from each computer is labeled so the network can route information to its proper destination. Ideally, a network can deliver information to all (broadcast), to a subset (multicast) or to only one recipient.

Such manifold computer interactions are often referred to as distributed computing. The term covers a multitude of applications and protocols. A

NETWORK CONTROL CENTER in the Philadelphia area from which AT&T monitors the flow of voice, data and entertainment traffic typifies the kind of communications system that will require significant enhancement to support growing computerization. Advances in the use of computers in business and professions, expanding consumer services and new entertainment media create the need for changes. The system must be able to handle many classes of traffic, which range in frequency from hundreds of bits per second to billions per second and which bear varying requirements for accuracy and confidentiality.

VINTON G. CERF is vice president of the Corporation for National Research Initiatives (CNRI), where he is responsible for the Digital Library System, Electronic Mail Interconnection and Internet research programs. He received his B.S. in mathematics from Stanford University and his Ph.D. in computer science from the University of California, Los Angeles. He taught at Stanford and worked for the Defense Advanced Research Projects Agency and MCI before taking up his present position in 1986.

Scientific American 265 (3), September 1991, pp. 72-81. Reprinted with permission.

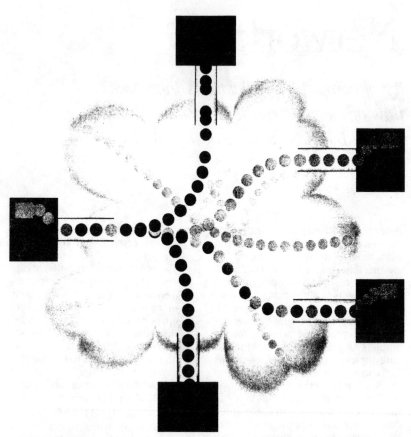

WIDE-AREA NETWORK moves data among computers through high-speed links. (The network is represented as a cloud, which is the term for it used among computer scientists.) Information packets from several programs running on the same computer may be multiplexed together. In addition, the network can deliver the same message simultaneously to several different addresses, a process known as multicasting.

popular distributed computing concept is called the client-server model. In this model, one computer provides a service, which another computer accesses as a client. For example, one or more computers might be dedicated to storing files of information for all the other computers. Various machines in the network can ask the "file servers" to deliver copies of files on demand. Another set of computers might be dedicated to providing laser-printing services. More generally, a number of computers might be dedicated to providing access to vast quantities of catalogued information in on-line data bases.

Autonomous, interprogram communication is being explored today in an even more general form under the rubric of knowledge robots (Knowbot is a registered trademark of the Corporation for National Research Initiatives), programs that move from machine to machine, possibly cloning themselves. Knowbots support parallel computations at different sites. They communicate with one another, with various servers in the network and with users. In the future, much computer communication could consist of the interactions of Knowbots dispatched to do our bidding in a global landscape of networked computing and information resources.

In any kind of multiplex network, there are two means of relaying information: circuit switching and packet switching. Circuit switching, the familiar technique that links telephones to one another, can make sense whenever two computers need to be connected for a long time to transfer large amounts of information. Its speeds typically range from a few hundred bits per second to a few million. Nonswitched dedicated data circuits can operate at speeds of nearly 45 million bits per second, but the expense of such a system must be justified by a nearly continuous need to transmit data between computers.

Circuit-switched systems suffer from a severe drawback: they often do not prove satisfactory for applications requiring that multiple programs running concurrently in one machine communicate with programs running in different machines. In such cases, it would be necessary to reconfigure the switching system from one computer to the others in turn, a process that takes an inordinate amount of time. Compared with the few microseconds (millionths of a second) or less it takes a computer to finish a computation, setting up and tearing down circuits can take hundreds of milliseconds (thousandths of a second) or more—enough time to complete thousands of computer transactions.

Packet switching avoids this drawback: it is expressly designed to accommodate the bursty, multiprocess communication commonly found in distributed computing environments. Packets, or chunks of data, produced at the originating computer are prefixed with headers containing routing information that identifies the source and destination computers. Small computers, called packet switches, are linked to form a network. Each packet switch examines each header and decides where to send the packet to move it closer to its final destination. When circuit-switched systems cannot accept new traffic, they refuse to set up new circuits. Packet-switched systems, however, exchange this behavior for variations in delay resulting from storing and forwarding packets. Thus, traffic is not refused, only momentarily delayed.

Packet-switched systems offer another bonus. In circuit-switched systems, the sending and receiving computers must usually be able to exchange data at the same rate, such as 9,600 bits per second or 64,000 bits per second. In packet-switched systems, by contrast, the sender might be able to transmit at very high speeds, such as 10 million bits per second, while the receiver might be able to receive only at low speeds, such as 1,200 bits per second. The automatic speed-matching feature of packet-switched systems allows different types of computer systems, such as supercomputers and personal computers, to communicate. Of course, when two very mismatched computers communicate, the faster one must adapt its average rate of transmission to accommodate the slower.

In addition, because the packet switches are programmable computers, they can detect when the trunk lines linking them have failed and select alternate routes for passing packet traffic without disturbing the source and destination computers. A circuit switch can detect similar failures, but the entire circuit has to be reconstructed in order to recover.

Although packet-switched systems can support communication among processes running in many different computers concurrently, they are not without their problems. In some systems, packets may be routed over multiple paths and arrive in a different order from the one in which they were sent. The receiving computer has to make sure packets are put back in the original sequence (in some systems this service is provided by the receiving packet switch). A disorderly arrival can also occur if a packet is retransmitted because of a detected error.

Another problem is congestion. The packet flow may overtax the storage and forwarding capacity of the switches. If that happens, the switches may be forced to discard packets that cannot be stored or delivered. Detection and prevention of congestion is an important area of packet-switching research.

To avoid disorderly arrivals, some packet-switched systems offer a virtual circuit service. In this system the network appears to provide a dedicated circuit to deliver information from one computer to another. In reality, the circuit is virtual, delivering packets in order but with variable delay. Usually the traffic routes are fixed and change only if a failure takes place. If the traffic on

Layers of Communication

APPLICATION	Detailed information about data being exchanged
PRESENTATION	Conventions for representing data
SESSION	Management of connections between programs
TRANSPORT	Delivery (reliable or otherwise) of sequences of packets
NETWORK	Format of individual data packets
LINK	Access to and control of transmission medium
PHYSICAL	Medium of transmission (electronic, optical or other)

each virtual circuit is variable—if the packets emerge from the source in a bursty fashion—then route selection to minimize congestion can still present a challenge. An international standard for virtual circuit packet switching has been codified by the Consultative Committee for International Telephony and Telegraphy (CCITT), an arm of the International Telecommunications Union (ITU). The ITU, which is affiliated with the United Nations, is an international treaty organization.

One of the first packet-switched systems was developed in 1969 under contract to the U.S. Defense Advanced Research Projects Agency (DARPA). Called the ARPANET, the system used minicomputers as packet switches and dedicated 50-kilobit-per-second telephone lines to connect them. Similar projects were also started in other countries, notably the U.K. (the National Physical Laboratory) and France (Institut National Recherche d'Informatique et d'Automatique). Since then, a great many private and public packet-switched networks have been deployed. They typically operate using trunk lines at 56,000, 64,000 or 1.5 to 2 million bits per second.

Concurrent with its research on the ARPANET, DARPA also explored packet-switching methods in mobile radio systems and synchronous satellite systems. The ARPANET and its satellite-based counterpart were early examples of so-called wide-area networks (WANs).

Packet-switched systems are used on a variety of transmission media, including local-area networks, metropolitan-area networks, integrated-services digital networks (ISDNs) and networks that operate at gigabit (one billion bits) speeds. One of the first local-area networks to use packet switching was developed in the early 1970s by the Xerox Palo Alto Research Center [see "Networks for Advanced Computing," by Robert E. Kahn; SCIENTIFIC AMERICAN, October 1987]. The system, called Ethernet, is still used today. An Ethernet network transmits signals, which are heard by all receivers (in a broadcast), by coaxial cable over distances of a kilometer or two. Initially operating at three million bits per second, modern Ethernets now work at 10 million bits per second, taking 100 nanoseconds (billionths of a second) to send each bit. Electric signals propagate on the coaxial cable at roughly half the speed of light, or 150,000 kilometers per second. Consequently, one bit can propagate through a 1.5-kilometer network in 10 microseconds.

Each transmitter on the Ethernet listens before it transmits. If another transmission is detected, it ceases and waits for a random interval before retrying. This method of channel sharing is called carrier-sense multiple access (CSMA). The Ethernet design cleverly in-

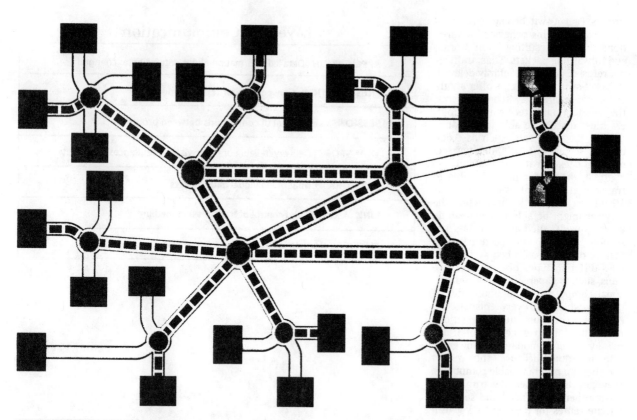

CIRCUIT SWITCHING creates an end-to-end path through the network for data flowing between two computers. This technique, based on methods developed for connecting telephone calls, simplifies data transmission. Yet it is not efficient, because setting up the connection typically takes far more time than transmitting the desired message.

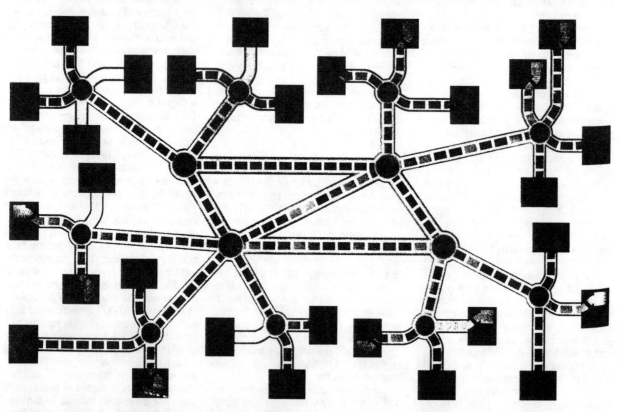

PACKET SWITCHING reduces data transmission overhead by attaching codes (*shown as different colors*) to each item of data sent through the network. The codes identify the source and the destination of each item, so that no end-to-end connection needs to be established. Thus, packets from many different computers can travel easily over the same network links.

cluded a test for competing transmissions *during* transmission so that a collision at the start of sending would cause all colliding senders to stop and wait for a random length of time. The deleterious effect of simultaneous transmissions was thus minimized. If the maximum span of an Ethernet is kept under 1.5 kilometers, collisions, or conflicting transmissions, will be quickly detected and will not consume much capacity on the network. A larger network, however, would suffer a much higher incidence of collision.

A development made in parallel with Ethernet was based on the idea of a ring of computers in which a token, or a short series of bits, is passed from computer to computer. A computer receiving the token is free to transmit one or more packets; other computers must wait until they receive the token to transmit. Token-based systems, which can also broadcast and multicast messages, generally operate at four million to 16 million bits per second.

More recently, packet technologies based on fiber-optic transmission have been developed. They operate at higher speeds and are better suited to larger, metropolitan-area networks. One example is the Fiber Distributed Data Interface (FDDI), which operates at 100 million bits per second and uses a token-based approach to sharing the fiber capacity. The system is organized in a dual ring, so that if a section fails, full operation can be rapidly recovered [*see illustration on this page*]. Token systems can span larger distances than broadcast Ethernets, but the price paid is a longer delay to access the ring. Care must be taken not to introduce more than one token on the ring at a time, although some variations permit multiple tokens to circulate.

A recent development is a fiber-based network technology called Distributed Queue Dual Bus (DQDB) networking. In this design, which works over tens of kilometers or more, nodes are connected to two different fibers, one for each direction. At the originating ends of each fiber, a special node sends out empty packets. The first node that has a packet of data to send fills the empty packet and sends it on its way. When a node has data to send to another node, it sends a request indicator on packets flowing on both fibers. In this way, upstream nodes learn that a downstream node has a packet to send. As empty packets appear, each upstream node allows them to propagate downstream to the node that needs to send data. Each node thus keeps track of the queue of packets awaiting transmission downstream.

The DQDB technology, which was developed by the University of Western Australia in the mid- to late 1980s, is undergoing trials by local exchange carriers in the U.S. and by telephone administrators in other countries. Because the service is expected to operate at speeds up to 600 million bits per second, it may figure prominently in metropolitan-area networks.

Another recent networking technology is Frame Relay. It is similar in nature to the virtual circuit system, except that the virtual circuits are determined at the time subscribers are connected to the system. No error checking is done as the packets move from switch to switch; there is only end-to-end error checking and retransmission, thereby reducing the delay through the network. Frame Relay, expected to operate in the range of 64,000 to 45 million bits per second, can be used in local-, metropolitan- or wide-area networks.

Over the past 15 years, the telephone carriers have been developing a wide-area digital communications technology, the ISDN, that would permit both voice and data to be carried in digital form across an international, switched digital backbone. ISDN offers two kinds of access to the digital transmission medium. The first, called Basic Rate Interface (BRI), gives a subscriber two bearer (B) channels that operate at 64,000 bits per second each and one data (D) and signaling channel that operates at 16,-000 bits per second. The D channel is used to signal the network where to connect each of the B channels. The second is called Primary Rate Interface and operates at 1.5 to 2 million bits per second, providing 23 to 30 B channels.

Unfortunately, the service has not been widely deployed, nor has there been a great demand for it. One reason for the cool reception may be that it has been possible to use the voice network to support data communications at speeds up to 19,200 bits per second by employing a device called a modem (modulator-demodulator). The modem turns digital binary signals into modulated sound signals that can be propagated anywhere in the voice network. The difference between 19,200 and 64,-000 bits per second is a factor of three, but apparently this difference has not been attractive enough to overcome the cost barrier of having to purchase special equipment to interface with the ISDN network.

An exciting recent development is the emergence of the gigabit-speed network. Local networks operating at speeds in the range of a billion bits per second are now being designed by running parallel connections between com-

DUAL RING (*top*) of the Fiber Distributed Data Interface network helps to safeguard connections against failure. If one of the FDDI optical fibers fails (*middle*) or if a network node ceases operation (*bottom*), the adjacent nodes can readily reconfigure the system to restore full operation.

puters. For example, a ribbon cable containing 64 conductors could sustain an effective data rate of a billion bits per second if each cable carried 16 million bits per second. (Cables carrying 10 to 20 million bits per second are commonplace.) One such system is marketed by Ultra Network Technologies for

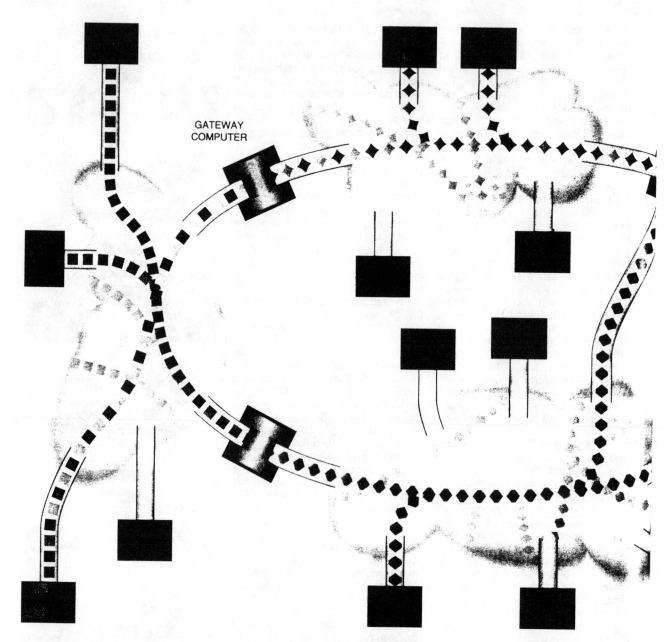

GATEWAY
COMPUTER

INTERNET is a network of networks. Each subsidiary net adheres to a minimal set of common protocols that allow data to pass transparently among computers attached to the Internet, even though the various networks may use different data formats, transmission rates or low-level routing algorithms (represented here schematically by differing data packet shapes).

the purpose of linking supercomputers.

For the past few years, fiber-based technologies have been emerging from the laboratory and making their appearance in experimental wide-area settings. These transmission and switching technologies are designed to operate at speeds in excess of a billion bits per second. On the transmission side, the Synchronous Optical Network (SONET) supports a multiplexed hierarchy of transmission speeds ranging from 51 million to 2,400 million bits per second. The SONET system allows data streams of varying transmission speeds to be combined or extracted without first having to break down each stream into its individual components.

Complementing this new transmission technology is a fast packet technique, Asynchronous Transfer Mode (ATM) switching, which can switch short packets called cells at extremely high rates. Cells, which contain up to 48 octets (an octet is eight bits) of data and five octets of addressing and control information, can carry digitized voice, arbitrary data and even digitized video streams.

Conceived as part of a Broadband ISDN (BISDN) system design, ATM switches and SONET fiber transmission technologies may well become the 21st-century equivalent of the 20th-century telephone network. BISDN offers the promise of a common network for all information and communications services, rather than special networks for different services, such as voice, data and video. Already several experimental test-beds, sponsored by DARPA and the National Science Foundation, are exploring applications and architectures for building wide-area gigabit networks.

In addition to the high-speed network developments under way, researchers are working on wireless digital networks that will permit mobile workstations to be part of the global

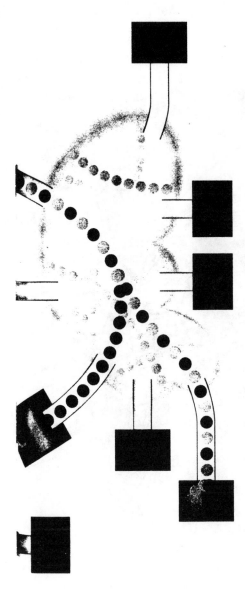

network. Wireless local-area networks capable of transmitting 10 megabits per second within a room or building are already available, and experimental systems offer far greater bandwidth.

The wireless component of the global net will bear some resemblance to a cellular telephone network—computers carried in trucks, ships or briefcases will be able to maintain connections and send and receive data wherever they go—but current cellular technology is not appropriate for wireless data transmission. First, cellular telephones rely on analog broadcast techniques, so that using them to move digital data would be inherently inefficient. Digital information would have to be converted to analog form for wireless transmission, much as computers now em-

ploy modems to send data over ordinary telephone lines.

Second, existing cellular networks are already unable to process the full load of calls that their users desire, much less additional data traffic. A single telephone "cell," typically several miles across, can handle only 59 connections at a time. A few dozen cellular modems could easily block out almost all other callers.

Third, even under the best of circumstances, the frequencies assigned to the cellular telephone network can provide data transmission rates of no more than 100,000 bits per second—insufficient for many potential mobile applications. A wireless complement to existing and future global networks will require new technology, massive capital investment and regulatory changes to allocate sufficient space for data transmission in the electromagnetic spectrum.

Although it may not be apparent, the various technologies I have described can be organized into an architectural hierarchy. Such a conceptual base helps in designing new computer communications technology. Since any computer communications system is based on its protocols, it is not surprising that the conceptual structure is a protocol hierarchy. From the bottom up, the layers can be labeled physical, link, network, transport, session, presentation and application [see top illustration on page 75].

The physical layer has to do with the actual medium of electronic, radio frequency or optical transmission and the way in which bits are signaled on the medium. The link layer determines how sequences of bits are framed into chunks. The network layer deals with packet communication and is typically the lowest level at which computer programs can communicate.

The transport layer is the first one at which end-to-end flow and congestion control between communicating programs are regulated. Some applications require that data be delivered in sequence, with high reliability. Others require only that data be delivered expeditiously—some information can be lost. For example, voice or video packets can be made to work if the delays are minimal and the arrival time between packets is short. A lost speech or video packet might introduce a brief gap, but if gaps are infrequent, listeners and viewers can ignore the problem. On the other hand, a file containing a computer program must arrive intact, and an accurate and sequenced delivery is essential.

The layers above transport are closer

to the applications and often reflect their needs. Associations between communicating programs are established at the session layer. Conventions for representing information to be exchanged are determined at the presentation layer. Spanning all the layers is the management layer, since management pervades all aspects of networking, from the lowest level to the highest.

In nearly all the discussion so far, I have focused on the first three protocol layers—physical, link and network. I now move to the higher layers—and straight into the important concept of networking the networks, a procedure called network interconnection, or internetting.

Internetting was first explored in the early 1970s by DARPA. The agency sought ways to interconnect different kinds of packet networks so that the computers using them could communicate without concern for which kind of and how many networks made the interconnections. Special processors called gateways were developed to connect two or more networks and to pass packet traffic from one network to the next. Gateways were also responsible for dealing with network differences, such as speed, maximum packet length and error rates [see illustration on these two pages].

An internet gives each of its users an address and defines a standard packet format. To send information, a computer creates packets including the source and destination addresses and encapsulates the packets in the format required by the underlying network. The computer then routes the packets to the appropriate gateway or host for further processing, and this series of operations is repeated until the packets reach their final destination.

Many of the same problems that arise in ordinary networks arise in internets. Gateways need routing algorithms so that they can determine the topology of the relevant parts of the internet and decide where internet packets should be sent. Changes in topology caused by network failures and gateway crashes must be accommodated. Control of flow and congestion in an internet pose as much of a challenge as they do in lower-level networks.

In the boiling ferment of modern telecommunications technology, a critical challenge is to determine how the internetting architecture developed over the past 15 years will have to change to adapt to the emerging gigabit-speed ATM, BISDN and SONET technologies of the 1990s. DARPA and the National Science Foundation are sponsoring

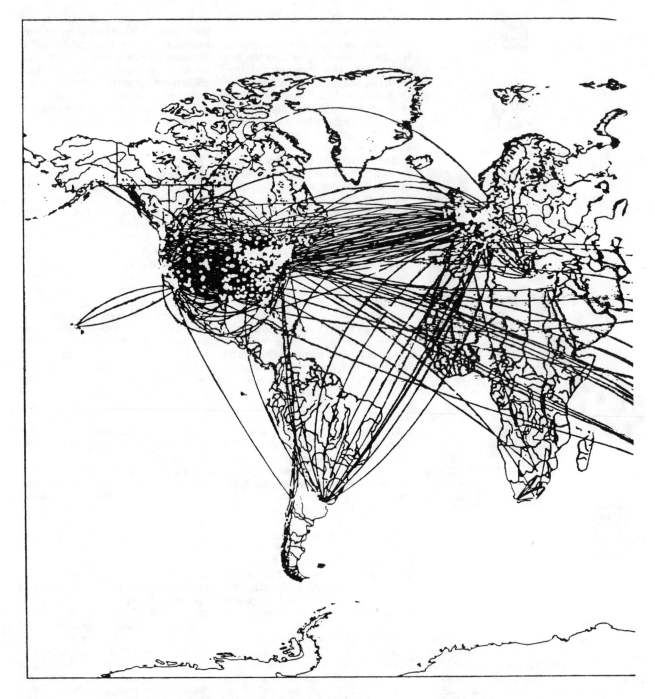

USENET, a worldwide, voluntary member network, has approximately 37,000 nodes (about one tenth the size of the Internet). Accessing electronic mail and other network services requires only finding another Usenet site that is willing to supply a connection.

a major test-bed program to examine this problem through the exploration of experimental applications requiring such superhigh-speed networking. Supercomputer simulation imagery ("visualization"), multiple supercomputer computations and medical and geo-

physical image generation are all being used to test protocol designs, architectural alternatives and programming environments.

A number of proprietary internetting technologies have been developed by Xerox (the Xerox Network System), Digital Equipment Corporation (DECnet Network Architecture, or DNA) and IBM (Systems Network Architecture and Systems Network Interconnection). DARPA initiated one of the largest open-network systems, the Internet. It operates in 26 countries, comprises more than 5,000 networks and supports several

million users on more than 300,000 computers in several thousand organizations. In the U.S., the Internet system has strong support from DARPA, the National Science Foundation, the National Aeronautics and Space Administration and the Department of Energy.

Operating a complex and large-scale computer network or collection of computer networks is a complicated enterprise. As the number of devices involved in the system increases, the system's complexity grows exponentially. Detecting and repairing software, machine and communications

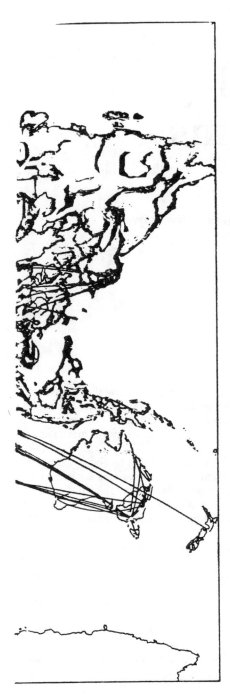

link failures are extremely difficult. As might be expected, network management is a major target for research and development.

A crucial area of network management concerns the security of the system at all levels. Users of remote resources must be satisfactorily identified—typically, by means of a password. Unfortunately, this approach is weak, in part because passwords are not chosen well (they are often last names, names of spouses, license plates and birth dates, for exam-

ple) and in part because passwords are carried without special protection across the network and thus may be observed by those technically equipped to do so.

The need for security and, in particular, authentication arises at all levels of the protocol hierarchy. At the top level, users may want assurance that electronic mail is coming from the person purported to be the sender; processors may need to know, for accounting purposes, which other systems are consuming resources or, for access-control purposes, which systems are accessing information. In financial transactions, it is critical to assure integrity (that is, to make sure there has been no tampering with a message). For example, one would like to be certain that a deposit is not surreptitiously transferred to another account. In business transactions in which orders are placed, it would be helpful if it were difficult to repudiate confirmed orders.

At lower layers, gateways and routers need to know that control commands are coming from legitimate network management stations. In addition, sometimes information exchanged on the network, such as medical records and electronic mail, needs to be kept confidential. In other cases, it is critical that information such as financial transactions, business orders, network-control information and accounting records not be altered in transit.

Digital cryptography can often satisfy these various requirements. The National Institute of Standards and Technology sponsored the development of a Data Encryption Standard (DES) in the mid-1970s for commercial and government users who did not require military-level cryptography. During the same period, the concept of public key cryptography (PKC) was developed.

In conventional cryptographic systems, a single key encrypts and decrypts messages between parties who wish to keep their communication private and who want assurance that only parties who hold the keys are able to communicate. The DES algorithm is a conventional system: any party holding the key can encrypt or decrypt messages. Such a system is sometimes called a symmetric keying system, since all parties use the same keys, and the same cryptographic algorithm serves for both encryption and decryption.

Public key systems, in contrast, use a pair of keys [see "The Mathematics of Public-Key Cryptography," by Martin E. Hellman; SCIENTIFIC AMERICAN, August 1979]. Messages encrypted in one key can be decrypted only with the other key. It does not matter which key is used to encrypt, only that the other key must be used to decrypt. This form of cryptography is sometimes called an asymmetric keying system.

Typically a user of a public keying system will keep one key private and publicize the other (hence the term "public key system"). To transmit a confidential message to a recipient, the sender encrypts the message in the recipient's public key. Only the recipient can decrypt the message, since only the secret key is useful for that purpose.

An interesting twist to public key cryptography is the digital signature. To "sign" a message, the sender encrypts the message in the secret key. The recipient is given the encrypted message and the advice that it came from the sender. The recipient looks up the sender's public key and uses it to decrypt the message. If the decryption is successful, the recipient knows that the message came from the sender, since only the sender has the secret key that matches the public one. Clearly, digital signatures can be exploited for various transactions (including network management exchanges) in which it is important to verify the source of the message. More important, they allow commerce that would otherwise suffer from serious threats of abuse.

In its book on computer and network security, *Computers at Risk*, the National Research Council opens the first chapter with the alarm, "We are at risk." This is a fair assessment for heavily networked computer systems operating in many countries and with large numbers of programs running concurrently. Technologies for ameliorating that risk are emerging from the research community. If we are at risk, we are also forewarned and, increasingly, forearmed with powerful methods for protecting the system.

FURTHER READING

NEW DIRECTIONS IN CRYPTOGRAPHY. Whitfield Diffie and Martin E. Hellman in *IEEE Transactions on Information Theory*, Vol. IT22, No. 6, pages 644–654; November 1976.

PACKET COMMUNICATION NETWORKS. Special issue of *IEEE Proceedings*, Vol. 66, No. 11; November 1978.

THE MATRIX: COMPUTER NETWORKS AND CONFERENCING SYSTEMS WORLDWIDE. John S. Quarterman. Digital Press, 1989.

COMPUTERS AT RISK: SAFE COMPUTING IN THE INFORMATION AGE. National Research Council System Security Study Committee Staff. National Academy Press, 1990.

COMPUTERS UNDER ATTACK: INTRUDERS, WORMS AND VIRUSES. Edited by Peter J. Denning. Addison-Wesley, 1990.

Advances in Interactive Digital Multimedia Systems

Edward A. Fox, Virginia Polytechnic Institute and State University

Progress in hardware, algorithms, and standards has facilitated interactive access to digital multimedia information. This tutorial introduces basic concepts in digital multimedia systems and surveys recent literature.

Humans communicate using a variety of senses and capabilities, especially in face-to-face situations. We should aim to emulate the bandwidth, fidelity, and effectiveness possible in those situations when we develop interactive multimedia computing systems, especially as we move from analog to digital processing environments.

That movement, a part of the evolution of information technology since the early days of computing, gained momentum with the widespread use of compact discs, which demonstrated the accurate reproduction and superb quality of digital audio. Bilevel (black-and-white) image handling, especially facsimile, has demonstrated the potential for rapid communication of documents, changing in a few years the way organizations operate.

Methods for managing computer graphics, color images, and motion video will lead to even greater changes. When fully digital multimedia computing systems are readily available, we will have powerful tools for improving human-human collaboration and human-computer symbiosis.

Televisions, CD players, telephones, and home computers will evolve and be combined, yielding systems with stereo speakers, high-resolution color displays, megabytes of RAM, fast processors for video and audio, fiber-optic network connections, hundreds of megabytes of disk capacity, CD-ROM drives, and flexible input devices, including stereo microphones, pointing devices, and text-entry units. True programming of video will be possible for personalized presentations.

High-resolution images, high-fidelity audio, nicely typeset text, and high-definition video will be available on demand, as versatile alternatives to conventional photographic, audio, newspaper, and television services. Home shopping, cottage industries, delivery of professional services, supplemental adult and child education, surrogate travel to real or artificial sites, video mail and conferencing, and diverse modes of entertainment will be supported.

Many areas of computer science and electrical engineering are aiding these developments. Fast processors, high-speed networks, large-capacity storage devices, new algorithms and data structures, graphics systems, innovative methods for human-computer interaction, real-time operating systems, object-oriented programming, information storage and retrieval, hypertext and hypermedia, languages for scripting, parallel processing methods, and complex architectures for distributed systems — all are involved.

To understand interactive digital multimedia computing systems, it is necessary to see how relevant aspects of these fields relate. The references cited in this article are a small assemblage of quality writings covering much of this broad spectrum.*

First, I provide background regarding developments in interactive videodiscs, which first made images and video accessible through computer systems. Then, I deal with digital storage media, including optical, magnetic, and network options, which allow digital multimedia to be preserved, shared, and distributed. I also discuss the characteristics of audio and video and their digital representations. Because these media are so demanding of space and channel bandwidth, I review compression methods.

Technology is not all that is necessary. Vendors must follow standards — discussed in their own section — to ensure that the economics and usability of digital multimedia help this industry grow. Building on existing de facto standards and an emerging suite of international standards, digital multimedia systems (for example, from Intel, Commodore, and Philips) are already available, and the future for digital multimedia in general looks bright.

Interactive videodiscs

Computer handling of large quantities of audio and video information became possible with the advent of the videodisc in the late 1970s. Each side of these optical discs can hold 54,000 im-

ages, or 30 minutes of motion video if the images are played in sequence at the standard rate of 30 frames per second and they run concurrently with 30 minutes of stereo sound, all recorded in an analog format. Although seek time is on the order of a second, the random-access capability allows computers to control playback in interactive videodisc systems. Videodisc output usually goes directly to a monitor; with additional boards the computer system can overlay text or graphics on the video output, or even digitize the video signal as it is received.

Preparation of videodisc applications is typically a relatively expensive process, requiring a team for design, video and audio production, graphic art, programming, project management, and content specialist_duties.[1] While mastering and replication cost several thousand dollars, complete projects may cost $100,000 per disk. Recordable videodiscs are available but not common, so preparing videodiscs is essentially a publication process. When interactive videodiscs are coupled with high-quality software and a good user interface, powerful educational experiences for thousands of people can result.[2]

Videodisc applications presenting neuroanatomy and supporting surrogate or simulated travel, language study, and video research work have been developed at MIT in connection with Project Athena and the Media Lab,[3] thanks to an elaborate cable plant for analog video. Electronic books, manuals, magazines, and visual databases also have been prototyped there, showing the potential of combining interactive computer systems with videodiscs, graphics, and digitizer boards. However, similar cable systems are too expensive for widespread deployment. Instead, the shift is to digital storage and communication systems.

Digital storage media

In the jargon of the international standards community, "digital storage media" refers to both storage and communication capabilities. These have increased in capacity more than a thousandfold in the past decade, allowing digital multimedia to emerge as a cost-effective competitor for analog approaches. In 1985, CD-ROM (compact-disc read-only memory) with a capacity

of more than 600 Mbytes but a manufactured cost under a dollar was first applied to electronic publishing.[4,5] Similarly, fiber-optic cable now makes gigabit-per-second communication channels a reality worldwide.

Storage. CD-ROMs, the most cost-effective storage medium for distributing large quantities of digital data, are related to regular compact discs — that is, CD-DA, or compact-disc digital-audio. Both support direct access to individual sectors of data that can store 1/75 second of CD-quality digital audio in CD-DA format, using 2,336 bytes, or 2,048 bytes of arbitrary digital data in CD-ROM format, with the rest of the space for error correction. Thus, CD-ROM data transfer speed is 150 Kbytes per second or 1.2 Mbits per second.

An elaborate system of optics, servos, and signal decoding circuits allows data to be accessed within a second.[6] International Organization for Standardization (ISO) 9660 (based on the High Sierra standard[7]) specifies the volume and file characteristics, allowing access through nearly any CD-ROM drive and operating system. Efforts of the Rock Ridge Group have extended the utility of ISO 9660 for Unix systems and servers.

Compact discs are part of the family of optical media.[8,9] There are prospects for further improvement, including write-once and erasable discs of varying sizes.[10] For example, announcements indicate that in 1992, write-once CD-ROM drives will cost under $3,000, and minidisk (2.5-inch, 128-Mbyte) drives will cost about the same as those for CD-ROMs, handling both formats. Further information on optical disc-publishing and access is available in the literature.[4,5]

Magnetic disks are readily available with capacities on the order of a gigabyte, but they are not low-cost, removable, or produced by mass replication. Use of caching, memory hierarchies, and minimal perfect hashing will make all storage units even more effective contributors to digital multimedia.

Networking. While fiber-optic connections are the most cost-effective scheme for rapidly transmitting large volumes of digital data, a great deal of research regarding networked multimedia is required. The Fiber Distributed Data Interface operates at 100 Mbps,

---

* This tutorial provides an introduction to the basic concepts and an overview of the literature; a longer version is available from the author, whose address appears after his biography on p. 21.

Table 1. Multimedia publishing.

Medium	Collecting	Preparing
Video	Video edit list	Digitize, enhance, compress
Image	Selection	Digitize, enhance, compress
Audio	Audio edit list	Filter, digitize, enhance, compress
Text	Text filing	Text processing, tool use
Graphics	(Composite) Object selection	Rendering, drawing, animating tool use

Publishing: ordering, correlating multiple representations, organizing (layout, order), hypermedia linking, adding interactive scripts.

Using: network distribution, optical publishing, on-line use, hypermedia enhancement by users.

and connection costs dropped below $5,000 in the early 1990s. Gigabit-per-second networks are being tested, and will form the backbone for national telecommunication. However, research regarding network protocols, local area network and workstation architectures, and operating-system support software for digital multimedia is still in its infancy. The first international workshop exclusively on these topics was held late in 1990.[11]

Asynchronous transfer mode networks support both variable and constant bit rate services at very high speeds and serve as the basis for the Broadband Integrated Services Digital Network.[12] Streams of digital multimedia, including uncompressed live video, can use the constant bit rate services. These types of fast packet switching can support real-time communication with reduced jitter. (Jitter is caused by delays of packets.) Yet many questions remain regarding synchronization of related data types, dynamic adaptation to different terminal and network services, and real-time requirements for hypermedia.[13] Research is also needed on rate structures, spectrum and channel allocation, and handling of scalable representations of video streams.[14]

Network and operating-system concerns coalesce because of the need for open systems, synchronization ("lip-sync" of audio and video), and fast transfer from network to presentation unit. High performance and reliability are also important. Research is proceeding on object-oriented models to handle the various classes of multimedia,[15] abstractions for continuous media (for example, an audio stream) I/O,[16] and connection architectures for networks and workstations.[17,18] There is a trade-off between network reliability, how closely the network approximates providing a constant rate stream, and other factors. Without buffering, the stream of data must be carefully prepared, such as by interleaving data on storage units.[19] That is especially important with CD-ROM, where seek times are one to two orders of magnitude slower than with magnetic disks. As memory prices decline, however, buffering of multimedia data will allow fast processors to compensate for many performance problems in digital storage media.

Adding audio and video capabilities

While issues of text and graphics processing have continuing importance in standard information systems, the current wave of development in digital multimedia deals mainly with audio and video. Luther[20] discusses many important issues, and Bottoms and Helgerson[21] and Adkins[22] cover ways to manage data-conversion projects including these media. The goal is integrated capabilities encompassing cameras, slide and filmstrip projectors, camcorders and VCRs, tape recorders, television broadcast and reception units, and postproduction studios.

Many tools are required to fully support both commercial and end-user multimedia publishing. Table 1 illustrates some key issues for important media types. First, suitable multimedia objects must be collected. These come from natural or artificial sources — for example, a captured image or a synthesized sound. While many people know how to file text documents, select a graphic object while drawing, or choose slides for a presentation, most people have had no experience editing audio or video files. Nevertheless, tens or hundreds of hours of raw footage are often edited to produce a single hour of a video production.

After collection comes preparation. For use with computers, audio and video are digitized and then stored in the minimum amount of space suitable for subsequent use. Specialized tools for each medium are required to enhance or add new materials. Multimedia publishing then involves ordering the pool of accumulated resources and tying together the various representations of each object (for example, audio and video synchronization or sequencing of images obtained at different times). Publications must be organized both spatially and temporally, and associational links must be provided, as with hypermedia.[23] Suitable sequences of interaction must be scripted.[2] The resulting publication is shared over a network, distributed on CD-ROM, or enhanced into an even better publication as part of a hyperbase (a database of hypermedia documents).

Multimedia publications stretch the capabilities of modern computers. Enormous requirements for storage make compression necessary. Computers must provide facilities for accurate control of playback, flexible editing, and signal processing or enhancement. Combinations such as warping video onto graphic structures must be supported.

Audio. On a computer, digital sounds can supplement video, communicate when the user's other senses are engaged, or provide a suitable background or stimulus. Brewer discusses uses of audio as well as technical issues relating to CD-ROM.[24] While special VLSI chips have been developed for various digital signal processing tasks, the related matter of digital representation is a particular concern.

When sound is digitized, it is usually

sampled and quantized using a scheme called *pulse code modulation*. According to sampling theory, samples should be taken at least twice for each cycle of the highest frequency component to be recovered. Because the human ear is not sensitive to sounds higher than 20 kHz, the 44.1-kHz sampling rate used for CD-DA permits fairly accurate reproduction. Each sample uses 16 bits to indicate the amplitude — that is, to quantize the sound — yielding a large dynamic range and a signal-to-noise ratio of over 95 dB. The main disadvantage of this approach is that roughly 10 Mbytes of storage are consumed by each minute of audio (171 Kbytes per second). In other words, a communication channel of about 1.4 Mbps must be allocated to handle a single stereo source.

Several approaches are commonly used to reduce the need for storage, but they reduce the quality of reproduction. Storage decreases when a system uses

- mono instead of stereo;
- fewer samples, reducing the frequency range covered; or
- fewer bits per sample, reducing the quality of waveform reconstruction.

Thus, with Compact Disc-Interactive, or CD-I, level A stereo sound requires 85 Kbytes per second, level B 42.5 Kbytes per second, and level C 21.3 Kbytes per second to give sound quality comparable to an LP record, FM radio, or AM radio, respectively. Significant further reductions are possible with *adaptive differential pulse code modulation* schemes, which use fewer bits for quantization. The differential approach involves recording the difference from the previous sample and often requires fewer bits than the actual current value. The adaptive feature involves computing parameters, so the scale for values changes as the rate of amplitude shift varies. Often, 4 bits per sample is adequate for good-quality reproduction, as in the ADPCM scheme used in the CD-ROM XA (extended architecture) standard promulgated by Philips and Sony.

Graphics, images, and video. Doherty and Apperson survey graphics, images, and video.[25] Many issues relate to all forms of graphics, images, and video, but there are differences in origin, storage, and presentation. Generally, graphics components of multimedia programs originate on computer systems. It is

> **Most current representations of images assume that descriptions are a two-dimensional array or raster, and that video is a sequence of such images.**

possible for natural images to lead to graphics, such as when line-tracking algorithms are applied to digitized versions of engineering diagrams, or when scanned images are converted to a "draw" representation by software that tries to fit lines and filled shapes. Sophisticated conversions to the structured representation characteristic of graphics or to higher level forms managed by artificial intelligence routines also take place in the context of computer vision.

Ultimately, images and video will be analyzed and stored in high-level and storage-efficient representations that identify and characterize objects, relationships, distances, and movement. This will facilitate "virtual reality" investigations, support model-based compression, and allow truly scalable presentations for displays varying in size from wristwatch monitors to wall panels.[26]

Most current representations of images assume that descriptions are a two-dimensional array or raster, and that video is a sequence of such images. The "resolution" of an image is crucial as it defines the raster size. Still images that are closely examined should be stored using at least 512×480-pixel resolution, according to experiments we have conducted at Virginia Polytechnic Institute and State University; but, in such applications as menu selection or image database browsing, low-resolution picture icons or "picons" may suffice.

With video, the key issue is the enormous bandwidth and storage required for digital representations. NTSC television (the US standard established by the National Television System Committee) has 525 horizontal lines to define the vertical resolution or height. The theoretical width or horizontal resolution limit, based on the allowed bandwidth of 4.5 MHz, is 360 vertical lines. However, because of the scanning meth-

od and television construction constraints, the "safe" region on a television is even smaller, so 360×240 pixels is often the resolution achieved. This is called "normal resolution" for CD-I.[27]

Recommendation 601 of the International Radio Consultative Committee, or CCIR, specifies the international standard for digital video as 720 lines. The number of pixels per line varies depending on the television scheme used: There are 480 pixels for NTSC and 576 for PAL[28] (phase alternating line, the European standard). The International Telegraphy and Telephony Consultative Committee, or CCITT, uses the Common Intermediate Format (CIF) for video telephony, which has a resolution of 360×288 pixels, and Quarter-CIF (QCIF), which has a 180×144-pixel resolution.[29] Super VHS camcorders achieve 400 lines, and high-definition television about 1,000 lines.

Images have a third dimension, pixel depth, which refers to the number of bits used for each picture element. While monochrome uses a single bit, gray scale often uses 8 bits to get 256 levels. For color graphics, 4 or 8 bits may suffice, while for color images, 8, 9, 16, or 24 bits are standard. With 32-bit color, 24 bits are used for color and 8 bits for the "alpha channel," which indicates degree of transparency or mixing with other image planes.

Pixel depth relates to the choice of color space. Cameras or scanners will often separate the red, green, and blue (RGB) components and quantize them with a certain number of bits each. Examples are RGB 5:5:5, which is used with CD-I,[8] or 8:8:8, which produces 24-bit color. However, the human visual system is not as sensitive to color (chrominance) as it is to intensity (luminance), so color spaces other than RGB have been developed. Mappings between these color spaces can be done with linear transformations.[20] For PAL, the YUV space was chosen, and that has been adopted for use with both CD-I and Intel's Digital Video Interactive, or DVI. For analog television, 4.5 MHz can be used for luminance (Y), and 1.5 MHz each for the two chrominance channels (U and V).

Home televisions and VCRs, which are considered acceptable by many viewers, often use only 0.5 MHz for the chrominance channels. Similarly, with CCIR Recommendation 601, chrominance is subsampled, yielding a 4:2:2

scheme that provides twice as many samples for luminance. DVI's 9-bit compressed video format uses 4:1 subsampling in each dimension, yielding 1 bit of chrominance for every 8 bits of luminance.[20]

Smooth motion video requires at least 25 to 30 frames per second. PAL and Secam (Sequentiel Coleur avec Memoire, the standard used in France) use 25 frames per second; NTSC uses 30 frames per second. These are usually interlaced, so each frame is made of two fields containing alternating lines, and two fields are shown during each frame time. Eventually, noninterlaced displays like computer monitors could be refreshed with a full image 60 times per second.

To estimate bandwidth requirements, however, we can concentrate on total samples per second for various schemes. If digital video is uniformly quantized at 8 bits per sample, according to CCIR Recommendation 601, with a sampling rate of 13.5 MHz for luminance, the total bit rate is 216 Mbps. The bit rate for NTSC "network-quality" video is about 45 Mbps.[28] For CIF and QCIF the uncompressed bit rates are approximately 36 and 9 Mbps.[29] Contrast these rates with the 150-Kbps data rate of CD-ROM!

Compression methods

Clearly, compression is essential if audio, images, and video are to be used in digital multimedia applications. A megabyte of space would be filled by roughly six seconds of CD-quality audio, a single 640 × 480-pixel color image stored using 24 bits per pixel, or a single frame — 1/30 second — of CIF video. Nevertheless, videodisc applications often have more than 20 minutes of video, perhaps 10,000 slides, and 30 minutes of stereo sound on each laser disc side. And with the tremendous volume of data that will be received each day from planned NASA missions[30] and other scientific ventures, the need for proven compression techniques is obvious.

Happily, there has been a great deal of research and many implementations using software, hardware, or both for a variety of compression methods. Research continues, with further improvements expected using wavelet and other time- and space-domain schemes. Elsewhere, I have published a brief intro-

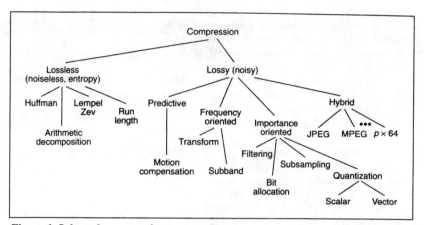

Figure 1. Selected compression approaches.

duction with a glossary and references.[31] Rao and Yip provide a comprehensive treatment of compression for images and video.[32] A set of useful articles appears in conference publications by NASA[33] and the IEEE Computer Society,[34] with many good references included in the bibliographies.

Compression of digital data involves computational algorithms that can be implemented in software. Some involve digital versions of signal processing methods, others involve pattern recognition, and still others use statistics or characteristics of particular data types or samples. High-speed implementations involve VLSI chips, such as for audio digital signal processing, discrete cosine transform, or vector quantization approaches. I discuss these in a later section.

Approaches. At the boundary of image processing, computer vision, and graphics is the area of model-based compression.[26] Models of faces can be analyzed, yielding facial motion parameters that can be transmitted at low bit rates and synthesized at a receiver for "talking head" video telephony. Other approaches involve feature detection at the encoder and rendering at the decoder.

Fractals (images that can be described by a set of rules specified with a relatively small number of bits) allow compression of natural scenes where the underlying structure matches this type of model.[35] Very high compression ratios can be achieved, sometimes on the order of 1,000:1 (size of the uncompressed form versus the compressed form). How-

ever, extensive computation is required for encoding. While decoded images may be acceptable to human judgment, there is usually some quality loss. Nevertheless, several companies — for example, Barnsley Communications — are marketing boards and software for fractal compression and decompression. Commodore has announced plans for software-based fractal decompression in their CDTV system.

Figure 1 shows a taxonomy of compression approaches. In *lossless* schemes, the original representation can be perfectly recovered. For text, lossless methods may achieve a 2:1 reduction. For bilevel images, 15:1 is a good figure. (A new international standard for bilevel image coding, referred to as JBIG, improves on CCITT Group 3 and 4 approaches for facsimile transmission, and in some situations achieves more than 50:1 compression.)

These approaches are also called *noiseless* — because they do not add noise to the signal — or *entropy coding* — because they eliminate redundancy through statistical or decomposition techniques. For example, Huffman coding uses fewer bits for more common message symbols, and run-length encoding replaces strings of the same symbol with a count/symbol pair. Discussions of research on lossless compression appear elsewhere.[36,37]

The other approach, *lossy* compression, involves encoding into a form that takes up a relatively small amount of space, but which can be decoded to yield a representation that humans find similar to the original.

Table 2. Standards for multimedia and hypermedia.

Short Name	Official Name	Standards Group	Group Designation	Approval Status
JPEG	Digital compression and coding of continuous-tone still images	Joint Photographic Experts Group	JTC1/SC2/WG10	Committee draft balloting in 1991
H.261	Video coder/decoder for audio-visual services at $p \times 64$ Kbps	Specialist Group on Coding for Visual Telephony	CCITT SG XV	Approved Dec. 1990
MPEG	Coding of moving pictures and associated audio	Moving Picture Experts Group	JTC1/SC2/WG11	Video committee draft balloting in 1991
MHEG	Coded representation of multimedia and hypermedia information	Multimedia and Hypermedia Information Coding Expert Group	JTC1/SC2/WG12	Working document
HyTime	Hypermedia/Time-Based Structuring Language	Standard Music Representation Work Group	ANSI X3V1.8M	Committee draft balloting in 1991

Lossy compression. Lossy or noisy compression may add artifacts that can be perceived.[33] Careful study of the human visual system has focused attention on approaches that cause little perceived loss in quality, but achieve high compression ratios.

Prediction. Predictive approaches like ADPCM involve predicting subsequent values by observing previous ones, and transmitting only the usually small differences between actual and predicted data. An example involves motion compensation. Successive frames in a video sequence are often quite similar or have blocks of pixels shifted from one frame to the next — for example, as the camera pans or a person moves.[20] Although it is computationally expensive to analyze images and yield motion vectors, parallel computers[38] or neural networks can help with the processing.

Frequency-oriented compression. Subband coding can exploit the fact that humans have different sensitivities to various spatial and temporal frequency combinations.[39] The idea is to separate (for example, using a series of filters) the different frequency combinations, and then to code with greater fidelity the frequencies that humans pay particular attention to. Without subband coding, all frequency combinations would be coded identically, so the technique achieves high perceived quality with fewer total bits.

Another approach relating to humans'
handling of frequency is transform coding. This usually involves spatial frequencies, as in single images. The most common approach applies the *discrete cosine transform*, which is related to the fast Fourier transform. Rao and Yip cover DCT approaches thoroughly.[32] Lower spatial frequencies must be carefully coded, while higher frequencies need less detailed coding. If we think of a block (say, an 8×8-pixel section) of a two-dimensional image as a square with rows and columns numbered from the top-left corner, then the DCT of that block will also be a similarly numbered square. Consider a zigzag sequencing of the values in transform space, starting at the top-left corner and covering the nearest cells first. Run-length encoding and coarse quantification of cells later in the sequence both lead to good compression. The encoder applies DCT in the forward direction, and the decoder uses an inverse mapping from transform to image space.

Importance-oriented compression. Other characteristics of images besides frequency are used as the basis for compression. The principle is to consider as more important those parts of an image that humans are better attuned to. An example of this approach is to filter images, getting rid of details that cannot be perceived, as in the low-pass filtering done for real-time video with DVI systems. Another technique is to allocate more bits to encode important parts of an image, such as where edges occur,
than to encode large homogeneous regions, such as those depicting clouds.

Color lookup table use, as in CD-I and DVI, applies the principle of indirection. Instead of letting the bits that describe a pixel refer to a location in color space, the bits identify a table location, and the table entry refers to color space. Color spaces often cover a palette of size 2^{24}, which means 24 bits are needed. On the other hand, lookup table size may be only 256 (2^8). The reduction is 24 to 8 bits per pixel. The challenge is to select for each lookup table the most important colors to be accessed by the display processor.

Subsampling, also based on characteristics of human vision, was discussed in an earlier section. It involves using fewer bits for chrominance than luminance. Interpolation, which can be carried out in hardware,[40] results in a full but approximate reconstruction of the original. We can think of this process as that of taking one matrix and generating from it another matrix four or 16 times larger — by interpolating values horizontally, vertically, and diagonally. Related to interpolation is line doubling, used in some DVI systems to go from the 256 lines that result from video decompression to 512 lines.

Importance also relates to patterns in an image representation. Clearly, higher level descriptions where symbols refer to large structures can take much less space than raster forms. In coding theory, this translates into the fact that vector quantization can lead to higher compression than scalar quantization.[39] Scalar quantization is often just called quantization, and was discussed in an earlier section in connection with pulse code modulation and audio encoding. It takes values and maps them into a fixed number of bits.

Vector quantization, on the other hand, usually takes two-dimensional vectors of values — for example, 4×4 — and maps them into a code symbol. Thus, code books are developed for images, recording the most important vectors, and all data vectors are mapped to the nearest code-book entry, minimizing mean square error. Decoding involves fast table lookup to replace coded entries with vectors from the code book.

Vector quantization is discussed in depth in the literature.[41,42] There are many algorithms and some VLSI implementations. Encoding usually takes a good deal of computation, so near optimal code books can be developed.

Hybrid coding. Various compression approaches can be combined, for example, DCT and differential pulse code modulation, subband coding and DCT, or differential pulse code modulation and vector quantization. Generally, subband coding is coupled with vector quantization. Systems and standards for video compression often apply motion compensation for temporal compression, transform coding for spatial compression, and Huffman or arithmetic coding for statistical compression.

Standards

Initially, standards for digital multimedia were established by fiat. Thus, Philips and Sony developed CD-I, with its formats for images and audio.[8] Similarly, as a step toward CD-I and a way to incorporate audio more easily into CD-ROM applications, the companies specified CD-ROM XA. It uses ADPCM, with three different sample rates (levels A, B, C). Since the specification of CD-ROM XA, manufacturers have produced interface boards for CD-ROM-based playback. Very widespread use of CD-ROM XA is expected, such as through joint efforts involving Philips and Nintendo systems.

Recently, important new international standards for images, audio, and video have been accepted by electronics, computer, and communications organiza-

---

Important new international standards for images, audio, and video have been accepted through consensus.

---

tions through consensus, with the standards groups actually pushing the limits of state-of-the-art research. Table 2 presents summary details; explanations follow in subsequent sections. Two types of standards are particularly important: low-level coding or compression standards for data streams and hardware processing, and higher level standards for network and software operation.

Coding. The first standard listed in Table 2 is JPEG,[43] named for the Joint Photographic Experts Group, which developed it. This work is technically complete. The committee draft was sent for balloting early in 1991, and it will be approved as ISO/IEC (International Electrotechnical Commission) Standard 10918 by 1992. Processing usually involves sequential encoding using forward DCT scalar quantization, and either Huffman or arithmetic coding for compression. The decoder simply reverses the process. Applications control the quantization and Huffman tables.

JPEG also includes optional modes of compression and decompression. Progressive encoding is supported, where the image is encoded in multiple scans and the viewer can see the image build up in successively more detailed versions. This operation is important when communication bandwidth is low, or users need to browse through an image collection. Hierarchical encoding is also specified, where lower resolution images can be accessed before higher resolution images, again useful for browsing or low-resolution displays. JPEG also specifies a lossless encoding scheme, which involves a predictor and entropy coder.

A second international standard, CCITT Recommendation H.261, is referred to as $p \times 64$.[29] The p is a parameter since the standard can be used to pro-

---

duce compressed video streams at rates of $p \times 64$ Kbps, with p ranging from 1 to 30. Given CIF or QCIF input, $p \times 64$ codecs (coder/decoders) will support video telephony. For $p = 1$ or 2, only QCIF and videophone applications at low frame rates will be possible, but for p over 5, use of CIF and video conferencing is possible.

The coding is a hybrid of DCT using 8×8 blocks, and differential pulse code modulation with motion estimation[29] involving 16×16 luminance blocks, using picture memory for macroblock comparisons. Spatial coding involves DCT followed by scalar quantization. The loop filter removes high-frequency noise. Depending on the fullness of the output buffer, the quantizer step size can be varied to decrease or increase the bit rate. Statistical coding takes place in the multiplexer.

A third important standard is referred to as MPEG, for the Motion Picture Experts Group.[44] The ISO/IEC committee draft was assigned standard number 11172. There are actually three parts to the effort: MPEG-Video, MPEG-Audio, and MPEG-System. The first refers to work with video compression of television resolution — 360×240 pixels — down to a bit rate of approximately 1.2 Mbps. This rate is suitable for use with CD-ROM, digital audio tape, and T1 communication channels. All MPEG decoders should be able to operate with a "core" bit stream that has the following upper bounds[44]: resolution of 720×576 pixels, speed of 30 frames per second, bit rate of 1.86 Mbps, and decoder buffer of 46 Kbytes. Another MPEG project is to investigate compression for CCIR Recommendation 601 video at bit rates up to 10 Mbps.

While there is overlap between $p \times 64$ and MPEG capabilities, and some of the VLSI components involved can be used for both, $p \times 64$ has a goal of broad coverage for varying channel capacity, while MPEG has the goal of high-quality coverage at an important but narrower range of bit rates.

MPEG-Video specifies a layered bit stream that consists of a video sequence header and layers for sequence, a group of pictures, pictures, slices, macroblocks, and blocks.[44] The lower two levels include motion compensation and DCT data. The algorithm ensures features desirable for a range of applications: random access, fast forward and reverse searches, forward and reverse playback,

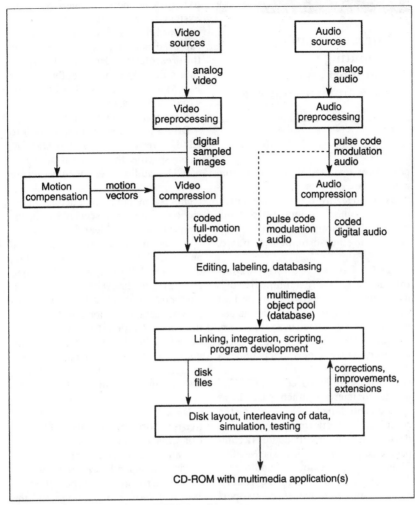

Figure 2. MPEG-based CD-ROM development.

will be coded according to the MPEG-Audio standard. Application development will then proceed, involving editing, labeling, and cataloging of the audio/video resources into a pool of "objects." Higher level activities of linking, integrating media streams, scripting interaction, and developing programs all lead to stored files. For CD-ROM, disc layout of possibly interleaved data allows simulation to ensure proper real-time operation of finished applications. After enough cycles of testing and refinement, a finished CD-ROM master can be used for replication.

With these several standards, it is imperative that headers and descriptors for video streams be created so coding methods can be easily distinguished.[14] This is particularly important for multimedia electronic mail.[46] These standards will certainly be further developed to better support users of digital multimedia.[26]

High level. In addition to coding, standards are needed for higher layers of the multimedia application development process. This work is just beginning, and it will require a few years to reach maturity. One effort is coordinated by the Multimedia and Hypermedia Information Coding Expert Group, or MHEG, whose aim is to allow bit-stream specifications for multimedia and hypermedia applications on any platform, leading to good real-time performance drawing on object-oriented methods. Version 2, July 1990, of the MHEG Working Document S includes useful definitions regarding multimedia and hypermedia. It gives a partial object hierarchy of both basic and composite objects, covering input, output, interaction, and linking. Methods include editing, operating, and presenting, with a state model including combinations of not ready versus stopped ready, running versus suspended, and exposed versus concealed. MHEG covers synchronization (between objects, or using marks or conditions), buffer memory, input objects like buttons or menus, and interactive objects like prompts.

A higher level but related effort involves extending ODA (Office Document Architecture) standards to include hypermedia. Further along, however, is work in applying the Standard Generalized Markup Language (SGML, ISO 8879) to multimedia and hypermedia. This approach led to HyTime,[47] ballot-

audio/video synchronization, robustness against errors, delays limited to 150 ms, and editability.

The MPEG-Video algorithm uses motion compensation on 16×16 blocks and DCT coding of 8×8 blocks, followed by quantization and entropy coding. Motion compensation involves predictive and interpolative coding. As in JPEG, reference frames are fully coded using DCT-based methods. Predicted (interpolated) frames are determined on the basis of the nearest reference or predicted frame (on both sides). Finally, the motion information is statistically coded.

The MPEG-Audio standard[45] is being fully specified in 1991. While CD-quality audio requires two channels of 706 Kbps, the compressed bit rate will be two channels of 128 kbps or possibly

64 Kbps — that is, a reduction from 1.412 Mbps to 0.256 Mbps. Input sampling rates of 32, 44.1, and 48 kHz with 16 bits per sample will be supported; delays will be no more than 80 ms; and addressing will be to units no longer than 1/30 second. Sound quality close to the original is expected.

Ultimately, MPEG-System work will produce a complete approach to encoding television-quality audio and video into a single stream operating at about 1.5 Mbps. Figure 2 shows how this may lead to development of digital multimedia applications for CD-ROM. Video will be converted to digital form and then compressed using motion compensation and other processing specified in MPEG-Video. Audio will be digitized. While limited amounts of pulse code modulation audio can be stored, most

ed in 1991 as ISO/IEC Committee Draft 10744. HyTime allows a complete digital multimedia application to be encoded in a linear stream, including all details regarding "document" structure, hypermedia linking, synchronization, and timing. For interchange, Abstract Syntax Notation 1 (ASN.1, ISO 8824) allows bit string representation. A pool of multimedia objects can be referenced from the main part of the document. Also, there are series of events and "batons" to control the timing, with mapping from virtual time units to real time. The Text Encoding Initiative has drawn on HyTime for describing multimedia and hypermedia documents and performances.

Further standards work will facilitate interchange and transcoding of multimedia,[14] integration of object pools with scripting languages, interoperability of applications on heterogeneous platforms connected by fiber networks, conversions between storage units, and other requirements called for by a growing community of users.

Systems

Interactive multimedia computing systems must support application development and use. At present, there is a tight coupling of hardware, software, and applications, but that coupling will gradually loosen. Here, I deal with a variety of platforms and related software.

Next. Next systems with a Nextdimension board support 32-bit color (24-bit color plus an alpha channel). The board was designed to include an i860 processor for graphics and a JPEG compression chip[48] from C-Cube Microsystems. While 640 × 480-pixel image compression in software requires almost 10 seconds using the Motorola MC68040 microprocessor, the special board must do that in 1/30 second. This allows full-motion compression and decompression, using the 600-Kbps speed achieved by some hard disks to achieve moderate-quality playback.

MediaView is a digital multimedia communication software system built with Nextstep, the interface used on Next systems, to handle graphics, audio, video, animations, mathematics, and so on.[49] It uses an object-oriented approach to documents. Searching is sup-

---

Interactive multimedia computing systems must support application development and use.

---

ported for text, and digital darkroom methods are used for images. Annotations include Draw-it and Hear-it notes, as well as object- or image-based animations. Full-motion video will be supported using the Nextdimension board.

CD-I, CDTV. Compact Disc-Interactive was the first interactive digital multimedia technology targeted for the consumer market. First announced in 1986, CD-I is defined in a proprietary standard, the "Green Book," which Philips provided to developers under a license arrangement.[8] The first prototype disks were prepared in 1987. The official commercial launch of CD-I was delayed until fall of 1991, reflecting the complexity of software and application development. Each unit includes a compact disc player, a Motorola M68000 family microprocessor, an audio processing unit, audio and video decoders, a clock, a pointing device, and an operating system, CD-RTOS, derived from OS-9, with real-time capabilities. There will be optional MPEG-compliant full-motion video support. The minimal system, the CD-I Base Case Decoder, will connect to an external monitor and external speakers. The decoder supports a variety of visual effects, including single-plane effects like cuts, scrolling, mosaics, and fades, as well as two-plane effects like transparency, chroma key, matte, dissolve, and wipe.

The challenge of CD-I has been to build a carefully defined hardware, software, and storage environment for interactive multimedia computing that can be sold as a package for under $1,000. Such systems would serve the needs of consumers and the low-end education/training marketplace. Careful design is required, since "hit" CD-I discs, selling for perhaps $40, might establish a large consumer electronics market, as did compact disc players and Nintendo units. Toward that end, Optimage Interactive Services Company has developed tools

to help developers, and there is Starter System software that works with the standard decoder, allowing previously captured materials to be reorganized for presentations. However, full application development currently calls for PC-, Macintosh-, and/or Sun-based networks and a variety of software tools and programming expertise.

Bruno gives a short introduction to CD-I.[27] Brewer describes CD-ROM XA, which specifies the use of various levels of CD-I audio in an open hardware environment.[24] Philips' work with MPEG compression and related details on the video decoder are discussed by Sijstermans and van der Meer.[38]

In the spring of 1991, Commodore announced CDTV (Commodore Dynamic Total Vision), with pricing and an approach similar to those of CD-I. Commodore uses CD-ROM with proprietary representation schemes rather than the CD-I format, so CDTV is positioned as a related but competing technology, building on Commodore's experience with real-time operating systems and the Amiga 500 computer.

DVI. Intel's Digital Video Interactive is a more open approach than CD-I or CDTV, emphasizing digital video and audio compression, chip sets, and machine-independent audio/video software environments. Luther gives an excellent short introduction[50] and the best overall description.[20] Included in a series of articles in a special section in *Communications of the ACM*[51] is an overview of the technology and applications, a short history of the development and graphics-based prototyping, a description of parallel encoding, and details of an exciting application to training. Elsewhere, Harney et al. described the new "B" chip set,[40] and Green described the new software design.[52]

Current DVI technology uses a 25-MIPS pixel processor, the 82750 PB. Although in some ways it is like a conventional microprocessor, the 82750 PB is five to 10 times faster because of its specialized architecture. It is programmable and can support various standards.[40] The 82750 PB can

- perform graphics operations rapidly;
- use special effects to highlight image or video transitions;
- decode a 640 × 480-pixel JPEG compressed image in less than a second;

Table 3. Classes of multimedia systems.

Component	Multimedia PC	Typical Current System	Typical Advanced System
Storage	CD-ROM, 30-Mbyte disk	CD-ROM, 100-Mbyte disk	CD-ROM, gigabyte disk
Host processor	80286	80386 or MC68030	80486 or MC68040
Display	VGA	768 × 480	1,024 × 768
Extra board	Audio board	Nextdimension, CD-ROM XA, DVI	MPEG system
Networking	None	Ethernet, token ring	Fiber Distributed Data Interface
Software	Windows 3.0	Authology: Multimedia, Mediascript, MediaView	Athena Muse, Integrator

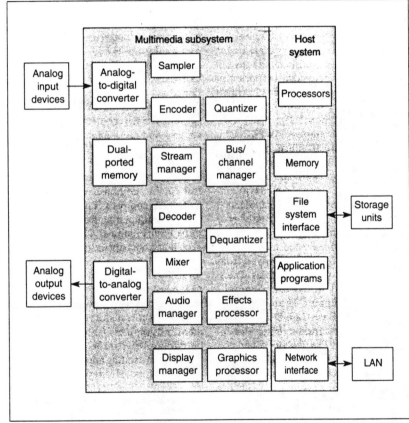

Figure 3. Logical components of a future multimedia workstation.

warping textures selected from an image database onto graphic objects selected from a wireframe database.

Intel has published a bit-stream specification. DVI will support MPEG standards when they are fully specified, and Intel has an even faster pixel processor planned for 1993.

The companion display processor, the 82750 DB chip, supports pixel interpolation, genlocking, an alpha channel, reconfigurable color lookup tables, conversion from YUV to RGB, and triple 8-bit digital-to-analog converters, for resolutions at least through 640 × 480 pixels. Intel provides the ActionMedia 750 board set for AT or Micro Channel Architecture 80386-based computers. Boards using the chip set have been developed for Macintosh computers as well.

The present DVI audio/video subsystem software, called AVSS, will be replaced by AVK, the audio/video kernel.[52] Instead of the current single environment for DOS, AVK has been designed to work with at least Microsoft Windows, OS/2, and Unix. Instead of implementing only the simple VCR metaphor supported by AVSS, AVK uses the metaphor of a digital production studio, managing a variety of streams with sampling, mixing, and effects. More attention is given to interfacing with the host operating system and handling real-time operations. Saturation of processors, memory, and I/O is avoided with flexible buffering. Scheduling is handled by the pixel processor instead of the host system, streams are synchronized into groups, and windows are supported.

Third-party developers have provided higher level software support. For

- compress or decompress images using a proprietary format at up to 768 × 480-pixel resolution in a fraction of a second;
- compress 128 × 120-pixel resolution motion video at 30 frames per second with fair quality into a special representation (RTV, or real-time video) on hard disk; and

- play back video compressed on a 64-processor Intel computer into another special representation (PLV, or production-level video) at 30 frames per second with good quality at 256 × 240-pixel resolution.

Combinations of these operations are fast and effective for such effects as

example, Mediascript[20] is a high-level language interpreter that eliminates much of the need for programming in C. Other tools support painting (for example, Lumena), animation building (Authology: Multimedia), and hypermedia. Our efforts at Virginia Polytechnic Institute and State University (VPI & SU) have led to a "hot spot" tool for managing buttons and a prototype "integrator" that uses the metaphor of a musical score and concepts covered by the MHEG and HyTime standards as the basis for direct manipulation to develop interactive multimedia applications.

Prospects

Clearly there are opposing forces in the future of digital multimedia systems: closed versus open systems, low cost versus high cost, performance versus flexibility, and stand-alone systems versus distributed systems. Table 3 illustrates two key dimensions of systems: components and power. Companies like Microsoft and Tandy have promulgated multimedia PCs (MPCs), but these are fairly minimal systems. As the table shows, most serious offerings go beyond these minimal specifications, possibly adding Ethernet or token ring networking.

The next generation of digital multimedia systems will be at the level shown in the last column of Table 3. Not only CD-ROM but also large-capacity writable local storage will allow capture and development as well as use of applications. Faster host processors and full support for the MPEG standard will be required. Networking will provide access to image, audio, and video servers at high speeds. Tools like our integrator or systems building on the Athena Muse system at MIT[3] will provide flexible support for a variety of application classes.

Figure 3 illustrates one type of future workstation. Access to network and storage units as well as analog input and output devices must be supported. Inside the workstation (the workstation itself may be physically distributed) will be the standard host system components and a comprehensive multimedia system. The multimedia system may be part of the host motherboard, but we can think of it as logically separate. Hardware and software components must carry out the multiple functions shown for the multimedia subsystem.

Table 4: Reference model, upper layers.

Layer	Description/Contents
Application	Hypertext, hypermedia, interactive multimedia
Presentation	Devices: keyboard, mouse, speakers, windows
	Media: animations, audio, graphics, images, video
	Operations: accessing, editing, sequencing, transforming
Session	History management, user identification, versioning
Base	Searching and inferencing with data, information, and knowledge bases
View	Frames, graphs, lists, relations
Link	Labels, link identifiers, types
Anchor	Anchor identifiers, span descriptions
Node	Basic and composite media objects, object identifiers
Communication	File systems, messages, processes

Table 4 illustrates how these advanced workstations might relate to current views of interoperability. Above the bottom layer shown here, which represents the lower levels of the Open Systems Interconnection reference model, are four layers related to multimedia and hypermedia, followed by the usual three top layers of the OSI reference model. Thus, the view layer provides convenient abstractions that support data, information, and knowledge bases, which fit into the next layer. In our work at VPI&SU on the Large External Network (object-oriented) Database, we have implemented parts of these top five layers. Altogether, Table 4 provides a partial conceptual framework for digital hypermedia systems, emphasizing how they must fit into the overall picture of open networks, information processing, and flexible access.

The future for digital multimedia systems is bright, but calls for thoughtful discussion and planning.[14] Already, there have been demonstrations of how hypermedia news services can construct and deliver overnight issues in all-digital format.[23] Based on successes of prototypes at MIT, we can conclude that electronic magazines, manuals, and movie services will be developed. Hypermedia publishing and computer-supported cooperative work will use digital multimedia.

Hardware costs will continue to decline, standards will evolve and become more widely adopted, software systems and tools will mature, and publishers and end-users will learn to work creatively with a range of new capabilities.[53] Interactive computing will benefit from the development of the audio and television industries, leading to exciting new possibilities for interactive digital multimedia computing. ■

Acknowledgments

The anonymous reviewers provided helpful comments. NCR Corp. supported some of our work on interactive digital video. Gregory Fox and Mahesh Ursekar provided secretarial assistance. I extend special thanks to Deborah Hix, Edward Schwartz, and the many students working with us on digital video at VPI&SU.

References

1. *Managing Interactive Video/Multimedia Projects*, Educational Technology Publications, R. Bergman and T. Moore, eds., Prentice Hall, Englewood Cliffs, N.J., 1990.

2. *Learning with Interactive Multimedia*, S. Ambron and K. Hooper, eds., Microsoft Press, Redmond, Wash., 1990.

3. W. Mackay and G. Davenport, "Virtual Video Editing in Interactive Multimedia Applications," *Comm. ACM*, Vol. 32, No. 7, July 1989, pp. 802-810.

4. *CD-ROM, Vol. 2: Optical Publishing*, S. Ropiequet, J. Einberger, and B. Zoellick, eds., Microsoft Press, Redmond, Wash., 1987.

5. *The CD-ROM Handbook*, C. Sherman, ed., McGraw-Hill, New York, 1988.

6. J. Nadler and R. Wiesenberg, "CD-ROM Hardware," in *The CD-ROM Handbook*, C. Sherman, ed., McGraw-Hill, New York, 1988, pp. 79-106.

7. J. Einberger and B. Zoellick, "High Sierra Group Format Description," in *CD-ROM, Vol. 2: Optical Publishing*, S. Ropiequet, J. Einberger, and B. Zoellick, eds., Microsoft Press, Redmond, Wash., 1987, pp. 195-216.

8. Philips International Inc., *Compact Disc-Interactive*, McGraw-Hill, New York, 1988.

9. D. Traub, "An Historical Perspective on CD-ROM,"in *The CD-ROM Handbook*, C. Sherman, ed., McGraw-Hill, New York, 1988, pp. 17-50.

10. D. Davies, "Future Possibilities of CD-ROM," in *The CD-ROM Handbook*, C. Sherman, ed., McGraw-Hill, New York, 1988, pp. 209-239.

11. *Proc. First Int'l Workshop on Network and Operating System Support for Digital Audio and Video*, Tech. Report TR-90-062, D. Anderson et. al., eds, Int'l Computer Science Inst., Berkeley, Calif., 1990.

12. R. Sansom and E. Cooper, "The Impact of Broadband Integrated Services on the Structure of Systems and Application Software," *Proc. First Int'l Workshop on Network and Operating System Support for Digital Audio and Video*, Tech. Report TR-90-062, Int'l Computer Science Inst., Berkeley, Calif., 1990.

13. D. Wybranietz, R. Cordes, and F. Stamen, "Support for Multimedia Communication in Future Private Networks," *Proc. First Int'l Workshop on Network and Operating System Support for Digital Audio and Video*, Tech. Report TR-90-062, Int'l Computer Science Inst., Berkeley, Calif., 1990.

14. M. Liebhold and E. Hoffert, "Toward an Open Environment for Digital Video," *Comm. ACM*, Vol. 34, No. 4, Apr. 1991, pp. 103-112.

15. R. Steinmetz et al., "Compound Multimedia Objects — Integration into Network and Operating Systems," *Proc. First Int'l Workshop on Network and Operating System Support for Digital Audio and Video*, Tech. Report TR-90-062, Int'l Computer Science Inst., Berkeley, Calif., 1990.

16. D. Anderson, R. Govindan, and G. Homsy, "Design and Implementation of a Continuous I/O Server," *Proc. First Int'l Workshop on Network and Operating System Support for Digital Audio and Video*, Tech. Report TR-90-062, Int'l Computer Science Inst., Berkeley, Calif., 1990.

17. P. Momtahan and R. Kamel, "PX Connection Architecture," *Proc. First Int'l Workshop on Network and Operating System Support for Digital Audio and Video*, Tech. Report TR-90-062, Int'l Computer Science Inst., Berkeley, Calif., 1990.

18. H. Katseff et al., "An Overview of the Liaison Network Multimedia Workstation," *Proc. First Int'l Workshop on Network and Operating System Support for Digital Audio and Video*, Tech. Report TR-90-062, Int'l Computer Science Inst., Berkeley, Calif., 1990.

19. C. Yu et al., "Efficient Placement of Audio Data on Optical Discs for Real-Time Applications," *Comm. ACM*, Vol. 32, No. 7, July 1989, pp. 862-871.

20. A. Luther, *Digital Video in the PC Environment*, second edition, McGraw-Hill, New York, 1991.

21. J. Bottoms and L. Helgerson, "The First Step Toward Publishing on CD-ROM," in *The CD-ROM Handbook*, C. Sherman, ed., McGraw-Hill, New York, 1988, pp. 269-307.

22. A. Adkins, "Data Preparation and Premastering," in *The CD-ROM Handbook*, C. Sherman, ed., McGraw-Hill, New York, 1988, pp. 343-396.

23. E. Hoffert and G. Gretsch, "The Digital News Systems at Educom: A Convergence of Interactive Computing Newspapers, Television, and High-Speed Networks," *Comm. ACM*, Vol. 34, No. 4, Apr. 1991, pp. 113-116.

24. B. Brewer, "Using Audio," in *CD-ROM, Vol. 2: Optical Publishing*, S. Ropiequet, J. Einberger, and B. Zoellick, eds., Microsoft Press, Redmond, Wash., 1987, pp. 169-183.

25. G. Doherty and R. Apperson, "Displaying Images," in *CD-ROM, Vol. 2: Optical Publishing*, S. Ropiequet, J. Einberger, and B. Zoellick, eds., Microsoft Press, Redmond, Wash., 1987, pp. 121-168.

26. A. Lippman, "Feature Sets for Interactive Images," *Comm. ACM*, Vol. 34, No. 4, Apr. 1991, pp. 92-101.

27. R. Bruno, "Compact Disc-Interactive," in *The CD-ROM Handbook*, C. Sherman, ed., McGraw-Hill, New York, 1988, pp. 131-185.

28. B. Haskell, "International Standards Activities in Image Data Compression," *Proc. Scientific Data Compression Workshop*, NASA Conf. Pub. 3025, NASA Office of Management, Scientific and Technical Information Division, Washington, DC, 1989, pp. 439-449.

29. M. Liou, "Overview of the px64 Kbit/s Video Coding Standard," *Comm. ACM*, Vol. 34, No. 4, Apr. 1991, pp. 59-63.

30. A. Fleig, "The EOS Data and Information System," *Proc. Scientific Data Compression Workshop*, NASA Conf. Pub. 3025, NASA Office of Management, Scientific and Technical Information Division, Washington, DC, 1989, pp. 73-83.

31. E. Fox, "Guest Editor's Introduction: Standards and the Emergence of Digital Multimedia Systems," *Comm. ACM*, Vol. 34, No. 4, Apr. 1991, pp. 26-29.

32. K. Rao and P. Yip, *Discrete Cosine Transform — Algorithms, Advantages, Applications*, Academic Press, London, 1990.

33. *Proc. Scientific Data Compression Workshop*, NASA Conf. Pub. 3025, H. Ramapriyan, ed., NASA Office of Management, Scientific and Technical Information Division, Washington, DC, 1989.

34. *Proc. DCC 91, Data Compression Conf.*, J.A. Storer and J.H. Reif, eds., IEEE CS Press, Los Alamitos, Calif., Order No. 2202, 1991.

35. M. Barnsley and A. Sloan, "Fractal Image Compression," *Proc. Scientific Data Compression Workshop*, NASA Conf. Pub. 3025, NASA Office of Management, Scientific and Technical Information Division, Washington, DC, 1989, pp. 351-365.

36. A. Blumer, "Noiseless Compression Using Non-Markov Models," *Proc. Scientific Data Compression Workshop*, NASA Conf. Pub. 3025, NASA Office of Management, Scientific and Technical Information Division, Washington, DC, 1989, pp. 367-375.

37. M. Cohn, "Performance of Lempel-Ziv Compressors with Deferred Innovation," *Proc. Scientific Data Compression Workshop*, NASA Conf. Pub. 3025, NASA Office of Management, Scientific and Technical Information Division, Washington, DC, 1989, pp. 377-391.

38. F. Sijstermans and J. van der Meer, "CD-I Full-Motion Video Encoding on a Parallel Computer," *Comm. ACM*, Vol. 34, No. 4, Apr. 1991, pp. 81-91.

39. A. Lippman and W. Butera, "Coding Image Sequence for Interactive Retrieval," *Comm. ACM*, Vol. 32, No. 7, July 1989, pp. 852-860.

40. K. Harney et al., "The i750 Video Processor: A Total Multimedia Solution," *Comm. ACM*, Vol. 34, No. 4, Apr. 1991, pp. 64-78.

41. R. Gray, "Vector Quantization," *Proc. Scientific Data Compression Workshop*, NASA Conf. Pub. 3025, NASA Office of Management, Scientific and Technical Information Division, Washington, DC, 1989, pp. 205-231.

42. R. Baker, "AVLSI Chip Set Real-Time Vector Quantization of Image Sequences," *Proc. Scientific Data Compression*

Workshop, NASA Conf. Pub. 3025, NASA Office of Management, Scientific and Technical Information Division, Washington, DC, 1989, pp. 419-437.

43. G. Wallace, "The JPEG Still Picture Compression Standard," *Comm. ACM*, Vol. 34, No. 4, Apr. 1991, pp. 30-44.

44. D. Le Gall, "MPEG: A Video Compression Standard for Multimedia Applications," *Comm. ACM*, Vol. 34, No. 4, Apr. 1991, pp. 46-58.

45. H. Musman, "The ISO Audio Coding Standard," *Proc. Globecom 90*, IEEE, New York, 1990.

46. N. Borenstein, "Multimedia Electronic Mail: Will the Dream Become a Reality?" *Comm. ACM*, Vol. 34, No. 4, Apr. 1991, pp. 117-119.

47. S. Newcomb, N. Kipp, and V. Newcomb, "HyTime: The Hypermedia/Time-Based Document Structuring Language," to appear in *Comm. ACM*, Vol. 34, No. 11, Nov. 1991.

48. G. Cockroft and L. Hourvitz, "Nextstep: Putting JPEG to Multiple Uses," *Comm. ACM*, Vol. 34, No. 4, Apr. 1991, p. 45.

49. R. Phillips, "MediaView: A General Multimedia Digital Publication System," *Comm. ACM*, Vol. 34, No. 7, July 1991, pp. 74-83.

50. A. Luther, "Digital Video Interactive," in *The CD-ROM Handbook*, C. Sherman, ed., McGraw-Hill, New York, 1988, pp. 187-207.

51. Special section on interactive technologies, E. Fox, ed., *Comm. ACM*, Vol. 32, No. 7, July 1989.

52. J. Green, "The Evolution of DVI System Software," to appear in *Comm. ACM*, Vol. 35, No. 1, Jan. 1992.

53. M. Liebhold, "Hypermedia and Visual Literacy," in *Learning with Interactive Multimedia*, S. Ambron and K. Hooper, eds., Microsoft Press, Redmond, Wash., 1990, pp 99-110.

Edward A. Fox is associate director for research at the Computing Center and associate professor of computer science at Virginia Polytechnic Institute and State University. He directed the Virginia Disc series of CD-ROMs and Virginia Tech work on interactive digital video. His interests, research projects, and publications are in the area of information storage and retrieval, library automation, hypertext/hypermedia/multimedia, computational linguistics, CD-ROM and optical disc technology, electronic publishing, hashing, and expert systems.

Fox received a BS in electrical engineering from MIT and an MS and a PhD in computer science from Cornell University. He serves ACM as a member of the Publications Board, chairman of the Special Interest Group on Information Retrieval (SIGIR), and associate editor of *ACM Transactions on Information Systems*.

The author can be reached at the Department of Computer Science or the Computing Center, Virginia Polytechnic Institute and State University, Blacksburg, VA 24061-0106; e-mail fox@vtopus.cs.vt.edu.

Proceedings of the Second European Conference on Computer-Supported Cooperative Work
Bannon. L.. Robinson, M. & Schmidt, K. (Editors)
September 25-27, 1991, Amsterdam, The Netherlands

Sound Support For Collaboration

William W. Gaver

Rank Xerox EuroPARC, England

Shared work often involves fluid transitions between relatively focussed collaboration, division of labour, general awareness and serendipitous communication. This leads to a tension in the design of software systems meant to support shared work: focussed collaboration implies the need to coordinate people's views of work objects, while division of labour requires individual control over views. A similar tension exists in the office environment as well: group engagement in the workplace depends on a shared context, but individual work is facilitated by privacy and freedom of action. Auditory cues have the potential to reduce these tensions because graphics and sound can provide two independent ways to present and obtain information. I illustrate the potential of sound in collaborative systems with observations drawn from two systems: the ARKola simulation, which explores the effects of sound on collaboration within a workstation environment; and EAR, in which auditory cues are used to increase general awareness of events and encourage group engagement within the workplace itself. These examples suggest useful functions sound can play in collaborative systems.

Introduction

The shift from computer systems that support a single user working alone to those supporting a group of users working together is a profound one. It leads to a consideration of the ways people work together in the everyday world and possible ways to extend and support their interactions. Perhaps more importantly, it suggests that the unique capabilities of computers should be embedded more firmly in ordinary work practises, so that the distinctions between the world of the computer and the workaday world are blurred (Moran & Anderson, 1990).

Developments in collaborative systems are promising, but if traditional models of human computer interaction seem to assume that we work in isolation, the new model sometimes seems one of people spending the totality of their working lives in

meetings. To date, most software systems designed to support shared work seem aimed at supporting relatively intensive periods of collaboration – for instance, in meetings (Mantei, 1988), creating structured outlines (Ellis et al., 1988), or simultaneously developing documents (CSMIL, 1989).

But just as most people don't work alone at all times, nor do they always work together. Often people are merely aware of each other – aware of others' presence, perhaps their activities and progress. Occasionally people meet randomly in the course of day to day work, and these meetings are serendipitously fruitful, as when casual conversation leads to some question being answered or a longer term collaboration being started. And even when collaborating, people often divide their labour, meeting one another to share results and plan the future. Only occasionally do we actually join and work together closely on the same task.

People shift from working alone to working together, even when joined on a shared task. Building systems that support these transitions is important, if difficult. One promising approach is to embed collaborative software in a larger system of audio and video interconnectivity that allows people to be virtually co-present even if not working closely with one another (e.g., Buxton & Moran, 1990; Root, 1988; Goodman & Abel, 1987). Such systems have had some success, but it also seems important for such transitions to be supported by software systems themselves.

In this paper, I discuss the potential for auditory cues to support relatively casual and serendipitous forms of collaboration, both in software and office environments. First, I explore the movement between awareness and focussed collaboration, and discuss the reasons auditory cues seem appealing for support of smooth transitions in the degree of engagement on a common task. The potential of auditory cues is illustrated with examples from two systems that use sound to support collaboration. The first example comes from the ARKola bottling plant simulation, which explores the effects of auditory cues on a collaborative task in a workstation environment. The second system, called EAR (for Environmental Audio Reminders), is a system in which sound helps users maintain awareness of one another and events within the workplace itself. These two examples complement one another in focussing on the effects of auditory cues on collaboration in the workstation environment and the more general office environment; together they point the way towards many possible future developments.

Moving among ways of working

Figure 1 is a simple representation of the complex process of working together. Although simplistic, it provides a useful orientation to the extremes of the experience. Four major landmarks are indicated here. Underlying all is *general awareness*. This is a pervasive experience, one of simply knowing who is around and something about what they are doing; that they are busy or free, meeting or alone, receptive to communication or not. Awareness is necessary for all collaborative work, but the degree to which its focus is shared varies. An intense sharing of awareness characterizes *focussed collaboration* – those occasions in which people work closely together on a shared goal. Less is needed for *division of labour*, that common work practise in which a shared goal is divided and component tasks addressed separately. Finally, more casual awareness can lead to *serendipitous communication*, in which people realize the potential for productive work through chance encounters.

People move among these ways of working together along many trajectories. Simple awareness may lead to serendipitous communication, which in turn may lead to division of labour or focussed collaboration. Alternatively, a period of focussed collaboration may be followed by a division of labour. All of these forms of working together are likely to be important at one time or another in a shared project; supporting fluid movements among them is an important goal for collaborative software.

Yet the design of systems with the flexibility necessary to support many styles of shared work is not an easy task. One problem seems to be the tension between the need to maintain a common focus for collaborators and the desire to allow individuals freedom to work on their own. Bellotti et al. (1991) make this tension explicit in a Design Rationale based around studies of a shared editor (cf. MacLean et al., 1989). Two of the criteria they identify as pervasive in the choice of design options are the seemingly contradictory ones of "maintaining shared work focus" and "allowing individual work."

In the design of shared software systems, the tension between shared and individual work is reflected in issues concerning the degree of control over work objects afforded users. Individual work is supported by giving people complete control over their view of a work object: over its screen placement, the parts of it made visible, their appearance, etc. But shared focus is supported by *reducing* individual control over their view. From this perspective, focussed collaboration is most likely to occur when all participants can be assumed to be viewing the same thing. Although enforcing an identical focus on a given task may be helpful for supporting focussed collaboration, it is likely to hamper the smooth flow to other, less close forms of shared work (Bellotti et al., 1991).

Similar issues arise in offices, where the shared contexts necessary for group engagement compete with the privacy needed to concentrate on individual work – it is difficult to get work done when constantly in meetings about work. Providing ubiquitous audio-video interconnectivity may encourage awareness, but one must monitor a video screen at the expense of attention to one's work. Using video windows on a workstation is only a partial solution, since they must vie for valuable screen real-estate with other graphical tools.

In sum, systems which seek to support both shared work and individual flexibility suffer from the need to compete for control over the same display resources and limited visual attention. Clearly these issues can be dealt with by increasing the size and number of displays and relying on the time-honored panacea of social control. In this paper, however, I suggest that sound can provide a valuable alternative to vision as a means of providing the contextual information that allows free movement among more and less intense forms of collaboration.

Auditory icons and collaborative work

There are a number of reasons to think that sound has the potential to complement visual displays in supporting the transitions between focussed collaboration and more casual and separate forms of shared work. Primary among these reasons is hearing's status as a distance sense secondary only to vision. By distance sense, I mean that we are able to listen to information about events at a distance. Just as we can see a tree fall from far away, so can we hear it. We hope, on the other hand, neither to feel or taste the falling tree; and though we may smell it the experience is not likely to provide us with much useful information.

Because we can listen to as well as look at distant events, we can divide information about computer events between the two senses. On the one hand, we may provide redundant information about an event, so that we can both see and hear it. More interesting, we can disassociate the two, so that we may hear what we don't see.

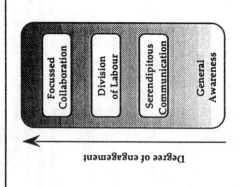

Figure 1: Shared work involves fluid transitions among focussed collaboration, division of labour, serendipitous communication, and general awareness (which supports them all).

Hearing also complements vision in that listening to an event does not necessarily interfere with the maintenance of a visual focus on another event. As I write this, for instance, I might hear a colleague walk by my office. The sounds of footsteps, doors opening, etc., provide information about what is going on around me, but I can nonetheless maintain my focus on my work. This should carry over quite well to collaborative systems, so that individual control can be granted users while sufficient cues as to the activities and whereabouts of others are still available. By splitting information about a shared workspace between sound and vision, we may reduce the tension between the desire to maintain a shared focus and that of allowing individual work.

Of course, no matter how attractive sound may be as a medium, it must be able to convey relatively complex information about events if it is to be useful. Clearly a collaborative system relying on the beeps and buzzes currently used in computers to increase awareness of colleague's activities would entail too high a cognitive overhead to provide valuable support to users (not to mention the irritation it would cause). It is not only necessary that sound complement vision, but that it provide information in subtle and intuitively obvious ways.

I have been developing a strategy for using sound to convey complex information that is based on the ways people listen to events in the everyday world (Gaver, 1986). From this perspective, we listen not to sounds and their attributes (such as pitch, loudness and timbre) but rather to events and theirs (e.g., footsteps, force and size). *Everyday listening* refers to the experience of listening to events. Taking this experience of listening as primary allows the development of a framework for analyzing and manipulating sounds that is based on attributes of events rather than the parameters of sound *per se*. These attributes, in turn, may be mapped to attributes of computer events, giving rise to *auditory icons*. Auditory icons are environmental sounds (like taps, scrapes, etc.) designed to convey information by analogy with everyday sound-producing events.

Auditory icons have several appealing qualities as a method of providing feedback about events. First, sound as a medium is a valuable way to provide information that is not constrained to a single location (e.g., I can hear a sound without facing my computer monitor). Second, non-speech audio is often less distracting, less susceptible to masking, and more efficient than is speech. Third, everyday sounds can often be mapped more closely to the events they are meant to represent than can musical sounds. Finally, auditory icons can be designed to present information in an almost subliminal way – just as we are likely to get a great deal of information without conscious attention from the sounds of colleagues working, so can auditory icons convey a great deal of information without being overly distracting.

Experience with systems employing auditory icons has suggested that such cues can be useful for individual work (Gaver, 1989). In particular, sound can convey information about events and objects that is difficult to convey visually – for

instance, about the timing of events or the nature of interactions – as well as information that is inconvenient to present and obtain visually, for instance about the progress of relatively long lasting processes. Finally, informal experience with sound in a large-scale, collaborative system called SoundShark (Gaver & Smith, 1990) suggests that sound can support general awareness of collaborators' whereabouts and activities.

What I am suggesting, then, is that a smooth flow from focussed collaboration to division of labour can be facilitated by using well-designed auditory icons to increase awareness of activities and events. In the next two sections, I expand and support this notion by detailing experience with two collaborative systems which employ auditory icons. The first is the ARKola bottling plant simulation, a system in which sound provides cues designed to aid users collaborating in a workstation environment. The second is EAR, a system that uses designed audio cues to support awareness of events and activities within the entire work environment.

The ARKola bottling plant simulation

The ARKola bottling plant is a simulation designed expressly to explore the functions of auditory cues in complex, collaborative software systems. The simulation was developed to serve as a domain for testing that would satisfy a number of constraints:

- We hypothesized that sounds would aid in monitoring multiprocessing systems, so many simultaneous processes should be involved in the task.
- Sound should enable people to track hidden or invisible events, so the task domain should be too big to entirely fit the computer screen.
- Auditory cues are likely to be most evidently useful when tasks are demanding, so we wanted a task that was simple to understand yet difficult to perform.
- We expected sound to affect collaboration, and so wanted a task that would encourage shared work.
- Finally, we wanted a task that would seem natural and engaging for participants, so they would not be bored or confused during our studies.

The ARKola simulation seemed to fulfill these requirements quite well. We stress, however, that though this simulation may seem more representative of video games or process control tasks than of traditional workstation domains, we believe it shares many features with – and thus our results are relevant to – more traditional domains. Although we were interested in testing several functions for auditory icons within this environment, for the purposes of this paper I focus primarily on aspects directly relevant for collaborative work (for a more complete description of this work, see Gaver et al., 1991).

people could coordinate their views to work with a shared focus, or use separate views and divide their labour.

Observing collaboration on the plant

We observed eight pairs of people using the system for two one-hour sessions apiece; one session with and one without auditory feedback. Half the participants had auditory feedback on their first sessions and half did not. Partners worked on the system from different offices in the building, working together in the "same" factory shown on different workstations and communicating via a two-way audio and video link. Figure 3 shows the experimental set-up for the two offices.

We collected video-taped data upon which we based our observations of plant usage both from the subjects' audio-video links and from cameras pointing at each of their screens. Our observations are informal, relying mainly on occasions when participants explicitly referred to the sounds. We were able to cull a number of suggestive examples of the use of sounds. We take our data, then, as providing hypotheses for further testing and exploration.

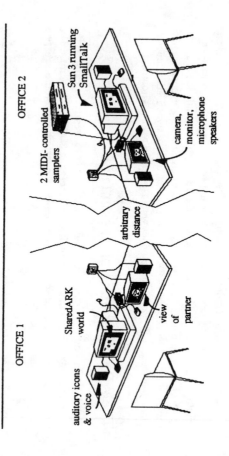

Figure 3. Setup for the ARKola experiment. Subjects worked in separate offices, collaborating on the ARKola simulation and communicating via an audio-video link. Data was collected from their camera and from cameras pointing at the computer screens.

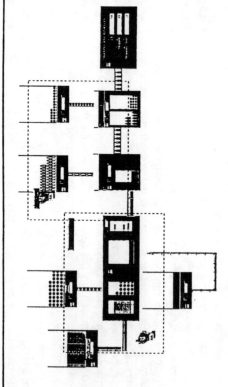

Figure 2: The ARKola bottling plant simulation. Nine machines mix, cook, bottle, cap, and count bottles of simulated cola. Mouse-driven hands are used to move and press buttons, control machines, etc. Dotted rectangles show the approximate extent of the view each user could have of the plant. (This figure is approximately one-fifth actual size.)

The plant, shown in Figure 2, consists of a virtual assembly line for producing a simulated softdrink. Users control the plant using mouse-driven "hands" to activate machine controls and to move and activate "buttons" which order new supplies or repair broken machines. Completed bottles of cola add funds to a virtual "bank account" at the end of the line; buying supplies or repairs deplete funds. The goal of participants, then, was to make money by producing as much cola as possible as efficiently as possible.

The simulation was implemented in SharedARK, a collaborative version of the Alternate Reality Kit (Smith, 1987); thus the simulated softdrink was called ARKola and the plant named accordingly. SharedARK, a fascinating environment in its own right, was used here as a foundation for developing the visual appearance and actions of the plant and participants' interactions with it.

Feedback about the status of the plant was provided by visual and auditory cues. Supplies could be heard as they moved along: cooking cola burbled, the capping machine clanged, and wasted supplies crashed and spilled audibly. Although some attempt was made to equate the information presented audibly with that displayed graphically, the purpose of the experiment was not to compare the two media in terms of effectiveness, but rather to understand their different characters.

The bottling plant was designed to be too large to fit on a computer screen, so each participant could only view part of the plant at a given time. However, participants could move their view by "sliding" their screen over the plant. Thus

Collaboration in the ARKola Simulation

We were struck with the great degree to which participants divided the labour of running the system in this study. We had not expected this, but our observations indicated that division of labour was encouraged by the design of the simulation. The plant divides rather neatly into two halves, with the four machines on the left (which produce cola) connected to the five on the right (which bottle and cap it) by only one pipe. In addition, the operation of the cooking half did not depend on bottling at all, while incoming cola was buffered by the bottling machine, reducing time dependency on the cooking half. Because the two sides were relatively independent, then, and because there was only one connection between them, each could be run without much care for the other – though of course successful performance on the task itself required that both sides be well run.

The tendency for participants to divide the task was made apparent by the large amounts of time that they spent using different views on the system. After an initial period during which the partners would usually wander over the plant together in order to orient themselves to the machines, they almost always separated and seldom shared views again. (For instance, participants M. and H. made this explicit M: *"Maybe this is a good strategy, actually, to look after half of the world each..."* H: *"Yes, then we can... keep an eye on machines and see them break straight away."*) This division of labour was also made evident in their conversations. Although each would comment to the other about events and progress on their respective sides of the plant, longer conversations were relatively rare.

The addition of auditory cues seemed to change this pattern of division of labour to a noticeable extent. Although subjects still maintained separate views to a great degree, their conversations seemed to reflect a greater degree of concern for events on their partner's side. (For instance, in one tape E is working on the cooker half and P on the bottling half. P remarks on a sound made by a machine on the other side of the plant: *"Isn't that the fizzy water that's leaking?"* E: *"I don't think it's leaking... I think it's just going into the tank."* Caps start spilling on P's side. P: *"Ok, I'm losing, uh..."* E: *"That's the caps."* P: *"caps..."* P turns off cap dispenser.) While joint problem-solving was relatively rare without sound, it became common with auditory feedback.

The ability for both partners to hear events seems to be the key to sounds' effect on their collaboration in this task. Running the ARKola simulation was relatively demanding, requiring constant attention to the state of supply hoppers and the flow of materials through the plant. Leaving one's area of responsibility was risky in that some disaster was liable to occur; without auditory feedback this would go unnoticed until one's return. Because partners could not see each others area of the plant, joint problem-solving required verbal descriptions of plant status and made problem solving much more difficult for the distant partner. Each participant tended to focus on his or her own responsibilities, without the possibility of direct awareness of other events.

Auditory feedback allowed users to be aware of parts of the plant that were not visible on the screen or at the focus of their visual attention. Thus participants could refer directly to sounds from their partner's half of the plant and hear problems occurring in areas on which they were not focussing. (For example, when bottles started breaking on T's side of the plant, his partner, S, said: *"Bottles are breaking!"* T: *"Where?"* S: *"I don't know, but they're breaking..."*) Being able to hear the status of the plant also reduced the risk of venturing to other areas of the plant. If problems did occur during one's absence, they were likely to be heard. In providing a new dimension of reference for partners running the plant, auditory cues seemed to ease the transition between division of labour and collaboration in this system.

Of course, the sounds we used were not without their problems. Care was needed to ensure that the auditory feedback was loud enough to be heard without preventing conversation, for example – though this is not a difficult task, it is a crucial one. In addition, designing the sounds to work together so that all could be heard was quite demanding (see Gaver et al. 1990 for a description of our approach to this problem). Finally, some of the sounds were more effective than others. Most notably, when a supply hopper ran out of supplies its sound simply stopped. We had expected that participants would notice the cessation of sound and refill the hopper; instead the sound's absence often went unnoticed. Nonetheless, the majority of sounds seemed informative and useful to subjects.

In sum, the auditory feedback used in this system had important effects on participants' collaboration. Sound provided a new dimension of reference for subjects. By increasing ways to maintain awareness it smoothed the transition between division of labour and focussed collaboration. Being able to hear the status of offscreen machines allowed a dissociation of focussed visual attention and more general awareness, so that each participant could have an area of primary responsibility and still join together to solve problems.

It is important to stress that we expect these findings to be relevant to a broad range of shared software, not just the sort of process control simulation described here. As systems become more powerful, they are increasingly likely to demand the scheduling and control of simultaneous tasks which are often hidden or invisible – and collaborative as well. The ARKola simulation was designed as it was precisely to embody these features in a self-motivating task domain, so that our results would be broadly relevant.

Our observations of the ARKola simulation in use are indicative of the potential for auditory cues in collaborative software systems. Such cues can also support awareness of events and activities beyond the computer in the encompassing workplace. I explore these possibilities in the next section.

Ambient audio in the workplace

A great many collaborative activities take place in the office environment, ranging from relatively formal meetings to more casual encounters. Just as there is a tension in collaborative software systems between enforcing a shared focus and allowing individual activities, so are there tensions in the workplace between encouraging group engagement and providing for individual work. As with collaborative software, group engagement in the workplace depends on a shared context – meeting rooms, open spaces, and established office hours. But individual work is facilitated by individual control over the environment – private offices, work at home, or work during off-hours.

In the everyday world, this tension is mitigated to some degree by the naturally-occurring auditory environment. We often listen to ambient sounds in the workplace in order to maintain awareness of our colleagues' activities. As I write this, for instance, I can hear automobiles and buses pass by on the street below, people walking by outside my office, and the sudden roar of the copier machine being used. As with collaborative software, these sounds may provide the sorts of awareness useful for moving in and out of close collaboration. For example, hearing Paul enter his office next door may prompt me to ask him about some project of mutual interest. Hearing the murmur of voices from outside my office may encourage me to join in an informal discussion with my colleagues. Hearing nearby events in the building can support casual awareness of others or indicate ongoing meetings, whether serendipitous or formal.

Hearing events in the workplace can draw us into them; but in large buildings many will go unheard. In addition, many potentially relevant events don't make informative sounds. For instance, hearing Paul leave his office may tell me he is unavailable, but not whether he is going to a meeting, to fetch some coffee, or to the pub. And of course, naturally-occurring sounds can be irritating, as sounds of the rush of traffic, the roar of the copier, and the blare of Paul's stereo often are. Such sounds are annoying because they are not informative or relevant: Noise is uninformative sound. In general, the ambient audio environment of the workplace can be useful, easing the tension between group and individual work. But sound can also pose problems: not all events may be heard, some important events may not make sounds, and the sounds events do make may be annoying.

EAR: Environmental Audio Reminders

For the past year and more, we have been using a system at EuroPARC which allows us to design informative ambient audio environments in our workplace. Called EAR, for Environmental Audio Reminders, this system triggers short, unobtrusive audio cues which are transmitted to offices around the building in order to inform people about ongoing events or to remind them about upcoming ones. Using this system, we can smoothly expand the naturally-occurring office ambience so that we can hear events out of earshot, and events which don't ordinarily make sounds. This work can be seen as moving auditory icons out of the workstation and into the world, so that the working environment itself becomes the interface. From this perspective, the strategy guiding the use of sound to facilitate collaboration in workstation environments can be applied to the overall work environment as well.

The EAR system relies on two interesting features of EuroPARC's environment. The first is a data-base of events called Khronika (Lövstrand, 1991) which allows a wide range of events to be browsed, edited and indicated by various cues. Khronika controls the generation of audio cues which are routed to speakers in particular rooms by the second system, a computer-controlled audio-video network (Buxton & Moran, 1989). The net result of this environment is that events generate designed audio cues that can be heard remotely.

As with the design of auditory icons for workstation environments, two design constraints are important in shaping the auditory cues used in EAR. First, the sounds must be semantically related to the messages they are meant to convey. This is achieved by using sampled environmental sounds that are either causally or metaphorically related to their referents. The second constraint is that they be acoustically shaped to avoid distraction and annoyance. Our strategy for creating unobtrusive sounds has been guided by work on designing sets of auditory alert sounds of appropriate perceived urgency (Patterson, 1989). For instance, most of the sounds we are designing have relatively slow onsets, which means they do not startle or distract listeners but instead slowly emerge from the natural auditory ambience of the office. In general, we try to maintain a balance between designing auditory cues that have clearly recognizable semantic content and designing them to be acoustically appropriate.

EAR in action

EAR is used to play audio cues which support casual awareness of one another, indicate opportunities for casual (and perhaps serendipitous) communication, and inform us about more focussed and formal events in our working environment. For instance, meetings are signalled by the sound of murmuring voices slowly growing in number, ended by the sound of a gavel. The sound interrupts individual work discreetly, reminding the listener about a prior engagement to join with other members of the lab. We view teatime, on the other hand, as an opportunity for informal communication. Each afternoon people in the building are invited to take tea by the sound of boiling water, followed by sounds of pouring water and spoons stirring in teacups. This sound serves as a more gentle reminder to those of us concentrating on our work that we might want to join our colleagues. Finally, sounds have evolved to indicate even very informal meetings. For instance, in the evening one of us is likely to trigger the pub-call, which plays the sounds of a pint being poured in a background of people talking and laughing.

These sounds serve as unobtrusive yet effective announcements of events in the workplace. They don't interrupt ongoing work, and can easily be ignored (though meeting sounds are likely to be heeded). Because they are stereotypical versions of the sorts of sounds we might hear around the building every day, the auditory cues used in EAR provide an effective and intuitive way to call people together and keep them informed of events around the building.

The EAR system also uses a number of auditory cues to indicate events in the electronic environment. For instance, the arrival of email can be accompanied by the sound of several pieces of paper falling on a surface, like letters falling through a mail slot. Other auditory cues are valuable in maintaining our awareness of the status of our audio-video network. This network allows people to connect their monitors to cameras around the building to gain a sense of "virtual co-presence" with distant colleagues. Because there is no visual indication when somebody accesses the signal from a camera (and video symmetry is not enforced), a pervasive sense of monitoring might be expected to result. But the EAR system allows audio feedback about connections, so that when somebody connects to my camera I hear the sound of a door creaking open; when they disconnect I hear the door shut. These simple audio cues provide invaluable feedback about the state of the audio-video network and seem to bolster feelings of privacy control to a significant degree. In addition, they can serve to tell us about a wider context of activities than is revealed by the network alone. For instance, auditory cues are used to distinguish the purpose of an audio-video connection: Different sounds indicate "vphone" calls; casual, one-way glances; and camera accesses by our framegrabber service.

Many of the sounds we use in EAR may seem frivolous because they are cartoon-like stereotypes of naturally-occuring sounds. But it is precisely *because* they are stereotyped sounds that they are effective. Using sounds that mimic those made by actual events means that the mapping between the information to be conveyed and the sound used to represent it can be quite close, and thus easy to learn and remember. While the sounds we use must be introduced to new users, they are quickly understood and seldom forgotten. It seems unlikely that more "serious" sounds – such as electronic beeps or sequences of tones – would be as effective at providing information in an intuitive and subtle way.

Like the sounds in the ARKola simulation, the cues about our electronic environment indicate computer events without demanding visual attention. But because the primary purpose is to provide cues about events in the workplace, the system has the further effect of bringing the two environments closer. The workstation is no longer the sole source of information about the electronic environment; instead electronic events are made an integral part of the general environment.

EAR is an installed system, constantly evolving to reflect our current needs and opinions about the auditory cues. Thus we have taken a strategy of "evaluation by use," in which cues which do not seem useful or which are annoying are discarded or redesigned. Generally this evolution has involved the introduction of subtle variations between cues. For instance, soon after the door-opening sound was introduced to indicate camera accessing, new sounds appeared which differentiate between short connections made by colleagues and connections made by an application which digitizes images and makes them available to colleagues overseas.

In sum, the auditory cues used in the EAR system can be unobtrusive, informative, and valuable. They serve to indicate events in the same way that they might be heard in everyday life, with the added advantage that the events cued are chosen by users. They allow us to hear distant events, or events that don't naturally produce informative noises, helping to blur the distinction between the electronic and physical environments. Perhaps most importantly, by informing us about ongoing events in the building they help to ease the transition between working alone and working together.

Discussion

The ARKola simulation and EAR system complement one another as examples of the use of auditory cues in collaborative systems. Where the ARKola simulation explored the design of auditory cues that support collaboration within the workstation environment, the EAR system demonstrates that similar principles can guide the design of useful auditory cues in the more general working environment as well. In ARKola, auditory cues were crucial sources of information, whereas in the EAR system sounds generally support a relatively unconscious awareness of ongoing events.

But though the two systems are different in many ways, parallels can be drawn in the functions auditory cues perform in each. In both the ARKola simulation and the EAR system, auditory cues make use of sound as a new medium for increasing awareness of events and activities which are not visually available. The effect of this new dimension of reference seems to be that users can simultaneously maintain visual attention on a potentially shared focus of work while remaining aware of a wider context of interest. This ability, in turn, seems to lead to smoother transitions between different ways of sharing work.

The functions auditory cues play in the ARKola simulation and the EAR system should be broadly applicable to a number of CSCW systems. The tension between maintaining a shared focus and allowing individual control over work seems common in the class of collaborative tools that allow synchronous editing of objects (Bellotti et al., 1991). Our observations of the ARKola simulation suggest that this tension may be reduced by exploiting sound as an alternative medium for presenting and receiving information. So, for instance, users of a shared document editor might hear their partners' editing operations even when such activities are offscreen. Such sounds could be useful in coordinating activities ("...it sounds like you're making major changes up there – should I hold off on this section?").

Similarly, experiences with EAR suggest that using auditory cues to communicate contextual information in the workplace itself can facilitate the flow of engagement among colleagues. For example, just as EAR allows us to hear activities in distant parts of our building, so might users of systems supporting virtual co-presence hear activities in distant environments. Such sounds could provide a natural means for indicating potentials for casual or focussed engagement by conveying contextual information which might otherwise be lost.

I have shown in this paper some of the functions sound can perform in collaborative systems. But it should be stressed that our work on the use of auditory cues to facilitate collaboration has only just begun. Both the ARKola simulation and EAR are suggestive, but neither is definitive; the potential of sound as an intuitive, unobtrusive medium for communication promises to be much richer than either of these applications can show.

Acknowledgements

The ARKola study was done in collaboration with Randall Smith and Tim O'Shea; the EAR system with Lennart Lövstrand. I thank Allan MacLean for his many insightful comments on this work, and give particular thanks to Victoria Bellotti and Paul Dourish for many helpful discussions about the nature of sharing.

References

Bellotti, V., Dourish, P., & MacLean, A. (1991). From users themes to designers DReams: Developing a design space for shared interactive technologies. EuroPARC/AMODEUS Working Paper RP6-WP7.

Buxton, B., & Moran, T. (1990). EuroPARC's integrated interactive Intermedia Facility (IIIF): Early experiences. *Proceedings of the IFIP WG8.4 Conference on Multi-user Interfaces and Applications*, Heraklion, Crete, September.

CSMIL (1989). ShrEdit: A multi-user shared text editor: Users manual. Cognitive Science and Machine Intelligence Laboratory, The University of Michigan.

Ellis, C., Gibbs, S., & Rein, G. (1988). Design and use of a group editor. MCC Technical Report Number STP-263-88.

Gaver, W. W. (1986). Auditory icons: Using sound in computer interfaces. *Human-Computer Interaction*. 2, 167 - 177.

Gaver, W. W. (1989). The SonicFinder: An interface that uses auditory icons. *Human-Computer Interaction.* 4 (1).

Gaver, W. W., & Smith, R. B. (1990). Auditory icons in large-scale collaborative environments. *Human-Computer Interaction – Interact'90.* D. Diaper et al. (eds.) Elsevier, North-Holland.

Gaver, W. W., Smith, R. B., & O'Shea, T. (1991). Effective sounds in complex systems: The ARKola simulation. *Proceedings of CHI 1991*, New Orleans, April 28 - May 2, 1991, ACM, New York.

Goodman, G., & Abel, M. (1987). Communication and collaboration: Facilitating cooperative work through communication. *Office: Technology and People, 3* (2), 129 - 146.

Lövstrand, L. (1991). Being selectively aware with the Khronika system. In the Proceedings of ECSCW91, Amsterdam, The Netherlands.

MacLean, A., Young, R., & Moran, T. (1989). Design Rationale: The argument behind the artifact. *Proceedings of CHI'89: Human Factors in Computing Systems*, April 30 - May 4, Austin, Texas, 247 - 252. New York: ACM.

Mantei, M. (1988). Capturing the Capture Lab concepts: A case study in the design of computer supported meeting environments. *Proceedings of the Conference on Computer-Supported Collaborative Work*. Portland, Ore., September 1988, 257 - 270.

Moran, T. P., & Anderson, R. J. (1990). The workaday world as a paradigm for CSCW design. *Proceedings of CSCW 90* (Los Angeles, U.S., October 1990).

Patterson, R. D. (1989). Guidelines of the design of auditory warning sounds. *Proceedings of the Institute of Acoustics 1989 Spring Conference. 11* (5), 17 - 24.

Root, R. (1988). Design of a multi-media vehicle for social browsing. *Proceedings of the Conference on Computer-Supported Collaborative Work*. Portland, Ore., September 1988, 25 - 38.

Smith, R. B. (1989). A prototype futuristic technology for distance education. *Proceedings of the NATO Advanced Workshop on New Directions in Educational Technology.* (Nov. 10 - 13, 1988, Cranfield, U.K.)

Smith, R. B. (1987). The Alternate Reality Kit: an example of the tension between literalism and magic. *Proceedings of CHI + GI 1987* (Toronto, Canada, April 5 - 9, 1987) ACM, New York, 61 - 67.

Hypertext: An Introduction and Survey

(Excerpts)

Jeff Conklin

Microelectronics and Computer Technology Corp.

Most modern computer systems share a foundation which is built of directories containing files. The files consist of text which is composed of characters. The text that is stored within this hierarchy is linear. For much of our current way of doing business, this linear organization is sufficient. However, for more and more applications, a linear organization is not adequate. For example, the documentation of a computer program* is usually either squeezed into the margins of the program, in which case it is generally too terse to be useful, or it is interleaved with the text of the program, a practice which breaks up the flow of both program and documentation.

As workstations grow cheaper, more powerful, and more available, new possibilities emerge for extending the traditional notion of "flat" text files by allowing more complex organizations of the material. Mechanisms are being devised which allow direct machine-supported references from one textual chunk to another; new interfaces provide the user with the ability to interact directly with these chunks and to establish new relationships between them. These extensions of the traditional text fall under the general category of *hypertext* (also known as *nonlinear text*). Ted Nelson, one of the

Documentation is the unexecutable English text which explains the logic of the program which it accompanies.

> **Hypertext systems feature machine-supported links—both within and between documents—that open exciting new possibilities for using the computer as a communication and thinking tool.**

pioneers of hypertext, once defined it as "a combination of natural language text with the computer's capacity for interactive branching, or dynamic display . . . of a nonlinear text . . . which cannot be printed conveniently on a conventional page."[1]

This article is a survey of existing hypertext systems, their applications, and their design. It is both an introduction to the world of hypertext and, at a deeper cut, a survey of some of the most important

design issues that go into fashioning a hypertext environment.

The concept of hypertext is quite simple: Windows on the screen are associated with objects in a database, and links are provided between these objects, both graphically (as labelled tokens) and in the database (as pointers). (See Figure 1.)

But this simple idea is creating much excitement. Several universities have created laboratories for research on hypertext, many articles have been written about the concept just within the last year, and the Smithsonian Institute has created a demonstration laboratory to develop and display hypertext technologies. What is all the fuss about? Why are some people willing to make extravagant claims for hypertext, calling it "idea processing" and "the basis for global scientific literature"?

In this article I will attempt to get at the essence of hypertext. I will discuss its advantages and disadvantages. I will show that this new technology opens some very exciting possibilities, particularly for new uses of the computer as a communication and thinking tool. However, the reader who has not used hypertext should expect that at best he will gain a perception of hypertext as a collection of interesting features. Just as a description of electronic spreadsheets will not get across the real elegance of that tool, this article can only hint at the potentials of hypertext. In fact, one must work in current hypertext environments for a while for the collection of fea-

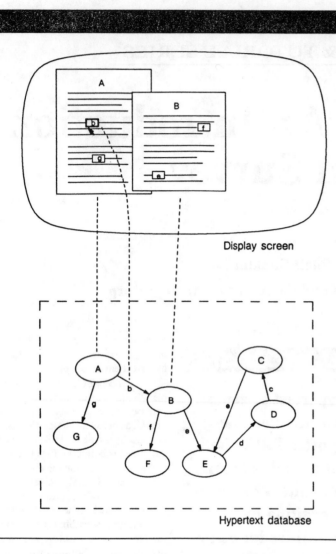

Display screen

Hypertext database

Figure 1. The correspondence between windows and links in the display, and nodes and links in the database. In this example, each node in the hypertext database is displayed in a separate window on the screen when requested. The link named "b" in window A has been activated by a pointing device, causing a new window named "B" to be created on the screen and filled with the text from node B in the database. (Generally, links can have names that are different from the name of the node they point to.)

that is common to many hypertext systems is the heavy use of windows that have a one-to-one correspondence with nodes in the database. I consider this feature to be of secondary importance.

One way to delimit hypertext is to point out what it is not. Briefly, several systems have some of the attributes of hypertext but do not qualify. Window systems fall into this category; while window systems do have some of the interface functionality, and therefore some of the "feel" of hypertext, window systems have no single underlying database, and therefore lack the database aspect of hypertext. File systems also do not qualify as hypertext; one could claim that a file system is a database, and that one moves among *nodes* (files) by simply invoking an editor with their names. However, to qualify as hypertext, a system must use a more sophisticated notion of links and must provide more machine support for its links than merely typing file names after a text editor prompt. Similarly, most outline processors (such as ThinkTank) do not qualify. They provide little or no support for references between outline entries, although their integrated hierarchical database and interface do approximate hypertext better than the other systems that I have mentioned. Text formatting systems (such as Troff and Scribe) do not qualify. They allow a tree of text fragments in separate files to be gathered into one large document; however, this structure is hierarchical and provides no interface for on-line navigation within the (essentially linear) document. Similarly, database management systems (DBMSs) have links of various kinds (for example, relational and object-oriented links), but lack the single coherent interface to the database which is the hallmark of hypertext.

As videodisc technology comes of age, there is growing interest in the extension of hypertext to the more general concept of *hypermedia*, in which the elements which are networked together can be text, graphics, digitized speech, audio recordings, pictures, animation, film clips, and presumably tastes, odors, and tactile sensations. At this point, little has been done to explore the design and engineering issues of these additional modalities, although many of the high-level design issues are likely to be shared with hypertext. Therefore, this survey will primarily address the more conservative text-based systems.

A glimpse of using hypertext. It is use-

tures to coalesce into a useful tool.

One problem with identifying the essential aspects of hypertext is that the term "hypertext" has been used quite loosely in the past 20 years for many different collections of features. Such tools as window systems, electronic mail, and teleconferencing share features with hypertext. This article focuses on machine-supported *links* (both within and between docu-

ments) as the essential feature of hypertext systems and treats other aspects as extensions of this basic concept.* It is this linking capability which allows a nonlinear organization of text. An additional feature

---

*While this article seeks to establish the criterion of machine-supported links as the primary criterion of hypertext, this is by no means an accepted definition. Therefore I will also review and discuss some systems which have a weaker notion of links.

ful to have a sense of the central aspects of using a hypertext system, particularly if you have never seen one. Below is a list of the features of a somewhat idealized hypertext system. Some existing systems have more features than these, and some have fewer or different ones.

• The database is a network of textual (and perhaps graphical) nodes which can be thought of as a kind of *hyperdocument*.

• Windows on the screen correspond to nodes in the database on a one-to-one basis, and each has a name or title which is always displayed in the window. However, only a small number of nodes are ever "open" (as windows) on the screen at the same time.

• Standard window system operations are supported: Windows can be repositioned, resized, closed, and put aside as small window icons. The position and size of a window or icon (and perhaps also its color and shape) are cues to remembering the contents of the window. Closing a window causes the window to disappear after any changes that have been made are saved to the database node. Clicking with the mouse on the icon of a closed window causes the window to open instantly.

• Windows can contain any number of *link icons** which represent pointers to other nodes in the database. The link icon contains a short textual field which suggests the contents of the node it points to. Clicking on a link icon with the mouse causes the system to find the referenced node and to immediately open a new window for it on the screen.

• The user can easily create new nodes and new links to new nodes (for annotation, comment, elaboration, etc.) or to existing nodes (for establishing new connections).

• The database can be browsed in three ways: (1) by following links and opening windows successively to examine their contents, (2) by searching the network (or part of it) for some string,** keyword, or attribute value, and (3) by navigating around the hyperdocument using a *browser* that displays the network graphically. The user can select whether the nodes and links display their labels or not.

The browser is an important component

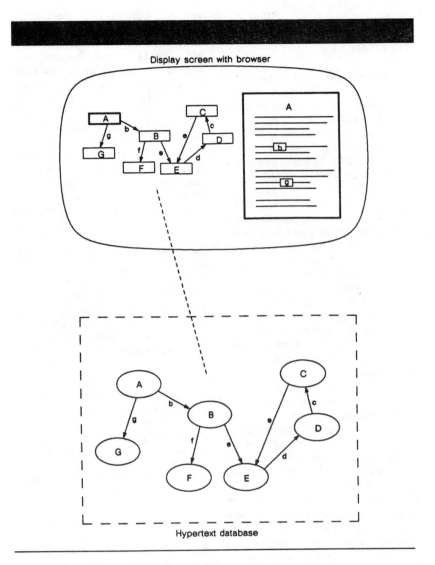

Display screen with browser

Hypertext database

Figure 2. The screen at the top illustrates how a hypertext browser provides a direct two-dimensional graphic view of the underlying database. In this illustration, the node "A" has been selected for full display of its contents. Notice that in the browser view you can tell not only which nodes are linked to A but also how the subnetwork fits into the larger hyperdocument. (Of course, hyperdocuments of any size cannot be shown all at once in a browser—only portions can be displayed.)

---

*Note that I am are describing two uses of icons: those that function as placeholders for windows that have been temporarily put aside, and those within windows that represent links to other nodes.

**A *string* is a series of alphabetic and numeric characters of any length, for example "listening" or "G00274."

of hypertext systems. As the hyperdocument grows more complex, it becomes distressingly easy for a user to become lost or disoriented. A browser displays some or all of the hyperdocument as a graph, providing an important measure of contextual and spatial cues to supplement the user's model of which nodes he is viewing and how they are related to each other and their neighbors in the graph. (See Figure 2.) Using a browser can be likened to using

visual and tactile cues when looking for a certain page in a book. Sometimes we remember the general way the page looked and about how far it was through the book, although we don't recall the page number or even which keyword terms would help us find it by using the index or table of contents. The browser display can be similarly scanned and scrolled when the user has forgotten all but the appearance or location of a node.

The Essence of Hypertext

It is tempting to describe the essence of hypertext as its ability to perform high-speed, branching transactions on textual chunks. But this is a little like describing the essence of a great meal by listing its ingredients. Perhaps a better description would focus on hypertext as a computer-based medium for thinking and communication.

The thinking process does not build new ideas one at a time, starting with nothing and turning out each idea as a finished pearl. Thinking seems rather to proceed on several fronts at one, developing and rejecting ideas at different levels and on different points in parallel, each idea depending on and contributing to the others.

The recording and communication of such entwined lines of thought is challenging because communication is in practice a serial process and is, in any case, limited by the bandwidth of human linguistic processing. Spoken communication of parallel themes must mark items with stresses, pauses, and intonations which the listener must remember as the speaker develops other lines of argument. Graphical forms can use lists, figures, and tables to present ideas in a less than strictly linear form. These visual props allow the reader/viewer to monitor the items which he must understand together. One of the challenges of good writing, especially good technical writing, is to present several parallel lines of a story or an argument in a way that weaves them together coherently.

Traditional flat text binds us to writing and reading paragraphs in a mostly linear succession. There are tricks for signalling branching in the flow of thought when necessary: Parenthetical comments, footnotes, intersectional references (such as "see Chapter 4"), bibliographic references, and sidebars all allow the author to say "here is a related thought, in case you are interested." There are also many rhetorical devices for indicating that ideas belong together as a set but are being presented in linear sequence. But these are rough tools at best, and often do not provide the degree of precision or the speed and convenience of access that we would like.

Hypertext allows and even encourages the writer to make such references, and allows the readers to make their own decisions about which links to follow and in what order. In this sense, hypertext eases the restrictions on the thinker and writer. It does not force a strict decision about whether any given idea is either within the flow of a paper's stream of thought or outside of it. Hypertext also allows annotations on a text to be saved separately from the reference document, yet still be tightly bound to the referent. In this sense, the "linked-ness" of hypertext provides much of its power: It is the machine processible links which extend the text beyond the single dimension of linear flow.

At the same time, some applications demonstrate that the "node-ness" of hypertext is also very powerful. Particularly when hypertext is used as a thinking, writing, or design tool, a natural correspondence can emerge between the objects in the world and the nodes in the hypertext database. By taking advantage of this object-oriented aspect, a hypertext user can build flexible networks which model his problem (or solution). In this application the links are less important than the nodes. The links form the "glue" that holds the nodes together, but the emphasis is on the contents of the nodes.

From a computer science viewpoint, the essence of hypertext is precisely that it is a hybrid that cuts across traditional boundaries. Hypertext is a *database method*, providing a novel way of directly accessing data. This method is quite different from the traditional use of queries. At the same time, hypertext is a *representation scheme*, a kind of semantic network which mixes informal textual material with more formal and mechanized operations and processes. Finally, hypertext is an *interface modality* that features "control buttons" (link icons) which can be arbitrarily embedded within the content material by the user. These are not separate applications of hypertext: They are metaphors for a functionality that is an essential union of all three.

The power of linking. In the next two sections of this article, I will explore links and nodes in more detail as the basic building blocks of hypertext.

Link following. The most distinguishing characteristic of hypertext is its machine support for the tracing of references. But what qualifies a particular reference-tracing device as a link? How much effort is permissible on the part of a user who is attempting to trace a reference? The accepted lower limit of referencing support can be specified as follows: To qualify as hypertext, a system should require no more than a couple of keystrokes (or mouse movements) from the user to follow a single link. In other words, the interface must provide links which act like "magic buttons" to transport the user quickly and easily to a new place in the hyperdocument.

Another essential characteristic of hypertext is the speed with which the system responds to referencing requests. Only the briefest delay should occur (one or two seconds at most). Much design work goes into this feature in most systems. One reason for this concern is that the reader often does not know if he wants to pursue a link reference until he has had a cursory look at the referenced node. If making this judgement takes too long, the user may become frustrated and not bother with the hypertext links.

However, not all link traversals can be instantaneous. Perhaps as important as rapid response is providing cues to the user about the possible delay that a given query or traversal might entail. For example, some visual feature of the link icon could indicate whether the destination node is in memory, on the disk, somewhere else on the network, or archived off line.

Properties of links. Links can be used for several functions. These include the following:

• They can connect a document reference to the document itself.

• They can connect a comment or annotation to the text about which it is written.

• They can provide organizational information (for instance, establish the relationship between two pieces of text or between a table of contents entry and its section).

• They can connect two successive pieces of text, or a piece of text and all of its immediate successors.

• They can connect entries in a table or figure to longer descriptions, or to other tables or figures.

Links can have names and types. They can have a rich set of properties. Some systems allow the display of links to be turned on and off (that is, removed from the display so that the document appears as ordinary text).

The introduction of links into a text system means that an additional set of mechanisms must be added for creating new links, deleting links,* changing link names or attributes, listing links, etc.

---

*Link deletion is problematical. For example, what should the policy be for nodes which are stranded when all their links have been deleted? Should they be placed in "node limbo" until the user decides what to do with them?

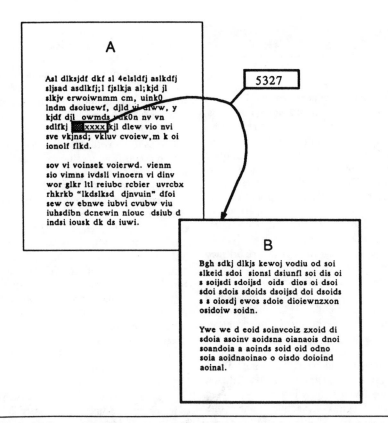

Figure 10. An example of a link with a point source and a region destination. The source of the link is a token in the text of document A which contains a textual identifier ("xxxx"). The identifier may be (1) the name of the destination node (in this case it would be "B"), (2) the name of the link, or (3) an arbitrary string which is neither the name of the link nor the destination node. The destination of this link is node B which is a region. The link has an internal name (5327) which is normally visible to the user.

Referential links. There are two methods for explicitly linking two points in hypertext—by reference and by organization. The reference method is a nonhierarchical method. It uses referential links that connect points or regions in the text.

Referential links are the kind of link that most clearly distinguishes hypertext. They generally have two ends, and are usually directed, although most systems support "backward" movement along the link. The origination of the link is called the "link source," and usually acts as the *reference*. The source can logically be either a single point or a region of text. At the other end, the "destination" of the link usually functions as the *referent*, and can also be either a point or a region. (See Figure 10.)

A *link point* is some icon indicating the presence of the link. It usually shows the link's name and perhaps also its type. Or it may show the name and/or type of the destination node. In systems such as Neptune which support links with both point

source and point destination, the icon also indicates which type of link is indicated. In some systems, the display of links can be suppressed, so that the documents appear linear.

A *link region* is a set of contiguous characters which is displayed as a single unit. In Figure 10, the link destination is a link region, namely, an entire node. Figure 10 illustrates the most common form of hypertext link, in which the source is a point and the destination is a region. This example typifies many of the link applications listed above, because it shows how a chunk of text—a region—is written about or referenced by some smaller chunk of text, often a sentence. Since most readers are accustomed to single point references to sentences (i.e., footnotes), they have no problem accepting a link with a point source. There can be regions in graphics as well—either bordered regions or collections of graphic objects in a figure.

Link regions can pose difficult design problems. They are easiest to implement

as whole nodes, since setting a region off from its neighboring material within the same node raises a tough implementation issue—how to display the selected region to the user. It must be highlighted somehow, using reverse video, fonts, or color, but each of these options poses difficulties in keeping overlapping regions clearly highlighted. The Intermedia designers propose to draw a light box around regions and a darker box around region/region overlaps, thus showing a single level of overlapping[15]; however, this technique is not effective if there are more than two overlapping regions.

Another difficulty posed by link regions is how to show the name of the link. Unlike a link point, a link region has no obvious position for a title, unless it is placed arbitrarily at the beginning or end of the region.

Link regions can also be difficult to manipulate. Designers must devise a system for copying, moving, modifying, and deleting the region and the substrings within it. The movement of regions involves logistical dilemmas which are not easy to resolve: For example, when one moves a major portion of the text in a destination region to someplace else in the node, should the link destination move with it or stay with what remains? Also, designers must make special provisions for deleting, moving, or copying the defining end points of a region.

Organizational links. Like reference links, organizational links establish explicit links between points in hypertext. Organizational links differ from referential links in that they implement hierarchical information.

Organizational links connect a parent node with its children and thus form a strict tree subgraph within the hypertext network graph. They correspond to the *IS-A* (or *superconcept*) links of semantic net theory, and thus operate quite differently than referential links.* For example, rather than appearing as explicit highlighted tokens in each node, organizational links are often traversed by a separate mechanism at the node control level (i.e., special *goto-parent*, *goto-first-child*, and *goto-next-sibling* commands). In other cases, there are organizational nodes (such as toc nodes in Textnet and FileBoxes in NoteCards) which record the organizational structure.

*Note that organizational links are distinct from the class hierarchy links that would be used (in the object-oriented programming paradigm) to define types and subtypes of nodes in the hypertext system.

Keyword links. In addition to the explicit linking performed by referential and organizational links, there is a kind of implicit linking that occurs through the use of keywords. This type of linking is yet to be fully explored.

One of the chief advantages of text storage on a computer is the ability to search large and complex documents and sets of documents for substrings and keywords.* Naturally, this ability is also a valuable aspect of hypertext. Indeed, most users of large hyperdocuments insist on having some mechanism for scanning their content, either for selected keywords (which can apply to nodes, links, or regions) or for arbitrary embedded strings.

From a functional standpoint, link following and search are similar: Each is a way to access destination nodes that are of possible interest. Link following usually yields a single node, whereas search can yield many; hence, a keyword is a kind of implicit computed link. The value of this insight is that it may allow design of a hypertext interface which is consistent across all link-tracing activities.

To tree or not to tree. Some hypertext systems (for example, Emacs INFO) support only hierarchical structures, others (such as Xanadu and Hyperties) provide no specific support for hierarchical structures, and others (such as Textnet and NoteCards) support both kinds of structures.

One could question just how sufficient strictly hierarchical structures are, and for which applications they are sufficient and for which they are not. On the one hand, abstraction is a fundamental cognitive process, and hierarchical structures are the most natural structures for organizing levels of abstraction. On the other hand, cases obviously exist where cross-hierarchical links are required. Frank Halasz, one of the developers of NoteCards, has gathered statistics on the *hyperspace* of a single representative NoteCards user; this person had 1577 nodes (cards) in all, 502 of which were File-Boxes (hierarchical nodes). Connecting these nodes were a total of 3460 links, 2521

---

*There is some controversy over the relative merits of keyword retrieval as opposed to full text search. On the one hand, keyword retrieval is only as good as the skill and thoroughness of the person selecting the keywords. On the other hand, full text search does not find all the relevant documents, nor does it always find only the relevant documents. Its shortcomings are due in part to the commonness of synonyms in English. In addition, full text search can be computationally prohibitive in large networks.

(73 percent) of which connected FileBoxes to each other or to individual notecards, 261 (7.5 percent) of which were nonhierarchical referential links, and the remainder of which were mail links (used by the system to tie mail messages to other nodes). This example, for what it is worth, suggests that hierarchical structure is very important in organizing a hypertext network, and that referential links are important but less common.

One advantage of a strictly tree-oriented system is that the command language for navigation is very simple: From any node, the most one can do is go to the parent, a sibling, or a child. This simplicity also diminishes the disorientation problem, since a simpler cognitive model of the information space will suffice.

Of course, the great disadvantage of any hierarchy is that its structure is a function of the few specific criteria that were used in creating it. For example, if one wishes to investigate what sea-based life forms have in common with land-based life forms, one may find that the traditional classification of life forms into the plant and animal kingdoms breaks up the information in the wrong way. The creator of a hierarchical organization must anticipate the most important criteria for later access to the information. One solution to this dilemma is to allow the information elements to be structured into multiple hierarchies, thus allowing the world to be "sliced up" into several orthogonal decompositions. Any hypertext system which has hierarchy nodes, such as Textnet (toc nodes) and NoteCards (FileBox nodes), can perform this operation quite easily. These are the only systems which explicitly claim to support multiple hierarchies. Indeed, one early user of NoteCards used the system in doing the research and writing for a major project paper; he imposed one organization on the data and his writings while doing the research, and then quite a different (yet coexistent) organization on the same material to produce his paper. As a generalization, it seems that engineering-oriented hypertext users prefer hierarchical organizations, whereas arts- or humanities-oriented users prefer cross-referencing organizations.

Extensions to basic links. Certain features of the link enable it to be extended in

several ways. Links can connect more than two nodes to form *cluster links*. Such cluster links can be useful for referring to several annotations with a single link, and for providing specialized organizational structures among nodes. Indeed, the toc nodes of Textnet and the FileBoxes of NoteCards are both forms of cluster links.

One useful way to extend the basic link is to place attribute/value pairs on links and to query the network for them. The Neptune system, for example, has an architecture that is optimized for this function. Coupled with specialized routines in the database interpreter (the HAM), these attribute lists allow users to customize links in several ways, including devising their own type system for links and performing high-speed queries on the types.

It is also possible to perform procedural attachments on a link so that traversing the link also performs some user-specified side effect, such as customizing the appearance of the destination node. This ability is provided in Neptune and Boxer.

Hypertext nodes. Although the essence of hypertext is its machine-supported linking, the nodes contribute significantly to defining the operations that a hypertext system can perform. Most users of hypertext favor using nodes which express a single concept or idea, and are thus much smaller than traditional files. When nodes are used in this fashion, hypertext introduces an intermediate level of machine support between characters and files, a level which has the vaguely semantic aspect of being oriented to the expression of ideas. But this sizing is completely at the discretion of the hypertext writer, and the process of determining how to modularize a document into nodes is an art, because its impact on the reader is not well understood.[21]

The modularization of ideas. Hypertext invites the writer to modularize ideas into units in a way that allows (1) an individual idea to be referenced elsewhere, and (2) alternative successors of a unit to be offered to the reader (for instance, more detail, an example, bibliographic references, or the logical successor). But the writer must also reckon with the fact that a hypertext node, unlike a textual paragraph, tends to be a strict unit which does not blend seamlessly with its neighbors. Some hypertext systems (Notecards, CREF, Boxer, FRES, NLS) allow nodes to be viewed together as if they were one big node, and this option is essential for some applications (for example, writing and reading prose). But the boundaries around nodes are always discrete and require sometimes difficult judgements about how to cleave the subject matter into suitable chunks.

The process of identifying a semantically based unit, such as an idea or concept, with a syntactic unit, such as a paragraph or hypertext node, is not unique to hypertext. Manuals of style notwithstanding, traditional text has rather loose conventions for modularizing text into paragraphs. This looseness is acceptable because paragraph boundaries have a relatively minor effect on the flow of the reading. Paragraph boundaries are sometimes provided just to break up the text and give the eye a reference point. Thus, decisions about the distribution of sentences among paragraphs is not always critical.

Hypertext, on the other hand, can enforce a rather stern information hiding. In some systems, the only clue a user has as to the contents of a destination node is the name of the link (or the name of the node, if that is provided instead). The writer is no longer making all the decisions about the flow of the text. The reader can and must constantly decide which links to pursue. In this sense, hypertext imposes on both the writer and the reader the need for more process awareness, since either one has the option of *branching* in the flow of the text. Thus hypertext is best suited for applications which require these kinds of judgements anyway, and hypertext merely offers a way to act directly on these judgements and see the results quickly and graphically.

Ideas as objects. While difficult to document, there is something very compelling about reifying the expression of ideas into discrete objects to be linked, moved, and changed as independent entities. Alan Kay and Adele Goldberg[22] observed of Smalltalk that it is able to give objects a perceptual dimension by allocating to them a rectangular piece of screen real estate. This feature offers enhanced retrieval and recognition over computer-processed flat documents, because to a much greater degree abstract objects are directly associated with perceptual objects—the windows and icons on the screen.

Paragraphs, sections, and chapters in a book, viewed through a standard text editor or word processor, don't stand out as first-class entities. This is particularly apparent when one can view one's docu-

ment hierarchically (i.e., as an outline) at the same time that one adds new sections and embellishes existing ones. People don't think in terms of "screenfulls"; they think in terms of ideas, facts, and evidence. Hypertext, via the notion of nodes as individual expressions of ideas, provides a vehicle which respects this way of thinking and working.

Typed nodes. Some hypertext systems sort nodes into different types. These *typed nodes* can be extremely useful, particularly if one is considering giving them some internal structure, since the types can be used to differentiate the various structural forms.

For example, in our research in the MCC Software Technology Program, we have been implementing a hypertext interface for a design environment called the Design Journal. The Design Journal is intended to provide an active scratchpad in which the designer can deliberate about design decisions and rationale, both individually and in on-line design meetings, and in which he can integrate the design itself with this less formal kind of information. For this purpose we have provided a set of four typed nodes for the designer to use—*notes*, *goals/constraints*, *artifacts*, and *decisions*. Notes are used for everything from reminders, such as "Ask Bill for advice on Module X," to specific problems and ideas relating to the design. Goals/constraints are for the initial requirements as well as discovered constraints within the design. Artifacts are for the elements of the output: The Design. And decisions are for capturing the branch points in the design process, the alternatives considered by the designer, and some of the rationale for any commitment (however tentative) that has been made. The designer captures assumptions in the form of decisions with only one alternative. Our prototype of the Design Journal uses color to distinguish between note types in the browser, and we have found this to be a very effective interface.

Hypertext systems that use typed nodes generally provide a specialized color, size, or iconic form for each node type. The distinguishing features help the user differentiate at a glance the broad classes of typed nodes that he is working with. Systems such as NoteCards, Intermedia, and IBIS make extensive use of typed nodes.

Semistructured Nodes. So far I have spoken of the hypertext node as a structureless "blank slate" into which one might put a word or a whole document. For some applications, there is growing interest in *semistructured nodes*—typed nodes which contain labelled fields and spaces for field values. The purpose of providing a template for node contents is to assist the user in being complete and to assist the computer in processing the nodes. The less that the content of a node is undifferentiated natural language (for example, English) text, the more likely that the computer can do some kinds of limited processing and inference on the textual subchunks. This notion is closely related to Malone's notion of semistructured information systems.[23]

To continue with the example of the Design Journal, we have developed a model for the internal structure of decisions. The model is named ISAAC. It assumes that there are four major components to a design decision:

(1) an *issue*, including a short name for the issue and a short paragraph describing it in general terms;
(2) a set of *alternatives*, each of which resolves the issue in a different way, each having a name and short description, and each potentially linked to the design documents or elements that implement the alternative;
(3) an *analysis* of the competing alternatives, including the specific criteria being used to evaluate them, the trade-off analysis among these alternatives, and links to any data that the analysis draws upon; and
(4) a *commitment* to one of the alternatives (however tentatively) or to a vector of preferences over the alternatives, and a subjective rating about the correctness or confidence of this commitment.

Without getting into the details of the underlying theory, I merely wish to stress here that the internal structure of ISAAC suggests that the author of an ISAAC decision is engaged in a much more structured activity than just "writing down the decision," and the reader is likewise guided by the regularity of the ISAAC structure.

Of course, it may not be clear why we do not treat each of the elements listed above as its own typed hypertext node. The reason is that the parts of an ISAAC frame are much more tightly bound together than ISAAC frames are bound to each other. For example, we could not have an analysis part without an alternatives part; yet if we treat them as separate hypertext nodes, we have failed to build this constraint into the structure. The general issue here is that some information elements must always occur together, while others may occur together or not, depending on how related they are in a given context and how important it is to present them as a cluster distinct from "surrounding" information elements. This problem is recursive: An element that is atomic at one level may turn out on closer inspection to contain many components, some of which are clustered together.

In hypertext this tension presents itself as the twin notions of semistructured nodes and composite nodes.

Composite nodes. Another mechanism for aggregating related information in hypertext is the *composite node*. Several related hypertext nodes are "glued" together and the collection is treated as a single node, with its own name, types, versions, etc. Composite nodes are most useful for situations in which the separate items in a bulleted list or the entries in a table are distinct nodes but also cohere into a higher level structure (such as the list or table). This practice can, however, undermine the fundamental association of one interface object (window) per database object (node), and thus must be managed well to avoid complicating the hypertext idiom unduly.

A composite node facility allows a group of nodes to be treated as a single node. The composite node can be moved and resized, and closes up to a suitable icon reflecting its contents. The subnodes are separable and rearrangeable through a subedit mode. The most flexible means of displaying a composite node is to use a constraint language (such as that developed by Symbolics for Constraint Frames) which describes the subnodes as *panes* in the composite node window and specifies the interpane relationships as dynamic constraints on size and configuration.

Composite nodes can be an effective means of managing the problem of having a large number of named objects in one's environment. Pitman described the problem this way:

> In this sort of system, there is a never-ending tension between trying to name everything (in which case, the number of named things can grow quickly and the set can become quickly unmanageable) or to name as little as possible (in which case, things that took a lot of trouble to construct can be hard to retrieve if one accidentally drops the pointers to them).[19]

One problem with composite nodes is that as the member nodes grow and change the aggregation can become misleading or incorrect. A user who encounters this problem is in the same predicament as a writer who has rewritten a section of a paper so thoroughly that the section title is no longer accurate. This "semantic drift" can be difficult to catch.

Analogy to semantic networks. The idea of building a directed graph of informal textual elements is similar to the AI concept of *semantic networks*. A semantic network is a knowledge representation scheme consisting of a directed graph in which concepts are represented as nodes, and the relationships between concepts are represented as the links between them. What distinguishes a semantic network as an AI representation scheme is that concepts in the representation are indexed by their semantic content rather than by some arbitrary (for example, alphabetical) ordering. One benefit of semantic networks is that they are natural to use, since related concepts tend to cluster together in the network. Similarly, an incompletely or inconsistently defined concept is easy to spot since a meaningful context is provided by those neighboring concepts to which it is already linked.

The analogy to hypertext is straightforward: Hypertext nodes can be thought of as representing single concepts or ideas, internode links as representing the semantic interdependencies among these ideas, and the process of building a hypertext network as a kind of informal knowledge engineering. The difference is that AI knowledge engineers are usually striving to build representations which can be mechanically interpreted, whereas the goal of the hypertext writer is often to capture an interwoven collection of ideas without regard to their machine interpretability. The work on semantic networks also suggests some natural extensions to hypertext, such as typed nodes, semistructured nodes (frames), and inheritance hierarchies of node and link types.

The advantages and uses of hypertext

Intertextual references are not new. The importance of hypertext is simply that references are machine-supported. Like hypertext, traditional literature is richly interlinked and is hierarchically organized. In traditional literature, the medium of print for the most part restricts the flow of reading to follow the flow of linearly arranged passages. However, the process of following side links is fundamental even in the medium of print. In fact, library and information science consist principally of the investigation of side links. Anyone who has done research knows that a considerable portion of that effort lies in obtaining referenced works, looking up cross-references, looking up terms in a dictionary or glossary, checking tables and figures, and making notes on notecards. Even in simple reading one is constantly negotiating references to other chapters or sections (via the table of contents or references embedded in the text), index entries, footnotes, bibliographic references, sidebars, figures, and tables. Often a text invites the reader to skip a section if he is not interested in greater technical detail.

But there are problems with the traditional methods.

• Most references can't be traced backwards: A reader can not easily find where a specific book or article is referenced in a document, nor can the author of a paper find out who has referenced the paper.

• As the reader winds his way down various reference trails, he must keep track of which documents he has visited and which he is done with.

• The reader must squeeze annotations into the margins or place them in a separate document.

• Finally, following a referential trail among paper documents requires substantial physical effort and delays, even if the reader is working at a well-stocked library. If the documents are on line, the job is easier and faster, but no less tedious.

New possibilities for authoring and design. Hypertext may offer new ways for authors and designers to work. Authoring is usually viewed as a word- and sentence-level activity. Clearly the word processor *

---

*Actually, the term "word processor" is quite misleading. Most such tools accept input only at the character level, and manipulate characters, words, sentences, and paragraphs with equal facility. So these tools manipulate units of text, not words. But do they "process" these units? "Processing" implies that the computer performs some additional work, such as changing the verb form if the subject was changed from singular to plural, or performing real-time spelling and grammar correction. Since this is not the case, we really should return to the original term for these tools: "text editors".

is a good tool for authoring at this level. However, authoring obviously has much to do with structuring of ideas, order of presentation, and conceptual exploration. Few authors simply sit down and pour out a finished text, and not all editing is just "wordsmithing" and polishing. In a broad sense, authoring is the *design of a document*. The unit of this level of authoring is the idea or concept, and this level of work can be effectively supported by hypertext, since the idea can be expressed in a node. As the writer thinks of new ideas, he can develop them in their own nodes, and then link them to existing ideas, or leave them isolated if it is too early to make such associations. The specialized refinements of a hypertext environment assist the movement from an unstructured network to the final polished document.

New possibilities for reading and retrieval. Hypertext may also offer new possibilities for accessing large or complex information sources. A linear (nonhypertext) document can only be easily read in the order in which the text flows in the book. The essential advantage of nonlinear text is the ability to organize text in different ways depending on differing viewpoints. Shasha provides the following description of this advantage:

> Suppose you are a tourist interested in visiting museums in a foreign city. You may be interested in visual arts. You may want to see museums in your local area. You may only be interested in inexpensive museums. You certainly want to make sure the museums you consider are open when you want to visit them. Now your guidebook may be arranged by subject, by name of museum, by location, and so on. The trouble is: if you are interested in any arrangement other than the one it uses, you may have to do a lot of searching. You are not likely to find all the visual arts museums in one section of a guidebook that has been organized by district. You may carry several guidebooks, each organized by a criterion you may be interested in. The number of such guidebooks is a measure of the need for a nonlinear text system.[21]

Another advantage is that it is quite natural in a hypertext environment to suspend reading temporarily along one line of investigation while one looks into some detail, example, or related topic. Bush described an appealing scenario in his 1945 article:

> The owner of the memex, let us say, is interested in the origin and properties of the bow and arrow. Specifically he is studying why the short Turkish bow was apparently superior to the English long bow in the skirmishes of the Crusades. He has dozens of possibly pertinent books and articles in his memex. First he runs through an encyclopedia, finds an interesting but sketchy article, leaves it projected. Next, in a history, he finds another pertinent item, and ties the two together. Thus he goes, building a trail of many items. Occasionally he inserts a comment of his own, either linking it into the main trail or joining it by a side trail to a particular item. When it becomes evident that the elastic properties of available materials had a great deal to do with the bow, he branches off on a side trail which takes him through textbooks on elasticity and tables of physical constants. He inserts a page of longhand analysis of his own. Thus he builds a [permanent] trail of his interest through the maze of materials available to him.[2]

As we have seen, Bush's notion of the "trail" was a feature of Trigg's Textnet,[6] allowing the hypertext author to establish a mostly linear path through the document(s). The main (default) trail is well marked, and the casual reader can read the text in that order without troubling with the side trails.

Summary. We can summarize the operational advantages of hypertext as:

- *ease of tracing references*: machine support for link tracing means that all references are equally easy to follow forward to their referent, or backward to their reference;

- *ease of creating new references*: users can grow their own networks, or simply annotate someone else's document with a comment (without changing the referenced document);

- *information structuring*: both hierarchical and nonhierarchical organizations can be imposed on unstructured information; even multiple hierarchies can organize the same material;

- *global views*: browsers provide table-of-contents style views, supporting easier restructuring of large or complex documents; global and local (node or page) views can be mixed effectively;

- *customized documents*: text segments can be threaded together in many ways, allowing the same document to serve multiple functions;

- *modularity of information*: since the same text segment can be referenced from several places, ideas can be expressed with less overlap and duplication;

- *consistency of information*: references are embedded in their text, and if the text is moved, even to another document, the link information still provides direct access to the reference;

- *task stacking*: the user is supported in having several paths of inquiry active and displayed on the screen at the same time, such that any given path can be unwound to the original task;

- *collaboration*: several authors can collaborate, with the document and comments about the document being tightly interwoven (the exploration of this feature has just begun).

The disadvantages of hypertext

There are two classes of problems with hypertext: problems with the current implementations and problems that seem to be endemic to hypertext. The problems in the first class include delays in the display of referenced material, restrictions on names and other properties of links, lack of browsers or deficiencies in browsers, etc. The following section outlines two problems that are more challenging than these implementation shortcomings, and that may in fact ultimately limit the usefulness of hypertext: *disorientation* and *cognitive overhead*.

Getting "lost in space." Along with the power to organize information much more complexly comes the problem of having to know (1) where you are in the network and (2) how to get to some other place that you know (or think) exists in the network. I call this the "disorientation problem." Of course, one also has a disorientation problem in traditional linear text documents, but in a linear text, the reader has only two options: He can search for the desired text earlier in the text or later in the text. Hypertext offers more degrees of freedom, more dimensions in which one can move, and hence a greater potential for the user to become lost or disoriented. In a network of 1000 nodes, information can easily become hard to find or even forgotten altogether. (See Figure 11.)

There are two major technological solutions for coping with disorientation—graphical browsers and query/search mechanisms. Browsers rely on the extremely highly developed visuospatial processing of the human visual system. By placing nodes and links in a two- or three-dimensional space, providing them with

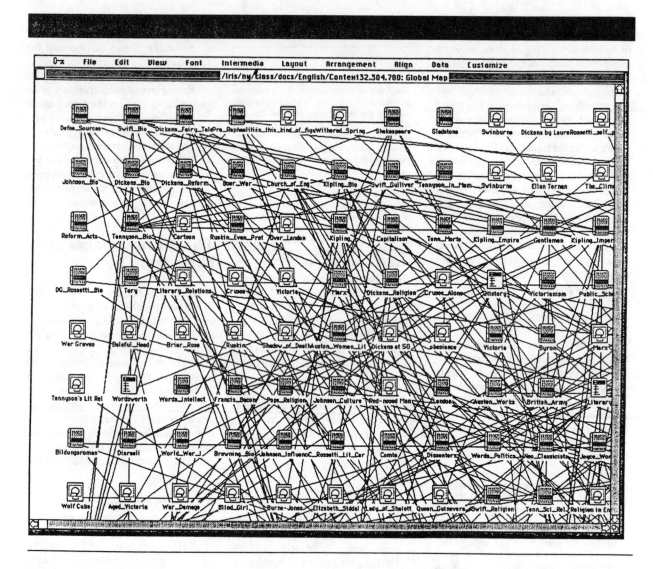

Figure 11. Tangled web of links. This experimental implementation of a global map in the Intermedia system shows the difficulty of providing users with spatial cues once a linked corpus contains more than a few dozen documents. This global map only represents about one tenth of the documents in a corpus designed for a survey of English literature course.

properties useful in visual differentiation (color, size, shape, texture), and maintaining certain similarities to our physical environment (for example, no two objects occupy the same space, things only move if moved, etc.), browser designers are able to create quite viable virtual spatial environments. Users orient themselves by visual cues, just as when they are walking or driving through a familiar city. However, there is no natural topology for an information space, except perhaps that higher level concepts go at the top or on the left side, so until one is familiar with a given

large hyperdocument, one is by definition disoriented. In addition, an adequate virtuality is very difficult to maintain for a large or complex hypertext network. Such parameters as (1) large numbers of nodes, (2) large numbers of links, (3) frequent changes in the network, (4) slow or awkward response to user control inputs, (5) insufficient visual differentiation among nodes and/or links, and (6) nonvisually oriented users combine to make it practically impossible to abolish the disorientation problem with a browser alone.

One solution to this dilemma is to apply

standard database search and query techniques to locating the node or nodes which the user is seeking. This is usually done by using boolean operations to apply some combination of keyword search, full string search, and logical predicates on other attributes (such as author, time of creation, type, etc.) of nodes or links. Similarly, one can filter (or *ellide*) information so that the user is presented with a manageable level of complexity and detail, and can shift the view or the detail suppression while navigating through the network. However, much research remains to be done on effective and standardized methods for ellision.

The cognitive task scheduling problem. The other fundamental problem with using hypertext is that it is difficult to become accustomed to the additional mental overhead required to create, name, and keep track of links. I call this "cognitive overhead." Suppose you are writing about X, and a related thought about Y comes to mind and seems important enough to capture. Ideally, hypertext allows you to simply "press a button" (using some mouse or keyboard action) and a new, empty hypertext window pops onto the screen. You record Y in this new window, then you press another button, the Y window disappears, and you are in the X window right where you were when Y occurred to you.

Unfortunately, the situation is a bit more complex than this scenario implies. If Y has just occurred to you, it may still be hazy and tentative; the smallest interruption could cause you to lose it. Coming up with a good word or short phrase to summarize Y may not be easy. You have to consider not just what is descriptive but also what will be suggestive for the reader when he encounters the link to Y within X. In addition, you must determine whether you should name the link to Y to suggest the contents of Y or to show Y's relationship to X. Some systems (for example, NoteCards) provide that links can have both a *type* (such as "idea") and a *label* (such as "subsume A in B"). Coming up with good names for both can impose even more load on an author struggling with an uncertain point. (One way to reduce this problem is for the authoring system to support immediate recording of the substance of the idea, deferring the creation and labeling of the link and/or the node until after the thought has been captured.)

Beyond that, you must also consider if you have provided sufficient links to Y before returning to work on X. Perhaps there are better ways to link Y to the network of thoughts than at the point in X where Y came to mind.

The problem of cognitive overhead also occurs in the process of reading hypertext, which tends to present the reader with a large number of choices about which links to follow and which to leave alone. These choices engender a certain overhead of metalevel decision making, an overhead that is absent when the author has already made many of these choices for you. At the moment that you encounter a link,

how do you decide if following the side path is worth the distraction? Does the label appearing in the link tell you enough to decide? This dilemma could be called "informational myopia." The problem is that, even if the system response time is instantaneous (which it rarely is), you experience a definite distraction, a "cognitive loading," when you pause to consider whether to pursue the side path. This problem can be eased by (1) having the cross-referenced node appear very rapidly (which is the approach of KMS), (2) providing an instantaneous one- to three-line explanation of the side reference in a pop-up window (which is the approach of Intermedia), and (3) having a graphical browser which shows the local subnetwork into which the link leads.

These problems are not new with hypertext, nor are they mere byproducts of computer-supported work. People who think for a living—writers, scientists, artists, designers, etc.—must contend with the fact that the brain can create ideas faster than the hand can write them or the mouth can speak them. There is always a balance between refining the current idea, returning to a previous idea to refine it, and attending to any of the vague "proto-ideas" which are hovering at the edge of consciousness. Hypertext simply offers a sufficiently sophisticated "pencil" to begin to engage the richness, variety, and interrelatedness of creative thought. This aspect of hypertext has advantages when this richness is needed and drawbacks when it is not.

To summarize, then, the problems with hypertext are

- *disorientation*: the tendency to lose one's sense of location and direction in a nonlinear document; and
- *cognitive overhead*: the additional effort and concentration necessary to maintain several tasks or trails at one time.

These problems may be at least partially resolvable through improvements in performance and interface design of hypertext systems, and through research on information filtering techniques.

In this article, I have reviewed existing hypertext systems, the opportunities and problems of hypertext, and some of the top-level design issues of building hypertext systems. It has been my intention to give the reader a clear sense of what hypertext is, what its strengths and weaknesses are, and what it can be used

for. But I also intended something more: that the reader come away from this article excited, eager to try using hypertext for himself, and aware that he is at the beginning of something big, something like the invention of the wheel, but something that still has enough rough edges that no one is really sure that it will fulfill its promise.

To that end, I mention one more book that might be considered to belong to the literature on hypertext. *Neuromancer*[24] is a novel about a time in the distant future when the ultimate computer interface has been perfected: One simply plugs one's brain into the machine and experiences the computer data directly as perceptual entities. Other computers look like boxes floating in three-dimensional space, and passwords appear as various kinds of doors and locks. The user is completely immersed in a virtual world, the "operating system," and can move around and take different forms simply by willing it.

This is the ultimate hypertext system. The basic idea of hypertext, after all, is that ideas correspond to perceptual objects, and one manipulates ideas and their relationships by directly manipulating windows and icons. Current technology limits the representation of these objects to static boxes on a CRT screen, but one can easily predict that advances in animation, color, 3D displays, sound, etc.—in short, Nelson's *hypermedia*—will keep making the display more active and realistic, the data represented richer and more detailed, and the input more natural and direct. Thus, hypertext, far from being an end in itself, is just a crude first step toward the time when the computer is a direct and powerful extension of the human mind, just as Vannevar Bush envisioned when he introduced his Memex four decades ago. □

Acknowledgements

I wish to thank Les Belady, Bill Curtis, Susan Gerhart, Raymonde Guindon, Eric Gullichsen, Frank Halasz, Peter Marks, and Andy van Dam for their thoughtful reading of previous drafts.

References

1. T.H. Nelson, "Getting It Out of Our System," *Information Retrieval: A Critical Review*, G. Schechter, ed., Thompson Books, Wash., D.C., 1967.

2. V. Bush, "As We May Think," *Atlantic Monthly*, July 1945, pp.101-108.

3. D.C. Engelbart, "A Conceptual Framework for the Augmentation of Man's

Intellect," in *Vistas in Information Handling*, Vol. 1, Spartan Books, London, 1963.

4. D.C. Engelbart and W.K. English, "A Research Center for Augmenting Human Intellect," *AFIPS Conf. Proc.*, Vol. 33, Part 1, The Thompson Book Company, Washington, D.C., 1968.

5. T.H. Nelson, "Replacing the Printed Word: A Complete Literary System," *IFIP Proc.*, October 1980, pp. 1013-1023.

6. R.H. Trigg, *A Network-based Approach to Text Handling for the Online Scientific Community*, PhD. Thesis, University of Maryland, 1983.

7. H. Rittel and M. Webber, "Dilemmas in a General Theory of Planning," *Policy Sciences*, Vol. 4, 1973.

8. D.G. Lowe, "Cooperative Structuring of Information: The Representation of Reasoning and Debate," in *Int'l. J. of Man-Machine Studies*," Vol. 23, 1985, pp. 97-111.

9. J.B Smith et al, "WE: A Writing Environment for Professionals," Technical Report 86-025, Department of Computer Science, University of North Carolina at Chapel Hill, August 1986.

10. W. Hershey, "Idea Processors," *BYTE*, June 1985, p. 337.

11. D. McCracken and R.M. Akscyn, "Experience with the ZOG Human-computer Interface System," *Int'l J. of Man-Machine Studies*, Vol. 21, 1984, pp. 293-310.

12. B. Shneiderman and J. Morariu, "The Interactive Encyclopedia System (TIES)," Department of Computer Science, University of Maryland, College Park, MD 20742, June 1986.

13. J.H. Walker, "The Document Examiner," *SIGGRAPH Video Review*, Edited Compilation from *CHI'85: Human Factors in Computing System*, 1985.

14. F.G. Halasz, T.P. Moran, and T.H. Trigg, "NoteCards in a Nutshell," *Proc. of the ACM Conf. on Human Factors in Computing Systems*, Toronto, Canada, April 1987.

15. N.L. Garrett, K.E. Smith, and N. Meyrowitz, "Intermedia: Issues, Strategies, and Tactics in the Design of a Hypermedia Document System," in *Proc. Conf. on Computer-Supported Cooperative Work*, MCC Software Technology Program, Austin, Texas, 1986.

16. N. Yankelovich, N. Meyrowitz, and A. van Dam, "Reading and Writing the Electronic Book," *Computer*, October 1985.

17. N. Delisle and M. Schwartz, "Neptune: A Hypertext System for CAD Applications," *Proc. of ACM SIGMOD Int'l Conf. on Management of Data*, Washington, D.C., May 28-30, 1986, pp. 132-143. (Also available as SIGMOD Record Vol. 15, No. 2, June 1986).

18. A. diSessa, "A Principled Design for an Integrated Computational Environment," *Human-Computer Interaction*, Vol. 1, Lawrence Erlbaum, 1985, pp. 1-47.

19. K.M.Pitman, "CREF: An Editing Facility for Managing Structured Text," A.I. Memo No. 829, M.I.T. A.I. Laboratory, Cambridge, Mass., February 1985.

20. P.J. Brown, "Interactive Documentation," in *Software: Practice and Experience*, March 1986, pp. 291-299.

21. D. Shasha, "When Does Non-Linear Text Help? *Expert Database Systems, Proc. of the First Int'l Conf.*, April 1986, pp. 109-121.

22. A. Kay and A. Goldberg, "Personal Dynamic Media," *Computer*, March 1977, pp. 31-41.

23. T.W. Malone et al, "Intelligent Information-Sharing Systems," *Communications of the ACM*, May 1987, pp. 390-402.

24. W.Gibson, *Neuromancer*, Ace Science Fiction, 1984.

A more detailed version of this article, including an extended bibliography, is available from the author. To obtain a copy, circle number 181 on the Reader Service Card at the back of the magazine.

E. Jeffrey Conklin is a member of the research staff and GE's liaison to the Software Technology Program in the Microelectronics and Computer Technology Corporation (MCC). His research centers on constructing information systems for the capture and use of design rationale.

Conklin Received his BA from Antioch College and his MS and PhD from the University of Massachusetts at Amherst.

Readers may write to Conklin at MCC Software Technology Program, P.O. Box 200195, Austin, TX 78720; (512) 343-0978.

What is Coordination Theory and How Can It Help Design Cooperative Work Systems?

Thomas W. Malone and Kevin Crowston

Center for Coordination Science (E53-333)
Massachusetts Institute of Technology
Cambridge, MA 02139

It is possible to design cooperative work tools based only on "common sense" and good intuitions. But the history of technology is replete with examples of good theories greatly aiding the development of useful technology. Where, then, might we look for theories to help us design computer-supported cooperative work tools? In this paper, we will describe one possible perspective—the interdisciplinary study of coordination—that focuses, in part, on how people work together now and how they might do so differently with new information technologies.

In one sense, there is little that is new about the study of coordination. Many different disciplines—including computer science, sociology, political science, management science, systems theory, economics, linguistics, and psychology—have all dealt, in one way or another, with fundamental questions about coordination. Furthermore, several previous writers have suggested that theories about coordination are likely to be important for designing cooperative work tools (e.g., [Holt88], [Wino86]).

We hope to suggest here, however, that the potential for fruitful interdisciplinary connections concerning coordination is much greater than has as yet been widely appreciated. For instance, we believe that fundamentally similar coordination phenomena arise—unrecognized as such—in many of the fields listed above. Though a single coherent body of theory about coordination does not yet exist, many different disciplines could both contribute to and benefit from more general theories of coordination. Of particular interest to researchers in the field of computer-supported cooperative work is the prospect of drawing on a much richer body of existing and future work in these fields than has previously been suggested.

In this paper, we will first describe what we mean by "coordination theory" and give examples of how previous research on computer-supported cooperative work can be interpreted from this perspective. We will then suggest one way of developing this perspective further by proposing tentative definitions of coordination and analyzing its components in more detail.

What is coordination?

We all have an intuitive sense of what the word "coordination" means. When we attend a well-run conference, when we watch a winning basketball team, or when we see a smoothly functioning assembly line we may notice how well coordinated the actions of a group of people seem to be. Often, however, good coordination is nearly invisible, and we sometimes notice coordination most clearly when it is lacking. When we spend hours waiting on an airport runway because the airline can't find a gate for our plane, when the hotel room we thought had been reserved for us is sold out, or when a company fails repeatedly to capitalize on innovative ideas its researchers develop we may become very aware of the effects of poor coordination.

In order to proceed it is helpful to have a more precise idea of what we mean by "coordination." Appendix A lists a number of definitions that have been suggested for this term. The diversity of these definitions illustrates the difficulty of defining coordination, and also the variety of possible starting points for studying the concept. For our purposes here, however, we believe it is most useful to start with the following "common sense" definition of coordination taken from a dictionary [Amer81]:

> *the act of working together harmoniously.*

We will refer to this as the "broad" definition of coordination, and will suggest a more restrictive "narrow" definition below. It is important to note here, however, that we intend for working together "harmoniously" to include conflict as well as cooperation. Even when a group of actors has strong conflicts of interest or belief, they may still produce results that observers would judge to be "good" or "harmonious." For example, different groups in a company often compete for budget resources and people, and this competition sometimes contributes to the company's ability to produce useful products.

What is coordination theory?

We define *coordination theory* as a body of principles about how activities can be coordinated, that is, about how actors can work together harmoniously. It is important to realize that there is not yet a coherent body of theory in this domain. However, there are theories, concepts, and results from many different fields that could both contribute to and benefit from the development of such general theories.

For instance, it is clear that questions about how people coordinate their activities are central to parts of organization theory, sociology, social psychology, anthropology, linguistics, law, and political science. Important parts of economics and management science also analyze how people can coordinate their work with a special focus on rational ways of allocating resources. Computer science does not deal primarily with people, but different computational processes must certainly "work together harmoniously," and as numerous observers have pointed out, certain kinds of interactions among computational processes resemble interactions among people (e.g., [Fox81], [Hewi86], [Hube88], [Mill88], [Smit81]).

These potential overlaps suggest that coordination theory will be like other interdisciplinary fields that arise from the recognition of commonalities in problems that have previously been considered separately in different fields. For instance, the field of cognitive science grew out of the recognition by researchers in several different fields (e.g., psychology, computer science, and linguistics) that they were dealing separately with similar problems: how can information processing systems (people or computers) do things like use language, learn, plan, remember, and solve problems (e.g., see [Gard85], [Norm80])? Most observers would agree that progress in the new field has benefitted significantly from emergent cross disciplinary connections, and the paradigms used have in turn been quite influential in the older fields [Gard85].

In coordination theory, the common problems have to do with coordination: How can overall goals be subdivided into actions? How can actions be assigned to groups or to individual actors? How can resources be allocated among different actors? How can information be shared among different actors to help achieve the overall goals?

In its attempts to find generalizations that apply across disciplines and across levels of analysis, coordination theory resembles earlier work on systems theory and cybernetics (e.g., [Beer67], [Boul56], [Emer69], [Forr80], [vonB50], [Wien61]). We are significantly better equipped for the task of identifying and analyzing coordination processes now, however, than systems theorists were several decades ago. For instance, new qualitative languages from computer and cognitive sciences (such as object inheritance networks and Petri nets) seem especially promising as tools for formalizing "mid-level theories" like Winograd and Flores' [Wino86] "conversations for action." These qualitative mid-level theories are more specific than the quantitative abstractions of systems theory, but more general than specific case studies.

What isn't coordination theory?

If coordination theory can draw upon so many different fields, is it any more than just the union of these fields? How can we look at a theory and decide whether it is or is not an example of coordination theory? While it is certainly not helpful to include everything in coordination theory, neither do we think it is essential to draw sharp boundaries between what is and is not coordination theory. Instead, as in cognitive science and many other fields, we think certain characteristic questions and approaches will come to typify central examples of coordination theory. For example, theories that apply to only one kind of actor will probably be less important to coordination theory than theories that can be applied to several kinds of actors.

Previous examples of coordination theory and CSCW

With the definition of coordination theory we have just presented, it is clear that some of the work already done in the field of computer-supported cooperative work can be viewed as examples of the use of coordination theory. Even though these authors did not use the term "coordination theory," each of the following examples involves using ideas about coordination from other disciplines to help develop cooperative work tools:

(1) Holt [Holt88] describes a theoretical language used for designing coordination tools that is based, in part, on ideas about Petri nets, a formalism widely used in computer science to represent process flows in distributed or parallel systems. This language is part of a larger theoretical framework called "coordination mechanics."

(2) Winograd and Flores ([Flor88], [Wino87], [Wino86]) have developed a theoretical perspective for analyzing group action based heavily on ideas from linguistics (e.g., [Sear75]) about different kinds of "speech acts," such as "requests" and "commitments." This perspective was a primary basis for designing the Coordinator, a computer tool that helps people make and keep track of requests and commitments to each other.

(3) Malone [(Malo90] describes how ideas from organization theory about flexible organizational structures called "adhocracies" [Mint79] and ideas from artificial intelligence about "blackboard architectures" for sharing information among program modules ([Erma80], [Nii86]) contributed to the design of the Information Lens, a system for helping people share information in organizations [Malo87].

(4) Conklin & Begeman [Conk88] and Lee [Lee90a] describe systems to help groups of people record the structure of arguments (e.g., positions, arguments, and counterarguments) that are based in part on ideas from philosophy and rhetoric about the logical structure of decision-making.

(5) Turoff [Turo83] used ideas about prices and markets to suggest a computer-based system to help people to exchange services within organizations.

Clearly, drawing a line around these examples and calling them "coordination theory" does not, in itself, provide any benefit. Nor does using ideas about coordination from other disciplines provide any guarantee of developing useful cooperative work tools. Nevertheless, we feel that considering these examples within the common framework of coordination theory provides two benefits: (1) it suggests that no one of these perspectives is the complete story, and (2) it suggests something about how we might look for more insights of the sort that many people feel have resulted from these previous examples.

In particular, the perspective of coordination theory suggests (1) that we should look to previous work in various disciplines for more insights about coordination, (2) that we should attempt to develop frameworks or concepts that will facilitate such interdisciplinary transfers, and (3) that we should attempt to develop new concepts and theories focused specifically on the questions of coordination that seem central to building cooperative work tools. In the next section, we will take a step in this direction.

TOWARD A FRAMEWORK FOR COORDINATION THEORY

So far, we have claimed that many different disciplines can contribute to our understanding of coordination and that better understanding of coordination will help build useful cooperative work tools. But is it really sensible to use the term "coordination" in describing all the different kinds of phenomena to which we have alluded? For that matter, is there anything in common among these different phenomena, other than some occasional similarities in terminology? As a first step toward answering these questions, we will present in this section our preliminary efforts toward developing a framework for analyzing coordination. This framework is not a "theory of everything;" it is only one approach which we have found helpful in seeing the relationships between different views of coordination.

Components of coordination

According to our broad definition of coordination above, coordination means "the act of working together harmoniously." What does this broad definition of coordination imply? First of all, what does the word "work" imply? The same dictionary defines "work" as "physical or mental effort or activity directed toward the production or accomplishment of something" [Amer81]. Thus there must be one or more *actors*, performing some *activities* which are directed toward some ends. In what follows, we will sometimes refer to the ends toward which the activities are directed as *goals*. By using the word "harmoniously," the definition implies that the activities are not independent. Instead, they must be performed in a way that helps create "pleasing" and avoids "displeasing" outcomes, that is, that achieves the goals. We will refer to these goal-relevant relationships between the activities as *interdependencies*. These components and the coordination processes associated with them are summarized in Table 1. (See [Bali86], [Bali81], [Barn64;], [Malo87b], [Malo88], [McGr84], [Mint79] for related decompositions of coordination.)

Components of coordination	Associated coordination processes
Goals	Identifying goals
Activities	Mapping goals to activities (e.g., goal decomposition)
Actors	Selecting actors Assigning activities to actors
Interdependencies	"Managing" interdependencies

Table 1. Components of coordination.

For example, an automobile manufacturing company might be thought of as having a set of goals (e.g., producing several different lines of automobiles) and a set of actors (e.g., people) who perform activities that achieve these goals. These activities may have various kinds of interdependencies such as using the same resources (e.g., an assembly line) or needing to be done in a certain order (e.g., a car must usually be designed before it is built).

One use of this set of components of coordination is to help facilitate conceptual transfers between disciplines. For instance, elsewhere [Malo88], we have shown how research in selected areas of economics and artificial intelligence can be compared in terms of these dimensions. This comparison suggested a novel insight for economic theorists about the importance of product descriptions, as well as prices, in coordinating resource allocation in markets.

Coordination is attributed to a situation by observers

It is important to realize that the actors involved in a situation may or may not all agree on the identification of all these components. Instead, one or more of these components may be attributed by an observer in order to analyze the situation in terms of coordination. For instance, we may sometimes analyze everything that happens in a manufacturing division as one "activity", while at other times, we may want to analyze each station on an assembly line as a separate "activity."

One very important case of this occurs when the actors have *conflicting goals*, but we choose to analyze the results of their behavior in terms of how well it achieves some goals in which we are interested. For instance, even though two designers on a project team may have strongly opposing views about how a product should be designed, we can evaluate their collective behavior in terms of the quality of the final design. Another important example of conflicting goals occurs in market transactions: All the participants in a market might have the goal of maximizing their own benefits, but we, as observers, can evaluate the market as a coordination mechanism in terms of how well it achieves some global goal such as allocating economic resources to maximize consumer utilities (e.g., [Debr59]).

In practice, situations in which actors have at least partly conflicting goals are nearly universal, and mixtures of cooperation and conflict are quite common (e.g., [Cibo87], [Will85], [Sche69]). When we analyze the coordination in these situations, we must (at least implicitly) evaluate the actors' collective behavior in terms of how well it achieves some overall goals (which may or may not be held by the actors themselves).

A narrow definition of coordination

The broad definition of coordination we have been using includes almost everything that happens when actors work together: setting goals, selecting actors, and performing all the other activities that need to be done. For some purposes, it is useful to be able to focus explicitly on the elements that are unique to coordination, that is, on the aspects of "working together harmoniously" that are not simply part of "working." In our analysis of the broad definition above, the element of coordination that was implied by the word "harmoniously" was interdependencies. Therefore, when we want to focus specifically on the aspects of a situation that are unique to coordination, we will use the following narrow definition of coordination:

> *the act of managing interdependencies between*
> *activities performed to achieve a goal.*

Clearly, many important coordination situations involve multiple actors, and in our previous work (e.g., [Malo88]), we defined coordination as something that occurs only when multiple actors are involved. Since then, however, we have become convinced that the essential elements of coordination listed above arise whenever multiple, interdependent activities are performed to achieve goals—even if only one actor performs all of them.

Kinds of Interdependence

Both our definitions of coordination give a prominent role to interdependence: If there is no interdependence, there is nothing to coordinate. There is also a long history in organization theory of emphasizing the importance of interdependence in determining how organizations are structured (e.g., [Thom67], [Galb73], [Lawr67], [Pfef78], [Rock89], [Har90]). This suggests that one useful way to extend the theory of coordination is to ask what kinds of interdependence between activities are possible and how different kinds of interdependence can be managed.

Our preliminary investigations of this question have led us to believe that interdependence between activities can be analyzed in terms of *common objects* that are involved in some way in both actions. For example, the activities of designing and manufacturing a part both involve the detailed design of the part: the design activity creates the design and the manufacturing activity uses it.

These common objects constrain how each activity is performed. Different patterns of use of the common objects by the activities will result in different kinds of interdependences. For example, the parts can be manufactured only after the design is complete and the actor doing the manufacturing has received a copy. We call this pattern of usage (one task creating an object that is used by others) a *prerequisite* constraint. In general, the common object may constrain any or all of the activities that use it. In this case, for example, it might make sense for a designer to consider the constraints that the manufacturing process places on the design and to create a design that will be easier to manufacture.

Table 2 presents a preliminary list of types of interdependencies and coordination processes that can be used to manage them. The table includes both generic kinds of interdependence and specific examples of interdependence that arise in particular situations. We labeled this list "preliminary" because we suspect that there is more structure in the space of kinds of interdependence and processes than is currently reflected in the table.

One use of this table (especially the generic parts of it) may be to help show the relationships between previous work in different disciplines. For instance, much of economics is focused on analyzing market mechanisms for resource allocation, and parts of computer science have focused on questions of synchronizing activities to meet simultaneity constraints.

An even more important use of the approach suggested by this table may be to help generate possible alternative ways of coordinating in a particular situation. For instance, it may be possible to characterize a situation in terms of the kinds of interdependence it involves, and then use a "catalog" of interdependencies and their associated processes to generate a set of alternative processes that could be used to manage the interdependencies. This ability to characterize a space of possible coordination processes for a given set of activities would be useful in understanding how new kinds of coordination tools could lead to new ways of organizing cooperative work.

Kinds of Interdependence	Common object	Example of interdependence in manufacturing	Examples of coordination processes for managing interdependence
Generic:			
Prerequisite	Output of one activity which is required by the next activity	Parts must be delivered in time to be used	Ordering activities, moving information from one activity to the next
Shared resource	Resource required by multiple activities	Two parts installed with a common tool	Allocating resources
Simultaneity	Time at which more than one activity must occur	Installing two matched parts at the same time	Synchronizing activities
Domain-specific:			
Manufacturability	Part	Part designed by engineering must be made by manufacturing	Decision-making (e.g., negotiation, appeal to authority)
Customer relations	Customer	Both field service and sales personnel deal with same customer	Information sharing (e.g., sharing problem reports)

Table 2. Preliminary examples of kinds of interdependence.

Example: Coordinating interdependencies between design and manufacturing

This example illustrates how knowing the interdependencies in a situation may suggest alternative ways to manage them. The example is based, in part, on extended field studies of engineering change processes in several manufacturing organizations [Crow90]. In the case of design and manufacturing, an important kind of interdependence results from the common object that is the design of the product to be manufactured.

One simple way technology can help manage these interdependencies is simply by helping to detect them in the first place. For instance, one of the applications we have investigated for the Information Lens and Object Lens systems ([Lai88], [Malo87]) is routing engineering change notices to engineers to whose work is likely be be affected by a given change, even when the person making the change does not know who else it will affect.

Whether all the interdependencies are recognized or not, there seem to be at least four basic ways to manage them:

(1) At a minimum, the designer must create a design and give it to the manufacturer to build. One simple effect of CAD systems, for example, is to make this transfer process easier.

(2) The designer and the manufacturer can negotiate what the design should be, for example, by iterating the design process or in joint meetings. A variety of electronic meeting support and communication tools could help this process and could make it more desirable relative to alternative ways of managing the same interdependencies.

(3) Sometimes the need for explicit negotiation can be eliminated by moving some of the knowledge about the constraints of either task from one engineer to another. For instance:

   (a) Some of the manufacturer's knowledge (the knowledge about the manufacturing constraints, not about how to do the manufacturing) can be made available to the designer, for example, by training the designer in methodologies such as design for manufacturing or by embodying the knowledge in an intelligent CAD system.

   (b) Some of the designer's knowledge can be transferred to the manufacturer. For example, if a system like gIBIS [Conk88] is used to capture more of the designer's intent as well as the details of the part, the manufacturing engineer might be able to change some details of the design to make the parts easier to build while preserving the intent.

(4) A third party, such as a common superior, may be able to resolve problems as they arise or to give enough initial direction that problems do not arise.

This analysis seems to be easily transferred to other domains. For example, a bank and a potential borrower have to agree on a common object, a loan. The typical approach seems to be case (1) above: the bank offers a loan with its standard terms and a person who wants the loan takes it or leaves it. In some cases, the bank and the borrower negotiate the details of the loan, case (2) above. Finally, one can imagine transferring some of the bank's knowledge about making loans, for example, to a computer program that a potential borrower could run to explore possible loan conditions (case (3a)), or to a third party who would suggest which bank would be best for a given applicant (case (4)).

Processes underlying coordination

In attempting to characterize more precisely different coordination processes, we have found it useful to describe them in terms of successively deeper levels of underlying processes, each of which depends on the levels below it. Table 3 shows a preliminary diagram of the levels we have used. For instance, most of the coordination processes listed in the last column of Table 2 require that some decision be made and accepted by a group (e.g., what goal will be selected or which actors will perform which activities). Group decisions, in turn, require members of the group to communicate in some form about the goals to be achieved, the alternatives being considered, the evaluations of these alternatives, and the choices that are made. This communication requires that some form of "messages" be transported from senders to receivers in a language that is understandable to both. Finally, the establishment of this common language and the transportation of messages depends, ultimately, on the ability of actors to perceive common objects such as physical objects in a shared situation or information in a shared database (e.g., see [Such87]). These layers are analogous to abstraction levels in other systems, such as protocol layers for network communications.

Even though the strongest dependencies appear to be downward through these layers, there are also times when one layer will use processes from the layers above it. For instance, a group may sometimes use decision-making processes to extend the common language it uses to communicate (e.g, see [Lee90b]), or a group may use coordination processes to assign decision-making activities to actors.

Process Level	Components	Examples of Generic Processes
Coordination	goals, activities, actors, resources, interdependencies	identifying goals, ordering activities, assigning activities to actors, allocating resources, synchronizing activities
Group decision-making	goals, actors, alternatives, evaluations, choices	proposing alternatives, evaluating alternatives, making choices (e.g., by authority, consensus, or voting)
Communication	senders, receivers, messages, languages	establishing common languages, selecting receiver (routing), transporting message (delivering)
Perception of common objects	actors, objects	seeing same physical objects, accessing shared databases

Table 3. Processes underlying coordination.

Example : Selecting actors to perform activities

To see how this framework can be used to analyze coordination processes, let us consider the part of the activity assignment process that involves selecting which actors will perform which activities. For this example, we will analyze one particular method that can be used for this process: a competitive bidding scheme like that used in many kinds of markets. Our analysis will draw upon the version of this process formalized by Smith and Davis [Smit81] and extended by Malone ([Malo87b], [Malo88]).

In this scheme, a client first broadcasts an announcement message to all potential contractors. This message includes a description of the activity to be performed and the qualifications required of potential contractors. The potential contractors then use this information to decide whether to submit a bid on the action. If they decide to bid, their bid message includes a description of their qualifications and their availability for performing the action. The client uses these bid messages to decide which contractor should perform the activity and then sends an award message to notify the contractor that has been selected.

In this case, the decision to be made is which contractor will perform a specific action. The choice results from a multi-stage process in which contractors decide whether to propose themselves as alternatives (by submitting bids) and clients decide which contractor to select based on their evaluations of the contractors' bids. The actors communicate by exchanging messages, and we can regard these messages as including representations of common objects (such as activities and bids) which both senders and receivers can perceive.

Viewing the activity assignment process in this way, immediately suggests other possibilities for how it can be performed. For instance, an authority-based decision-making process might be used in which a manager simply assigns activities to people who have implicitly already agreed to accept such assignments. This view also suggests how computer tools could be used to support a bidding process for task assignments in human organizations (e.g., see [Malo87a], [Turo83]).

CONCLUSIONS

In this paper, we have argued that many different disciplines can contribute to our understanding of coordination and that a better understanding of coordination can help us build useful cooperative work tools. In order to support these claims, we have shown examples of interdisciplinary transfers of ideas about coordination that have already provided useful insights for cooperative work tools, and we have sketched out the beginnings of a framework that can facilitate such interdisciplinary transfers and lead to the development of new general theories about coordination.

Clearly there is much left to be done. We hope, however, that the perspective we have suggested here will help build tools that enable people to work together more effectively and more enjoyably.

ACKNOWLEDGEMENTS

This work was supported, in part, by Digital Equipment Corporation, the National Science Foundation (Grant Nos. IRI-8805798 and IRI-8903034), the MIT International Financial Services Research Center, and General Motors/Electronic Data Systems.

Parts of this paper were included in a previous working paper [Malo88] and in proposals submitted to the National Science Foundation. We are especially grateful to Deborah Ancona, John Carroll, Michael Cohen, Randall Davis, John Little, and Wanda Orlikowski for comments on earlier versions of the paper, and to participants in numerous seminars and workshops at which these ideas have been presented.

APPENDIX:
PREVIOUSLY SUGGESTED DEFINITIONS OF COORDINATION

"The operation of complex systems made up of components." [NSF89]

"The emergent behavior of collections of individuals whose actions are based on complex decision processes." [NSF89]

"Information processing within a system of communicating entities with distinct information states." [NSF89]

"The joint efforts of independent communicating actors towards mutually defined goals." [NSF89]

"Networks of human action and commitments that are enabled by computer and communications technologies." [NSF89]

"Composing purposeful actions into larger purposeful wholes." [Holt89]

"Activities required to maintain consistency within a work product or to manage dependencies within the workflow." [Curt89]

"The additional information processing performed when multiple, connected actors pursue goals that a single actor pursuing the same goals would not perform." [Malo88]

REFERENCES

[Amer81]   American Heritage Dictionary. Boston: Houghton Mifflin, 1981.

[Bali86]   Baligh, H. H. Decision rules and transactions, organizations and markets. *Management Science, 32,* 1480–1491, 1986.

[Bali81]   Baligh, H. H., Burton, R. M. Describing and designing organizational structures and processes. *International Journal of Policy Analysis and Information Systems, 5,* 251–266, 1981.

[Barn64]   Barnard, C. I. *The Functions of the Executive.* Cambridge, MA: Harvard University, 1964.

[Beer67]   Beer, S. *Cybernetics and Management* (2nd ed.). London: English Universities Press, 1967.

[Boul56]   Boulding, K. E. *The Image.* Ann Arbor, MI: University of Michigan, 1956.

[Cibo87]   Ciborra, C. U. Reframing the role of computers in organizations: The transaction costs approach. *Office Technology and People, 3,* 17-38, 1987.

[Conk88]   Conklin, J., Begeman, M. L. gIBIS: A hypertext tooling for exploratory policy discussion. In Tatar, D. (Ed.), *Proceedings of the 2nd Conference on Computer-supported Cooperative Work* (pp. 140–152). New York: ACM, 1988.

[Crow90]   Crowston, K. *Modeling Coordination in Organizations.* Ph.D. Dissertation, Sloan School of Management, Massachusetts Institute of Technology, Forthcoming (1990).

[Curt89]   Curtis, B. Modeling coordination from field experiments. In *Organizational Computing, Coordination and Collaboration: Theories and Technologies for Computer-Supported Work.* Austin, TX, 1989.

[Debr59]   Debreu, G. *Theory of value: An axiomatic analysis of economic equilibrium.* New York: Wiley, 1959.

[Emer69]   Emery, J. C. *Organizational Planning and Control Systems: Theory and Technology.* New York: MacMillan, 1969.

[Erma80]   Erman, L. D., Hayes-Roth, F., Lesser, V. R., Reddy, D. R. The HEARSAY-II speech understanding system: Integrating knowledge to resolve uncertainty. *Computing Surveys, 12*(2), 213–253, 1980.

[Flor88]   Flores, F., Graves, M., Hartfield, B., Winograd, T. Computer systems and the design of organizational interaction. *ACM Transactions on Office Information Systems, 6*(2), 153–172, 1988.

[Forr80]   Forrester, J. W. *Systems dynamics.* New York: North-Holland, 1980.

[Fox81]   Fox, M. S. An organizational view of distributed systems. *IEEE Transactions on Systems, Man and Cybernetics, 11*(1), 70–79, 1981.

[Galb73]   Galbraith, J. R. *Designing Complex Organizations.* Reading, MA: Addison-Wesley, 1973.

[Gard85]   Gardner, D. *The Mind's New Science: A History of the Cognitive Revolution.* New York: Basic, 1985.

[Hart90]   Hart, P. & Estrin, D. Inter-organization computer networks: Indications of shifts in interdependence. *Proceedings of the ACM Conference on Office Information Systems,* Cambridge, MA, April 25-27, 1990.

[Hewi86]   Hewitt, C. Offices are open systems. *ACM Transactions on Office Systems,* 4(3), 271–287, 1986.

[Holt89]   Holt, A. *Personal communication.,* 1989.

[Holt88]   Holt, A. W. Diplans: A new language for the study and implementation of coordination. *ACM Transactions on Office Information Systems,* 6(2), 109–125, 1988.

[Hube88]   Huberman, B. A. (Eds.). *The Ecology of Computation .* Amsterdam: North-Holland, 1988.

[Korn81]   Kornfeld, W. A., Hewitt, C. The scientific community metaphor. *IEEE Transactions on Systems, Man, and Cybernetics, SMC-11,* 24–33, 1981.

[Lai88]   Lai, K. Y., Malone, T., Yu, K.-C. Object Lens: A spreadsheet for cooperative work. *ACM Transactions on Office Information Systems,* (Oct), 1988.

[Lawr67]   Lawrence, P. R. & Lorsch, J. W. *Organization and Environment.* Boston: Graduate School of Business Adminsitration, Harvard University, 1967.

[Lee90a]   Lee, J. Sibyl: A qualitative decision management system. In Winston, P. (Ed.), *Artificial Intelligence at MIT: Expanding Frontiers* Cambridge, MA: MIT Press, 1990.

[Lee90b]   Lee, J., Malone, T. W. Partially Shared Views: A scheme for communicating among groups that use different type hierarchies. *ACM Transactions on Information Systems, 8,* 1-26, 1990.

[Malo87a]   Malone, T. W. Computer support for organizations: Towards an organizational science. In Carroll, J. (Ed.), *Interfacing Thought: Cognitive Aspects of Human Computer Interactions* Cambridge, MA: MIT Press, 1987.

[Malo87b]   Malone, T. W. Modeling coordination in organizations and markets. *Management Science, 33,* 1317–1332, 1987.

[Malo88a]   Malone, T. W. *What is coordination theory?* (Working paper #2051-88). Cambridge, MA: MIT Sloan School of Management, 1988.

[Malo90]   Malone, T. W. Organizing information processing systems: Parallels between organizations and computer systems. In Zachary, W., Robertson, S., Black, J. (Ed.), *Cognition, Computation, and Cooperation* (pp. 56–83). Norwood, NJ: Ablex, 1990.

[Malo87c]   Malone, T. W., Grant, K. R., Turbak, F. A., Brobst, S. A., Cohen, M. D. Intelligent information-sharing systems. *Communications of the ACM, 30,* 390–402, 1987.

[Malo88b] Malone, T. W., Smith, S. A. Modeling the performance of organizational structures. *Operations Research, 36*(3), 421–436, 1988.

[McGr84] McGrath, J. E. *Groups: Interaction and Performance.* Englewood Cliffs, NJ: Prentice-Hall, 1984.

[Mill88] Miller, M. S., Drexler, K. E. Markets and computation: Agoric open systems. In Huberman, B. A. (Ed.), *The Ecology of Computation* (pp. 133–176). Amsterdam: North-Holland, 1988.

[Mins87] Minsky, M. *The Society of the Mind.* New York: Simon and Schuster, 1987.

[Mint79] Mintzberg, H. *The Structuring of Organizations.* Englewood Cliffs, NJ: Prentice-Hall, 1979.

[Nii86] Nii, P. The blackboard model of problem solving. *The AI Magazine,* (Spring), 38–53, 1986.

[Norm80] Norman, D. A. Twelve issues for cognitive science. *Cognitive Science, 4,* 1–32, 1980.

[NSF89] NSF-IRIS. *A report by the NSF-IRIS Review Panel for Research on Coordination Theory and Technology.* Available from NSF Forms & Publications Unit, 1989.

[Pfef78] Pfeffer, J. & Salancik, G. R. *The External Control of Organizations: A Resource Dependency Perspective.* New York: Harper & Row, 1978.

[Sche60] Schelling, T. C. *Strategy of Conflict.* Cambridge: Harvard University Press, 1960.

[Sear75] Searle, J. R. A taxonomy of illocutionary acts. In Gunderson, K. (Ed.), *Language, Mind and Knowledge* (pp. 344–369). Minneapolis, MN: University of Minnesota, 1975.

[Rock89] Rockart, J. F. & Short, J. E. IT and the networked organization: Toward more effective management of interdependence. In M. S. Scott Morton (Ed.), *Management in the 1990s Research Program Final Report.* Cambridge, MA: Massachusetts Institute of Technology, 1989.

[Smit81] Smith, R. G., Davis, R. Frameworks for cooperation in distributed problem solving. *IEEE Transactions on Systems, Man and Cybernetics, 11*(1), 61–70, 1981.

[Such87] Suchman, L. A. *Plans and Situated Actions: The Problem of Human Machine Communication.* Cambridge: Cambridge University Press, 1987.

[Thom67] Thompson, J. D. *Organizations in Action.* New York: McGraw-Hill, 1967.

[Turo83] Turoff, M. *Information, value, and the internal marketplace* (Unpublished manuscript). New Jersey Institute of Technology, 1983.

[vonB50] von Bertalanffy, L. The theory of open systems in physics and biology. *Science, 111,* 1950.

[Wien61]   Wiener, N. *Cybernetics: Or Control and Communication in the Animal and the Machine* (2nd ed.). Cambridge, MA: MIT Press, 1961.

[Will85]   Williamson, O. *The Economic Institutions of Capitalism*. New York: Free Press, 1985.

[Wino87]   Winograd, T. A language/action perspective on the design of cooperative work. *Human Computer Interaction, 3*, 3–30, 1987.

[Wino86]   Winograd, T., Flores, F. *Understanding computers and cognition: A new foundation for design*. Norwood, NJ: Ablex, 1986.

Proceedings of the Second European Conference on Computer-Supported Cooperative Work
Bannon, L., Robinson, M. & Schmidt, K. (Editors)
September 25-27, 1991, Amsterdam, The Netherlands

CSCW and Distributed Systems: The Problem of Control

Tom Rodden   Gordon Blair
Lancaster University, U.K.

The user-centred philosophy of CSCW challenges the established principles of many existing technologies but the development of CSCW is dependent on the facilities provided by these technologies. It is therefore important to examine and understand this inter-relationship. This paper focuses on distributed computing, a technology central to the development of CSCW systems. The nature of both CSCW and distribution are compared by using a common framework. In this discussion, control emerges as the major problem in supporting CSCW systems. It is argued that existing approaches to control in distributed systems are inadequate given the rich patterns of cooperation found in CSCW. A number of recommendations are made for improving distributed support for CSCW.

1. Introduction

Computer support for cooperative working (CSCW) has emerged over the last five years as a research discipline in its own right (Bannon, 1991). The growing interest in CSCW reflects the demands of industry for improved tools to aid the coordination and control of group activities. The majority of CSCW applications are fundamentally distributed and are dependent on the facilities provided by existing distributed systems platforms. It is therefore important to assess the support that such systems provide.

The aim of this paper is to evaluate distributed system support for CSCW. In particular we wish to consider the particular requirements of CSCW and the interaction between distributed systems and CSCW. To achieve this two

dimensions of CSCW are introduced in section 2. These dimensions provide a basis for the our discussion. This is followed in section 3 with an examination of distributed system support for CSCW based on the above dimensions. Control, an additional and important feature of both CSCW and distributed systems, is introduced in section 4. The impact of control on distribution is examined and techniques to support control are also discussed. Distributed transactions are presented in section 5 as an illustrative case study of the problem of control. Finally some concluding remarks are presented in section 6.

2. Dimensions of CSCW

A wide variety of CSCW systems have been developed reflecting the many different views of cooperation. The nature of cooperation has been an on-going debate within the CSCW community (Schmidt, 1989). Two principal characteristics have emerged from this debate *the form of cooperation* and *the geographical nature*. We shall use these characteristics as the basis for examining both CSCW systems and the underlying support provided by distributed systems.

2.1 The Form of Cooperation

CSCW systems are primarily concerned with supporting a number of users cooperating to address a particular problem, or range of problems. People cooperate in a variety of ways depending on a range of circumstances. The nature of this cooperation can be distinguished by the way in which the group members interact. People can either interact and cooperate *synchronously* or *asynchronously*. Synchronous interaction requires the presence of all cooperating users while asynchronous cooperation occurs over a longer time period and does not require the simultaneous interaction of all users.

Figure 1 shows how a number of classes of CSCW systems fit into this division.

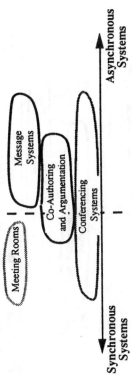

Figure 1 Forms of cooperation in CSCW systems

From this classification three general classes of CSCW system can be highlighted.

i) Purely synchronous systems
Purely synchronous systems need the simultaneous presence of all users. This general class of system is used for investigative and creative problems. Systems which typify this approach include real-time conferencing systems (Lauwers, 1990) using shared screen techniques (Stefik, 1987b) and the brainstorming tools found in meeting rooms (Stefik, 1987a)

ii) Purely Asynchronous systems
Asynchronous systems are designed to allow cooperation without the simultaneous presence of all group members. Cooperative message systems are a primary example of this type of system where users take on independent roles which produce and consume messages. Similarly, traditional conferencing systems assume an asynchronous mode of cooperation with users reading and adding articles to conferences independently of other users.

iii) Mixed Systems
Mixed systems contain elements of support for both synchronous and asynchronous cooperation. They allow real-time synchronous cooperation to take place within the same framework as time-independent asynchronous working. The primary examples of this type of systems are computer conferencing and co-authoring and argumentation systems. Modern computer conferencing systems provide a central asynchronous conferencing systems often augmented with facilities such as real-time conferencing (Sarin, 1985).

2.2. Geographical Nature

Computer support for group interaction has traditionally considered the case of geographically distributed groups who work asynchronously to each other. More recent research (Stefik, 1987a) has complemented this emphasis by considering the support of face to face meetings. As a result cooperative systems can be considered as being either *remote* or *co-located*. In this classification the division between remote and co-located is as much a logical as a physical one and is concerned with the accessibility of users to each other rather than their physical proximity. A range of CSCW systems are divided in terms of their geographical nature in figure 2.

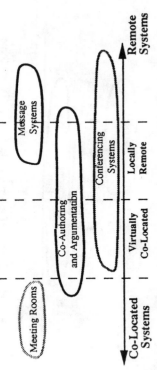

Figure 2 Geographical nature in CSCW systems

Four general divisions can be highlighted.

i) Co-Located.
Purely co-located systems require the local presence of all users. This class of system normally takes the form of a purpose built meeting room with a large projected computer screen and a number of personal computer linked by a local area network (Kraemer, 1988).

ii) Virtually co-located
Systems which are virtually co-located are similar to co-located systems but do not have the requirement that participants need to be in one room. This is often achieved by the use of Multimedia technology, allowing real-time multimedia audio and video links to be maintained. Systems in this class include real-time multimedia conferencing systems such as those been developed for MMConf (Crowley, 1990) and Mermaid (Watabe, 1990).

iii) Locally Remote
Locally remote systems are those systems which provide high-bandwidth real-time accessibility between users often using shared screen techniques.. Argumentation and co-authoring systems such as CoAuthor (Hahn, 1991) or gIBIS (Conklin, 1987) and real-time conferencing facilities such as RTCAL (Sarin, 1985) can be considered in this way.

iv) Remote
Remote cooperative systems are those that assume the existence of only minimal accessibility between users. These include message systems which assume only the simplest of communication systems and computer conferencing systems which assume only rudimentary "dial-in" mechanisms.

3. CSCW and Distributed Systems

Distributed systems have been one of the major growth areas in computing over the past decade. Products such as ETHERNET (Shoch, 1982) and MACH (Jones, 1986) are available in the market place and standards to provide open communications are generally agreed.

It can be argued that distributed systems are entering a period of consolidation with techniques for implementing distributed systems relatively well understood, and that emphasis should be placed on issues such as promotion of standards, large scale experiments, and gaining of experience. However, a major problem in distributed systems is a lack of existing applications of the technology leading to technological solutions to technological problems.

Until recently, this feature of distributed computing has not posed many problems. However, the emergence of CSCW has led to more sophisticated demands on the underlying technology. This section reviews the ability of existing distributed system technologies to support the wide range of CSCW systems.

3.1. The Form of cooperation

Distributed systems have traditionally being viewed in terms of support for cooperation between a number of computers connected by a network. It is important to note that the term cooperation is used in this context to refer to how closely related the computers within the distributed systems are to each other, rather than the more general application of the term in section 2. This interpretation is used throughout this section.

The nature of support for cooperation varies greatly from system to system. A traditional problem with cooperation in distributed systems is the need to recognise the autonomy of individual sites in a network. Indeed, full cooperation and full autonomy are actually two extremes in a spectrum of possibilities with most practical systems found between these two extremes.

Increasing the autonomy of a system inevitably decreases the support for cooperation and vice-versa. Much of the research in distributed systems has been concerned with resolving this design tension and establishing a compromise between the two extremes. A number of distinct classes of system, each taking a particular approach to this issue, have been developed:-

i) autonomous systems with mailing capabilities

This is an important class of system where personal computer environments are interconnected by electronic mail allowing users to interact asynchronously via (usually) text based messages.

ii) resource sharing systems

Resource sharing systems allow resources to be accessed whether they are local or remote to a workstation. The motivation for resource sharing systems is that many resources are expensive and hence it is economical to share such resources across a network.

iii) distributed operating systems

Distributed operating systems are operating systems which manage resources across a distributed environment (Tanenbaum, 1985). They provide global management of such resources with the consequent loss of node autonomy. Most distributed operating systems are based on the *client-server* model of interaction with clients requesting remote operations from *servers* on other nodes.

More recent distributed operating systems have also tended to provide more sophisticated support for interaction. For example, several systems have developed protocols to provide general group interaction (e.g. ISIS (Birman, 1989)) as opposed to the one to one patterns encouraged by the traditional client-server model.

The need to support autonomy has proved to be more important than the support for cooperation. Most commercially available computer systems support a mailing capability and this has become accepted as a standard means of cooperation in a distributed system and provides adequate support for the development of asynchronous cooperative systems.

Systems with resource sharing capabilities provide access to networked resources such as printers and remote files. More sophisticated resource sharing systems will provide the user with a global file system accessible from anywhere in the network. Resource sharing systems provide an ideal platform for developing *mixed cooperative systems* with asynchronous cooperative working as the norm and rudimentary synchronous support being provided as an expensive shared resource.

There has been much less commercial interest/ exploitation of distributed operating systems. Distributed operating systems have been an area of intense research activity (Mullender, 1986); however, this has yet to be mapped on to a real demand for the technology.

Distributed operating systems represent the maximum support available for cooperation. They support reasonably sophisticated modes of interaction and often mask out the problems of distribution (e.g. locating objects and handling failure). However, most distributed operating systems allow some recognition of the autonomy of individual nodes and the cooperative end of the spectrum has not been explored fully. There are a few notable exceptions , for example, the work of the ISIS project on group interaction could be viewed as supporting more sophisticated levels of cooperation.

This spectrum of support corresponds quite closely to the forms of cooperation described in section 2.1. Synchronous systems require highly cooperative distributed systems while asynchronous systems tend to be much more autonomous in nature. Basic asynchronous cooperative systems need only the facilities provided by electronic mail systems, the most autonomous of distributed systems. Fully synchronous systems test the facilities provided by the most cooperative of distributed operating systems. Most distributed systems are found at the lower end of the spectrum, i.e. supporting a high degree of autonomy. This may account for the lack of highly interactive synchronous cooperative systems. The two views of a cooperative system are shown together in figure 3

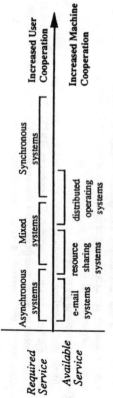

Figure 3 Comparison of Models of Cooperation

A strong correspondence can be seen between the two categories in figure 3. However, there appears to be a gap when considering more sophisticated forms of synchronous working. It is not clear how best to support highly synchronous cooperative systems such as meeting rooms and real time multimedia conferencing with existing distributed technology.

3.2. Geographical Nature

As discussed in section 2.2, the geographic nature of CSCW systems is concerned with the *logical* concept of co-location. In contrast, distributed computing has been solely concerned with the *physical* transmission and processing of specialised, computer-oriented, media such as numerical and textual data. Most distributed computing environments have been connected by a range of local or wide area networks providing a reasonable handling of such media types. The characteristics of each type of network is summarised in figure 4.

Network	Throughput	Classification
Ethernet	10 Mbits/Sec	Local Area Network
1Base5 CSMA/CD	1 Mbits/Sec	Local Area Network
PSS (UK)	64 KBits/Sec	Wide Area Network
Arpanet (USA)	64 KBits/Sec	Wide Area Network

Figure 4 Local vs Wide Area Networks

The performance characteristics listed above have proved sufficient to support a range of distributed computing environments. The table also highlights the quantitative difference that currently exists between local and wide area technologies. Local area networks have been used to implement the full range of systems described in section 4.1 including distributed operating systems supporting varying degrees of cooperation. Wide area networks have generally been restricted to mailing systems and, occasionally, resource sharing systems.

Recently, there has been great interest in high speed networks and, in particular, their capability to handle a greater variety of media types. The capabilities of these multimedia networks are summarised in figure 5.

Network	Throughput	Classification
FDDI	100 Mbits/Sec	Local Area Network
DQDB	upto 100 Mbits/Sec	Metropolitan Area Network
Basic Rate ISDN	64 KBits/Sec	Wide Area Network
Primary Rate ISDN	2 MBits/Sec	Wide Area Network
Broadband ISDN	155 MBits/Sec	Wide Area Network

Figure 5 High Performance Networks

Networking technology is increasing at a rapid rate but there is still a long way to go before such networks can provide support for sophisticated forms of multimedia cooperation. The problems are most acute when considering the group interactions demanded by CSCW. Considerable research is also required in issues such as synchronisation of different multimedia channels and the integration of high performance protocols into multimedia workstations (Hopper, 1990).

The existing spectrum of communications technologies in distributed systems can be compared directly with the geographical nature CSCW systems (figure 6).

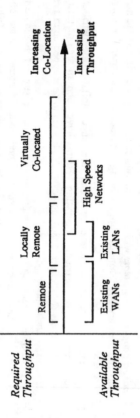

Figure 6 Geographic Dispersion Comparison

As in the case of cooperation distributed systems seem to provide good support for asynchronous cooperative systems. However, there are limitations with existing technology in supporting more synchronous styles of work. This is particularly true in CSCW applications supporting a high degree of co-location. Communication networks simply cannot cope with the logical 'bandwidth' demanded by this class of application. It is likely that high performance multimedia networks will have some impact on CSCW systems. The extent of this impact will depend on the development of protocols suitable for CSCW systems.

4. The Importance of Control

The previous sections have examined the styles of interaction and the geographical nature of both CSCW and distributed systems. However, a critical element is still missing from our discussion. The distinguishing feature of CSCW systems is their approach to representing and controlling cooperation. This section examines this issue in more depth. In effect, the authors see this issue as crucial to future success of CSCW systems.

4.1 CSCW and Control

People work together to solve a wide variety of problems using different forms of cooperation for each class of problem. Cooperative problems can be though of as existing at some point on a spectrum ranging from *unstructured* problems at one end to *prescriptive* tasks at the other. Unstructured problems are those requiring creative input from a number of users which often cannot be detailed or described in advance; software design is a good example of such an activity. Prescriptive tasks, on the other hand, represent the routine procedural cooperative mechanisms used to solve problems which have existing group solutions. Prescriptive tasks respond well to detailed control of cooperation while unstructured problems require a significant degree of freedom to be exercised by the cooperative system.

The amount of control provided by cooperative systems is an additional means of classifying cooperative systems. This classification is significant in that it highlights the level of automation each cooperative system provides.

CSCW systems exhibit two major forms of control, *explicit* or *implicit* control. In systems which provide explicit control users may both view and tailor group interaction and cooperation. In contrast, systems exhibiting implicit control provide no techniques for representing or coordinating group interaction. These systems dictate cooperation by the styles of interaction they allow.

A simple classification of the representation and control of cooperation in CSCW systems yields five classes of system.

i) Speech act or conversation based systems
Speech act systems apply a linguistic approach to computer supported cooperation based on speech act theory which considers language as a series of actions. Cooperation is represented and controlled within this class of system using some form of network structure detailing the patterns of message exchange. Speech Act theory has been forms the basis of several computer systems including the Coordinator system (Winograd, 1987) and the CHAOS project (De Cindio, 1986).

ii) Office procedure systems
Office procedures describe tasks performed within an office in terms of the combined effect of a number of small sub-tasks or procedures. Research has concentrated on developing languages which allow the specification of office procedures and a description of their interaction. This class of system is characterised by the use of a procedural language to describe and control cooperation by defining roles and activities. Approaches of this form include the AMIGO (Danielson, 1986) and COSMOS (Wilbur, 1988) projects.

iii) Semi-formal active Message systems
Semi-formal or active message systems provide supportive mechanisms for automatic message handling including the concepts of roles and autonomous agents. Systems of this form include the OBJECT LENS (Malone, 1988), the Strudel project (Sheperd 90), and the ISM system (Rodden, 1991)

iv) Conferencing systems
Conferencing systems provide basic control mechanisms which are minimal and fixed within applications. In traditional conferencing systems this takes the form conferences and moderators who control the addition of information to these topics. In real time conferencing systems control centres around the floor control mechanism imbedded in the conferencing application which dictates who has access to a shared conference space at any given time.

v) Peer-group meeting or Control free systems
Peer meeting systems such as the Colab system (Stefik, 1987a) deliberately do not provide any control mechanisms and rely on the meeting participants to formulate their own meeting protocols. All users have equal status and may amend and use the systems freely. In turn the systems keeps no track of the nature or form of group work being undertaken and provide limited support for these work processes.

The first three classes listed above are all examples of systems which exhibit *explicit* control allowing the representation and editing of control information. In contrast, conferencing and control free systems are *implicit* control systems which contain no representation of control.

4.2 Control requirements for CSCW

CSCW encompasses a wide range of control techniques. In many ways this is to be expected; CSCW is essentially about supporting the rich patterns of inter-personal cooperation. This richness should be reflected in the provision of control within CSCW systems, and the underlying technology should support rather than constrain this process. This latter point highlights the importance of the relationship between CSCW and distributed systems design. It is difficult to derive precise requirement from the list of control techniques presented above. However, some important observations can be made:

- The organisational context of the work needs to be captured.
- The many different forms of cooperation need to co-exist.
- The structure and organisation of groups need to be explicitly recognised.
- Groups work in dynamic and unexpected ways and are themselves dynamic
- Control should be enabling rather than constraining

Collectively these issues demand a *user-centred* approach to the control of cooperation within CSCW systems. This poses fairly fundamental questions for distributed system designers and highlights significant deficiencies in existing technology.

4.3 Supporting Control in Distributed Systems

Traditionally, distributed systems have taken a *systems-oriented* approach to control. They view control as dealing with the problems of distribution and masking such problems from applications (*distribution transparency*). Unfortunately this focus on transparency has tended to re-inforced the bottom-up development of distributed systems. For example, consider the problem of shared access to resources. In most distributed systems this is dealt with by masking out the existence of other users. Hence sharing is transparent with each user unaware of the activity of others. This clearly contradicts the needs of CSCW.

Recent work on distributed systems has clarified the meaning of the term distribution transparency (ANSA, 1989). Distribution transparency is now seen as a collective name for the masking out of various features of a distributed computation. In effect, there are a number of individual transparencies corresponding to each of these features (figure 7).

Transparency	Central Issue	Result of Transparency
Location	The location of an object in a distributed environment	User unaware of the location of services
Access	The method of access to objects in a distributed system	All objects are accessed in the same way
Migration	The re-location of an object in a distributed environment	Objects may move without the user being aware
Concurrency	Shared access to objects in a distributed environment	Users do not have to deal with problems of concurrent access
Replication	Maintaining copies of an object in a distributed environment	System deals with the consistency of copies of data
Failure	Partial failure in a distributed environment	Problems of failure are masked from the user

Figure 7 The Forms of Transparency in Distributed Systems

The prevalent view in distributed computing is to implement each of these transparencies to mask out *all* the problems of a distributed system. This is particularly true in the distributed operating system community. The problem with this approach is that presumed control decisions are embedded into the system and hence cannot be avoided or tailored for specific classes of application. This is the root of the problem in supporting CSCW. Because of the dynamic requirements of CSCW applications, it is very unlikely that such prescribed solutions will be suitable.

It is important to consider alternatives to this complete distribution transparency. System designers are currently aware of the problems that can be caused by full distribution transparency. Consequentially, a number of alternative approaches have already been explored:

i) Non-transparency

In non-transparent systems, all the features of distribution are visible to the programmer. They must therefore deal directly with issues such as failure and migration. This allows more flexibility since individual applications can deal with the management of objects in a distributed environment. However, the handling of distribution can become an intolerable burden on the programmer.

ii) Selective Transparency

Selective transparency allows the application developer to opt for transparency or non-transparency for each of the issues in distributed computing (figure 7). It is therefore possible to have location and access transparency, for example, but request non-transparency for the other issues. This approach provides some of the flexibility required for CSCW applications, however, existing solutions do not include user selection.

None of these provide complete solutions to the problem of controlling CSCW applications. The option of transparent control is too prescriptive for the needs of CSCW applications. However, the alternative of non-transparency imposes too high a burden on application developers. Selective transparency does appear more promising but does not address the fundamental user issues within control in cooperative working. CSCW demands a fresh approach to control which is specifically tailored for cooperative working. There has been very little work in this area. However, it is possible to identify a number of features of such an approach.

i) Clean separation of mechanisms and policies

The first requirement for control in CSCW applications is that there should be a clean separation between the mechanisms required for distribution management and the policies which govern the use of these mechanisms. To appreciate this distinction, consider the case of migration. There is a clear distinction between the ability to move an object (the mechanism) and the decisions about when the object should be moved and to which site (the policy). Distributed systems can provide the mechanisms required to manage distribution leaving higher level authorities to impose the policy. This separation of concerns is implicit in both non-transparency and selective transparency.

ii) Tailored Mechanisms

Current mechanisms have been developed in the classical bottom-up tradition of distributed systems. Such mechanisms may not be suitable for the particular semantics of CSCW applications. It is therefore important to consider existing mechanisms for the various transparencies and whether they are suitable for the demands of CSCW. Returning to the discussion of section 4.1 mechanisms delimit the *implicit control* exhibited by CSCW systems. A single set of mechanisms is unlikely to be suitable for all manifestations of implicit control in CSCW applications and the co-existence of a range of mechanisms needs to be considered.

iii) Tailored Policies

Distribution policies provide the representation necessary for *explicit control* in CSCW systems. It is important that these policies meet the control requirements identified in 4.2. It is equally important that policies can be tailored to allow support across the range of explicit control techniques identified in section 4.1. The provision of the policies will require input from all areas of CSCW. It is important to avoid these policies overly inhibiting the cooperation of users. As described in (Armstrong, 1990) when considering good practice in management science: "Policies are both restrictive and permissive at once. They spell out the limits to actions, but at the same time they give freedom to act within the limits specified".

5. A Case Study in Control: Distributed Transactions

Transaction mechanisms are concerned with the maintenance of consistency in a distributed system (Spector, 1989). In particular, they deal with concurrent access to data and partial failure of the system. Traditional approaches to distributed computing. More specifically, transaction mechanisms realise both concurrency and failure transparency, masking out problems associated with these features of a distributed system. Transparency is achieved by *prescribing* the following principles:-

i) serialisability

Transactions handle concurrent access to shared information by enforcing a regime where concurrent operations are allowed only if their combined effect is equivalent to a serial sequence of operations.

ii) recoverability

Systems recoverability is supported by the creation of a set of consistent *snapshops* which can be returned to in the event of failure. Effectively, this allows transaction to be undone if an error occurs.

The provision of both serialisability and recoverability has been examined in detail and a wide range of algorithms have been proposed (Kohler, 1981). The general approach adopted is to restrict access to data by *locking* out other operations. This gives the impression of shared access being carried out in isolation. The problem with this approach is that it embeds one particular view of cooperation. This is unacceptable for CSCW giving the rich patterns of cooperation identified above (section 4.1). For example, consider the case of a co-authoring system. If a group member is updating a section of text, then it might make sense for an interested colleague to "read over their shoulder". This would not be supported by a simple locking strategy.

Several researchers have started to focus on transactions for group working (Ellis, 1989). This research is still at an early stage. However, some interesting results are starting to emerge. For example, a paper by Skarra (Skarra, 1988) challenges traditional transaction models and proposes an alternative approach more

closely tailored for group work. They explicitly identify the notion of a *transaction group* which co-ordinates access to shared data for a number of co-operating members. Within a transaction group, the notion of serialisability is replaced by access rules based on the semantics of the cooperation. Access rules provide the *policy* of cooperation as discussed in the previous section. Policies can thus be *tailored* for a particular application by amending access rules.

Transaction are symptomatic of the mismatch between distributed systems platforms and CSCW systems. It is clear that traditional approaches to transactions are not well suited to group work and hence many group applications have chosen to by-pass the system support. This places unacceptable burdens on developers of CSCW systems. It is therefore important to continue the work on group transactions and to identify suitable user-centred mechanisms and policies. Similar examinations are required across the field of distributed systems.

6. Concluding Remarks

Existing distribution technology currently has shortfalls in supporting CSCW systems both in terms of the cooperation between users and the geographic nature of these users. However, it is possible to see how particular shortfalls can be overcome by current developments in technology, e.g. high speed networks. More seriously, the traditional approach to control in distributed systems seems to be inadequate. It is difficult to foresee how distribution transparency can provide the highly flexible and tailorable facilities needed to represent the process of cooperation within CSCW applications.

The provision of appropriate facilities will almost certainly require a careful re-examination of distributed systems architectures and the provision of control within these architectures. It is important to avoid prescriptive and often unsuitable solutions to issues such as migration, concurrency and failure. Rather, both the mechanisms and policies of distribution should be tailored more closely to the demands of group working. This raises some fundamental and, as yet, unresolved questions:-

i) what are the most suitable *mechanisms* to support group working,
ii) what are the appropriate control *policies* for CSCW, and
iii) how are cooperation and control *represented* in CSCW systems?

A solution to these problems will require a detailed understanding of *both* the behaviour of distributed systems and the behaviour of interacting user groups. This problem therefore illustrates the inherently cross-disciplinary nature of CSCW research. The problem compounded further by the fact that existing distributed systems already provide adequate support for a range of applications. It is important that distributed systems continue to support these applications and any mechanisms for supporting CSCW systems need to smoothly integrate with these existing distributed applications.

7. References

ANSA (1989): *ANSA: An Engineer's Introduction*, Release TR.03.02, Architecture Projects Management Limited. November 1989.

Armstrong, M (1990): "Management Processes and Functions", in Armstrong, M., Farnham, D. (eds): *Management Studies Series*, ISBN 0 85292 438 0.

Bannon, L., Schmidt, K (1991): "CSCW: Four Characters in Search of Context", in J.M. Bowers and S.D. Benford (eds): *Studies in Computer Supported Cooperative Work. Theory, Practice and Design*, North-Holland, Amsterdam, 1991, pp 3-17.

Birman, K., and K. Marzullo.(1989): "ISIS and the META Project." *Sun Technology No.: Summer*, Pages: 90-104.

Conklin, J (1987): "gIBIS: A Hypertext Tool for Team Design Deliberation", *Proceeding of Hypertext 87*, November 1987,pp 247-251.

Crowley, T., Milazzo, P., Baker E., Forsdick H., Tomlinson R.(1990):"MMConf: An Infrastructure for Building Shared Multimedia Applications", *in proceedings of CSCW 90*, Los Angeles, CA, October 7-10 1990, ACM press , ISBN 0-89791-402-3.

Danielson, T., Panoke-Babatz, U., et al. (1986): "The AMIGO project: Advanced Group Communication Model for Computer-based Communication Environment", *in proceedings of CSCW 86*,Austin,Texas,December 1986.

De Cindio, F., De Michelis, G., et al (1986): " CHAOS as a Coordinating Technology", *in proceedings of CSCW 86*, Austin, Texas, December 1986.

Ellis, C.A., Gibbs.SJ. (1989): "Concurrency Control in Groupware Systems." *ACM SIGMOD International Conference on the Management of Data*, SIGMOD Record, Pages: 399-407.

Hahn, U., Jarke, M., Kreplin, K.et al.(1991): "CoAuthor: A Hypermedia Group Authoring Environment", in J.M. Bowers and S.D. Benford (eds): *Studies in Computer Supported Cooperative Work. Theory, Practice and Design*, North-Holland, 1991, pp 79-100.

Hopper, A. (1990): "Pandora - An Experimental System for Multimedia Applications", *ACM Operating Systems Review*, Vol. 24, No. 2, April 1990.

Jones, M.B. and R.F Rashid. (1986): "Mach and Matchmaker: Kernel and Language Support for Object-Oriented Distributed Systems." *Proceedings of the Conference on Object-Oriented Programming Systems, Languages and Applications (OOPSLA '86);*, Portland, Oregon, 1986. Editor: N. Meyrowitz, Special Issue of ACM SIGPLAN Notices, Vol: 21, Pages: 67-77.

Kohler, W.H (1981): "A Survey of Techniques for Synchronisation and Recovery in Decentralsied Computer Systems". *ACM Computer Surveys*, Vol. 13, No. 2, June 1981.

Kraemer, K L, Kling, J L (1988): "Computer Based Systems for Cooperative Work and Group Decision Making". *ACM Computing Surveys*, Vol 20, No 2, June 1988.

Lauwers, J.C., Lantz, K.A. (1990): "Collaboration Awareness in Support of Collaboration Transparency: Requirements for the Next Generation of Shared Window Systems", *Proceedings of CHI '90* Seattle, Washington April 1-5, 1990, ACM press, ISBN-0-201-50932-6.

Malone, T W, Lai, K (1988): "Object Lens: A Spreadsheet for Cooperative Work", *in proceedings of CSCW 88*, Portland, Oregon, September 1988.

Mullender, S.J., and A.S. Tanenbaum. (1986): "The Design of a Capability-Based Distributed Operating System." *The Computer Journal* Vol: 29 No.: 4, pp 289-299.

Rodden T., Sommerville I. (1991): "Building Conversations using Mailtrays", in J.M. Bowers and S.D. Benford (eds): *Studies in Computer Supported Cooperative Work. Theory, Practice and Design*, North-Holland, Amsterdam, 1991, pp 79-100.

Sarin, S., Grief, I.(1985): "Computer-Based Real time Conferencing Systems", *IEEE Computer* October 1985, pp 33- 45.

Schmidt, K. (1989): "Cooperative Work: A Conceptual Framework", FCI Publication #89-1, The Informatics Centre of the Danish Trade Union Movement, June 1989, ISBN 87-89369-00-9.

Sheperd A, Mayer N., Kuchinsky A. (1990): "Strudel- An Extensible Electronic Conversation Toolkit", *in proceedings of CSCW 90*, Los Angeles, CA, October 7-10 1990, ACM press , ISBN 0-89791-402-3.

Shoch, J.F., Y.K. Dalal, D.D. Redell, and R.C. Crane.(1982): "Evolution of the Ethernet Local Computer Network." *IEEE Computer*, August 1982. Pages: 10-26.

Skarra, A.H. (1988): "Concurrency Control for Cooperating Transactions in an Object-Oriented Database." *Proceedings of the ACM SIGPLAN Workshop on Object-Based Concurrent Programming*, San Diego. September. Editor: Gul Agha, Peter Wegner and Akinori Yonezawa, SIGPLAN Notices, Pages: 145-147.

Spector, A. (1989):"Distributed Transaction Processing Facilities", in Mullender, S. (ed):, *Distributed Systems*, Addison-Wesley, New York, 1989.

Stefik M, Bobrow D.G., et al. (1987b): "WYSIWIS Revised: Early Experiences with Multiuser Interfaces", *ACM transactions on Office Information Systems*, Vol 5, No 2, April 1987, pp 147-168.

Stefik M., Foster G., et al. (1987a): "Beyond the Chalkboard: Computer Support for Collaboration and Problem Solving in Meetings", *Communications of the ACM* Vol 30, No 1, January 1987.

Tanenbaum, A.S., and R.V. Renesse, (1985): "Distributed Operating Systems." *ACM Computer Surveys* Vol: 17 No.: 4, December 1985, Pages: 419-470.

Watabe K., Sakata S, Maeno K et al. (1990): ' Distributed Multiparty Desktop Conferencing System: MERMAID', *in proceedings of CSCW 90*, Los Angeles, CA, October 7-10 1990, ACM press , ISBN 0-89791-402-3.

Wilbur S.B., Young R.E.(1988): "The COSMOS Project : A Multi-Disciplinary Approach to Design of Computer Supported Group Working", in R. Speth(ed): *EUTECO 88: Research into Networks and Distributed Applications*, Vienna, Austria, April 20-22,1988.

Winograd T. (1987): "A Language/Action Perspective on the Design of Cooperative Work", Stanford University Department of Computer Science Technical Report, STAN-CS-87-1158.

Part III
Asynchronous Groupware

Having completed our presentation of background material to aid the understanding of group processes and groupware technologies, we can now examine specific classes of these technologies, the ways in which they are used, and some impacts of their use. We begin with the class that has to date achieved the greatest prominence and the greatest success—asynchronous groupware. We divide the space of approaches into three categories:

- Electronic mail and computer conferencing systems

- Systems that support structured messaging, agents, and workflow management

- Cooperative hypertext and organizational memory systems.

We begin in Chapter 7 with *electronic mail (e-mail)*, arguably the most successful form of groupware to date. Typically, electronic mail begins as a substitute for traditional, physical mail ("snail mail"), in that messages are directed at a single individual or very small number of individuals. When messages are directed at large numbers of individuals who belong to a group, or at a large number of individuals who share a common inter-est, the nature of the communications process and the technology usage changes. Such systems, also discussed in Chapter 7, are then known as *computer conferencing* or *electronic bulletin board* systems.

The dramatic success of e-mail has also led to a number of problems such as an overabundance of e-mail and electronic "junk mail." *Structured messaging systems* represent an attempt to provide users with better methods of organizing, classifying, filtering, and managing messages. One goal of these efforts may be viewed as the creation of "intelligent" messaging systems in which useful tasks are delegated to computer processes typically known as *agents*. In some cases the role of messages is to define, embody, and manage *workflows* in a corporation. Chapter 8 discusses these approaches.

In both Chapters 7 and 8, the focus is on the process of messaging and on messages that define process. Yet sometimes applications focus instead on the corpus of messages or other computer documents and their interrelationships. They may then best be described as *cooperative hypertext systems*, in which a web of complex information is recorded and structured into a hypertext. Applications of such systems include collaborative knowledge building, asynchronous collaborative writing, and *organizational memory*. These approaches are the topic of Chapter 9.

Electronic Mail and Computer Conferencing

The most pervasive groupware technology developed to date is that of electronic mail. The short "A Lesson in Electronic Mail" by Robert Sproull (1991), an Appendix excerpted from *Connections* by Lee Sproull and Sara Kiesler (1991a), helps us understand how networking and communications technology can be applied to allow the creation, storage, transmission, and retransmission of messages. After sketching issues of *access*, *naming*, *transport*, and *interface*, he then lists six key characteristics of electronic mail:

- E-mail is asynchronous

- E-mail is fast

- E-mail is text-based

- E-mail can be addressed to multiple receivers

- E-mail has a built-in external memory

- The external memory can be processed by computer.

He closes by using these characteristics to compare electronic mail to face-to-face meetings, the telephone, a letter, a telex, a facsimile, and voice mail.

Sproull's paper briefly mentions the use of electronic mail for group communications. The original intent of electronic mail was to facilitate point-to-point communication very much in the spirit of conventional postal mail, although with greater speed. Because e-mail can be addressed to multiple receivers, the identical base technology can also facilitate communication among and discussion by groups or networks of individuals. This technology, variously known as *computer conferencing systems* or as *electronic bulletin boards*, organizes user access and message transmission by topic or time rather than by the names of individual recipients. Bulletin board messages are usually organized by *time*; the emphasis is on the broadcasting of information to a community where there may be interest. Conferencing system messages are usually organized by *topic*; the emphasis is on the dialogue that is facilitated among members of a community. "Computer-Mediated Communication Requirements for Group Support" is by one of the pioneers of computer conferencing, Murray Turoff (1991). Turoff begins (in an excerpt omitted from this volume due to space limitations) by reviewing the history of the technology, emphasizing the unique contributions of each important early system in the 70s and the 80s. From this perspective, he synthesizes a number of design principles which are necessary for a *computer-mediated communications (CMC) system* to enable a group to exhibit "collective intelligence." He closes by outlining the design of recent CMC systems developed by his group which leverage their 20 years of experience building such systems.

"Increasing Personal Connections," an excerpt from *Connections* by Sproull and Kiesler (1991a), focuses on the role of electronic communication in increasing the informational and emotional connections of employees, particularly those who are "peripheral," that is, geographically and hierarchically distant from the center of things. The authors show how passive connections (receiving information) can provide a "window on the corporation" and how active connections (sending information) can give "a voice for the voiceless." After discussing the role of electronic discussion groups, they hypothesize that electronic communication may provide greater benefits for peripheral employees than for centrally-located employees because the latter already know more and are more active in the corporation.

Concrete evidence on the nature and role of electronic group mail in organizations is provided in Finholt and Sproull (1990). Group behavior in organizations is described in terms of group attributes, such as physical settings, member characteristics, and membership criteria; the resulting group processes of *interaction*, *influence attempts*, and *identity membership*; and organizational consequences of *participation*, *performance*, and *learning*. Hypotheses about the impacts of electronic communication on group processes and organizational consequences are studied by examining 1248 messages, 985 of which were distribution list messages, sent to 96 employees in a Fortune 500 office products firm over a 6-week period. Distribution lists included those required for work, work-related discretionary lists, and extracurricular discretionary lists. Analysis of the messages showed that the electronic groups exhibited the group processes of interaction, influence, and identity.

Additional evidence for "increasing personal connections" through electronic communication is provided by "Work Group Structures and Computer Support: A Field Experiment" by Eveland and Bikson (1988). Two matched groups consisting both of active workers and retirees spent a year planning a company's retirement policy. One task force had the option of using electronic communication; the second task force did not. The electronically supported group developed a structure significantly different from that developed by the one not using e-mail, achieving greater breadth of access and opportunity to participate as well as to be a leader.

The group using e-mail maintained a significantly higher degree of contact than did the control group, and experienced considerably more involvement in the work of the group and significantly less communication isolation.

Notes and Guide to Further Reading

Tanenbaum (1988) provides more detail on the technology of e-mail. A good source to begin the study of the use and impacts of electronic mail and computer conferencing is the book by Sproull and Kiesler (1991a; see also Kiesler, 1986, and Sproull and Kiesler, 1991b), from which we have provided two excerpts above. Other chapters of the Sproull and Kiesler book cover issues such as the coordinating effects of computer-mediated communications (CMC), "electronic etiquette" in CMC, changes in group dynamics between face-to-face meetings and electronic meetings, and the problems of authority, control, and influence that arise through the use of CMC.

Problems of authority and control are highlighted in a paper by Perin (1991), who shows how CMC can create *electronic social fields* that challenge and stress conventional bureaucratic structures within organizations. A classic case of this documented by Zuboff (1988, Ch. 10) is that of "DrugCorp," where enthusiastic use of CMC for "access to information, thoughtful dialogue, and social banter" seriously threatened management when the content of supposedly *closed* conferences became public knowledge. The result was the demise of the vitality of the system (Zuboff, 1988, p. 363):

> Managers' critical and sometimes punitive attitude had stung the more innovative participants in the system and gradually succeeded in shifting the emphasis of the new medium from one of inquiry and dialogue to one of perfunctory messages and routine electronic mail.

Other important papers from a decade of social science research on e-mail and conferencing led by Sara Kiesler and Lee Sproull are Kiesler, Siegel, and McGuire (1984), Sproull and Kiesler (1986), and Finholt, Sproull, and Kiesler (1990). An interesting recent review paper is "Group Decision Making and Communication Technology" by Kiesler and

Sproull (1992), which summarizes a body of experiments on the impact of electronic mail (broadly defined) on individuals, groups, and organizations. They begin by distinguishing between *first-level effects* of technology, such as planned efficiency or productivity gains, and *second-level effects*, such as enabling people to do things that were impossible or infeasible without the new technology. They contrast modern technology-based communications with face-to-face communications, and discuss how social context cues are typically attenuated through communications technology. They then present a summary of seven experiments on computer-mediated small group decision making, which typically show longer decision times, more equal participation, more difficult consensus-building processes, and more willingness to choose risky options than is the case in face-to-face meetings. After cautioning the reader that their results may not scale up to large groups in real contexts, they conclude with a discussion of the appropriateness of decision making using CMC.

The extensive research on computer conferencing systems carried out at the New Jersey Insitute of Technology is reviewed in Hiltz and Turoff (1978), Hiltz and Turoff (1981), Kerr and Hiltz (1982), and Hiltz (1984). Hiltz and Turoff (1985) discuss the problem of information overload that often arises in CMC. Other results on electronic communications and on its uses and effects include Fanning and Raphael (1986), Eveland and Bikson (1987), Mackay (1989), and Fafchamps, Reynolds, and Kuchinsky (1991). An interesting study of conferencing in a text-based *virtual reality* environment is Curtis (1992). Brothers, Hollan, Stornetta, Abney, Furnas, Littman, and Nielson (1992) explore *ephemeral interest groups* as a means of supporting informal communication (see also Hollan and Stornetta, 1991, included in Chapter 13 of this volume).

The commercial use of electronic mail is expanding rapidly. Rosall (1992) cites data indicating that, as of the end of 1991, the worldwide count of the most popular e-mail applications worldwide was: DEC All-in-1, 3.5 million users; IBM Office Vision/Profs, 1.5 million users; Lotus cc-Mail, 1.5 million users; Microsoft MS Mail, 1.4 million users; and Verimation, 1.2 million users. Increasingly, there are now *gateways* between systems making use of the *X.400* communications standard (Rosall, 1992). Another trend is toward the *mail enabling* of existing applications (Smith, 1992), through which programs can create and send "messages" to other applications as easily as they can now create and store documents in file systems. Wolfe (1992) discusses the provision of an electronic mail and collaboration infrastructure as part of Apple's *Open Collaborative Environment (OCE)* for the Macintosh.

The last decade has also seen increasing interest in the use of electronic mail and computer conferencing in the classroom. Good sources to begin studying this phenomenon are the papers by Hiltz and her collaborators on the *virtual classroom* (Hiltz, 1986, 1988; Hiltz, Shapiro, and Ringsted, 1990); the book edited by Mason and Kaye (1989), which focuses on the use of CMC for distance education; the special issue edited by Koschmann (1992), which looks more broadly at computer-supported cooperative learning; and the volume edited by Waggoner (1992).

Ehrlich (1987a, b) presents some early results on the introduction of voice mail. A more recent study is documented in Rice and Shook (1990) and Rice and Steinfield (1991, in press). Resnick (1992) presents a set of software tools for constructing phone-based cooperative work applications. Hindus and Schmandt (1992) discuss the use in collaborative work applications of conversation that has not been understood by a machine, but which has been processed in order to derive some of the structure of the utterance, which they call *semi-structured audio*.

Of particular interest in Rice and Steinfield (1991, in press) is a method of characterizing communication media in terms of four dimensions of media attributes:

- *Constraints*, such as limits on message length, ability to store the message, ability to reprocess the message, anonymity, and privacy

- *Bandwidth*, including the ability to represent gestures or *paralinguistics* (such as tone and volume), and the ability to convey social presence and information richness

- *Interaction*, such as quickness of response, and control over the pace of the reception and the sequencing of the messages and replies

- *Network factors*, such as whether the communication is one-to-one, one-to-many, few-to-few, or many-to-many, and whether critical mass is required for success.

Reprinted from L. Sproull, L. and S. Kiesler, *Connections: New Ways of Working in the Networked Organization*, pp. 177-184. © 1991, The MIT Press. Reprinted with permission.

A Lesson in Electronic Mail

By Robert F. Sproull

Electronic communication technology uses computer text processing and communication tools to provide a high-speed information exchange service. Anyone with a computer account can create and send information to anyone who has a mailbox on that computer or on any other computer to which it is connected through a computer network. The networked computers might be physically proximate and connected to a local area network, or they might be in different states, countries, or continents and connected via long-distance telecommunications that form a permanent network or a transient dial-up link. Depending on software sophistication, the mailed information can be a message, a document, a computer program, statistical data, or even a collection of organized messages—a computer discussion—forwarded from some other mailbox. At the recipient's convenience, he or she can read the information, edit it, save it, delete it, move it to another computer file, and/or reply to the sender.

Access

The utility of an electronic mail system depends heavily on who has access to it and how convenient the access is. If only a few people have access to the system, it won't serve an appreciable fraction of anyone's communication needs and may become an unused curiosity. Barriers to use arise if people have to share computer terminals, or walk "to the computer room" to get access, or learn a complex set of instructions to send and receive mail. Electronic mail can be as convenient and uninhibiting as picking up the telephone, or it can be one more piece of office drudgery.

For people who already have terminals on their desks, electronic mail can be offered as one of the services available on the terminal. Whether these

terminals connect to large computers or are part of personal computers, they can all deliver the mail.

An initial implementation of electronic mail often identifies clusters of users who already have computer access for another purpose and equips their computers with sufficient software and communication capabilities to send and receive mail. This user group can then be grown by offering mailboxes to new users, perhaps with incentives for joining. Deciding on a rate of growth and corresponding expense is one of the key parts of designing an organization's electronic mail system.

Naming

Each electronic mail message must name precisely the mailbox to which it is destined. It would be nice to use names like "John Smith," but names are rarely unique, and the electronic mail system has insufficient information to resolve ambiguities properly. Some systems assign a unique number to each mailbox, just as a unique number is assigned to each telephone line, but this technique forces each sender to remember or look up mailbox numbers in a directory and gives people the impression they are just numbers to a computer—hardly conducive to smooth communication. A better solution is to add addresses to names, much the way addresses are placed on envelopes, so that the name and address together identify a unique mailbox. For example, "John Smith at Computer Science at Carnegie Mellon University" may suffice to identify a unique mailbox and to give the electronic mail system enough information to transport the message from the sender to the recipient. (Issues surrounding naming and addressing in electronic mail are much more complex than this discussion implies. Devising a scheme that can gracefully handle worldwide use by millions of people has taxed the committees setting electronic mail standards. Supporting "white pages" directory services for millions of users is especially challenging.)

Transport

How is electronic mail delivered from a sender to one or more receivers? There are two basic methods and combinations of them.

At one extreme, all electronic mail terminals communicate with a single computer, where the electronic mail software runs. A person signs on to the computer and uses the software to compose a message or to read messages from a disk file that serves as a mailbox. For delivery, the text of the message is simply copied into the recipient's mailbox file. Because all mailboxes are on the same computer, a message can be routed to anyone just by copying it to the proper mailbox. If the users of such a system are geographically distant, telecommunications must be used to link the terminal to the single "mail computer." Commercial electronic mail systems, such as CompuServe, operate essentially in this way.

At the other extreme, each person operates a separate computer, which runs electronic mail software and holds on its disk a single mailbox file for its user. To send a message to another person, the computer uses a computer-to-computer communications network and an associated electronic mail protocol to transport the message text from the sender's computer to the receiver's computer and thence into the receiver's mailbox. Alternatives to a network are also possible, such as dedicated communications links between computers used only for electronic mail traffic or dial-up links that are used only when mail transmission is required.

In practice, electronic mail systems usually operate between the two extremes. A local group of users will all have mailboxes on one computer and can send mail to each other by simply copying messages directly into mailboxes. Messages for distant users are transported through the computer network to the computer where the recipient's mailbox is located. Each local site has such a computer, holding mailboxes for all local users. These computers are linked via a network in order to transport mail from one local site to another. If a site's computer becomes overloaded, a new computer can be added to the network to share the load at the site.

Today electronic mail systems cannot always send mail to other electronic mail systems because software from different vendors uses different formats and conventions. Dissimilar systems can sometimes be connected by mail gateways, whereby one computer's mail system can format and deliver messages to a foreign system. For example, Digital's All-In-One mail system can send mail to a gateway that in turn sends the mail to IBM's SNADS mail system. Eventually the need for gateways will be obviated by using standard electronic mail protocols, a single set of rules for formatting messages that flow between computers, so that all computers use one format. A worldwide standard for this purpose, called X.400, *Recommendations for Message Handling Systems*, has been defined and is beginning to be implemented.

Different electronic mail systems also provide different facilities for ensuring privacy and security. The transport and storage of electronic mail messages can be as secure as sensitive military communications or as public as waving a banner at a football game. Encryption can be used to obtain security so that a message can be read only by the sender and receiver who know a secret code that scrambles and unscrambles the message. Today very few electronic mail systems will encrypt messages. A computer system's access controls, such as log-in procedures and passwords, may help ensure that a mailbox and other computer data are not accessed by other people. But many personal computers lack these controls; a night visitor can read anyone's mail. Facsimile machines also have poor security: the telephonic transmission is not secure, and the receiving machine may be accessible to many people. The rather poor state of electronic mail security is likely to improve only slowly; for now, people are concentrating on making mail easier to use for wider audiences.

Group Communication

Electronic mail transmits messages to individuals by copying messages to their personal electronic mailboxes. A single message will be copied to several mailboxes if the sender lists the name of each recipient explicitly. One message may also be delivered simultaneously to many mailboxes by sending the message to a group name or distribution list (DL)—for example, PC Users, Strategy Group, or Movie Reviews. The sender does not specify, or need to know, the names and addresses of group members. The computer automatically mails a copy of the communication, which is addressed to the group as a whole, to the personal mailbox of each group member. Electronic bulletin boards (bboards) and conferences transmit messages to a single named mailbox that is accessible to more than one person. The distinction between these forms of group communication is that in DLs, messages come to recipients' own mailboxes, intermixed with personal communications, whereas in bboards and conferences, people have to take a bit more initiative to find messages. Bboards and conferences differ from one another in that bboards simply display messages in chronological order as they are received; conferences group messages by topic and display grouped messages together.

Interface

A person sends and receives electronic mail by using a computer program designed to manage mail. These mail programs may provide only primitive mechanisms for sending and receiving mail, or they may offer a rich set of facilities. Here is a list of features sometimes found in these programs:

• Composing a message using a word processor or text editor. Other text files can be copied into the message. The mail program may check the names and addresses of recipients to detect typographical errors. The mail program dispatches the message.

• Extracting incoming mail from a mailbox and displaying a short summary of each message.

• Selecting one or more messages and displaying them on the terminal or printing them on a printer.

• Searching a mailbox or a set of saved messages by date, keyword, or sender's name.

• Deleting a message.

• Copying a message to a computer file for permanent storage or some other use.

• Replying to a message, using conventional message-preparation tools, but without having to specify the name of the recipient. Some systems allow one to reply by annotating the original message, distinguishing original and reply text.

• Displaying messages by category, such as name of sender or subject.

• Determining whether a message has been read by its recipient—a form of "return receipt requested."

• Finding mail addresses for individuals or groups in directory services.

• Maintaining a group list—for example, adding or removing a name from distribution lists.

• Directing a mail agent to process mail automatically—for example, to reply to each message received with a message announcing you are on vacation for two weeks.

Some of these features depend not only on the mail program but on features of the underlying mail system and mail transport protocols, such as distribution lists.

Social Features

Despite differences in particular implementations, electronic mail technologies share six characteristics that differentiate them socially from other communication technologies. First, electronic mail is asynchronous. Senders and receivers do not need to attend to the same communication at the same time. They can send and receive at their convenience. Asynchrony is not only a matter of personal convenience; it means communication crosses time as well as space. Although there are electronic communications programs for simultaneous communication ("TALK"), they are little used in organizations at present.

Second, electronic mail is fast. An electronic message can be transmitted in seconds or minutes down a hall, across a continent, or around the world. Replies can flow back just as rapidly. Speed is not just a matter of convenience either. Speed makes possible long-distance conversation, decision making, and almost any other interaction requiring give and take.

Third, electronic mail is text-based. Messages convey typographic characters, not video images or speech. Only a few of today's mail programs allow pictures or forms to be transmitted. The text in electronic communication makes it useful for exchanging documents, as well as messages. But more important, electronic communication looks pretty much alike no matter what is sent. It lacks social information and reminders of the social rules and statuses that usually regulate communication.

Fourth, electronic mail has multiple-receiver addressability: someone can send a message to one, twenty, or hundreds of people wherever they may be. This attribute means that without respect to physical, temporal, or social location, people can delegate work, collaborate, form new groups, and make collective decisions.

Fifth, electronic mail has built-in external memory. The contents of electronic messages can be stored and retrieved later. This property is important for social memory. For instance, people can participate in a group project over months or years and save in memory all of the interactions of the group. At any time, this group memory can be accessed by members who want to trace the history of an issue or by newcomers who want to learn about the group's activities.

Finally, the external memory is computer processable. It can be conveniently searched, edited, partitioned, and shared with others. This attribute extends the power of social memory by allowing analyses of issue trends, participation patterns, consensus points, and other social memory characteristics.

Other communication technologies have some of these attributes, as we show in table A.1, but the six attributes taken together comprise a unique and peculiarly social technology. We avoid considering cost as an attribute here because the assumptions one must make to compare costs are quite arbitrary. For instance, a face-to-face conversation is cheap—unless the parties are separated by a continent and must travel to their meeting place. An electronic network is typically expensive to install, but electronic mail is inexpensive to operate insofar as one considers the cost of an additional message or of putting an additional person on the network. Hence cost is closely tied to scale of use. Furthermore, many electronic networks are installed and maintained principally to support remote access to databases and processing power. In these settings, electronic mail adds function with relatively low marginal cost.

The explosion of facsimile machines in recent years provides an alternative to electronic mail, but one with quite different properties. Facsimile has some advantages over electronic mail: images of all sorts can be transmitted, and any fax machine can talk to any other fax machine because they are connected to the pervasive dial telephone network rather than to isolated computer networks and because they all transmit images in a compatible format. But today's facsimile lacks some important properties that we consider essential for electronic communication. The documents sent or received by facsimile are hard to manipulate: on a personal computer, one can't receive a facsimile document, add three sentences in one paragraph, revise a chart, reformat the results, and then send the revised document onward to a group of reviewers. Facsimile images are expensive to store and hard to search, edit, send to groups, or process by other computer programs (McCarthy 1989). And most fax images never make it into a computer; they are printed on paper and destroyed. Thus fax is convenient for one-time, one-to-one communication, especially when handwritten material or images are required, but it is not as good as electronic mail for collaborative or ongoing efforts. This is changing; improved image quality will allow techniques like optical character recognition to extract computer-processable text from facsimile messages, more personal computers will be outfitted with facsimile interfaces, and we can generally expect electronic mail and facsimile capabilities to fuse into a general form of computer-based communication.

References

McCarthy, J. (1989). Networks considered harmful for electronic mail. *Communications of the ACM*, 32 (12), 1389-1390.

Table A.1
Comparing communication on a computer network with other communication technologies

	Technology Attributes					
	Asynchrony	Fast	Text content only	Multiple address-ability	Externally recorded memory	Computer-processable memory
Meeting	no	yes[a]	no	yes	no[b]	no
Telephone	no	yes[a]	no	no[b]	no[b]	no
Letter	yes	no	no	no[b]	yes	no[c]
Telex	yes	yes	yes	no	yes	no[c]
Facsimile	yes	yes	no	no[b]	yes	no[c]
Voice mail	yes	yes	no	yes	no[b]	no
Electronic mail	yes	yes	yes	yes	yes	yes

a. Although conversation is instantaneous, meetings are fast only if people do not have to travel to the meeting place. Telephone conversations are fast only when both parties are simultaneously available to talk and don't have to play telephone tag.

b. Special actions can be taken to approximate the attribute in question. For example, memory can be provided by recording or transcribing meetings or telephone conversations. Voice messages can be stored. Multiple addressability is achieved with conference calls, certain facsimile machines that can be programmed to dial multiple telephone numbers, and letters that are copied and mailed to several people.

c. Special actions can be taken to improve retrieval properties of paper-based technologies. Vertical filing systems improve the retrievability of paper documents. Imaging systems that "annotate" facsimile images make the resulting documents easier to search. When facsimile or other image-handling technologies are integrated with computers, their retrievability capabilities approach those of electronic communication.

JOURNAL OF ORGANIZATIONAL COMPUTING, 1, 85–113 (1991)

Computer-Mediated Communication Requirements for Group Support (Excerpts)

Murray Turoff

New Jersey Institute of Technology

This article presents an overview of the historical evolution of computer-mediated communication (CMC) systems within the context of designing for group support. A number of examples of design features to support specific group tasks are illustrated. The result of this is the synthesis of a number of observations on the assumptions and goals for the design of CMC systems. An emphasis is placed on the advantages offered groups by asynchronous support of the communication process, self-tailoring of communication structures by users and groups, and the integration into the communication system of other computer resources and information systems. The systems that have been developed recently at New Jersey Institute of Technology (EIES2, TEIES, and Personal TEIES) are used to illustrate the translation of design objectives into specific features and functions.

---

computer-mediated communications,   groupware,   GDSS,
    CSCW,   computerized conferencing,   message systems,
        electronic meeting systems,   hypertext

"The mighty telescope looks afar.

But finds no place to park a car."

—Samuel Hoffenstein, *Pencil in the Air*

This article was originally an invited paper for the Conference on Organizational Computing with respect to Theories and Technologies for Computer Supported Work, held at the University of Texas, Austin, November 1989.

The work on the EIES2, TEIES, and Personal TEIES systems described in this report has been made possible by funding from a variety of sources, including the Annenberg/CPB Project, IBM, AT&T, Hewlett Packard, the N.J. Commission on Science and Technology, the N.J. Office of Telecommunications and Information Services, and the New Jersey Department of Higher Education.

Also, acknowledgment is due to Starr Roxanne Hiltz, James Whitescarver, and John Foster for their contributions to the thoughts in this article.

Correspondence and requests for reprints should be sent to Murray Turoff, Computerized Conferencing and Communications Center, New Jersey Institute of Technology, Newark, NJ 07102.

- The same interface that allows individuals to communicate with other individuals can also allow individuals to communicate with other computer and information resources. A communications-oriented interface is an ideal systemwide interface for accessing data bases and running analysis routines [38, 46].

- Both individual and group problem-solving requirements imply that one must integrate computer resources as part of the communication process for many real-world problem situations [38].

- Individuals and groups must be able to exercise a high degree of selective tailoring in using CMC systems [45].

- Groups evolve their use of the CMC systems, and the development of new facilities must be part of a planned feedback process [44].

- Human roles, and the computer support of human roles, are key factors in the success of group activities [15]. Providing system privileges that reflect the flexibility of human communication processes is essential to supporting human roles.

- The privacy and security (as well as reliability) of human communications are essential to the acceptance of the system [40].

- Information overload and the ability to deal with large user populations and large group size are the driving forces for the appropriate design of CMC systems [14].

- There are numerous difficult design trade-offs, in terms of conflicts in control and structure of communications. These conflicts revolve around differences in individual and group behavior and objectives in the communication process [40, 43].

- The appropriate metaphor in CMC systems for experienced users in a "list processing" one. A single communication is only one item in a set related to one or more tasks. Each task results in a list of relevant communications [46].

- The future of CMC systems lies in the degree of tailoring that is possible within a single interface metaphor and the degree of integration with other computer resources [46].

For example, one of the standard design exercises this author gives students is the design of a "group calendar." It gives students a difficult problem because it does not take them very long to realize that the issues of communication structure, and the control of communication structure within the group calendar are closely tied to organizational culture and norms. Under what conditions and who has access to what information? One cannot design a single system that would be acceptable across a wide range of organizations.

3.0 Asynchronous Group Operations.

Much of the current work in the area of groupware and GDSS is carried out under the chronic fallacious assumption that has always plagued the development of information systems: the presumption of automation. It is assumed that

2.0. ASSUMPTIONS FOR AND GOALS OF CMC SYSTEMS

Based on almost two decades of activity in the design and evaluation of CMC systems, the following conclusions are offered on desirable goals and objectives for future research and development for CMC, GDSS, Groupware, CSCW, EMS, Coordination Systems, or whatever jargon one wishes to use:

- The objective of a CMC system is to provide an opportunity for a group to exhibit "collective intelligence" [15]. This means that the results of the group communication process are better than the result any single member of the group could have obtained alone. Collective intelligence is a very significant objective, because it is measurable in real situations and across the use of different communication alternatives.

- A CMC system needs to support group communications 24 hours a day and offer the flexibility of being used synchronously or asynchronously [42]. Individuals do not deal with problems only when they meet together as a group. Nor do they operate, in most situations, as only one group. In real organizations, groups are very fluid in their nature, and the process is one of overlapping and intersecting subgroups.

- The benefits offered by CMC result from the ability to utilize the computer to tailor the communication structure to fit the nature of both the application and the group [38].

- Appropriate communication structures are extremely sensitive to group norms and organizational culture [11].

- Individuals have a great deal of leeway in organizations as to what mode of communication they will use for what purpose. Individuals and groups cannot be ordered to use CMC technology [11].

Figure 1.
Asynchronous Group Process Factors

1.1 Group Problem Solving

Process	Clarification
Orientation	of an issue
Recognition	of related considerations
Exploration	of a strategy or approach
Formulation	of specific ideas
Generation	
Evaluation	
Focusing	on an item
Specification	of an item
Introspection	evaluating an item
Review	considering the results
Solution	
Closure	completion of an item
Presentation	finalizing expression of results

1.2 Individual Problem Solving

Process	Clarification
Orientation	of an issue
Identification	of a consideration
Acquisition	of an item
Reformulation	Reduction and dividing
Segmentation	
Exploration	
Abstraction	developing a generality
Search	finding related items
Structuring	considering relationships
Interpretation	gaining an understanding
Conceptualization	arriving at a concept
Evaluation	
Induction	empirical extrapolation
Deduction	logical relationships
Analogical reasoning	by analogy
Creation	leaps of inference
Selection	making decisions or choices
Scaling	relative evaluation of items
Introspection	consistency evaluation

1.3 Meta Individual and Group Processes

Process	Clarification
Regulation	
Sequencing	of tasks
Iteration	to prior tasks
Synchronization	of group process
Participation	by group members
Tracking	of status of process
Assignment	of tasks

the best way to do something is the way it was originally done manually. Although that may be the easiest thing to sell, it has been demonstrated consistently that this is among the worst ways to design a system to gain the benefits that computerization can offer.

The most misunderstood concept in CMC systems is the view that an asynchronous (or nonsimultaneous) communication process is a problem, because it is not the sequential process that people use in the face-to-face mode. The approach of "How do we make CMC feel to the user like face-to-face processes?" is incorrect. The real issue is how do we use the "opportunity of asynchronous communications" to create a group process that is actually better than face-to-face group communications?

The primary advantage of using CMC to support group processes is not that people can engage in the process whenever it is convenient for them. It lies in the very fundamental asynchronous nature of the communication medium. Many of the current design philosophies are trying to maintain the sequential nature of the process that groups go through in face-to-face settings, and assuming this is the right way to go. Quite the contrary, the potential for real improvement in the group processes lies in the fact that individuals can deal with that part of the problem they can contribute to at a given time, regardless of where the other individuals are in the process.

The advantages of groups are that individuals with very different psychology, expertise, and resulting approaches to problem solving contribute their "differences" to the group problem. It is well known that different people approach complex problems from very different directions. The potential for the computer is in the ability to allow people to do this, and to integrate the results for the group as a whole. The recognition of this was at the core of most good Delphi designs, and was one of the reasons that the paper-and-pencil communication structures of Delphi produced many underlying insights that would not be expected to occur in face-to-face processes for the same ends.

Figure 1 is a collection of tables from many different sources [7, 10, 17, 18, 27, 30, 35, 36, 49, 52] of the factors, processes, and dimensions that can be involved in both individual and group problem-solving activity. Most real situations may involve only a much smaller portion of this morphology. For individuals, there is the natural tendency to approach a problem with those cognitive processes at which they excel. For groups, the problem, and the nature of the group and its leadership, dictates some selection of an appropriate sequence of problem solving.

The specification of a group process may very well be in conflict with the ways in which specific individuals can best contribute to dealing with the problem. The resulting opportunity for asynchronous approaches to group problem solving is to free the individual to deal with the problem in ways consistent with his or her cognitive style. The resulting challenge for design is the communication structures and facilities to allow for synchronization of the group process, and the organization of the material for the benefit of the group.

Another important observation is that, for each and every group or individual process, one can hypothesize possible computer-based tools and facilities

1.7 Outcome Variables

Variable	Clarification
Consensus	Degree of group agreement
Agreement	Match between individual view and group view
Quality	Goodness of results
Confidence	In the results
Comprehension	Of the results
Efficiency	Relative effort in arriving at result
Commitment	of members to group results
Satisfaction	with group process
	with technology
	with own performance
	with other individuals
	with group results
	with leadership

1.3 Cont.

Process	Clarification
Facilitation	
Organization	classification of material
Abstraction	developing generalities
Summarization	coding and abbreviation
Filtering	eliminating noise
Exposure	of hidden factors
Retrieving	of related material
Integration	modeling
Social-Emotional	
Socialization	Cooperation and friendship
Signaling & Cueing	of status
Consensus Formulation	of group results
Conflict Exploration	reasons for disagreements
Value Exposure	Interest conflict exploration
Conflict Resolution	resolving disagreements

1.4 Objects of Discourse

Object	Clarification
Problems, Issues, Questions	main concerns
Goals, Objectives, Plans	Normative formulations
Strategies, Policies, Agendas, Approaches	Solution management
Concerns, Criteria, Arguments, Assumptions, Viewpoints, Opinions, Values, Interests	Underlying factors
Consequences, Scenarios, Impacts	Evaluative factors
Tradeoffs, Compromises, Proposals, Solutions, Allocations, Decisions, Projects, Tasks	Possibilities

1.5 Dimensions of Human Communication

Factor	From	To
Cooperation	Cooperative, Friendly	Competitive, Hostile
Intensity	Intense, Engrossed	Superficial, Uninvolved
Dominance	Democratic, Equal	Autocratic, Unequal
Formality	Personal, Informal	Impersonal, Formal
Orientation	Productive, Task Oriented	Unproductive, No Objective

1.6 Other Intervening Factors

Factor	Clarification
Norms	Of group and organization
Values	Of individuals
Pressures	Status, biases, hidden agendas
Task type	The nature of the problem
Technology	Interface and facilities
Leadership	Type and quality
Density	Size, relationships
Group type	Cooperative, Negotiating, etc.

that might be an aid in that step of the process. Many of these are very dependent on the nature of the problem. Hence, we are driven to the concept of a "toolbox" metaphor for group support. The toolbox should be tailorable by the individual in his or her individual examination of a problem, and by those holding appropriate roles in the group dealing with the problem.

4.0. EIES2, TEIES, and PERSONAL TEIES

For the past three years at NJIT, we have been working on what we feel is a new generation of technology for CMC systems. Our design is based, in large part, on the experiences of the past two decades and the assumptions and goals we have formulated as a result of these experiences. The basic CMC metaphor we are utilizing is summarized in Figure 2.

Many of these objects should be clear to anyone who has had some experience with this technology. Our discussion will focus on those areas where there are new specifics in the functionality of a given object. Two of the concepts that are very new, not explicitly present in current CMC systems, are "notifications" and "activities." These will be discussed in some detail. The final discussion will be of some of the underlying technical factors that make the functionality we are incorporating feasible.

4.1. Conferences

The heart of the working space for a group is a conference or a set of conferences. There may be many different conferences for a group, each serving a slightly different subobjective. Some of the classical types of conferences that require unique forms of tailoring are listed next.

A conference, as a working space to meet a specific objective, can be structured in a number of ways. The resulting structure influences the efficiency of the conference communication facilities for reaching the specific conference objectives. The typical types of parameters that one can adjust and tailor when setting up a particular conference for a specific objective are the following:

• The memberships and roles of individual members are established and modified by the owner.
• Conference comments usually have a number of association and/or reply levels. For example, comment 24.5 would be the fifth reply to root comment 24. The owner of a conference should be able to specify the number of levels allowed and the size of the comments at each level. In a composition conference, fairly large comments are allowed. In a discussion conference, one wants to limit size to a few screens, because long comments break up the cognitive flow of the comments.
• In a composition conference, one should be able to restrict roles to fixed ranges of root comments. This way, one can assign selective composition and review responsibilities for different sections of a document.
• Determining the nature of the specific "activities" that occur in given conferences, when they should be activated, and who may activate them.
• The introduction of specific forms, to allow the gathering of structured information from members of the group and controlling the organization of the resulting data base.
• Specifying the degree of control on the incorporation of index keys.

The major mechanism for selective tailoring of the conference structure is the introduction of activities. By choosing the types of activities and when they are used, the owner or organizer of a conference has considerable flexibility, both in assigning what has to be done and in providing the ability of the group to track the progress of the effort.

4.2. Comment and Message Structure

The core of CMC systems is the communication objects that carry actual content between the members of a group or team. These are messages and conference comments. There are four distinct parts that can exist for a given message or comment. These are:

• *Abstract:* The abstract is all the status information associated with a message or comment. It includes:
—Name and identification of author and any modifier, and date and time item was created or modified.
—Identification of the item, size of item, number of replies, and pointers to related items.
—Title of the item, key words for indexing of item, and status with respect to attachments and/or activities.

Figure 2.
CMC Metaphor

Component	Explanation
Members	The users of the system
Personal Index	To track items
Roles	Privilege collections
Tickets	Privilege exceptions
Groups	Super members of the system
Membership List	Status of all members
Group Index	Shared by all members
Group Conference	Owned by group
Group Messages	Sent and received to group
Messages	Private, Group, and Public
Conferences	Topic communication space
Membership List	Status of all members
Conference Index	Comment keys
Comments	Entries in a conference
Directory	Of members, groups & conferences
Interest Index	Member interests & message sending key
Topic Index	Group and conference topics
Activities	Executable programs
Notifications	Transaction notices
Forms	Structured data collection
Attachments	File attachments
Lists	Collections of items (e.g. marked list)
Index Entries	
Reference Keys	pointers to items
Filters	Screening terms
Labels	Substitutions for commands or strings

• *General discussion:* Conferences structure to facilitate active participation by all members of a group or subgroup.
• *Tracking conferences:* Oriented to tracking events such as the status of a project, bug reports, etc.
• *Information exchange:* Oriented to organizing and categorizing information based on unpredictable inquiries and responses.
• *Planning conferences:* Oriented to structuring subjective viewpoints on complex situations.
• *Collaborative composition:* Oriented to structuring the creation of a document by a group of members.
• *Data collection and validation:* Organized to gather structured data, check the correctness of the data, and discuss the implications.
• *Games:* Use of role playing and event-oriented simulations for learning and exploring complex situations.
• *Training and education:* Use of Virtual Classroom™ structures for communications in a learning situation.

- *Content*: This is the actual content of the communication item. In most CMC systems, members are able to designate whether they want to see the content after reviewing the abstract of an item.
- *Attachments*: Attachments or appendages serve a wide variety of functions. They may represent an attached graphic or binary file produced by a special software package. The types of attachments that are possible are listed next.
  — Any type of file that is to be transferred to the member's workstation or personal computer before they can be viewed or utilized.
  — Very long text items that the sender describes in the contents, in order to give the receiver the opportunity to decide whether to display the longer attachment.
  — Appendages to the original text item made by various readers: expressions of reactions (such as agreement, disagreement, or approval), with the content of the item. Such expressions are identified by who in the group added the appendage. Canned notifications may be attached as well.
- *Activities*: These are described subsequently in detail. They are executable procedures that aid in the structuring of the activities of a group, or which facilitate the ability of individuals to handle large amounts of information. While one may "view" a comment or message, one would "do" the linked activity. For activities, the content of the comment or message would usually provide information about the activity.

Clearly, a great deal of the adaptability of structures in a CMC environment rests with the ability to use a text item in a significant number of different ways. Associated with this variety of utilization is the concept of notifications. For example, when someone modifies another person's item, the original author should be notified by the system of the occurrence.

4.3. Activities

One of the necessities for a CMC system to service group-oriented objectives is the integration of other computer resources within the CMC environment. This means the following types of available capabilities:

- Decision support tools collect and process and display "votes," such as weighting, ranking, or yes-no "straw votes" on options.
- Members of a CMC system should be able to bring data from other data bases into the communication environment.
- One must be able to trigger the execution of programs that support the group process and obtain the results of those programs within the conferencing environment.

The future direction for group support in the computer environment is toward the integration of communications and all other computer resources into a single interface structure. There is no reason why the same interface process utilized to communicate with other humans cannot be utilized to communicate with other computer- or network-based facilities. A communication system is the ideal concept for a user-oriented executive system.

There are many approaches to integration with the underlying technology. We utilize the metaphor of an "activity" that can be attached to any communication item, such as a comment or message. This activity, when triggered or done, will execute a program or procedure on the host computer or the network of computers. Such an activity could ask the person using it to supply input data, and generate a new communication item to receive the output of the resulting program.

As long as the preceding is implemented as a general facility, it can be used to easily trigger requests and searches of data bases, execute analysis programs, or make changes to data bases. The original communication item containing the attached activity can provide a description of the activity or a summary of its current status.

LIST GATHERING ACTIVITY

An example of a necessary activity is the ability to collect collaboratively a list of structured items and to treat this collection of items as one type of list. One list is the table of contents of a document, such as the document the group is trying to create. Another type of list is a set of tasks to be accomplished. In addition, there could be lists of issues to address, terms to define, alternative criteria for a decision, possible solutions to a problem, etc.

How to handle the contributions to a list varies with the nature of the objective:

- Any member can add an item to the list at any time, such as a list of issues to address.
- Only one, or a certain select set of individuals, can contribute to the list, as in a table of contents or a set of tasks to be done.
- Some individuals can add to only certain parts of the list, as in adding subheadings to certain sections of a table of contents.
- Individuals can be assigned to various items in the list, or they can volunteer to be associated with various items in the list. For example, who is to write a particular section of a document? Or, who is to handle a certain task?
- A status can be associated with items on the list, such as whether a task has been done and the date completed.

The person creating an activity has to have control over when certain actions are allowed. For example, if people are contributing to the list, the owner of the activity should be able to do things such as "close" it to further contributions, if

Figure 3.
Activity Commands

Command	Explanation
View	Content of a message or comment. Would usually explain nature of activity
Review	Displays status of activity (e.g., Done or Undone)
Do	To execute the activity (e.g., vote, read document, etc.)
Organize	Control the activity
Notify	Trigger associated notifications

it has sufficient contributions. The owner should be able to open, at the right time, certain other actions that can take place on an existing list:

- Associate a voting scale with items on the list, which may be of a number of different types. For example, a simple yes/no vote or an arbitrary 1–7 scale, which can be used to measure consensus on such dimensions as agreement, feasibility, importance, etc.
- Allow other text items to be associated with the items on the list, such as in the actual drafting of entries for the table of contents.
- Freeze contributions at any time, and perform editing and reorganization of the list.
- Allow selections of responsibility for items on the list, such as in a voluntary task assignment.
- Control whether a person has access to the activity before they have made a contribution to it.
- Open the activity to access by others who are not part of the original group developing the contents of the activity.

There are many types of activities possible, both of a very general and very specific nature. Whatever is the nature of a specific activity, it is important that this facility provide the tracking of status of activities for both individuals and the group. The system must provide individuals' organized reviews of what activities they have and have not done. The leaders or facilitators of a group need to know the status of who in the group has or has not completed a given activity. Also, they should have facilities for such things as sending automatic reminder notifications to anyone who has not done a particular activity.

In some types of tasks, it is important, for psychological motivation, that all the group members are able to perceive who in the group has and has not contributed to the group-oriented activities.

The concept of activities, within a CMC system, is open-ended and represents one of the primary mechanisms whereby future extensions will be made to EIES2 and TEIES. What is crucial is that the incorporation of a wide range of tailored facilities to support an application be provided via a common interface metaphor, with the same command functions and object definitions applying to the whole set. This is the only way that all the members of the group can quickly acquire and learn the tools as they are carrying out the application.

Once the members learn the commands (Figure 3) that apply to any and all activities, they are able to manipulate any type of activity. The related concept of notifications provides a single facility through which the progress of any type of activity can be tracked by the members of the group.

4.4. Notifications

Notifications are short one- or two-line messages intended to reduce the amount of effort necessary to communicate about complex tasks. These objectives are listed next.

- Generate automatic alerts based on transactions that have taken place. For example, a reply to an "urgent" item might notify the readership of that item that a reply exists. Most automatic alerts are optional in nature.
- Provide a direct manipulation handle, since one may point to a notification and retrieve the material to which it is referring.
- Provide a data base to the member for tracking the actions associated with a particular task. Each member has a cyclic file of the notifications delivered to him or her.
- Providing the interface function of "closure" on processes that the member or group have triggered. Each activity defined for the system may incorporate its own set of tailored notifications and the conditions under which they are triggered.
- Alerting members to changes of status, such as a vote summary being viewable.
- Reminders such as the controller of an activity triggering automatic sending of reminders to those who have not made their contribution.
- Reducing the need for messages or comments by the use of "canned" notifications. A member may point to an item and trigger a standardized notification expressing any of a large number of common communication tasks, such as expressing agreement or disagreement, desirable or undesirable, responsibility for taking care of, etc.

These notifications may be incorporated as attachments to the original message or comment.

- Enhance communication awareness though notifications, such as announcements about new members being added to a private conference or the introduction of new classification categories for use by the group.

As an example, if an individual sends a message that is a "planned decision," the receiver can respond with a canned notification by merely pointing to the message and triggering the "notify" command. This provides a menu of canned notifications, among which are the following:

AGREE (I agree with your decision.

DELAY (Wait until I respond before taking the action.)

Notifications represent a general open-ended concept and provide a great deal of flexibility as to how they may be used in association with groups, conferences, and activities.

The importance of the concept of notifications is that a wide variety of applications for alerting, closure, and tracking is served by one interface metaphor, and not by a variety of interfaces for different applications.

4.5. Roles, Privileges, and Tickets

One aspect that makes a CMC system more difficult to design and develop is that the system must incorporate the software to support the roles that humans take on in both facilitating and leading groups. In synchronous systems, this aspect is largely ignored.

Roles on our systems are built out of a subset of the primitive privileges that we have defined as being crucial to the human communication process. These are operations that allow people to do things such as adding something to someone else's file folder without being able to see what is there. One can do this in the physical world, and clearly systems that are going to offer the same flexibility must go far beyond the basic privileges of read and write. Based on empirical observation of human communications, we have defined some 25 such privileges. Some of these are also associated with maintaining a high degree of privacy and security with respect to the communication process. Some examples of such privileges are listed next.

• APPEND: which only allows material to be added to such objects as a conference comment, or message, without any necessary access to what is there unless one also has a READ privilege. It does not allow any modification of what is there, unless a separate MODIFY privilege is part of the privilege set.
• LINK: to be allowed to link someone else's object to another object.
• ASSIGN: to be able to establish a member for an activity such that the activity becomes required for the member.
• USE: allows user's machine to use data and/or code in a different user machine but does not allow transfer.

Clearly, users do not normally deal with individual privileges. Rather, they deal with roles. Some examples of the sort of roles that can be created out of the basic privileges are listed next.

• Indexer: the person in a conference or group who can modify and update the index, including the changing of keys on associated communication items.
• Organizer: the person who can create activities in a conference.
• Contributor: a person who can add comments to a conference, or send group messages, but cannot see any of the others that have been created.

The final component of this facility is the concept of TICKETS. A ticket is the ability of a user to pass a specific privilege that they possess to another user. For example, one could give a secretary a privilege to edit an authored comment in a conference, even though the secretary has no access to the rest of the conference. Tickets can be made conditional on such things as the number of times they can be used and the interval of time during which they may be used. A ticket can be canceled by the issuer at any time. Usually, tickets will generate notifications back to the issuer when they are used. They can also be designated as transferable, if the situation warrants it. Tickets are a mechanism to handle the unpredictable needs for the usage of privileges.

5.0. APPROPRIATE TECHNOLOGY FOR CMC

For the past three years, we have been developing a new generation of CMC systems. EIES2 is now available for installation at other sites. It is a fully distributed CMC system that operates under UNIX in any TCP/IP or X.400 network, with distributed "group" and "user" agents [50]. The IBM/VM system called TEIES (Tailorable EIES [46]) is currently in alpha test. Internally, both systems utilize a very similar design philosophies, based on what we have come to feel are natural consequences of the requirements for group support in a communications environment.

There are a large number of factors that lead one quite naturally to the necessity of an object-oriented data base as the foundation for any CMC system. These are as follows:

• Members and groups are represented in the data base and must be linked to the communication objects with which they have some association.
• Maintaining the security of communications along with the flexibility of a wide range of alternative communication-oriented privileges of access,
• Minimizing user-interface learning by the use of generic commands that may have somewhat different functionality, as a result of the type of object on which they are used.
• In any collaborative environment, communicators may make use of communications produced by others. Creators of items must be made aware that their items are being used by others if they seek to modify such items.
• The need to integrate other computer and information resources with the CMC system in such a way as not to violate security and privacy requirements.

The security and privacy of communications must be maintained rigorously in a communication system that supports organizational communications and the activities of various intersecting and overlapping groups. A second fundamental requirement is that the system must allow the same sort of communication flexibility humans have available with other communication media. A third is the necessity to integrate other computer resources that the individuals and groups need to support dealing with their tasks and problems.

The preceding considerations lead to a number of important technical requirements that form the basis for our current systems:

- The data base must be self-contained with respect to privileges of access to communication objects by the users of the system.
- Members must be objects defined in the data base.
- Groups, which are collections of members, must also exist as objects, so that linkages between communication objects may be made to groups as well as to members.
- The essence of a link is the specification of a bit mask that indicates the set of primitive privileges associated with the connection between a communications object and the member or specific groups to which he or she belongs.
- Each object type must have its own set of associated functions, so that generic user commands can be interpreted in terms of the object on which they are working.
- Links between objects must be two-way, so that actions on one object can be transmitted, as appropriate, to other linked objects. As a result, an object-oriented data base is a very natural approach to handling many of the requirements for CMC systems. In addition, object-oriented systems allow the behavior of an object to be defined independently from the rest of the system. This allows for the efficient evolution of the system through the introduction of new object types. Both EIES2 and TEIES have been designed around the basic object-oriented data-base concept.

With the addition of privileges within the data base, it is possible for the data base alone to determine whether or not to honor a request for data from any other system or application program. The EIES2 data base can be accessed from C programs or the UNIX shell. The TEIES data base can be accessed utilizing REXX. This means that other application programs can be created that make use of the CMC data base, without the application programmers having to be concerned with any aspect of security or privacy. In addition, any such application program can be triggered through the use of an "activity," within the CMC interface itself. This provides for the integration of other computer resources, either through an internal (e.g., activities) or external interface.

Both TEIES and EIES2 are distributed systems. EIES2 is designed around the ISO model and is composed of separate user and group agents, which may be located on separate machines. Each agent has its own Remote Operation Server, based on the X.400 standards. There is a Communication Language Processor,

which accepts X.409 language specifications to create new objects for the data base. In EIES2, a single conference has a master copy on a single group agent, but the distributed nature of the system is completely transparent to a user. In principle, EIES2 can support a very large user population, given a sufficient number of machines within a TCP/IP or X.400 network. At the moment, we have three HP machines and a SUN machine at NJIT, and an HP machine in Denmark, all operating as one system.

TEIES is designed to be distributed as a single master virtual machine, with multiple user and data-base machines. The master machine provides a directory service for all objects in the system, and it also validates the establishment of a link between a given user machine and a given data-base machine with a specific set of access privileges. TEIES is designed to be very compatible with the IBM/VM environment. REXX can be used as the integration language.

Given the perspective of the evolution of a CMC system within an organizational context, the next obvious requirement is to minimize the effort involved in creating new functionality and interface capabilities. EIES2 utilizes a fully distributed SMALLTALK interpreter, developed at NJIT to create both the interface and user functionality. The applications programmer does not have to be concerned about the location of objects in the network of user and group agents. The TEIES interface is written in a version of SGML (Standard General Markup Language) developed at NJIT, which has implicit knowledge of the TEIES objects through the defined object and data variable names in the TEIES data base. It is our view that SGML is ideal as an interface specification language, given the proper functional extensions. It allows the interface specification to be stored in the text items that are a part of the CMC system. This also means that different users can be using interfaces in different languages on the same operational version of the system.

The final component of the NJIT development effort in CMC systems is PERSONAL TEIES™. This MS/DOS-based system serves as a graphics composition and display system, as well as a communications front end to TEIES and EIES2. One may view PERSONAL TEIES as, in part, a GKS to NAPLPS translator. GKS is used to drive the workstation, and NAPLS is the communication format for the graphics, as well as the data storage specification. PERSONAL TEIES™ is designed to allow a group to exchange and modify conceptual diagrams. It is intended to provide a form of "group graphics," where members in the group may make modifications to each other's diagrams. An important functionality of PERSONAL TEIES™ is that users may create their own icon sets. These could be anything from math symbols to symbolic representations of parts of an organization or project. Therefore, a group can develop its own diagrammatic jargon for representing graphical relationships of interest. As a result, many situations (e.g., laying out a new manufacturing process using a set of machines) can be reduced to the process of layouts and icons developed by the group. We plan to transfer PERSONAL TEIES™ to the Macintosh environment in the future.

All our software systems are being developed with the C language as the primary foundation language. As one might guess, there is a strong emphasis on utilizing standards wherever possible. These systems have been designed to be both usable production systems and provide a foundation for research and development in CMC and the related areas of Groupware, GDSS, and CSCW. Furthermore, the facilities have been provided to make it easy for organizations to incorporate their own tailoring and integration with other information systems and resources. We expect their evolution to stretch over the next decade, and to see other organizations making their own extensions to the basic foundation.

6.0. SUMMARY

The asynchronous group support problem is an order of magnitude more difficult than working with synchronous groups. The system must be able to aid in the organization of the material over long periods of time. It must also provide support for human roles and communication signaling and cueing. However, in the asynchronous approach, it is possible to integrate individual problem-solving processes with group problem-solving processes in such a manner that one can hope for true "collective intelligence" by taking advantage of both processes. Systems need to be designed based on appropriate models and theories of both processes.

The role of a well-designed CMC system is to support the human roles dedicated to synchronizing the individual and group processes, and to integrate the toolbox needed to support dealing with complex problems. For example, a typical planning effort for a new product or production process may involve the specification and analysis of anywhere from a few hundred to a few thousand subprojects and tasks. This has to be accomplished by a multitude of individuals and groups with overlapping and shifting membership. Such efforts need the benefits of support tools in such areas as structural modeling that will deal with collaborative and conflicting estimates of costs, effort, time to accomplish, relative significance, alternatives, objectives, etc.

There is no reason why a CMC system cannot support synchronous as well as asynchronous use. The focus on only synchronous systems is very much the classical "Drunkard's Paradox" of providing an easy solution to the wrong problem. A great deal of the current synchronous work seems to be oriented at building the "telescope." There is a tremendous social technology of small group problem solving, and it is not clear that the claimed effectiveness of elaborate and expensive decision rooms outperforms a well-structured "focus" group with normal meeting room facilities. At least, this sort of controlled experiment is not common in the literature.

The real advantages of computer technology lie in the integration into the group process of the powerful analysis techniques that can aid the solution of complex problems. These include:

• Scaling methods, such as Multi-Dimensional Scaling, to aid in the understanding and organization of human judgments [19, 27, 37].

• Structural modeling methods, such as Interpretive Structural Modeling and Cross Impact Analysis [25, 27], to aid in dealing with large-scale complex problems.
• Modeling, simulation, and gaming methods [20, 27] to aid in the forecasting of long-term implications.

The incorporation of techniques in these areas is what will bring about, in the long run, sizable benefits for group processes. However, they all require learning curves and facilitation in interpretation that mean availability of these aids on a continuous asynchronous basis. Complex group problems, such as "parking cars," already exist, and the need is to focus on those problems.

Furthermore, individuals will not tolerate, in the long run, a host of different systems for dealing with the same tasks. They will also not tolerate being constrained to one sequential approach for solving all problems. CMC systems have to be viewed as "toolboxes" that can be tailored by the users, both on an individual and group basis, for dealing with a specific type of problem. The ability of users to "self-tailor" the system and the integration of the tools a computer network can provide are the primary challenges for the designers of CMC systems.

To date, CMC systems have been designed and utilized to support real applications in such areas as project management, crisis management, planning and budgeting, collaborative learning, collaborative composition, group therapy and meditation, gaming, data-base validation, large-scale information exchange, decision support, and Delphi exercises. The key to good design is as much the understanding of the task as it is understanding the technology. Designers should be aware that they are not merely designing a computer system, they are designing a "social system" [40]. Perhaps even more important, management needs to be aware that this is what is occurring. These systems have and will continue to change the nature of management and the behavior of the organization by providing an evolutionary approach to the development of these systems by coupling an evaluation program [23].

7.0 REFERENCES

1. Bahgat, A. *A decision support system for zero-base capital budgeting: A case study*, Ph.D. in Management Thesis, Rutgers Graduate School of Management, Newark, N.J., 1986.
2. Bernstein, L.M., Siegel, E.R., and Goldstein, C.M. The hepatitis knowledge base: A prototype information transfer system. *Annals Internal Medicine 93*, 2 (1980), 169–181.
3. Cashman, P.M. A communication-oriented approach to structuring the software maintenance environment, ACM SIGSOFT. *Software Engineering Notes 5*, 1 (1980), 4–17.
4. Churchman, C.W. *The Design of Inquiry Systems*. Basic Books, New York, 1971.
5. Conklin, J., and Begeman, M. gIBIS: A Hypertext tool for team design deliberation. *ACM Trans. Office Info. Systs. 6*, 4, (1988), 303–331.
6. Daft, R.L., and Lengel, R.H. Organizational information requirements, media richness and structural design. *Manage. Sci. 32*, 5 (May 1986), 554–571.
7. Delbecq, A.L., VandeVen, A., and Gustofson, A. *Group Techniques for Program Planning: A Guide to Nominal Group Techniques and Delphi Processes*. Scott-Foresman, 1975.

8. Englebart, D.C. Coordinated information services for a discipline or mission oriented community. In *Proceedings of the 2nd Annual Computer Communications Conference*. SRI, San Jose, 1973.

9. Englebart, D.C., Watson, R.W., and Norton, J.C., The augmented knowledge workshop. In *Proceedings of the AFIPS National Conference 42*. 1976.

10. Ericsson, K.A., and Simon, H. *Protocol Analysis: Verbal Reports as Data*. MIT Press, Cambridge, Mass., 1984.

11. Hiltz, S.R. *Online Communities: A Case Study of the Office of the Future*. Ablex Press, Norwood, N.J. 1984.

12. Hiltz, S.R. The "Virtual Classroom": Using computer-mediated communication for university teaching. *J. Commun. 36*, 2 (Spring 1986), 95–104.

13. Hiltz, S.R., Johnson, K.J., and Turoff, M. Experiments in group decision making, 1: Communication process and outcome in face-to-face vs. computerized conferences. *Human Commun. Res. 13*, 2 (Winter 1986), 225–253.

14. Hiltz, S.R., and Turoff, M. Structuring computer-mediated communications to avoid information overload. *Commun. ACM 28*, 7 (July 1985), 680–689.

15. Hiltz, S.R., and Turoff, M. *The Network Nation: Human Communication via Computer*. Addison-Wesley, Reading, Mass., 1978.

16. Hiltz, S.R., Turoff, M., and Johnson, K. Using a computerized conference system as a laboratory tool. *SIGSOC Bull. 13*, 4 (1982), 5–9.

17. Hirokawa, R.Y., and Poole, M.S. *Communication and Group Decision-Making*. Sage Publications, Beverly Hills, Calif., 1986.

18. Hoffman, L.R. *The Group Problem Solving Process: A Valance Model*. Praeger Publishers, New York 1979.

19. Hopkins, R.H., Cambell, K.B., and Peterson, N.S. Representations of perceived relations among the properties and variables in a complex system. *IEEE Trans. Syst. Man, Cybern. 17*, 1 (Jan./Feb. 1987), 52–60.

20. Hsu, E. Role-event gaming-simulation in management education: A conceptual framework and review. *Simulation and Games 20*, 4 (Dec. 1989), 409–438.

21. Johnson-Lenz, P. and T., Kerr, E., and Hiltz, S.R. Groupware: The process and impacts of design choices. In *Computer Mediated Communication Systems*, E., Kerr and S.R. Hiltz, (Eds.). Academic Press, New York, 1982.

22. Johnson-Lenz, P. and T., and Hessman, J.F. JEDEC/EIES computer conferencing for standardization activities. In *Electronic Communication: Technology and Impacts*, M. Henderson (Ed.). AAAS Selected Symposium 52. Westview Press, Boulder, Colo. 1980.

23. Kerr, E., and Hiltz, S.R. *Computer-Mediated Communication Systems*. Academic Press, New York, 1982.

24. Kupperman, R.H., Wilcox, R.H., Smith, H.A. Crisis management: Some opportunities. *Science 187* (1975), 404–410.

25. Lendaris, G. Structural modeling: A tutorial guide. *IEEE Trans. Syst., Man, Cybern. 10*, 12 (Dec. 1980), 807–840.

26. Lerch, I.A. Electronic communications and collaboration: The emerging model for computer aided communications in science and medicine. *Telematics and Informatics 5*, 4 (1988), 397–414.

27. Linstone, H., and Turoff, M. *The Delphi Method: Techniques and Applications*. Addison-Wesley, Reading, Mass., 1975.

28. McKendree, J.D. Decision process in crisis management: Computers in a new role. In *Encyclopedia of Computer Science and Technology*, J. Belzer (Ed.), Volume 7. Marcel-Dekker, 1977.

29. Mitroff, I.I., Nelson, J., and Mason, R. On management myth—Information systems. *Manage. Sci. 21*, 4 (1974), 371–382.

30. Pinsonneault, A., and Kraemer, K. The impact of technical support on groups: An assessment of the empirical research. *Decis. Support Syst. 5* (1989), 197–216.

31. Renner, R., et al. EMISARI: A management information system designed to aid and involve people. In *Proceedings of the International Symposium on Computer and Information Science (COINS)*. Dec. 1972.

32. Schneider, S.J., and Tooley, J. Self-help computer conference. *Computers and Biomedical Research 19* (1986), 274–281.

33. Schneider, S.J. Trial of an on-line behavioral smoking cessation program. *Computers in Human Behavior 2* (1986), 277–296.

34. Siegel, E.R. The use of computer conference to validate and update MLM's hepatitis data base. In *Electronic Communications: Technology and Impact*, H. Henderson and J. MacNaughton (Eds.). AAAS AAAS Selected Symposium 52. Westview Press, Boulder, Colo. 1980.

35. Sternberg, R.J. Human intelligence: The model is the message. *Science 230*, 4730 (Dec. 6, 1985), 1111–1118.

36. Sternberg, R.J. (Ed.). *Handbook of Human Intelligence*. Cambridge University Press, Cambridge, 1982.

37. Torgerson, W.S. *Theory and Methods of Scaling*. Wiley, 1958.

38. Turoff, M. Delphi and its potential impact on information systems. In *AFIPS Conference Proceedings 39*, (1971), 317–326.

39. Turoff, M. Delphi conferencing: Computer based conferencing with anonymity. *J. Technol. Forecasting and Social Change 3*, 2 (1972) 159–204.

40. Turoff, M. Management issues in human communication via computer. In *Emerging Office Systems*, R. Landau et al. (Eds.). Ablex Press, Norwood, N.J. 1982.

41. Turoff, M. Information and value: The internal information marketplace. *J. Technol. Forecasting and Social Change 27*, 4 (July 1985), 257–373.

42. Turoff, M. The anatomy of a technological innovation: Computer mediated communications. *J. Technol. Forecasting and Social Change 36*, (1989), 107–122.

43. Turoff, M., and Hiltz, S.R. Computer support for group versus individual decisions. *IEEE Trans. Commun. 30*, 1 (Jan. 1982), 82–90.

44. Turoff, M., and Hiltz, S.R. Office augmentation systems: The case for evolutionary design. In *Proceedings of the 15th Hawaii International Conference on Systems Science*. Jan. 1982, 737–749.

45. Turoff, M., and Hiltz, S.R. The electronic journal: A progress report. *J. ASIS 33*, 4 (July 1982), 195–202.

46. Turoff, M., and Hiltz, S.R., Foster, J.F., and Ng, K. Computer mediated communications and tailorability. In *Proceedings of the Twenty-Second Annual Hawaii Conference on Systems Science*. Vol. III. IEEE Computer Society, Jan. 1989, 403–411.

47. Turoff, M., Whitescarver, J., and Hiltz, S.R. The Human-machine interface in a computerized conferencing environment. In *Proceedings of the IEEE Systems, Man and Cybernetics Annual Conference*. 1977, 145–157.

48. Vallee, J., Johansen, R., Lipinski, H., and Wilson, T. Pragmatics and dynamics of computer conferencing: A summary of findings from the forum project. In *Proceedings of the International Conference on Computer Communications*. IEEE, 1976, 208–213.

49. Wang, C.H., and Hwang, S.L. The dynamic hierarchical model of problem solving. *IEEE Trans. Syst., Man, Cybern. 19*, 5 (Sept./Oct. 1989), 946–954.

50. Whitescarver, J., et al. A network environment for computer supported collaborative work. In *Proceedings of ACM SIGCOMM Workshop: Frontiers in Computer Communications*. Aug. 1987, 230–244.

51. Wilcox, R.H., and Kupperman, R., An on-line management system in a dynamic environment. In *Proceedings of the First International Conference on Computer Communications*. IEEE, 1972, 117–120.

52. Wish, M., and Kaplan, S.J. Toward an implicit theory of interpersonal communication. *Sociometry 40*, 3 (1980), 234–246.

53. Zinn, K.L., Parnes, R., and Hench, H. Computer-based educational communication at the University of Michigan. In *Proceedings of 31st ACM National Conference*. 1976.

Reprinted from *Connections: New Ways of Working in the Networked Organization*, pp. 79-101. © 1991, The MIT Press. Reprinted with permission.

Increasing Personal Connections

Lee Sproull and Sara Kiesler

Not everyone can be the boss, have a big office, make important decisions, be the center of attention. Many employees are geographically and hierarchically distant from the center of things. Whenever an organization has more than two people in it, someone will be out of the center. The larger the organization, the greater the number and proportion of peripheral employees. "Peripheral," however, does not mean unimportant. Peripheral employees in the commercial and service sectors are the first, and often the only, contact that customers have with an organization. Their behavior can make the difference between keeping customers or clients and losing them. Peripheral employees in manufacturing and construction perform and inspect the actual production work. Their behavior can make the difference between acceptable and unacceptable product quality. Yet peripheral workers pose problems for organizations. They may not know what's going on—an information problem—and they may not care—a motivation problem.

Advertisements that encourage us to "reach out and touch someone" reflect the belief that we strengthen relationships when we communicate with others. Every relationship is both informational and emotional. All other things being equal, the more you talk with someone, the more you learn from that person (and vice versa). Additionally, the more you talk with someone, the more you like and feel committed to that person (and vice versa).[1] Participation through communication is an old principle of management. It has recently revived in the United States as managers look to Japan and the industrial democracies of Western Europe for "new" management practices.

Participation plans typically rely on communications initiated from the center and representation of the periphery to the center. Management initiates most participation plans. Employees receive participation overtures rather than initiate them. For instance, management may ask employees to get more involved through such mechanisms as quality circles, or employee representatives may be named to various management committees. Much of the internal communications apparatus of modern organizations is designed to "get the word to the troops," to ensure that employees have current information on policies, procedures, and other relevant topics. Devices ranging from televised messages from the company president to routine policy manual updates are intended to reduce the information distance between peripheral employees and the center. Even so, peripheral employees may be operating with outdated information, unaware of new initiatives or policies.

Even if peripheral employees have the information they need to do their jobs, they may not have any great desire to do so. (Motivation, of course, can interact with how informed an employee is. Highly motivated employees will figure out ways to learn what is going on.) Unmotivated employees' relationship with their employer is strictly letter of the law. Their information connection may be adequate, but their emotional connection is weak. Motivation and commitment can affect both work quality and work satisfaction. When people are "marking time" or "going through the motions," their behaviors and attitudes are qualitatively different from those in which people are "gung ho" or "going all out." Episodes of working to rule, as in, for instance, an air traffic controllers' slowdown, show the importance of employees who do more than they have to do. Organizations employ a host of motivating techniques to reduce the emotional distance between peripheral employees and the center: employee recognition awards, spirit campaigns, company-sponsored social occasions, and community events. Like information procedures, the center initiates most of these for the periphery.

Electronic communication may offer peripheral employees new opportunities to initiate connections within the organization to reduce the information gap and increase motivation. If connectivity is high, there are potentially many people accessible via the network. Because of the social processes described in chapters 3 and 4, employees should feel somewhat uninhibited about "meeting" new people electronically. If management policies permit or encourage such interactions, employees can increase their information and emotional connections. These interactions can increase both connections between the periphery and the center of the organization and connections among peripheral workers.

In the first section of this chapter, we show how employees can benefit from increasing their electronic connections with other employees. These increasing connections could benefit all employees, but peripheral employees are likely to see a relatively greater benefit than are central employees. We show how both passive and active connections (receiving information and sending it, respectively) can be beneficial. Passive connections offer employees the opportunity not only to learn from other employees but also to discover similarities they share with people who have different jobs and are located in different places. Active connections provide a new opportunity for employees to have a voice in their work group and with their boss. In the second section of the chapter we consider performance implications of having peripheral members increase their connections.

Increasing Information and Commitment Through New Connections

Window on the Corporation

Receiving mail can affect employees' attitudes toward their organization by increasing their informational and emotional connections to other employees. This can be particularly true for peripheral employees who participate in large electronic distribution lists (DLs), bulletin boards, or conferences.

In one Fortune 500 firm, we noted several instances of these benefits. One secretary described several DLs to which she belonged by saying that she liked seeing what people had to say on various topics, including "important people who you would never talk to me in person." She said she would never send a message to any of these DLs, but they were her "window on the corporation." Another employee used the mail system to describe his feelings about his employer, which had recently sold one of its subsidiaries. In a message sent to a large DL, the sender explained that another employee had told him: "It's a firm policy that [the corporation] won't make anything that will hurt anyone; they're getting pretty close, and that's probably why we're selling it." The sender then confided (to several hundred people), "That made me feel awfully good." As Martha Feldman (1987) pointed out in analyzing this message, "Though not all people who hear about the reason for selling the operation will agree on whether it is good or bad, the knowledge, by itself, provides organizational members a

better understanding of the organization" (p. 97). In a third case, another secretary used the electronic mail system to organize a get well gift for an employee (box 5.1). Tokens of appreciation are common in many organizations. What made this one interesting is that the message went to three hundred people, presumably most of whom had never before heard of Benny, the ailing employee. Probably most people paid little conscious attention to this message. But even with a quick scan and delete, the subliminal message was, "I work for a company with caring people."

Corporate communications offices and human resources offices are in the business of sending employees information designed to increase informational and emotional connections. How could ad hoc communications among employees be any more effective than professionally designed ones? Messages share several characteristics that distinguish them from professional communications and that may make them particularly potent. First, most are from voluntary or discretionary DLs. People choose to belong to these DLs and therefore perceive that they receive messages by their choice, not because they must do so. Second, because these DLs have widespread membership, they can reflect information and feelings from throughout the organization, not just from one communication office. Third, the overt contents of these messages pertain to a variety of topics and

---

Box 5.1. Benny hurt his back

```
Date:      19 May 1983 10:37 am PDT  (Thursday)
From:      Sandi Colman
Subject:   Benny Schrinka
To:        [All employees, about 300 people, working in one location]
cc:
Reply To:  Sandi Colman
     Benny Schrinka hurt his back last week and will be unable to
work for at least 3-4 weeks or more......depends on how he
responds to physical therapy.
     Several of his friends are putting together a surprise
"goodie basket" for him, hoping to cheer him and ease his pain.
We hope to include a ham, some wine, maybe a good book or two
for him to read..suggestions welcome.
If you care to make a contribution toward the basket...I am
collecting $$$; John Devon has volunteered to coordinate
getting the goodies and basket.
I am in "Area 2" of ABC Bldg. 10....x1111; John Devon is in
room 76, same building.
     Thanks to you all....Sandi
```

interests, not just to official company news or boosterism. These characteristics can make these messages more persuasive than professional ones because of a process psychologists call insufficient justification (Aronson 1966).

When people receive a message, they evaluate the sender's motivation so that they know how to interpret the message. If a recipient knows that the sender was paid for sending the message or was coerced into sending it, the recipient discounts the sender's sincerity. The recipient believes that the sender has "sufficient justification" for sending the message even without sincerely believing its contents. By contrast, if a sender lacks obvious external incentives for sending the message, the recipient does not discount the sender's sincerity. When unsolicited messages appear on large, discretionary distribution lists, readers have little reason to doubt their sincerity. Peripheral employees who frequently receive such messages build information connections over time to other employees of the corporation.

Cognitive processes of everyday inference also can magnify the influence of these messages in the minds of their recipients. Because people commonly ignore base rates and remember singular instances, they overestimate the frequency of rare events (Lichtenstein et al. 1978).[2] For instance, people typically overestimate the frequency of death by lightning. (Similarly they tend to underestimate the frequency of death by motor vehicle accidents, which are more frequent and less memorable.) Suppose a person who read the message in box 5.1 were to ask, "How kind to one another are people who work for this company?" The best answer, without any other similar information, is "About as kind as the people who work for any similar company." The Benny message should carry very little weight in changing that assessment, increasing the kindness score by only $1/n$th, where n is the total number of employees. Because the message has memorable features—the ham, the bottle of wine, the books—it is likely to be overweighted (in a statistical sense) in its contribution to the person's assessment.

Reading messages gives employees the opportunity to make connections with other employees who would otherwise be invisible or unknown. Because electronic communication can be independent of geographic and organizational distance, these connections cut across conventional organization boundaries. In this way, employees can learn about people whose experiences are different from theirs because they have different jobs or work in different locations. They also can learn that, despite these differences, they have much in common. Such lessons are reinforced by the

nature of the communication—the free exchange of unofficial information. Research on the relationship between electronic connections and feelings of affiliation shows that if you have a choice of face-to-face contact with people exactly like you or meeting via electronic communication, then you will like each other more if you meet in person (Kiesler et al. 1985). The situation is different for meeting people you would otherwise not see in person, whom you might avoid, who are different. Here there is a positive association between electronic connections and affiliation.

It is possible that people communicating electronically could become attached to specific other people or even to favorite bulletin boards or electronic groups without these positive attachments generalizing to the larger organization. No research directly tests the impact of "windows on the corporation" on attachment to the organization. If the process works as it has in other settings, then whether affiliation extends to the larger organization will depend on the orientation of the individuals' communications. If messages about the larger organization are mainly negative, recipients will increase their affiliation with the communicators but decrease it with the larger organization. If the communications are mainly positive toward the larger organization, recipients will increase both affiliations.

A Voice for the Voiceless

Sending messages also can increase information and emotional connections. An experiment conducted by the Rand Corporation demonstrated that peripheral people who communicated electronically became better integrated into the organization (Eveland and Bikson 1988). Two corporation task forces were formed to investigate how employees make the transition to retirement and to develop a set of recommendations about preretirement planning. Each task force had forty members—half recently retired from the company and the other half still employed but eligible for retirement. The only difference between the two groups was that one of them was given electronic communication technology and the other was not. At the outset, the retired people in both task forces were judged by themselves and others to be more peripheral to the group than their employed counterparts. On standard sociometric measures of recognition, knowing, and contact, retirees had lower scores than those who were still employed. Halfway through the year's work, the retired members of the electronic communication group had become intensely involved in the project by electronic mail. They knew more people, had more interactions, belonged to more subgroups, and felt more involved than their retired counterparts in the nonelectronic task force. They even decided to continue meeting after the year's work was completed and the task forces had been officially disbanded.

We found a similar story in a city government (Huff, Sproull, and Kiesler 1989). Over 90 percent of the city employees used electronic mail routinely. We discovered that the more they used it, the more committed they were to their employer—measured by how willing they were to work beyond the requirements and hours of their jobs, how attached they felt to the city government, and how strongly they planned to continue working for the city. The connection between electronic communication and commitment is not explained by employees' total amount of communication across all media, by their technical ability, or by their seniority and hierarchical status (although the later two variables predicted commitment independently). One explanation of our findings is that using electronic mail caused commitment to increase. Another explanation is that already committed people used the modern, symbolically important technology of electronic mail. To compare these alternatives, we proposed that if communicating by electronic mail increased commitment, then the correlation between using electronic mail and commitment should be especially strong among shift workers who are routinely separated from the mainstream of work and decision making in the organization. We reasoned that the technology would be somewhat more useful to them than to employees in the mainstream. By contrast, if commitment caused people to use electronic mail, then shift work should have no differential effect. We found that the relationship between using electronic mail and commitment was much higher for shift workers than for other workers, supporting the idea that electronic mail can increase commitment among those who otherwise might feel somewhat peripheral in an organization.

Once we knew that total volume of an employee's electronic mail predicted that person's level of commitment, we wondered if receiving mail or sending it (or both) contributed to feelings of commitment. It might be that receiving more mail would cause people to feel more informed, as was the case with the large corporation, and therefore more committed. We found, however, that neither the amount of electronic mail received nor a person's reporting that he or she felt "in the know about what is going on in the city" predicted commitment. Rather, the amount of electronic mail

a person sent predicted commitment. In this city government, computer communication seems to have increased commitment primarily because it allowed employees to participate actively in the life of the organization by sending messages that they would not otherwise have sent, not primarily because it increased the amount of information they received. One police officer wrote to us, "Working the night shift, it used to be that I would hear about promotions after they happened though I had a right to be included in the decision making. Now I have a say in the discussion." Electronic communication gave peripheral employees the chance to have a voice.

We found a similar relationship between commitment and sending mail in the software development teams that we described in chapter 2. Recall that the teams using electronic mail the most produced the best systems because they could better coordinate their activities than could the teams that relied on more conventional means of communicating. We also looked at how committed each member felt to his or her team. For this analysis, we categorized each person by how much he or she talked in meetings and how much electronic mail he or she sent. We discovered that people who sent much mail were just as committed to their team as were the people who talked a lot in meetings. Also, as is true of the city government, there was no relationship between the amount of mail a team member received and his or her commitment to the team, although receiving mail was related to performance. (See table 5.1.) Thus electronic mail can provide an alternate route to letting people have a voice if they are low contributors to face-to-face meetings.

Face-to-face groups consistently show a positive relationship between how much a person talks and how satisfied that person is with the group and how committed he or she is to it (McGrath 1984; Forsyth 1983). Yet

Table 5.1
Attitudes and performance of individuals as a function of communication behavior

	Performance[a]	Commitment[b]
High communicators[c]	17.4	9.1
High talkers only	17.5	8.7
High mailers only	17.0	8.9
Low communicators[c]	12.3	7.8

a. Performance was measured on a scale from 0-20.
b. Commitment was measured on a scale from 1-10.
c. High or low frequency of both talking and using electronic mail.

Management reluctance may actually stem from confusing a commitment to listen to employees with a commitment to act on what they say.

Electronic communication offers the possibility of increasing the amount of communication from lower to higher levels of the hierarchy and solving the logistics problems of collecting information from distant employees. Workers can send messages at their convenience, without having to wait for an appointment or to catch the manager in the hall. It also can alleviate employee reluctance to talk. Workers feel less intimidated about talking to the boss electronically than they do about talking to him or her face-to-face, particularly if what the worker wants to say is in any way negative. Because there are few reminders of status differences, the fear of evaluation or criticism declines.

In one corporation we studied, people who used electronic communication extensively reported that they preferred this form when communicating up the hierarchy to negotiate or solve problems (Sproull and Kiesler 1986). Box 5.2 displays an example of a message from a first-level manager to a vice-president located four levels above him in the hierarchy. This message

air time in meetings is an extremely limited commodity—only one person can talk at a time—and total meeting size is physically constrained. With electronic communication, air time and meeting size are less constrained resources, and so more people can enjoy the benefits of active participation. These benefits may especially accrue to those who, by virtue of geographic or organizational position, would otherwise be peripheral contributors.

Talking to the Boss

Most managers talk more than they listen and issue more directives, make more organizational announcements, and promulgate more policy statements than do lower-level employees. When managers do listen, it's mostly to people close to them. Most talking and listening occurs among people who are physically and hierarchically close to each other. This means managers often don't hear new news; they may be ignorant of information they need that is in the heads or on the desks of lower-level or distant employees—and lower-level employees may feel that no one listens to them.

Giving people a voice is a strong value in our culture. Its embodiment ranges from constitutional principles of freedom of speech and assembly and parliamentary rules of order to public opinion polls, Dale Carnegie's rules for success, and radio call-in shows. Although work organizations are not democracies and free speech does not prevail, giving peripheral people a voice is an important means of binding them to the organization, and it may yield information important for performance.

Managers face three kinds of problems in giving people a voice. One is straightforward logistics problems. By definition, peripheral people are far from the center. Physically collecting their opinions can be time-consuming and expensive. This is one reason that conventional participation mechanisms usually rely on representation rather than direct participation; collecting information from employee representatives is easier than listening to all employees. A second problem is motivational. Although peripheral employees may have a lot to say, they may be reticent, distrustful, or fear recrimination. A third problem is also motivational—but on the receiving end rather than the sending end. Central management may not want to hear what peripheral employees have to say. Given the cultural value we put on being good listeners, this reluctance is not likely to be expressed publicly. Instead it is more likely to be expressed as confidence in the existing ways of hearing from employees and a need to avoid information overload.

Box 5.2. Talking with the boss

```
DATE:     20 May 89  07:29:24
FROM:     Sam.Marlowe
SUBJECT:  Messages from on high
TO:       Bill.Hargrave  John.East
CC:       Don.Dulane , Bob.Bilk, Sam.Marlowe
```

This is to inform you of some small personnel problems you have been causing at lower levels of the organization. I hope that being informed, you will do the right thing in the future. I have made a suggestion at the end.

I like your (electronic) open-door policy; anyone can send you a message on anything, and you will read (and maybe respond to) it. I hope that we do not misuse this policy by sending you so many messages that you will have to close the door, and I would ask that you not misuse this policy by running the organization with it.

There are many good ideas floating around this organization. We do not have enough resources to work on all of them, so managers have to allocate their resources to the most important one (which sometimes are not the most ingenious ones). When a person has a good idea, and it is not worked on, that person tends to be disappointed. Usually, he understands the situa-

> tion, and respects the decision of his boss(s). sometimes when he thinks a mistake is being made, or when he is just plain angry, he uses your open-door policy to sell his good idea. This is just what the policy is for, and I see no harm done.
>
> The problems arise when you, with all your weight and authority, endorse the good idea to the point where the originator believes he now has your blessing to start work on it. He believes that you have/will over-rule his boss, and [the organization] will implement his idea because you think it is so good.
>
> SUGGESTION
>
> When someone sends you an idea, and you are willing/want to respond, please continue to give your opinion (for/against) of the idea, but please make sure that you indicate that the decision to work on the idea will be made by the normal processes in the organization (like release planning or chain of command). I am not suggesting that you stop responding altogether.

illustrates how status imbalance can be reduced in computer communication both in the style of communication from subordinate to superior and in the behavior about which the subordinate is complaining. Although both had offices in the same building, the sender almost never talked with the vice-president directly; most of the occasions on which they were in the same room were formal or ceremonial ones in which the vice-president was making a speech or conducting a large meeting. Yet the sender felt he could send this frank complaint electronically. Notice that the topic of the sender's message is electronic mail behavior. The sender liked the vice-president's electronic open-door policy but did not like what he saw as an electronic endorsement policy.

Managers notice that the nature of the conversation often changes when they walk in the room.[3] One manager calls this the "social Heisenberg effect." "With electronic communication people can forget that I'm their manager when they talk to me," he told us. The manager did not mean this literally, but in our terms many cues to status differences disappear with electronic communication. For this manager, that produced benefits. The cliché is that the boss is always the last to hear the bad news. Electronic communication may convey it sooner.

Why should managers want to encourage more communication from their subordinates, particularly if it's likely to be bad news, negative opinions, or complaints? Obviously, smart managers may prefer to know sooner, rather than later, that all is not well. That justification assumes a view of managers as problem finders and problem solvers. Another view of managers as involvement increasers also suggests benefits from encouraging more communication from lower-level employees. In this view, managers elicit communication because they believe it increases involvement and improves morale. High morale may be sought for its own sake, because it has some direct link with performance, or both. It may turn out that what is most important is letting people talk, not acting on what they say. In the city government we described, we have no evidence that anyone acted on the messages sent by the shift workers, but the electronic communication gave peripheral employees the opportunity to communicate more actively with the boss.

Electronic Discussion Groups

Electronic discussion groups offer the opportunity to consolidate and magnify the effects of passive and active electronic participation. Most employees belong to few groups at work—a primary work group, perhaps a committee or two, and perhaps a social group. (Group membership is positively associated with hierarchical position; high-level managers belong to many more groups than do lower-level employees.) Except for committee assignments, these memberships are relatively stable and enduring, and they lead to important benefits for their members. Electronic group communication makes it possible for more people to belong to many groups and to tailor their group memberships to their changing interests. The groups are not constrained by physical location or fixed-length meetings and can enroll anyone who wants to participate, either actively or passively.

Employees in one Fortune 500 firm received an average of twenty-one DL messages per day from over seven hundred DLs (Finholt and Sproull 1990). The majority of the average person's DL mail came from strangers (company employees unknown to the recipient), and a high percentage came from remote locations. Thus DLs represented a way for people to receive information and make connections that otherwise would have been difficult or impossible. About half the DLs were required ones: an employee's name was placed on a required DL as a function of his or her job or work

Box 5.3. Electronic discussion groups

UserFeatureForum

UserFeatureForum was a work-related discretionary DL for employees interested in discussing interface features of company products. UFF had 125 members and received a mean of 2 messages a day (max = 8, min = 0). Many of the messages on UFF were mildly pedantic, as people demonstrated their technical opinions or virtuosity.

```
Regarding contention resolution in Graphics:  I like meaning 1
(option 2) of the next key (next item in the contenders list).
Meaning 2 would seem to me to be very unpredictable from a
user's point of view. The internal sibling structure could not
in general be predicted from the image they see whereas the
next contender would be much more natural. Regarding how
frames behave during pagination:  both alternatives have
undesirable qualities. Data should never be intentionally
thrown away (as in alt1). And alt2 would more than likely
result in an unacceptable positioning of the frame. Given the
current of document structure in [product], I don't see any
better pagination heuristic that what we do now. One possibil-
ity might be to post a message when one of these guys is
encountered and let the user decide what to do such as abort
pagination. then the user could change the page props of the
problem page and repaginate.
/Joe
```

Still, UFF was not all bland discourse on "contention resolution problems" or "multinational user interfaces." Personal rivalries sometimes surfaced. For example, toward the end of one particularly arcane exchange, one member pointedly observed in a message that "some people" on UFF spent more time talking about user interfaces than building them. On the whole, though, talking about interfaces was the raison d'être of UFF. It had no identity outside the mail system. UFF was an arena for people to display their knowledge before their superiors and peers—although this knowledge was rarely acted upon (in our sample of messages, only two UFF communications resulted in actual changes to an interface). In the words of one UFFer:

```
To paraphrase a famous saying about economists, which pretty
much summarizes my feeling about all this endless user-inter-
face niggling that's been going on for the last six years, and
shows every indication of continuing out to eternity:

If all the user interface experts in the world were laid end to
end, they wouldn't reach a conclusion.
```

location. The employee had no choice about belonging to required DLs, which ranged from ten-person DLs for subunit groups to six-hundred-person site lists for all employees working in a particular city. The discretionary DLs, which people joined by choice, covered a wide spectrum of topics, some about work and some extracurricular. They ranged from the exotic to the mundane: Oenologists for wine fanciers, NetSpecs for computer network designers, GoPlayers for students of the Japanese strategy game Go, Classifieds for selling things, and ChildCare for locating babysitters.

Some discretionary DLs, such as Classifieds and ChildCare, merely served as a convenient way to broadcast information; others functioned as interacting discussion groups. (See box 5.3 for descriptions of three electronic discussion groups and sample messages from each of them.) The discretionary discussion groups were large and geographically dispersed, averaging 260 members located in seven different cities, and they inter-acted regularly. Four days out of five, messages went to these groups, week after week—an average of four messages a day. Messages were sent by an average of 41 different people in each discussion group over a two-week to one-month period. Although most of these members were not personally known to one another and had no common tasks, most messages were not simply disconnected broadcasts unrelated to one another but explicit replies to previous messages. These groups sustained involving discussions over distance and time among strangers. Each discretionary group also worked at being a group. They sent messages discussing the purpose and procedures of the group and membership criteria for it. Although group members were physically invisible and unknown to one another, the groups took on personalities and lives of their own.

Membership in any group confers informational and emotional benefits to the member, including increased information resources, emotional resources, and the opportunity to take on different roles and identities. These processes are so powerful that peoples' mental health status is positively associated with the number of groups they belong to (Thoits 1983). It is plausible, although only a hypothesis at this point, that membership in multiple electronic groups has similar beneficial effects, particularly for people who belong to few face-to-face groups. For those who belong to a great many face-to-face groups, we would expect much less effect; the costs in demands on their time and energy might well outweigh the benefits.

In response to this complaint, though, another member responded with a hoary mail system adage: "If you don't like talking about user features, drop out of UserFeatureForum."

Cinema

Cinema was an extracurricular discretionary DL, with over 500 members—managers, professionals, technicians, and secretaries. Cinema members received a mean of 4 messages a day from this DL (max = 31, min = 0). Messages were related to movie reviews—highly subjective commentaries on everything related to the movie, including the ambiance in the theater and the quality of the popcorn.

John,
I just saw flashDance, you were very right. I stopped by Tower Records on the way home and picked up the sound track. I am taping it now. I am not a big movie goer and I am at odds with Mann and AMC theaters but this film was well worth the trip to my local corporate theater. Fortunately I was spared the newspaper ads by arriving 5 minutes late.

Well, I did not start this as a flame about corporate theaters. I wanted to say that FlashDance is a clever, well filmed, moving musical that runs around your head for a long time after leaving the theater. Go see it and check out the sound track on Casablanca Records. It's a Polygram Record with a few built in flaws.
Later...
/PRL

V was a mashed-up composite of about twenty science-fiction stories. Not a single original idea in it. And besides that it wasn't very good.
Save Joe-Bob!

Rowdies

Rowdies, a discretionary extracurricular DL, had 98 members, 73 percent of them male technicians or professionals. Typically Rowdies was the source of over 20 "RowdieMail" messages per day (max = 50, min = 0). Although some work issues occasionally crept into Rowdies discussions, most messages concerned gossip (mostly about other Rowdies), group activities (such as organizing softball teams or writing electronic novels), and crude humor.

Squnds to me like you have quit while you were ahead!! Has anyone else noticed that we've actually been getting messages from 666 lately, and most of them have times on them like 3:05 a.m.-5:42 a.m., etc., etc. Do you think he's trying to impress us with his devotion to duty? I'll bet his boss gets a message every day at that time as well...even if 666

has nothing much to say to him. He also lets us know that he is working a 13 hour day — he has stated that more than once.

I mean, we enjoy your messages 666, but, really, impressing us isn't going to change the fact that there are no merit increases this year — unless, of course, they change their mind in June or July after re-evaluating this situation.

And by the way, 3:00 a.m. to 12:30 p.m. is only a 9-1/2 hour day..........
2
GeezSomePeople

Rowdies regularly sent messages to organize afternoon beer busts, which were the focus of elaborate preparation. These outings were documented in full, and their histories were carefully indexed and archived for future reference in secure Rowdie disk space.

John and Phil,
I have room for both of you in my car plus one more RowdieLuncher. I'm pretty sure the luncheon is still on for 12:30 pm.
44

....zzzzzzzzzzzzzzzzzz.Hmmph. Burp...huh? who me....what column? miss a deadline...what day is it? ohmygod it's wednesday already. What? somebody wrote it? Joe, who? Oh yes, JOE! - he's the one I had always thought was bald.
zR722

Was a great party, in fact I'm still smiling.
...that whipped cream was good stuff

Rowdies messages displayed complex stylistic conventions, including closing messages with a Rowdy number and a run-on commentary that often took the form of sarcastic observations on previous messages or continued observations from other messages. Rowdies sometimes referred to fellow Rowdies by using Rowdy "handles," such as "Colt45" or "Mr. Toon-toon," an important part of Rowdy identity. Periodically Rowdies issued a membership list indicating numbers, handles, birthdates, and favorite "RowdieDrinks." During our observation, the membership list contained the names of honorary Rowdies, including several waitresses at Rowdy hangouts, and Divine, the transvestite star of *Pink Flamingos* and *Polyester*.

Rowdies messages expressed clear opinions about Rowdies and the larger electronic community. On one occasion a prominent Rowdy noted, after three new Rowdies members dropped out after only two days, "They weren't Rowdy material. Keep up the good work!"

Source: Adapted from Finholt and Sproull (1990).

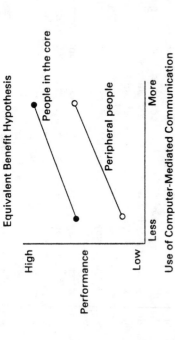

Equivalent Benefit Hypothesis

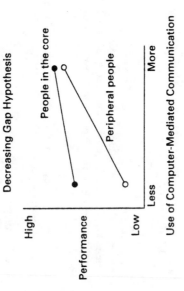

Decreasing Gap Hypothesis

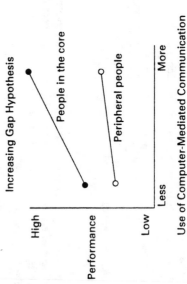

Increasing Gap Hypothesis

Figure 5.1
Some hypothetical relationships between computer-mediated communication and employee performance

Performance Implications

This chapter emphasizes the information and motivation benefits of increasing peripheral employee participation through electronic communication. Do these connections also differentially benefit the performance of peripheral workers? There are almost no data to help us answer this question; we can only lay out the basic reasoning underlying why we might expect to see a differential benefit and report some tantalizing bits of evidence.

Differential Performance Benefits for Peripheral Employees

The basic argument suggests that peripheral employees have more to gain from electronic communication than do more central employees. We assume that peripheral employees start out at an information disadvantage. In principle, both groups of employees could benefit equally, illustrated as "equivalent benefits" in figure 5.1. But central employees are likely to experience ceiling effects on their communication. That is, each new communication benefits them relatively less because they already know a great deal and are already active contributors. Peripheral employees, by contrast, derive more benefit from each additional communication both because they know less and because they have fewer other opportunities to participate actively. This relationship is illustrated as the "decreasing gap hypothesis" in figure 5.1: peripheral employees' performance increases more than central employees' performance does, closing the gap between the two groups. Of course, there could be other relationships as well. Both groups could be equivalently harmed by electronic communication. This outcome could be produced by a simple information overload process in which each new communication distracts attention or confuses the recipient. Or central employees could benefit much more than peripheral employees. This "gap-increasing" benefit (shown at the bottom of figure 5.1) could most plausibly occur if central employees had better access to computer-based information resources, or if they communicated only with one another or communicated entirely different kinds of information. We believe, however, that when access is open the effects are mainly positive, with differential benefit to peripheral workers.

We have found evidence of differential benefits to peripheral workers in an investigation of how physical oceanographers use computer networks (Hesse et al. 1990). We examined how the use of electronic communication affected the relationship between age and professional recognition (scientific awards, appointment to editorial boards, professional committees, and advisory committees). In this kind of analysis, younger scientists are considered more peripheral than older scientists. We found that while older scientists generally received more professional recognition than younger scientists (and scientists who used electronic communication more received more professional recognition), electronic communication benefited younger scientists more than it did older scientists in receiving professional recognition.

John Earls has discovered a similar pattern of advantage for people with physical handicaps. He directed a multiyear program for participants in a rehabilitation program designed to teach confidence and positive attitudes toward the disabled among both disabled people and human service professionals. He compared a control group with an equivalent experimental group that used a computer bulletin board for communication over several years. Each group had thirty members: ten disabled people, ten therapists, and ten university students. The experimental group did not differ from the control after six months in the program, but after two years there were highly significant differences. By then the experimental group was more positive in its attitudes about disability and the disabled than the control group was. The disabled members were even more positive in their attitudes than other experimental group members were. Also, the disabled people in the experimental group participated more actively. They logged onto the network and read and sent more messages than the professionals or students did (box 5.4.)

Short-run versus Long-run Implications

Even if increasing affiliation and commitment through increasing electronic connections is feasible, the direct link between increased commitment and increased performance has not been demonstrated. Happy workers are not necessarily more productive workers.[4] Nor are more informed workers necessarily more productive workers. Charles O'Reilly (1980) looked at the relationship between employees' attitudes toward and use of information and the quality of their job performance as rated by their supervisors. He found a positive association between how much information people had to do their jobs and their satisfaction with the amount of information they had. That is, people who reported they had more information were also more satisfied with the amount of information they had. But he also found a negative association between how much information people had to do their jobs and the quality of their actual performance. The more information people had, the worse was their performance. These findings

---

Box 5.4. Differential benefits of computer-based communication

T is a 30-year-old man whose disability is cerebral palsy. He works in the office area at Centrecraft Industries, a sheltered employment facility. In the last year he has been nominated as a representative of the disabled people working at his work facility.

T states that one of the personal benefits of his participation in the Bulletin Board project has been the opportunity to resume communication with people with whom he had lost contact. In addition, he sees that being able to talk to other people with disabilities about work issues as well as his own thoughts and feelings is being a great strength of the Bulletin Board. The fact that he is able to talk to individuals using their private mail box is particularly good; especially when he wants to discuss a problem at work and wants to be assured of privacy. Its use as a public forum, allowing the discussion of issues relevant to the disabled consumer group, has been very helpful in his role as a consumer representative. It has enabled him to get different people's ideas, discuss matters with them and report them to the consumer group at Industries.

In T's opinion, his involvement in the Bulletin Board has enabled him to better express his thoughts and opinions. In effect, it has made him more confident in talking to groups both via the Bulletin Board and also face to face. In addition, it has made him more willing to consider other people's viewpoints. He reported that prior to his use of the Bulletin Board, he was probably "one sided" in his attitudes. Now, he is more able and prepared to consider the attitudes and feelings of the group as a whole. In addition, T feels that his involvement with the Bulletin Board has resulted in staff looking at him "in a much more positive light."

During his participation in the Bulletin Board project, T was initially loaned a computer, modem and communications software by the organisation. He has subsequently purchased his own computer and equipment and reports that this is a direct consequence of his involvement with the Bulletin Board. He uses the computer not only for communication purposes but also for word processing. He is currently writing a book and has begun to see other possible uses for his computer.

T is now accessing a community bulletin board as well as that run by the organisation. T reported that this board extends his information capability and there is more opportunity to communicate with people you do not know. It also has a variety of different interest areas covering topics such as sports, politics and hobbies. Although T has not yet communicated with people in these areas, he enjoys reading the comments of others and feels that one day he will want to share his own thoughts on some of the different areas.

Source: Earls (1990: 204–205).

are consonant with the view of economists who point out that people often overinvest in information; they acquire more information or more costly information than they need to do their work. In this view any strategy that seeks to increase information and motivation connections among employees should be viewed with suspicion. This view is typically characterized by an extremely short-run perspective, considering the relationship between performance and amount of information or amount of satisfaction at only one time. Companies or managers that have primarily a short-run orientation can use similar reasoning to forbid or minimize widespread use of a computer-based communication system.

Companies and managers with a longer view, however, may think of increasing employee participation by electronic communication as a capacity-building strategy with implications for long-term performance. They might consider three components of such a strategy: creating connections among employees, building new skills, and increasing employees' ability to absorb new ideas. Increasing employee participation increases links among employees. Although most of the time these links are irrelevant to routine performance, they are available when needed, in times of crisis or opportunity. A case from Manufacturer's Hanover Trust (MHT) illustrates the point. Several years ago, MHT launched a new financial product in the Far East under extremely tight time deadlines governed by impending regulatory changes. MHT lawyers in Washington, corporate officers in New York, and marketing personnel in California used the MHT electronic mail system to coordinate their activities with one another and with the Hong Kong office to bring out the product under the deadline. Employees told us this story to illustrate how much they depend on their mail system. It also illustrates a capacity-building strategy. At the time of this opportunity, MHT personnel already "knew" many employees through communicating with them electronically. They could use these connections because they already existed.

Research on teaching and learning shows that people don't learn new ideas or skills just by being exposed to them.[5] Learners must be prepared to learn; they must have the mental scaffolding and requisite skills to understand and master new ideas (Cohen and Levinthal 1990). Listening to network discussions may help produce this "absorptive capacity" in employees, both old-timers and newcomers. It is easier to join and be socialized to electronic groups than to face-to-face ones (Moreland and Levine 1982). When group members are physically invisible, as is true with

electronic interaction, the high salience and potential stress associated with the newcomer identity decline. Putting new employees on the mail system, especially if they can join large discretionary distribution lists, can help bring them quickly up to speed on how and what their fellow employees are thinking. It can get them more oriented toward the organization.

What about Extracurricular Mail?

Although some companies discourage any electronic discussions, many permit or encourage discussions related to company business for the reasons noted. Extracurricular messages and groups are a more difficult issue. It is easy to dismiss them as a waste of company resources—both network resources and employee time. The question of extracurricular mail is not one to be settled in a vacuum. It is simply an instance of a much more general view of human resource management. Some companies subsidize extracurricular benefits for their employees. Exercise facilities, discount entertainment tickets, office celebrations, softball teams—all could be viewed as a waste of resources. Companies that invest in them do so as a way of building employee enthusiasm, loyalty, or commitment. A recent study of employees in a high-technology service sector firm showed that "socializing with coworkers and supervisors, either on or off the job or both" was correlated with positive organizational attitudes (Kaufman et al. 1988). Allowing extracurricular messages and groups may serve a similar function. Where we have systematic data, it seems lower-level employees more often send and receive extracurricular messages and participate in extracurricular electronic groups.

Allowing extracurricular mail also can contribute to a capacity-building strategy. A steely-eyed controller might frown on a company DL called ChocolateLovers. Yet that DL might be just the means to get peripheral employees motivated to increase their network connections and skills. In the accounting department of one large organization, a new employee was enrolled in a ChocolateLovers DL by another employee as a friendly orientation gesture. (She was also enrolled in all of the DLs required for her job and location.) After reading ChocolateLovers for a month or so, the new employee decided she wanted to print out some recipes she had read, so she had to learn various commands for manipulating and printing text. She then decided that she would compile recipes from the DL into a book to give as a Christmas present. To illustrate the book, she learned color desktop graphics by experimenting during her lunch hour. Over an eighteen-month period, this accounts payable supervisor became the office guru on desktop publishing and color graphics because she had joined ChocolateLovers. These skills were not directly applicable to accounts payable supervision, but they represented an increase in her skill repertoire and an increase in the skill capacity of the entire office.

Conclusion

It may seem paradoxical that computers, stereotyped as cold and impersonal, can be used to increase personal connections and affiliation. Electronic communication is not a substitute for face-to-face relationships, but for many peripheral employees, satisfying face-to-face relationships are hard to come by in the workplace. Electronic communication can increase the informational and emotional connections of these employees. The benefits to individual employees are immediate. The organization can additionally benefit by increasing employee capacity to work beyond the letter of the employment contract.

From the organization's perspective, giving a voice to the voiceless and opening a window on the corporation can produce bad effects as well as good ones. If the previously voiceless employees use the mail system to complain or to mobilize protest, managers might prefer that they had remained mute. And even if increasing participation by electronic means does not lead to riot or revolution, it still costs money. Some managers may be unwilling to support communication services that are not directly tied to task performance even if they do increase employee motivation and commitment. That decision, however, is one that should be taken in the light of more general human resource strategies.

References

Aronson, E. (1966). The psychology of insufficient justification: An analysis of some conflicting data. In S. Feldman (Ed.), *Cognitive consistency* (pp. 115-133). New York: Academic Press.

Cohen, W., and Levinthal, D. A. (1990). Absorptive capacity: A new perspective on learning and innovation. *Administrative Science Quarterly, 35*, 128-152.

Earls, J. (1990) Social integration by people with physical disabilities: The development of an information technology model based on personal growth and achievement. Unpublished doctoral dissertation, The University of Wollongong, Wollongong, Australia.

Eveland, J. D., and Bikson, T. K. (1988). Work group structures and computer support: A field experiment. *Transactions on Office Information Systems, 6*(4), 354-379.

Feldman, M. S. (1987). Electronic mail and weak ties in organizations. *Office: Technology and People, 3*, 83-101.

Finholt, T., and Sproull, L. (1990). Electronic groups at work. *Organization Science, 1*(1), 41-64.

Forsyth, D. R. (1983). *An introduction to group dynamics*. Monterey, CA: Brooks/ Cole Publishing Co.

Hesse, B., Sproull, L., Kiesler, S., and Walsh, J. (1990). *Computer network support for science: The case of oceanography*. Unpublished manuscript, Carnegie Mellon University, Pittsburgh.

Huff, C., Sproull, L., and Kiesler, S. (1989). Computer communication and organizational commitment: Tracing the relationship in a city government. *Journal of Applied Social Psychology, 19*, 1371-1391.

Kaufman, R. L., Parcel, T. L., Wallace, M., and Form, W. (1988). Looking forward: Responses to organizational and technological change in an ultra-high technology firm. In I. H. Simpson and R. L. Simpson (Eds.), *Research in the sociology of work, 4* (pp. 31-67). Greenwich, CT: JAI Press.

Kiesler, S., Zubrow, D., Moses, A. M., and Geller, V. (1985). Affect in computer-mediated communication: An experiment in synchronous terminal-to-terminal discussion. *Human Computer Interaction, 1,* 77-104.

Lichtenstein, S., Slovic, P., Fischhoff, B., Layman, M., and Combs, B. (1978). Judged frequency of lethal events. *Journal of Experimental Psychology: Human Learning and Memory, 4,* 33-35.

McGrath, J. E. (1984). *Groups: Interaction and performance.* Englewood Cliffs, NJ: Prentice-Hall.

Moreland, R. L., and Levine, J. M. (1982). Socialization in small groups: Temporal changes in individual-group relations. *Advances in Experimental Social Psychology, 15,* 137-192.

O'Reilly, C. (1980). Individuals and information overload in organizations: Is more necessarily better? *Academy of Management Journal, 23,* 684-696.

Sproull, L., and Kiesler, S. (1986). Reducing social context cues: Electronic mail in organizational communication. *Management Science, 32*(11), 1492-1512.

Thoits, P. (1983). Multiple identities and psychological well-being. *American Sociological Review, 48,* 174-187.

ELECTRONIC GROUPS AT WORK*

TOM FINHOLT AND LEE S. SPROULL

Department of Social and Decision Sciences, Carnegie Mellon University, Pittsburgh, Pennsylvania 15213-2833

This paper considers how computer-based communication technology, specifically electronic group mail, might affect group behavior in organizations. It proposes a framework for analyzing groups formed by electronic distribution lists. It describes the scope and nature of electronic group mail in one organization, illustrates how members of electronic distribution lists can exhibit fundamental group processes, and compares behavior in different kinds of electronic groups. It suggests that the electronic group at work is a new social phenomenon that may contribute importantly to organizational behavior.
(ELECTRONIC WORK GROUPS; INFORMAL ELECTRONIC ORGANIZATIONS)

Introduction

Groups, not individuals, are the fundamental unit of work in modern organizations. On-going work and routine work are organized in formal organizational subunits. Nonroutine work and new work are accomplished through teams, committees, or ad hoc work groups. Groups and group behavior are consequential for organizational performance and for individual group members.

New computer-based technology may affect groups and group behavior in organizations. For instance, robotics technology may alter how production work groups are organized (e.g., Argote, Goodman, and Schade 1983). Office automation technology may alter how office groups are organized (e.g., Matteis 1979). This paper considers how computer-based communication technology, specifically electronic group mail, might affect group behavior in organizations.[1]

Electronic mail has several characteristics that condition its use as a communication medium (see Culnan and Markus 1987, for a recent review). For instance, it is *fast*. It is *text-based*. Additionally, in most systems mail *can be sent to a group of people as easily as to one person*. This attribute makes possible our focus on group communication. In many systems, a list of people's names and computer addresses, sometimes called a distribution list (DL), is given a name. A sender mails one communication to the group name (e.g., to Sales.Group or to ScienceFictionLovers.Group). The sender does not specify, indeed need not know, the names and addresses of group members. The computer automatically mails a copy of the communication to all group members. Every member receives the communication, which has been addressed to the group as a whole, in his or her own mailbox.

How might electronic communication affect groups in organizations? It might simply speed up on-going communication. That is, existing groups might use it to accomplish their existing information activities more quickly than they could with more conventional channels. In this case the technology would produce efficiency effects but no other changes. Alternatively, the technology might lead to new or different forms of group organization with organizational consequences beyond efficiency changes. This paper explores that alternative. Five sections follow. The first proposes a framework for understanding how electronic communication could affect group behavior in organizations. The second section enumerates research questions derived from that framework. The third describes the methodology used to address them. The fourth presents results. And the fifth suggests some future research and management opportunities.

Group Communication in Organizations

A social group is two or more people who influence one another over time through direct communication among group members (Forsyth 1983). Social groups in organizations benefit their members by providing information resources, emotional resources, and identity support. Social groups benefit the organization by coordinating individual participation, organizing productive work, and providing a mechanism for specialized learning (e.g., Goodman and Associates 1986; Hackman 1987; McGrath 1984, pp. 137–245). In order for groups to perform any of these functions, members must communicate with one another.

Previous research on social groups in organizations has emphasized three classes of variables relevant to communication: group attributes, group processes, and organizational consequences. Their relationships are displayed in the top half of Figure A. The bottom half of Figure A summarizes how electronic communication technology may affect these variables.

Group Attributes

A group's physical setting regulates the group's behavior and communication (Baum and Valins 1977; Oldham and Rotchford 1983). Variation across kinds of settings can have even stronger effects: the same group of people behaves quite differently in a bar and in a funeral parlor. Physical setting influences group communication even when the communication is asynchronous. For instance, a physical bulletin board conveys cues about what should be posted or can be read on it. The boss's office late at night is still the boss's office and suggests some kinds of messages would be less appropriate to leave on his desk than others.

Electronic mail creates communication situations with no shared physical setting. Physical setting is not shared because there is no singular place at which group communication occurs and there are no shared artifacts of the communication. Group members can send or read group mail while physically in their office, their secretary's office, a public workstation cluster, a laboratory, home, or (by using portable computers and the telephone) in a client's office or on the road. Furthermore, messages appear on and disappear from video terminals, apparently leaving no trace behind. Thus people should be less reminded of shared context in electronic communication than in other communication situations.

Member characteristics also regulate group behavior. Members' physical appearance and location within the group influence group interaction—who talks and who listens (Berscheid and Walster 1975). So do the members' social status, including their

---

* Accepted by Robert W. Zmud; received January 14, 1988. This paper has been with the authors 5 months for 1 revision.

[1] Most organizational predictions and research about how computing will affect work and worklife have focussed on what happens when individual workers begin interacting with a computer on the job (e.g., Glenn and Feldberg 1977; Guiliano 1982; Hartmann 1987; Morton and Huff 1980; Wallace and Kalleberg 1982). The explicit focus on group effects by organizational researchers has been less common. Communication researchers have examined how computer communication affects behavior in extraorganizational groups. For instance, experimental laboratory studies have compared computer-mediated groups with face-to-face groups; see Rice (1984) for a review. Field studies have examined special interest electronic conferences whose members come from different organizations (e.g., Vallee et al 1974; Hiltz and Turoff 1978; Kerr and Hiltz 1982; Rice 1982; Freeman 1984; Palme 1981) and conferences within organizations (Vallee and Wilson 1976; Lipinski and Adler 1982; Zuboff 1988). Some computer scientists are beginning to build special purpose hardware and software for group work (e.g., Stefik et al. 1987; Malone et al. 1987; Grief 1987).

1047-7039/90/0101/0041$01.25
Copyright © 1990, The Institute of Management Sciences

FIGURE A. Comparing Conventional Group Behavior with That of Electronic Groups.

Group Attributes	Conventional Group Behavior in Organizations — Group Processes	Org. Consequences
(1) Physical settings	(1) Interaction: Synchronous	(1) Participation
(2) Member characteristics	(2) Influence: Multiple social cues	(2) Performance
(3) Membership criteria	(3) Identity maintenance: Multiple physical & social cues	(3) Learning
(4) Task type		

Group Attributes	Hypothesized Electronic Group Behavior in Organizations — Group Processes	Org. Consequences
(1) No shared physical settings	(1) Interaction: Asynchronous	(1) Participation: Larger groups, dispersed groups, rel. equality across members
(2) "Invisible" members	(2) Influence attempts: Few social cues	(2) Performance: Reduced process loss, increased information access
(3) Membership criteria	(3) Identity maintenance: Through text primarily	(3) Learning: New information buffers, rapid feedback, rapid diffusion
(4) Topic		

in more ceremonial communication—hazings, graduations, retirement parties, official memoranda, and the like.

The membership distinction between formal and informal groups may be either required or discretionary. In required groups, an authority controls whose names are on the group DL; employees have no choice about belonging to required DLs. Required DLs typically mirror formal organizational units. Discretionary lists are open to anyone; a list of discretionary lists is usually available on-line. Anyone can join a discretionary DL simply by asking that his or her name be added to the list; similarly anyone can exit by asking that his or her name be removed. We may expect behavior to vary between required and discretionary DLs as it does between formal and informal groups.

Group behavior is also affected by the type of task the group is performing (McGrath 1984, pp. 51–136). Most organizational group research focusses on groups whose primary task is work-related. Even informal groups, whose members socialize with one another on and off the job, are usually analyzed in terms of work performance. Organizational researchers have paid little attention to nonwork groups. However, recent research on Japanese organizations suggests that organizationally-based extracurricular groups—such as sports teams, clubs, and hobby groups—may contribute to organizational socialization and commitment even though they perform no overt organizational tasks (Lincoln and Kalleberg 1985).

The distinction between work topics and nonwork topics is also found in electronic DLs. Because there has been little prior organizational research comparing work groups with extracurricular ones, it is difficult to predict how electronic work groups might differ from electronic extracurricular groups. Conceivably work groups might be more active because members would have shared work topics and perhaps assignments and deadlines to motivate their interaction. Alternatively extracurricular groups might be more active because they would provide a "break" from the workday and because their members would have fewer nonelectronic occasions to interact with one another.

Group Processes

All social groups, no matter what their particular attributes, exhibit three communication-related processes over time: interaction, influence attempts, and identity maintenance. Interaction means that, at a minimum, group members have information contact with one another. Influence attempts means that, through this interaction, group members exchange new information, attitudes, or behaviors. Identity maintenance means that the group differentiates itself from its environment both physically through such mechanisms as uniforms and gestures and socially through such mechanisms as rituals and outsider denigration (Trice and Beyer 1984).

Because electronic mail is asynchronous, "interaction" in the electronic group must also be asynchronous. The speed of electronic mail means that one message can follow another with very little delay. However electronic communication cannot include the simultaneous exchange of nonverbal feedback or awareness of shared circumstances that synchronous communication can provide. From the perspective of a DL member, messages from many sources and DLs simply appear on a video screen one after another. If messages are perceived as a stream of disconnected one-way broadcasts, there would be little motivation to answer them, little continuity of topics over time, and little sense of interaction among members.

Influence attempts may be problematic. Social context cues, which emanate from physical settings and member attributes, regulate influence attempts. When physical settings are not shared and members are invisible, influence can emanate only from the text of messages. Furthermore, because group members do not necessarily see the reaction of other group members to an influence attempt, social validation of influence

hierarchical position, gender, and task expertise (Cohen and Roper 1972; Kanter 1977; Watson 1982). Physical and social attributes also influence how people's contributions to the group are valued (Festinger 1950). And they influence how the group's identity is perceived by members and outsiders (Sherif et al. 1961).

Electronic mail not only lacks a physical shared setting—it also lacks visible participants.[2] Participants are invisible in three ways. One: message recipients are not named. A person sending a group message knows that everyone whose name is on the group list will receive it, but he or she may not know which names are on the list. Similarly, a recipient of a group message will not be told who else has received it. Two: there is no indication of which recipients actually read a message. Thus, even if someone knows who belongs to a DL, he or she will not know who has read a particular message. Three: even when participants are known to one another, there are few reminders of their presence in the communication situation. Thus people should be relatively less aware of the attributes of others in electronic communication than in other communication situations.

In conventional groups, membership criteria also regulate group behavior. They underlie one of the oldest distinctions among types of organizational groups: formal groups versus informal groups. The distinction is important because researchers discovered that informal groups could have as much impact on performance as formal ones (Dalton 1959; Mayo 1945; Roethlisberger and Dickson 1939). Formal groups correspond to organizational units and include everyone working within the unit boundaries. Informal groups, which can develop within or across formal groups, emerge through voluntary association. They typically display different patterns of communication and member motivation. For example, people in formal groups engage

[2] Various electronic mail systems can make participants more or less invisible based on software or policy choices. This topic is discussed further in the concluding section of this paper.

attempts is weak. In conventional groups information influence occurs for instrumental purposes to direct attention, coordinate activity, and solve problems (March and Simon 1958, p. 161), to symbolize competence (Feldman and March 1981), and to have fun (March and Sevon 1984). Can these purposes be detected solely through the text of electronic messages?

Identity maintenance may be even more problematic. Messages simply scroll down a screen in most systems. Can one DL's messages be differentiated from another's? Membership criterion (required versus discretionary) and topic (work versus nonwork) may help differentiate DLs. Beyond that, if differentiation occurs at all, it should be visible in the text of the messages themselves. Electronic DLs have no way to tangibly differentiate themselves but they may do so linguistically through text style. They may also do so through text content, explicitly discussing the purpose or nature of the DL in group messages.

Organizational Consequences

Groups influence employee participation by providing information that helps people know how to behave, by affecting how people regard their work, by shaping attitudes toward the larger organization, and by channeling their contributions (e.g., Van Maanen and Schein 1979). It should be relatively easy to join and be socialized to electronic groups in contrast with face-to-face ones (Moreland and Levine 1982). Thus we would expect people to join relatively more electronic groups than face-to-face ones. Assimilating new electronic group members should also be relatively easy. The only behaviors necessary for electronic group members to know are the appropriate occasions for sending messages and their style and content. Models of these behaviors (i.e., actual messages) are fully visible to all group members.

Electronic group membership may affect members' sense of self, as does conventional group membership. Research on face-to-face groups has demonstrated that a group benefits its members by increasing their information and enhancing their self-identify (Forsyth 1983; McGrath 1984). The net consequences of multiple group membership are also positive, because membership roles provide meaning and rules for behaving (e.g., Thoits 1983). In organizations a person's group position affects his or her perceived influence and commitment (Blau and Alba 1982; Brass 1984; Eisenberg, Monge, and Miller 1983; Fombrun 1982; Tichy, Tushman, and Fombrun 1979). If electronic groups offer employees additional opportunities for group membership over and above conventional ones, they may also confer additional benefits.

Because participants are invisible, conventional social regulators of participation such as gender or hierarchical status should not constrain contribution to electronic groups as much as they constrain face-to-face discussions. Thus electronic groups sometimes have more equal participation than their nonelectronic counterparts of the same size (Siegel et al. 1986; Hiltz and Turoff 1978, p. 111). Because electronic group members do not share a common setting, situation regulators of participation should also be attenuated. Thus the content of electronic group communication may be more idiosyncratic than that of face-to-face groups (McGuire et al. 1987; Hiltz and Turoff 1978, p. 90).

Conventional groups affect organizational performance by coordinating individual performance and by helping people learn about how they can best work with others to meet organizational goals (Hackman and Morris 1975). Electronic group membership may affect employees' task performance. Theories derived from observation of traditional groups explain that above a certain size, group performance becomes increasingly inefficient as a result of process loss (Steiner 1972). Process loss can occur because one individual monopolizes the floor or because too many people are talking

at once. Process loss should be reduced in electronic groups because there is no physical meeting space, specified meeting length, or constraints on how many people can speak at once. Further, people who are disadvantaged in face-to-face meetings because they are reticent or of lower status can contribute more equally in the electronic setting (Finholt, Sproull and Kiesler 1988). Electronic group membership should also benefit employees' performance outside the electronic arena because electronic groups can be sources of information that people would otherwise find it difficult to access (Feldman 1987).

Groups affect organizational learning by providing occasions, procedures, and repositories for specialized memory (Levitt and March 1988). It is technically easy to ask for and provide information in electronic groups. A requestor can send a message to the group asking, "Does anybody know ...?" An answerer can reply to the entire group. If electronic groups actually do behave this way, then individual expertise and experience is turned into shared knowledge; electronic groups become information buffers (Kmetz 1984), devices for pooling current information in a readily accessible form. Furthermore, they also provide a way to share feedback by making both an initiating message and all responses visible to the entire group. If group mail is automatically archived, then the electronic record remains available to people who join the group in the future. If electronic groups are large in comparison with conventional ones, the rate of diffusion of ideas across people should be relatively fast. And, if people belong to many electronic groups, the rate of diffusion across groups should be relatively fast as well.

We have suggested ways that electronic group attributes and processes may differ from those in conventional groups in organizations. Some of these differences can be (and have been) explored in laboratory research. But many of our claims can be investigated only within the context of on-going work organizations. The purpose of the study reported below is to look for evidence of electronic groups in the on-going electronic mail traffic of one work organization.

Research Questions

The first empirical task is to demonstrate that electronic groups exist in work organizations. The empirical starting point for this paper was the observation that employees in one organization received DL messages every day. But conceivably they could all have come from one DL and one sender and been on one topic, resembling a company newsletter more than a collection of social groups. Thus the first research question is:

1. What is the nature and scope of DL activity within the study organization?

The answer to this question will demonstrate how one large organization uses electronic group mail. Additionally, assuming the description reveals some variation across DL activity then we can investigate whether any of the DLs behave like social groups. That is:

2. Do DLs exhibit the fundamental social group processes of interaction, influence attempts, and identity maintenance?

If such processes are at all evident in DLs, they should be most prevalent in DLs whose members interact only electronically. If DL members meet as a group face-to-face, they need not concentrate their group behaviors in the electronic medium because they have other opportunities to engage in interaction, influence attempts, and identity maintenance. These DLs might be labelled "augmenting DLs" because they function in addition to other group interaction media. Furthermore, "pure" electronic groups are less likely to be subject to the physical constraints of size and geographic colocation that may characterize the electronic counterparts of face-to-face groups.

Thus:

3a. Do pure electronic groups exhibit a higher degree of interaction than do augmenting ones?

3b. Do pure electronic groups exhibit more influence attempts?

3c. Do pure electronic groups exhibit more identity maintenance?

3d. Are pure electronic groups larger than required ones?

3e. Are pure electronic groups more geographically dispersed?

We return to questions of organizational consequence in the concluding section.

Methodology

The study organization is a Fortune 500 office products firm employing over 100,000 people, which we call the Porter Hall Corporation (PHC).[3] We collected data in two units of this firm, each employing about 300 people, located within the R & D division and the Business Products division. A stratified random sample of employees (n = 96) saved a hard copy of all incoming and outgoing electronic mail for a three-day period. Respondents were asked a series of questions about a subsample of those messages (up to 15 messages on one of the days for each person resulting in a total of 1248 messages, 985 of which were DL messages). The questions included: What is this message about? Would you have received this information in some other way if there were no electronic mail system?[4]

The mail system used by PHC supported over 3700 users, handled over 8000 messages each working day (many of which were sent to hundreds of people), and had been in place for over a decade. On average, people in our sample had used electronic mail for more than four years, found that the organization's policies and procedures encouraged electronic mail use, and believed that the mail program was easy to use. In addition, access to the system was good and there were few sending restrictions.

We addressed the first research question by reanalyzing data from all respondents in the original sample survey to characterize their DL mail behavior. We addressed the second and third research questions by means of illustrative descriptions of a small number of DLs. For these descriptions we relied on both the subset of message data from the previous analysis as well as on other messages from the respondents' entire three-day sample of messages.

To select the example groups, we had to characterize membership criterion, topic, and activity level for each DL in our sample. The corporation provided us with a list of all required DLs. Every DL not on that list was categorized as a discretionary one. DL topics were categorized as work-related or extracurricular based on respondents' answers to the question (for each subsample message), "What is this message about?" A message and its DL were categorized as work-related if its contents had anything at all to do with the corporation, its employees, or their activities; otherwise it was categorized as extracurricular. We then selected from each category the DL (or DLs) with the greatest number of messages in our sample. We chose high activity DLs from each category (rather than random ones) because we wanted to maximize the likelihood of finding DLs that exhibited interaction, influence attempts, and identity maintenance. We reasoned that if these processes occurred at all in electronic DLs they would be most likely to do so in high activity ones. Based on message volume, we selected two required DLs with work-related topics, one discretionary work-related DL, and two discretionary extracurricular DLs.

Because every group message was sent to every group member, we were able to use sequential sampling of group messages across people as an approximation of continuous sampling from each DL as a whole. The original data were collected over a six-week period with each respondent providing three consecutive days worth of mail during that period. Each group members' three-day period was noted to calculate the total number of days during which group messages could appear in our sample. (For instance, if one group member provided messages on April 1, 2, and 3, a second provided messages on April 2, 3, and 4, and a third provided messages on April 19, 20, and 21, then the total number of days on which group mail could appear in our sample would be seven.) We knew that if one group member received a group message on a particular day that the same message had been delivered to every group member on that day. We also knew that if one member received no group message on a particular day then no member received a group message on that day. This sampling yielded 616 messages from the five groups, which became the primary source for the group descriptions.

Results

We first present summary data on the scope and nature of electronic mail use and DL behavior across the organization as a whole to address the first research question. We then present more detailed descriptions of behavior within and across the five selected DLs to address the second and third research questions.

Nature and Scope of DL Mail Across the Organization as a Whole

PHC employees received mail from 700 DLs during our observation; 80% of their daily mail (a mean of 21 messages a day) was DL mail. Fifty-six percent of the DLs were required ones, ranging from DLs for ten-person subunit groups to site lists for all employees working in a particular city. The discretionary DLs covered a wide spectrum of topics, ranging from the exotic to the mundane such as Oenologists for wine-fanciers, NETSpecs for computer network designers, GoPlayers for students of the Japanese strategy game Go, PHCToday for company news, Classifieds for selling things, and ChildCare for locating babysitters.

DL mail dominated as a percentage of total mail in each stratum and in the entire organization. (See Table 1 for summary characteristics.) Thirty-four percent of the group mail came from required DLs. Fifty-seven percent of the mail came from work-related DLs. Conceivably DLs could be serving only as a way to speed up the circulation of information that people would otherwise have received more slowly through more conventional means. To check this we looked at the proportion of DL mail that respondents characterized as "nonredundant" (that is, the respondent reported he or she would not have received this information any other way). In all strata, respondents described the majority of their DL mail as "nonredundant."[5] The majority of DL mail (58%) came from strangers (i.e., senders described as "unknown" by their recipients). The majority (68%) came from remote locations, i.e., somewhere other than the recipient's own building.

[3]Names of all organizations, locations, groups, and people are pseudonyms.

[4]See Sproull and Kiesler (1986) for a more detailed description of the study design and data collection protocol.

[5]This finding could simply be an artifact of variation in the level of activity across DLs. That is, a small number of high volume DLs could have produced most of the nonredundant messages. To rule out this possibility we characterized each DL by its proportion of nonredundant messages; any DL with over 50% nonredundant messages (as described by respondents) was categorized as a nonredundant DL. Forty-nine percent of the work-related DLs were nonredundant and 78% of the extracurricular DLs were nonredundant by this categorization. One cause of the lack of redundancy in the electronic mail traffic might be reduced barriers to communication. That is, much of the traffic may appear nonredundant because it consists of messages that, previously, were not perceived to be worth the effort required to send them.

TABLE 2
Communication Characteristics of Illustrative Groups

	Required Work		Work	Discretionary Non-Work	
	CSG	CD	UFF	Cinema	Rowdies
Number of people	35	25	125	500	98
Number of messages	32	110	69	62	343
Interactions					
Daily activ. rate[a]	76%	90%	66%	63%	87%
Av. daily mssgs.	2	4	2	4	23
Max. daily mssgs.	5	11	8	31	50
Active participants					
Proportion	53%	92%	28%	8%	49%
Total number	18	23	35	41	48
Gini coefficient	.22	.52	.37	.24	.52
Information exchange					
Query/response	Yes	Yes	Yes	Yes	Yes
Implicit formats	Yes	Yes	No	Yes	No
Influence Attempts					
% replies	3%	6%	62%	50%	73%
New information	No	Yes	Yes	Yes	Yes
Primary purpose	Instru.	Instru.	Instru./Symbolic	Fun	Fun
Identity Maintenance					
"Who we are"	No	No	Yes	Yes	Yes
Norm statements	No	No	Yes	Yes	Yes

Notes:

a % sampled days in which at least one message is sent to group.

The hiring meeting for Jane Smith has been rescheduled for 9:30 am on Thursday, March 31 in the Commons. Please mark your calendars.
Thanks Karen

The third-floor printer is acting up. Use at your own risk. Martin will be out this afternoon to see what the problem is.
Darlene

During the sample period CSG was used to announce personnel changes, coordinate job interviews, present trip reports, organize informal research colloquia, describe research results, and post information about outside speakers. Underlying these messages was a high degree of familiarity among the members of CSG; they saw one another everyday. Hence, although many matters discussed on CSG were quite serious (e.g., related to hiring and firing personnel or to the quality of PHC research in comparison with that of other research groups), they were pursued in an informal style resembling the breezy collegiality found in university settings.

A couple of interesting graphs depicting the performance of [two research projects] are pasted on my whiteboard in my office (room 642). Drop by and have a look.
Ray....

CSG was mostly an adjunct to everyday business, characterized by a high proportion of bureaucratic notices, some witticisms, and a few requests for information.

TABLE 1
Characteristics of Group Mail for Each Hierarchical Stratum and for the PHC as a Whole

	Male Non-Exempt N = 17	Female Non-Exempt N = 18	Male Prof. N = 20	Female Prof. N = 20	Male Mngrs. N = 21	PHC N = 9
Percentage of daily mail that is group mail:						
	90%	73%	82%	89%	67%	80%[a]
Percentage of daily group mail from:						
work related groups	49%	53%	56%	53%	82%	57%[b]
required groups	40%	27%	35%	34%	49%	34%
nonredundant groups	83%	72%	82%	74%	64%	78%[c]
Percentage of daily group mail received from senders located:						
within 100 yds	10%	14%	21%	19%	19%	19%
in the same bldg	12%	17%	13%	17%	20%	13%
in the same city	15%	29%	18%	17%	25%	20%
in other cities	27%	29%	23%	32%	23%	27%
at unknown sites	36%	11%	25%	15%	13%	21%
Percentage of daily group mail received from senders in:						
same chain of command	6%	24%	22%	21%	25%	19%
another chain	34%	39%	40%	45%	59%	44%
an unknown chain	60%	38%	40%	34%	17%	37%[d]
Percentage of daily group mail from senders reported as:						
strangers	72%	53%	58%	57%	49%	58%
slight acquaintances	10%	17%	10%	18%	19%	13%
acquaintances	8%	11%	17%	12%	20%	14%
friends	10%	16%	14%	12%	9%	13%
close friends	0%	2%	2%	2%	3%	2%

Notes:

a) Scheffe comparison of means shows that managers are significantly different ($p < .05$) from male nonexempts and female professionals.

b) Scheffe comparison of means shows that the percent of group work messages received by managers is significantly different from that for all other strata.

c) Scheffe comparison of means shows that managers are significantly different from male professionals and male professionals

d) Scheffe comparison of means shows that the difference between managers and male nonexempts is significant.

While everyone in PHC read DL mail, they did not read the same amount or kinds of DL mail. Managers received less DL mail than did members of other strata. Also managers' daily DL mail had a higher percentage of work-related messages, redundant messages, and messages from within their chain of command.

Illustrative Group Descriptions

We describe five high activity DLs and the nature of their electronic communication. In each case we use the actual text of messages sent to the group to illustrate the groups' behavior.

ComputerScienceGroup. The ComputerScienceGroup (CSG) was a required work-related DL. CSG included the 35 members of the Computer Science Department within the R & D division—managers, professionals, secretaries, and technicians. On an average day, 2 messages were sent to CSG (max = 5, min = 0). (Table 2 summarizes communication characteristics of each group.) CSG conveyed official announcements, reports, and notices.

CaptainDevelopers. CaptainDevelopers was a required work DL for 25 people building a new operating system called Captain. CD averaged 4 messages per day (max = 11, min = 0). Its membership reflected the structure of a conventional working group with multiple levels of managers and professionals who had specific responsibilities. CD was actively engaged in building systems, so its members faced actual design dilemmas and real deadlines. The conversation on CD was succinct.

Clearing house stub has been [linked] to Int. Mary

Ten percent of the messages in CD had no message text; all information was conveyed in the topic field. For example, the topic field of one message said, "*abc* < – Hamlet," meaning a new program named Hamlet had just been stored in *abc*. There was no message text following the topic field.

Messages on CD always referred to the task at hand: making the Captain Operating System work. But CD was not sterile. Within the scope of building Captain, triumphs were celebrated and failures were disparaged with high feeling. For instance new performance figures showing that Captain was running much faster were accompanied by a flourish of exclamation marks. That message prompted a senior manager to reply:

Congratulations folks! Let's hope this means some of Captain's clients will get correspondingly faster. /George

Still, CD emphasized efficiency. CD was not a recreational pastime; there were no messages about nonwork topics. Nor was it tangential to regular work; there were no messages about work issues other than the Captain operating system. CD was a vital and central part of making Captain a functioning software system.

UserFeatureForum. UserFeatureForum was a work-related discretionary DL for PHC employees interested in discussing user-interface features on PHC products. UFF had 125 members and received a mean of 2 messages a day (max = 8, min = 0). Many of the messages on UFF were mildly pedantic, as people demonstrated their technical opinions or virtuosity.

Regarding contention resolution in Graphics: I like meaning 1 (option 2) of the next key (next item in the contenders list). Meaning 2 would seem to me to be very unpredictable from a user's point of view. The internal sibling structure could not in general be predicted from the image they see whereas the next contender would be much more natural. Regarding how frames behave during pagination: both alternatives have undesirable qualities. Data should never be intentionally thrown away (as in alt1). And alt2 would more than likely result in an unacceptable positioning of the frame. Given the current limitations of document structure in [product], I don't see any better pagination heuristic than what we do now. One possibility might be to post a message when one of these guys is encountered and let the user decide what to do such as abort pagination. Then the user could change the page props of the problem page and repaginate. /Joe

Still, UFF was not all bland discourse on "contention resolution problems" or "multi-national user-interfaces." Personal rivalries sometimes surfaced. For example, toward the end of one particularly arcane exchange one member pointedly observed in a message that "some people" on UFF spent more time talking about user-interfaces than building them.

On the whole, though, talking about user-interfaces was the raison d'etre of UFF. UFF had no identity outside of the mail system, unlike CD and CSG. UFF was an arena for people to display their knowledge before their superiors and peers—although this knowledge was rarely acted upon (in our sample of messages only two UFF communications resulted in actual changes to a user-interface). In the words of one UFFer:

To paraphrase a famous saying about economists, which pretty much summarizes my feelings about all this endless user-interface niggling that's been going on for the last six years, and shows every indication of continuing out to eternity:
If all the user interface experts in the world were laid end to end, they wouldn't reach a conclusion.

In response to this complaint, though, another member responded with a hoary PHC adage: If you don't like talking about user features, drop out of UserFeatureForum.

Cinema. Cinema was an extracurricular discretionary DL, with over 500 members. Membership consisted of managers, professionals, technicians, and secretaries. Cinema members received a mean of 4 messages a day from this DL (max = 31, min = 0). Messages were related to movie reviews—highly subjective commentaries on everything related to the movie including the ambiance in the theater and the quality of the popcorn.

John,
I just saw FlashDance, you were very very right. I stopped by Tower Records on the way home and picked up the sound track. I am taping it now. I am not a big movie goer and I am at odds with Mann and AMC theaters but this film was well worth the trip to my local corporate theater. Fortunately I was spared the newspaper ads by arriving 5 minutes late.
Well, I did not start this as a flame about corporate theaters. I wanted to say that FlashDance is a clever, well filmed, moving musical that runs around inside your head for a long time after leaving the theater. Go see it and check out the sound track on Casablanca Records. It's a Polygram Record with few built in flaws.
Later...
/PRL

————

V was a mashed-up composite of about twenty science-fiction stories. Not a single original idea in it. And besides that, it wasn't very good.
Save Joe-Bob!

During our sampling period a flurry of activity occurred after a Cinema member sent the group "Joe Bob Briggs" reviews copied from a Dallas newspaper. Joe Bob Briggs had a colorful style, devoted mostly to drive-in fare and frequently skirting propriety: one of his criteria for evaluating a movie favorably was the amount of blood shed—measured in gallons. These reviews set off a storm of reaction, both pro and con, ranging from cool rage to verbose harangues. One Cinema member concluded a 2-line vote for JBB with the blunt suggestion that objectors should "f–k themselves." During this period, there were two Cinema message styles. One, associated with those against JBB, was relatively formal, reasoned, and disdainful.

Just because not many people type in Movie reviews is no reason to put stuff on this DL that is better suited to Trash (a catchall DL). Perhaps all the people that complain that this DL is all but dead should go out to the movies and give us a review or two.
—Jim

The other, associated with those favoring JBB, was relatively emotional, combative, and abusive.

Look I don't have time to read all your messages about not wanting extra messages on this dl. If you don't like the idea of this dl getting some use and want to keep all that so-called 'garbage' off of same, then please send a message to yourself and I promise you we won't even notice.

I object strongly to censorship. If he stops sending Joe Bob, I'll start...doo dah, doo dah!

Kyle

Rowdies. Rowdies, a discretionary extracurricular DL, had 98 members, 73% of whom were male technicians or professionals. Typically, Rowdies was the source of over 20 "RowdieMail" messages per day (max = 50, min = 0). Although some work issues occasionally crept into Rowdies discussions, most messages concerned gossip (mostly about other Rowdies), group activities (such as organizing softball teams or writing electronic novels), and crude humor.

Sounds to me like you should have quit while you were ahead!!

Has anyone else noticed that we've actually been getting messages from 666 lately, and most of them have times on them like 3:05 a.m.–5:42 a.m., etc. Do you think he's trying to impress us with his devotion to duty? I'll bet his boss gets a message every day at that time as well...even if 666 has nothing much to say to him. He also lets us know that he is working a 13 hour day–he has stated that more than once.

I mean, we enjoy your messages 666, but, really, impressing us isn't going to change the fact that there are no merit increases this year–unless, of course, they change their mind in June or July after re-evaluating this situation.

And by the way, 3:00 a.m. to 12:30 p.m. is only a 9-1/2 hour day...

2

GeezSomePeople

Rowdies regularly sent messages to organize afternoon beer busts, which were the focus of elaborate preparation. These outings were documented in full, and their histories were carefully indexed and archived for future reference in secure Rowdie disk space.

John and Phil,
I have room for both of you in my car plus one more RowdieLuncher. I'm pretty sure the luncheon is still on for 12:30 pm.
44

...zzzzzzzzzzzzz. Hmmph. Burp... huh? who me... what column? miss a deadline...what day is it? ohmygod it's wednesday already. What? somebody wrote it? Joe, who? oh yes, JOE!:he's the one I had always thought was bald.
qR-722

Was a great party, in fact I'm still smiling. ...that whipped cream was good stuff.

Rowdies messages displayed complex stylistic conventions, including closing messages with a Rowdy number and a run-on commentary. The run-on commentaries often took the form of sarcastic observations on previous messages, or continued observations from other messages. Rowdies sometimes referred to fellow Rowdies by using Rowdy "handles" such as "Colt45" or "Mr. Toon-toon." Like RowdieNumbers, these handles were an important part of Rowdy identity. Periodically, Rowdies issued a membership list indicating numbers, handles, birthdates, and favorite "RowdieDrinks." During our observation the membership list also included the names of honorary Rowdies including several waitresses at Rowdy hangouts, and Divine, the transvestite star of "Pink Flamingos" and "Polyester."

Rowdies messages expressed clear opinions about Rowdies and about the larger electronic community. On one occasion a prominent Rowdy noted, after three new Rowdies members dropped out after only two days, "They weren't Rowdy material. Keep up the good work!"

Group Processes

One of the purposes of the illustrative groups descriptions was to discover whether naturally occurring electronic DLs could exhibit properties of real social groups, namely interaction, influence attempts, and identity maintenance. This section addresses each of those processes in turn.

Interaction. The groups were selected to be high activity groups. Their daily activity rate (% of days in which at least one message was sent) ranged from 63% to 90%. The mean number of messages sent per day ranged from 2 to 21. The daily minimum for all groups was 0; the daily maximum ranged from 5 to 50.

Interaction is partly characterized by level of participation, that is, the proportion of group members who contribute actively by sending messages. We defined "active participants" as those who sent at least one message to the group. The proportion (and total number) of active participants for the groups were CSG, 53% (18); CD, 92% (23); UFF, 28% (35); Cinema, 8% (41); Rowdies, 49% (48). Active participants may exhibit different sending patterns ranging from complete equality in the number of messages sent to dominance by one person with all others contributing only a single message. We calculated Gini coefficients for each group to obtain a rough measure of equality of participation. (Alker 1979); the Gini coefficient varies between 0 and 1 where 0 means perfect equality. The Gini coefficients for active group participants were: CSG, 0.22; CD, 0.52; UFF, 0.37; Cinema, 0.24; Rowdies, 0.52.[6]

Interaction implies more than sending messages one way. Although we did not know the total number of people who actually read any messages, we could characterize the extent to which messages provoked at least one person to reply. "Explicit replies" were messages whose header included a line saying "in-reply-to" and designating a specific prior message. The proportion of explicit replies for the groups in this study were: CSG, 3%; CD, 6%; UFF, 62%; Cinema, 50%; Rowdies, 73%.

Several processes encouraged information exchange in these groups. One was an explicit process of query and response in which someone asked the group a question of the form, "Does anybody know...?" Any answer to that question was sent to the entire group. A message sent to CSG said:

Alas, we need to board our cat for a short period. Any recommendations?

[6]In practical terms, the Gini coefficient describes the difference between ideal (equal) participation and actual participation by plotting cumulative participation percentages against cumulative membership percentages. If participation is equal, this plot will form a 45-degree line. For example, in an equal participation 10-person group Person A, who is 10% of the group membership, sends 10% of the messages, and the cumulative plot at this point is 10% vs. 10%; Person B also sends 10% of the messages, and the cumulative plot at this point is 20% vs. 20%; and so forth. The Gini coefficient measures divergence from this ideal by calculating the area between the 45-degree line and the actual participation curve. Studies of face-to-face groups commonly include passive participants, as well as active ones, in calculating equality of participation measures. Had we done so in this study the coefficients would have been much larger for UFF, Cinema, and Rowdies because of the large absolute number of passive members in each of these groups. This illustrates how electronic groups may offer both theoretical and methodological challenges for researchers. In conventional groups it is easy for every member to see the total number of active and passive participants. Thus including both in calculating participation measures is certainly appropriate. But when members are invisible, then each passive participant may perceive that the total group size is equal to the number of active participants plus him/herself. If so, then Gini coefficients calculated for active participants may closely reflect group members' perceptions of total participation patterns. Of course this is a question for future research.

A message sent to CD said:

I am in the midst of trying to integrate a [product] disk into Captain. How does one go about following the changes to Captain and the Captain code?

A UFF message solicited input on a proposal for a new product feature:

I'm putting together a proposal to the Product Review Board to add a 'try again' feature for pointing and am soliciting additional ideas before I make a formal proposal.

Questions about the location of a theater showing "Return of the Jedi" were answered on Cinema, requests for help in locating a spreadsheet program were made and answered on Rowdies.

Information exchange was also encouraged through implicit reporting formats. On Cinema individuals shared information with the group by using a movie review format. CSG had a format for document abstracts (e.g., journal articles about new programming languages) and a format for trip reports (e.g., a description of visiting a research lab in another firm). CD had a format for reporting error corrections and program updates. These were not formal "fill-in-the-blanks" templates, but rather were informal conventions for the form of such messages.

DL members exchanged information on a wide variety of topics. The CSG message about boarding cats was followed on the same day by a detailed critique of an operating system, a message inviting people to view a new product in operation, and an announcement of the time and place for the weekly group meeting. Conversations were opportunistic and short-lived: topics on CSG, CD, UFF, and Rowdies were typically discussed for less than a day. Thus, on any given day, information exchange could have seemed sporadic and incomplete. Yet groups did accumulate information over them. A sequence of messages on UFF illustrated how this could occur. One day a UFF member told the group he wanted rapid response when making large movements with a pointing device. Another UFF member provided a temporary solution (2 messages and 38 hours later) based on changing default settings for the device. Finally, another member announced that he had written a new software routine to produce a faster device (7 messages and 84 hours later).

Information exchange also occurred across DLs. One manager, who wanted PHC products to support a spreadsheet package, asked several likely DLs (including UFF) their opinions on the value of building such a package for PHC products. Within 48 hours 25 people had responded from several cities with suggestions on the spread-sheet idea. In fact, a new DL was soon created called PHCSpreadSheetForum for people interested in this topic.

Influence. One way in which groups influence their members is by giving them new information. In the original subsample of messages we had asked each respondent how, if at all, he or she would have received the message if there were no electronic mail. CSG members reported that over half of the information in their CSG messages could have been received in other ways—primarily in face-to-face conversations and hard copy memos. In the other four groups, members reported that over half of the group messages contained information that they would not have received in any other way.

Each group emphasized one of the three information exchange purposes (instrumental, symbolic, fun), although all groups exhibited all of them. CD and CSG exchanged information to direct attention, coordinate activities, and solve problems. For instance,

Since Don Garvin has transferred to CSG, we have assigned a new OAD Liasion for EP. This person is Jake Chapman.MPLS, formerly of OAD, at mail stop PH-319F. Please put his name on all

your distribution lists to liaison personnel. Jake will be interfacing with you with EP questions and problems. He is also the person who will receive the manuals, etc.

On Tuesday at 10 AM there will be internal hearings for both [product] releases. The purpose of these hearings is to adjust the published priorities to reflect our own needs, and to identify missing, uninteresting and completed tasks.

UFF exchanged information to direct attention and to symbolize competence. For instance as part of a discussion on path-name conventions, and in reply to a specific message on that topic, one person said:

"there is nothing particularly 'logical' about the 'most-significant-first' order, however."

That is a remarkable statement for a computer scientist. Do you think computer science is based on ad hoc conventions that have no logical foundation? The logical order of identifying things is to progress from general categories to more specific ones. This is a basic principle of logic and of science, not just of computer science.

Many business conventions and most political laws are neither logical nor consistent. I do not necessarily accept conventions imposed on us by the U.S. Snail Service as the highest standard, worthy of universal imitation. However, I am sure that even USPS wishes addresses were specified in the opposite order so that it would be easier to automate mail handling. How many forms have you seen that ask for last name first? Why do you suppose they do that?

"consistency is inherently better than inconsistency"

I believe that those of us who know what we are doing should try to make our products and our environments more consistent and more logical whenever we have the opportunity. What could be a better opportunity than the choice of naming conventions for a system we have designed and created ourselves? We have no one to blame for the inconsistencies but ourselves.
Neil

Rowdies and Cinema exchanged information to have fun.

Another way in which groups influence their members is by influencing their behavior. One such behavior (which is also an indicator of interaction) is inducing people to respond to previous messages. As reported above, induced responses (as measured by explicit replies) ranged from 3% for CSG to 73% for Rowdies.[7]

Identity. There are no tangible ways to differentiate one electronic group from another—messages simply appear on a person's screen. Yet group identity is important in letting people know what topics will be discussed in what ways and in attracting members to discretionary groups. Electronic groups did manage to establish unique identities by using names, norms, and message content.

The name of a DL was one differentiating cue. All DLs in the PHC were named and all DL messages were addressed to DL names. At the coarsest level the name of a DL indicated appropriate topics for that DL. Thus people expected to talk about the Captain operating system on CD and movies on Cinema.

Yet, DL names do not answer all identity questions. Norms were also important (Bettenhausen and Murnighan 1985; Fulk, Steinfield, Schmitz, and Power 1987). Norms were usually conveyed by example. Only when groups are new, take on many new members, or during periods of conflict do people discuss norms explicitly. The JBB incident on Cinema provided an example of conflict-induced norm statements. Initially, opponents and proponents of JBB simply sent diatribes stating their views on JBB. Three hours (and 9 messages) after the original post, one Cinema member proposed that all further diatribes on JBB be accompanied by a legitimate movie

[7]While it is possible to measure influence *attempts* by looking only at messages, assessing influence *effects* is better done by directly observing or asking about the behavior of people who are the targets of influence attempts.

FIGURE B. Two Examples of Adopting a Distinctive Group Voice.

Person A

To UserFeatureForum-
I cannot imagine a pathname standard that does not reserve * as a wildcard. It's much more than PHC we're dealing with here—I think most other major operating systems use the same conventions: TOPS-20, RSX-11W—Users of these systems are exactly the few hundred thousand people who are most likely to be our first customers—people who'll be talking to these other operating systems via TTY emulation.

To Cinema:
an' I likes Joe Bob. Shucks, I thought all the humorless prigs had already migrated to Review. If'n ya dun lak it, y'all kin CLICK DELETE once a week on any msg with "Joe Bob" in the header. AH HAS SPOKEN! I suggest directing your brickbats, kudos, etc. to me rather than subjecting the whole list to any further meta-discussion.

Person B

To UserFeatureForum:
The easiest interface to learn and use would seem to be the multiple click for contention resolution, since it is what most people already do. However, I would think the inevitable small movements of the mouse in the course of clicking would make implementation difficult, with nonredundant ambiguities introduced between an unintentional movement while intending to continue on the contenders list, and an intentional movement to start somewhere nearby.

To Rowdies:
By the way, there's this convention on TV that flashers run around in raincoats with no pants. Now, if memory serves, the men I've seen more of than I would normally expect were generally just hanging around near the bottom of the subway steps or something, with their fly open and their whatever hanging out. So what I want to know, is whether there really are flashers that run around without any pants on, or whether that's just something someone made up for TV so people would get the idea without getting the picture, so to speak. Anyone know? Anyone have personal experience in the matter? ~1492~

Note: All names and numbers are pseudonyms.

review. Gradually, JBB messages were accompanied by reviews, although opponents of JBB followed the norm more than did proponents.

Another explicit statement of norms emerged as a result of a suggestion made to UFF, which led to a new DL for "informal sharing of tips on use of Louise [a PHC product]." The message announcing the new DL included three rules:

(1) This DL is for disseminating information, not for asking for help. Use Helpline.La to ask questions.

(2) "Just the facts, ma'am." Please try to avoid flaming about how bad/good a system is that requires/allows the described workaround/capability.

(3) Especially around release time, when different versions of Louise are in use at once, be sure to mention what version you are talking about.

Explicit statements reiterating "who we are" were found in discretionary group messages (Cinema, Rowdies, and UFF). For instance, the JBB incident provided an occasion for Cinema members to debate the nature of their group's identity. One member opposed to further JBB reviews on Cinema recommended that they be posted on a different DL. The conflict became a dispute between those who viewed Cinema as a forum for discourse on "films," and those who felt that anything associated with "movies" was OK. The founder of Cinema even asserted that the "prigs" who didn't like JBB should move to Criticism (a more high-brow review DL), and leave Cinema alone. In another case, a query by a newcomer elicited the following description of Rowdies by a non-Rowdy: "If the PHC network were Star Wars, Rowdies would be Darth Vader." Naturally, a Rowdy responded to this challenge with his own analogy: "If the PHC network were a porn movie theater, Rowdies would be the sticky substance under the seats."

The style or "voice" that people use when talking to a group also signals and supports group identity. Sociolinguists have long known that use and mastery of a dialect indicates membership in a social organization (Labov 1967; Gumperz 1982, p. 38). Figure B displays pairs of messages sent by the same person to two different groups. In each case, the first mesage was taken from UserFeatureForum. The second message in each pair is quite different in voice. In the Cinema case, the reasoned professional UFF voice became the vernacular voice of Joe Bob Briggs, the cowboy reviewer. Similarly, the detached UFF voice discussing "contention resolution implementation" became a highly personal Rowdy voice.

Group Comparisons

The previous section illustrated that DLs can exhibit the fundamental social group processes of interaction, influence attempts, and identity maintenance. We reasoned that if such processes were at all evident in DLs, they would be more prevalent or pronounced in "pure" electronic groups—ones with no interaction outside the mail system. In our sample groups, thus, they should be more prevalent in the discretionary DLs (UFF, Cinema, and Rowdies) than in the required ones (CSG, CD). Remember that we compare the most active DLs of each type; they are not necessarily representative of all DLs of each type.

The discretionary groups were almost nine times larger on average (260 members) than required ones (30 members). The discretionary DLs were more geographically dispersed than the required ones. Members of discretionary DLs were located in at least seven different cities; members of required DLs were located in only one city.

There were no differences in active participation between required and discretionary groups. There was no difference in the median daily volume of messages (4 for discretionary and 3 for required), the daily activity rate (72% for discretionary and 83% for required), the daily proportion of active participants (2% for discretionary and 3% for required), or the equality of participation (mean Gini coefficient for both group types was .37).

The discretionary groups displayed a higher interaction rate than did required groups. The explicit reply rate for the discretionary groups averaged 62%; it averaged 4% for the required groups.

In each discretionary group over half of the group messages contained information that would not have been received without electronic communication. This was also true of one of the required groups (CD), but not the other (CSG).

The discretionary groups displayed more identity maintenance behavior. Each discretionary group and neither required group displayed "the purpose of this group is..." messages. Each discretionary group and neither required group displayed "how-we-do-things on this DL" messages. These differences are not an artifact of more activity on the discretionary DLs; the levels of activity, as we note above, were comparable.

We had no specific research questions about differences between work groups and extracurricular groups. But we note that the extracurricular groups were larger (five times larger on average) than the work groups. The extracurricular groups were more geographically dispersed (members were located in seven different cities on average; while members of work groups were located in three different cities on average). They had a greater average number of messages per day (13 for extracurricular groups; 3 for work groups). There was no difference in the daily proportion of active participants (2% for each kind of group) or the equality of participation (0.38 for nonwork groups and 0.37 for work groups). Extracurricular groups displayed a higher explicit reply rate (61%) than did work groups (21%). The use of identity statements in the extracurricular groups was similar to that in the discretionary work-group (but not the required work groups).

Discussion

Summary and Generality of Findings

Two observations stand out in this study. One is the extensive scope and diversity of DL activity in the organization. Electronic group mail was used throughout the organization for many kinds of group communication. The second observation is that at least some of these groups behaved like real social groups—despite the fact that they shared no physical space, their members were invisible, and their "interaction" was asynchronous. This observation is even more striking when we note that groups may have had a hundred or more members in different cities—all sharing the same group mail.

Because our data were not originally collected to study electronic groups, our analyses were not definitive. Our description of the scope of group mail was based on message data, not membership data. Thus, we characterized the 700 DLs that were active during our six-week period of observation, but we had no information on DLs that were inactive during that period. Our measures of influence and identity were also taken solely from the messages. Augmenting these measures with other kinds of data from group members would better portray the influence and identity processes.

Our illustrative groups were drawn from high activity DLs only. They were not representative of all DLs. Nor was the PHC representative of all organizations using electronic mail. It is a "mature" electronic mail community, and thus an appropriate organization for studying group mail behavior. But not all mature electronic mail communities have the same kind of group mail behavior nor would they necessarily exhibit the same kind of group mail behavior as this one. Policy choices and organizational norms make a difference (Fulk et al. 1987). For instance, it is possible to implement an electronic mail system that makes it difficult to send group mail or that forbids discretionary groups or extracurricular groups. Such a system would surely generate group structures and behaviors different from those in PHC.

Despite its limitations, this study identifies and begins to characterize a new social phenomenon in organizations—the large-scale electronic group. Given an appropriate mail system and social context, these groups cut across conventional organizational boundaries of geography and work unit. They provide a way to tap and pool the expertise of individual employees no matter where they are located. And they provide a way for employees to discover others with similar interests.

Research and Management Issues

If electronic groups become widespread in organizations, the research opportunities and management challenges will be extensive. People have begun thinking about how electronic group communication can augment or change patterns of coordination and performance in small face-to-face work groups (e.g., Kraemer and King 1988; Gallegher, Kraut, and Egido forthcoming). While augmenting face-to-face group performance with technology will surely be important for organizations, this section emphasizes the large-scale discretionary electronic group.

A fundamental question is, why do such groups exist at all? They depend upon the interest and goodwill of organizational members to join and contribute over time. Why do people do it? We speculate that peoples' motivation is more likely to be found in the pleasures of gossip and feeling in-the-know than in any calculation of the instrumental utility of information acquired from these groups. (See March and Sevon 1984, for this argument in the nonelectronic context; see Thorn and Connolly 1987, for the counterargument.) We do not imply that DLs traffic in useless information, but rather that the immediate job relevance of any particular message for any particular employee is low. As one secretary told us, DLs are her "window on the corporation." The benefits may be particularly high for lower level employees who otherwise have the fewest opportunities to make connections across the organization. This speculation is consistent with our finding that managers' DL traffic was significantly less wide-ranging than that of nonmanagerial employees.

The vitality of the discretionary groups in our study suggests a second fundamental question: why are these groups so lively? Research on conventional groups suggests that with large size comes formality and specialization. That was not the case with the electronic groups we saw. One possibility is that the groups we looked at were populated by "lively" people (e.g., young people, newcomers, extroverts, "joiners"). Our data cannot refute this possibility. Another possibility is that, to their members, large electronic groups seem small. Perhaps because members are invisible and share no tangible setting, every member significantly underestimates the number of others who belong to the group. Members' behavior may be more a function of how big (or small) they perceive the group to be than of its objective size.

The lack of information about members and their social context is sometimes portrayed as a negative feature of electronic communication. There is a nice irony in the possibility that this feature may make it possible for big groups to feel small. There is also a caution here for software designers who want to increase member visibility by, for instance, enumerating members' names, attaching pictures to names, or notifying senders of who has read their messages. Perhaps, in large-scale groups, reminding members of others would decrease their willingness to participate rather than increase it.

Organizationally, the implications of increasing the participation of lower-level employees through electronic communication are intriguing. Prior research on participation has primarily considered the work-group, with mixed results. Electronic groups offer a new opportunity, that is participating in groups that are larger, more heterogeneous, and less structured than the work-group. As such, they may afford the opportunity to rapidly share working-level expertise across subunits. Furthermore, if they give people the impression that otherwise inaccessible people are now accessible to them, they may also lead to an increase in commitment to the organization as a whole (e.g., Huff, Sproull, and Kiesler 1988).

The likely consequences of electronic groups need not all be positive. For instance, group membership may benefit individual members. But, if groups are negative toward the larger organization, individual disaffection may be magnified as people realize others are also dissatisfied with the organization. Electronic groups may then be used to mobilize discontent (e.g., Emmett 1982; Zuboff 1987, pp. 362–386). As groups increase in size, the probability of junk mail may also increase. Although some writers worry about "information overload" (e.g., Hiltz and Turoff 1985), members of the PHC community seemed relatively untroubled by this problem. People deleted unwanted messages without reading them just the way they might throw away third-class postal mail without opening it. They also dropped out of groups if they felt the volume of irrelevant mail was too high. The PHC administration took no official action to limit junk mail; the system was self-policing and each user determined how much of what kind of mail to read each day. Perhaps more troublesome than junk mail is that electronic mail can easily promulgate erroneous information to large numbers of people. For example, one day a message was sent to PHCToday, a DL for company news, announcing that the PHC research division had just been sold to a competitor. It explained how the division would be organized in the new company, who would have management responsibilities, and how the transition would proceed. Twelve days later, the sender of this April Fool's day message sent another message apologizing for his joke.

As we have noted, management policies will strongly influence the nature of electronic group activity and the ratio of positive to negative consequences within any organization. Both technical and social features of the electronic communication environment are appropriate design targets for managers. On the technical side managers may endorse experiments with a variety of mechanisms to help people find information and groups that would be helpful or interesting to them. Filters, group directories, and group performance data (the electronic group equivalent of Nielson ratings) are obvious candidates for experiments. On the social side managers may endorse a variety of norms and incentives encouraging people to participate responsibly in electronic groups. In any case managers should realize these experiments entail important questions of organizational design; they should not be left, by oversight or intention, to programmers and technicians.

Understanding electronic groups may help us better understand some of our theories about organizations. For instance, some theorists have proposed that communication media vary along a "richness" continuum with electronic mail residing somewhere between telephone calls and written memoranda (e.g., Daft and Lengel 1984; Steinfeld and Fulk 1987). It would seem, however, based on variation across the groups described in this study, that "richness" is as much a function of the social definition of a medium as it is of any inherent properties of it (Fulk et al. 1987). Our study suggests that, for any person, the definition can vary from minute to minute as messages from different DLs scroll down the screen. It also suggests that the social definition of any one medium depends upon the extent to which other media are also accessible. Thus, in perhaps, our required groups could define their DLs primarily as a way to communicate one-way updates because they had other opportunities to interact more extensively. By contrast, our discretionary groups defined their DLs as their only way to interact extensively.

Understanding electronic groups at work may also help us understand play at work. In our study, over 40% of peoples' mail came from extracurricular DLs. This suggests several possibilities. One is that the medium brings out playfulness in people, perhaps because it is relatively disinhibiting. A second is that the kinds of people who use electronic mail extensively, such as researchers and product developers, are less serious-minded than other people. A third, and most intriguing to us, is that play abounds in organizations but, because our theories are about work, we do not see it. Electronic communication simply makes it visible.

Play at work is substantively interesting in its own right. It also has obvious management implications. Some organizations prohibit employees from using electronic mail for "nonwork purposes," presumably because such uses would consume network resources such as disk space and would interfere with peoples' work activities. Conceivably extracurricular electronic groups might distract employees from their jobs and thereby reduce both the quality of their work and their affiliation with the organization. Alternatively such groups could ultimately increase the quality of work through providing new information resources and increase affiliation with the organization through providing new opportunities for employees to discover things they have in common with other employees.

Modern organizations are generally structured to locate routinely interdependent activities in close proximity. While this strategy increases the efficiency of routine behavior, it can disadvantage organizations facing nonroutine problems and opportunities that cut across conventional structures. Electronic groups may help organizations create more flexible structures so that the experience and expertise of employees can be

mustered wherever it is needed. The company whose groups we studied did not view electronic communication and electronic groups as tools for organizational design (Huber 1986). Yet, they became the de facto tools as people discovered they could easily create new groups cutting across geographic and department lines. The electronic group at work is a new organizational phenomenon. In the future it may afford significant research opportunities and contribute importantly to organizational behavior.[8]

References

ALKER, HAYWARD R. JR. (1979). "Measuring Sociopolitical Inequality," In J. Tanur (Ed.), *Statistics: A Guide to the Unknown*, Holden-Day, San Francisco, 405–413.

ARGOTE, LINDA, PAUL GOODMAN AND DAVID SCHADE (1983). "The Human Side of Robotics," *Sloan Management Rev.*, 24, 3 31–40.

BAUM, ANDREW AND STUART VALINS (1977). *Architecture and Social Behavior*, Erlbaum, Hillsdale, NJ.

BERSHEID, E. AND E. WALSTER (1975). *Interpersonal Attraction*, (Second ed.), Addison-Wesley, Reading, MA.

BETTENHAUSEN, KENNETH AND J. KEITH MURNIGHAN (1985). "The Emergence of Norms in Competitive Decision-Making Groups," *Admin. Sci. Quart.*, 30, 350–372.

BLAU, JUDITH AND RICHARD D. ALBA. (1982). "Empowering Nets of Participation," *Admin. Sci. Quart.*, 27, 363–379.

BRASS, DANIEL (1984). "Being in the Right Place. A Structural Analysis of Individual Influence in an Organization," *Admin. Sci. Quart.*, 29, 518–539.

COHEN, ELIZABETH AND SUSAN ROPER (1972). "Modification of Interracial Interaction Disability," *Amer. Sociological Rev.*, 37, 643–665.

CULNAN, MARY AND LYNNE MARKUS (1987). "Information Technologies," In Fredric M. Jablin et al. (Eds.), *Handbook of Organizational Communication*, Sage Publications, Newbury Park, CA, 420–443.

DAFT, RICHARD AND RICHARD LENGEL. (1984). "Information Richness: A New Approach to Managerial Behavior and Organizational Design," In Larry Cummings and Barry Staw (Eds.), *Research in Organizational Behavior.* Vol. 6, JAI Press, Greenwich, CT, 191–233.

DALTON, MELVILLE (1959). *Men Who Manage*, Wiley, New York.

EISENBERG, ERIC, PETER MONGE AND KATHERINE MILLER (1983). "Involvement in Communication Networks as a Predictor of Organizational Commitment," *Human Communication Res.*, 10, 179–201.

EMMETT, R. (1982). *Datamation*, 48.

FELDMAN, MARTHA (1987). "Electronic Mail and Weak Ties in Organizations," *Office: Technology and People*, 3, 83–101.

—— AND JAMES G. MARCH (1981). "Information in Organizations as Signal and Symbol," *Admin. Sci. Quart.*, 26, 171–186.

FESTINGER, LEON (1950). "Informal Social Communication," *Psychological Rev.*, 57, 271–282.

FINHOLT, TOM, LEE SPROULL AND SARA KIESLER (1989). "Communication and Performance in ad hoc Task Groups," To appear in Jolene Galegher, Robert Kraut, and Carmen Egido (Eds.), *Intellectual Teamwork: Social and Technical Bases of Collaboration*, Erlbaum, Hillsdale, NJ.

FOMBRUN, CHARLES (1982). "Strategies for Network Research in Organizations," *Acad. Management Rev.*, 7, 280–291.

FORSYTH, DONELSON R. (1983). *An Introduction to Group Dynamics*, Brooks/Cole, Monterey, CA.

FREEMAN, LINTON C. (1984). "The Impact of Computer-Based Communication on the Social Structure of an Emerging Scientific Specialty," *Social Networks*, 6, 201–221.

FULK, JANET, CHARLES STEINFIELD, JOSEPH SCHMITZ AND GERARD POWER (1987). "A Social Information Processing Model of Media Use in Organizations," *Communication Res.*, 14, 529–552.

GLENN, EVELYN AND ROSLYN FELDBERG (1977). "Degraded and Deskilled: The Proletarianization of Clerical Work," *Social Problems*, 25, 52–64.

GOODMAN, PAUL AND ASSOCIATES (1986). *Designing Effective Work Groups*, Jossey-Bass, San Francisco.

GRIEF, IRENE AND SUNIL SARIN (1987). "Data Sharing in Group Work," *ACM Trans. Office Information Systems*, 5, 187–211.

[8]The research reported in this paper was supported by the System Development Foundation and by the National Science Foundation Graduate Fellowship program. The paper was written while the authors were at the Xerox Palo Alto Research Center. We are grateful for helpful comments from Robyn Dawes, Rob Kling, Robert Zmud, and three anonymous reviewers. We also appreciate assistance, both electronic and face-to-face, from our research group: Kathleen Carley, Karen Hartman, Sara Kiesler, Jane Siegel, Suzanne Weisband, and David Zubrow.

SIEGEL, JANE, VITALY DUBROVSKY, SARA KIESLER AND TIM MCGUIRE (1986). "Group Processes in Computer-Mediated Communication," *Organizational Behavior and Human Decision Processes*, 37, 157–187.

SPROULL, LEE AND SARA KIESLER (1986). "Reducing Social Context Cues: Electronic Mail in Organizational Communication," *Management Sci.*, 32, 1492–1512.

STEFIK, MARK, GREGG, FOSTER, DANIEL G. BOBROW, KENNETH KAHN, STAN LANNING AND LUCY SUCHMAN (1987). "Beyond the Chalkboard: Computer Support for Collaboration and Problem-Solving in Meetings," *Comm. ACM*, 30.

STEINER, IVAN D. (1972). *Group Processes and Productivity*, Academic Press, New York.

STEINFIELD, CHARLES AND JANET FULK (1987). "New Information Technology and Media Choice in Organizations," Manuscript submitted for publication.

THOITS, PEGGY (1983). "Multiple Identities and Psychological Well-Being," *Amer. Sociological. Rev.*, 48, 174–187.

THORN, BRIAN AND TERRY CONNOLLY (1987). "Discretionary Data Bases: A Theory and Some Experimental Findings," *Communication Res.*, 14, 512–528.

TICHY, NOEL, MICHAEL TUSHMAN AND CHARLES FOMBRUN (1979). "Social Network Analysis for Organizations," *Acad. Management Rev.*, 4, 507–520.

TRICE, HARRISON AND JANET BEYER (1984). "Studying Organizational Cultures through Tires and Ceremonials," *Acad. Management J.*, 4, 653–669.

VALLEE, JACQUES, ET AL. (1974). *Group Communication Through Computers: A Study of Social Effects*, Vol. 2, R-33, Institute for the Future, Menlo Park, CA.

VALLEE, JACQUES AND THADDEUS WILSON (1976). "Computer-Based Communication in Support of Scientific and Technical Work," March, NASA CR 137879.

VAN MAANEN, JOHN AND EDGAR SCHEIN (1979). "Toward a Theory of Organizational Socialization," In B. Staw (Ed.), *Research in Organizational Behavior*, JAI Press, Greenwich, CT, 209–264.

WALLACE, MICHAEL AND ARNE L. KALLEBERG (1982). "Industrial Transformation and the Decline of Craft: The Decomposition of Skill in the Printing Industry," *Amer. Sociological Rev.*, 47, 307–324.

WATSON, KATHLEEN (1982). "An Analysis of Communication Patterns: A Method of Discriminating Leader and Subordinate Roles," *Acad. Management J.*, 25, 107–120.

ZUBOFF, SHOSHANA (1988). *In the Age of the Smart Machine: The Future of Work and Power*, Basic Books, New York.

GIULIANO, VINCENT (1982). "The Mechanization of Office Work," *Scientific American*, 247, 3, 148–165.

GUMPERZ, JOHN J. (1982). *Discourse Strategies*, Cambridge University Press, Cambridge.

HACKMAN, J. RICHARD AND CHARLES G. MORRIS (1975). "Group Tasks, Group Interaction Process, and Group Performance Effectiveness: A Review and Proposed Integration," In L. Berkowitz (Ed.), *Advances in Experimental Social Psychology*, Academic Press, New York, 45–99.

HARTMANN, HEIDI (Ed.) (1987). *Computer Chips and Paper Clips: Technology and Women's Employment*, National Academy Press, Washington, D.C.

HILTZ, STARR ROXANNE (1984). *Online Communities*, Ablex, Norwood, NJ.

―― AND MURRAY TUROFF (1978). *The Network Nation*, Addison-Wesley, Reading, MA.

HUBER, GEORGE AND REUBEN MCDANIEL, JR. (1986). "Exploiting Information Technologies to Design More Effective Organizations," In Jarke, M. (Ed.), *Managers, Micros and Mainframes*, Wiley, New York.

HUFF, CHARLES, LEE SPROULL AND SARA KIESLER (1988). "Communication and Commitment in a City Government," Carnegie Mellon University working paper.

KANTER, ROSABETH (1977). "Some Effects of Proportions in Group Life: Skewed Sex Ratios and Responses to Token Women." *Amer. J. Sociology*, 82, 965–990.

KERR, ELAINE AND STARR ROXANNE HILTZ (1982). *Computer-Mediated Communication Systems: Status and Evaluation*, Academic Press, New York.

KMETZ, JOHN (1984). "An Information Processing Study of a Complex Workflow in Aircraft Electronics Repair," *Admin. Sci. Quart.*, 29, 255–280.

KRAEMER, KENNETH L. AND JOHN LESLIE KING (1988). "Computer-Based Systems for Cooperative Work and Group Decision Making," *ACM Computing Surveys*, 20, 115–146.

LABOV, WILLIAM (1967) *The Social Stratification of English in New York City*, Center for Applied Linguistics, Washington, D.C.

LEVITT, BARBARA AND JAMES MARCH (1988). "Organizational Learning," *Ann. Rev. Sociology*, (in press).

LINCOLN, JAMES R. AND ARNE L. KALLEBERG (1985). "Work Organization & Work Force Commitment: A Study of Plants and Employees in the U.S. and Japan," *Amer. Sociological Rev.*, 50, 738–760.

LIPINSKI, HUBERT AND RICHARD P. ADLER (1982). "The HUB Project: Computer-Based Support for Group Problem Solving," R-51, Institute for the Future.

MALONE, THOMAS W. ET AL. (1987). "Intelligent Information-Sharing Systems," *Comm. ACM*, 30, 5, 390–402.

MARCH, JAMES G. AND GUJE SEVON (1984). "Gossip, Information and Decision-Making," In L. Sproull & P. D. Larkey (Eds.), *Advances in Information Processing in Organizations*, JAI Press, Greenwich, CT, 95–108.

―― AND HERBERT SIMON (1958). *Organizations*, Wiley, New York.

MATTEIS, RICHARD J. (1979). "The New Back Office Focuses on Customer Service," *Harvard Business Rev.*, 57, 146–159.

MAYO, ELTON (1945). *The Social Problems of an Industrial Civilization*, Harvard University Press, Cambridge, MA.

MCGRATH, JOSEPH E. (1984). *Groups: Interaction and Performance*, Prentice-Hall, Englewood Cliffs, NJ.

MCGUIRE, TIMOTHY W., SARA KIESLER AND JANE SIEGEL (1987). "Group and Computer-Mediated Discussion Effects in Risk Decision Making," *J. Personality and Social Psychology*, 52, 917–930.

MORELAND, RICHARD L. AND JOHN M. LEVINE (1982). "Socialization in Small Groups: Temporal Changes in Individual-Group Relations," *Adv. in Experimental Social Psychology*, 15, 137–192.

MORTON, MICHAEL SCOTT AND SIDNEY HUFF (1980). "The Impact of Computers on Planning and Decision Making," In Smith and Green (Eds.), *Human Interaction with Computers*, Academic Press, London, 177–202.

OLDHAM, GREG AND NANCY ROTCHFORD (1983). "Relationships between Office Characteristics and Employee Reactions: A Study of the Physical Environment," *Admin. Sci. Quart.*, 28, 542–556.

PALME, JACOB (1981). *Experience with the Use of the COM Computerized Conferencing System*, Forsvarets Forskningsanstalt, Stockholm, Sweden.

RICE, RONALD E. (1982). "Communication Networking in Computer-Conferencing Systems: A Longitudinal Study of Group Roles and System Structure." *Communication Yearbook*, 6, Sage, Beverly Hills, CA, 925–944.

―――― (1984). "Mediated Group Communication," In R. E. Rice (Ed.), *The New Media*, Sage, Beverly Hills, CA, 129–154.

ROBERTS, KATHLEEN AND CHARLES O'REILLY (1979). "Some Correlates of Communication Roles in Organizations," *Acad. Management J.*, 22, 42–57.

ROETHLISBERGER, FRITZ J. AND WILLIAM J. DICKSON (1939). *Management and the Worker*, Harvard University Press, Cambridge.

SHERIF, MUSTAFAH ET AL. (1961). *Inter-Group Conflict and Cooperation*, Institute of Group Relations, Norman, OK.

Work Group Structures and Computer Support: A Field Experiment

J. D. EVELAND and T. K. BIKSON
The Rand Corporation

It is frequently suggested that work groups that have computer technology to support activities such as text editing, data manipulation, and communication develop systematically different structures and working processes from groups that rely on more conventional technologies such as memos, phone calls, and meetings. However, cross-sectional or retrospective research designs do not allow this hypothesis to be tested with much power. This field experiment created two task forces, each composed equally of recently retired employees and employees still at work but eligible to retire. They were given the identical tasks of preparing reports for their company on retirement planning issues, but they were randomly assigned to different technology conditions. One group had full conventional office support; the other had, in addition, networked microcomputers with electronic mail and routine office software. Structured interviews were conducted four times during the year-long project; in addition, electronic mail activity was logged in the on-line group. Although both groups produced effective reports, the two differed significantly in the kind of work they produced, the group structures that emerged, and evaluations of their own performance. Although the standard group was largely dominated by the employees through the extensive reliance on informal meetings, the electronic technology used by the other task force allowed the retirees to exercise primary leverage. We conclude that use of computer support for cooperative work results in both quantitative and qualitative changes but that effective participation in such electronically supported groups requires significant investments of time and energy on the part of its members to master the technology and a relatively high level of assistance during the learning process.

Categories and Subject Descriptors: H.4.3 [**Information Systems Applications**]: Communications Applications—*electronic mail*; K.4.2 [**Computers and Society**]: Social Issues—*employment*; K.4.3 [**Computers and Society**]: Organizational Impacts

General Terms: Experimentation, Human Factors, Management

Additional Key Words and Phrases: Communication, Computer-Supported Cooperative Work (CSCW), group processes, social structures

1. INTRODUCTION

What happens when task groups attempt to couple the advantages of on-line text preparation or data analysis and decision support with computer-based communication capabilities? How, if at all, does networked information technology affect group structures and interaction processes? And do positive answers to these questions depend on having a technology-rich environment with computer-sophisticated individuals to start with, or could almost anyone reap significant advantages if provided with basic computer and communications technology?

For the last several years, Rand's Institute for Research on Interactive Systems has been pursuing research about the ways electronic information media may influence work groups—their structures, patterns of individual interaction, and experiences of task and social involvement.[1] Among the questions that have recurred are the following:

—When work groups get access to computer-based media for handling information and communication tasks, do their structures change? Do they move closer to or further from formally established organizational structures? Do group positions (e.g., leader roles, assistant roles) stay the same or change?

—Do computer-supported groups overcome physical barriers to interaction (e.g., space or time constraints)? Do they overcome preexisting social barriers (e.g., status differences)? Do they form tight clusters ("electronic islands"), or are they overlapping and not sharply defined ("loose bundles")?

—How, if at all, do networked information technologies affect the amount or density of interaction in a group? How do they affect the extent of members' integration within a group? Or centralization? Or communication across groups?

—How do these new technologies affect social communication among group members? How do they affect experienced task involvement? Do these media tend to "diffuse," that is, to spread and include other users and other uses? Do these media supplant or supplement other means for exchanging information and coordinating group tasks?

Our research to date has focused largely on the work group as the critical unit of analysis and on the overall context in which such units are embedded. Our findings support Kling and Scacchi's view [12] that any interactive technology introduced into a work group will be more like a "web" than like a discrete entity. When a web of interactive technology is introduced into a work group, the sociotechnical system is altered; work groups increasingly become "directly dependent on their material means and resources for their output" [2, 11, 16, 21, 22]. That is to say, individuals become interdependent not only on one another but also on the technology for accomplishing their tasks; access to and control over the "means of production" assume greater importance [9, 23]. New communication channels can introduce new ways of productive interaction; they can also exacerbate existing differences and force confrontations (they can also, of course, be largely ignored) [17, 18]. Although the avenues for group work and the means for managing it may have multiplied, new challenges are introduced, along with the technology that preexisting social structures may be ill-prepared to handle. New patterns are likely to emerge.

---

[1] We have previously reported on a number of aspects of this research, including a large cross-sectional study of work groups using computer-based tools [1, 4]; case studies of new information technology introduced into single organizations [5, 20]; and a developmental project to design, implement, and track an electronic message-handling system [3, 7].

Authors' address: The Rand Corporation, 1700 Main St., Santa Monica, Calif. 90406.

ACM Transactions on Office Information Systems, Vol. 6, No. 4, October 1988, Pages 354-379.

Our previous studies of the effects of electronic communication [7] allowed us to control the type of communications hardware and software, as well as its relationship to other computer-based tools, but it did not permit us to evaluate the extent to which network structures and interaction patterns that emerged over time were influenced by the new technology in comparison to ongoing social relationships, task differences, and other factors. It could not reveal how, if at all, computer-supported work group structures and processes differed from those that would be observed in groups employing standard interaction media.

The most effective method of trying to untangle the causal inferences we sought and still have the exercise carried out in a real-world rather than laboratory context is, of course, the classical field experiment. This procedure would allow us to randomly assign group members to computer-based versus traditional support in the completion of identical work goals, as well as to design and control the introduction of new information and communications technology. An effective experimental design, it seemed to us, should also have the following characteristics:

If individuals are expected to become familiar with new information technology, accomplish a meaningful goal, and in the process have an opportunity to form or reform work structures and social relations, it would require an intervention of about a year's time.

—Further, if individuals in both the "electronic" and "standard" conditions were to participate in a year-long effort, a strong mission focus was essential—the goal for group activity and the role of communication would have to be highly motivating.

—Also, for noncollocated individuals to agree to take part (and to continue their participation) in randomly assigned groups, they should be selected from a common "community"; that is, they should come from a common culture, share some concerns, and have some reason to think they might want to work with one another (cf. [14]).[2]

2. FIELD PROCEDURES

From one of the older and larger corporations in the greater Los Angeles area, we recruited volunteers for two task forces. Members, half retired and half actively employed, were to work together over the course of a year to consider, deliberate, and develop a set of recommendations about preretirement planning to be addressed to persons nearing retirement, to organizations (including, but not limited to, their own), and to professionals involved in preretirement planning. Meetings, phone calls, duplication, postage, and other supplies were provided by Rand or supported for both groups.

In addition, members of one of the two task forces had the option of communicating with each other and conducting their business with the aid of new

technology. Each member of this "electronic group" had access to networked microcomputers, communications software adapted from the interface to RAND-MAIL, built-in modems and hard disks, and local printers. Limited additional software was supplied, including full-text editing and formatting capabilities, a spreadsheet, a database management system, games, and Basic. (A more complete system description is available in [6].)

Because we were interested in the possible advantages and disadvantages of electronic communication compared with more standard media, we randomly appointed task force volunteers to either group. The project enrolled 79 members, all of them male professionals or managers with prior problem solving or decision-making responsibility. The mean age was 62 for retired participants and 60 for employees. Those who were retired had done so in the past four years, and the employees were all currently eligible to retire.

The distribution of participants thus was as follows:

	Computer	No Computer
Retired:	n = 20	n = 20
Not Yet Retired:	n = 20	n = 19

Although both groups received the same general orientation to and support for task force work, members of the electronic group additionally were taught to use the computer system. The three-hour training session (and the user manual developed by the research team) focused on fundamentals of operating the computer and using it to send and receive messages as well as to draft and print textual material.

The focus on electronic mail reflected several assumptions. First, the field experiment was concerned with communication and cooperative activity. Although using electronic mail has much in common with other activities users perform with computers, the difference is that electronic mail is a mechanism for dealing with others (most applications involve communication between users and programs within their own computers). Second, we supposed that communication is intrinsically motivating, so that when provided with that capability task force members would be likely to use it. Third, we regarded electronic mail as analogous to wrapping an envelope around whatever other information the user might want to share; although we could not anticipate just what else the task force might want to do, we equipped members with a number of general information handling tools to be used as they thought appropriate.

Highly structured individual interviews were administered to all subjects at the beginning of the project, with interim interviews conducted twice during the task force year and a final interview at its end. Interviews gathered detailed sociometric data about interactions among group members in addition to information about other aspects of subjects' work and social lives, attitudes, and evaluations of task force activity. In addition, for the electronic group, we collected automated usage logs and detailed network data of the sort obtained in the RANDMAIL study, as well as user assessments and diffusion and extension of use.

---

[2] Last, and definitely not least, we needed to find a funding source willing to support a rather costly experiment of this sort! This research is funded through a grant from a nonprofit organization whose two programmatic interests are aging and adult development and social uses of the media—The John and Mary R. Markle Foundation—for whose cooperation we are deeply indebted.

3. EXPERIMENTAL RESULTS

This research has produced two general kinds of findings. First, it yields the experimental results per se: what differences, if any, can be observed between the standard and electronic task forces? Second, it generates a profile of the electronic group's use of technology: an account of how a group initially unfamiliar with interactive systems adapts to and makes use of computer-based work tools. The short answer to the first question is that technology really does make a difference; the two groups differ significantly in many aspects of how they structure and carry out their tasks. Second, although virtually all members of the electronic task force adjusted in one way or another to the system, the adaptation took its toll. Thus, the standard task force was able to begin work on its task immediately, while members of the electronic group spent much of their time in the first project months just learning to use the tools. On the other hand, once a sizeable proportion of the electronic task force had acquired basic skills, the ease of coordination and interaction afforded by the system seemed to permit the group to undertake fairly ambitious substantive efforts, to involve a larger number of its members in carrying them out, and to move fairly rapidly to completion. In the remainder of this paper, we discuss some of the differences between the experimental groups, as well as characteristics that distinguished the emergent electronic network.

Findings from the research are qualified by a number of limitations that may bear on their generalizability. First, the sample size is small; resource constraints limited us to only two task forces of about 40 members each. Second, all the members are older men whose careers led to midlevel management or professional positions; we do not know how the inclusion of younger employees, women members, or representatives of the top or bottom of the organizational hierarchy might have affected the results. Third, participation in the task force was voluntary; results might not be the same for collaborative activities that are part of regular job assignments. As we see it, the main strength of the research design comes from random assignment to experimental conditions plus control over other potentially interfering variables (type of task, type of technology, prior experience with electronic mail, preexisting group structures, and the like). Any differences between the two task forces on the dependent measures reported here can, we believe, validly be interpreted as effects of networked interactive systems.

3.1 Baseline

The random assignment to experimental conditions, in fact, produced two quite similar groups. In both electronic and standard task forces, over 50 percent of participants had attained a college degree or higher level of education. Standard task force members appeared to have slightly higher incomes and occupation levels than their counterparts in the electronic group (especially within the employee category); however, this difference seems to be purely an artifact of random selection, and there is no evidence that it materially affected most of the outcomes. Prior computer experience was much the same across conditions. About half in each task force had had some sort of contact with batch-processing mainframe computers at work, and about a quarter had tried using a small home computer (typically for games). None had ever used computer-based communications.[3]

Both the conventionally supported and the computer-supported task forces had the same general charge and initially structured their approaches to it in much the same way. Each divided the basic mission into smaller issue areas for work by subgroups; the subgroups elected chairs, with the chairs forming a task force steering committee.[4] Interestingly, although both task forces generated six subcommittees related to specific concerns (health, finances, and so on), the standard task force spent considerable time arriving at a felicitous assignment of members to subgroups (e.g., balancing size and employee–retiree representation while accommodating individual interests).

In the electronic task force, by contrast, subgroup assignment did not arise as a problem. We suspect it was assumed that, given electronic means for overcoming space and time constraints on multiperson activity, members could work on as many subgroups as interested them. No one in the standard task force became a member of more than one subgroup, while most of those in the electronic task force started off with two or more subgroup assignments; the mean size of the subgroup in the standard task force initially was 6+ (range = 6–7), while it was 10+ (range = 6–15) in the electronic task force. It is reasonable to suppose that the availability of electronic media can affect people's expectations about how group work will proceed.

From items in the interview tapping relationships among respondents, we constructed three measures reflecting varying degrees of interpersonal attachment.[5]

(1) Recognition, or reflecting other task force members with which a subject is familiar at least by recognizing the name or face;

(2) Knowing, or a reciprocal acknowledgement between pairs of subjects in the task force that they know each other well;

(3) Contact, or having been in touch with any of the other task force members (in person, by phone, by memo, and/or by computer) in the past two weeks. At baseline (i.e., prior to the experiment), subjects on average "recognized" over a third of the other members of their task force but "knew" only about ten percent of them. Very few instances of actual contact were reported.

In general, we found few differences between the two experimental groups on these measures. Members of the standard task force tended to be slightly more widely recognized and better known, which we interpreted as a reflection of their

[3] An open-ended item at the end of the initial interview asked subjects why they had agreed to participate in the project. In both conditions a similar pattern emerged: Retirees were interested in giving information, and employees were interested in getting information about the transition to retirement; the task force topic itself was thus a strong incentive. Another often cited motivation was curiosity about research procedures. Access to the technology was infrequently cited—only ten percent of the standard group and five percent of the electronic group mentioned they were interested in computers.

[4] An experienced group facilitator was retained to help the task forces get started. She worked with both groups at several points during the study.

[5] See the Appendix for details on how these and other measures were constructed and used.

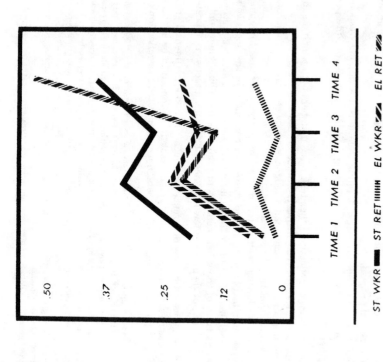

ST WKR ▰▰▰ ST RET ▥▥▥ EL WKR ▨▨▨ EL RET ▨▨▨

Fig. 1. Recognition density. Standard and electronic groups overall.

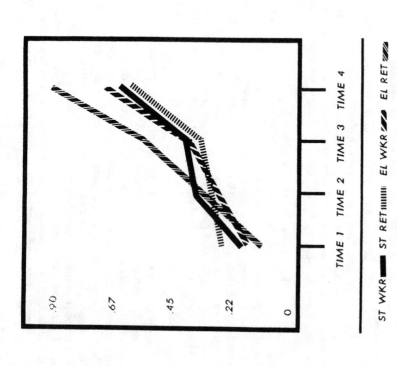

ST WKR ▰▰▰ ST RET ▥▥▥ EL WKR ▨▨▨ EL RET ▨▨▨

Fig. 2. Contact density. Standard and electronic groups overall.

higher status in the parent organization (differences were not statistically significant). Much stronger differences, however, were notable between employed and retired members across the task forces; measures of recognition and knowing, and especially of contact, were lower for retirees than for those still employed. Retirees in both electronic and standard groups were relatively peripheral.[6]

3.2 Structural Changes During the Project

The issues-oriented subcommittee structure persisted for both task forces throughout the project. In the electronic group, however, a second procedurally based work structure was also created to facilitate task completion. For instance, each subgroup sent members to a content coordinating committee whose job it was to determine how the issues examined by each subgroup fit together, to

locate overlaps, and to eliminate redundancies. Eventually six such groups were matrixed through the original six subcommittees. No structural additions or changes were instituted within the standard task force.[7]

An overall look at network patterns (based on the three measures outlined above) indicates increasing amounts of communication (measured by the "density" index; see the Appendix) over time for both task forces. Figure 1, for instance, shows changes in recognition density; for all groups, recognition increased by Time 4 to well over 50 percent. The increase is most striking for the electronic retirees, who went from recognizing less than 10 percent of their group at baseline to over 90 percent by the project's end. Figure 2 shows the changes in actual contacts. Again, electronic retirees evidence the greatest overall change with contact density increasing to over 50 percent.[8]

---

[6] "The proportion of the population with whom contact is reported (the "integrativeness" index—see the Appendix) for retirees in both groups averaged about .08. This contrasts with about .12 for electronic workers and about .20 for standard workers. An analysis of variance shows the only significant difference to be that due to employee-retiree status ($F = 15.87, p < .001$); neither condition nor interaction effects are significant).

[7] See Section 4 for further data on the evolution of this group.

[8] Figure 2 shows declines in actual contacts between Time 2 and Time 3. The Time 3 interviews were conducted in late summer when vacation schedules had significantly reduced participation in the project for the two-week period surveyed.

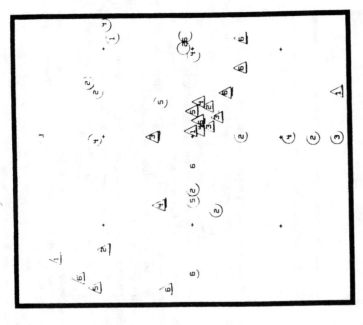

Fig. 4. Contact relationships. Electronic group—time 1 (at baseline).

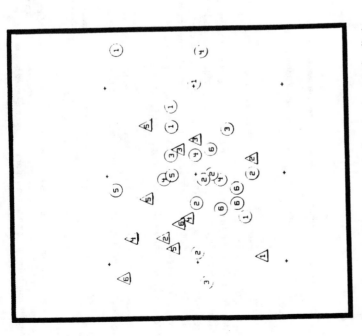

Fig. 3. Contact relationships. Standard group—time 1 (at baseline).

A repeated measures analysis of variance confirms the significance of these trends. The largest main effect, not surprisingly, is for time (recognition: $F = 22.4$, $p < .001$, contact: $F = 28.5$, $p < .001$). For recognition, the electronic-standard condition is also a significant source of variation ($F = 9.9$, $p < .01$), as is the time/status/condition interaction ($F = 3.5$, $p < .05$). For contact, condition is significant ($F = 3.9$, $p < .05$), as is status (employee–retiree)—($F = 18.9$, $p < .001$) and the condition–status interaction ($F = 15.6$, $p < .001$).

Both task forces saw their patterns of interpersonal contacts quickly change in response to task group activity. Figures 3 and 4 show "contact maps" (see the Appendix for details on how these "maps" were constructed and interpreted) representing the pattern of interactions at baseline; no particular clustering of members emerges within either task force. That is, there is no evidence that individuals chose to join particular issue-oriented subcommittees because of prior relationships to others in their task force.[9] In both tables, the relatively peripheral position of retired members is apparent.

By Time 2, only three months later, the patterns of contact shifted substantially. In the standard task force (Figure 5), what had begun as a rather formless collection now exhibited relatively well-defined relationship clusters that tended to reflect subcommittee boundaries. In the electronic task force, in contrast, the map shows much less sharply defined clusters (Figure 6), probably reflecting overlapping subcommittee memberships plus new group formation.[10]

The task forces also differed in terms of overall levels of contact their members experienced during the experiment. Figure 7 shows the number of people an average task force member reported contact with at each time period. Again, there is a strong interaction effect. At baseline, workers in both task forces reported contacts with 5–6 others on average; retirees reported contacts across the 1–2. For the standard group, both levels remain essentially static across the experiment, with retiree contacts actually declining somewhat. For the electronic group, worker contacts also remain basically stable, but retiree contacts increase

---

[9] The numbers on the figures indicate the location of persons as well as their subcommittee membership (subgroups are arbitrarily numbered 1–6). Workers are indicated as circles; retirees are shown as triangles.

[10] Contact maps for Times 3 and 4 are generally similar to those for Time 2. By Time 4, the tightness of clusters in the standard group has decreased somewhat but not so much as to resemble the electronic group.

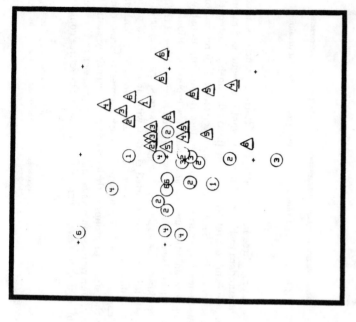

Fig. 5.   Contact relationships. Standard group—time 2 (about three months).

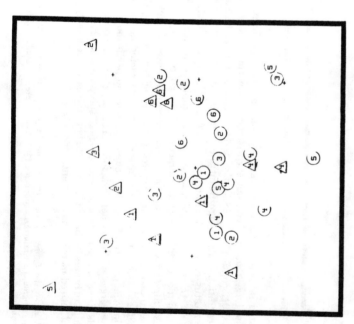

Fig. 6.   Contact relationships. Electronic group—time 2 (about three months).

dramatically. This is consistent with other evidence about the salience of retiree participation in the electronic task force.[11]

Different individuals often prefer to interact through different communication modes at different times, depending partly on personal preferences and partly on situation and task characteristics. No single mode is likely to be effective in all circumstances. As noted, both task forces had access to a full range of meeting, correspondence, and telephone capabilities, as well as electronic mail for the electronic group. Table I shows the number of contacts reported involving various media.[12]

For the standard group in this last time period, contacts tended to take the form of unscheduled meetings. Not surprisingly, retirees tended to be out of the

unscheduled meeting loop since these apparently took place largely at corporate headquarters; retirees participated in only 12 percent of the unscheduled meetings in the standard group and 25 percent of those in the electronic group. For the electronic group, by contrast, contacts tended to be primarily in the form of scheduled meetings with less reliance on unscheduled meetings and relatively heavy use of electronic mail. Retirees participated in 19 percent of the scheduled meetings in the standard group and 75 percent of those in the electronic group. Retirees also used 80 percent of the electronic mail that was sent.[13]

The standard group experienced significantly greater stability of leadership roles during the experiment than did the electronic group. Table II provides intercorrelations among "betweenness" scores obtained for the four time periods.[14] A repeated measures ANOVA shows significant main effects for task

---

[11] Repeated measures of analyses of variance (ANOVAs) confirm the significance of these trends. For task force by time, $F = 6.81, p < .001$; for status by time, $F = 6.35, p < .001$; for task force by status by time, $F = 5.51, p < .001$. There are also main effects for task force by status $(F = 19.9, p < .001)$ and for time $(F = 6.07, p < .001)$.

[12] Unfortunately, the question about media use was only asked at Time 4. See the Appendix for details on question wording. The table shows the number of actual contacts reported as using each medium; a few contacts were reported as using more than one medium and are logged here as separate contacts. The maximum possible number of contacts in any one cell would be $(N(N-1)/2)$ or 780 for the 40 individuals in each group.

[13] The electronic group set up a series of scheduled in-person meetings at the end of the study to coordinate preparation of their final report. This emphasis on scheduled meetings is probably not representative of the entire period of work.

[14] *Betweenness* is a measure of the relative centrality of a person in a network (see the Appendix for the construction and interpretation of this index). Because of high skewness in betweenness scores, logs of raw scores were used in these correlations.

Table I. Frequency of Use of Different Media for Contacts (Time 4)

	Standard N = 178		Electronic N = 408	
Scheduled Meetings	N = 36	.45	N = 220	.80
Unscheduled Meetings	N = 116	.83	N = 84	.47
Telephone	N = 23	.36	N = 41	.32
Letters/Memos	N = 2	.11	N = 8	.14
Electronic Mail			N = 55	.38

Table II. Continuity of Leadership Structure. (Pearson Correlations)

	Standard	Electronic
Time 1 To Time 2	.47	.19
Time 2 To Time 3	.69	.28
Time 3 To Time 4	.57	.21

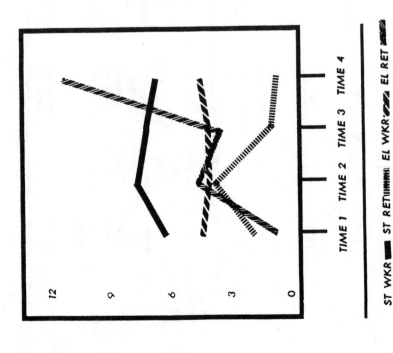

TIME 1   TIME 2   TIME 3   TIME 4

ST WKR ▬   ST RET▥   EL WKR▨   EL RET▨

Fig. 7. Average contacts per group member. Standard and electronic groups overall.

force ($F = 7.7$, $p < .01$) and for status ($F = 33.9$, $p < .0001$), as well as for task force by time interaction ($F = 4.6$, $p < .01$). For the standard group, the betweenness scores at each time point are significantly predicted by the betweenness scores at the preceding point (F's range from 11.5 to 18.6, $p < .01$). For the electronic group, this is not the case; betweenness scores are not significantly related to the previous period's scores.

If we take the 5 most central people in each contact network at each period to be a sort of "leadership cadre" for that time period, there are a total of 20 possible leader slots. For the standard group, 13 people fill those 20 leader slots (with 7 repeating the role at more than one time period); all but 1 are workers. For the electronic group, there are 16 leaders (4 repeaters); 7 are workers and 9 are retirees. The basic point of all these analyses is that the leadership of the electronic group is a much more fluctuating and diverse group and much less dominated by the workers than is that of the standard group.

3.3 Satisfaction

To understand the perceived effectiveness of computer-based and conventional media for carrying out group tasks, we asked subjects to make a number of evaluations using 5-point rating scales. In particular, task force members were asked to judge the level of their own task involvement, the effectiveness of their subcommittee(s), how well the task force as a whole was working, and the extent to which their experimental condition helped or hindered the accomplishment of the task force mission.

Repeated measures ANOVAs show that the electronic group became increasingly more positive about task involvement as well as subgroup and task force effectiveness, even though the standard group initially scored higher on most measures. The effect is primarily attributable to retirees in the electronic condition. Most informative, perhaps, are responses to the very direct question about the influence of the medium on the task (Table III). Ratings yielded a very strong work status-by-condition effect, with retirees in the electronic condition and employees in the standard condition giving their experimental assignments very high marks. Assessments were just the opposite for employees in the electronic condition and retirees in the standard condition, with the latter judging themselves by far the most disadvantaged.[15]

When asked about their general satisfaction with the overall accomplishments of their task force, participants showed the same pattern (Table IV). That is, the

---

[15] Repeated measures ANOVAs show a significant main effect for task force ($F = 7.6$, $p < .01$), as well as for task force by status ($F = 16.5$, $p < .001$) and task force by time ($F = 10.3$, $p < .001$).

Table III. Evaluation of Experimental Condition

	MEANS		
	TIME.2	TIME.3	TIME.4
Retirees			
Electronic	3.9	4.0	4.6
Standard	3.1	2.9	2.7
Employees			
Electronic	3.3	3.5	3.9
Standard	3.8	4.1	3.7

Condition: $F = 7.58$***
Condition x status: $F = 16.51$***
Condition x time: $F = 10.32$***

Note: Higher numbers mean the condition is perceived as more helpful to task completion.

Table IV. Evaluation of Overall Task Force Performance

	MEANS		
	TIME.2	TIME.3	TIME.4
Retirees			
Electronic	2.8	3.2	3.7
Standard	3.5	3.4	3.3
Employees			
Electronic	2.8	2.9	3.8
Standard	3.7	3.6	3.4

Condition: $F = 2.99$†
Time: $F = 5.53$**
Condition x time: $F = 13.7$***

Note: Higher numbers mean better performance ratings.

Table V. Correlations Between Involvement, Satisfaction, and Contact (Integrativeness Index)

Time 2	Involvement	.17
Time 2	Satisfaction with task-force performance	-.09
Time 3	Involvement	.21*
Time 3	Satisfaction with task force performance	-.15
Time 4	Involvement	.33
Time 4	Satisfaction with task force performance	.32

Table VI. Total Message Traffic Over Project Year

Recipients	Messages Sent	Messages Received
Individuals (total)	1,745	2,906
Single	1,160	1,160
Multiple	585	1,746
Staff (total)	1,266	—
Aliases (total)	1,080	11,590
Task Force Alias	434	—
All Chairs	407	—
Task Force	239	—
Overall Sum of Totals	4,091	14,496

electronic group showed increases, while the standard group showed stagnation or even declines.[16]

Correlating network participation (integrativeness[17]) with these effectiveness assessments in Table V shows, not surprisingly, that those who participate more in the communication network feel more involved in the task force. Effectiveness ratings do not, however, always follow involvement. Rather, the association between participation and perceived task force effectiveness is essentially zero at Time 2 and has become negative by Time 3; that is, those taking more active roles judge their task force as a whole to be less effective than do members who are less involved. By Time 4, the pattern is reversed, and task force effectiveness is again positively associated with participation.

[16] Repeated measures ANOVAs here showed significant main effects for task force ($F = 2.99$, $p < .05$) and time ($F = 5.53$, $p < .05$), as well as the time by task force interaction ($F = 13.7$, $p < .001$).

[17] Integrativeness, as noted earlier, is a measure of involvement (the proportion of actual links reported to possible links).

4. ELECTRONIC NETWORK STRUCTURE

As we explained, the project retained a log of the headers of all network messages exchanged among electronic task force participants over the project year. This log included the sender's ID, the receiver's ID, the message date and time, and, if the message was a reply, the date and time of the original message. Topic identifiers were not retained for confidentiality reasons.[18]

Table VI describes how many messages were involved. During the project year, 4091 messages were sent by the 40 people taking part in the electronic network.[19] Given the various "aliases" (multiple recipients addressed by a single name that expands into a distribution list) employed, this number translates into 14,496 messages received. About 40 percent of these messages were sent point-to-point, sometimes to multiple addresses; and about 30 percent were messages to project staff, either for substantive assistance or computer help.

These messages were not evenly distributed across group members. As several similar studies have reported, approximately 25 percent of the people accounted for about 75 percent of the messages sent. The 10 "high senders" in this case included the 6 subcommittee chairs (all retirees); only one employee emerged as a heavy sender. Figure 8 shows percent of participation (i.e., percent who sent at

[18] Advance consent to message header logging was obtained prior to the start of the project.

[19] This figure does not include messages sent by the project staff to task force members either as originals or replies; they were routed through another host and were not logged.

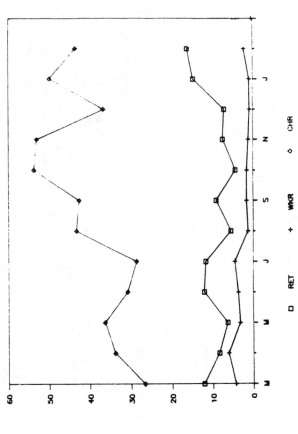

Fig. 9. Messages sent per capita by group.

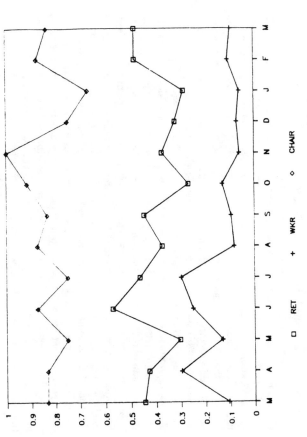

Fig. 8. Participation in network. Percent of groups participating.

least one message) during each project month by employment status. Retirees averaged nearly 50 percent participation each month; workers averaged closer to 20 percent, dropping to only about 10 percent during the last months.

Figure 9 shows the messages sent by the average individual in each group by month. On average, chairs sent 4 to 5 times as many messages as other participants. Of course, as Figure 10 indicates, chairs also received considerably more messages than other people; much of this information was apparently exchanged among themselves. Figure 10 also shows that, while retirees tended to send more messages than workers, they tended to receive just about the same number.[20]

In our first electronic mail study [7], we noted that users tend to divide early into heavy and light senders, with heavy senders getting heavier and light senders, lighter. Figure 11 shows sending patterns for the 10 "high users" in contrast to the remaining 30 network members. Here, too, this pattern is observed: High users got off to a fast start initially and their usage increased over time; light users started slow and changed little over time. The consistency of these trends suggests that they should be taken into account in implementation and training plans for electronic communication systems.

The availability of logged data for the electronic task force provides an opportunity to examine the relationship between computer-based communication and overall contact (structured self-report data). In general, we expected total reported contacts to exceed electronic contacts—and it would not have been

surprising to obtain reports of contact between people who do not exchange electronic messages. However, it is quite surprising to find the reverse. Figure 12 shows the proportions of contacts that are associated with the exchange of electronic messages.[21] The first part of this figure shows that, if we look at all messages exchanged, about 8 percent of the individuals reported having NO contact with people with whom they had in fact exchanged electronic communication.

If we look only at "message loops" (i.e., messages that have received an answer), the proportion in this category drops to about 5 percent. Further restricting the definition of "what constitutes an exchange"—to a message loop that is addressed to only one person rather than a group—does result in largely, though not entirely, eliminating this category.[22]

In any event, we believe that this question of just what it is about an electronic exchange that defines it as a "contact" for reporting purposes is an interesting one. The issue is significant, particularly in terms of the presumed ability of logging systems to capture the electronic message exchange. Although logging systems clearly can capture the messages actually exchanged, the question

---

[20] This figure is based on the 14,000+ expanded-alias message set.

[21] These data are from Time 4; however, similar patterns exist in each of the preceding time periods. The proportions are based on the 780 contacts possible among a group of 40 people. The first two parts of the figure are based on the expanded message set; the third part is based on the point-to-point limited message set.

[22] The overall contact matrix and the "all loops" matrix correlate at .03 only. The point-to-point electronic loop matrix and the overall contact matrix correlate at .15.

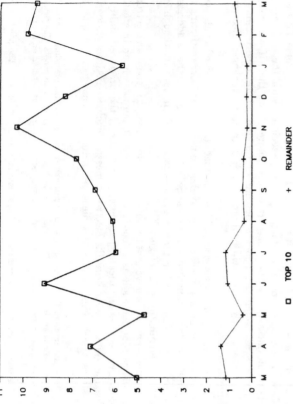

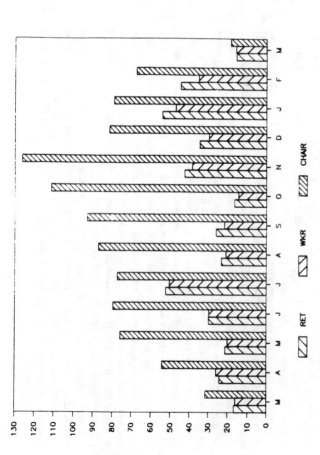

Fig. 10.   Messages received by the average person by month.

Fig. 11.   High versus low users over time. Average messages sent per week.

remains what has actually been measured. Certainly it is not contact as perceived by the messagers. The issue of the relationship between perceived contact and electronic message exchange, we believe, deserves further investigation.

On balance, we think the task force experiment demonstrates that an electronic network can provide an effective infrastructure for sustained collaborative activity, even among people who are not computer sophisticated initially. We believe, however, that we have much to learn about how and why it works and about networked interactive systems generally. First, electronic mail does not serve as a replacement for other interaction media; rather than substituting for them, it may reinforce them instead of reducing their use (see Table I). Second, providing electronic communication cannot be construed just as the provision of an application; it might better be regarded as providing a way of sharing other applications that are individually used (see Section 2).

As a multipurpose avenue of exchange, the system played a significant role in the administration and coordination of task force activities (as evidenced by its use in arranging scheduled meetings shown in Table I). It also figured heavily in the shared development, review, and dissemination of the group's substantive work. For example, the task force decided to survey a broad range of retirees and employees so that its white paper would be more representative than its own membership: questionnaire items were prepared on-line and iterated for review until a final version was accepted; responses to the survey were entered into the database program, datasets were divided and distributed for analysis to the

appropriate subgroup, and results were made available to the task force as a whole. The issue of the relationship between perceived contact and, after each subgroup had an approved draft of its topic area, the several sections were concatenated to create the final white paper.

These examples should help clarify why there was such a high level of interaction within the electronic task force: It had undertaken a very ambitious route to fulfilling its charge. The course it set upon required intensive use of the technology and substantial work commitments from the members. In facilitating their frequent contact, the network seemed also to enable subgroup restructuring as the subtasks at hand required (e.g., to arrive at a final nonoverlapping set of items for the survey, the task force thought the most efficient course was to form a committee composed of representatives from each subgroup; they would negotiate a draft among themselves and then circulate it more broadly after redundancies had been removed, wordings agreed upon, and so on). In that process, it seemed relatively easy for individual members to change roles (e.g., some people were not particularly interested in defining and wording issues for the questionnaire, but they were extremely interested in developing a database and analyzing its contents. They, therefore, acquired the necessary DBMS skills and led this effort). Finally, while different activities dominated task force work at any point in time, there was always need for within-group expertise; although the research team provided a help line, there is no substitute for the local "guru" who speaks the language of the group, is in touch with its tasks, and has a special affinity for

perhaps because the former seems more like a social interaction. In any case, analyses of variance (see above) confirm that those in the electronic task force think they have formed significantly more lasting social ties than those in the standard condition.

The picture that emerges of the electronic network is one of a vigorous and effective group in which some individuals take the lead and others take part in differing degrees. There is extensive communication both within and across specific subgroup lines. Patterns that emerged early in its evolution characterized its later operation, but not rigidly; individuals moved both into and out of active messaging over time. In short, it looks very much like a computer-supported cooperative group in which a lot of work gets done.

5. DISCUSSION

At the beginning of the paper we posed a series of questions that we hoped this experiment would illuminate. Although not all of them have been answered definitively even within the compass of this study, we think the following conclusions have been corroborated:

—The electronically supported group developed a structure significantly different from that developed by the standard group, one that appears to take advantage of electronic media in terms of both breadth of access and opportunity to participate. While maintaining its formal organization, it developed a set of alternative structures not apparent in the standard group. The standard group had a generally consistent set of leaders, mainly employees; the electronic group had a much more fluctuating leadership pattern, dominated largely by retirees.

—The electronically supported group allowed different people to work at different times of the day according to their own schedules and certainly increased the ability of noncollocated retired members to take an active role in the project.

—The electronically supported group maintained a significantly higher degree of contact than did the standard group and had considerably less communication isolation. It was generally less centralized both overall and in its task group interactions, although the extent of centralization fluctuated over the project year. Further, in the electronic group, not everyone uses the medium with equal facility, and early experiences with it tend to be carried over into later time periods.

—Members of the electronically supported group appear to experience significantly more involvement in the work of the group, and to be more satisfied with its outcomes. But electronic communications are not simply substituted for traditional media; rather, the electronic task force maintained higher levels of communication in general through all channels.

—Keeping an electronically supported work group up and running is a relatively labor-intensive effort. A good deal of staff time was required to devise and maintain the hardware–software configuration; even more effort was required to respond to user needs and support them as they made the technology their own. The "humanware" demands of such systems cannot be discounted.

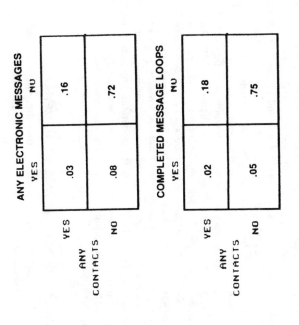

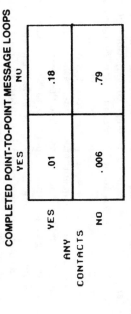

ANY ELECTRONIC MESSAGES

		YES	NU
ANY CONTACTS	YES	.03	.16
	NO	.08	.72

COMPLETED MESSAGE LOOPS

		YES	NU
ANY CONTACTS	YES	.02	.18
	NO	.05	.75

COMPLETED POINT-TO-POINT MESSAGE LOOPS

		YES	NU
ANY CONTACTS	YES	.01	.18
	NO	.006	.79

Fig. 12. Proportion of contacts associated with exchange of electronic messages.

the tools. Such local experts emerged within the electronic task force and provided a strong complement to official Rand help.

For all these reasons, a sizeable proportion of network interactions crossed initial subgroup boundaries, and their members had many opportunities both to maintain old social ties and to form new ones. Although the discussion above emphasizes instrumental exchange, it was evident that the network also became an important avenue of social exchange. Messages shared with the research team made it clear that even task-oriented interactions were conducted in a highly sociable manner, and the system was also used for interactions of an exclusively social nature. It is worth mentioning that the Bulletin Board facility remained notably underused—participants seemed to prefer sending a message to the electronic task force alias rather than to a Bulletin Board accessible by all,

What this project demonstrates is that electronic media can constitute a major component of the "means of production" for an information-intensive work group. Control of the means of production tends to mean control of the group's directions and purposes. In the standard group, production-relevant resources (e.g., colleagues, meeting opportunities) were more readily accessible to employees on a regular and usually informal basis; retirees had a more limited ability to shape the work process. In the electronic group, by contrast, the computer-based information and communication system offered a major new production technology, one that proved critical in the emergence of quite different work group structures. Employees, for varied reasons including job demands and time pressures, generally lacked the opportunity to acquire the level of knowledge of this technology that many of the retirees developed; accordingly, it was the retirees in that task force who controlled work group production processes.

Access to tools also clearly shaped the products of the task forces. Although both groups produced effective and insightful reports on the transition to retirement, the standard group's product was about 15 pages in length, composed largely of anecdotal advice gathered through conversations. The electronic group's report, by contrast, was about 75 pages in length, composed primarily of tables describing the results of an opinion survey that the group designed and analyzed on-line. This is not to say that one product is better as a function of length or of its qualitative or quantitative nature; rather, it is to suggest that work tools really do condition how groups define their work goals.

It is also interesting to note that although the task forces have achieved their goals and the field experiment has formally ended, the electronic group is continuing with a communication network. Although the network operates officially under the auspices of the parent organization, it will be managed and supported (and, perhaps, controlled) by electronic task force participants themselves. Additionally, there is considerable demand on the part of some former standard task force participants to become part of the electronic network, and plans are underway to broaden its membership as soon as feasible.

There are, we believe, a host of important questions to be answered about how a computer-supported cooperative work tools shape and interact with task demands. This research has contributed clear evidence that both the outcomes and the processes of cooperative work are significantly and directly affected by the tools themselves, and that these effects are systematic and pervasive. We have also established that it is feasible to conduct controlled field experiments in computer-supported cooperative work and to develop a substantial base of information about the structure and performance of such groups through relatively unobtrusive methods. We think the understanding to be gained from such procedures outweighs the effort they entail. Consequently, we hope that future research in this arena includes careful field experimentation with work groups and computer tools.

APPENDIX. RESEARCH AND ANALYTICAL METHODS

The bulk of the specific measures used in this study were derived from the four rounds of questionnaires. At each time point, respondents were shown pictures (ID photos) of each of the other participants.[1] They were asked first to indicate how well they "knew" the person, scaled as "know well," "know a little," or "don't know." "Know a little" was defined as "recognized by name or by face." If they "knew" the person at all, they were then prompted for whether they had had any "contact" with the person in the last two weeks, where contact was defined as including in-person interaction (in meetings or by classes), phone calls, memos, or electronic mail. If a contact was reported, they were asked if the purpose of the contact was "chance," "social," "general business," or "task force business" (more than one response was acceptable). In addition, at the last interview, respondents were asked how the contact took place: "scheduled meeting," "unscheduled face-to-face encounter," "telephone," "written letter or memo," or (for the electronic group) "electronic mail."

The three attachment measures were constructed from 40-by-40 matrices summarizing the knowledge degree and contact responses. Each matrix had the individuals as both row and column headers. Each row represented the answers of a given individual; each column, the people with whom that attachment was being reported. For "knowledge," values could range from 0 (no knowledge) to 2 (know well). For contact, values were either 0 (no contact) or 1 (contact). The matrices were initially not symmetric, since it was not necessarily the case that the two parties would agree on their connection.

The matrix of "recognition" relationships was constructed as a symmetric matrix by allowing the relationship between two people to be coded as "1" if *either* person reported knowing the other even a little ("0" otherwise). The matrix of "knowing" relationships was constructed by coding "1" only if *both* parties reported knowing the other "well." The contact matrix was merely made symmetric; that is, a contact was presumed to exist if *either* party reported it. There were thus three matrices of relationships for each task force for each of four time periods.[2]

The structural indices were largely constructed from these matrices. The "density" of a network of interconnections summarized in a matrix is simply the proportion of actual relationships reported relative to the total possible (in a 40×40 matrix, this would be 780 or $(N(N-1)/2)$. If everyone were connected to everyone else, the index value would be "1.0"; if there were no relationships, it would be "0" [13].

Integrativeness and *betweenness* are indices relating to an individual's position relative to others in the network (matrix). Integrativeness is related closely to density and is simply the proportion of others in the network to whom one is connected. Betweenness is a related but distinct concept reflecting one's centrality in a network; specifically, it measures the proportion of all the links between network members that pass through a given person [8]. It is an approximate measure of power or control vested in a given person. Both measures reflect higher values for a person the more significant that person's participation in the

[1] At Times 2 and 3 they were asked only about their own task force; at Times 1 and 4 they were queried about the participants in the other task force as well.

[2] Matrices reflecting the purposes of contacts were also constructed but are not reported here. For Time 4, five matrices, reflecting the contacts through different media, were also constructed by coding "1" if a contact was reported and a given medium was mentioned.

network might be. Scalar values for each individual in the network were calculated for each matrix and time period and used in correlational and regression analyses. The satisfaction and involvement measures used in these analyses were derived from questionnaire items that used a 5-point scale from high to low.

The "network maps" or "sociograms" (Figures 3–6) were constructed by decomposing the various matrices through multidimensional scaling, resulting in a two-dimensional representation of the more complex matrix [19]. In these "maps" people more central to the network tend to be closer to the center, while those less involved tend to be toward the periphery. People who interact with each other, and with others in similar ways, tend to be closer together in clusters on the map. For most purposes, visual inspection of the map is enlightening. For more rigorous analyses of social structure, there are tests for clustering and group formation; this stage in our analysis is still under way at this reporting.

The message header analyses are based partly on the "expanded" message set and partly on the more limited set of original address messages (see Table VI for how aliases translate into expanded messages). Figures 8, 9, and 11, dealing with message sending, use the limited set; Figure 10 (receiving messages) is based on the larger set. Figure 12 uses the expanded set for the "any message" section and the limited set for the communication-loop data.

Any other inquiries on data or analytical issues are welcomed by the authors.

REFERENCES

(Note: References [10] and [15] are not cited in text.)

1. BIKSON, T. K. Understanding the implementation of office technology. *Technology and the Transformation of White-Collar Work*, R. Kraut, Ed. Lawrence Erlbaum Associates, Inc., Hillsdale, N.J., 1987, pp. 155-176; also The Rand Corporation, N-2619-NSF, June 1987.
2. BIKSON, T. K., AND EVELAND, J. D. *New Office Technology: Planning for People*, Work in America Institute's Series in Productivity. Pergamon Press, New York, 1986.
3. BIKSON, T. K., EVELAND, J. D., AND GUTEK, B. A. Flexible interactive technologies for multiperson tasks: Current problems and future prospects. In *Technological Support for Work Group Collaboration*, M. Olson, Ed. Lawrence Erlbaum Associates, Inc., Hillsdale, N.J., pp. 89—112.
4. BIKSON, T. K., GUTEK, B. A., AND MANKIN, D. Implementing computerized procedures in office settings: Influences and outcomes. The Rand Corporation, R-3077-NSF, Oct. 1987.
5. BIKSON, T. K., STASZ, C., AND MANKIN, D. A. Computer-mediated work: Individual and organizational impact in one corporate headquarters. The Rand Corporation, R-3308-OTA, Nov. 1985.
6. BIKSON, T. K., EDEN, R., GILLOGLY, J., HAHM, W., PAYNE, J., AND SHAPIRO, N. How to use the task force microcomputer. The Rand Corporation, N-2670-MF, Sept. 1987.
7. EVELAND, J. D., AND BIKSON, T. K. Evolving electronic communication networks: An empirical assessment. In *Office Technology and People*, Elsevier Science Publications, Amsterdam, The Netherlands, 1987, pp. 103-128.
8. FREEMAN, L. A set of measures of centrality based on betweenness. *Sociometry 40* (1976), 35-41.
9. HILTZ, S. R. *On-Line Research Communities: A Case Study of the Office of the Future.* Ablex Publishing, Norwood, N.J., 1983.
10. HUFF, C., SPROULL, L., AND KIESLER, S. Computer communication and organizational commitment: Tracing the relationship in a city government. *J. Applied Social Psychology*, In press.
11. JOHNSON, B. M., AND RICE, R. *Managing Organizational Innovation: The Evolution from Word Processing to Office Information Systems.* Columbia University Press, New York, 1987.
12. KLING, R., AND SCACCHI, W. The web of computing: Computer technology as social organization. *Advances in Computers 21* (1982), 2-60.
13. KNOKEM, D., AND KUKLINSKI, J. H. *Network Analysis.* Sage Publications, Beverly Hills, Calif., 1982.
14. MARKUS, M. L. Toward a 'critical mass' theory of interactive media: Universal access, interdependence and diffusion. *Communication Research 14*, 5 (Oct. 1987), 491-511.
15. McEVOY, B., AND FREEMAN, L. *UCINET: A Microcomputer Package for Network Analysis.* University of California, Irvine, Calif., 1986.
16. PAVA, C. H. P. *Managing New Office Technology.* The Free Press, New York, 1983.
17. RICE, R. E. Mediated group communication. In *The New Media: Communication, Research and Technology*, R. E. Rice and Associates, Sage Publications, Beverly Hills, Calif., 1984, pp. 129-154.
18. RICE, R. E., AND CASE, D. Computer-based messaging in the university: A description of use and utility. *Journal of Communication 33*, 1 (1983), 131-152.
19. ROGERS, E., AND KINCAID, D. L. *Communication Networks: Toward a New Paradigm for Research.* Macmillan, New York, 1981.
20. STASZ, C., BIKSON, T. K., AND SHAPIRO, N. Z. Assessing the Forest Service's implementation of an agency-wide information system: An exploratory study. The Rand Corporation, N-2463-USFS, May 1986.
21. TAYLOR, J. C. Job design and quality of working life. In *Technology and the Transformation of White Collar Work*, R. Kraut, Ed. Lawrence Erlbaum Associates, Inc., Hillsdale, N.J., 1987, pp. 211-235.
22. TRIST, E. L. The sociotechnical perspective: The evolution of sociotechnical systems as a conceptual framework and as an action research program. In *Perspectives on Organization Design and Behavior*, Andrew H. Van de Ven and William F. Joyce, Eds. Wiley and Sons, New York, 1981, pp. 19-75.
23. ZUBOFF, S. *In the Age of the Smart Machine.* Basic Books, New York, 1988.

Received June 1988; revised September 1988; accepted September 1988

CHAPTER 8
Structured Messages, Agents, and Workflows

Another way in which e-mail is being extended is through the embedding of "intelligence," which aids in the structuring, routing, and *filtering* of messages. The motivation for structuring and routing e-mail gets stronger each year as the quantity of information available in electronic messaging and bulletin board systems continues to grow, and as we have more and more difficulty finding what we want. The motivation for filtering e-mail also gets stronger as individuals get bombarded with greater amounts of "junk e-mail." Malone, Grant, Lai, Rao, and Rosenblitt (1989) have developed the Information Lens as an environment for intelligent e-mail management. "The Information Lens: An Intelligent System for Information Sharing and Coordination" describes the concept of *semi-structured messages*, the Information Lens system based on it, the methods of tailoring it through the specification of rules for processing messages, and a variety of applications such as computer conferencing, calendar management, project management, engineering change notice distribution, software bug report tracking, and access to external information sources. The paper closes with a discussion of potential problems such as excessive filtering, imperfect information finding, and threats to personal privacy.

Malone et al. of the MIT group later began to generalize the Information Lens in ways that would allow the description of a greater variety of cooperative work procedures than just electronic mail. The result is described in "Object Lens: A 'Spreadsheet' for Cooperative Work" (Lai, Malone, and Yu, 1988). Object Lens enables unsophisticated computer users to create their own cooperative work applications using simple, powerful building blocks. These include the representation of "passive" information as *semi-structured objects* with template-based interfaces, the summarizing of "aggregate" information from collections of objects in *customizable folders*, and the representation of "active" rules for processing information as *semi-autonomous agents*. The paper illustrates how Object Lens integrates hypertext, object-oriented databases, electronic messaging, and rule-based *intelligent agents* to create applications such as task tracking, intelligent message routing, and database retrieval.

Both Object Lens and the Andrew Message System (Borenstein and Thyberg, 1991) are environments for building "intelligent" message systems. "Power, Ease of Use and Cooperative Work in a Practical Multimedia Message System" by Borenstein and Thyberg (1991) describes the design, development, and use of the Andrew System. Emphasis is placed on the underlying architecture and functionality, on its multimedia mail capabilities, on its *active messages* which carry out a particular interaction with their recipients in addition to transmitting information, on aspects of the design intended to ease the transition from novice to expert, and on the evolution of the Andrew Advisor system. Of particular interest is the combining of human capabilities and "intelligent" mail filtering to solve the problems of distributed support for a diverse user community in a geographically dispersed and heterogeneous computing environment.

Borenstein and Thyberg suggest that the concept of active messages can be substantially generalized. One such development is the work of Goldberg, Safran, Silverman, and Shapiro (1992), described in "Active Mail: A Framework for Integrated Groupware Applications." This short paper proposes *active mail* as a tool for maintaining persistent interactive connections, lists some applications of the concept, and discusses one possible architecture for active mail.

One way in which interdependencies among coworkers are managed and mediated and coordination is achieved is through language. A *language/action perspective* on the design of cooperative work has been presented by Winograd (1987–88). Basing his approach on the *speech act theory* of Searle (1975), Winograd defines *conversation* "to indicate a coordinated sequence of acts that can be interpreted as having linguistic meaning." A request, for example, can be followed by accepting that request, or by declining, or by making a counter-offer. Each of these conversation steps is followed by other steps in a "conversation for action." In "Computer Systems and the Design of Organizational Interaction" Flores, Graves, Hartfield, and Winograd (1988) explain the language/action perspective—their theory of "language as social action," show how it was made the basis for an early commercial groupware product (The Coordinator), and discuss its use in the context of organizational culture.

A classic process that seems ripe for automation through structured messages, agents, and/or workflows is meeting scheduling. Yet Grudin (1990, included in Chapter 2 of this volume) cautions us that this is not a trivial matter. Early attempts foundered—a sufficient critical mass was not reached in part because managers were seen to receive the primary benefit while workers had to invest the time to maintain electronic calendars without receiving substantial benefit. "Electronic Group Calendaring: Experiences and Expectations" by Lange (1992a) documents one case where bene-

fits were perceived to be widespread and the technology was therefore adopted. The keys in this case were that the groupware solved a serious problem for the group—scheduling a set of critical and scarce resources such as meeting rooms and presentation technology, and that the electronic calendars allowed principals to simplify what had previously been an onerous task—providing their secretaries weekly with their calendars so that they could be found when phone calls came in from clients (Lange, 1992b, personal communication). Once again, we see that groupware technology needs to be evaluated, adopted, and deployed with a sensitivity to the organizational context in which it is to be used.

Notes and Guide to Further Reading

Information Lens is further described in Malone, Grant, Turbak, Brobst, and Cohen (1987), Malone, Grant, Lai, Rao, and Rosenblitt (1987), and Malone (1987v). Systems such as Object Lens are similar to those in the intelligent office systems field, where researchers attempt to develop formal descriptions of office procedures and systems which embody these procedures; pointers to this literature may be found in the Notes section of Chapter 11. A successor to Object Lens called Oval is presented in Malone and Lai (1992).

The Andrew System is further described in Morris, Satyanarayanan, Conner, Howard, Rosenthal, and Smith (1986), Borenstein (1990), and Carnegie Mellon University (1989v). A pioneering multimedia communications system was Freestyle from Wang Laboratories, which is described and illustrated in Francik (1989v), Francik, Rudman, Cooper, and Levine (1991), and Levine and Ehrlich (1991). There is increasing interest in multi-media electronic mail, for example, Karmouch, Orozco-Barbosa, Georganas, and Goldberg (1990), Olson and Atkins (1990), Borenstein (1991), Palaniappan and Fitzmaurice (1991), Crowley (1992), and Magee and Cox (1992v).

Borenstein (1992) calls the active mail concept *computational mail* and defines it as "the embedding of programs within electronic mail messages." His paper discusses the promise of this technology and key problems such as security and portability. Work on active messages is also presented in more detail in Goldberg, Safran, and Shapiro (1992).

The concept of an *intelligent agent* is compelling to many working in the computer industry (see, for example, the bow-tied character Phil in the *Knowl-*

edge Navigator video tape, Apple Computer, 1988v), although the reality lags far behind the dream. Ramer (1992) defines three common characteristics of intelligent agents: that they are *programmable*, that their actions are *automatic*, and that they have an *identity*. McGregor (1992, p. 229) charmingly imagines an intelligent agent as a sort of administrative assistant much like Radar O'Reilley, the company clerk in the movie and TV show "M*A*S*H":

> Radar O'Reilley exemplifies the way changes to the user interface can support management of complexity and interaction with others. We frequently saw the colonel heading into the outer office to tell Radar to take care of something only to be greeted at the door by Radar, who already held not only the files and forms the colonel was about to request but also files he hadn't even realized he'd need. Other times we'd see Radar finding out what was going on elsewhere in Korea by talking on the phone with Sparky, the local telephone operator. Later we might see Radar telling everyone to get ready for incoming wounded before anyone else heard the approaching helicopters. In the TV series, Max Klinger later replaced Radar as company clerk. In contrast with Radar, Klinger was rarely able to find the requested files and often suggested that officers rummage through the files themselves. This is how most computer interfaces are today.

In a recent paper, "Groupware and the Emergence of Business Technology," Winograd (1992, pp. 70–71) briefly summarizes the essentials of the theory of work structure as language action:

> 1) Language acts, classified according to a theory of communications known as "speech-act theory".
> 2) Conversations (or "workflows"), which are coherent sequences of language acts with a regular structure of expectations and completions.
> 3) Explicit time points associated with completions of conversations.
> 4) Explicit mutually-visible representations of acts, conversations, and times, represented in computer systems as a way of facilitating communication in an organization.

In this paradigm, organizations do not consist of collections of physical objects, structures of authority, fiscal entities, or information flows. Instead, an organization is a network of interleaved 'workflows.' The atomic and molecular structures of organizations, in this new interpretation, are made up of observable events that occur when people take certain classes of linguistic actions which have the effects of defining and fulfilling conditions of satisfaction with the organization's internal and external customers. These events, in addition to being observable, make up the permanent structures that make individual organizations what they are, including three key structures:

> 1) The declarations, appointments and authorizations in which roles and features of organizations are defined and people given the authority to take action on behalf of the organization
> 2) The offers and acceptances in which agreements are made with customers and suppliers, and
> 3) The requests and promises in which projects are constituted and carried out.

Each workflow constitutes a basic unit of work. In each, a 'performer' commits to produce "conditions of satisfaction" defined in the workflow by the performer and a 'customer,' on or by a specified time. Four essential distinctions operate in each workflow:

> 1) Request and offers start all the crucial actions and frame what is to be produced in terms of "conditions of satisfaction" defined by a customer.
> 2) Agreements (or promises) tie together the actions of customer and supplier with commitments to future action.
> 3) Assertions allow the participants to speak to each other in terms of standards and evidence that can be witnessed. This allows recurrence and continuous improvement to be built into designs of business processes.
> 4) Assessments allow the participants to speak with each other about consequences, to speculate about the best paths for resolution, and to interpret what may be causing difficulties or affording new opportunities.

The origins of The Coordinator are described in more detail in Winograd (1987–88; see also Winograd and Flores, 1986; Winograd, 1988). Recent descriptions of their approach may be found in Medina-Mora (1992) and Medina-Mora, Winograd, Flores, and Flores (1992). Related work on project management systems is described in Sluizer and Cashman (1985) and Cashman and Stroll (1989).

There have been great controversies resulting from what appears to many individuals to be the authoritarian nature of The Coordinator (see, for example, Robinson, 1991a, included in Chapter 1 of this volume). Even Flores et al. (1988, p. 168) recognize that use of the system can be problematic:

> . . .The Coordinator has been most successful in organizations in which the users are relatively confident about their own position and the power they have within it . . . [where] there is clarity about what is expected of people and what authority they have (e.g., what requests can be clearly declined without fear of negative impact. . . . it does depend on basic assumptions that the overall interests are shared and that the parties recognize that honest dealings with one another will be for their shared benefit. . . .

Yet these conditions do not apply in many organizations. Reder and Schwab (1988) assert that there are serious problems with two tacit assumptions made in the design of The Coordinator. The first is that "the conversational routines of the office may be effectively transposed to a computer-mediated format." They argue that this does not hold true for many "oral traditions" of organizations. They also question the second tacit assumption, that "workgroup effectiveness will inevitably increase by prompting members '. . . to take clearer actions in declaring and following up on their commitments'" (Winograd, 1986, p. 219).

Nonetheless, influence of The Coordinator has been substantial. There are currently a number of products that it has inspired, marketed under the label of *workflow management*. The goal of work process automation is, according to Cruse (1992), the "coordination of tasks, data, and people to improve the effectiveness and efficiency of organizations." Palermo and McCready (1992) define workflow software as "the tool which empowers individuals and groups of individuals in both structured and unstructured environments to automatically manage a series of recurrent or non-recurrent events in a way which achieves the business objectives of the company." Marshak (1992) presents a comprehensive list of requirements for workflow products.

Ryan (1992) discusses group scheduling technology. Egger and Wagner (1992) use a case study of the scheduling of operations in a large surgery department to explore the prospects for computer support of collaborative time management.

THE INFORMATION LENS: AN INTELLIGENT SYSTEM FOR INFORMATION SHARING AND COORDINATION

Thomas W. Malone, Kenneth R. Grant, Kum-Yew Lai, Ramana Rao, and David A. Rosenblitt
Massachusetts Institute of Technology

INTRODUCTION

One of the key problems when any group of people cooperates to solve problems or make decisions is how to share information. Thus one of the central goals of designing good "organizational interfaces" (Malone, 1985) should be to help people share information in groups and organizations. In this chapter, we describe a prototype system, called the Information Lens, that focuses on one aspect of this problem: how to help people share the many diverse kinds of qualitative information that are communicated via electronic messaging systems. We also show how the same general capabilities that help with information sharing can be used to support a variety of more specific coordination processes such as task tracking and meeting scheduling.

It is already a common experience in mature computer-based messaging communities for people to feel flooded with large quantities of electronic "junk mail" (Denning, 1982; Hiltz & Turoff, 1985; Palme, 1984; Wilson, Maude, Marshall, & Heaton, 1984), and the widespread availability of inexpensive communication

capability has the potential to overwhelm people with even more messages that are of little or no value to them. At the same time, it is also a common experience for people to be ignorant of facts that would facilitate their work and that are known elsewhere in their organization. The system we describe helps solve both these problems: It helps people filter, sort, and prioritize messages that are already addressed to them, and it also helps them find useful messages they would not otherwise have received. In some cases, the system can respond automatically to certain messages, and in other cases it can suggest likely actions for human users to take.

The most common previous approach to structuring information sharing in electronic messaging environments is to let users implicitly specify their general areas of interest by associating themselves with centralized distribution lists or conference topics related to particular subjects (e.g., Hiltz & Turoff, 1978). Because these methods of disseminating information are often targeted for relatively large audiences, however, it is usually impossible for all the information distributed to be of interest to all recipients.

The Information Lens system uses much more detailed representations of message contents and receivers' interests to provide more sophisticated filtering possibilities. One of the key ideas behind this system is that many of the unsolved problems of natural language understanding can be avoided by using semi-structured templates (or frames) for different types of messages. These templates are used by the senders of messages to facilitate composing messages in the first place. Then, the same templates are used by the receivers of messages to facilitate constructing a set of rules to be used for filtering, categorizing, and otherwise processing messages of different types.

Examples

Before describing the Information Lens system itself, we briefly describe a few examples of situations in which systems like this might be useful. Later, we discuss in more detail how the capabilities of the Lens system could help in these situations.

Distributing engineering change notices. Almost all organizations that design and manufacture complex physical products (such as cars, televisions, or computers) have some system for distributing information about changes in design specifications. The forms that contain this information are often called "engineering change notices" or "engineering change orders." A particular engineering change may be of interest to a variety of people including (1) design engineers working on related parts of the product, (2) manufacturing engineers designing the manufacturing process, and (3) procurement specialists who must purchase the component parts to be used in the product. Early in the design process, an engineering change may be made by an individual engineer. As the design progresses, ap-

Reprinted from *Technological Support for Work Group Collaboration* (pp. 65–88), edited by M. H. Olson, 1989, Hillsdale, NJ: Lawrence Erlbaum. ©1989 Lawrence Erlbaum Associates. Reprinted by permission.

SYSTEM DESCRIPTION

There are five key ideas that, together, form the basis of the Information Lens system. Though some of these ideas are empirically testable hypotheses, we treat them here as premises for our system design. We list and briefly describe these ideas here. In the next sections, we describe in more detail how the Lens system uses them:

(1) A rich set of semi-structured message types (or frames) can form the basis for an intelligent information sharing system. For example, meeting announcements can be structured as templates that include fields for "date," "time," "place," "organizer," and "topic," as well as any additional unstructured information. There are three reasons why this idea is important:

(a) Semi-structured messages enable computers to automatically process a much wider range of information than would otherwise be possible. By letting people compose messages that already have much of their essential information structured in fields, we eliminate the need for any kind of automatic parsing or understanding of free text messages while still representing enough information to allow quite sophisticated rules to process the messages.

(b) Much of the processing people already do with the information they receive reflects a set of semi-structured message types. In our informal studies of information sharing in organizations (Malone, Grant, Turbak, Brobst, & Cohen, 1987), we found that people often described their filtering heuristics according to categories of documents being filtered (e.g., "This is a brochure advertising a seminar. I usually throw these away unless the title intrigues me or unless it looks like a brochure I could use as a model for the ones I write.")

(c) Even if no automatic processing of messages were involved, providing a set of semi-structured message templates to the authors of messages would often be helpful. Two of the people in our informal interviews mentioned simple examples of this phenomenon: one remarked about how helpful it would be if any memo requesting some kind of action included, in a prominent place, the deadline by which the action needed to be taken; a second commented about how wonderful it would be if all the meeting invitations he received included a field about why he was supposed to be there. We see later how message templates can be provided in a flexible way that encourages, but does not require, their use.

proval from group or division managers might be necessary. After the product is actually in production, some engineering changes may require approvals from very senior executives such as vice presidents.

How should this process be managed? How does the engineer who originates a change know who else will be interested? How can engineers designing one part of the product know that they have seen all the changes to other parts that might affect their work? What happens when incompatible changes are not detected until the product is actually in production? Many organizations today still use a primarily paper-based system to manage this process and they rely on official organizational channels and informal personal networks to disseminate information. We see later how systems like the Information Lens may dramatically improve the speed and effectiveness of this process.

Handling software bug reports. In any multi-person software development project, there must be some way of handling bug reports from users and testers. For example, who should screen out or respond to incomprehensible or erroneous bug reports? How is a bug report distributed to developers who should know about it or who might have information related to fixing it? Who insures that someone takes responsibility for fixing legitimate bugs? How are others notified when a bug is fixed? In many organizations today, this process relies heavily on communication by electronic mail, but we see later how a system like the Information Lens could help manage the process more effectively.

Distributing news and rumors to traders in financial institutions. In modern financial markets, perhaps as much as anywhere else in the world, "time is money"; that is, differences of a few minutes in getting access to the right information can make the difference between gains or losses of millions of dollars. How can traders find out quickly about news stories or rumors that will affect their markets without being overwhelmed by far too much irrelevant information? Athough there are already various forms of market quotation and news wire services used to support traders in these environments, we see later how ideas like those incorporated in the Information Lens might be even more helpful.

Sharing "lore" about repair problems in field service groups. Many manufacturing companies have widely distributed networks of field service offices that are responsible for maintaining and repairing their products for customers. Even though, in some ways, each customer's site and product is unique, there are many commonalities in the kinds of problems that arise at different customer sites and at different field service offices. We see later how systems like the Information Lens could help repair personnel share their experiences with different kinds of problems without overloading each other with too much irrelevant information. Such systems could also help people quickly find the company-wide experts on particular kinds of problems or the answers to specific questions.

(2) Sets of production rules (that may include multiple levels of reasoning, not just Boolean selection criteria) can be used to conveniently specify automatic processing for these messages.

(3) The use of semi-structured message types and automatic rules for processing them can be greatly simplified by a consistent set of display-oriented editors for composing messages, constructing rules, and defining new message templates.

(4) The definition and use of semi-structured messages and processing rules are simplified if the message types are arranged in a frame inheritance lattice.

(5) The initial introduction and later evolution of a group communication system can be much easier if the process can occur as a series of small changes, each of which has the following properties: (a) individual users can continue to use their existing system with no change if they so desire, (b) individual users who make small changes receive some immediate benefit, and (c) groups of users who adopt the changes receive additional benefits beyond the individual benefits.

System Overview

In order to provide a natural integration of this system with the capabilities that people already use, our system is built on top of an existing electronic mail system. Users can continue to send and receive their mail as usual, including using centrally maintained distribution lists and manually classifying messages into folders. In addition, the Lens system provides four important optional capabilities: (1) People can use structured message templates to help them compose their messages; (2) Receivers can specify rules to automatically filter and classify messages arriving in their mailbox; (3) Senders can include as an addressee of a message, in addition to specific individuals or distribution lists, a special mailbox (currently named "Anyone") to indicate that the sender is willing to have this message automatically redistributed to anyone else who might be interested; and (4) Receivers can specify rules that find and show messages addressed to "Anyone" that the receiver would not otherwise have seen. By gradually adding new message types and new rules, users can continually increase the helpfulness of the system without ever being dependent on its ability to perfectly filter all messages.

System architecture. The Lens system was written in the Interlisp-D programming environment using Loops, an object-oriented extension of Lisp. The system runs on Xerox 1100 series processors connected by an Ethernet. We use parts of the Lafite mail system and the XNS network protocols already provided in that environment. The message construction aids and the individual filtering rules all operate on the users' personal workstations.

As Figure 4.1 illustrates, messages that include "Anyone" as an addressee will be delivered by the existing mail server directly to the explicit addresses as well as to an automatic mail sorter that runs on a workstation and periodically retrieves messages from the special mailbox. This automatic mail sorter may then, in turn, send the message to several additional recipients whose rules selected it.

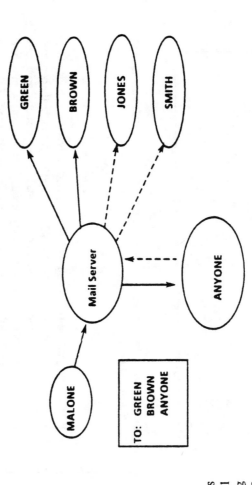

Figure 4.1. The Lens system includes components in the users' workstations and in a central server (called "Anyone"). Messages that include "Anyone" as an addressee are automatically distributed to all receivers whose interest profiles select the messages as well as to the other explicit addressees.

Implementation status. The Information Lens system as described in this chapter currently exists in prototype form. As of this writing, the system has been in regular use by about five members of our research group for over a year, and a larger scale test at an industrial research center has begun.

Messages

The Lens system is based on a set of semi-structured messages. For each message type, the system includes a template with a number of fields or slots for holding information. Associated with each field are several properties, including the default value of the field, a list of likely alternative values for the field, and an explanation of why the field is part of the template.

Figures 4.2 and 4.3 show a sample of the highly graphical interaction through which users can construct messages using these templates (see Tou, Williams, Fikes, Henderson, & Malone, 1982, for a similar approach to constructing database retrieval queries). After selecting a field of a message by pointing with a mouse, the user can point with the mouse again to see the field's default value, an explanation of the field's purpose, or a list of likely alternatives for filling in the field. If the user selects one of these alternatives, that value is automatically inserted in the message text. The user can also edit any fields directly at any time using the built-in display-oriented text editor. For example, the user can add as much free text as desired in the text field of the message.

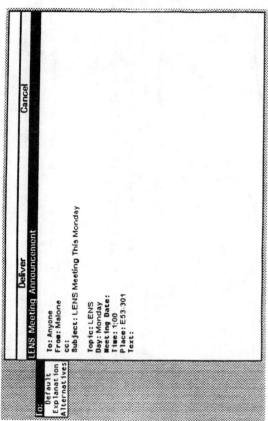

Figure 4.2. Messages are composed with a display-oriented editor and templates that have pop-up menus associated with the template fields.

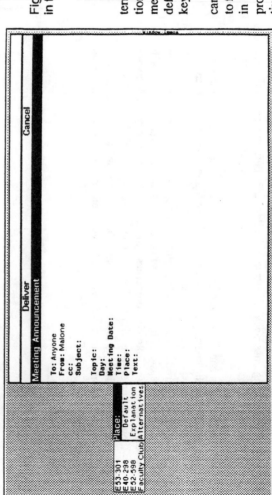

Figure 4.3. Some templates already have a number of default values filled in for different fields.

By providing a wealth of domain-specific knowledge about the default and alternative values for particular types of messages, the system can make the construction of some messages much easier. For example, Figure 4.3 shows how some message templates, such as a regular weekly meeting announcement, may have default values already filled in for most of their fields and require only a few keystrokes or mouse clicks to complete and send off.

Users who do not want to take advantage of these message construction aids can simply select the most general message type (message) and use the text editor to fill in the standard fields (To, From, and Subject) just as they would have done in the previous mail system. We expect, however, that the added convenience provided to the senders by semi-structured templates will be a significant incentive for senders to use templates in constructing some of their messages. This, in turn, will greatly increase the amount of information receivers can use in constructing automatic processing rules for incoming messages.

Message Types

To further simplify the construction and use of message templates the templates are arranged in a network so that all subtypes of a given template inherit the field names and property values (e.g., defaults, explanations, and alternatives) from the parent template. Any subtype may, in turn, add new fields or override any of the property values inherited from the parent (e.g., see Fikes & Kehler, 1985). For example, the seminar announcement template adds a field for speaker that is not present in its parent template meeting announcement. The Lens meeting announcement (Figure 4.3) adds a number of default values that are not present in its parent. The inheritance network eliminates the need to continually re-enter redundant information when constructing new templates that resemble old ones, and it provides a natural way of organizing templates, thus making it easier for senders to select the right template.

The message type lattice is made visible to the user through the message type browser. Figure 4.4 shows this lattice browser for our sample network of message types. Users select a template to use in constructing a new message by clicking with the mouse on the desired message type in this browser. By clicking with a different mouse button, users can view or modify the rules (see below) associated with a particular message type. Like the other message type characteristics, these rules are inherited by the subtypes of a message template. Thus, for example with the network shown in Figure 4.4, the rules for processing "notices" and "messages" would be applied to incoming "meeting announcements" as well as the rules specifically designed for meeting announcements.

The network shown in Figure 4.4 includes some message types that we believe will be useful in almost all organizations (e.g., meeting announcements) and some that are important only in our environment (e.g., Lens meeting announcement). Different groups can develop detailed structures to represent the information of specific concern to them.

We have developed another display-oriented editor, like the message editor shown in Figures 4.2 and 4.3, for creating and modifying the template definitions themselves. We expect that in some (e.g., rarely used) regions of the network anyone should be able to use this "template editor" to modify an existing message type or define a new one, whereas in other regions, only specifically designated people should have access to this capability. In the current version of the system people can use a simple version of this editor to personalize the default, explanation, and alternatives properties of the fields in existing message types.

Group use of message types. Individuals who begin using this system before most other people do can get some immediate benefit from constructing rules using only the fields present in all messages (To, From, Subject, Date). Groups of individuals who begin to use a set of common message types can get much greater benefits from constructing more sophisticated rules for dealing with more specialized message types. For example, a general rule might try to recognize "bug reports" based on the word "bug" in the subject field, but this would be a very fallible test. A community that uses a common template for bug reports can construct rules that deal only with messages the senders classify as bug reports. These rules can use specialized information present in the template such as the system in which the bug occurred, the urgency of the request for repair, and so forth. From the viewpoint of organization theory, we know that "internal codes" are among the most important productive assets of an organization (Arrow, 1974; March & Simon, 1958). In effect, the Lens system provides a medium in which this collective language of an organization can be defined and redefined.

Rules

Just as the structure of messages simplifies the process of composing messages, it also simplifies the process of constructing rules for processing messages. For instance, Figure 4.5 shows an example of the display-oriented editor used to construct rules in the Information Lens system. This editor uses rule templates that are based on the same message types as those used for message construction, and it uses a similar interaction style with menus available for defaults, alternatives, and explanations. We expect that this template-based graphical rule construction will be much easier for inexperienced computer users than more conventional rule or query languages. For example, the users of most typical database retrieval sys-

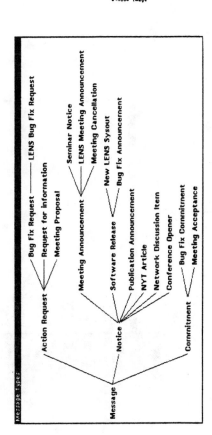

Figure 4.4. The message templates are arranged in a network with more general types at the "top" (shown at the left) and more specific types shown at the "bottom" (shown at the right).

tems must already know the structure of the database fields and their plausible values in order to construct queries. Users of our system have all this information immediately available and integrated into the rule-construction tools (Tou et al., 1982).

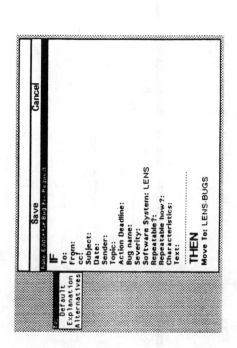

Figure 4.5. Rules for processing messages are composed using the same kind of editor and the same templates as those used for composing messages in the first place.

Local rules. There are currently two kinds of rules in the Lens system: "local rules" and "central rules". Local rules are applied when messages are retrieved from the mail server to a user's local workstation. Typical rule actions possible here include: moving messages to specific folders (Figure 4.6a), deleting messages (Figure 4.6b), and automatically "resending" messages to someone else (Figure 4.6c). Both "move" and "delete" mark a message as deleted, but do not physically expunge it. Thus, subsequent rules can move different copies of the same message to different folders. "Resending" a message is similar to "forwarding" it, except that instead of copying the entire original message into the body of a new message, the new message preserves the type and all but the "To" and "cc" fields of the original message. The new value of the "To" field is a parameter the user specifies for the automatic rule action, and the user whose rule does the resending is added as the "Sender" of the new message.

(a) IF   Message type: Action request
          Action deadline: Today, Tomorrow
   THEN *Move to:* Urgent

(b) IF   Message type: Meeting announcement
          Day: Not Tuesday
   THEN *Delete*

(c) IF   Message type: Meeting proposal
          Sender: Not Axsom
   THEN *Resend:* Axsom

(d) IF   From: Silk, Siegel
   THEN *Set Characteristic:* VIP

    IF   Message type: Action request
          Characteristics: VIP
   THEN *Move to:* Urgent

(e) IF   Message type: Request for information
          Subject: AI, Lisp
   THEN *Show*

(f) IF   Message type: NYT Article
          Subject: Computer
   THEN *Move to:* Computers

    IF   Message type: NYT Article
          Subject: Movies
   THEN *Move to:* Movies

    IF   Message type: NYT Article
          Article date: < Today
          Characteristics: Not MOVED
   THEN *Delete*

    IF   Message type: NYT Article
          Characteristics: Not MOVED and Not DELETED
   THEN *Move to:* NYT Articles

Figure 4.6. Sample Rules.

When the local rules have finished processing all incoming messages, the numbers of new messages that have been automatically moved into different folders because the last time the folder was viewed are shown on a hierarchical display of the folder names. Messages that were not moved anywhere remain in the "root" folder.

By combining conditions within and between fields, users can construct arbitrary Boolean queries. More interestingly, users can also construct elaborate

mitment" message being constructed to answer the message. Figure 4.7 shows a selection of message types and their default reply types.

Original message	Suggested reply types
Message	Message
Action request	Commitment, Request for information
Notice	Request for information, Action request, Message
Bug fix request	Bug fix commitment, Bug fix announcement, Request for information
Meeting proposal	Meeting proposal, Meeting acceptance
Meeting announcement	Request for information

Figure 4.7 Sample of Message Types Automatically Suggested as Replies

multi-step reasoning chains by having some rules set characteristics of messages and then having other rules test these characteristics (Figure 4.6d; see Malone, Grant, Turbak, Brobst, & Cohen, 1987, for details). It is also possible to have different kinds of actions available for different kinds of message. For example, rules for "meeting proposal" messages have an automatic action available to "accept" a meeting.

Central rules. In addition to the local rules applied when messages are retrieved to a user's workstation, an individual user can also specify central rules to select messages addressed to "anyone" that the user wants to see. Only two kinds of rule action are possible for central rules: "show" (Figure 4.6e) and "set characteristic". "Show" causes a message to be sent to the user, unless the user would have already received it as one of the original recipients. When these messages arrive at the user's workstation they are processed, along with all the other messages, by the user's local rules.

Rule interactions. Our early experience with the system suggested the importance of being able to give users some control over the interactions between local rules (e.g., having certain rules fire only if no other rules have fired on a message) and of being able to explain to users why certain messages were processed as they were. Accordingly, we added several simple features to the rule system. First, the rules for a given message type are applied in the order they appear in the "rule set editor" for that message type, and the rules pertaining to a specific message type are always applied before the rules inherited from more general message types. Also, rules that take actions (such as moving or deleting a message), always set a characteristic of the message (such as "MOVED" or "DELETED"). Thus subsequent rules can include conditions such as "the message has not yet been moved or deleted" (see Figure 4.6f). Finally, in order to help users understand and modify their rules, a simple explanation capability allows users to see a history of the rules that fired on a given message.

Intelligent Suggestions for Responding to Messages

The presence of recognizable types of semi-structured messages also simplifies the task of having the system intelligently present options for what a user might want to do after seeing a message. Almost all electronic mail systems provide standard actions (such as "answer" and "forward") that can be taken after seeing a message. We have recently generalized this capability in two ways.

Suggested reply types. First, since either answering or forwarding a message creates a new message, our system suggests options for the type of new message to be created. For instance, when a user selects the "answer" option for a "bug fix request", a pop-up menu appears with three choices: "bug fix commitment", "request for information", and "other". Selecting commitment results in a new "com-

Suggested response actions. Even more important than suggesting reply types, our system is also able to suggest other actions a user might want to take after seeing a message of a given type. For example, when a user reads a message of type "meeting announcement" another option, "add to calendar" is automatically presented, in addition to the standard options like "answer" and "forward." If the user selects this option, the information already present in the message in structured form (e.g., date, time, and meeting topic) are used to add an appropriate entry to the user's on-line calendar. As another example, when a user reads a message of type "software release" (or any of its subtypes such as "bug fix announcement"), an option called "load file" is automatically presented, and if this option is chosen, the file specified in the message is automatically loaded into the user's system. This saves the user from having to type the "load" command and the (often long) file designation.

APPLICATIONS

Our first, and most fully developed, application of these ideas is the intelligent information sharing system described above. In order to demonstrate the generality of the ideas, we now describe several other simple applications we have implemented in the same framework. The most important point here is not that it is possible to implement these other applications—in fact, we have chosen applications that have already been implemented in other systems. Instead the point is that a wide variety of applications for supporting cooperative work can all be implemented in a way that is (1) smoothly integrated from the user's point of view, and (2) much easier to implement because it takes advantage of the basic capabilities for supporting structured messages.

Computer conferencing. Many of the capabilities of a computer conferencing system (e.g., Hiltz & Turoff, 1978), can be easily incorporated in the Information Lens system. We have done this by adding (1) a new message type called "conference opener" that includes the name of the conference and (optionally) its parent conference, and (2) a response option called "join" for this type of message that, if chosen, will automatically create (a) a new folder by this name, (b) a new rule to select messages addressed to "Anyone" that contain this name in the topic field, and (c) a new rule to move all messages received about this topic to the new folder.

Our system thus includes the capability that computer conferencing systems have for structuring communication on the basis of flexibly defined sets of topics and subtopics. It is also easy to see how our system goes beyond these customary capabilities of a computer conferencing system by allowing, for example, more sophisticated rules that filter not only on topic but also on other characteristics such as sender.

The primary computer conferencing capability that is not included in our system so far is the ability for a user to retrieve messages that were sent before that user joined the conference. This capability is clearly important, and it would be quite desirable to add a shared database to our system. The addition of such a shared database of semi-structured messages could be done within the same general framework and would make possible much more sophisticated retrieval possibilities than are possible with only unstructured messages (e.g., see Tou et al., 1982).

Calendar management. We have already seen how a very simple form of calendar management is included in the system by providing users with a response option that will automatically insert incoming meeting announcements into the user's on-line calendar. We have also implemented a more sophisticated protocol for semi-automated meeting scheduling. This protocol uses several new message types, including "meeting proposals" and "meeting acceptances." Proposals and acceptances both include all the fields that "meeting announcements" do, but the values may often be nonspecific (e.g., "sometime this week" for the date field). People can schedule meetings by sending a sequence of proposals (and possibly counterproposals) until a proposal is accepted.

Our system provides automated support for this process in several ways. First, some people may want to automatically resend all messages of certain types (e.g., meeting proposals) to other people (e.g., their secretaries) for a response. Second, users the system helps people construct replies to these messages. For instance, users can choose to reply to a "meeting proposal" with a "meeting acceptance" and all the information (such as time, place, and topic) will be automatically copied from the proposal to the acceptance. When a meeting acceptance is received, one of the action options presented is to "confirm" the meeting. Selecting this option automatically adds the meeting to the user's calendar and sends a meeting announcement to the other participant(s) confirming the scheduled time.

Although we have not done so yet, this general framework also makes it possible to have some meetings scheduled completely automatically (e.g., see Greif, 1982). For example, meeting proposals from certain people (e.g., members of one's own work group) might be automatically accepted if they fall within regular working hours and do not conflict with other meetings already scheduled. Any messages that are exceptional (e.g., a request to meet outside of regular working hours or a request to meet at a time when a conflicting meeting is already scheduled) will then be brought to the attention of the human user for special handling.

These systems are, by no means, a complete solution to the meeting scheduling problem. For instance, because people can find out about each other's schedules only through messages, the system may require a number of iterations just to eliminate times in which they have conflicts due to publicly scheduled meetings. Adding shared databases might help solve this problem, but it brings up other problems about who has access to which parts of other people's calendars. Even in a system with partially shared databases, the semi-structured approach we have described has the desirable property that some cases (e.g., some meeting requests) are handled automatically while others are handled by human users in a smoothly integrated way. We believe this "graceful degradation" property will be especially important to the acceptance of systems—like those for calendar management—that involve subtle interpersonal and political issues about which people are reluctant or unable to be explicit.

Project management and task tracking. Systems based on structured messages can support project management and other coordination processes by helping to keep track of what tasks have been assigned to whom (e.g., see Sathi, Fox, & Greenberg, 1985; Sluizer & Cashman, 1985; Winograd & Flores, 1986). One simple way for users to do this in the current system is simply to set up rules that move copies of all action requests and commitments into special folders. For example, action requests a user receives might be categorized in folders by the project to which they relate, whereas action requests a user sends might be categorized by the people to whom they are sent.

To illustrate how more elaborate capabilities can be built up within the same framework, we have implemented a simple task tracking system for software maintenance activities similar to the example described by Sluizer and Cashman (1985). In this application, "users" of a software system send "problem reports" to a "work assigner." The work assigner first sends an "acknowledgment" to the user and then sends the problem report to a "developer." When the developer fixes the problem, the developer sends the "fix report" to the work assigner who, in turn, sends a "user report" to the original user noting that the problem has been fixed.

This application was implemented in our system by defining the three message types (two of which already existed under different names) and adding several new response options. Users who play the role of work assigners have two possible response actions suggested when they view problem reports. If the problem report has not been acknowledged, the option presented is to acknowledge it. Selecting this option prepares a standard acknowledgment message with the appropriate fields filled in from the information on the original problem report. When the acknowledgment message is sent, the token "acknowledged" is added to the "characteristics" field in the problem report message. Whenever a problem report that includes "acknowledged" in its "characteristics" field is displayed, a response action of "assign" is suggested. Selecting this option prepares the problem report message for forwarding to a developer whose name the work assigner selects from a list of alternatives.

Clearly this task-tracking system is quite limited. The original XCP system, for example, used a set of primitive actions to define protocols involving a number of roles, message types, and actions. A similar capability would be desirable in our system. Another obviously desirable capability would be more elaborate database facilities for sorting, displaying, and modifying the status of tasks. For example, the current system can sort messages into folders according to various criteria and it can display the header information (e.g., date, sender, and subject) for the messages in a folder. But it would also be quite useful to be able to display the tasks one had committed to do in a report format, sorted by due date, that summarized the task names and the task requestors. If these database capabilities are implemented in a general way for structured objects, then they should be useful for developing many other coordination-supporting applications as well.

Connections with external information sources. One of the desirable aspects of the system architecture we have described is its versatility in dealing with external information sources. As previously indicated, messages that are sent to users of the Lens system from people who do not use the system are simply represented by Lens as messages of type "message." When Lens users send messages to others outside the system, all the fields in the template that are not part of the standard message header are sent as part of the text field.

It is also possible to do more intelligent translation into and out of certain message types. For instance, we currently receive daily on-line transmission of selected articles from the New York Times (via the system developed by Gifford, Baldwin, Berlin, & Lucassen, 1985). When the Anyone server receives these messages, it parses out the fields already present in the wire service feed (e.g., "title", "subject", "category", and "priority") and formats these messages as Lens templates with the same fields. Users of our system are then able to construct elaborate sets of production rules to select the articles they wish to see and sort them into categories.

One of the most interesting possibilities for such systems occurs in the formation of computer-based markets (e.g., see Malone, Yates, & Benjamin, 1987). For example, techniques like those described here can be used to screen advertising messages and product descriptions according to precisely the criteria that are important to a given buyer. Air travellers, for instance, might specify rules with which their own "automated buyers' agents" could examine a wide range of possible flights and select the ones that best match that particular traveller's preferences. The preferences might include decision rules for trading off between factors such as cost, convenient arrival and departure times, window seats versus aisle seats, minimum number of stops, and so forth. A fairly simple set of such rules could, in many cases, do a better job of matching particular travellers' preferences than all but the most conscientious and knowledgeable human travel agents.

Natural language processing and information retrieval techniques. It is easy to imagine even more sophisticated facilities in this framework that could use whatever natural language understanding capabilities are available to parse unstructured documents into the templates used by Lens. The fields extracted in this way could then be used for automatic filtering or other processing after which human readers could look at the full text of selected articles to do more accurate processing themselves. This approach appears particularly promising for natural language documents about highly restricted domains (e.g., letters of credit—see Dhar & Ranganathan, 1986).

We have already seen how the Lens facilities can be used without any automatic natural language understanding capabilities. However, as natural language parsers become more powerful and accurate, rules like those specified in Lens will become more useful for processing a much wider range of documents.

Examples of Uses

Now that we have described the Information Lens and several applications implemented within it, we will return to the possible uses mentioned at the beginning of the chapter.

Distributing engineering change notices. It is easy to imagine semi-structured templates for different kinds of engineering change notices. The templates might include information such as: part changed, type of change (e.g., size, shape, material, vendor, weight, cost, etc.), subsystems affected by change (e.g., electrical, mechanical, etc.), description of problem being fixed, severity of problem, and explanation of change. With this kind of information structured in templates, different users could specify their own rules for selecting change notices they wanted to see and for sorting and prioritizing the change notices they receive. The change notices could still be addressed to people based on official organizational channels (e.g., "everyone in the power supply engineering group") and on the basis of informal personal networks (e.g., "I know Joe is interested in this because we talked about it in the hall last week"). In addition, however, change notices can also be addressed to "Anyone" and thus reach other people who are interested in the change but who wouldn't otherwise have received it. Notice that this approach has the desirable property that part of the responsibility for routing information falls on the receivers of the information (those who will actually use it and are therefore motivated to have it routed correctly) rather than on the senders (who are distributing the information primarily for the benefit of others).

In addition to the routing of change notices, systems like Lens could also help manage the approval process. Managers who must approve changes could have suggested response options to approve, disapprove, or ask for more information. Rules could be used to automatically sort change requests into categories based on type of request, whether it was approved or not, and so forth.

Handling software bug reports. We saw earlier how Lens could be used to help manage the process of assigning software bug reports to developers. With additional fields in bug reports such as "severity of failure" and "subsystem in which failure occured", Lens could also help developers prioritize the bugs that have been assigned to them and to select messages on other bugs they would like to know about. Also as we saw above, when a bug is fixed, the patch can be distributed to other people in the development group using a "bug fix announcement" message that has a suggested response option to load the file that contains the patch.

Distributing news and rumors to traders in financial institutions. We have seen how retrieval from external information sources, such as news wires, can be integrated into our framework. This approach could give traders access to news stories selected according to their interests, and this information would be integrated with the rest of the traders' electronic communications. At present, however, news wires provide only a limited amount of structuring (e.g., title of article, author of article, general subject area, and perhaps specific topic keywords). At least two other possibilities might make these services even more useful in the future.

First, improved natural language understanding capabilities might allow computers to parse the text of the news articles into templates (e.g., DeJong, 1979) that would allow traders to specify more useful rules. For instance, there might be templates for news events such as (1) takeover bids (with fields for the takeover target, the acquiring company, the amount, etc.), (2) oil price change (with fields for cause, old price, and new price), and (3) political upheaval (with fields for country, parties involved, etc.). This approach could lead to much more intelligent filtering of stories, but the technical problems involved in doing such natural language understanding are still quite difficult.

The second possibility is less obvious, but quite feasible technically: Human editors could append content-based templates to the news stories, just as they now

append topic keywords. In this case, one human editor appends a template once for a news story that can then be processed automatically by rules for thousands of receivers. The cost of this would presumably be much less than having highly fallible natural language understanding programs operating on the same story in each of the thousands of receivers' workstations.

A final possibility for improving traders' information access does not rely on news stories at all, but instead on creating more efficient channels for diffusing the informal gossip, rumors, and other "word-of-mouth" communications that are already pervasive in financial markets. For instance, traders might use a system like Lens to inform other traders in their own firm about rumors they hear about impending price changes, political upheavals, and so forth. Instead of flooding each other with mostly irrelevant information (or relying on yelling across the trading floor), different traders could specify rules about the kinds of "rumors" they wanted to see.

Sharing "lore" about repair problems in field service groups. One simple possibility for sharing field service "lore" is to have computer conferencing systems, like those described earlier, that let repair personnel at widely distributed sites set up conference topics to discuss different kinds of problems and their experiences in solving them. Not only could people "subscribe" to the conference topics in which they were most interested, but they could specify rules to, for example, highlight discussion contributions from people who often make useful remarks.

A more interesting possibility involves using the capabilities of a system like Lens to create "inquiry networks." For instance, people thoughout the organization with specific questions could send these "requests for information" to "Anyone." Also, different people could set up "Anyone" rules to select "requests for information" and other messages about topics in which they were interested. These people might or might not themselves be the most knowledgeable experts on the topics, but they could quickly become expert at referring questions in their general topic areas to the best experts or others who could answer the questions.

One of the key ideas here is that Lens-like features allow people with questions to broadcast them to a potentially large and unknown set of people, but without running the risk of inundating the receivers with unwanted information. Receivers will only get these questions when they have specifically indicated a willingness to see questions on this topic. By providing tools to create such highly differentiated "expertise nets," Lens-like systems have the potential to greatly improve the speed and effectiveness of "organizational memories."

POTENTIAL PROBLEMS WITH SYSTEMS OF THIS TYPE

Almost any powerful technology that has the potential to benefit people also has potentials for misuse or unintended negative consequences. The system we have described is intended to help avoid some potential negative consequences of computer-mediated communication systems (e.g., information overload for individuals) and at the same time to take advantage of some even greater potential benefits (e.g., selective sharing of much more information in organizations as a whole). In order to use a new technology wisely, it is important to try to anticipate and encourage beneficial uses and to anticipate and avoid possible negative consequences. Because much of this chapter has been devoted to describing potential benefits from systems of this type, in this section, we briefly describe a few potentials for misuse and some possible remedies.

Excessive filtering. Some people, on hearing descriptions of this system, worry that it might be used to decrease the flow of information in an organization. For instance, people might use it to filter out messages personally addressed to them and thus become less responsive to information from other people in their organization. While this is, in fact, a possible use of the capabilities we have described, we believe it is an unlikely one. The system leaves completely up to each user the decisions about how cautious or how reckless to be in specifying rules for automatic deletion of the messages they receive. There are already many social forces at work in organizations that affect how responsive people are to each other's communications, and in many cases, these forces would strongly discourage people from automatically deleting messages addressed to them personally. A much more likely scenario, we believe, is that people will use the capabilities of the system to sort and prioritize messages addressed to them personally and will use automatic deletion primarily for non-personal messages addressed to large numbers of people via distribution lists, conference topics, or bulletin boards.

In this case, of course, the ability of receivers to filter out "public" messages that are unlikely to be interesting to them increases the usefulness of the public communication channel in two ways: (1) receivers are more likely to attend to communication channels whose "richness" (i.e., probability of being interesting) is greater, and (2) senders are likely to send out more information if they are not worried about incurring the displeasure of many uninterested receivers whose mailboxes would be cluttered.

Imperfect finding. Another concern occasionally expressed about systems like this is that people may have difficulty knowing what they want and don't want to see until they have seen it. How, for instance, can you find out that another group in your organization is doing something of great interest to you if they use keywords for describing it that are unfamiliar to you? Here, of course, the relevant comparison is not an omniscient and perfect system, but the plausible alternatives that are available. No system, including the one described here, can do a perfect job of finding all and only the information in which a given user is interested. We believe, however, that capabilities like those we have described increase the likelihood that people will find useful information they would not otherwise have encountered.

One simple mechanism for helping people find messages they don't know they want is to give them the option of seeing some number of randomly chosen messages each day. (These messages should, of course, be chosen from the "public" messages addressed to "Anyone" not from private messages between individuals.) Some of the random messages may, in fact, be of interest and may lead their recipients to establish filters that select other similar messages in the future. A slightly more sophisticated version of this approach is to have each user's rules assign a "probable interest value" to all messages. Techniques used for document ranking (such as term weighting) could be helpful for this purpose (Noreault & McGill, 1977; Salton & McGill, 1983). The system could then show a user all the messages above some "interest threshold" and a sample of other messages that are below that threshold but are randomly selected in a way that favors messages of higher probable interest.

Excessive processing loads. In the prototype version of the Lens system, there is only one "Anyone" server for all the users of the system. Clearly, when systems like this are used on a larger scale, such a single server could easily become overloaded. It is a straightforward matter, however, to have multiple "Anyone" servers spread throughout an organization, each one, for example, serving a different group, department, or division. Each of these servers can, in turn, have rules that determine when to forward messages they receive on to other "Anyone" servers elsewhere in the organization.

Privacy concerns. Many important issues of privacy and security are raised by any computer-mediated communication system that carries personally or organizationally sensitive information. These issues are, of course, important in systems like the one we have described, but they are not unique here. For instance, it is already common in electronic mail systems to restrict the audience for certain messages by addressing the messages only to specific individuals or to distribution lists whose membership is restricted. The Information Lens system uses the underlying mail system in this way and adds one more level of "public" information (i.e., messages addressed to "Anyone"). We have also implemented a simple extension to the system that allows messages to be addressed to "Anyone-in-<distribution list name>." A message addressed in this way can be received only by people in a specific distribution list whose rules select it.

There are also some intriguing new possibilities raised by intelligent information sharing systems that are not present in all computer-mediated communication systems. For example, the rules about how people filter, select, and prioritize their messages represent a new kind of potentially sensitive information that is stored in the system. Would employees, for instance, want their supervisors to know that they had filters selecting notices about job opportunities in other parts of the company? It is not clear, however, that people's rules should always be kept completely confidential. Sometimes, for instance, people may want others to know that they are interested in certain topics to encourage the formation of interest groups. There may also be times when it is desirable to tell the senders of messages addressed to "Anyone" how many people's rules actually selected the messages, without revealing the names of the recipients. Similarly, there may be times when it is desirable to display the numbers (but not the names) of people interested in different topics. Devices like this could thus provide a new kind of nonintrusive and (in some cases) nonobjectionable method for conducting instant "opinion surveys" or "market research." Clearly, careful thought is needed about when and how these possibilities are desirable, but we think the possibilities are quite intriguing.

Conflicts of interest. Most of the capabilities for information sharing that are included in the current Information Lens system can be expected to work best in communities where people share goals and where there are not strong conflicts of interest about whether certain kinds of information are worthy of attention. When there are such conflicts, for example, when an "advertiser" wants you to pay attention to something that you will in fact regard as "junk mail," then filtering capabilities like those we have described can sometimes be defeated. For instance, someone who wants many people to read a particular message can indicate that the message is about a topic that is widely interesting when, in fact, the message is not about that topic at all. It is, of course, possible to evolve filters to combat such maneuvers (e.g., "delete all messages from X, regardless of the topic indicated"), but this kind of "game" can continue to escalate with each side adopting more and more subtle techniques to filter out (or filter in) the messages. We believe that situations involving conflicts of interest like this are probably better handled by the social and economic approaches to information filtering we have discussed elsewhere (Malone et al., 1987).

RELATED WORK

There are several other previous approaches to structuring information sharing in electronic communities that have been used much less widely than distribution lists, conference topics, and keyword retrieval methods. These include: (1) using associative links between textual items to represent relationships such as references to earlier (or later) documents on similar topics, replies to previous messages, or examples of general concepts (e.g., Engelbart & English, 1968; Halasz, Moran, & Trigg, 1987); and (2) representing and using detailed knowledge about specific tasks such as calendar management or project management (e.g., Sathi, Fox, & Greenberg, 1985; Sluizer & Cashman, 1985). Our system is, in some sense, at an intermediate level between these two approaches. It includes more knowledge about specific domains than simple associative links, but it can be used for communicating about any domain, even those for which it has no specific knowledge. A few systems (e.g., McCune, Tong, Dean, & Shapiro, 1985) have

used AI techniques such as production rules to reason about the contents of messages based on the presence or absence of keywords in unstructured text.

We have not focused here on facilitating the kind of real-time information sharing that occurs in face-to-face meetings (e.g., Sarin & Greif, 1985; Stefik et al., 1987) or teleconferencing (e.g., Johansen, 1984). We believe, however, that the aids we described could be useful in some real-time meetings (especially those involving very many people), and that these aids could eliminate the need for some meetings altogether.

CONCLUSION

In this chapter, we have seen how a combination of ideas from artificial intelligence and user interface design can provide the basis for powerful computer-based communication and coordination systems. For instance the use of semistructured messages can simplify designing systems that (1) help people formulate information they wish to communicate, (2) automatically select, classify, and prioritize information people receive, (3) automatically respond to certain kinds of information, and (4) suggest actions people may wish to take on receiving certain other kinds of information. We believe that systems like this illustrate important—and not yet widely recognized—possibilities for collaboration between people and their machines. The power of this approach appears to be due partly to the fact that it does not emphasize building intelligent, autonomous computers, but instead focuses on using computers to gradually support more and more of the knowledge and processing involved when humans work together.

ACKNOWLEDGMENTS

Much of this chapter appeared previously in Malone, Grant, Turbak, Brobst, and Cohen (1987), and Malone, Grant, Lai, Rao, and Rosenblitt (1987). This research was supported by Xerox Corporation; Wang Laboratories, Inc.; Citibank, N.A.; Bankers Trust Co.; General Motors/Electronic Data Systems; the Management in the 1990's Program at the Sloan School of Management, MIT; and the Center for Information Systems Research, MIT.

References

Arrow, K. (1974). *Limits of organization.* New York: Norton.

DeJong, G. F. (1979). Prediction and substantiation: A new approach to natural language processing. *Cognitive Science, 3,* pp. 251-273.

Denning, P. (1982). Electronic junk. *Communications of the ACM, 23*(3), 163-165.

Dhar, V., & Ranganathan, P. (1986 October). Automating review of forms for international trade transactions: A natural language processing approach. *Proceedings of the Third International Conference on Office Information Systems* (61-69). New York: Association for Computing Machinery.

Englebart, D. C., & English, W. K. (1968). Research center for augmenting human intellect. *Proceedings of the AFIPS National Conference* (9-21). Washington, DC: AFIPS Press.

Fikes, R., & Kehler, T. (1985). The role of frame-based representation in reasoning. *Communications of the ACM, 28*(7), 904.

Gifford, D. K., Baldwin, R. W., Berlin, S. T., & Lucassen, J. T. (1985, December). An architecture for large scale information systems. *Proceedings of the 10th ACM Symposium on Operation Systems* (161-170). New York: Association for Computing Machinery.

Greif, I. (1982). *Cooperative office work, teleconferencing, and calendar management: A collection of papers (unpublished technical memo).* Cambridge, MA: Laboratory for Computer Science, Massachusetts Institute of Technology.

Halasz, F., Moran, T., & Trigg, R. (1987). Notecards in a nutshell. *Proceedings of the ACM Conference on Computer Human Interaction* (45-52). New York: Association for Computing Machinery.

Hiltz, S. R., & Turoff, M. (1985). Structuring computer-mediated communication systems to avoid information overload. *Communications of the ACM, 28*(7), 680-689.

Hiltz, S. R., & Turoff, M. (1978). *The network nation: human communication via computer.* Reading, MA: Addison-Wesley.

Johansen, R. (1984). *Teleconferencing and beyond: Communications in the office of the future.* New York: McGraw-Hill.

Malone, T. (1985). Designing organizational interfaces. *Proceedings of the ACM Conference on Computer-Human Interaction* (66-72). New York: Association for Computing Machinery.

Malone, T., Grant, K., Lai, K., Rao, R., & Rosenblitt, D. (1987). Semistructured messages are surprisingly useful for computer-supported coordination. *ACM Transactions on Office Information Systems, 5*, 115-131.

Malone, T., Yates, J., and Benjamin, R. (1987). Electronic markets and electronic hierarchies. *Communications of the ACM, 30*, 484-497.

Malone, T. W., Grant, K. R., Turbak, F. A., Brobst, S. A., & Cohen, M. D. (1987). Intelligent information sharing systems, *Communications of the ACM, 30*, 390-402.

March, J. G. & Simon, H. A. (1958). *Organizations.* New York: John Wiley & Sons.

McCune, B. P., Tong, R. M., Dean, J. S., & Shapiro, D. G. (1985). RUBRIC: A system for rule-based information retrieval. *IEEE Transactions on Software Engineering, 11*, 939-944.

Noreault, M. K., & McGill, M. J. (1977). Automatic ranked output from boolean searches in SIRE. *Journal of the ASIS, 28*, 333-339.

Palme, J. (1984) *You have 134 unread mail do you want to read them now?* Paper presented to IFIP Conference on Computer Based Message Services, Nottingham University.

Salton, G. & McGill, M. (1983) *Introduction to modern information retrieval.* New York: McGraw-Hill.

Sarin, S., & Greif, I. (1985, October). Computer-based real-time conferencing systems. *IEEE Computer, 18*, 33-49.

Sathi, A, Fox, M., & Greenberg, M. (1985). Representation of activity knowledge for project management. *IEEE Transactions on Pattern Analysis and Machine Intelligence PAMI-7, 5*, 531-552.

Sluizer, S., & Cashman, P. (1985). XCP: An experimental tool for supporting office procedures. *Proceedings of the Office Automation Conference* (73-80). Los Alamitos, CA: Institute of Electrical and Electronics Engineers.

Stefik, M., Foster, G., Bobrow, D., Kahn, K., Lanning, S., & Suchman, L. (1987). Beyond the chalkboard: Using computers to support collaboration. *Proceedings of the Conference on Computer-Supported Cooperative Work* (221-228). Austin, TX: Microelectronics and Computer Technology Corp.

Tou, F. N., Williams, M. D., Fikes, R. E., Henderson, D. A., & Malone, T. W. (1982). RABBIT: An intelligent database assistant. *Proceedings of the National Conference of the American Association for Artificial Intelligence*, Pittsburgh, Pennsylvania.

Wilson, P., Maude, T., Marshall, C., & Heaton, N. (1984). *The active mailbox- Your on-line secretary.* Paper presented to IFIP Conference on Computer Based Message Services, Nottingham University.

Winograd, T., & Flores, F. (1986). *Understanding computers and cognition: A new foundation for design.* Norwood, NJ: Ablex Press.

Object Lens: A "Spreadsheet" for Cooperative Work

KUM-YEW LAI, THOMAS W. MALONE, and KEH-CHIANG YU
Massachusetts Institute of Technology

Object Lens allows unsophisticated computer users to create their own cooperative work applications using a set of simple, but powerful, building blocks. By defining and modifying templates for various semistructured objects, users can represent information about people, tasks, products, messages, and many other kinds of information in a form that can be processed intelligently by both people and their computers. By collecting these objects in customizable folders, users can create their own displays which summarize selected information from the objects in table or tree formats. Finally, by creating semiautonomous agents, users can specify rules for automatically processing this information in different ways at different times.

The combination of these primitives provides a single consistent interface that integrates facilities for object-oriented databases, hypertext, electronic messaging, and rule-based intelligent agents. To illustrate the power of this combined approach, we describe several simple examples of applications (such as task tracking, intelligent message routing, and database retrieval) that we have developed in this framework.

Categories and Subject Descriptors: H.1.2 [**Models and Principles**]: User/Machine Systems; H.2.1 [**Database Management**]: Logical Design—*data models; schema and subschema*; H.2.3 [**Database Management**]: Languages—*data description languages (DDL)*; H.2.4 [**Database Management**]: Systems—*distributed systems*; H.3.1 [**Information Storage and Retrieval**]: Content Analysis and Indexing; H.3.4 [**Information Storage and Retrieval**]: Systems and Software; H.4.1 [**Information Systems Applications**]: Office Automation; H.4.3 [**Information Systems Applications**]: Communications Applications; I.2.1 [**Artificial Intelligence**]: Applications and Expert Systems—*office automation*; I.2.4 [**Artificial Intelligence**]: Knowledge Representation Formalisms and Methods—*frames and scripts; representations*; I.7.2 [**Text Processing**]: Document Preparation—*format and notation*

General Terms: Design, Economics, Human Factors, Management

Additional Key Words and Phrases: Computer-supported cooperative work, hypertext, information lens, intelligent agents, object-oriented databases, semiformal systems

1. INTRODUCTION

It is common in the computer industry today to talk about the "next spreadsheet"—to claim that a particular application will be the "next spreadsheet" or to wonder what the "next spreadsheet" will be (e.g., [7]). Usually the term "spreadsheet" is used in this context simply to connote a product that embodies some kind of design breakthrough and is very successful.

We will focus here on a more specific property of spreadsheet programs: They make a restricted, but nevertheless, very flexible and useful, set of computational capabilities extremely easy to use. It is, of course, possible to do any computation a spreadsheet can do in a general purpose programming language. But because doing these things with a spreadsheet program is so much more convenient, the number of people who can use computers to do them increases by orders of magnitude.

In this paper, we describe an early prototype of a system, called Object Lens, which we believe shares this property of spreadsheets: It makes accessible to unsophisticated computer users a set of computational and communications capabilities that, although limited, are quite flexible and useful for supporting a wide variety of cooperative work activities. In other words, we use the term "spreadsheet" here, not to connote financial modeling or constraint languages, but to connote a flexible infrastructure in which people who are not professional programmers can create or modify their own computer applications.

In the remainder of this paper we (1) describe the key ideas used in the design of Object Lens, (2) show how these ideas are realized in Object Lens features, and (3) illustrate the flexibility and usefulness of these ideas in several examples of cooperative work.

1.1 Three Views of Object Lens

Before proceeding, it is useful to point out three ways of viewing the Object Lens system.

(1) *Object Lens is the "second generation" of the Information Lens system.* Object Lens is based on our experience with using and enhancing the Information Lens [13, 14], an intelligent system for information sharing and coordination. A very large number of the enhancements that we and others have suggested for the Information Lens are included in Object Lens. Like the Information Lens, Object Lens uses ideas from artificial intelligence and user interface design to represent knowledge in such a way that both people and their computational agents can process it intelligently. Object Lens, however, is a significant generalization of the Information Lens. It potentially goes far beyond the Information Lens in the kinds of knowledge that can be represented and the ways that information can be manipulated.

(2) *Object Lens is a user interface that integrates hypertext, object-oriented databases, electronic messaging, and rule-based intelligent agents.* Object Lens does not include all the capabilities of all these different classes of systems, but we have been surprised at how cleanly a large portion of these diverse capabilities can be integrated. The key contribution of Object Lens is thus not the completeness of its implementation, but the integration of its user interface. Since the capabilities of these different kinds of systems are no longer separate applications, each capability is more useful than it would be alone, and the resulting system is unusually flexible.

(3) *Object Lens is a knowledge-based environment for developing cooperative work applications.* In the original Information Lens system, we developed specific

The work described in this paper was supported, in part, by Wang Laboratories, Xerox Corporation, General Motors/Electronic Data Systems, Bankers Trust Company, the Development Bank of Singapore, and the Management in the 1990s Research Program at the Sloan School of Management, MIT.

Authors' current addresses: K.-Y. Lai, 10-174 Block 129, Bukit Merah View, Singapore 0315, Republic of Singapore; T. W. Malone and K.-C. Yu, Sloan School of Management (E53-333), Massachusetts Institute of Technology, Cambridge, Mass. 02139.

applications for information sharing, meeting scheduling, project management, and computer conferencing. From the viewpoint of knowledge-based systems, these applications only included knowledge about different types of messages: the kinds of information the messages contained and the kinds of actions they could evoke. Object Lens, by contrast, can include explicit knowledge about many other kinds of objects such as people, tasks, meetings, products, and companies. We expect that the flexible tools Object Lens provides for dealing with these diverse kinds of knowledge will significantly increase the ease of developing a much wider range of applications. This last view of Object Lens, which emphasizes its flexibility, is our primary focus in this paper.

2. KEY IDEAS

One of the most important characteristics of Object Lens is that it is a *semiformal system*. We define a semiformal system as a computer system that has the following three properties: (1) it represents and automatically processes certain information in formally specified ways; (2) it represents and makes it easy for humans to process the same or other information in ways that are not formally specified; and (3) it allows the boundary between formal processing by computers and informal processing by people to be easily changed.

Semiformal systems are most useful when we understand enough to formalize some, but not all, of the knowledge relevant to acting in a given situation. Such systems are often useful in supporting cooperative work where we believe they are especially important in supporting individual work, and there are usually some well-understood patterns in people's behavior and also a very large amount of other knowledge that is potentially relevant but difficult to specify.

In order to create such a flexible semiformal system, the knowledge embodied in the system must be exposed to users in a way that is both *visible* and *changeable* (cf., [20]). That is, users must be able to easily see and change the information and the processing rules included in the system. In Object Lens, there are three key ideas about how to represent and expose knowledge to users:

(1) "Passive" information is represented in *semistructured objects* with template-based interfaces;
(2) "Aggregate" information from collections of objects is summarized in *customizable folders*; and
(3) "Active" rules for processing information are represented in *semiautonomous agents*.

In the remainder of Section 2, we provide an overview of how these three components allow us to expose knowledge to users in a way that is both visible and changeable. Detailed descriptions of the system features are in Section 3.

2.1 Semistructured Objects

Users of the Object Lens system can create, modify, retrieve, and display objects that represent many physically or conceptually familiar things such as messages, people, meetings, tasks, manufactured parts, and software bugs. The system provides an interface to an object-oriented database in the sense that (1) each object includes a collection of fields and field values, (2) each object type has a set of actions that can be performed upon it, and (3) the objects are arranged in a hierarchy of increasingly specialized types with each object type "inheriting" fields, actions, and other properties from its "parents" [4, 16, 17]. For example, a TASK object may have fields like Requestor, Performer, Description, and Deadline; a PERSON object may have fields like Name, Phone, Address, and Job title; and a STUDENT object may add fields like Year and Advisor to the fields present in all PERSON objects. Some objects (e.g., MESSAGES) have specialized actions defined for them (e.g., Answer and Forward). As described in more detail below, we have provided rudimentary facilities for saving and sharing objects, and we are currently exploring ways to link our interface to remote databases.

The objects in Object Lens, like messages in the Information Lens, are *semistructured* in the sense that users can fill in as much or as little information in different fields as they desire, and the information in a field is not necessarily of any specific type (e.g., it may be free text such as "I don't know").

2.1.1 *Template-Based User Interfaces.* Users can see and change objects through a particularly natural form of template-based user interface. These interfaces have a number of virtues. For instance: (1) they resemble forms, with which users are already familiar; (2) they conveniently inform users about the likely alternatives for different fields; and (3) their use is consistent across many different kinds of objects. We discuss later how this interface approach, which was used for messages and rules in the Information Lens, can be easily generalized to many different kinds of objects.

2.1.2 *Relationships Among Objects.* Users can easily see and change the relationships among objects by inserting and deleting *links* between the objects. For instance, the Requestor and Performer fields of a Task object might contain links to the Person objects that represent, respectively, the person who requested that the task be done and the person who performs the task. Then, for instance, when the user looks at the Task object, it is easy to get more information (e.g., the phone numbers) about the people involved with the task. We discuss later how this capability of linking objects to each other provides a rudimentary *hypertext* system as a special case (see [1] for an extensive review of hypertext systems). We also show how it is also possible for an object, to which a link appears, to be displayed as an *embedded template* inside the original template.

2.1.3 *Tailorable Display Formats.* Users have several options for changing the ways they see objects. For instance, they can easily (1) select which fields are to be shown and which are to be suppressed, (2) rename selected fields, and (3) specify the default and alternative values the system presents for individual fields.

2.1.4 *Inheritance Hierarchy for Objects.* The creation and modification of type definitions is simplified by arranging object types in an inheritance hierarchy (e.g., [17]). New types of objects are defined as specializations of existing object types, and they automatically "inherit" all properties of the existing objects except those which are specifically "overridden." Since most of the information about new object types can thus be "inherited" from existing types, rather than having to be reentered each time, creating new object types becomes simpler. Also, when an object type definition is changed later, the changes are automatically "inherited" by the specializations of that object type.

2.2 Customizable Folders

Users of Object Lens can group collections of objects together into special kinds of objects called Folders. For instance, folders can be created for groups of people (e.g., project teams, company directory), tasks (e.g., those completed, those to be done by you, those to be done by others), messages (grouped according to topic or urgency), and so forth. Users can also easily customize their own displays to summarize the contents of objects in a folder. For instance, they can select certain fields to be displayed in a *table* with each row representing an object in the folder and each column representing a field. They can also select fields from which the links between objects can be used to create a *tree* (or graph) display with each object represented as a node in the tree and each link in the selected field represented as a line between nodes.

2.3 Semiautonomous Agents

Users of the Object Lens system can create rule-based "agents" that process information automatically on behalf of their users (see [2] for an extended discussion of agents). These agents provide a natural way of partitioning the tasks performed automatically by the system. As discussed later, agents can be "triggered" by events such as the arrival of new mail, the appearance of a new object in a specified folder, the arrival of a prespecified time, or an explicit selection by the user. When an agent is triggered, it applies a set of rules to a specified collection of objects. If an object satisfies the criteria specified in a rule, the rule performs some prespecified action. These actions can be general actions such as retrieving, classifying, mailing, and deleting objects or object-specific actions such as loading files or adding events to a calendar.

The agents in Object Lens are *autonomous* in the sense that once they have been created, they can take actions without the explicit attention of a human user. They are only *semiautonomous*, however, in the sense that (a) they are always controlled by their human user (that is, all their rules can be easily seen and changed by their human user), and (b) they may often "refer" objects to their human user for action (e.g., by leaving the object in the user's inbox) instead of taking any actions on their own.

2.3.1 *Descriptions*. Since agents and rules are themselves objects, users can see and modify them with the same template-based user interface that is used for all other kinds of objects. To specify the criteria for when rules should act upon a given object, users create *descriptions* of the objects to which the rules apply. A description is simply a partially filled-in template for an object of a particular type. Descriptions can also include *embedded descriptions* that specify characteristics that must be satisfied by objects to which the original object is linked. For instance, a description of a Task might include an embedded description of the person who performs the task. These embedded descriptions (like

those in the Rabbit system [19]), allow users to easily specify object retrieval operations that are equivalent to "joins" followed by "selects" in a relational database.

3. SYSTEM FEATURES

In this section, we describe in more detail the basic system features of Object Lens and illustrate them with simple examples (see [10] for more details about an earlier version of the system). The Object Lens system is implemented in Interlisp-D on Xerox 1100 series workstations connected by an Ethernet. The system makes heavy use of the object-oriented programming environment provided by Loops and the built-in text editor, Tedit. Except where otherwise noted, everything described here has been implemented, but many features have not yet been extensively tested. As of this writing, the basic mail handling capabilities have been used regularly by two people in our development group for about six months, and the other facilities have received limited testing.

3.1 Terminology: Objects and Templates

Before proceeding it is helpful to clarify some terminology concerning objects and templates. First, we distinguish between *object types* (or "classes") and specific *object instances* (e.g., see [5]). We use the term *object type* to refer to a kind of object (such as Person or Task) and the term *object instance* (or simply "instance") to refer to a specific example of one of these object types (e.g., "Joe Smith" or "Task No. 17"). In contexts in which the distinction between object types and object instances is not critical, we use the term *objects* to include both.

We also use the term *template* in two ways. First, in a general sense, we use the term *template* to mean any semistructured collection of fields and field contents. Most of a user's interactions with Object Lens are based on such templates. Second, in the Object Lens screen displays, we use the word Template to mean object type definition. (When we use Template in this specialized sense, we always capitalize it.) For instance, users can change the display format for all Person objects by editing the Template that defines the Person object type.

3.2 Editing Instances

Figure 1 shows a template for an instance of a Person. Using the built-in text editor, users can insert text or bitmaps in any field. In addition, when users click on a field name with the mouse, a list of likely alternative values for that field appears in a pop-up menu. The alternatives may be links to other objects or just text strings. Selecting one of these alternatives causes the alternative to be automatically inserted in the field. For instance, the figure contains a link to the Person object representing Kum-Yew Lai's supervisor. To insert links to objects that are not in the alternatives list, the user (a) positions the cursor at the place in the template where the link is to be inserted, (b) selects the Add Link option from the menu at the top of the window, and then (c) points to the object to which the link should be made. After a link is inserted, clicking on it with the mouse causes the object it points to to appear on the screen.

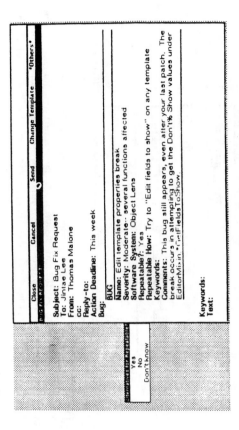

Fig. 2.   Embedded templates allow related objects to be viewed and edited simultaneously.

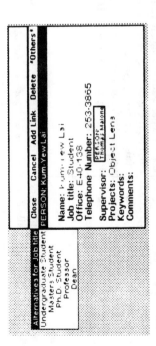

Fig. 1.   Objects can be edited with a simple template editor. Fields can include text, graphics, or links to other objects.

In the current version of Object Lens, users can insert any combination of text, numbers, links, and bitmaps in any field. Then, in some cases, type checking is done when the editing window for the instance is closed or when certain kinds of processing are done. For instance, the To and cc fields are checked for valid addresses before sending messages and the "move to" field in rule actions is checked for valid folders (see Sections 3.5 and 3.7 for descriptions of rules and folders). In future versions of Object Lens, we may experiment with more restrictive type enforcement in certain fields. For instance, it should probably be impossible to even insert something other than a folder in the "move to" field of a rule action.

Figure 2 shows a slightly more complex template; this one is for a Bug Fix Request message. One of the fields of this template is the Bug to be fixed, and the value of this field is a link to a Bug object. In this case, instead of simply showing a link to the Bug object, the template contains an *embedded template* for the Bug object itself. The fields in this embedded template can be edited just like the rest of the fields in the template. We later discuss how users can specify whether links to other objects should be displayed as *link icons* (as in Figure 1) or as *embedded templates* (as in Figure 2).

3.3 Creating New Instances

To create and display a new instance of an object type that already exists, users click with the mouse on the definition (i.e., the Template) for that object type. Figure 3 shows the Templates currently included in our system. For instance, to send a new message, users click on the Template for the type of message they want to create; to create a new person object, users click on the Person Template. Then an object instance, like those shown in Figures 1 and 2, appear, and the user can fill it in.

3.4 Creating New Object Types

To create a new object type, users click (with both mouse buttons instead of the left one) on the Template for the "parent" object type (see Figure 3). This causes a menu to appear showing alternative actions that can be performed on a Template. One of these actions is to Create a subtemplate. When the

user selects this action, a new Template is created with all the fields and properties of its "parent." Then users can add fields to the new Template or change its display format and other properties.

In the current version of Object Lens, all Things have three fields: Name, Keywords, and Comments. All objects inherit these fields, though as discussed below, some objects rename these fields or suppress their display. For instance, Messages, rename the Name field to be Subject and the Comments field to be Text.

3.5 Changing the Display Format and Other Properties of Object Types

To change the display format or other properties of an object type, users "edit" the Template that defines the object type. Users make these changes by selecting actions from the menu that appears when they click on the Template (as shown in Figure 3) with both mouse buttons. In this way, users can change (a) which fields of the objects are actually displayed, (b) the names of the fields that are displayed, (c) the alternative values that are displayed for each field, (d) the default values that are displayed in each field when new instances are created, and (e) whether the links in a field should be shown as link icons (see Figure 1) or as embedded templates (see Figure 2). In this mode, users can also add or delete fields from a template. All the changes made to a template are applied to old instances of an object type as well as to newly created ones. For example, if a user changes the name of a field, then the new name is shown when any old instances are redisplayed.

We anticipate that this system will be used with a core set of object types shared by the users in a group, and that the fields in these types will be modified only by an "authorized view administrator." Other users will be able to change the display format of these types (e.g., suppress the display of a field or change its name), but they would not be able to delete or add fields to these "official"

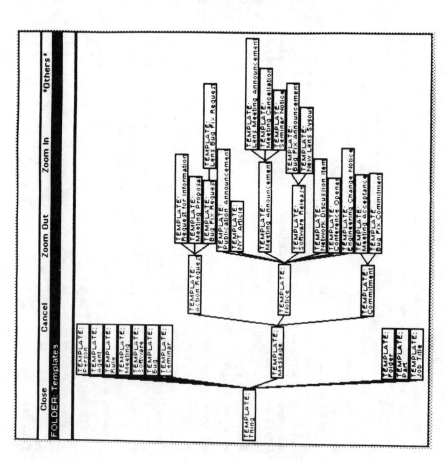

Fig. 3.   Object types are defined by a set of Templates.

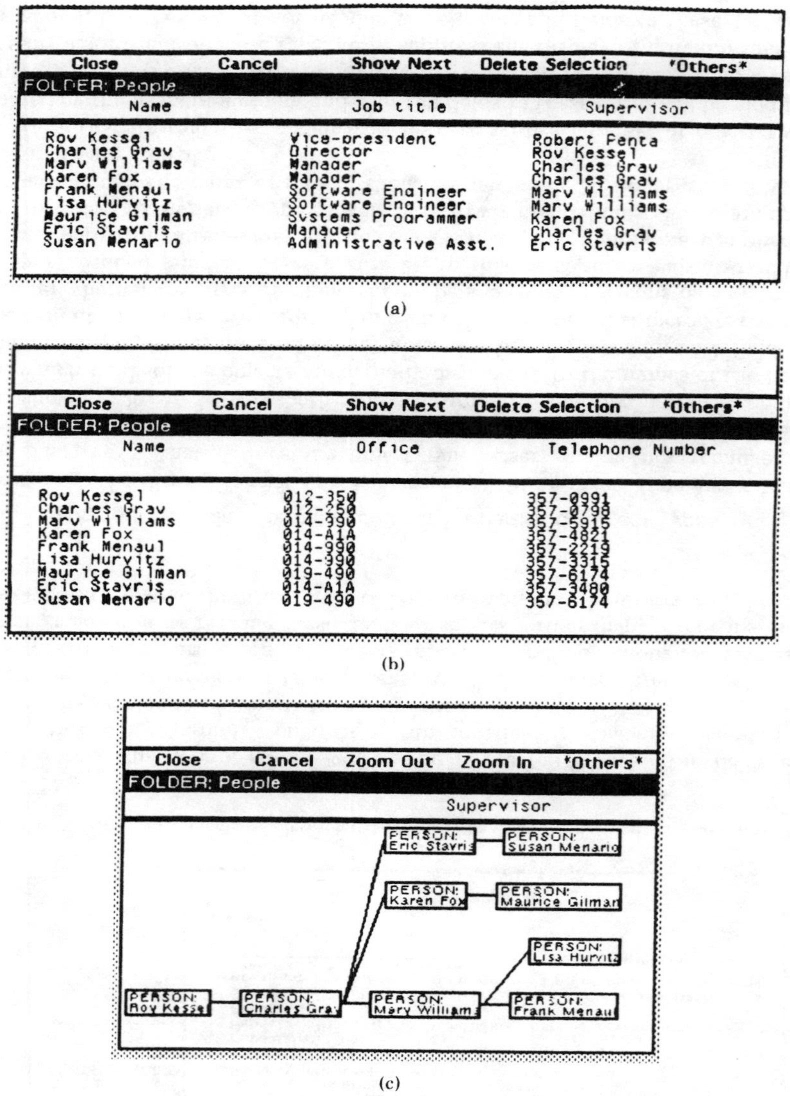

types. All users would, however, be able to create their own types as specializations
of the official types, and for these types they could add and delete new fields as
desired. Elsewhere [11, 12], we have proposed a scheme for letting an arbitrarily
large number of groups share partially overlapping sets of type definitions in
arbitrary ways. One of the key ideas of this scheme is that specialized types
created by one group can be interpreted by members of another group as instances
of the most specific "ancestor" type that both groups share. For instance, a
"Student" object created by one group might be interpreted as a "Person" object
by another group that does not have a definition for "Student."

3.6 Folders

As previously noted, Object Lens users can group collections of objects together
into special kinds of objects called Folders (see Figure 4). An object can be

added to a folder in two ways: (1) automatically, as the result of a rule action, or
(2) manually using the Add Link action from the *Others* submenu on the
folder. In both cases, the folders contain links to the objects, not the objects
themselves. Therefore, the same object can appear in more than one folder. Other

Fig. 4.   Users can select which fields to display in tables that summarize a collection of objects.

actions for moving, copying, and deleting both objects and links are described in Section 3.7.

Object Lens currently provides two formats for displaying the contents of objects folders: *tables* and *trees*. Tables show the values of selected fields from the objects contained in the folder. For instance, Figure 4(a) shows a folder that contains objects representing people with the fields for a simple office directory displayed. Users can easily tailor the format of these displays by selecting from a menu the fields they want to have included in the table. For instance, Figure 4(b) shows the same folder, but with the display format changed to include a different set of fields.

Trees are graphs that show the objects in a folder and the links that connect these objects. Just as users can select the fields to be shown in a table, they can also select the fields from which links are shown. For instance, Figure 4(c) shows the same folder again, but this time in tree format with the "Supervisor" field selected as the one from which links are displayed. In this case, the display resembles a simple organization chart. In the current version of Object Lens, only the links in one field at a time can be displayed in a tree. In future versions, we plan to allow links from multiple fields to be shown with the links from different fields being displayed as different types of lines (e.g., solid, dotted).

When a new folder is created, the user is asked to select the default object type to be contained in the folder. The user is then allowed to choose from the fields of this default object type when selecting the fields to show in a table or when selecting the fields from which links are to be shown in a tree. Even though all folders have default object types, no strict type checking is enforced. If an object of an unexpected type is inserted into a folder, only the fields it shares with the default type are displayed in tables and trees.

3.7 Performing Actions on Objects

In addition to editing the contents of objects, users can also perform predefined actions on them. The actions that can be performed at any time depend on two primary factors: (1) the type of object being acted upon, and (2) the context in which the action is invoked.

3.7.1 *Object Specific Actions.* Each object type has a set of actions that can be performed on it. Some of these actions are "inherited" directly from the "parents" of the object type. Others may be modified or added specifically for this object type. For instance, there are some actions, such as Hardcopy and Save, that can be performed on all objects (i.e., all instances of Thing and all its subtypes). (Some of these actions, such as Hardcopy, are not yet implemented for all object types.) In addition, more specialized types of objects have other actions defined for them. For instance, agents have a Run action that triggers them to start running, and folders have a Change Display Format action that changes them from table format to tree format or vice versa.

In a few cases, the object specific actions depend, not just on the type of the object, but also on its state. For instance, messages created on the local workstation have a Send action, and messages received from elsewhere have actions such as Answer and Forward. So far these state-specific actions on objects are implemented as special cases. However, we would like to experiment with a more general mechanism for representing state-specific actions and perhaps making this representation accessible to users. In some ways, this mechanism would be a generalization of the conversation manager in the Coordinator [21], which restricts the types of messages that a user can send at a given point in a conversation on the basis of the conversation state.

3.7.2 *Context Specific Actions.* There are some actions that can be applied to any kind of object but which can be invoked only from certain contexts. The primary contexts are (1) from an editor (like the one in Figure 1), (2) from a folder that contains the object, (3) from a rule operating on the object, and (4) from a link icon for the object.

For instance, when an object is being displayed in an editor, there are several kinds of actions, such as Close, Move, and Shape, that apply to the editing window. Other actions in an editor include (a) Add Link (insert at the current cursor position a link to another object selected by the user) and (b) Cancel (close the window without saving any of the changes made since the window was last opened).

When an object is displayed in a folder, other context-specific actions can be applied to it such as (a) Show (open an editor on the object) and (b) Select (select the item for some later folder action such as Delete Selection).

The actions that can be applied to an object by rules are discussed in Section 3.8. The actions that can be applied to link icons include Show (open an editor on the object) and Delete (delete this link to the object).

3.7.3 *Displaying and Invoking Actions.* Users invoke the above actions in slightly different ways depending on the context in which the object is displayed. If the object is displayed in an editor (like the one in Figure 1), then several of its most common actions are shown across the top of the editor, and all the other actions are shown in a menu that pops up when the *Others* action is selected.

When a link to an object is displayed (either as a link icon or as a row in a table), users can invoke actions in two ways. First, if users click on the link with both mouse buttons, a menu pops up showing all possible actions on the object. In addition, simply clicking on the link with the left mouse button invokes the most common action. For instance, clicking with the left button on a row in a table Selects the object for subsequent folder actions, whereas clicking with the left button on a link icon inside an editor Shows the object in another window on the screen.

3.8 Creating Agents and Rules

In some cases, agents can take actions automatically on behalf of their users. For instance, Figure 5 shows an example of a simple agent designed to help a user process incoming mail. When an agent is triggered, it applies a set of rules to a collection of objects in a folder. The agent in Figure 5 is applied to objects in the New Mail folder and is triggered by the arrival of new mail. That is, when mail is brought to the workstation, the mail program automatically inserts links to the new messages into the user's New Mail folder, and these New Links trigger the agent. In the current version of Object Lens, two other kinds of automatic triggers are available: Daily at Midnight and On the Hour.

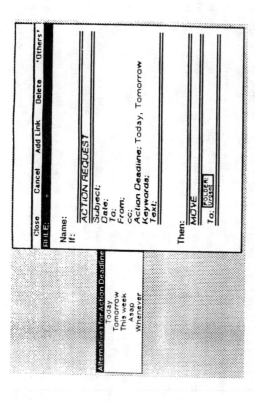

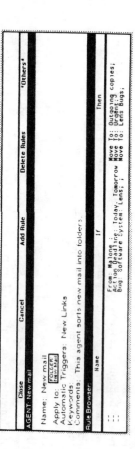

Fig. 5.   Agents include a collection of rules and specifications for when and where to apply them.

Fig. 6.   Rules describe the objects that satisfy them and specify what action to perform on those objects.

The agent shown in Figure 5 includes several rules, one of which is shown in Figure 6. A rule contains an IF field (predicate) and a THEN field (action). Both parts of the rule contain links to other objects which are shown as embedded templates. The IF part of the rule is a *description*, a special kind of template that describes a set of instances in terms of the values of their fields. The THEN part of the rule is an Action object.

To construct the IF part of a rule, a user (a) clicks on the IF field with the middle mouse button, (b) selects "Descriptions" from the menu presented, and then (c) selects an object type from the tree of object types presented. This causes a description of the appropriate type to be inserted in the rule as an embedded template, and the user can then fill in the fields in this description to specify the values that must appear in particular fields for an object to satisfy the rule. As in the Information Lens, more complex specifications for a field can be constructed by combining strings with *and*, *or*, *not*, and parentheses (i.e., arbitrary Boolean combinations are possible within a field). If specifications appear in more than one field, then all specifications must be satisfied at once for the rule to succeed (i.e., specifications in different fields are implicitly *and*-ed). As in the other template-based editors in Object Lens, pop-up menus listing likely alternatives for a field are available in editing descriptions.

To specify the THEN part of a rule, a user simply clicks on the THEN field and selects an action from the menu of alternatives presented. These actions are applied to the *current object* (the object matched by the IF part of the rule) in the context of the *current folder* (the folder specified in the "Apply to" field of the agent). In some cases (such as the "Move" action shown here), the user also needs to fill in some fields in the embedded template for the action (e.g., the field specifying where the object is to be moved). The actions currently implemented in rules include the following: copy (add the current object to a different folder without removing it from the current folder), move (add the current object to a different folder and delete it from the current folder), delete (remove the object from the current folder), and add keyword (add the specified keyword to the Keywords field of the object). In addition, rules can invoke object specific actions, including the actions that apply to all objects such as hardcopy and save. We view the addition of more rule actions (and possibly the refinement of the rule syntax) as one of the important directions for our ongoing research.

The rules are applied in the order in which they appear in the agent's rule folder. Users can create extended reasoning chains by having some rules set characteristics of objects (using the Add Keyword action) which other rules test (by checking the Keyword field).

3.8.1 *Embedded Descriptions*. With the capabilities we have described so far, all rules must depend only on information contained in the objects to which they are being applied. For instance, a rule about a message can depend only on information contained in the message itself. It is often desirable, however, to be able to specify rules that also depend on other information contained elsewhere in the knowledge base. For instance, in the Information Lens system, if a user wanted to specify a rule that applied to all messages from vice presidents, the rule would have to include the names of all the vice presidents in the From field.

In Object Lens, it is possible to draw upon other information by having descriptions embedded within other descriptions. For instance, the rule shown in Figure 7 is satisfied if the message is from any person with a job title that includes "vice president." To apply this rule, the system checks to see whether the string in the From field of the message is the same as the Name of any Person object in the knowledge base that satisfies the description.

3.9 Navigating Through the System

The starting point for navigation through the Object Lens system is the Object Lens Icon, a window that shows whether the user has new mail waiting and includes a menu item to Show Basics (show the basic folders included in the system). The system folders accessible through the Show Basics action include (1) a folder containing all the other folders in the system, (2) a folder containing all the Templates defined in the system (Figure 3), (3) a folder containing all the agents defined in the system, (4) a folder for each object type containing all the instances of that type in the system, and (5) the New Mail folder, into which new mail retrieved from the mail server is automatically inserted. In addition, we have designed but not fully implemented two other folders: (6) Everything, a virtual folder containing all objects in the system, and (7) Orphans, a virtual folder containing all objects to which no links exist.

These basic folders provide users with convenient starting points for locating any object in the system. In relatively small systems, users can browse through these folders directly. In larger systems, we expect users to let their agents search through the system folders to find objects that meet certain criteria. It is also possible for (a) individual users to create their own customized directory folders that contain the folders and other objects they most often use, and (b) application developers to create folders containing the objects used in their application.

3.10 Saving and Sharing Knowledge

One of the important research directions we plan to pursue in the Object Lens system involves different ways for people to save and share the kinds of knowledge described above. For instance, we are currently experimenting with linking Object Lens to a remote database server which contains large shared relational databases. This work is still at an early stage, but it is clear that the usefulness of Object Lens is significantly enhanced if it includes access to shared databases.

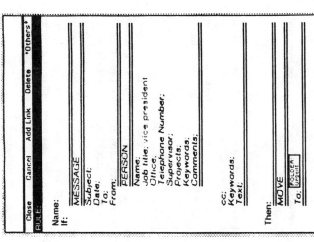

Fig. 7. Rules can use embedded descriptions to create complex queries.

In the current version of Object Lens, we have preliminary solutions to the problems of saving and sharing knowledge that meet some, but not all, of the needs people have in this area.

3.10.1 Saving Knowledge. Users can save an object (or a collection of objects in a folder) at any time by performing the Save action on the object (or the folder). This action uses the file package commands from the underlying Loops and Lisp systems to store the objects in permanent files in a form that can be reloaded at any time. There is also a Save action on the main Object Lens icon that saves all the instances in the workstation.

The potential disadvantages of this approach to saving knowledge are that (1) it requires explicit user actions to save objects in permanent storage and (2) it requires all knowledge used by the system to be loaded onto the local workstation. Sharing remote databases, of course, helps solve these problems, but we expect that systems like Object Lens can be of value even without shared databases. For example, many users are already accustomed to explicitly saving their work in applications such as word processing, and even this task can be simplified by creating agents to run periodically (e.g., every night) and do automatic backups of selected objects.

3.10.2 Sharing Knowledge by Sending Messages. There are two ways users of Object Lens can share objects with each other: (1) by sending messages, and (2) by transferring files. In this subsection, we discuss sending messages; in the next, we discuss transferring files. When an Object Lens user sends a message, the message object is converted into text and sent via the existing mail system. Any connected electronic mail users can receive and read this textual message. When an Object Lens user receives the message, it is added as a new object in the receiver's knowledge base.

When a user sends a message containing an embedded object that is expanded (as in Figure 2), the embedded object is converted into (indented) text in the message in a form that (a) can be easily read by any receivers who are not using Object Lens, and (b) is reconverted into another embedded object when it is received by Object Lens users. When a user sends a message containing embedded objects that are *not* expanded (e.g., that are shown only as link icons), the names of the objects are included in the message in place of the link icons, but these names are not resolved back into link icons at the receiver's end.

One intriguing research direction here involves how to communicate embedded objects in such a way that they can be resolved into preexisting objects at the receiver's end. For example, if the sender's message contains a link to a person object, it would be nice for the receiver's system to be able to automatically resolve this link into the receiver's object representing the same person.

3.10.3 Sharing Knowledge by Transferring Files. The second way for users to share objects is by transferring files. As described above, it is easy for users to store on a file server the current state of a set of objects. Other users can then load these files to create (or update) the objects in their own workstations. Saving and loading these files can often be done automatically. For example, we expect that a common way for users to keep current versions of shared information such

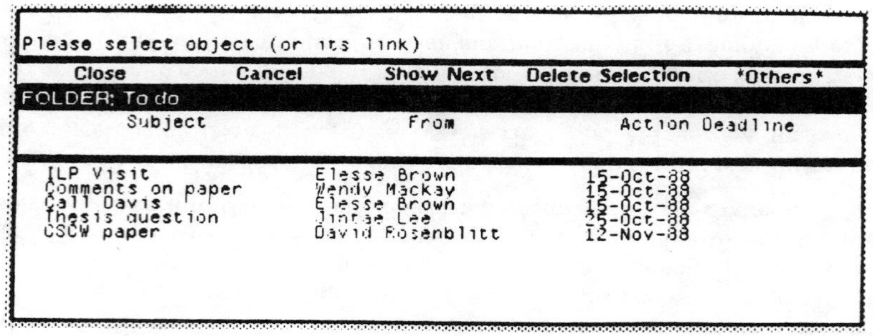

Fig. 8.   Tables can be used to summarize selected fields from Action Request messages.

as names, addresses, and job titles of people in their organization is to have someone maintain the official version of this information and periodically distribute updates to other users in the organization. Distributing these updates could be done in several ways: (1) the maintainer could have automatic agents that periodically store the current versions on a file server, and the other users could have automatic agents that periodically load the most recent versions, or (2) the maintainer could explicitly send out messages announcing the availability of files containing updated objects, and the other users could have agents that automatically load the files announced in such messages (e.g., a rule might load all files specified in "Official file update" messages from the official maintainer).

One potential problem with this approach is that any changes users have made to their local copies of objects (e.g., any notes they had added in the Comments field) are lost when a new version of the object is loaded. To help solve this problem, we are currently investigating more specialized updating actions for agents to use. With this approach, the official maintainer will be able to distribute update messages that specify changes in particular fields of particular objects. Users can then set up agents that make these updates automatically under most conditions, but under certain conditions the user might be notified before the update is made (e.g., if the field about to be modified has previously been changed by the user). In some cases, the user might want to have the change made automatically but also want to be notified (e.g., if someone in the user's group is changing phone numbers).

4. OTHER APPLICATIONS

In this section, we give more examples of how the above features can be combined to create a variety of cooperative work applications.

4.1 Task Tracking

One frequently mentioned capability for cooperative work applications is the ability to keep track of the tasks people are supposed to do (e.g. [18, 22]). For instance, such systems can help answer questions like: What tasks have other people requested me to do? Are any of these tasks overdue? What tasks have I requested other people to do for me?

Supporting capabilities like this in Object Lens is a straightforward matter. For instance, the system already includes message types for action requests and commitments. Even in the Information Lens, it was possible to automatically sort these messages into folders according to who is to perform the task, which project it involves, and so forth. In the Information Lens, however, the summary display of a folder's contents shows only the standard message header fields: From, Date, and Subject. To see more about the tasks, individual messages have to be displayed, one at a time. In Object Lens, the messages within a folder can easily be summarized by displaying whatever fields the user chooses. For example, Figure 8 shows a table display of action request messages that includes the action deadline.

4.2 Intelligent Message Sorting: Engineering Change Notices

As we have described in more detail elsewhere [15], an intriguing example of a cooperative work problem involves disseminating information about changes in product specifications (often called "engineering change notices") to the appropriate people in an organization. It was already possible in the Information Lens to sort engineering change notices according to the contents of fields such as Part Affected, Type of Change, and Severity. In Object Lens, it is possible to use additional knowledge to do even more intelligent sorting. For instance, Figure 9 shows a rule that uses a doubly embedded description to select all change notices that involve parts for which anyone reporting to a particular manager is responsible.

4.3 Database Retrieval

There are clearly many cases in both individual and cooperative work when it is useful to be able to automatically retrieve objects that satisfy certain conditions from a database. Object Lens provides a simple way to perform database queries: Users can simply create agents that scan the objects in one folder and insert links to selected objects into another folder. The rules in the agents specify the criteria for selecting objects.

For instance, suppose you wanted to find all the technical staff members who were assigned to both the project code-named "Dragon" and the one code-named "Lancelot." Figure 10 shows a rule that would retrieve all such people. Instead of listing all the technical job titles by name ("software engineer," "systems programmer," etc.), the rule includes an embedded description to determine whether a particular job title is on the technical, as opposed to the managerial or administrative, career ladder.

In addition to this general interface for database retrieval, we have also implemented a specialized feature in Object Lens for determining the recipients of messages. With this feature, descriptions (like that shown in the IF field of Figure 10) can be embedded in the To and cc fields of a message. Then, when the message is sent, these descriptions are automatically applied to all the Person objects in the local knowledge base, and the resulting people are inserted in the To and cc fields. This feature allows senders to create distribution lists that are dynamically computed at message-sending time on the basis of current information about people in their database (see [23] for a similar capability).

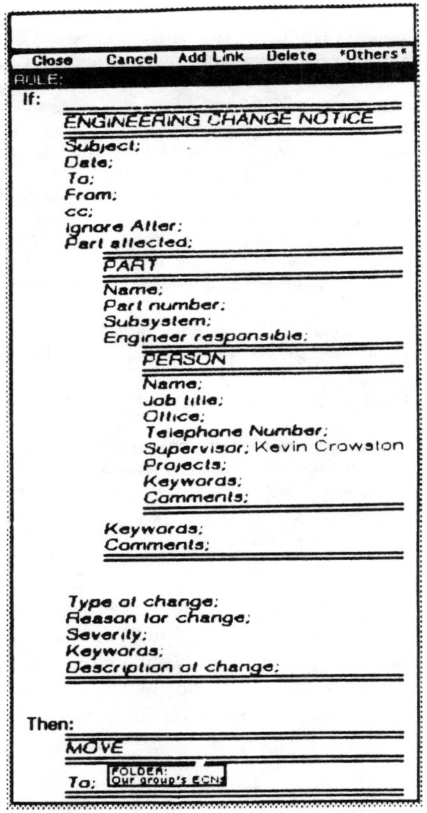

Fig. 9. Rules can include multiple levels of embedded descriptions that refer to linked objects throughout the knowledge base.

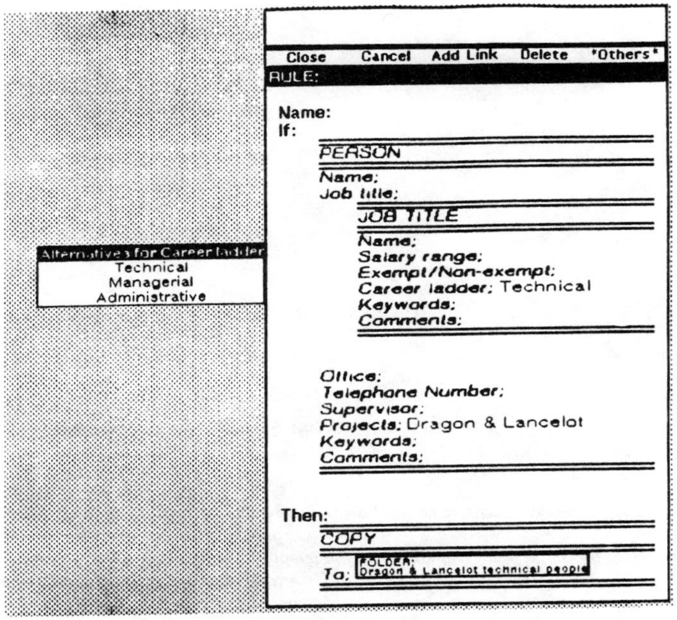

Fig. 10. Agents can retrieve all the objects from a database that satisfy certain criteria.

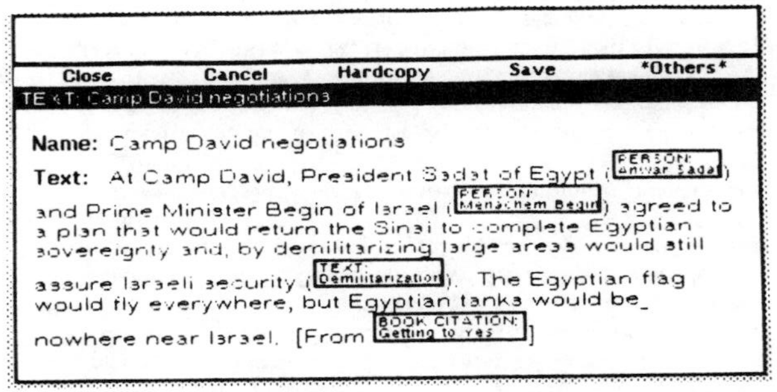

Fig. 11. Hypertext documents can include links, not only to other text passages, but also to other object types such as people and bibliographic citations.

4.4 Hypertext

As noted above, it is a straightforward matter to use many of the features of a hypertext system in Object Lens (e.g., [3, 6, 9]). For instance, our system currently contains an object type called Text that displays only two fields: Name and Text. The Text field of a Text object can contain links to as many other objects as desired. For example, Figure 11 shows a sample Text object that contains links to people and bibliographic citations as well as to another Text object.

In addition to the usual benefits of hypertext systems, Object Lens derives additional benefits from its integration of hypertext with other database, messaging, and computational capabilities. For instance, in order to insert a link to another node in a hypertext system, a user must first find the node to which the link will be made. In Object Lens, the database retrieval capabilities described above can be used to automatically find objects (such as people or bibliographic citations) that satisfy certain criteria. Then links to these objects can be inserted into the text. One desirable feature found in some hypertext systems that is not yet included in Object Lens is the ability to show and follow the incoming links

to an object. We would like to implement this capability as another action available on all objects.

Even though the relationship between Object Lens and previous hypertext systems is not the primary focus of this paper, it is interesting to observe that Object Lens appears to have some functionality in at least four of the seven areas that Halasz [8] listed as being needed in the next generation of hypermedia systems (search and query, computational engines, collaborative work, and tailorability).

5. CONCLUSION

In this paper, we have described a system called Object Lens that integrates facilities for hypertext, object-oriented databases, electronic messaging, and rule-based agents. Using the basic primitives provided by this system, we believe it is relatively easy to create a wide variety of cooperative work applications. We have shown several such applications here, and an important focus of our ongoing research will be to test the generality of the framework further by implementing more applications within it.

Object Lens is an example of a semiformal system, a system that represents knowledge in a way that both people and their computational agents can process intelligently. We believe that much of the power and flexibility of this system results from its choice of primitives (semistructured objects, customizable folders, and semiautonomous agents) and from the template-based interfaces that make these primitives both visible and changeable by inexperienced computer users.

ACKNOWLEDGMENTS

We would especially like to thank Ken Grant who suggested some of the earliest ideas that led to Object Lens and Jin Lee who helped debug the most recent version. The Object Lens system and this paper have also benefited from conversations with Cheryl Clark, Kevin Crowston, Randy Davis, Frank Halasz, Mitch Kapor, Stan Lanning, Wendy Mackay, Ramana Rao, Randy Trigg, David Rosenblitt, and Franklyn Turbak.

REFERENCES

1. CONKLIN, J. Hypertext: An introduction and survey. *IEEE Computer 20*, 9 (1987), 17–41.
2. CROWSTON, K., AND MALONE, T. W. Computational agents to support cooperative work. Working Paper No. 2008-88, Center for Information Systems Research, Massachusetts Institute of Technology, Cambridge, Mass., 1988.
3. DELISLE, N., AND SCHWARTZ, M. Contexts—a partitioning concept for hypertext. *ACM Trans. Off. Inf. Syst. 5*, 2 (Apr. 1987), 168–186.
4. DITTRICH, D., AND DAYAL, U., Eds. In *Proceedings of the International Workshop on Object-Oriented Database Systems* (Asilomar, Calif., Sept. 23–26). IEEE Computer Society, Washington, D.C., 1986.
5. FIKES, R., AND KEHLER, T. The role of frame-based representation in reasoning. *Commun. ACM 28*, 9 (Sept. 1985), 904.
6. GARRETT, L. N., SMITH, K. E., AND MEYROWITZ, N. Intermedia: Issues, strategies, and tactics in the design of a hypermedia document system. In *Proceedings of the Conference on Computer-Supported Cooperative Work* (Austin, Tex., Dec. 3-5). ACM, New York, 1986, 163–174.
7. GREIF, I. Computer-supported cooperative work: Breakthroughs for user acceptance (Panel description). In *Proceedings of the ACM Conference on Human Factors in Computing Systems (CHI '88)* (Washington, D.C., May 16–19). ACM, New York, 1988, pp. 113–114.
8. HALASZ, F. G. Reflections on NoteCards: Seven issues for the next generation of hypermedia systems. *Commun. ACM 31*, 7 (July 1987), 836–855.
9. HALASZ, F. G., MORAN, T. P., AND TRIGG, R. H. NoteCards in a nutshell. In *Proceedings of the 1987 ACM Conference on Human Factors in Computer Systems (CHI + GI '87)* (Toronto, Ontario, Apr. 5–9). ACM, New York, 45–52.
10. LAI, K. Y. Essays on Object Lens: A tool for supporting information sharing. Master's thesis, Sloan School of Management, Massachusetts Institute of Technology, Cambridge, Mass., 1987.
11. LEE, J., AND MALONE, T. W. How can groups communicate when they use different languages? Translating between partially shared type hierarchies. In *Proceedings of the ACM Conference on Office Information Systems* (Palo Alto, Calif., Mar. 23–25). ACM, New York, 1988, pp. 22–29.
12. LEE, J., AND MALONE, T. W. Partially shared views: A scheme for communicating among groups that use different type hierarchies. Sloan School of Management Working Paper, Massachusetts Institute of Technology, Cambridge, Mass., Sept., 1988.
13. MALONE, T. W., GRANT, K. R., LAI, K.-Y., RAO, R., AND ROSENBLITT, D. Semistructured messages are surprisingly useful for computer-supported coordination. *ACM Trans. Off. Syst. 5*, 2 (Apr. 1987), 115–131.
14. MALONE, T. W., GRANT, K. R., TURBAK, F. A., BROBST, S. A., AND COHEN, M. D. Intelligent information-sharing systems. *Commun. ACM 30*, 5 (May 1987), 390–402.
15. MALONE, T. W., GRANT, K. R., LAI, K.-Y., RAO, R., AND ROSENBLITT, D. The Information Lens: An intelligent system for information sharing and coordination. In *Technological Support for Work Group Collaboration*, M. H. Olson, Ed. Lawrence Erlbaum, Hillsdale, N.J., 1989.
16. SHRIVER, B., AND WEGNER, P. *Research Directions in Object-Oriented Programming*. MIT Press, Cambridge, Mass., 1987.
17. STEFIK, M., AND BOBROW, D. G. Object-oriented programming: Themes and variations. *AI Magazine* (Spring 1986), 40–62.
18. SLUIZER, S., AND CASHMAN, P. M. XCP: An experimental tool for supporting office procedures. In *IEEE 1984 Proceedings of the 1st International Conference on Office Automation* (Silver Spring, Md). IEEE Computer Society, Washington, D.C., 1984, pp. 73–80.
19. TOU, F. N., WILLIAMS, M. D., FIKES, R. E., HENDERSON, D. A., AND MALONE, T. W. RABBIT: An intelligent database assistant. In *Proceedings of the National Conference of the American Association for Artificial Intelligence* (Pittsburgh, Pa., Aug. 18–20). American Association for Artificial Intelligence, Philadelphia, Pa., 1982, pp. 314–318.
20. TURBAK, F. A. Grasp: A visible and manipulable model for procedural programs. Master's thesis, Department of Electrical Engineering and Computer Science, Massachusetts Institute of Technology, Cambridge, Mass., 1986.
21. WINOGRAD, T. A language/action perspective on the design of cooperative work. *Human Computer Interaction 3*, 1 (1988), 3–30.
22. WINOGRAD, T., AND FLORES, F. *Understanding Computers and Cognition: A New Foundation For Design*. Ablex, Norwood, NJ, 1986.
23. ZLOOF, M. M. QBE/OBE: A language for office and business automation. *IEEE Computer 14*, 5 (May 1981), 13–22.

Received June 1988; revised October 1988; accepted October 1988

Power, ease of use and cooperative work in a practical multimedia message system

NATHANIEL S. BORENSTEIN†

Bellcore, Room MRE, 2A274, 445 South Street, Morristown, NJ 07960, USA

CHRIS A. THYBERG

Room 3017, Hamburg Hall, Carnegie Mellon University, Pittsburgh, PA 15213, USA

(Received April 1990 and accepted in revised form August 1990)

The "Messages" program, the high-end interface to the Andrew Message System (AMS), is a multimedia mail and bulletin board reading program that novices generally learn to use in less than an hour. Despite the initial simplicity, however, Messages is extremely powerful and manages to satisfy the needs of both experts and novices through a carefully evolved system of novice-oriented defaults, expert-oriented options, and a help system and option-setting facility designed to ease the transition from new user to sophisticated expert. The advanced features of the system facilitate types of cooperative work that are not possible with other mail or bulletin board systems, but which would also be impossible in large heterogeneous communities if the system were not so easily used by both novices and experts. A major example of such cooperative work is the Andrew Advisor system, a highly-evolved and sophisticated system that uses the AMS to solve the problems of distributed support for a very diverse user community in a heterogeneous computing environment. The evolution of the Advisor system and its uses of the AMS mechanisms are considered as a detailed example of the power and limitations of the AMS.

Introduction

This paper describes one notably successful user interface program for reading and sending mail and bulletin board messages, the "Messages" interface to the Andrew Message System. This system is currently in use at hundreds of sites, and at some sites its use has become virtually ubiquitous. In such environments, where its advanced features can be universally relied on at both ends of the communication, it has facilitated new kinds of computer-based cooperative activities. In this paper, we will describe the Messages program in order to understand the factors underlying its success, both its popularity with users and its effectiveness as a tool for cooperative work. In particular, we will focus on the question of how it manages to accommodate the diverse needs of novices and experts alike. Finally, we will look at an example of how the system has been successfully used by an independent group to support a rather complex form of cooperative work, the Andrew Advisor system.

† This paper describes work carried out while the author worked at the Information Technology Center, Carnegie Mellon University, Pittsburgh, Pennsylvania.

A good user interface is, of course, always good news to the people who have to use it. All too often however, it has proven difficult or impossible to determine after the fact, what has made a user interface successful or popular. The lessons of popular user interfaces are often idiosyncratic and difficult to generalize, or just plain obscure, as noted in Borenstein and Gosling (1988). In the case of the Messages program, as with all others, a great deal of debate could be made over the reasons for its strengths and weaknesses, or indeed over the precise nature of those strengths and weaknesses. In this case, however, the program was initially built and subsequently remodeled on a clear foundation of assumptions and beliefs about user interface technology, so that the end product may justifiably be viewed as the result of an experiment, an empirical application of one set of user interface design principles. We will make these principles explicit before describing the program itself.

The principles put forward here were not explicitly stated or committed to print prior to the Andrew project, but they were certainly strongly held beliefs that were often expressed in conversation. One of the authors has recently produced an expanded attempt to enunciate these as general principles for user interface design (Borenstein, in press a). In that book, arguments are made to justify the principles. Here however, we will treat the principles as axioms, and will consider the resulting artifact, the Messages program, as empirical result of the application of these axioms. Or, to put it more simply, we describe the principles and the result in the hope that the connection between the two will tend to support the validity of the basic design principles involved.

Assumption 1: The actual utility of applications that promise to support Computer-Supported Cooperative Work (CSCW) cannot be judged in the absence of a real user community. Any system, therefore, that claims to make a contribution to CSCW, but has no significant base of regular users, is making an empty or unverifiable claim.

Assumption 2: Usability is an essential prerequisite for any software system with a significant user interface component, which includes all systems to support cooperative work. Even in "research" systems, if the focus of the research is on doing something for end users, as it necessarily must be in all CSCW research, then a highly polished and usable interface is essential. The absence of such an interface will make it nearly impossible to obtain a realistic user community, and will thus necessarily skew any research results in such a way as to make it nearly impossible to evaluate the underlying ideas.

Assumption 3: In user interfaces, there is *no* fundamental trade-off between power, complexity and usability. The most complex and powerful systems can also be the easiest to use, if designed properly, subject to ongoing, consciously evolutionary development.

Assumption 4: In a complex user interface, all defaults should be carefully tuned for the most common novice user responses and expectations.

Assumption 5: Powerful but potentially confusing user interface features should be turned off by default, so as to not conflict with novice learning.

Assumption 6: Mechanisms must be provided to ease the transition from novice

© 1991 Academic Press Limited

Reprinted from *International Journal of Man-Machine Studies*, 34(2), pp. 229-259. Reprinted by permission of Harcourt Brace Jovanovich Limited.

to expert, especially in systems where powerful expert-oriented features are not made available without explicit user action to request them.

Assumption 7: Good user interfaces grow and evolve. The most essential part of the design process is the evaluation of, and improvement upon, previous versions of the interface, based on feedback from, and observation of real users of the system.

This paper views the Messages program as an uncontrolled field test of the above assumptions. The successes and failures of the system cannot be absolutely demonstrated to have resulted directly from these assumptions, but it is the authors' belief that a substantial connection does exist. At the very least, the principles provide the philosophical background against which the system should be understood.

Andrew and its message system

Besides the philosophical background, there is also a technical background that must be understood in order to have a clear understanding of the Messages program. Messages was produced as a part of the Andrew project, about which a brief explanation is in order.

The Andrew Project (Morris, Satyanarayanan, Conner, Howard, Rosenthal & Smith, 1986; Morris, 1988; Borenstein, in press b) was a collaborative effort of IBM and the Information Technology Center at Carnegie Mellon University. The goal of the Andrew project was to build a realistic prototype of a university-wide distributed computing environment. That is, particular emphasis was paid to the needs of the academic and research communities. The success of that effort can be measured in part by the fact that the prototype has been taken up and is now fully supported by the University's central computing organizations.

As the project evolved, it concentrated on three main parts. The Andrew File System (Howard, 1988; Howard, Kazar, Menees, Nichols, Satyanarayanan, Sidebotham, & West, 1988; Kazar, 1988; Kazar & Spector, 1989) is a distributed network file system designed to provide the illusion of a uniform central UNIX file system for a very large network (10 000 workstations was the design goal).†
The Andrew Toolkit (Palay, Hansen, Kazar, Sherman, Wadlow, Neuendorffer, Stern, Bader, & Peters, 1988; Borenstein, 1990) is a window-system-independent programming library to support the development of user interface software. It currently supports a number of applications, including a multi-media editor that allows seamless editing of text, various kinds of graphics, and animations.
The third main piece of Andrew is the Andrew Message System, or AMS. The AMS, which makes heavy use of the file system and the toolkit, provides a large-scale mail and bulletin board system. It transparently supports messages which include text, pictures, animations, spreadsheets, equations, and hierarchical drawings, while also supporting "old-fashioned" text-only communication with low-end machines such as IBM PCs and with the rest of the electronic mail world. The Andrew Message System has in recent years become widely available. While the Carnegie Mellon installation is still the largest by some measures, there are other

† The Andrew File System technology, AFS 3.0, is a product of Transarc Corporation.

large Andrew sites, one of which has a bulletin board system at least twice as large as Carnegie Mellon's. This paper primarily reflects experience with the system at Carnegie Mellon however, as that is where the system was developed, has been used for the longest time, and has been most readily observed by the authors.

There are many parts to the Andrew Message System, including several non-multimedia user interfaces for reading mail and bulletin board messages from low-end terminals and PCs. There are also several AMS subsystems that have relatively small user interface components, such as the distributed message delivery system. A detailed description of the Andrew Message System is beyond the scope of this paper and can be found elsewhere (Rosenberg, Everhart & Borenstein, 1987; Borenstein, Everhart, Rosenberg & Stoller, 1988; Borenstein & Thyberg, 1988; Borenstein, Everhart, Rosenberg & Stoller, 1989). This paper will concentrate on the high-end user interface, the "Messages" program, and on the manner in which it has proven to be particularly conducive to cooperative work.

Messages: the system functionality

Although the AMS is a complex system made of many parts, to most users the "AMS" is virtually synonymous with the Messages user interface program, which is all they actually see of the AMS. Messages presents a basic user interface that is quite similar to many other mail and bulletin board readers, easing the learning process for many users. Hidden behind the superficial similarity, however, is a wealth of powerful features that await the interested user.

THE MESSAGES WINDOWS

Messages runs under any of several window management systems, the most common of which is the X11 window system from MIT (Scheifler & Gettys, 1987). The program can open multiple windows on the screen, but typically the novice user is confronted with the single window shown in Figure 1, in which the screen is divided into several subwindows for message bodies, message "captions" (one-line summaries), and the names of message "folders" (collections or directories of messages analogous to mail classes in some other systems).

Within this main window, the novice user can do everything one might need to do in the course of *reading* mail and bulletin board messages. The most common actions—selecting a new message or folder—are accomplished by pointing and clicking. Other actions, such as deleting messages, are available via the standard Andrew pop-up menu mechanism. For the novice user, there is never any reason to touch the keyboard in the course of reading messages.

To send a message, a user may either choose the Send Message menu item or one of the *Reply* menus. This will cause a new "messages-send" window to appear on the user's screen, as pictured in Figure 2.

MULTIMEDIA FEATURES

A major area in which Messages offers more functionality than most mail and bulletin board systems is in the integrated manner in which it includes formatted text and multimedia objects. In Figure 3, for example, the user is reading a message that

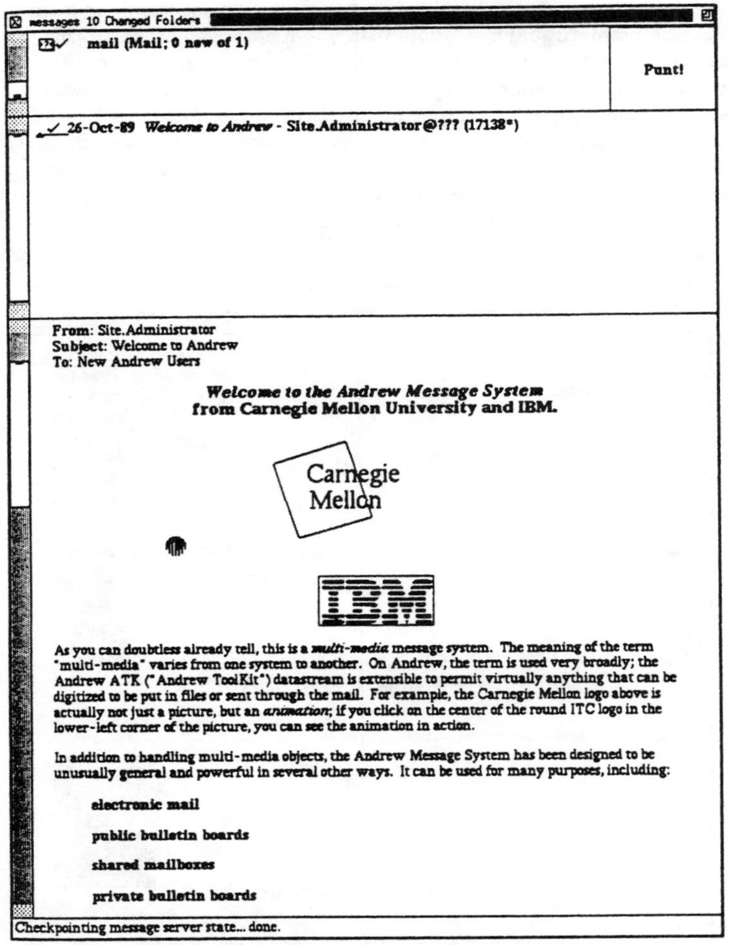

FIGURE 1. The main window of the Messages user interface as it might look to a new user receiving his first piece of multimedia mail.

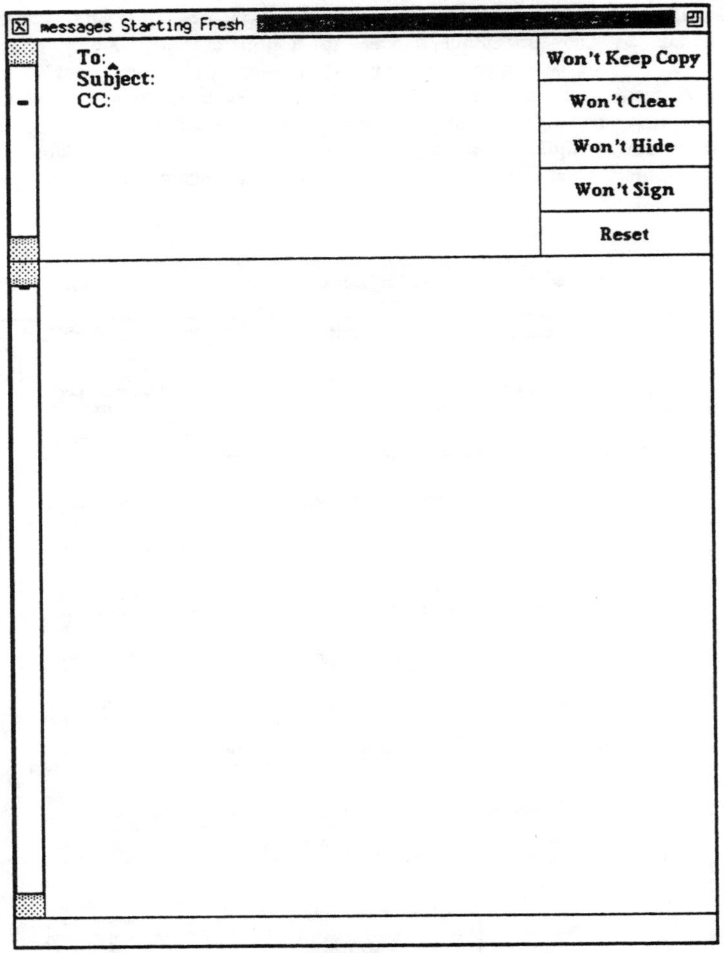

contains a picture within formatted text. It is important to note that users can read, print, and otherwise manipulate such messages with absolutely no knowledge about the multimedia system. Multimedia messages are fundamentally no different from the user's perspective, to any other messages in the system, and the user need learn nothing new in order to read most of them, and only a few new things in order to compose them.

The multimedia capability of Messages has, perhaps not surprisingly, proven to be one of its most admired and successful features. Crucial to its success has been the

FIGURE 2. The message-sending window.

fact that novices can receive and appreciate multimedia features with essentially no extra effort or learning. Also critical has been the ease with which new and casual users can master a subset of the multimedia authoring capabilities and still get substantial benefit from that subset. Nearly all Messages users quickly learn, for example, the ease and value of using multiple fonts within mail messages.

ACTIVE MESSAGE FEATURES

Another aspect of Messages that has proven extremely useful and popular is a set of features known collectively as "active messages". These are a set of specialized

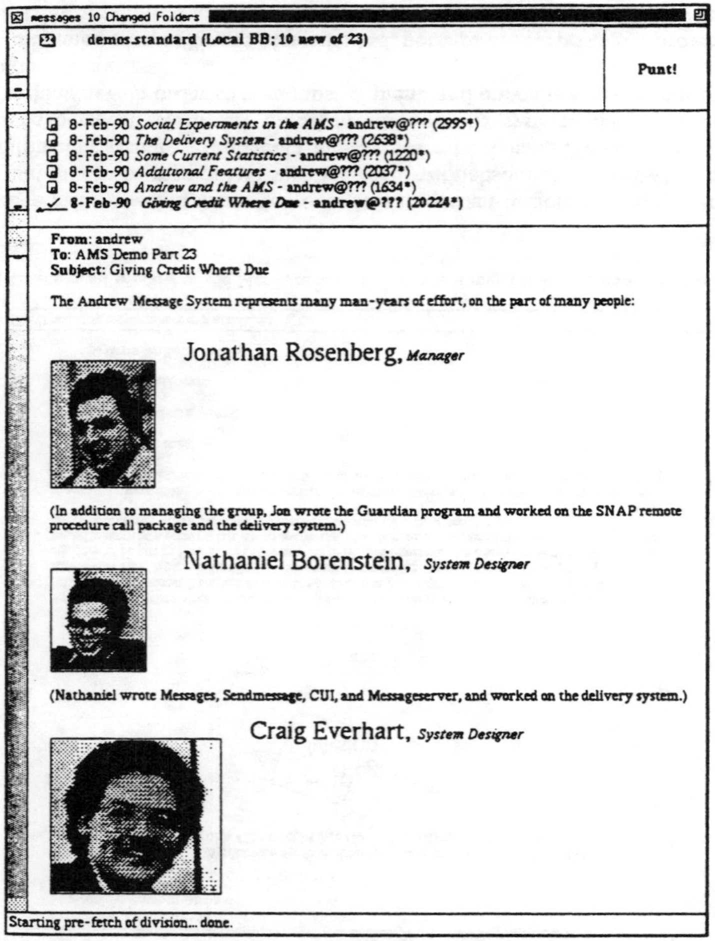

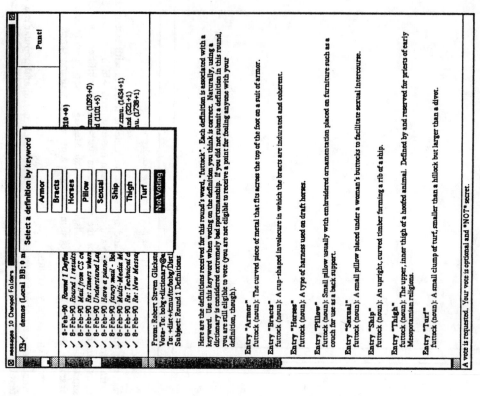

FIGURE 4. A "vote" message, inviting the reader to answer a question and have that answer automatically sent back to a specified destination.

FIGURE 3. A mail message in which a raster image is embedded within formatted text.

message types that carry with them, in addition to a normal (and possibly multimedia) message body, information that directs a particular interaction with the user. For example, one type of active message is the "vote" message. Here special headers direct the user interface to ask the user a multiple choice question, the answer to which will be mailed to a designated address for collection and tabulation. Figure 4 shows a user reading a vote message. In addition to votes, the Andrew Message System supports four other types of active messages: return receipt requests, enclosures, folder subscription invitations, and redistribution notices. (See Borenstein et al., 1989, for details on active messages).

As with multimedia messages, active messages require no special training to be of value to the receiver. For the receiver, they appear simply as messages that magically bring up dialog boxes and ask questions using mechanisms that are easily understood. The amount of expertise required to create an active message is also surprisingly small and is easily mastered by new users of the system.

It seems likely that the notion of "active messages" can be generalized substantially. This is the subject of recent research by Borenstein, unpublished data.

THE FLAMES MESSAGE FILTERING LANGUAGE

The AMS provides an embedded LISP-like language called FLAMES (Filtering Language for the Andrew Message System) that can be used to automatically classify new mail when it arrives. By default, new mail is placed in an automatically-created folder called "mail". However, a FLAMES program can sort incoming mail by keywords, by sender, or by any other aspect of the mail message, and can automatically place mail in the correct folder. (It is important, however, that the system will not automatically show the user the new messages in those folders.) Indeed, a FLAMES program can even reject mail by returning it to its sender, or it can automatically process the mail and send out an answer. The most common use for personal FLAMES programs is to automatically sort new incoming messages into folders. Beyond this, however, several complex FLAMES-based applications have been developed, and the Advisor system, to be described later in this paper, relies heavily on FLAMES for message processing.

PRIVATE BULLETIN BOARDS AND NEW BULLETIN BOARD CREATION

The Andrew Message System supports a rich and flexible set of protection and configuration options that facilitate group communication. In particular, the protection mechanisms permit the creation of public bulletin boards, private boards (readable and postable only by members of a group), official bulletin boards (readable by all, postable only by a few), administrative and advisory bulletin boards (postable by all, readable by only a few), administrative and advisory bulletin boards (postable by all, readable by only a few), and various hybrids thereof. In addition, the protection mechanisms can be (and are) used to allow, for example, a secretary to read and process someone else's electronic mail. (Indeed, a secretary could create something like a magazine for an employer, containing only those pieces of the employer's mail that the secretary thought the employer would really want to see.) The rich protection options make it possible to use message "databases" in innovative ways, as will be illustrated later in this paper.

CUSTOMIZATION OPTIONS

Most of the optional features that have been described are relatively easy to learn. Beyond this however, the Messages program is radically customizable using mechanisms that require substantially more expertise. The Andrew Toolkit, on which Messages is based, provides several such mechanisms, on several levels. In particular, it includes an "init file" mechanism, which offers a simple macro facility for creating compound commands. For situations where such a simple facility is inadequate, the toolkit includes Ness, an extension language described in Hansen (1990), which allows fully programmable customizations and extensions to the behavior of AMS, as well as the creation of powerful interactive objects that can be sent and received with Messages.

Though these mechanisms are complex enough to require substantial time and expertise to master, they are sufficiently useful and accessible to have been used on many occasions to create customized or extended versions of the AMS for specialized purposes, one of which will be discussed at some length later in this paper.

OTHER ADVANCED FEATURES

The AMS supports many other advanced features, too many to describe in detail here. These include:

- Electronic "magazines" which allow one user to act as an "information filter" for many other users and thus reduce the problem of "information flood".
- An unusually rich set of mechanisms for replying to messages.
- Support for easily including excerpts from one message in another in an aesthetically pleasing way.
- Heuristic validation of destination addresses.
- A rich set of variants on the basic notion of "subscribing" to a message folder.
- A large amount of functional support for manipulating message folders.
- Mechanisms for marking groups of messages and manipulating them as a group.

LEARNING ABOUT AND USING THE OPTIONAL FEATURES

As the Messages interface evolved, in every case where a choice had to be made between the needs of novices and the needs of experts, the default behavior of the program was targeted at novice users. The resulting program is undeniably easy for novices to use. For experts, the desire for extended functionality is accommodated through the use of options.

This in general, is a tricky and risky enterprise, because there is really no difference between a non-existent feature and a feature that the expert doesn't know about or can't figure out how to use. In order to successfully meet the needs of experts, it was important to ensure that no major expertise would be required in order to use the expert-oriented features.

The most important mechanism by which this is accomplished in the Messages program is the "Set Options" interface. In any message-reading window, the user can choose the Set Options menu option. When this menu action is initiated, the display is altered, as shown in Figure 5. Here the contents of the "captions" area have been replaced with a scrollable list of user-settable options, and the "bodies" area now displays a scrollable set of option-related information, including interaction objects that can be used to actually change the options.

Using the "Set Options" interface, users can easily learn about and use a large number of sophisticated options. By the time they have exhausted the potential of this interface, they are already expert Messages users by any reasonable definition. Beyond this point, further customization is still possible using more complex mechanisms, as previously mentioned. Although the Andrew help system provides significant assistance to users who want to master these mechanisms, they remain significantly harder than the "Set Options" mechanism. Most users never even attempt to learn to use the other mechanisms, so it is important that the needs of the majority of sophisticated and expert users be satisfied by the use of "Set Options".

The myth of the power/usability trade-off

There is a popular and widespread belief among programmers and end users alike that a fundamental trade-off exists between easy-to-use, novice-oriented programs on the one hand and very powerful and customizable expert-oriented programs on the

difficult in practice. Basically, only three things are required:

(1) An easy-to-use, novice-oriented default interface.
(2) A large set of powerful features and options that are not visible or enabled for new users.
(3) A smooth, obvious and easy-to-use mechanism by which users can gradually learn about the more advanced features.

Of course, all three requirements are much more easily stated than done. In the case of Messages, these three requirements were successfully obtained only after a great deal of evolution, user testing, and independent evaluation. But it is important to understand that the popularity and success of the Messages interface was not attributable to any particular intuitive genius on the part of the builders, but rather to the process and environment in which the interface was developed.

The initial public releases of the Messages program in particular, satisfied almost none of the users. Novices found the screen layout of the initial version, which mixed folder names and the new messages within each folder in a single scrollable text region, to be confusing and unintuitive. Experts, meanwhile, were frustrated by the many features that had been omitted in the name of usability (and also expediency). In fact, the initial version was met with such hostility that it would have been reasonable to consider simply abandoning the whole project. The fact that the program was able to evolve into the popular interface described in this paper, is indicative of the fact that something did go right in the process by which the system evolved.

The first salient feature of that evolutionary process was the fact it was long and painful. It took about four years of full-time programming work by one person, with additional work by many others at many points. Most of this time was spent trying to get a great number of details right. It is not at all obvious how the process could have been significantly streamlined. There may simply be no substitute for sweat and hard work.

Another aspect of the evolution worth noting is that, from the second version on, the Messages program always had a large community of experienced users as a well as a continuous influx of novice users (in the form of incoming freshman students at CMU). The expert users helped guarantee the continuing accretion of expert oriented features, while the steady stream of new users ensured that the default settings would continue to be refined towards ease of use for novices.

Also crucial during this period, was the fact that Messages captured the attention of a number of non-technical specialists who helped to guide its evolution. The Andrew project was able to hire as consultants, a graphic designer to study the visual aspects of the program, technical writers to improve the documentation and interaction messages, and a human factors expert to study how novices and experts actually used the system and where they got stuck.

Most important, the Messages interface was able to evolve successfully because of the tenacity or stubbornness of many of the parties involved. The author bullheadedly proceeded from the assumption that nothing could possibly be wrong with the interface that couldn't be fixed with enough work—an attitude which, while it produced a good interface in the end, may well have produced a much bigger system than was strictly necessary. The managers supported the project un-

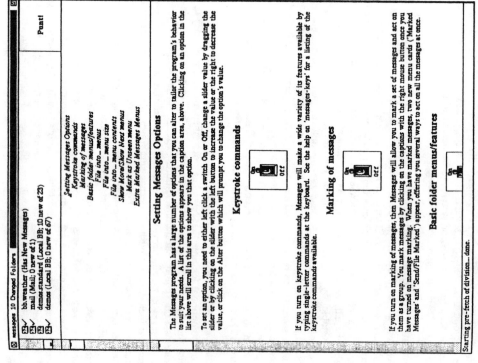

FIGURE 5. The "Set Options" interface, by which users gradually learn about and enable some of the more advanced capabilities of the system.

other. This belief persists in the absence of any really compelling evidence, and in spite of the existence of at least a few examples of programs that successfully "have it both ways".

Along with a handful of other programs, the Messages interface can be viewed as a proof-by-example of the fact that this is not a fundamental trade-off. There is no reason *in principle* why an interface cannot meet the needs of both experts and novice users. Indeed, doing so is startlingly simple in theory, though exceedingly

flaggingly, possibly fearing that the failure of the flagship application would produce domino-like conclusions of failure for the Andrew File System and the Andrew Toolkit, on which the message system was based. The funding had been secured for several years by the initial CMU/IBM contract, so there was essentially no one inclined to put the brakes on the project. Thus, a project that might have appeared to be headed for failure in the early years succeeded in some measure because it was given enough time to evolve naturally. Many other promising projects have surely died due to the absence of such patience and stability.

One useful practice that helped ensure that changes to Messages would be viewed as *positive* was that the author kept a permanent log of all functional changes made to the system. As the system matured through over one hundred releases of the software, this list became increasingly important. When changes were contemplated, the list could be used to determine why the current functionality worked the way it did. Without this list, it is easy to imagine an endless cycle of changes that undid each other to please diverse audiences. The list made it easier to relate new user feedback to the earlier feedback that had shaped the prior evolution of the system.

It is interesting to note that while the Messages interface grew into a form pleasing to experts and novices alike, it did not do this smoothly or continuously. After the disastrously unpopular first release in the spring of 1986, the next few versions were targeted explicitly at increasing the satisfaction of those who were currently using the system, and thus displayed an increasing bent towards expert users. Later, with the influx of new students in the fall, concern shifted abruptly to the difficulties experienced by new users of the system. This pattern continued for several years—expert-oriented refinements occurred in the spring and summer, and novice-oriented work was concentrated in the fall and winter. Good user interface projects are often driven by the needs of their users; in this case, the structure of the academic year was a fortunate coincidence that helped keep the Messages interface balanced between novice and expert concerns.

As the system developed, one of the last major pieces to be put in place was the "Set Options" interface. The evolutionary process just described had created a somewhat schizophrenic user base, with an artificially strong division between the novices and experts. Experts would request a new feature, it would be added, and an announcement would tell them explicitly what magic operation they had to perform in order to enable the new feature. But while established experts were able to assimilate one new bit of magic at a time, the growing body of such magic gradually became a major hurdle that prevented new users from growing into experts. That problem was substantially solved with the introduction of "Set Options".

Probably the hardest part of the evolutionary process was determining, whenever an expert-oriented change was made or contemplated, how that change would affect novices who were rarely part of the discussion about the functional change. It is very difficult for experts to predict how novices will react. Thus it is often hard to determine whether or not a new feature should be available by default. Indeed, the wrong decision was made on more than one occasion, though this was only found out via feedback from later novices. The only useful principle in this regard is to at least make an effort to view each new feature through novice eyes; this will catch many, though not all of the potential problems. The remainder simply have to be caught by experience with future novices.

To the authors, in hindsight at least, much of this appears to be little more than the application of common sense to practical user interface design. It is worth pausing, therefore, to consider why the myth of the power/usability trade-off is so widespread. Here too, the answer is mostly common sense: the above approach to interface evolution is quite costly, frustrating and time-consuming. It is so sufficiently hard and rare to build an interface that is exceptionally good for novices, or exceptionally good for experts, that most projects are more than satisfied with either achievement. For that reason, many users have rarely, if ever, been exposed to an interface that works well for both categories of user. The myth, then, is a simple case of unjustified extrapolation: "if I've never seen an elephant, then elephants must not exist".

Unfortunately, the analogy may apply equally to the future prospects for interfaces that work well for novices and experts. Like the elephants, which are being slaughtered wholesale for their ivory, such interfaces may be almost doomed to extinction by the laws of economics. It is far from clear that there is any substantial economic advantage to building programs that are tuned for both novices and experts, but it is all too clear that building them in such a way entails substantial extra costs. It seems sadly unlikely, therefore, that we will see a proliferation of such programs in the near future.

Putting it all together: cooperative work in the Andrew Message System

The Andrew Message System has proven to be exceptionally popular with its user community in general. Weekly statistics indicate that roughly 5300 people use it at Carnegie Mellon to read bulletin boards regularly. Even more users read their personal mail with the system. The AMS is also in use at over a hundred other universities and research sites. This would be indication enough that the system is a success; however, the greatest enthusiasm has in fact been found among those who are using the AMS for substantial cooperative activity. Most notable among these devoted users are the people who provide support services on Andrew at CMU. The Andrew Advisor is a singular example of real-life cooperative work, conducted with the Andrew Message System.†

THE ADVISOR SYSTEM

Centrally supported and distributed UNIX computing at CMU has a long and diverse history. The most recent milestone is the Andrew Project, as described above. Quite apart from the Andrew project is the much longer tradition of departmental UNIX computing, especially among such UNIX sophisticates as are to be found in the School of Computer Science. This tradition is a major influence on the development of centrally supported, distributed UNIX computing. Indeed, "collaboratively supported" is a better phrase than "centrally supported" since it indicates the (sometimes stormy) marriage of departmental and central facilities, systems administration, and user services.

† Substantially different versions of the following discussion of the Advisor electronic mail consulting service have appeared in Borenstein and Thyberg (1988) and Thyberg (1988).

The central computing organizations at Carnegie Mellon face unusual challenges in supporting their computing constituency. Four factors complicate the task. First, the distributed UNIX computing environment we provide has grown substantially beyond the Andrew project, and is now a complex assemblage of vendors' operating systems, the Andrew File System (now provided by Transarc Corporation), the X11 windowing environment from M, the Motif user interface offerings from the Open Software Foundation, third-party and campus-contributed software and, of course, the components of the Andrew project: ATK and AMS. Furthermore, this environment is provided for and supported by hardware from many manufacturers. Second, although the environment has been widely deployed and promoted, it is an ever developing, rapidly changing environment. As a result, it is not too inaccurate to characterize the computing environment as a 9000-user beta-test site. Third, campus computing expertise is widely, but unevenly, distributed. The users span the entire spectrum from technophobe to technophile. Fourth, the people involved in software development and maintenance, system administration, and user services belong to several organizations and work in different buildings.

To cope with these challenges, members of the Distributed Workstation Services group (DWS), with the help of the AMS group, developed an extensive electronic mail consulting service called "Advisor". Advisor presents the user with a single, private, and personal help resource for every conceivable problem a user might encounter in the complex system described above. The user simply mails a query to Advisor's account. In 24 to 48 hours, private mail comes back to the user from Advisor's account, prepared by a DWS staff member. In fact, however, Advisor is the front-end of a vast network of bulletin boards that enlist the cooperative efforts of all the professional staffs in the central computing organizations.

ADVISOR I

Advisor has been in use since January 1985. In the earliest days, it was simply another Andrew account. One person logged in as "advisor", read the incoming mail, handled it with what limited tools were available (online lists, hardcopy lists, hand written notes, and a good memory for the status of a given request), gathered information by talking with the programmers, and sent out replies to the user. This worked reasonably well during the deployment of Andrew when there were a small number of carefully selected users and the Andrew consultant had an office among the Andrew developers.

The first public Andrew workstation lab appeared in the spring of 1986. Shortly thereafter, Andrew accounts were made generally available. Advisor was immediately overwhelmed with mail. An additional consultant picked up Advisor duties, but there were always problems with how to divide the work between the two staff members and how to keep track of the status of any given message. A rudimentary method for classifying messages did exist, but the mechanism was clumsy, time-consuming and not that useful because all the messages were lumped together in one large, flat mail directory. The combination of the large volume of the easy questions and the genuine difficulty of the hard questions made it difficult to process Advisor mail in a timely fashion. We clearly required some way of getting almost immediate assistance from the right people in other organizations.

In the fall of 1986, the first version of what is now the Andrew Message System was released to campus. It marked a major advance in the integration of electronic communication. Personal mail and bulletin boards, though conceptually distinct, were now no longer different in kind. A public bulletin board and a user's private mailbox are both examples of message databases. The only real difference is the degree of accessibility to other users. As indicated above, the AMS supports a rich and flexible set of protection options that permit the creation of public bulletin boards, private bulletin boards, official bulletin boards, semi-private bulletin boards and shared mailboxes, and other variations on the theme. Furthermore, since message databases are built on top of the UNIX hierarchical directory structure, bulletin boards could now be nested within each other.

One of the authors hit on the idea of using bulletin boards as folders for classifying Advisor's mail. The authors created a suite of semi-private bulletin boards, postable by the whole community, but readable only by those in the central computing organizations, and wrote a program in a primitive stack-oriented language for automatically filing messages. (The stack-oriented language was the predecessor to the FLAMES language described earlier). The result was Advisor II.

ADVISOR II

Tom Malone, in his discussion of the Information Lens system (Malone, Grant, Turbak, Brobst & Cohen, 1987), has identified three fundamental approaches for handling large volumes of electronic information. The first approach, *cognitive filtering*, attempts to characterize the contents of a message and the information needs of the recipient. The system then matches messages about XYZ with readers who have expressed an interest in XYZ. The second approach, *social filtering*, focuses on the relationships between the sender and the recipient. In addition to the message's topic, the status of the sender plays a role in the reader's interest in the message. The final approach, *economic filtering*, looks at implicit cost-benefit analyses to determine what to do with a piece of electronic mail. Advisor II relied heavily on both cognitive and social filters as the criteria for automatic message classification.

Each message to Advisor that did not come from a member of a known set of Advisor "helpers" was assumed to be from a user requesting assistance. The message was then placed on a bulletin board called "*advisor.open*". The Advisor staff subscribed to this bulletin board and used it as an inbox for new questions. A copy of mail from the user was also placed in *advisor.trail*, to assist the staff in keeping track of requests, and to *advisor.qa*, to which answers would also eventually go, thus forming a repository of useful past work. Thus, the first criterion for sorting the mail was a social one—is the sender a helper or a user? The list of the helpers, that is, the staffs of the various computing organizations, had to be kept current as constants within the stack language program that did the automatic filing of messages.

An incoming question from a user was also copied to one of a series of subject-specific bulletin boards, according to keywords in the subject line. For example, if a subject line was "mail bug", the message was copied to *advisor.mail*. These bulletin boards, though not open to the public, were readable by the developers, system administrators, etc. who subscribed to the bulletin boards covering their areas of interest and responsibility. To continue the example, the AMS group members subscribed to *advisor.mail*, thereby increasing the likelihood of seeing only those messages generally relevant to them. Uninformative or nonexistent subject lines caused the message to be copied to *advisor.misc*. All good Advisor helpers were expected to subscribe to *advisor.misc*, in addition to their other subscriptions. Thus, the second criterion for sorting mail was a cognitive one—is the mail likely to be of interest to a particular group of people?

Cognitive and social filtering were combined at several critical junctures. For example, when the Advisor staff requested more information from the user, Advisor received a blind carbon copy of that request. Because the message was from Advisor, it did not go into *advisor.open* by virtue of the social filter which stipulated that Advisor was never to be taken as a user asking for help. Instead the message went to *advisor.trail* and to the relevant subject-specific bulletin board by virtue of cognitive filtering of the subject line. Another example was in the processing of contributions from Advisor helpers. A helper would see a question on some topical bulletin board. By choosing the Reply to Readers menu option (which prepends "Re:" to the same subject line as the user's initial post), the helper sent the answer, not to the user, but directly back to that subject-specific bulletin board. By virtue of social filtering, mail from helpers never went into *advisor.open*, but only to some topic-oriented bulletin board. And when a final answer was sent to the user, the blind carbon receipt once again bypassed *advisor.open* because it was from Advisor and ended up on *advisor.trail* and the correct topical bulletin board. In addition, the Advisor would carbon copy the final answers to the *advisor.qa* bulletin board. Unfortunately, the questions and answers were not paired, but in chronological order, due to early limitations in the AMS.

To summarize: the Advisor staff answered questions from *advisor.open* as they were able. They kept an eye on the relevant subject-specific bulletin boards for help with the difficult problems. Having collected the information from the helpers, the Advisors sent polished answers back to the users. As far as the users could see, they had sent mail to Advisor and received an answer from Advisor. The fact that there was additional internal consultation was kept behind the scenes.

EVALUATION OF ADVISOR II

The key feature of the first automated Advisor mechanism was the automatic filing of messages into subject-specific bulletin boards. The positive effect of this was two-fold. First, messages came to the immediate attention of the other technical groups. Often, the Advisor staff found that someone in another group had already answered the question before Advisor had even looked at it. This kind of pro-active assistance was greatly appreciated. Second, because requests for more information and final answers passed back to the subject-specific bulletin boards, the other groups could provide problem-solving advice and assure technical accuracy.

However, the negative effects outweighed the positive. First, poorly phrased questions from the users led to many "misclassifications". The message filing algorithm worked quite well, but so many subject lines were virtually contentless, e.g. "Help!", that far too many messages ended up on *advisor.misc*: close to 50%

of all mail to Advisor, according to the authors' estimate. Without better characterization of the message's content in the subject line, the Advisor staff were helpless to get the right mail to the right parties. The designers of Advisor considered the possibility of also searching the body of a message for sort keys, but the pre-FLAMES filtering language was not powerful enough to support free-text information retrieval techniques. Advisor settled for pattern matching on the subject line, rather than suffer too many false keyword hits.

Second, with every question going to a subject-specific bulletin board, the Advisor helpers had no easy way to distinguish between the questions the Advisor staff knew how to answer and those they didn't. Hence, they wasted time answering some questions unnecessarily and neglected other questions for which help really was required. In retrospect, it seems like a truism, but actual use of the mechanism vividly showed that cooperative work disintegrates if what is expected, and from whom, is not clearly articulated. Computer-supported methods can just as easily exacerbate the problem of undefined expectations as alleviate it.

Third, because every blind carbon from Advisor and every message from an Advisor helper also went to the subject-specific bulletin boards, these soon became too cluttered to be of much use. On the one hand, helpers got tired of wading through them. On the other, Advisor, at that time, had no way to show a message and all the replies to it in a single chain, so it was sometimes very hard to find the answers that were already available. There is nothing so deadly to cooperation as seeming to ignore another's efforts. Despite Advisor's best intentions, this problem appeared far too often.

Fourth, because every question and every answer went to *advisor.qa*, but the question and the answer were not adjacent messages, *advisor.qa* proved to be virtually worthless as a resource for the Advisor staff.

These four failings were compounded by the rapidly growing amount of mail being sent to Advisor. More staff were needed, contributing to difficulties working from a single inbox, and the helpers were becoming frustrated beyond their willingness to assist in the support of Andrew. It was clear that Advisor needed a significant overhaul.

ADVISOR III

The third version of the Advisor system was implemented in 1988, and, with the exception of the recent changes described below, Advisor III represents the current state of the system. In Advisor III, the only automatic sorting of incoming mail is by the day it arrived. This sorting is done by a FLAMES program. Mail goes into one of *advisor.inbox.monday*, *.tuesday*, etc. Student Advisors are each responsible for a particular day's worth of Advisor mail. They acknowledge every piece of user mail, handle most of the requests, and then cross-post the tough questions on topic-oriented bulletin boards with names like "*advisor.helpbox.mail*". Figure 6 gives a sampling of the current suite of helpboxes. They are very similar to the "magazines" mentioned previously—they are, in essence, journals compiled by the Advisor staff of just those questions that require the help of some other group to answer. The technical staffs subscribe to appropriate helpboxes and to the parent bulletin board, *advisor.helpbox*. Posts to the parent bulletin board notify Advisor helpers of the

question came in collects the information posted to the helpbox and sends a well-crafted reply to the user.

In addition to the helpboxes, there are *advisor.questions* and *advisor.trail* which provide rudimentary measurement and tracking. Copies of the incoming user mail get placed in *advisor.questions* and *advisor.trail* automatically, thanks to the FLAMES program. Monthly daemons take messages off these bulletin boards and archive them in date-stamped subsidiary bulletin boards, for example, *advisor.questions-Apr-1990*. There is even an Advisor bulletin board, *advisor.daemons*, where the daemons report their activities.

To assist Advisors in getting good answers to the users, a collection of interesting questions and their answers is generated on *advisor.outbox*, which replaces *advisor.qa* from Advisor II. The Advisor uses improved message-filing commands to move back-to-back question/answer pairs to the *advisor.outbox*. Also, there are two bulletin boards for internal dialog; *advisor.discuss*, for meta-Advisor debate and general Advisor information, and *advisor.official* where official pronouncements from other groups can be posted. *Advisor.official* is how Advisor receives such technical and policy "FYI" ("For Your Information") items, insuring that every Advisor sees the information, not just the Advisor on the day the FYI was sent.

It is important to note that Advisor III no longer applies any social filtering to separate the folks who are likely to be qualified to send us official FYIs from those who are not. Staff in other groups who wish to send us an official FYI are simply told to send it directly to the address "*advisor + official*".† We apply social pressure on our peers should we ever get information on this channel that is not accurate or useful. In fact, what usually happens is that the Advisors themselves and their supervisors see official pronouncements elsewhere and resend them to *advisor + official*. Another benefit of removing Advisor II's social filtering mechanism is that we no longer discriminate against staff; our peers are able to ask questions of Advisor just as our users do. And by no longer having to maintain lists of who are the helpers, we have been able to expand our assistance base significantly since it is trivial to create and maintain an access group for a particular helpbox using the protection mechanisms mentioned earlier.

EVALUATION OF ADVISOR III

By putting human intelligence to work at the heart of the system, the Advisor staff solved in one stroke several of the problems that troubled Advisor II. First, Advisor can support a far more fine-grained suite of helpboxes than it could with automatic filing. Poorly phrased subject lines are less of a concern because humans read the mail and digest its contents before passing it to a topical bulletin board. Second, when an Advisor staff member puts a question on a helpbox bulletin board, everyone knows this means help is genuinely needed. Third, because clutter does not automatically accumulate in the helpboxes, these have become "high-content" bulletin boards that the programmers and administrators feel are worth

---

† The Andrew Message System interprets any address of the form "userid + text" to be deliverable to the user named on the left of the "+" character. It is up to the FLAMES program processing that user's mail box to take whatever action the user would like, keying off the text to the right of the "+" character. If the user has no FLAMES program, or his FLAMES program doesn't recognize the text, the message is dropped off into the user's mail folder.

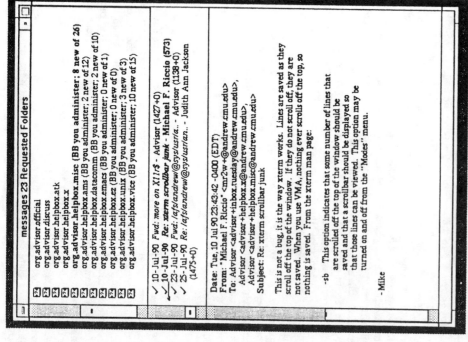

messages   23 Requested Folders

```
  org.advisor.official
  org.advisor.discuss
  org.advisor.helpbox.atk
  org.advisor.helpbox.x
  org.advisor.helpbox.misc (BB you administer; 8 new of 26)
  org.advisor.helpbox.ams (BB you administer; 2 new of 12)
  org.advisor.helpbox.datacomm (BB you administer; 2 new of 10)
  org.advisor.helpbox.emacs (BB you administer; 0 new of 1)
  org.advisor.helpbox.ez (BB you administer; 0 new of 0)
  org.advisor.helpbox.unix (BB you administer; 3 new of 3)
  org.advisor.helpbox.vice (BB you administer; 10 new of 15)

  10-Jul-90  Fwd: more on X11/$ - Advisor (1427+0)
  10-Jul-90  Re: xterm scrollbar junk - Michael F. Riccio (573)
  23-Jul-90  Fwd: [afs/andrew/@sys/usr/a... - Advisor (1138+0)
  25-Jul-90  Re: [afs/andrew/@sys/usr/an... - Judith Ann Jackson
             (1475+0)
```

```
Date: Tue, 10 Jul 90 23:43:42 -0400 (EDT)
From: "Michael F. Riccio" <mr2w+@andrew.cmu.edu>
To: Advisor <advisor+inbox.tuesday@andrew.cmu.edu>,
  Advisor <advisor+helpbox.x@andrew.cmu.edu>,
  Advisor <advisor+helpbox.misc@andrew.cmu.edu>
Subject: Re: xterm scrollbar junk

This is not a bug, it is the way xterm works. Lines are saved as they
scroll off the top of the window. If they do not scroll off, they are
not saved. When you use VMA, nothing ever scrolls off the top, so
nothing is saved. From the xterm man page:

  -sb  This option indicates that some number of lines that
       are scrolled off the top of the window should be
       saved and that a scrollbar should be displayed so
       that those lines can be viewed. This option may be
       turned on and off from the "Modes" menu.

  -Mike
```

FIGURE 6. A partial listing of the Advisor suite of bulletin boards; a sampling of helpboxes.

---

creation of a new helpbox, give a synopsis of its purpose, and invite them to subscribe. All this is done automatically, via folder subscription invitations, one of the "active message" features mentioned above.

Some members of the technical staff prefer to receive as personal mail the postings to the helpbox they've agreed to monitor. FLAMES makes it trivial to combine any helpbox with a distribution list of interested individuals: these helpers get direct mailings while the bulletin board serves as a shared archive. The helpers' replies go back to Advisor' mailbox, where the FLAMES program processes them and, on the basis of a special reply-to header, places them on the correct helpbox and sends them to any associated distribution lists. The Advisor on whose day the

reading regularly. The pay-off for Advisor is a much more reliable information resource. And just in case there are a number of items pending on a given helpbox, the AMS now has a Mark Related Messages menu option which puts a marker beside all the messages in a given reply-chain. Advisor rarely misses a helper's contribution in the new scheme. Fourth, advisor.outbox is a useful repository of previously answered queries because the Advisors themselves decide to post only those question/answer pairs that are likely to be of future use. The questions are now adjacent to their answers with the addition of the message filing command, Append to Folder, which takes a set of marked messages and adds them to the end of a folder, rather than shuffling them into the folder in chronological order.

In summary, though Advisor III lacks the pro-active help and the quality assurance that was evident in Advisor II, the Advisor staff is better equipped to handle the load than before. Currently, Advisor receives, on average, 450 new messages per month; 714 messages received is the current single-month record. Note that these are new requests from users; the total number of messages that pass through the Advisor system, including help from Advisor helpers, requests for more information, and replies to users, averages 50 messages per day, or 1500 per month. The student Advisors do an admirable job of performing triage on incoming mail. Full-time DWS staff now function much more as Advisor supervisors, taking areas of technical responsibility, expediting helpbox requests, and insuring that the answers that go out from Advisor are timely and accurate. Messages in Advisor III filter up "manually" through different levels of expertise: the simplest questions are answered by the students, the harder ones are answered by the full-time consultants, and the hardest are tackled by the programmers and administrators themselves. At each level, humans work diligently and efficiently to minimize time-delays inherent in the system. But all parties involved feel that the Advisor scheme focuses and streamlines their efforts.

There were, however, some aspects of Advisor III that cried out for significant improvement. First, there was the problem of correctly routing follow-up mail to the inbox where the initial mail was placed. For example, if the first piece of mail about a particular problem came on Monday and thus was placed in advisor.inbox.monday, how would Monday's Advisor continue a dialog with the user on Tuesday, without having all that mail end up in the inbox of the Tuesday Advisor? If the follow-up mail is delivered to the Tuesday Advisor, parallel processing or deadlock can occur as both Tuesday's and Monday's Advisors try to figure out what's going on.

Second, we had no good way of tracking requests to Advisor. We would have liked to have been able to find out quickly, for any particular piece of mail from a user, when that mail arrived, who on the Advisor staff first handled it, who in some other organization was then working on it, what the current status of the item was. This was just one aspect of a larger need for good monitoring tools on Advisor. We needed ways to measure the flow of questions, their types, the steps taken to answer them, and the mean time to find an answer for a user.

Third, Advisor handles a huge load of routine items like requests for more disk quota. These are matters that rarely require attention from the Advisor staff, save to pass them along to a system administrator and send the users an acknowledgment of receipt. It would have been nice if it took little or no effort to handle such requests.

Fourth, routine filing operations were tedious and error-prone. For example when closing an interesting exchange with a user, the Advisor had to move mail one by one, into advisor.outbox. The messages that constituted the dialog were likely to be spread around in the inbox and were not necessarily connected by the same subject line. The Advisor would have to rummage around and find all the relevant messages, get them over to advisor.outbox in the correct order, and then delete the entire set from the inbox.

How the designers of Advisor have addressed these concerns, and what issues remain for future exploration, is discussed in the remainder of this paper.

ADVISOR TODAY

The Advisor III system was sufficiently successful to leave the basic scheme unaltered. Incoming messages are still classified primarily by the date of receipt, and then filtered upward as necessary through human action, allowing the simplest questions to be responded to by the least-expert Advisors. However, the authors believe that the powerful automatic classification features Messages provided encouraged over-automation. in Advisor II and that Advisor III was in large part a reaction against such over-automation. The further development of Advisor has been evolutionary, incremental, and in the direction of adding more automation back into the system. This time, automatic mail handling features have been added in a much more selective, principled, and informed way than was the case in the crude keyword-classification mechanisms of Advisor II. Automation has been added where it could solve specific problems in the Advisor mechanism, rather than attempting to automate the entire process at once.

Structuring routine advisor actions

While the Advisor designers were concerned to solve in a piecemeal fashion particular shortcomings with Advisor III, the authors believe that a pattern of development has been emerging which can be characterized as the application of the language-as-action paradigm (explicated in Winograd & Flores, 1986; Winograd 1988) to various aspects of the Advisors' actual work practices. This paradigm, along with the Information and Object Lens work of Malone, Grant, Lai, Rao and Rosenblitt, (1987) and Lai and Malone, (1988), has guided the Advisor staff toward the semi-formalizing of certain linguistic "steps" that Advisor frequently makes in the "language dance" from initial query to final answer.

We mentioned earlier that sorting Advisor mail by day creates the problem of how Monday's Advisor continues a dialog with a user on Tuesday, without getting in the way of the Tuesday advisor. This problem is solved with the Messages customization facilities mentioned earlier. The designers of Advisor have developed a suite of specialized message sending/replying commands on the Advisor menu card of the "messages-send" window as shown in Figure 7. These commands, which are also bound to keys, insert a special reply-to message header on the outgoing mail. That mail, and all mail in reply to it, get sorted into the correct day's inbox by virtue of that header. So even though the follow-up reply from the user comes in on Tuesday, it still goes to the Monday inbox, where Monday's Advisor is waiting for it. This mechanism is not foolproof. For example, a user may send in a piece of mail

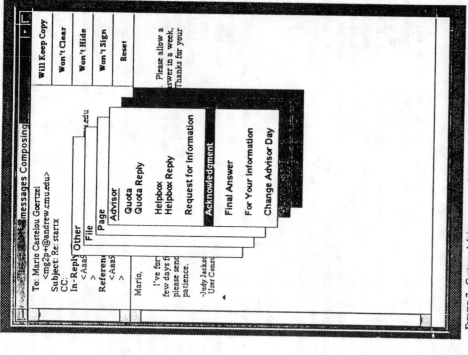

FIGURE 7. Custom Advisor commands for sending or replying to users' mail.

at 11:59 pm on Monday and follow it at 12:01 am on Tuesday with another piece of mail about the same matter, but with a completely different subject line. Since no reply from Advisor has come to the first message to provide the hook on which to hand subsequent dialog, the two messages are going to end up on different inboxes and the Monday and Tuesday Advisors are going to have to work it out. Still, the special reply-to header works in most cases to route extended mail exchanges correctly.

Notice in Figure 7 that these commands make no mention of any particular day of the week. The day-specific special message header is correctly inserted by virtue of an environment variable, *DAY*, which conditions the behavior of this single set of commands automatically and appropriately. This variable is set for each Advisor in a personal setup file he invokes whenever he logs into the Advisor account. Should this setup mechanism fail and the *DAY* variable be undefined, the sending/replying commands will prompt the Advisor for which day of the week it is that he is now answering. The Advisor can enter the day on the fly and can also set *DAY* for the rest of the session with the Change Advisor Day menu action. Staff members who work on more than one day's worth of incoming messages can, in a single Advisor session, trivially switch back and forth between, say, their identity as the "Tuesday advisor" and their identity as the "Wednesday advisor". With a single operation, they change all of the special header information that identifies and tracks their correspondence in these roles.

The second problem, tracking the actions that have been taken in response to a user's request for assistance, is one that Advisor continues to wrestle with. To provide the hooks for a solution, the Advisor staff introduced the notion of special message headers that indicate the "state" of each piece of Advisor mail in the progression from initial acknowledgment to closure. State is automatically set by use of the four sending/replying commands shown in Figure 7: Acknowledgment, Request for Information, For Your Information, and Final Answer, each of which marks the outgoing message with a distinct state message header: "ACK", "RFT", "FYI", and "ANS", respectively. A reply from the user to an Advisor message of a particular state can inherit the same state message header, which in turn can be processed by either Ness or FLAMES to generate rudimentary tracking and measurement. For example, one could go to advisor.trail, start with a user's initial request, and trace the entire exchange, noting Advisor's acknowledgment of the query, all requests for and provision of further information, and what Advisor believed to be the closing message. If the user replies to that "final answer" it indicates that the matter is still open. Unfortunately, there is currently no way to go back and change the state of Advisor's first "final answer" to something like "first try at an answer", "second try at an answer", and so on. As we have said, tracking a user's request is not yet fully developed in the current Advisor system.

The third area of concern in Advisor III is that of quickly handling the large volume of mail that requires nothing more than "message-shuffling" on Advisor's part. The most frequent request of this sort is the request for more disk quota. The Advisor neither dictates nor applies the quota policy and does not have the privileges required to actually change a user's quota. Thus, the Advisor does little more than acknowledge the user's request and pass it along to the Accounts group,

who makes the judgement whether additional quota should be granted and perform the necessary steps required to increase the user's quota. To streamline handling quota requests, the Advisor staff created the pair of menu actions Quota and Quota Reply, also shown in Figure 7. First the Advisor chooses the Forward menu action to create a message-sending window with the user's mail in it, giving the Advisor the opportunity to make annotations if warranted. Then the Advisor chooses Quota. The user's message is automatically addressed to *advisor.helpbox.quota*, and a command is run to generate some information about the requester's current disk usage. The results from this command, which are captured in a distinctive font, are prepended to the user's text and the resulting message is sent off with the state

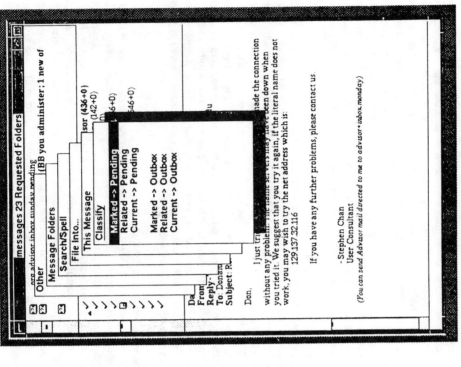

FIGURE 8. Custom commands for transferring Advisor mail into the *advisor.outbox*.

message header, "Quota", which gives us a hook for measuring the number of quota requests Advisor processes. The message also has a modified reply-to header so that both the user and Advisor will be notified by the Accounts group when the user's quota request has been processed. The Advisor acknowledges the user by using Quota Reply, which sends a message containing a prepared text about policy and current resource constraints.

The pair of commands, Helpbox and Helpbox Reply, are simply generalizations of the quota operation. After choosing the Forward menu action, addressing the mail-to-be-forwarded to the correct helpbox, and adding any commentary the Advisor thinks will be useful to the readers of that helpbox, the Advisor chooses the menu action, Helpbox. The state message header "Helpbox" is added to the message and the message goes to the specified helpbox. The state message header is a hook both for tracking Advisor's actions in getting an answer for the user, particularly to remind one of pending requests for assistance, and for measuring the frequency with which Advisor asks for help from the technical staff.

The fourth problem with Advisor III was the clumsiness of certain filing operations that Advisor frequently performed. Compound commands on the *Classify* menu card of the messages-reading window, shown in Figure 8, were created to make these actions easy. The menu action Current → Outbox appends the currently displayed message to *advisor.outbox* and removes it from the inbox. The menu action Related→Outbox gathers the messages that are in the same reply-chain as the currently displayed message, appends them to the outbox, and removes them from the inbox. If necessary, the Advisor can generate a reply-chain with the Mark Related Messages menu action, mark additional relevant messages by pointing and clicking, and then use the menu action Marked→outbox to move the entire group of messages to the outbox, deleting them from the inbox.†

In summary, the four problem areas for Advisor III have been attacked by putting some structure into common Advisor behaviors. The designers of Advisor have made some investigation of the varying illocutionary implications of such linguistic actions as sending an acknowledgement or requesting more information. Though there is much more fruitful development to be done in this area. the authors are satisfied that this kind of approach is the right one for the principled addition of automation to the Advisor service.

Linking support groups

The Distributed Workstation Services group has for some time been exporting the Advisor concept and connecting the Advisor system to other help groups on campus. The most mature example to date is a bridge between the *advisor.helpbox.datacomm* bulletin board and a suite of bulletin boards attached to an account, dc0m, belonging to the Network and Communications group. Rather than have these folks subscribe to the Advisor helpbox as a second source of input to their group, the Advisor designers created a "hot link" between the two groups. When Advisor puts mail into its datacomm helpbox, it is automatically resent to dc0m with a special header. When someone in Data Communications replies to that mail, by virtue of that header, it comes back directly to Advisor's helpbox, just where the Advisor expects to find it. There are similar links to other groups who employ Advisor-like systems that we have exported for both academic and administrative use. In this way, DWS hopes to provide these groups with a common front-end to the community—mail to Advisor—while allowing them to use whatever internal consulting structures suit them best. It is our belief that a large part of Distributed Workstation Services' role is to enable this kind of distributed support.

† Another evolutionary change in the Advisor system has been the development of customized environments for each of the Advisor staff members. Staff members have developed their own auxiliary sub-systems, including additional bulletin boards for their own pending Advisor items, and have elaborately customized compound operations defined as well. The move-to-pending menu actions in Figure 7 are examples of a "personal" extension of the Advisor mechanism which has been adopted by all the Advisors.

Revealing Advisor's inner workings to users

Another subtle but useful change has been in making the hidden structure of the Advisor system more visible to sophisticated users. The Advisor system was heavily oriented from the very beginning to the notion that users would simply send mail to "advisor" and the right thing would happen automatically. That this is ideal for novice users is virtually self-evident. However, it has come to seem desirable to give expert users the ability to direct certain kinds of requests more specifically. (This is an interesting parallel to the general effort, in the Messages interface, to accommodate novices by default but to provide powerful and sophisticated features to those who want them.) Thus, for example, an expert can now send a security-related message to "advisor + security", and it will be delivered directly to the Advisor staff members concerned with security issues. In this case, not only is the message delivered more directly, it is also more private—fewer staff members will see what may be a rather sensitive message.

ADVISOR'S FUTURE

Structuring routine user actions

It would be nice if the Advisors did not have to handle such commodity services as quota requests, but had them forwarded immediately to the staff who do take care of such matters. However, the experience with automatic classification by keywords in Advisor II suggests that a simple keyword-based approach to routing such messages might well backfire. Instead, the Advisor staff is developing a combination of mail templates, Ness extension programs, and FLAMES programs that permit users to create semi-structured messages, similar in spirit though not in detail, to those of the Information Lens system (Malone, Grant, Turbak et al., 1987), which can then be reliably routed automatically. For example, a user might type a command such as "more-quota" and be presented with a new mail-sending window, containing an interactive form containing various headers, fields, and relevant information, some of which may be filled in automatically. The data thus generated is then used by Advisor's FLAMES program to send an appropriate acknowledgment automatically and route the mail directly to the right place, rather than have it filter through the normal Advisor mechanism. Once we work out the kinks in a limited domain like quota requesting, the Advisor developers hope to follow this prototype with interactive templates and FLAMES parsings for bug reports, requests for new features, and the like.

Automatic Advisor "claim checks" and social filtering

We indicated earlier that we have not completely solved the problem of routing all mail from a user about a given problem to a single Advisor's inbox. It has been proposed that the FLAMES file which processes incoming Advisor mail immediately sends back to the user a confirming message which will ask the user to send Advisor any further messages about the matter at hand by replying to this "claim check" message. While such a claim check could be implemented today, the Advisor staff feel it makes more sense to introduce this after we have supplied some Advisor-submission templates, because then the claim check that is returned can be made apropos of the type of query Advisor received. It is here Advisor may introduce social filtering again. For example, if the submission mechanism can automatically generate information about the status of the sender (e.g. faculty, staff, student, which department, etc.), then the handling of this mail, including the initial claim check, can be sensitive to the different needs of these constituencies and the (possibly) different computing policies that apply to various groups.

Structuring routine helper actions

Those who cooperate with Advisor by reading helpboxes and posting information there do so on a voluntary basis. It would be useful to develop tools for the helpers that semi-formalize their uptake of Advisor's requests for assistance. To design such tools will require careful thought about various illocutionary categories like directives—Advisor messages that attempt to get the helpbox reader to do something (e.g. answer the forwarded question), and commissives—helper messages that commit the helper to some action (e.g. fix some bug by a certain date). Furthermore, the helpers need some way to transfer ownership of a commitment, and both Advisor and the helpers need tools to facilitate the negotiation of help commitments, especially if they are subject to change as new information and technical and resource feasibilities warrant. Similarly, if the staffing model for Advisor changes significantly from that of an Advisor taking an entire day's worth of Advisor mail to a queue of requests that all the Advisors draw from, then there may be much greater need for internal mechanisms whereby different Advisor staff members can take up, transfer, and close responsibility for individual user requests. The work of Winograd and Flores, especially as it has begun to appear in software products like The Coordinator, is fundamental to our explorations in this area.

Tracking and measurement revisited

An experiment has been conducted with the Advisor database to use our FLAMES program to automatically generate an Informix database of tracking information about all the traffic through the Advisor system. This database, which was a course project for a group of students in the Social and Decision Science department, never went into full-scale use, largely due to a lack of programming resources. Nevertheless, the idea seems very promising, and also points strongly to the lack of database facilities as an underlying weakness in AMS. The Advisor staff is looking for additional resources to take up this project in earnest. The result will be a system parallel to Advisor's myriad bulletin boards that both the Advisors and their supervisors can use to get status on a particular user request, as well as to generate routine statistical measures and reports.

Question/answer service for users

The advisor.outbox is a fairly useful collection for Advisor's own use. But the notion of a database or a hyper-document of commonly asked questions and expert answers that grows in step with Advisor's question-answering is what we are aiming for. Such a tool would be enormously valuable to the Advisors themselves, their helpers, and other computing consultation services around campus. With careful user-interface design and expert system intelligence, it could also be most beneficial to the end user, provided that the information was timely, accurate, and easy to navigate. A recent example of the sort of system we would like to graft onto Advisor is the Answer Garden (Ackerman & Malone, 1990).

Other engines behind the AMS front-end

The infrastructure for the Advisor service was put together using AMS bulletin boards as much for the reason that was the tool we had available as for any intrinsic virtues of bulletin boards. Exploring other computer-based communication technologies would be a useful exercise. For example, computer conferences are a different breed of animal to bulletin boards. It would be very instructive to re-implement Advisor's helpboxes using an advanced conferencing system, one rich in mechanisms for assigning various roles and passing control of "the floor", in order to see how many of the tools for semi-formalizing Advisor and helper behaviors simply fall out as a consequence of the particular strengths of computer conferencing.

At a more fundamental level, it is clear to the authors that the Advisor service has nearly reached the limits of what current AMS bulletin boards can do as information repositories—AMS does not provide a general database mechanism, but Advisor often needs one. Then again, without AMS and its powerful kit of features and customization and extension mechanisms, the Advisor staff, who are neither academics nor researchers, but practising consultants and service providers, would likely never have pursued the vision of computer-supported cooperative consulting to the point where such limitations become apparent. When the son-of-AMS is available, whatever that might be, the designers of Advisors ars poised and ready to investigate the avenues of development outlined above.

Conclusions

The Messages interface has been highly successful as a user interface, easily learned and appreciated by novices, easily extended by experts, and powerful enough to support major cooperative work applications. Although one such program cannot be considered proof, it lends support to the notion that power and usability are not fundamentally incompatible. It demonstrates one approach to reconciling power and usability, which entails tailoring all default behavior to novices while providing a simple and graceful mechanism by which experts can extend its power.

The evolution of the Advisor system has taught its designers a great deal about computer-supported cooperative work. Our failed experiments have been the most instructive of all our experiences. But with each incarnation, Advisor feels more and more like an enduring technology for user support in times when central consulting services are lean and everyone looks to some form of distributed consulting to ease the load. We realize that we have only begun to scratch the surface, but we feel we are taking the right steps to exploit the ever-increasing power and sophistication of distributed computing in higher education. The Advisory staff, most of whom are not programmers, have proven able to use the expert-oriented features of the Andrew Message System to develop FLAMES programs, customized compound commands, hot links between support systems, Advisor-templates, and interfaces to alternative engines largely independent of the AMS developers. It is by virtue of putting these tools in the hands of cooperating workers that the Advisor system continues to be an interesting example of how the AMS supports a large, important, complex, "real-life" cooperative work application.

Messages is a part of the Andrew Message System, which was developed by Nathaniel Borenstein, Jonathan Rosenberg, Craig Everhart, Bob Glickstein, Adam Stoller, Mark Chance and Mike McInerny. Substantial parts of the Messages user interface reflect the suggestions and experiences of thousands of users, but most especially the suggestions of Dan Boyarski, Chris Haas, Chris Thyberg and Pierette Maniago, who devoted substantial time and effort to studying, deploying and extending the system. The Andrew Message System was built on top of the rich infrastructure provided by the Andrew File System and the Andrew Toolkit, which are themselves the product of a great deal of work by a great many top-notch software developers. The Andrew Message System and the Andrew Toolkit are part of the Andrew software as distributed on the X11R4 tape from MIT. They are freely available to all interested parties.

Advisor II was conceived by Chris Thyberg and implemented by Pierette Maniago, with help from Nathaniel Borenstein. Advisor III was designed and implemented by Chris Thyberg, Pierette Maniago, and Adam Stoller. Recent Advisor extensions are the work of Chris Thyberg, Wallace Colyer, Judith Jackson, Bob Glickstein and Michael Riccio. Continued thanks also go to our frontline Advisors over the years. They are the real answer-givers and they have been an unfailing source of useful suggestions for the improvement of the Advisor mechanism and of distributed user support in general.

Finally, none of the work described here would have been possible without the encouragement and support of some very enlightened and visionary management at both CMU and IBM. This paper was written with the support of equally enlightened management at Bellcore.

Judith Jackson helped substantially with the description in this paper of the Advisor system. The paper also benefited greatly from the comments of several anonymous reviewers, as well as Terilyn Gillespie, Peter Clitherow, Bob Kraut and Steve Rohall.

References

ACKERMAN, M. & MALONE, T. (1990). Answer garden: A tool for growing organizational memory. In *Proceedings of the Conference on Office Information Systems*, Cambridge, Massachusetts. New York: ACM Press.

BORENSTEIN, N. S. & GOSLING, J. (1988). UNIX Emacs as a test-bed for user interface design. In *Proceedings of the ACM SIGGRAPH Symposium on User Interface Software*, Banff, Alberta.

BORENSTEIN, N. S., EVERHART, C. F., ROSENBERG, J. & STOLLER, A. (1988). A multi-media message system for Andrew. In *Proceedings of the USENIX 1988 Winter Technical Conference*, Dallas, Texas. Dallas, TX: USENIX Association.

BORENSTEIN, N. S. & THYBERG, C. (1988). Cooperative work in the Andrew Message System. In *Proceedings of the Conference on Computer-Supported Cooperative Work, CSCW 88*, Portland, Oregon.

BORENSTEIN, N. S., EVERHART, C. F., ROSENBERG, J. & STOLLER, A. (1989). Architectural issues in the Andrew Message System. In E. STEFFERUD, O.-J. JACOBSEN & P. SCHICKER, Eds. *Message Handling Systems and Distributed Applications*. Amsterdam: North-Holland.

BORENSTEIN, N. S. (In press a). *Software Engineering and Other Delusions*. Englewood Cliffs, NJ: Prentice Hall.

BORENSTEIN, N. S. (In press b). CMU's Andrew project: a report card. *Communications of the ACM*.

BORENSTEIN, N. S. (1990). *Multimedia Applications Development with the Andrew Toolkit*. Englewood Cliffs, NJ: Prentice Hall.

HANSEN, W. (1990). Enhancing documents with embedded programs: how Ness extends insets in the Andrew Toolkit. In *Proceedings of IEEE Computer Society 1990 International Conference on Computer Languages*, New Orleans.

HOWARD, J. (1988). An overview of the Andrew File System. In *Proceedings of the USENIX 1988 Winter Technical Conference*, Dallas, Texas.

HOWARD, J., KAZAR, M., MENEES, S., NICHOLS, D., SATYANARAYANAN, M., SIDEBOTHAM, R. & WEST. M. (1988). Scale and performance in a distributed file system. *ACM Transactions on Computer Systems*, **6**, (1).

KAZAR. M. (1988). Synchronization and caching issues in the Andrew File System. In *Proceedings of the USENIX 1988 Winter Technical Conference*, Dallas, Texas.

KAZAR, M. & SPECTOR, A. (1989). Uniting file systems, *UNIX Review*, March.

LAI. K.-Y. & MALONE, T. (1988). Object lens: a spreadsheet' for cooperative work. In *Proceedings of the conference on computer-supported cooperative work*, CSCW 88, Portland, Oregon.

MALONE, T., GRANT, K. TURBAK, F., BROBST, S. & COHEN, M. (1987). Intelligent information-sharing systems. *Communications of the ACM*, **30**, (3).

MALONE, T., GRANT, K., LAI, K.-Y. RAO, R. & ROSENBLITT, D. (1987). Semi-structured messages are surprisingly useful for computer-supported coordination. In I. GREIF, Ed., *Computer Supported Cooperative Work: A Book of Readings*. San Mateo, CA: Morgan Kaufman.

MORRIS, J., SATYANARAYANAN, M., CONNER, M., HOWARD, M., ROSENTHAL, D. & SMITH, F. (1986). Andrew: a distributed personal computing environment, *Communications of the ACM*, **29**, (3).

MORRIS, J. (1988). Make or take decisions in Andrew. In *Proceedings of the USENIX 1988 Winter Technical Conference*, Dallas, Texas.

PALAY, A., HANSEN, W. KAZAR, M., SHERMAN, M., WADLOW, M., NEUENDORFFER, T., STERN, Z., BADER, M. & PETERS, T. (1988). The Andrew Toolkit: an overview. In *Proceedings of the USENIX 1988 Winter Technical Conference*, Dallas, Texas.

ROSENBERG, J., EVERHART, C. & BORENSTEIN, N. (1987). An overview of the Andrew Message System. In *Proceedings of SIGCOMM '87 Workshop, Frontiers in Computer Communications Technology*, Stowe, Vermont.

SCHEIFLER, R. & GETTYS, J. (1987). The X window system. *ACM Transactions on Graphics*, **5**, (2).

THYBERG, C. (1988). Advisor—an electronic mail consulting service. In *Proceedings ACM SIGUCCS User Services Conference XVI*, Long Beach. California.

WINOGRAD, T. & FLORES, F. (1986). *Understanding Computers and Cognition*. Norwood, NJ: Ablex Publishing Corp.

WINOGRAD, T. (1988). A language perspective on the design of cooperative work. In I. Grief, Ed. *Computer Supported Cooperative Work: A Book of Readings*. San Mateo, CA: Morgan Kaufman.

Active Mail: A Framework for Integrated Groupware Applications

Yaron Goldberg, Marilyn Safran, William Silverman and Ehud Shapiro
Department of Applied Mathematics and Computer Science
The Weizmann Institute of Science, Rehovot 76100, Israel

Abstract

What do conversations, legal contracts, technical papers, meeting schedules, and the game of Tic-Tac-Toe have in common with electronic mail? How can a multi-user application cause a new user to "get on board" in a way which is non-intrusive, can tolerate delayed response, and require little effort on the user's part?

A system for computer-mediated interaction, Active Mail provides a solution to both questions. Receivers of *active* messages can interact with the sender, with future recipients, and with remote, distributed multi-user applications. Persistent active connections are maintained in hierarchical, notifiable folders.

Our presentation of applications implemented within this framework includes a text conversation tool, a collaborative writing facility with a floor passing protocol and revision control management, an interactive meeting scheduler — and some distributed multi-user interactive games.

1 Introduction

Active Mail is a framework for implementing groupware, designed to support more effective computer-mediated interaction. Active Mail extends ordinary electronic mail with *active messages*, which are active entities that contain communication ports. An active message, manifested as a window on the user's screen, contains facilities that allow communication and cooperation with other users. In particular, it allows its receiver to interact with its sender, with other users to whom a copy of the message was sent, as well as with remote, distributed multi-user applications connected to a communication port in the message.

2 The Different Views of Active Mail

An Extension to Ordinary Electronic Mail

Electronic mail is convenient for human interaction because of its non-intrusive, informal nature, its ability to support both asynchronous and more immediate communication needs, and its ability to interoperate with other computer-based tools. It assumes no predefined roles for its users, both sender and receiver gain from using it, and no rigid format is required [4]. The universal nature of electronic mail is the source of its power, but also prevents it from supporting the specific needs of the two main modes of interaction for which it is used: computer-mediated conversations, and document exchange.

When electronic mail is used for computer-mediated conversation, users often find it hard to maintain continuity. To which message does the current one respond? What was the sequence of messages exchanged on a particular topic? When participants join a conversation, how can they be brought up to date?

When Active Mail is used, an instance of its *conversation agent* supports an ongoing asynchronous discussion among a dynamically changing group of users distributed across a network of client processors, and maintains a conversation log. A user can initiate an *active conversation* which can be sent to others (by the originator or by any of the current participants) at any stage of the discussion. When new participants join in by opening the relevant *active conversation* message in their input folders, they receive a copy of the log which (by definition) details the history of the conversation.

When electronic mail is used for exchanging documents, users often find it hard to maintain document consistency. What is the most recent version of the document? How can one distribute an update and maintain previous versions? How are multiple authors coordinated?

When Active Mail is used, an instance of its *document agent*, like a conversation agent, allows a dynamically changing group of users to collaborate by creating, sending, and modifying automatically updated *active documents*. A current *floorholder* status and queue of pending floor requests are maintained, and

Reprinted from D. Coleman (Ed.), *Groupware '92*, pp. 222-224. Morgan Kaufmann Publishers.

revisions are managed by interoperating with a Revision Control System (RCS) agent.

A Protocol for Computer-Initiated Interaction

The problem of computer-initiated interaction is of fundamental importance to groupware; the design of any groupware application must provide an answer to: *How can a multi-user application cause a new user to "get on board" in a way which is non-intrusive, can tolerate delayed response, and requires little effort on the user's part?* Active Mail offers a protocol and a user interface to achieve just that. When users of its *meeting scheduler agent*, for example, wish to schedule a meeting, they simply send an active "meeting scheduler" message to desired participants. The system places it in the appropriate input folders, and recipients can choose to interact whenever they wish. The interaction mimics the usual human meeting scheduling process by supporting negotiations between expected participants[1]. Note that these same people can discuss the meeting agenda on-line, and/or collaborate on related documents without leaving the Active Mail environment. The conversations, documents, and meeting scheduler itself are all simply specific instances of active messages.

A Tool for Maintaining Persistent Interactive Connections

When handling passive messages in electronic mail, two kinds of storage facilities are involved: the user mail-spool (or *in-tray*) where incoming mail resides, and the local file system, where old messages are saved in *folders*. Both forms are persistent, in that they survive logging out or computer shutdown.

Maintaining active messages is more of a challenge, as the messages can still communicate with the outside world. Active Mail provides a hierarchy in which the user's persistent *active* connections are maintained. Thus users may hold multiple connections to various agents in their private folders and yet not lose them when logging out. Each user's folder system consists of two components: the *input folder* where incoming active messages are placed—with a functionality similar to the user's ordinary mail-spool—and a folder hierarchy which functions like a private file system hierarchy.

In contrast to electronic-mail, active messages *change*, and the user should be alerted about those changes (e.g., a new contribution to a conversation has arrived, or the user's opponent in a chess game has moved). Hence the Active Folder system incorporates a *notification mechanism* [6]. An agent becomes *notified* after a modification has occurred; if its window is closed, the icon changes and beeps. A folder becomes notified if any of its member agents (including subfolders) becomes notified. Thus the modification of an agent may reach the root folder (and hence change the Active Mail icon if it is closed). Notification also affects open windows.

3   Active Mail Architecture

An Active Mail *configuration* consists of *agents*, interconnected via two-ported bidirectional *communication channels*. There are two types of agents: *users* and *applications*. An example of an Active Mail configuration is given in Figure 1.   We say that a user is a *participant* in an application if there exists a port connecting it to the application. Figure 1 shows two users, *User A* and *User B*, participating in two applications *Application 1* and *Application 2*. *User B* participates in an additional application not shown in the figure, and *Application 2* has an additional participant, also not shown in the figure.

An Active Mail agent with a given set of ports may change the configuration it is in by creating a new application agent, by sending a copy of one of its ports to a user, and/or by discarding one of its ports. It may also send messages to, and receive messages from, any of its ports. A participant in an application (*i.e.*, a user with a port *p* to an application) may initiate another user into the application by sending that user a copy of its port *p*. A user can leave an application by discarding its port to it.

Similarly, an application *A* having a port to some other application *B* may initiate an interaction between a user and the application *B* by sending to the user a copy of its port to *B*. Abstractly, users interact with applications via a bidirectional communication port. This abstraction is realized via windows on the user's screen. Each application comes with one or more application-specific windows, and all support a uniform way to view and interact with participants. Users are provided with an interface that allows them to spawn new application agents, as well as with a folder system, to manage their application ports.

---

[1] One of the main criticisms [4] of existing meeting schedulers is that they require all participants to maintain their schedule on-line using the same tool, and let various algorithms search through their calendars for vacant slots. Many consider this to be a breach of privacy, quite bothersome, and of little benefit to anyone but the meeting coordinator.

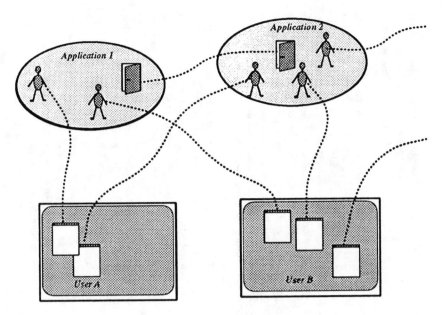

Figure 1: An Active Mail Configuration

4 Implementation and Future Directions

Active Mail is implemented under the Logix [7] distributed programming environment in a subset of the concurrent logic programming language FCP [7] which employs directed logic variables [5]. Its main aspect which requires support from the language is the need for communication ports to migrate. Concurrent logic languages are particularly suitable for supporting dynamic port migration, and the Directed Logic Variables (DLV) algorithm described in [5] provides a practical implementation of this capability over the datagram communication protocol of the Internet [1].

FCP has been interfaced with the X window system using the XView library (conforming to the OpenLook standard). An FCP transformer was also built to convert the output of an interface design tool (Sun Microsystems's Dev-guide) to FCP, enabling semi-automatic creation of new applications.

Active Mail can accommodate a wide range of applications. We are planning to refine the currently available applications and to provide additional ones.

The implementation of Active Mail is based on a single server. Although the DLV algorithm [5] may support a multi-server implementation, the lack of a recovery protocol that can sustain server failure prevents us from using it. We are working on such a recovery protocol, following ideas from [2].

The Active Mail architecture provides a powerful generalization of electronic mail, but does not provide a similar generalization of shared file systems. Its folders are private, and it has no notion of public, or shared, folders. We are working on a more general abstract architecture which supports such a notion of sharing.

References

[1] Comer D., *Internetworking with TCP/IP*, Prentice-Hall, second edition, 1991, pp. 434-435.

[2] Gaifman, H., Maher, M.J., and Shapiro, E., Replay, Recovery, Replication, and Snapshots of Nondeterministic Concurrent Programs, *Proc. ACM Conference on Principles of Distributed Computing*, ACM,1991.

[3] Goldberg Y., *Active Mail: A Framework for Implementing Groupware*, M.Sc. Thesis, The Weizmann Institute of Science, November 1991.

[4] Grudin J., *Seven Plus One Challenges in Understanding Social Dynamics for Groupware Developers*, CHI Conference, Tutorial Notes, 11, 1991.

[5] Kleinman A., Moscowitz, Y., Pnueli, A., Shapiro. E., *Communication with Directed Logic Variables*, In ACM conference of Principles of Programming Languages, 1991.

[6] McCarthy J. C. et al, *Four Generic Communication Tasks Which Must Be Supported in Electronic Conferencing*, To appear in acm/SIGCHI Bulletin, January 1991.

[7] Shapiro, E. (Editor), *Concurrent Prolog: Collected Papers*, Vols. 1 and 2, MIT Press, 1987.

Computer Systems and the Design of Organizational Interaction

FERNANDO FLORES
Action Technologies
MICHAEL GRAVES
Logonet, Inc.
BRAD HARTFIELD and TERRY WINOGRAD
Stanford University

The goal of this paper is to relate theory to invention and application in the design of systems for organizational communication and management. We propose and illustrate a theory of design, technology, and action that we believe has been missing in the mainstream of work on office systems. At the center of our thinking is a theory of language as social action, which differs from the generally taken-for-granted understandings of what goes on in an organization. This approach has been presented elsewhere, and our aim here is to examine its practical implications and assess its effectiveness in the design of The Coordinator, a workgroup productivity system that is in widespread commercial use on personal computers.

Categories and Subject Descriptors: H.4.1 [**Information Systems Applications**]: Office Automation; H.4.3 [**Information Systems Application**]: Communications Applications—*electronic mail*

General Terms: Design, Human Factors, Management

Additional Key Words and Phrases: Conversation, coordination, language/action, ontology, speech act, The Coordinator

1. INTRODUCTION

In using the word "technology" people are generally concerned with artifacts—with things they design, build, and use. But in our interpretation, technology is not the design of physical things. It is the design of practices and possibilities to be realized through artifacts. Computer technology involves machines, but that is not what is ultimately significant. It encompasses the design of new practices (including those of word processing, electronic communication, printing, accounting, and the like), and beyond that it opens the possibility for new realms of practice.

Computer technology can change what it means to manage and to act in an organization. In fact, such a change is happening and is going to happen regardless of what the designers think they are doing. When we accept the fact that computer technology will radically change management and the nature of office work, we can move toward designing that change as an improvement in organizational life.

At one level this is a paper about a particular system designed to provide computer support for communication in organizations. At another level, it is about the design of computer systems in general, and beyond that about the nature of the design process and its relation to theory. We argue that careful, conscious theorizing at a foundational level should precede design and can increase the likelihood of its effectiveness. We begin by expanding on what we mean by "theory."

2. THEORY AND DESIGN

The design of new technology is always an intervention into an ongoing world of activity. It alters what is already going on—the everyday practices and concerns of a community of people—and leads to a resettling into new practices, which in turn create new future design possibilities.

The designer is someone who steps back from what is already going on to create an intervention. In doing this he or she applies, implicitly or explicitly, a background orientation toward the activity in which the technology is to be employed. This orientation may rest on taken-for-granted conventional wisdom or may emerge from an explicit theoretical articulation of what it is that is going to be facilitated. For example, the design of a tool for communication and management in an organization will embody an orientation toward action and the management of action. As one possibility, the designer may assume that the relevant activity can be characterized as the generation and movement of objects (papers, reports, products, etc.) through some space (the office or a network of offices and receiving and dispatching points).

One can increase the coherence of a design by developing a theoretical "ontology," which lays out basic dimensions and distinctions. In saying that this explication is theoretical we are not attributing to it a predictive structure like that of mathematical theories of physics. What we mean is that it clarifies the preunderstanding of what kinds of things exist, what kinds of properties they can have, and what kinds of events and relationships they can enter into. The "objects," "forces," "velocities," and the like of Newtonian physics provide this kind of basis for the more quantitative aspects of the theory.

A theory, as an ontology, is a set of key distinctions for observing, participating, and designing. It is (to use a metaphor) the eyes with which we see what is going on. For example, one distinction in our common sense ontology of organizations is that of "messages" that people send to one another. As observers in this ontology we see messages going back and forth; as participants, we send and receive messages; and as designers we may design systems for facilitating message composition and transmission. But "messages" is only one possibility for constituting ourselves as observers, participants, and designers. We might, as theorizers, offer other interpretations of what is happening on the basis of other key distinctions, such as those of shared tasks and goals or of speech acts.

Every theory or every ontology of distinctions will allow us to make some observations, actions, and designs and prevent us from making others. Designers who work with "messages" can devise systems for making the preparation and passing of messages more efficient. But the possibilities are also limited by this ontology—they cannot escape designing something to do with messages. The question is what ontology of distinctions—what theory of management and organizational action—will prove effective in designing systems for organizations.

The effectiveness of a work of design, and of a theory as a basis for design, must be assessed in the context of the consequences of the intervention. Some theories will prove better as a basis for design than others. That is to say, some will be more effective for orienting us toward new possibilities that can be developed into useful artifacts. For some purposes, the understanding we already experience will be a satisfactory basis. In others, reorientation can open new and better possibilities.

Two prominent orientations underlie most of the computer systems in common use today. Each of them offers distinctions from which users and designers observe and participate in the activities of concern. The most prevalent, which underlies traditional electronic data processing, has been based on an ontology of "data" and "information." Its distinctions are those of data, formatting, and algorithms for data storage and manipulation. A computer system contains and manipulates information and is related to the "real world" through operations of "data entry" and "reporting" or "data access."

This orientation is embodied in the design of "management information systems" (MISs), which focus their intervention on the task of providing quantities of accurate, up-to-the-minute data to managers. They carry the assumption that the greater the quantity and accuracy of the information available, the more able are people to consider alternatives and make decisions. These systems have largely failed in their attempt to improve management because the problem is not one of insufficient or stale data. Management is not management of information. Information is only important to managers because they need to take actions, for which they sometimes require grounding that can take the form of statements, summaries, and reports. By focusing on an ontology defined in terms of data, MISs operate in a secondary domain and more often than not swamp the manager in distracting information.

A second orientation takes "decision making" as the central task of managers and is expressed in the design of "decision support systems" and more recently of "expert systems." Here the focus moves away from the data itself to the process of problem solving and decision making. This process can be roughly characterized as a series of steps, which include defining the problem space, listing alternatives within that space, assessing the consequences of each alternative, and finally selecting from among them. Decision, evaluation, search, and cognition are taken as the key distinctions.

Hidden within this ontology is a focus on evaluation and search for solutions that rest on a relatively well-established and formalizable problem space. We believe that much of the work in this area is foundering because this assumption is rarely appropriate in practice. Coming to terms with the ill-defined background within which we feel there is a problem or state of irresolution is one of the fundamentally unsolved central issues in this line of research.

Both traditional data-processing and problem-solving orientations convey an attitude that there is an "objective" external world that can be neutrally observed and fully characterized in symbolic representations. This kind of approach (which we have labeled "rationalistic" in [6]) has a long and useful history, but it is not the one best suited to design in the office. The more urgent need is to understand the role of background and language in setting the dimensions of the space in which people interpret and generate their possibilities for action.

In line with this, a third theoretical orientation underlies our own work, with "action through language" as the key domain of distinctions. The design of conversational systems focuses on interventions into the recurrent patterns of communication in which language provides the coordination between actions.

3. A LANGUAGE/ACTION PERSPECTIVE

Our principal theoretical claim is that human beings are fundamentally linguistic beings: Action happens in language in a world constituted through language. What is special about human beings is that they produce, in language, common distinctions for taking action together. Language then is not a system for representing the world or for conveying thoughts and information. Language is ontology: a set of distinctions that allows us to live and act together in a common world.

The orientation within which we go about design is one that allows human beings to observe their producing and acting in a world linguistically, to design their actions together, and to recognize and respond to breakdowns. The designer's job is to identify recurring breakdowns, or interruptions in ongoing activities, and prepare interventions to resettle the activities in ways that cope with or avoid those breakdowns.

In using the term "breakdown" here, we do not intend it to have a tone of "upset" or "catastrophe." A breakdown is any interruption in the smooth unexamined flow of action. It includes events that participants might assess as negative (as when the pen you are writing with runs out of ink) or as a positive new opportunity (e.g., a stray useful thought that interrupts your flow of writing or a friend knocking at the door).

In turning our attention to this ontology, we are not designing something new for human beings to do. People already produce a world together in language and they already coordinate their actions in that world. A fundamental condition of human action is the ability to affect and anticipate the behavior of others through language. Design can improve the capacity of people to act by producing a reorganization of practices in coherence with the essential, ineliminable nature of human interaction and cooperation. The crucial distinctions—the ontology—of our design are the fundamental linguistic actions: requests, promises, assertions, and declarations. A brief summary of the dimensions of linguistic action is given by Auramäki et al. (pp. 126–152, this issue) and is based on a taxonomy developed by Searle [3]. We do not lay out all of the distinctions here but indicate the direction of our theory with the cases of requests and promises.

When you request that someone perform an action in the future, you anticipate the fulfillment of certain conditions. The conditions explicitly stated in the request are interpreted within an implicit background of standard practices—what is "normally" done in your community in similar situations—and within the shared understanding of speaker and hearer. Not all conditions will be or need be explicitly stated when the background itself is sufficient. For example, in requesting "Meet me tomorrow at two o'clock," you specify an action and a description of those conditions of fulfillment that are not taken for granted. In this case, the time is explicit, whereas the place and any other conditions are implicit in the preunderstanding of the speaker and listener. We speak of the "conditions of fulfillment" of a request as including not just the explicit statement, but the larger interpretation (which may differ between speaker and hearer) of the conditions under which the requester will declare that the request has been satisfactorily fulfilled.

People promise actions to one another. That is, they offer to perform some action in the future, or they agree to perform some future action that has been requested of them. This act need not involve any mention of "promise." A promise might be "Okay," or "You're the boss," a nod, or even in some contexts just a mutually recognized silence.

A request and promise (or a declining) make up an initial segment of a "conversation for action," which initiates a simple structure of possibilities for continuing to some kind of completion. The promiser may later report performance of the action, and the requester may declare the conversation and the action completed. Alternatively, the request or promise may be canceled, or a further request made (by either party) to clarify or modify the conditions of fulfillment.

Organizations are structures for the social coordination of action, generated in conversations based on requests and promises. These distinctions of linguistic action are crucial to building technology for organization and management. They are also universal with respect to time and culture. So long as people live and work together, they will coordinate their actions in requests and promises and the expectations that derive from them.

It is important to separate out these basic constitutive phenomena of social action from the particular cultural and linguistic forms in which they appear. As mentioned above, many different kinds of utterances (or nonutterances) can be interpreted as promises in a particular cultural background. The same words may lead to very different interpretations in different contexts.

In some cases the forms depend on the details of the situation. "It's cold in here" may be a request for action in some situations and not in others. In other cases there are cultural norms. In adapting The Coordinator to Italian, the programmers were told to avoid the term corresponding to "request" because "Only the government requests." Other people 'invite.' Similarly, a popular observation about Japanese culture concerns a reluctance to appear to offend the listener. It is said that the Japanese will "never decline a request." In the immediate visible sense, this may be true: A direct expression of a request is never (in polite discourse) answered with "No." But in the deeper interpretation there must be recognizable means for conveying all of the basic possibilities of promising, declining, and negotiating. If I enter into a conversation with you about meeting at two o'clock tomorrow, I need to go away from that conversation knowing whether it is worth my effort to show up at the appointed time on the expectation that you will be there. Without the fundamental distinctions of social coordination, we cannot carry out activity that involves other people in anything but the immediate present or in predictable recurrent patterns.

These distinctions will be implemented with different tools and regularized practices, depending on context and culture and on what technology is available. Much of our own work has concerned computer-based tools for conversation. We have also implemented our theory of language as action in other areas, such as the design and presentation of courses in management and effective communication, and for generally allowing people to learn and embody new distinctions for observing, assessing, and designing social actions.

By teaching people an ontology of linguistic action, grounded in simple, universal distinctions such as those of requesting and promising, we find that they become more aware of these distinctions in their everyday work and life situations. They can simplify their dealings with others, reduce time and effort spent in conversations that do not result in action, and generally manage actions in a less panicked, confused atmosphere.

4. COMPUTER TOOLS FOR ACTING IN LANGUAGE

As computer networks become more widely available and easier to use, they are generating new phenomena relevant to management. They introduce more than just the connectivity of being able to send, store, and receive information. Via networking, one can extend the effective reach of actions, record them, and structure them. Although this new potential rests on the technology of computer networks, that is not where the relevant understanding lies. The potential for designing new and more effective tools and practices lies in the domain of networks of people engaged in conversation and in the networks of actions that connect them. This is where the fundamental distinctions are made and where the salient breakdowns occur.

As we described above, the rationalistic tradition leads people to think that as they become more electronically connected, the ensuing availability of information will greatly improve the effectiveness of organizations and the execution of management. It is tacitly assumed that information quantity can somehow be correlated with enhancement of alternatives and hence more effective decision making. But productivity in the office is not quantity of information—it concerns the effectiveness of people getting things done. As more and more databases, electronic bulletin boards, online query systems, and the like become routinely available, people often become less rather than more certain of what actions are appropriate. The breakdown that arises is one of overload. It becomes more difficult to assess the available information in a meaningful way: to determine what is relevant to actual and potential concerns, what legitimacy to grant to the information and its speaker, and what structure to impute or assign to it.

Electronic mail, for example, has led to new possibilities for communication that cuts across many of the older structures in organizations [4]. At the same time, it has created a new source of breakdown for many people, who find themselves swamped by messages that demand their attention. As Kiesler observes, "If you just add technology to the office, you may wind up having more communications to monitor, more things to type, and more projects initiated that don't get completed; you may not improve performance" [2, p. 48). In the authors' personal experiences working within a community of researchers dedicated to the design and use of computer systems, we are continually jolted back to reality by statements like "Oh, sorry I didn't get to that—I'm two weeks behind in getting through my e-mail."

For older media, specialized roles and institutions have evolved to deal with this breakdown. Libraries, universities, publishers, editors, commentators, and the media marketplace help to digest information for us. Receptionists, secretaries, and assistants manage the flow in a variety of organizational situations. The range and quantity of information readily accessible via the computer appears to have temporarily outpaced the growth of new roles and institutions for handling information. And so, to view networks as simply a mechanism for information connectivity leads to a fundamental breakdown. The management of information becomes an additional task—a burden, not a support.

Tools continually emerge to handle this flow as people attempt to cope with the breakdowns they experience. A survey of the software available for use in offices reveals a great potential for innovative practices. Calendar programs, project management tools, spreadsheets, and the like can be used effectively to associate information with the human environment that makes the information meaningful. Users adapt generic technologies such as spreadsheets to the immediate tasks at hand in a pragmatically effective way (often in ways other than those anticipated by their designers) without a theoretical foundation.

If design is based on a theoretical framework, a unified and coherent approach can be developed. The vast number of specialized and idiosyncratic tools and practices can be incorporated into a coherent theory that leads to an effective redesign of already existing tools and to fruitful new possibilities. Database systems offer an example of this process in a different domain. The jumble of practices for storing structured data in computer-accessible files has gradually evolved into a relatively small and coherent theory on which powerful generic tools such as relational databases and query languages can be built and standardized, thereby not only providing a way to clean up existing systems, but, as these database tools become standard in operating systems, offering new possibilities for their use.

We propose that the language/action theory offers such a unified foundation for designing the support of interactive work in organizations. We illustrate the relevance of this analysis to computer systems by describing The Coordinator,[1] a workgroup productivity system currently used on IBM PC-compatible machines for everyday operations in sales, finance, general management, and planning in organizations of a variety of sizes and types. The Coordinator provides facilities for generating, transmitting, storing, retrieving, and displaying records of moves in conversations. However, unlike electronic mail systems that take messages and information as their starting points, it is based on the language/action theory outlined above. The description here focuses on the "conversation manager," which is one part of an integrated system that also includes word processing, formatting, calendar maintenance, and connectivity over phone lines and local-area and wide-area networks.

4. THE COORDINATOR

The Coordinator is a system for managing action in time, grounded in a theory of linguistic commitment and completion of conversations. Conversations are essentially temporal, both as a sequence of acts and in the wider context of conversations and actions in a community or organization.

In making a request or promise, the speaker brings into a shared domain of interpretation a set of conditions to be fulfilled through action in the future. A conversation that develops from this opening can be viewed as a kind of "dance" in which particular linguistic steps move toward completion: If an action has been requested of you, you promise or decline; if you have promised to complete the action, you report completion or revoke your promise; if you have requested an action, you cancel your request, ask for a progress report, or declare that your conditions have been fulfilled and the action completed. What drives the design here is our theoretical claim that social action happens through language. The conversational dance is a social dance of bringing forth conditions of fulfillment, commitment to fulfill them, and completion.

The user interface of The Coordinator is based on menus that reflect the underlying theory. The primary menu for conversing is shown in Figure 1. Some of the menu items initiate new conversations. Others bring up records of existing conversations.

Instead of providing a uniform command to initiate a new message, The Coordinator provides options that identify different linguistic actions. When "Request" is selected, the user is prompted to specify an addressee, recipients of copies, a domain (a keyword that groups related conversations under a common concern), and a brief action heading (corresponding to the subject header in traditional mail systems). The body of the message is prompted with the phrase "What is your request?" to which the user enters any text whatsoever. The system makes no attempt to interpret this text but relies on the user's understanding and cooperation that the message is properly identified as a request. This is a key design issue: Let people interpret the natural language, and let the program deal with explicit declarations of structure (such as the user's declaration that this is a request). The conditions of fulfillment rest in the interpretations of speaker and hearer, not in the structure of the text. A perfectly understandable request (one with mutually understood conditions of fulfillment) might contain the single word "Noon?" if the participants have a shared understanding (e.g., they often go to lunch together).

When the user signals that the text is complete, the system prompts for three dates associated with the completion of the action: a "respond-by" date, a "complete-by" date, and an "alert" date. Date entries are optional, but experienced users almost always include one or more of them. Not only do they provide the primary structure for retrieval and for monitoring completion, but the identification of completions with specific dates plays a surprisingly large role in producing effective conversations. A requester will specify a completion time for the action based on assessing when this action is crucial in dealing with wider concerns, preparations for other actions, and so on. The response time will reflect an assessment of how soon other actions need to be taken if the request is declined. For example, suppose that someone requests preparation of a financial

[1] "The Coordinator" is a registered trademark of Action Technologies.

a standard reply informing the requester that the request was received. "Free-form" allows any kind of communication relevant to the conversation—most frequently, notes, comments, and questions—that does not fit into the formal structure. "Commit-to-commit" would be conveyed in natural language with sentences like "I'll let you know by Thursday if I can do it." That is, the speaker is committing to take the next conversational step (promising or declining) by a specific time.

When any answering action is selected, a new message is automatically generated with markers corresponding to the choice of act and with a generic text. For example, if the response is "Promise," the initial message is "I promise to do as you request," whereas for "Counter-offer" it is "No; I counteroffer: . . ." The user can augment or replace this text using embedded word processing facilities. Experience has shown that a surprising number of messages need only the initial pro forma composition. The message initiating a request or offer needs to contain text that sets forth the action such as "This is a reminder to send me that report we were talking about at lunch." But often the subsequent steps are made by simply selecting the appropriate menu item and hitting the button that sends a message.

Whenever "Answer" is selected, the menu displays only those actions that could sensibly be taken next by the current speaker, given the direction of the conversation toward completion of action. For example, after making a commitment, the next time the promiser answers in that conversation (assuming no intervening action by the requester), the menu offered will be as shown in Figure 3. At this point, there is no longer an option to decline, but the promiser can "Report-completion" or "Cancel" with or without initiating a new promise.

The Coordinator has no magic for coercing people to come forward with their promises, but it provides a straightforward structure in which they can review the status of their commitments, alter commitments they are no longer in condition to fulfill, anticipate coming breakdowns, make new commitments to take care of breakdowns and opportunities appearing in their conversations, and generally be clear (with themselves and others) about the state of their work. The structure and status of conversations is the primary basis for organizing retrieval and review in the system. To put it simply, the structure is organized to provide straightforward and relevant answers to the implicit question "What do I have to do now?"

Several things are of note:

—The basic unit of work in the system is a conversation, not a message. In conventional electronic mail systems, messages are often linked by conventions such as the use of "Re: . . ." in headers. For The Coordinator, each message (including a Free form) belongs to a particular conversation. The retrieval structure is a two-level one with the user first identifying a conversation, then selecting particular messages within it to be displayed.

—The explicit use of conversation theory in the generation of messages makes it possible for retrieval to be based on status. There is a way to display answers to questions such as "In which conversations is someone waiting for me to do something?" or "In which conversations have I promised to do things?" Note

```
          C O N V E R S E

OPEN CONVERSATION FOR ACTION          REVIEW / HANDLE
  Request                               Read new mail
  Offer                                 Missing my response
                                        Missing other's response

OPEN CONVERSATION FOR POSSIBILITIES
  Declare an opening                    My promises/offers
                                        My requests
ANSWER                                  Commitments due: 24-May-88

NOTES                                   Conversation records
```

Fig. 1. Converse menu from The Coordinator. (Reprinted by permission from F. Flores, C. Bell, M. Graves, and J. Ludlow. *The Coordinator Workgroup Productivity System I. Version 1.5 P.* Action Technologies, Emeryville, Calif., 1987.)

```
SPEAKING IN A CONVERSATION FOR ACTION

Acknowledge       Promise
Free-Form         Counter-offer
Commit-to-commit  Decline
Interim-report    Report-completion
```

Fig. 2. Menu for responding to a request. (Reprinted by permission from F. Flores, C. Bell, M. Graves, and J. Ludlow. *The Coordinator Workshop Productivity System I. Version 1.5 P.* Action Technologies, Emeryville, Calif., 1987.)

report that is crucial to a meeting on Thursday. The request includes, as a condition of its fulfillment, that it be satisfied by the meeting time, and the response must be soon enough to find another way to get the report or alternative information for the meeting.

When a request is received, the recipient responds by selecting "Answer" from a menu of mail-reading operations, which calls forth a subsidiary menu as shown in Figure 2. This menu is automatically generated by a conversational state interpreter that keeps track of the current state of the conversation (as determined by the preceding acts). For a detailed description of conversation structure and its embodiment in The Coordinator see [5] and [6].

The first three items in the right-hand column (Promise, Counter-offer, and Decline) represent the standard actions available in response to an initial request. The fourth choice (Report-completion) is also possible, since in some cases, it will turn out that the recipient of a request has already done what was requested. The left-hand column introduces conversation acts concerned with the conduct of the conversation itself, which do not advance its state. "Acknowledge" sends

is reconstructing constitutive distinctions of human social action. These are distinctions for generating any socially coordinated actions: bringing, in a request, a future action and its conditions of fulfillment into a publicly shared world and producing, in a promise, a commitment to complete the action. These distinctions are simple, universal, and generative of the complex organizational and management phenomena with which we need to deal.

Managers are often faced with apparently overwhelmingly complex projects and sets of actions to manage, recurrent miscoordinations of action (misunderstandings of requests, conditions of fulfillment, and promises), and information overload. By interpreting the situation as a network of requests and promises with certain regular logical and temporal structures, we can help bring order. Information is information that appears within a conversation with relevance to action: It is not piled up as contextless facts. The activity of management is the creation and development of conversations for completing action. These constitutive distinctions give managers an improved awareness of what they are managing and an increased capacity to observe, monitor, and intervene in the flow of activity.

Everyone makes requests and promises, but we are not typically aware of them in a fashion that helps to identify breakdowns or intervene in the constitutive dimension of our actions. The Coordinator expands the individual's capacity to observe and assess a situation and intervene into what is already going on. When you make a request with The Coordinator, you are presented with the fact that you are making a request—you choose "request" from its menu for conversations. When you make a promise, it is the same. And, more important than the names on the screen, the request or promise you make in the conversation sets in motion a conversational structure and a structure for observing your conversation that is defined by the linguistic move you have made. You have tools, in other words, for anticipating and identifying breakdowns on the way to the completion of action, for intervening consistently with breakdowns that have occurred, and generally for making the next appropriate moves in the conversation.

What is crucial, we are saying, to the effectiveness of The Coordinator is that it produces in its user a capacity to observe action in its constitutive dimension. The system will "coach" its user to operate in a system of distinctions that constitute and promote effective coordination of action. The effectiveness of the tool is not limited to its actual occasions of use. The Coordinator also has an educational dimension. By operating consistently within the distinctions embodied in it, people begin to acquire a "new common sense" about social action. Even away from The Coordinator itself, they will begin to observe and act in ways that are consistent with the theory. Their taken-for-granted understanding or way of observing will embody those distinctions on which The Coordinator is designed, and they will learn to observe, assess, identify, and intervene in accordance with them.

5. THE SOCIAL ENVIRONMENT

Since The Coordinator embodies an orientation toward language as social action, its effects must be examined beyond the context of a single user—in the social interaction of an organization as a whole. The key observation about a tool like

---

```
SPEAKING IN A CONVERSATION FOR ACTION

Free-Form        Cancel/New-Promise
Interim-report   Cancel
                 Report-completion
```

Fig. 3. Answer menu generated in continuing a promise. (Reprinted by permission from F. Flores, C. Bell, M. Graves, and J. Ludlow. *The Coordinator Workshop Productivity System I, Version 1.5 P.* Action Technologies, Emeryville, Calif., 1987.)

that these two queries are different. For example, if you make an offer to me, then our conversation is in a state in which the next move characteristically belongs to me, but I have made no promise to you.

—The distinction of "completion" is central to monitoring the progress of conversations. An "open" conversation is one in which additional steps are required to reach a state of closure. Note that completion is not the same as satisfaction. If I withdraw a request, the conversation is complete even though the request was never satisfied. The distinction between open and closed conversations is one of the primary ones used to filter out those to be retrieved. Unless the user designates otherwise, The Coordinator will display only those conversations that are still open to further action.

—Explicit response, completion, and alert dates identify potential breakdowns in the progress toward completion and are used for time-oriented retrieval. The calendar subsystem is integrated, so that all of these items can optionally appear at the appropriate places in a personal calendar, along with more conventional entries such as meetings and appointments.

—The Coordinator applies theories of language without attempting to automate language understanding. All of the interpretations (e.g., that a particular message is a request, or that it should be done by a certain time) are made by the people who use the system, guided by appropriate menus and prompts. This is not experienced by users as an extra job of annotating but in fact replaces typing parts of the contents.

—It is a generic tool in the same sense as a word processor or a spreadsheet, but in a different domain of elements, that is, a different ontology. A word processor is not equally well suited to generating all kinds of character sequences but is specially designed for the words, sentences, and paragraphs of ordinary written text. Similarly, The Coordinator is not built for arbitrary sequences of messages, but for the requests, promises, and completions that are at the heart of coordinated work.

We want to reiterate our point that, although The Coordinator exemplifies a new design and a new theory of action and management as a basis for design, the distinctions of linguistic acts and completion of action are not those of new entities or new proposals for doing something. What we are doing in our theory

The Coordinator is that it intervenes and creates change by making explicit a structure of conversation that was already there.

The most visible impact is to facilitate the shared clarity of communication. Participants who share a grounding in observing, assessing, and intervening in conversations for action will have the basis for a more effective mutual understanding of actions to be taken. A request is a request, with a well-understood structure of consequences, in the understanding of all participants. They share a language of distinctions for attacking ambiguity and ensuring that they share an understanding of what they are doing together.

In a sense, this clarity is something that needs to be recovered as we move from older social forms to the complex computer-mediated modern organization. In a simple closely knit society, there is a tremendous degree of overlap in people's backgrounds. They share a common set of social mores and understandings and can anticipate close similarity in their interpretations. In a small group, furthermore, each individual is familiar and everyone's behavior can be frequently anticipated on the basis of prior personal experience. In such a context, there is a relative clarity of knowing what people really mean by what they say.

In today's modern society, there is much less cultural commonality, and organizations tend toward being collections of nameless and faceless "functional roles." Communication structures are mechanized and regularized in order to regain some degree of predictability. Kiesler describes how "computer-mediated communication can break down hierarchical and departmental barriers, standard operating procedures, and organizational norms" [2, p. 48]. She documents a number of ways in which the use of electronic messages can lead to breakdowns in the face of the relative absence of what she terms "static and dynamic personal information" and argues that "the real challenge is to build electronic communication facilities so that it is easy for people to negotiate and to implement procedures and norms—in other words, to design systems that somehow give back the social context that computer mediation wipes out" [2, p. 54].

In a way, the drive toward "computerization" is an overreaction in this direction. A rigidly specified set of procedures can help ensure context-independent predictability at the cost of a mindless lock-step pattern in which the individual cannot vary from the prescribed routines. In contrast, by making the network of requests and promises explicit in its structure and temporality, systems such as The Coordinator can provide a means of improving the degree to which people have adequately shared interpretations of their commitments and actions, while leaving them the individual choice and responsibility for dealing with them.

The success of systems based on the language/action ontology depends on the development of a new shared culture or "tradition" in which the commitment dimension of language is taken seriously within a shared interpretation of explicitly marked language acts. Although the dance of request and promise is universal, doing it and being explicit about it are two very different things. In all areas of social interaction, the experienced phenomenon of acting is very different from what happens when we make an interpretation of our acts explicit by describing or characterizing them. If I discreetly behave in a way that I hope will make you want to leave (e.g., looking at my watch and stacking up things on my desk while we talk), my act is socially different from directly saying "I request that you leave." These kinds of subtleties are extremely important in maintaining the network of relationships and assessments of other people.

In some contexts, standard practices lead us to associate indirectness with politeness. A request to have the window closed can be "Close the window!" or "My, but it's chilly in here." The explicit prefacing of a request with a marker ("I request that you close the window") is an additional act, which in the background of everyday interaction has a stiff and rather formal sound. The same explicitness as signaled by the message type in a Coordinator request can be heard (especially by new users) as having a less-than-friendly tone. But as practices evolve in a group, the listening evolves to suit the medium.

By explicitly marking the action structure, The Coordinator changes the space of possibilities for communication—the form of the dance. It is not possible, for example, to be ambiguous as to whether or not a message is intended to convey a request. It is hard to "suggest" an action to test whether it is taken as something you want the hearer to do. Each message carries a label that distinguishes it as a request or as not-a-request (e.g., a conversation for possibilities). The labeling itself constitutes part of the meaning. Even the need for the sender to consider "Am I making a request here?" changes the situation.

New users who interpret The Coordinator as a "message system" are sometimes frustrated by what they perceive as undue restrictiveness or regimentation; they see it as restricting the range of possibilities for communication by imposing categories such as "offer" and "request." At a superficial level, it is easy to refute this by noting that these categories are not forced on all messages: It is always possible to send a "free-form" which has no status in the conversation structure, and there are "conversations for possibilities" in which no pattern of request and promise is expected or made possible. But it should be clear that this is not the whole story. The fact that there is a conversation initiated with "request" means that when a sender chooses to label something as "free-form" or "possibilities" it can be interpreted as not making a request. The overall space of possible choices conditions the interpretation of everything made within it.

Relative to a seemingly unstructured language such as that associated with standard electronic mail systems, conversation systems such as The Coordinator present constraints. This is not surprising; all language always does that by creating a space of distinctions in which to interpret the world and our actions. The questions are then, "Relative to what is it constraining?" and "What is gained by these constraints?"

There is a spectrum having at one end unstructured message systems and at the other traditional information systems, that are limited to a particular conversation that they help to administer effectively (e.g., customer service requests). Information systems impose significant constraints and provide efficient tools for dealing with the specified conversations. There is little confusion about which set of conversations can best be mediated by the particular system and which are best dealt with in some other way.

Electronic messaging systems seem quite unstructured, but in fact they do impose some structure, such as forcing explicit declaration of recipients and, sometimes, of the subject. They do not provide, for example, the potential found in ordinary conversation for making a remark without making it clear whether a particular person was supposed to hear it. Even though this could be seen as a limitation in the design of mail systems, it is a limitation that people are accustomed to and which for the purpose of most conversations is not serious. The Coordinator comes in the middle. It offers more structure than conventional mail systems in order to better organize and more rapidly assess the conversations one is engaged in, that is, to deal with the barrage of messages that can be quickly produced and transmitted with computer networks. On the other hand, it is less confining than the customer-order system.

The underlying claim of The Coordinator is that such explicitness is beneficial, overall, for the kinds of conversations that go on among managers and other workers in settings like offices. This claim can be refined in several dimensions as outlined in the following sections.

5.1 Conversation Types

With The Coordinator, we are only dealing with some of the conversations in an office setting. It is misleading to see the future "electronic office" as one in which all communication is mediated by computers. There is a vital place for everything from highly structured messages to the open-ended discourse that thrives around the coffeepot or in chance encounters in the corridor. In fact, an important question is what aspects of language in the office should be incorporated into computer systems at all. The medium is well suited to some types of conversation (especially those in which structured records and recall are important) and ill suited to many types that have traditionally been carried on face-to-face or by voice.

As we move from face-to-face encounter, to telephone, to written text, to online data, we progressively narrow the basis for interpretations. A shrug and a smile may be a perfectly adequate response to a request in face-to-face conversation because the listener (who listens with eyes as well as ears) has a wealth of observations on which to ground assessments of what to expect. On the other hand, not everything can be done face-to-face. The airplane, postal system, telephone and telegraph coexist. We select the medium on the basis of its suitability, cost, and convenience.

The Coordinator is a machine for conducting conversations for action and also provides facilities (equivalent to conventional electronic mail) for other types of conversation. For a broad range of work-related interactions we believe much can be gained from the introduction of commitment management in conversations for action. There are also interesting new possibilities for different kinds of machines that would provide support for conversations with different structures. But computer-based communication cannot take over the wide range of spoken communications, including those in which vagueness serves an important social purpose and in which the (often unconscious) interpretation of "tone of voice" and "body language" are essential to understanding. It may well be that as office communication systems evolve, there will be a mix in which computer-based text is used for the more explicit forms, while recorded and transmitted voice and video images become the preferred mode for less structured types of conversation that must occur at a distance.

5.2 Stability of Role Structure

We are primarily designing for settings in which the basic parameters of authority, obligation, and cooperation are stable. The typical office presents a structure of recurrent patterns of conversation in mutually understood domains of possibilities associated with formally declared roles such as "group manager," "assistant," and "programmer." The issue here is not whether the role structure is hierarchical, democratic, or whatever, but whether it is basically agreed upon and is not itself a matter of ongoing active negotiation. In an unstable organization, for example, it might be very useful to be able to "suggest" an action without explicitly requesting that anyone do it in order to gauge people's responsiveness.

This is not to imply the absence of such negotiations within the structure of The Coordinator, since they always occur in every social setting. For example, authority roles are negotiated as people judge whether it is acceptable for them to decline (or even counter) a request of a given kind from a particular party, upon considering the consequences of doing so. But successful functioning depends on this not being the primary concern in the bulk of interactions.

An observation that goes along with this is that The Coordinator has been most successful in organizations in which the users are relatively confident about their own position and the power they have within it. This does not mean that the organization is democratic or that power relations are equal. It means that there is clarity about what is expected of people and what authority they have (e.g., what requests can be clearly declined without fear of negative impact). In such an environment, people can be comfortable with making (and then possibly changing) commitments and accepting commitments from others in the same spirit.

5.3 Cooperation and Competition

We are primarily concerned with work settings in which the cooperative aspects of achieving mutually declared results dominate over the competitive aspects of interpersonal or intergroup conflict. Of course, no setting, no matter how visibly "cooperative," can be understood without recognizing the internal conflicts of interest and the ways in which they generate the space of actions. The Coordinator's successful use does not depend on an idealized cooperative spirit in which everyone is working for the good of all. But it does depend on basic assumptions that the overall interests are shared and that the parties recognize that honest dealings with one another will be the best for their shared benefit. This is true, for example, in successful market structures in which each party competes with the others, but recognizes the joint advantage in maintaining (through legal systems and the like) a communication mechanism based on mutual trust.

Our philosophy of communication rests on an interpretation of individual responsibility and autonomy in which people take responsibility for their language acts and behave in accordance with shared standards. This does not mean a utopia in which people always tell the truth or always come through with what they promise. We can design to facilitate the positive aspects of social interaction but we cannot magically change human nature. People can use any communication device whatsoever to lie, deceive, and manipulate. They will always promise things they cannot or will not do and will generate further conversations to deal with the consequences.

With The Coordinator, we are not proposing a change in the nature of action and cooperation in the office. What we are doing is laying bare the constitution of action and cooperation in order to open the way to diagnosing breakdowns, increasing effectiveness, and in general designing the workplace as an effective, healthy environment. To do so requires building and implementing practical tools on the basis of a theory of organizational life. We believe it is imperative that constitutive theories of organization and cooperation be embodied in tools and practices. Only in that way can our understandings shape the reality of work. Work, and the organization of work, can be designed only when practices are designed and implemented on the basis of sound theory.

6. TECHNOLOGY, CHANGE, AND LEARNING

Our view of design is consciously oriented toward improving the quality and effectiveness of organizational life, not just providing computer support for current practices. As we emphasized in the first section, all innovative technology leads to new practices, which cause social and organizational changes whether anticipated or not. Some of these will be effective and others may be counterproductive. Our firm belief is that this process can be done with awareness. Although we can never fully anticipate the changes a technology will trigger, we can make conscious choices in the directions of change we facilitate.

This attempt to do conscious design in this domain is both worthwhile and difficult. A system that is intended to have certain positive impacts (as assessed by the designer and/or the users) may turn out to do quite the opposite when it is put into practice. Although all aspects of design gain from being done in collaboration with the users (see [1]), it is especially essential that the explicit interpretation and implementation of social changes be generated jointly with the people who participate in them.

There needs to be a shared understanding within the organization that there is an ongoing breakdown in the domain of conversation and commitment that is relevant to productivity. There is wisdom in the aphorism "If it ain't broke, don't fix it"; people only seek change when they experience breakdown. The problem is that it is relatively easy for people to identify small-scale breakdowns ("I can't get invoices to the branch offices fast enough") and difficult to recognize the large-scale breakdowns of organization and communication that pervade their work. Most people (including most managers) do not experience "lack of coordination" as a breakdown even though they face the consequences of it every day under a variety of names.

In addition to recognizing the problem, people must understand the intervention well enough to identify and anticipate the new breakdowns it will create when integrating with preexisting structures, practices, and tools. The use of an explicit conversation manager will lead to changes in the social practices with potentially complex ramifications. In every organization a background of practices has evolved in conjunction with the mixture of previous technologies and circumstances. Any change to this background, planned or not, will affect power relations, stability of roles, and individual satisfaction. With the introduction of any new technology (hardware, software, or practices), some people will see themselves as gaining and others will anticipate (often appropriately) being put at a relative disadvantage. Education cannot eliminate the underlying power struggles but can be the basis for dealing with them explicitly in the context of potential changes.

It must be understood that a system can be used as the basis for an ongoing process of mutual education in which the people who use the system envision possibilities for new ways of working, interpret those possibilities in light of their own experience, and choose what will be implemented. The technology in turn can play a role in "coaching" the users. We are all aware of cases in which our verbal understanding of what we should do is not effective in generating the acts we want. For example, understanding the advantages of getting things done on time is rarely sufficient to prevent procrastination. An effective reminder system cannot prevent it either, but it can help us by offering opportunities for self-examination, that is, by getting us to ask the question "When am I really going to work on this?"

In the domain of commitment and conversation, this kind of coaching is offered by the structure of The Coordinator. The simple need to characterize a message as an "offer," "request," or "opening for possibilities" leads the user to ask "What am I trying to do here?" At a later stage in a conversation, the need to explicitly declare it "complete" or to choose a speech act that leaves it "open" leads the user to ask questions about what is still missing and who is responsible for resolving it. Our experience in introducing The Coordinator has convinced us that this kind of coaching can be valuable and that it leads to a kind of continuing education that goes well beyond training for technical facility in using software. As people use the system they develop their understanding of the acts that go with it.

Programs like The Coordinator, which are based on an explicit theory of organizations and of directions for change, have at times been referred to pejoratively as "missionary software." The implication is that organizational or social change is being imposed on an unwilling populace by outsiders with a dogmatic theology. Although this kind of manipulation is possible in principle, the technology is likely to be rejected, ignored, or subverted in practice. But from a different perspective, The Coordinator is a new kind of "educational software" in which the everyday use of its communication tools serves to educate users in the principles of conversation and action. Learning is integrated into the practice of working so that the skills for understanding the organization as a network of negotiated commitments for operating within it can be developed.

7. CONCLUSION

In this paper, we have been talking primarily about The Coordinator. Here we want to reemphasize that the Coordinator design, with its particular screens, buttons, and so forth, is an initial example of a large family of potential tools, based on some fundamental theoretical claims about design and organizational action:

—Design is for transparency of action and expansion of possibilities. It is always an intervention into the practices, breakdowns, and possibilities already present in a community: an intervention that will shift and resettle practices, breakdowns, and possibilities. All design embodies an ontology, a set of constitutive distinctions, of the domain in which the design is an intervention. Good design is an ontologically grounded intervention that allows work to flow smoothly with a minimum of breakdowns in completing an action and that expands positive possibilities for participants and production in the domain.

—The ontology in which we are designing is one of action happening through language. The constitutive dimension of social and organizational interaction can be laid out as a structure of linguistic actions in a temporal dance. The key distinctions in this structure, as we have interpreted it, are requests, promises, assertions, and declarations as moves in conversations for the completion of action.

The Coordinator is a generic tool for conversations for action. Many customizations and extensions of the design are possible. For example, in The Coordinator people make requests and promises by typing in English text. But this is not the only possibility; the interpretation of linguistic acts can be based on embodiments that include figures, drawings, oral content, symbols, and formalized data relations. In another direction, tools can be developed to fit particular organizational situations, standard practices, and domains of work. The actions can be tailored to particular recurrent conversations that include the ones handled in traditional data processing such as order entry, inventory, and accounting.

By taking language/action theory as a basis, we are asking people to go about their business with a different awareness. We design in a fundamental domain of social interaction, which calls for the explicit recognition of the autonomy and responsibility of communicating individuals within a social network that is defined and maintained through the action of language. The evolving nature of computers and of work in organizations will inevitably lead to the widespread development and use of computer tools grounded in this domain of design.

REFERENCES

1. BJERKNES, G., EHN, P., AND KYNG, M. *Computers and Democracy*. Avebury, Aldershot, England, 1987.
2. KIESLER, S. Thinking ahead: The hidden messages in computer networks. *Harvard Bus. Rev.* (Jan.-Feb. 1986), 46-60.
3. SEARLE, J. R. A taxonomy of illocutionary acts. In *Language, Mind and Knowledge*, Minnesota Studies in the Philosophy of Science, Vol. 11, K. Gunderson, Ed. University of Minnesota Press, Minneapolis, 1975
4. STASZ, C. AND BIKSON, T. K. Computer supported cooperative work: Examples and issues in one federal agency. In *Proceedings of the Conference on Computer Supported Cooperative Work* (Austin, Tex., Dec. 3-5).
5. WINOGRAD, T. A language action perspective on the design of cooperative work. *Human-Computer Interaction 3*, 1 (1987-88), 3-30.
6. WINOGRAD, T., AND FLORES, F. *Understanding Computers and Cognition: A New Foundation for Design*. Ablex, Norwood, NJ., 1986 and Addison-Wesley, Reading, Mass., 1987.

Bibliography

FLORES, F.C. Management and communication in the office of the future. Unpublished Ph.D. dissertation, Univ. of California at Berkeley, 1981.
FLORES, F. C., AND LUDLOW, J.J. Doing and speaking in the office. In *DSS: Issues and Challenges*, C. Fick and R. Sprague, Eds. Pergamon Press, London, 1981.

Received February 1988; revised March 1988; accepted May 1988.

Electronic Group Calendaring: Experiences and Expectations

Beth Marcia Lange
Center for Strategic Technology Research
Andersen Consulting
100 S. Wacker Drive, Suite 900
Chicago, IL 60606
lange@andersen.com

ABSTRACT

Our organization began using an electronic group calendaring system in April, 1991. We found that there are two highly-related elements to the use of groupware: the set of features and capabilities these products provide, and the integration of these products into the corporate environment. The right set of features can make the use of groupware possible, while the basic ingredients for corporate adoption can maximize the benefit of groupware for an organization. Our experience provides an example of the steps to follow to successfully introduce groupware technology into an organization.

1 INTRODUCTION

It is not an easy task for organizations to adopt new technologies. There are many cited examples [Grudin, Ehrlich, Kiesler, Sproull] of the challenges presented to organizations including technical, social, and organizational issues. Our experience shows that introducing an electronic calendaring system into a corporate environment can be successful by providing these elements:

- Expected Uses: providing a baseline set of expected uses of the calendaring product

- Guidelines: establishing examples and guidelines for the social protocols of using the product

- Key Users: finding champions who lead by example and encourage adoption of the product

- Modifying Procedures: creating a process for modifying communication patterns and processes as styles of work change through use of the product

- Styles of Use: supporting the various styles of usage that will emerge.

This paper describes our experiences and findings, and identifies some requirements for group calendaring products.

2 EXPECTED USES

In April 1991 we began a pilot program to introduce the use of a Macintosh-based group calendaring product at our site. Our initial goal was to address the problem of coordinating the use of shared meeting room facilities. In addition, several people wanted to improve coordination and communication across the organization. We began our program with a core group of eighteen people and now support approximately seventy users.

One executive assistant had held the responsibility for scheduling the conference rooms. She maintained a paper calendar and coordinated the reservations. This system was ineffective as she was not always available and did not always have the necessary information for resolving conflicts.

Our goal was to replace the paper procedure with a more efficient and decentralized process, which we defined as the ability to carry out the process in a more timely manner and provide more information about the meetings scheduled. Through the use of electronic scheduling we hoped to eliminate the need for assigning a person to be responsible for this task.

3 PRODUCT FUNCTIONALITY

We selected On Technology's Meeting Maker™ product.** It is a network-based Macintosh desk accessory that allows individuals to maintain their personal calendars, propose meetings with other people, and access the calendars of shared resources, such as conference rooms.

** No endorsement of the product is implied by the author or the author's organization.

Reprinted from D. Coleman (Ed.), *Groupware '92*, pp. 428-432. Morgan Kaufmann Publishers.

A block of time on a calendar can be scheduled in two ways, as meetings or as activities. A meeting has several attributes: a specific date (or series of dates if it is a recurring meeting), time, and duration, a meeting proposer (often the meeting sponsor), a list of proposed attendees, a location, a title which is displayed on the calendar, and an agenda. An activity is private to an individual's calendar and like a meeting is created for a specific date and time.

A user controls which meetings and activities are added to his/her calendar. While colleagues can invite a user to attend, the user chooses to accept or decline the invitation. The software does not prevent a user from scheduling overlapping events. Resources (such as conference rooms, computers, and audiovisual equipment) accept proposals automatically, on a first-come, first-served basis, and scheduling conflicts are not allowed.

A user may grant other users proxy privileges, giving them access to the grantor's calendar. The privileges may be read only, or read and write. A user can also control the degree to which a proxy can view activity details. A proxy user with write privileges can act on behalf of the grantor by proposing meetings and responding to proposals.

The product is based on a client/server architecture. A central server maintains the database, and distributes messages representing events and state changes, such as responses to proposals. Upon login, a user receives the current week's calendar from the server. Proposing a meeting requires server interaction, as well. For example, a proposer can suggest a meeting time and the server will indicate any attendee conflicts, although specific details are not provided. In "auto-pick," the server searches for a time when all of the proposed attendees are available.

4 GUIDELINES

While the product is versatile, we wanted to establish a common framework among all the users. We introduced the product by choosing a task that would motivate people to use it. We expected users to discover the multitude of product features on their own, as they used the product for reserving rooms.

We developed a four page document outlining the guidelines for using Meeting Maker. We wanted to encourage a consistent format for reserving rooms, which would provide sufficient information to anyone looking at the calendars. The document outlined the steps for viewing a resource's calendar and proposing a meeting to reserve it. Users were reminded that resources would not accept proposals for conflicting meetings and they were asked to negotiate conflicts through other means (telephone, electronic mail, voice mail etc).

The document included a glossary of terms used in the product (such as "activities," "auto-pick," "proxy," "resources," and "frequency"). It also included hints for interpreting icons and navigating around the calendar, a description of known bugs and product limitations, and the names of people to contact for help.

In addition to publishing the document we suggested that each user attend an informal demonstration of the product, at which time we reviewed the procedures, provided helpful hints, and entertained questions.

5 KEY USERS

We chose eighteen people to pilot the use of Meeting Maker. We selected people who most frequently reserved the meeting rooms, and we included the entire management team. These eighteen users represented a cross-section of the seventy people in two departments (Research and Technology Transfer). Included were one partner, four directors, four executive assistants, one part-time librarian, two network administrators, one business manager, four researchers, and one program development/marketer. All of these users had Macintosh computers in their offices; typical uses include word processing, building spreadsheets, preparing presentations, and using electronic mail. Everyone else in these two departments was informed of the new procedures and was asked to reserve meeting rooms through their executive assistants.

The current user base includes sixty-three people and seven resources (3 meeting rooms, 2 computers, 1 VCR, and 1 videocamera). Thirty-six users have Macintosh computers in their offices, the remaining 27 have other types of computers (Unix workstations or PCs).

6 USER FEEDBACK

The product does not provide tools for collecting data on usage patterns, such as frequency of use, number of meetings and activities scheduled, or communication patterns. So, instead, we relied on data collected from the users. After using the product for four months the original eighteen users completed an informal questionnaire about their uses of electronic calendaring. They answered up to twenty-three questions about their use of the product, frequency of use, significance of our procedures, meetings they propose, and use of activities. We collected data on styles of use, perceived benefits, suggestions for new features (as a way of exploring new ways in which people would use electronic calendaring systems), problems, and other comments. The remaining forty-five users were asked to submit comments on these topics in an informal manner.

7   MODIFYING PROCEDURES

We eliminated the meeting room paper calendars shortly after we started using Meeting Maker. Users' apprehensions about converting to the electronic system focused on product reliability and availability, not on the value of using electronic systems or the appropriateness of the procedures we established.

Traditionally, conference rooms were always booked on a first-come, first-served basis subject to change based on the priority of competing needs. This policy did not change when Meeting Maker was installed. Some users were initially concerned that meeting room reservations would not be based on the "right" priorities or that the process of conflict negotiation would not work as well under our new process. These concerns appear to be unfounded; users have not complained or experienced unsolvable problems. Users can view a room's calendar, and have access to all the relevant information about a scheduled meeting. [Ehrlich] describes a paper calendar maintainer's function as the "role of problem solver." In fact, we were able to eliminate the need for a single person to maintain the calendar. The electronic calendar provides distributed access to the information, removing the centralized control, which had provided no tangible functionality.

According to the users, the process for scheduling meetings and reserving conference rooms is more efficient because we are using electronic calendaring - the timeliness of the process is improved, and there is better access to information about a meeting (at a minimum who proposed it or who is the sponsor). The benefits they cited include:

- "eliminates telephone tag (or email tag)"
- "ease of scheduling meetings with standardized protocol"
- "asynchronous communications about meetings and schedules"
- "save time and energy arranging a meeting - it does the work for you"
- "it's a better way than email to communicate meeting agendas and location"
- "easy to change meetings"
- "can schedule the room simultaneously"

We asked the users how the guidelines influenced their decision to use the electronic group calendar. Most said they followed the guidelines the first time they tried using the product. This was the main motivation for people who reserve the rooms frequently. Several said they immediately experimented with the product. One user said "I knew there were guidelines but I didn't find out what they were since Meeting Maker worked fine for me and no one told me I was violating rules."

8   STYLES OF USE

Responses to our questionnaire (and informal communications with the entire user community) revealed four distinct styles of usage of the group calendaring system. We classified the users according to their answers to questions about frequency of use, reactions to the product and new process, use of activities for tracking tasks, and customized, individual utilization of the product features. All of the users honored the new process we put in place. They differed, however, in the extent to which they personally use the system.

The four styles are:
- as-needed: they use the product for discrete tasks, not on a routine basis.
- proxy: this group uses the product on behalf of others including those with user accounts and those without.
- indirect: they have accounts but do not personally use the product. They abide by the established procedures, but rely on their assistants to handle all of their proposals and responses.
- advocates: users who embraced the product and use it on a daily basis. These users, in general, stopped using paper calendars (as much as possible given that most users' computers are not portable). These users experimented with the product and identified important issues regarding product acceptance.

The 18 users who answered the survey were classified as: 9 advocates, 3 as-needed, 4 proxy, 2 indirect. Over half of the current users are as-needed or indirect users (mostly because many of these people do not have Macintosh computers). The existence of these styles is consistent with the findings in studies of strategies and styles of use of various systems, including electronic mail and Information Lens, which reveal personalized approaches to adopting to the use of these systems [Mackay].

As-Needed Users: Most of their usage is for the purpose of reserving a conference room, as outlined in the guidelines. These users login infrequently and logout after short bursts of use. They generally schedule few meetings a week, and said their schedules are generally unstructured (few formally scheduled meetings).

Proxy Users: The executive assistants all use the product primarily as proxy users for other users or to reserve the conference rooms on behalf of the people in the organization who do not have user accounts. These users do not, as a rule, use the product to maintain their own personal calendars. Like the "as-needed" users, their personal schedules include few meetings or other regularly scheduled activities. Typical use is to login for short periods of time to handle specific tasks such as proposing meetings, checking someone's calendar using proxy privileges, or checking on the availability of resources.

Indirect: These people do not personally use the calendaring system, but abide by the procedures. Either they do not have Macintosh computers in their offices, or they expect their assistants to maintain their calendars.

Advocates: This group of users gave many reasons why they use group calendaring on a routine basis. For example, eight out of nine (of the original eighteen users) mentioned increased productivity. Four of them set up recurring meetings, and six said it is more effective than scheduling by telephone. Five people said they like using an electronic calendar more than a paper calendar.

Specific examples of benefits include: "Before using [the electronic calendar] I would often not keep track (not write down) scheduled meetings or activities and just keep them in my head. It helps me be a bit more organized," "especially setting up meetings. It is light years faster than me doing it by phone and much less intrusive on my time compared to having my EA [executive assistant] do it," "reduces time spent finding when people and rooms are available," "allows my staff to save time they would otherwise spend finding out when I am available," "saves time I used to spend sending my schedule to my assistant," and "don't have to notify and catalog separately".

The advocates were motivated to create personalized uses of the product, beyond the ones outlined in the guidelines. There is diversity in the use for group calendaring (meetings) versus activities, as seen in Table 1. The percentages in the columns "group entries %" and "personal entries %" indicate how they use the calendar, not how they spend their time. The third column "work week % time scheduled" is the percentage of their time, for the week of the questionnaire, scheduled with activities and meetings. The users who indicated the highest percentage of group entries were the same people who said they had structured schedules.

person	group entries %	personal entries %	work week % time scheduled
A	35	65	>75
B	40	60	50-75
C	50	50	<50
D	60	40	<50
E	20	80	50-75
F	10	90	<50
G	70	30	>75
H	30	70	50-75
I	50	50	50-75

Table 1

These users created activities to track a wide variety of items including reminders and personal appointments, and to block out time for various tasks. In addition to typical entries such as vacation, dates out of the office, training classes, and planned lunches, users created activities for reminders on upcoming deadlines (such as submitting papers to conferences), morning reading, biweekly timesheet reminder notices, evening tasks at home, administration, and research. The advocates, in general, believe they are more organized because they are using the calendaring tool, as summarized by one user who said "It is particularly useful to me as a personal time manager. I deal with lots of due dates and deadlines and I can input an activity on the due date so I can keep track of them."

Over time some users adapted their styles of use, in part due to pressure from colleagues. For example, one person who travels frequently wanted to avoid maintaining multiple calendars. He used the application one day to check on the availability of a meeting room and "had about a dozen meeting messages. I now keep MM [Meeting Maker] active on my screen just in case one of the `group´ meetings changes." One advocate said "You work for me and I want you to use it"; next to the comment he noted "only half kidding." He actively encouraged others to use the electronic system. Another user commented that the questions we asked about use of activities prompted him to consider developing some personalized uses of his calendar.

Users were asked how they adapted to the [non-]use of the calendar by others. Responses include communicating with "indirect" users' executive assistants, or relying on other communication means, such as electronic mail. The infrequent or indirect users were asked if they missed meetings because they didn't used the product.- some of them said "yes" or "probably," but did not reflect on the consequences.

9 ADDITIONAL USES FOR GROUP CALENDARING

Through our continued use of the product we have collected suggestions for features and functionalities to include in a group calendaring product. While the product's use in our organization can be characterized as successful, missing features prevent users from always effectively communicating, sharing information, and meeting their goals. Arranging meetings, maintaining calendars, coordinating activities, and time-management are dynamic processes in the corporate world. Groupware products that support these tasks will enable organizations to work more effectively. In addition to the need for portability (by allowing a user to detach from the server and work with a snap-shot view of the database, for example) and performance improvement, suggestions include improved access to data, tools for negotiating conflicts, features for enhanced communication, and features for tracking time and using reminder notifications. Data collection tools would enable organizations to study their patterns of usage, monitor software performance, and provide valuable data to demonstrate the need for new product features.

Difficulties arise from the lack of information about the state of a proposal. Users requested improved access to:
- View users' calendars: the ability to see free times for a week or month, improving access to information such as when people are out of the office for extended periods of time.
- Status of meeting proposal: publish proposal responses for all attendees to view. Invitees' are interested in who has confirmed attendance. Proposers want the ability to set response deadlines, and view the status of responses as the deadline approaches. They want an easy way to poll users about changing the date of a meeting - the cost of rescheduling a meeting is usually assessed before making the change.
- Improve notifications: users must intentionally look for notification of conflicts and comments from invitees. Improved notifications would enable users to easily observe the status of a proposal.

Users requested these features:
- Wait list: establish a waiting-list for resources. Users often want to reserve rooms, should they become free.
- Proposal enclosures: send notes to individual attendees, include documents, circulate minutes after a meeting, enclose a note in a meeting cancellation notice.
- Forwarding: users want to forward proposals, just as they can forward electronic mail.
- Interface to electronic mail: electronic mail is used to communicate meeting proposals to potential attendees who are not using the calendaring system.
- In/Out board: a feature to quickly view team members' schedules at a high-level. For example, the In/Out board might indicate who is in town, who is on vacation, how to locate people out of town etc.
- Time management: features to track deadlines with reminders, and use the calendar for time reporting.
- Printing: users want to generate reports, calendar summaries, time-reports from the data in their calendars.

10 CONCLUSIONS

By including each of the key elements described above we have successfully introduced the use of group calendaring into our business environment. These five important elements are: defining expected uses for the product, establishing guidelines for usage, finding key users, encouraging the organization to modify procedures as a result of using the product, and supporting multiple styles of use. Our experience suggests that other organizations can have similar results if they introduce groupware by planning for each of the elements we have cited. In this new area of personal and group productivity tools we can expect individuals and groups to invent new ways of using technology to improve work coordination and communication.

ACKNOWLEDGMENTS

I greatly appreciate the comments I received on drafts of this paper from Gail Rein, Anatole Gershman, and Bill Martin.

REFERENCES

Ehrlich, S. F. 1987. Strategies for encouraging successful adoption of office communication systems. *ACM Transactions on Office Information Systems* 23, 2:340-357.

Ehrlich, S. F. 1987. Social and psychological factors influencing the design of office communication systems. *Proceedings of CHI+GI 1987 Human Factors in Computing Systems and Graphics Interface.* New York: ACM, pp. 323 - 329.

Grudin, J. 1988. Why CSCW applications fail: problems in the design and evaluation of organizational interfaces. *Proceedings of the Conference on Computer-Supported Cooperative Work.* New York: ACM, pp. 85 - 93.

Kiesler, S., Siegel, J., and McGuire, T.W. 1988. Social psychological aspects of computer-mediated communication. *Computer-Supported Cooperative Work: A Book of Readings*, I. Greif (ed). San Mateo: Morgan Kaufmann Publishers, Inc., pp. 657 - 682.

Mackay. W.E. 1988. More than just a communication system: diversity in the use of electronic mail. *Proceedings of the Conference on Computer-Supported Cooperative Work.* New York: ACM, pp. 344 - 353.

Sproull, L., and Kiesler, S. 1988. Reducing social context cues: electronic mail in organizational communication. *Computer-Supported Cooperative Work: A Book of Readings.* I Greif (ed). San Mateo: Morgan Kaufmann Publishers, pp. 683 - 712.

## CHAPTER 9

Cooperative Hypertext and Organizational Memory

One of the earliest uses of cooperative hypertext systems was in education. We include as our first reading in this chapter some excerpts from "Hypertext and Collaborative Work: The Example of Intermedia" by Landow (1990), which describes some uses of Brown University's Intermedia system. Intermedia was for several years the largest and most fully developed hypertext and *hypermedia* system being used in university-level education. Landow shows how hypertext, by "blurring the distinction between authors and readers," enables new kinds of reading, writing, teaching, and learning. A variety of examples are given from the Context32 project, a set of 2000 electronically-annotated and -linked Intermedia documents dedicated to humanities courses.

A parallel project in which cooperative hypermedia are used in elementary and secondary school education is described in a reading which consists of excerpts from "Higher Levels of Agency for Children in Knowledge Building: A Challenge for the Design of New Knowledge Media" by Scardamalia and Bereiter (1991). The goals of the Computer-supported Intentional Learning Environments (CSILE) project are to design an environment in which children are encouraged and supported in producing and recognizing educationally productive questions and in which they can use such questions to guide their building of knowledge. The latter part of the paper discusses cooperative knowledge building in the CSILE environment.

Another typical application of cooperative hypertext is writing. A number of investigators have developed systems primarily intended to facilitate the process of writing by a group of collaborators working at different times and possibly also in different places. Neuwirth, Kaufer, Chandhok, and Morris (1990) discuss "Issues in the Design of Computer Support for Co-authoring and Commenting." Their design seeks to provide three kinds of support: support for social interaction among co-authors and commenters, support for cognitive aspects of co-authoring and commenting, and support for some of the practical aspects of document creation. Their paper then sketches how these goals inform the design of the "work in preparation" (PREP) editor, which introduces a spreadsheet-like notation as a novel means of constraining and displaying what normally becomes a complex arbitrarily-linked hypertext. New sections of a document are arrayed vertically; plans, document versions, and each individual's annotations and comments are arrayed horizontally.

"Building an Electronic Community System" by Schatz (1991–92) takes the process of cooperative knowledge building one step further, moving from the knowledge of a small group to that of a large community. The goal of the Community Systems project is to build an electronic scientific community by collecting "all" of that community's scientific knowledge into a digital library and then making it transparently available and manipulable over nation-wide networks. The paper explains the philosophy of the Telesophy system and its planned use by a community of 500 researchers studying the nematode worm *C. elegans*, a model organism in molecular biology. Next is discussed the enabling technology of information spaces which is used to represent the community library, and the enabling sociology dealing with editorial and quality control, and privacy and rewards. The paper concludes with sample sessions that illustrate the system, and a discussion of the relationship of the concept of *community memory* to that of *organizational memory*.

Conklin (1992) proposes stronger criteria for organizational memory in his paper "Capturing Organizational Memory." He argues that organizations must shift from a document- and artifact-oriented paradigm to one that embraces *process* as well. (See also Chapter 8.) He suggest that this can be done with software that integrates three technologies—hypertext, groupware, and a *rhetorical method*, such as the *Issue-Based Information System (IBIS)* method to be discussed below. The rhetorical method can improve the quality of the dialogue process within an organization by providing a structure for the discussion of complex problems, and can provide an improved "conversational record" in which conversations are structured according to issues instead of chronology.

Researchers at the Microelectronics and Computer Technology Corporation (MCC) have explored the development and use of Issue-Based Information Systems, such as gIBIS, itIBIS, and rIBIS, to capture and manage the rationale behind large and complex systems. The IBIS rhetorical method deals with Issues (questions or problems), Positions (possible resolutions of an Issue), and Arguments (pros and cons of Positions). "Report on a Development Project Use of an Issue-Based Information System" by Burgess Yakemovic and Conklin (1990) describes the use of itIBIS and gIBIS by a group of software engineers in a commercial development environment as they attempted to manage the data arising

from 2200 requirements analysis and design decisions arising over a period of 18 months. Although gIBIS is a workstation-based graphical editor and browser of IBIS networks (the "g" stands for "graphical"), itIBIS is humble groupware that can be implemented on any stand-alone personal computer using an outline processor or text editor (the "it" stands for "indented text"). The authors describe their experiences during the field trial, noting the detection of errors during requirements analysis and design, the increased productivity in project team meetings, and the improvement in inter-organizational communication. They assert that they found great value in the process of review of their design rationale, "more than paying for the cost of capturing and organizing the rationale."

Notes and Guide to Further Reading

Modern work on cooperative hypertext owes much to the pioneering work of Engelbart (1963, 1982). An early influential system was NoteCards (Trigg, Suchman, and Halasz, 1986; Trigg, 1988). Issues about hypertext are explored at depth in Halasz (1988). Yankelovich, Meyrowitz, and van Dam (1985) and Yankelovich, Haam, Meyrowitz, and Drucker (1988) provide more detailed descriptions of Intermedia. Haake and Wilson (1992) describe a collaborative hypertext authoring system that supports synchronous as well as asynchronous work.

Scardamalia, Bereiter, McLean, Swallow, and Woodruff (1989) is another reference on the CSILE system. Brown (1985) explores a variety of individual and collaborative tools for the use of computers in learning.

There is increasing interest in systems for collaborative writing. An early and influential prototype of an asynchronous system is described in Fish, Kraut, Leland, and Cohen (1988), Leland, Fish, and Kraut (1988), and Egido, et al. (1987v). Another interesting approach is that of Smith, Weiss, and Ferguson (1987). The origins of the PREP editor are discussed in Neuwirth and Kaufer (1989) and Cavalier, Chandhok, Kaufer, Morris, and Neuwirth (1991). Neuwirth, Kaufer, Morris, Chandhok, Erion, and Miller (1992) analyze the problem of the automatic and flexible generation of differences ("diffs") between versions of text. Musliner, Dolter, and Shin (1992) describe a system that aids collaborative authoring by maintaining a consistent shared bibliography. A comparison of speech and text as media for expressing revision annotations is Chalfonte, Fish, and Kraut (1991).

The Telesophy System is further described in Schatz (1991) and Schatz and Caplinger (1989). Another system for organizational memory is described by Lynch, Snyder, and Vogel (1990). Making use of capabilities drawn from relational databases, information retrieval systems, hypertext, and decision support systems, the Arizona Analyst Information System facilitates entry, retrieval, analysis, and inter-researcher communication about large volumes of textual information. Of particular interest is their emphasis on the need for organizational guidelines to achieve consistency in data and procedures. Duff and Florentine (1992) also discuss collaboration and document databases.

A distributed, multimedia hypertext system developed for research is the Virtual Notebook System (Shipman, Chaney, and Gorry; 1989; Burger, Meyer, Jung, and Long, 1991; Gorry, Long, Burger, Jung, and Meyer, 1991; Long, 1991v; see also MacIntosh and Yalcinalp, 1992).

Work with IBIS falls within what is now known as *design rationale* research within the human-computer interaction community. A recent special issue of Human-Computer Interaction (Carroll and Moran, Eds., 1991) is devoted to this topic. The editors describe the importance of this field as follows (Carroll and Moran, 1991, p. 198):

> There are several motivations for constructing explicit design rationale: (a) to support reasoning processes in design, (b) to facilitate communication among the various players in the design process (designers, implementers, maintainers, users, etc.), and (c) to further the cumulation and development of design knowledge across design projects and products. Design rationale research addresses the issues involved in capturing, articulating, representing, and using explicit rationale for these various purposes. The goal of this research is to provide improved concepts, methods, and tools for design.

Lee and Lai (1991) develop a framework for evaluating the expressive adequacy of design rationale representations. The work of Conklin and his collaborators is described in far more detail in Conklin and Begeman (1988) and Conklin and Burgess Yakemovic (1992).

As of the date of completion of this manuscript (August 1992), by far the dominant technology for organizational memory is Lotus Notes. Notes is "an integrated communications and database network application, designed to gather, organize and distribute information among work groups, regardless of individual members' physical locations" (Connor, 1992). It is also (Marshak, 1990) "a platform for developing workgroup applications." Notes can be used for message routing, report distribution, idea discussion, and for the tracking and management of projects, sales leads, and customer support information. Notes achieves this through the use of a unique replicated database algorithm designed for an environment in which servers are "rarely connected" (Kawell, Beckhardt, Halvorsen, Ozzie, and Greif, 1988). A number of applications and uses of Notes are documented in Karon (1991), Connor (1992), Goulde (1992), Press (1992), Wilke (1992), and Wozny (1992).

The most substantial and longest term use of Notes other than at Lotus itself has been at Price-Waterhouse. Laube (1992) states that there were three major business issues confronting their corporation that motivated the purchase of tens of thousands of Notes licenses:

- Nobody knew who had the knowledge needed to solve a particular problem.

- Price-Waterhouse professionals were constantly reinventing the wheel, solving, on a worldwide scale, the same problems over and over again.

- There was a need for better communcations throughout the corporation.

Unlike many technology adoptions, Notes at Price-Waterhouse was introduced from the top down rather than from the bottom up, and there is now virtually 100% penetration among the roughly 1000 partners, including the chairman of the corporation! Laube describes the results as dramatic:

- Retention of knowledge, a "filing cabinet in the sky"

- Support for global collaboration and global discussions

- Enhanced communication.

For a somewhat less enthusiastic view, see Orlikowski (1992), who analyzes the adoption of Notes within "Alpha Corporation," an organization that appears to be Price-Waterhouse, in terms of the mental models of users of Notes and the reward systems and workplace norms which motivate these users.

Reprinted from *Intellectual Teamwork: Social and Technological Foundations of Cooperative Work* (pp. 407-415, 423-428), edited by J. Galegher, R. Kraut, and C. Egido, 1990, Hillsdale, NJ: Lawrence Erlbaum. ©1990, Lawrence Erlbaum Associates. Reprinted by permission.

Hypertext and Collaborative Work: The Example of Intermedia

(Excerpts)

George P. Landow
Brown University

Abstract

Hypertext, by blurring the distinction between author and reader, allows, encourages, and even demands new modes of reading, writing, teaching, and learning. Because hypertext permits a reader both to annotate an individual text and also to link it to other, perhaps contradictory texts, it destroys one of the most basic characteristics of the printed text—its separation and univocal voice. In so doing it creates new understanding of collaborative learning and collaborative work. These themes are developed in a description of Intermedia, the networked hypertext system developed at Brown University by its Institute of Research in Information and Scholarship.

HYPERTEXT, COLLABORATIVE WORK, AND THE HUMANITIES

Intermedia, the networked hypermedia system developed at Brown University by its Institute of Research in Information and Scholarship (IRIS), allows, encourages, and even demands new modes of reading, writing, teaching, and learning. In so doing it creates new understanding of collaborative learning and collaborative work. Hypertext changes the relation of teacher and student and of author and reader (Yankelovich, Meyrowitz, & van Dam, 1985) just as it also changes the relationship of text and commentary (or the relationship of one text to other texts) (Landow, 1988a). All these changes contribute to changing notions of authorship and authorial property.

Hypertext, a term coined by Theodor H. Nelson in the 1960s, refers to text in an electronic medium designed to be read nonsequentially. One can easily comprehend what is meant by nonsequential reading if one recalls how one proceeds through a scholarly or technical article. The reader begins at the top of the text, encounters a number or symbol that indicates the presence of a footnote, endnote, or bibliographical citation outside the main body of text, and then leaves it to investigate this material. Articles and books in the humanities often contain extensive discussion of issues, presentations of additional evidence, and statements of indebtedness to other authors or disagreement with them. All writing that makes use of reference conventions, however, leads the reader to exit the main text, consider additional material, and return to it. In some cases, material contained in the referenced section leads the reader outside the particular article or book entirely, and the reader may investigate other printed texts before returning to the original one. Imagine if one could simply touch the reference symbol and the indicated additional text appeared. Then imagine if one could touch the title of a work or body of research data mentioned in that additional text and it appeared, too. That is hypertext.

According to Nicole Yankelovich, one of the designers of Intermedia, a hypertext system is "both an author's tool and a reader's medium." It permits authors or groups of authors "to *link* information together, create *paths* through a corpus of related material, *annotate* existing texts, and create notes that point readers to either bibliographic data or the body of the referenced text" (Yankelovich, Meyrowitz, & van Dam, 1985, p. 18). Intermedia is a *networked hypermedia system*. It is *hypermedia* and not just hypertext, because it links images, graphic documents, and sound to text. It is *networked* because individual workstations join together to share a large body of information, thus making material created or modified at any one workstation available at all others.

Before looking at Intermedia and discussing in detail how it encourages collaborative work, let us examine the various forms that such collaboration might take. The word, which derives from the Latin for *working* plus that for *with* or *together*, conveys suggestions of working side by side on the same endeavor. I suspect that most people's conceptions of collaborative work take the form of two or more scientists, songwriters, or the like continually conferring as they pursue a project in the same place at the same time. I have worked on an essay with a fellow scholar in this manner. One of us would type a sentence, at which point the other would approve, qualify, or rewrite it, and then we would proceed to the next sentence. Far more common a form of collaboration, I suspect, is a second mode described as *versioning* (Morrell, 1988), in which one worker produces a

Most of our intellectual endeavors involve collaboration, although we do not always recognize it. The rules of our intellectual culture, particularly those that define intellectual property and authorship, do not encourage such recognitions, and furthermore, information technology from Gutenberg to the present—the technology of the book—systematically hinders full recognition of collaborative authorship. Intermedia and other hypertext systems, however, emphasize the collaboration suppressed by other technologies of cultural memory. Thus, even though print technology is not entirely or even largely responsible for current attitudes in the humanities toward authorship and collaboration, a shift to hypertext systems may well change them. If we can make ourselves aware of the new possibilities created by these changes, at the very least we can take advantage of the characteristic qualities of this new form of information technology.

Networked hypertext systems characteristically produce a sense of authorship, authorial property, and creativity that differs markedly from those associated with book technology. Intermedia changes our sense of authorship and creativity (or originality) by moving away from the constrictions of page-bound technology. In so doing, it promises to have an effect on cultural and intellectual disciplines as important as those produced by earlier shifts in the technology of cultural memory that followed the invention of writing and printing (Bolter, 1988; McCluhan, 1962).

By blurring the distinction between authors and readers as well as between teachers and students, networked hypertext systems create powerful shifts in the politics of reading (Landow, 1989a; Yankelovich, Meyrowitz, & van Dam, 1985). One corollary of this change appears in the radically different notions of authorship and authorial property generated by networked hypertext systems. Throughout this century the physical and biological sciences have increasingly conceived of scientific authorship and publication as group endeavors. The conditions of scientific research, according to which many research projects require the cooperating services of a number of specialists in the same or (often) different fields, bear some resemblances to the medieval guild system in which apprentices, journeymen, and masters all worked on a single complex project. The financing of scientific research, which supports the individual project, the institution at which it is carried out, and the costs of educating new members of the discipline, nurtures such group endeavors and consequent conceptions of group authorship. In general, the scientific disciplines rely on an inclusive conception of authorship: anyone who has made a major contribution to finding particular results, occasionally including specialized technicians and those who develop techniques necessary to carry out a course of research, can appear as authors of scientific papers. Similarly, those in whose laboratories a project is carried out may receive authorial credit if an individual project and the publication of its results depend intimately on their general re-

draft that another person later edits by modifying and adding. The first and second forms of collaborative writing tend to blur, but the distinguishing factor here is the way versioning takes place out of the presence of the other collaborator and at a later time.

Both of these models require considerable ability to work productively with other people, and evidence suggests that many people either do not have such ability or do not enjoy putting it into practice. In fact, according to those who have carried out experiments in collaborative work, a third form proves more common than the first two: the *assembly-line* (Morrell, 1988) for segmentation model of working together, according to which individual workers divide up the overall task and work entirely independently. This last mode is the form that most people already engaged in collaborative work choose when they work on projects ranging from programming to art exhibitions.

Networked hypertext systems like Intermedia offer a fourth model of collaborative work that combines aspects of the previous models. By emphasizing the presence of other texts and their cooperative interaction, networked hypertext makes all additions to a system simultaneously a matter of versioning and the assembly-line mode. Once on Intermedia, a document no longer exists by itself. It always exists in relation to other documents in a way that a book or printed document never does and never can. Two principles derive from this crucial shift, which in turn produce this fourth form of collaboration: (a) any document placed on Intermedia (or on any other networked system that supports electronically linked materials) potentially exists in collaboration with any and all other documents on that system; (b) any document electronically linked to any other document collaborates with it. The examples provided in the following pages will make clear how collaboration takes place on Intermedia.

According to the *American Heritage Dictionary of the English Language*, *to collaborate* can mean either "to work together, especially in a joint intellectual effort" or "to cooperate treasonably, as with an enemy occupying one's country." The combination of labor, political power, and aggressiveness that appears in this dictionary definition well indicates some of the problems that arise when one discusses collaborative work. On the one hand, the notion of collaboration embraces notions of working together with others, of forming a community of action. This meaning recognizes, as it were, that we all exist within social groups, and it obviously places value on contributions to that group. On the other hand, collaboration also includes a deep suspicion of working with others, something both aesthetically as well as emotionally engrained since the advent of romanticism, which exalts the idea of individual effort to such a degree that it often fails to recognize or even suppresses the fact that artists and writers work collaboratively with texts created by others.

that in turn stimulated the ultimate triumph of the vernacular and fixed spelling (McLuhan, 1962, pp. 229–33), so, too, the fixed nature of the individual text made it possible for each author to produce something unique and identifiable as property.

Hypertext, which links one block of text to myriad others, destroys that physical isolation of the text as well as the attitudes created by that isolation. As Walter J. Ong (1982) pointed out, books, unlike their authors, cannot be challenged:

> The author might be challenged if only he or she could be reached, but the author cannot be reached in any book. There is no way to refute a text. After absolutely total and devastating refutation, it says exactly the same thing as before. This is one reason why "the book says" is popularly tantamount to "it is true." It is also one reason why books have been burnt. A text stating what the whole world knows is false will state falsehood forever, so long as the text exists. (p. 79)

Because hypertext systems permit a reader both to annotate an individual text and link it to other, perhaps contradictory texts, it destroys one of the most basic characteristics of the printed text—its separation and univocal voice. Whenever one places a text within a network of other texts, one forces it to exist as part of a complex dialogue. Hypertext linking, which tends to change the roles of author and reader, also changes the limits of the individual text.

As I have pointed out elsewhere, electronic linking radically changes the experience of a text by changing its spatial and temporal relation to other texts (Landow, 1989a). Reading a hypertext version of Dickens's *Great Expectations* or Eliot's *The Waste Land,* for example, one follows links to predecessor texts, variant readings, criticism, and so on. Following an electronic link to an image of, say, the desert or wasteland in a poem by Tennyson, Browning, or Swinburne takes no more time than following one from a passage earlier in the poem to one near its end. Therefore, readers experience these other, earlier texts outside *The Waste Land* and the passage in the same work as if they existed equally distant from the first passage. Hypertext thereby blurs the distinction between what is "inside" and what is "outside" a text. It also makes all the texts connected to a block of text collaborate with that text.

CONTEXT32 AND INTERMEDIA

For the past two years Intermedia has supported the teaching of four English courses plus one each in biology, anthropology, political science, and the Program in Liberal Medical Education. Recent publications by other mem-

search. In the course of graduate students' research for their dissertations, they may receive continual advice and evaluation. When the student's project bears fruit and appears in the form of one or more publications, the advisor's name often appears as coauthor.

Not so in the humanities, where graduate student research is supported largely by teaching assistantships and not, as in the sciences, by research funding. Although an advisor of a student in English or Art History often acts in ways closely paralleling the advisor of the student in physics, chemistry, or biology, explicit acknowledgements of cooperative work rarely appear. Even when a senior scholar provides the student with a fairly precise research project, continual guidance, and access to crucial materials that the senior scholar has discovered or assembled, the student does not include the advisor as coauthor. Part of the reason for the different conceptions of authorship and authorial property in the humanities and sciences, it is clear, derives from the different conditions of funding and the different discipline-politics that result.

Technology, specifically page-bound print technology and the attitudes it supports, is also responsible for maintaining exaggerated notions of authorial individuality, uniqueness, and ownership that often drastically falsify the conception of original contributions in the humanities and convey distorted pictures of research. The sciences take a relatively expansive, inclusive view of authorship and consequently of text ownership. The humanities take a far more restricted view emphasizing individuality, separation, and uniqueness—often at the expense of creating a vastly distorted view of the connection of a particular text to those that have preceded it. Neither view possesses an obvious rightness. Each has on occasion proved to distort actual conditions of intellectual work actually carried out in a particular field.

Whatever the political, economic, and other discipline-specific factors that perpetuate noncooperative authorship in the humanities, print technology has also contributed to the sense of a separate, unique text that is the product—and hence the property—of one person, the author. Intermedia and other networked hypertext systems promise to change all this, in large part because they do away with the separation of one text from all others that characterizes the book. As McCluhan (1962) and other students of the influence of print technology on culture have pointed out, modern conception of intellectual property derive both from the organization and financing of book production and from the uniform, fixed text that characterizes the printed book. Printing a book requires a considerable expenditure of capital and labor, and the need to protect that investment contributes to notions of intellectual property. But these notions would not be possible in the first place without the physically separate, fixed text of the printed book. Just as the need to finance printing of books led to a search for the large audiences

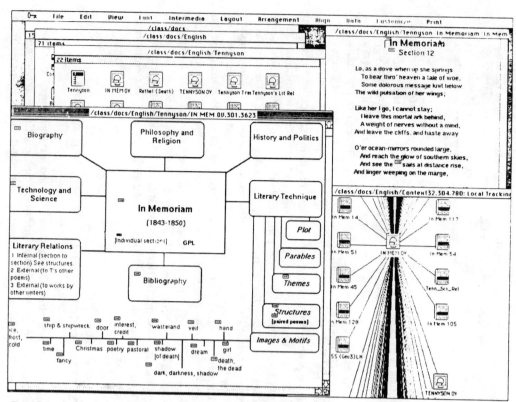

Fig. 15.1. In Memoriam OV (overview or directory file). Within folders the titles of OV files appear in full caps to make them easier to locate. The Tennyson folder appears above (and behind) the overview, and the local tracking map, which shows what documents link to the active window (here the overview), appears on the right.

bers of IRIS have described the design, underlying theories, and development of Intermedia (Meyrowitz, 1986; Yankelovich, Haan, Meyrowitz, & Drucker, 1988), and I have similarly described its use in English courses (Landow, 1987a, 1989a). Undergraduate and graduate students in English employ *Context32*, that part of the Intermedia-based corpus specifically dedicated to humanities courses, to supplement assigned readings. The full corpus at present contains 4,700 electronically linked documents in various forms, and *Context32* contains 2,000 documents. The Intermedia system and the body of documents it links make up the largest as well as the most fully developed hypertext and hypermedia system thus far used for teaching at the college and university level.

Context32 consists of a mixture of primary materials, study guides, and questions to individual works, summaries of state-of-the-art scholarship ("Dickens Biography") introductions to basic critical concepts ("Satire," "The Sonnet"), and original scholarly and critical contributions ("Feminist Views of the Literary Canon," "Biblical Typology"). These essays contain biographies of individual authors, brief essays on literary technique, both general and specific (e.g., "Narration and Point of View" and "Imagery in D. H. Lawrence's 'Prussian Officer'"), and discussions of nonliterary topics related to more than one author (e.g., "Social Darwinism," "Ages of Technology," "Biblical Typology," and "Freud and Freudianism"). Most essays contain questions that refer students back to the reading, ask them to apply their newly acquired information to an included portion of text, or encourage them to follow links to other files.

In addition to these text documents, *Context32* also contains graphic documents in various forms, including digitized reproductions of paintings, maps, photographs, architectural drawings, and the like. Furthermore, using InterDraw, the graphics editor in the Intermedia system, we have created many index diagrams. These graphic presentations of intellectual relationships, one of the most educationally important parts of *Context32*, serve as directories or overviews that inform the user about various information on individual authors, works, and topics, and also include links that provide quick access to that information. By surrounding an individual phenomenon, say, Tennyson's poem *In Memoriam* (Fig. 15.2), with a range of phenomena, including biographical information, contemporary science, and history, these overview diagrams immediately enforce one of the main educational points of the course—that any literary or other phenomenon exists surrounded by relatable contributing phenomena. This graphic presentation simultaneously shows existing links, thus directing the reader to more information, and cultivates the habit of making such connections, thus developing a particular intellectual skill. *Context32* also contains graphic representations of literary influence and interrelations that take the form of diagrams of vector forces. Unlike over-

THE *IN MEMORIAM* PROJECT

The *In Memoriam* project, which employs all the forms of collaborative work described thus far, takes advantage of the capacities of hypermedia to do things virtually impossible with book technology. In particular, the dual capacity of hypertext to record relations between text blocks and allow readers quickly to navigate these links offers enormous possibilities to the humanistic disciplines. As an experiment in collaboration to determine precisely how one goes about creating, maintaining, and using hypertext to study the internal and external connections implicit in a major literary work, the members of the graduate seminar and I placed a particularly complex poem on *Context32* and then linked to it (a) variant readings from manuscripts, (b) published critical commentary, as well as (c) that by members of the seminar, and (d) passages from works by other authors. Tennyson's *In Memoriam*, a radically experimental mid-Victorian poem, perfectly suits this experiment, in part because in its attempt to create new versions of traditional major poetic forms from 133 separate sections, each a poem that can stand on its own it makes extensive use of echoing, allusion, and repetition, all of which are perfectly suited to hypertext linking.

The *In Memoriam* project made use of documents created as an exercise for the undergraduate seminar in Victorian poetry that directed students to take a single section of Tennyson's *In Memoriam* and "show either by an essay of no more than two pages (typed) or by a one-page diagram its connections or relations to other sections of the poem." Kristen Langdon's "Relations of In Memoriam 60 to Other Sections" (Fig. 15.6), which relies on a wheel diagram in which blocks of text connect by spokes to a center, reinvents the Intermedia concept map by making a more concrete use of it. Langdon demonstrates how Tennyson enriches his straightforward, simple diction by linking individual phrases, such as "dark house," "some poor girl," and "sphere," to other sections of the poem. This author's decision to link partial blocks of text to a complete one and avoid generalizing statements or summaries distinguishes her approach from most previous material on the system. Her solution to the assignment, which was paralleled by those of several other students, manages to convey on one page or screen information that would take many more words in an essay format.

Between January and April 1988, the six members of the graduate seminar added links and documents to the body of materials already on-line. In addition to the 133 sections of the poem, the students in the course encountered several dozen files on the poet and his other poems, as well as relevant

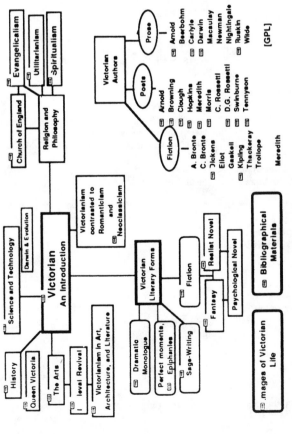

Fig. 15.2 Victorianism OV.

view files, literary relation files and similar analyses of complex historical and cultural phenomena emphasize unidirectional flow of forces.

materials on Victorian religion, science, history, and art. Students from the undergraduate seminar had created approximately a dozen graphic or text documents and linked them to individual sections of *In Memoriam.* I had already created an overview file (Fig. 15.1) for the poem itself, basing it on the one for Tennyson, and to this file student consultants, room monitors, and I linked individual sections and a few of the relevant motifs.

In the course of the next few months the members of the graduate seminar added more than a hundred documents, each commenting specifically on one or more sections of the poem and on one another's work. The first assignment for the project required them to create five documents to

FIG. 15.7.   Local Tracking Map for the fourth section of *In Memoriam* (In Mem 4). The active file appears at the center of the linked files. On the left, the top icon represents a clean copy of the poem without any link markers in the text. Since particular phrases in the preceding (In Mem 3) and following (In Mem 5) sections link to this one, icons indicating them appear (at upper left, second from the top, and lower right). Third from the top on the left appears the icon indicating an essay on the allusion to contemporary geology in section 4, and the last item on the left indicates commentary on lines 11–12. In Memoriam OV appears at the top right, and below that appears the icons for an essay comparing sections 1 and 4, two poems by Rossetti, and the already mentioned earlier section 5.
The number of words required to explain these documents suggests how much more efficient are the Intermedia tracking maps as a means of quickly conveying such information.

In 60 concern is more for passing of the friend and the earthly loss; Compare: 95:33-36 "So word by word, and line by line/The dead man thoughed me from the past."

116:15-16 "Less yearning for the friendship fled Than some strong band which is to be."

129:9 "Strange friend, past, present, and to be"

environmental description reflects speaker's mood:

7:1-2. "Dark house, by which once more I stand/Here in the long unlovely street
No. 119 shows same setting with happier mood, thus reflecting a change of attitude. [follow for discussion by R. Fletcher] ▭

Others around the girl of 60 and women of 97 question her position in love:

97:13-16 "Their love has never past away. . . Whate'er the faithless people say."

BUT with spiritual awakening in 95, he can see friendship in both present and future terms (Cp 116, 129)

60

He past, a soul of nobler tone;
  My spirit loved and loves him yet,
  Like some poor girl whose heart is set
On one whose rank exceeds her own.

He mixing with his proper sphere,
  She finds the baseness of her lot,
  Half jealous of she knows not what,
And envying all that meet him there.

The little village looks forlorn;
  She sighs amid her narrow days,
  Moving about the household ways,
In that dark house where she was born.

The foolish neighbours come and go,
  And tease her till the day draws by;
  At night she weeps, "How vain am I!
How should he love a thing so low?"

9:18 "Till all my WIDOW'D race be won"

85:113 "My heart, tho' WIDOW'D, may not rest"

52:13 "So fret not, like an idle GIRL"

97:7 "And of my spirit as a WIFE"

(In 48 and 49, sorrow is identified as "she" when the speaker is overwhelmed by sorrow. Likewise, knowledge and wisdom are females in 114)

Imagery of circles and spheres:
61:3 "With all the CIRCLE of the wise"
63:11-12 "The CIRCUITS of thine ORBIT ROUND"

97:31 "She knows but matters of the house"

Fig. 15.6.   "Relations of In Memoriam 60 to Other Sections," by Kristen Langdon '88.

append to individual sections of the poem. Each week members of the seminar read the contributions of others, added more documents, and then made links. The final assignment directly involving the *In Memoriam* project required each student to put on-line the texts of poems by another poet, Christina Rossetti, that had obvious relevance to individual sections of Tennyson's work. Members of the class had earlier added texts from work by writers other than Tennyson, and this assignment was intended to explore hypertext presentation of interauthor relations in specific terms. The local tracking map (Fig. 15.7), which represents the documents linked to whichever open document is active, shows those connected to a single section of *In Memoriam*.

Although the project has just begun, it already rivals in size and complexity the first version of *Context32*. Working independently and yet together, the members of the seminar have created a presentation of a major nineteenth-century literary work that makes obvious many of its internal and external relations. Equally interesting, graduate students in English have worked collaboratively in a manner rare in their discipline, and because their work has taken the form of contributions to Intermedia, those who follow them will have access to what they have created.

CONCLUSION

One can argue, of course, that all writing inevitably follows this form of collaboration however much book-bound technology hides or obscures it. Such is precisely the argument made by Roland Barthes and other structuralists who continually emphasize that each speaker or writer manipulates a complex semiotic system containing layers of linguistic, semantic, rhetorical, and cultural codes with which one always collaborates. Unlike book technology, hypertext, however, does not hide such collaborative relationship. Even if all texts (however defined) always exist in some relation to one another, before the advent of hypertext technology, such interrelations could only exist within individual minds that perceived these relations or within other texts that asserted the existence of such relations. The texts themselves, whether art objects, laws, or books, existed in physical separation from one another. Networked hypermedia systems, in contrast, record and reproduce the relations among texts, one effect of which is that they permit the novice to experience the reading and thinking patterns of the expert. Another result of such linking appears in the fact that all texts on a system like Intermedia potentially support, comment on, and collaborate with one another. To repeat what I said in the first section: Once placed on Intermedia, a document no longer exists alone. It always exists in relation to other documents in a way that a book or printed document never does and never can. From this follows two corollaries. First, any document placed on Intermedia (or on any other networked system that supports electronically linked materials) potentially exists in collaboration with any and all other documents on that system. Second, any document electronically linked to any other document collaborates with it.

Intermedia is the outstanding example of a system in which the whole is far *greater* than the sum of its parts, for each works synergistically with others. The idea that any text placed on Intermedia potentially collaborates with any other and that any link between texts in fact makes them work collaboratively may take some getting used to. Can technology so radically change the status and conditions of work? Can technology so challenge established notions of writing, authorship, and authorial property? Yes. The technology of printing and book production clearly created current notions of grammar, fixed orthography, national languages, copyright, and so on, so one should expect that a technology that again shifts the relations of author, reader, and work would again have equally powerful effects.

To create a document or a link on Intermedia is to collaborate with all those who have used it previously and will use it in future. The essential connectivity of Intermedia encourages and demands collaboration. By making each document in *Context32* exist as part of a larger structure, Intermedia places each document in what one can term the "virtual presence" of all previously created documents and their creators. This electronically created virtual presence transforms individual documents created in an assembly-line mode into documents that also exist as if they had been produced by several people working at the same time. In addition, by permitting individual documents to contribute to this electronically related overarching structure, Intermedia also makes each contribution a matter of versioning. In so doing, it provides a model of scholarly work in the humanities that better records what actually takes place in such disciplines than traditional book technology.

ACKNOWLEDGMENTS

Intermedia is the culmination of two years of intense effort by a large team of developers at IRIS led by Norman Meyrowitz. I would especially like to thank Nicole Yankelovich, our Project Coordinator, for her continual resourcefulness, tireless effort, and unfailing good humor as well as for her assistance with this chapter. I would like to thank David Cody, Tanuja Desai, Laurelyn Douglas, Glenn Everett, Suzanne Keen Morley, Kathryn Stockton, and Robert Sullivan for their contributions to *Context32*. Finally, I wish to thank the students in my graduate seminar in Victorian literature—Maryanne Ackershoek, Chatchai Atsavapranee, Mark Gaipa, Laura Henrickson,

Helen Kim, and Mark McMorriss—for their contributions to the *In Memoriam* project.

The work described in this chapter was sponsored in part by a grant from the Annenberg/CPB Project and a joint study-contract with IBM.

REFERENCES

Bolter, J. (1988). *Writing space: Computers in the history of literacy.* Unpublished manuscript.

Landow, G. P., Cody, D., Everett, G. Stockton, K., & Sullivan, R. (1986). *Context32: A web of English literature.* Providence, RI: Institute for Research in Information and Scholarship, Brown University.

Landow, G. (1987a). *Context32:* Using Hypermedia to Teach Literature. Proceedings of the 1987 IBM Academic Information Systems University AEP Conference. Milford, CT: IBM Academic Information Systems, 30–39.

Landow, G. (1987b). Relationally Encoded Links and the Rhetoric of Hypertext. *Hypertext '87* (pp. 331–344). Chapel Hill, NC: Department of Computer Science, University of North Carolina.

Landow, G. (1989a). Hypertext in literary education, criticism, and scholarship. *Computers and the Humanities, 23,* 173–98.

Landow, G. (1989b). Course assignments in Hypertext: The example of Intermedia. *Journal of Research on Computing in Education, 21,* 349–65.

McLuhan, M. (1962). *The Gutenberg galaxy: The making of typographic man.* Toronto: University of Toronto Press.

Meyrowitz, N. (1986). Intermedia: The architecture and construction of an object-oriented Hypermedia system and applications framework. *OOPSLA '86 Proceedings* (pp. 186–201). Portland, OR.

Morrell, K. (1988). Teaching with *Hypercard:* An Evaluation of the Computer-Based Section in Literature and Arts C-14: The Concept of the Hero in Hellenic Civilization. Perseus Project Working Paper 3, Department of Classics, Harvard University.

Ong, W. (1982). *Orality and literacy: The technologizing of the word.* London: Methuen.

Yankelovich, N., Meyrowitz, N., and van Dam, A. (1985). Reading and writing the electronic book. *IEEE Computer, 18,* 15–30.

Yankelovich, N., Landow, G., & Cody, D. (1987). Creating Hypermedia materials for English literature students. *SIGCUE Outlook, 19,* 12–25.

Yankelovich, N., Haan, B. Meyrowitz, N., & Drucker. (1988). Intermedia: The concept and the construction of a seamless information environment. *IEEE Computer, 21,* 81–

Higher Levels of Agency for Children in Knowledge Building: A Challenge for the Design of New Knowledge Media

(Excerpts)

Marlene Scardamalia and Carl Bereiter

Centre for Applied Cognitive Science
Ontario Institute for Studies in Education

⋮

BACKGROUND OF CSILE

CSILE grew out of earlier research on writing processes and on intentional learning. Both in writing and in learning from text, we found evidence that more expert students engage in a kind of dialectical process that enhances their knowledge and understanding (Scardamalia & Bereiter, 1985, in press). In learning from reading, the dialectic may be thought of as taking place between construction of the *textbase* and construction of the *situation model*; in van Dijk and Kintsch's (1983) terms—that is, between representing what the text says and representing the world, as referred to by the text. When given a text passage asserting that germs are not really trying to harm us, less able readers might accept or reject the statement, ignore it, or even miscomprehend it, whereas more able readers would recognize and try to deal with the disparity between this assertion and what they normally thought—for instance: "That's hard to believe. Let's see. Then I always thought [of] germs moving around and raise a family. That's not exactly my idea of a germ" (Bereiter & Scardamalia, 1989, p. 375).

In writing, the dialectic can be represented as taking place between two problem spaces—a *content space*, in which problems of knowledge and belief are worked out, and a *rhetorical space*, in which problems of

presentation are dealt with. By translating problems arising in one space into problems to be solved in the other, both the writer's understanding and the emerging composition are enhanced. Less skilled writers, however, do not usually exhibit this knowledge-transforming approach but instead gave evidence of a knowledge-telling process, in which knowledge is little influenced by its translation into text (Bereiter & Scardamalia, 1987b).

The original intent of CSILE, and the reason it was called an *intentional learning* environment, was to provide computer supports for this dialectical process. In an earlier classroom instructional experiment in writing (Scardamalia et al., 1984), we obtained encouraging gains in planfulness and reflectivity by providing children with procedural supports in the form of sentence openers reflecting the kinds of thinking skilled writers had been observed to do in planning (e.g., "This isn't very convincing because . . .," "My own feelings about this are . . .," and "No one will have thought of . . ."). The experimenter demonstrated planning aloud using these supports and individual children then volunteered to do so, with their planning processes (rather than the outcomes) becoming a focus of class discussion. The two principles illustrated here that we sought to generalize through CSILE were (a) providing external supports for higher level cognitive processes and (b) making metacognitive activity, which is normally hidden and private, overt and a subject for public consideration. This attention to both the private and the public aspects of cognitive activity remains characteristic.

The public aspect of knowledge-building centers on a student-generated community database, which is CSILE's most distinctive feature (Scardamalia, Bereiter, McLean, Swallow, & Woodruff, 1989). The database is accessed via networked microcomputers (currently, eight per classroom). At the beginning of the year, the database is empty. Text and graphical notes in all curriculum areas go into the same database, where they can be retrieved by pseudo-natural language searches involving topics, keywords, authors, thinking types, and status. These last two note attributes illustrate the twin concerns of encouraging higher level processes and making knowledge-construction public:

- Thinking types. Notes are labeled, using student-designed icons, as *high-level questions, new learning, plans,* and *what I know.* (The list changes as curriculum emphases shift.) These icons are displayed along the left side of Figure 1, which shows a typical screen on which a student is reading one of a retrieved set of notes and is creating a related note. Teachers work thinking types into class assignments in various ways. One unit, on human biology, began by having students produce what I know and high-level question notes; then, after class discussions, students, individually or in teams, produced plans for how

THE JOURNAL OF THE LEARNING SCIENCES, *1*(1), 37-68
Copyright © 1991, Lawrence Erlbaum Associates, Inc.

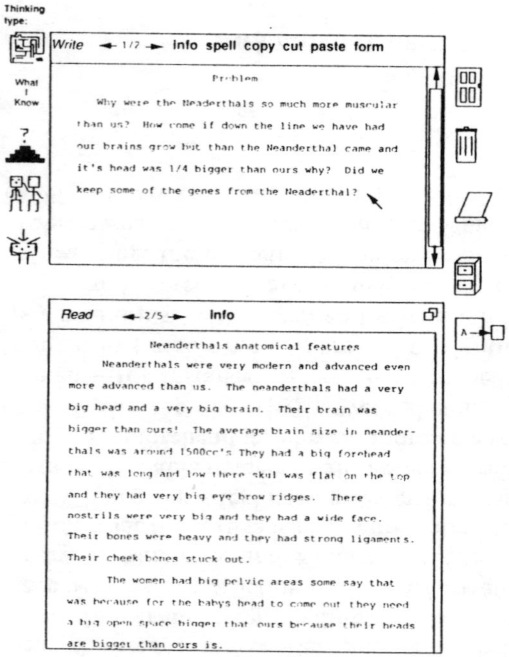

TABLE 1
Notes by a Grade 6 Student Illustrating Four Thinking Types

I know

I know that Charles Darwin developed the theory of evolution by natural selection. Darwin could not explain how the parents gave their characteristics to their children, or why the features sometimes changed. Modern scientists can answer these questions with the study of genetics.

Defects in the appearance of the body are also mainly controlled by genes.

High-level questions
1. What are genes?
2. How do genes work?
3. How do genes control defects in birth?
4. What were some of the theories, old and new, about the genetic code controlling appearance?

Plan

I will read parts of two books on genes. Take notes and use them to make my draft copy. I will then talk about it with my dad and find how I can change it in any way. After I have made all the changes, I will fix the spelling. Then fix the spelling again and hand in the note.

Problem

I will be focusing on the genetic code. I will try and find information on the following problems:

Why do genes determine defects in appearance? How do gene defects occur? What are the most common gene defects? Are we immune to some defects, and if so does this immune system ever break down to cause defects.

· · ·

FIGURE 1 CSILE screen showing read-a-note and write-a-note windows. Arrows in read-a-note window permit stepping through a set of notes retrieved through pseudonatural language Boolean search. Arrows on write-a-note window permit stepping through a set of notes in process.

they were going to pursue some of their questions; they then proceeded with study of the unit, using a variety of library materials and entering new learning notes to report and share what they had found out. Table 1 gives examples of notes produced by a child in a Grade 6 class at each stage of this sequence.

· **Note status.** Students have a choice of several different statuses for their notes. *Private* notes are not accessible to other students. *Public anonymous* and *public named* notes make up the bulk of the community database. However, students may also designate a note as *candidate for publication.* This means they believe the note to make some distinctive contribution to the knowledge base. Candidate notes are reviewed by peer committees or the teacher, may be returned for revision; if accepted, they become "published" and have a distinctive appearance on the screen. Students searching for notes on a topic may limit their search to published notes. Publishing, thus, is intended to play the role in classroom knowledge building that it plays in the learned disciplines.

COOPERATIVE KNOWLEDGE BUILDING IN A COMPUTER-SUPPORTED INTENTIONAL LEARNING ENVIRONMENT

Evidence on children's questioning indicates that, even in areas where they have little prior knowledge, children can produce questions that could profitably guide inquiry and study. This evidence suggests, therefore, one kind of potential for students to assume a higher level of agency in their

· · ·

zones of proximal development. That this potential is seldom exploited in school curricula goes without saying. But what would it take to use children's competence in question asking effectively? The ability to ask a question does not imply the ability to find an answer to it. We have already seen evidence that when students generate questions that they expect they will have to try to answer, they sensibly opt for text-based questions whose answers they can be fairly sure they will find in the material available. These questions tend to be of a low order, inferior to questions provided in published curriculum materials. The high-order questions children ask tend to come when they are free to wonder and under no threat of having to seek answers for the questions they raise. But, then, how can students' wondering be put to use?

We do not have an explicit answer to that question. Instead, we report hopeful observations about knowledge-building activities of students in a computer-supported environment. To provide a context for these observations, it is important that students' questions be seen in a broader perspective of knowledge-building activities. There is much more to acquiring an understanding of endangered species or fossil fuels than finding the answers to a list of questions, no matter how good those questions may be. Knowledge should have a structure that makes it possible to see how one proposition or question relates to another. Furthermore, there is a time course to learning, which can make the answer to one question depend on the answers to preceding ones; new questions can be expected to emerge as inquiry proceeds, or old questions may be reinterpreted. In a cooperative learning environment, such as we are trying to achieve with CSILE, questions will ideally form part of a dialogue that moves progressively toward deeper levels of explanation.

Accordingly, the observations that follow do not represent children pursuing answers to a list of questions. Rather, they represent children engaged in cooperatively developing and extending their knowledge, within an activity structure that allows children's questions, discoveries, and ideas to interact cooperatively and to give direction to their efforts.

How Cooperative Knowledge Building is Supported in CSILE

CSILE-related research currently in progress, dealing with cooperation and group work, indicates the importance of distinguishing between the two.[3] In ordinary classrooms, because small group work presents the only practical

[3]This research is being carried out as doctoral thesis work by Earl Woodruff (on cognitive cooperation) and Elaine Coleman (on effects of group work on problem solving and conceptual change).

way for students to cooperate in learning, the two are almost inevitably conflated. But with an information medium like CSILE, there are ways for students to cooperate that do not involve their working together as groups. On a given unit, some students may work as a group, deciding which questions to pursue and assigning individual responsibilities, whereas other students may pursue their own questions independently, cooperating only through commenting on or using information from other students' notes. Or the teacher may prescribe a way of proceeding, based on considerations of difficulty of the topic, availability of resources, and so on. It appears that children as early as the first grade understand and appreciate the value of cooperation, but by the fourth grade many students have acquired serious reservations about working in groups. They are aware of the variety of things that can go wrong: rivalries and domination, the suppression of novel ideas, time wasting, and the plain nastiness that often infects preadolescent social relations.

In CSILE, students can cooperate with one another by means of comments on one another's notes—by comments that raise questions, suggest information sources, provide constructive criticism or counter-arguments, or that simply provide praise and encouragement. In a larger sense, they can cooperate the way people who are doing related work in a scholarly discipline cooperate to advance knowledge—by paying attention to what one another has found out and by trying to extend it or go beyond it. More directly, they can work together off-line preparing material that eventually goes into CSILE as notes. It may be asked what will induce students to cooperate in these ways? Initial findings from research in progress by Earl Woodruff suggest the following:

1. Without any urging, some students spontaneously engage in a considerable amount of cooperative activity of the kinds indicated, although others do little or none of it. The commenting that occurs spontaneously appears to be generally cooperative in intent, although limited in variety.

2. Simply by introducing a cooperation icon so that students can mark notes that involve or intend cooperation and discussing the value of cognitive collaboration, a significant rise in the frequency of commenting and other cooperative efforts can be observed.

3. Further gains in quantity and quality can be obtained by discussions of ways to cooperate—by making cooperation an overt goal of classroom efforts.

Communicating through a public written medium probably in itself does much to encourage a higher level of civility. When CSILE was first introduced into classrooms nasty anonymous notes began to appear, but ceased abruptly when the students were reminded that teachers had access

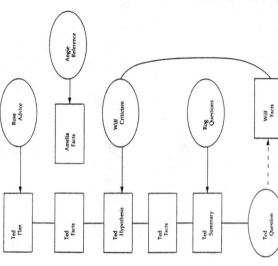

FIGURE 2   Cooperative commenting. Schematic representation of a set of related notes and comments. Rectangles represent notes; ovals represent comments. Time proceeds from top to bottom. See text for discussion of note content.

to authors' names. Following the example of Lampert (1988), however, we have been trying to coach children in the spirit and language of constructive commenting—going so far as to provide a menu of sentence openers, as indicated earlier.

A common problem with cooperative group work in classrooms is keeping the less able and less aggressive students from being sidelined. Woodruff's research should show to what extent this is a problem in CSILE. One thing we do know, however, is that CSILE provides ways for less able students to participate. Learning disabled students, who would have difficulty producing original text, find that they can copy text from someone else's note or from a combination of notes and edit it to have it say what they want. We also find some less able students playing the role that Miyake (1986) found less knowledgeable pair-members playing in efforts to explain how a mechanical device worked: They prevent the premature closure of inquiry by asking questions or requesting fuller explanations.

CSILE is now undergoing major redesign to provide the additional tools and supports that 4 years of experience with the initial version suggest will help children assume higher levels of agency in their zones of proximal development. Among other things, the new version will provide continuous monitoring of many aspects of student participation, so that questions about excluded students and about the frequency of various kinds of cooperative action can be readily answered. In the observations that follow, we point out the needs for enhancement of CSILE and show what children have been able to do with the existing facility.

An Example of Cooperative Commenting

As illustrated in Figure 1, CSILE students can have "read a note" and "write a note" windows open on the same screen. This encourages students to write comments on each others' notes. The system calls comments to the attention of the author of the original note, but they are also available to anyone else who reads the original note.

Figure 2 shows connections among a set of notes and comments produced by six students working on a unit on "human evolution." Most of the notes are produced by Ted, one of the lower achieving students in the class, who studies skulls. His first note indicates nine information sources he plans to use, with the nearby Royal Ontario Museum being first on the list. A comment from Rose suggests an exhibit at the museum that deals with skulls. Ted's next note lists names and ages of hominid skeletons he has noted. There follows a note with a hypothesis about evolution: "When a baby was born 4 million years ago and it had one change of its body closer to man like standing up straighter or having a different skull shape, that

could be why our ancestors changed to be us."[4] A comment by his friend, Wilf, points out the speculative nature of Ted's note, saying "The only real fact in it is that a baby was born 4 million years ago. That's not really much information." Ted subsequently produces a richly factual note and then summarizes his findings about skulls in a note that is commented on by Rog. Rog praises the note and asks six rather stimulating questions, including "Do you think that we might ever become apes again and why?" and "Why don't apes turn into humans anymore?" In the meantime, Wilf produced a note of his own, summarizing his findings on the early history of tool use. Ted comments on this note, suggesting questions that would lead to a deeper analysis of the topic: "First you could add some information like about how the neanderthals could live through the ice ages and how could they make the fire in the cold?" Unconnected with Ted and his colleagues is a note by Amelia on *Homo erectus*. Angie comments on this note, "I found the part about *Homo erectus's* appearance very interesting. That's something that not many people know about. The part you wrote about fire was also quite interesting." Angie then mentions a clipping about Peking man that she thinks Amelia might find useful.

These notes and comments indicate the potential for students, even relatively low-achieving students, to assist one another and to upgrade one

---

[4]Spelling and punctuation have been corrected in quotations from student notes.

another's inquiry through suggestions and questions. They also indicate two needs, which we are trying to meet in the redesign of CSILE:

1. More ways to link students with common interests. It is clear to us that Amelia and Angie would have had much to contribute to the work centering around Ted and Wilf; but the students themselves were probably unaware of this. Although students can search for notes on the basis of keywords, topics, author, along with other criteria, the usefulness of such searches is limited both by the competence of authors in assigning identifiers to their notes and by the competence of readers in delimiting a search. Students tend to rely heavily on search by author, which means that they tend to make connections with others already known to share their interests. In redesigning CSILE, two avenues are being pursued to facilitate the linking of students on thematic bases. One is the design of graphical keyword-organizing interfaces.[5] Keywords are organized into diagrams or attached as labels on scenes, and from the interface students can pull keywords to attach to their notes, retrieve other notes bearing the keyword, obtain definitions, or see a list of other keywords that have been associated with the keyword in question. Preliminary observations suggest this kind of interface greatly increases the number of keywords assigned to notes and results in fewer idiosyncratic keyword assignments. It should therefore increase the likelihood of students using keywords rather than authors as a search criterion. The other avenue is inspired by the Analog Retrieval by Constraint Satisfaction (ARCS) program of Thagard, Holyoak, Nelson, and Gochfeld (in press), which retrieves analogs. ARCS identifies potential analogs by computing semantic similarities, using an automated thesaurus. This much of ARCS should be applicable to comparison of notes. Because such comparisons are computationally intensive, our plan is to run them as overnight operations, which would present students the next day with pointers to the notes most likely to be closely relevant to notes of their own. By such a process, we would expect Ted and Wilf to be made aware of Angie's work and vice versa.

2. Support for pursuit of convergence and coherence. In the note sequence depicted in Figure 2, Rog raised several provocative questions, which, however, seem not to have been followed up. In general, we find students engaging readily in the divergent processes of knowledge building—generating questions, hypotheses, and relevant information—but needing help in the convergent processes—pruning hypotheses, weaving information together into coherent accounts, pressing beyond

superficial explanations, and so on. Correspondingly, CSILE in its current version lends itself nicely to divergent processes but lacks support for convergence. Plans for the new architecture include special knowledge-building environments. One will provide tools for describing and simulating processes, specifically supporting the kind of constructive interaction that Miyake (1986) found to go on when pairs of people are trying to work out an understanding of a process. Another environment will focus on explanatory coherence, providing an interface for organizing networks of facts needing explaining and hypotheses explaining the facts, based on Thagard's (1989) computer implementation of his theory of explanatory coherence.

We expect that through these enhancements to CSILE, there will be more opportunities for the best ideas to work their way to the front and for them to be pursued to the point where they result in substantive gains in understanding.

An Example of Cooperative Elaboration

Somewhere between divergence and convergence is organized elaboration, where students assemble information within some organizing structure. Having students work to a prescribed outline is a didactic way of structuring such elaboration. The jigsaw classroom, as implemented by Brown and Campione (in press), organizes the social arrangement rather than the product, designating different knowledge to be acquired by different students, and a way for them to interact to produce products that combine and organize that knowledge. In the example that follows, organized elaboration takes place spontaneously, supported by the functionality of CSILE's *charts* program.

Charts incorporates conventional graphics software into a system that permits charts to be hierarchically linked via labels attached to the parent chart. Thus users can "zoom in" or "zoom out" through any number of levels of hierarchy, with the levels representing part–whole relationships, levels of detail, or any other relationship the students may think of. Although students cannot edit each other's charts, they can freely connect new charts to them. This provides a structure for cooperative elaboration that will tend naturally to have a hierarchical structure.

Figure 3 shows a few examples from a much larger network of charts, all linked ultimately to the kitchen scene at the center of the figure. This network was originated by a group of four students working on the fossil fuels unit mentioned earlier in this article. The idea that gives coherence to the network is the challenge they set themselves, to show all the ways that

---

[5]The idea for these interfaces came from Jacques Viens, who is studying their effects in doctoral research.

be commented on the way text notes can. In the new version of CSILE all notes, regardless of medium, will have both capabilities.

References

Bereiter, C., & Scardamalia, M. (1987b). *The psychology of written composition.* Hillsdale, NJ: Lawrence Erlbaum Associates, Inc.

Bereiter, C., & Scardamalia, M. (1989). Intentional learning as a goal of instruction. In L. B. Resnick (Ed.), *Knowing, learning, and instruction: Essays in honor of Robert Glaser* (pp. 361-392). Hillsdale, NJ: Lawrence Erlbaum Associates, Inc.

Lampert, M. (1989). *The teacher's role in reinventing the meaning of mathematical knowing in the classroom.* (Research series No. 186). East Lansing: Michigan State University, Institute for Research on Teaching.

Miyake, N. (1986). Constructive interaction and the iterative process of understanding. *Cognitive Science, 10,* 151-177.

Scardamalia, M., & Bereiter, C. (1985). Development of dialectical processes in composition. In D. R. Olson, N. Torrance, & A. Hildyard (Eds.), *Literacy, language, and learning: The nature and consequences of reading and writing* (pp. 307-329). Cambridge, England: Cambridge University Press.

Scardamalia, M. Bereiter, C., McLean, R. S., Swallow, J., & Woodruff, E. (1989). Computer-supported intentional learning environments. *Journal of Educational Computing Research, 5*(1), 51-68.

Scardamalia, M., Bereiter, C., & Steinbach. R. (1984). Teachability of reflective processes in written composition. *Cognitive Science, 8*(2), 173-190.

Thagard, P. (1989). Explanatory coherence. *Behavioral and Brain Sciences, 12*(3), 435-502.

Thagard, P., Holyoak, K., Nelson, G., & Gochfeld, D. (in press). Analog retrieval by constraint satisfaction. *Artificial Intelligence.*

van Dijk, T. A., & Kintsch, W. (1983). *Strategies of discourse comprehension.* New York: Academic.

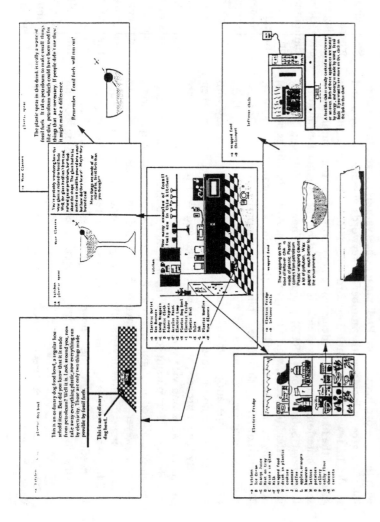

FIGURE 3 Cooperative elaboration. Students elaborate the theme of fossil fuel consumption by producing charts hierarchically descending from a parent chart (kitchen scene). Each chart (only a few examples shown) explains how fossil fuels are used in relation to the selected object. All texts and drawings are original.

fossil fuels are used in an ordinary kitchen. Thus, fuels used in plastics, in manufacturing processes, and in generating electricity to power appliances are all noted. Recall that most of the students initially had little idea what fossil fuels are. That being the case, this kind of systematic elaboration of facts about fossil fuels, their uses, and their conservation, in a realistic context, would seem to build up just the kind of basic knowledge the children showed, by their questions, that they needed. In fact, the whole project can be seen as addressing the same basic-information question that six students in the other class asked in the knowledge-based condition, "What are the uses of fossil fuels?"

An unfortunate limitation of the present version of CSILE is that the charts program and the text-notes program are only weakly linked. Text notes cannot be hierarchically linked the way charts can, and charts cannot

Issues in the Design of Computer Support for Co-authoring and Commenting

Christine M. Neuwirth
David S. Kaufer
Ravinder Chandhok
James H. Morris

Carnegie Mellon University
Pittsburgh, PA 15213

ABSTRACT

This paper reports on a project to develop a "work in preparation" editor, or PREP editor, to study co-authoring and commenting relationships. As part of the project, we have identified three issues in designing computer support for co-authoring and commenting: (1) support for social interaction among co-authors and commenters; (2) support for cognitive aspects of co-authoring and external commenting; and (3) support for practicality in both types of interaction. For each of these issues, the paper describes the approach the PREP editor takes to address them.

GOALS OF THE RESEARCH

The goal of this project is to develop a "work in preparation" (PREP) editor, a multi-user environment to support a variety of collaborative and, in particular, co-authoring and commenting relationships for scholarly communication. In our research, we do not focus on collaborations in which co-authors or commenters interact at the same time, though systems that support research into the issues such collaborations raise are clearly valuable [Stef87]. Our focus is on enhancing the effectiveness of loosely-coupled collaboration. We focus on co-authoring because it represents an interesting challenge for collaborative work over networks: co-authors, after all, must share a planning environment that often relies on, but is nonetheless richer than a working draft. We focus on commenting because it poses a challenge for communication within authoring groups as well as between external readers and such groups. We focus on scholarly communication because scholarly communities as they exist today are already collaborative work groups. They are not explicitly organized around single, concrete goals, but members of groups share the common goal of advancing the state of knowledge. Such work groups are organized in local settings, but they also interact intensively at a distance, as members of a common "invisible college" [Cran72].

ISSUES IN SUPPORTING CO-AUTHORING AND COMMENTING

The PREP editor we are developing addresses three issues: (1) support for social interaction among co-authors and commenters; (2) support for cognitive aspects of co-authoring and external commenting; and (3) support for practicality in both types of interaction.

Issue 1:   Support for the social aspects of collaboration

Generally speaking, we know very little about the social aspects of long-term collaborative writing relationships. Several researchers have conducted observational studies and developed initial frameworks to help define a set of requirements for supporting collaborative writing groups [Gere87; Krau87; Luns90]. Despite limited knowledge about social aspects of collaboration generally, one of the social aspects of collaborative work that we do understand to some extent involves problems of coordination. Coordination issues arise in answer to the question "What activities do writers need to perform by virtue of the fact that they are working together rather than alone?" [Malo88].

Support for the definition of social roles

One response to the coordination problem is to support the definition of social roles: Defining roles reduces the coordination problem by specifying "proper functions" (e.g., responsibilities and patterns of interaction) of the various collaborators. The Quilt system exploits this strategy [Fish88; Lela88]. In Quilt, three social roles are defined (co-author, commenter and reader) as well as six objects (base document, suggested revision, public comment, directed message, private comment, history) and a set of actions (create, modify, delete, attach a suggested revision, attach a public comment, attach a directed message, attach private message, and read). It is then possible in Quilt to specify which roles can perform which actions on the various objects. Quilt further defines three collaboration types: *exclusive*, in which only the author of a section in the base document can modify it; *shared*, in which any author can modify any section; and *editor*, in which a designated editor can modify any section and other authors may only make suggested revisions. In addition, Quilt supports user-defined types of collaboration.

Providing user-defined types is a crucial feature of Quilt. Without it, defining permissible actions on objects in terms of abstractions such as "author" and "commenter" would be problematic. This is because the systemic features of these roles vary in different contexts [Kauf*ms*]. For example, the APA [APA83] defines authors to be "not only those who do the actual writing but also those who have made substantial scientific contributions to a study." Thus, it is possible to imagine a collaboration in which the abstract roles and collaboration types predefined by Quilt would be at odds with the wider social meanings of those abstractions in the particular context. For example, a group of three authors may want to define permissions so that two of them--the ones actually doing the writing--can change the base document. The third, let us say, will not change the base, but will simply comment on the piece for accuracy. No predefined combination of role/collaboration type would suffice.

Our experience supporting user-annotations in Comments, a hypertext tool developed in order to study computer support for response to writing [Neuw88], also affords some insight into other crucial features involved in the definition of social roles, especially the interaction of social roles with writing processes.[1] For example, we have found that, regardless of their social role (either as co-author or commenter), some commenters want

---

[1] Users were students at Carnegie Mellon University enrolled from Fall, 1987 to Spring ,1989 in computer-based tools sections of a freshmen writing course and their teachers. We conducted user tests and interviewed users about their use of the program. We also conducted more formal evaluations [Hart*ms*]. The Comments program also has a menu option that allowed users to report problems to us via a compus-wide network and we maintained a campus-wide bulletin board where users could discuss reactions, problems, and so forth. Some users were paid for their participation in our studies. Users' previous computer experience ranged from experienced to hardly any experience.

the ability to rewrite the written text and not simply attach annotations.[2] This phenomenon may be due to the fact that many significant problems in texts (e.g., voice, persuasiveness, organization), though easy for an experienced writer to detect, cannot be easily described. For such problems, rewriting is often a more efficient strategy than trying to diagnose the problem, and writers often choose this strategy when revising others' texts [Haye87]. In any case, writers in the role of commenters often copied a region of the base document into a commenting box and proceeded to rewrite the copy. Writers who worked in this fashion, however, reported difficulties in revising because their revisions were physically separated from the larger body of text. More specifically, they reported needing a "sense of the whole text" even when commenting on a part. One exasperated commenter went so far as to copy an *entire* document into a comment box and to revise it from there. Whether a commenter is able to modify the base document or not should certainly depend on his or her rightful relationship (co-author, commenter) to the text. An optimal design, however, would not collapse cognitive needs and social roles, but give commenters the ability to rewrite his or her *view* of the text and deal with the effects of this revision on the original base document independently.

There is a potential problem in systems which support the definition of social roles: "premature" definitions of these roles could lead to undesirable consequences. For example, it is not always clear at the outset of a project who is going to make a "significant contribution" and therefore who should get authorship. But if authorship is defined at the outset, then it may reduce the motivation of someone who has been defined as a "non-author" and the person may not contribute as much. Just as we need more research into the social aspects of writing, we need more research with writers actually using systems that define social roles.

Despite potential problems, role specification is likely to be a useful strategy for managing some coordination problems; however, roles such as "co-author" and "commenter" substantially underspecify the activities involved in coordinating complex tasks such as collaborative writing.[3] Writers also need support for coordination activities that fall outside role boundaries. Discussing the full range of these activities is beyond the scope of this paper, but we will briefly sketch two that are especially acute in writing tasks: support for communication about plans and support for communication about comments.

Support for communication about plans

Talk about dividing the labor of writing is likely to include plans for the paper [Krau87]. Writers, however, to not "execute" plans in the same sense that programs do. Instead, writers use a plan as a resource in deciding what to do while they are writing [cf. Agre89]. Often, the partially completed product plays an important role in this process: The partially completed product becomes part of the task environment and constrains the subsequent course of the design [Flow81; Kauf86]. In addition, writers set new goals for themselves as they discover what it is they want to say [Haye80]. When writers work alone, they may not need to articulate the constraints that they have imposed and the new goals they have set. Not surprisingly, co-authors often need to communicate about the constraints in order to refine their views of the goals that co-authors have generated and increase the likelihood that they will generate compatible products. In addition, communication about evolving plans and constraints may improve performance by saving co-authors and commenters from having to infer the other's plans. For example, here is

---

[2] Unlike Quilt, the Comments program does not define social roles explicitly, but like Quilt, collaborators can be granted or denied permission to modify the base document.

[3] Of course, it is possible to define more specific roles. For example, we have been experimenting with Devil's Advocacy, among others [Neuw89a].

an excerpt from a co-author we recently observed communicating about constraints in a paper entitled, *Structure Editors: Evolving Towards Appropriate Use*:

> *In the title I want to stress that we have spent time discovering, sometimes the hard way, when structure editors are useful.*

If a co-author understands the goal, he or she is more likely to be able to produce revisions to the title that are compatible with the other author's goal.

Our approach accepts that plans do not control writing, indeed, that plans will not be made completely in advance of writing and concentrates instead on supporting communication about plans.

Support for the communication about comments

The problems with comments, that is, critical notes on texts, are well-known and legion: writers don't understand comments, they think the comments reflect confused readings rather than problems in their texts, they are frustrated by perceived lack of consistency in comments and contradictory comments [Neuw88]. The problems in author/commenter relationships become even more pressing if authors solicit comments from multiple readers. The interesting empirical question for the author/commenter relationship is how best to help the authoring group manage and make good use of the comments coming in?

Our approach to comments acknowledges that confusions and difficulties abound in the communication among commenters. By providing a system that facilitates communication about comments, we hope to provide one promoting more helpful interactions.

Issue 2: Support for the cognitive aspects of collaborative writing

Supporting the cognitive aspects of collaborative writing involves two things: task specific support for cognitive activities of writing *per se*, and support for the cognitive activities involved in collaborative writing.

Task specific support for cognitive activities of writing

There have been some attempts to understand the task-specific activities (e.g., jotting, drawing, writing, gesturing) that occur in collaborative tasks in order to inform the design of specialized tools to support those tasks [Cook87; Stef87; Tang88]. But because there is a tendency to equate the substantive work of writing with a written draft, most text annotators support only communication about the working draft or outlines of a draft. Experienced writers, however, typically produce intermediate external representations that have no direct relation to the text product [Flow89]. When working with environments that do not support the the creation of arrows, boxes, or other diagrams for displaying conceptual relationships among ideas and the suppression of detail, writers report frustration [Brid87] and important planning activity is curtailed [Haas89].

Our experience with the Comments program also indicates that the written draft is an essential though in many respects incomplete representation for supporting communication about writing. For example, many of the writers we have observed using our tools resort to paper to produce intermediate representations, such as plans for drafts, two-dimensional grids depicting similarities and differences across sources, and trees depicting structural characteristics of an outline or draft. These writers typically like to create (and discard) such intermediate representations quickly, often relying on them only as temporary "sketches" "doodles" or "scribblings" for getting their bearings or adjusting their bearings with those of their co-authors. They further report that drawing editors are too slow to serve these "coordinative" functions and consequently they do not use them for these purposes. So they turn to hardcopy and pass hardcopy drafts to one another for review. The result is that much of their significant planning as co-authors is not done on-line.

Thus, research in writing processes as well as our own observations of writers working with annotation tools suggest that cognitive issues such as supporting the jotting, drawing and note-taking that writers engage in as they write are especially important in writing and that cognitive aspects must be taken into account when designing computer support for co-authoring and commenting.

External commenters differ from co-authors in that they are normally not privy to the informal planning leading up to the working draft. Nor can they claim ownership of the working draft or any future draft. Nonetheless, tools to support more of the writing process than just drafts allow us to define a host of potential new relationships for the external commenter in relation to an authoring group. An important goal of the current project is build a set of tools that will help us explore the interesting roles that external commenters can play vis-a-vis co-authors. Among the leading candidates for interesting roles are the following:

Allowing commenter access to planning objects

Suppose that co-authors use computer tools not only to write their working drafts, but to plan them as well. Then much of their planning environment could be recoverable and open to the scrutiny of external readers. Will external readers have any incentive to explore these planning environments as a context for commenting on a working draft? If so, then the boundaries between original co-author and external reader may grow less distinct. For us, it is an interesting empirical question to consider how much information about the co-authoring interaction the external commenter will seek when computer tools make larger amounts of that interaction available for inspection. The tools we build will allow studies that examine commenting situations of this type and observe what happens to the author/commenter relationship.

Allowing commenters to perform "authoring tests"

External commenters are not likely to involve themselves in the planning environment of the co-authors beyond that which is revealed in the working draft. External commenters, however, have been known to interrogate a text in some of the ways that co-authors expect one another to. Some journal editors, for example, advise their editorial boards to try to "outline" a text submitted for publication if it seems unclear. Doubtless, external commentators keep in mind some of these interrogation tests as they read. Whether they actually perform them and the extent to which they perform them is another matter. But if computer tools can make it easier for co-authors to perform these tests on their drafts, will they also make it cost-effective enough for the external reader to be willing to perform them as well? If so, then the external reader will be assuming some of the conventional duties of the author, much like the external reader described in the previous section who suggests actual revisions.

Requesting or requiring commenters to perform "authoring tests"

Commenters in this situation are requested to make a set of responses about the working draft (or required by a set of defined responses) and these responses function for the authoring group as a test of how well the draft is functioning. For example, the commenter may be asked to identify the "point" of the draft, gist it, or index the key words. This author/commenter relationship has potential efficiencies not shared by the others since commenters are given a specific task to perform on the working draft.

Indeed, experienced writers using the Comments program often asked their commenters to perform a specific type of reading.

Support for the cognitive activities involved in collaborative writing

The cognitive activities involved in collaborative writing are too numerous to detail here. We focus, therefore, on one: accessing comments. Most text annotation systems are based on a hypermedia model and the primary method for accessing information in hypermedia systems is following link icons from node to node. Typically the user brings a node (e.g., a text node) onto the screen, reads its contents and notes any links, then chooses to traverse some of the links. Such localized link following is adequate for browsing tasks but has been problematic for others [Hala87]. For example, we have found that co-authors and commenters want to visually scan a set of comments quickly and resent the time required by the "search and click" interface to call up each comment, inspect it and put it away. Some researchers have worked to tailor the navigational linking system of hypermedia systems to meet user's writing needs [Catl89; Neuw87], but the access problem remains to be addressed. Our approach calls for a tailoring the program to match user's cognitive activities [Norma86].

Issue 3: Support for the practical aspects of collaboration

Most annotation systems for writers assume that all collaborators can basically look at the same text. This assumption is impractical when members of a working group are working at remote sites. Since many academic co-authoring groups are members of the same "invisible college" [Cran72] who work at a distance, we need to worry about the practical obstacles of remote collaboration. The lack of document standards makes feedback over a network impractical even within highly-motivated co-authoring groups. There are two important problems involved in making collaborative authoring practical: compatibility and permeability.

Compatibility

In a study based on interviews with one partner from each of fifty pairs of collaborative researchers in social psychology, management science, and computer science, Kraut, Galegher, & Egido [Krau87] note that "[M]ost collaborators had difficulties with the incompatibilities among programs and computing environments.... this incompatibility was one reason why a single partner in the collaboration typically controlled the manuscript and incorporated the other's handwritten annotations and changes into an electronic version of the text."

Although many existing systems for computer support for collaborative work have addressed the issue of multi-user access to manuscripts [Deli86a, b; Edwa86; Fish88; Grei87; Lela88], none has adequately addressed the issue of access by those with incompatible systems. Potential collaborators' resources (time; money; support environment, for example, computer consultants, printers), however, often preclude them from adopting such systems [Cara88; Ehrl87]. Instead, real collaborators work with some more cost-effective combination of electronic manuscripts and hardcopy, and the collaborative system remains a laboratory rather than a field system. But as Grudin [Grud88] observes [cf. Malo85], "it is difficult or impossible to create a group in the lab that will reflect the social, motivational, economic, and political factors that are central to group performance." As a result, we fail to gain the accumulated experience in using collaborative systems in real-world tasks that is crucial to the evaluation and development of support for collaborative work [Hala87]. A "systems rationalist" perspective [Klin80] may discount the important of the failure of systems to address these issues, but researchers do so at the risk of developing systems that will never be used.

Permeability

Current computer tools for collaborative work are relatively *impermeable*--that is, the boundary between electronic text and hardcopy is difficult to cross. As a result, there is a mismatch between the requirements for successful use of the system and the work habits and requirements of users. It is not unusual, for example, for researchers to annotate hardcopy manuscripts on plane trips. It is unlikely, however, that a busy researcher would be willing to do the extra work required to enter those annotations in an electronic form upon his or her return. Indeed, an examination of applications in several areas (automatic meeting scheduling, project management, group decision support) indicates that when a system requires participants to engage in additional work, it is unlikely to be used [Grud88]. Since it is unlikely that participants' needs for hardcopy input and output will diminish significantly in the near future, failure to address this issue will result in the same negative consequences as failure to address the compatibility issue. Thus, an issue for the next generation of computer tools to support collaborative work will be to make the systems more permeable--that is, to reduce to a minimum the effort required to move from the electronic medium to hard copy and from hard copy to electronic.

Serious bottlenecks in scholarly communication arise, we believe, because pre-publication protocols for scholarly activity have yet to be seriously worked out or standardized. Authors often lack the means to share formatted text over a network, and readers often lack the resources to make hard-copy. Thus, a crucial requirement of the PREP editor is that it be prepared to accept input and produce output in a variety of standard forms including voice, paper, print file, and editable file. At base, we believe that paper is a durable commodity for scholarly exchange and that systems which cannot handle paper (either on the input or output stream) will remain isolated from real users. The best case, of course, in one in which both a user and a correspondent are on an electronic network and use the same document editor. Then it is relatively easy to communicate and the main contribution of the PREP editor will be to help organize the discussion. However, even in the hardest case -- in which the correspondent forwards a handwritten draft and can accept only paper in return -- we still want the PREP editor to be useful, to let the receiving correspondent at least scan the paper in, annotate it, print it, and send it back.

New potentials for interaction

Addressing the practical issues of compatibility and permeability enables us to consider new potentials for co-authoring and commenting interaction, enabling authoring groups to explore increasing the number of readers over national networks.

THE PREP EDITOR

The PREP editor[4] approaches these issues of collaboration and co-authoring by emphasizing communication, planning, and organized annotation. Central to the PREP editor is a focus on providing a usable, visual representation of the information that will allow new kinds of communication in addition to supporting existing styles.

---

4 This section describes the PREP editor as it is currently implemented. Since we are using a prototyping, formative design methodology to develop the PREP editor [Goul88], the system will continue to evolve in response to behavioral observations. The system is implemented on MAC IIs running MacApp. We have also currently restricted ourselves to monochrome displays, since we expect students to use the system on low-end machines.

Basic constructs

At the structural level, the PREP editor shares basic features with many of the hypermedia systems reported in the literature, for example, Intermedia [Meyr86], Neptune [Deli86] and NoteCards [Hala87]. The system defines chunks, which roughly correspond to ideas. Chunks can contain text, grids, trees or arbitrary images. The system specifically targets several chunk types (synthesis grids, synthesis trees) that we have argued are useful external representations for writers building arguments [Neuw89]. Although the workspace includes drawing tools to help users make visual connections as they are formulating their early ideas and arguments, we intend to explore to what extent these targeted chunk types alleviate the need for full-blown drawing tools. The system also defines links between chunks, so that networks of concepts can be built. During the process of planning, when concepts are being formulated and relationships among them defined, authors can choose to work with the chunks as free floating objects in a workspace, which roughly corresponds to the "network mode" in Smith *et al.*'s Writing Environment [Smit87].

Chunks are stored in a database that is shared among the collaborators. But merely having shared access to a network of ideas does not make for a collaboration. Perusing a collaborator's entire scratch space typically makes as much sense as having to sift through the clutter of books, file folders and papers on his or her desktop. To facilitate mutual intelligibility, the PREP editor provides conventions for communicating about parts of the workspace. Specifically, the system allows authors to define "drafts." A draft defines an area in the workspace that an author intends others to access and consists of a sparsely filled grid of chunks. Typically, each column in the grid is used to store different workspace content. The columns can be related to each other (or all to a main column). For example, one column might be the content of a paper and another column the plan that is guiding the construction of the content. Commenters might add columns to hold their own comments as they read. Figure 1 depicts a draft with three columns: a paper plan, the content of a paper, and a co-author's comments. The difference between a column in a draft and some chunks in the workspace is the ordering of workspace content that the columns require. At first, a PREP editor draft might not look much like the traditional linear, text-based draft, but as work progresses, it typically begins to look more and more like a traditional draft--the content typically becomes more important than the plans and comments.[5]

Using the constructs provided by a workspace and a draft built upon a sharable database, co-authors and commenters can create plans and communicate about plans and comments, in addition to simply annotating the content of the paper.

---

[5] Although it is possible to produce the final copy of a paper in the PREP editor, we have not concentrated on general page layout. We include a spelling checker and simple type manipulations (bold, italic, etc.) in the list of supported features, however.

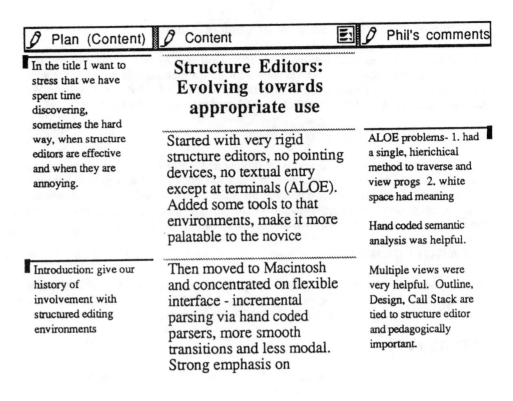

Figure 1. PREP editor with three columns in a "draft."

The interface

Much of our current work has focused on the interface, specifically on the visual representation of the draft and an optimized action grammar. For the visual representation, we are pursuing a path that could be called "dynamic glossing," since we support annotation in a style similar to old, glossed scholarly texts. While in some sense this means that we are mimicking the static annotation process, we are also taking advantage of the dynamic nature of the computer to use visual cues such as font size and spatial relationship to show the interconnections among chunks in the system. To create a visual system that will lend itself to providing and accessing comments easily, the visual grammar must be capable of supporting writers' needs. We have found, for example, that visual alignment of comments is a useful feature for allowing collaborators to see comments "at a glance" (see Figure 1), but in a flexible system, the general case requires a constraint-based layout algorithm that can handle arbitrary shapes and complex interconnections among dynamically selected items [Smol87]. This is an area we are pursuing vigorously. We have also worked on the action grammar, optimizing actions that are used frequently. For example, to create a comment, a writer need only click and drag the mouse.

Versioning

One of the most common events in a co-authoring relationship is the "edit-review-incorporate" cycle where an author gives the draft to another and the second reviews it, leaving the first author to incorporate the new material. Some systems aid this process by supporting "change bars" or other history mechanisms to indicate the points where the text has changed [Iris89]. The PREP editor will go further than this, allowing revisions to exist as distinct versions of the draft. In addition, by virtue of the inherent planning space, the reasoning behind the revisions will be communicated. This revision by versioning will allow expert writers to use operate in the space of the draft without the worry of losing old material.

Relation of the PREP editor to existing systems

The PREP editor does *not* provide a better general linking (i.e. hypertext) system. Instead, it supports linked chunks via somewhat new structural and visual constructs. These constructs would be possible to build on top of some other hypertext system. We are concentrating on improving the usability of hypertext--not its functionality.

CONCLUSION

Designing a computer tool to support co-authoring and commenting requires more than providing users with a hypermedia tool with a sharable database. Our approach has been to draw on the social and cognitive research literature in writing and upon our experience with prototype tools to identify social, cognitive and practical issues that we are attempting to address with a formative-evaluation-based prototype.

ACKNOWLEDGMENTS

The work reported here has been supported by NSF under grant number IRI-8902891. We thank Dale Miller for work on programming the PREP editor prototype and Todd Cavalier for work on graphic design for the PREP editor interface.

REFERENCES

[Agre89]   Agre, P. E., & Chapman, D. *What are plans for?* MIT AI MEMO 1050a, MIT, Oct., 1989.

[APA83]   American Psychological Association. *Publication manual of the American Psychological Association.* APA, Washington, DC, 1983.

[Brid87]   Bridwell-Bowles, L. S., Johnson, P., & Brehe, S. Computers and composing: Case studies of experienced writers. In A. Matsuhashi (Ed.), *Writing in real time: Modeling production processes.*, pp. 81-107. Norwood, NJ: Ablex, 1987.

[Cara88]   Carasik, R. P. & Grantham, C. E. A case study of computer-supported cooperative work in a dispersed organization. In M. Mantei and P. Orbeton (Eds.), *Proceedings CHI '88 Human Factors in Computing Systems*, pp. 61-66. ACM SIGCHI, Washington, D.C. May 15-19,1988.

[Catl89]   Catlin, T., Bush, P., & Yankelovich, N. InterNote: Extending a hypermedia framework to support annotative collaboration. In *Hypertext'89 Proceedings*, pp. 365-378. ACM, Pittsburgh, PA, Nov. 5-8,1989.

[Cook87]   Cook, P., Ellis, C., Graf, M., Rein, G., & Smith, T. Project Nick: Meetings augmentation and analysis. *ACM Transactions on Office Information Systems 5* (2):132-146, April, 1987.

[Cran72]   Crane, D. *The invisible college.* University of Chicago Press, Chicago, IL, 1972.

[Deli86a]   Delisle, N. M., & Schwartz, M. D. Neptune: A hypertext system for CAD applications. In *Proceedings of the ACM SIGMOD '86 International Conference on Management of Data*, pp. 132-143. ACM SIGMOD, Washington, D.C., May 28-30, 1986.

[Deli87b]   Delisle, N. M., & Schwartz, M. D.   Contexts--a partitioning concept for hypertext.   In *Proceedings of the Conference on Computer-Supported Cooperative Work*, pp. 147-152.   ACM SIGCHI SIGOIS, Austin, TX, December 3-5, 1986.

[Edwa86]   Edwards, M. R., Levine, J. A., & Kurland, D. M.   *ForComment*. Broderbund, 1986.

[Ehrl87]   Ehrlich, S. F.   Strategies for encouraging successful adoption of office communication systems.   *ACM Transactions on Office Information Systems 5*:340-357, 1987.

[Fish88]   Fish, R. S., Kraut, R. E., Leland, M. D. P., & Cohen, M.   Quilt: A collaborative tool for cooperative writing.   In *Proceedings of COIS '88 Conference on Office Information Systems*, pp. 30-37. ACM SIGOIS, 1988.

[Flow81]   Flower, L. and Hayes, J. R.   The pregnant pause: An inquiry into the nature of planning.   *Research in the Teaching of English 15*:229-243, October, 1981.

[Flow89]   Flower, L., Schriver, K. A., Carey, L., Haas, C., & Hayes, J. R. *Planning in writing: The cognition of a constructive process*. Technical Report 34, Center for the Study of Writing, Carnegie Mellon University, July, 1989.

[Gere87]   Gere, A. R.   *Writing groups: History, theory and implications*. Southern Illinois University Press, Carbondale, IL, 1987.

[Goul88]   Gould, J. D.   How to design usable systems.   In M. Helander (Ed.), *Handbook of human-computer interaction*.   Elsevier Science Publishers B. V., North-Holland, Amsterdam, 1988.

[Grei87]   Greif, I., & Sarin, S.   Data sharing in group work.   *ACM Transactions on Office Information Systems 5*(2):187-211, April, 1987.

[Grud88]   Grudin, J.   Why computer-supported cooperative work applications fail: Problems in the design and evaluation of organizational interfaces.   In *Proceedings CSCW '88 Conference on Computer-Supported Cooperative Work*, pp. 85-93.   ACM SIGCHI & SIGOIS, Portland, OR, September 26-29, 1988.

[Haas89]   Haas, C.   How the writing medium shapes the writing process: Effects of word processing on planning.   *Research in the Teaching of English, 23* (2):181-207, May, 1989.

[Hala87]   Halasz, F. G.   Reflections on NoteCards: Seven issues for the next generation of hypermedia systems.   In *Hypertext'87 Proceedings*, pp. 345-365.   ACM, Chapel Hill, NC, November 13-15, 1987.

[Hala87a]   Halasz, F. G., Moran, T. P., & Trigg, R. H.   NoteCards in a Nutshell.   In *Proceedings of the 1987 ACM Conference on Human Factors in Computer Systems* (CHI+GI '87), pp. 45-52.   Toronto, Ontario, Apr 5-9, 1987.

[Hart*ms*]   Hartman, K., Neuwirth, C. M., Kiesler, S., Sproull, L., Cochran, C., Palmquist, M., & Zubrow, D. Patterns of social interaction and learning to write: Some effects of network technologies. Manuscript under review.

[Haye80]   Hayes, J. R., & Flower, L. Identifying the organization of writing processes. In L. Gregg & E. Steinberg (Eds.), *Cognitive processes in writing: An interdisciplinary approach.* Lawrence Erlbaum, Hillsdale, N.J., 1980.

[Haye87]   Hayes, J. R., Flower, L., Schriver, K. A., Stratman, J., & Carey, L. Cognitive processes in revision. In S. Rosenberg (Ed.), *Advances in applied psycholinguistics, Volume II: Reading, writing, and language processing.* Cambridge University Press, Cambridge, England, 1987.

[Iris89]   Irish, P. M., & Trigg, R. H. Supporting collaboration in hypermedia: Issues and experiences. In E. Barrett (Ed.), *The Society of text: Hypertext, hypermedia, and the social construction of information,* pp. 90-106. MIT, Boston, MA, 1989.

[Kauf86]   Kaufer, D. S., Hayes, J. R. & Flower, L. Composing written sentences. *Research in the Teaching of English* 20(2):121-140, May, 1986.

[Kauf*ms*]   Kaufer, D. K., & Carley, C. *Interaction at a distance.* ms.

[Klin80]   Kling, R. Social analyses of computing: Theoretical perspectives in empirical research. *Computing Surveys, 12*`(1): 61-110, 1980.

[Krau87]   Kraut, R. E., Galegher, J., & Egido, C. Relationships and tasks in scientific research collaboration. *Human-Computer Interaction* 3:31-58, 1987.

[Lela88]   Leland, M. D. P., Fish, R. S., & Kraut, R. E. Collaborative document production using Quilt. In *Proceedings of CSCW '88 Conference on Computer-supported Cooperative Work,* pp. 206-215. ACM SIGCHI & SIGOIS, Portland, OR, September 26-28, 1988.

[Luns90]   Lunsford, A., & Ede, L. *Singular texts/plural authors: Perspectives on collaborative writing.* Southern Illinois University Press, Carbondale, IL, 1990.

[Malo85]   Malone, T. W. Designing organizational interfaces. In *Proceedings CHI '85 Human Factors in Computing Systems,* pp. 66-71. ACM, San Francisco, April 14-18, 1985.

[Malo88]   Malone, T. W. What is coordination theory? In *Coordination Theory Workshop.* National Science Foundation, Feb., 1988.

[Meyr86]   Meyrowitz, N. Intermedia: The architecture and construction of an object-oriented hypermedia system and applications framework. In *Proceedings of the Conference on Object-oriented Programming Systems, Languages, and Applications* (OOPSLA '86), pp. 186-201. Portland OR, Sep. 29-Oct. 2, 1986.

[Neuw87] Neuwirth, C. M., Kaufer, D. S., Chimera, R., & Gillespie, T. The Notes program: A hypertext application for writing from source texts. In *Hypertext'87 Proceedings*, pp. 345-365. ACM, Chapel Hill, NC, November 13-15, 1987.

[Neuw88] Neuwirth, C. M., Kaufer, D. S., Keim, G., & Gillespie, T. *The Comments program: Computer support for response to writing.* CECE-TR-3, Center for Educational Computing in English, English Department, Carnegie Mellon University, January, 1988.

[Neuw89] Neuwirth, C. M., & Kaufer, D. S. The role of external representations in the writing process: Implications for the design of hypertext-based writing tools. In *Hypertext '89 Proceedings* , pp. 319-342. ACM, Pittsburgh, PA, November 5-8, 1989.

[Neuw89a] Neuwirth, C. M., Palmquist, M., & Gillespie, T. Role playing in peer review: The Devil's Advocate exercise. In D. Beil (Ed.), *Teacher's guide to using computer networks for written instruction*, pp. 157-164. Realtime Learning Systems, Washington, DC, 1989.

[Norm86] Norman, D. A. Cognitive engineering. In D. A. Norman & S. W. Draper (Eds.), *User-centered system design*, pp. 31-61. Lawrence Erlbaum Associates, Hillsdale, NJ, 1986.

[Smit87] Smith, J. B., Weiss, S. F., & Ferguson, G. J. A hypertext writing environment and its cognitive basis. In *Hypertext'87 Proceedings*, pp. 345-365. ACM, Baltimore, MD, Chapel Hill, November 13-15, 1987.

[Smol87] Smolensky, P., Bell, B., Fox, B., King, R., & Lewis, C. Constraint-based hypertext for argumentation. In *Hypertext'87 Proceedings*, pp. 215-246. ACM, Chapel Hill, November 13-15, 1987.

[Stef87] Stefik, M., Foster, G., Bobrow, D. G., Kahn, K., Lanning, S., & Suchman, L. Beyond the chalkboard: Computer support for collaboration and problem solving in meetings. *Communications of the ACM 30*(1):32-47, January, 1987.

[Tang88] Tang, J. C., & Leifer, L. J. A framework for understanding the workspace activity of design teams. In *Proceedings CSCW '88 Conference on Computer-Supported Cooperative Work*, pp. 244-249. ACM SIGCHI & SIGOIS, Portland, September 26-29, 1988.

Building an Electronic Community System

BRUCE R. SCHATZ

BRUCE R. SCHATZ is Director of the Community Systems Laboratory and is a research scientist in molecular and cellular biology and in MIS at the University of Arizona. He spent ten years in industrial research laboratories at Bell Labs and Bellcore as a lead architect on a variety of research and development projects in information and communications systems. He came to the University of Arizona in 1989 to found a laboratory to construct novel science information systems and propagate them to large-scale communities. The funding for this laboratory includes a grant (on which he was Principal Investigator) that was one of the winners of the NSF National Collaboratory competition. He earned an M.S. in artificial intelligence from Massachusetts Institute of Technology and a Ph.D. in computer science from the University of Arizona. His research interests include community systems, electronic libraries, computational biology, and network applications.

ABSTRACT: An *electronic community system* encodes and manipulates the range of knowledge and values necessary to function effectively in a community or organization. The knowledge includes both formal data and literature and informal results and news. The manipulation includes both browsing through the available knowledge, and recording and sharing interrelationships between the items. A large-scale experiment is underway to build an electronic community system for the community of scientists studying the nematode worm *C. elegans*, a model organism in molecular biology. This paper discusses a model for community systems and previous such systems in science, the biology experiment and a previous system, the enabling technology for handling the knowledge, the enabling mechanisms for handling the values, the state of the prototype, and speculations on future applications in supporting organizational memory.

KEY WORDS AND PHRASES: electronic community systems, electronic communities, scientific applications, information spaces, telesophy, organizational memory.

TO FUNCTION EFFECTIVELY IN AN ORGANIZATION, one needs access to a wide variety of knowledge. This knowledge includes not only the archives of financial data about

An earlier version of this paper was originally published in the *Proceedings of the Twenty-Fourth Hawaii International Conference on System Sciences* (IEEE Computer Society Press, 1991). This paper is partially based upon a grant proposal written with Samuel Ward, who introduced me to the worm community and has supported me at the University of Arizona. Many people worked on the implementation of the prototype, including Terry Friedman, Ed Grossman, Scott Hudson, Kevin Powell, and Andrey Yeatts. Mark Edgley and John Sulston provided much of the worm data. John Wooley provided helpful advice. Planning for this project was supported by a Small Grant for Exploratory Research DIR–9003540 from the National Science Foundation. The project itself is now supported by NSF IRI–9015407 through the Special Initiative in Coordination Theory and Collaboration Technology.

Journal of Management Information Systems / Winter 1991–92, Vol. 8, No. 3, pp. 87–107.

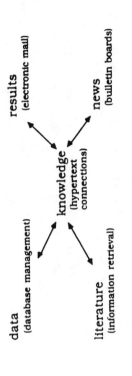

results
(electronic mail)

news
(bulletin boards)

knowledge
(hypertext connections)

data
(database management)

literature
(Information retrieval)

Formal ←——→ Informal

Figure 1. An Electronic Community System Records and Manipulates All the Knowledge of a Community or Organization

products and technical information about designs, but also test results, meeting reports, and other informal sources. To integrate this knowledge, one must understand the relationships between the available items in the context of the company values and culture. Productivity would be greatly enhanced if a substantial fraction of this integrated knowledge were easily available from the employee's desktop computer. Traditional management information systems have only supported a small portion of this functionality.

It is now possible to build substantial prototypes of information systems that handle such a wide variety of integrated knowledge. These can be termed *electronic community systems*, which encode and manipulate formal and informal knowledge and their interrelationships. A large-scale experiment is being carried out to encode the knowledge of a community of scientists and to build a software environment to manipulate this knowledge from their laboratories. The community includes those scientists studying the nematode worm *C. elegans*, a model organism in molecular biology. This paper discusses a model for community systems and previous such systems in science, the biology experiment and a previous system, the enabling technology for handling the knowledge, the enabling mechanisms for handling the values, the state of the prototype, and speculations on future applications in supporting organizational memory.

A Model for Electronic Community Systems

THE WORD "COMMUNITY" IS CLOSELY ALLIED WITH THE WORDS "common," meaning "the same," and "communicate," meaning "to exchange information." Originally, *community* referred to the people residing in some small physical location and more generally to their shared values. The meaning of the word has been extended to groups of people with common interests and shared values who may reside in geographically separate places. Thus, one may refer to the scientific community or the physics community or the relativity community. This section discusses a general model for a community and its support by a computer system.

To support a community electronically, it is necessary to encode as much of its knowledge as possible. Figure 1 illustrates the range of possible knowledge that might be supported by a computer system. To live effectively within a community, one must have available both the formal archival material and the informal transient folklore. This includes the fundamental items of data for the community, for example, as maintained by database management systems, and the intermediate results, for example, as contained in electronic mail messages. This includes the archival literature for the community, for example, as maintained by information retrieval systems, and the intermediate news, for example, as contained in electronic bulletin boards. Finally, it includes support for the shared values as well as the common interests. The mores of the community can be supported by means of a variety of mechanisms for recording the relationships between the data and information, for example, by providing hypertext documents.

An *electronic community system* is a computer system that encodes the knowledge of a community and provides an environment that supports manipulation of that

knowledge. Different communities have different knowledge but their environments have great similarities. The community knowledge might be thought of as being stored in an electronic library. Much of the material originates within external sources. The environment must accordingly provide software for building a library to access these sources, for example, convenient mechanisms for encoding and browsing what is available. But, unlike existing physical libraries, a community library is dynamic and the members will actively add items to it. The environment must also provide software for updating this library, that is, convenient mechanisms for refereeing and sharing added items. The environment thus provides support for both the knowledge and the mores of the community.

The functionality of an electronic community system can be motivated by considering the analogy of doing research in a physical library. Consider the analogy of a physical library in order to write a book. You start with references from a paper or colleagues, look the references up in the card catalog, go to an appropriate section of the library, and scan your eye along the titles on the spines of the books. If any books look relevant, you pull them off the shelf for detailed examination of the pages. If some pages look relevant, you make a copy for later use. After some scanning and examining, you go to another section of the library, often using references found in the previous section. When the research phase is finished, you write your book, utilizing references to copied pages, and submit your book to be published (and subsequently placed itself into the library).

In the model of a community library, the books are distributed multimedia objects. There are three basic stages in the interaction process: browsing, filtering, and sharing. In *browsing*, the user can rapidly examine the items in the library. This can be accomplished via search, by giving an associative specification and viewing matching items, or via navigation, by following the connections from a given item. The results can be displayed at a variety of summary levels. Multiple searches and navigations can be issued and cross-compared to located desired items.

The next stage is *filtering*, where the user culls the items located by browsing into some desired set, relevant to the current need. If the browsing speed is sufficiently fast, user view of displays may be sufficient to select relevant items manually. If the items are too numerous or too complex, manual examination may not be sufficient. In this case, a set of selected items can be passed into an external analysis program for automatic filtering. Such a program might sort the items by date or perform a complicated computation to determine rank ordering against some similarity metric.

After a set of desired existing items have been found, the user may wish to add this set with comments back into the library. *Sharing* is the support for publishing in the electronic library. A variety of mechanisms are supported within an electronic community system for grouping the items to record their relationships, for example, storing a set with a description of its relationship or forging a connection link between related items. Mechanisms are also supported for writing hyperdocuments, which incorporate other items into the text via embedded links. Once a sufficiently important new group or document has been composed, facilities are available for releasing this to the community. A variety of mechanisms are supported to provide editorial and privacy control of the release process. These mechanisms are the attempt to encode the mores of the community, by permitting members of the community to control the quality of the material in the library and who may view the material.

Electronic Scientific Communities

THE BUSINESS OF SCIENTIFIC RESEARCH IS AN UNUSUALLY GOOD DOMAIN to investigate the development of an electronic community system. Practicing scientists need access to a wide variety of knowledge to carry out their research. Much of this knowledge resides in formal published literature, but much also resides in informal community knowledge. Some of this informal community knowledge, such as preliminary results, will eventually become published, but other knowledge, such as details of methods and the "lore" of experimental systems, never reaches the formal literature. The scientist who shares a community's current informal knowledge and has rapid access to the formal knowledge can do better research. This is particularly true in the biological sciences, which are largely data-driven, because the choice and design of experiments depend on familiarity with the most current methods and knowledge. As the pace of science increases, only a small number of insiders who lead each field, the "invisible college" [2], have enough knowledge to perform seminal research efficiently. If the informal community knowledge could be captured and disseminated more widely, the quality and efficiency of scientific research would improve. This is because the invisible college would be larger and because it would be open to scientists from diverse disciplines, which would encourage novel interdisciplinary research.

The existence of nationwide networks has fostered electronic scientific communities. The ARPANET was the first nationwide computer network widely available to the scientific community in the United States. It was constructed during the late 1960s and reached its potential throughout the 1970s. The original motivation for the network was to support remote access to the large "supercomputers" constructed and purchased by ARPA-funded researchers. What emerged as the most important service, however, was the new facility of *electronic mail*, which provided a new communications medium. The ability to convey informal information rapidly caused a new feeling of closeness among the researchers on the network and the emergence of the first widespread electronic community, the ARPANET community [7]. Researchers on the ARPANET could get essential information more quickly than those not on the net and many collaborations took place without the collaborators ever physically meeting.

Early users of electronic mail in the ARPANET noted the convenience of being able to send items to many others on a distribution list. Standardized lists became established to distribute messages to people interested in a wide variety of topics. These lists evolved into the next generation of community system, the *electronic bulletin board*. An illustrative current-day bulletin board system is Netnews [10], which distributes messages over USENET [9]. USENET is not a centrally planned and maintained network, but a loose collection of computers running the Unix™ operating system connected by a wide variety of physical transmission lines from high-speed leased lines to ordinary telephone lines. It operates today with more than 250,000 users on more than 10,000 machines spread throughout the world. Netnews contains more than 650 boards across a wide variety of topics, ranging from comments about existing computers to technical science to popular culture to job positions to movie reviews to cooking recipes. The software functionality has evolved to support streamlined posting to the appropriate boards, comments on previous messages, reading of selected boards, and saving of selected messages.

Everyday operation of Netnews shows the benefits of community sharing. When you post a technical question, you often get a detailed technical answer from somewhere out in the Net, often from a place you would never have thought of looking. Frequently, your posting stimulates a series of postings, each illuminating the problem from a different point of view. It is common to see the understanding of a problem evolve over a week through comments from a series of different postings from different parts of the world. For example, a recent query by the author concerning radio interference on laptop computers elicited helpful comments and critiques from people at sites in Massachusetts, California, Wisconsin, Oregon, Hawaii, Ontario, Germany, and Sweden. There is a real feeling of community interaction to solve shared problems on the many responsible boards. As with the ARPANET boards, Netnews tends to be self-policing. The users tend to be responsible individuals who understand that the system is supported by the generosity of their employers. People who abuse the Net (by posting inflammatory or irresponsible messages) are quickly dealt with by peer pressure. There are elaborate documents on appropriate Net etiquette: what boards are suitable for what topics, what content is appropriate for a posting, how to be terse and polite, and so on. Different board types have evolved a spectrum of editorial control, ranging from boards where anyone can post anything to ones where all messages pass through a human moderator for topic and quality control.

As the speed of networks increases, so does the range of information that can be effectively encoded within an electronic community. The dream of an all-encompassing science information system is an old one, since the possibility of being able to sit in front of a computer and be able to access all the knowledge you need for your research is so attractive. This dream has resurfaced periodically whenever the computing and communications technology makes a dramatic increase in functionality. See, for example, the "future of libraries" study after the advent of minicomputers in the 1960s [6], the "world scientific information system" study after the advent of computer networks in the 1970s [16], and the "national collaboratory" study after the advent of workstations and supercomputer networks in the 1980s [8]. The forthcoming NREN (National Research and Educational Network) will provide network speeds fast enough to support interactive manipulation of a wide variety of material across the national scientific network. This leads to the possibility of realizing an all-encompassing information system with the next generation of community systems.

Building an Electronic Community System

COMMUNITY SYSTEMS OF THE NEAR FUTURE will support the complete range of knowledge and functionality discussed in the Model section above. They will support a wide variety of database management and information retrieval functions to support a wide variety of formal experimental data and literature information. In addition, they will support a wide variety of electronic mail and bulletin board functions to support a wide variety of informal results and news.

The Community Systems Laboratory is building an electronic community system in the domain of scientific research and evaluating its use within the community as a large-scale experiment. The resulting system is meant to serve a wide variety of communication needs within the community, both retrieval and analysis, as well as rapid sharing of knowledge with others. It will permit researchers, who have common interests and shared values but are geographically dispersed, to browse and share the community knowledge. The scientific community chosen for this experimental project is the community of molecular biologists united by their common use of a model organism, the nematode worm *Caenorhabditis elegans* [11].

The Worm Community

Building an electronic scientific community in today's largely nonelectronic world requires a specialized community with an appropriate set of characteristics. It must have a large amount of data, both formal and informal, and a real need to manipulate these data extensively. The data must be freely available and already largely in electronic form. There must be many interested users who are willing to experiment with new technology and who have adequate computer equipment and network connections. There must be real support for data administration and software development, which implies that the community must be an important one scientifically so that adequate funding is available.

A scientific community that exhibits these properties is the *worm community*, the molecular biologists who utilize the nematode worm *Caenorhabditis elegans*. Molecular biology is a largely data-driven experimental science and, due to such efforts as

the Human Genome Initiative, its data are growing rapidly and being stored in databases. Communities in molecular biology often form around organisms, rather than techniques or problems. *C. elegans* is a nonparasitic worm found in the soil, which has been extensively studied, with a wide range of experimental data available on its genetics, anatomy, and development [17]. The "worm" has become a primary model organism and will likely become one of the first to be completely sequenced.

The worm community itself is young, but growing rapidly, with more than 500 researchers at the last large meeting in June 1991. It has a close-knit and communicative group of "insiders," the postdoctoral fellows of Sydney Brenner who initiated the modern genetics of *C. elegans* in the late 1960s. It has a strong community tradition of free sharing of unpublished data, unlike the competitive nature of many other areas of science. Substantial bodies of data are already in electronic form, and there is an adequate level of computer literacy and interest in electronic communication.

Two examples of widely shared unpublished data within the worm community illustrate its suitability as a cooperative experimental electronic community. The *Worm Breeder's Gazette* is a newsletter analogous to a moderated electronic bulletin board, which consists of short research items and has been published several times a year for more than ten years in an unrefereed open format. The physical map database is an electronic recording of an ordered set of cloned DNA fragments that constitute the genetic material of the worm [1]. Its curators map new fragments and distribute the database as a service to the community; the easy availability has dramatically facilitated molecular analysis of genes.

The worm community is an excellent candidate for an electronic scientific community due to a number of unusual characteristics. It is the right size—big enough so that newcomers no longer know the pioneers directly but small enough so that fierce competition has not yet set in. It is the right age—old enough so that there is extensive knowledge already discovered but young enough so that the insiders still remember the original days and want to preserve their closeness. It has the right importance—significant enough so that discoveries make a scientific difference but offbeat enough so that researchers do not hoard their data.

Finally, the worm community has always had a special tradition of sharing knowledge. Reasons include the fact that many members of the worm community were trained in the phage group where openness was encouraged and that there has always been a primary goal of understanding everything about the worm. The worm community's informal network of communication is becoming inadequate as the community grows, and there is concern among the insiders about losing the community's unique flavor. Thus, there is an immediate need for an electronic worm community and a favorable set of conditions for an experiment in electronic communication.

Worm Community Knowledge

One major advantage of the worm community as a community system testbed is the large amount of important data available. The most significant available sources are listed below. The categories for these materials span the range of editorial control: published literature is refereed; archival data are edited (checked for quality); informal information is moderated (checked for topic); and unpublished data are posted (no checking). Archival data are typically maintained by a central curator, whereas unpublished data are maintained by individual researchers. Similarly, much of the informal information is unrefereed literature.

Archival Data

Gene Descriptions. These are text descriptions of the phenotypes of worm mutations and other genetic effects. About 1,200 of perhaps 5,000 genes are known.

Genetic Map. This represents the relative positions of genes on the chromosomes, based on how often two genes recombine during sexual reproduction. The display is a line drawing with marks denoting the gene positions.

Physical Map. This represents cloned fragments of worm DNA and how they overlap to form the chromosomes. Genes known to be within a fragment thus have a known absolute position. The display is a drawing with many overlapping lines and located genes. About 11,000 clones nearly cover the chromosomes.

DNA Sequences. These are the nucleotide codes for the genes, with only a few known at present. They display as strings of ACGT.

Cell List. This table and text identify every one of the 959 cells and their location in the worm.

Wiring Diagram. This table gives the complete connection pattern of all 302 neurons. It is displayed as a line drawing.

Cell Lineage. This table and line drawing give the complete developmental history of every cell, i.e., which cell develops into which other cells during growth.

Formal Literature

Bibliography. This text gives citations for most of the *C. elegans* literature. The current list of some 1,400 articles is maintained by a central curator.

Abstracts. Text abstracts for most of these articles are available in on-line literature databases such as Medline, Biosis, and Agricola.

Full-text. Text of the complete contents of all the papers would be preferable for a complete community library. If copyright permission were available, it would be possible to scan and recognize the characters in worm journal articles.

Page Images. The most desirable storage would be complete article contents, including drawings, figures, tables, graphs, and equations, in addition to text. The most practical approach is to digitally scan page images of the nontextual material. After an article is located by searching the full-text, the text can be displayed in formatted form along with the images of the figures.

Worm Book. This is the standard reference book *The Nematode Caenorhabditis Elegans* [17], which contains review articles on all aspects of *C. elegans* biology as well as the existing data, nearly 700 pages total.

Informal Literature

Newsletters. The *Worm Breeder's Gazette* has been published for ten years and is a rich source of one-page notes about items of interest from experimental results to methods to news.

Conferences. The biannual *C. elegans* Meeting publishes one-page abstracts of presented papers that can be cited as personal communications.

Unpublished Data

Lab Directory. This is the list of current researchers with their addresses.

Strain List. This is the list of the worm mutations available from the centralized stock center.

Useful unpublished data are also maintained in the laboratories of individual researchers. They include: experimental methods (text), genomic maps (drawings), micrographs (images), and strain lists (text).

Analysis Software

There are a variety of programs available for analyzing the biological data, such as comparing sequence similarity. The environment provides a facility for selecting a set of items and passing this set into an external analysis program. Some of these programs also provide sophisticated displays of the data, for example, genetic and physical maps.

Community Lore

Much of the knowledge about the worm is not currently recorded anywhere. The Worm Community System will support facilities for entering annotations, specifying relationship links, and writing documents. This new material will be added to the shared community library.

The Telesophy System

AS AN INTRODUCTION TO THE TECHNOLOGY required to implement an electronic community system, its predecessor will be briefly discussed. Then the specific support for technology and for sociology will be described. Finally, the existing prototype will be discussed, along with future plans.

During the 1960s, Douglas Engelbart's NLS project carried out a pioneering effort to build a tool to "augment the human intellect," a single computer system that enabled a researcher interactively to manipulate all their knowledge [3]. The resulting system could manipulate collections of documents consisting of a hierarchy of paragraphs, which were interconnected on the basis of similar words. There was extensive support for collaboration, such as a shared journal that kept a record of annotations and revisions [4], and support for remote access over ARPANET. The project gathered a group of devoted users, eventually totaling several hundred, and attempted to support a few small specialized communities [5]. Typical users were information specialists whose jobs involved examining and writing large formal bureaucratic documents with detailed hierarchical structure.

During the 1980s, the present author carried out a project to investigate whether sufficient technology was available to build a complete community system [12, 13]. Much infrastructure had already matured—for example, hardware technology such as large-memory graphics workstations and high-speed fiber networks and software technology such as bibliographic information search and object-oriented programming systems. This project was called *telesophy*, or wisdom at a distance, to indicate that the system was intended to support transparent manipulation of knowledge across computer and communications networks. The concept of telesophy as an all-inclusive network system was intended to be analogous to the concept of telephony, with the ultimate goal of supporting transparent manipulation of "all the world's knowledge" just as the telephone system supports transparent connection of "all the world's telephones."

As part of the Telesophy project, a prototype of a complete community library was constructed, including both data and software [13, 14]. The system forms a distributed digital library, which enables fast browsing across a wide range of data physically distributed across a network. Data are collected from external sources and transformed into uniform objects, which can be manipulated by a uniform set of commands, regardless of the original physical data type. The set of objects is called the *information space* and may be distributed across many machines within a network. Retrieval takes place transparently, regardless of the actual physical location, and is done either by associative search or by following links between objects. The software runs on Sun workstations and has been distributed to more than forty-five sites. The software contains a custom window manager, object system, network handler, and text searcher.

In the main configuration, a wide variety of data was collected and transformed into units in the information space. This collection represented a good sample of what is currently available electronically. It also spanned the range of different media types, from text to graphics to image to video, as a test of the system's ability to support type transparency. The prototype space consisted of some 300,000 items from some twenty data sources. The informal material were short text messages that included bulletin boards, electronic mail, wire services, and notes. The formal material included bibliographic citations with abstracts covering computing from INSPEC™ and biology from Medline™, and also full text of magazine articles and movie reviews. The pictorial material included line drawing graphics, black and white images, color magazine figures, glossy photographs, and videodisc stills. Finally, the video material included played segments from a variety of educational and entertainment videodiscs. The data thus spanned the range from informal to formal material, as well as including material such as pictures and graphics. A few materials with code were also collected, including playing of videodisc segments and stored queries that are executed on-the-fly to provide a different result each time.

The software supports transparent, distributed information retrieval. Every data item is searchable by combinations of phrases on all the text associated with the item, such as the abstract, body of text, or picture captions. Searches can be done across all the different databases and all matching items returned. The databases can be physically distributed across machines in a network. In the prototype configuration, the twenty databases were spread across three large file servers connected by a building Ethernet so that any appropriate workstation (i.e., a Sun-3) could access them. The database searching takes place on the file servers, while the user interface and information manipulation take place on the user's workstation. The Telesophy system concentrated on supporting associative search as in information retrieval systems rather than following of links as in NLS or hypertext systems; tradeoffs between search and navigation are discussed in [15].

The software implementation is tuned to support fast browsing. The data are fully indexed so that processing a query typically takes one to two seconds. The resulting items are then downloaded from the remote file server over the network to the local workstation. The interaction is "instantaneous" (less than one second) for displaying and page flipping one-line summaries of query results or zooming into the complete items. This same speed has been maintained for the vast majority of the items (text and line drawings) across a variety of physical networks: building Ethernet, campus Ethernet, and a WAN (wide-area network) consisting of two building Ethernets forty miles apart connected by a private T1 line.

In addition to supporting library browsing, the Telesophy system also supports kinds of community sharing. All of the external data items are represented as information units (IUs), the collection of which forms the information space. There is a single set of commands for basic manipulation of any information unit, independent of type and location. The user can perform an exploratory browsing session, issue multiple queries, and save a collection of selected items as a new information unit that can be indexed and placed back into the space. These collections are a simple form of "metalevel" grouping, of classifying sets of items of different types from different databases into new semantic groupings, which can arise by saving the results of a simple query or from the results of considerable searching and analysis. Since all users, regardless of their physical location, access the same information space, these new composite IUs, which form regions in the space, are automatically shared with other members of the community.

Proving the viability of a new communications medium requires demonstrating that its implementation is technically feasible and its deployment causes a sociological change. The Telesophy system demonstrated the technical feasibility of building a community system, but failed to achieve widespread usage due to the difficulty of obtaining suitable data in electronic form for the needs of the user community—electrical engineers in an industrial research laboratory. Experience with physical libraries has shown that one of their most important features is complete coverage, that is, essentially all materials on the covered subjects are available. Coverage is even more important in an electronic community library since a key feature is rapid annotation of existing material. During the course of the Telesophy project, it became clear that demonstrating the requisite sociological change would require carrying out a large-scale trial with a specialized community, thus prompting the beginnings of the Worm Community System project.

Enabling Technology

THERE ARE A NUMBER OF TECHNOLOGIES REQUIRED to implement an electronic community system effectively. This section discusses one of the most important—the representation for the knowledge in the community library. This builds upon the experience from the Telesophy system.

Information Spaces

The data model for a community system must support uniform commands for browsing and sharing across the complete spectrum of community knowledge. This requires supporting features not well supported by the models underlying traditional database management systems. Community knowledge spans a wide range of types, each requiring its own operations for search and display. Community knowledge is interconnected and needs an efficient representation for making relationship links between items. Community knowledge exists across many sources, which can be distributed across a network. The relational model, for example, cannot easily support multiple types or arbitrary links between arbitrary groupings. An appropriate object-oriented model can, since each type of object can have its own set of operations and each object can have its own set of pointers to other objects. A community system uses a particular kind of federated heterogeneous distributed object-oriented database, called an *information space*.

Information spaces support uniform manipulation of heterogeneous data items by transforming them into homogeneous information units. The generation of an information space begins with data already existing in some external source. The format of this data is administratively transformed into a canonical internal representation called an *information unit*, or *IU*. An information unit is an encapsulated object, in the sense of an object-oriented programming language, which has an associated set of operations to provide manipulation capability for its particular data type. Every "database" thus has a set of transformation routines and every "data type" has a set of data operations. Once the data items have become information units, there are a set of generic operations available for performing on them. These generic operations support uniform commands at the user level for such functions as search, display, and grouping. Thus, a user of an information space need only learn one set of commands to manipulate information units, which operate uniformly across a wide range of external data types. Each information unit may be connected to other units to represent a semantic relationship and collections of information units may be grouped into new composite units. An *information space* is a set of information units and their connections. Logically, it is a single uniform graph structure, although physically it may be composed of many different sources of data of many different types stored on many different machines in many different locations spread across a network.

There are several levels of representation in an information space. Data exist in the external sources and are transformed into information within the space. Knowledge, in the sense of *community knowledge*, is represented by the different components of information units. Any IU can be annotated; a typical *annotation* is a note stating some additional feature of the encapsulated data, for example, this gene may encode this function. Any two IUs can have a relationship specified between them; a typical *connection* is a link to another IU supplying additional information, e.g. this article discusses this gene. Any collection of IUs can be grouped into a single composite IU which forms a region in the information space; a typical *region* is a set of IUs on the same topic, for example, all genes coding for mechanosensory deficiencies. Since every IU has a unique identification within the entire space, it is possible to implement a uniform mechanism for forging and maintaining these groupings, even across sources. As discussed below, every IU also has specification to provide publication control over the sharing of these groupings.

Forming the Space

Anything accessible may potentially be incorporated into the space. That is, all data reachable via the underlying network for which appropriate transformation routines exist can reside logically within the information space. When administration is done to bring data physically into the space depends on ease of reliability and maintenance. In many cases, maintaining the data directly in an external database is the most convenient; in this case, data items are transformed into information units only when they are actually retrieved (and then only temporarily during use so that any updates must be written back into the database itself). If the data are to be maintained directly in the information space itself, the data items are transformed once into information units when they are brought into the space and then any updates are performed by operations within the space. Since maintaining consistency and correctness of large amounts of data requires considerable system support, initial implementations of information spaces will likely rely on existing database management systems to provide maintenance, transforming external data items into internal information units on-the-fly or periodically whenever the database has been significantly updated.

In the worm information space, for example, there are a variety of methods for incorporating external data and software. The support for these may be handled internally (as objects brought into the system) or externally (as objects existing outside the system). Some external data are read in from text files, then handled by internal software. For example, the gene list is a text description kept in a file, then supported by the built-in text display. Some external software is invoked as a separate process with arguments. For example, the sequence map display is called as an external program. Some external software is invoked with objects passed in and out. For example, a sequence analysis program is passed sequences in a canonical textual format and returns text that is transformed back into sequence objects. Finally, some external software supports its own classes which are directly communicated with, providing internal software with direct interactive access to external objects. For example, the genetic map displayer is an external program that implements an annotation command that invokes the internal support for annotating the objects belonging to the external program.

The major generic operations built into the system, as part of the IU class definition, are the support for grouping. These include connection links and region sets. Other operations, which provide support for the uniform user commands, are implemented at the individual subclass level, for example, those for search and display. This enables the system to support many different types of search (e.g., text and sequences), and of display (e.g., text and maps). Some of the type classes are available in essentially every community—for example, an atomic class for text and a composite class for some kind of hyperdocument. Other types are specific to individual communities—for example, an atomic class for gene and a composite class for genetic map containing gene positions. The object structure of information units enables an electronic community library to be extensible, with a base set of classes that can be augmented by specific classes for a specific community.

Enabling Sociology

THE ABOVE DISCUSSIONS HAVE INDICATED THAT IT IS TECHNICALLY POSSIBLE to collect a significant amount of community knowledge and make this easily available to community members. Ensuring their active participation in this electronic experiment requires resolution of the following sociological problems, among others.

Editorial and Quality Control

Published literature typically goes through a careful refereeing process. This is also true of the archival data, where there is typically a trusted central administrator who performs editorial quality control. With informal information or unpublished data, especially when entered by the users, quality control becomes significant,

The solution to quality control in the printed literature is to have a range of editorial review that leads to a spectrum of documents ranging from lab notes to working documents to internal memoranda to newsletter announcements to conference papers to journal articles to research monographs to textbooks. A similar spectrum has emerged in electronic bulletin boards. In public boards, anyone can post any message. In moderated boards, all messages go first to a moderator who eliminates those that are on wrong topics, redundant, or inflammatory. In edited boards, the editor passes judgment not only on topic but also on quality and format. There has been talk of true refereed boards with long articles, but not many examples exist.

A community system should provide a mechanism for "levels of editorial release," that is, how carefully checked an item is before it is released to the community. Following on the experience of electronic bulletin boards, the spectrum of editorial control should include: posted, moderated, edited, refereed. The system does not, however, determine the policy of which level an author chooses for a particular item or who performs the function of the editor for which items. An appropriate set of conventions will have to evolve for the electronic community library, just as such a set of conventions has already evolved for electronic bulletin boards. Based on experience with the worm community in the past, editors will emerge who can provide appropriate levels of quality control for each data source and who are sufficiently respected by the community so that their blessing of the data is trusted.

The level of editorship should be recorded on each item in the information space, because this is of interest to the researchers who are evaluating the suitability of particular information units for their current purposes. This is a form of policy that permits the individual users to choose for themselves whether they are currently interested in refereed facts and data or in rumors and notes.

Privacy and Reward Considerations

Another problem in extending the community library beyond formal data is whether the members are willing to share the data before it has been formally published. The tradition of freely sharing unpublished data is a primary reason for choosing the worm community for the initial experiment. But there is a significant problem in any scientific community for establishing credit and priority, particularly as competition becomes more intense.

The community system should provide the mechanism of "levels of privacy release," that is, who is permitted to view which material. Sample levels include: private (user only), colleagues (local), colleagues (global), community. As with the editorial release, the policy for each item is individually determined by the author and can be changed as the item evolves in maturity and quality. Each researcher can also determine who is permitted to view each level of release, that is, who their colleagues are.

Conversely, for searching purposes, each researcher can use the privacy level to help determine the appropriateness of those items in the information space that they have permission to access. It should be noted that the privacy levels enable the community system to support services equivalent to electronic mail and bulletin boards.

An issue related to privacy is rewards. What reward does the author of an information unit receive? It will be a long time before the prestige of making a connection in information space rivals that of publishing a paper in a journal. The system can provide the mechanism of a super citation index, by keeping track of the frequency that an item is retrieved and the number of times a connection is made to it. Hopefully, these usage statistics will aid in establishing policies for electronic publishing. Also note that every information unit has complete attribution of its creation, that is, author and date. In fast-moving fields with extensive electronic coverage, this could provide a method for establishing priority and credit.

Prototype Community Systems

THE FIRST RELEASE OF THE WORM COMMUNITY SYSTEM was completed during the summer of 1991 and is now in the labs of the initial test users, who are using it to browse the data and beginning to add annotations.

The current community knowledge spans the potential range. It includes fairly complete archival data, such as the list of gene descriptions, the genetic map, the physical map, and many DNA sequences. It includes abstracts of most of the archival

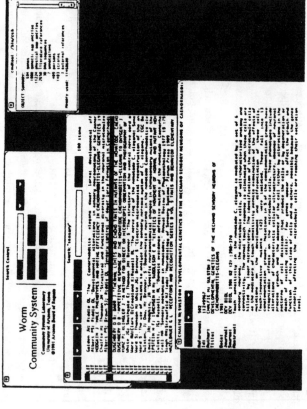

Figure 2.   Search

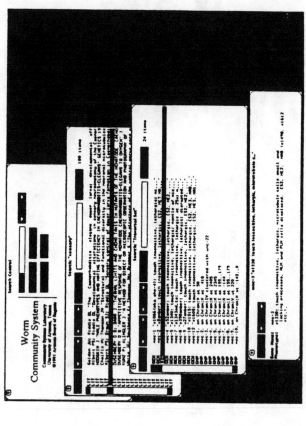

Figure 3.   Navigation

worm literature. The worm newsletter has been completely scanned and the text recognized, so that articles can be searched for, then displayed as formatted text with accompanying images for the figures. Unpublished data are available, such as standard strains and a person directory, plus a sampling of other data from individuals.

The software functionality also spans the potential range. Searches can be done across all the sources for text phrases. An extensive set of links has been made between information units by a variety of automatic and manual means. These links can be followed from any IU to the related set of IUs. Sets of IUs can be selected and grouped. Several external analysis programs can be called to provide displays of worm data for the genetic map and the sequence coding map. Finally, an annotation facility is available which permits a note to be added to a set of IUs giving additional information about the group. This note may include embedded links as well as text. When saved, annotations are released into the information space, where they can be manipulated as ordinary information units.

Sample Session

Figure 2 is a screendump from a sample session with the Worm Community System. This session is a summary of the interaction with a biologist, interested in sensory neurons, who is attempting to discover which genes in *C. elegans* control the sense of touch, mechanosensation. The information space enables the biologist rapidly to locate all such known genes and retrieve information about them.

The session starts with the user entering a search for the keyword "sensory" as shown in the topmost Search Control window. The search is performed across all objects of any type contained in the information space; the number of objects is shown in the upper right. The window below Search Control labeled Search: "sensory" contains a summary of the set of objects in the worm information space matching this keyword (containing that text string). Each object has a one-line summary (uniform for all types) that can be zoomed into by pointing with the mouse and double-clicking. The selected object is displayed in the bottom window. It is a literature object containing a citation and abstract from the journal articles about the worm.

In addition to associative search, units in the information space are interconnected and the user can follow links to navigate to related units. For the worm space, literature objects are linked to all genes described in the article. Figure 3 shows a link following. In the window labeled Search: "Traversal Set," the user has requested all objects linked to the selected literature object and the system displays one-line summaries of the set of matching gene objects. The user selects one gene "mec–3" and zooms into its description, which is displayed in the bottom window. This description shows that mutations in the gene indeed make the worm insensitive to touch.

The user now wants to see where the gene is located physically on the DNA of the worm and issues the "show physical map" command on the selected gene in the Traversal Set. Figure 4 displays a section of the physical map of the chromosome showing the known locations for a variety of cloned DNA fragments. The window labeled Contig #423 displays the region containing mec–3. This window is not just a

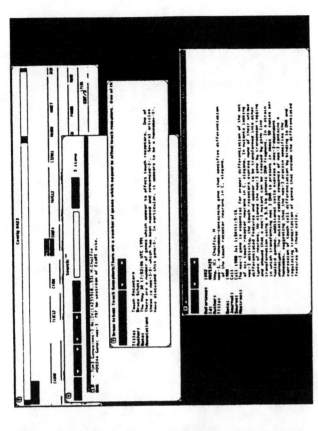

Figure 4. Data Displays

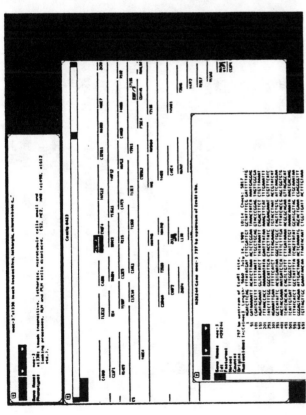

Figure 5. Annotation

line drawing but a live first-class graphical display of a composite object "physical map" that contains many subobjects of type "clone." Thus, the individual objects can be manipulated and interacted with. In this session, the user zooms into the clone on the map containing mec–3 and displays its DNA sequence in the window at the bottom of the screen. An external analysis program might now be invoked (but not yet in this prototype) to compare this gene controlling touch in worms to a library of the sequences for genes in all organisms to identify similar genes in humans.

Finally, the user checks whether other community members have added any informal information about the gene of interest. Figure 5 shows the result of zooming into the physical map entry for mec–3. Three IUs are displayed, corresponding to the gene, the clone, and the DNA sequence. The gene has a checkmark by its summary line indicating that an annotation is available. Issuing "show annotations" brings up the window discussing "Touch Receptors." This has a number of embedded references denoted by -%-. Zooming into the reference stating that mec–3 is a homeobox retrieves the paper in the bottom window. The user has thus made good use of the value-added informal knowledge to find a relevant specific paper concerning the gene of interest.

Future Plans

The current prototype system is written in GNU C++ and runs under the Unix™ operating system, typically on a Sun SPARCstation™. The external sources are maintained in files in text form and transformed into information unit objects when

the system starts up. All the software is custom written, including the object manipulation. The current system runs all in memory and takes about 11 megabytes when loaded. This comprises some 18,000 objects, the bulk of which are physical map entries, while the bulk of the size is literature items. Some of the test sites run the system on a local Sun workstation directly. Since the display uses X-windows, others run it remotely on an Apple Macintosh™ II running MacX™, with acceptable response over a local area network.

This first release is now in the labs of the initial users, on the order of ten laboratories. Initially the goal is to recruit enough users to support a "fair test" of this kind of system. These users must be enthusiastic enough to use a preliminary system and influential enough to have their reactions taken seriously by community members. In addition, geographical distribution is important since the experiment is a test of a nationwide electronic scientific community.

The feedback from this release is being used to design the second release. This version will be a distributed system with separate modules for database searching, for object manipulation, and for user interface. Computer scientists associated with the project will be experimenting with what caching and protocol technology is necessary to provide interactive retrieval across the NSFNET. The plan is for this version to be a fully featured system that is propagated to a significant fraction of the worm community. Sociologists associated with the project will be investigating its usage to understand the effects on the community's communication patterns.

In the longer term, as the system for supporting the worm community becomes functional, the software will be made available to other communities. The next

and product information is available only on a need-to-know basis. There may be other controls to support the policies and procedures, and to regulate the flow of information within the organizational structure. Finally, there may be other types of functionality necessary to capture some degree of the company culture. For example, there may be precise style and content constraints on hyperdocuments in the organization's information space.

Large-scale experiments in real organizations will be necessary to assess the value of electronic community systems for supporting organizational memory. Preliminary evidence indicates that this technology will be valuable to the scientific community, so great potential exists for its value to the business community as well.

References

1. Coulson, A.; Sulston, J.; Bremner, S.; and Karn, J. Towards a physical map of the genome of the nematode *Caenorhabditis elegans*. *Proceedings of the National Academy of Science*, 83 (1986), 7821–7825.
2. D. Crane. *Invisible Colleges: Diffusion of Knowledge in Scientific Communities*. Chicago: University of Chicago Press, 1972.
3. Engelbart, D., and English, W. A research center for augmenting the human intellect. *Proceedings of the AFIPS Fall Joint Computer Conference*. 33 (1968), 395–410.
4. Engelbart, D. Collaboration support provisions in AUGMENT. *Proceedings of the AFIPS Office Automation Conference*, Los Angeles, February 1984, pp. 51–58.
5. Engelbart, D. Coordinated information services for a discipline- or mission-oriented community. In *Computer Communications Networks*, R. Grimsdale, ed. NATO Series, vol. 4, Noordhoff, 1975, pp. 89–99.
6. Licklider, J. *Libraries of the Future*. Cambridge, MA: MIT Press, 1965.
7. Licklider, J.; Taylor, R.; and Herbert, E. The computer as a communication device. *Science and Technology* (April 1968), 21–31.
8. National Science Foundation. Towards a national collaboratory. Report of an Invitational Workshop. March 1989. Directorate for Computer and Information Science and Engineering.
9. Quarterman, J. *The Matrix: Computer Networks and Conferencing Systems Worldwide*. Englewood Cliffs, NJ: Digital Press/Prentice-Hall, 1989.
10. Reid, B. The USENET cookbook—an experiment in electronic publishing. *Electronic Publishing*, 1 (1988), 55–76.
11. Roberts, L. The Worm Project. *Science*, 248 (June 15, 1990), 1310–1313.
12. Schatz, B. *Telesophy*. Technical Memorandum TM-ARH-002487, Bell Communications Research, August 1985.
13. Schatz, B. Telesophy: a system for manipulating the knowledge of a community. *Proceedings of IEEE Globecom '87*, Tokyo, November 1987, pp. 1181–1186.
14. Schatz, B. A prototype information environment. *Proceedings of the 2nd IEEE Workshop on Workstation Operating Systems*, Pacific Grove, CA, September 1989, pp. 118–124.
15. Schatz, B. Searching in a hyperlibrary. *Proceedings of the 5th IEEE International Conference on Data Engineering*, Los Angeles, February 1989, pp. 188–197.
16. UNESCO. *UNISIST: Study Report of the Feasibility of a World Science Information System*. Paris: United Nations Educational, Scientific, and Cultural Organization, 1971.
17. Wood, W., ed. *The Nematode Caenorhabditis elegans*. Cold Spring Harbor, NY: Cold Spring Harbor Laboratory Press, 1988.

electronic communities will probably be molecular biologists whose communities are also organized around experimental organisms, including the bacterium *E. coli*, the fruit fly *Drosophila*, the weed *Arabidopsis*, the slime-mold *Dictyostelium*, the alga *Chlamydomonas*, yeast, mouse, and man. The problem for many of these communities will be the lack of coverage of available data in electronic form, but much of the software should prove transferable.

As attempts to build more electronic community systems begin, more will become known about the characterization of communities. Many factors play a role in the suitability and usefulness of such a system to a community. These include: data (extent of coverage and vitalness of need); maturity (size and age of the community); competitiveness (readiness to share, pace and stakes); sophistication (computer literacy, tolerance for new technology); and many others. It may eventually prove possible to tailor an electronic community system to be more effective for a given set of community characteristics.

Toward Electronic Systems for Organizational Memory

AN ORGANIZATION IS IN MANY RESPECTS SIMILAR to a community. It consists of people with common interests and shared values. So the knowledge in an organization is similar to the knowledge in a community. This knowledge might be termed *organizational memory*, that is, the knowledge that enables the organization to continue to function effectively. This is the permanent knowledge, as opposed to the transient knowledge generated during meetings. As with communities, organizational memory includes not just the tangible information in designs and memoranda, but also the intangible information in company procedures and values. The permanent memory in an organization that can enable it to outlive its founders is contained in both the company products and the company culture. Recording this memory and making it easily accessible electronically would clearly be of enormous use to the functioning of organizations.

The knowledge-encoding and software-system techniques developed for an electronic community system will likely be relevant to building electronic systems for organizational memory. An industrial organization, for example, has similar knowledge to the scientific community described in this paper. There are archival data, such as design specifications and product evaluations, and intermediate data, such as test results and market surveys. There is formal literature, such as technical memoranda and progress reports, and informal literature, such as design notes and meeting minutes. An organization also has similar needs to manipulate this knowledge. There is a need to browse the knowledge, to filter out selections relevant to the problem, then to share annotations of these selections with other members of the organization.

The sociology of an organization tends to be somewhat more rigid than a scientific community. Thus, although the faster pace will likely require the fast distribution of the knowledge, greater control over its dissemination is likely to be important. A finer granularity of specification and tracking of the editorial and privacy controls is likely to be necessary. For example, a design must be approved by a specified series of people

Capturing Organizational Memory

E. Jeffrey Conklin, PhD
Corporate Memory Systems, Inc.
8920 Business Park Drive
Austin, Texas 78759
512 795 9999

Abstract

Contemporary organizations have only a weak ability to remember and learn from the past, and are thus seeking to gain the capacity for "organizational memory." Networked computers might provide the basis for a "nervous system" that could be used to implement the capacity for organizational memory, but the technology (software and hardware) must provide for easy capture, easy recall, and learning. Moreover, for an organization to augment its memory it must shift from the currently pervasive document- and artifact-oriented paradigm (or culture) to one that embraces *process* as well. This process-oriented paradigm requires a new kind of computer system which integrates three technologies: **hypertext**, **groupware**, and a **rhetorical method**. Groupware allows the organizational record to be built in the course of everyday communication and coordination. Hypertext provides the ability to organize and display this rich informational web. And a rhetorical method, such as IBIS, structures the memory according to content, not chronology. In addition to the computer technology, a **shift in organizational culture** toward an appreciation of process is required to implement organizational memory.

1 What is organizational memory?

By "organizational memory" I mean the record of an organization that is embodied in a set of documents and artifacts. Note that collective memory (i.e. the pooled memory of individuals) is excluded from this definition. Organizational memory has become a hot topic recently due to the growing recognition that it appears to be so thoroughly lacking in contemporary organizations. (As M. Graham as pointed out in Graham 1991, organizations in the first half of this century were not so amnesic.) The problem is not a scarcity of documents and artifacts for the organizational memory, but rather the quality, content, and organization of this material. For example, an effective organizational memory would be able to answer such often asked questions as "Why did we do this?" and "How did such and such come to be the case?" Rarely is this possible now.

Organizational memory is perhaps most clearly missing in industries where large numbers of people engage in the design and construction of large, complex systems over long periods of time, such as defense, aerospace, utilities, pharmaceuticals, and telecommunications. Engineering organizations in these industries have serious limitations in transferring previous learning to current problems. The design rationale of large, complex systems is thoroughly and systematically lost. Such phrases as "reinventing the

From D. Coleman (Ed.), *Groupware '92*, pp. 133-137. Morgan Kaufmann Publishers.

wheel", "going in circles", "having the same discussion over and over," often heard in large engineering organizations, point to a striking phenomenon: while organizations don't seem to learn or remember very well, this limitation was, until recently, regarded as normal and inevitable.

2 Why is organizational memory so poor?

It is thus highly desirable to increase the capacity of organizations to remember and to learn. According to our definition, this means capturing more of the "documents and artifacts" of the organization in a way that they can be effectively recalled and reinterpreted. The growth of networked computers for all phases of information work promises to provide the "nervous system" that would support this increased capture and reuse.

However, within the current "artifact-oriented" paradigm (see Figure 1), the only thing we have to capture is that in which we are already drowning: more "data", documents, and artifacts. These are not what is missing from organizational memory -- what is missing is the *context* (i.e. the sense or rationale) that lay behind these documents when they were created. In short, organizations fail to capture any record of the *process* behind the artifacts.

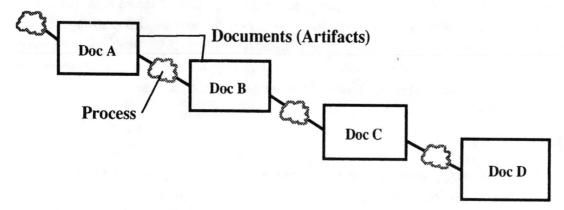

Figure 1: In the artifact-oriented view of work the artifacts (such as diagrams, documents, letters, reports, etc.) are the focus of management attention. Moreover, tools and methods are solely for the production and modification of these artifacts. The process by which this work is done is regarded as secondary.

This is because the current paradigm of work focuses almost solely on the artifacts (or products) of work. For example, in software engineering it is the documents (e.g. requirements, functional specifications, designs, code, etc.) that really count -- the process of creating and revising these artifacts is only recently receiving any attention.

This artifact-oriented paradigm is slowly giving way to a new "process-oriented" paradigm (see Figure 2). Organizations are finding the artifact-oriented way of capturing work to be too impoverished a model to support the complexity of work in the information age. They are turning to a richer, more complete view which embraces the messy (and sometimes chaotic) nature of *process*. No longer ignored are the assumptions, values, experiences, conversations, and decisions which lead to and constitute the context and background of the artifacts. Still, few tools exist for supporting and capturing these elusive but critical aspects of design and action.

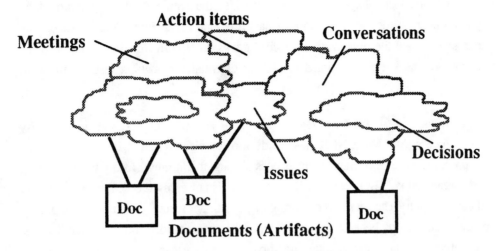

Figure 2: In the process-oriented paradigm there are still artifacts, but they are seen as being no more important than the interactions between *people*.

3 Tools for organizational memory

The most immediate barrier to capturing more of the process of work and making it part of organizational memory is that it seems to present an insurmountable and onerous documentation burden on the people doing the work. *The key to overcoming this perception is to shift the notion of capturing the process data from being an additional documentation burden to "tapping into" the flow of communication that is already happening in an organization. Not surprisingly, this shift is also a shift from an artifact-oriented to a process-oriented perspective.*

For example, one might argue that electronic mail (email) already provides a kind of organizational memory for organizations which use it, and that it does so at no additional documentation cost to the members. While email does indeed have an acceptably low capture cost, it does not provide an effective record because email messages are strictly personal and are stored that way, and because the email record, even for an individual, is so poorly organized and structured that it cannot effectively augment even an individual's memory. So, with email the cost of capture is low, but so is the value of that record for organizational memory.

During 6 years of research on gIBIS (in the MCC Software Technology Program) we learned much about the necessary characteristics of a technology that could provide acceptable capture *and* recall costs for organizational memory (Conklin & Yakemovic 1991). This technology embraces hypertext, groupware (or computer-supported cooperative work), and a rhetorical method. In addition, we learned that computer technology is not enough -- the organization itself must embrace the technology adoption process as part of a larger shift in the corporate culture.

The first element of the computer technology is **hypertext**, because the nature of the process-oriented approach is essentially non-linear, so the representation for capturing and organizing it must also be that rich. Moreover, as time goes by and the organizational record grows more convoluted and complex, the unlimited flexibility of hypertext as a representational medium is essential for ongoing restructuring and summarization.

The second element is **groupware** -- for the same reason that email is a natural first step toward easy capture of organizational process. An MCC/NCR field study showed clearly that it is critical that the technology of used to capture rationale be as transparent as possible, and that it must closely fit the existing practices and tools of the organization. Groupware by its very nature is not focused on capture, but rather on communication and coordination. The secret to capturing organizational memory, then, is to "tap into" the existing flow of process interactions between the members of the organization, and to crystallize this, ongoingly, into the key elements of the organizational memory. Groupware can provide the medium for organizational dialogues which, because they occur via the computer, create a computable record of semi-structured documents. The ability then exists to manipulate, distribute or share this information and intelligence throughout the organization or team, effectively and ongoingly creating a memory and learning tool.

The third element of the technology for capturing organizational memory is the use of a **rhetorical method**, or conversational model, for structuring the conversations occurring with the technology. The reason for this is twofold. A simple rhetorical method provides a structure for discussion of complex problems which can immediately improve the quality of the dialogue process. The IBIS (Issue-Based Information System) method (Kunz & Rittel 1970) provides this kind of process improvement. Secondly, such a model provides a basis for structuring the conversational record which is not simply chronological (as in an email or bulletin board type system). For example, conversations in the IBIS method are structured according to the *issues* being discussed. This provides a *content-based* indexing structure within which the cumulative record of the organizational process is preserved and organized.

The technology for organizational memory must, at a minimum, incorporate hypertext, groupware, and a rhetorical model. But this computer technology is not sufficient to create an effective organizational memory. While the technology must be very good and the user interface transparent, the *organization must also shift* to making capture and use of organizational memory an important and natural practice. This shift towards a process-oriented paradigm and culture requires organizational commitment, and it is the most challenging part of establishing a capacity for memory and learning in an organization.

However, this shift is consistent with the trend already under way in organizations toward quality, customer service, reducing time to market, and all of the other forms of process awareness and improvement. Thus, a new symbiosis is emerging between the human and technological aspects of work: tools for organizational memory and learning can support and maintain a beneficial culture shift, and the culture shift highlights the value of the new tools and promotes their use.

Corporate Memory Systems, Inc. is now offering CM/1, which combines software and consulting technologies based on our MCC gIBIS experience. CM/1 is a groupware system developed to support organizational learning, better decision making, and collaborative work group productivity.

References

Conklin, E. Jeffrey and KC Burgess Yakemovic. 1991. A Process-Oriented Approach to Design Rationale. *Human-Computer Interaction,* Vol. 6, pp. 357-391.

Graham, Margaret. 1991. Notes on Organizational Memory: Practice and Theory. Unpublished Xerox PARC working paper.

Kunz, W. & H. Rittel. 1970. Issues as elements of information systems. Working Paper No. 131, Institute of Urban and Regional Development, University of California at Berkeley, Berkeley, California, 1970.

Report on a Development Project Use of an Issue-Based Information System

K.C. Burgess Yakemovic

NCR Human Interface Technology Center,
500 Tech Parkway,
Atlanta, Georgia 30313
USENET: kcby@atlanta.ncr.com

E. Jeffrey Conklin

MCC Software Technology Program,
P.O. Box 200195,
Austin, Texas, 78720
INTERNET: conklin@mcc.com

ABSTRACT

It has long been recognized that certain kinds of vital information -- usually informal and unstructured, often having to do with *why* certain actions are taken -- are usually lost in large projects. One explanation may be that this kind of information, while important, is too unstructured to be readily captured and retrieved. We report on a field study in which a simple structuring method (IBIS, for Issue-Based Information System) was used over an extended period of time to record and allow retrieval of a significant quantity of precisely this kind of information, using very simple technology. We draw some implications for hypertext and groupware, and for the prospect of supporting the design process with technology.

INTRODUCTION

There is a growing recognition that there is a need during development to capture the *rationale* -- the *why* that underlies the *what* -- behind large and complex computer systems [Sche83], [Most85], [MacL89]. More precisely, there is a growing appreciation of the cost of *failing* to capture this information. In current practice, for example, it is normal to rehash design decisions several times during development simply because no one can recall how the decisions were resolved previously [Walz89]. Similarly, the maintainers of large systems can not reliably make changes to the code without understanding the reasoning, or plan, that was used by the system developers [Leto86], [Wild88]. Finally, software engineering research deals more and more with how to detect errors and misunderstanding as early in the development process as possible, including errors of reasoning that might be avoided if rationale were dealt with more explicitly [Boeh81].

The great difficulty, of course, is that it is costly to capture design rationale, particularly in terms of manual effort, and once captured it is expensive to keep it organized and difficult to access any given piece of rationale when it is needed. Some efforts have been reasonably successful[1], but in large projects the sheer amount of information and its inherent lack of structure[2] make it clear that very powerful technology will be needed to make the capture, analysis and reuse of design rationale normal industrial practice.

Broadly speaking, inventing this design rationale technology involves two critical research problems: how to get the rationale into some kind of database, and how to get it back out effectively. Much of the research currently underway in hypertext and large textual databases offers solutions to the retrieval problem. Our approach to the "data entry" problem is to consider a CSCW technology for supporting the *existing* conversations and information flows as a source of design rationale.

This paper reports on a field trial of a method for capturing design rationale. Our approach is based on the IBIS (Issue-Based Information System) method, and exploits several key features of that method:

• The IBIS structure of Issues (which state questions or problems), Positions (which state possible resolutions of an Issue), and Arguments (which state pros and cons of Positions) is one form of the natural, intuitive structure of decisions: some choice to be made, some set of alternatives, some tradeoff analysis among the alternatives (optional), and a commitment to some resolution. (We note that there are other rhetorical models which have been incorporated into systems, e.g. ARL [Smol87] and Toulmin [Stor89].)

• The IBIS method has been tested and used for design and planning [Kunz80]. It has been shown to be effective in structuring exploratory thinking, providing clarity and rigor on such projects as civic and policy planning.

• The method allows for relatively "low tech" support, such as using an outline processor to provide hierarchical structure among the IBIS elements.

The structure of this paper is: the *background* for the field trial, our *observations* and interpretation about what happened in using the IBIS method, and our *conclusions* about the implications of this field trial for gIBIS, a tool supporting IBIS, and other CSCW systems. Because of the limitations of conducting this experiment within a commercial development group, much of the "data" we present here is anecdotal. However, since the trial spanned a period of over 18 months and generated documentation on over 2200 requirements analysis and design decisions (Issues), we feel it is important to publish these results. We have tried to provide enough detail and examples that the reader can have a sense of how IBIS was used, what problems it solved, and what new problems developed from trying to use it.

Figure 1 presents a rough overview of the field trial, showing the relationship between the number of people using the method, key events in the observed project, time of observation, and the amount of data in the IBIS.

---

[1] For example, the ANSI graphics standards groups have for years recorded each issue, the competing alternative solutions, the tradeoffs of each alternative, and the final decision and voting record of committee members.

[2] More precisely, by "lack of structure" we mean that the information generated in the course of ongoing activity is heterogeneous, ad hoc and imbedded in the activity of its production and use.

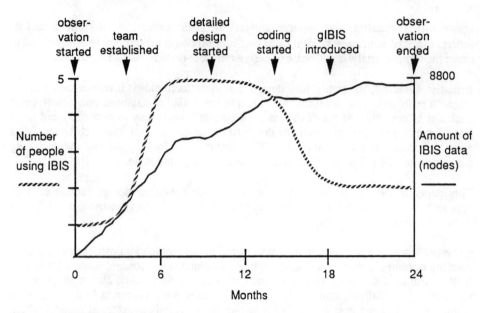

Figure 1 - Field Trial Overview

THE EXPERIMENT

One of the authors (Conklin) has been involved for the last few years at MCC in the development of a workstation-based hypertext groupware tool, called gIBIS, which applies computer technology to the problems of capture and retrieval of IBIS information. It became apparent that there is a large gap between the environments in which the current version of gIBIS can, and would be, used and those in which the capture of design rationale is economically important: commercial development groups with scarce resources, hard deadlines, and a central accountability to produce industrial strength products at a profit. The difference in the environments includes both available computer platforms and organizational practices and attitudes.

The other author (Burgess Yakemovic) had worked many years as a systems analyst in the software development environment at NCR, and during this time collected information about the decisions made during software development projects by keeping detailed handwritten notes on most meetings she attended. Moreover, she acquired a reputation for being good at retrieving this information and other informal documents from the 3-ring binders in which she stored them, thus helping the projects she was on to avoid wasting time and loosing information. Having been exposed to the IBIS method and the gIBIS tool, when she began the requirements analysis for a new commercial application development project, she decided to see if the IBIS method could be used without special tools to help structure the information she normally collected. After she had used the method for a few months, she persuaded the rest of the team of five developers to try to use the method with her.

Thus two issues were addressed by observing the use of the method at NCR; a) could the IBIS method be used, over an extended period of time, in a commercial environment *with minimal alteration of the existing practices of the trial group?*, and b) could the method improve a process of capturing design rationale that was already in place and *extend the use of the process beyond a single individual?*. After using the method without a tool specifically designed for issue-base management, we decided that the gIBIS tool should be introduced, to see if it would solve some of the data management problems encountered.

The next section describes the use of the method without an issue-base management tool: following that, we describe the use of gIBIS during this study.

Indented Text IBIS (itIBIS) and How it was Used

To allow the method to be used with "off the shelf" software and hardware, Indented Text IBIS (itIBIS) was developed. It uses indentation to represent the hierarchical relationships among the "nodes", and can be implemented with an outline processor or text editor on generally available personal computers. Issues are labeled with "I", Positions with "P", supporting Arguments with "AS", and objecting Arguments with "AO". Issue resolution is marked using "*" to show that an Issue had been resolved or that a Position had been selected, "?" to show that no decision has been made, and "-" for rejected Positions. The following example shows what a simple Issue deliberation might look like.

> *I: Which processor should be used?
>   ?P: Processor A.
>   AS: Fast
>   *P: Processor B.
>   AS: Already in use, thus cheaper.
>   -P: Processor C.
>   AO: Won't be available in time

itIBIS was used to collect and structure information during three activities: formal document analysis, requirements analysis and design meetings, and personal brainstorming.

Initially, the method was used to extract issues and other information from the requirements document, as well as from the product management group (interactively). Although not explicitly stated in the document, the root issue it addressed was *What is required for this product?* This root issue was specialized into sub-issues, such as *What is required for the product hardware?* and *What is required for the product software?* The document itself contained mostly positions (again, not explicitly stated as such), and some arguments supporting these positions. When creating the IBIS network which represented the product requirements, additional supporting arguments were supplied through discussion with the document author.

Next, the IBIS method was used by the entire team to capture the content of the discussions that occurred at many meetings, in which the team discussed not only hardware, software, and user requirements, but also design approaches, interfaces with other systems and other departments, and so on. In meetings of this type, there was usually a central issue which was the reason for the meeting, such as *What do we need to supply? What does the hardware need to do? How should we solve this design problem? What information is needed for a particular interface? Who should perform system integration test?*

In addition, two of the developers made use of the method for a variety of individual analysis tasks. These tasks included preparation of presentations, creation of trip reports, and analysis of design options for particular modules within the application.

During the 18 months when itIBIS was used, 66 files containing IBIS networks were created. A single file contained a group of related issues, positions and arguments: for example, the set derived from the hardware portion of the product requirements document, those from meetings held to verify the design against a particular set of user events, or issues relating to the software requirements from a meeting with marketing. The files contained approximately 16,000 lines of text in total and required 780 KB of disc space. For the purpose of analysis, the files were divided into four categories:

Platform - information about the hardware and operating system platform
Requirements - total system requirements
Design - application design
Process - development process

Figure 2 shows the total nodes by category. The entire set of itIBIS files contained approximately 8000 nodes and addressed 2260 Issues.

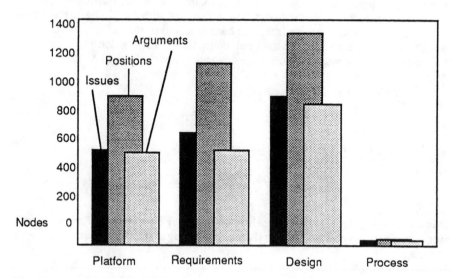

Figure 2 - Nodes by Category

Graphical IBIS (gIBIS)

gIBIS is a SUN workstation-based tool which provides a graphical interface for building and browsing IBIS networks [Conk88], [Conk89]. Because IBIS is a rhetorical model, gIBIS has "groupware" features which support a bulletin-board style interaction among its users. As Figure 3 shows, the basic gIBIS interface is divided into four tiled windows: a graphical browser on the left, a structured node index on the top right, a control panel below the index window, and an inspection window in which the attributes and contents of nodes and links can be viewed.

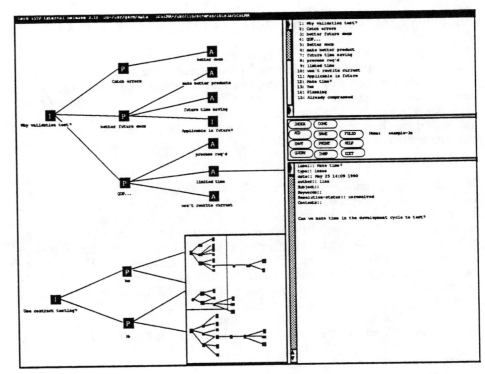

Figure 3: The gIBIS tool screen

After 18 months of using itIBIS, the indented text files were converted to gIBIS format, through a semi-automated process. There were two major manual processes required for conversion; one to create the labels used in the graphical browser, and the other to clean up the results of the automated layout which placed the nodes in the graphical view. While working with itIBIS, the users often made both status and new node updates on the printed copy of the network, but did not update the electronic version (file). Thus, in addition to the updates required by conversion, the resolution status of issues was examined and updated as needed, and additional rationale was added to the networks.

Because of the amount of time required to perform this conversion and manual processing, we made a decision to concentrate the update primarily on the design category material. As a result, only the design issues were reviewed in detail. Our decision was based on two factors: many design issues were still open, and the design issues in general were the most relevant to the other project activities at the time. In addition, there had been a complete change in direction with regard to the product platform which meant that platform category could be archived.

Of the 66 itIBIS files, 47 were converted to gIBIS format: 29 of these were design, 12 requirements and 6 platform. After conversion, 25 of the design files and 4 of the requirements files (representing 35% of the original network) were reviewed and updated. Within this set, the resolution status of the issues went from 36% open to 12% open. Approximately 800 nodes, including new Issues, were added during the update process. But overall, the great majority of the experience reported here is with itIBIS.

OBSERVATIONS

In this section we describe our observations and interpretations of the field trial of itIBIS, covering four aspects of usage: the introduction of the method to the development team, the collection of the IBIS data in itIBIS, the problems and benefits accessing this data, and how using itIBIS and gIBIS influenced the software development process.

Introducing the Method and itIBIS

There are several factors which contributed to the acceptance of the method and itIBIS on this project. One factor was the historical commitment of the system's analyst to the capture of information for later use, which meant that for her the IBIS method was an improvement on an *existing* process. Another factor may have been the timing of the introduction to the team -- had the project been in progress for 6 months, this particular tool would not have made sense. We also were able to secure the support of management, which is necessary to allow any new technique to be used in a commercial environment.

Providing training seems to have been a key factor in the acceptance of the method. Training involved presenting three types of information: first we explained why the method was being introduced and what we hoped to accomplish by using it, second we defined the itIBIS "keywords", the structure of indentation to be used, and how the status of an issue was indicated, and third we gave examples of how to 'reduce' normal conversations to Issues, Positions, and Arguments. This introduction, which allowed a trainee to read an itIBIS document, could be accomplished in 15-30 minutes. For individuals who would be using the method to *create* the itIBIS material, the next step involved actually using the technique to record a discussion, with the results critiqued by another individual who had already been trained. Using the method to record 2 or 3 meetings was sufficient to bring the trainees to a level consistent with the trainers.

Another factor which may have influenced the introduction of the method to this team was the decision to use familiar tools (personal computers and text editors) for the initial implementation. Had the technology been too big of a jump from what they were already using, acceptance would have been less likely [Grud88]. Also, itIBIS was presented as a refinement of an existing practice, producing minutes of meetings, but one that was easier than producing minutes in English prose.

Finally, we note that convincing someone of the value of itIBIS was easier if they had previous experience doing commercial software development. The experience level of the project team varied from first project to 10 years experience, with an average at 4 years. We speculate that more experienced engineers were more receptive because they perceived a need for this kind of documentation.

Information Capture

One effect we noted during the use of itIBIS was the consistency in the quality of notetaking when this format was used. During training, there were two "designated" note takers at several meetings who compared their results, for critiquing purposes. Once both indicated they felt "comfortable" with the technique, the networks they produced were in structure and content almost identical, though of course, variations in the specific wording of a node occurred. Another observation which pointed to improved consistency was made by the project manager, who commented that where, in the past, he could easily identify who had produced meeting minutes from the style and content, with the use of itIBIS he had to look for the author's name to tell.

The team also indicated that of the more "important" information was captured, basing this opinion on their experience with previous projects. The project manager provided some confirmation that this occurred, by indicating that when reading itIBIS meeting minutes produced for meetings he did not attend, he was able to tell what was *discussed*, not just what was decided. Of course, these claims are quite subjective -- it may be, for example, that simply by securing management interest and by providing *some* structure for notetaking, similar increases in quality and quantity of information capture might have been achieved.

While building the itIBIS, a new file was created for each new topic. After several months there was an unmanageable amount of data scattered across many files. Because of the difficulty associated with finding the information, few of the files were updated in their electronic form. Loading this data into gIBIS provided new mechanisms for organizing the information, which allowed issues to be located so that they could be updated.

Information Access

When the team began using itIBIS, they expected that the information would be used primarily during the maintenance phase of the project by the maintenance organization. However, as they progressed beyond the initial months of the project, they found that the information was useful to themselves as developers. For example, one of the team members, a design methodology expert who played a central role in initial design discussions, *quit* before the detailed design was complete. Under normal circumstances, by the time a developer was working on the code which was dependent on those early decisions, no one would have been able to remember *why* they had been made. Because the early design rationale was captured using itIBIS, and made available to all the team members shortly after it was recorded, when the expert left, much of the logic behind his design was retrained. This *"why"* information turned out to be critical to implementing the system correctly.

One effect of using IBIS to capture the information was that it was easier to find out what had been discussed earlier, and in what context that discussion was held, e.g., what other issues were discussed at the time. It was also easier to determine *why* a decision was made without replaying the discussion. In one case, for example, the team knew that they had (months before) decided to use string format, rather than numeric format, for a certain buffer. There were now some new reasons to switch to numeric format, but no one could remember why string format had been chosen in the first place. The IBIS record revealed that, in this case, there had not been a strong reason for the earlier decision, so the team reversed the decision (and noted the change in the IBIS), confident that there were no hidden dependencies on the earlier choice.

Although itIBIS was used for capturing many discussions, not everything that might have been useful was captured. For example, at one point two documents (on different aspects of the system) which should have been in agreement were found to disagree. No account of the difference could be found in the itIBIS record. There were at least two factors which lead to information not being captured: schedule pressure, and failure to recognize "important" information the first time it was discussed. One signal we used to determine that a particular discussion was "important" was noting that the same *why* question had been asked (and answered) more than once. And, as with many software development projects, when schedule pressure occurred, all forms of documenting were abandoned, in favor of getting code written.

Even within the relatively short time period that itIBIS has been used (18 months), we have seen one of the standard problems which occurs when using textual databases: changing terminology poses a problem for retrieval based on string search. As the team came to understand the problem better, they refined their terminology. Therefore, searching for a given node or subnetwork by string match has a higher risk of missing important targets as time goes by. For example, the term "screen number " was used in some early design discussions. Later the team determined that "screen number" had been used in two different ways; to identify a particular piece of hardware and to identify a location for data routing. The term "screen number" was then dropped in favor of "workstation number" and "logical destination". There are techniques (in this case, use of a synonyms table in the search engine) currently available which could be incorporated into an IBIS tool to help to reduce this problem.

Observations Relating to the Development Process

The use of IBIS on this project influenced detection of errors during requirements analysis and design, effectiveness of project team meetings, and inter-organizational communication. It also suggested a simple extension of the method to better support project management.

Requirements Analysis and Design

During requirements analysis, we found that the technique helped the team to more quickly understand the problem they were trying to solve. When itIBIS was used to restructure the information contained in the requirements definition document, *explicitly* stating the issues to be addressed provided a framework not only for the discussion of the document, but also for the entire development. By stating the requirements in terms of Issues, Positions and Arguments, weak or missing supporting arguments were made apparent, and assumptions made by the document creator which were not common knowledge were frequently exposed. The approach allowed the group to propose solutions which satisfied the rationale more clearly than seemed to have been the case on earlier projects. (Of course, using the method required more work on the part of the development team to extract information from the document creator, and any effort in this direction would likely have improved the final solution.)

One of the most important and exciting results of this study is that the maintenance of the IBIS *paid for itself* by helping the project team detect design elements that had "fallen through the cracks", even though both high and low level design reviews were held. During the process of inspecting and updating nodes following the conversion to gIBIS, eleven problems were found with the existing design; without this examination, it is most likely that seven of these problems would not have been discovered until the related code was written and four not until integration test was occurring. Based on industry statistics [Albe], the early detection of problems resulted in a substantial savings for the project. The savings was *3-6 times greater* than the cost of using gIBIS, calculated from the actual number of hours spent working with the tool reviewing the itIBIS information and performing updates.[3]

The information captured in an IBIS provides a different view of the software design than is presented by usual design documentation, so reviewing the issue-base allows the design to be reviewed from a 'different angle', exposing different problems than traditional design reviews. And though during this field trial the IBIS was reviewed and updated during a short period of time (because these actions occurred simultaneously with the conversion from itIBIS to gIBIS), if there were suitable tools for browsing and maintaining a project issue-base, less concentrated review of the IBIS would occur as information is added or the issue-base is used for inquiries. The results of this study suggest that if design rationale is documented in an IBIS, the process of performing the review and update of this information may pay for itself, by allowing more problems to be found earlier in the development cycle, when they are less costly to repair.

---

[3] Our calculation does not include the cost of initial entry of data into the IBIS. We excluded this cost, because for the most part, the itIBIS was built by creating text files in IBIS format which *replaced* documentation (such as meeting minutes) which would have been produced anyway.

Meetings

Once the entire development team was trained in the IBIS method, we noticed that team meetings seemed to be more productive. We propose that a knowledge of the underlying form of the dialog allowed the team to determine when the discussion had wandered from the intended topic. By recording the discussion, they were able to 'save' any open issues raised during tangential discussions - so that they could be addressed later - and were able to return to the original topic quickly, by reviewing what had been recorded prior to the tangent. (It should be noted that while making use of IBIS during meetings, the team members spoke normally, and did not preface their with "My Issue/Position/Argument is...".)

The IBIS method was also used for setting meeting agendas: the attendees were provided with a set of issues and, if the topic had been discussed before, any existing positions and arguments. This proved particularly useful when the issues being discussed were inter-related in ways that were not obvious. For example, in one case the team had been struggling for several months to resolve some key issues dealing with a particular technical problem. While examining the IBIS during the conversion from itIBIS to gIBIS, the analyst discovered that there were *seven* design decisions[4] which needed to be resolved 'simultaneously', in order to produce a consistent system design. Until that point, each issue had been considered separately, and with different people involved. Having now determined *what* needed to be discussed (the seven decisions), and *who* needed to be at the meeting, an agenda was prepared, listing the set of issues, with all previously discussed positions and arguments. This allowed the attendees to come to the meeting prepared to discuss any issues where they were personally involved, with an awareness of the related issues, and the prior discussions. The team successfully resolved all seven issues in one meeting -- in a way that would have been unlikely had all the attendees not been aware, beforehand, of the whole set of issues. Further, the final positions on the issues, while incorporating the *arguments* from the prior discussions, were in six cases *not* in the original set of positions: better solutions had been found.

Inter-organizational Communication

In the commercial environment responsibility for the complete development of a product often crosses organizational boundaries. For this team, working within the software development organization, a significant amount of interaction occurred with marketing, product management, and the organization providing the application platform (hardware and system level software). Two of these organizations were geographically remote from the software developers. Communication between these organizations was further impeded by differing priorities -- the other organizations were simultaneously working on other projects, and had changing personnel.

The team found that the IBIS method was helpful in supporting communications between organizations. For example, the requirements analysis process, discussed earlier, was essentially a communications process between the product management group, who wrote the formal requirements definition document, and the software development team, who needed to implement a system to those requirements. Historically, this communication had been difficult, but in this case it was much smoother. The hard copy of the itIBIS network was accepted as a record of the discussion, including the issue resolution. The member of the product management organization who was responsible for this development's requirements document has commented that he wished he'd had an IBIS

---

[4] The seven design decisions referred to here are different from the seven problems referred to above.

record of his discussions with the other organizations he had to deal with, because he spends a lot of time reconstructing previous conversations.

Quite by accident, the development team performed an informal experiment in the level of training required. In the case of the product management organization, the IBIS method was introduced to them and some training provided before it was used. However, when the development team used the method to prepare minutes of their first meeting with the marketing organization, no introduction beyond a brief written one, was provided. Unfortunately, the members of the marketing group were overwhelmed by the nomenclature of itIBIS and refused to read the minutes. Rather than risk alienating other organizations, the group decided not to use this format for communication outside of the software team. Hindsight has shown that these inter-organizational meetings *were* situations where a significant benefit from the structured, issue based approach could have been derived. In one case, recording issue status in an explicit form would have made issues which remained unresolved for more than six months evident. In another case, where new personnel were brought into the platform organization twice during a ten month period -- having a record of past discussions between the organizations would have simplified the "training" required to bring the new people up to the former level of understanding.

Project Management

The project manager suggested some very natural ways in which the IBIS approach could be extended to assist in project management. During a project, some issues are resolved promptly, but other issues remain open for a long time. Tracking these open issues is an obvious benefit of using the IBIS method. However, many open issues require additional activity, such as a phone call, another meeting, or the creation of a prototype before they can be resolved. Also, it turned out that the most important of these action items were the ones that required action from someone not on the software development team -- for example, someone from the hardware development team, marketing organization, or product management. These action items tended to hold up the design progress, and tracking them appears to be a natural adjunct to the IBIS activity. This also suggests the use of an IBIS tool to coordinate action across project groups.

CONCLUSIONS

What does this field trial tell us about CSCW? [Joha88] lists 17 approaches to team support technology. Our observations lead us to propose that issue-based technology directly addresses three of these:

- group decision support
- conversational structuring, and
- management of group memory

Software design for any system of significant size requires lots of decisions to be made. To date, most decision support tools have concentrated on helping the users pick between existing solutions. We noticed that the team using IBIS had little difficulty picking a solution: there was more difficulty trying to define *possible* solutions from which to pick. An issue-based approach can help frame a problem and help the users invent new solutions, giving them options to which they can then apply their decision making talents. IBIS creates no restriction as to "how" a problem may be solved, but it does help point out where alternatives have not been considered and where particular solutions are strong or weak, based on the supporting and objecting arguments. Thus IBIS can be thought of as "qualitative group decision support".

Regarding conversational structuring, [Joha88] says

> *Communication among team members is a critical aspect of a team's performance, even though most groups do not consider how to structure this communication most effectively.... Structuring people's conversations is a risky business. It can be perceived as intrusive or worse.*

If a tool for conversational structuring is to be widely accepted, it must not change the way people normally work. Based on the experience reported there, we believe that the issue-based approach may help provide a framework for structuring conversations which is non-intrusive. While using IBIS as a structure to contain the discussion can be a useful technique among trained users, it is important to note that we also found that IBIS could be used to structure information "after the fact", even if this information developed during the typically anarchistic process associated with many meetings.

Finally, one might consider an IBIS containing design rationale to contain a type of shared memory for the project team. Although the information to be stored in this memory is generated in a serial manner (across time), we want it to be well organized and cross-linked in the memory - so that we do not always have to extract it in the sequence in which it was generated. The conversion process we used to go from itIBIS to gIBIS is an example of this linear to hypertext process. Although the itIBIS files were hierarchically organized, in gIBIS the IBIS elements could be arbitrarily grouped and cross-linked. This resulted in a much richer, more "associative" structure, although most of the cross-linking was done manually. The gIBIS query facility has been useful in finding missing links within the graph. It is obvious that additional capabilities will be required before gIBIS will truly support a group memory; however, the ability of the team to find information within the IBIS indicates that the issue-based approach is a promising structuring technique.

We have pointed out some of the implications of this study for the field of groupware, but there are two important questions that we have not addressed: *How is the software development process like other kinds of teamwork?* and *How does itIBIS relate to other more and less structured models in terms of cost and effectiveness?*

The first question is a standard issue that any study which focuses on a specific application domain must address. We have little to offer on this point except to note that, within the DeSanctis and Gallupe GDSS classification framework [DeSa87] (p. 591), software engineering spans most of the categories for Task Type, Member Proximity, and Group Size. This would suggest that even if software engineering is not representative of the "average" work setting, it is one of the most demanding domains for CSCW support.

The second question might be rephrased *Is there any magic in IBIS?* Why was this particular rhetorical model so useful, and would another model be even more so? Would simply organizing the same kinds of information in an outline format, without the IBIS classifications, have been just as valuable? We think not. Although it is difficult to prove, the exercise of separating questions (issues in IBIS) from answers (positions) seems to be a challenging but useful intellectual exercise (which goes back as far as Aristotle). Separating the objections from the supporting claims (both of which are IBIS arguments) exposes an initial *qualitative* tradeoff analysis, without demanding the quantization typical of decision support, e.g. multi-attribute utility matrices.

On the other hand, it may be that a more articulated rhetorical model than IBIS, such as that of Toulmin [Toul58], offers even more power to structure the intellectual and communicative process. However, there is a delicate balance between complexity of the model and ease of learning and use: our experience indicates that IBIS itself, while easy to learn, approaches the upper limit of complexity for a rhetorical model that will be realistically used in an industrial environment. More articulated models demand a high level of "meta-processing" by the user/thinker in terms of both solving the problem at hand and analyzing the problem solving process in terms of the model. In any case, further studies will be necessary to explore what, if any, the magic is in IBIS.

The IBIS method was used on a commercial development project over a two year period, initially with the support of existing, non-specific software and later with the gIBIS tool. The method was seen as an improvement to the existing process of capturing design rationale (unstructured notes), and was successfully used by developers not previously accustomed to using any process for this purpose. The rationale recorded during the use of itIBIS was used during the development to support the process of requirements analysis and design. The gIBIS tool was introduced after 18 months, and the review of the design rationale which occurred while converting the information made a number of design problems evident relatively early in the development process, *more than paying for the cost of capturing and organizing the rationale.* The use of IBIS on this project suggested several changes to gIBIS which might make it more useful in commercial environments. One, which has already been incorporated, is extending the tool to support action items as distinct node types. Others include making the tool usable during meetings (to prevent the need for batch data entry after a meeting) and across wide area networks (to improve inter-organizational communications in distributed corporations).

ACKNOWLEDGEMENTS

Many thanks to Peter Marks (NCR/MCC), who introduced the authors, and thus was "grandfather" to this work. We particularly appreciate the efforts of Allison Kemp, Tom Klempay, David Pynne, and David Witherspoon at NCR, who were trying to get their *real* work done while this study was taking place. Thanks also to Jim Brown, Hildegarde Gray, Ed Krall and Roy Kuntz of NCR who provided management support and David Cremer and Charles Sandel at MCC, who provided technical support. Finally, thanks to the CSCW reviewers for their constructive comments.

REFERENCES

[Albe]   Albertson. Figures used were from a graph on page 21 of course material accompanying Computer-Aided Software Engineering Environment, USC Institutional Television Network. Dr. Ellis Horowittz, professor.

[Boeh81]   Boehm, B. W., **Software Engineering Economics**, Prentice-Hall, Englewood Cliffs NJ, 1981.

[Conk87]   Conklin, J. , **Hypertext: a Survey and Introduction.** *I E E E Computer,* Vol. 20, No. 9, 1987.

[Conk88]   Conklin, J. and M. Begeman gIBIS: **A Tool for Exploratory Policy Discussion.** *Proceedings of CSCW '88* (Portland, Oregon, September, 1988), and ACM *Transactions on Office Information Systems* (TOOIS), October, 1988.

[Conk89]   Conklin, Jeff and Michael Begeman. **gIBIS: A Tool for all Reasons,** *Journal of the American Society for Information Science (JASIS),* pp. 200-213, May 1989. Also, MCC TR STP-252-88

[DeSa87]   DeSanctis, Geradine and Brent Gallupe. **A Foundation for the Study of Group Decision Support Systems.** *Management Science* 33.5 pp. 585-609 May 1987

[Grud88]   Grudin, Jonathan, **Why CSCW Applications Fail: Problems in the Design and Evaluation of Organizational Interfaces**, MCC Technical Report ACA-HI-211-88, 1988.

[Joha88]   Johansen, Robert, **Groupware: computer support for business teams**, Free Press, New York, 1988.

[Kunz80]   Kunz, W. and Rittel, H., **Issues as elements of information systems**, Working Paper No. 131, Institute of Urban and Regional Development, University of California at Berkeley, 1970. (See also Rittel, H., APIS: a concept for an argumentative planning information system. Working Paper No. 324, Institute of Urban and Regional Development, University of California at Berkeley, 1980.)

[Leto86]   Letovsky, Stanley, and Elliot Solloway. **Delocalized Plans and Program Comprehension**, *IEEE Software*, pp. 41-49, May 1986

[MacL89]   MacLean, Allan, Richard M. Young, and Thomas P. Moran, **Design Rationale: The Argument Behind the Artifact**, in Proceedings of CHI '89, Austin Texas, April 30-May 4 1989 ACM Press, 1989

[Most85]   Mostow, Jack, **Toward Better Models of the Design Process**, *The AI Magazine*, pp. 44-57, Spring 1985.

[Sche83]   Scherlis W. and D. Scott, **First steps towards inferential programming**, invited paper, IFIP Congress 83, North-Holland.

[Smol87]   Smolensky, Paul, Brigham Bell, Barbara Fox, Roger King, and Clayton Lewis, **Constraint-Based Hypertext for Argumentation**, Proceedings of Hypertext '87, ACM Press, November 1987.

[Stor89]   Storrs, Graham, **Group Working in the DHSS Large Demonstrator Project**, Proceedings of the First European Conference on Computer Supported Cooperative Work, Computer Sciences Company, Slough UK, September 1989.

[Toul58]   Toulmin, Stephen E., **The Uses of Argument**, Cambridge University Press, Cambridge, England, 1958.

[Wild88]   Wild, Chris, and Curt Maly, **Towards a Software Maintenance Support Environment**, *Proceedings of the Software Maintenance Conference*, Phoenix AZ, October 1988. Also, TR-88-04 Department of Computer Science, Old Dominion University, Norfolk, Virginia, USA.

PART IV
Synchronous Groupware

Groupware intended to facilitate live interaction and real-time collaboration among several individuals who may be co-located or physically remote is known as *synchronous groupware*. We shall introduce, both in terms of technology and social impact, four classes of software:

- Workstation-based systems for collaborative work at a number of desktops, for example, outlining, writing, sketching, drawing, or building a spreadsheet

- System software and programming tools for implementing distributed synchronous groupware across workstations, for example, via shared screens or shared windows

- Software for creating electronic meeting and decision rooms such as group decision support systems

- Systems and software for creating the computer-controlled audio-visual networks and meeting spaces which have come to be known as *media spaces*.

The former two topics, covered in Chapters 10 and 11, deal with synchronous groupware on workstations, first at the application level, then at the development tool level. As we have seen in Chapter 6, implementing synchronous groupware across a network forces one to deal with difficult problems in distributed processing such as keeping replicated databases consistent and dealing with subtle issues of synchronization and concurrency control. We can choose to attempt the usage of *collaboration transparent* single-user applications by a group, or modify or rewrite them to be *collaboration aware*; both cases, however, force us to confront serious issues of design and implementation. We shall do so in Chapter 11.

The latter two topics concern themselves with the physical and virtual environments in which collaboration can take place. We first look at specialized meeting rooms designed to support CSCW in Chapter 12, and then at media-based meeting and collaboration spaces in Chapter 13.

CHAPTER 10
Desktop Conferencing

One of the earliest demonstrations of a variety of synchronous multi-user interfaces was carried out by Xerox PARC's Colab project. Tools for collaborative brainstorming (Cognoter), argument development (Argnoter), and freestyle sketching (Boardnoter) were used by small groups of two to six individuals working in the Collaboration Laboratory meeting room. Each individual had a workstation which was linked to all other workstations and also to a large touch-sensitive screen at the front of the room. "WYSIWIS Revised: Early Experiences with Multiuser Interfaces" by Stefik, Bobrow, Foster, Lanning, and Tater (1987) describes Boardnoter and Cognoter, raises issues discovered in system use, and suggests design solutions in response to the issues. A central theme is that of *WYSIWIS (What You See Is What I See)*, an idealization of multi-user interfaces in which everyone sees exactly the same image of the shared meeting workspace and can see where everyone else is pointing. WYSIWIS is axiomatic to screen sharing approaches, but more general multi-user interfaces have difficulty achieving it and often relax the abstraction consciously to allow for private workspaces and individual activities that need not always be in lockstep with the group.

More recently, Tatar, Foster, and Bobrow (1991) have taken another look at their experiences in "Design for Conversation: Lessons from Cognoter." In observing two groups work with Cognoter, they noticed some unexpected and serious communication breakdowns. They describe these breakdowns and then analyze them in terms of Clark's interactive model of conversation (Clark and Wilkes-Gibbs, 1986; see also Clark and Brennan, 1991, included in Chapter 4 of this volume). The basic problem is that users had trouble coordinating their conversational actions because they had difficulty in determining whether or not they were talking about the same objects and actions in the workspace. The suggested design solutions consist of moving the system somewhat closer to one that adheres to a pure WYSIWIS model.

Another interesting class of synchronous groupware consists of systems for collaborative sketching, drawing, and design. Two such systems are described by Greenberg, Roseman, Webster, and Bohnet (1992) in "Issues and Experiences Designing and Implementing Two Group Drawing Tools." Their designs were heavily influenced by the pioneering work of Tang (1991, included in Chapter 5 of this volume), and utilize Tang's descriptive framework of actions of listing, drawing, and gesturing, and functions of storing information, expressing ideas, and mediating interaction. The paper presents the interface design of a multi-user sketchpad and an object-based multi-user draw package and justifies the designs in terms of design criteria developed by Tang (1989). It then lists some observations about use of the two systems. Finally, a number of implementation issues are discussed—replicated versus centralized architecture (see Chapter 11), registration, multiple cursors, communications, and drawing primitives.

We conclude this chapter with a paper that fits thematically with the design of desktop conferencing systems, although the implementation does not satisfy our criteria for "synchronous": changes to the state of each copy of a shared document must be explicitly transmitted to collaborators working on the other copies. Of greatest interest in "Designing Group-enabled Applications: A Spreadsheet Example" by Greif (1992) is the discussion of technical and business issues involved in extending existing desktop tools such as word processors, spreadsheets, and presentation creation systems. The paper examines group spreadsheet applications such as budget planning and consolidation, presents some extensions to spreadsheet concepts to facilitate group work, recounts experiences in discussing these ideas with existing customers, and suggests an approach to implementation. We concur with the author's assessment that the next few years will see a "wave of innovation" which will come from integrating existing desktop tools with the communications and data sharing capabilities of groupware technology.

Notes and Guide to Further Reading

Further details about Colab and about its computational meeting tools may be found in Stefik, Foster, Bobrow, Kahn, Lanning, and Suchman (1987). An important video tape discussing this work is Xerox PARC (1988v). Another tool for brainstorming through the creation of outlines is the Grove system described in Ellis, Gibbs, and Rein (1991, included in Chapter 1 of this volume).

The Boardnoter prototype for collaborative sketching, drawing, and design has been followed by a number of interesting research projects at Xerox PARC. These are described in Bly and Minneman (1990), Tang and Minneman (1990), Tang (1990v), and Minneman and Bly (1990, 1991). Greenberg's work is documented further in Greenberg and Bohnet (1991; 1992v). Also of great interest is the work described in Gerrissen and Daamen (1990), Lu and Mantei (1991, 1992; see also Mantei, 1992v), and Brinck and Gomez (1992; see also Brinck, 1992v). The significant developments of Hiroshi Ishii (Ishii, 1990; Ishii and Ohkubo, 1990, included in Chapter 13 of this volume; Ishii, 1990v; Ishii and Arita, 1991; Ishii and Miyake, 1991; Ishii and Kobayashi, 1992, included in Chapter 13 of this volume, Ishii, Kobayashi, and Grudin, 1992; and Ishii, Arita, and Kobayashi, 1992v) are presented in some depth in Chapter 13. Shu and Flowers (1992) discuss a real-time group editor for three-dimensional computer-aided design.

In the last few years, attention has also been turned towards collaborative writing tools for synchronous work. An interesting example is the the ShrEdit system (Olson, Olson, Mack, and Wellner, 1990; Olson and Olson, 1991). There have been several studies of its use for collaborative brainstorming and design (Dourish and Bellotti, 1992; Hymes and Olson, 1992; Olson, Olson, Storrøsten, and Carter, 1992;). A commercial product for shared drawing and writing is demonstrated in Group Technologies (1991v). Mawby (1991), Nastos (1992), and Baecker, Mawby, Nastos, and Posner (1992, submitted for publication) document the iterative design of a collaborative writing tool that supports both synchronous and asynchronous work over local and wide area networks. Design of their system, called SASSE, was informed by the study of collaborative writing carried out by Posner and Baecker (1992, included in Chapter 5 of this volume).

WYSIWIS Revised: Early Experiences with Multiuser Interfaces

M. STEFIK, D. G. BOBROW, G. FOSTER, S. LANNING, and D. TATAR

Xerox Palo Alto Research Center

WYSIWIS (What You See Is What I See) is a foundational abstraction for multiuser interfaces that expresses many of the characteristics of a chalkboard in face-to-face meetings. In its strictest interpretation, it means that everyone can also see the same written information and also see where anyone else is pointing. In our attempts to build software support for collaboration in meetings, we have discovered that WYSIWIS is crucial, yet too inflexible when strictly enforced. This paper is about the design issues and choices that arose in our first generation of meeting tools based on WYSIWIS. Several examples of multiuser interfaces that start from this abstraction are presented. These tools illustrate that there are inherent conflicts between the needs of a group and the needs of individuals, since user interfaces compete for the same display space and meeting time. To help minimize the effect of these conflicts, constraints were relaxed along four key dimensions of WYSIWIS: display space, time of display, subgroup population, and congruence of view. Meeting tools must be designed to support the changing needs of information sharing during process transitions, as subgroups are formed and dissolved, as individuals shift their focus of activity, and as the group shifts from multiple parallel activities to a single focused activity and back again.

Categories and Subject Descriptors: D.2.2 [**Software Engineering**]: Tools and Techniques—*user interfaces*; H.1.2 [**Models and Principles**]: User/Machine Systems—*human factors; human information processing*; H.4.2 [**Information Systems Applications**]: Types of Systems: H.4.m [**Information Systems Applications**]: Miscellaneous

General Terms: Design, Human Factors

Additional Key Words and Phrases: Collaborative systems, computer-supported collaboration, computer-supported group work, computer-supported meetings, multiuser interfaces, WYSIWIS

1. INTRODUCTION

The Colab is an experimental meeting room at Xerox PARC in which computers support collaborative processes in face-to-face meetings. The Colab is designed for small working groups of two to six people (see Figure 1) using personal computers connected over a local-area network.

Fig. 1. View of the ISL Colab. The Colab is an experimental meeting room that provides computational support for collaboration in face-to-face meetings. It is designed for typical use by two to six persons. Each person has a workstation connected to a personal computer. The computers are linked together over a local area network (Ethernet) which supports a distributed database. In addition to the workstations, the room is equipped with a large touch-sensitive screen and a stand-up keyboard. (Photograph by Brian Tramontana).

Some simple observations prompted the formation of the Colab project. Office workers spend 30 to 70 percent of their time in meetings and office automation does not reach people who are away from their offices [8]. Although we have been developing computer tools and programming environments for several years, whenever we enter a conventional meeting room we must abandon them and fall back on using a chalkboard.

Computational meeting tools are being designed and used in the Colab for a range of informal and formal meeting processes. These tools, which are described elsewhere [5, 10], support various kinds of meetings, such as meetings for organizing ideas and meetings for developing and evaluating competing design proposals. *Multiuser interfaces* are essential to these tools. Multiuser interfaces provide meeting participants with simultaneous and shared access to the meeting database.

The Colab project is supported in part by grant N00140-87-C-9258 from the Defense Advanced Research Projects Agency.
A previous version of this paper was published in the *Proceedings of the Conference on Computer-Supported Cooperative Work* (Dec. 3–5, 1986), pp. 276–290.
Authors' address: Intelligent Systems Laboratory, Xerox Palo Alto Research Center, Palo Alto, CA 94304; stefik.pa@xerox.com

WYSIWIS (What You See Is What I See—pronounced "whizzy whiz") is an abstraction that guides the design of multiuser interfaces. It is an abstraction of some of the functional properties of a chalkboard in a meeting. In "strict" WYSIWIS, everyone sees exactly the same image of the written meeting information and can see where anyone else is pointing. Colab tools support this abstraction by maintaining synchronized views across workstations and providing facilities for telepointing with publicly visible cursors.

Although strict WYSIWIS is an important abstraction for multiuser interfaces in the Colab, it is too inflexible, and all of the meeting tools need some relaxed interpretation. For example, many tools provide both private and public windows, that is, single-user and multiuser windows. By providing personal access to information, private windows mimic the concept of a personal notepad more than a public chalkboard. Strict WYSIWIS would outlaw private windows.

This paper is about the ways in which the WYSIWIS abstraction for multiuser interfaces needs to be relaxed in order to accommodate important interactions in meeting processes. There are four dimensions, with corresponding constraints following relaxations have proved useful. Strict WYSIWIS applies to everything on the displays; applying it to only a subset of the visible objects (e.g., windows and cursors) relaxes the space constraint. Strict WYSIWIS requires that images be synchronized; allowing delays in updating or viewing relaxes the simultaneity constraint. Strict WYSIWIS requires shared viewing to apply to everyone in the full meeting group; allowing sharing to be limited to subgroups relaxes the population constraint. Strict WYSIWIS requires that images be identical; allowing alternative views (including visual variations) relaxes the congruence constraint.

The presentation is organized around two case studies that deal with progressively more subtle interactions. We begin with a multiuser interface for freestyle sketching. This case raises issues that are preliminary to the main study of this paper: multiuser interfaces for a group collaborating on the organization of ideas. The design issues raised in this paper are the result of our reflections on our use of the first generation of collaborative meeting tools. They illustrate how the computer media must accommodate the needs of a group, as well as the needs of individuals.

2. CASE 1: THE HUMBLE CHALKBOARD

In the Colab we sometimes refer to the chalkboard[1] as the competition, that is, the competing technology for meetings. Chalkboards are quite effective for many things, such as flexible placement of text and figures, ease and familiarity of use, and providing a central focus for group attention. Chalkboards can be used to support a wide range of meeting processes. The WYSIWIS abstraction comes

from our observation of the role of a chalkboard as a recording center and focus of group attention in meetings. Our primary assumption is that this abstraction is useful for multiuser interfaces.

Chalkboards also have some flaws. Space on a chalkboard is limited. Rearranging items is awkward and is done by copying items by hand and then erasing the originals. Information storage is unreliable because chalkboards are often erased between meetings. Information cannot be changed, except by the person at the chalkboard, or carried away by meeting participants, unless they copy it manually. Indeed, information on a chalkboard is isolated: It cannot easily be copied, transmitted, transformed, or accessed by computers.

Computer tools can maintain the strengths of the chalkboard while improving on some of its shortcomings. Text and figures in a computer medium can be made legible and easily movable. In window systems, one can quickly reorganize the information on display. Data can be stored reliably in databases between meetings. Computer programs can put information in reach of all meeting participants. Best of all, the computer medium is active and can enable many kinds of operations that are unthinkable with a chalkboard.

This is not to say that the issues about computer support of meetings are understood and solved. Many issues arise in finding ways to understand tradeoffs between conflicting needs for use of limited display space. In this paper we try to articulate and separate the issues that arise in a multiuser context and to propose some solutions to fit available technology and our meeting processes.

Before starting the report of the case studies, we need to identify one more important assumption that underlies our work. It derives from widespread practice in single-user interfaces but takes on special importance in a multiuser setting. In many of our childhood and everyday situations, collaboration skills are acquired around the joint manipulation of physical objects. Examples include passing a ball in sports, passing a tool or a part in a collaborative assembly or repair task, and handling paper and staplers in a collaborative collating task with an old-fashioned copier.

The Colab meeting tools attempt to draw on this familiar kinesthetic and spatial experience of teamwork by representing information and operations in terms of visible, manipulable objects. Our designs of multiuser interfaces are based in part on widely known examples of single-user interfaces in which one can treat icons in a display as objects, and manipulate them by moving them around. This approach, sometimes called direct manipulation, draws on much previous work and contrasts with more limiting linear representations of information, such as streams of characters for text [9].

2.1 Freestyle Sketching

Of all the Colab meeting tools, Boardnoter is the one that most closely imitates the informal functionality of a chalkboard. Our goal has been to make Boardnoter as easy to use as a chalkboard. Hoping to capitalize on habits acquired in elementary school, we decided further that drawing with Boardnoter should be similar to drawing on a chalkboard. For example, to sketch a square with Boardnoter one can just "pick up the chalk" and make four strokes.

Figure 2 illustrates the general layout of this meeting tool. The main feature is a large writing area (the board). To draw on the board one uses the chalk; to

---

[1] We use the term chalkboard to refer to any of the wall-mounted eraseable writing surfaces, commonly used in meeting rooms, which are white, black, or some other color and upon which the marks are made with chalk, crayon, or ink. We chose this term to avoid misunderstandings about the word blackboard, which means, among other things, a commercially available teleconferencing product and which means, among other things, a programming organization for artificial intelligence systems. We also avoid the term whiteboard, a white metal writing surface on which colored felt-tipped pens are used, and a particular graphical database tool developed at Xerox PARC [4].

pen), we shall consistently refer to the tool's writing implement as the *chalk*. Moving the pen moves the chalk cursor. If the pen button is depressed while being moved, a trace of the movement (the "chalk mark") is left on the screen. The shape and size of the chalk can be adjusted by separate controls.

—To use the eraser, one clicks on the eraser icon, causing the cursor to appear as an eraser. Moving the pen across the screen causes items near the eraser to fade—shifting from black to gray. If the pen is clicked, the gray items disappear. This action by the eraser is different from that of a chalkboard eraser: The computational equivalent of a chalkboard eraser would treat a board as a collection of pixels. However, each stroke of the Boardnoter chalk is remembered as a single item. When an eraser is near, an entire item is grayed out. This makes many erasing tasks easier. For example, it eliminates the need for small motions to erase particular pixels when two items are very close together.

—To use the keyboard, one clicks on its icon, causing the cursor to appear as a miniature keyboard. The cursor can then be moved. Clicking again causes the cursor to flash, and one can use the workstation keyboard to enter text that is then displayed at the cursor position.

—To use the pointer, one clicks on the pointer icon, causing the cursor to appear as a large pointing arrow. In contrast with the pen, moving the pointer around does not leave behind chalk marks. However, it does cause a pointer image to move around on the displays of the other meeting participants. We call this *telepointing*. ("Lookee here!") In addition, clicking the mouse while pointing causes an image of the pointer icon to be deposited on the board. This image is analogous to the small magnetic arrows that are sometimes used on whiteboards. Like chalk marks and typewritten text, these deposited pointers can later be erased.

The tangibility of these implements and displays marks is a simple example of the direct manipulation abstraction mentioned earlier. Implements are picked up, moved about, and used. The pictorial moding of the cursor draws on a natural moding of the chalkboard: We can have only one implement in our writing hand at a time, and generally we use only one hand.

2.2 WYSIWIS Considerations

The Colab provides separate workstations for each participant in a meeting. A workstation provides a kind of immediate access that a chalkboard across the room cannot. One can call up particular information or add or change information without leaving one's chair. One motivation for this is to enable parallel activity.

All of the Colab tools are based on WYSIWIS as a foundational abstraction for supporting parallel activity with multiuser interfaces. We have found WYSIWIS useful both as a basis for the initial designs of interfaces and as a guide to revising and changing them. We have discovered that WYSIWIS, although crucial, is too inflexible if strictly interpreted, and must be relaxed to better accommodate important interactions in meetings. Our thinking about meeting tools is focused by the four key dimensions of WYSIWIS: display space, time of display, subgroup population, and congruence of view.

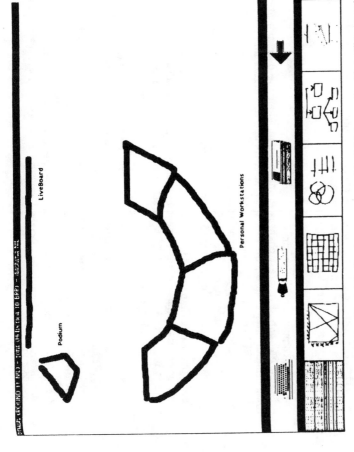

Fig. 2. Screen image of Boardnoter. The Boardnoter meeting tool in Colab is operational but still in its early stages of development. A key feature of the tool is that it can provide a large area for free-style sketching. Below the writing area is a "chalk tray" on which several implements appear: a piece of chalk, an eraser, a keyboard, and a pointer. To draw on the board, one uses the chalk (picked up by clicking the mouse or pen over the chalk icon); to erase one uses the eraser; to point one uses the pointer. More than one boardful of information may be needed in the course of a meeting. One can shrink the current board to a miniature version, save it in the "stampsheet" at the bottom, and replace it with a clean slate or one previously stored.

erase one uses the eraser; to type one uses the keyboard; to point one uses the pointer. Collectively we shall refer to these as *implements*; they are stored in the chalk tray below the board. Following the WYSIWIS abstraction, all of the actions with these implements that change the image on the board are replicated on the displays of the other meeting participants.

Interaction with Boardnoter can be through different kinds of physical pointing devices such as a mouse or a cordless pen. In either case, clicking on an implement icon causes the screen cursor to display that implement and makes Boardnoter ready to work as follows:

—To use the chalk, one clicks on the chalk icon, causing the cursor to appear as a piece of chalk. For familiarity at PARC, we actually depict the chalk as a whiteboard pen. However, to maintain the chalkboard terminology in this paper and to avoid ambiguity with the physical pointing device (preferably a cordless

In Boardnoter, parallel activity is enabled by giving participants their own implements. A strict interpretation of WYSIWIS would require that all of the implements and their movements be visible to all of the participants. However, we quickly discovered that the movement and flickering of multiple cursors became distracting when multiple participants were active.

Issue. The WYSIWIS display of cursors from multiple users is unacceptably distracting.

Design Solution. Display only local implements and those used for telepointing. This relaxes the WYSIWIS constraint on display space and recognizes the distinction between cursors being used to provide focus for a group and their use only for the pointing needs of individuals.

With our current technology, Colab participants coordinate by voice and the display of information. This brings us to our next WYSIWIS issue. At what grain-size should changes to a display be updated? For example, when one participant is drawing with the chalk, should the other participants see every small movement being made? When one participant is typing text on the chalkboard, should other participants see every keystroke? The current version of Boardnoter shows only the drawing of a completed stroke and the typing of a completed text entry. As noted by Greif, choice of grain size can be important for system performance by greatly reducing the rate of changes to the database and the rate of updates to the displays [6]. But large grain-size updating also restricts interaction to a large grain size. For example, a participant must complete typing while phrasing. However, after the text has been entered, it can be edited by any participant.

Issue. Small grain-size transmission of data allows small grain-size collaboration but is computationally expensive.

Design Solution. Broadcast changes to information when the user indicates completion or after a reasonable time interval. Although this argues for relaxing the WYSIWIS simultaneity constraint to achieve performance, there are other reasons in meeting situations for being able to control the granularity of interaction. For example, it may be useful to allow moments of privacy while a participant works out the spelling of a word or a turning of phrase.

Sometimes it is important to make certain suboperations visible to enable small grain-size collaboration. For example, in collaborative editing, we have found it useful to show publicly items selected for deletion or rearrangement before the operation is carried out.

Issue. Object selection is sometimes a natural breakpoint in operations for collaborative editing, such as in moving, copying, and deleting objects.

Design Solution. Provide transmission of teleselection on demand. This recognizes that there may be important "joints" in public processes that need to be visible in order to accommodate discussion.

Issue. Teleselections can be confusing if they are displayed in the same way as local selections. Confusion is especially likely in the middle of local operations that require their own selections.

Design solution. Modify the display of teleselected objects so that they are distinguishable from objects locally selected, for example, by using different shades of gray. This solution relaxes the WYSIWIS congruence constraint by reflecting the fact that multiple operations can be taking place at the same time.

One of the important characteristics of real chalkboards is that they are large enough to display a substantial amount of pictorial and written information. Their size is limited mostly by human reach. When we take into account the size that text characters need to be drawn to be visible in a standard-sized conference room, it turns out that the amount of information (measured in number of text characters) that can be usefully placed on a chalkboard requires a large portion of a high-resolution computer display.[2]

To bring more writing space within reach, classrooms are sometimes fitted with sliding chalkboards. Many conference rooms are fitted with multiple flip-charts so that a large amount of information can be scanned at once. Analogously, icons enable more effective use of display space by providing recognizable reminders in shrunken form [2, 3]. In addition, icons can be arranged in arrays for easy reference, much like paned windows [1]. We use the term *stampsheet* for such arrays of icons.

Issue. Meetings often need multiple chalkboards, but there is room to show only one on a computer display.

Design Solution. Boardnoter provides multiple visible boards by arranging shrunken versions of them as icons in a stampsheet below the chalk tray. (See Figure 2).

Clicking on a stamp causes the current large board to be redrawn in miniature scale in its own place in the stampsheet and causes the selected stamp-size board to be expanded and made available for use as a full-size chalkboard. Using the stamp marked "new board," one can obtain a fresh chalkboard. Since the stamps portray the contents of the boards in shrunken form, it is easy to recognize them and to return to a previous board. By itself, the stampsheet concept is not a relaxation of WYSIWIS because all participants continue to see the same information, shrunken or not. But as we will see later, stampsheets and their extensions lead to a family of WYSIWIS relaxations.

Issue. Pixel-based computations for shrinking boards are computationally expensive and do not always produce recognizable images.

Design Solution. Images are represented in terms of scaled projections of objects, rather than raw pixels, and provide specialized shrinking methods for

[2] To compare the amount of space on a computer display with a standard 4-by-5-foot chalkboard, we carried out a simple, informal measurement. We filled both media with text at the smallest size that was easily readable. We required that the text appear approximately the same size if viewed from a distance of 10 feet from the chalkboard or from a distance of 2 feet from the computer display. This corresponded roughly to characters in 12-point font on the computer displays and characters 15 millimeters in height on the chalkboard. The chalkboard could display approximately 3520 characters (32 × 110). The current Colab uses displays that are 808-by-1024 pixels, which were able to display 9520 characters (56 × 170). Even allowing for the space-displaying implements and the stampsheet, Boardnoter provides the same spaciousness as a chalkboard in less than half of the computer screen.

different kinds of graphics objects. This solution relaxes WYSIWIS congruence by allowing systematic distortions, in addition to changes of scale.

Our wish to have recognizable small versions of boards is another argument for maintaining graphics objects with specially tuned techniques for redrawing them at different scales (e.g., letters in smaller fonts). However, our experience with this is quite limited, and we are not sure that this technique will work with all images.

2.3 Beyond the Chalkboard

Our initial focus on Boardnoter was to imitate the capabilities of a real chalkboard. In the next phase of development we will add to Boardnoter capabilities beyond those of the conventional chalkboard. For the operations described so far, we want to preserve the analogy to the familiar chalkboard. The next version of Boardnoter will add capabilities for copying, moving, resizing, linking with rubber-band lines, grouping, and smoothing (neatening), and also for using and scaling selections from a set of predrawn images. Our experience with other Colab meeting tools suggests that several of these features raise questions related to WYSIWIS.

Although a meeting participant will usually focus on one board at a time, being able to see several of them simultaneously is important for both reference and copying. Imagine conferences at which chalkboards were kept in separate rooms so that participants had to run back and forth. That would get in the way of operations in which more than one board must be visible, such as when the contents of two boards are being compared or information is being copied across boards.

We have considered several different models for copying items between chalkboards. One model is the register model, which provides a constantly accessible place into which items can be moved intermediately during transit between boards. A variation of this general approach is the clipboard on the Macintosh.[3]

Following the direct manipulation abstraction, we prefer an alternative approach in which one can pick items up and move them around. This requires that multiple chalkboards be made accessible at the same time, for example, in a two-by-two arrangement of half-size boards. From this arrangement one can pick up copies of items from one chalkboard and deposit them in another.

Raising the possibility of multiple accessible chalkboards in Boardnoter highlights some assumptions and issues about its design so far. If one participant switches to a two-by-two format, should the displays of all the participants be switched? Having display space for four boards could allow different people to display different boards at the same time. Should WYSIWIS congruence and subgroup population constraints be relaxed to allow participants to view different boards?

We cannot answer these questions from our limited experience with Boardnoter and its associated formal and informal meeting processes. Although Boardnoter is operational, we need to extend its capabilities in order to carry out the necessary

experiments. Nevertheless, a very similar set of questions arises in the redesign of a Colab tool with which we now have several months of experience: our Cognoter meeting tool for organizing ideas. That experience and interface redesign is discussed next.

3. CASE 2: COLLABORATION IN THE ORGANIZATION OF IDEAS

Cognoter, a meeting tool for organizing ideas for a presentation, supports a meeting process in which participants come together, usually without having prepared any materials. They determine the audience and goals for their presentation, the topics to be included, and the overall organization. The output of Cognoter is an annotated outline. Cognoter has been used for preparing many presentations and papers, including this one.

Since Cognoter is described elsewhere in detail [5, 10], the discussion here will be brief. We focus on the breakdown of WYSIWIS in the first design, and trade-offs in the redesign.

In organizing ideas for a presentation, several things can reduce the quality of the results. The presentation could fail to include some important topics; it could dwell on irrelevant or unimportant topics, or it could address the topics in an incoherent order. Cognoter separates these concerns by organizing the available actions into stages.

Cognoter is more formal than Boardnoter in both its representations of information and its meeting process. It organizes its meeting process into a sequence of stages: brainstorming, ordering and grouping, evaluation, and outline generation. These stages are additive in several senses. The database of decisions becomes more complete as a group advances through the stages. Although each stage is intended for completion of a particular part of the task, it is always possible to use the operations of previous stages to wrap up loose ends. One need not decide that some part of the process is absolutely completed before moving on. In addition, the operations in Cognoter are small and incremental.

3.1 The Stages of Cognoter

Each stage in a Cognoter meeting focuses attention on one part of the task of organizing ideas for a presentation. We originally adopted this structure because a similar one has proved useful in noncomputational settings; however, there are significant differences in the uses and effects of the stages when computers are introduced.

3.1.1 Brainstorming Ideas. The brainstorming stage is designed to foster the free-flowing contribution of ideas. There is one basic operation: A participant selects an empty space in a public window and types in a catch word or phrase characterizing an idea.

Unlike brainstorming in meetings without computers, there is no waiting for turns in Cognoter; any participant can enter an item at any time. Often the inspiration for an idea is triggered by another participant's actions—either saying something or entering an item in a public window. All items appear on everyone's screens. In addition, participants can augment an item with a longer description to help clarify its meaning.

---

[3] Macintosh is a trademark of McIntosh Labs., Inc.

3.1.2 Organizing Ideas. The order of ideas for the presentation is established in Cognoter by incremental and local steps. There are two operations: linking items into presentation order, and putting items into delineated subgroups. If item *A* is linked to *B* (meaning *A* comes before *B*), and *B* is linked to *C*, then *A* comes before *C*. If item *A* is linked to a subgroup, then it comes before every item in the group. By means of these transitive and distributive operations, a small number of explicit links can tightly constrain the total order of items.

The linking operation often takes place in conjunction with an oral justification. For example, if "expenses" and "bottom line results" were items, a participant might argue "We have to talk about expenses before bottom line results" because otherwise the reader will not understand the results." This relation is represented visually in Cognoter as an arrow linking the item labeled "expenses" to the one labeled "bottom line results." It is also possible to move related ideas to a separate window. Before moving items, it is common practice to put them in a spatially compact cluster. This allows comment on the coherence of the proposed grouping.

In Cognoter, organizing becomes a richer task than in the traditional brainstorming paradigm. Not only do participants put ideas in a particular order, but they also tend to form subgroups that focus on the development of particular aspects of the subject matter. Since subgroups of ideas are usually put into separate windows, each subgroup of people tends to be focused around one window or another. We characterize these subgroups as *lightweight collaborations* because they are quickly formed and usually last only a few minutes.

Although there is parallel activity, there is also communication between subgroups. For example, one group may decide that some of the ideas in its windows do not fit with the others after all and may put them back into the general pool or offer to give them to another subgroup. Further assignment of responsibility for organizing sets of ideas requires additional communication. Finally, some activities require the attention of the whole group. When subgroups rejoin, participants recap the changes made in the subgroups.

3.1.3 Evaluation of Ideas. During the evaluation stage of Cognoter, the subgroup boundaries tend to dissolve, and the meeting participants function again as a single group. Participants try to understand the organization of the presentation as a whole. During this phase, ideas that seem irrelevant or less important than others can be deleted. Tentative outlines are generated by Cognoter upon request, and ambiguities in the ordering of ideas can be highlighted. Arguments are made about whether particular ideas are irrelevant or unimportant when compared with other ideas.

3.2 Some Problems with the First Cognoter

The use of the WYSIWIS abstraction in the first version of Cognoter was conceived in terms of the contents of individual windows and ignored issues of window placement. This approach drew on our experience with systems in which window shape, size, and position are completely under user control. We gradually came to appreciate an inherent conflict between our style of screen management and the needs of multiuser interfaces. Failing to address overall display layout issues explicitly created the following unpredictable results for routine window manipulation:

—In Cognoter sessions, the displays of the participants often became crowded and cluttered with windows. In attempting to deal with this clutter, participants could close individual windows on their own displays. However, these windows reappeared whenever another participant made a change in them.

—When a participant changed the shape or position of a public window in Cognoter (e.g., to make more room for items), they were changed on all of the displays. This sometimes obscured private work on other's screens.

—The telepointer in Cognoter worked in terms of absolute screen coordinates but was used to point to items positioned relative to particular windows. Depending on the operations that have been done, a remote pointer could point to the wrong part of a display.

—For all these reasons, participants needed to fiddle with window sizes and placements too much. The problem was exacerbated by the fact that participants could have a mix of public and private windows. The private windows could be in different places on different displays, and participants were unaware of the different window placements. This caused unexpected occlusion.

The apparent bugs in Cognoter's original user interface resulted in part from a lack of principles for understanding inherent conflicts between the needs of an individual and the needs of a group. In a way, these conflicts reflect the combined use of the display for both private and public media—conventionally kept separately as a notepad and a chalkboard.

The following sections present a more detailed analysis of the differing needs of a group and its individuals in a face-to-face meeting. They suggest how the computer media can better accommodate the needs of both by relaxing the WYSIWIS constraints. The conflicts arise in part because the elements (e.g., windows) needed to support any of the activities must compete for the same display space and meeting time. In the following we compare two proposals for organizing the displays and use them in thought experiments to expose design principles for our second generation of meeting tools. The examples illustrate how the dimensions of WYSIWIS can be used to provide a guide for such thinking.

3.3 A WYSIWIS Stampsheet Approach

Even with single-user applications, the space on a workstation display is limited and often crowded with windows. In WYSIWIS situations, contention for display space is even more problematic because the same area is shared by multiple participants. In Boardnoter, stampsheets are used to create more space for those windows that are actively being used. Although stampsheets relax WYSIWIS by reducing scale, they provide a simple means for locating information since it is generally still recognizable when displayed in miniature.

Issue. The screen can be crowded with windows used mainly by other participants.

Design Solution. Allow participants to select independently which windows are at full scale. This relaxes WYSIWIS space and congruence constraints and allows participants to reclaim display space for private use as they withdraw from parts of the public discussion.

One of the important properties of the Cognoter meeting process is the tendency to form lightweight collaborations of one to three people. Unfortunately, when active windows are reduced to static shrunken icons, participants lose the ability to follow the action. They can no longer quickly determine which information is being worked on.

Issue. When windows are shrunk to the miniature scale of stamps, it is no longer possible to assess quickly the locus of activity or which information has changed since the windows were last viewed at full scale.

Design Solution. Unlike conventional icons, stampsheet icons should *actively* indicate when information is changing. Stamps can be augmented with specialized indicators that show different measures of change. Making the stamps less similar to the full-size windows relaxes the congruence constraint beyond miniaturization. Adding the activity indicators compensates in part for the diminished WYSIWIS of stampsheets and provides visual clues to the participant both to monitor meeting progress and to guide a transition back to full WYSIWIS participation in the meeting.

Accordingly, stamps can be made to flicker when changes are made in the corresponding full-scale windows. This makes it easier to see at a glance the locus of activity at any given moment. To minimize the distraction of flickering, shades of gray in limited regions can be used, rather than blinking or inverting the entire stamp.

To make it easier to determine how much information has changed, one can attach a bar along an edge which is initially white and becomes progressively darker as changes accumulate. Alternatively, the bar could be in the format of a thermometer that fills as changes accumulate.

Issue. Identifying recent changes is also important for full-size windows, when participants refocus on a window.

Design Solution. Provide a facility for highlighting recent changes. This relaxes the WYSIWIS congruence constraint because the indications show only on the requestor's display. This relaxation of WYSIWIS makes it possible to superimpose privately needed information on top of public windows, without distracting other members of the group.

Notification of change supports parallel activity by enabling individuals and subgroups to catch up with work done by others. Shared windows support parallel activity by enabling subgroups to share common information. By limiting sharing to a subset of windows, subgroups can focus on particular shared information and filter out that which is distracting. Thus notification and window sharing are two sides of support for subgroups.

Issue. Subgroups need to cause other group members to attend to a particular item without interfering with the activities of other subgroups.

Design Solution. Provide a way of using the telepointer to show only within subgroup boundaries. This solution relaxes the WYSIWIS population constraint

by recognizing that the demarcation of public versus private or group versus individual is too inflexible. Meetings can operate productively with subgroups of different sizes. This is an example of where the flexibility of the computer-based tools enables styles of activity that are less convenient when there is a single shared medium. It is analogous to the use of separate flipcharts by subgroups in a large meeting.

This raises the issue of membership in subgroups. One possibility is to have explicit actions for defining and modifying subgroups. A problem with this is that it presupposes notification that would not already be part of a meeting. One does not normally need to make a note on a blackboard in a small meeting to announce that a subgroup is being formed. Explicit notification places a continuing burden on the participants to keep this information up-to-date.

The WYSIWIS stampsheet proposal does not support subgroups as a *formally selected* set of people. Instead, communication is based on the interests of the participants. All viewers of a window see the same information. Subgroups are those who have a common focus. People can play bridging roles between subgroups or monitor activities in several subgroups by maintaining views of windows being used by several groups.

Subgroups can also encounter situations in which they want to momentarily get the attention of the larger group, even though the windows containing the information may not be visible on everyone's screen.

Issue. Subgroups need to be able to bring information to the attention of a full meeting, even though the windows containing the information may not be visible on everyone's screen.

Design Solution. Provide both subgroup and full-group telepointing. A full-group pointer signals a *remote window fault* in the corresponding stamps, causing it to be expanded for any participant who does not already have the window at full scale. Having two kinds of telepointing makes it possible to relax the congruence and population constraints of WYSIWIS in a controlled way, reflecting the varying needs of the group. Here the computer technology simplifies the transition to full WYSIWIS participation in a way that shared flipcharts cannot.

Issue. Sometimes a participant wants to join a subgroup but cannot find the stamp corresponding to a subgroup window. Asking a member of the subgroup to identify the window using a full-group telepointer would be disruptive for other members of the full group.

Design Solution. Two ideas help fix this. One is to provide labels for windows and their corresponding stamps so that participants can refer to them by name both verbally and visually. Another idea is to extend the subgroup telepointer to flash an indicator on remote stamps. The latter helps to support a transition in a meeting process during which WYSIWIS becomes more strictly enforced as a group becomes more cohesive.

We have now distinguished two kinds of telepointing. Subgroup telepointing displays the remote cursor in the windows of all other participants who already have the window at full scale and flickers a remote pointing indicator in the stamps of participants not viewing full-scale windows. Full-group telepointing causes the corresponding stamps of all participants to expand and show the telepointer. The distinction reflects the differing needs for coordination in subgroups of different sizes.

One of the important operations for organizing ideas in Cognoter is clustering. As discussed earlier, this operation is typically begun by first moving the items near each other in a public window and calling for discussion. The items can then be formed into an explicit subgroup that is displayed in its own window. When a subgroup of ideas is created and placed in a new window, it is necessary to decide which participants will see the new window on their displays. If it is shown only on the display of the creating participant, then all other members of the subgroup must individually find the corresponding stamp and expand it. If the window is displayed on the screens of all the meeting participants, it will appear unexpectedly and may disrupt the activities of other subgroups.

Issue. When a new public window is created to support joint action on new information, putting the window on all of the displays may disrupt the activities of other subgroups.

Design Solution. New windows are spawned from existing ones. They are automatically placed on the displays of those participants for whom the original window is at full scale. For participants having the original window at stamp scale, the windows are added to the stampsheet. Limiting the sharing of information to a subgroup relaxes the population dimension of WYSIWIS and reflects the fact that discussion and the formation of subgroups tend to be continuous processes. Strict WYSIWIS can be relaxed to support this by displaying the new window on the screens of participants known to be interacting actively.

Returning to the issue of screen management, when a participant places a public window, it is done without knowledge of the placement of any private windows on the other screens. This leads to the possibility of unexpected window occlusions for other participants.

Issue. Although stampsheets reduce the contention, public and private windows still compete for display space. When a participant adds a new public window to a subgroup, it can occlude windows of other participants.

Design Solution. Participants can control the placement of all windows on their displays. New public windows may be repositioned after they appear. By convention, certain regions are used primarily for the placement of private windows. Allowing personalized window placement relaxes the similarity dimension of WYSIWIS. Another idea would be to provide a density map of screen usage that would guide a participant to place the new window in a place where it might provide the least occlusion. Again, the density map would relax WYSIWIS by balancing the needs of a subgroup—showing an individual where private windows tend to be located without revealing their contents.

3.4 A WYSIWIS Rooms Approach

Windows on the display of a participant can arise from several sources. They can result from the direct action of the participant, from the actions of other members of a subgroup, and from remote telepointing from a separate subgroup. Displays can become cluttered with windows. In this regard, it is interesting to compare the WYSIWIS stampsheet mechanisms proposed so far to the Rooms mechanisms, suitably extended for multiuser situations [7].

The Rooms concept was designed to help with a problem that already arises in single-user applications: Displays provide quite limited space for holding information, when compared with the amount of information that can be placed on a large table using sheets of paper. The analysis of this approach draws on an analogy to memory paging systems for computers in which most of the action during short working periods typically occurs in small subsets, called working sets, of the total pages.

Rooms organize collections of windows into related screenfuls of information. Each screenful is a room. To work well, the approach requires that each room be big enough to hold a working set of windows. Performance of the system can be determined in part by measuring the rate of *window faults*—occasions on which a user needs to access information not visible on the display. In general, a user is expected to organize rooms around tasks. For example, there can be a mail room with electronic mail windows, a writing room with text editors and related tools, a programming room, and so on. Windows needed for more than one task can appear in as many rooms as needed.

In the following we revisit the WYSIWIS relaxation issues that were introduced in our discussion of the stampsheet approach. We propose alternative solutions based on multiuser extensions of Rooms. The basic approach is to associate subgroups of participants with separate rooms. In Cognoter, different rooms would be formed around subtopic areas.

Issue. The screen can be crowded with windows used mainly by other participants.

Design Solution. Provide separate rooms for each subgroup. Rooms are connected by *doors*. New rooms and doors between them are created as needed. Rooms relax the space and congruence constraints by accommodating the need for subgroups and individuals to maintain their workspaces.

Issue. When subgroups are located in separate rooms, it is no longer possible to assess quickly where group activity is, or what information has changed since the rooms were last viewed at full scale.

Design Solution. Create an overview room from which one can watch the overall activities of the meeting. Following the miniaturization technique from stampsheets, the overview room can contain miniaturized active images of the rooms. Augment the room images with indicators that show how much change there has been and where the activity is from moment to moment. This solution relaxes the WYSIWIS congruence constraint by providing more graceful transitions as participants join parts of an ongoing discussion.

Issue. Identifying recent changes is also important when a participant reenters a room.

Design Solution. Provide a facility for highlighting recent changes in a room. This relaxation of the WYSIWIS congruence constraint makes it possible to overlay privately needed annotations on information in public windows.

Issue. Subgroups need to cause other group members to attend to a particular item without interfering with the activities of other subgroups.
Design Solution. Provide a subgroup telepointer that shows only within a room. This solution relaxes the WYSIWIS population constraint by recognizing temporary independence of multiple subgroups.

Issue. Subgroups need to be able to bring information to the attention of a full meeting, even though the windows containing the information may not be visible on everyone's screen.
Design Solution. Provide a full-group telepointer that *teleports* all participants of the meeting into the room of interest. A "backdoor" would be provided to take participants back to the meeting rooms they were using before the interruption. An alternative solution, which may be less disruptive, is to add the referenced window into the rooms of all of the participants. The window can be closed afterward. In either case the mechanisms provide a transition to full WYSIWIS for that window for participation by the entire group.

Issue. Although rooms reduce the contention, public and private windows still compete for display space. When a participant adds a new public window to a subgroup, it can occlude windows of other participants.
Design Solution. Establish conventions so that certain regions of rooms are used primarily for the placement of private windows or a room-limited density map. Both approaches recognize that there is a tension between the public and private use of display space.

3.5 Comparison of Approaches

The WYSIWIS stampsheet and Rooms proposals have been developed in response to shortcomings of the multiuser interfaces in the first generation of Cognoter. In the following comparisons we treat them as separate and competing proposals in order to articulate some of the issues and trade-offs. A reliable evaluation of the ideas requires further implementation and experimentation.

The WYSIWIS stampsheet and WYSIWIS Rooms proposals provide mechanisms to alleviate window crowding, resulting from the use of the same display space for multiple meeting participants and from the use of the same space for private and public purposes. Both proposals depend on patterns of window access. At any stage in a meeting, participants focus their attention on a relatively stable subset of the windows.

The two approaches differ in their assignment of responsibility for placing public windows. In WYSIWIS stampsheets, public window placements are privately determined; in WYSIWIS Rooms, public windows are in the same place for everyone. This reflects a difference in attitude: Rooms creates a more formal division of information, and it seems natural to expect a room to be set up when one enters. In both cases, telepointing is window relative.

Compared with stampsheets, the WYSIWIS Rooms approach creates harder boundaries between subgroups. Participants in a room are more isolated from the rest of the group because they have to leave the subgroup room in order to see the activities of other subgroups. To get an overview of activity, participants must go to the overview room.

There are some differences in the quality of activity overviews for stampsheets and Rooms. Since rooms keep subgroups more isolated, miniature images will be less recognizable to other subgroups that did not watch them evolve. Balancing this, the recent change indicators in both approaches may compensate by helping people to more gracefully join an ongoing discussion.

Sometimes, in the course of a Cognoter meeting, it is important to reconsider the division of items between two sets of ideas being worked on by two subgroups of people. For this purpose, a participant needs to make the relevant windows for the two subgroups simultaneously visible. In the WYSIWIS stampsheet approach, a participant can just open the relevant windows. In a WYSIWIS Rooms approach, there is a greater overhead because a participant must either create a new room for the comparison, or involve all the other members of one of the subgroups with the extra windows. With stampsheets, subgroups can more easily have ragged boundaries, with some participants playing bridging roles between subgroups.

In the WYSIWIS Rooms approach, rooms stay around even after participants finish working on a subgroup or subgroup of ideas. In contrast, windows just return to their places in a stampsheet in the WYSIWIS stampsheet approach: no permanent record of subgroups is kept.

We conjecture that extra overhead will inhibit both the formation and dissolution of subgroups. Inhibiting the formation of subgroups will diminish the likelihood of lightweight collaborations. Inhibiting the dissolution of subgroups may encourage too much independence and dilute the sense of coherence for the group as a whole, leading to a greater difficulty in reintegrating ideas.

This section has focused on the differences between WYSIWIS Rooms and WYSIWIS stampsheets as independent approaches. Actually, the next generation of our tools may combine the ideas, such as providing rooms with stampsheets. Other fundamental assumptions of the proposals may also be reexamined. For example, both proposals have been written as if the only available displays were on the workstations of the participants. The Colab actually includes a large public display on one wall of the room as shown in Figure 1. This wall display could be used for public windows, which participants could also access from their workstations. Combining the wall display with WYSIWIS Rooms could enable a less jarring technique for full-group telepointing: Instead of teleporting participants to the appropriate room, the tools could simply direct their attention to the large public display.

Many of the design decisions for Colab meeting tools turn fundamentally on expectations for the size of the meeting group. The Cognoter tool was designed for a meeting process that involves 2 to 6 people. Meetings of this sort tend to last from 1 to 2 hours and yield outlines that require 2 to 5 pages of text. Since 20 stamps occupy less than 25 percent of the screen, ample space is still left for working windows. For larger groups or tasks, the approach may not work as well.

We hypothesize that WYSIWIS Rooms will prove increasingly effective with larger groups and larger tasks—just as larger physical rooms and breakout rooms are advocated in meetings not supported by computers.

4. SUMMARY

Our design of meeting tools begins with the assumption that multiuser interfaces should imitate the essential properties of a chalkboard as summarized by the WYSIWIS abstraction. Strict WYSIWIS means that everyone sees exactly the same image of the meeting information and also can see where anyone else is pointing. This paper examined our experience with our first Colab meeting tools. We argued that these tools need to relax the strict application of WYSIWIS to accommodate important interactions in meetings, especially those involving the different and competing needs of individuals, subgroups, and the full group. Relaxations to WYSIWIS were categorized as constraints on space, time, population, and congruence.

We introduced several basic mechanisms for relaxing WYSIWIS in the design of Boardnoter, a meeting tool that most resembles a chalkboard and which has no process model for meetings. We then considered Cognoter, a tool for organizing ideas for a presentation. Cognoter supports a richer and more formal meeting process, which we have used in the Colab for several months. Several problems with Cognoter's ad hoc approach to WYSIWIS were identified.

Two approaches for organizing display space and systematizing the application of WYSIWIS were presented: one based on WYSIWIS stampsheets and the other on multiuser extensions of the Rooms approach developed by Henderson and Card [7]. Our separation of ideas for multiuser interfaces into two competing approaches was for the pedagogical purposes of helping us uncover the underlying tensions and principles. By no means are WYSIWIS Rooms and stampsheets mutually exclusive: actual systems would benefit by combining them.

In considering these proposals, we introduced several concepts for meeting tools and multiuser interfaces besides WYSIWIS, WYSIWIS stampsheets, and WYSIWIS Rooms. One important notion was the idea of lightweight collaborations—collaborations that are formed quickly in the context of a meeting and which persist for just a few minutes. Supporting lightweight collaborations was an important goal for our meeting tools. They are an important source of potential parallelism in computer-supported meetings.

We argued that meeting tools need to model subgroups explicitly and to provide services that respect subgroup boundaries. In the stampsheet approach, we suggested that subgroup boundaries can be determined by an analysis of window use: in the room model, subgroup formation follows explicit user action in which subgroups are assigned their own conference rooms. In both cases we argued the need for a variety of mechanisms to support the changing needs of information access as process transitions occur, as subgroups are formed and dissolved, as individuals shift their focus of activity, and as the group shifts from multiple parallel activities to a single focused activity and back again.

Early observations of Cognoter use have shown that, for lightweight collaborations, subgroups are transient, and it is important to be able to get an overview of what other subgroups are doing. To this end, we proposed miniaturization as a way of compressing images, both for Rooms and in stampsheets. In both cases we extended the concept of static icons in ways that allow participants to get an overview of the activities. The extensions include active icons, as well as flashing activity indicators, subgroup telepointing indicators, and cumulative change indicators. These mechanisms relax the constraints of strict WYSIWIS to help participants adjust the degree to which they participate in various parts of the discussion and allow a kind of progressive disclosure for scanning parts of the discussion for changes.

Telepointing is an example of one of the new concepts that arise when interfaces are extended to support multiple users in meeting situations. Another example is teleselection, the indication to collaborators of those objects on which an editing operation is being performed. Teleselection recognizes that certain joints in the operations on public information must be made visible in order to admit comment. Mechanisms for displaying teleselection must recognize that multiple activities (including private ones) can be occurring simultaneously, and therefore WYSIWIS must be relaxed to disambiguate the display.

The WYSIWIS stampsheet and WYSIWIS Rooms approaches present us with several trade-offs. Our preliminary hypothesis is that the next generation of Cognoter design will need to pick a combination of features from these approaches that provides low overhead for lightweight collaborations. We also predict that the Rooms approach will scale better for meetings and processes associated with larger groups.

There has been much less experience with multiuser interfaces than with single-user interfaces. This paper represents experience with our first generation of meeting tools and presents speculations about design issues for the next generation. In the next phase of our work, there will be an opportunity to test some of these hypotheses and revisions experimentally.

ACKNOWLEDGMENTS

The authors wish to thank John Seely Brown for creating in PARC's Intelligent Systems Laboratory a rich, multidisciplinary environment in which projects like the Colab can flourish, and Austin Henderson and Stuart Card for reading and critiquing early drafts of this paper.

REFERENCES

1. BLY, S. A., AND ROSENBERG, J. K. A comparison of tiled and overlapping windows. In *Human Factors in Computing Systems: CHI'86 Conference Proceedings* (Boston, Apr. 13–17, 1986), pp. 101–106.

2. CARD, S. 'Windows: Why they were invented, how they help. *The Office* (Mar. 1985), 52–54.

3. CARD, S., PAVEL, M., AND FARRELL, J. E. Window-based computer dialogues. In *Proceedings of the IFIP Conference on Human-Computer Interaction—INTERACT '84.* North-Holland, Amsterdam, 1985, pp. 239–243.

4. DONAHUE, J., AND WIDOM, J. Whiteboards: A graphical database tool. *ACM Trans. Off. Inf. Syst.* 4, 1 (Jan. 1986), 24–41.

5. FOSTER, G., AND STEFIK, M. Cognoter, theory and practice of a colab-orative tool. In *Proceedings of the Conference on Computer-Supported Cooperative Work* (Austin, Tex., Dec. 3–5), 1986.

6. GREIF, I., SELIGER, R., AND WEIHL, W.   Atomic data abstractions in a distributed collaborative editing system (extended abstract). In *Proceedings of the 13th Annual ACM Symposium on Principles of Programming Languages* (St. Petersburg Beach, Fla., Jan.). ACM, New York, 1986, pp. 160–172.

7. HENDERSON, D. A., AND CARD, S. K.   Rooms: The use of multiple virtual workspaces to reduce space contention in a window-based graphical user interface. Intelligent Systems Laboratory, Tech. Rep., Xerox Palo Alto Research Center, Palo Alto, Calif., July 1986.

8. PANKO, R. R.   Office work. *Office: Technol. People 2*, 1964, 205–238.

9. SCHNEIDERMAN, B.   Direct manipulation: a step beyond programming languages. *IEEE Comput.* (Aug. 1983), 57–69.

10. STEFIK, M., FOSTER, G., BOBROW, D. G., KAHN, K., LANNING, S., AND SUCHMAN, L.   Beyond the chalkboard: Computer support for collaboration and problem solving in meetings. *Commun. ACM 30*, 1 (Jan. 1987), 32–47.

Received November 1986; revised December 1986; accepted February 1987

Design for conversation: lessons from Cognoter

DEBORAH G. TATAR,† GREGG FOSTER‡ AND DANIEL G. BOBROW

System Sciences Laboratory, Xerox Palo Alto Research Center, 3333 Coyote Hill Road, Palo Alto, CA 94304, USA

(Received April 1990 and accepted in revised form August 1990)

When studying the use of Cognoter, a multi-user idea organizing tool, we noticed that users encountered unexpected communicative breakdowns. Many of these difficulties stemmed from an incorrect model of conversation implicit in the design of the software. Drawing on recent work in psychology and sociology, we were able to create a more realistic model of the situation our users faced and apply it to the system to understand the breakdowns. We discovered that users encountered difficulties coordinating their conversational actions. They also had difficulty determining that they were talking about the same objects and actions in the workspace. This work led to the redesign of the tool and to the identification of areas for further exploration.

Introduction

The Colab project was an ambitious attempt to provide computational support for group work, particularly for the support of small design teams working together in the same room. The project coordinated several technologies, including networked computers, video network facilities, and a specially designed room. Moreover, Colab had an elaborate and articulated model of the meeting processes it tried to support (Foster, 1986; Foster & Stefik, 1986; Stefik, Foster, Bobrow, Kahn, Lanning & Suchman, 1987a; Stefik, Bobrow, Foster, Lanning & Tatar, 1987b). This approach was exciting and important because it promised significantly to permit significantly more effective ways of working. However, the observation of users working with Cognoter, the most developed Colab tool, showed that there were serious breakdowns in the system.

While trying to understand these breakdowns, it came to our attention that there was a potential conflict between the "interactive" model of communication proposed by recent work in psychology and sociology and the "parcel-post" model implicit in Cognoter. However, the importance of the difference between the two was initially unclear because the interactive model was created to describe situations (two-person, purely verbal communication, often without visual contact) that differed in important respects from the situation we had created in Cognoter. We drew upon sociological work studying the use of traditional representational media such as whiteboards to extrapolate from the interactive model and argue about its significance for our system. This analysis guided the redesign of the system.

This paper starts with an overview of Colab and Cognoter. We then describe

some of the difficulties that our users had working with the system. Next, we present elements of the interactive and parcel-post models of conversation. To extend appropriate expectations to the Cognoter situation, we discuss the use of traditional representational media in meetings. This allows us to create a picture of the problems our users faced. Lastly, we talk about the implications of this line of thinking for the redesign of the system, for understanding more about communication, and as embodying techniques which are important for CSCW systems in general.

Colab and Cognoter

The Colab room was designed to enable the use of computers in meetings of two to five people. The room consisted of three specially designed tables arranged in a U-shape facing a large screen at the front of the room (Figure 1). Each table had on it a display, keyboard and mouse. Each display was connected to a separate processor. The processors were connected to one another by an Ethernet network. Additionally, the displays were connected to one another and to the large screen ("Liveboard") by a video network. The video network could be used to project any of the small displays on the Liveboard, as well as allowing any user to project another user's screen on her own display.† When the video network was being used to look at another station's display, the user lost access to the input devices and computational facilities of her own workstation.

Cognoter was software designed for the Colab to aid small work groups in the creation of a plan or outline. Cognoter "implemented" a three-part process of brainstorming, organizing the brainstormed ideas into sequences and groups, and evaluating them. As originally conceived, Cognoter was supposed to be a fairly

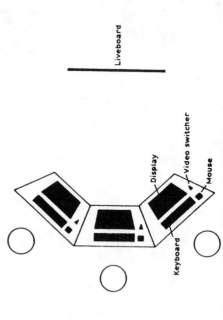

FIGURE 1. A diagram of the Colab room. An Ethernet network connected the computers, and a video network connected the displays and the large display ("Liveboard") at the front of the room.

† This video facility was intended primarily for use with software outside the Colab project.

From International Journal of Man-Machine Studies, 34(2), pp. 185-209. Reprinted by permission of Harcourt Brace Jovanovich Limited.

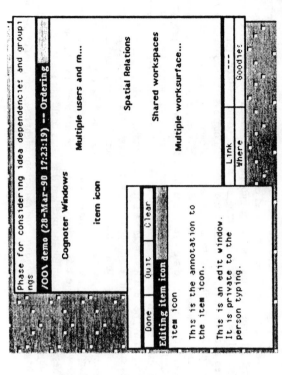

Phase for considering idea dependencies and group
ings

/OOV demo (28-Mar-90 17:23:19) -- Ordering

Cognoter Windows

item icon

Multiple users and m...

Spatial Relations

Shared workspaces

Multiple worksurface...

Link
Where

Goodies

Done   Quit   Clear

Editing item icon

item icon

This is the annotation to
the item icon.

This is an edit window.
It is private to the
person typing.

FIGURE 2. Item organization and edit windows. Item organization windows were shared and allowed users to arrange item icons. Edit windows were used to create and modify items.

direct translation of a process that we ourselves used in meetings with the whiteboard and other static representational media.

However, Cognoter took advantage of the Colab setting in several ways. To increase the effectiveness and efficiency of the meeting, the software allowed participants to work on their computers in parallel. They could each use their keyboard and mouse at any time to make contributions. We hoped that this would reduce the "production blocking" (Diehl & Stroebe, 1987) that is an impediment to group idea generation.

The fundamental unit in the Cognoter user interface was the item. Each Cognoter item consisted of an icon made up of a short catchphrase, usually limited to about 20 characters. Additional text could be associated with the item to explain the catchphrase. We thought of this additional text as an annotation to the item icon, although it could also be thought of as the content of an item. A special kind of item, a *group* item, could have other nested items associated with it.

Cognoter had two kinds of windows: *item organization windows*, whiteboard-like spaces used to display and move the icons, and *edit windows*, used to create and change both the catchphrases displayed in the item icons and the annotations associated with the items.

A major innovation of the project over other computerized brainstorming tools was to use the item organization windows to give users *shared workspaces*. The item organization windows appeared on every user's display at the same time. Each user's copy of an item organization window contained the same information and behaved the same way as every other user's copy. This approach and the many possibilities it raises are discussed in Stefik *et al.* (1987*a*).

To create an item, a user opened an edit window. When she completed the entry of the item, the system created an icon to be placed in an item organization window for everyone to see (Figure 2). Once created, the item was equally available to all users. By clicking on the icon, a user could either drag it to a different location or open an edit window and change it. A user could make a group item expand so that its associated group of sub-items appeared in a new item organization window. Icons could be moved within and across item organization windows. Items, nested groups and annotations allowed users to create what may be thought of as an annotated graph of ideas, with items and annotations at the leaves and groups at the nodes (Figure 3). This graph could be useful in its own right as a way of representing a complex problem space, or it could be used to generate a linear outline.

In theory, the computational representational medium seemed to combine the features of several tools in current use (Tang, 1989; 1990). As on a whiteboard, each person shared the same up-down orientation or perspective on the material. As on large sheets of paper (as used by architects and other designers), each person shared a close physical relationship to the representational medium. Lastly, as on a computer, information could be handled flexibly; even if the amount of material was quite large, editing, saving, restoring and printing were all possible and easy.

We believed that Cognoter changed people's patterns of work and even what happened in each person's head: "Cognoter...divides the thinking process into smaller and different kinds of steps that are incremental and efficient" (Stefik *et al.*, 1987*a*, p. 35). We also expected it to change the way people relate to one another in meetings. However, initially we considered design trade-offs with regard to meeting

processes only as they seemed to fix problems such as overlooked ideas and inefficiency. We did not consider whether the interventions we proposed manipulated resources at the level of basic human communication.

Experiences working with Cognoter

We had substantial experience using Cognoter in a series of working sessions with one or more members of the Colab group participating. Reports from these experiences were mixed, with a number of positive responses, but many unhappy comments. However, meetings can be good or bad for many reasons not related to the technology. Although preliminary observations of Cognoter use (Stefik *et al.*, 1987*a*) anticipated the problems detailed here, these observations were hampered by the impossibility of seeing the details of work between three or four users working on separate machines. The observations were also, as it turned out, hampered by the ability of people who were very familiar with the performance characteristics of the software to compensate for its problems.

To gain an understanding of what happened to "real" people, we asked two outside groups to work with Cognoter. Each group consisted of three long-term collaborators who were familiar with the editor, window system, and mouse conventions Cognoter used. Each group was asked to brainstorm about a subject of their own choosing that would be useful for their own work. Both groups worked for two two-hour sessions. To solve the observational problem, we videotaped them at work and kept a record of all messages sent between the different machines in the session.

ultimately threatened to walk out. They expressed astonishment that anyone would build such a system.

There are many reasons why prototype computer systems can be frustrating, especially to novices, but our users were experienced with computers and expected certain kinds of difficulty. Furthermore, the Cognoter developers were available to help them with any problems that arose, and there were three of them to try to figure out difficulties. Bugs and lack of familiarity notwithstanding, the degree of their frustration was surprising. Some sources of frustration were straightforward once observed and led immediately to design solutions, reported by Foster, Tatar and Bobrow (Unpublished data). However, there were two major classes of problems that seemed connected with the worst frustrations and whose implications required more thought. The first kind of problem was that our users felt a need to see things in the workspace that the system would not let them see. The second was that they mistook references in one another's speech or actions and could not resolve the difficulty satisfactorily.

Before the second group found a viable mode of working using the video network, they made five attempts to work in the private editors. Four of the five attempts evoked a complaint from the people who were not typing about what could and could not be "seen." User objections (leaving out the tone of voice, gesture and surrounding detail which are what lead us to think of these as particularly important reactions) included:

- "Why can't I see that?"
- "I don't see what use it is to have a big screen if we can't all contribute to it."
- "Click DONE so I can see it."
- P1: "P2, do you have anything you want to say?" P2: "I won't be able to see it up there, right?"†

These objections are united by participant confusion and difficulty in seeing what they needed to see. Even the second comment, which looks at first glance like a complaint about the distribution of information between the large screen and the individual displays, reflects confusion about what could be seen. (Since the large screen at the front projected one of the individual displays, they could contribute to it simply by contributing to the shared workspace. The fundamental objection concerned what could be seen in the shared workspace and it is particularly telling that they did not immediately recognize that a shared workspace was projected.)

The fifth case, although relatively unproblematic, is still instructive. In this case, one user started to take notes on what the other two were talking about. Subsequently, he read his notes back to them, adding "Well, you can all see this" They could indeed all see it by looking at the large screen at the front of the room, which had been set so that it displayed his screen. Yet, even in this unproblematic usage, the user felt he had to read aloud what could have been read by each participant separately, and to comment on the fact that they could have seen it. In other words, he had to take action to bring it back into the conversation.

These objections establish the problem that users could not see things. However, the objections also raise questions. What exactly do the users expect to see? In a meeting involving a whiteboard, one participant might be looking out of the window.

† "P" followed by a number is used to denote participants.

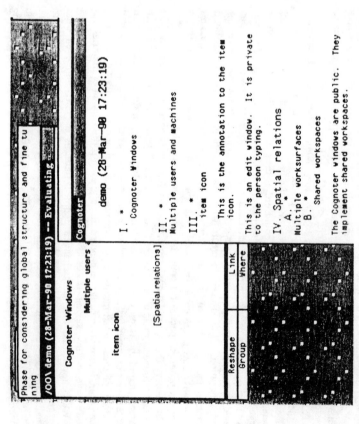

FIGURE 3. Items, annotations, and groups created an annotated graph. The graph could be used to generate a linear outline.

Our trial groups encountered serious problems. In one group, work proceeded in two phases. In the first, each person started an edit window and worked in it. They hardly talked at all and did not look at one another's work. In the second phase, they stopped using the system altogether and resorted to working together with a pad of paper. The other group managed to find a successful way of using the tool by using the video network to look at the screen of whoever was typing, thus employing the shared video workspace instead of the shared computational workspace. This solution worked rather well for them, and they ended up pleased with some aspects of the tool. However, this meant that they lost one of the chief features of the system, the ability to switch typists easily. Far from attaining the expert, fluid trade-off, seen in designers working around a large sheet of paper, they had to spend quite a bit of effort negotiating who would type next.

Both groups bypassed the computational shared workspace either by working privately and then doing the group work on paper, or by giving up on their input devices and using the video connection to create a visually shared workspace. When they tried to use the shared workspace created by the software, they found it so frustrating that they put their heads in their hands, raised their voices, and

or be taking notes, or whispering to someone else, and not see a gesture or drawing as it is put up. Yet this lack of attention does not usually cause extreme frustration or a breakdown of the situation. What was significantly different in the Colab situation?

We also saw a second kind of problem that required explanation. This was a problem with mistaken reference. As Bly (1988) has documented, deictic references, such as pointing to the screen and saying "there", "this", or "that", persist even when such behavior has limited utility, as when we are on the phone. However, any ambiguity raised by this practice is by and large handled without remark. In fact, deictic reference is often ambiguous even in face-to-face conversation. Nonetheless, the ambiguity our users experienced appeared to be more extreme than in these other cases. For example, our users had a problematic breakdown in which they appeared to have quite different interpretations of the word "that". A summary account of what happened follows:

(1) P2 was using the video network to look at P1's machine. There was a general discussion about creating a new item;
(2) P1 hit a mouse button, thereby creating an edit window for entering a new item;
(3) P3 suggested that P2 should type instead of P1;
(4) P2 went to switch her display back to her own machine;
(5) P1 looked at her screen, appeared surprised, typed four characters (the title of the item) and moused the DONE button, thus sending it to the others.
(6) P2 found that her display had gone black (into idle) and was confused, "What! Who did that?" At virtually the same time, the item that P1 had created appeared on P2's and P3's screens.
(7) P3 "P1";
(8) P2 (hitting a space bar which caused the machine to come out of idle) "Oh, it was my fault".
(9) P1 "I did not!"
(10) P3 "P1. Let P2 type!"
(11) P1 "I am!"
(12) P2 "I've forgotten what I was going to type".

P2 said "Who did that?" referring to the fact that her machine had gone into idle. P3 interpreted "that" to mean the thing that had changed in his environment, which was the appearance of a new item. He had not caused this new item to appear, so he replied that P1 had caused it. P3 ended up with the wrong picture of P2's complaint and therefore P1 was unjustly accused of not permitting P2 to type.

In fact, the participants/collaborators moved on without sorting out what had happened, and it was only through careful reconstruction that we as analysts came to understand the sequence. Since both our trial groups consisted of long-term collaborators, the amount of interpersonal damage was probably small, but it did represent a substantial disruption to their work. Furthermore, the incident, combined with the fact that both groups declined to use the computational shared workspace, was telling. It suggested that in this situation people could not rely on familiar mechanisms for coordinating or managing ambiguity. The technology was not increasing their efficiency in this respect.

To proceed, we needed to understand what was causing the difficulties our users experienced. We needed to understand what they needed to see and what factors contributed to the increase in ambiguity. However, since this was not intended as our major line of research, but rather as enabling work for other more central interests, we faced the challenge of trying to work as much as we could with materials already in the literature (rather than constructing a research project to explore this one set of issues). The challenge that we faced is a general one because CSCW systems almost always touch on many different research areas, not all of which can be pursued actively. Designers need approaches that maximize their use of appropriate existing research.

Models of conversation

The fields of conversation analysis (see Goodwin & Heritage, 1990 for an overview of the field) and psycholinguistics (see Clark & Wilkes-Gibbs, 1986; Clark & Schaefer, 1987, 1989; Schober & Clark 1989; for the most relevant aspects) offer a model of conversation which seems highly pertinent to the difficulties our users faced. They present what we may term an "interactive" model of communication. The interactive model emphasizes the notion that conversation is a highly coordinated activity in which meaning is attained and affirmed using a number of mechanisms that have context dependent functions. By contrast, Cognoter implemented and thus supported what we may term a "parcel-post" model in which communication is delivered in parcel-like units.

INTERACTIVE MODEL

The starting point of the interactive model of conversation is the observation that conversation does not consist of one person making a complete utterance while the other person waits passively. Both participants are active even when only one is actually speaking. Thus people nod, complete or reshape one another's phrases, and say "uh-huh" (Duncan, 1973).

A second major point of the interactive model is that the function of an utterance is context dependent. Each conversational move involves not only its own contents but a projection of what the next move will be. For example, one of the resources that people have available in conversation is the *noun phrase*. There are different types of noun phrases (Clark & Wilkes-Gibbs, 1986), the most common being the *elementary* noun phrase, as in "the green cup on the bookshelf" uttered as one tonal sequence. When a person utters "the green cup on the bookshelf", she is projecting that the phrase will be accepted without comment. Other types of noun phrases, e.g. "the whatchamacallit", set up other expectations. If she alters the phrase by the use of a *try-marker* (Sacks & Schegloff, 1979), a tonal, non-lexical request for judgement about its acceptability,† she is indicating that the preferred next move is a listener response indicating whether his meaning is clear. In the case of an unmodified elementary noun phrase, a non-response complies with the projection and asserts that the phrase has been understood. If the phrase is modified with a try-marker, a non-response indicates trouble, perhaps that the other person is no

† A try-marker sounds similar to a question, but it is not a request for agreement on contents, just agreement that the phrase is understood.

longer listening. Furthermore, a response after a pause is not the same as an immediate response. For example, it may set up a question about whether the listener is attending or beginning to signal dissention (Pomerantz, 1984; Pomerantz, 1978; Goodwin, 1980).

Listeners have the ability to make statements explicitly or implicitly which add to, accept, reject, question or modify what the speaker has just said. In the interactive model, this listener response is a crucial part of conversation. In fact, Clark and Schaefer (1987, 1989) have gone so far as to advance the notion that the basic unit of conversation consists of two parts, a *presentation* and an *acceptance* phase. Together the two constitute a *contribution*. Since, as mentioned above, non-response is in fact a statement, the ability to perform the acceptance portion actively is crucial.

The interactive model also draws our attention to the importance of mid-course corrections (Goodwin, 1981; Schegloff, 1981; Clark & Wilkes-Gibbs, 1986). Mid-course corrections happen when speakers or listeners adjust in midstream, either of their own accord or in response to something in the environment. For example, while uttering the phrase "the green cup on the bookshelf", the speaker may note the listener's confused expression and attempt to clarify by adding "in the library". We know that people can succeed in conversing without some elements of this because they succeed in conversing over half-duplex phone lines and with computer TALK systems which may be serial. However, most people find this quite unpleasant and, in face-to-face conversation, mid-course corrections, whether by the speaker or the listener are endemic. According to Clark and Wilkes-Gibbs, mid-course corrections are yet another way that conversationalists obey the general goal of "reducing the collaborative work" of holding the conversation.

In the interactive model, conversation is structured around the work that both participants must do to establish that they are talking about the same things. One aspect of this is establishing what objects they are referring to. To study this problem, Clark and Wilkes-Gibbs (1986) asked pairs of subjects to sort a deck of cards with non-representational pictures on them. The subjects each had their own deck and could not see one another or the other person's deck. The *matcher* was supposed to put the deck in the same order as the *director*. On average, the first references to each card took close to four turns at speech by the director. However, people's ability to refer verbally to particular objects developed through shared experience. As they repeated the task, the references they used to the cards become more compact. They were simplified and/or narrowed at close to the crucial components. Thus, the second trial took on average two turns and the third averaged at close to one. Furthermore, the number of words per turn at talk declined over time; "the one that looks like a skater with one leg kicked back" turned into "the skater" (Clark & Wilkes-Gibbs, 1986).

Furthermore, in general people preferred to refer to the task items with permanent descriptions rather than temporary views. A permanent reference is one such as describing a drawing as "the rabbit". This contrasts with temporary sorts of references such as "the one we got confused on last time". A reason for this preference may be that permanent descriptions permit successive refinement of the reference.

In the interactive view, conversation is a complex, highly coordinated process in which conversants seek mutual understanding through the coordinated presentation and acceptance of a variety of lexical and non-lexical statements. Projections of the next conversational move and active listener response are crucial for this activity. The abilities to make mid-course corrections and abbreviated references are highly desirable. Time plays a crucial role.

PARCEL-POST MODEL

Although Cognoter permitted people to talk with one another, and thus employ their normal resources, its textual component may be described as embodying a parcel-post model of communication. The qualities of a parcel-post model are that items are packaged and sent by the speaker, and then unpackaged and decoded by the receiver. An additional component of the model is that if the receiver does not open his "mail" right away, he may end up with a bunch of stuff with no particular order.

The differences between these models suggest that one class of problems may occur in coordinating such interactive features as mid-course corrections, projections of the next move, and listener response. A second class of problems may occur in determining that both people are talking about the same thing.

Problems applying the interactive model to Cognoter

The differences between the interactive and parcel-post models suggest that our users had difficulty because they could not accomplish necessary or highly desirable activities described by the interactive model. However, we cannot immediately conclude that this explains our users' problems, because the interactive model arose from studying situations that differed in two important respects from the situation we created in Cognoter: the number of people involved in an interaction, and the type of communication involved. To understand whether and how we would expect the interactive model to generalize to Cognoter, we must understand the impact of these differences.

The first issue arises because most of the work that led to the interactive model studied conversation between only two people. Our Cognoter experiences involved three people. In recent years, there have been some studies of multi-party interaction which extend but do not refute the two-person model (Goodwin & Goodwin, 1990). While these studies provide some assurance of continuity between the situations, they have not concentrated on identifying the differences between the two party and multi-party conversation. They leave open the possibility that, for example, the expectation of response is lessened in the multi-party case. Nonetheless, conversation with three people is, by and large, unlikely to simplify the possibilities or render resources for achieving shared reference less necessary. Although there are unanswered questions, we may safely assume that any factors that seem likely to cause difficulties in the two-person situation will be only more likely to do so in the three.

The second problem originates in the recognition that many forms of communication exist which are not conversational. For example, the parcel-post model works perfectly well for letters. Since people are creating text in Cognoter, we initially assumed that the parcel-post model would suffice. Why should we now attribute their difficulties to conversational impediments?

Clark and Wilkes-Gibbs (1986) propose a highly relevant distinction between conversation and literary communication. They propose that the principle of *mutual responsibility* holds in conversation:

> The participants in a conversation try to establish, roughly by the initiation of each new contribution, the mutual belief that the listeners have understood what the speaker meant in the last utterance to a criterion sufficient for current purposes (Clark & Wilkes-Gibbs, 1986, p. 33).

They contrast this with the principle of *distant responsibility*:

> The speaker or writer tries to make sure, roughly by the initiation of each new contribution, that the addressees should have been able to understand his meaning in the last utterance to a criterion sufficient for current purposes (Clark & Wilkes-Gibbs, 1986, p. 35).

The principle of distant responsibility applies in the many situations—writing a paper, sending e-mail, giving a lecture, broadcasting on TV, dictating a tape to be sent in the mail—that are distinguished from conversation less by the medium carrying the communication (paper, airwaves, Ethernet) as by a relative lack of co-production and therefore of time constraints in the preparation of the communication. In other words, conversation is distinguished from literary forms of communication by the amount of work to ensure understanding that is done *within the time frame* of the actual communication. Cognoter differs from literary communication because Cognoter is not the sole or primary carrier of the communication. Cognoter differs from conversation as we have described it because it involves writing activity. In fact, Cognoter is neither of these, but rather a medium for representation in relationship to the conversation.

A large body of work has been done exploring the relationship between conversation and writing activity in traditional representational media such as whiteboards and large sheets of paper. This work provides evidence that similar constraints apply when working with representational media as with unadorned conversation, and that similar resources are necessary or desirable.

Traditional representational media

Suchman (1988) and Tang (1989, 1990) and Bly (1988) have studied traditional representational media such as whiteboards and large sheets of paper. We can draw on their work to extrapolate from the interactive model to understand how we might expect the parcel-post model of Cognoter to cause users trouble.

Suchman and Tang give evidence that, since writing and drawing activity interacts with conversation, coordination is as important when using these media as it is in conversation without them. Suchman (1988) describes the way in which turns at "... the board may be used in taking and holding the floor, or in maintaining some writing activity while passing up a turn as talk. Writing done during another's talk may (a) document the talk and thereby display the writer's understanding, (b) continue the writer's previous turn or (c) project the writer's next turn. providing an object to be introduced in subsequent talk". The writing actions are neither appendages to the verbal conversation nor independent of it. Writing and talking is intricately bound together in a similar fashion to the way a statement and its response are bound

together. However, the coordination issues are even more complex because a person can write while talk is occurring. There are therefore more kinds of moves to be made.

The fact that textual items persist makes it tempting to believe that time is less relevant in shared writing and drawing activities than in purely verbal conversation. "Recording information" is usually accounted the chief reason to use a whiteboard and this activity is considered to be independent of the conversation. However, in practice, only a small percentage of the activity in relationship to a whiteboard is recording information (Tang 1989). It is important therefore to look at other functions of work in the shared medium.

Suchman (1988) distinguishes between those actions in reference to the whiteboard that involve the production of textual or graphical objects and those that involve the use. Our construction of this distinction is that whiteboard items hold a dual status as elements *in* the conversation and elements that may be conversed *about*. During production (when they are being created) they are typically, but not always, elements in the conversation and, like verbal conversation, understood according to precise context. Thus, the moment a person starts to write helps determine whether the writing action acknowledges what has already been said (or written) or ignores it, and whether the writing represents agreement, clarification, informed disagreements, a side activity, or an attempt to bring up a new topic. Once created, the textual items are similar to other physical objects such as tables and chairs in the environment and may be conversed about.† As objects in the world, they are not subject to timing considerations. However, participants may have to do work to ensure that they are talking about the same objects in the world, and time is a factor in that work.‡

Recording information for future use is certainly an important function for representational media. However, even while recording information, participants are not free from timing considerations. Tang (1989) reports that the length of time recording information takes, presents a "challenge" for the group. This challenge can be handled in a number of different ways. They may wait for the recorder to finish, occupy the pause with individual work, or move on to another topic. Any of these activities may be accompanied by talk, preceded by it, or followed by it, or free of it. Drawing upon the Clark and Wilkes-Gibbs distinction between conversation and literary communication, we may speculate that the challenge arises because the person doing the recording has in an important sense stepped out of the conversation. She is engaged in an essentially literary endeavor in which she must take the time to anticipate what the group or someone else will need to know later on. Meanwhile, the other participants may compensate, e.g. by monitoring the activity (but not always).

A further issue arises when we consider whiteboard items as elements to be referred to, as objects in the world. In everyday conversation and in whiteboard use,

† The situation is a bit more complex than this. Since production takes time and items once created may be modified, which is a kind of production, a given item on the whiteboard has the potential to be both an element in the conversation and to be conversed about as an object. People intermix actions in relationship to these different aspects of whiteboard elements smoothly.

‡ Furthermore, we expect that work to be increased over the work people have to do to talk about tables and chairs, because the objects which are in general not familiar, represent other complex ideas, and may not be as easily recognized.

deixis, the ability to point or say "this" or "that" with reference to the objects in the environment, is omnipresent. The success of a deictic reference depends on shared knowledge about the position of an object. This suggests that one reason that whiteboards are so useful is they give a highly salient quality or position to an idea.

The salience of position is demonstrated by instances of people referring to the spot on the whiteboard where a particular idea, now erased, once was represented (Suchman, 1988). Clark and Wilkes-Gibbs do not discuss deixis. However, they do note that people prefer permanent qualities to temporary ones. In their study, location was considered a temporary feature. This makes sense because they were talking about stacks of cards that were being continually moved in the course of the task. However, the prevalence of gesture in relation to whiteboard objects and the salience of position, provides evidence that the location of whiteboard objects is regarded as a permanent quality for the purposes of the conversation. Thus, threats to positional information will make object identification more difficult.

The study of traditional representational media contains ample evidence that people use the basic "interactive" conversational paradigm. It is highly structured and dependent on both time and context. While there may be interesting modifications in response to different representational media, we have every reason to believe that the same resources are available for projecting the next move, for making and obtaining listener response, and for mid-course correction. The whiteboard provides increased facilities for determining what objects are being discussed, and the success of this facility appears to be dependent on positional information, as well as on the contents of whatever is written.

Cognoter problems

Cognoter differs from whiteboards and large sheets of paper in important respects: items may be easily rearranged; people work with keyboards; and the participants have not only displays instead of boards, but separate displays. Still, Cognoter is like a whiteboard or large sheet of paper in several important respects: crucially, it allows the visual presentation and inspection of all items by all participants; it allows items to be created and pointed at; and it allows items, though of a limited nature compared with whiteboard elements, to be arranged freely within the available space.

We have drawn a picture of conversation in relationship to a representational medium that emphasizes interactivity and coordination. This picture also contains the notion that an important utility of the representational medium lies in the ability to refer to objects in a succinct way. We have evidence from Cognoter that users could not "see" what they wanted to see, and some evidence about mistaken reference.

To have enough confidence that the differences between the interactive model and the parcel-post model substantially account for the difficulties our users faced, we want to have a picture of how we might expect the interactive processes that the users were engaged in to play out against the system with which they were working. We cannot have a complete model because we don't know all the resources that people have available or their significance at all moments. Nonetheless, demonstrating a severe blockage of the process components that we have identified, both

argues for the significance of these processes and highlights specific implementation decisions in the system.

In light of this, eight design decisions which we must consider as possible contributors to the difficulties our users had are as follows:

• Separate screens: We gave each user a separate screen. They were not in fact looking at the same place. This meant that gaze and gesture information was reduced.
• Lack of sequentiality: There was no marked position where the next icon would appear or any way of determining the order of contributions.
• Short labels: Icons could only be short phrases. This meant only a small amount of information per item could be viewed by the group together.
• Anonymity: All changes were anonymous. The results were delivered to others with no indication of who had made them.
• Private editing: Editing of item text was accomplished in private editor windows. The results were delivered to the others wholesale. The catchphrase (and therefore the icon) could be changed entirely. Alternatively, the item could retain the same catchphrase but the annotations which gave it a particular meaning could have changed.
• Unpredictable delay: Changes showed up on other people's screens after an unpredictable delay. Sometimes they showed up as quickly as a third of a second but at times it took as long as 20 seconds.
• Private moving: Moving icons was accomplished privately. On other people's screens, an icon would disappear from one position and appear in another. The object could lose its identifiable position.
• Tailorable windows: Users could tailor their screen individually by moving windows around and by changing their size and shape. Item organization windows could appear in different places in different sizes on each person's screen.

With these design issues in mind, we revisit the Cognoter situation and attempt to describe what we believe the users faced and why these factors contribute to a problem for them. We divide this discussion into two sections: coordination problems and reference problems.

For the purposes of this discussion, the person making the contribution is referred to as "he" and the person responding as "she". The "speaker" is used for the person making the contribution, while "listener", "recipient", and "responder" are used for the person responding.

COORDINATION

Cognoter users are presented with a choice of media; they can choose to communicate: verbally, through text, or by using a combination of the two.† Like all participants in a conversation, they collectively face the need to (1) produce contributions,‡ (2) recognize contributions as such, and (3) make responses. Although by definition making a contribution must be a positive action, response may be made either by positive action or by a non-response. Verbal and writing activities need to be coordinated with one another if made by the same person, and

† For the purposes of this discussion, we treat these as distinct choices. However, people presumably intermix them smoothly.

‡ Although Clark and Schaefer (1987, 1989) have used the term "contribution" to refer to the whole process of saying something and getting a response, we are using the term contribution more colloquially to refer to the spoken or written utterance. They use the term "presentation" for the utterance. "Presentation" is unsatisfactory for our purposes because it sounds as though there is a slice of time in which the listener is purely an "audience".

responses need to be understood in relationship to the contributions that evoked them.

Producing contributions

A person making a contribution in Cognoter has a choice of media. Making a spoken contribution in the Cognoter situation is hardly different from making a spoken contribution in the other situations we have discussed.† However, if the user attempts to include Cognoter in his action, he faces certain difficulties. A purely textual contribution, since it is made privately (private editing), does not in itself contain the elements of a bid for the floor, in the way starting to write at a whiteboard sometimes does.

The speaker may attempt to remedy this by accompanying his writing activity with speech. However, private editing and unpredictable delay mean that the textual and verbal elements of the contribution will be extremely hard to coordinate. On a whiteboard, users can perform different kinds of actions. We've observed that one whiteboard, users can perform different kinds of actions. We've observed that one participant, namely recording information, presents a challenge for the other participants, which they handle with a variety of strategies. In Cognoter, even acts which do not involve recording information present a similar challenge insofar as they are invisible. It is as if the person, rather than making a bid for the floor, had simply dropped out of the conversation in the same way they have to when recording information in traditional media.

While the challenge of coordinating talking and writing is similar to the challenge the group faces when handling recording information on traditional media, their resources are not in all cases the same. If the speaker speaks as he starts to type and is timed if his speech succeeds in capturing the attention of the group (i.e. if it is timed carefully enough despite the distraction of typing), then the group faces options similar to the traditional case (although the listeners may be waiting in situations which would not normally require them to wait: recall that our users asked unhappily "Why can't I see it?"). However, if the speaker waits until he has finished typing to speak, he risks losing any projectible connection between the time he initiated the typing and the time the message is received. Furthermore, because of separate screens, unpredictable delay, and lack of sequentiality, there will never be a particular moment at which the speaker knows that his text item has been received by everyone and is being looked at.‡ Lastly, even if the recipients see the item come up, if more than one person was typing, they must figure out who's commentary matched the new (anonymous) item.

This lack of coordination means that the speaker is hampered in several ways. First, he cannot make or obtain mid-course corrections. Even if the speaker does adjust his writing activity in response to something the listener has said or done, this adjustment loses any meaning as acknowledgement or anticipation of listener reaction. The inability to evoke mid-course corrections increases the speaker's burden to complete the work of the phrase by himself, and increases the total work of the group since his extra work could in many cases be avoided.

Second, even once the contribution is complete, he encounters difficulties

† Contributions are not, in general, really made against a clean slate.
‡ As with response, overt work can be done to make everyone look at the item, but this is a far cry from increasing the efficiency of the conversation or the meeting.

projecting a preferred response. Two resources we have identified as important in conversation are try-markers and pauses. These are strictly verbal. The absence of coordination between talk and writing means that try-markers and pauses are ineffective in relation to the computational medium.

Mid-course corrections, try-markers and pauses certainly do not represent the complete set of resources that speakers have available in conversation. However, their absence is quite a significant loss.

Recognizing contributions

We expect from the analysis above that the speaker will have to do more work to make a contribution in relation to Cognoter, than with traditional media or in simple conversation. However, the situation is even worse for the person who attempts to use the system to respond to another's contribution. First, she must know what to respond to and-that itself presents difficulties.

The ability to know what to react to and when is reduced. If the speaker is typing and talking, the listener can respond at the appropriate time to either the verbal or the textual component of the turn. Since these are not coordinated, she must choose between them. If she has enough information to respond to the verbal component, then she has the difficulty of timing her response to avoid competing with the typing. If she waits to receive and assess the text, she has the difficulty of spotting it on the screen (lack of sequentiality). If she does spot the item, she must determine that no one else has priority making a response (lack of sequentiality, private editing, unpredictable delay). Furthermore, since people may well occupy their time making their own contributions, even when one contribution is detected, she may have trouble deciding on an order for response.

Additionally, since it is extremely difficult for the speaker to establish a connection between verbal and textual matter, the listener is likely to see the item in the absence of mid-course corrections, try-markers and pauses. This means that the phrase will be seen as "elementary", that is projecting assurance that it can be understood. She will therefore work hard to make sense out of it. This increase in her work is significant because even in everyday conversation, "the heavier burden usually falls on the listener, since she is in the best position to assess her own comprehension" (Clark & Wilkes-Gibbs, 1986, p. 34). Furthermore:

When the speaker utters I just found the keys, marking the noun phrase as elementary...the listener is under strong pressure to accept it. After all, the speaker marked it as elementary; so he must believe it to be adequate for current purposes. If she rejects it, she risks offending him by indicating that it wasn't adequate. She also risks revealing her own incompetence if indeed it should have been adequate. Finally, like the speaker, the listener wants to minimize collaborative effort—to avoid extra steps in the acceptance process—and that too puts pressure on her to accept. All this encourages her to tolerate a certain lack of understanding, even to feign understanding when it is not justified. She may do this trusting that the holes will be filled in later, or that they won't have serious consequences (Clark & Wilkes-Gibbs, 1986, p. 34).

Making a response

Once the listener has identified something she wishes to respond to, she must carry out the response. A non-response becomes extremely ambiguous; it is difficult to distinguish lack of attention from confirmation that all is well from a deliberate snub. If she chooses to make a positive response, she must choose her media. Here she faces the same problems coordinating speech and text that the speaker faced in making the contribution. However, the problems play out a bit differently.

If she responds verbally to a verbal presentation, all is well. If she responds verbally to a textual item, not using the tool at all, she may have to do more work, because she does not know that other people have received the item and consider it an active element in the conversation. She may have to establish what she is talking about, for example, by reading the item aloud.

If a listener responds in text to either a verbal or a textual contribution, then there is a considerable chance for her act or the meaning of her act to be lost. For example, a person could acknowledge agreement by building upon one idea with a related idea or by writing down the idea just mentioned. Alternatively, the same act of beginning to write could signify an attempt to propose a new topic. The lack of coordination between the contribution and the response means neither the fact that one is making a response nor the particular meaning of the response will be fully available to others. In the absence of speech, even if the others notice that the responder has begun to type, there will be nothing to mark her action as a response to a particular contribution. Furthermore, if the recipients are not monitoring exactly the right space on their screen (lack of sequentiality) some unpredictable amount of time after she finishes (unpredictable delay), they may well fail to register that any change was made at all. If the change is made in an annotation, then not only must they each wait for it but they must perform an extra action to find it in the text of the item (short labels). It is quite possible for someone to re-open something that they typed originally and find that the annotations are quite different and no longer make sense to them.†

Just like the speaker, the recipient can also hope to improve on this difficult situation by including both written and verbal components in her response. However, she cannot just say "yes" and begin to write, but must say "yes, I'll write that down" or "yes, even better" to let the other's know the meaning of her beginning to type at that instance. Even if she does this extra work, the others will not necessarily know that what she has written down is consistent with her "yes" until they see it. (She could also tell them what that she is writing, but since she is typing, she is in no position to pursue subsequent discussion. This behavior would represent yet more work that had to be done just to manage the logistics of the technology.) By the time she has finished typing, they may well have moved on to other things and the value of the response built on what was said, making a bid for the floor, or in any way guiding the discussion, is lost.

While the burden on the recipient is increased, her ability to respond effectively is curtailed. One way she could handle this increased burden is by inserting some sort of meta-comment, such as a question about why the item looks the way it does, into the text of the item. However, this behavior has strong consequences. For the query to carry enough information for whoever in turn receives it to know how to answer in the absence of sequential order, whatever was typed has to obey the principle of distant responsibility. That means that the responder has to take the time to anticipate what others in the future will need to see to be reminded of the issue. To

† Someone may well open an item just to see the annotations and not as a conversational act at all. The mere fact that there is activity does not signify change.

make such a response, the responder might well have to drop out of the conversation. If people drop out of the conversation too much, it is no longer a conversation, and they are no longer working collaboratively. Indeed, we may speculate that something like this is what happened in our first group in which each person worked separately until they turned to pencil and paper for the work they really needed to do together.

Thus, there are difficulties in both making contributions and in making responses. The contribution phase could probably be handled. However, the burden on the listener seems to be too great. Our users complained that they couldn't see enough. Our interpretation of those complaints is that users probably could have waited for the representational content of the items. They did this in the one case that seemed unproblematic for the group, when the text was reintroduced by being read aloud. What they needed to "see" immediately was the written component coordinating the interaction. The absence of coordination between speech and writing led to a highly frustrating experience.

CO-REFERENCE

Clark and Wilkes-Gibbs (1986) point out that shared reference is something that must be achieved. We had hoped that the differences between the displays at Cognoter stations would be transparent to the users or at least be accepted without too much difficulty. However, in fact people were not looking at the same surface (separate screens). This meant that they lost most of the gaze and gesture information and their base-level knowledge of what was being talked about was less than with other representational media. These losses would probably not be crippling since people manage to talk and even work (Bly, 1988) over the phone. Nonetheless, built on top of this basic situation are several discontinuities which combine to make effective co-reference difficult.

Trying to find previously entered items is potentially difficult. By design, windows may be in different places and have different shapes and sizes on different people's screens (tailorable windows). Indexical descriptions such as "It's in the upper left" do not work under these circumstances. To locate an item, you must first determine that you and your colleagues are referring to the same window, then locate the item within the window. Since windows cannot be identified by position or shape, the user must fall back on searching for their titles. Windows may be moved very quickly and invisibly. Therefore, this already time-consuming work may have to be performed repeatedly.

Additionally, trying to keep track of changes to the items presents new difficulties. First, moving or substantially changing items can be done very abruptly. When a user clicks on an item icon to move it, the item greys out on other people's screens, just as it does when an item is being edited. When the user puts the item down elsewhere, it suddenly disappears from its original location on everyone else's screen and reappears somewhere else. Even if one is looking for the flash of its reappearance, it can be hard to find on a busy screen. Furthermore, given the privacy of moving and editing, it is not very interesting to look at the screen while waiting to spot something new. Lastly, unlike with traditional media, an item is not necessarily fully displayed. Therefore, someone may change the text shown in the icon. Subsequently, another person might want to look at the annotations attached to the item and not be able to find the item because the icon has changed.

In the case of other technologies comparable to Cognoter, we have seen that position is treated as a highly salient quality and that compact reference is desirable. In Cognoter the ability to use positional information to achieve compact reference is jeopardized in part by the new facilities we are providing and in part because we provided them in a way that undermines the work that people have to do to be able to refer to positioned items efficiently.

The combination of the eight design decisions mentioned at the beginning of this section with the conversational processes involved in using the tool, made Cognoter items more difficult both to create and to use than whiteboard objects. Our users could not "see" vital portions of the conversation and they could not make sure that each one was seeing the same objects in their representational world. Although people are in general good at compensating, there are limits to their abilities and willingness to do so. Cognoter posed too hard a communicational puzzle for our users in a conversational, time-constrained situation.

Consequences for Cognoter

An important outcome of this work was the development of a second generation tool, Cnoter. The redesign was oriented towards improving the system without giving up those features, such as the ability to move and edit items, that seem to be major benefits of computation for this kind of application. As shown in Table 1, the redesign attempted to fix four out of the eight problems we have discussed.

The major problems we tried to fix were those of private editing, private moving, unpredictable delay, and tailorable windows. We introduced shared editing and moving facilities, a significant speed-up of communication between machines, and consistent positioning of windows across machines. When someone creates a new item in Cnoter, they still open an edit window, but that window opens on everyone else's screen as well. Updates are broadcast every second. Only one person can type in a shared edit window at a time; however, control can be transferred from one person to another by clicking the mouse in the window. Thus, everyone has visual access to items while they are being created, and they can even contribute actively to that creation when appropriate. Likewise, the activity of moving icons is broadcast several times a second, so that icons no longer disappear from one place and appear suddenly somewhere else.† We not only sped up communication between the machines, but added some more checking to balance out the times at which the text arrived at different machines. We eliminated the occasional very long delay for information to get from machine to machine. Thus, users should not be confused by having a particular text object and not knowing whether or not others can see it. Lastly, we made window position and shape consistent across all machines. This means that people can rely on positional information for resolving the uncertainties of reference.

We have not changed our decisions about short labels, lack of sequentiality and anonymity. With the addition of shared editing and moving, the short labels found in the idea organization windows carry much less communicative weight. They seem to be adequate for the purpose of reminding users of item contents.

The lack of sequentiality interacted poorly with attempts both to coordinate the conversation and to keep track of where items were; however, whiteboards and large sheets of paper function well without maintaining explicit evidence of sequentiality. This suggests that we should distinguish between process and product when considering our design. We had failed to give users sufficient evidence of sequentiality during the process of creating items; however, we did not need to preserve this information after the fact, when the textual contributions became simple objects in the world. The addition of shared editing and moving probably provides enough sequence information, and we do not need to change the basic whiteboard metaphor.

The issue of anonymity is similar to that of sequentiality in that one can have anonymity in the process of creation and anonymity of the eventual product. As we have pointed out, the issue of who has written text on the whiteboard is of primary importance during the process of writing, when it is a component in the conversation. There is not usually a need for a permanent label of authorship. With shared editing, anonymity no longer really exists for groups our size. If people are watching the process of creation, they will see who is doing what. This can be considered a loss, since anonymity in creating an item might permit shy or low status people to make more contributions. However, to implement process anonymity viably, we would need to move away from a basically conversational paradigm.

One of the chief benefits of the forgoing analysis is that it limits what we perceive as the sources of user difficulties. Users had problems that interacted with our decisions about sequentiality and anonymity. However, we came to believe that the designs we had in these areas were not themselves the cause of the problems. This thinking also applies to what is from some perspectives the fundamental problem with Cognoter: that we give users separate screens.

The thought that separate screens are the root of the problem is a very serious one, since they were a premise of the original system and the multiple arrangement is one of the most promising features of Colab. It is extremely flexible and presents the possibility of moving between private and public work. Furthermore, with the multiple screen/multiple keyboard setup, people can type at the same time, which means that, as with a whiteboard, the controls over whether they choose to do so are social and decided upon in response to the situation.

---

† We believe that this improvement allows perceptual rather than cognitive processing of positional changes, as described in Robertson, Card & MacKinlay (1989).

TABLE 1
Summary of changes motivated by the extended interactive model

Cognoter design issue	Cnoter status
Separate screens	Unchanged
Short labels	Unchanged
Sequentiality	Unchanged
Anonymity	Unchanged
Private editing	Shared editing
Unpredictable delay	Sped up communication
Private moving	Shared moving
Tailorable windows	Windows same on all screens

Although the analysis we have presented is by no means exhaustive, having a rich account of how the users probably came to have the difficulties they did, gives us reason to believe that the difficulties were not inherent in the multiple screen arrangement, but had limited, identifiable causes in what information was displayed on the screens. This means that, rather than giving up on the whole idea, we can try to address the problems in a more local fashion.

The new system has yet to be tested and evaluated. However, preliminary use by non-members of the Colab project suggests that users are much happier. At least one group has been able to work in the system using the computational shared workspace without the distress that we saw in our previous groups.

Other consequences

These changes fix the immediate problem. Since the Colab project's ultimate interest is in higher-level processes such as brainstorming and argumentation built on top of this fundamental conversational level, we needed to fix other difficulties as quickly as possible. Getting conversation right enables us to ask the questions about working with the system that we started with. For example, do the facilities we provide decrease "production blocking"? Do shy people contribute more or less when given a keyboard? Do people actually have a greater shared understanding of the material due to the less cryptic notes that get taken?

However, in our solutions, we tried not to experiment but simply to provide the facilities to enable successful conversation. The conversational mechanisms themselves provide another interesting source of technological experimentation and development. For example, although we now coordinate each participants' window size and shape, and make editor windows as well as item organization windows public, it would be interesting to see what happened if we made this user-tailorable. We might find out under what circumstances it is necessary or desirable for everyone to see the same things in the same way. We might also find out whether there are a class of situations in which it is not necessary for everyone to see the same things in the same way.

Another issue is that we have made Cognoter more conversational, rather than less. However, there is nothing about the Cognoter technology that intrinsically demands that it be used for closely coordinated work. In our studies, we set up a situation in which people would use the technology conversationally. We asked them to bring a task that they wanted or needed to work on together in the course of their own work. Presumably there are reasons why these tasks needed group solution. Our description of the technology revolved around its cooperative nature and its benefits for collaboration. Users were driven by the task, by our set-up, and by their own expectations to attempt to work by minimizing the least collaborative effort and by enjoying the benefits of mid-course correction and listener response. This must always be the case when people are actually working together. However, instead of trying to support activities already done in meetings, we could have tried to make it easier to bring activities normally done in isolation at least partially into a public forum, as when one wanders down the hall and asks a colleague about a word or a paragraph, or the outline of an algorithm, or the arguments to a function without actually involving them in the central work that is being done. The challenge here is to provide easy flow back and forth between the public and the private at the right grain-size. This requires strategies for getting people's attention and agreement about moving from private work to collaboration. These strategies, whether provided through the computer or verbally, must be conversationally viable.

This analysis also has benefits in terms of the study of conversation and interaction. Several questions have been raised: one is how a more complete description of the relationship between talk and action in traditional representational media, might look. What are the mechanisms and resources available to people for incorporating written items into the conversation? Does some more subtle kind of try-marker occur in whiteboard use? Are there certain categories of communications that are never written on whiteboards? Why do we ordinarily not see marks like "???" on whiteboards? Some of these questions have technical implications. For example, would it be helpful to render our notions of certainty about particular items visible in some fashion?

Conclusions

We realize that there were aspects of the original Cognoter system which did not work, and we have given some account of why. We claim that many of the serious problems in Cognoter stem from a culturally prevalent, easy-to-make assumption that communication consists of bits of verbal or textual material passed whole from one person to the next. Under this model, messages could be created, packaged, and sent by one person, unpacked, interpreted, changed, and sent on by others without regard for the exact moments of their creation and distribution. We also believe that we underestimated the problem for users of determining shared reference and therefore allowed too much activity that undermined its reliability. These underlying assumptions permitted a small but crucial number of design decisions in Cognoter that were responsible for much of the difficulty.

While it is possible that given enough time people could, as we did ourselves, learn to work with the system better than our users did, the initial difficulty was too great for a useful tool. Furthermore, whatever efficiency we gained by avoiding "production blocking" through parallel typing, this was certainly lost in the increased amount of work that had to be done to maintain communication.

We had reason to continue work on Cognoter. For one thing, we learned that certain aspects of the system were positively received. Promisingly, the group that used the video network to work around the problems discussed, was quite happy with the system. Although they used only a fraction of its functionality, some felt it could become "addictive", and commented with enthusiasm on the ease of bringing a fourth colleague up to speed on the work they had done in their Cognoter sessions.

Furthermore, we have yet to evaluate the features that we imagine as the most important contributions of the tool. By and large, the qualities we sought to promote in patterns of work are untouched by this analysis. Brainstorming, organizing and evaluating is still an interesting process to support. The ability to use the keyboard, the ability to save, printout, and recall organizations, the ability to rearrange material, and to handle large amounts of material are all important features.

However, we now see that the process we first identified at the whiteboard and later brought to the computer was built on conversational abilities. This affects some of our ideas. For example, we promoted the notion that it would be more efficient to work in parallel. That idea remains; however, it now rests on a deeper notion of what working in parallel means. It does not mean merely working at the same time as someone else, which is after all, what we do when we work alone. Instead, it means giving participants the ability to judge when it is appropriate to overlap, just as they judge the efficacy of other possible moves in a conversation. In other words, to work successfully in parallel, we must have resources for working together.

What happened with Cognoter has significance for CSCW beyond the boundaries of this particular project because Colab was a highly innovative project that encountered serious difficulty because it did not recognize that it had entered a new arena. It slipped up on implicit aspects of the system, places where the system designers didn't realize they were making choices. Although these problems were suspected in preliminary observations, two factors common to CSCW research conspired to make them difficult to pin down convincingly. One is that the problems are at such a fine level of coordination that is not possible to capture and recreate specific incidents of problems without electronic means. The second is that considerable knowledge of the system and its rationale does seem to allow people to function without overt distress, perhaps by causing them to reduce their criteria for understanding what is happening at particular moments.

Human–machine studies are done typically to examine those aspects of systems that are already deemed important for success. In a field that is as new and as complex as computer-supported cooperative work, and equally as liable to fail as undirected observation. Furthermore, system designers must draw on and reason about social science results such as the interactive model that are not necessarily predictive and which do not necessarily describe the exact situation that they are designing. This is a risky but potentially rewarding strategy.

The ability to use whatever social science insights we have to feed into careful thought about the situation we are trying to create is crucial because, as designers of novel technologies, we must judge whether the technologies we envisage are likely to work. While it is easy to judge failure by the distress expressed by users, it is much harder to judge the success and potential of a system that has encountered difficulty. Although this analysis has focused on problems and addressed potential only incidentally, it also suggests that Cognoter was close to being able to create a multi-user system that people would be able to use with the ease, range of expressive behaviors, and mastery that they employ in conversation. Furthermore, experience suggests that perhaps we can give users much more facility due to the potentially greater expressive power of the computerized representational medium.

Many thanks are due to Sara Bly, Frank Halasz, Steve Harrison, Leigh Klotz, Cathy Marshall, and John Tang for reading early drafts and giving excellent comments. Robert Anderson, Liam Bannon, Marjorie Goodwin, Jonathan Grudin, Susan Newman, Wendy Mackay, Lucy Suchman, and Mark Stefik all contributed through comments and extensive discussion. As usual, Stan Lanning was indispensable in helping us implement the software. Additional thanks to the anonymous reviewers. We were grateful for their suggestions and hope they are pleased with the results.

References

BLY, S. (1988). A use of drawing surfaces in different collaborative settings. In *Proceedings of the Conference on Computer-Supported Cooperative Work*, pp. 250–256, Portland, Oregon, September 26–28.

CLARK, H. H. & SCHAEFER, E. F. (1987). Collaborating on contributions to conversations. *Language and Cognitive Processes*, **2**, 19–41.

CLARK, H. H. & SCHAEFER, E. F. (1989). Contributing to discourse. *Cognitive Science*, **13**, 259–294.

CLARK, H. H. & WILKES-GIBBS, D. (1986). Referring as a collaborative process. *Cognition*, **22**, 1–39.

DIEHL, M. & STROEBE, W. (1987). Productivity loss in brainstorming groups: toward the solution of a riddle. *Journal of Personality and Social Psychology*, **53**, 497–509.

DUNCAN, S. D. (1973). Toward a grammar for dyadic conversation. *Semiotica*, **9**, 29–47.

FOSTER, G. (1986). Collaborative systems and multiuser interfaces. PhD. thesis, University of California, Berkeley.

FOSTER, G. & STEFIK, M. (1986). Cognoter, theory and practice of a Colaborative tool. In *Proceedings of the Conference on Computer-Supported Cooperative Work*, pp. 7–12. Austin, Texas, December 3–5.

GOODWIN, C. (1981). *Conversational Organization: Interaction Between Speakers and Hearers.* New York: Academic Press.

GOODWIN, C. & HERITAGE, J. (1990). Conversation analysis. *Annual Review of Anthropology*, **19**, 283–307.

GOODWIN, C. & GOODWIN, M. H. (1990). Context, activity, and participation. In P. AUER & A. DI LUZO, Eds. *The Contextualization of Language.* Amsterdam: Benjamins.

GOODWIN, M. H. (1980). Processes of mutual monitoring implicated in the production of description sequences. *Sociological Inquiry*, **50**, 303–317.

GRUDIN, J. (1988). Why CSCW system fail. In *Proceedings of the Conference on Computer-Supported Cooperative Work*, pp. 85–93, Portland, Oregon.

POMERANTZ, A. (1978). Compliment responses: notes on the co-operation of multiple constraints. In J. SCHENKEIN, Ed. *Studies in the Organization of Conversational Interaction*, pp. 79–112. New York: Academic Press.

POMERANTZ, A. (1984). Pursuing a response. In J. M. ATKINSON & J. HERITAGE, Eds. *Structures of Social Action*, pp. 152–164. Cambridge. UK: Cambridge University Press.

ROBERTSON, G. G., CARD, S. K. & MACKINLAY, J. (1989). *The Cognitive Co-processor Architecture for the Interactive User Interfaces*, Xerox PARC Technical Report #SSL-89-28.

SACKS, H. & SCHEGLOFF, E. A. (1979). Two preferences in the organization of reference to persons in conversation and their interaction. In G. PSATHAS, Ed. *Everyday Language: Studies in Ethnomethodology.* New York: Irvington.

SCHEGLOFF, E. A. (1981). Discourse as an interactive achievement: some uses of uh-huh and other things that come between sentences. In D. TANNEN, Ed. *Analyzing Discourse: Text and Talk.* Georgetown University Roundtable on Languages and Linguistics 1981, pp. 71–93. Washington, DC: Georgetown University Press.

SCHEGLOFF, E. A. & SACKS, H. (1973). Opening up closings. *Semiotica*, **8**, 289–327.

SCHOBER, M. F. & CLARK, H. H. (1989). Understanding by addressees and overhearers. *Cognitive Psychology*, **21**, 211–232.

STEFIK, M. J., FOSTER, G., BOBROW, D. G., KAHN, K., LANNING, S. & SUCHMAN, L. (1987a). Beyond the Chalkboard. *Communications of the ACM*, **30**, 32–47.

STEFIK, M. J., BOBROW, D. G., FOSTER, G., LANNING, S. M. & TATAR, D. G. (1987b). WYSIWIS revised: early experiences with multiuser interfaces. *ACM Transactions on Office Information Systems*, **5**, 147–167.

SUCHMAN, L. (1988). Representing practice in cognitive science. *Human Studies*, **11**, 305–325.

TANG, J. C. (1989). *Listing, Drawing and Gesturing in Design: A Study of the Use of Shared Workspaces by Design Teams*, Xerox PARC Technical Report #SSL-89-3 (Ph.d. thesis Stanford University).

TANG, J. C. (1990). *Observations of the Use of Shared Drawing Spaces*. Videotape, Xerox PARC Technical Memo.

Issues and Experiences Designing and Implementing Two Group Drawing Tools

Saul Greenberg
Mark Roseman
Dave Webster

Department of Computer Science, University of Calgary, Calgary, Canada T2N 1N4

Ralph Bohnet

MPR TelTech Ltd, 8999 Nelson Way, Vancouver, Canada

Abstract

Groupware designers are now developing multi-user equivalents of popular paint and draw applications. Their job is not an easy one. First, human factors issues peculiar to group interaction appear that, if ignored, seriously limit the usability of the group tool. Second, implementation is fraught with considerable hurdles. This paper describes the issues and experiences we have met and handled in the design of two systems supporting remote real time group interaction: GroupSketch, a multi-user sketchpad; and GroupDraw, an object-based multi-user draw package. On the human factors side, we summarize empirically-derived design principles that we believe are critical to building useful and usable collaborative drawing tools. On the implementation side, we describe our experiences with replicated versus centralized architectures, schemes for participant registration, multiple cursors, network requirements, and the structure of the drawing primitives.
Keywords: *shared workspace, real time remote conferencing, computer supported cooperative work.*

1: Introduction

Most research efforts in geographically distributed conferencing have been in the field of *tele-presence*—a way of giving distributed participants a feeling that they are in the same meeting room (Egido 1988; Johansen & Bullen 1984; MIT 1983). The goal of tele-presence is to transmit both the explicit and subtle dynamics that occur between participants. These include body language, hand gestures, eye contact, meta-level communication cues, knowing who is speaking and who is listening, voice cues, focusing attention, and so on. Tele-presence facilitates effective management and orchestration of remote meetings by the natural and practised techniques used in face to face meetings. *Tele-data*, on the other hand, allows participants at a meeting to present or access physical materials that would normally be inaccessible to the distributed group (Greenberg & Chang 1989). These include notes, documents, plans and drawings, as well as some common work surface that allows each person to annotate, draw, brainstorm, record, and convey ideas during the meeting's progress. Given that an individual's work is commonly

centered around a computer workstation, the networked computer can become a valuable medium for people to share on-line work with each other.

In this document, we will focus on tele-data that provides small groups (2 to ~4 people) with real-time access to a shared drawing space via multi-user equivalents of the now-common paint and draw programs. We describe the issues encountered and experiences gained in the design of two systems supporting real time group interaction: *GroupSketch*, a multi-user sketchpad; and *GroupDraw*, a prototype object-based multi-user drawing program. The intent is to highlight human factors issues critical to the design of real time collaborative drawing tools, and to pass on our own experiences building such systems.

We begin the paper with a literature summary of research studies of face to face design teams and the resulting design principles generated from them. We then explain how these principles were incorporated into our groupware design, and the early experiences people had using the systems. The next section then describes our implementation experiences, concentrating on our choice of a replicated over a centralized architecture, handling of participant registration, displaying of multiple cursors, the network requirements, and the underlying structure of the drawing primitives.

2: Designing for the human factors of small group design meetings

Almost every group process begins with a set of initial design meetings, where participants express, discuss, and develop ideas. It is a creative forum where people are encouraged to present their thoughts to the group, to build upon the ideas presented by fellow members, and to problem-solve. Participants typically use some large communal *work surface*—a group drawing area—to facilitate their interactions. Typical media now used include whiteboards, flipcharts, large sheets of paper, as well as a variety of coloured pens for drawing.

Our aim is to apply the human factors knowledge of face to face design meetings to the design of workstation conferencing tools supporting remote work surfaces. This section will describe how people use conventional work surfaces, the implications for the design of a workstation-based work surface, and how our systems instantiated the design recommendations.

2.1: Understand collaboration.

In order to design a software-based work surface, we must have an adequate understanding of how traditional ones are used in group meetings. Indeed, Grudin has identified a lack of understanding of group behaviour to be one of the reasons why groupware has not been generally successful (Grudin 1989). He asserts that designers rely too heavily upon their own intuition, which is often based upon experiences that may not be applicable to the target group as a whole.

For example, an intuitive "conventional" view of the communal work surface would consider it merely as a medium for creating and storing a drawing artifact (Tang 1989). Bly disproves this naive view (Bly 1988). She studied two designers communicating through three different media offering different access to a drawing surface: face to face including a shared sketchpad; over a video link that included a view of the other person and their personal drawing surface; and over the telephone. From her observations, she asserts that the drawing process—the actions, uses, and interactions on the drawing surface—are as important to the effectiveness of the collaboration as the final artifact produced. Bly also noticed that allowing designers to share drawing space activities increases their attention and involvement in the design task. When interaction over the drawing surface is reduced, the quality of the collaboration decreases.

Tang refined Bly's findings even further through his ethnographic study of eight short small-team design sessions (Tang 1989; Tang 1991; Tang & Leifer 1988). Each team used large sheets of paper as a shared work surface and were given problems to solve. Some teams placed the paper on a table, others tacked it to a whiteboard. Even this simple difference had a profound effect on how the group used the shared work surface. When participants were huddled in close proximity around the table-mounted paper, the sketchpad played a key role in mediating the conversation, and simultaneous access to the work surface was a normal occurrence (45–68% of all activity). This role was lessened in the whiteboard situation where people were seated several feet away.

Tang built a descriptive framework to help organize the study of work surface activity, where every user activity was categorized according to what action and function it accomplished, as listed below (Tang 1989).

Actions:
- *listing* produces alpha-numeric notes that are spatially independent of the drawing;

- *drawing* produces graphical objects, typically a 2-dimensional sketch with textual annotations that are attached to the graphic;
- *gesturing* is a purposeful body movement that communicates specific information eg pointing to an existing drawing.

Functions:
- *storing information* refers to preserving group information in some form for later recall;
- *expressing ideas* involves interactively creating representations of ideas in some tangible form, usually to encourage a group response;
- *mediating interaction* facilitates the collaboration of the group, and includes turn-taking and focusing attention.

Tang's classification of small group activities within this framework revealed that the "conventional" view of work surface activity—storing information by listing and drawing—constitutes only ~25% of all work surface activities. Expressing ideas and mediating interaction comprised the additional ~50% and ~25% respectively. Gesturing, which is often overlooked as a work surface activity, played a prominent role in all work surface actions (~35% of all actions). For example, participants enacted ideas using gestures to express them. Gestures were used to signal turn-taking and to focus the attention of the group. Information can be cognitively chunked and preserved through gestures.

2.2: Implications for design of a work surface

Tang's observations led him to derive six design criteria that shared work surface tools should support. He stresses the importance of allowing people to gesture to each other over the work surface, and emphasises that the process of creating a drawing is in itself a gesture that must be shown to all participants through continuous, fine-grained feedback. Another key point is that the tool must not only support simultaneous activity, but also encourage it by giving participants a common view of the work surface. The six design criteria plus a summary of the reasons why each is offered are listed in the first two columns of Table 1 (condensed from Tang, 1989). These form the foundation for the rest of this paper.

2.3: The *GroupSketch* interface

GroupSketch is a simple group sketching tool that allows an arbitrary number of people to draw on a virtual piece of paper (the screen) (Greenberg & Bohnet 1991). It is designed around the criteria listed in Table 1. Its main features are:
- a what you see is what I see (WYSIWIS) display
- multiple, active cursors that identify their owners are always visible on all displays
- simultaneous interaction is fully supported; any user can do anything at any time
- any user action (cursor movement or drawing), no matter how small, is immediately visible on all screens

Design Criteria	Reasons	How criteria were met in *GroupSketch*
Provide ways of conveying and supporting gestural communication. Gestures should be clearly visible, and should maintain their relation with objects within the work surface and with voice communication.	• gestures are a prominent action • gestures are typically made in relation to objects on the work surface • gestures must be seen if they are to be useful • gestures are often accompanied by verbal explanation	Physical gestures are conveyed via specialized multiple cursors synchronized with voice. • Since gestures must be seen in order to convey information, all cursors within a work surface are always visible to all participants. Cursors are also made prominent on the display by their larger than normal size. • Cursors change their shape to reflect a natural action. Four gesture modes are supported (Figure 1). The default cursor shape is the pointing hand, while the large arrow allows users to point at and direct the group's attention with greater emphasis than the normal hand. • Cursors are unique, each identifying the person it belongs to by labelling it with the user's name. In addition (and more subtly) each cursor is orientated at different angles (Figure 1). • Cursor movements appear with no apparent delay on all displays, which means that they remain synchronized with verbal communication. • Cursors always maintain their same relative location on every display so that they retain their relation to the work surface objects.
Minimize the overhead encountered when storing information.	• only one person usually records information • other participants should not be blocked from continuing private or group work while information is being stored	Any person may store a snapshot of the current work surface into their own private directories at any time. While that particular workstation display will 'freeze' for a short period, other workstations remain unaffected. Any person may restore their private images back to the public work surface at will.
Convey the process of creating artifacts to express ideas.	• the process of creation is in itself a gesture that communicates information • speech is closely synchronized with the creation process • artifacts in themselves are often meaningless	• In *GroupSketch*, any work surface action, no matter how small, is visible with no apparent delay on all participants' screens. Every movement of the cursor, every pixel that is drawn, and every letter typed is immediately broadcast to other screens and are therefore immediately visible. • As with cursors, all details of artifact creation and manipulation is transmitted in real time and remains synchronized with accompanying speech.
Allow seamless intermixing of work surface actions and functions	• a single action often combines aspects of listing, drawing and gesturing • writing and drawing alternates rapidly • actions often address several functions	• The simplicity of *GroupSketch* allows it to have a nearly modeless interface. When no mouse buttons are depressed, the cursor is in the pointing gestural state. Drawing occurs as long as the left button is depressed, which also turns the cursor into a pen. Typing immediately inserts text at the current cursor location. The cursor image changes to the pen, and automatically reverts back to the hand-shaped cursor after a reasonable pause in typing is detected One can even enter text and draw simultaneously by holding one hand on the keyboard and the other on the mouse!
Enable all participants to share a common view of the work surface while providing simultaneous access and a sense of close proximity to it.	• people do not see the same things when orientation differs • simultaneous activity is prevalent • close proximity to the work surface encourages simultaneous activity	• Advantages of a common view were considered more beneficial than the lesser advantages of differing orientations. *GroupSketch* uses a what you see is what I see (WYSIWIS) display and the presence of all participants' cursors to promotes a close sense of proximity. As participants track other cursors, they naturally associate actions in the work surface with people who are executing those actions. • Simultaneity is fully supported. All participants have free and equal access to the work surface. Any one can do anything at any time.
Facilitate the participants' natural abilities to coordinate their collaborations	• people are skilled at coordinating communication • we do not understand the coordinating process well enough to mechanize it	As *GroupSketch* does not enforce any style of social protocol and as all participants are in direct control of their actions, the group is free to use whatever coordination method suits them (an argument favouring this approach is presented by Dykstra 1991.

Table 1. Criteria for designing a communal work surface (after Tang 1989), and how they were met in *GroupSketch*

- drawing, gesturing and listing are as modeless as possible.

Column 3 of Table 1 provides detail of *GroupSketch*'s user interface features and how they were designed around Tang's criteria.

Figure 1 displays a typical *GroupSketch* screen with four participants engaged in a design session. On the left is the shared work surface where people draw, enter text, or gesture. Every person has a cursor labelled with their name. All participants see the same work surface on their display, and every movement of the cursor and change in the drawing is immediately visible on all displays. Each participant is represented by a unique labelled caricature located outside the work surface on the right of the screen. While audio is not directly supported, we expect a full duplex audio channel to be available by other means (eg speaker phones).

Four action modes are supported: gesturing through cursors, drawing, textual listing, and erasing (Figure 1). With no mouse buttons or keyboard keys pressed, the cursor portrays the image of a pointing hand (Sandy's cursor). To draw freestyle, the user depresses the left mouse button of a three-button mouse, changing the cursor from a hand to a pen (Saul's cursor). The pen-shaped cursor also appears automatically when typing. Pressing the middle mouse button changes the cursor into a large arrow to draw participants' attention (Irene's cursor). Users can erase graphics or text in the work surface by holding down the right mouse button, which changes the shape of the cursor into an eraser (Wilf's cursor).

The menu on the right of Figure 1 allows a person to privately save an image, retrieve a previously stored image to the group display, clear the public work surface, or leave the collaboration (leaving other participants in the meeting). Menu selections and cursor movements outside the work surface are private and are not broadcast to other workstations. Loading an image or clearing the work surface affects all participant's screens.

We have performed limited usability studies on *GroupSketch* under relatively informal conditions (Greenberg & Bohnet 1991). In a typical *GroupSketch* scenario, participants converse and interact as they would over a shared piece of paper. Yet it is not identical to a face to face meeting. People tend to concentrate intently on the group work surface (they cannot see each other), not only for tele-data but for the limited sense of tele-presence provided via gestures. People focus attention to objects in the display by pointing at them or by circling objects with the cursor. Drawing and listing are both independent (one person responsible for a drawing) and cooperative (multiple people working together on a drawing). People can—and often do—work simultaneously on any part of the display, and anyone can be actively gesturing, creating, or editing

the drawing artifact. The specific observations we had made about *GroupSketch* are summarized in Table 2. We feel it fair to say that *GroupSketch*, in spite of its primitive functionality, is reasonably effective as a distributed work surface.

2.4: The GroupDraw interface

While *GroupSketch* is a simple paint program where one can only make and erase marks on a bit-map surface, *GroupDraw* is an object-oriented drawing program with features approaching those of most structured drawing and drafting packages (such as Claris MacDraw). *GroupDraw* is currently under development (a working prototype now exists). While its design is based upon our experiences with *GroupSketch*, we are using it as an experimental platform to study different interface and architecture features. *GroupDraw* supports the multiple active cursors and simultaneous activity that we have seen in *GroupSketch*. However, users can now create, move, resize, and delete drawing objects (rectangles, lines, circles, text, etc). Also, WYSIWIS has been relaxed to provide a scrollable work surface; this is a concession to the limited screen real estate available, and also provides users with room to work on private drawings. Figure 2 illustrates a *GroupDraw* screen with three users working on a design. The smaller registration window lists conference participants, their physical location, their phone numbers, and buttons that will dial that number.

The effect of having objects that can be selected and modified by different people raises a surprising number of issues in terms of interface design. The most obvious is what to do when several people try to manipulate a single object. The simplest strategy is to let only one person at a time acquire a particular object—others are prevented from accessing it. Even so, feedback must be supplied to the user differentiating the act of selection from actually acquiring the object, for there could be a time lag between these two states. In the current implementation, users can actively grab an object and start manipulating it—the system assumes optimistically that there will be no conflict. If an acquisition conflict does occur and permission is denied to manipulate the object, the object will snap back to its original position. In practice, system response time is so fast that the selection/acquisition process occurs almost instantly—a rejected acquisition appears as a momentary flicker. We are also experimenting with other visual cues, such as grey-scale coloring, to indicate acquisition status during this transition period.

Another issue relates to Tang's fourth design criteria (Table 1) recommending a seamless intermixing of workspace actions and functions. The fact that users must now select from a variety of object types and go into a particular drawing mode makes this recommendation difficult to fulfil. Selecting an object from a palette or a menu can detract from the fluidity of group interaction. We do not yet

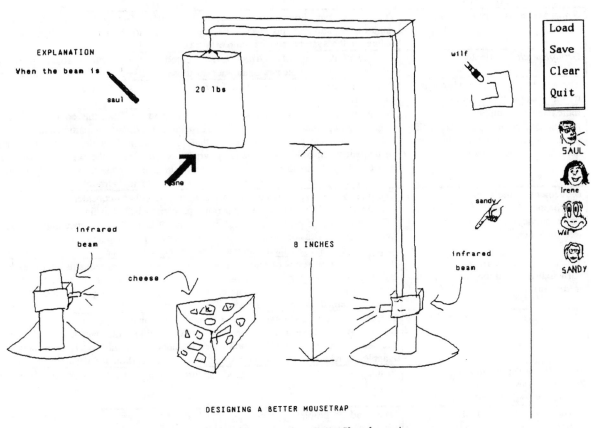

Figure 1: A sample *GroupSketch* session

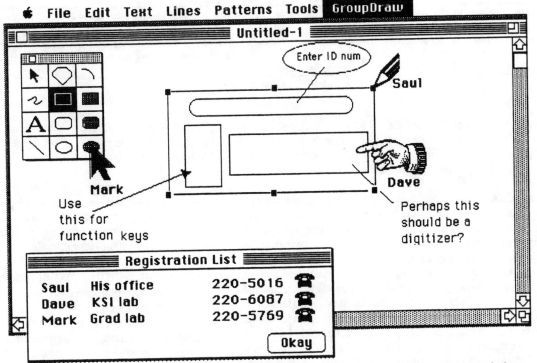

Figure 2: A sample *GroupDraw* session, showing the work surface and the registration window

Observation	Details
GroupSketch is very easy to learn.	People with even limited computer experience learnt *GroupSketch* in moments (ie less than a minute). We attribute this ease to its direct analogy to the paper sketchpad, the modeless nature of the system, and its simple syntax.
GroupSketch is effective.	In spite of its simplicity, *GroupSketch* worked. Participants were able to pursue their tasks effectively, using strategies analogous to those observed in face to face design meetings.
The worst part of *GroupSketch* is trying to draw with a mouse.	People expressed frustration when drawing with a mouse. A stylus would have been a large improvement.
Increasing the number of participants in an open floor policy increases parallel activity but also decreases focused attention.	We observed much simultaneous activity. As noted by Tang, this comes at the price of reduced group attention (Tang 1989). For example, when four participants were collaborating, one person commented that she found it difficult to listen to another participant when others were actively writing or drawing in the communal work area. We expect this problem to be exacerbated as group size increases. Yet most participants agreed that restricting access to the work surface or introducing turn-taking would be unacceptable.
Movement of the cursor synchronized with a participant's voice provides the greatest sense of tele-presence.	The presence of even idle cursors in the work surface was considered important by participants. People did not have serious problems distinguishing who was doing what. Still, the quality of presence did not match that of a face to face meeting. For example, we observed two occasions when visually separated but co-located participants involved in an intense discussion left their computers to speak face to face.
The shared work surface captured participants' attention and focused interaction.	There is a strong focus of attention on the work surface. Participants' eyes remained fixed on the shared area for long periods of time, as if they did not want to miss any of the actions occurring in the work surface. The ease of drawing and talking simultaneously around artifacts seemed to provide a focused interaction.
Participants desired greater functionality.	People familiar to computer systems wanted functionality greater than a simple sketchpad could provide. These included object-oriented drawing tools over free-hand bit-mapped sketching, editable text fields, and other features commonly available in single-user graphical packages. This finding was our main motivation for designing *GroupDraw*.
Intermixing listing and drawing (text and graphics) occurred frequently and naturally.	Resulting artifacts contained a good mixture of graphics and textual lists of points.
Vertical orientation of the work surface removed the physical limitations of the table top.	Users had no problem recognizing objects on the display. As people could literally draw on top of one another, we observed people working together on objects in quite close proximity (examples include multiple people erasing different parts of a single line and cooperative construction of a drawing artifact).
Saving only one image is not enough.	*GroupSketch* only allowed any one user to save one image at a time. This was not enough to allow rapid switching between drawings.
The work surface is too small.	The work surface quickly becomes cluttered during long design sessions, especially with larger group sizes. Larger displays, windowing strategies, or better storage and retrieval facilities are required.

Table 2. Observation of *GroupSketch* use.

have an acceptable solution. Rather, we are using *GroupDraw* as a platform to test methods for minimal impact mode-switching. These include palettes, menus, hot keys, and gesture recognition.

Another issue is private drawings, which Tang had observed as a positive resource. These drawings are often worked on and then presented to the group at a later time. *GroupDraw* implements privacy in two ways. The first is by providing a scrollable drawing surface; a user can scroll and work in their own area of the screen, and then move the image to the main view (a split screen may work well here). Second, an object's "coupling status" can be specified (Dewan & Choudhary 1991). Here, a user can indicate whether an object can be manipulated by all others, can only be viewed by others, or can be private. One interface issue here is how to indicate the object status to the group. Although an

obvious scheme includes identifying object status by colors, it means that it will no longer be available as a drawing resource.

In summary, our early experience with the *GroupDraw* interface raises more questions than it answers. We know for certain that some of the interaction techniques now found in conventional drawing programming will not transfer well to a multi-user domain.

3: Implementation experiences

GroupSketch is implemented on Sun workstations running Unix connected together via Ethernet. *GroupDraw* is built upon the Macintosh/AppleTalk platform. The design of both systems contain two features unusual in single-user interface design. First, they are distributed programs—resulting issues are the tradeoffs between a replicated or centralized architecture; the network communication demands; and how users can dynamically register with an existing electronic meeting. Second, both systems support multiple cursors and simultaneous activity—issues here are how multiple cursors are implemented, and how the graphics primitives are structured to support multiple synchronized access.

The internal architecture of *GroupSketch* and *GroupDraw* are briefly described in this section, indicating how the issues listed above were addressed.

3.1: Replicated vs Centralized Architecture

Two architectural alternatives for constructing distributed groupware are the *centralized* and *replicated* approach (Ahuja, Ensor & Lucco 1990; Lauwers, Joseph, Lantz & Romanow 1990; Lauwers & Lantz 1990). In the centralized approach, a single program called the *central agent* mediates all distributed work surfaces. Each person's workstation runs a *participant process* that just collects user input and passes it to the central agent. After processing this information, the agent tells each participant process what to display on their screens. In effect, the central agent acts as one large program managing users. An example is *WScrawl*, a public domain group drawing program that runs on the X window system. The single *WScrawl* program acts as the central agent that decides what to do with user events and where to display the output. In *WScrawl*, the participant process is simply the X window server. The advantage of a centralized scheme is that synchronization is easy, as state information is consistent since it is all located in one place. The disadvantages are that the complete system is now vulnerable to the failure (either machine or network) of the central agent, and that the central agent could be a network bottleneck as all activity must be channelled through it.

In the replicated approach, there is no central agent. Instead, the participant processes replicated on every machine are totally responsible for maintaining the integrity of the drawing surface. Rather than passing information to a central agent, the participant processes communicate directly with each other. The advantages are that network traffic is reduced because communication does not go through a central mediary, and that the system is more robust to network and machine failure. The catch is that it becomes more difficult to keep the work surfaces and user requests synchronized.

Hybrid approaches are also possible. For example, the participant processes may use a central agent only for synchronization and for mediating conflicting user requests. All other activities are performed within and between participant processes.

Both *GroupSketch* and *GroupDraw* use fully replicated architectures, with the participant process running as a single process on every workstation. Taking *GroupSketch* as an example, participant processes communicate via Unix stream sockets using only eight primitive events, as listed and explained in Table 3. Since the only actions that can be done by a process are to either draw/erase on a bit mapped surface or to move the cursor, there is no need to synchronize user activities[1].

Event	Information passed
Registering a new user	host name, port number, name of participant, caricature
Unregistering a user	Id of participant
Moving cursors	Id of participant, cursor shape, new coordinates
Drawing a line	Id of participant, start and end coordinates
Erasing a region	Id of participant, coordinates of region
Listing	Id of participant, string location, string, cursor shape, location of cursor
Clearing screen	—
Image transfer	binary data of the work surface image

Table 3. Communication protocol between processes

The interaction between replicated participant processes in *GroupDraw* is more complex. As we have seen, one of the advantages of an object-based drawing system such as *GroupDraw* is the ability to not merely view, but to interact with the entities in the shared workspace in a structured way. However, we must ensure that the object's behavior is managed consistently between users, so that (for instance) two people grabbing and dragging the same point on a line do not both succeed. This poses concurrency problems that are not encountered in the simpler *GroupSketch* situation. Central architectures, by their very nature, can easily resolve this problem. However, there are effective approaches to dealing with this under a replicated architecture as well, which we employed in *GroupDraw*. We define an *owner* for each object drawn, who has final authority on all operations affecting the object. The owner of a single object is one of the replicated participant processes in the *GroupDraw* conference[2], and each process may be the owner of more than one object. The responsibility of the owner is to maintain object

---

[1] This is not quite true, for it is possible to get out of step. For example, if a user draws on a surface that is simultaneously being erased by someone else, the final appearance of the bitmap could look different depending upon the order in which these events arrive at each participant process. In practise, this is not a problem due to the scarcity of this occurring, and the minimal visual disruption to the drawing.

[2] Initially, the owner will be the process supporting the participant who creates the object, whether by drawing it, restoring it from a file, or copying it from another source. The ownership may change during the course of a conference or between conferences by various means.

consistency across all sessions. This is best illustrated by an example.

Suppose three users userA, userB and userC are part of a conference, each running processA, processB, and processC. Within the conference's workspace there is a line object owned by processA. UserB and userC, simultaneously select the same end point of the line object—this is a situation where object consistency could be compromised as only one person should be allowed to select the object. Both processB and processC then send a message to processA requesting control of the end point. ProcessA then assigns permission on a first come, first served basis. If processB's request arrives first, processA will send a message to processB granting permission to grab the object, while processC will receive a message denying permission.

Under this approach, object ownership is distributed through all participant processes; it is only the *GroupDraw* session as whole that maintains full state information for its objects. The result is a fairly robust system. If a participant process leaves (eg when the participant leaves or their node fails), its objects are systematically transferred to other participant processes. When the last person leaves the conference, ownership need not be retained—it is relevant only during a single conference.

3.2: Registration

We believe that any participant should be able to join and leave the conference at any time. Yet how do people "register" with the shared drawing session, and how is this managed internally? How does each participant process know about and adjust to the comings and going of other participants?

In *GroupSketch*, a central *registrar* process performs dynamic registration functions. The following example indicates how the registrar incorporates new participants into a *GroupSketch* session.

1 An incoming participant or late-comer connects to the registrar, opens its own communication port for other connections, and sends the port address along with the participant's name and caricature data to the registrar (see Table 3).
2 The registrar acknowledges the newcomer and informs other participants' *GroupSketch* process of the newcomer's address in the network.
3 Each *GroupSketch* process connects to the newcomer, with the nearest sending it the current state of the work surface image. The registrar is now out of the loop.

In contrast, *GroupDraw* uses a distributed registration scheme. Each workstation's registrar maintains an AppleTalk socket listener. Whenever a new *GroupDraw* participant enters a session, it announces its arrival over the network. The announcement is heard by every registrar, and

connections are made directly. The new entrant then asks one of the other participant processes to send it a display list of the current work surface.

Both schemes work reasonably well. *GroupDraw's* method has the advantage that it is not tied to a single central registrar. But what is most important in both schemes is that the registrar is fairly independent of the underlying application. It is a high-level toolkit component that should be reusable in other groupware applications requiring registration. In fact, we were able to reuse in part a registrar that we had originally designed for a completely different application (Greenberg 1990; Greenberg 1991).

3.3: Multiple Cursors

Multiple cursors present a significant problem, for current window systems only support single cursors. As a result, multiple cursors are usually implemented independently from the system-supplied cursors.

In *GroupSketch* we eschewed window systems completely in favour of a graphical library that allowed us to manipulate the bit-map display directly (we used Sun's Pixrect library). Large multiple cursors are implemented directly by exclusively OR'ing bitmaps. The general algorithm for handling multiple cursors follows. After initial variable setup and participant registration, the participant process executes a main loop that acts on events arriving from four different sources: the keyboard, the mouse, the registrar, and from other participant processes. A participant's activity is detected through keyboard events for character insertion; and mouse events for specifying cursor gesture movement, drawing and erasing. Modifications are then broadcast to the remote processes where it appears to them as an "other participant event"; their workspaces are then updated.

As an example of managing cursor movements, assume two *GroupSketch* participants: userA and userB. When userA moves the cursor, the change is updated immediately on the local screen the coordinates of the new position broadcast to userB. UserB's participant process receives an 'other participant interrupt' event, and reads the new mouse location. From an internal table, it looks up the old location of userA's cursor, erases it via an XOR operation, and then redraws it in its new position. The internal table is then updated.

Reading directly from the mouse device driver and writing to the screen provided efficient and fast cursor performance in *GroupSketch*. However, this approach is costly in terms of implementation effort, for we had to design a graphical interface from the ground-up (eg to manage cursors, menus, simple drawing). We also made a design error in our choice of handling local events differently from remote events. For example, *GroupSketch* now has a bug that will cause it to leave a spurious mark on the screen if one cursor is erasing on top of another person's cursor. While we understand why the problem occurs, it has proven difficult to fix due to the different ways local and remote cursor events are handled; a complete overhaul of the code would be required.

In contrast, *GroupDraw* multiple cursors are built in part on top of the Macintosh interface toolkit. While we use standard Macintosh events to determine where the mouse cursor is, we do not use the toolkit routines to display the cursor. Instead, the standard cursor is made invisible, and an XOR scheme similar to the one mentioned above is used in its place. The other difference is that all local and remote events are handled in exactly the same way—the same cursor redrawing function is notified when any cursor is moved (whether local or remote), and the display is updated accordingly.

While the standard cursor could have been used to display the local cursor position, we believe it not worth the effort. First, the local cursor has to be treated as a special case from the remote cursors, leading to more complex coding and debugging problems. Second, there are often limitations and system dependencies in application cursors that may conflict with design goals. For example, our cursors are larger than the cursors provided by some window systems. Finally, we have found that our scheme works well in practice—tracking is fairly smooth and occurs in real time.

3.4: Communications

People designing real time groupware systems are concerned that the communication channel will be the primary system bottleneck, and often go to great lengths to minimize the information transmitted over the channel. We believe it has been used as a reason *not* to implement multiple cursors, and for choosing some architectural styles over others (eg Ahuja, Ensor & Lucco 1990; Lauwers, Joseph, Lantz *et al* 1990; Lauwers & Lantz 1990).

Our experiences with *GroupSketch* and *GroupDraw* shows that communication throughput is not a problem over typical local area networks (Ethernet runs at 10Mbps, Appletalk at ~250Kbps). Our communication requirements were modest. Both *GroupSketch* and *GroupDraw* use a standard stream-oriented connection that guarantees in-order, error free delivery (Unix Stream Sockets and Appletalk Data Stream Protocol respectively). When we ran profiling tools on our systems, we were surprised to find that it was the processor speed that was the performance bottleneck. While the network comfortably accommodated the events we had sent over the network, the slower processors had difficulty interpreting all of them in real time.

To get a feel for the network traffic, we traced the number of packets sent by three *GroupSketch* participants on several short but active design sessions. On average, a total of 15–25 packets/second were transmitted, with an average packet length (ignoring packet overhead) of 5–20 bytes long. This gives a network utilization ranging from 600 to 4000 bits per second. This rate is easily handled by LANs, but could be demanding for a low-speed telephone link. About 75% of the packets sent indicated a "cursor moved" event. Another thing we noted is that each user's network demands are unequal, for active users generated many more events than inactive users.

Because in our situation CPU processing and not network bandwidth seemed to be the limiting constraint, we adopted the following philosophy. Each participant process sends out as much information as possible to the other processes. For example, cursor information is broadcast as often as possible. On the receiving end, decisions must be made about what information to process when backlogs in the event queue occur. A slower machine, for example, might ignore all cursor updates received from a particular process except for the last. While this can result in jerky cursor motion, it is far less disconcerting than waiting for the cursor to "catch up".

One final point worth mentioning is the relation of bandwidth to the number of participants. In the current setup, network demands will increase factorially (worst case) with every new participant, for each participant process must broadcast the same message to all others[1]. If a multi-cast network were available instead, then the communication demands would be linear to the number of participants, for only a single message need be broadcast by the sender.

3.5: Drawing primitives

A structured drawing package provides its users with a set of drawing primitives: lines, circles, rectangles and so on. While these are familiar to most simple graphics packages, the property that they are shareable is still fairly novel. This section shows how object-oriented programming is used in *GroupDraw* to isolate most multi-user characteristics into a prototypical drawing object. Subclasses, which inherit these characteristics, need only specify the actual graphical properties of the drawable object. This prototypical object will be discussed in terms of its properties and operations. We will indicate how its subclasses can be implemented.

All drawable objects have certain properties which we isolate as much as possible into a root object called *GroupGraphicalObject*. Table 3 provides some detail of the instance variables and methods it contains. Each graphical object has an *ownerProcess*, which is by default the creator of the object. The ownerProcess serves to arbitrate contention in manipulating the object. Objects also have a

---

[1] The factorial relation only occurs if every person is actively doing something on the work surface. In practise, some people will be idle.

GroupGraphicalObject, the root object of all graphics primitives

instance variables	
int couplingStatus	*-indicates if object is private, public, or shareable*
int ownerProcess	*-indicates who the owner of the process is*
int id	*-a unique reference that identifies the object across the whole system*
boolean acquired	*-indicates if the object is currently being manipulated by a participant*
point whereGrabbed	*-a logical point indicating the position where the object was acquired*
methods for initializing and destroying an object, and for sending its description to others	
initializeGroupObject()	*-initializes the object, filling in any defaults*
destroyObject()	*-destroys the object and frees its space*
makeDescription()	*-make a complete description of the object suitable for transmission over the network*
sendDescription()	*-send the description to a requestor*
methods for changing object attributes	
requestChangeStatus()	*-request the object owner to change the coupling status*
doChangeStatus()	*-actually change the status, and broadcast change over network*
requestChangeOwner()	*-request the object to change its owner*
doChangeOwner()	*-actually change the owner, and broadcast change over network*
methods for graphically manipulating and drawing the object	
draw ()	*-a place holder for a routine that will draw the object on the screen*
requestToGrab()	*-request the object for permission to acquire it*
doGrab()	*-permission is granted or denied*
endGrab()	*-an acquired object is relinquished*
saveOriginal()	*-the original position of a selected object*
restoreOriginal()	*-restore a moved object to its original position*
drag()	*-high level drag handler; checks permission, broadcasts changes, etc*
doDrag()	*-a place holder; this routine will actually drag the object*
whereGrabbed()	*-a place holder; checks to see where object was grabbed*

LineObject, a sub-class of GroupGraphicalObject

instance variables	
point startPoint	*-the start point of the line*
point endPoint	*-the end point of the line*
methods	
initializeGroupObject()	*-initializes attributes specific to a line, then calls the super-class' initializeGroupObject*
makeDescription()	*-specialized to include line descriptions, then calls the inherited method*
saveOriginal()	*-specialization line-aware form of the inherited method*
restoreOriginal()	*-specialization line-aware form of the inherited method*
doDrag()	*-actually drags the object*
draw()	*-actually draw the object*

Table 3. The GroupGraphicalObject and its LineObject sub-class.

couplingStatus (Dewan & Choudhary 1991) that indicates the extent to which graphical objects are shared. As mentioned in Section 2.4, *GroupDraw* defines three coupling levels: private, public, and shareable. Each object is also referenced by a unique *id*, which is used in all network messages to identify the object being manipulated.

To create a new object, whether it be in response to a local or remote drawing action, we provide a standard initialization method *initalizeGroupObject()*, which will set the instance variables mentioned above. Subclasses will specialize this method to initialize any extra properties it may have eg zeroing out the endpoints of a line (see *LineObject*, Table 3). For communication and storage purposes, each object must be able to construct and interpret a string representing itself (*make/send-Description()*); this is used to save and restore images and to send update information to new users in the conference.

The latter is implemented by requesting each object to tell the new user about itself.

Next, we look at operations dealing with changing the coupling status of an object. *GroupDraw* insists that the owner approves status changes; processes request permission by the *requestChangeStatus()* method. If the owner grants permission, the *doChangeStatus()* method will actually change the object status and broadcast the change to all participants. Table 3 lists several other methods that follow this request/do form of arbitration.

Because multiple users may select and start to drag an object asynchronously, the object may be in slightly different places on different screens. Yet each selected object will want to tell the other processes where it had been selected. Passing the precise pixel coordinates is often meaningless, since that point may not match its partner on the remote object. Instead we define a "logical" point for each object. For example, the logical points of a line will be the two endpoints (*start/endPoint*). Dragging a point within an object would then be described in relation to these logical points (*whereGrabbed*). Most of the group interaction algorithms are handled within the *GroupGraphicalObject*. The root methods handle arbitration for object selection (*requestToGrab(), doGrab(), drag(), endGrab()*) The *doDrag()* method, specialized for each subclass, actually does the dragging— it does not need to know how other users are manipulating the object. The actual drawing of the object by *draw()* will, of course, be specialized to each sub-class.

What must a sub-classed object such as *LineObject* be responsible for? First, it needs to create or interpret the description string it defines if it is to send a complete object description over the network. Second, given a physical point, it must determine the corresponding logical point. Third, it must handle the object-specific graphical activities, including methods to draw and erase itself, to drag itself around, and to save enough state information to undo the dragging operation if the object's owner refuses dragging permission (*save/restoreOriginal()*). Object status, ownership, contention, and other issues need not be dealt with by the sub-class.

4: Summary

This paper introduced some human factors issues and implementation experiences we have had designing two multi-user systems: *GroupSketch* and *GroupDraw*.

On the human factors side, it may appear that some of the design principles mentioned in Section 2 are self-evident eg multiple cursors for gesturing, allowing simultaneous activities, and so on. Yet there are many examples of related groupware systems that have failed to live up to these seemingly self-evident criteria. Consider Xerox PARC's *Boardnoter*, a computerized whiteboard used to support face to face meetings (Stefik, Bobrow, Foster, Lanning & Tatar 1987; Stefik, Foster, Bobrow, Kahn, Lanning *et al* 1987). While a single large tele-pointer could be seen by all, individual cursors were not. Neither did participants see each others actions as they occurred, for actions were not broadcast until a complete graphical stroke was made or a complete text line entered. *Xsketch*, a recent object-based group drawing package suffers a similar lack as its objects are only transmitted after they are created (Lee 1990). *WScrawl*, a group sketchpad in the public domain, does not show multiple cursors. Group Technologies' *Aspects* does not necessarily show multiple cursors, nor can the process of creating or manipulating an object be seen by participants. We have also seen several other systems now under development that fail in the same manner to provide the basic necessities of a group drawing area.

On the positive side, there are several systems (including *GroupSketch* and *GroupDraw*) that do support the kinds of interactions people expect from a group drawing surface. All have one thing in common: they were derived from Tang's design principles as listed in Table 1. While these systems are quite diverse, they all share a common feel, and observations of use are strikingly similar. Two systems, for example, are video based: *VideoDraw* (Tang & Minneman 1990) and *TeamWorkStation* (Ishii 1990). Both are limited by scalability, for serious image deterioration results when too many video images are fused. In contrast, *Commune* is a workstation-based multi-user sketchpad built independently but in parallel with *GroupSketch* (Bly & Minneman 1990; Minneman & Bly 1990 and 1991). Although the interface to the two systems are remarkably similar, there are some minor differences. In *Commune*, people use a stylus to write directly on top of the horizontally-oriented monitor—the resulting artifacts are superior to the ones generated on our mouse-based system.

We have also shared our implementation experiences, concentrating on where a multi-user drawing application would differ from its single-user counterparts. We found that while there are some tradeoffs between replicated versus centralized architecture, there is no compelling reason to choose one style of another. We recommended that conference registration be managed as independently as possible from the underlying application, and that it is best handled as a high-level toolkit component. Multiple cursors are considered fundamental to these systems; we recommended that future interface toolkits and window systems support these directly. We have also found that communication bandwidth on moderate speed local area networks is not a problem. While we recognize that slow-speed telephone lines are still a fact of life, we suggested that in general the underlying system functionality should not be compromised for communications problems that may not exist. Finally, we outlined how a multi-user graphics library can be created by having most of its collaborative-aware properties reside within a root prototypical graphics object. By sub-classing, it should be fairly straight forward to extend the library via conventional graphics procedures.

Note and acknowledgements. GroupSketch is available from the author at no cost through anonymous ftp. This research is supported by the National Science and Engineering Research Council of Canada.

References.

Ahuja, S. R., Ensor, J. R. and Lucco, S. E. (1990) "A comparison of applications sharing mechanisms in real-time desktop conferencing systems." In *Proceedings of the Conference on Office Information Systems*, p238-248, Boston, April 25-27.

Bly, S. (1988) "A use of drawing surfaces in different collaborative settings." In *Proceedings of the*

Conference on Computer-Supported Cooperative Work (CSCW '88), p250-256, Portland, September 26-28, ACM Press.

Bly, S. A. and Minneman, S. L. (1990) "Commune: A shared drawing surface." In *Proceedings of the Conference on Office Information Systems*, p184-192, Boston, April 25-27.

Dewan, P. and & Choudhary, R. (1991) "Flexible user interface coupling in collaborative systems." In *ACM SIGCHI Conference on Human Factors in Computing Systems*, p41-48, New Orleans, April 28-May 2, ACM Press.

Dykstra, E. A. and Carasik, R. P. (1991) "Structure and support in cooperative environments: The Amsterdam Conversation Environment." In *Computer Supported Cooperative Work and Groupware*, S. Greenberg ed. Academic Press. Also in *Int J Man Machine Studies*, **34**(3), p419-434, March.

Egido, C. (1988) "Video conferencing as a technology to support group work: A review of its failures." In *Proceedings of the Conference on Computer-Supported Cooperative Work (CSCW '88)*, p13-24, Portland, September 26-28, ACM Press.

Greenberg, S. (1990) "Sharing views and interactions with single-user applications." In *Proceedings of the ACM/IEEE Conference on Office Information Systems*, p227-237, Cambridge, Massachusets, April 25-27.

Greenberg, S. (1991) "Personalizable groupware: Accomodating individual roles and group differences." In *European Conference of Computer Supported Cooperative Work (ECSCW '91)*, Amsterdam, September 24-27, Klewar Press.

Greenberg, S. and Bohnet, R. (1991) "GroupSketch: A multi-user sketchpad for geographically-distributed small groups." In *Proceedings of Graphics Interface '91*, Calgary, Alberta, June 5-7.

Greenberg, S. and Chang, E. (1989) "Computer support for real time collaborative work." In *Proceedings of the Conference on Numerical Mathematics and Computing*, Winnipeg, Manitoba, September 28-30. Available in Congressus Numerantium vol 74 and 75.

Grudin, J. (1989) "Why groupware applications fail: Problems in design and evaluation." *Office: Technology and People*, **4**(3), p245-264.

Ishii, H. (1990) "TeamWorkStation: Towards a seamless shared space." In *Proceedings of the Conference on Computer Supported Cooperative Work (CSCW '90)*, p13-26, Los Angeles, October 7-10, ACM Press.

Johansen, R. and Bullen, C. (1984) "Thinking ahead: What to expect from teleconferencing." *Harvard Business Review*, p4-10, March/April.

Lauwers, J. C., Joseph, T. A., Lantz, K. A. and Romanow, A. L. (1990) "Replicated architectures for shared window systems: A critique." In *Proceedings of the Conference on Office Information Systems*, p249-260, Boston, April 25-27.

Lauwers, J. C. and Lantz, K. A. (1990) "Collaboration awareness in support of collaboration transparency: Requirements for the next generation of shared window systems." In *Proceedings of the ACM/SIGCHI Conference on Human factors in Computing*, Seattle Washington, April 1-5, ACM Press.

Lee, J. J. (1990) "Xsketch: A multi-user sketching tool for X11." In *Proceedings of the Conference on Office Information Systems*, p169-173, Boston, April 25-27.

Minneman, S. L. and Bly, S. A. (1990) "Experiences in the development of a multi-user drawing tool." In *The 3rd Guelph Syposium on Computer Mediated Communication*, p154-167, Guelph, Ontario, Canada, May 15-17, by University of Guelph Cont Education.

Minneman, S. L. and Bly, S. A. (1991) "Managing a trois: A study of a multi-user drawing tool in distributed design work." In *ACM SIGCHI Conference on Human Factors in Computing Systems*, p217-224, New Orleans, April 28-May 2, ACM Press.

MIT (1983) "Talking heads." In *Discursions*, Boston, Mass, Architecture Machine Group, MIT. Optical disc.

Stefik, M., Bobrow, D. G., Foster, G., Lanning, S. and Tatar, D. (1987) "WYSIWIS revised: Early experiences with multiuser interfaces." *ACM Trans Office Information Systems*, **5**(2), p147-167, April.

Stefik, M., Foster, G., Bobrow, D., Kahn, K., Lanning, S. and Suchman, L. (1987) "Beyond the chalkboard: Computer support for collaboration and problem solving in meetings." *Comm ACM*, **30**(1), p32-47.

Tang, J. C. (1989) "Listing, drawing, and gesturing in design: A study of the use of shared workspaces by design teams." PhD thesis, Department of Mechanical Engineering, Stanford University, California, April. Also available as research report SSL-89-3, Xerox Palo Alto Research Center, Palo Alto, California.

Tang, J. C. (1991) "Findings from observational studies of collaborative work." In *Computer Supported Cooperative Work and Groupware*, S. Greenberg ed. Academic Press. Also in *Int J Man Machine Studies*, **34**(2), p143-160, February.

Tang, J. C. and Leifer, L. J. (1988) "A framework for understanding the workspace activity of design teams." In *Proceedings of the Conference on Computer-Supported Cooperative Work (CSCW '88)*, p244-249, Portland, Oregon, September 26-28, ACM Press.

Tang, J. C. and Minneman, S. L. (1990) "Videodraw: A video interface for collaborative drawing." In *ACM SIGCHI Conference on Human Factors in Computing Systems*, p313-320, Seattle, Washington, April 1-5, ACM Press.

Designing Group-enabled Applications: A Spreadsheet Example

Irene Greif
Lotus Development Corporation
1 Rogers Street
Cambridge, MA
email: igreif@lotus.com

1. Introduction

To date, the most successful groupware products have been products that facilitate general group communication.   Email systems and Lotus Notes are examples. But there are many situations in which a workgroup's business is already conducted using products that support the individual -- spreadsheets, word processing, graphic design. Communication and sharing happen outside those products and often off-line entirely. We believe that the next wave of innovation in workgroup computing will come from integrating such desktop tools with the communications and data sharing capabilities of groupware systems. The result will be products that encourage collaboration in the application domain.

In order to leverage existing successful software, both the communications infrastructure of the general purpose groupware tools and the application-specific software need to change. Groupware products must be "opened up" to provide communications and data storage infrastructure to applications. Trends towards this kind of architecture are evident in the race among system vendors to offer new system services for object stores and standard messaging interfaces. Application software then needs to be modified to interface with groupware infrastructure, and to make it possible to share the objects created in the application. As we group-enable today's products, the design challenge is to introduce these changes in ways that naturally extend the product metaphor while substantially changing the ways the product can be used.

At Lotus, we've learned that there is an unmet need for what could be termed a "workgroup spreadsheet."   This paper is a case study of the design of the series of products that will respond to that need. The paper describes the original target application -- budget planning -- and explains how spreadsheet characteristics and user input influenced the design.   The next three sections cover the three main threads of the design: application analysis; software design;

In D. Coleman (Ed.),   *Groupware '92*, pp. 515-525. Morgan Kaufmann Publishers.

and user input.   The result is a product very different from our initial prototypes: instead of a new "workgroup spreadsheet" product, we have group-enabled 1-2-3 and are incrementally adding group support by using Lotus Notes technology.

A significant outcome has been that customers find the group-enabling features very attractive for individual use. Not only will our group spreadsheet be based on the standard 1-2-3, but the new features that we add will have a very good chance of becoming part of the standard repertoire for individuals who use spreadsheets. We expect that this will play an important role in increasing customer acceptance of workgroup spreadsheet technology, since people will not need to learn the features solely to participate in the group process.   There is also some basis for expecting this kind of incidental pay-off for the individual to emerge in other personal productivity products as they are group-enabled. An individual working over time often needs assistance remembering what they were up to -- this can be provided by the same features that help the user understand a new contribution from a co-worker.

2. Group Spreadsheet Applications

2.1. Consolidation and Budget Planning

Budget planning is the quintessential group financial application.   At most large corporations, people across the organization are involved in discussions, negotiations, planning and approval cycles for corporate budgets for months out of every year.   During the rest of the year, changes to plan result in *ad hoc* adjustments to budget -- rarely is a complete revision of the corporate budget done more than annually.

For spreadsheet users, budget planning is equated with a batch process called "roll-up" and is supported through data entry templates. A financial officer builds a model for the whole organization. Sections to be filled in by departments are extracted and sent to each department. These sections are spreadsheets in their own right usually with some data filled in. For example, the formulas for computing results would be typed in ahead, as would some basic assumptions about target headcount, expenses, etc. Spreadsheet protection features are often used to ensure that data can be entered only in certain areas, leaving formulas and assumptions protected and unchangeable. In some organizations, macros are written that guide data entry into the sheet.

As the templates are completed, they are collected and consolidated.   Typically, data collection is done completely off-line through exchange of files on floppy disks. Occasionally exchange happens through email, by attaching spreadsheet files, or by placing files in shared directories on file servers. When files are all collected in one place, a "roll-up" macro is invoked. It brings in each section, places it in the spreadsheet, and triggers calculations as each is read in. For a large organization, this can be a lengthy process. Mainframe spreadsheet programs have been developed in part to help these massive roll-ups run more efficiently.

2.2. Limits of this process: Departmental Consolidation

While roll-up is a very successful application of spreadsheets, it supports only a small segment of the work involved in developing a budget for an organization. Much more work happens as each department in the organization prepares its own contribution to the budget. This preparation involves complex interactions among groups of people before they are ready to "fill in" the corporate template.

A large department will need to divide up its own "template" budget, request numbers from subgroups, roll them up, consider the results and iterate the process. Few departments will institute a formal roll-up -- the overhead is too high and not all of the contributors use spreadsheets. What is more, the process requires people to work in many different settings -- alone at their desks, on the road, in meetings, by phone. Since the spreadsheet program is not used in some settings -- for example, while in a meeting room -- even experienced spreadsheet users revert to the "lowest common denominator" of paper. Confusion results when each participant at a meeting leaves with private notes on paper which may reflect differing ideas of what's been agreed to. There's delay after the meeting while a transcriber tries to reconstruct what happened into a new spreadsheet version. Finally, the new spreadsheet printed on paper is different from the old, but there are no easy ways to make a comparison and find out what has changed.

There's a missed opportunity here, not just for the department, but for the organization as a whole. An on-line budget can become a strategic tool in an organization. It can be reviewed and revised to reflect changing circumstances throughout the year. The main obstacle is that no one has time to keep up with it. The departments that spend several months of each year in the "budgeting exercise" can't spend more time on it. If the process could be made more efficient through more extensive use of technology, the budget could be a more dynamic and reliable part of business operation.

Quality of decisions could also be affected by introduction of spreadsheet sharing technology. Today, people work privately on their own sections of the budget. Department resources like headcount must be allocated by central authority who can put target figures into each template. Shared spreadsheet technology would *allow, not require*, more flexible resource allocation. Using this technology, target figures for the whole department could be put in a shared spreadsheet and groups could negotiate allocation, as long as total for department met the overall target number. Even if the manager continued to set group targets, a shared spreadsheet would allow individuals to see more contextual information as input to their planning. Sharing the full budget would of course depend on good access control that could protect sensitive information such as current salaries. With the right tools, not only would today's process run more efficiently, but also innovative uses of spreadsheets would be facilitated making new work processes practical.

2.3. Integration of Information Management Tools and Spreadsheet

This broad picture of the full budget planning process emerged as we interviewed planners from several companies about their budget processes.[*] A full workgroup spreadsheet system would support people as they:

- ask for numbers for parts of the sheet (distribute templates);

- share parts of the sheet, or the entire sheet, with ways of focusing attention to specific sections;

- set access control on sections of shared sheets;

- collate sheets after they are filled in;

- compare alternative versions;

- look at partial roll-ups with assistance from the system in understanding what's "good" data, "partial" data and "inconsistent" data;

- monitor progress: assign responsibility; review list of outstanding requests; send reminders;

- discuss and comment on parts of the sheets.

The requirements amount to identifying a set of "communication gaps" in today's process that inhibit spreadsheet use in a group setting. Integration of spreadsheets with communications and data sharing technologies fills these gaps:

- email: easy exchange of spreadsheets;

- database: spreadsheet sharing and concurrency;

- access control: hiding sensitive information;

- annotations: document reasoning;

- versioning: track changes and alterative suggestions (supports meetings, both in conference rooms and at-a-distance);

- workflow: tracking requests for information; iteration.

Most of the communication gaps described above can be filled using email, shared database and workflow technology. However, there are application-specific aspects to access control and versioning that require some support directly in the application product.   For spreadsheets, the internal structure of the sheet must be enriched so that components can have their own version histories and so that users can work in separate parts of the sheet at the same time. Today, the spreadsheet is a relatively unstructured object: that's its strength for the

---

[*]The budget planning analysis was done in collaboration with Kate Ehrlich of Sun Microsystems.

individual, but may be a weakness in the group setting. Our design challenge was to add some structure to the sheet without impinging on spreadsheet usability.

3. Designing the Group Spreadsheet

3.1. Objects in Spreadsheet: Named Ranges

Group spreadsheet applications strongly motivate versioning, so we were particularly interested in how versioning of objects would work out. Since cells are the "objects" of which the spreadsheet is composed, we considered an automatic versioning mechanism that tracked changes to cells throughout the sheet. However we found such cell tracking would have little value to users who were trying to go back to known states that cut across these versions. We needed a "transaction mechanism" -- a way for the user to indicate that a group of values made sense together and were worth saving as a version. This led to the idea of working with *named ranges* within the spreadsheet.

In the spreadsheet, structure is implicit in the layout of a model -- in the labels on rows and columns. But that structure is in the minds of the designers and reader of the sheet, not in the internal data structure of the spreadsheet. A range is a rectangular block of cells in a sheet defined by two cells -- the top left and bottom right cells. By selecting and naming ranges, the user makes explicit the structure of the spreadsheet.

We also let the user indicate when a range contains a set of values worth saving as a new version. At the time the user saves these versions, they can be given a name and an annotation about the reason they are of interest. The system automatically adds a user id, date, and time stamp.

3.2. Named Versions, Range Alternatives and Scenario Management

Source control systems for software and CAD have sophisticated version control and configuration management features. This was a lot of new functionality to consider adding to the spreadsheet, particularly as it is apparently unrelated to current use of spreadsheets for model building and analysis. The features are needed only at certain points in the process and would also be of greatest benefit to the manager of the budget planning process, rather than to the individual contributor. We needed to simplify configuration management and looked for ways to make it natural for the end-user to manage the versions themselves.

Our solution came out of considering how an individual would work with the range versions. If each version has a meaningful name, they become "alternative versions" that represent different cases. (See Figure 1.) They are no longer just being saved for historical reasons and back-up, but rather to represent several different meaningful situations that should be evaluated, analyzed and perhaps even shared. Sharing is enhanced by adding annotations,

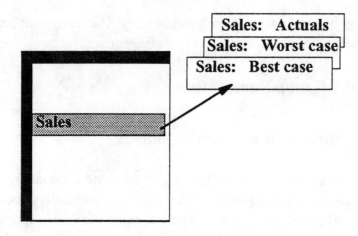

Figure 1: Ranges have Alternatives

timestamps and user names (See Figure 2). (Alternatives also appear in configuration management system as distinct from automatically generated revisions.)

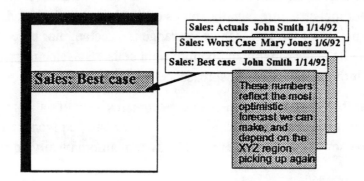

Figure 2:   Alternatives have Name, Date & Annotation

The individual will use these "alternatives" in "what-if" experiments and will want to mix and match alternatives from different parts of the sheet to form "scenarios" for the model. For example, a user might define alternatives for ranges SALES and EXPENSES. They might include "best case" for SALES, "moderate expectations" for SALES, "Joe's forecast" for EXPENSES and "Sally's thoughts" for EXPENSES. A planning and analysis phase might involve mixing and matching these to build new scenarios, such as "best case" for SALES combined with "Sally's thoughts" for EXPENSES. Today, scenarios are built by making changes directly in the spreadsheet and saving to files with cryptic names. If two scenarios -- say one with all high numbers, and another with all low numbers -- contain numbers that ought to be looked at in another combination -- say HIGH SALES and LOW EXPENSES -- the new scenario has to be created manually by cutting and pasting, then saved to yet another file. With range alternatives and scenario management, users can keep all the scenarios in one file and can mix and match easily.

3.3. Email versus Database Integration

With the additional structure added through range alternatives, spreadsheet information can be made available for sharing. We mentioned integration with email and shared databases. Email is the natural communication medium for automating today's central process. Group members will send sections of spreadsheet in emails, collect them over email, use email filters and email-based workflow tools to track progress.

We would expect a shared spreadsheet to be used by a group that wants to collaborate on building a model. Concurrency and access control would be set relative to component ranges. Sections of the model common to all group members would be shared this way with confidence that updates would be seen by all group members. The shared spreadsheet would be implemented by using database technology rather then email.

As we designed out first prototype, we stayed closer to current practices in which spreadsheets are exchanged rather than shared. Thus we integrated with email first.

4. Testing the Ideas with Customers

4.1. Customer Reaction

The analysis of budget consolidation took a broad view of financial applications. Instead of focusing on spreadsheet usage alone, we examined a full process that had impact on both spreadsheet users and non-users. This kind of analysis is different from the traditional feature-driven customer input. For example, Lotus has worked with customers for some time to understand how to make our products more useful on their networks. Customer requests have led us to introduce features that make our products easier to load over networks, and to modify our licensing scheme to accommodate sharing of licenses. In addition, all of our products share a common "file reservation" scheme for managing conflicting updates to files.

The budget planning analysis gave us a new perspective on product requirements. We shared that perspective with customers at focus groups where we showed a "Chronicle" prototype. The prototype consisted of a separate Chronicle product that worked with 1-2-3. Chronicle saved alternatives and scenarios, and managed some email-based support for requesting information from group members.

It was interesting that even among the more "network aware" of the focus groups, customers were initially cautious about the idea of the broad value of a workgroup spreadsheet. This came across in distrust of their networks and file servers and a nervousness about what other people would do to their work. However, their comments after seeing the first prototype were more open and positive.

Customers understood and liked the "what-if" and scenario management application. We received very strong feedback that this was a feature that could be used right away, to solve a common problem for the individual doing "what-if" analysis and scenario management. They wanted that feature to be more closely integrated into 1-2-3, and they did in fact appreciate that it would help them manage the input of multiple users to the spreadsheet.

Once they saw this feature, they started to explore its uses and slowly returned to the workgroup theme. By the end of the sessions several customers were telling us that they could see how these features might serve as a gentle first step towards sharing. One group talked about the opportunity for "consensus building" if a model could be on a network for all to see. As the groups started to see the potential for sharing, they also became more creative in generating additional requirements, particularly in the area of security and information hiding. They could see the value of sharing if they could be assured of the ability to hide sensitive information.

4.2. Impact on Design

Overall, the focus groups had a strong influence on our product strategy. It was their strong positive reaction to "scenario management" for the individual that resulted in making this a standard feature of 1-2-3, rather than a part of a separate workgroup spreadsheet product. The fact that they became more open to spreadsheet sharing after seeing Chronicle led us to accelerate the use of database technology to facilitate sharing (see section on Chronicle with Notes).

Design partners have contributed ideas for further applications such as sales forecasting, acquisition analysis and resource monitoring. Like budget planning, these are workgroup activities that use today's spreadsheets and currently get no explicit support for sharing.

The response from our design partners indicates that we are designing a smooth migration path for current spreadsheet users to workgroup spreadsheets. The scenario management features will be incorporated as a valuable addition to the standard spreadsheet repertoire. Because the features include name and time stamping and annotations, they make spreadsheets more shareable, even when exchanged through file transfer or floppy exchange. Follow-on versions or companion products will offer additional workgroup features and will be targeted at the users who will benefit the most -- the consolidators and the decision makers who have responsibility for managing the workflow and sharing aspects of financial applications. Their satisfaction with the product will be enhanced by the ease of getting group members to participate: other group members will already have the basic tools in hand for participating in group projects.

5. Chronicle Products

5.1. Implementation Approach

The design project we have described is code-named Chronicle. It has resulted in a multi-stage plan for workgroup-enabling spreadsheets and integrating the spreadsheet with communications software. Thus, several "Chronicle Products" will be developed. In the first phase, we are building an alternative scenario manager that will be part of the standard spreadsheet package. The second phase is to use database technology to upgrade from file sharing to sharing with concurrency and access control. By leveraging existing database technology, spreadsheets can be stored on secure network servers and shared across wide area networks. Users can update spreadsheets concurrently, set access constraints, and query spreadsheet information. In later stages, additional workflow support can be added in complementary products and alternative user interfaces provided for individual roles in the group process. We describe the first two stages in the following sections.

5.2. Chronicle in 1-2-3 for Windows

The first implementation of Chronicle is a scenario management capability in Lotus 1-2-3 for Windows 2.0. It allows spreadsheet analysts to save alternative values for sections of the sheet -- named ranges -- and to combine them into alternatives "scenarios" for the overall spreadsheet model. Values may be data or formulas. Alternatives are created by typing directly in the spreadsheet. Scenarios are created by selecting an alternative for each of several ranges and naming the combination.

Alternatives and scenarios are marked with name and time stamp at creation and whenever modified. The name used for the user identification is taken from the best available source on the machine -- either Notes ID, ccMail name or network name. Each alternative also carries with it an annotation provided by the user to document reasoning about the values in the alternative.

Alternatives and scenarios can be viewed by placing the numbers in the sheet causing recalculation of other formulas. The user can also browse through an index of these alternatives viewing them by range name, by user name, by time, or organized as scenarios. In all views, the user can also read the annotations, and select alternatives to place in the spreadsheet. For example, it might be useful to collect a set of alternatives all by the same person into one scenario.

The scenario management features are integrated in to Lotus 1-2-3. Users can flip between alternatives directly on the sheet. Spreadsheet sharing is at the file level -- users will take turns updating files on servers. The workgroup that chooses to share files on file servers will find the name and time stamps and the documentation of reasoning in annotations helpful for auditing changes and understanding each other's contributions. Design partners frequently discussed the value of auditing or tracking "who did what to the sheet, when they did it and why."

Chronicle will provide a number of report formats. Information from alternatives will be put back into a spreadsheet file and formatted for printing. One report format might highlight differences between alternatives for each range. Another might be organized to collate all annotations together for each range. Report formats specifically designed for auditing will be available.

5.3. Chronicle with Notes

Using database technology for storing ranges and alternatives, we can add new functionality that lets users:

- see new and unread alternatives contributed since they last viewed the spreadsheet;

- work concurrently on the same spreadsheet;

- be notified of changes (when more than one user is working on the spreadsheet, a user can be notified as new alternatives are added);

- control access.

We are working first with the Lotus Notes database technology, because there is an especially good match between the versioning support Chronicle adds to spreadsheets and the Notes replication mechanism. Lotus Notes technology provides a document store with a unique replication scheme that supports sharing information over wide-area networks. Applications that work best with Notes technology are ones in which communication is accomplished primarily through additions of new information. Because Chronicle will encourage people to make changes through additions of alternatives rather than by directly overwriting data in the sheet, spreadsheets stored in Notes databases can be replicated over wide area networks. Users at any site can add changes concurrently. The effect will be to meet a long-standing customer request for finer grained concurrency, but without introducing yet another kind of lock that must be explicitly set and unset in order to manage updates. What is more, the version history implicit in a set of alternatives supports communication about the changes, allowing people to see what used to be in the sheet as a way to understand the new numbers.

One important benefit of using the Lotus Notes technology is that we now have a common data representation between two applications: the spreadsheet and Lotus Notes. Lotus Notes is a flexible application development environment for workgroups. New "forms" and "views" can be added to the database through the Notes user interface without affecting the 1-2-3 view. These new views can include review of requests, automatic notification of overdue information and other management support. The forms can also be used for data entry, as an alternative to typing into the spreadsheet. Data entered this way is made available immediately to anyone looking at the database through 1-2-3.

6. Conclusion

A significant lesson of Chronicle is the importance of looking beyond current use to view products in the workgroup setting. Even though customers can quickly appreciate the value of the Chronicle features for sharing, their current work practices had not led them to ask for these features as enhancements to 1-2-3. What is especially interesting about their reaction, is the enthusiasm with which the basic group-enabling feature -- range alternatives -- has been received by individual users. The value of this feature to individual users should significantly ease overall group acceptance: it means that the consolidator who decides to use the product will find group members already comfortable with the basic features because they use them in everyday work for their own scenario management and "what-if" analysis.

Once the broad requirements were established, group-enabling was a two-step process: first the application-specific changes were introduced; then the application began leveraging workgroup technologies -- email and shared databases -- to support groups. The first step added value for the individual, even before the connection was made to the communication infrastructure. Customers say that a file that contains alternative scenarios, documentation of assumptions, and history of cases analyzed, is much easier to understand and is, therefore, more shareable. The second step is actually a sequence of planned enhancements as the product is used with different kinds of groupware software from email, to databases, to workflow engines.

We expect that much of what we did for spreadsheets will generalize to other applications. Other applications will also have new requirements for structure, versions and user identity as part of the initial step of group-enabling. These enhancements to the application extend its functionality for the individual even if it's only a matter of making it easier to manage one's own revisions and reworking of data. Just as 1-2-3 users will create scenarios and do "what-if" experiments with named alternatives, a word processor user could write alternative paragraphs to be used in different "editions" of their document for different audiences. In a product like Lotus' Freelance Graphics for Windows, alternatives for slides and scenarios can be used to assemble presentations on the same topic for different audiences. We anticipate the wide appearance of such features in the future as group-enabled products appear on desktops of individuals.

CHAPTER 11
System and Language Support for Desktop Conferencing

The most straightforward way of enabling the synchronous collaborative use of interactive software is to provide a mechanism that distributes the display of a conventional single-user application program to multiple workstations and that accepts input from any one of the workstations as the program's input. To do this requires running the program on each of the workstations under control of a *screen sharing* system. The advantages of this approach are that one can run existing *collaboration-transparent* applications without modification to the software and without the user needing to learn anything new, and that the more ambitious development of *collaboration-aware* applications is not required. Although the software cannot acknowledge and take advantage of the fact that there are multiple users, this approach will likely be the dominant technology for synchronous collaborative work in the near future (Greenberg, 1990; Crowley, 1992).

An alternative to screen sharing is *window sharing*, which has the advantage that each user can continue to work in his or her own private workspace while collaborating within the window that represents the public workspace. One of the first groups to tackle the problem of window sharing was at Bolt Beranek and Newman Inc., as originally reported by Forsdick (1985). "MMConf: An Infrastructure for Building Shared Multimedia Applications" by Crowley, Milaz-zo, Baker, Forsdick, and Tomlinson (1990) is a recent report on their attempt to support both single-user applications and new collaboration-aware applications in a networked windowing environment. The authors discuss the advantages and disadvantages of a *replicated architecture* versus a *centralized architecture* and present the design of a system in which relatively simple modifications to toolkits and applications allow them to function robustly under a replicated architecture.

Keith Lantz and his colleagues have carried out almost a decade of research on these issues; results of this work are summarized in the two papers included as our next readings. "Replicated Architectures for Shared Window Systems: A Critique" by Lauwers, Joseph, Lantz, and Romanow (1990) is a deep analysis of the serious implementation challenges that must be tackled in order to keep copies of shared synchronous applications running under a replicated architecture synchronized with one another. In order to achieve this, one must guarantee *input consistency*, *output consistency*, and *start-up consistency* for the applications. One way to do this is to make some system components, such as the underlying window managers, collaboration aware.

Yet existing window managers are not well suited to supporting groupware. "Collaboration Awareness in Support of Collaboration Transparency: Requirements for the Next Generation of Shared Window Systems" by Lauwers and Lantz (1990) suggests the changes that will be required of window systems if they are going to support adequate *spontaneous interactions*, *shared workspace management*, *floor control*, *annotation*, and *telepointing* in collaboration-transparent applications.

Increasingly, researchers are moving beyond the investigation of operating system issues for supporting groupware to the design and construction of environments, toolkits, and languages for building groupware. An outstanding example of this approach is the Rendezvous collaborative *user interface development environment* (usually known in the literature as a user interface management system; see, for example, Beaudouin-Lafon, 1991) built by a group at Bellcore. Unlike the previous three papers, the Bellcore group chose a centralized rather than a replicated architecture. They identified (Patterson, 1991) three dimensions of programming complexity that seriously affect multi-user applications. These are *concurrency*, which enables parallel activities, *abstraction*, which allows separation of the user interface from the underlying application, and *roles*, which addresses the need to provide different interfaces for different users. In "Languages for the Construction of Multi-user Multi-media Synchronous (MUMMS) Applications," Hill (1992) describes the Rendezvous language, in which Common Lisp has been extended to include an object system, light-weight processes, non-blocking message passing, a simple language for handling incoming events, a simple 2.5 dimensional declarative graphics system, and a fast, multi-way constraint maintenance system. The paper discusses these concepts and their implementation experience in detail.

Another approach to the design of a language and system for programming both collaboration-transparent and collaboration-aware multi-user programs is described by Dewan and Choudhary (1991a) in "Primitives for Programming Multi-user Interfaces." The authors first present some unique single-user features of their Suite user interface toolkit: *active variables*, *attributes*, and *value groups*. They then describe in detail their multi-user extensions to support collaboration transparency, *group awareness*, *user/session awareness*, *environment awareness*, and *coupling awareness*. Stress is placed on the concept of *coupling*, which determines which user actions are seen by other users and when they are seen. The paper concludes with a discussion of implementa-

tion experience and ideas about applying their approach in other system and language contexts.

Notes and Guide to Further Reading

An early and insightful presentation of implementation issues for real-time conferencing systems is Sarin and Greif (1985). Greenberg (1990) reviews the history of screen sharing applications, presents an architecture for implementing such systems, and discusses technical problems that must be solved in order to achieve viable implementations, particularly if the goal is the sharing of individual windows as opposed to entire screens. He identifies four key aspects of view sharing software: *view management*, *floor control*, *conference registration* by participants, and handling of *meta-level communications*. A variety of floor control mechanisms are discussed in Greenberg (1991b) in the context of the concept of *personalizable groupware*. Roseman and Greenberg (1992) describe the design of a groupware toolkit for building real-time conferencing applications.

References on windowing managers that display information on a screen and manage screen real estate are listed in the Notes section of Chapter 6. A number of systems now provide window sharing. The pioneering Rapport window sharing system is described in Ensor, Ahuja, Horn, and Lucco (1988), Ahuja, Ensor, and Horn (1988), AT&T Bell Labs (1989v), Ahuja, Ensor, and Lucco (1990), and Ensor, Ahuja, Connaghan, Horn, Pack, and Seligmann (1991). The Ahuja, Ensor, and Lucco (1990) paper is particularly interesting in that it described both centralized and replicated implementations of Rapport.

The MMConf prototype has recently been commercialized as the BBN/Slate family of products (Crowley, 1992). Other architectures and implementations are described in Bonfiglio, Malatesta, and Tisato (1991), Patel and Kalter (1992), Newman-Wolfe, Webb, and Montes (1992; see also Newman-Wolfe and Montes, 1992), Rodden, Bentley, Sawyer, and Sommerville (1992), Hopper (1992v), and Helms (1991), who presents an interesting architecture for multi-point desktop conferencing over heterogeneous networks. Zellweger, Terry, and Swinehart (1988) and Vin, Zellweger, Swinehart, and Rangan (1991) describe the Etherphone environment for multimedia conferencing. Vin and Rangan (1992) present an abstract formulation of system support for multimedia collaboration.

Rendezvous and its design and use is further described in Patterson, Hill, Rohall, and Meeks

(1990), Patterson (1991), and Rohall, Patterson, and Hill (1992v). Patterson (1991) describes some of the programming challenges in the development of collaboration-aware multi-user applications. Patterson (1990) discusses "the good, the bad, and the ugly" of implementing window sharing under the X window manager. Garfinkel, Gust, Lemon, and Lowder (1989) is a users' guide for the Shared X environment which allows the sharing of existing X-based applications by replicating the window interface among users.

Kaplan (1990), Kaplan, Carroll, and MacGregor (1991), and Kaplan, Tolone, Bogia, and Bignoli (1992) describe the Conversation/Builder system for supporting collaborative work. The underlying theoretical framework of this system is the language/action model presented in Flores and associates (1988, included in Chapter 8 of this volume). Bier and Freeman (1991; see also Bier, Freeman, and Pier, 1992v) present a user interface architecture for shared editors working on single or multiple screens. Other languages for building collaborative applications are described in Graham and Urnes (1992) and Jeffay, Lin, Menges, Smith, and Smith (1992).

Precedents for some of these approaches can be found in the office information systems literature. A comprehensive and scholarly review of the early work in this field is presented in Ellis and Nutt (1980). One example is the Diplans formalism and language (Holt, 1988), intended for the study and implementation of coordination, which was inspired in part by the mathematics of Petri nets (see, for example, Peterson, 1977 and Reisig, 1985). Influential European coordination models and implementation environments include Domino (Kreifelts, Victor, Woetzel, and Woitass, 1991; Kreifelts, Hinrichs, Klein, Seuffert, and Woetzel, 1991; Kreifelts, 1991; Martial, 1991), CHAOS (DeCindio, DeMichelis, Simone, Vassallo, and Zanaboni, 1986; Bignoli and Simone, 1991), Cosmos (Bowers and Churcher, 1988), and Amigo (Pankoke-Babatz, 1989). Two interesting recent North American projects are described in Sarin, Abbott, and McCarthy (1991) and Martens and Lochovsky (1991).

A number of recent papers focus on key issues in the design of system and language support for desktop conferencing. Narayanaswamy and Goldman (1992) present the "lazy" consistency approach to maintaining relationships between multiple versions of a document under distributed cooperative development. Shen and Dewan (1992) discuss the issue of access control. When multiple actors are working on a document concurrently, it is no longer obvious what it means to *undo* the last action; Prakash and Knister (1992) present an abstract formulation of this very important problem in collaborative work. The kind and degree of sharing or coupling among various views or windows displaying a shared workspace is treated in some depth in Dewan and Choudhary (1991b) and Dewan (1992v).

MMConf: An Infrastructure for Building Shared Multimedia Applications

Terrence Crowley, Paul Milazzo, Ellie Baker, Harry Forsdick, and Raymond Tomlinson

Bolt Beranek and Newman Inc.
10 Moulton Street
Cambridge, MA 02138

1 INTRODUCTION

Computers affect powerfully how we interact and collaborate. Traditionally, computers have allowed asynchronous group work through shared file systems, explicit file transfer, and electronic message exchange. In contrast, the MMConf project explores how computers can support distributed, real-time group interaction.

Computer teleconferencing allows individuals scattered near and far to collaborate in writing a paper, negotiate over a budget spreadsheet, or cooperate in debugging a program. Our project focuses on applications that bring subject matter into a meeting, not on applications—such as voting or brainstorming tools—that aid the meeting process itself. We attempt both to support single-user applications running in the shared environment, and to provide a base for developing inherently shared applications.

So far, the MMConf project has:

1. designed an architecture that supports shared, real-time applications,

2. implemented that architecture on UNIX systems, partly as a user interface toolkit and partly in a separate *conference manager* process, and

3. created a number of applications that support real-time cooperative work.

The MMConf project's ultimate goal is to determine how computers can break down the barriers, imposed by distances long or short, that limit the possible kinds of collaboration.

Some of the assumptions that have guided our work include:

1. MMConf must operate across wide-area networks with a wide range of bandwidth and latency characteristics.

2. It must support highly graphical, highly interactive applications. Interactive performance of an application within a conference should be as good as when used alone. It should also be fair: all sites should see roughly equal performance.

3. MMConf must support conferences many hours long as well as *lightweight* conferences analogous to a quick phone call.

4. A conventional voice or video teleconference will normally accompany the computer teleconference. We have used MMConf both with traditional telephone conference calls and with a packet-switched voice and video conferencing system [Scho89] that uses the Wideband network.

A description of the MMConf architecture, its implementation, and some of its dependent applications follows, along with a comparison of alternative approaches to building shared applications.

2 OTHER WORK

The MMConf project has a number of antecedents as well as contemporaries with similar goals.

Terminal linking in NLS (later Augment) allowed one user's screen image to be displayed on other "linked in" terminals [Enge68, Enge75]. Linked users could view or interact with any application running on the screen. NLS was limited to terminals connected to a single system, only allowed text conferencing, and took over the entire screen; Augment supported multiple windows and graphics [Enge85].

Forsdick at BBN [Fors85] reports on the earliest incarnation of MMConf. That version was limited to a single special-purpose conferencing application but identified many of the requirements of wide-area multimedia conferencing.

Lantz and Lauwers's work [Lant86, Lauw90a, Lauw90b], initially with the V-System at Stanford and later with Mach and X11 at Olivetti, addressed the issue of replicated architectures for *shared window systems* and had many of the same goals as our work. Their primary concern was supporting unmodified applications. A number of other implementors have based shared window systems on X11 [Gust88, Ahuj88, Patt89]; again, all have primarily concentrated on supporting unmodified applications.

The Colab project at Xerox PARC [Stef87] is the most notable effort in computer-based support for face-to-face meetings; it concentrated on applications specifically designed for multiple users in a meeting environment. Although confined to a single room, the Colab architecture addresses many of the issues faced in wide-area conferencing.

Finally, several projects at MCC [Elli88, Elli89] have concentrated on the special architectural and user-interface issues raised by group applications.

3 DESIGN ISSUES

Conventional graphical user interfaces assume a single user. Any architecture that distributes such an interface among several users must address whether to use a centralized or replicated computation model, whether to manage each participant's entire screen or only certain windows, and how to reconcile multiple pointing devices while still allowing meta-discussions.

3.1 Centralized or Replicated Architecture

The primary design decision in a computer conferencing architecture is whether it should be centralized or replicated. The difference lies in where the applications execute.

In a centralized architecture, a single copy of the application exists. The central server distributes output to all conference sites, including the local screen; servers at each site send input back to the central server, which forwards it to the application.

In a replicated architecture, a copy of the application runs at every site in the conference. Servers at each site distribute input to each copy, using some control mechanism to ensure that every copy sees the same sequence of input events. Output from each copy only appears locally; because all copies see the same input, their states remain synchronized, yielding identical output at each site.

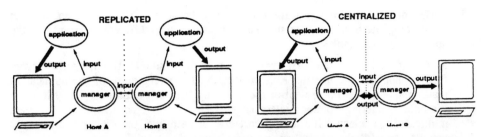

Figure 1: Replicated and Centralized Architectures. The dotted vertical line represents a machine boundary. The replicated architecture sends only input events across the boundary; the centralized architecture must distribute both input and output.

Of the two, the centralized architecture is intrinsically simpler. It requires no changes in the applications, just a new conferencing window server inserted between the application and the workstation.

MMConf uses a replicated architecture; while they are more complex, replicated architectures have three striking advantages:

1. **Performance.** Two properties of replicated architectures result in substantially better performance. First, they require lower bandwidth because only input, rather than input and output, must be distributed among the sites. Second, replicated systems are less sensitive to variations in network latency; all participants in the conference receive good interactive performance because they interact with local copies of the application. Because of network latency, remote observers may see somewhat "sticky" playback—as any remote user would in the centralized case—but our experience indicates that it is far more important that the active user get good performance.

2. **Versatility.** Centralized architectures work best with server-based window systems. In a server-based system, input events and output requests pass through a network connection, which provides a good handle for obtaining the output to distribute.

   Replicated architectures, on the other hand, work equally well with server-based or kernel-based systems. In a kernel-based window system, library or system calls handle input events and output requests, leaving no handle on the output. Replicated architectures need only a handle on the input, which is much easier to intercept; window systems typically offer a single entry point for obtaining input, but a multitude of entry points for generating output.

   Local generation of output also simplifies operating in heterogeneous environments; replicated teleconferences among sites running entirely different window systems need only translate the input events. Centralized architectures must struggle even to adapt to minor discrepancies in display geometry or color maps.

3. **Easy Site-specific Interaction.** With a replicated architecture, new applications can easily perform local interactions in the shared environment. Centralized applications that allow individual interactions must maintain separate event-processing threads for each conferee. The replicated application remains single-threaded, simply multicasting to the other conferees occasional announcements of its state (MMConf currently simulates multicasts with multiple point-to-point connections).

The primary disadvantage of a replicated architecture is the difficulty of maintaining the identical state across all copies of an application; the impediments take four forms: differences in initial application state, misordered input events, nondeterministic applications, and latecomers to the conference.

Crowley [Crow89] and Lauwers [Lauw90a] discuss most of these effects; a summary follows:

1. **Differences in initial application state** arise because of differences in the host filesystem, per-user and per-site customization, and different versions of the application executables.

   MMConf addresses the first two causes with a simple file-multicast library facility; applications use it to ensure that the file every copy of the application reads matches the file present at the currently active user's site. The MMConf file-name-gathering dialog interacts privately with the active user, then multicasts the selected file to all conferees; at each site, the dialog returns some name that yields the proper version of the file.

   MMConf currently provides a simple way for applications to compare their version identifiers. A future version will perform this task automatically.

2. **Misordered input events** occur either because the conference software assigned some site an incorrect portion of the event sequence number space, or because of uncontrolled communication among applications. MMConf ensures that only the active user's site can generate event sequence numbers, and makes it natural for child processes to join their parent's conference and thus share the same sequence numbers. Nevertheless, applications must exercise caution in connecting to uncontrolled event sources such as network servers.

3. **Nondeterminism** usually results from timing-dependent interactions. For example, applications might scroll continuously while a button is depressed, or discard all pending events upon reaching some part of their code. During a conference, MMConf automatically disables any such actions that appear inside the user-interface library, but the application programmer must also avoid any application-level timing-dependent behavior. Fortunately, few applications have such needs.

   In many cases nondeterminism simply reflects application bugs.

4. **Latecomers to the conference** are perhaps the least tractable problem. Replaying the entire existing event sequence would be unwieldy; downloading a summary of the program state is easier, but requires explicit support in each application. Currently, MMConf does neither.

   Centralized architectures also face this problem, because the window servers themselves have state.

Aside from the fatal inconsistencies described above, replicated architectures experience temporary inconsistencies because of differences in processor and filesystem speeds. A common example is that conferees read a document into an editor and then enter a verbal negotiation about whether the document is visible on all the screens ("do you see it yet?").

While centralized architectures can also experience inconsistent display output because of network and local window-server latencies, these delays tend to be smaller because they involve neither file system access nor arbitrary amounts of computation.

3.2 Screen Workspace Management

A computer conferencing architecture must choose whether to manage the user's entire screen or only certain windows; if the latter, it must also choose which window controls affect only the local screen. Window controls include window size, position on the screen, position relative to other conference windows, stacking order, and iconification. Window controls might also affect the conference windows as a group, raising or iconifying all of them together.

Managing only the conference windows allows users to pursue independent activities on their workstations; it is also crucial to lightweight conferences, which appear and disappear without affecting existing windows. MMConf follows this model.

Given that participants will have differing layouts for private windows and may be working in those private windows while a conference is going on, we felt it important that window position and stacking order be local decisions. Allowing independent control of iconification would reduce shared context: many applications behave differently depending on whether they are iconified or open. In MMConf, iconification affects all copies of a given application. Window size is often critical to the interpretation of application events; in MMConf, all copies of a given window change size together.

Finally, though managing conference windows as a group could be an important function for some styles of use, it seemed far more important that conferencing be perceived as a lightweight facility that does not preempt other tasks. There should be no separate "conference workspace;" it should be easy to mix shared and private windows.

3.3 Meta-discussions

The final issue in distributing graphical user interfaces is reconciling multiple pointers while retaining the ability to conduct *meta-discussions*: pointing or sketching to draw attention to some conference element. Computer teleconferencing systems could allow only a single pointer in the conference, or as many simultaneous pointers as there are conferees; both approaches have precedents.

3.3.1 The Telepointer

Our experience suggests that the correct number of pointers in a lightweight teleconference architecture is two: the user's own pointer and a shared *telepointer*. Allowing only a single pointer would preempt other users' activities; numerous pointers do not match the voice-mediated teleconference model, in which individual participants tend to speak in turn rather than in concert.

Design decisions for a telepointer include whether it differs in appearance from the normal pointer, how a user invokes it, and whether the invoker must be the active user.

MMConf's telepointer is a very large, conspicuous arrow that only appears within conference windows. Currently, the active user invokes the telepointer by holding down the middle mouse button. To avoid preempting application functionality, the telepointer also sends normal pointer events; all our applications assign the middle mouse button a harmless function, or none at all.

In some situations and applications, separating the telepointer from the active user, requiring no explicit action to invoke the telepointer, and not overloading a standard mouse button would be better; we consider our current approach to be a compromise at best.

3.3.2 Sketching

A transparent window would allow a simple, consistent sketching function that could overlay any window. Unfortunately, no window system we support offers transparent windows.

Instead, we have added sketching support directly within several discussion-oriented applications. The *Presenter*, a tool that manages a set of applications in a conference, also provides the ability to freeze any application it is managing, then sketch over the frozen image; nevertheless, it cannot sketch over live applications, and obtaining the frozen image is slow.

4 THE MMCONF ARCHITECTURE

The MMConf architecture consists of five parts:

1. conference management and communications,

2. an application programming model,

3. a method of intercepting input to applications,

4. window-system-specific implementations of the programming model, and

5. a mapping between window-system-specific input events and MMConf generic event descriptions.

The UNIX implementation of MMConf puts everything but the conference management and communications in a user interface toolkit linked with all teleconference applications; conference management resides in a separate process.

4.1 Terminology

The remainder of this description uses the following terms:

- A *conference* is two or more identical collections of application processes, all in synchronized execution states. Each collection belongs to one conferee.

- The *conference manager* is a special application process that embodies the conference management and communications functions; a single conference manager represents each conferee.

- *Application peers* are all the copies of a given application process.

- A *conversation* is a single top-level set of application peers started by the conference manager, and all the sets of application peers the top-level set creates.

- The *floor* identifies the active user in a conversation; every conversation has exactly one floor. *Floor control* is a mechanism and policy under which users exchange possession of the floor.

- Software is *conference-aware* if it takes special action when it detects that it is running in a conference.

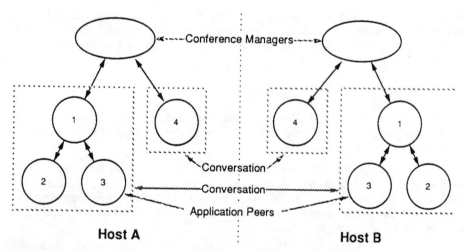

Figure 2: Process Structure and Terminology. This diagram shows the basic process structure in a conference. The *conference managers* handle communication among machines. Matching processes within a tree are *application peers*. Matching trees are *conversations*.

4.2 Purposes of Conference Awareness

MMConf's user interface toolkit contains many functions whose behavior changes under conferencing; some MMConf applications also have their own conference-aware components. Conference awareness serves four purposes:

1. **Ensuring synchronization.** Our toolkit and certain applications must take note of membership in a conference to prevent the possible loss of synchronization. For example, the toolkit disables continuous scrolling and some applications ignore user customizations.

2. **Sharing data among sites.** The toolkit automatically provides all applications with certain data-sharing functions, usually because the application's data may not be available at all sites. For example, the user interface function that gathers the name of a file to be read will enter a local interaction with the floor holder to select and transmit the file; all other members of the conversation block until notified that their copy of the file has arrived.

   Similarly, the library that reads menu configuration files explicitly multicasts them so that all sites display the same menus, while the text-editing buffer multicasts the active user's copy of a selection to be pasted from another window. Some applications explicitly multicast their initialization files rather than simply ignoring them. In general, MMConf chooses the active user's version of any input data that must be identical everywhere.

   These modifications are not simply "fixes" to make conferencing work under the replicated model; they are significant functional improvements. They allow private data from any site to be easily and transparently incorporated into the conference; in many cases, the conference awareness exists entirely within the toolkit and is transparent to the application.

3. **Limiting side-effects.** Some applications have side-effects that should not be replicated at every site. One example is mailing a message: a naive implementation would mail n copies of the message; the conference-aware implementation sends one. Writing or printing files should often be similarly restricted. In most cases, the necessary conference awareness consists simply of skipping the operation if a conference is underway and this peer does not have the floor.

4. **Facilitating parallel activity.** A significant advantage of the replicated model is the ease of supporting parallel activity. Conference aware applications that allow parallel activity simply turn off floor control; some also disable automatic distribution of input events.

4.3 Mechanisms for Conference Awareness

The toolkit offers applications three basic conference awareness mechanisms: state queries, floor policy control, and multicast functions:

1. **Conference Information.** The simplest query is whether the application is running under conferencing. Other queries reveal which conferee generated the most recent event, whether the local application peer has the floor, and how many participants the conference contains. A special query returns a number that identifies the local conferee.

2. **Floor-policy Control.** When floor control is active, an application can lock the floor, preventing it from changing hands during certain interactions; the application can also decide whether the system should distribute events while the floor is locked. Applications typically lock the floor during some private interaction at one site, for example while gathering a file name.

   To support parallel activity, the toolkit allows an application to disable floor control and specify whether events are distributed automatically. An application that maintains no floor allows all conferees to interact with the application at the same time; each application peer will see events arrive in a different order. For normal applications this will cause havoc, but a conference-aware application could use the origin of each event to maintain separate threads of control for each conferee.

Another approach to parallel activity is to disable event distribution as well, passing completed interactions through a private application-specific protocol over the message transfer path described below.

3. **Message Transfer.** The basic transfer mechanism for application-specific protocols is the ability to multicast a message to all application peers. Layered atop this basic facility is the ability to invoke one of a family of registered functions, passing arbitrary data as arguments. This ability is not a full remote-procedure call facility; invoked functions cannot return values.

   Both transfer mechanisms are asynchronous: the sending process does not block waiting for a response. The receiving process sees the message as just another event in its input queue.

4. **File Transfer.** One of the disadvantages of a replicated architecture is the need to replicate data files as well. Requiring files to be distributed before the conference begins would discourage spontaneous conferences and the introduction of new material into a planned conference. We included a file transfer capability in MMConf so that applications can easily introduce new files, and to ensure that every conferee gets the same file.

   The basic mechanism allows an application at one site to request that a file be transferred. The remote sites receive a message containing either the name of the transferred file or an error indication.

The event passing mechanism is flexible but certainly less powerful than many applications require. In general, handling communication among cooperating processes is a distributed database problem; the solutions developed for distributed databases are applicable to a toolkit for conferencing applications. Nevertheless, Ellis, Gibbs, and Rein [Elli88] show that many database solutions are inappropriate in the context of a real-time conference.

For example, if a locking protocol is used, large-grained locking may interfere with the natural flow of group communication, while fine-grained locking has unacceptable overhead and attendant diminished responsiveness. In contrast, long transactions are inappropriate for interactive use because the results of the transaction are not apparent until it has been committed, while short transactions are too expensive. Mechanisms that abort conflicting transactions have the unfortunate behavior that user actions may appear to take effect and then vanish.

Some applications of teleconferencing have a natural division of responsibility that allows simpler approaches to managing concurrency and cooperation. Card games, for example, inherently divide control of the data; users can only manipulate the cards in their hand. Similarly, an editor that only allows insert and delete can eliminate any possibility of conflict by properly defining the operations; insert and delete need never conflict if the context in which they are executed is understood [Elli89].

5 IMPLEMENTATION

Under UNIX, MMConf consists of a user-interface toolkit linked into every application, and a conference manager process with which routines within the toolkit communicate. The conference manager represents the conferee to the conference, handles all communication among conferees, and provides the user interface through which the conferee joins and leaves the conference and initiates new conversations.

A single data stream, currently implemented over TCP/IP, connects the local conference manager to each of the remote conference managers; another data stream connects the local manager to each of the local application peers. Applications send all conference traffic to the conference manager, which multicasts it by writing copies into each outgoing conference stream.

5.1 Conference Startup

To start a conference, one user—the *conference initiator*—invokes the conference manager, specifying the user and host names of the other conferees and the name of the top-level application in the first conversation. The initiator's conference manager connects to a well-known port on each of the other conferees' hosts, which then start their own copies of the conference manager.

The remote conference managers display on each conferee's screen a dialog box identifying the initiator and requesting that the user accept or reject the conference invitation. Once all the invitees have responded or timed out, the initiator's conference manager sends each remaining manager the complete list of conferees, then starts the first conversation.

5.2 Application Startup

A conference manager starting a given conversation first assigns it a unique identifier (ID). The manager then multicasts the ID, the name of the top-level application, and any command-line arguments.

Each manager then forks a copy of the application, placing in the application's environment a variable that contains both the ID and the name of an IPC port on which the manager is listening. The first time the application calls a toolkit function, that function will notice the environment variable and quietly open an IPC connection to the manager's port.

Should that application create another, its version of `fork()` will concatenate a small integer onto the ID in the child's copy of the environment variable; this integer increments after every `fork()`. The ID thus describes the child's complete ancestry and is identical for every copy of the child; the first element of every ID identifies the conversation to which the child belongs.

5.3 Floor Control

Every conversation has exactly one floor; it identifies the conferee currently providing events to the conference. The floor consists of a token and a sequence count; the count is used to prevent misordered events during a floor transition in a conference among more than two participants.

MMConf separates the concept of floor control into mechanism and policy. The mechanism handles the low-level activities of passing the floor token and maintaining a synchronized event stream for all participants; the policy determines how conferees request and grant the floor. Each conversation can use a different floor policy, which the conferees can change at any time.

5.3.1 Floor Mechanism

To acquire some conversation's floor, an inactive conferee generates a request in a manner determined by the conversation's current floor policy; that conferee's manager then multicasts a floor request to all other managers. If it does not already have a stream to some manager, it opens one.

When the manager holding the floor in question receives the request, it either processes it directly or, if required by the current floor policy, waits for its conferee to relinquish the floor. Once the manager can relinquish the floor, it must ask all the local applications to do likewise, because:

1. Toolkit code within an application may be directly enqueuing local events; when it loses the floor it must cease doing so.

2. The application can lock the floor, usually during private interactions such as gathering a file name from the user.

If the applications also agree to relinquish the floor, their manager transmits the floor to the requesting manager, which informs all applications within the conversation that they may begin generating events. If some application refuses to relinquish the floor, its manager drops the floor request.

There are two reasons a requester might not receive the floor: first, because some application refused to relinquish it, and second, because the floor was in transit at the time of the request and thus no manager held it. Should the requester receive no reply, it eventually retransmits the request.

Should the apparent floor-holder's site become inaccessible, the least-recently created remaining conference manager regenerates the floor token. This protocol is not foolproof; there is a small chance that the regenerating manager's record of the current floor holder is out of date.

5.3.2 Floor Policy

Floor policy determines how the user requests the floor and how it is granted:

1. **Implicit Request, Implicit Grant** policy is the simplest from the user's perspective. Here an inactive user requests the floor by taking some action such as typing a character or depressing a mouse button. Upon noticing the event, the toolkit places a floor request, leaving the event unread. The request is always granted, and the user's action eventually takes effect.

   Blocking the events that triggered the floor request and then handling them when the floor is received has the advantage that floor passing is transparent; the user simply interacts with the application as if running alone. One disadvantage is that the user, misinterpreting the delayed feedback, may invoke the operation multiple times.

   In our experience, this policy works best when mediated by voice interactions. When several users simultaneously contend for the floor, they tend to become confused.

2. **Explicit Request, Implicit Grant** policy requires users explicitly to request the floor, which is always automatically granted. This policy seems to work well when users contend for the floor because it prevents the floor from bouncing back and forth by mistake, especially during sketching activities. A request for the floor requires an explicit action but is acknowledged immediately, making the system seem responsive.

3. **Explicit Request, Explicit Grant** policy requires an inactive user explicitly to request the floor, and the active user explicitly to relinquish it. An early version of the system provided only this policy; we found it awkward under normal conditions.

   We believe conversations will only use this policy to lock the floor for a short time rather than as their normal mode, but we have little experience to validate this belief.

4. **No floor** policy means that all conferees can simultaneously be active. Because MMConf also uses the floor to manage the sequence number space, an application that enables this policy must be prepared for input events to arrive in a different order at each site.

The natural interactions simultaneously taking place on the voice channel aid each of these policies.

Under implicit-request policy, inactive users block between requesting and receiving the floor; we do not believe the combination of {implicit request, explicit grant} would be useful because applications could block for an arbitrarily long time.

Adding hysteresis by ignoring floor requests received either within a few seconds of obtaining the floor or while the holder is continuously active might prevent inadvertent floor bounce. Nevertheless, any policy that delays response in implicit-request mode is probably unacceptable.

5.4 Distributing Input Events

Code within the toolkit receives all the application's input events. When the application has the floor, the toolkit first enqueues the event to the application, short-circuiting any interaction with the conference manager and thereby ensuring good interactive performance. Next, the toolkit translates the event into a window-system-independent form and forwards it to the conference manager, which in turn stamps it with the application peer ID and multicasts it to the other conferees.

If the application does not have the floor, the toolkit's actions upon receiving an event depend on the current floor request policy. Under implicit-request policy, the toolkit places a floor request and blocks the input queue; under explicit-request policy, it discards the event.

The conference managers buffer incoming remote events, ordering them by sequence number; out-of-order reception is possible during floor transfers. The managers then dispatch the ordered events to the local applications by ID.

Upon receiving an event from the manager, the toolkit within each application translates the event back into window-system-specific form and enqueues it as if it were locally generated. Nevertheless, a conference-aware application can always determine the actual participant who originated the event.

6 APPLICATIONS

Building useful shared applications is major goal of the MMConf project. Descriptions of several applications that provided both experience in computer teleconferencing and insight into the requirements of a teleconferencing architecture follow:

6.1 BBN/Slate Document Editor

With the BBN/Slate Document Editor [Liso90], users can view and edit documents containing text, graphics, images, spreadsheets, and voice. Using BBN/Slate—originally a single-user application—in teleconferences provided us with a number of insights:

1. It is important that the tools used in conferencing be familiar. For most people, teleconferences are still rare events; having to learn new interfaces for a sporadic task will discourage many users.

2. It is important that the transition into conferencing be simple. For example, BBN/Slate users need only press a button on the document browser interface to confer over the current document.

3. It is important that introducing new information into the conference be easy. During the conference of the previous example, any participant can introduce a new document through the standard document browser interface.

Each of these features simplifies the transition from working alone to working together.

6.2 ViewShell

ViewShell is a terminal emulator that demonstrates some of the flexibility of the MMConf architecture. The emulator itself is a normal replicated program that uses floor control and event distribution to manage user input, while the command interpreter (shell) and all programs it starts only run at one site. The emulator at that site uses application-specific messages to distribute program output to its peers. All application peers receive user input, but only the site running the shell actually uses it.

Essentially, ViewShell creates a centralized conference architecture for terminal-based programs; it shares all the advantages of centralized architectures, offering MMConf users access to unmodified and even hardware-dependent applications. Nevertheless, ViewShell's only conference awareness is code to forward program output and discard unneeded input.

6.3 Video Tools

Bringing video information into distributed meetings is an important facet of the MMConf project; the *Video Information Server* [Crow90] and various video applications provide a powerful environment for sharing video resources among nearby workstations. Like the file-name-gathering function in the user interface toolkit, facilities in the video toolkit provide all of the conference awareness most video applications need.

For example, during a conference these facilities automatically partition conferees into clusters around local, replicated Video Information Servers. Application peers within the same cluster share access of the same physical video medium; across clusters, peers simultaneously gain access to replicated copies of the medium, avoiding the very large bandwidth requirements of transmitting high-quality digital video.

Video applications include:

1. **vide**, a video editor that directly controls remote video resources from a workstation, and creates and manipulates *edit decision lists* that specify video clips.

2. **vlens**, a video database browser with which users can locate and view video clips by keyword. Database entries identify a variety of video sources: LaserDiscs, write-once videodiscs, videotape, framestores, and live broadcasts; all are treated identically. Users can select subsets of the clips and paste them, as edit decision lists, into other applications.

3. **Xnavigate**, a map browser based on a graphical interface that overlays images of maps recorded on videodisc.

6.4 Sketch

Sketch is a simple graphical editor that operates without floor control or automatic event distribution; all conferees can interact with the drawing at the same time. Sketch announces each conferee's changes to the drawing using application-specific messages; it also implements screen-grab and text-grab facilities that allow conference participants to import images or text from private windows. Sketch only allows additions to the drawing; we have not addressed the question of synchronizing replicated copies of the drawing.

6.5 The Presenter

The *Presenter* implements a slide show in a teleconference. Each slide names an application and associated data files; selecting it starts the application, which reads and displays its data. The Presenter helps organize a complicated exhibition that uses multiple tools and files into a unified talk; it also allows sketching atop any slide (Section 3.3.2).

7 CONCLUSIONS AND FUTURE DIRECTIONS

Our experience leads us to several fairly firm conclusions:

1. A shared window system using a centralized architecture is a more robust platform for sharing arbitrary applications built with unmodified toolkits than one that uses a replicated architecture. It is almost impossible for a replicated architecture to assure correct behavior in an unmodified single-user application. Nevertheless, Lauwers and Patterson [Lauw90a, Patt89] show that it is very difficult to build a centralized architecture atop the current generation of window systems.

2. Relatively simple modifications to toolkits and applications allow them to function robustly under a replicated architecture. Because the use of standard user interface toolkits is becoming the norm, it should soon be possible to import many popular applications into replicated teleconferencing environments.

3. Replicated architectures have significant performance and device-independence advantages over centralized ones. The performance advantages are most important when communicating across wide areas or running applications that frequently generate voluminous output.

4. Users prefer lightweight teleconferencing architectures that do not preempt private activities.

5. With a replicated architecture, it is easy to confer over private data from any participating site; a conferee at that site loads it, and the standard file-multicast facility distributes it to everyone else.

6. Replicated architectures make it easy to write applications that allow multiple active users; many such applications can retain the simple, single-threaded structure of a single-user application. In contrast, even trivial centralized multi-user applications must be multiply threaded.

Possible improvements to the MMConf infrastructure include:

1. Graceful addition of latecomers; currently MMConf does not support latecomers in any way.

2. Adapting to significant configuration differences among sites; for example, some participants might have severe restrictions in screen size or font selection.

3. Recording conferences and exploring uses of such recordings.

4. Supporting very large conferences, which would involve exploring the use of true network multicasting and new user-interface paradigms.

5. Supporting long-running conferences, which would require much easier transitions between asynchronous and synchronous interaction, better failure recovery, and, again, new user-interface paradigms.

8 ACKNOWLEDGEMENTS

This work was sponsored by the Defense Advanced Research Projects Agency under contract N00140-88-C-8006. Many thanks to the reviewers for their insightful comments and to the members of the Collaboration Technology Research Group of the Internet Activities Board for stimulating discussions of many of these ideas.

9 REFERENCES

[Ahuj88]   S.R. Ahuja, J.R. Ensor, D.N. Horn, and S.E. Lucco. "The Rapport Multimedia Conferencing System: A Software Overview". In *Proc. 2nd IEEE Conference on Computer Workstations*, pp. 52-58. IEEE, March 1988.

[Crow89]   T. R. Crowley and H. C. Forsdick. "MMConf: The Diamond Multimedia Conferencing System", In *Proc. Groupware Technology Workshop*. IFIP Working Group 8.4, August 1989.

[Crow90]   T. R. Crowley, H. C. Forsdick, P. Milazzo, R. Tomlinson, and E. Baker. "Final Report on Research in Real-time Multimedia Communications Applications", BBN Report #7325, July 1990.

[Gust88]   Phil Gust. "Shared X". *Presentation at the X Conference*, MIT, January 1988.

[Elli88]   MCC Technical Report Number STP-414-88 "Groupware: the Research and Development Issues", Clarence A. Ellis, Simon J. Gibbs, Gail L. Rein.

[Elli89]   C. Ellis, S.J. Gibbs, and G.L. Rein. "Design and use of a Group Editor." In *Working Conference on Engineering for Human-Computer Interaction*. IFIP Working Group 2.7, August 1989.

[Enge68]   Douglas C. Engelbart and William K. English, "A Research Center for Augmenting Human Intellect", In Proc. Fall Joint Computing Conference, pp. 395-410. AFIPS Conference Proceedings Vol. 33, December 1968.

[Enge75]   Douglas C. Engelbart, "NLS Teleconferencing Features: the Journal, and Shared-Screen Telephoning." In Fall COMPCON 75 Digest of Papers, pp 173-177. September 1975.

[Enge85]   Douglas C. Engelbart, "Collaboration Support Provisions in Augment", in "OAC '84 Digest", Proceedings of the 1984, AFIPS Office Automation Conference, Los Angeles, Ca., February 20-22, pp. 51-58.

[Fors85]   H.C. Forsdick, "Explorations in Real-Time Multimedia Conferencing". In *Proc. 2nd International Symposium on Computer Message Systems*, pp 299-315. IFIP, September 1985.

[Lant86]   Keith Lantz, "An Experiment in Integrated Multimedia Conferencing", in *Proceedings of the Conference on Computer-Supported Cooperative Work*, December 1986, pp. 267-275.

[Lauw90a] J. Chris Lauwers, Thomas A. Joseph, Keith A. Lantz and Allyn L. Romanow, "Replicated Architectures for Shared Window Systems: A Critique", in *Proceedings of the Conference on Office Information Systems*, ACM, March 1990.

[Lauw90b] J. Chris Lauwers and Keith A. Lantz. "Collaboration Awareness in Support of Collaboration Transparency: Requirements for the Next Generation of Shared Window Systems", in *Proceedings of the Conference on Human Factors in Computer Systems*, ACM, April 1990.

[Liso90]   Herb Lison and Terrence Crowley, "Sight and Sound", in Unix Review, October 1989, pp. 76-86.

[Patt89]   John Patterson, "The Implications of Window Sharing for a Virtual Terminal Protocol", in *Proceedings Groupware Technology Workshop*. IFIP Working Group 8.4, August 1989.

[Scho89]   E.M. Schooler and S.L. Casner, "A Packet-switched Multimedia Conferencing System", *ACM SIGOIS Bulletin*, pp.12-22 (Jan 1989).

[Stef87]   Mark Stefik, Gregg Foster, Daniel G. Bobrow, Kenneth Kahn, Stan Lanning, Lucy Suchman, "Beyond the Chalkboard: Computer Support for Collaboration and Problem Solving in Meetings", Communications of the ACM, 30-1, January 1987, pp. 32-47.

Replicated Architectures for Shared Window Systems: A Critique

J. Chris Lauwers, Thomas A. Joseph, Keith A. Lantz and Allyn L. Romanow*

Olivetti Research California
2882 Sand Hill Road
Menlo Park, CA 94025

Abstract

Replicating applications in a shared window environment can significantly improve the performance of the resulting system. Compared to a completely centralized approach, a replicated architecture offers superior response time and reduces network load. To date, however, these advantages have been overshadowed by the equally significant synchronization problems associated with replication. In this paper we document these problems and show that the most frequent synchronization problems can be solved without changing existing software. We further indicate how some of the limitations of the resulting system can be removed by making applications or system servers collaboration-aware. Finally, we point out where general system support is needed to address the remaining deficiencies.

1 Introduction

A central aspect of computer support for group work is desktop teleconferencing. In the ideal, desktop teleconferencing enables geographically distributed individuals to collaborate, in real time, using multiple media (in particular, text, graphics, facsimile, audio, and video), from their respective offices. In addition, conferees are able to *share* applications, so that, for example, they can collaborate on the writing of a paper, the preparation of a budget, or the debugging of a program. One approach to application sharing is to develop special-purpose (*collaboration-aware*) applications designed for simultaneous use by multiple users (see, for example, [7, 17, 22, 26]). In many cases, however, it would be better if conferees could simply share existing single-user (*collaboration-transparent*) applications. In contemporary window-based environments, this requirement has led to the development of *shared window systems* [1, 5, 11, 13, 15, 20].

At the highest level of abstraction, a shared window system consists of a *conference agent* that is interposed between *applications* and the *window system* (Figure 1). The principal function of the conference agent is I/O multiplexing. Specifically, the conference agent distributes output streams from applications onto the users' window systems and merges the input streams from all users into a single input stream directed at the appropriate application(s). This activity enables participants in a teleconference to see the same view of every shared application and to interact with shared applications through their local input devices.[1] In contrast to terminal linking or shared-screen teleconferencing facilities [8], which require that users share everything on their screens, shared window systems permit a user to retain access to private applications during a teleconference. Shared window systems may also allow a user to take part in a number of teleconferences simultaneously, sharing different subsets of his applications (and associated windows) with different sets of users.

Most shared window systems have been implemented using variants of two basic architectures. Figure 2(a) presents the canonical *centralized* architecture: there is one instance of the conference agent and one instance of each shared application. All user input to a shared application is forwarded to the single instance of the application, and the application's output is sent to all the window systems for display. Figure 2(b) presents the *fully replicated* architecture: a copy of the conference agent and a copy of every shared application is executed locally on each user's

---

*E-mail: {lauwers,joseph,lantz,romanow}@orc.olivetti.com
[1]We refer to applications running under a shared window system as "shared applications." Similarly, windows associated with such applications are referred to as "shared windows."

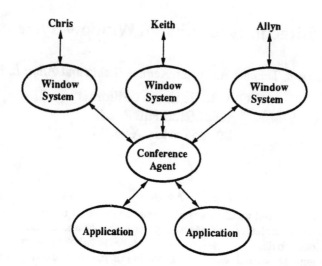

Figure 1: Abstract architecture of a shared window system.

workstation. User input to a shared application is distributed from the user's window system to all instances of that application. The output from each copy, however, is delivered only to the local window system. Although many variants of these basic architectures are possible, the remainder of this paper only deals with full application replication as in Figure 2(b).

Replication can significantly improve the performance of shared applications, as originally suggested by Sarin and Greif [21, 23]. Compared to a completely centralized approach, a replicated architecture offers superior response time and reduces network load. These benefits are sufficient to justify experimentation with replication and, indeed, motivated our work on VConf [15] and its successor, Dialogo [6]. The one other shared window system that employs application replication is MMConf, developed at BBN [5, 9]. The Colab project at Xerox PARC also adopted a replicated architecture for their collaboration-aware tools [10, 26].

Adopting a replicated architecture requires dealing with all the synchronization problems associated with replicated execution. Many solutions to these problems have been suggested [3, 4, 14, 25], all of which require extensive modifications to existing system software and applications. As a principal goal of shared window systems is to minimize modification to existing software, these approaches were originally deemed unacceptable. Rather, we decided to investigate how far we could push application replication without modifying any existing software.

The goal of this paper, then, is to document the synchronization problems associated with application replication in shared window systems. This discussion is based on our own experience with VConf and Dialogo, together with our understanding of the experiences of the MMConf team. We will show that the most frequent synchronization problems can be solved and that a usable system can be built without changing existing software. We will further indicate how some of the limitations of such a system can be removed by making applications or system servers collaboration-aware. Finally, we will point out where general system support is needed to address the remaining deficiencies.

The body of the paper is organized as follows. Section 2 reviews the motivations for adopting replicated architectures for shared window systems. Section 3 gives an overview of the challenges that application replication imposes on system designers. These challenges are discussed in detail in sections 4-6. Section 7 concludes with a summary of our approaches to the difficulties associated with replicated architectures.

2   Motivations for Application Replication

The main advantage of application replication is performance. Response time is better than in a centralized system because each user always receives output from a local copy of shared applications. Furthermore, depending on the window system, this output may not even have to go through the local conference agent, as was the case with VConf. This results in a further improvement in response time.

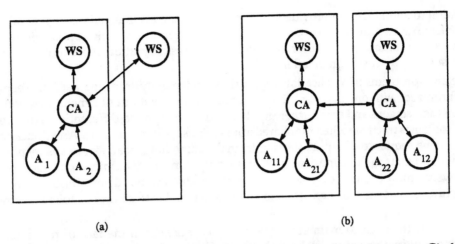

(a)   (b)

Figure 2: (a) Canonical centralized architecture. (b) Canonical fully replicated architecture. Circles should be interpreted as module instances—typically processes in separate address spaces. Boxes represent machine boundaries. The use of two subscripts in (b) indicates that the applications are replicated, with the first subscript identifying the application and the second the replica of that application.

Another performance benefit of application replication is that it typically lowers network traffic. In a centralized architecture, output data must be sent across the network to all window servers. When applications are replicated, each copy sends output only to the local window server, and no output data need be distributed across the network. The effect of this reduction in network traffic is magnified in typical workstation-based environments where the volume of output data sent to the window system dwarfs the volume of the input data received from it. Experiments performed on VConf and on Rapport [2] have verified these observations in the context of two different window systems—TheWA [16] and X [24], respectively. This reduction in bandwidth requirements suggests that a replicated architecture is particularly suited for teleconferencing across long-haul or slow networks.

A replicated architecture is also more versatile than a centralized one. In kernel-based window systems, such as SunWindows, the display hardware of a particular machine cannot be accessed by remote clients, so that a centralized architecture is not possible in such an environment. With kernel-based window systems, window sharing can only be achieved by adopting a replicated architecture.

More importantly, however, replicated architectures appear much better suited to accommodating heterogeneous hardware environments. Differences in hardware or other resources cause problems for any shared window system, whether based on a centralized or replicated architecture. In particular, X's imaging, color, and input models are neither consistent nor hardware-independent. Sizes and distances are measured in screen pixels, which vary from display to display. Keycodes are reported in vendor-specific terms. Applications can gain access to hardware-dependent information through objects called *visuals*, which abstract the properties of various displays. A companion paper [19] discusses this issue at length. In general, however, it should be easier to accommodate these differences using a replicated architecture because each instance of a shared application can (automatically) tailor itself to the display capabilities of its window server.

The same rationale applies when collaboration-aware applications must allow conference participants to use personalized interaction techniques or display different views on shared applications [17, 23, 26]. Again, these requirements are most easily handled in a replicated environment where each replica of a shared application can adapt its presentation to one participant's preferences.

3 Disadvantages of Application Replication: Overview

Application replication is not without its drawbacks. Indeed, some of these appear to be intractable under current technology. In particular, a replicated architecture will not work if an application to be shared is not available at all sites, or if it requires more resources (e.g. memory, devices, or licenses) than a particular participant's workstation can offer. Furthermore, it is difficult to add new participants to an ongoing teleconference, to move a participant from one workstation to another, or, to provide support for spontaneous interactions in general. With a replicated architecture, these features require the ability to create up-to-date replicas of active applications on a new workstation. Thus, unless we have ubiquitous support for logging or process migration, these problems are likely to remain unsolved. These issues are discussed in detail in [18].

The more tractable problems of application replication arise mainly from the need to keep copies of shared applications synchronized with one another. If applications were to get out of synchronization, users would see different images on their screens and any further input would be interpreted differently on different machines. The synchronization problem is tractable when the shared applications are deterministic. An application is deterministic if, when given the same sequence of inputs starting from the same initial state, it always responds with the same sequence of outputs, and ends in the same final state. Also, output from a deterministic application does not depend on the timing between input events. In general, applications that are not deterministic cannot be handled in a replicated architecture. However, we shall see below that it is possible to control or tolerate certain forms of non-determinism.

A related problem is the need to maintain *single-execution semantics* in the face of replicated execution. This means that executing multiple replicas must have the same effect on global system state as running a single replica.

How these problems manifest themselves depends greatly on the underlying window system. Since our discussion is based primarily on Dialogo, the solutions we present apply mainly in the context of X (Version 11). Nevertheless, the types of problems we describe are relevant to any replicated shared window system, and most of our solutions can be adapted to any underlying window system.

4   Input Consistency

The first step in keeping all replicas of a shared application synchronized is to ensure that they are started up in equivalent initial states and receive equivalent inputs. We say "equivalent" rather than "identical" because the inputs may have to be reinterpreted at each replica because of their different contexts. For example, window identifiers, sequence numbers and timestamps have to be remapped at each machine. This problem is complicated by the fact that an application may receive input from many sources besides the user. An application may read data from files, obtain the values of environment variables, communicate with the local window manager, receive messages from other applications, or access system servers. The conference agent guarantees that the same user input is delivered to all sites, but does not ensure the equivalence of input from other sources.

We can divide the problem of input equivalence into two parts: ensuring that applications receive the same (or equivalent) inputs from each individual source, and ensuring that inputs from the various sources are interleaved in the same order at all replicas. First, we describe how shared window systems guarantee equivalent user input. Then, we discuss how input from other sources can be handled. Finally, we discuss input ordering.

4.1   User Input

As discussed before, shared window systems use conference agents to distribute equivalent user input to all replicas of shared applications. Figure 3 shows the conference agent implementation for Dialogo, where conference agent functionality is distributed between a single conference manager and several conferee's agent processes, one per participant. Like VConf and MMConf, Dialogo uses the notion of a floor holder to regulate concurrent access to the shared workspace. Equivalence of user input is ensured by broadcasting input events generated by the floor holder to all replicas of conference applications. In the remainder of this paper, we refer to the floor holder's conferee's agent as the *active agent*, whereas all other conferee's agents are referred to as *passive agents*. Naturally, the floor holder changes as the conference progresses.

Generating consistent user input does not imply distributing the entire window system input stream to all participants, since not all events may be generated in response to user actions. X, for example, includes many events that are only used for *inter-client* communication. These events are generated by the X server in response to requests made by a client and inserted in the input stream of the intended receiver. For the remainder of this discussion, we classify X events in two classes:[2] user-input events (like the ButtonPress event), and inter-client events (like the

---

[2]For the discussion in this paper, events responsible for window refresh (like the Expose event) are not relevant and will not considered further.

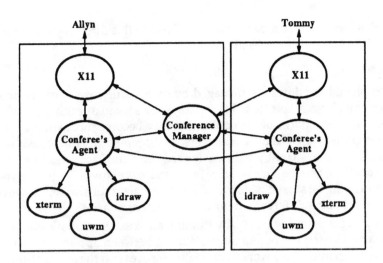

Figure 3: Architectural overview of Dialogo

`MapRequest` event). In general, a shared window system distributes user-input events only and does not broadcast inter-client events.

4.2   Input from Other Sources

There are two general approaches to ensuring that external sources generate the same input for all replicas. One is to replicate the external environment (or at least the parts of it used in a teleconference) and ensure that it remains the same at all sites. The other approach is to modify the external environment or its interface to make it *collaboration-aware*. In the latter approach, some of the entities in the external environment are modified so that they know when they are communicating with shared applications, and they generate consistent input to all replicas. However, one of the goals of a shared window system is to minimize modifications to existing software, so the solutions we describe below follow the first approach.

4.2.1   Files

At first glance, it may appear that the problem of reading input from files can be avoided by using a shared file system. However, if an application then *writes* to a file, each replica of the application would perform a write on the same file, and these multiple writes could lead to incorrect behavior (see Section 5). Dialogo, MMConf and VConf all address this problem by creating a separate "conference directory" for each participant. Dialogo and MMConf provide tools for creating and placing files in the conference directory. These tools ensure that any file placed in a user's conference directory is automatically copied into the other users' conference directories. In VConf, the user has to do this manually. As long as participants work within the conference directory and use relative path names to refer to files, they will all access identical copies of files.

Although this approach of copying working files into a conference directory is sufficient for most applications, it still has some shortcomings. If an application uses absolute path names to reference files, a different mechanism is needed to guarantee file consistency. Also, if a file copied into the conference directory contains a reference to another file, this reference may not be handled correctly. Under VConf and Dialogo it is up to the user to take care of these situations; MMConf circumvented some of these problems by adopting a collaboration-aware file system browser.

4.2.2   Environment Variables

Dialogo starts the first conference application (usually a window manager) with a standard set of environment variables, which will be inherited by all child applications. Participants in a teleconference may later change these values and add or delete environment variables. Since this action occurs on all workstations, the environment variables remain consistent. Dialogo also sets the value of the HOME environment variable to be the conference directory and copies a standard set of user customization files into this directory, ensuring that shared applications will be customized the same way on all workstations.

4.2.3 Window Managers

Problems arise when shared windows are managed by each participant's private window manager. When a user resizes a shared window, for example, only his replica of the shared application will be notified of this change by his window manager, and the replicas of the application may become inconsistent. The general solution to this problem is to use collaboration-aware window managers, as discussed in [18]. These would coordinate between themselves to resize all instances of shared windows. Indeed, MMConf achieves this basic effect by broadcasting changes in window size to all conference agents. Since SunWindows allows clients to invoke window management functionality, these agents can adjust shared windows to keep their sizes consistent. However, under X, this becomes a problem when conferees are using different window management policies.

In contrast, Dialogo manages shared windows by running an existing window manager as a shared (replicated) application in a conference. Consequently, all communication between applications and the conference window manager is replicated on each participant's workstation. This ensures that the application and the window manager receive the same input and take the same actions on all workstations. One result of this approach is that Dialogo implements strict WYSIWIS workspaces—users have identical views of the shared workspace, including window placement and size.

4.2.4 Communication with Other Processes

Applications may also receive input from other applications and/or system servers. In fact, communication with the window manager, as described above, is just a special case of inter-process communication. In X and TheWA, clients communicate through the window server to implement functions like cut and paste. In MMConf, the folder browser application and the Diamond editor communicate directly when a file is opened through the browser. The way to ensure that the same input is received from other applications or system servers is the same as before—either replicate these processes or make them collaboration-aware. The more difficult problem, however, is to ensure that input from these sources is interleaved in the same order at all replicas. This is discussed next.

4.3 Ordering Input from Multiple Sources

Merely ensuring that all replicas of a shared application receive equivalent inputs from all sources is not sufficient, since events originating from different sources may be arbitrarily interleaved. Correct operation requires the entire input stream to be equivalent, meaning that all input events have to be delivered to replicated instances of shared applications in the same order.[3] The ordering problem usually does not occur for interactions with the file system, since applications typically use synchronous requests to read data from files. A problem occurs when multiple sources deliver input asynchronously. As an example, consider what happens under X when an application is started up. Applications typically create a new window and request that it be mapped, which results in a MapRequest event being sent to the window manager application. The window manager then waits for a ButtonPress event from the user to select the window position and size. Thus, the window manager is receiving input from both the application and the user. In a replicated environment, the MapRequest is generated in a replicated fashion on each participant's workstation, whereas the ButtonPress is generated by the floor holder and distributed to all replicas of the window manager. We have to ensure that the locally generated MapRequest and the floor holder's ButtonPress events are delivered in the same order to all replicas of the window manager.

Again, the general solution to this problem requires that applications be made collaboration-aware. In window-based systems, however, inter-process communication is often mediated through the window system. In both X and TheWA, for example, cut and paste operations are managed by the window server. Moreover, in X, all interactions between clients and the window manager application go through the server. The window server provides such *inter-client* communication by translating requests from one client into inter-client events sent to the destination client. These inter-client events are distributed over the same input stream as used for user-input events, and are therefore intercepted by the conference agent. This is an important observation, since it allows us to address ordering problems by implementing a synchronization algorithm in the conference agent.

---

[3]This requirement can be relaxed if application semantics are known [12]. We do not assume that shared window systems have knowledge about application semantics.

Dialogo takes the following approach (see [6] for a more detailed description). Since there is only one floor holder for the conference at any given time, Dialogo uses the event order on the active workstation as the unique ordering for all event packets. A naive implementation would distribute all event packets (inter-client events as well as user-input events) from the floor holder to passive agents, since this guarantees consistent ordering. However, this approach introduces another kind of synchronization problem: it could violate the causal relationship between the action that initiates an inter-client communication and the delivery of the corresponding inter-client event. In the example above, it was the application's call to XMapWindow that caused the delivery of the MapRequest event to the window manager. A passive agent could violate causality by delivering the floor holder's MapRequest event to the window manager before the application calls XMapWindow at that site. The window manager could then attempt to map the window even before it was created by the application, and would fail. If this happened on some sites but not on others, the system would get out of synchronization.

Therefore, Dialogo distributes both user-input and inter-client events from the floor holder to all passive agents, but the passive agents use the floor-holder's inter-client events only to impose an ordering relation on each participant's locally generated event stream. To achieve this ordering, passive agents queue locally generated inter-client events and deliver them to the application only as they are matched by corresponding inter-client events generated by the active agent. This guarantees that inter-client events are ordered consistently with respect to each other and with respect to user-input events. In the above example, then, this means that the passive conferee's agents queue the locally generated MapRequest event until the corresponding event is received from the floor holder, so that the correct order of delivery with respect to the ButtonPress can be determined.

Note that this solution is made possible by the existence of a single floor for the entire conference. If there is more then one floor per conference—as in MMConf, where there can be several *conversations*, each with its own floor—it is much more difficult to find a unique ordering relation for the event stream. The designers of MMConf have realized this, and require that communicating applications (like the folder browser and the editor) be part of the same conversation.

A final issue that needs to be addressed is the synchronization of input with respect to changing the floor. For example, if the current floor holder loses the floor while typing some input, it is important that all workstations agree whether that input occurred before or after the floor change. Dialogo employs a 2-phase protocol that guarantees that all participants agree on when a floor change occurs relative to the application input streams. Details of the algorithm may be found in [6].

4.4 Accommodating Non-Deterministic Input

As discussed earlier, applications that are non-deterministic cannot, in general, be run with a replicated architecture. However, disallowing all non-deterministic applications would be too drastic. A common source of non-determinism occurs when input queues are used by application programs to buffer events delivered by the window system. In particular, we refer to input queues implemented by the window system libraries, although this discussion applies to all queuing mechanisms that are not provided by the window server (pseudo ttys used by terminal emulators, for example, are input queues for terminal-oriented applications). Since most window-based applications are event-driven, the window system deposits events in these queues asynchronously, while at the same time the application processes queued events. This introduces the potential for race conditions between event delivery and queue manipulation operations, which results in non-deterministic behavior. Since the input queues and the routines that manipulate them are not implemented in the window server, a shared window system cannot prevent such race conditions. However, there are situations where these non-determinisms can be tolerated. This section discusses two common examples.

4.4.1 Polling the Input Queue

Many interactive applications contain code fragments that repeatedly execute the body of a loop until a particular input event arrives. After every iteration through the loop, the application program polls the input queue to check if the terminating event has arrived. Since there is no synchronization between the application polling the queue and the window system delivering the terminating event, the number of iterations through the loop is non-deterministic. The Diamond editor, for example, exhibits this behavior: holding down the mouse button in the scroll icon causes the editor to scroll through the document as long as the mouse button is depressed. In a computer conference, this mode of operation can cause replicated instances of the Diamond editor to scroll a variable number of pages. The

```
while(XCheckTypedEvent(display, ButtonPress, ...) == FALSE)
{
    XQueryPointer(display, rootWindow, ... );
    MoveOutline( ... );
}
```

Figure 4: A typical code fragment for rubber banding.

general solution to this problem is to modify all applications that exhibit this behavior. This is in fact the approach taken by the MMConf project.

However, if the body of the loop has no effect on application state, this form of non-determinism can be tolerated without modifying applications. A common example is the implementation of rubber-banding—the interactive display of an outline of an object being moved or resized. A typical code fragment for X is shown in figure 4; window managers often use code like this to draw an outline of a window as it is being moved. Although such code exhibits non-deterministic behavior, it can generally be tolerated since the body of the loop is only responsible for intermediate display actions and does not change application state.

In Dialogo, however, the code fragment causes the synchronization algorithm described in Section 4.3 to break. If different replicas of an application do not make exactly the same number of QueryPointer requests, different numbers of QueryPointer replies will be generated. This means that for some locally generated QueryPointer replies, there will be no matching reply coming from the floor holder. As a result, the locally generated replies will remain queued in the conferee's agents.

Therefore, to accommodate rubber banding, we slightly modified Dialogo's synchronization algorithm such that QueryPointer replies are not queued. Rather, whenever a QueryPointer reply is received from the floor holder, passive conferee's agents cache the latest information about the floor holder's pointer position. When a local QueryPointer reply is generated, pointer information in the reply packet is replaced by the cached information, and the reply passed on immediately to the local replica of the application.

4.4.2 Discarding Input Events

Another race condition occurs when application programs discard input events from the input queue. Since event delivery is asynchronous, input queues kept by different instances of shared applications may be different when the discard operation is performed, so that a different set of events will be discarded. The different replicas of the application may thus receive different input streams, and may take inconsistent actions as a result. A typical application that exhibits this behavior is rn, a Unix news reader program, which discards incoming events while its display is being updated. Using applications like rn in a computer conference will most likely result in inconsistencies.

Dialogo exhibits this problem because the XSync function provided by the X library. XSync allows an application to discard events that are pending in its input queue. For example, the twm window manager uses this feature to disable click-ahead when positioning a newly created window (presumably in order to prevent erroneous input). Since XSync is implemented completely in the window system libraries (there is no XSync request in the X protocol), a shared window system cannot prevent the resulting race conditions. On the other hand, if there were an explicit XSync request as part of the X protocol, the XSync reply could be used to delineate exactly the set of events that need to be flushed.

5   Output Consistency

Just as an application may receive input from many sources, it may also send output to various objects in the environment. For example, an application may write to a file, send a document to a printer, invoke a mailer, or turn on an actuator. Single-execution semantics need to be maintained when multiple copies of shared applications issue output requests to the same external object. For example, if the participants in a teleconference decide to send mail to someone, it is almost always the case that they intend only one copy of the mail to be sent. In contrast, if each replica of a shared application invoked a mailer, multiple copies would be sent. Moreover, if we replicate an external object that receives output from many applications concurrently, these replicas might become inconsistent unless we ensure that output is delivered to each replica in the same order. (This is similar to the ordering requirement on input to shared applications.)

Fortunately, the applications typically used in a teleconference interact mainly with the window system and any external output is almost exclusively to the file system. Furthermore, these applications rarely write to the same files concurrently. In such situations output requests from different applications impose no ordering problems, and no concurrency control is required. The remaining problem is how to accommodate redundant output requests from replicas of the same application. The solution is to replicate the relevant files and have each application replica write to its own copies—that is, precisely the conference directory approach introduced in Section 4.2.1. These observations imply that a large class of applications can be used in a replicated system with no modification to system or application software.

However, if it is necessary to support concurrent access to the same file, then access to the file system must be regulated by a concurrency control mechanism that ensures that output operations are serialized in the same order on all copies of the file. Traditional replicated databases would *not* solve this problem. Such databases all assume that there is a single source for each write request, whereas here each write request is issued once from each copy of any application. One approach to solving this problem is to extend an existing replicated database to accommodate multiple instances of the same request. Another approach would be to modify the offending applications.

Similar observations hold with respect to objects other than files. That is, in the general case either the applications or the relevant object managers have to be modified to intercept redundant output requests and perform the operation only once. This approach was adopted by MMConf, which provides a collaboration-aware mailer and video information server, among other tools.

6 Start-up Consistency

The mechanism described in Section 4.3 synchronizes the input streams of applications that are already part of a teleconference. We also need to synchronize the starting up and introduction of new applications into a teleconference. If the workstations involved have different speeds, an application may start up on one workstation before it does on another. In this situation, the latter workstation may begin to receive events for an unknown application. To avoid this, Dialogo delays reading from or writing to a new application at the floor holder's site until all the passive agents have opened connections to replicas of the application.

A more difficult synchronization problem arises when applications are started up by a mechanism external to the conferencing system and there is no foolproof way for a server to identify new applications. With X on Unix, for example, a new application is started up when an existing application (usually a shell or a window manager) forks a new process—an action external to the conferencing system. The new application opens a connection to the conference agent using a well-known port. However, the conference agent has no way of identifying the application at the other end of a connection. This can lead to a problem when two (or more) applications are started at about same time (say by typing "xterm; emacs" to a shell). Each conference agent will receive two new connection requests, but there is no guarantee that the two applications will request connections in the same order at all workstations, and there is no simple way to tell which connection belongs to which application. If the conference agent makes the wrong choice, the input/output of one application at one site could be fed into the other application at another site, which would be disastrous.

Fortunately, this situation rarely occurs in practice. Participants in a teleconference typically spend most of their time browsing through shared windows and only occasionally start up new applications. They almost never start up multiple applications simultaneously. So, little damage is likely to result from leaving this problem unresolved, as we did in Dialogo.

For the sake of completeness, however, we indicate how the problem of start-up synchronization can be addressed. One general solution would be to somehow uniquely identify applications that open new connections. The conference agents could then use this information to synchronize application start-up. Unfortunately, it is not possible to uniquely identify applications without extensive support from the underlying system. While the application name or the command line arguments may suffice to differentiate between applications in most situations, a general solution should be able to disambiguate between multiple invocations of the same application, possibly with the same arguments. Such an approach would also require changing the underlying window system protocol.

No current protocol includes a mechanism for a new application to identify itself when it connects itself to a server. Hence, a solution based on identifying applications is impractical in the short term.

Another approach to start-up synchronization is to force the user to start up new applications only through the conference agent, as in MMConf, or through a conference-aware shell. The conference agent or shell then imposes the necessary synchronization. However, with this approach it is necessary to disallow users from themselves starting up any kind of shell application, lest they bypass the synchronization mechanism by starting applications from within their own shell.

7   Conclusions

Despite the potential benefits of replicated architectures for shared window systems, most groups have avoided them due to the significant synchronization problems that are associated with replicated execution. In this paper we have documented these problems, based primarily on our experience with VConf and Dialogo.

Keeping replicas of a shared application consistent requires that each replica receive (semantically) equivalent input from each input source and that input events originating from different sources be delivered to all replicas in the same order. The conference agent can guarantee equivalence for input generated by the base window system in response to user actions, but other mechanisms are required to guarantee input equivalence from other sources—file systems or window managers, for example. Two approaches are possible:

1. Replicate all relevant input sources.
2. Build collaboration-aware input sources, so that those sources can multicast their input to all replicas of shared applications.

The more difficult problem is to deliver input events originating from different sources in the same order to all replicas. In the most general case—where every source is generating input asynchronously, direct to the application—this requires that the application be made collaboration-aware.

As one of the principal goals of shared window systems is to minimize modifications to existing software, our intent with Dialogo was to investigate how far we could push application replication without changing existing software. Although conference agents can only guarantee equivalent user input, we have found that it is possible to replicate most other input sources—in particular the file system and the window manager. Moreover, in the case where the asynchronous input streams are all being mediated by the base window system (as is the case in a typical X environment), the conference agent can guarantee consistent input ordering. It is possible, therefore, to build a usable system without modifying existing software. Such a system, however, is not guaranteed to be robust when non-deterministic applications are used or when shared applications interact extensively with external entities that are not monitored by the shared window system.

To remove the constraints of such a basic system, it is necessary to make some system components collaboration-aware. This is in fact the approach taken by the MMConf team. Trivial modifications to applications or to system servers can often eliminate or prevent non-deterministic behavior. Building collaboration-aware window managers can remove the WYSIWIS-workspace constraint that results from replicating the window managers [18]. Collaboration-aware shells can prevent race conditions that arise when two conference applications are started simultaneously. Moreover, such shells can prevent users from running applications that are not robust in a replicated environment. Finally, single-execution semantics can often be preserved by modifying existing servers or by employing conference agent-like frontends to them.

Introducing collaboration-awareness into existing applications and/or servers can eliminate most of the problems associated with application replication. Solving the remaining problems—however rare—requires extensive additional support from the underlying operating system and from the available system servers. Input sources that cannot be replicated need to be modified and general system support for ordering events from arbitrary sources is required. Moreover, extensive system support is needed to support spontaneous interactions.

In general, we believe that the benefits of application replication are significant enough to warrant further attention, but that collaboration transparency cannot be maintained with current technology.

8   Acknowledgments

Thanks to Terry Crowley for his comments on an earlier version of this paper.

References

[1] S.R. Ahuja, J.R. Ensor, D.N. Horn, and S.E. Lucco. The Rapport multimedia conferencing system: A software overview. In *Proc. 2nd IEEE Conference on Computer Workstations*, pages 52–58. IEEE, March 1988.

[2] S.R. Ahuja, J.R. Ensor, and S.E. Lucco. A comparison of application sharing mechanisms in real-time desktop conferencing systems. Technical report, AT&T Bell Labs. To be presented at the COIS '90 Conference on Office Information Systems, ACM, April 1990.

[3] K.P. Birman, T.A. Joseph, T. Raeuchle, and A. El-Abbadi. Implementing fault-tolerant distributed objects. *IEEE Transactions on Software Engineering*, SE-11(6):502–508, June 1985.

[4] E.C. Cooper. Replicated distributed programs. In *Proc. 10th Symposium on Operating Systems Principles*, pages 63–78. ACM, December 1985.

[5] T. Crowley and H. Forsdick. MMConf: The Diamond multimedia conferencing system. In *Proc. Groupware Technology Workshop*. IFIP Working Group 8.4, August 1989.

[6] Desktop Teleconferencing Group. The Dialogo shared window system. Technical report, Olivetti Research California, in preparation.

[7] C. Ellis, S.J. Gibbs, and G.L. Rein. Design and use of a group editor. In *Proc. Working Conference on Engineering for Human-Computer Interaction*. IFIP Working Group 2.7, August 1989.

[8] D.C. Engelbart. NLS teleconferencing features: The Journal, and shared-screen telephoning. In *Proc. Fall COMPCON*, pages 173–176. IEEE, September 1975.

[9] H.C. Forsdick. Explorations in real-time multimedia conferencing. In *Proc. 2nd International Symposium on Computer Message Systems*, pages 299–315. IFIP, September 1985.

[10] G. Foster. *Collaborative Systems and Multi-User Interfaces*. PhD thesis, University of California - Berkeley, 1986.

[11] P. Gust. SharedX: X in a distributed group work environment. Presentation at the 2nd Annual X Conference, MIT, January 1988.

[12] M. Herlihy. *Replication Methods for Abstract Data Types*. PhD thesis, Massachusetts Institute of Technology, 1984. Published as Laboratory for Computer Science Technical Report MIT/LCS/TR-219.

[13] B. Janssen. Personal communication. February 1988.

[14] L. Lamport. The implementation of reliable distributed multiprocess systems. *Computer Networks*, 2(2):95–114, May 1978.

[15] K.A. Lantz. An experiment in integrated multimedia conferencing. In *Proc. CSCW 86 Conference on Computer-Supported Cooperative Work*, pages 267–275. MCC Software Technology Program, December 1986. Reprinted in I. Greif (editor), *Computer-Supported Cooperative Work: A Book of Readings*, pages 533–552. Morgan Kaufmann Publishers, 1988.

[16] K.A. Lantz. Multi-process structuring of user interface software. *Computer Graphics*, 21(2):124–130, April 1987. Presented at the SIGGRAPH Workshop on Software Tools for User Interface Development, ACM, November 1986.

[17] K.A. Lantz, J.C. Lauwers, B. Arons, C. Binding, P. Chen, J. Donahue, T.A. Joseph, R. Koo, A. Romanow, C. Schmandt, and W. Yamamoto. Collaboration technology research at Olivetti Research Center. In *Proc. Groupware Technology Workshop*. IFIP Working Group 8.4, August 1989.

[18] J.C. Lauwers and K.A. Lantz. Collaboration awareness in support of collaboration transparency: Requirements for the next generation of shared window systems. Technical report, Olivetti Research California. To be presented at the CHI '90 Conference on Human Factors in Computing Systems, ACM, April 1990.

[19] J.C. Lauwers and K.A. Lantz. Desktop teleconferencing and existing window systems: A poor match. Technical report, Olivetti Research California, in preparation.

[20] S. Piccardi and F. Tisato. Conference Desk: An experiment and model for application sharing. Technical report, Systems Software Laboratory, Direzione Olivetti Ricerca - Milan, January 1989.

[21] S.K. Sarin. *Interactive On-line Conferences*. PhD thesis, Massachusetts Institute of Technology, 1984. Published as Laboratory for Computer Science Technical Report TR-330.

[22] S.K. Sarin and I. Greif. Software for interactive on-line conferences. In *Proc. 2nd Conference on Office Information Systems*, pages 46–58. ACM, June 1984.

[23] S.K. Sarin and I. Greif. Computer-based real-time conferencing systems. *Computer*, 18(10):33–45, October 1985. Reprinted in I. Greif (editor), *Computer-Supported Cooperative Work: A Book of Readings*, pages 397-420. Morgan Kaufmann Publishers, 1988.

[24] R.W. Scheifler and J. Gettys. The X Window System. *ACM Transactions on Graphics*, 5(2):79–109, April 1986.

[25] R.D. Schlichting and F.B. Schneider. Fail-stop processors: An approach to designing fault-tolerant computing systems. *ACM Transactions on Computer Systems*, 1(3):222–238, August 1983.

[26] M. Stefik, G. Foster, D.G. Bobrow, K. Kahn, S. Lanning, and L. Suchman. Beyond the chalkboard: Computer support for collaboration and problem solving in meetings. *Communications of the ACM*, 30(1):32–47, January 1987. Reprinted in I. Greif (editor), *Computer-Supported Cooperative Work: A Book of Readings*, pages 335-366. Morgan Kaufmann Publishers, 1988.

COLLABORATION AWARENESS IN SUPPORT OF COLLABORATION TRANSPARENCY: REQUIREMENTS FOR THE NEXT GENERATION OF SHARED WINDOW SYSTEMS

J. Chris Lauwers and Keith A. Lantz

Olivetti Research California
2882 Sand Hill Road
Menlo Park, CA 94025
415-496-6200,{lauwers,lantz}@orc.olivetti.com

ABSTRACT

Shared window systems enable existing applications to be shared in the context of a real-time teleconference. The development and successful use of several such systems, albeit within limited user communities, testifies to the merits of the basic idea. However, experience to date has suggested a number of areas that have not been adequately addressed, namely: spontaneous interactions, shared workspace management, floor control, and annotation and telepointing. This paper focuses on the ramifications, for the software designer, of various user requirements in these areas. While the recommendations that result are motivated by the desire to enable continued use of *collaboration-transparent* applications, addressing them involves the development of systems software that is distinctly *collaboration-aware*.

KEYWORDS: computer-supported cooperative work, shared window systems, desktop teleconferencing.

1 INTRODUCTION

Numerous efforts are currently underway to develop computer support for group work. One technology that has commanded particular attention for over 20 years is computer-supported real-time teleconferencing, the ultimate goal of which is to integrate contemporary (non-computer-supported) audio/video teleconferencing technologies with workstation-based network computing environments. The resulting system would enable geographically distributed individuals to collaborate, in real time, using multiple media (in particular, text, graphics, facsimile, audio, and video) and all available computer-based tools, from their respective offices. We refer to such a facility as *desktop teleconferencing*.

The *data conferencing* aspect of desktop teleconferencing requires applications that support multi-user interfaces, so that, for example, two users can collaborate on the writing of a paper, the preparation of a budget, or the debugging of a program. In some cases, the most effective way of accomplishing this is to develop special-purpose (*collaboration-aware*) applications designed for simultaneous use by multiple users (see, for example, [7, 19, 25, 28]). In many cases, however, it would be better if conferees could simply share existing single-user (*collaboration-transparent*) applications. In contemporary window-based environments, this requirement has led to the development of *shared window systems*.

The purpose of a shared window system is to enable existing (window-based) applications to be invoked from within a teleconference. Moreover, each user may participate in any number of teleconferences simultaneously—sharing different subsets of her applications (and associated windows)—as well as retain private access to other applications. These latter features distinguish shared window systems from terminal linking or shared-screen teleconferencing facilities, which require that the user share everything on her screen (refer, in particular, to Engelbart's seminal work on NLS [8]).

One of the first shared window systems, VConf [18], was developed by the authors at Stanford University, based in part on ideas originally proposed by Sarin and Greif at MIT [26] and by Forsdick at BBN [9]. We have since developed a new system, Dialogo, at Olivetti [5]. Numerous similar systems have been developed elsewhere, including Rapport at AT&T Bell Labs [1], SharedX at HP Labs [14], VISEX at MCC [16], Conference Desk at Olivetti-Milan [22], and the latest incarnation of MMConf [1] at BBN [3]. The development and successful use of all of these systems, albeit within limited user communities, is ample testimony to the merits of the basic idea.

---

[1] The original version of MMConf, which helped inspire VConf, was embedded in a specific application (the Diamond multi-media editor) and therefore did not constitute a shared window system as defined herein.

However, experience to date has also suggested a number of areas for improvement. Space limitations prohibit us from giving a comprehensive overview, so this paper focuses on the ramifications, for the software designer, of several perceived user requirements. The reader is referred to two companion papers [20, 21] for more detailed discussion of our current opinions with respect to environmental factors—in particular, the inadequacies of the X Window System as a basis for a shared window system—and structural issues—specifically, the long-running debate over replicated architectures.

This paper, then, will address the following specific issues:

- **spontaneous interactions**: How can a shared window system support spontaneous interactions (as opposed to pre-planned meetings)? For example, how can conference startup overhead be minimized? How can private windows be brought into the conference? How can late-comers be supported?

- **workspace management**: How can a shared window system provide better management of windows associated with a conference? For example, how can it ensure that instances of a shared window are kept consistent, or that the user, if she wishes, can easily distinguish private windows from shared windows or all windows associated with a particular conference?

- **floor control**: How can a shared window system assist in "moderating" a conference? For example, if anyone is to be permitted to "speak" at any time, how might the system assist in recovering from any conflicts that occur? How might it adapt to increases in communications delay or number of participants, where running open floor may not be acceptable?

- **annotation and telepointing**: How can a shared window system support pointing at and annotation of shared objects?

- **performance**: Quite simply, the system must be responsive; in particular, the user should notice no difference from running under the base window system. This is a requirement that spans all other issues and will be dealt with accordingly, that is, in the context of the discussions associated with each of the issues presented above.

As suggested in the phrasing of the above issues, our discussion focuses on *how* to achieve desired behaviors, where what is desired has been determined by evaluation of our own informal observations and the observations, both anecdotal and experimental, of other research groups (e.g. [6, 12, 17, 24, 27]). The discussion is further biased by the intent to limit the impact on existing applications, that is, to continue to support collaboration-transparent applications. An interesting result, however, is that the new "systems software" we are calling for is distinctly collaboration-aware.

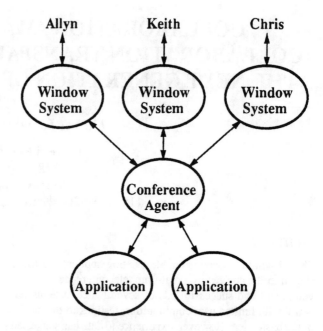

Figure 1: Abstract architecture of a shared window system. Ovals should be interpreted simply as modules, which may or may not be implemented as separate processes or reside in separate address spaces.

The body of the paper is organized as follows. In Section 2 we present a brief overview of shared window systems. This is followed, in order, by a discussion of the issues noted above, specifically, support for spontaneous interactions (Section 3), shared workspace management (Section 4), floor control (Section 5), and annotation and telepointing (Section 6). Section 7 concludes with a summary of our recommendations for designers of the next generation of shared window systems.

2   SHARED WINDOW SYSTEMS: AN OVERVIEW

At the highest level of abstraction, a shared window system consists of a *conference agent* that is interposed between *applications* and the *window system* (see Figure 1). The principal function of the conference agent is to multiplex output streams from applications onto the participants' window systems and demultiplex the input streams from all participants into a single input stream directed at the appropriate application(s). This activity both creates a *shared workspace* wherein each participant sees the same view of every window associated with the shared applications—although the layout of those windows may vary (see Section 4)—and permits each participant to interact, through their local input devices, with shared applications.[2]

In addition to I/O multiplexing, the conference agent is also responsible for:

---

[2]We refer to applications running under a shared window system as "shared applications" even though they have not been modified in any way. Similarly, we refer to the windows associated with those applications as "shared windows."

- **floor control:** Processing user input with respect to whether or not that user is currently authorized to generate input for a particular application or applications. Architecturally, one can think of a floor control module being invoked on every user input. A companion set of mechanisms is needed for changing the floor.

- **workspace management:** Determines the manner in which shared windows are "grouped" within the shared workspace, including window layout. Architecturally, one can think of a workspace management module similar to contemporary window managers.

- **dynamic reconfiguration:** Handling latecomers and the departure of participants prior to termination of the conference. Architecturally, one can think of a reconfiguration module being invoked whenever someone joins or leaves a conference.

- **secretarial functions:** These include conference initialization and termination, pre-staging, and logging. Architecturally, one can think of these functions as being provided by a conference secretary module.

These functions form the core of discussion in the remainder of the paper.

Implementation Strategies

The interposition of conference agent functionality can be achieved in a variety of ways, depending in part on the underlying architecture of both the window system and the operating system. For example, in the context of a server-based window system such as X or NeWS the conference agent can itself be implemented as a server (or collection of servers); it appears to be an application from the viewpoint of the window system and a window system from the viewpoint of the applications. The alternative is to modify either the window system library linked with applications or the window system itself. Indeed, in the case of a kernel-based window system such as SunWindows, at least some of the conference agent functionality must be implemented in the run-time libraries (see, for example, [3]).

A related decision is whether or not to replicate applications. Figure 2(a) presents the canonical centralized architecture, wherein there is one instance of each application and one instance of the conference agent. Figure 2(b), on the other hand, presents the fully replicated architecture, wherein there are as many instances (or replicas) of each application and the conference agent as there are participants in the conference.

Application replication offers two key advantages over the centralized architecture: performance and versatility. On the other hand, it requires that all replicas of the application be synchronized at all times. Consequently, of the shared window systems developed to date, only VConf, Dialogo, and

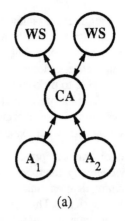

(a)

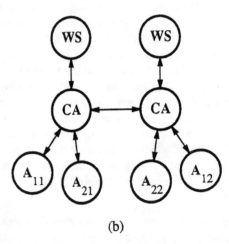

(b)

Figure 2: (a) Canonical centralized architecture. (b) Canonical fully replicated architecture. In both cases, circles should be interpreted as module instances—typically processes in separate address spaces. The use of two subscripts for applications in the replicated architecture indicates that the applications are replicated, with the first subscript identifying the application and the second the replica of that application.

MMConf have adopted a replicated architecture.[3] We will discuss some of the ramifications of application replication in this paper; further details may be found in [2, 3, 18, 20].

3 SUPPORTING SPONTANEOUS INTERACTIONS

Not all group interactions occur in the context of scheduled meetings. In fact, many interactions between collaborators are spontaneous and unplanned. This means that users can not always predict who they will be interacting with, nor can they anticipate which windows need to be shared. For example, consider debugging: "Something went wrong. It's here on my screen now. I'd like you to take a look at it and help me debug it."

Shared window systems need to accommodate these types

---

[3] The Colab project at Xerox PARC also adopted a replicated architecture for their collaboration-aware tools [10, 28].

of interactions. This requires that initiating a conference be a *light-weight* operation, so as not to be a deterrent to spontaneity. In addition, it should be possible for latecomers to join an ongoing conference. Moreover, a shared window system should allow users to pick up private windows and move them onto a different display (to allow co-workers to work on them asynchronously) or to bring private windows into a shared workspace (for synchronous collaboration).[4]

In order to share or transfer private windows, it must be possible to *dynamically* interpose a conference agent in the existing communication link between the application and the window system. This allows the conference agent to intercept and translate subsequent application requests and redirect them to different displays. Although more recent message-based operating systems support facilities for dynamic reconfiguration of communication links—Accent [23], for example, used such a scheme to interpose a debugger between applications and the user—they are not commonly available in commercial Unix systems. If the system does not support such dynamic reconfiguration, users must create all private windows in the context of a conference agent if they want to share or move them later. Once the presence of a conference agent is assumed, the problem of moving private windows reduces to the problem of bringing latecomers into an ongoing conference. The remainder of this section, therefore, will focus on dealing with latecomers.

In order to bring a latecomer into a shared session, shared state needs to be replicated on the newcomer's workstation. In a shared window system, shared state is distributed between the applications, the conference agent, and the window server. Which of these entities need to be brought up to date depends on the system architecture. The centralized architecture only requires the transfer of window server state. As a result of this state transfer, replicas of all shared windows will be created on the newcomer's display. The replicated architecture, on the other hand, also requires the creation of new replicas of the applications and the transfer of application state into these new replicas.

Three basic mechanisms are available for transferring system state:

1. The system can replay to the new replica (application, conference agent, or window server, depending on the architecture) the history of events that led to the current state.[5]

2. The system can upload the shared state from an existing replica and download it directly into the new replica.

3. Process migration techniques can be applied to copy rather than move an existing replica.

Histories

Replaying event histories is the most straightforward approach for bringing latecomers up to date. It works well with both the centralized and the replicated architectures. In a replicated environment, the input event stream to applications is logged and replayed to newly created application replicas. Window system state is updated automatically by the applications in response to the input events. In a centralized environment, on the other hand, output requests are logged and replayed to the window system on the latecomer's workstation.

Although this approach is straightforward, it suffers from three significant drawbacks. First, it simply may not be possible to replay the log accurately. If any event depends on state external to the window system, and that state differs at the time of the replay from the time the event originally took place, then replay may lead to different results. Second, histories may require a lot of disk space, especially in a centralized environment, since output traffic is typically an order of magnitude larger than input traffic. Third, replaying the log of events is a time consuming process that could disrupt the ongoing conference.

Direct State Transfer

A faster way to bring latecomers up to date consists of directly downloading the entire shared state vector into new replicas. This requires, however, that the entity being replicated support mechanisms for uploading and downloading state information. Unfortunately, most existing applications do not support such mechanisms, so this approach is not feasible in a replicated environment (where application state needs to be replicated).

In a centralized environment, where application state need not be replicated, this approach requires window system state to be transferred from one window server into another. Ideally, the relevant state would be represented in a single state vector and expressed in a device-independent way, so that the shared state vector could simply be passed along to the appropriate window server without interpretation by the conference agent. Regrettably, existing window servers neither store state in an appropriate manner nor provide the requisite query and set facilities.

Therefore, to implement direct state transfer with existing window systems, conference agents need to maintain redundant copies of shared window system state so that a latecomer can be brought up to date by *projecting* the conference agent's state vector onto the latecomer's window server.[6]

---

[4] Our discussion is focused on making the state S' associated with person B consistent with the state S associated with person A. It ignores the utility of and mechanisms required for B to see everything that happened to reach state S in the first place.

[5] This is analogous to log-based recovery in database management systems.

[6] This is the approach taken by SharedX. In fact, SharedX is a complete X11 server implemented on top of itself: the low-level graphics routines are implemented using X11 library routines. SharedX, therefore, is referred to as a *nested server*.

This approach, however, is troublesome for performance and efficiency reasons.

Process Migration

Since direct state transfer is not possible in a replicated environment, an alternative approach consists of extending process migration facilities to allow shared applications to be duplicated on latecomers' workstation. Such facilities, however, are extremely complex. The main difficulties arise from the need to rebind connections to external services (like connections to the conference agent, file descriptors, etc.) to corresponding services on the workstation of the new replica. Moreover, shared files need to be replicated on the new workstation. Although most of these problems have been addressed in the context of message-based distributed operating systems (see, for example, [29, 30]), it is unlikely that these facilities will become widespread in the near future.

Summary

In summary, this discussion suggests two clear guidelines for supporting spontaneous interactions in the near term:

1. It seems unlikely that without additional operating system support, the replicated architecture can provide *light-weight* mechanisms for supporting spontaneous interactions. When there is a pressing need to support such interactions, a more centralized architecture—possibly a hybrid architecture as suggested in [18]—needs to be adopted. Specifically, applications introduced into an ongoing conference should be grafted onto an existing instance of a conference agent, and latecomers should share an existing instance of a conference agent and each application.

2. Existing window systems do not provide adequate mechanisms for uploading and downloading the state vector associated with client connections. As a result, too much window system state and functionality must be duplicated in the conference agent. This is inefficient and expensive. Steps should be taken to organize state in a more effective manner and to provide associated set and query operations.

In the long term, we believe that even these steps are inadequate, indeed, that providing the most effective support for spontaneous interactions requires the implementation of conference agent functionality within the base window system.

4   WORKSPACE MANAGEMENT

One architectural component of shared window systems that has received relatively little attention so far is workspace management. Workspace managers are very much like window managers, since they control the layout and size of a user's windows. Traditional window managers, however, are inadequate in a shared window system environment where both shared and private windows need to be managed. As demonstrated later in this section, achieving acceptable behavior typically requires that all instances of a shared window have identical size. Workspace managers, therefore, need to coordinate between themselves to guarantee consistent sizes of shared windows. Moreover, additional functionality may be necessary that does not apply to traditional single-user environments and that cannot be provided by existing window managers. For example, a shared workspace manager should allow conferees to distinguish:

- shared windows from private windows,

- all windows associated with a given conference, and

- which of several conferences a window is associated with.

These facilities can consist of simple visual cues to identify shared windows (for example, use different colors for window borders), or mechanisms for bringing all windows of a session to the top. Alternatively, shared workspace managers can provide mechanisms to organize shared windows into shared workspaces, separate from each user's private workspace.

Very few shared window systems built to date have addressed these issues. In SharedX, for example, shared workspace management functionality is subsumed by each participant's private window manager. Since existing window managers don't distinguish between shared and private windows, collaborators can freely mix shared and private windows on their display. No mechanisms are provided to identify shared windows. Moreover, collaborators can move and resize shared windows independently of other participants. Unfortunately, rather awkward displays may result when users privately resize shared windows. The Emacs text editor, for example, keeps a command-input line at the bottom of its window. This line (as well as part of the displayed text) may be clipped if a collaborator privately reduces the size of her Emacs window.

In a replicated environment, the use of private window managers can lead not only to appearance problems, but to incorrect operation due to inconsistencies in application state. Consider again the Emacs text editor. Emacs keeps track of the size of the window that it displays its buffers in. This information is used, for example, to determine how many lines to scroll when going to the next page in the document. If different participants use different sizes for shared Emacs windows, they lose mutual consistency of their displays after scrolling one page. MMConf solves this problem by broadcasting notifications of changes in window size to all application peers.

A radical way to distinguish private from shared windows is to employ grouping facilities similar to Rooms [15]. In this approach, a separate workspace is created for each shared session—in X11, for example, by creating a pseudo-root window. All shared windows are organized within this workspace. Both Dialogo and Rapport currently take this *conference room* approach.

The question here is to what extent does the system allow users to lay out windows in the shared workspace independently from other participants. Dialogo implements strict WYSIWIS (What You See Is What I See [27]): all participants have identical layouts of the shared workspace. Considerable opinion supports this approach: WYSIWIS workspaces can make a conference more effective by providing a common frame of reference to conference participants. This is important, for example, when trying to use telepointing facilities (like those described in Section 6) that span the entire shared workspace.

Strict WYSIWIS in Dialogo is guaranteed by delegating control over the shared workspace to a separate window manager that runs as a shared application within the workspace. In theory, this approach solves the consistency and presentation problems that arise when private window managers control shared windows. In practice, however, resolving all the synchronization problems involved has proven exceedingly difficult [20]. Moreover, the WYSIWIS approach has one important limitation from a user's point of view: As a result of sharing a single conference window manager, concurrent operation within the shared workspace is not possible; that is, it is impossible for different collaborators to work on different conference applications at the same time. This is a direct consequence of the fact that there exists only one *input focus* per conference (maintained by the conference window manager and shared by all collaborators). This limitation is not present in systems like SharedX, MMConf and Conference Desk, which do not adopt the WYSIWIS approach, but those systems in turn do not provide the visual advantages of a conference room metaphor.

It appears, then, that none of the approaches implemented to date are sufficient and that addressing their limitations requires the development of new collaboration-aware window managers. This would allow each window manager to coordinate with other window managers in its conference to guarantee consistent sizing of shared windows. Moreover, it would allow window managers to provide visual cues to distinguish shared from private windows, and to perform stacking operations on all windows in the same session. Finally, in the context of conference rooms, collaboration-aware window managers could better support concurrent activities—for example, by providing a separate input focus for each participant and a separate conference floor for each conference application.

Thus, we again see a need to introduce conferencing functionality into the base window system, in this case the window manager. Unfortunately, existing standards for communication between applications and window managers do not support the necessary mechanisms. Changing these standards to accommodate window sharing may require existing applications to be changed also in order to conform to the new standards.

5 FLOOR CONTROL

One of the issues raised in the preceding discussion of workspace management was that of permitting different participants to interact with different shared applications at the same time. This is one manifestation of the general problem of *floor control*: who can communicate, with whom (or what), when, and how? In a true multi-media conference, it is possible to distinguish a separate floor for each medium. In this section, however, we address audio and video only in the context of how they can assist us in managing access to the shared workspace.

Floor control is an extremely contentious area of debate, with policies ranging from permitting only one person at a time to control the entire shared workspace, to running "open floor" with anyone generating input at any time to any window. These policies can be characterized along three dimensions:

1. the number of floors—one for the entire conference, one per shared application, or one per window;

2. the number of people who can "hold" a floor at the same time; and

3. how the floor is passed (or handed off) between floor holders. This includes the potential use of auxiliary communication channels, specifically audio.

The arguments over the first two dimensions amount to arguments over the amount of concurrent activity to be permitted. Separate floors correspond to sub-conferences and number of holders per floor corresponds to how the meeting is being run ("floor control" in its most restricted sense). Concurrency was touched on briefly in Section 4. The reader is left to imagine further arguments for or against concurrency, using his or her own experience in meetings (face-to-face or teleconferences) as a guide.

With respect to how the floor is passed, this is where technology can clearly be used to improve upon traditional social protocols. For example, the system can maintain lists of people who have asked for the floor, and can optionally introduce hysteresis by selecting from this list at random rather than from the head of the queue. Or, when the basic algorithm is preemptive—the requester gets the floor on demand—the system can ensure that a request for the floor is not granted unless the current floor holder has been inactive for some (tunable) delta [11].

All arguments considered, the only certainty is that no one policy will suffice for all groups, in all situations. For example, one geographically distributed team of programmers using SharedX has reported the need to alternate between open floor when "brainstorming" to one-person-at-a-time when wanting to make sure a particular piece of code is coded correctly [13]. In general, running open floor becomes increasingly difficult as the number of participants increases, as anyone who has participated in a large meeting (especially a multi-party audio conference) can attest.

Moreover, experience indicates that even a shared window system tailored to a particular group's behavior will require different mechanisms (and policies) depending on the operating environment in which a conference takes place. In particular, running open floor becomes increasingly difficult as communications delay increases. Anyone who has engaged in a telephone conversation over a satellite link can appreciate the types of conflicts that arise.

Finally, the availability of audio and video links may significantly influence the floor control mechanisms required in the conference agent. In particular, if a high-quality audio link is available, and is synchronized with the data channel, there may not be a need for rigid floor handoff policies, since conference participants can use traditional social protocols over the audio link to negotiate access to the shared workspace. Indeed, rigid floor control mechanisms might even obstruct these negotiations. However, as suggested in our allusions to satellite communications and multi-party audio conferences, access to the audio link can itself be a problem—the solution to which may well be mechanisms in the conference agent.

What, then, would the ideal shared window system provide by way of mechanisms? In a nutshell, support for a broad range of policies indicated above, in an architecture capable of switching between different policies depending on user preferences and operating environment. Moreover, in support of running open floor, the ideal system would provide mechanisms to enable recovery from conflicting input—that is, to prevent or compensate for data corruption resulting from simultaneous input. [7] Given that people running open floor are already prepared to account for some conflicts and to prevent them from occurring via social protocols, these mechanisms should almost certainly be *optimistic*—there to recover from the presumably rare conflicts that do occur rather than to limit availability (hence response) by preventing conflicts from occurring [4]. It remains for further research to determine the details of how all these mechanisms can be incorporated in a coherent fashion, and without modifying existing applications.

6 ANNOTATION AND TELEPOINTING

In a real-time conference, the ability to point at shared objects on the display can greatly enhance communication between conference participants. It allows users to make references like "let's move this there". Most shared window systems (including Dialogo, SharedX, MMConf, and Rapport) include a *telepointing* facility that displays an arrow-shaped pointer in the shared workspace. Conference participants can grab this pointer and move it around the shared workspace to direct attention to specific objects. Equally

valuable is the ability to make graphical annotations, for example, to say (and draw): "I think it should look like this ..." This simulates real-life presentations where overlays are used to annotate presented materials.

Telepointing and annotation facilities are most easily implemented if the underlying window system supports transparent windows. In that case, the annotation and telepointing tools can create transparent windows on top of existing windows, and use these transparent windows as their drawing canvases.[8] Unfortunately, no existing window system supports transparent windows.

Without transparent windows, it is still possible to implement a telepointing facility. In Dialogo, for example, the telepointing application draws its pointer directly in the shared conference windows (by XORing). Telepointing is achieved by repeatedly erasing the pointer and redrawing it in its new position as it tracks the controlling user's mouse movements. However, this method can result in incorrect displays if the window being XORed is associated with an application that is simultaneously generating output to that window.

7 CONCLUSIONS

We have discussed a set of user requirements that require attention in order for shared window systems to mature and become more widely used. Rather than offering an experimental evaluation of how different approaches to each requirement measure up in actual use, we have focused on the tradeoffs involved in implementing those approaches that have been deemed "reasonable" by the community at large. The following is a summary of our recommendations:

- If spontaneous interactions are to be supported, a fully replicated architecture is impractical in the short term. Rather, an application introduced into an ongoing conference should be grafted onto an existing instance of a conference agent, and latecomers should share an existing instance of a conference and each application. Moreover, steps should be taken to organize application state internal to the window system in a more effective manner and to provide associated "global" set and query operations.

- Window managers (and the conventions to communicate with them) need to be extended to support shared windows. This would enable experimentation with new strategies for managing shared workspaces, including the use of visual cues to distinguish shared windows from private windows and implementation of conference rooms whose layout can vary with the participant.

- Conference agents should support a range of floor control strategies and be able to switch between them depending on other communication channels available,

---

[7] This problem does not exist for true audio/video teleconferencing.

[8] These tools can be built as simple single-user applications, since the shared window system allows them to be shared like any other existing application.

user preferences, and operating environments. It is not sufficient, particularly in high-delay environments, to rely exclusively on social protocols. On the other hand, certain floor handoff policies are not acceptable in many environments.

- Window systems may need to support features that are of little use in single-user environments but are extremely valuable in a collaborative setting. One example is transparent windows, which enable efficient implementation of annotation and telepointing facilities.

- Finally, and related to all the previous requirements, many problems could be avoided or more easily solved if conferencing functionality were implemented directly in the underlying window system. This is only practical, however, if the necessary modifications become part of the "standard" distribution.

In closing we observe that while these recommendations are motivated by the desire to make shared window systems more convenient to use—and therefore to promote continued use of collaboration-transparent applications—addressing them involves the development of systems software that is distinctly collaboration-aware.

ACKNOWLEDGMENTS

Tommy Joseph and Allyn Romanow have contributed greatly to the Dialogo effort. They, along with Terry Crowley, Phil Gust, and John Patterson have also influenced many of the ideas presented in this paper. Barbara Fredrickson provided much useful input from the "human factors" perspective. Finally, thanks to the User Interface Task Force of the Internet Activities Board for the engaging discussions that contributed to the observations in Section 5.

REFERENCES

[1] S.R. Ahuja, J.R. Ensor, D.N. Horn, and S.E. Lucco. The Rapport multimedia conferencing system: A software overview. In *Proc. 2nd IEEE Conference on Computer Workstations*, pages 52–58. IEEE, March 1988.

[2] S.R. Ahuja, J.R. Ensor, and S.E. Lucco. A comparison of application sharing mechanisms in real-time desktop conferencing systems. Technical report, AT&T Bell Labs. Submitted for publication.

[3] T. Crowley and H. Forsdick. MMConf: The Diamond multimedia conferencing system. In *Proc. Groupware Technology Workshop*. IFIP Working Group 8.4, August 1989.

[4] S.B. Davidson. Optimism and consistency in partitioned distributed database systems. *ACM Transactions on Database Systems*, 9(3):456–481, September 1984.

[5] Desktop Teleconferencing Group. Dialogo: A replicated shared window system. Technical report, Olivetti Research California, in preparation.

[6] C. Egido. Videoconferencing as a technology to support group work: A review of its failure. In *Proc. CSCW 88 Conference on Computer-Supported Cooperative Work*, pages 13–24. ACM, September 1988.

[7] C. Ellis, S.J. Gibbs, and G.L. Rein. Design and use of a group editor. In *Proc. Working Conference on Engineering for Human-Computer Interaction*. IFIP Working Group 2.7, August 1989.

[8] D.C. Engelbart. NLS teleconferencing features: The Journal, and shared-screen telephoning. In *Proc. Fall COMPCON*, pages 173–176. IEEE, September 1975.

[9] H.C. Forsdick. Explorations in real-time multimedia conferencing. In *Proc. 2nd International Symposium on Computer Message Systems*, pages 299–315. IFIP, September 1985.

[10] G. Foster. *Collaborative Systems and Multi-User Interfaces*. PhD thesis, University of California - Berkeley, 1986.

[11] J.J. Garcia Luna Aceves, E.J. Craighill, and R. Lang. Floor management and control for multimedia computer conferecning. In *Proc. Multimedia '89: 2nd International Workshop on Multimedia Communications*. IEEE Communications Society, April 1989.

[12] J. Grudin. Why CSCW applications fail: Problems in the design and evaluation of organizational interfaces. In *Proc. CSCW 88 Conference on Computer-Supported Cooperative Work*, pages 85–93. ACM, September 1988.

[13] P. Gust. Personal communication. February 1989.

[14] P. Gust. SharedX: X in a distributed group work environment. Presentation at the 2nd Annual X Conference, MIT, January 1988.

[15] D.A. Henderson Jr. and S.K. Card. Rooms: The use of multiple virtual workspaces to reduce space contention in a window-based graphical user interface. *ACM Transactions on Graphics*, 5(3):211–243, July 1986.

[16] B. Janssen. Personal communication. February 1988.

[17] R. Kraut and C. Egido. Patterns of contact and communication in scientific research collaboration. In *Proc. CSCW 88 Conference on Computer-Supported Cooperative Work*, pages 1–12. ACM, September 1988.

[18] K.A. Lantz. An experiment in integrated multimedia conferencing. In *Proc. CSCW 86 Conference on*

Computer-Supported Cooperative Work, pages 267–275. MCC Software Technology Program, December 1986. Reprinted in I. Greif (editor), *Computer-Supported Cooperative Work: A Book of Readings*, pages 533-552. Morgan Kaufmann Publishers, 1988.

[19] K.A. Lantz, J.C. Lauwers, B. Arons, C. Binding, P. Chen, J. Donahue, T.A. Joseph, R. Koo, A. Romanow, C. Schmandt, and W. Yamamoto. Collaboration technology research at Olivetti Research Center. In *Proc. Groupware Technology Workshop*. IFIP Working Group 8.4, August 1989.

[20] J.C. Lauwers, T. Joseph, K.A. Lantz, and A. Romanow. Replicated architectures for shared window systems: A critique. Technical report, Olivetti Research California. Submitted for publication.

[21] J.C. Lauwers and K.A. Lantz. Desktop teleconferencing and existing window systems: A poor match. Technical report, Olivetti Research California, in preparation.

[22] S. Piccardi and F. Tisato. Conference Desk: An experiment and model for application sharing. Technical report, Systems Software Laboratory, Direzione Olivetti Ricerca - Milan, January 1989.

[23] R.F. Rashid and G.G. Robertson. Accent: A communication oriented network operating system kernel. In *Proc. 8th Symposium on Operating Systems Principles*, pages 64–75. ACM, December 1981. Proceedings published as *Operating Systems Review* 15(5).

[24] R.W. Root. Design of a multi-media vehicle for social browsing. In *Proc. CSCW 88 Conference on Computer-Supported Cooperative Work*, pages 25–38. ACM, September 1988.

[25] S.K. Sarin and I. Greif. Software for interactive on-line conferences. In *Proc. 2nd Conference on Office Information Systems*, pages 46–58. ACM, June 1984.

[26] S.K. Sarin and I. Greif. Computer-based real-time conferencing systems. *Computer*, 18(10):33–45, October 1985. Reprinted in I. Greif (editor), *Computer-Supported Cooperative Work: A Book of Readings*, pages 397-420. Morgan Kaufmann Publishers, 1988.

[27] M. Stefik, D.G. Bobrow, G. Foster, S. Lanning, and D. Tatar. WYSIWIS revised: Early experiences with multiuser interfaces. *ACM Transactions on Office Information Systems*, 5(2):147–167, April 1987. Presented at the CSCW'86 Conference on Computer-Supported Cooperative Work, December 1986.

[28] M. Stefik, G. Foster, D.G. Bobrow, K. Kahn, S. Lanning, and L. Suchman. Beyond the chalkboard: Computer support for collaboration and problem solving in meetings. *Communications of the ACM*, 30(1):32–47, January 1987. Reprinted in I. Greif (editor), *Computer-Supported Cooperative Work: A Book of Readings*, pages 335-366. Morgan Kaufmann Publishers, 1988.

[29] M.M. Theimer. *Preemptable Remote Execution Facilities for Loosely-coupled Distributed Systems*. PhD thesis, Stanford University, 1986.

[30] M.M. Theimer, K.A. Lantz, and D.R. Cheriton. Preemptable remote execution facilities for the V-System. In *Proc. 10th Symposium on Operating Systems Principles*, pages 2–12. ACM, December 1985. Proceedings published as *Operating Systems Review* 19(5).

Languages for the Construction of Multi-User Multi-Media Synchronous (MUMMS) Applications

Ralph D. Hill

9.1 Introduction

At Bellcore we are studying the design, construction, and use of MUMMS interfaces—user interfaces that allow multiple users to simultaneously interact with a single instance of an application from multiple workstations using multiple media. Our group has focused on the problems of constructing MUMMS interfaces and has developed the RENDEZVOUS language for MUMMS interface construction. The RENDEZVOUS language is based on Common Lisp. We have extended Common Lisp with our own object system, light-weight processes, non-blocking message passing, a declarative graphics system, and a fast, multi-way constraint maintenance system. This chapter describes the design rationale behind the RENDEZVOUS language and explains how the features in this language meet the needs of programmers building MUMMS interfaces.

Reprinted from B.A. Myers (Ed.), *Languages for Developing User Interfaces*, pp. 125-143. © 1992, Boston: Jones & Bartlett Publishers. Reprinted by permission.

9.2 Background

Multi-User Multi-Media Synchronous (MUMMS) interfaces are user interfaces that allow multiple users working from multiple workstations to simultaneously interact with the same instance of the same application [Patterson 90]. This interaction may use multiple media, such as text, graphics, audio, and video, for both input and output. We are studying the design, implementation, and use of MUMMS applications, so that we can provide advice on when, where, and how to use MUMMS technology. In addition, we hope to provide both interface design guidelines and tools to help implement the designs.

We are focusing on MUMMS applications because, like Dertouzos in Chapter 2, we believe that the next steps in the evolution of computer-based tools will both help spatially separated people work and play together, and increase the richness of input and output modalities. Traditional user interface design and construction are tasks well-known for their difficulty. By choosing the MUMMS focus we make our task even more difficult.

Most of our effort to date has gone into the design and construction of the RENDEZVOUS programming language [Hill 91]. This is a language specifically designed for the implementation of MUMMS interfaces. Our goal is to produce a language and supporting tools that can be used by programmers to implement MUMMS applications of commercial size and complexity. To date, we have built two non-trivial interfaces with RENDEZVOUS, and have a third under active development.

One application that we have built with RENDEZVOUS is a multi-user CardTable. This application allows up to four people to interact with a deck of cards on a card table. Figure 9.1 shows Ralph's view of a two-person blackjack game. Louis, the other player, sees a different interpretation of the same information. In Louis's view, the card table and the cards on it (but not the command buttons in the corners) are rotated so that Louis's hand is at the bottom. Also, in Louis's view, the card in Louis's hand is face up, while the card in Ralph's hand is face down.

Users can interact with the cards via both direct manipulations that are initiated by pointing to a card and clicking the appropriate mouse button, and indirect manipulations that are initiated by clicking on a command button and then pointing to the cards to act on. The supported operations

9.3 The Importance of Language Structures

While we believe that direct manipulation interface builders, as proposed in Chapters 2 and 3, can and should hide much of the complexity of programming languages from interface implementors, they cannot completely hide the programming model. Basic programming model properties, such as whether it is object-oriented, and whether objects are processes, will show through the direct manipulation interface builder to the person who is trying to build an interface. These properties (and lower-level language properties as well) will become apparent when debugging, linking in the application, or when it is necessary to manually program interface features that the direct manipulation interface builder does not support.

Further, we claim, and state as a goal, that there should be a range of programming languages, from a powerful but detailed language used by programmers to build fundamental widgets, to an easily used (but restrictive) direct manipulation interface builder that can be used by non-programming interface design experts. In order to facilitate migration of personnel and experience among languages within this range, the languages should have some commonality in their underlying model.

Because the programming model will, at some level, become apparent to the people building and maintaining interfaces, and the model will be shared by a number of languages, we believe it is important to begin by designing a model that is well-adapted to the task to be performed. We claim (without proof) that, in practice, we can derive a well adapted model by minimizing the mental effort the interface implementors must go through when translating from a user's view of the interface to a programmer's view of the implementation of the interface. This measure varies with programmers, their experience, and the task. The technique for computing the measure will vary with the level of the language. Despite these sources of variability, this measure is something that can be (at least informally) measured, and should be minimized.

In order to begin designing a programming model, we must first understand the tasks involved in interface implementation. Since our interest is in MUMMS interfaces we will concentrate on the tasks we believe are needed to construct MUMMS interfaces.

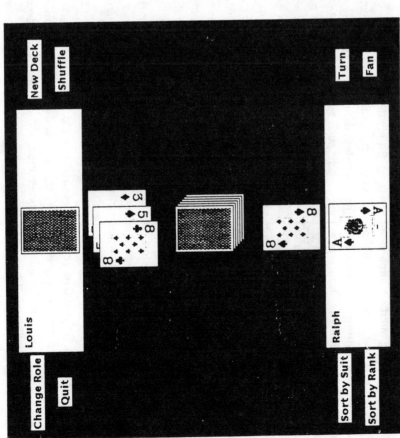

Figure 9.1: Multi-user CardTable implemented in RENDEZVOUS.

include shuffling, dealing, flipping and turning cards, gathering cards into piles, and moving cards into and out of hands. Currently the only media used in this interface are 2.5-D color graphics for output and mouse for input. The CardTable is already a compelling example of a multi-user synchronous application. We plan to add audio and video extensions that will make it a compelling multi-media example as well.

inheritance using mix-in classes [Stefik 86] is a powerful technique for constructing graphical interactive objects. Mix-ins are a programming discipline for using multiple inheritance. When using mix-ins, there are two basic types of classes: the base classes and the mix-in classes. Instances of the base classes are complete objects in themselves. Instances of mix-ins classes would not be complete objects—the mix-ins are intended to be added to the base classes to customize or specialize them. To create specialized classes, a programmer creates a class that is a subclass of a base class and one or more mix-in classes. This new class has the properties of the base class and the mix-ins.

Using a paint store analogy, the base classes are like tinting base—it is paint and can be used as paint, but it is bland. The pigments are the mix-ins. Pigments are added to the tinting base to create the many hundreds of colors most paint stores advertise. By themselves, the pigments, like mix-in classes, have little practical use.

Multiple inheritance and mix-ins allow the construction of a basic class hierarchy of graphical classes that can then be customized by mixing in specialized behavior classes or classes that customize graphical appearance. Using this approach, it is possible to have a small and easily developed set of base classes and mix-ins that can be used to create a very large number of customized classes. Again, consider the paint store analogy. A paint store can offer hundreds of colors, in each several qualities and types (exterior vs. interior, gloss vs. matte) of paint, for a total of thousands of combinations. This is all from a small stock of tinting bases and pigments. A well designed set of base classes, mix-ins, and composition techniques can give similar flexibility to a user interface construction environment.

In addition to multiple inheritance, the object system must have features to support the description of important properties of graphical interactive objects that may not be found in other objects. For example, graphical objects are often arranged in hierarchies. The substructure of an instance of a class (its child objects) should be considered part of the class's definition, and be inherited like other class attributes (Myers also advocates this in Chapter 10). Also, there must be mechanisms for describing: their abstract relation to

9.4   MUMMS User Interface Implementation

MUMMS interface implementation is very different from many traditional programming tasks such as sorting, merging, and numerical computations. The behavior of many traditional programs can be described in terms of some number of input and output files, and the computations that must be performed on the input to get the output.

On the other hand, MUMMS interfaces are likely to be described in terms of the objects visible to the user (e.g., cards, hands, and control buttons in the CardTable), their appearances (e.g., color, size, position, and shape), and the manipulations the user is allowed to perform on them (e.g., click left mouse button to drag).

The interface implementation must display these visible objects to the users, wait for input from any of the users directed at any of the objects, and react to the input. The reaction may include updating all users' displays, and maintaining relationships among objects, such as keeping several objects attached as one of them is dragged, so that the whole group is moved. Internally, the basic actions of MUMMS interfaces are: *display* objects, *maintain* relations among objects, and *react* to user input. This is very different from the read–compute–write cycle that is common in many forms of programming.

Since user interfaces are often designed and implemented using an iterative approach, it is important that the interface implementor be able to quickly and easily change an interface implementation and see the effects of the change on the running interface. Ideally, changes that are small changes in appearance or behavior should be small changes in the implementation.

This brief discussion (and a lot of experience) leads to the list of required features presented below. Each feature is marked as being a *basic* language requirement, or supporting *display* of objects, *maintenance* of state, or *reaction* to user input.

Object Orientation (basic). Most user interfaces can be easily described in terms of objects (such as the cards and hands of the CardTable). Thus, we consider object orientation, with all the features described in Chapter 7, to be a requirement.

One of these features, multiple inheritance, is particularly important, but is often considered difficult to use. We have found that multiple

other objects (e.g., part-of), their appearance (and how it changes over time), and their interactive behavior. Language features that address these requirements are presented below.

Objects as Processes (reaction). The objects on the display must be able to respond to a user independent of the other currently active objects and users. This requires multiple processes and some way of scheduling them so that all users are given equal access to the processor and receive rapid feedback in response to their input. Making each object a process is a conceptually simple approach that can be implemented without distorting the object-oriented programming model. This greatly simplifies the implementation of the behavior of the objects. This approach requires a very lightweight process mechanism as there may be thousands of objects. Scheduling is also an important issue—resources must be fairly allocated, without impeding responsiveness.

Interprocess Communication (reaction). Since we assume that objects are processes, inter-object communication is also interprocess communication. Thus, it is important that there be an interprocess communication mechanism that is easy to use, and, as far as possible, protects the programmer from races, dead-locks, and other concurrency problems. In particular, although user interface implementors will be writing concurrent programs, we do not want to require them to have a deep understanding of concurrency issues.

Event-Based Input (reaction). The input mechanisms of traditional programming languages, such as blocking reads, are not appropriate in an environment where input may come from any of a number of users and input devices, as well as the application program, at any time. The 'select' system call in the UNIX operating system makes it possible to implement non-blocking reads from multiple sources, but it is far too inconvenient to use. An event-driven mechanism, with a language that makes it easy to build event-handlers, would be far better (e.g., [Hill 86, Green 86]).

Declarative Output (display). The programmer should never have to call a drawing primitive, such as draw-line, directly. Instead, the graphics system should detect changes to the descriptions of objects (say, changes to the value of the color slot or position slot of a line, in addition to the creation and destruction of objects), and automatically and efficiently update the display. This automatic display update must include redrawing any other objects that must be redrawn to keep the display consistent. For example, when an object moves, any objects that were obscured by the moved object at its old position must be redrawn.

Given a declarative output system like this, the programmer only has to describe the display that is wanted. There is no need to determine how to draw it—that is the job of the declarative graphics system.

Declarative output should be supported for other media as well—see Section 9.4.1 below.

Constraint Maintenance (maintenance). Interactive programs do not read input and compute outputs. Most of their effort goes into maintaining state. For example, they keep the display consistent with underlying data and maintain relative sizes and positions in screen layouts. Hence, user interface construction would be better supported by programming constructs that support maintenance of state consistency than the traditional language constructs that are designed to support branching, looping, and data manipulation. We believe that a constraint maintenance system should be considered an essential element of any language for user interface construction.

Our experience suggests that the constraint system must support (at least) these features: multi-way constraints, indirect references (such as the pointer variables of Chapter 12), structural constraints (or some variation thereon, see Chapter 12), and temporal constraints [Duisberg 88]. (Chapter 11 proposes a constraint system with similar capabilities, but employing a different model.)

The more restrictive the constraint solver, the more likely it is that the programmers will have to be careful to avoid exceeding the limits of the constraint solver. Our experience, and that of the developers of DeltaBlue, suggest that a multi-way constraint maintainer can be just as fast as a one-way constraint maintainer. Thus, a multi-way constraint maintenance system should be supported.

Some simple real-time clock support will be needed to trigger help and advice systems. This might be needed, for example, to prompt the user with advice when he or she pauses for some minimum amount of time in the middle of an action that is normally one continuous action (see also Chapter 8).

Libraries and Component Reuse (basic). It must be easy to construct and use parameterized interface components. Normally, this is a consequence of using a good object-oriented language. When the language is extended with constraints and other features listed above, it is important to ensure that ease of code reuse is not sacrificed. This implies (among other things) thinking carefully about how to inherit, and override inheritance of, constraints, event-handlers, and process control mechanisms.

Assistance Dealing with Large Numbers of Parameters (basic). Relatively general and easily reused classes of graphical interactive objects tend to have large numbers of slots (easily 30 or more) and a similarly large number of parameters to their creation methods. The language should support some mechanism for providing default values for parameters, and making it easy to specify only some of the parameters (using the defaults for the others). Common Lisp [Steele 90] provides a mechanism for doing this in the form of keyword parameters. This mechanism allows parameters to be given as parameter-name, parameter-value pairs. Any parameter not explicitly named and given a value gets its default value. This makes simple things easy and complex things just a bit harder. For example, to create a circle of default size, color, position, etc., you need only say '(create 'Circle)'. Creating a circle of specific size and color requires a slightly more complex expression: '(create 'Circle :radius 6 :fillColor "blue")'.

Rapid Prototyping (basic). Since interfaces are often designed and built by iterative refinement, the programming environment must support rapid program refinement (see Chapter 7). This implies support for dynamic loading, and an interpreter or very fast compiler (see also Chapter 8). We also believe that automatic storage management (i.e., garbage collection) simplifies rapid prototyping by reducing the

Indirect references are very important when using constraints to link objects. Indirect references in constraints allow the variable that is set by the constraint, or the variables that the constraint depends on, to be determined by pointers to objects. For example, an object, **A**, may have a slot, **p**, whose value is a pointer to another object. **A** could arrange to always be the same color as the object pointed to by **p** by installing a constraint that sets the color of **A** to be the color of the object pointed to by **p**. The constraint system ensures that whenever the value of **p** changes, or the color of the object pointed to by **p** changes, the color slot of **A** is updated. This relation could also be reversed—if **A** is a color selection object, and **p** points to an object the user is picking a color for, a constraint can be installed that sets the color of the object pointed to by **p** to the color of **A**.

Along with indirect references in constraints, structural constraints are an important aid in maintaining structural consistency (e.g., keeping the user interface data structures consistent with the application data structures, see Chapter 21). The structure of the data is an aspect of state, just as the values are. Thus, just as constraints are used to maintain value consistency, constraints should be used to maintain structural consistency.

As we get more experience with animations and temporal media like sound and video, we are beginning to make use of temporal constraints. Temporal constraints are much like ordinary constraints, but they depend on the current value of real-time. In the case of animations, they can be used to establish a relationship between time and the position of an object on a display. This naturally leads to rates of motion that are unaffected by system performance. Using temporal constraints to drive animations is natural and easy.

Real-Time Requirements (basic, reaction). As a general user interface quality requirement, it must be possible to predict approximate response times and guarantee response within a certain time. The requirements, and the consequences of failure to meet them, are not as severe as for true real-time programming, so we hope that the elaborate techniques used in modern real-time languages are not needed. If possible, we would like to avoid adding this complexity.

programmers' burden. The alternatives—forcing the programmer to manually manage storage or letting the garbage accumulate—put too much load on the programmer or the hardware.

9.4.1   Emerging Problem Areas

While we have been able to derive the list of requirements presented above, we know this list is not complete. We have learned that the following are problem areas to be considered, but we are not yet able to map them into a set of requirements. We expect to encounter other problem areas as time goes on.

Synchronization of Media. When building multi-media interfaces it is important to synchronize multiple media sources. For example, in video games, it is important to synchronize the presentation of a sound effect with its corresponding video effect. We fear it may be impossible to achieve the tight synchronization required using common workstation software such as UNIX and the X Window system [Scheifler 88]. The UNIX scheduler and the unpredictable performance of X make it hard to know when a request to draw an image on the display will be honored. Similarly, any audio server in a UNIX environment would likely have unpredictable latency. This will be a common problem for virtual reality interfaces.

Declarative Specification of Non-Graphical or Mixed Media. Just as it is important to have declarative specification of graphics, declarative specifications of other media, such as audio and video, should be supported. Since we do not yet have experience attempting declarative specification of temporal media, other than animation of structured graphics, we do not know what the exact implications of this will be.

9.5   The RENDEZVOUS Programming Model

The RENDEZVOUS programming model has been derived by iteratively refining and extending it, while actively building interfaces. We are confident that it is a solution to the problems we have encountered. This does not imply that it is a good solution to all user interface construction problems.

The model continues to evolve as we (and our clients) try to build new and different interfaces and discover new problems.

The current RENDEZVOUS programming model is based on an object system that is extended with:

- a simple 2.5-D declarative graphics system,

- a fast multi-way constraint mechanism with the additional features listed above,

- a lightweight process mechanism that allows each object to be a separate process,

- a non-blocking message passing mechanism, and

- a simple language for handling incoming events.

All these features have been smoothly integrated so, for example, constraints and event-handlers are inherited like slots and methods. As a result of this smooth integration elaborate RENDEZVOUS classes are easily parameterized and reused.

To help control the complexity of dealing with large numbers of objects, and to allow some optimizations, the RENDEZVOUS run-time architecture requires that the graphical objects in an interface be arranged (by the programmer) into an explicit tree which represents a part-of hierarchy, and implies a stacking order for overlapping objects on the display. If there really are no part-of relationships to represent, the tree can be broad and flat. But, in practice, we have found that often the graphical objects are naturally arranged into a part-of hierarchy. This hierarchy can then be used in a variety of ways, including: optimization of redrawing and picking (the part-of hierarchy is usually a graphical containment hierarchy), and run-time inheritance of graphic properties (the parts of an object often want to inherit information like color and position from their parent in the run-time hierarchy).

The graphics system builds off of the constraint system and the run-time hierarchy. RENDEZVOUS programmers never write code to update the display, they simply change the graphical parameters of objects (e.g., color, position), and edit the run-time hierarchy by adding, moving, and removing objects. The graphics system monitors changes to the objects

The constraint system also provides some support for structural constraints, that is, constraints that can maintain structural consistency by creating, deleting, and moving objects within a tree. While the current model needs refinement, it is being heavily used. The experience of programmers using structural constraints so far has been that they are essential for building large multi-user applications.

In the RENDEZVOUS run-time architecture, we make extensive use of indirect references to communicate between user interfaces and underlying applications. We are experimenting with the use of interprocess constraints as a declarative mechanism for assembling applications from modules. (This is related to problems identified in Chapter 3 and is discussed in more detail in Chapter 21.)

Currently, the RENDEZVOUS constraint system also has experimental support for temporal constraints, that is, constraints that relate values in objects to the value of a real-time clock. We have done some preliminary testing of these constraints with some simple animations. While our model of temporal constraints needs to be refined, we are convinced that temporal constraints are a very powerful tool for constructing a wide range of animations, and must be supported.

The RENDEZVOUS model requires that every object be a (very) light-weight process. We find that this makes it much easier to control and specify the interactive behavior of objects. It would be impractical to use, say, a UNIX process for each object (since we may have thousands of objects). Instead, we partition a single UNIX process into many light-weight processes using a model derived from Sassafras [Hill 86].

Non-blocking message passing is primarily intended for communication with outside (non-RENDEZVOUS) processes, although it could be used as a general interprocess (or inter-object) communication mechanism. Input events (e.g., mouse button activity) are treated as messages that are sent to objects. Within each object, a rule-based language (derived from Sassafras) is used to define event-handlers that implement the objects' responses to the events. The responses normally do some simple computations and set local values (possibly invoking the constraint maintenance system). The responses may also include sending events to other objects. The event dispatcher is (by definition) a key component of the process

and the hierarchy and updates the display as needed. The graphics system tries to optimize redisplay, by trying to minimize the number of objects that must be redrawn, while preserving overlapping relationships on the display. While careful hand coding can produce faster display update under some conditions, the ratio of programmer effort (zero) to performance (typically, very good) of the current automatic approach is vastly preferable to hand optimizing redisplay algorithms. (This is probably analogous to the compiled language vs. assembly language arguments of one or more decades ago. Given enough time, highly skilled programmers using low-level tools can produce more efficient code—but how often do real programmers working with real dead-lines have the time and the skill?)

The RENDEZVOUS multi-way constraint system is designed to support fast implementations and to be easy to use. The constraints are used to specify relations among slots in the objects. Constraints can be used strictly within objects, or can link values in different objects. In the latter case, the constraints are acting as a form of inter-process communication as each object is a lightweight process. To ensure correctness, this use of constraints between processes requires that any constraint propagation must happen as an indivisible operation. This is easy to implement by protecting a single constraint evaluator that is shared by all processes with a monitor or semaphore. Unfortunately, this approach may make achieving good parallelism on a multi-processor very difficult.

The constraint system includes a unique feature we find essential—the slot that a constraint updates, and the slots a constraint depends on, can both be indirectly referenced, through variables that can be set by the constraint system. For example, objects in the RENDEZVOUS run-time hierarchy have pointers to their parents. This allows the objects to inherit color information from their parent by installing a constraint that sets their color to be the color of the object pointed to by their parent field. The constraint system ensures that whenever the parent changes (possibly as a result of constraint evaluation), or the color of the parent changes, the local color slot is updated. Garnet has a similar, but slightly less general, facility; see Chapter 10. What is unique about RENDEZVOUS is this relation can be reversed—an object can set the value of the color slot of the object pointed to by its parent field. This facility could be used to have a color selector object update the color of an object it is currently attached to.

scheduler. Thus, careful design can all but eliminate races and dead-locks, and allow the scheduler to minimize latency when responding to user input.

9.6 The RENDEZVOUS Language Implementation and Experience

The RENDEZVOUS language is built on top of Common Lisp [Steele 90]. The current version uses a simple object system that we built ourselves on top of the Common Lisp structure mechanism. We now have a fast implementation of CLOS, the Common Lisp Object System [Bobrow 88], and are building a new version of RENDEZVOUS on top of it. The new version is, as far as possible, syntactically and semantically consistent with CLOS. We have found that the CLOS Metaobject Protocol [Kiczales 91], a feature of CLOS designed to simplify extending CLOS, makes it very easy to seamlessly and portably add constraints and event-handlers to CLOS classes. Based on our experience with the two versions of REN-DEZVOUS, we believe it would be foolish for researchers, or builders of prototype language implementations, to attempt to add inheritable features like constraints and event-handlers to classes in any object system that does not support a metaobject protocol.

We use the X Window system as a device independent networked graphics system for input and output. X makes it easy to connect one UNIX process running a collection of user interfaces implemented in REN-DEZVOUS, to a number of workstations or X terminals—this is a key requirement of multi-user applications that use a centralized model like RENDEZVOUS. We are experimenting with using the audio capability of SUN SPARCstations for audio input and output.

The use of Common Lisp helps us meet our rapid prototyping requirements. It provides dynamic loading, mixed execution of interpreted and compiled code, good debugging support, and automatic garbage collection. The keyword argument feature of Common Lisp is crucial to effective support of easily overridden defaults. Common Lisp syntax supports very strict static type checking (of the level described in chapter 7), but we know of no compiler that fully implements static checking. (This may be because static checking based on full source text analysis is not part of the Lisp culture.)

Currently, there are five programmers actively using RENDEZVOUS to build user interfaces. Four of the programmers joined the team after the initial version of RENDEZVOUS was implemented. All were able to build interfaces quickly and easily. Their biggest impediments were bugs in the implementation and lack of documentation. We found only minimal difficulties with the extended object-oriented model. We hope to have fixed these problems in version 2 of the RENDEZVOUS language, in addition to adding some extensions to the existing model.

Most programmers have some initial confusion about when to use inter-object constraints, and when to send messages. We have found that the provision of a simple guideline—use events for communication with the outside world (e.g., X and the audio server), use constraints for communication within the interface—and some examples, helps resolve this confusion. This problem does leave us with some concerns though—the constraint system and message passing are two different mechanisms to communicate and synchronize among processes. Is it good to have two ways of doing the same thing? We are leaning toward yes in these cases, because one approach is event-oriented and the other has a state maintenance orientation. Each approach has its place.

Using our current (non-CLOS) system, we are pleased with the performance we are getting. Often, our bottleneck is X, not the Lisp process running RENDEZVOUS. Initial tests of our new, CLOS-based, implementation suggest that it will be at least as fast as the current version of RENDEZVOUS. CLOS probably costs us some performance, but we use better algorithms and optimization techniques we developed as we worked with the initial version of RENDEZVOUS.

Our biggest impediments to consistent real-time response are swapping and contention from other processes running on our workstations. Like X, these things are outside our control, so it is unlikely we will be able to make guarantees about responsiveness or performance. While we are still learning about responsiveness and performance issues, we believe that most currently available variations on the UNIX operating system do not provide real-time features that would allow guaranteed responsiveness, nor synchronization of media. Within the current implementation of REN-DEZVOUS we partially overcome this problem by having everything run as a single UNIX process. This way, we have good control over process scheduling and synchronization for all RENDEZVOUS processes. When we have to rely on the operating system for synchronization with other processes (e.g., X server, sound server) or resource allocation (swapping), there are serious synchronization problems. We believe that, ultimately, operating systems and languages that support MUMMS interfaces will have to provide much better real-time support features, in order to ensure responsiveness and to ensure that independently generated acoustic and visual media can synchronized.

9.7   Future Work

The current version of RENDEZVOUS meets all of the requirements we list in Section 9.3, except it has limited support for the use of real-time to drive animations and other time-dependent interface features. We plan to add temporal constraints to help overcome this weakness.

Once we complete the second version of RENDEZVOUS, we plan to work in three directions:

- build more multi-media interfaces, to begin understanding the requirements of synchronizing media and declaratively specifying output for temporal media like audio and video,

- build higher-level tools in RENDEZVOUS, such as a multi-user, graphical debugger and a multi-user, graphical interface builder, for RENDEZVOUS, and

- informally study typical programmers building interfaces with RENDEZVOUS, to gain insights to improve RENDEZVOUS and make it more useful to large program development organizations.

Throughout the implementation of RENDEZVOUS, we have tried to use algorithms and data structures that provide good performance. In general, we are pleased with the performance we get; however, when running the CardTable on one of our current processors, we cannot provide adequate response if four users simultaneously drag one card each. This requires one processor to track four mice and update four displays, each with four moving objects! In general, we cannot simultaneously run many high-quality graphical interfaces on a single processor. Since we expect

interfaces to become more elaborate at least as fast as processors get faster we will have to find ways to distribute our multi-user interfaces across multiple processors.

Acknowledgements

John Patterson implemented the CardTable. John Patterson and Steve Rohall have assisted with the design and implementation of RENDEZVOUS. They, along with Debbie Bloom and Tom Brinck, have thoroughly tested RENDEZVOUS by using it to implement a variety of interfaces.

References

[Bobrow 88] Bobrow, D. G., DeMichiel, L. G., Gabriel, R. P., Keene S. E., Kiczales, G., and Moon, D. A. (1988). *Common Lisp Object System Specification*. X3J13 Document 88-002R, June 1988.

[Duisberg 88] R. A. Duisberg. Animation Using Temporal Constraints: An Overview of the Animus System. *Human-Computer Interaction*, 3(3): 275-307, 1987-1988.

[Green 86] Mark Green. A Survey of Three Dialog Models. *ACM Transactions on Graphics*, 5(3):244-275, July 1986.

[Hill 86] Ralph D. Hill. Supporting Concurrency, Communication and Synchronization in Human-Computer Interaction - The Sassafras UIMS. *ACM Transactions on Graphics*, 5(3):179-210, July 1986.

[Hill 91] R. D. Hill. A 2-D Graphics System for Multi-User Interactive Graphics Based on Objects and Constraints. In E. Blake and P. Wisskirchen, editors, *Advances in Object Oriented Graphics I*, pages 67-91. Springer-Verlag, Berlin, 1991.

[Kiczales 91] Kiczales, G., Des Rivieres, J., and D. G. Bobrow. (1991). *The Art of the Metaobject Protocol*. MIT Press, Cambridge, MA, 1991.

[Patterson 90] Patterson, J. F., Hill, R. D., Rohall, S. L., and Meeks, W. S. (1990). Rendezvous: An Architecture for Synchronous Multi-User Applications. In *Proceedings CSCW '90*, pages 317-328, Los Angeles, October 1990.

[Scheifler 88] Robert W. Schiefler and Jim Gettys. The X Window System. *ACM Transactions on Graphics*, 5(2):79-106, April 1986.

[Steele 90] Steele, Guy L., Jr. ed. (1990). *Common Lisp: The Language*, 2nd Ed. Digital Press, 1990.

[Stefik 86] Stefik, D. and Bobrow, D. G. (1986). Object-Oriented Programming: Themes and Variations. *The AI Magazine*, 6(4): 40-62, Winter 1986.

Primitives for Programming Multi-User Interfaces

Prasun Dewan and Rajiv Choudhary

Department of Computer Sciences
Purdue University
W. Lafayette, IN 47907
pd@cs.purdue.edu *or* rxc@cs.purdue.edu

Abstract

We have designed a set of primitives for programming multi-user interfaces by extending a set of existing high-level primitives for programming single-user interfaces. These primitives support both collaboration-transparent and collaboration-aware multi-user programs and allow existing single-user programs to be incrementally changed to corresponding multi-user programs. The collaboration-aware primitives include primitives for tailoring the input and output to a user, authenticating users, executing code in a user's environment and querying and setting properties of it, and tailoring the user interface coupling. We have identified several application-independent user groups that arise in a collaborative setting and allow the original single-user calls to be targeted at these groups. In addition, we provide primitives for defining application-specific groups. Our preliminary experience with these primitives shows that they can be used to easily implement collaborative tasks of a wide range of applications including message systems, multi-user editors, computer conferencing systems, and coordination systems. In this paper, we motivate, describe, and illustrate these primitives, discuss how primitives similar to them can be offered by a variety of user interface tools, and point out future directions for work.

1. Introduction

Implementing user interfaces of interactive single-user applications is difficult [16]. Implementing user interfaces of multi-user applications is even more difficult since these applications must, in addition, perform several collaboration tasks such as dynamically making and breaking connections with (possibly remote) users, gathering input from and displaying output to multiple users, and providing concurrency and access control [4, 14].

The difficulty of user-interface implementation has prompted the development of a variety of general-purpose user interface tools (UITs) such as screen managers, window systems, toolkits, and user interface management systems [9]. However, most of these tools have been designed to support only single-user applications. The exceptions are shared screen systems such as NLS [5] and shared window systems such as Rapport [6] and VConf [10], which are extensions of single-user versions of these tools. These tools do not provide any new primitives for programming user interfaces— they simply extend the semantics of the primitives supported by the corresponding single-user UITs. They allow users to make and break connections with applications, create/destroy copies of interaction entities[1] when a user makes/breaks a connection with the application, inform the application of an input operation invoked on an interaction entity by any user without distinguishing among different users, manage all aspects of concurrency and access control for the application, and execute output operations on all copies of the interaction entities. They differ mainly in the interaction entities linked by them— shared screen systems link entire screens while shared window systems link only those windows on a screen that are created by multi-user applications.

Shared screen and window systems greatly increase the power of interactive systems. Since they do not extend the primitives of single-user UITs, multi-user applications supported by them are collaboration-transparent [11], that is, completely unaware of the fact that multiple users are interacting with them. As a result, these applications contain no code to handle collaboration tasks and existing single-user applications developed using the original UITs can be used by multiple users. Moreover, since they extend low-level UITs, they can be used to perform the collaboration tasks of not only direct clients of the UITs but also clients of higher-level UITs that use these low-level UITs. For instance, a shared X window system can

---

[1] We use the term interaction entity to refer to an entity such as a screen, window or scrollbar that is displayed to the user.

be used to perform the collaboration tasks of not only direct clients of the X window system but also the clients of the large number of toolkits and UIMSs developed on top of the window system.

However, the approach used by these systems suffers from two related limitations. First, applications cannot tailor the collaboration to their needs. For instance, a client of a shared window system cannot create both shared and private windows since it is collaboration unaware. As a result, applications that require any tailoring cannot use these systems and must handle collaboration tasks using other mechanisms. For this reason, several multi-user applications such as RTCAL [14], CES [8], and GROVE [4] have been developed almost from scratch despite the presence of shared window and screen systems. Second, it is not possible to add to these systems several useful high-level primitives for tailoring the collaboration. For instance, it is not possible to add primitives for defining high-level units of access control such as paragraphs or procedures, since they understand only low-level interaction entities such as pixels, windows, and screens.

We have developed a multi-user UIT that addresses these limitations of current multi-user UITs. Like these tools, it extends an existing UIT, but unlike them, it extends a high-level UIT, called Suite [2], and supports both collaboration -transparent and -aware applications, allowing them to choose the degree to which they wish to be collaboration aware. As a result, it supports a richer set of multi-user applications and incremental development of collaboration-aware applications.

The rest of the paper is organized as follows. Section 2 briefly describes the original single-user primitives supported by Suite. Section 3 describes how we extend these primitives to support multi-user interaction. Section 4 discusses how similar primitives can be supported by other systems. Finally, Section 5 gives conclusions and directions for future work.

2. Single-User Primitives

We give here only a brief summary of the primitives offered by Suite for programming single-user interfaces. More detailed descriptions of these primitives and motivation for supporting them are given in [2].

The Suite primitives are built around the abstractions of *active variables* (or *active values*), *attributes*, and *value groups*. An active variable is an application data structure displayed to the user that can be updated by the application to show results and edited by the user to input new values. An attribute is an interaction property of an active variable, which can determine, for instance, the presentation of the data structure or the procedures invoked when it is edited by the user. A value group is a group of related active values that stores attributes shared by these values. An inheritance relation is defined among value groups that allows a more specific value group to inherit attributes from a more general one.

The Suite primitives are divided into *Suite calls*, which are invoked by applications to perform user-interface operations, and *Suite callbacks*, which are procedures invoked in applications in response to user actions. The Suite calls consist mainly of:

(1) *Creation/Deletion Calls*: These calls allow users to create/delete displays of active variables and consist of the `Dm_Submit`/`Dm_Remove`[2] calls, which create/delete active variables, and the `Dm_Engage`/`Dm_Disengage` calls, which create/delete displays of these data structures.

(2) *Attribute Setting/Retrieving Calls*: These calls consist of the `Dm_SetAttr` and `Dm_GetAttr` calls, which define and retrieve, respectively, the value of an attribute in a value group.

(3) *Value Setting/Retrieving Calls*: These calls include the `Dm_Update` and `Dm_GetValue` calls, which update and retrieve, respectively, the value of an active variable.

(4) *Message Call*: The `Dm_Message` call displays a text message to the user.

The Suite callbacks inform the application of actions performed by the user. They consist mainly of the the *load callback*, which is invoked when the user connects to the application, *validate callbacks*, which check user changes to data structures for semantic consistency, and

---

[2]Suite calls are prefixed with `Dm` since they are executed by runtime agents called dialogue managers [2,3].

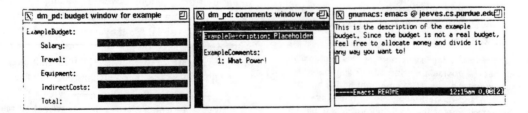

Figure 1: Single-User Interaction

update callbacks, which are invoked when the user commits semantically correct changes.

We illustrate these primitives using the example of an application that displays, in separate windows, a budget and comments on the budget (Figure 1), allows the user to change these data structures, and displays a description of the budget if the user selects a placeholder for it (Figure 1). Figure 2 shows the Suite primitives used by the application.

The `Load` procedure is the callback invoked when the user makes a connection to the application. It makes several Suite calls. It invokes `Dm_Submit` to create the active variables `ExampleBudget`, `ExampleComments`, and `ExampleDescription`, which store the budget, comments, and placeholder, respectively. The arguments of `Dm_Submit` specify the location, name, and type, respectively, of the active variable. It invokes the `Dm_SetAttr` calls to define attributes of value groups. The first `Dm_SetAttr` call defines the *update*

callback for a value of type `Budget`, which updates the dependent fields of the value and invokes `Dm_Update` to refresh the display of the value. The second `Dm_SetAttr` call defines the `select callback` of the variable, `BudgetDescription`, which is invoked when the user selects the value. This procedure invokes an operating system command to display a description of the budget. Both callbacks take two arguments, the first is the name of the active variable that was modified/selected and second is a pointer to the value of the variable. The last `Dm_SetAttr` call tells Suite that integer values should be displayed as scrollbars. Finally, the load callback invokes the `Dm_Engage` calls to ask Suite to display `ExampleBudget` in the graphics window `budget`, and `ExampleDescription` and `ExampleComments` in the text window `comments`.

3. Multi-User Extensions

We have extended these primitives to support multi-user applications. The windows, active variables,

```
/* Declarations */
    ...
typedef struct {
    int Salary, Travel, Equipment;
    int IndirectCosts, Total;
    } Budget;
String ExampleDescription;
StringList ExampleComments;
Budget ExampleBudget;

void UpdateBudget(name, val)
    char *name; Budget *val;
{
    val->IndirectCosts = (val->Salary + val->Travel) * OVERHEAD;
    val->Total = val->Salary + val->Travel + val->IndirectCosts;
    Dm_Update ("ExampleBudget", "Budget", val);
}
void DescribeBudget(name, val)
    char *name; Budget *val;
{
    system ("gnumacs README &");
}


Load ()
{
    Dm_Submit (&ExampleBudget, "ExampleBudget", "Budget");
    Dm_Submit (&ExampleDescription, "ExampleDescription", "String");
    Dm_Submit (&ExampleComments, "ExampleComments", "StringList");
    Dm_SetAttr ("Type: Budget", AttrUpdateProc, UpdateBudget);
    Dm_SetAttr ("Value: ExampleDescription", AttrSelectProc, DescribeBudget);
    Dm_SetAttr( "Type: int", AttrGraphicWidget, AttrGraphicHorizontalScrollbar );
    Dm_Engage ("ExampleBudget", "budget", "Graphical");
    Dm_Engage ("ExampleDescription", "comments", "Text");
    Dm_Engage ("ExampleComments", "comments", "Text");
}
```

Figure 2. Single-User/Collaboration-Transparent Program

and value groups defined by an application are created for each user who starts a session with it. Continuing with the example, separate copies of ExampleBudget, ExampleComments, and ExampleDescription are created for different users, thereby allowing the users to edit them independently (Figure 3); and separate copies of the value groups Budget and int are created for different users, thereby allowing them to independently customize attributes of active variables. Figure 3 illustrates multi-user interaction in Suite. It shows the window displays of the screens of users pd and rxc, who have independently edited ExampleBudget and ExampleComments, respectively.

Strictly speaking, Suite supports "multi-session" applications rather than "multi-user" applications since a user can simultaneously start multiple sessions with an application. However, in the rest of the paper, we will use the terms "user" and "session" interchangeably unless we need to explicitly distinguish between them.

Our extensions were motivated by our experience with developing several experimental multi-user applications in Suite. We followed an iterative approach to defining these extensions, wherein we added concepts as we needed them to build our applications and then generalized them if we found examples that used the generalizations. Our presentation of these extensions reflects this approach.

3.1. Collaboration-Transparency

To support collaboration-transparent applications, we extended the semantics of the single-user Suite primitives using the following rules:

(1)   A Suite callback can be invoked as a result of an appropriate action by any user. For instance, the Load procedure in Figure 1 is invoked when any user starts a session with the application.

(2)   A Suite call made when no user is connected to the application is a no-op.

(3)   A Suite call other than a value setting call (that is, a creation/deletion, attribute setting/retrieving, value retrieving, or message call) made in a Suite callback refers to the *current user*, that is, the user whose actions resulted in the callback. For instance, the Dm_Submit calls in Figure 2 create the active variables ExampleBudget, ExampleComments, and ExampleDescription for the user who invoked Load.

(4)   A creation/deletion, attribute setting, or message call not made in a Suite callback refers to all users interacting with the application, since the call cannot be associated with a distinguished user. These semantics allow, for instance, the example application to display a new list of comments to all users in response to an external message.

(5)   An attribute/value retrieving call not made in a Suite callback refers to *any user*, that is, a user chosen non-deterministically by the system. We choose any user over all users since a (single-user) retrieving call returns a single value. Another alternative we considered is to choose the *previous user*, that is, the user whose actions caused the most recent callback to be executed. Choosing any user over previous user can lead to better performance when users are interacting from remote sites since the system can choose the user who is nearest to the application. However, both alternatives can cause the application to behave non-deterministically unless all user copies of the object retrieved are identical. Yet another alternative is to return the most recent version of the object cached in the application. This approach is more efficient but is not applicable when the object is not cached. Moreover, it can lead to non-deterministic behavior even when all user copies of the object are identical, since these values may be different from the value cached.

(6)   A value setting call always refers to all users. Thus, the invocation of Dm_Update in response

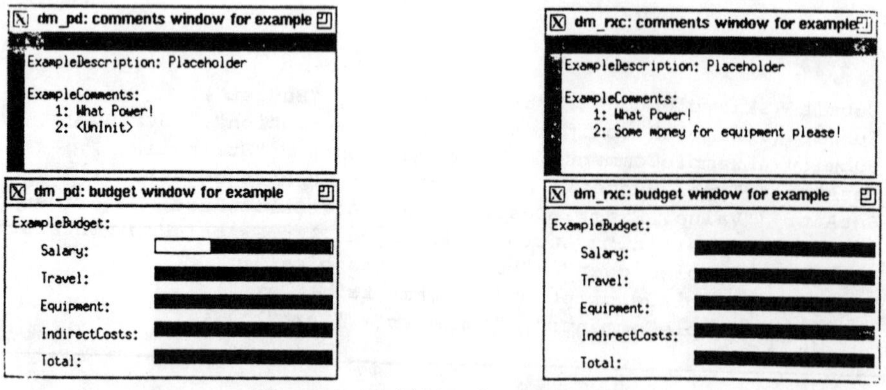

Figure 3: Multi-User Interaction

to a change made by one user (Figure 3) to Exam-pleBudget updates the value of all versions of the variable (Figure 4). We distinguish between value and attribute setting calls because we expect users to, typically, share values but not formatting and other attributes of these values.

(7) Changes made by a user to data structures are displayed to other users when the user commits them. For instance, user pd sees the contents of the comment made by user rxc when the latter commits them (Figure 4).

These are only the default semantics of the Suite primitives. They have been designed, based on our preliminary experience with developing and using multi-user applications, to allow existing single-user applications to be used in a reasonable way by multiple-users and keep the collaboration awareness low in typical multi-user applications. We describe below primitives that allow collaboration-aware applications to override these semantics.

3.2. Group Awareness

We identified above three groups of users to which a Suite call may be directed: *current*, *any*, and *all*. Two other such groups are the *others* group and the parameterized *session* group. The former refers to all users other than the current user and may be the target of a Suite call that, for instance, displays a message to all other users when a new user starts a session with the application. The latter is parameterized by an integer, n, and refers to the *n*th session in a list of sessions sorted by when they were started. This group may be used, for instance, by applications such as DCS [12] and a multi-user debugger we have built that check with the user of the first session with the application if a particular user should be allowed to enter the conference. Suite allows each of the original single-user calls to be explicitly directed to the various groups of users. For instance, in addition to the Dm_Message call, it provides the calls, Dm_Message_Current,

Dm_Message_Others, Dm_Message_Any, Dm_Message_All, and Dm_Message_SessionNo. Suite calls explicitly directed to the user groups *current* or *others* must be executed in callbacks.

We have modified the update callback of Figure 2 to illustrate the use of these calls:

```
void UpdateBudget(name, val)
  char *name; Budget *val;
{
#ifdef DEBUG
  Dm_Message_All ("UpdateBudget Starts");
#endif
  Dm_Message_Others ( "Budget Updated");
  val->IndirectCosts = (val->Salary +
                    val->Travel) * OVERHEAD;
  val->Total = val->Salary +
          val->Travel + val->IndirectCosts;
  Dm_Update ( "ExampleBudget", "Budget", val);
#ifdef DEBUG
  Dm_Message_All ("UpdateBudget Terminates");
#endif
}
```

The two Dm_Message_All calls allow all users of an application to together debug the application. The Dm_Message_Others call alerts all users other than the one who made the change that the budget has been modified (Figure 5).

We call applications that explicitly target calls at these five kinds of groups as *group aware*. These groups are general groups in that they are defined independently of specific applications and users. Moreover, they are dynamic groups in that they are formed at execution time. We discuss below primitives that allow applications to target Suite calls at application-defined groups based possibly on static properties of the application such as its owner and protection group.

3.3. User/Session Awareness

A multi-user application may need to be aware of the identities of specific users, for two main reasons: First,

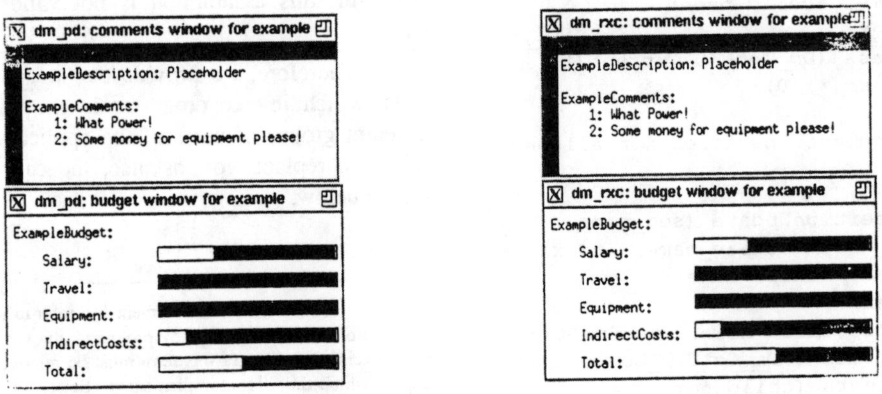

Figure 4: Collaboration Transparency

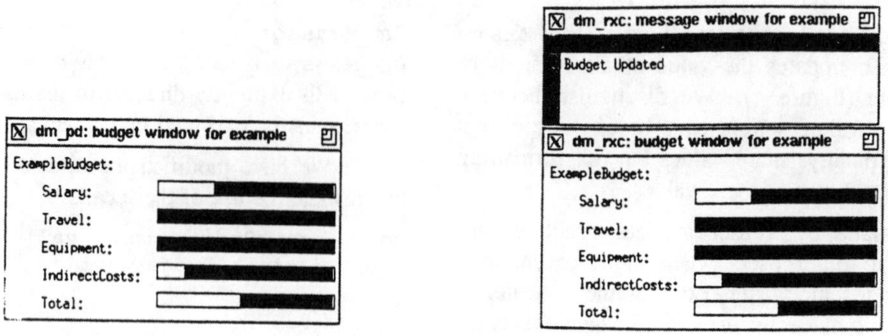

Figure 5: Group Awareness

it may want to implement access control. For instance, the example application may wish to allow certain users to add comments. Second, it may want to tailor its processing of input and displaying of output to the user. For instance, the example application may wish to use a user's favourite editor when displaying the budget description to him.

Therefore, the Suite primitives support *user aware* applications. It allows each of the original single-user calls to be targeted at a particular user. For instance, it provides the `Dm_Message_UID` call which displays the message to (all sessions of) a specific user. The call is a no-op if the specified user is not connected to the application.

Suite also allows the application to determine which users are interacting with it. It provides the `Dm_GetUID` family of calls, which can be used to get the user identifiers of various groups of users. These primitives allow applications to define their own groups and target Suite calls at them.

We illustrate user awareness by adding two callbacks to the example application, `CommentInsertion-Validate`, which is invoked by Suite to check if the addition of a new comment should be allowed, and `CommentInsertionUpdate`, which is invoked by Suite to inform the application of the new comment. These callbacks are outlined below:

```
char * CommentInsertionValidate (seq_name,
                            child_name, index)
  char *seq_name, *child_name;
  unsigned index;
{ if (CheckAccess (Dm_GetUID_Current ()))
    return ((char *) 0);
  else
    return ("Comment Insertion not allowed");
}

void CommentInsertionUpdate (seq_name,
                        child_name, index)
  char *seq_name, *child_name;
  unsigned index;
{ Dm_SetAttr_All (child_name, AttrPreString,
        NameFromId ( Dm_GetUID_Current ()));
  Dm_SetAttr_Others (child_name,
                AttrReadOnly, 1);
}
```

`CommentInsertionValidate` checks the access

rights of the user and `CommentInsertionUpdate` labels the comment with the name of the user (Figure 6) and makes it read-only for all users other than the current user.

A multi-user application may also need to be aware of properties of specific user sessions. For instance, the example application may wish to use an editor specified dynamically by the user during the interaction session. Therefore, Suite also provides *session aware* primitives. It provides the `Dm_GetSessionID` family of calls, which returns session identifiers of various groups of users, and allows calls to be targeted at sessions named by these identifiers. For instance, it provides the `Dm_Message_SessionID` call, which is targeted at the session specified by its argument.

3.4. Environment Awareness

The semantics of a multi-user application are sometimes dependent on the environments[3] of its users. To illustrate, consider the example application of Figure 2, which executes the `system` call provided by C for invoking user programs. The call invokes the `gnumacs` program, which needs to know the display (workstation) on which the budget description should be shown. In the single-user case, an application is bound to a particular user, so it is reasonable to assume that display inherited from the application is the one to be used by `gnumacs`. However, this assumption is not valid in the multi-user case.

Therefore, we provide the `Dm_System` family of calls, which invoke programs in the environment of the different groups of users of the application. One of these calls can replace, for instance, the call to `system`, as shown below:

---

[3]We use the term "environment" to refer to a set of properties of a user session that are inherited by programs invoked from that session. A more precise definition of this term must be relative to the operating system on which the UIT is implemented. Suite, which is implemented on the UNIX operating system, uses the UNIX definition of this term.

```
void DescribeBudget(name, val)
    char *name; Budget *val;
{
    Dm_System_All ("gnumacs README &");
}
```

The `Dm_System_All` call invokes the `gnumacs` program in the environments of all the users (Figure 7). The example above is *environment aware* in that it knows that it is being used by multiple users with different environments. However, it is not aware of specific properties of the environment— it simply executes the command in the current user's environment. In general, however, a multi-user application may need to directly refer to specific properties of the environments of its users, for at least three reasons. First, it may need to execute a command that uses properties of a user's environment even when the user is not connected to the application. For instance, the example application may wish to display a message on the displays of both past and current users of the application when a new user joins the conversation or the value of the budget is committed. Second, for access reasons, it may not be able to execute a command in the user's environment. For instance, a user of the application may not have rights to execute the `gnumacs` program. Finally, the application may need to compose properties of multiple environments. For instance, a user of the example application may not have `gnumacs` in his search path— therefore the application may wish to use its search path but the user's display when invoking `gnumacs`.

Therefore, Suite provides two additional primitives to support environment aware applications. It provides the `Dm_GetEnv` and `Dm_SetEnv` calls to set and get properties of the various groups of users. The modified `DescribeBudget` call below illustrates the use of one of these calls:

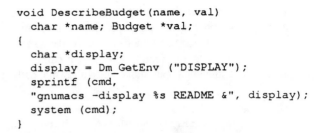

```
void DescribeBudget(name, val)
    char *name; Budget *val;
{
    char *display;
    display = Dm_GetEnv ("DISPLAY");
    sprintf (cmd,
    "gnumacs -display %s README &", display);
    system (cmd);
}
```

To support environment aware applications, it is necessary that the UIT execute for each user a *user agent* that defines the user's environment and executes commands in it. The Suite user agent is an extension of the Suite dialogue manager, which manages the syntactic details of the dialogue with the user [2,3]. Giving an application the capability of asking a user agent to execute programs raises an access control problem— it allows the application to execute malicious programs with the rights of the users of the program. We plan to address this problem by allowing the users to choose the programs their agents execute.

3.5. Coupling Awareness

An important issue in the design of multi-user applications is the coupling among the users of the application [3], which determines which actions made by a user are observed by other users and when they are observed by them. An application may need to tailor the coupling to its needs. For instance, a multi-user ''talk'' program may wish to transmit a user's change to other users as soon as it is made, while a ''mail'' program may wish to delay the transmission until the user explicitly executes a command to send the data.

Therefore, Suite allows applications to tailor the default coupling to their needs. It provides a fine-grained coupling model that associates the interaction entities (active variables, value groups, and windows) created for a

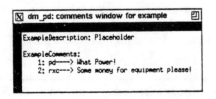

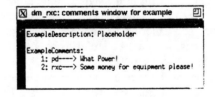

Figure 6: User Awareness

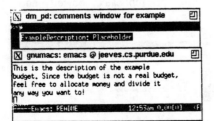

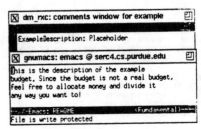

Figure 7: Environment Awareness

user with *coupling attributes*, which determine how these entities are coupled with the corresponding entities created for other users. An application can specify the value of these attributes using the regular SetAttr calls. Thus the example application can make the following call in Load

```
Dm_SetAttr ("Value: ExampleComments",
            AttrTransmitOn, AttrIncrement)
```

to ask Suite to broadcast changes to comments as soon as they are made (Figure 8). A detailed description of the Suite coupling attributes and motivation for supporting them is given in [3].

We refer to applications that define values of coupling attributes as *coupling aware* applications. It is important to note that while coupling awareness supports flexible coupling, these two concepts are not equivalent, since the coupling attributes can be interactively defined by users. For instance, the users of the example application can interactively make the attribute definition above. As a result, it is possible to tailor the coupling of coupling-transparent applications including existing single-user applications.

4. Extending other Systems

Many aspects of our approach to extending Suite to support multi-user interfaces can be applied to other systems. Here we briefly consider interactive programming languages, window systems, toolkits, and object-oriented frameworks for building user interfaces. In the rest of this paper, we shall use the general terms *UIT primitives*, *UIT calls*, and *UIT callbacks* to refer to the primitives, calls, and callbacks, respectively, provided by a UIT for programming user interfaces.

Conventional (Pascal-like) programming languages offer synchronous constructs such as the Pascal read and write constructs for programming user interfaces. The concepts of directing UIT calls at the various Suite groups, querying and setting users' environments and executing programs in them, and tailoring of coupling can all be applied to them. Thus, it would be useful to provide, for instance, calls such as WriteAll and WriteOthers in Pascal. Coupling can be specified using a mechanism similar to the one used for specifying formats. For instance, in Pascal, the statement

```
ReadAny (id#increment)
```

could be used to indicate that the input echo should be seen incrementally by all users.

Not all groupings proposed in § 3 are applicable or appropriate in this context. The *current* (and hence *other*) groups are no longer valid, since conventional languages do not support the notion of a callback. The *any* group is not appropriate since an input call targeted at this group can block for a long time if the system non-deterministically chooses, for instance, a user who is away from his terminal. It is more appropriate to define *current* as the last user who input a value, thereby allowing, for instance, a program to read a data item from the same user it read the previous item from. Moreover, in the case of an input call, it is useful to queue the values input by different users and define *any* as the first one of the values in the queue, thereby ensuring there is no starvation. (In a system that provides floor control, there would be only one user with pending input.) The default target groups of the input and output routines can now be defined as *any* and *all,* which is consistent with the semantics of these routines implemented on top of shared window systems. This approach to extending conventional synchronous I/O primitives can also be applied to languages such as EZ [7] that support unconventional synchronous I/O.

Our approach can be more directly used for extending window systems and toolkits, which, like Suite, support callbacks and calls that create and delete interaction entities (e.g: windows, widgets) and set and retrieve their interaction properties (e.g: font, colour) and state. However, it may not be as useful since these systems address user interaction at a lower level. For instance, the window system and toolkit concept of a state of an interaction entity may be different from the application concept of a state. For instance, a toolkit may consider the state of text widget to be the text buffer while the application may consider it to be the value displayed (along, possibly, with some syntactic sugar) by the text buffer. As a result, it is less useful to distinguish between calls that update interaction properties and those that update state.

Some of the aspects of our work can also be applied to systems such as Colab [15] and Rendezvous [13] that provide object-oriented frameworks for implementing multi-user interfaces. Colab supports the abstraction of an *association* of replicated objects and a facility for

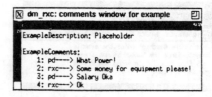

Figure 8: Coupling Awareness

broadcasting messages to all objects in an association. Rendezvous also supports such a facility but distinguishes between *underlying objects* (application-data) and *interaction objects* (views of application-data) and allows sharing of underlying objects without sharing of the corresponding interaction objects. These frameworks can be extended by providing facilities to send messages to *current*, *others*, *any* and other Suite groups of users.

5. Conclusions and Future Work

Multi-user applications are necessary for automating the large amount of time people spend in group activities [1]. The Suite multi-user primitives have been designed to support the easy construction of such applications. Unlike other multi-user systems, we have extended high-level single-user primitives and support both collaboration-transparent and collaboration-aware applications. Some of the components of our design such as broadcasting output to all users have been borrowed directly from earlier systems. The novel aspects of our design are:

(1) the distinction made in the definition of collaboration-transparent semantics of single-user primitives between (a) UIT calls that change the state of interaction entities and those that change interaction properties of them and (b) UIT calls that are made in callbacks and those that are made in other procedures;

(2) primitives for (a) defining application-specific access control, (b) tailoring the input and output to a user, (c) executing programs' in a user's environment and querying and setting properties of it, and (d) tailoring the user interface coupling;

(3) allowing UIT calls to refer to a variety of user groups that arise in a collaborative setting.

The Suite multi-user primitives have been used so far by 13 programmers at Purdue and the University of Minnesota to create several experimental multi-user applications including tools that display system data structures such as line printers and process lists to multiple users, a multi-user talk program, a multi-user debugger, a multi-user appointment service, a multi-user "visitor tool" that allows members of an organization to schedule meetings with visitors and view and manipulate information about them, a multi-user "expense service" that keeps the common expenditures of a group of users, a multi-user "library service" that allows users to borrow and return books, a multi-user "voting tool" that allows users to vote on some issue, a multi-user "version control tool" that allows users to edit the state of a version control system, a multi-user code inspector that allows users to together browse through code and annotate it, and a multi-user query interface that allows users to share results of queries interpreted by a database system. Our experience with building these applications helped us identify issues in the design of these primitives and choose approaches for addressing them. While these primitives were designed specifically for Suite,

similar primitives can also be added to other systems including window systems, toolkits, programming languages, and object-oriented frameworks.

We motivated our design using specific examples of multi-user tools. It is also possible to make some general statements about our design by describing the kind of multi-user applications it can support. Ellis et al [4] describe two alternate taxonomies for classifying multi-user applications—the *time space taxonomy* and the *application-level taxonomy*. The former classifies applications based on two considerations: (1) whether they support collaboration that is face-to-face or distributed over many locations, and (2) whether they support synchronous (real-time) interaction or asynchronous interaction. The coupling aware primitives allow Suite to support applications with a variety of synchronization needs including pure-synchronous and pure-asynchronous applications [3]. The ability of Suite to support distributed interaction depends on how many of the interaction tasks can be performed locally, which in turn depends on many factors including the collaboration awareness of the application. An application that is more collaboration aware may need to process more user events, and would thus be less suitable for distributed interaction. This problem can be reduced in an architecture that replicates the application [10].

The application-level taxonomy characterizes multi-user applications by their functionality. It divides these applications into various groups including message systems, multi-user editors, computer conferencing systems, and coordination systems. Our multi-user primitives together with the abstractions of distributed objects [2] can be used to easily implement many collaborative aspects of these applications. Indeed, several of the experimental applications we have built fall into one or more of these classes. To illustrate, consider the example application described in this paper. Like asynchronous multi-user editors and message systems, it allows users to asynchronously edit data structures (Figure 3); like computer conferencing and real-time multi-user editors, it allows them to also synchronously edit data structures (Figure 8); and like coordination systems, it automatically triggers users' actions by informing other interested users about them (Figure 5). The collaborative aspects of these applications were relatively easy to implement—Suite implemented most of these aspects and the applications contained very little code to customize the collaboration. The automation supported by Suite is illustrated by the example application described in this paper, which provides the functionality of a variety of multi-user applications with a few lines of code.

The Suite multi-user primitives are only a first step towards flexible, high-level primitives for programming multi-user interfaces. We are extending the flexibility of our work by providing applications with primitives for tailoring the concurrency control and undo/redo models. We also plan to increase its automation by providing applications with high-level attributes for specifying the access control policies. Finally, we also plan to write a general multi-user teletype emulator that uses the Suite multi-user primitives to implement the extensions to the traditional I/O primitives proposed in § 4. Like multi-user emulators built on shared window systems, such a tool would allow the large number of existing programs based on these primitives to be used by multiple users. In addition, it would allow programmers to incrementally tailor these collaboration-transparent programs.

Since Suite is a high-level UIT, it supports a limited set of user interfaces in comparison to lower-level UITs such as window systems and toolkits. In particular, it does not support multi-user applications that require highly application-specific graphical displays. Therefore, it would be useful to apply aspects of our approach to lower-level UITs and evaluate the practicality of this idea. Further study is also necessary to determine how the responsibilities of performing collaboration tasks should be divided among the various layers of an interactive system. One approach is to let every layer implement mechanisms for sharing of interaction entities it manages and provide user-interface mechanisms that can be used by higher-level layers to determine the policies on sharing the lower-level mechanisms. It would also be useful to explore implementation of Suite-like UITs using object-oriented frameworks such as Colab and Rendezvous.

Acknowledgments

Several of the collaboration-aware primitives described here were motivated by the applications developed by Bret Lane, Vahid Mashayekhi, and John Riedl. Bret Lane implemented some of these primitives. The referees gave helpful, in-depth comments. This research was supported in part by National Science Foundation grant IRI-9015442 and in part by a grant from the Software Engineering Research Center at Purdue University, a National Science Foundation Industry/University Cooperative Research Center (NSF Grant No. ECD-8913133).

REFERENCES

[1]   T. DeMarco and T. Lister, *Peopleware: Productive Projects and Teams*, Dorset House Publishing Co., New York, 1987.

[2]   Prasun Dewan, "A Tour of the Suite User Interface Software," *Proceedings of the 3rd ACM SIGGRAPH Symposium on User Interface Software and Technology*, October 1990, pp. 57-65.

[3]   Prasun Dewan and Rajiv Choudhary, "Flexible User Interface Coupling in Collaborative Systems," *Proceedings of the ACM CHI'91 Conference*, April 1991, pp. 41-49.

[4]   Clarence A. Ellis, Simon J. Gibbs, and Gail L. Rein, "Groupware: Some Issues and Experiences," *CACM* 34:1 (January 1991), pp. 38-58.

[5]   D.C. Engelbart, "NLS Teleconferencing Features," *Proceedings of Fall COMPCON*, September 1975, pp. 173-176.

[6]   J.R. Ensor, S.R. Ahuja, D.N. Horn, and S.E. Lucco, "The Rapport Multimedia Conferencing System: A Software Overview," *Proceedings of the 2nd IEEE Conference on Computer Workstations*, March 1988, pp. 52-58.

[7]   C.W. Fraser and D.R. Hanson, "High-Level Language Facilities for Low-Level Services," *Conference Record of POPL*, 1985, pp. 217-224.

[8]   Irene Greif, Robert Seliger, and William Weihl, "Atomic Data Abstractions in a Distributed Collaborative Editing System," *Conference record of POPL*, January 1986.

[9]   H. Rex Hartson and Deborah Hix, "Human-Computer Interface Development: Concepts and Systems," *ACM Computing Surveys*, March 1989, pp. 5-92.

[10]   Keith A. Lantz, "An Experiment in Integrated Multimedia Conferencing," *Proceedings of Conference on Computer-Supported Cooperative Work*, December 1986, pp. 267-275.

[11]   J.C. Lauwers and K.A. Lantz, "Collaboration Awareness in Support of Collaboration Transparency: Requirements for the Next Generation of Shared Window Systems," *Proceedings of ACM CHI'90*, April 1990, pp. 303-312.

[12]   R. E. Newman-Wolfe, C. L. Ramirez, H. Pelimuhandiram, M. Montes, M. Webb, and D. L. Wilson, "A Brief Overview of the DCS Distributed Conferencing System," *Proceedings of the Summer Usenix Conference*, June 1991, pp. 437-452.

[13]   John F. Patterson, Ralph D. Hill, Steven L. Rohall, and W. Scott Meeks, "Rendezvous: An Architecture for Synchronous Multi-User Applications," *Proceedings of the Conference on Computer-Supported Cooperative Work*, October 1990, pp. 317-328.

[14]   Sunil Sarin and Irene Greif, "Computer-Based Real-Time Conferencing Systems," *IEEE Computer* 18:10 (October 1985), pp. 33-49.

[15]   Mark Stefik, Gregg Foster, Daniel G. Bobrow, Kenneth Kahn, Stan Lanning, and Lucy Suchman, "Beyond the Chalkboard: Computer Support for Collaboration and Problem Solving in Meetings," *CACM* 30:1 (January 1987), pp. 32-47.

[16]   J. Sutton and R. Sprague, "A Study of Display Generation and Management in Interactive Business Applications," Tech. Rept. RJ2392(#31804), IBM San Jose Research Laboratory, November 1978.

CHAPTER 12
Electronic Meeting and Decision Rooms

One of the earliest computer-based meeting rooms was the Capture Lab at Electronic Data Systems. "Observation of Executives Using a Computer-supported Meeting Environment" by Mantei (1989) explores ways in which aspects of the room layout, the placement of people in the meeting room, and the method of user participation in the meeting can affect the effectiveness and usability of the entire system. Observations in the Capture Lab demonstrate that details such as the interior design and colors of the conference room, the shape of the conference table, the position of the workstations with respect to the table, and the nature of the participants' chairs had a substantial effect on participant interactions. Meeting in this new environment produced a new "power position" in the room—the seat opposite the screen—and managers quickly moved to take advantage of it. Because WYSIWIS meeting software often leads to total absorption in typing and a subsequent drop in verbal exchange and eye contact, and because of the technical difficulties in implementing WYSIWIS, the Capture Lab developers designed a serial access floor control protocol. Groups of users seemed to apply it in three different ways, the "Interactive Meeting," the "Rotating Scribe Meeting," and the "Designated Scribe Meeting."

If room layout impacts meeting dynamics, imagine the impact of a whiteboard-size interactive display being used by a speaker for activities such as sketching, gesturing, and presenting slides. Such technology is described in "Liveboard: A Large Interactive Display Supporting Group Meetings, Presentations and Remote Collaboration" by Elrod, Bruce, Gold, Goldberg, Halasz, Janssen, Lee, McCall, Pederson, Pier, Tang, and Welch (1992). The authors describe the construction of the system including the use of a liquid crystal display, rear projection screen, and cordless pen; the system software; and some of the application software. Among their observations based on initial usage is the need for new interaction paradigms such as *gestural input* (Buxton, 1986), which are better suited to working in front of a group at a whiteboard.

Electronic meeting rooms, including the *roomware*, hardware, and software, have often been designed by the management information systems (MIS) community with the explicit goal of supporting decision making. The software has come to be known as *group decision support systems* (GDSSs), sometimes also known as *electronic meeting systems* (EMSs). A GDSS has tools to facilitate brainstorming and idea generation, as well as idea organization, and also provides capabilities for ranking and voting.

In many cases, participants contribute their ideas and their votes anonymously, a technique which has been shown to encourage participation from those who might otherwise be too shy or too intimidated to speak up. (Connolly, Jessup, and Valacich, 1990; Jessup, Connolly, and Galegher, 1990). "Electronic Meeting Systems to Support Group Work" by Nunamaker, Dennis, Valacich, Vogel, and George (1991) describes a system developed by Jay Nunamaker and his colleagues at the University of Arizona that was one of the earliest GDSSs and that has since become one of the most influential and successful. Their paper begins by sketching the nature of an electronic meeting system and by presenting the theoretical foundations upon which they were conceived. For example, there is the desire to reduce meeting *process losses* such as domination by one person, pressure to conform to the majority, and information overload by providing *process support*, *process structure*, *task support*, and *task structure*. The University of Arizona GroupSystems EMS is then described in some detail, including its tools for idea generation, idea organization, prioritizing, and policy development. The paper concludes by reviewing some of the literature of empirical research evaluating GroupSystems, including both laboratory experiments and field research.

As of the summer of 1991, the Arizona system had been installed at more than 22 universities and 12 corporations, and had been used by over 5000 individuals at those sites. Additionally, more than 25,000 IBM employees had used GroupSystems at 36 installations within IBM, with 20 more scheduled to be operational within the following year. "Experiences at IBM with Group Support Systems: A Field Study" by Nunamaker, Vogel, Heminger, Martz, Grohowski, and McGoff (1989) presents an analysis of experiences over one year at an IBM manufacturing site with 6000 employees. Pre- and post-session questionnaires, facilitator observations, and followup interviews were used to evaluate outcome effectiveness, efficiency, and user satisfaction of several hundred users of GroupSystems. Users rated both the quality of session process and the quality of session outcome very highly, estimated a 55% average per session time savings compared to the *projected* time to have the same meeting and carry out the same functions in a traditional meeting environment, and were generally very satisfied with the systems and the process.

A more general and more critical review of the impacts of EMS technology and the research lit-

erature on these impacts appears as "The Impact of Technological Support on Groups: An Assessment of the Empirical Research" by Pinsonneault and Kraemer (1989). The authors distinguish between Group Communication Support Systems (GCSSs), which include electronic mail and computer conferencing systems, and Group Decision Support Systems (GDSSs), which include electronic meeting systems such as GroupSystems. Their approach is to cluster and review the empirical research results in terms of how each result portrays task- and group-related outcomes as a function of contextual variables such as *group structure*, *task structure*, and technological support and group process variables such as *decisional characteristics*, *communication characteristics*, and *structure* imposed by the GCSS or GDSS. They repeatedly caution the reader to beware of too great a reliance on certain reported research results because of methodological flaws such the lack of an adequate control group, the use of a small numbers of subjects, or the failure to look at groups at different stages of development.

Notes and Guide to Further Reading

Additional reports detailing and analyzing work with the Capture Lab are Centre for Machine Intelligence (1988v), Elwart-Keys, Halonen, Horton, Kass, and Scott (1990), Austin, Liker, and McLeod (1990), and Losada, Sanchez, and Noble (1990). Other approaches to meeting room design are presented in Ferwanger, Wang, Lewe, and Krcmar (1991) and Lewe and Krcmar (1991), and in Olson, Olson, Killey, Mack, Cornell, and Luchetti (1990, in press). Of particular interest in both projects is the special focus on the environmental and ergonomic aspects of teamwork room, furniture, and interface design.

Pioneering work on group decision support systems has been done at the University of Minnesota as well as at the University of Arizona. The Minnesota work is described in DeSanctis and Gallupe (1987), Watson, DeSanctis, and Poole (1988), Poole, Holmes, and DeSanctis (1988), and University of Minnesota (1988v). Among the large number of reports on the Arizona work, the reader is particularly referred to University of Arizona (1988v), Dennis, George, Jessup, Nunamaker, and Vogel (1988), and Valacich, Dennis, and Nunamaker (1991). Further details about the use of the Arizona GDSS at IBM may be found in Grohowski, McGoff, Vogel, Martz, and Nunamaker (1990). Another paper reporting on the process of adopting this technology within an organization is George, Valacich, and Nunamaker (1990).

Commercial development and adoption of GDSSs is now vigorous. The University of Arizona has licensed their technology for resale by both Ventana Corporation and IBM. A number of other systems are also available. Reports from enthusiastic adopters may be found in Di Pietro (1992) and Dallavalle, Esposito, and Lang (1992).

Bostrom, Watson, and Kinney (Eds.) (1992) and the forthcoming Jessup and Valacich (Eds.) (1993, expected) are two useful books that focus more generally on group decision support systems. Poole and DeSanctis (1990) propose that we need to understand the use of GDSSs in terms of the theory of *adaptive structuration*, where structuration "refers to the process by which systems are produced and reproduced through members' use of rules and resources." DeSanctis (1991) reviews five competing theories for GDSS research: theories of decision making, group process theories, communication theories, institutional theories, and coordination theory. McGrath and Hollingshead (1991) suggest that we need a new classification of systems for technological enhancements of group work: Group (Internal) Communication Support Systems (GCSS), Group External Communication Support Systems (GXSS), Group Information Support Systems (GISS), and Group Performance Support Systems (GPSS).

There have recently been efforts to go beyond the conventional GDSS paradigm in several new directions. *Negotiation support systems* are discussed in Jones and Sanford (1990) and Foroughi and Jelassi (1990). *Organizational decision support systems* are reviewed in King and Star (1990); *organizational information support systems* are reviewed in Weisband and Galegher (1990).

Despite the wealth of activity and the increasing number of new paradigms, we still know very little about the effects of these technologies. In a critical review of the research on computer-assisted groups, Hollingshead and McGrath conclude as follows (1991, p. 25 of manuscript):

> It is apparent that any generalization one might make from these results is very shaky. While each individual study may be methodologically strong and sound (many are, some are not!), the body of literature as a whole is burdened with a triple or quadruple confounding of communication system, task type, research strategy, and lab or research locale. Furthermore the literature virtually ignores all group and member variables. Finally, there is wide variation in dependent variable—and they tend to cluster within the confounded task-media-lab-strategy clusters.

Observation of Executives Using a Computer Supported Meeting Environment

Marilyn MANTEI

Center for Machine Intelligence, Electronic Data Systems Corporation and Computer Science Department, University of Toronto, Toronto, Ont., Canada M5S 1A4

Designing interactive interfaces for individual usage is a significantly hard task that is being surmounted by evolving theory and hours of trial and error. The task of designing interactive interfaces for cooperative work and group decision making is even more difficult. Not only is it necessary to deal with the individual's cognitive processes and their model of the computer aided task, but also to build software to support human - human communication with all the underlying socialization and group dynamics that this communication implies. In the development of the Capture Lab, a computer supported meeting environment, guesswork was coupled with a study of human behavior in meetings both electronic and conventional. Added to these approaches was an extrapolation of existing research studies on non-computerized meetings and a series of mini-experiments to test out various ideas about the design. The body of the paper describes the application of this mixture along with the design considerations at issue and the meeting behaviors we have since observed as a result of our design choices.

Keywords: Groupware; Group Decision Support Systems; Computer Supported Cooperative Work; Computer Supported Meeting Environments; Executive Meeting Behavior.

1. Introduction

In the design of individual computer interfaces, the software designer concentrates on the order and sequence of the information that appears on the screen. If the interface is to be part of a hardware product such as the basic operating system of a personal computer, the design of the interface extends to the design of the computer casing and the keyboard. When designing a meeting room supported by computers, the design situation changes dramatically. The interface becomes a room interface and consideration is given to the layout of the computers, the placement of the people in the meeting room, the sequencing of the user participation in the meeting and the visual accoutrements of the room.

As with screen layout, each of these details affects the interface and the performance of the group members using the interface. The computer supported meeting interfaces are extremely new and no literature exists on the efficacy of various

Marilyn M. Mantei received her Ph.D. [1982] in Communications Theory from the University of Southern California's Annenberg School of Communications. During her graduate years, she worked at Xerox Palo Alto Research Center and spent two years as a visiting scholar at Carnegie-Mellon University in the Psychology and Computer Science Departments. Dr. Mantei traveled from Carnegie-Mellon University to take a faculty position at the University of Michigan's Business School where she taught until 1986. While at Michigan, Dr. Mantei built a doctoral program in human-computer interaction and started the Human Computer Interaction Laboratory for the University. She is currently Associate Professor of Computer Science at the University of Toronto. During her stay in Michigan, Dr. Mantei was project director of a system development project for a startup microcomputer company and head of a collaborative work project at Electronic Data Systems Corporation's Center for Machine Intelligence. She has served as Secretary-Treasurer of the Association for Computing Machinery's Special Interest group on Computer Human Interaction and as Chair of their Advisory Board. She also chaired the CHI'86 Conference on Human Factors in Computing. Her current research interests include computer supported cooperative work, cognitive models of user interfaces to complex systems and user interface management systems.

North-Holland

Decision Support Systems 5 (1989) 153–166

designs. We describe three of the intuitive and partially tested design decisions we made in building a computer supported meeting environment, the Capture Lab. We based our decisions on the experiences we had in meeting in three other computer supported meeting environments, on our own trial meetings in prototype environments, on observations of meetings held by our intended user population, and on existing user interface design and group dynamics research.

Our basic design goal was to build a room environment that was close to the meeting environments our user population was accustomed to. We reasoned that large deviations from meeting environments that our users had already adapted to would create too large a learning task. We were concerned that a high learning threshold would cause meeting participants to reject the technology. Therefore, we opted for a strategy of small changes and a gradual evolution into the use of the computer support.

From our videotaped observations of individuals meeting in the Capture Lab, we find that our design choices have made the inclusion of the computers non-obtrusive and that meeting participants select to use the room for subsequent meetings. We also find that the addition of the computer support coupled with our methods of implementing the support generated a set of unpredicted behaviors in the meeting participants, behavior which we have not seen reported by other researchers. These behaviors are described in the next three paragraphs and discussed in considerable detail in the description of the Capture Lab design choices.

After much consideration, an oval conference table was selected over semi-circular seating arrangements. Oval seating worked fine for meetings in which everyone participated in the meeting, but when the meeting was clearly dominated by a senior manager, the seating arrangement moved from its oval format into a semi-circular format.

We found that the strong focal point caused by the dynamic behavior of the front screen changed the traditional seating positions of power. This disconcerted our managers until they found the location of the new "power" seat.

We expected that our serial access protocol would cause individuals to verbally negotiate access to the front screen. We believed that this access would switch constantly as each individual placed their spoken thoughts and opinions on the screen. Instead, meeting attendees created a new social exchange form where attendees agreed implicitly to type the spoken suggestions of each other.

2. The Capture Lab and its User Population

Before discussing the unique design choices we faced in building the Capture Lab, we briefly overview its main features and the hardware that supports it. Because meetings differ so widely depending on the task and types of individuals in attendance (DeSanctis & Gallupe, 1987), we also describe the types of managers that we observed in the Capture Lab and the tasks they were working on in their meetings.

2.1. The Basic Design

The Capture Lab is a computer-based system for cooperative work and group decision making. Kraemer and King (1988) describe the technology as a collaboration laboratory and characterize it as having a conference room with an electronic chalkboard, microcomputer workstations and a form of "e"-lectern from which a designated member of the meeting manages the meeting. The Capture Lab shares all these properties except the electern. It also includes an adjoining laboratory for unobtrusively recording and observing meetings. Fig. 1 presents a schematic drawing of the Capture Lab layout including the observation room.

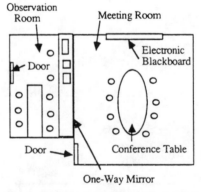

Fig. 1. Layout of the Capture Lab meeting and observation rooms.

The Capture Lab is contained in a 20 ft. deep by 19.5 ft. wide conference room and an adjoining 15 ft. by 10.5 ft. observation room. Eight Macintosh II computer monitors are tilted back and embedded in a formica topped oval conference table placed in the center of the room. Each of the monitors is connected to a Macintosh II computer with five Megabytes of memory and a 40 Megabyte internal hard disk. A ninth computer, similarly configured, sends its video output to a Hughes 700 projector which rear projects the Macintosh screen image on a 4 ft. by 6 ft. screen in front of the conference room. A tenth Macintosh II (also with 5 Megabytes of RAM and a 40 Megabyte hard disk) manages the communication software and access to the front screen. The ten computers communicate with each other via the Appletalk network.

Apple Macintosh II computers were chosen because the smaller monitors would fit into the conference table while still providing us with the needed computing power. We also wanted a bit-mapped screen for graphics capabilities. In addition we felt that the "direct manipulation" style of the Macintosh interface plus its consistent interface across many different software packages made the system easier to learn by meeting attendees.

Each of the ten computers in the Capture Lab runs autonomously. This means that users can run different programs on each computer. The shared focus for individuals meeting in the Capture Lab comes from using the front display screen or electronic blackboard. By typing a request at their own keyboard, any person in the room can move from working on their own computer to working on the computer driving the front screen. They are then using whatever program has been running on the front screen computer at the time they request access.

Individuals meeting together can agree on a program to run on the electronic blackboard computer and then share access to this program. For example, in a meeting on budget planning, a spreadsheet package could be invoked with each meeting member filling in their budget needs in the common spreadsheet displayed on the front screen.

The communications software also allows individuals to work alone at their own personal computers. They can share this work by copying it to a buffer (the Macintosh Clipboard) and requesting access to the front display screen. The work in the buffer is transferred with the access to the electronic blackboard computer and can be placed anywhere on the front screen.

The ten computers are connected to three file servers, each with eighty Megabyte hard disks. Large volumes of information that are not readily transferred through the use of the buffer are often brought to the front screen by way of the file server.

Except for the program managing the communications requests and a small background communications program residing in each workstation, all other software available to users is that which is commercially available for the Apple Macintosh II computer. Although the communications architecture was more difficult to build for this approach, we did not have to spend considerable coding effort on rebuilding wordprocessors and graphics packages which were already available commercially and of high quality. Lantz (1986) describes in detail both the difficult architecture problems and the gains made from this approach.

We find that this approach has significantly increased the types of software support we are able to offer our users. Our major disadvantage to this approach is the copyright law which requires us to purchase not one but ten copies of each new software package we add to the Capture Lab's repertoire. The software packages also suffer from having been designed as interfaces for a single user, preventing us from employing any group tools.

In addition to the monitor embedded in the table, users of the Capture Lab have an Apple Macintosh II keyboard and a mouse. Wires connect to these devices via an inkwell like hole near one side of the monitor. Only the monitors, keyboards and mice are inside the conference room. The computers are behind the front display screen and connected by cables running in a cable tray that leads to the inside of the conference table.

Cloth covered chairs with arms that swivel and tilt sit in front of each work area. To the left of the front screen, a screen folds back to review a whiteboard. A similar screen folds back on the right to reveal a pull down screen for front projection of slides or overheads.

All lighting fixtures were placed around the side of the room to reduce glare on the front screen and the monitors. Florescent fixtures were placed in the exterior and interior perimeters of a two foot wide dropped ceiling that circumnavigated the entire room. Light reflected from the fixtures was designed to scatter off the ceiling.

To gather data on meetings taking place in the room, three video cameras were embedded in the dropped ceiling behind one-way mirrors. Their signals were sent to an observation room located on the left-hand wall of the conference room. A one-way mirror spanning the entire left wall of the conference room permitted researchers to observe and document meeting behavior. Six directional microphones embedded in the wall of the meeting room picked up the meeting conversations both for the videotape records and for broadcast into the sound insulated observation room.

The observation room consisted of a two-tiered seating arrangement with writing workspace in front of each row of seats. The table for the front tier abutted on the lower edge of the one-way mirror. A third of the front table contained the video and audio control apparatus which permitted changing camera angles, zooming in on specific individuals in the meeting and mixing the video signals.

Above the front table, a television monitor and a large screen computer monitor were suspended from the ceiling for the viewing advantage of the back row of observers. This permitted them to see the VCR video signal being recorded and the information being displayed on the front screen of the meeting room. The equipment in the observation room was built to "capture" meeting behavior taking place in the primary meeting room. The name, Capture Lab, is derived from this purpose.

2.2. Meeting Participants

The Capture Lab is located at the Center for Machine Intelligence, a unit of Electronic Data Systems Corporation. Executives from EDS and from one of its customer accounts use the Capture Lab regularly for offsite meetings. It is these meetings that are discussed in relation to the specific design options presented in the body of the paper. Four separate meeting groups were observed and videotaped in a series of three to six meetings. Each member of the groups consented to be videotaped as long as the information and their identity were kept confidential.

The initial session for two of the four meeting groups began with an hour's introduction to the use of the Macintosh computers. Before the meetings took place, one of the members of the meeting group – either a secretary or a lower ranked staff member – either visited the Center for Machine Intelligence for two days or already was well-versed in the use of the Macintosh computer. These individuals were present to help others with the problems they might encounter in using the software, but they found that their expertise was soon usurped by other meeting members.

In the case of the other two groups each meeting member used a Macintosh computer frequently. They therefore received only a 15 minute introduction on the use of the Capture Lab access button and the software they intended to use.

In one set of meetings the members came from different but equal managerial levels of the corporation. Each of the managers controlled a major functional area of one of the company's divisions. The managers met to lay out a plan of responsibilities for the processing of the company's product at various stages of development. Each of the manager's contributed information on what his or her responsible areas were and negotiated the ambiguous areas of responsibility. A PERT charting software package and a wordprocessor were used for these meetings. This group met for 4–6 hours in three different Capture Lab meetings. They worked on a different set of responsibility assignments in each meeting.

A second set of meetings involved personnel in strategic marketing performing online preparation of slides for a presentation to be given to upper management. These individuals worked as staff for a vice president of the company. They used a slide making software package to generate their presentation. Each presentation preparation took approximately three hours. The staff members began each meeting with a clean slate and developed the sequence of slides for the presentation in the meeting.

A third set of meetings involved senior executives engaged in setting up a policy document describing the relations and authority lines their company would have with a third party vendor. The members of the meeting were either senior executives, staff to senior executives or corporate consultants. An initial document had been drafted by a staff member for the meeting. The individuals in the meeting negotiated details of the agreement and had these details typed into the document as the meeting progressed. They used a wordprocessing package as the electronic blackboard communication tool.

Meetings were held weekly and lasted 8–10 hours. Each meeting ended with resolution on a major section of the policy document. A Macintosh support person in the meeting was directed to clean up the document and distribute it to the meeting members. Their next meeting focused on the next policy section, and they continued to meet until the document was complete.

The fourth set of meetings consisted of staff meetings held by a product development group within the company. These meetings, held weekly, assessed the week's accomplishments and any problems. Meeting output consisted of new directions to take and solutions to current problems. Action items assigned to personnel at the meeting were typed on the front display screen. They used an outliner software package for most meetings, but occasionally employed a drawing package. Each meeting begain with a display of the agenda generated at the previous meeting. This was modified and ordered to reflect new items and new priorities. Each item was then assigned a time limit and discussed in the meeting. The meeting ended when all agenda items had been discussed or placed on next week's agenda.

Most groups traveled one hour to use the Capture Lab. The product development group met for the shortest period of time (approximately 2 hours), but had to travel the least distance to use the facility. All other groups met for half a day or the entire day. The reason given by each of the groups for taking the time to drive to the Capture Lab for a meeting was the enormous time saving they achieved in tasks which required negotiation or coordination. They gave estimates of a factor of ten in real time savings, citing the exchanges of multiple drafts of plans and documents before agreement could be reached using traditional meetings.

3. Computer Supported Meeting Design Choices

In building the Capture Lab environment we made many detailed design decisions. We report on three choices that are unique to the design of computer supported meeting environments. They are the seating arrangements of the meeting participants, the field of view between participants, and the protocols we used for the exchange of information typed on each of the individual workstations. We give the rationale for each design decision followed by an explanation of how we implemented the decision given the physical, technical and cost constraints of the environment. Since the Capture Lab has been operational, we have had a chance to videotape meetings of our user population using the room. The videotapes have given us a set of new insights into our design decisions. We present descriptions of the meeting behaviors we have observed that stemmed from our design choices. We also offer explanations for behaviors which were not necessarily the ones we expected.

3.1. Seating Arrangements

When we began the design of the Capture Lab, we envisioned two semi-circular rows of wedge-shaped desks facing a front screen. We were particularly pleased with the design of Colab (Stefik, Foster, Bobrow, Kahn, Lanning, and Suchman, 1987), Xerox PARC's meeting environment. We reasoned that the interchange between meeting participants would be primarily through the contents placed on the main viewing screen of the meeting room. Our plan was to enlarge their seating arrangement to accomodate eight users instead of four.

Groups from our user population regularly met in three different conference rooms. We noted that when our user population met around an oval conference table, more members participated in the meetings than when they met at tables arranged in a U-shaped fashion. This observation led us to rethink our design approach. We could not assume instant use of the computers as a replacement to verbal communication. Therefore, we needed to support the verbal exchange at meetings. A semi-circular seating setup is not conducive to eye contact, nonverbal exchanges and verbal interaction among meeting participants, exchanges which have been documented to be an important part of communication (Krauss, Garlock, Bricker and McMahon, 1977). Since we were interested in building an environment which supports meeting participation, we decided to have our participants seated around an oval conference table. We felt that a conference table also symbolized a typical meeting to most individuals and therefore matched our design criteria to build a conventional looking meeting room.

In designing the Capture Lab's conference table, we wanted to focus the meeting on the front screen of the meeting room. This design constraint arose from our decision on how to manage the computer exchange of information in the meeting. Because we chose the front screen as the display area for this exchange, we needed to design the seating arrangement to give easy visual access to this display.

We set up the seating around the table so that participants could face the front screen by rotating their chairs. We could not seat anyone at the head of the table in the way of the screen. The constraints of the physical placement of the computer monitors in the table also prevented us from seating a participant at the base of the table. This led to nearly equal seating for each member of our user population. Fig. 2 illustrates the seating arrangement we chose.

We use swivel, tilt and roll chairs for the meeting room. Meeting members turn their chairs to face forward, lean back and look at the front screen. They then swivel around to face the individuals in the meeting. There is constant eye contact and non-verbal communication between meeting members in addition to a high volume of verbal exchange. They verbally discuss their differences or ideas and then use the front screen to display and edit the results of their exchange. We have observed disagreements on issues but the disagreements are not extreme and discussion involves clarifying points rather than taking strong stands. This behavior occurs in meetings where members are of equal status in the organization.

Meeting members form a different seating arrangement with their movable chairs in meetings in which a person in a higher managerial position

Electronic
Blackboard

Fig. 2. Conference Table Seating Arrangement Used in the Capture Lab.

is present. The focus of the meeting members is only on the front display screen. Participants in the front of the room move their chairs away from the table and form a semi-circle. These individuals do not use the computer workstation to input their thoughts but rely on someone in the meeting to be a scribe.

We believe this occurs because of the intense focus of the group on the front screen and because of the constraints against individual computer input that are brought on by the control structure of the group. (Management explicitly directs meeting participants to stop typing their ideas on the front screen.) The visual angle and the lighting near the front of the meeting room make viewing the front screen more difficult. The table, because of the need to put the keyboard at a reasonable typing height and to support the weight of the monitors, does not allow sufficient leg room. The social constraints against using the computer terminals makes sitting next to the keyboard unnecessary. Meeting participants can therefore improve their viewing and comfort by moving away from the table into a semi-circle.

We cannot disambiguate the effect of the tasks brought to the meetings from that of the power structures in the meetings. It may be that the semi-circular groups have work which needs less interaction. However, we have observed a group that was engaged in active discussion over their differences move to a state of reduced verbal exchange and to a semi-circular arrangement when late arriving management entered the meeting. This suggests that different power structures in a meeting take on different seating arrangements in our environment with the oval seating used by parity participants and semi-circular seating used by participants who have unequal power positions in the meeting.

3.2. Inter-Viewing Arrangements Between Participants

Research on computer mail and teleconferencing systems has shown that the individuals using these systems often exchange more extreme communication than they would do in a face-to-face meeting (Siegel, Dubrovsky, Kiesler and McGuire, 1986; Kiesler, Siegel and McGuire, 1984). This includes such behavior as the reduction in comments which directly address the person in the

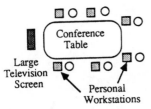

Fig. 3. Workstation placement and seating arrangement in SAAM, University of Minnesota's computer supported meeting environment.

communication, the use of socially indelicate words and the statement of more extreme positions.

Watson, DeSanctis and Poole (1988) have also found this to be true in the computer supported meetings they observed at the University of Minnesota. This behavior is believed to be caused by the loss of social controls that occur in face-to-face meetings. However, this explanation makes it difficult to understand Watson, DeSanctis and Poole's results which occurred in a face-to-face meeting. Only the presence of the computer terminals and the typing made their meetings different from conventional face-to-face meetings. One explanation for the occurrence of the behavior observed by Watson, et al. could be the positioning of their workstations (see fig. 3). Individuals work by facing their workstation and the front screen and not by facing each other.

Nunamaker, Applegate and Konsynski (1988) found that the anonymity designed into their PLEXSYS system tended to heighten conflict within the group as members became more blunt and assertive in their comments. Participants in SAAM meetings have some degree of anonymity but only if everyone is typing simultaneously. The PLEXSYS system has monitors which occlude the view of other individuals in the room, and participants in meetings are arranged in a semi-circle around the front display screen. It may be that anonymity is the cause of the loss of social controls, but the occluding terminals are a potential mitigating factor. We reason that it is the visual contact between people that brings on the enforcement of social norms at a meeting, perhaps, because of its immediate loss of anonymity. Because our user population has real corporate conflicts as part of their meetings, we did not want the environment to generate behavior that

would affect the negotiation of these conflicts. Based on the above reasoning, we decided to make the viewing of other meeting participants as easy as possible.

We were concerned about being able to achieve satisfactory interperson viewing arrangements for two reasons. First, most computer monitors are so large and bulky that they require additional depth on a desktop. This depth requirement places the opposing person seated at a table at a greater physical distance. Second, the size of the computer monitors is large enough to occlude the opposing person and, unfortunately, the occlusion is inversely proportional to the physical displacement of the monitors from the participants. The size of the monitors we planned on placing in the table limited the minimum distance at which we could seat people. This was larger than a normal conference table (5 feet as compared to 3.5 feet). When we sat at a table with this viewing distance, we felt that the person across the table was too far away. We observed meetings in which individuals were separated by 5 feet and 10 feet, and found that individuals turned to talk with their neighbors rather than having conversations with the person facing them. At 3.5 feet, conversations occurred more often across the table unless visual obstructions interfered with the viewing.

To make the visual distance look less, the conference table was built with a light colored formica oval covering in its center and a darker circle of 1.5 feet around the edge. See fig. 4 for an illustration of this. The darker circle was intended to visually make the light colored oval look smaller and to give individuals a sense of being closer together. We also carpeted the room in a lighter gray border with a darker blue gray center square in which the table was placed. We placed a violet blue band of wall paneling at seated head height between lighter gray tan wall paneling. The low dark centering area of the rug and the dark bands on the walls also served to enclose the group members and make them feel visually closer. We used the advice of our architect for generating these visual sensations and have not empirically tested the effect of these color arrangements.

To keep the meeting room computers from occluding other individuals in the meeting room, we purchased 12 inch monitors. We were not able to buy smaller monitors. We needed personal workstations that were powerful enough to run

Fig. 4. The use of colors to reduce the apparent visual distances in the Capture Lab.

our communications and meeting support software plus the applications of our user population. These workstations did not support small graphics monitors.

We felt that reducing the obtrusiveness of the monitor was an extremely important decision in the room design. We based our intuitions on two tests that we ran. First, we asked people to seat themselves in a comfortable arrangement in which 12 inch diagonal monitors were placed on the table in front of them. Each of the people chose a maximum distance (about 20 feet) to sit from the other individuals in the room. This gave them the least visual obstruction of the other individuals. When we stopped using the computer system, the individuals moved to the side of the monitors and to a closer distance of five feet.

In our second test, we placed Apple Macintosh Plus computers on a circular table in front of three seated individuals. They were asked to exchange computer mail messages on a topic undergoing some debate in the office. The computers partially occluded the view of each of the participants. The participants in the meeting did not look at each other nor did they exchange verbal messages although they were seated facing each other across a 3 foot table. One of the group members needed help with the use of the mail system, but did not ask for or receive help on using the system until messages had been exchanged for 20 minutes.

An individual in the meeting had been primed to type outrageous or irrelevant statements in the computer message exchange. Rather than generating computer moderated conflict these statements were responded to verbally with individuals bringing their chairs to the side of the person sending the outrageous messages. A dyadic exchange developed between these two individuals. When it ended, the displaced person returned to his or her computer. These anecdotes reinforced our belief that reducing the obtrusiveness of the monitors was an important part of the design.

The 12 inch monitors used in the Capture Lab interfered with the view of other meeting participants. For that reason, we tipped the monitors and lowered them into the conference table so that they were 4 inches above the table at their highest point. We colored the center part of the table to match the color of the monitors. Our architect indicated that this would cause them to visually become a part of the table and thus appear smaller and less obtrusive. In placing the monitors in the table, we had a variety of choices in how they could be arranged. We worked with two dimensions in laying out these choices, (1) the location of the monitor inside the individual's workarea, and (2) the orientation of the monitor. The moni-

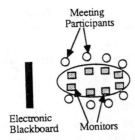

a. Monitors face perpendicular to conference table and are located in center of user's workarea.

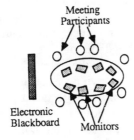

b. Monitors alternate orientation and placement, first facing forward then facing backward, first to left of work area, then to right of work area.

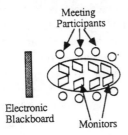

c. All monitors oriented toward front of meeting room and located to the side of user's work area.

Fig. 5. Examples of monitor orientations and placements possible in the layout of an oval conference table. Example c was used for the Capture Lab.

tor could either be located directly in front of the user or to one side. It could be oriented to face the front of the room, to face forward or in alternating orientations for each meeting participant.

Fig. 5 gives examples of the possible monitor arrangements that could be utilized. We chose the orientation and placement shown in Figure 5-c, i.e., the monitors oriented toward the electronic blackboard and placed to one side of the person's workspace.

We moved the monitors out of each individual's workspace to free up this space for papers, coffee and other items which are brought to meetings. The monitors were aligned so that open space occurred across the table between each dyad of meeting participants. This permitted full visual exchange of gestures and the ability to pass papers back and forth across the table. The monitors were placed to face the front screen because we wanted to encourage meeting participants to focus on the shared workspace of the electronic blackboard. We did not want the presence of monitors in the meeting to completely absorb each participant's attention.

The use of color to shorten distance and the placement of the monitors in the conference table appears to work. Participants in the meeting talk to all other members of the meeting.

People seated at the back of the table can view the screen and everyone seated at the table. People seated near the front miss looking at other meeting members when they are viewing the screen. Because of this, the rear seating has become a powerful position. Managers move to this seating after very little experience with the Capture Lab. Managers new to the room sit on the side of the table farthest from the door and in the seat closest to the front screen. In a conventional meeting environment a manager in this position can face the rest of the people at a meeting and also walk up to a blackboard or overhead projector screen and write or point to items being discussed.

In the Capture Lab environment control of the front screen lies in the individual keyboards of the meeting participants. The attention of the meeting participants is on the front screen and therefore the front area of the room. The information is rearprojected making the screen bright and giving front seated persons a visual sensation of being in shadow. A front seat does not give its owner control of the meeting input or the opportunity to draw attention (and therefore power) to his or her position. The sense of being at the head or leading position of the table is better achieved at the seats near the base of the table with the seat facing the door being more powerful because it observes entry into the room. It also causes other participants to turn their heads away from the screen in order to view the speaking person thereby drawing additional attention to the speaker.

Three managers bring their groups to meet in

the Capture Lab on a regular basis. The following behaviors have been videotaped at their meetings.

In his first meeting in the Capture Lab, Manager No. 1 took the front seat farthest from the door and closest to the screen. He became very uncomfortable in this position and engaged in a variety of behaviors. First, he walked around the room and looked at each individual's screen. Then he walked to a whiteboard positioned to the left of the main screen and began to write his ideas on this whiteboard. this maneuver did not draw the attention of the group away from the main screen.

Manager No. 1 then stood to the side of the main screen and pointed to elements on the screen. He requested different individuals in the room to type in his ideas on the main screen. It was difficult for the manager to see the text on the main screen at this proximity causing him to move to the side of the room to see what was being typed. He eventually left the room and came back with a chair which he placed between the two individuals seated at the base of the table. Although he did not have his own computer, he directed others in the meeting to type in his ideas. He now uses this seat in all Capture Lab meetings.

Manager No. 2 was told by Capture Lab support staff that the more powerful seats were at the base of the table. He took a seat with his back to the door at the table's base in his first meeting. Initially, Manager No. 2 typed in his ideas for display on the front screen along with other meeting participants. As the meeting progressed, he moved his chair between the two monitors at the base of the table and directed others to type in his comments. At subsequent Capture Lab meetings he continues to sit at this point of the table with no keyboard in front of him. By directing others to type in his ideas, he has complete verbal control over the meeting.

We do not have a videotape record of the initial meeting of Manager No. 3 and no-one can remember his initial seat choice. In recent Capture Lab meetings, if he arrives at a meeting at the same time or before other meeting participants, he always takes the chair at the base of the conference table, facing the door. If someone has already taken this chair, he will sit next to this person between the two monitors on the far side of the table. He will then slide his chair back and speak to the room. Because he has positioned himself behind the normal seating arrangement,

meeting participants are required to reorient their positions to view the speaker. He draws more attention to himself in this way.

When Manager No. 3 wishes to enter comments on the computer screen, he borrows a keyboard from the computer at the base of the table and places it on his lap. Gradually, the person at this position moves toward the base of the table giving up the monitor and keyboard control to the manager.

Our room, through the installation of the computers and the difficulty in viewing the main display screen at close proximity, has changed the "power" seats at the conference table. Our observed managers exhibited discomfort until they located the new power seat in the room. They then shifted over to always occupying this seat.

The placement of the monitors to face the front screen has caused another potential problem. Because these monitors are aligned in the same direction, the individuals can see what is typed on the screens of those seated just forward of them. This prevents participants from sending private messages or preparing personal work. We do not know what meeting impact this lack of privacy causes. Until recently our software tools only permitted work on the electronic blackboard, making the use of the monitors negligible. Individuals did use their personal monitor to explore different computer systems, to doodle and to play games when the meeting taking place began to "drag".

3.3. Participation Protocols

We did not want our meeting to be a teleconferencing style meeting where the only difference between the Capture Lab and teleconferencing would lie in the real time nature of the meeting. We wanted the meeting participants to interact verbally with each other and to sense each other's presence in the group. The difficulty in designing the user interface for this type of system was of deep concern to us. We needed to make the number of commands a user needed to know and the number of steps a user took to perform any type of communication task as low as possible. We were worried that even if we met this criteria, that the task of typing on a computer keyboard would make the cognitive load of meeting participants so high that they could not carry on useful conversations.

Before building the Capture Lab, we held meetings using a large screen projector and a single personal computer. The items discussed in the meeting were entered and displayed on a large screen. We passed the keyboard back and forth between individuals wanting to input information in the meeting. We met in this fashion with outside consultants, within our own group and with anyone else who felt comfortable using the microcomputer software we were using. Invariably, one individual became the scribe for the meeting. Instead of talking, the scribe typed other's ideas and everyone else talked. These early experiences did not alleviate our worries about the impact of typing.

The initial software plan for the Capture Lab was a distributed shared workspace on everyone's workstation in the fashion of the "What You See Is What I See (WYSIWIS) design of the Xerox Colab System (Stefik et al., 1987). In the WYSIWIS environment, what is typed on the personal workstation of one person in the meeting immediately shows up on the other meeting participant's workstations and on the front screen.

Our experience in meeting with the Colab System gave us a very positive impression of the WYSIWIS concept. The simultaneity of the input from each meeting participant allowed all persons to contribute to the meeting and removed the necessity of waiting to speak.

We reasoned that a considerable cognitive load is required of meeting participants wishing to speak. They need to rehearse what they are planning to say, to pay attention to the speech patterns of others so that they can grab an opening in which to speak and to constantly update what they are going to say to match the changing context of the meeting discussions. WYSIWIS removes these constraints, allowing participants to spend more cognitive effort on the problem under discussion and on hearing (reading) what others are saying (typing). The disadvantage that we perceived with using the Colab meeting environment was the total absorption of the participants in their typing with a subsequent drop in verbal exchange. We wanted to maintain the eye contact and verbal exchange. The drop in verbalizations in Colab and our observations of people using the large screen with a single computer led us to drop plans for a WYSIWIS interface. The very high software development cost for implementing a WYSIWIS system was also a major reason for our choice of a serial communications protocol.

We made the electronic blackboard (e.g., front screen) into the shared workspace and kept the personal workstations as private work areas. Access to the electronic blackboard is sequential. We reasoned that the sequential nature of the input would encourage a focus on the group product and establish time for verbal commentary on each piece of input.

We made access to the electronic blackboard available to any meeting participant via a function key on their keyboard. Whenever any participant wants to type something on the front screen, they press this function key and begin typing. They can be interrupted by any other meeting participant in the same way that a speaker at a meeting can be interrupted. Unlike a spoken interruption, the electronic interruption cannot be ignored. We call this a pre-emptive protocol. Many different protocols are possible for accessing the front screen. These are discussed in depth by Scott (1988). We chose the pre-emptive protocol because it permitted the group to verbally manage interruptions. We felt that current understanding of social exchange protocols was not sufficient to impose a particular set of electronic controls on meeting input.

If meeting participants wish to prepare information at their own workstation, they may do so at any time during the meeting. To display this information on the electronic blackboard, they must select the information on their personal screen they wish to display. When they press the access button for the front screen, the selected information is carried with them and copied to a buffer in the computer running the front screen. The information can then be copied from this buffer to the desired insertion point on the front screen.

We envisioned that group negotiated usage would regulate when the members engaged in simultaneous generation of input at their personal workstations and when they engaged in verbal interchanges. At the writing of this paper, the ability to transfer information to the front screen has only been made available to a small number of groups meeting in the Capture Lab. We have not observed sufficient meetings using this capability to draw any conclusions about how this capability is being used.

Using the electronic blackboard and not having a WYSIWIS capability has generated three different types of meetings in the Capture Lab; the Interactive Meeting, the Rotating Scribe Meeting and the Designated Scribe Meeting. The Interactive Meeting is what we expected to take place. All participants use the keyboard access key when they wish to contribute to the meeting. There is considerable verbal exchange about the items typed on the screen and a large number of changes are made to the items after they are put on the main screen. Verbal exchange usually occurs after the item is inserted. If a group member generates information in their private workstation and then inserts it on the front screen, this behavior is received negatively by the group which prefers to absorb the smaller volumes of information generated on the front screen. These meetings are rare and occur when everyone is equally comfortable with the software and types at approximately the same speed.

The second type of meeting, the Rotating Scribe Meeting is the most common meeting we observe. Whenever someone has access to the front screen, other meeting participants give this person their verbalized ideas to type on to the front screen. Discussion occurs before the item is typed, and often group members are involved in giving detailed task information such as, "enthousiasm is misspelled", or "move that up by one line". This individual usually maintains control of the front screen until they ask another member to take over. This request is made when they have suggestions they wish to have placed on the front screen or when they have tired of typing.

Rotating Scribe Meetings have a large amount of verbal exchange. Most of the exchange is task directed. Before an item is typed, the discussion focuses on the content of the item to appear on the screen. After the item is typed, the discussion focuses on detailed syntactic corrections to the item. The meeting participants show little anxiety or boredom during these meetings and mistakes made in using the electronic blackboard become a source of shared humor for group participants.

The individuals who become scribes in the meeting are those who are better typists or who are more skilled in using the personal workstations. Other members use the access to the front screen less frequently. When a meeting member is in scribe mode, they do not participate

with as high a verbal frequency in the meeting as when they are not acting as a scribe. Access to the front screen is taken by another group member when such a member has input that they do not want to take the time to relay to the current scribe. It also occurs when the scribe has made a spelling or insertion error that the incoming scribe wishes to correct. The outgoing scribe readily releases control of the front screen. Access is invariably preceded by a verbal indication of a desire for access.

In the third type of meeting, the Designated Scribe Meeting, a single person is designated to enter information on the front screen for the group. Each of the group members tells the scribe what they wish entered. The meeting looks like a single secretary taking dictation from many people at once. This type of meeting occurs by prior planning. A manager deciding to have a meeting in the Capture Lab will bring along a secretary or a staff member to record information suggested by the meeting participants. Often, the designated scribe visits the Capture Lab a week prior to the first meeting to become comfortable with the software.

The Designated Scribe Meeting is different from a blackboard meeting where someone is writing down meeting suggestions. The verbal behavior is directed at the front screen and not at the other meeting members. The discussion focuses directly on what is to be typed on the front screen and there is little pre-discussion of the issues before they are placed on the front screen. Meeting members begin to fidget during this type of meeting and exhibit other types of behavior associated with a drop in meeting attention, e.g., side discussions with neighbors, playing with the mouse on their personal workstation or getting up for a coffee refill.

We often observe a breakdown of the Designated Scribe Meeting into a Rotating Scribe Meeting. The designated scribe is not always as knowledgeable about the topics under discussion and other meeting members become frustrated with the amount of verbal detail they need to supply to the scribe. Eventually, the designated scribe has little to do in the meeting as other meeting members take the controls. Upper level management is often in attendance at Designated Scribe Meetings, but this does not deter the breakdown of these meetings into Rotating Scribe Meetings.

Because the shared workspace for the Capture Lab is on the front screen, all of the Capture Lab meetings proceed in sequential fashion. Information being displayed on the front screen captures people's attention so much in a meeting that even members who are speaking lose their train of thought if someone else is typing information on the front screen. We note that although there is considerable focus of meeting members on the task at hand and a lively discussion taking place, there is also fidgeting and yawning of meeting members who are not using the computer tools. We therefore believe that the shared workspace on personal workstations is a good idea because it allows meeting participants to generate input simultaneously. It is likely that the best type of meeting structure permits a meeting focus on the front screen for designated interactive portions of the meeting and a focus on individual workstations for designated individual effort portions of the meeting. Our prediction that this would occur as a natural group evolution in the use of the meeting tools was wrong. We are now planning to demonstrate this potential usage as part of our meeting room instruction.

4. Conclusion

Many detailed and important design decisions were made in the construction of the Capture Lab environment. We discussed three, the seating arrangements, the inter-viewing distances and the electronic blackboard access protocols. Our decisions were made with the goal of making the Capture Lab meeting environment as close as possible to the meeting environments that our user population was accustomed to. We adopted this goal because we did not know what impact our computer supported meeting environment would have on groups.

We felt that we would have a better chance of understanding the impact of the computer supported meeting environment on meetings if we limited the number of differences between the Capture Lab and our users' current meeting environments. Our goal implied that we reduce the visual presence of the computers in the meeting room, that we use a conference table and that we establish a communication protocol for the use of the computing system that followed the sequential verbal communication protocols that people use in ordinary, non-computer supported meetings.

Despite our desires to make few changes to a standard meeting environment, the addition of a dynamic shared workspace changes the capabilities of the meeting participants dramatically. We have observed meeting members change their seating arrangements and focus on the dynamic workspace when upper management is present and revert to their original seating arrangement when upper management leaves the meeting.

In placing the computers in the table with the goal of encouraging verbal interaction and a focus on the front screen, we observed the use of new power positions at the conference table. We built in the pre-emptive protocol for accessing the electronic blackboard with the concept that meeting participants would all share in the access. Instead, we have observed that a rotating scribe role evolves within the meetings even when meetings begin with a predesignated scribe.

We have observed four groups of individuals who met regularly in the Capture Lab. The participants are all from the same organizations and the groups are well-formed, i.e., they have been meeting together as a group (with some turnover in membership) for 1–5 years. Because of the limited number of groups we have studied and because of the strong impact of a particular corporate culture on meetings, the observations in this paper cannot be extrapolated to a more general population. They are described to provide the reader with insights into how small perturbations in the design of a meeting environment can interact with the meeting process.

In our Capture Lab environment we are observing participants in real meetings as they understand and adapt the tools we provide to their meeting needs. What we see in process is a change in the meetings taking place in order to incorporate the shared textual and graphics workspace and the ability of any meeting participant to provide input to the workspace. Some of these changes are unexpected. Each of them will help us to better understand how meetings work and how we can design the most useful and effective tools for meetings.

5. References

DeSanctis, G. and Gallupe, R.B. A Foundation for the Study of Group Decision Support Systems. Management Science, 1987, 33, 589–609.

Kiesler, S., Siegel, J. and McGuire, T.W. Social Psychological Aspects of Computer-Mediated Communication. American Psychologist, October 1984, 39 (10), 1123–1134.

Kraemer, K.L. and King, J. Computer-based Systems for Co-operative Work and Group Decision Making. ACM Computing Surveys, June 1988, 20 (2), 115–146.

Krauss, R.M., Garlock, C.M., Bricker, P.D. and McMahon, L.E. The Role of Audible and Visible Backchannel Responses in Interpersonal Communication. Journal of Personality and Social Psychology, 1977, 35, 523–529.

Lantz, K. An Experiment in Integrated Multimedia Conferencing. Proceedings of CSCW'86 Conference on Computer-Supported Cooperative Work, Austin, TX, December 3–5, 1986, 267–275.

Nunamaker, J.F., Applegate, L.M. and Konsynski, B.R. Computer-aided Deliberation: Model Management and Group Decision Support. To appear in Journal of Operations Research, 1988.

Scott, P.D. Formal Models of Protocols for Computer Supported Meetings. Working Paper, Center for Machine Intelligence, EDS, 2001 Commonwealth Blvd., Ann Arbor, MI, February 1988.

Siegel, J., Dubrovsky, V., Kiesler, S. and McGuire, T.W. Group Processes in Computer-mediated Communications. Organizational Behavior and Human Decision Processes, 1986, 37, 157–187.

Stefik, M., Foster, G., Bobrow, D.G., Kahn, K., Lanning, S. and Suchman, L., Beyond the Chalkboard: Computer Support for Collaboration and Problem-Solving in Meetings. Communications of the ACM, 1987, 30(1), 32–47.

Watson, R.G., DeSanctis, G. and Poole, M.S. Using a GDSS to Facilitate Group Consensus: Some Intended and Unintended Consequences. MIS Quarterly, 1988, 12(3).

Acknowledgements: The design decisions described in this paper benefited from the experience gained by the builders of the first computer supported meeting environments. We are grateful to Mark Stefik at Xerox PARC, Jay Nunamaker at the University of Arizona and Gerardine DeSanctis at the University of Minnesota who graciously let us meet in their electronic meeting rooms and formulate our ideas on the type of environment and design we needed for the Capture Lab. A special thank you goes to the CMI staff who supported the implementation of the Capture Lab design, lived through the noise and dust of its birth, worked through detailed equipment lists, programmed and reprogrammed, soldered and sewed, pulled cable and pushed schedules and coordinated the meetings, the training and the executive catering. They are John Gotts, Pete Gaston, Dave Halonen, Paul Scott, Gary Van Poperin, Andy Nolan, Mary Elwart-Keys, and Joyce Massey.

LIVEBOARD: A LARGE INTERACTIVE DISPLAY SUPPORTING GROUP MEETINGS, PRESENTATIONS AND REMOTE COLLABORATION

Scott Elrod, Richard Bruce, Rich Gold, David Goldberg, Frank Halasz, William Janssen, David Lee, Kim McCall, Elin Pedersen, Ken Pier, John Tang* and Brent Welch

Xerox Palo Alto Research Center
3333 Coyote Hill Road
Palo Alto, CA 94304
elrod@parc.xerox.com, (415)812-4224

ABSTRACT

This paper describes the Liveboard, a large interactive display system. With nearly one million pixels and an accurate, multi-state, cordless pen, the Liveboard provides a basis for research on user interfaces for group meetings, presentations and remote collaboration. We describe the underlying hardware and software of the Liveboard, along with several software applications that have been developed. In describing the system, we point out the design rationale that was used to make various choices. We present the results of an informal survey of Liveboard users, and describe some of the improvements that have been made in response to user feedback. We conclude with several general observations about the use of large public interactive displays.

KEYWORDS: interactive display, large-area display, cordless stylus, collaboration, group work, gestural interface.

INTRODUCTION

An integral part of most meetings is a central display or drawing surface which serves as a medium for presenting and capturing ideas. Examples include slides and viewgraphs projected onto a screen, whiteboards and flip-charts.

Recent work on computer-supported meeting environments [6,4,2] has recognized the importance of a central display surface. Meeting rooms such as Colab [6], Capture Lab [4] and Project Nick [2] all utilize one or more large displays as a major focus of the group work. For the most part, however, these displays function primarily to present information.

Drawing and recording ideas is usually accomplished with a keyboard and a mouse at a workstation adjacent to the large display. Although this configuration supports the interactive presentation and discussion of ideas, it still lacks the dynamic, direct interactivity of a whiteboard or flip-chart.

Recent work has explored the use of more directly interactive display surfaces. For example, VideoWhiteboard[7] used audio-video links to create a large-area interactive drawing surface that could be shared between remote locations. Commune [5] examined the use of a stylus-based computational sketchpad to support shared drawing at a distance. Although the drawing surfaces in these systems are more directly interactive, the technologies are not suitable as the central display in a fully networked computer-supported meeting room.

The Liveboard system described in this paper is an attempt to build a directly interactive, stylus-based, large-area display for use in computer-supported meetings. While still falling short of the ultimate wall-sized, flat-panel, high-resolution display, prototype Liveboards have enabled us to begin to develop and evaluate user interfaces for group meetings, presentations and remote collaboration.

The Liveboard project fits into the broader scheme of ubiquitous computing for the workplace of the future [9]. Liveboards complement other personal computing devices (i.e. office workstations and portable sketchpads) by providing a shared workspace around which groups can collaborate.

---

*Current address of John Tang is: Sun Microsystems Laboratories, Inc, 2550 Garcia Avenue, Mountain View, CA 94043, Tang@eng.sun.com, (415) 336-1636.

Figure 1: The Liveboard in use.

As can be seen in Fig. 1, the current Liveboard is a large display housed in a wooden cabinet. The display surface (46 x 32 inches) is approximately the size of an office whiteboard and has nearly 1 million pixels. Two features of the system allow the display to be viewed comfortably at very close distances. First, the Liveboard image is projected from a digitally addressed liquid crystal display. As a result, the image does not exhibit any of the jittering and wavering often found in CRT-based projection systems. Second, the Liveboard incorporates a rear-projection screen which widely disperses the image and can be easily seen at oblique angles. The result is a crisp, stable image which can be viewed comfortably by a group of people standing around the Liveboard.

The Liveboard incorporates an accurate cordless pen, a feature which is particularly important for group meetings. Allowing participants to interact directly with the display provides a natural point of focus for meetings. By contrast, it is difficult to maintain the focus of a meeting when interaction with the central display is mediated by an adjacent keyboard. In addition, the cordless pen is easy to pass among participants. For these reasons, the pen is a particularly appropriate technology for group interaction around a large display surface.

The pen has four distinct states which are controlled by buttons on its body, and by a pressure-sensitive tip switch. Under software control, these states are used for drawing, to pop up menus, or to provide other means of input control.

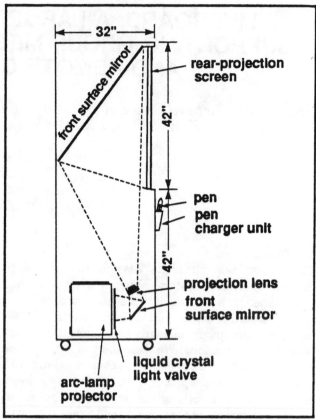

Figure 2: Optical and mechanical details.

The Liveboard is controlled by a high-performance workstation (Sun SPARCstation-2) and can run a large collection of UNIX-based software. Liveboards are fully networked, and can be used in a shared mode between remote locations.

SYSTEM HARDWARE: Display

The Liveboard image is produced by projecting a liquid crystal display (LCD) onto a rear-projection screen, as shown in the side view of Fig 2. The LCD's 1120 x 780 monochrome pixels are magnified to give an image that measures 46 x 32 inches and has a resolution of 25 lines per inch. The Liveboard optics can accommodate projected images with resolutions up to 50 lines per inch. In order to minimize the depth of the cabinet, the optical path is folded twice, as shown in Fig. 2. We found it necessary to exclusively use front surface mirrors in order to eliminate secondary reflection images. In order to make the image sufficiently bright, we chose a 600W arc-lamp overhead projector for the light source. This results in images which are bright enough (25-50 foot-lamberts) for use in a typical office or conference room.

Cordless Pen

The design of the Liveboard pens was driven by several requirements. They were to be cordless for ease of use and especially to avoid tangling when several pens were used simultaneously. They were to provide input at some distance from the board to allow for remote pointing and gestural input. Also, they were to provide the functionality of a three-button mouse so that they could be used with existing software. Human factors considerations dictated that the pens be as small and light as possible, and that the batteries be placed so that the weight was properly balanced.

Shown in Fig. 3 are functional details of the Liveboard pen. The pen emits a beam of optical radiation which is imaged onto a detector module located behind the screen near the LCD. After

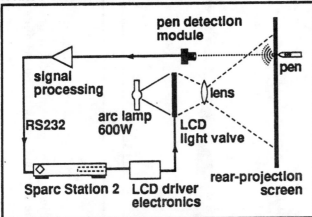

Figure 3: Functional diagram of optics and pen.

some signal-processing, the digitized pen position readings are sent through a serial port to the computer. The pen is capable of a marking accuracy of better than 1 mm, and produces 90 X-Y coordinate pairs per second.

Circuitry inside the pen allows for operation in four distinct states, one for cursor tracking and three that are controlled by the buttons on the body of the pen and by the pressure-sensitive tip switch. The front, middle and rear buttons on the pen body are configured to emulate the left, middle and right buttons of the standard mouse. The tip switch is redundantly mapped to the left mouse button.

In Fig. 4, a person is using the pen to pop up a menu by touching the tip to the screen. The pen can be used at distances of up to several feet from the screen, as can be seen in Fig. 5, where the user has depressed the front button to pop up a menu. The pen has rechargeable batteries, and charging

Figure 4: Popping up a menu by pressing the pen tip against the screen.

Figure 5: Operating the pen remotely to pop up a menu.

sockets are provided on the front of the Liveboard cabinet.

SYSTEM SOFTWARE: Pen Device Driver

In order to give the pen the widest possible applicability, we developed a custom software device driver. The driver serves to map readings from the pen detection electronics to genuine X-Y screen coordinates, and packages them in a form that can be readily integrated with window systems. With this device driver, the pen can be used as the pointing device in X windows (MIT X11R4 or XNeWS) or in SunView.

Walk-Up User Interface

The Liveboard is intended to be an information appliance with wide usage, rather than merely a large computer display. As such, it requires an

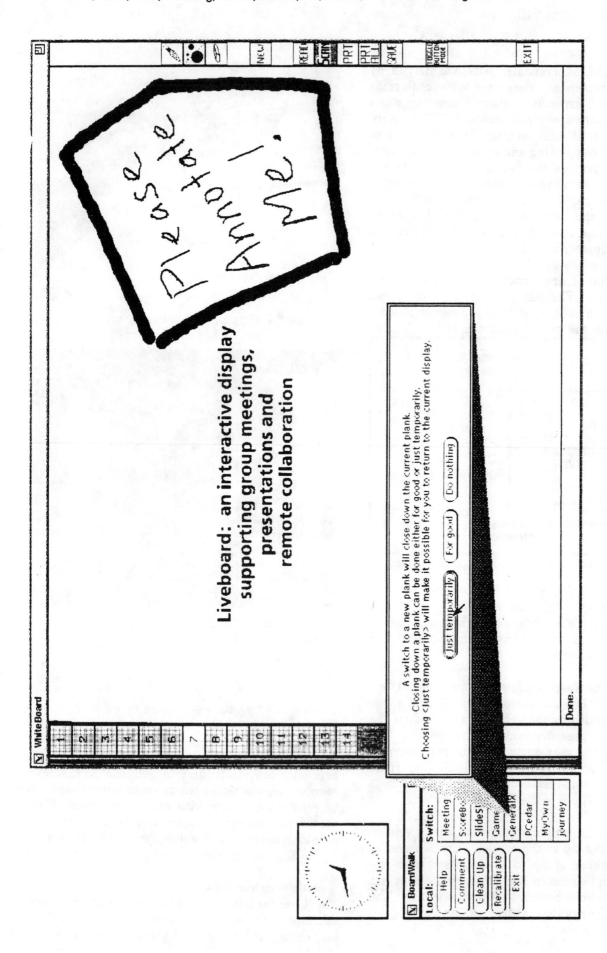

Fig. 6: The Whiteboard application, with a pre-loaded document and annotations made using the pen. The user has just initiated a change to another plank.

interface which the average meeting participant can use without knowing the intricacies of UNIX. Our solution to this requirement is a custom *walk-up* interface called the *BoardWalk*.

BoardWalk is implemented as a simple extension of the TWM window manager. It makes use of the basic mechanisms of the window manager, but hides the details with a layer of tailored environments, called *planks*. We chose not to use the well-known Rooms system [3] for this purpose because we believed that it was too powerful for novice users.

The BoardWalk control panel is shown in the lower left corner of Fig. 6. The control panel contains a list of planks that the user can choose among. The standard planks are:

1) *Meeting*--meeting tools, including a Whiteboard application, a text editor and a clock.
2) *Scoreboard*--a dynamic electronic bulletin board (under development [8].)
3) *SlideShow*--an application for versatile display of prepared slides.
4) *Games* ---what to do when the boss is away.
5) *General X*--a plain and unrestricted X/Unix environment.
5) *PCedar*--for applications written in PARC's PCedar [1] programming environment.

Choosing a plank automatically opens a set of applications. A dialogue box, shown in Fig. 6, asks whether the user wants to leave the current plank *for good*, or only *temporarily*. When the user logs in as *liveboard*, the Meeting plank comes up as the default environment.

In addition to the planks, there are utility functions like *Help, Comment, Clean up, Recalibrate* and *Exit*.

SOFTWARE APPLICATIONS: Whiteboard

One of the uses imagined for the Liveboard is as a meeting support tool, at which people can write down ideas and retrieve documents. Shown in Fig. 6 is *Whiteboard*, an application designed to support this use. The application provides whiteboard-like functionality, with an added flip-chart capability to handle multiple *sheets* that can be printed or saved for later use.

Whiteboard is a simple X11-based bitmap painting program. Features include a variable brush size and an eraser that can wipe out pixels. New sheets can be readily created by touching an icon with the pen. All sheets are remembered, and any sheet can be easily recalled. The sheets can be printed, or can be stored in a file and retrieved at a later time.

The Whiteboard program has been used both for taking notes at informal meetings, and for presentations. For meetings, two important features differentiate the Whiteboard program from conventional copy-boards. First, the meeting record can be stored and subsequently retrieved on any Liveboard. Having such a record has been found to be very useful in returning the collective attention of work groups to previous discussions. The Whiteboard has multiple sheets that can be rapidly switched, providing almost unlimited drawing space.

For presentations, people usually pre-load the Whiteboard with text or scanned images. With the Whiteboard, material is much more available than with conventional slides. One can circle important concepts while they are being discussed, draw connections between related ideas, and illustrate ideas as they are being explained. The final annotated version of the slides can be printed.

SlideShow

Another BoardWalk plank is for the SlideShow presentation tool, which combines the features of a slide projector and an overhead transparency projector. SlideShow presents a multi-page image file, encoded in a page description language such as PostScript, as a set of slides. The presenter, standing a few feet from the Liveboard, gestures with the pen at the SlideShow window. A sweeping gesture to the right is used to bring up the next slide, while vertical gestures are used for direct-manipulation scrolling. SlideShow also provides random access to slides via a gauge at the top of the window. Buttons can be tapped with the pen to adjust the scale of the displayed images. In Fig. 7, the user has chosen the *Fill* option (i.e. fill the SlideShow window) for the current slide, and has just gestured with the pen to bring up the next slide.

SlideShow uses a display graphics package with device-independent imaging, so scrolling, scaling and filling the screen are easily accomplished. Unlike conventional slides or overhead transparencies, each SlideShow slide may be individually scrolled and scaled for optimum viewing, or a common viewing transformation may be applied to all slides in a set. Finally, the presenter may use the pen to write directly on the slides.

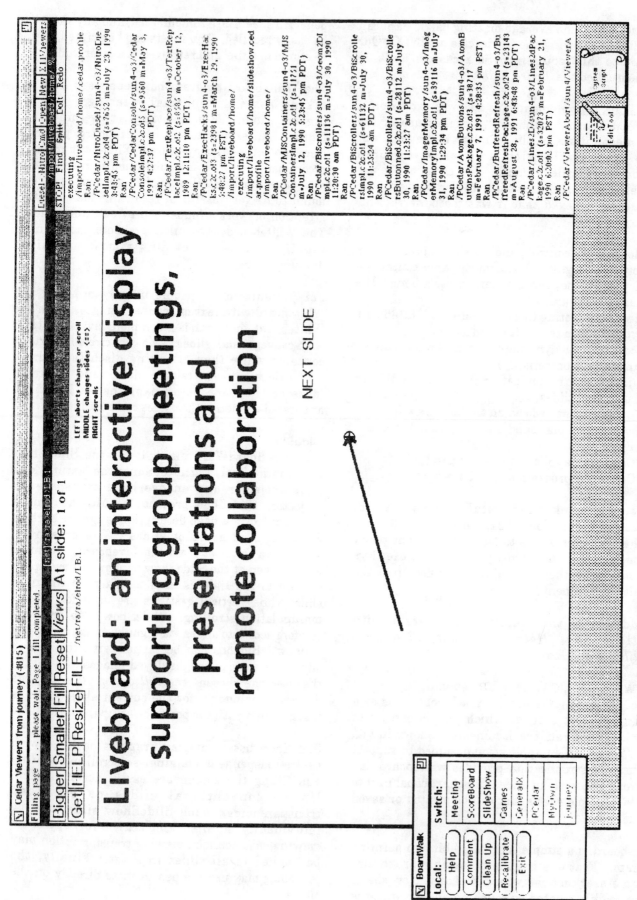

Fig. 7: The SlideShow presentation tool. The user has just made a sweeping gesture to the right to bring up the next slide.

SlideShow is motivated by the observation that default font sizes displayed on the Liveboard are generally too small to be easily viewed in meeting rooms. In addition, most editors do not provide bidirectional scrolling or scaling for presentation purposes. The SlideShow user interface is deliberately simple in an attempt to make it immediately available to novice users. After a few tries, people generally remember and use the gestures naturally.

LIVEBOARD USE: Informal Survey Results

Of the twelve prototype Liveboards that have been built, ten have been placed in conference rooms and open areas within PARC, while two have been sent to Xerox facilities overseas. During the year since they were installed, Liveboards have been used by diverse people for wide-ranging purposes: hardware researchers for meeting facilitation, managers for presentations, designers for remote collaboration, authors for collaborative writing of papers, and software developers for code reviews.

In order to better understand the situations in which Liveboards have been used, we conducted an informal survey of the PARC community. The survey consisted of an e-mail questionnaire sent out to everyone at PARC (250 researchers, managers and support personnel). The 60 respondents were self-selected, and while the survey was not conducted in a scientific manner, we believe that it raises important issues about the design of large, public, interactive display systems.

Table I summarizes the results of the survey. Perhaps most striking is the fact that while most respondents have used the Liveboard at least once, a significant number of those who have used it (34%) do not know how to turn it on. (This is despite the prominent display of an "ON" button on the front panel.) Users have reported general feelings of discomfort at the idea of walking up and just trying things. Some are intimidated by the size of the Liveboard, while others express fear of making a mistake and damaging it. Still others feel limited by their lack of UNIX knowledge.

Not surprisingly, the Liveboard is most often used for meeting facilitation (50% of respondents.) Of the different software applications that can be run on the Liveboard, the Whiteboard meeting tool is the oldest and most well publicized in the PARC community. In fact, it has had the favored status of being the default tool that comes up whenever the

Total number of respondents who:	Yes	No
1) know how to turn it on	32	16
2) have ever used one	46	3

Purposes for which respondents have used a Liveboard:	%Yes
1) in a meeting	50%
2) to randomly walk up and draw	48%
3) to show something to a friend	36%
4) to explain an idea	30%
5) in a presentation	26%
6) to write or look at code	18%
7) to write a paper	8%
8) to write a paper collaboratively	8%
9) for remote communication	8%

Items needing improvement, ordered from most to least as indicated by respondents:
1) image quality
2) accuracy of pen
3) size of cabinet
4) feel of pen
5) shape of cabinet
6) color of image (i.e. add color)
7) add printer
8) add scanner

Table I: Results of informal survey taken one year after Liveboards were installed. (60 respondents)

BoardWalk is started. Other common uses are casual drawing and explaining ideas to others.

Above all else, people would like to have better image quality on the Liveboard. While the number of pixels is high (1 million), there are still perceptible jaggies that degrade the appearance of handwriting. Next in importance to users is the accuracy of the pen. People are troubled by positional inaccuracies of the pen that can result from optical parallax in the screen and from long-term drift in the detection electronics. People are also concerned about the way the pen feels. They are concerned both about its size and shape, but also about having a tip which feels "right" as it moves across the screen surface (i.e. uniform friction of the proper amount.)

RESPONSE TO SURVEY FEEDBACK

We have begun to take steps to address the concerns raised by Liveboard users. First, we have attempted to reduce the barrier that users feel in getting started at the Liveboard. The PARC security staff now turns on all Liveboards before people arrive at work in the morning. A software script has been implemented which automatically starts up the BoardWalk whenever the Liveboard is rebooted. The script includes a loop which automatically restores the machine to the Meeting plank of the BoardWalk whenever the Liveboard is not being actively used. The result is that the Liveboards are more reliably in a state of readiness, where they look like a clean whiteboard.

Steps have also been taken to reduce the parallax of the Liveboard pen, and to improve the feel of the pen tip on the surface of the screen. In addition, a simple four-point pen recalibration has been implemented which allows users to correct for long-term drift in pen accuracy.

GENERAL OBSERVATIONS: Input to a Large Screen

Only by observing the Liveboards in use have we realized the extent to which stylus input on a large screen is different from a mouse at a workstation. Before building the current Liveboard pen, we constructed several prototypes in an effort to understand the optimal size, shape and placement of buttons. Despite these efforts, we have observed that while people readily use the pen for drawing, they find the buttons awkward and tend to avoid using them.

Clearly, a usable multi-state stylus will require semantics that are more intuitive than the current Liveboard pen. On the other hand, our early experience suggests that with more carefully designed user interfaces, most functions could be implemented using only two states (i.e. tracking and screen contact.)

Another important difference between the pen and a mouse is that the act of putting the pen down frequently causes the cursor to move across the screen. This makes it difficult for the user to define an input focus and then move to the keyboard. We have partially alleviated this problem by using a click-to-type mode in our window manager. A more

satisfactory solution might be to separate the tracking feedback and focus point functions that are commonly combined in mouse-based software. The tracking cursor would still follow the pen, but explicit action would be required to specify a new focus point.

The fact that the Liveboard pen is cordless, operates from a distance and interacts directly with the screen allows for types of input that make no sense with a mouse. As an example, we have found ways to use natural gestures (i.e. sweeping motions up or down) to accomplish various functions in a slide presentation (i.e scrolling).

Large Interactive Displays vs Workstations

Unlike workstations, Liveboards are frequently used by a group, often with one person standing at the screen and a larger number of people seated in the room. For the person working at the Liveboard screen, the user interfaces of most workstations and notebook computers are inadequate. The Liveboard is large enough that fixed buttons can be difficult to locate, and awkward to reach. We believe that either gestural input, or some type of floating or movable menus or buttons will be required for such large screens. For those people seated in the room, the default font size is often too small for comfortable viewing. Arbitrary scaling and scrolling will be needed to accommodate groups of different sizes.

While users may tolerate the intricacies of UNIX in the privacy of their offices, we have found that in group settings, people are much less willing to take the time to solve software mysteries. Typically, they will give up on using the Liveboard, and revert to a conventional whiteboard if they encounter problems with the software. To be accepted in group settings, systems like the Liveboard must have robust, easy-to-use software.

On the other hand, one of the virtues of Liveboards is that they are fully networked and, like workstations, can draw on a rich and complex set of applications and document formats. Finding the compromise between these two requirements (having both ease of use and the full power of networked workstations) will be central focus of much of our future work.

ACKNOWLEDGEMENTS

Many people have made valuable contributions to the Liveboard project. On the hardware side, we would like to thank R. Bell, T. Fisli, J. Gasbarro, W.

Jackson, E. Richley, G. Sander, D. Steinmetz and F. Vest. For their software contributions, we are indebted to N. Adams, R. Allen, P. Dourish, D. MacDonald, D. Nichols, M. Theimer, M. Toho and P. Wellner. For their contributions to early use studies, we are grateful to S. Bly, S. Harrison, S. Irwin and S. Minneman. Finally, we would like to thank a number of others for their creative suggestions and support of the project: R. Bauer, R. Beach, E. Bier, D. Bobrow, W. Buxton, R. Flegal, R. Gold, A. Henderson, C. Kent, S. Kojima, M. Krueger, J. Mackinlay, C. Marshall, M. Molloy, T. Moran, G. Robertson, Z. Smith, M. Stefik, and M. Weiser.

REFERENCES

1. Atkinson, R., Demers, A., Hauser, C., Jacobi, C., Kessler, P., and Weiser, M., Experiences creating a portable Cedar. In Proceedings of the 1989 ACM SIGPLAN Conference on Programming Language Design and Implementation, Portland, OR (June 1989), SIGPLAN Notices 24, 7 (July 1989), 322-329.

2. Cook, P., Ellis, C., Graf, M., Rein, G., and Smith, T. Project Nick: Meetings Augmentation and Analysis. ACM Transactions on Office Information Systems 5, 2 (April 1987), 132-146.

3. Henderson, D. A. Jr., and Card, S. K. Rooms: The Use of Multiple Virtual Workspaces to Reduce Space Contention in a Window-Based Graphical User Interface. ACM Trans. on Graphics, 5, 3 (July 1986) 211-243.

4. Mantei, M., Capturing the Capture Lab Concepts: A Case Study in the Design of Computer Supported Meeting Environments. Proceedings of the Conference on Computer-Supported Cooperative Work (Portland, OR, September 1988), 257-270.

5. Minneman, S. L., and Bly, S. A. Managing a trois: a study of a multi-user drawing tool in distributed design work. Proceedings of the Conference on Computer Human Interaction (CHI), New Orleans, LA (April 1991), 217-224.

6. Stefik, M., Foster, G., Bobrow, D., Kahn, K., Lanning, S., and Suchman, L. Beyond the chalkboard: Computer support for collaboration and problem solving in meetings. Communications of the ACM 30, 1 (Jan. 1987), 32-47.

7. Tang, J. C., and Minneman, S. L. VideoWhiteboard: Video Shadows to Support Remote Collaboration. Proceedings of the Conference on Computer Human Interaction (CHI), New Orleans, LA (April 1991), 315-322.

8. Theimer, M., and Nichols, D. Private Communication.

9. Weiser, M. The Computer for the 21st Century. Sci. Amer. 265, 3 (Sept. 1991), 94-104.

ELECTRONIC MEETING SYSTEMS TO SUPPORT GROUP WORK

"Almost every time there is a genuinely important decision to be made in an organization, a group is assigned to make it—or at least to counsel and advise the individual who must make it." [21, p. 459]. No one works completely independently. Almost everyone is part of at least one group, typically several groups at any point in time.

Groups communicate, share information, generate ideas, organize ideas, draft policies and procedures, collaborate on the writing of reports, share a vision, build consensus, make decisions, and so on.

However, group meetings are often not as effective as they could be [42]. Meetings may lack a clear focus. Group members may not participate because they are apprehensive about how their ideas will be received or because a few members dominate discussions. Hidden agendas may promote political decisions that are not in the best interests of the organization. Meetings may end without a clear understanding or record of what was discussed. Yet in spite of these problems, little computer support is available for meetings—which is somewhat surprising given the ubiquitous nature of computer support in modern organizations.

A new form of meeting environment, which we term an Electronic Meeting System (EMS), has emerged which strives to make group meetings more productive by applying information technology. EMS technology is designed to directly impact and change the behavior of groups to improve group effectiveness, efficiency, and satisfaction. Our definition of a meeting is broad—including any activity where people come together, whether at the same place at the same time, or in different places at different times (see Figure 1) [5, 12].

The purpose of this article is to present the research conducted at the University of Arizona in developing and using same-time/same-place and same-time/different-place EMS technology.[1] The Arizona research program includes two types of research defined by Ackoff et al.[1]. The first type is developmental, which attempts to create improved work methods. The second type is empirical, which attempts to evaluate and understand them. The initial phase of the research program focused on the development of tools and techniques to support groups of analysts

J.F. Nunamaker
Alan R. Dennis
Joseph S. Valacich
Douglas R. Vogel
Joey F. George

PHOTO 1. The Collaborative Management Room at the University of Arizona

PHOTO 2. The Electronic Meeting Room at IBM Decision Support Center, Boulder, Colorado

and users in the construction of information systems. The second phase began in 1984 with the construction of a special-purpose meeting room to support the same-time/same-place meetings of these groups. This meeting room and the ones that followed are based on a series of networked microcomputer workstations arranged in a U-shape, around a table, or in tiered legislative style (see Photo 1). A large-screen video display is provided at the front of the room, from where the meeting leader/facilitator guides the meeting. Other audio-visual support is also available—typically white boards and overhead projectors [5, 36, 51, 53].

The realization that this technology enabled groups to perform many tasks beyond system development (e.g., strategic planning), led to the third phase which began in 1986 with the establishment of four major research projects with IBM. The number of EMS facilities at Arizona grew from one in 1985 to the three we have now. Four additional facilities are scheduled to open later this year. Each of these new facilities addresses a different cell in Figure 1; one is a large group meeting room, one is a small group meeting room, one supports distributed large groups, and the fourth is a meeting room-to-meeting room teleconferencing facility.

During this phase, new software was developed (University of Arizona GroupSystems[2]) and was installed at EMS facilities at more than 22 universities and 12 corpo-

rations, such as BellSouth and Greyhound Financial Corporation. IBM has built 36 GroupSystems facilities (e.g., see Photo 2), with an additional 20 scheduled to be operational by January 1992. More than 25,000 people have used GroupSystems within IBM; more than 3,000 others from 200 public and private organizations have used the Arizona GroupSystems facilities. Another 2,000 have used GroupSystems in more than 20 laboratory experiments and 15 doctoral dissertations that have been conducted at Arizona.

While GroupSystems supports a variety of different tasks, many groups follow a common sequence of use. The group leader meets with a GroupSystems meeting leader/facilitator, who assists in developing an agenda and selecting the GroupSystems tools to be used. Meetings typically begin with participants generating ideas (e.g., "How can we double our sales over the next four years?" see Figure 2). As they type their comments, the results are integrated and displayed on the large screens at the front of the room, as well as being available on each workstation. Everyone can see the comments of others, but without knowing who contributed what. Participants can build on each others' ideas, independent of any positive or negative bias about who contributed them—ideas are evaluated on their own merits, rather than on the basis of who contributed them. These ideas are then organized into a list of key issues (e.g., "Stronger ties with customers"), which the group can prioritize into a short list. Next, the group could generate ideas for action plans to accomplish the important issues, followed by more idea organization and prioritization, and so on. The result of the meeting is typically a large volume of input and ideas, and a group consensus for further action. In many cases, final decisions are not made during the meeting, but are made later by the group leader and/or other participants after considering all the in-

formation, knowledge and opinions shared. The EMS meeting can enable wide participation so that broad input has been obtained, ownership established, and consensus developed.

For example, Greyhound Financial Corporation has used GroupSystems on several occasions for a variety of tasks, including the development of a mission statement, strategy formulation, evaluations of senior managers, and information systems (IS) planning.[3] One meeting was a one-day session to develop proposals to create competitive advantage, in which 30 managers from all departments used a structured idea generation

process (a variant on the value chain technique) to develop proposals. On post-session questionnaires, 88% of participants reported that particular meeting was more effective than previous non-EMS meetings [7]. Said CEO S.L. Eichenfield: "I found that we accomplished 100% of our objectives. People usually reluctant to express themselves felt free to take part, and we were surprised by the number of new ideas expressed. We also reached conclusions far more rapidly."

The experience of this group is typical of the other groups in our field research. Our laboratory research generally supports our findings in the field. In this article we shall argue that EMS facilities can improve group work in many situations because it:

- enables all participants to work simultaneously (human parallel processing);
- provides an equal opportunity for participation;
- discourages behavior that can negatively impact meeting productivity;

---

[1] Much valuable EMS and related research has been conducted elsewhere. However, space limitations preclude us from discussing it, since an attempt to compare findings across different EMSs is appropriate only with a careful consideration of the different functions they provide. We encourage readers to examine the contributions made by other developers and empirical researchers (see [5, 39] for reviews of this work).

[2] GroupSystems evolved from the Plexsys Research Program.

[3] See "Strategy on the Screen," An Open University Videotape, Production Centre, British Broadcasting Corp., 1991.

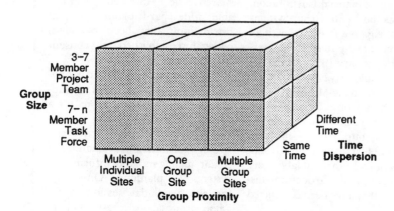

FIGURE 1. EMS Domain

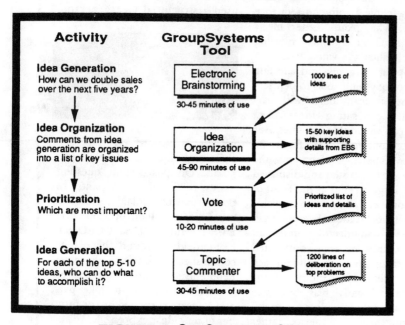

FIGURE 2. One Sequence of Use

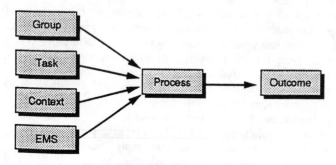

FIGURE 3. Research Model

- enables larger group meetings which can effectively bring more information, knowledge, and skills to bear on the task;
- permits the group to choose from a spectrum of structured or unstructured techniques and methods to perform the task;
- offers access to external information; and
- supports the development of an organizational memory from meeting to meeting.

We begin by discussing the theoretical foundations of GroupSystems. These foundations provide the basis for understanding the design and implementation of both our EMS software and facilities. We argue that EMS design is one of four contingencies, along with the group, the task, and the context, that affect the process of group meetings which in turn affects meeting outcomes [5]. We will then focus on the key elements in the design of GroupSystems, and how these elements interact with these contingencies. We examine one example of each type of contingency, using the findings from our empirical research to illustrate our arguments.

Theoretical Foundations

Prior research and theory with non-EMS-supported groups provides a rich starting point for EMS research. However, as information technology has the ability to profoundly affect the nature of group work [26], it becomes dangerous to generalize the *outcomes* or *conclusions* from research with non-supported groups to the EMS environment.[4] A better approach is to examine underlying theory that explains *why* these events occur and consider how EMS use and various situational characteristics may affect the theory to produce different outcomes.

---

[4]For example, such commonly accepted conclusions as larger groups are less satisfied than smaller groups, or that groups generate fewer ideas than the same number of individuals working separately (i.e., nominal groups [13, 27, 30] have been shown *not* to hold with EMS-supported groups [10, 11, 48, 49]).

Figure 3 presents a high-level view of the research model that has guided our work and has evolved with our research program. We contend that the effects of EMS use are contingent on a myriad of group, task, context and technology factors that differ from situation to situation [5]. Group characteristics that can affect processes and outcomes include (but are not limited to) group size, group proximity, group composition (peers or hierarchical), group cohesiveness, etc. Task characteristics include the activities required to accomplish the task (e.g., idea generation, decision choice), task complexity, etc. Context characteristics include organizational culture, time pressure, evaluative tone (e.g., critical or supportive), reward structure (e.g., none versus individual versus group), etc. Meeting outcomes (e.g., efficiency, effectiveness, satisfaction) depend upon the interaction within the meeting process of these group, task, and context factors with the EMS components the group uses (e.g., anonymity). Thus, it is inappropriate to say that EMS use "improves group task performance" or "reduces member satisfaction"; all statements must be qualified by the situation—the group, task, context and EMS to which they apply. One approach, then, is to conduct developmental research to build an EMS providing certain components that may improve meeting outcomes and empirical research to determine what effects these components have in what situations.

To understand these interactions, we need to examine group processes at a lower level of detail. Certain aspects of the meeting process improve outcomes (process gains) while others impair outcomes (process losses) relative to the efforts of the same individuals working by themselves or those of groups that do not experience them [22, 47]. Meeting outcomes are contingent upon the balance of these process gains and losses [3]. Situational characteristics (i.e., group,

task, and context) establish an initial balance, which the group may alter by using an EMS.

There are many different process gains and losses. Table 1 lists several important process gains and losses, but this list is by no means exhaustive. Each of these gains and losses vary in strength (or may not exist at all) depending upon the situation. For example, in a verbal meeting, losses due to *air time fragmentation,* the need to partition speaking time among members, depend upon group size [13, 27, 30]. Air time fragmentation is a greater problem for larger groups, as the available time must be rationed among more people. If everyone in a 3-member group contributed equally in a 60-minute meeting, each person would speak for 20 minutes, while each member of a 15-member group would speak for 4 minutes.

EMS Effects

There are at least four theoretical mechanisms by which the EMS can affect this balance of gains and losses: process support, process structure, task structure, and, task support (Figure 4). Process support refers to the communication infrastructure (media, channels, and devices, electronic or otherwise) that facilitates communication among members [12], such as an electronic communication channel or blackboard. Process structure refers to process techniques or rules that direct the pattern, timing or content of this communication [12], such as an agenda or process methodology such as Nominal Group Technique (NGT). Task support refers to the information and computation infrastructure for task-related activities [5], such as external data bases and pop-up calculators. Task structure refers to techniques, rules, or models for analyzing task-related information to gain new insight [12], such as those within computer models or Decision Support Systems (DSS).

For example, suppose a group was charged with generating a plan

to encourage more European tourists to visit the U.S. Providing each group member with a computer workstation that enabled him/her to exchange typed comments with other group members would be process support. Having each member take turns to contribute ideas (i.e., round-robin) or agreeing not to criticize the ideas of others would be process structure. Task support could include information on when, where and how many European tourists visited last year, or about tourist programs run by other governments. Task structure could include a framework encouraging the group to consider each U.S. region (e.g., New England,

California) or different types of tourists (e.g., tour clients, businessmen), or an economic model of potential impacts.

These four mechanisms are the fundamental means by which an EMS such as GroupSystems affects meetings. These mechanisms are not unique to EMS technology. The EMS is simply a convenient means by which to deliver process support, process structure, task support, and task structure. But in many cases, the EMS can provide a unique combination that is virtually impossible to provide otherwise. We hypothesize potential effects for each mechanism. These effects are those suggested most strongly by prior research, and again, this list is necessarily incomplete. As we will discuss, each mechanism can have many separate effects on process gains and losses, some positive, some negative. The combined effects are contingent on strength of the preexisting gains and losses and the strength of the EMS impact on them (e.g., if the EMS reduces a weak process loss, we would anticipate few effects on outcomes). For

TABLE 1.
Important Sources of Group Process Gains and Losses

Common Process Gains

More information	A group as a whole has more information than any one member (30, 42, 47)
Synergy	A member uses information in a way that the original holder did not because that member has different information or skills (38).
More Objective Evaluation	Groups are better at catching errors than are the individuals who proposed ideas (21, 22, 42)
Stimulation	Working as part of a group may stimulate and encourage individuals to perform better (30, 42)
Learning	Members may learn from and imitate more skilled members to improve performance (22)

Common Process Losses

Air Time Fragmentation	The group must partition available speaking time among members (13, 27, 30)
Attenuation Blocking	This (and concentration blocking and attention blocking below) are subelements of "production blocking." Attenuation blocking occurs when members who are prevented from contributing comments as they occur, forget or suppress them later in the meeting, because they seem less original, relevant or important (13, 27, 30)
Concentration Blocking	Fewer comments are made because members concentrate on remembering comments (rather than thinking of new ones) until they can contribute them (13, 27, 30)
Attention Blocking	New comments are not generated because members must constantly listen to others speak and cannot pause to think (13, 27, 30)
Failure to Remember	Members lack focus on communication, missing or forgetting the contributions of others (13, 27)
Conformance Pressure	Members are reluctant to criticize the comments of others due to politeness or fear of reprisals (21, 42)
Evaluation Apprehension	Fear of negative evaluation causes members to withhold ideas and comments (13, 27, 30)
Free Riding	Members rely on others to accomplish goals, due to cognitive loafing the need to compete for air time, or because they perceive their input to be unneeded (2, 13)
Cognitive Inertia	Discussion moves along one train of thought without deviating because group members refrain from contributing comments that are not directly related to the current discussion (27, 30)
Socializing	Nontask discussion reduces task performance, although some socializing is usually necessary for effective functioning (42)
Domination	Some group member(s) exercise undue influence or monopolize the group's time in an unproductive manner (27)
Information Overload	Information is presented faster than it can be processed (23)
Coordination Problems	Difficulty integrating members' contributions because the group does not have an appropriate strategy, which can lead to dysfunctional cycling or incomplete discussions resulting in premature decisions (21, 24)
Incomplete Use of Information	Incomplete access to and use of information necessary for successful task completion (24, 34)
Incomplete Task Analysis	Incomplete analysis and understanding of task resulting in superficial discussions (24)

simplicity, this discussion treats each mechanism separately; interactions are discussed later. This discussion assumes the group actually uses the mechanisms described; any mechanism that is provided by the EMS but is not used, obviously has few effects. In our discussion of these four mechanisms, the one that has been central to our research, process support, will be emphasized.

Task structure assists the group to better understand and analyze task information, and is one of the mechanisms by which DSS improve the performance of individual decision makers. Task structure may improve group performance by reducing losses due to incomplete task analysis or increasing process gains due to synergy, encouraging more information to be shared, promoting more objective evaluation or catching errors (by highlighting information). Methods of providing task structure include problem modeling, multicriteria decision making, etc. While task structure is often numeric in nature, it is not necessarily so. For example, Greyhound used a variant of the value chain technique. Many other non-numeric approaches to providing task structure are also available—e.g., stakeholder analysis [32].

Task support may reduce process losses due to incomplete use of information and incomplete task analysis, and may promote synergy and the use of more information by providing information and computation to the group (without providing additional structure). For example, groups may benefit from electronic access to information from previous meetings. While members could make notes of potentially useful information prior to the meeting, a more effective approach may be to provide access to the complete sources during the meeting itself. Computation support could include calculators or spreadsheets.

Task support is also important at an organizational level. Simon argues that technological support for organizational memory is an essential part of organizational functioning [45]. An EMS can assist in building this organizational memory by recording inputs, outputs and results in one repository for easy access for subsequent meetings. Although the importance of such an organizational memory has been recognized in system development (e.g., CASE tools), it has not yet been widely applied to other organizational activities.

Process structure has long been used by non-EMS groups to reduce process losses, although many researchers have reported that groups often do not follow the process structuring rules properly [21, 27]. Process structure may be global to the meeting, such as developing and following a strategy/agenda to perform the task, thereby reducing process losses due to coordination problems. The EMS can also provide process structure internal to a specific activity (local process structure) by determining who will talk next (e.g., talk queues) or by automating a formal methodology such as NGT. Different forms of local process structure will affect different process gains and losses. For example, the first phase of NGT requires individuals to work separately to reduce production blocking, free riding, and cognitive inertia, while subsequent phases (idea sharing and voting) use other techniques to affect other process gains and losses. Process structure has been found to improve, impair, and have no effect on group performance [cf. 21, 24, 42]. Its effects depend upon its fit with the situation and thus little can be said in general.

Process support can be provided by the EMS in at least three ways: parallel communication, group memory, and anonymity. With parallel communication, each member has a workstation that is connected to all

other workstations, thus providing an electronic channel that enables everyone to communicate simultaneously and in parallel [5]. No one need wait for someone else to finish speaking. Process losses from air time fragmentation, attenuation blocking and concentration blocking should be significantly reduced. Free riding may be reduced as members no longer need to compete for air time. Domination may be reduced, as it becomes difficult for one member to preclude others from contributing. Electronic communication may also dampen dysfunctional socializing [54]. Parallel communication increases information overload (as every member can

contribute simultaneously). Process gains may be enhanced due to synergy and the use of more information. Increased interaction may also stimulate individuals and promote learning.

The EMS can provide a group memory by recording all electronic comments, which is typically done by many, but not all EMSs [e.g., 43]. Participants can de-couple themselves from the group to pause, think, type comments and then rejoin the "discussion" without missing anything. This should reduce failure to remember, attention blocking and incomplete use of information, and may promote synergy and more information. A group memory that enables members to queue and filter information may reduce information overload. A group memory is also useful should some members miss all or part of a meeting, or if the group is subjected to interruptions that require temporary suspension of the meeting [34]. The EMS may also provide other forms of group memory that do not capture all comments. An electronic black-

A group memory that enables members to queue and filter information may reduce information overload.

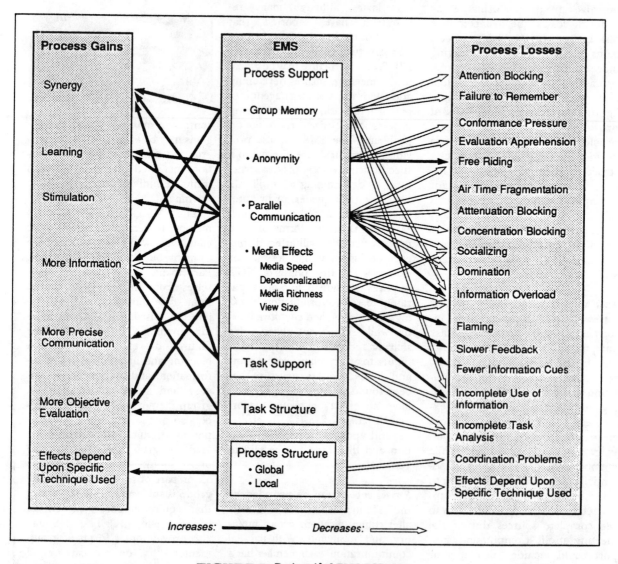

FIGURE 4. Potential EMS Effects

board, for example, may reduce failure to remember by presenting a summary of key information and reduce dysfunctional socializing by increasing task focus [46].

The electronic channel may provide some degree of anonymity. Anonymity may reduce the pressure to conform and evaluation apprehension, but may also increase free riding, as it is more difficult to determine when someone is free riding [2]. However, when the group meets at the same place and time, the lack of process anonymity (i.e., members can see who is and is not contributing) as opposed to content anonymity (i.e., members cannot easily attribute specific comments to individuals) may reduce free riding [50]. Anonymity may encourage members to challenge others, thereby increasing process gains by catching errors and a more objective evaluation. Anonymity may also provide a low-threat environment in which less skilled members can contribute and learn.

The use of electronic media may also introduce media effects that reflect inherent differences between verbal and electronic communication. These include *media speed, media richness, depersonalization/deindividuation* and *view size.* Media speed refers to the fact that typing comments to send electronically is slower than speaking (which can reduce the amount of information available to the group and introduce losses) while reading is generally faster than listening (gains) [54]. Electronic media are less rich than face-to-face verbal communication, as they provide fewer cues and slower feedback (losses), but typically promote more careful and precisely worded communication (gains) [4]. Depersonalization is the separation of people from comments, which may promote deindividuation, the loss of self- and group-awareness [54]. This may reduce socializing, and encourage more objective evaluation and more error catching—due to less negative reaction to criticism,

and increased group ownership of outcomes—(gains). But reduced socializing and more uninhibited comments like "flaming," may reduce group cohesiveness and satisfaction (losses). Workstations typically provide a small screen view for members (e.g., 24-line screen), which can encourage information chunking and reduce information overload (gains). But this can also cause members to lose a global view of the task [35, 36], increasing losses due to incomplete use of information.

The University of Arizona GroupSystems EMS

Here we summarize the developmental research conducted at Arizona. We have primarily focused on supporting large groups that meet at the same place and time—legislative sessions [5, 12]—although recent work has studied small project teams and distributed groups meeting at the same time in different places. This focus arose from our early work with a variety of organizations in which project teams of 10–20 members were typically assigned to address key issues.

What are the needs of large groups meeting at the same place and time? Research with non-EMS-supported groups has shown that larger groups have a greater need for process structure [42], particularly if members do not share the same information [21]. Large non-EMS-supported meetings are usually less effective and less satisfying than small group meetings [42], due to sharp increases in process losses as size increases [2, 47]. We concluded that, in general, high levels of global process structure and process support were appropriate.

Task structure and task support also depend on task characteristics. Since the groups with whom we worked often faced strategic issues, we developed several tools providing task structure and support for strategic planning (e.g., stakeholder analysis), as well as general-purpose tools capable of supporting a variety of task structure and support needs. As strategic tasks are often associated with political and highly competitive groups [32], process support components such as anonymity became important.

GroupSystems Architecture

The general design for GroupSystems builds on three basic concepts: an EMS meeting room, meeting facilitation, and a software toolkit. Although many different meeting room designs have been used, the minimum configuration provides a separate networked, hard disk-based, color graphics microcomputer workstation to each participant, with another one or

two workstations serving as the meeting leader/facilitator's console. A large-screen video display is provided as an electronic blackboard, with other audio-visual support also available (e.g., white boards and overhead projectors) [5, 36, 51, 53].

Meeting leader/facilitator: The person who chairs the meeting is the leader/facilitator. This person may be the group leader, another group member or, more commonly, a separate, neutral, individual who is not a group member. Using a non-member enables all group members to actively participate, rather than losing one member as the chair. A nonmember can be a specialist in EMS and group work, but may lack the task and group knowledge of a regular member. The meeting leader/facilitator provides four functions. First, this person provides technical support by initiating and terminating specific software tools, and guiding the group through the technical aspects necessary to work on the task. This reduces the amount of training required of group members by re-

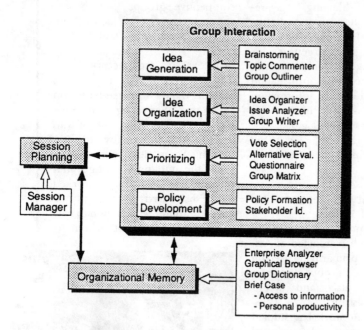

FIGURE 5. GroupSystems Tools

Chauffeured	Supported	Interactive
• One person enters group information	• All group members can enter comments	• All group members can enter comments
• Electronic blackboard can provide group memory	• Electronic blackboard can provide group memory	• All comments in group memory accessible via workstations
• Verbal communication predominates	• Both verbal and electronic communication	• Electronic communication predominates

FIGURE 6. Electronic Meeting Processes

moving one level of system complexity. In some cases, technical support is provided by an additional technical facilitator.

Second, the meeting leader/facilitator chairs the meeting, maintains the agenda and assesses the need for agenda changes. The meeting leader/facilitator may or may not take an active role in the meeting to improve group interaction by, for example, providing process structure in coordinating verbal discussion. This person also administers the group's knowledge. In EMSs designed without support for meeting leaders/facilitators, any member may change or delete the group memory. When disagreements occur, members' competition for control can become dysfunctional (e.g., "Scroll Wars" [46]). While this is manageable for small collaborative groups, it is much less so for larger groups with diverse membership, where competitive political motives and vested interests exist. With GroupSystems, members can view the group memory and add to it at their own workstation, but in general only the meeting leader/facilitator can modify and delete public information.

Third, the meeting leader/facilitator assists in agenda planning, by working with the group and/or group leader to highlight the principal meeting objectives and develop an agenda to accomplish them. Specific GroupSystems tools are then mapped to each activity. Finally, in on-going organizational settings where meeting leaders/facilitators are not group members, they provide organizational continuity by setting standards for use, developing training materials, maintaining the system, and acting as champion/sponsors, which is key to successful technology transfer [31]. The roles of the meeting leader/facilitator may also change over time. For example, after a group has some experience using EMS, the need for technical support and agenda planning advice may decrease.

Software toolkit: Many first-generation EMSs were task-driven, as defined by Huber [25], in that they were designed to support one single group task. Second-generation EMSs, such as GroupSystems, provide a software toolkit, similar to a DSS model base, which is a collection of generic tools for various group *activities* such as idea generation and voting rather than being one indivisible system to support the entire *task* like strategic planning. Such EMSs are activity driven.

The key advantage provided by a toolkit is flexibility. Each tool provides a different approach to support a particular activity, thus the EMS can provide various combinations and styles of process structure, process support, task structure and task support during any one meeting. Groups use many approaches and often do not proceed in a straightforward manner [40]. The tools can easily be mixed and matched and combined with non-EMS activities in whatever order the group believes is most effective. This philosophy also enables new tools to be easily added to the toolkit and existing tools to be customized to specific needs.

While flexibility is important, it is also important to restrict the number and type of functions available to participants [44]. Restrictiveness provides a more powerful intervention, increasing the liklihood that groups will use the EMS as intended by its designers; this has proved a problem with non-computerized techniques [21, 27]. Restrictiveness promotes the use of more effective techniques and prevents less effective ones, fosters learning, promotes consistency, and provides coordination to ensure that all group members are using the same tool at the same time. But it can also constrain creativity and exploration, limit the applicability of a system, promote user dissatisfaction, and be seen as manipulative, resulting in non-use of the system.

GroupSystems balances these issues by being both highly flexible *and* highly restrictive. The system is flexible in that a wide variety of tools are available, but each tool is locally restrictive so that users can perform only certain functions. The selection of which tools will be used for a specific meeting is done during a pre-meeting planning meeting. During the meeting itself, the system is restrictive, so that members use only those tools determined to be the most appropriate during pre-planning. While agendas sometimes change, it is the group leader or the group as a whole who makes changes, not individual members.

Development of GroupSystems tools has not followed either the Software Development Life Cycle model or the rapid prototyping model, although we do believe in prototyping as a means to determine requirements. GroupSystems tools have typically been "grown." The basic concept for a tool typically comes from prior group theory and research (e.g., NGT), from a specific task domain (e.g., stakeholder analysis [32]) or from our own experiences. The concept is first developed and tested within our research group, before being refined into an initial production version. This initial version is intentionally not a complete version of the tool, as it is difficult to determine exactly what functions are needed until the tool is actually used by groups. As the tool begins to be used, new functions are identified, and the capabilities of the tool grow. Significant changes are not unusual in the first few months after tools are added.

The GroupSystems toolkit provides tools in five areas:

1. session planning and management;
2. group interaction;
3. organizational memory;
4. individual work; and
5. research data collection.

Tools in the first three areas are discussed in Figure 5. Those in the latter two areas are not, because they are not central to our theme of improving group performance.

Tools for Session Planning and Management

The GroupSystems tool to support this activity, Session Manager (SM), has three components: pre-session planning, in-session management, and post-session organization. SM supports pre-session planning by providing an electronic questionnaire to ensure that important planning information is not overlooked, and an agenda tool to assist in agenda development. An expert system to assist this stage is currently under development. SM provides in-meeting management via

the control menu; all tools are initialized, started, and ended via SM. SM also provides a task assignment tool to record information about the tasks assigned to specific individuals. Members are provided read-only access to this list but only the facilitator is allowed to add to or modify its contents. Post-session organization involves the logical organization and physical storage of the session outputs as part of the organizational memory. Various components can be indexed and stored, task assignment reports generated and distributed, and paper printouts copied and distributed to better integrate information between this session and subsequent sessions.

Tools for Group Interaction

The purpose of these tools is to provide process structure, process support, task structure and task support for group interaction. While there are many possible combinations of the process support functions (i.e., parallel communication, group memory, anonymity), GroupSystems provides three dis-

As the tool begins to be used, new functions are identified and the capabilities of the tool grows. Significant changes are not unusual in the first few months after tools are added.

TABLE 2					
Group Interaction Tools					
	Activities Supported	Process Support	Process Structure	Task Support	Task Structure
Electronic Brainstorming	1,2	●	●	◐	○
Electronic Discussion*	1,2,3	●	○ to ●	◐	○
Topic Commenter	1	●	○	◐	○
Group Outliner	1,2	◐	○	◐	●
Idea Organizer	2,1	◐	◐	●	◐
Issue Analyzer	2	◐	●	●	◐
Group Writer	2,1	●	○	◐	○
Vote Selection	3	●	◐	◐	●
Alternative Evaluator	3	●	○	◐	●
Group Questionnaire	3	●	●	◐	●
Group Matrix	3	◐	○	◐	●
Stakeholder Identification	4	◐	●	◐	●
Policy Formation	4	◐	●	◐	●

Activities Supported:

1. Exploration and Idea Generation
2. Idea Organization
3. Prioritizing
4. Policy Development and Evaluation

*EDS is used for laboratory research only

Process & Task
Support & Structure
○ Low   ◐ Medium   ● High

tinct styles of process support which blend these functions with different amounts of electronic and verbal interaction: a *chauffeured* style, a *supported* style and an *interactive* style. These styles can be combined with each other and with non-EMS verbal discussion at different stages of any one meeting. We first describe these three styles (see Figure 6) and then consider the process gains and losses that each affects.

With a chauffeured style, only one person uses the EMS, either a group member or the meeting leader/facilitator. A workstation is connected to a public display screen, providing an electronic version of the traditional blackboard. The group verbally discusses the issues, with the electronic blackboard used as a group memory to record and structure information. A supported style is similar to a chauffeured style, but differs in that each member has a computer workstation that provides a parallel, anonymous electronic communication channel with a group memory. The meeting proceeds using a mixture of verbal and electronic interaction. The electronic blackboard is still used to present and structure information, but with each member able to add items. With an interactive style, the parallel, anonymous electronic communication channel with a group memory is used for almost all group communication. Virtually no one speaks. While an electronic blackboard may be provided, the group memory is typically too large to fit on a screen, and thus it is maintained so that all members can access it electronically at their workstations.

The interactive style is the strongest intervention (but not necessarily "the best") as it provides parallel communication, group memory and anonymity to reduce process losses due to air time fragmentation, attenuation blocking, concentration blocking, attention blocking, failure to remember, socializing, domination, interruptions, evaluation apprehension and conformance pressure. Informa-

tion overload may increase, and free riding may be reduced or increased. Process gains may be increased due to more information, synergy, catching errors, stimulation and learning. Media effects increase and decrease process gains and losses as noted previously.

The weakest intervention is the chauffeured style (but not necessarily "the worst"), for which the EMS does not provide a new communication channel, but rather addresses failure to remember by providing focus through a common group memory displayed on the electronic blackboard. An increased task focus promoted by this style may also reduce socializing. Few other process gains or losses are affected.

Between these styles is the supported style. When verbal interaction is used, the effects are similar to a chauffeured style; when electronic interaction is used, the effects are similar to an interactive style. But there are several important differences. First, while anonymity is possible with electronic communication, its effects on evaluation apprehension and conformance pressure are substantially reduced with the supported style because non-anonymous verbal communication occurs. Second, attention blocking (and possibly failure to remember and information overload) will be *increased* beyond that of a traditional meeting (or an interactive style) as members must simultaneously monitor and use both verbal and electronic communication channels. Third, process losses due to media speed, media richness and depersonalization will probably be less than with the interactive style, as members can switch media as needed (e.g., if media richness proves a problem when using the electronic channel, members can switch to verbal interaction).

Each GroupSystems tool was initially designed to use one of these meeting styles to support one specific type of group activity. There are many useful ways of classifying

group activities [42]. We use four categories. The first, exploration and idea generation, involves the development and exploration of issues relevant to the task. The second category, idea organization, involves the synthesizing, structuring, and organizing of ideas into specific alternatives which may follow the generation of ideas; if a group has previously discussed an issue, a meeting may begin with idea organization without idea generation. Tools in the third category, prioritizing, support the individual members in evaluating alternatives. The final category contains tools that provide formal methodologies to support policy development and

evaluation, such as stakeholder analysis. The tools may be used in whatever order the group chooses; there is no mandatory order, although many tasks follow a natural order of idea generation, idea synthesis, prioritizing, and exploration of important issues.

Table 2 summarizes the activities and process support, process structure, task support, and task structure of each group interaction tool. The levels of process support (low, medium, high) correspond to the three meeting styles (chauffeured, supported, interactive) respectively. While most tools can be used in chauffeured mode or in different ways according to the direction of the meeting leader/facilitator, they are described as they are normally used at Arizona. All tools provide at least a medium level of task support due to BriefCase, a memory resident organizational memory tool. For more information, see [7, 51].

Exploration and idea generation: The objective of these tools is to assist the group in exploring issues and generating ideas and alternatives.

Electronic Brainstorming (EBS) provides an interactive style in which participants enter comments into many separate discussions contained in separate files that are randomly shared throughout the group. The high degree of process structure from this random sharing of many discussions attempts to reduce cognitive inertia by precluding the group from focusing on one approach. Process support and structure are thus high, while task structure is low. Electronic Discussion System (EDS) was developed for laboratory research to support exploration and idea generation, idea organization and voting. Its support for exploration and idea generation works in a manner similar to EBS, except that it can also be configured to provide low process structure. All comments can be placed in one central file accessible by all participants at all times, thus providing only one discussion. Topic Commenter (TC), which uses an interactive style (high process support), provides a high level of task structure; comments are collected from participants using a task-specific framework. TC operates like a set of index cards, with each card having a name. Participants select a card, enter comments, and read comments entered by others. Group Outliner works similarly to TC, but enables the group to develop the set of cards (which may be hierarchically structured) using a supported style and then discuss them with an interactive style.

Idea organization: The purpose of idea organization is to identify, synthesize, formulate and consolidate ideas, proposals or alternatives— that is, to build a task structure for ideas. Idea Organizer (IO) provides a supported style, while Issue Analyzer (IA) provides a more structured two-phase approach that first *identifies* (via an interactive style) and then *consolidates* (i.e., achieves consensus on) ideas (via a chauffeured style). With both tools, each participant works separately to cre-

ate a private list of ideas which are submitted to the group. Comments from a previous idea generation activity may be available as task support and may be easily included. As the list grows, the meeting leader/facilitator assists the group in combining similar ideas to move to consensus. Group Writer is a multiuser word processor that enables a group to jointly write and organize documents. Most group interaction is electronic, but verbal communication is used to coordinate members' activities (e.g., who works on what).

Prioritizing: There are a variety of prioritizing methods available in Vote Selection (e.g., yes/no, multiple choice, 10-point scale rating or ranking in order), which employ an interactive style to collect votes, followed by a chauffeured style to discuss the results. Alternative Evaluator (AE) is a multicriteria decision-making tool that uses a similar interactive/chauffeured set of styles. With AE, the group rates each alternative on a 1-10 scale for each criterion. Criteria can be considered equally important, or can be assigned different weights. With Group Questionnaire each participant completes an electronic questionnaire, which may branch to different questions based on user responses. Group Matrix is a consensus-building tool that enables participants to dynamically enter and change numeric (or text) ratings in a two-dimensional matrix. Typically groups initially enter ratings with an alternative style. These ratings are then discussed and revised using a supported style.

Policy development and evaluation: Tools in this category implement formal methodologies to support policy development and evaluation. Stakeholder Identification and Assumption Surfacing (SIAS), based on the strategic assumption surfacing and testing techniques developed by Mason Mitroff [32], is used to assess the potential impact of a plan or policy by identifying those

individuals and organizations that affect (or are affected by) the plan (i.e., the "stakeholders"). SIAS provides a highly structured supported style, in which participants first identify stakeholders and then their assumptions, before rating assumptions for importance to the stakeholder and importance to the plan. Policy Formation (PF) provides a structured multi-phase supported style for reaching agreement in the exact wording of a policy statement. Each participant independently drafts one version of the policy, which is sent to the public screen at the front of the room. Each of the drafts is discussed verbally, and then the policy is sent out to be redrafted again by each participant.

Tools for Organizational Memory

The primary purpose of the organizational memory tools is to provide task structure and task support. Thus far, many EMSs have supported meetings as independent, autonomous events. Group-Systems views the meeting as one part of a larger whole. While improving meeting outcomes is important, it is also important to capture the additions to organizational memory and to provide access to them in subsequent meeting(s). The organizational memory tools provide this organizational memory. Some of the files it contains are knowledge bases in the artificial intelligence sense (e.g., semantic nets) while others are text files or databases.

Briefcase (BC), mentioned earlier, is a memory resident tool that provides immediate read-only access to any text file in the organizational memory at any point during the session. The user simply presses the appropriate keys and is presented with a menu describing each text file. BC also provides a calculator, notepad and calendar. Enterprise Analyzer (EA) facilitates the structuring and analysis of group information in a semantic net using a variety of user-defined modeling techniques (e.g., IBM's Business System Planning (BSP), Porter's

Value Chain). Information can be viewed in tabular form, or in graphical form with the Semantic Graphics Browser (SGB). SGB enables the user to move through the organizational memory and "zoom-in" on specific areas to view details, "zoom-out" to obtain a high-level view, or "explode" a view to display detail information under a node. Group Dictionary enables the group to develop and store formal definitions for use in current or subsequent meetings.

EMS in Practice: Lessons From Using GroupSystems

Our research strategy has been to build on theoretical foundations from prior research to develop EMS environments which are tested via empirical research. Our empirical research has included both laboratory experiments [e.g., 3, 10, 11, 14, 15, 18, 19, 28, 29, 48, 49, 50, 51, 55] and field research [e.g., 6, 7, 9, 20, 35, 36, 37, 51, 52], as we believe that both are important in understanding the impacts of EMS, and in developing the EMS components appropriate for various tasks, groups and organizations. While most studies have found EMS use to improve effectiveness, efficiency and satisfaction, they have also found different effects in different situations. Perhaps the most important conclusion is therefore that even within the same EMS, effects depend on the group, the task, the context, and the EMS components used. This should not be surprising; Figure 4 suggests that the effects depend on interactions among more than three dozen constructs in the meeting process.

We believe it will be difficult to find universal truths. In the meantime, we believe it is important to develop contingency theories to identify the best fit between specific EMS components and the specific group, task, and context characteristics. Isolating the individual effects of specific situational characteristics and EMS components is

difficult, as most studies have examined the combined effects of many factors simultaneously. In this section, we return to the contingency model in Figure 3, which hypothesizes that processes and outcomes depend upon the interaction of four sets of characteristics: context, group, task and EMS. There are dozens of potentially important contingencies. We consider only five: one from the set of EMS characteristics (anonymity), two from group characteristics (size and proximity), one from the context (evaluative tone) and one from task (task activities). For each, we present theoretical arguments and empirical evidence that lead us to hypothesize certain effects. In each case, however, more research is warranted.

Anonymity

Anonymity is possible in interactive styles and in the electronic component of supported styles, but not with the verbal component of supported and chauffeured styles. Anonymity can affect EMS use by reducing or eliminating evaluation apprehension and conformance pressure, as well as social cues. The reduction of evaluation apprehension and conformance pressure may encourage a more open, honest and free-wheeling discussion of key issues. However, the reduction of social cues can lead individuals to behave in ways that are outside of the realms of socially prescribed behavior. Some evidence of the de-individuation associated with the reduction of social cues has been found in some forms of computer-mediated communication, the most extreme form of which is "flaming" [cf. 43].

Changes in evaluation apprehension, conformance pressure and social cues brought about through anonymous communication should have some effect on the meeting process, which should in turn affect the meeting's outcomes. The relaxation of social cues in anonymous EMS groups has been found in varying degrees in five laboratory

experiments conducted at the University of Arizona. Groups using anonymous EMS have been found to generate more critical comments than groups using EMS where the author of each comment was identified [3, 28, 50]. Jessup and Tansik [29] also found that anonymous, non-proximate groups generated the most critical comments. However, only one of five experiments found anonymous groups to have increased performance compared to non-anonymous groups [3]; there were no performance differences in the other studies [19, 28, 29, 50].

Participants in field studies have usually reported that anonymity

was important, particularly in cases where there were power and status differences in the group (e.g., more than two management levels present) [6, 9, 35, 36]. We infer that student groups in the laboratory have lower evaluation apprehension and conformance pressure, and thus while anonymity may reduce these process losses, there are fewer noticeable effects on outcomes. In situations where evaluation apprehension and conformance pressure are high, anonymity appears to have a more significant impact on meeting outcomes.

In all of the laboratory studies referenced here, anonymity was treated as a discrete variable, i.e., communication was either anonymous or it was not. However, the Valacich, Dennis, and Nunamaker [50] study suggests that anonymity may be better thought of as a continuous variable—it may be more appropriate to think of degrees of anonymity. In this study, there were two independent variables, anonymity and group size. The small anonymous groups in this study were more critical than small identified groups, but there were no differences in the level of criticalness among small and large anonymous groups and large identified groups. Because the groups were composed of so many members, there was already a degree of anonymity built into the structure of the group. This was not the case in the smaller groups, where the relative intimacy of the group reinforced existing social cues.

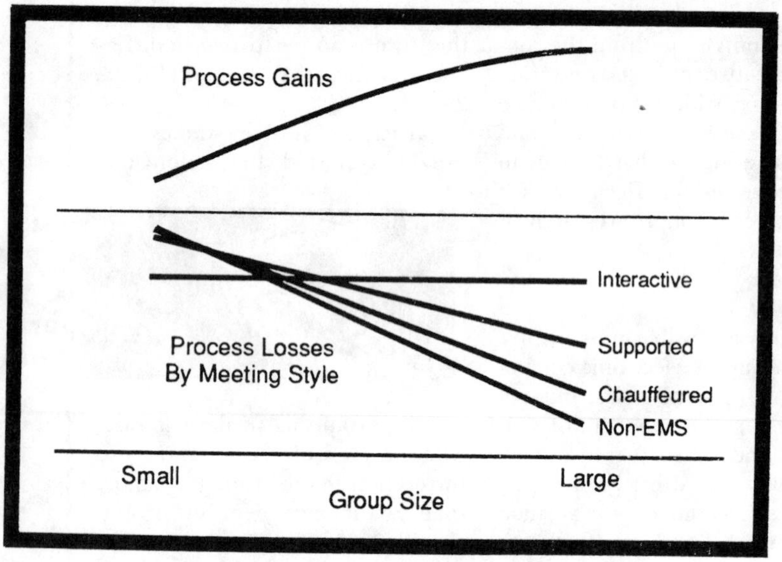

fast with group size (see Figure 7). A supported style introduces more fixed process losses initially (e.g., media speed), but reduces the rate at which losses increase with group size. An interactive style addresses most losses (and thus they should increase very slowly with size) but introduces more fixed losses initially. Thus we hypothesize that interactive styles will be preferred for larger groups, and supported or

process losses may remain relatively constant as size increases. Other experiments have found outcome measures such as effectiveness and member satisfaction to *increase* with size for interactive styles [10, 11, 49]. Another laboratory experiment built, tested and confirmed a model of group performance which proposed process losses from interactive styles to be relatively constant across group size [49]. Our field studies also provide some support for these hypotheses. Participants in studies with larger groups (i.e., 12–20 group members) have reported that interactive styles were more important than supported styles [37].

FIGURE 7. Gains and Losses

Group Size

In general without EMS, process losses increase rapidly with group size [47]. Previous non-EMS research has concluded that in general, regardless of the task, context or group, the "optimal" group size is quite small, typically 3–5 members [42], because process losses quickly overtake any process gains from increased group size. Our EMS research draws a different conclusion: the optimal group size depends upon the situation (group, task, context, EMS), and in some cases may be quite large.

In theory, each of the three EMS styles (chauffeured, supported, interactive) can reduce or increase process losses in varying degrees. A chauffeured style reduces a few process losses. Thus compared to traditional non-EMS meetings, process losses do not increase quite as

chauffeured styles for smaller groups.

There is some empirical evidence to support these hypotheses. One measure of process losses is participation, as it is directly affected by air time fragmentation, production blocking, free riding, etc. A laboratory experiment with small groups found that participation was the same between groups using a chauffeured style and non-supported groups [14], suggesting few differences between the two styles. Another experiment found participation to be more equal in groups using an interactive style than in non-supported groups, suggesting differences between the two [19]. Experiments studying interactive styles have found per-person participation levels to remain constant regardless of the size of the group [10, 48, 50], suggesting that

Task Activities

The type of activities that must be performed to accomplish the task (e.g., idea generation) [42] has a significant impact on the balance of gains and losses. One primary goal of most group activities is the exchange of information among members [12], and thus the form of this information will have significant effects. Zack and McKenney [56] contrast three general states of information [also see 4]. Ambiguity exists when there is both a lack of information and a lack of a framework for interpreting that information. Uncertainty exists when a framework exists, but there is a lack of information. Equivocality exists when there are multiple (and possibly conflicting) interpretations for the information or the framework.

Equivocality requires negotiation among group members to converge to consensus on one interpretation, and media providing information richness are preferred [4]. In contrast, ambiguity and uncertainty require someone in the group (or the group as a whole) to provide, locate, or create the needed information or framework components. Thus the degree of media richness is unimportant; the ability of the group to rapidly gather information and framework components becomes paramount, especially if members of the group have different information, perceptions, and viewpoints.

Exploration and idea generation is more often a problem of ambiguity or uncertainty than of equivocality. It is a divergent activity, as members work individually to report information, propose elements of the framework, and respond to the comments of others. Prioritizing is also a divergent activity, as members work individually. In contrast, synthesizing and organizing ideas, building consensus on a framework, or interpreting the meaning of vote to achieve consensus are primarily problems of equivocality, as the group focuses on the same issues at the same time to resolve different viewpoints to converge on one interpretation.

Therefore, for divergent activities that are problems of uncertainty, such as idea generation, we hypothesize that an interactive style is more appropriate as its parallelism and anonymity facilitate rapid development of ideas. For convergent tasks that are problems of equivocality (such as synthesis and consensus building), process losses from reduced media richness in the interactive style increase dramatically. In this case, the relatively horizontal line for the interactive style in Figure 7 would move beyond the lines for supported and/or chauffeured styles for most group sizes, making them more appropriate.

Our laboratory and field research provide weak support for this hypothesis. A laboratory experiment of idea generation—a task of uncertainty—found groups using an interactive style to generate more ideas and be more satisfied than verbally interacting groups [18]. A similar study using Group-Systems at Indiana University had similar findings [16]. Experiments using purely interactive style for generating and choosing tasks (tasks which begin with ambiguity but evolve into equivocality) have found no performance or satisfaction differences compared to verbally interacting groups [19, 55]. The EMS groups in one of these

studies also required longer to reach consensus [19]. Groups in our field studies have typically used interactive styles to generate ideas, options, and analysis framework components, but used supported or chauffeured style to resolve equivocality.

Group Member Proximity

In our definition of an EMS [5], we note that groups may be distributed with respect to both space and time, although the majority of our research to date has focused on groups interacting in a single room at the same time. Other researchers have also argued that advanced computer-assisted communication and decision technologies, such as an EMS, can be important for project-oriented work groups and temporary task forces that may be distributed geographically and temporally throughout an organization [e.g., 26].

From a theoretical perspective, group process and performance for distributed groups may be substantially different from proximate groups. Social facilitation research has shown that the presence of others can improve a person's performance for easy tasks and hinder performance for more difficult tasks [57]. Remoteness may also foster increased anonymity, and increased anonymity may have several effects on the group, ranging from reduced apprehension to increased social loafing and deindividuated behavior as noted previously. Further, several small group researchers have found that close group proximity may foster liking and fondness among group members [57], and in EMS environments, proximate groups have been as satisfied [48] or more satisfied than distributed groups [29].

.Our initial research in this area has built on our growing body of idea generation research (i.e., a problem of uncertainty not equivocality), where groups communicate only through electronic communication. One laboratory experiment found no difference in the number

of ideas generated between proximate and distributed groups, but found proximate groups to be more satisfied [29]. A second study using a similar research design found distributed groups to generate more ideas than proximate groups, with no satisfaction differences [48].

During these experiments, proximate groups were interrupted more often by disruptive movements or by laughter prompted by a humorous electronic comment. Social facilitation research suggests that such reaction will generally be stronger when a person is proximate to other group members than when working alone in a distrib-

uted group [57]. Thus, we believe that the primary explanation for these performance effects in the laboratory was that distributed groups remained more task-focused than proximate groups.

However, the effects of the proximity manipulation may have been different if this research had been conducted in the field. Our groups worked without outside interruptions. Yet, there are many potential interruptions for group members working alone in the privacy of their offices by events that cannot be helped (e.g., a call from the boss) or by purposely working on other tasks. As a result, distributed groups in the field may, or may not, be more task focused than groups working together in the same room, and thus may find different effects.

Evaluative Tone

Several researchers have advocated a supportive, non-judgmental atmosphere as a means to enhance group productivity by lowering evaluation apprehension and encouraging "freewheeling" stimulation. The withholding of criticism is a cornerstone of many idea generation techniques [38]. However, other researchers have proposed that group productivity may be stimulated by a more critical atmosphere where structured conflict (e.g., dialectical inquiry or devil's advocacy) is used to stimulate group members [e.g., 41]. In any event, there are two very distinct,

> # We are convinced that the use of EMS technology can improve group processes and outcomes in many cases...

and opposing, positions related to this construct.

Connolly, Jessup and Valacich [3] used a laboratory experiment which crossed anonymity (anonymous or identified groups) with the meeting tone (supportive or critical as manipulated by a confederate) to test whether the effects of evaluative tone were moderated by anonymity. Not surprisingly, anonymous groups and critical groups made more critical remarks than groups that were identified or supportive. Groups working anonymously and with a critical tone pro-

duced the greatest number of ideas of the highest quality. However, groups in supportive and identified conditions were typically more satisfied than groups in critical and anonymous conditions. This suggests that the combination of a critical tone and anonymity may improve idea generation, but also may lower satisfaction.

Observations from our field studies provide some insight into possible reasons for these effects. The anonymity may have encouraged group members to detach themselves from their ideas, allowing them to view criticism as a signal to suggest another idea:

"I noticed that if someone criticized an idea of mine, I didn't get emotional about it. I guess when you are face-to-face and everyone hears the boss say 'You are wrong' it's a slap to you, not necessarily the idea. . . . [Here] no one knows whose idea it is, so why be insulted? No one is picking on me. I think I'll just see why they don't agree with me." (manager, Hughes Aircraft).

This runs counter to the typical knee-jerk reaction that might occur in a traditional verbal meeting where a critical comment may be seen as directed at the contributor, not the idea (e.g., "I wasn't as uncomfortable when I saw someone being critical of someone else's idea, because I thought 'nobody's being embarrassed here at all.'" manager, Hughes Aircraft).

Conclusion

The Arizona EMS research program using the GroupSystems Concept has included both developmental and empirical research. Our developmental research has produced more than two dozen software tools currently in use at more than 70 EMS facilities worldwide. Our empirical research has studied EMS use in the laboratory and in the field by more than 30,000 individuals from more than 200 organizations. In this article, we have dis-

cussed several key aspects in the theoretical foundation of EMS, have illustrated how these aspects are reflected in the Arizona facility and software designs, and have highlighted the contingent nature of EMS effects. Nonetheless, much more research is needed to develop new group work methods embodied in facilities and software, and to empirically test the many contingencies involved in their use.

While still recognizing the need for future research, we are convinced that the use of EMS technology can significantly improve group processes and outcomes in many cases—but effects are contingent on the situation. For example, we would expect fewer benefits from EMS use for small cohesive groups in supportive contexts, as they face fewer process losses. Based on the theoretical foundation of process gains and losses, and our observations of EMS use in the field and the laboratory, we believe that EMS use may provide benefits because:

- Parallel communication promotes broader input into the meeting process and reduces the chance that a few people dominate the meeting;
- Anonymity mitigates evaluation apprehension and conformance pressure, so that issues are discussed more candidly;
- Group memory enables members to pause and reflect on information and opinions of others during the meeting and serves as a permanent record of what occurred;
- Process structure helps focus the group on key issues and discourages irrelevant digressions and unproductive behaviors; and
- Task support and structure provides information and approaches to analyze it.

We have drawn four general conclusions about conducting EMS developmental and empirical research. First, the effects of EMS use are contingent upon the situation. Thus we believe that it is critical to clearly document specifics about the group, task, context, and EMS in all research. Who were the group members and were they a cohesive team, strangers, or competitors? Exactly what did the task entail? Were group members motivated? What did the EMS provide at what points, and exactly how did the group use them? Without such detail, the contribution of a study cannot be clearly interpreted or extended.

Second, the results of any one study will not apply to all group work, so it is important to explicitly consider the bounds to which the findings can be generalized. Do they apply to large or small groups, chauffeured, supported or interactive styles, choice or idea generation activities, etc.? We agree with Huber [26] that even apparently subtle differences may have significant impacts. For example, in theory, slower system response time should increase process losses due to attenuation and concentration blocking; one experiment found groups using EBS with a few seconds slower response time to generate significantly fewer ideas than those using the standard version [17]. Only by carefully defining the scope of a study and interpreting the results within it can we extend our understanding of EMS effects.

Third, much EMS research to date has addressed the "what" of EMS technology; researchers have compared EMS and non-EMS groups to determine if there are differences between the two, which is typical of initial research into new technologies. From this research, we know that EMS and non-EMS meetings *are* different, but cannot completely explain *why*. While there is still a place for such research, we believe that it is now more important to understand why EMS encourages different effects in different situations. The research question becomes "does this factor explain why EMS use produces these results in this situation?" rather than "is there a difference?" To understand the "why," it is nec-

essary to compare situations that differ only in the one or two factors of interest. As EMS and non-EMS groups can differ in so many ways (e.g., production blocking, media richness), this research will typically not involve a comparison between EMS and non-EMS groups, as there are too many potential differences to draw conclusions. Field research presenting qualitative investigations of EMS effects on group process in different meeting situations and over the long term will also become important. Our future empirical research will continue to develop contingency models to isolate and explain why certain EMS features (i.e., types of process support, process structure, task support and task structure) are of value for certain groups, tasks and contexts.

Finally, we believe that in developing new EMS tools, it is important to strive to understand what EMS components are useful in what situations. A focus on these four mechanisms may help clarify the needs of specific situations. It will become increasingly important for developmental researchers to work closely with empirical researchers to best fit the components offered by different configurations of EMS technology to user needs. In the early years of EMS, there was little empirical research to guide developers. Developers built EMS environments, gave them to users to see what happened, and then redesigned them in an iterative cycle of design-test-redesign. Today, there is a growing base of empirical research, and while iterative development remains important, developers building on this empirical foundation can provide more successful initial environments requiring less redesign.

The study of EMS is still in its infancy. It is reminiscent of the early days of the automotive industry when a motor was put into a carriage giving the world a horseless carriage. We are now in the horseless carriage phase of EMS, having

installed computers into existing manual processes. We need to learn how best to support groups and group meeting processes, to build on these experiences to create systems that take better advantage of the abilities of technology and of groups. We may discover that many current EMS components (e.g., a facilitator) are the buggy whips of this horseless carriage phase. We are only beginning to discover what functions are robust and valuable, from which will emerge the next generation of EMS. Nonetheless, based upon research and experiences to date, we are convinced that this technology is fundamentally changing the nature of group work.

Acknowledgments

This research was partially supported by grants from IBM. Additional funding for several laboratory experiments was provided by the Social Sciences and Humanities Research Council of Canada. We would like to acknowledge the efforts of the following people who have been involved in the Group-Systems project: Erran Carmel, David Chappell, Kathy Chudoba, Bob Daniels, Mark Fuller, Glenda Hayes, Barbara Gutek, Bruce Herniter, Suzanne Iacono, Ben Martz, Jolene Morrison, Mike Morrison, David Paranka, Mark Pendergast, V. Ramesh, Ed Roberts, Bill Saints, Craig Tyran, Lee Walker, and Suzanne Weisband. We would like to thank Brent Gallupe, Karen Judson, the anonymous reviewers, and the editor for particularly helpful comments on earlier drafts of this article. ◪

References

1. Ackoff, R.L., Gupta, S.K. and Minas, J.S. *Scientific Method*, John Wiley & Sons, 1962.
2. Albanese, R. and Van Fleet, D.D. Rational behavior in groups: The

free riding tendency. *Academy of Management Review*, 10 (1985), 244–255.

3. Connolly, T., Jessup, L.M. and Valacich, J.S. Effects of anonymity and evaluative tone on idea generation in computer-mediated groups. *Management Science*, 36, 6 (1990), 689–703.

4. Daft, R.L. and Lengel, R.H. Organizational information requirements, media richness and structural design. *Management Science*, 32, 5 (1986), 554–571.

5. Dennis, A.R., George, J.F., Jessup, L.M., Nunamaker Jr., J.F. and Vogel, D.R. Information technology to support electronic meetings. *MIS Quarterly* 12, 4 (1988), 591–624.

6. Dennis, A.R., Heminger, A.R., Nunamaker Jr., J.F. and Vogel, D.R. Bringing automated support to large groups: The Burr-Brown Experience. *Information and Management*, 18, 3 (1990), 111–121.

7. Dennis, A.R., Nunamaker Jr., J.F. and Paranka, D. Supporting the search for competitive advantage. *Journal of MIS*, forthcoming.

8. Dennis, A.R., Nunamaker Jr., J.F. and Vogel, D.R. A comparison of laboratory experiments and field studies in the study of electronic meeting systems. *Journal of MIS*, 7, 2 (1991), 107–135.

9. Dennis, A.R., Tyran, C.K., Vogel, D.R. and Nunamaker Jr., J.F. An evaluation of electronic meeting support for strategic management. In *Proceedings of ICIS* (1990), 37–52.

10. Dennis, A.R., Valacich, J.S. and Nunamaker Jr., J.F. An experimental investigation of group size in an electronic meeting system environment. *IEEE Transactions on Systems, Man, and Cybernetics*, 20, 5 (1990), 1049–1057.

11. Dennis, A.R., Valacich, J.S. and Nunamaker Jr., J.F. Group, Subgroup and Nominal Group Idea Generation in an Electronic Meeting Environment, HICSS-24, 1991, III: 573–579.

12. DeSanctis, G. and Gallupe, R.B. A foundation for the study of group decision support systems. *Management Science*, 33, 5 (1987), 589–609.

13. Diehl, M. and Stroebe W. Productivity loss in brainstorming groups: Toward the solution of a riddle. *J. Personality and Social Psychology*, 53, 3 (1987), 497–509.

14. Easton, A.C., Vogel, D.R. and Nunamaker Jr., J.F. Stakeholder identification and assumption surfacing in small groups: An experimental study. HICSS-22, 1989, III 344–352.

15. Easton, G., George, J.F., Nunamaker Jr., J.F. and Pendergast, M.O. Using two different electronic meeting system tools for the same task: An experimental comparison. *J. of MIS*, 7, 1 (1990), 85–100.

16. Fellers, J.W. The effect of group size and computer support on group idea generation for creativity tasks: An experimental evaluation using a repeated measures design. Unpublished Ph.D. Thesis, Indiana University, 1989.

17. Gallupe, R.B., Cooper, W. and Bastianutti, L. Why is electronic brainstorming more productive than traditional brainstorming. Administrative Sciences Association of Canada Conference Proceedings, Information Systems Division (Whistler, Canada, 1990), 82–92.

18. Gallupe, R.B., Dennis, A.R., Cooper, W.H., Valacich, J.S., Nunamaker Jr., J.F., and Bastianutti, L. Group size and electronic brainstorming. Queen's University Working Paper, 1991.

19. George, J.F., Easton, G.K., Nunamaker Jr., J.F. and Northcraft, G.B. A study of collaborative group work with and without computer based support. *Inf. Syst. Res.*, 1, 4 (1990), 394–415.

20. Grohowski, R.B., McGoff, C., Vogel, D.R., Martz, W.B. and Nunamaker Jr., J.F. Implementation of electronic meeting systems at IBM. *MIS Quarterly*, 14, 4 (1990), 369–383.

21. Hackman, J.R. and Kaplan, R.E. Interventions into group process: An approach to improving the effectiveness of groups. *Decision Sciences*, 5 (1974), 459–480.

22. Hill, G.W. Group versus individual performance: Are N + 1 heads better than one? *Psychological Bulletin*, 91, 3 (1982), 517–539.

23. Hiltz, S.R. and Turoff, M. Structuring computer-mediated communication systems to avoid information overload. *Commun. ACM*, 28, 7 (1985), 680–689.

24. Hirokawa, R.Y. and Pace, R. A descriptive investigation of the possible communication based reasons for effective and ineffective group decision making. *Commun. Monographs*, 50 (1983), 363–379.

25. Huber, G.P. Issues in the design of group decision support systems. *MIS Quarterly*, (1984), 195–204.

26. Huber, G.P. A theory of the effects of advanced information technology on organizational design, intelligence, and decision making. *Acad. of Manag. Rev.*, 15, 1 (1990), 47–71.

27. Jablin, F.M. and Seibold, D.R. Implications for problem solving groups of empirical research on 'brainstorming': A critical review of the literature. *The Southern States Speech Commun. J.*, 43 (Summer 1978), 327–356.

28. Jessup, L.M., Connolly, T. and Galegher, J. The effects of anonymity on group process in automated group problem solving. *MIS Quarterly*, 14, 3 (1990), 313–321.

29. Jessup, L.M. Tansik, D.A. and Lasse, T.D. Group problem solving in an automated environment: The effects of anonymity and proximity on group process and outcome with a GDSS. *Decision Sciences*, forthcoming.

30. Lamm, H. and Trommsdorff, G. Group versus individual performance on tasks requiring ideational proficiency (brainstorming): A review. *European J. of Soc. Psy.*, (1973), 361–387.

31. Maidique, M.A. Entrepreneurs, champions, and technological innovations. *Sloan Manag. Rev.*, 21, 2 (1980), 59–76.

32. Mason, R.O. and Mitroff, I.I. *Challenging Strategic Planning Assumptions*, John Wiley & Sons, New York, 1981.

33. Miller, J.C. Information input overload and psychopathology. *J. of Psychiatry*, (Feb. 1960), 696–704.

34. Mintzberg, H., Raisinghani, D. and Theoret, A. The structure of 'unstructured' decision processes. *Administrative Sciences Quarterly*, 21 (1976), 246–275.

35. Nunamaker Jr., J.F., Applegate, L.M., and Konsynski, B.R. Facilitating group creativity with GDSS. *J. of MIS*, 3, 4 (1987), 5–19.

36. Nunamaker Jr., J.F., Applegate, L.M. and Konsynski, B.R. Computer-aided deliberation: Model management and group decision support. *J. of Operations Res.*, 36, 6 (1988), 826–848.

37. Nunamaker Jr., J.F., Vogel, D., Heminger, A., Martz, B., Grohowski, R. and McGoff, C. Experiences at IBM with group sup-

port systems: A field study. *Decision Support Systems, 5,* 2 (1989), 183–196.

38. Osborn, A.F. *Applied Imagination: Principles and Procedures of Creative Thinking.* 2nd edition, Scribners, New York, 1957.

39. Pinsonnault, A. and Kraemar, K.L. The impact of technological support on groups: An assessment of the empirical research. *Decision Support Syst., 5,* 2 (1989), 197–216.

40. Poole, M.S. Decision development in small groups II: A study of multiple sequences of decision making. *Communication Monographs,* 50 (1983), 206–232.

41. Schweiger, D.M., Sandberg, W.R., and Rechner, P.L. Experimental effects of dialectical inquiry, devil's advocacy, and consensus approaches to strategic decision making. *Academy of Management Review, 32,* 4 (1989), 745–772.

42. Shaw, M. *Group Dynamics: The Psychology of Small Group Behavior.* 3rd edition, McGraw-Hill, New York, 1981.

43. Siegel, J., Dubrovsky, V. Kiesler, S. and McGuire, T.W. Group processes in computer mediated communication. *Organizational Behavior and Human Decision Processes, 37* (1986), 157–187.

44. Silver, M.S. Decision support systems: Directed and non-directed change. *Information Systems Research, 1,* 1 (1990), 47–70.

45. Simon, H.A. *Administrative Behavior.* 3rd edition, Free Press, 1976.

46. Stefik, M., Foster, G., Bobrow, D.G., Khan, K., Lanning, S., and Suchman, L. Beyond the chalkboard: Computer support for collaboration and problem solving in meetings. *Commun. ACM, 30,* 1 (1987), 33–47.

47. Steiner, I.D. *Group Process and Productivity.* Academic Press, New York, 1972.

48. Valacich, J.S. Group size and proximity effects on computer mediated generation: A laboratory investigation. Doctoral dissertation, University of Arizona, 1989.

49. Valacich, J.S., Dennis, A.R., George, J.F. and Nunamaker Jr., J.F. Electronic support for group idea generation: Shifting the balance of process gains and losses. Arizona working paper, 1991.

50. Valacich, J.S., Dennis, A.R., and Nunamaker Jr., J.F. Anonymity and group size effects on computer

mediated idea generation. Proceedings of Academy of Management Meeting, 1991, forthcoming.

51. Valacich, J.S., Dennis, A.R. and Nunamaker Jr., J.F. Electronic Meeting Support: The Group-Systems concept. *Intern. J. of Man Machine Studies,* forthcoming.

52. Vogel, D.R., Martz, W.B., Nunamaker Jr., J.F., Grohowski, R.B. and McGoff, C. Electronic meeting system experience at IBM. *J. of MIS, 6,* 3 (1990), 25–43.

53. Vogel, D.R., Nunamaker Jr., J.F., George, J.F. and Dennis, A.R. Group decision support systems: Evolution and status at the University of Arizona. In R.M. Lee, A.M. McCosh, and P. Migliarese Eds. *Organizational Decision Support Systems,* Proceedings of IFIP WG 8.3 Working Conference on Organizational DSS, North Holland, 1988, 287–305.

54. Williams, E. 1977. Experimental comparisons of face-to-face and medidated communication: A review. *Psychol. Bull., 84,* 5, 963–976.

55. Winniford, M.A. The effect of electronic meeting support on large and small decision-making groups. Unpublished doctoral dissertation, University of Arizona, 1989.

56. Zack, M.H. and McKenney, J.L. Characteristics of organizational information domain: An organizational information processing perspective. Harvard Business School Working Paper 89-027, 1989.

57. Zajonc, R.B. Social facilitation. *Science,* 149 (1965), 269–274.

CR Categories and Subject Descriptors: H.1.2 [**Models and Principles**]: User/Machine Systems—*human information processing;* H.4.2 [**Information Systems Applications**]: Types of Systems—*decision support;* H.4.3 [**Information Systems Applications**]: Communications Applications—*computer conferencing and teleconferencing;* H.5.3 [**Information Interfaces and Presentations**]: Group and Organization Interfaces—*synchronous interfaces; theory and models;* J.1 [**Administrative Data Processing**]: General.

General Terms: Design

Additional Key Words and Phrases: Communication, computer-supportive cooperative work, electronic meeting systems, group decision support systems, groupware, group work, multi-user systems

About the Authors

J.F. NUNAMAKER heads the Department of MIS at the University of Arizona where he is a professor of MIS and Computer Science. His research interests include computer-aided support of systems analysis and design, and systems for management.

ALAN R. DENNIS is a doctoral candidate in MIS at the University of Arizona. His current research interests include electronic meeting systems, systems analysis and design, and business process re-engineering.

JOSEPH S. VALACICH is assistant professor of information systems at the University of Indiana. His current research interests include the design and investigation of communication and decision technologies to support collaborative group work, systems analysis and design, and group and organizational memory. **Authors' Present Address:** Decision and Information Systems Department, School of Business, Indiana University, Bloomington, IN 47405, valacich@iubacs.bitnet.

DOUGLAS R. VOGEL is an assistant professor of MIS at the University of Arizona. His research interests bridge the business and academic communities in addressing group support system development, implementation, and evaluation issues.

JOEY F. GEORGE is an assistant professor in the Department of MIS at the University of Arizona. His research interests focus on information technology in the work place, and currently include the study of group decision support systems.

Authors' Present Address for Nunamaker, Dennis, Vogel, and George: Department of MIS, Eller Graduate School of Management, University of Arizona, Tuscon, AZ 85721, nunamake@arizmis.bitnet, dennisa@arizmis.bitnet, vogel@arizmis.bitnet, george@arizmis.bitnet.

Experiences at IBM with Group Support Systems: A Field Study

Jay NUNAMAKER, Doug VOGEL,
Alan HEMINGER, and Ben MARTZ

Department of Management Information Systems, College of Business and Public Administration, University of Arizona, Tucson, AZ 85721, USA

Ron GROHOWSKI and Chris MCGOFF

IBM Corporation, Bethesda, MD 20817, USA

Although numerous laboratory studies have been conducted, virtually no attention has been given to how well an operational Group Support System functions in a real-world, organizational setting. This paper presents the results of a Group Support System field study conducted at an IBM site. Data collected included session pre- and post-session questionnaires and facilitator observations plus followup interviews with managers and participants. Process and outcome effectiveness, efficiency, and user satisfaction were consistently higher for Group Support Systems compared to no automated support. Further, those who had used the automated system before consistently had a higher mean score on questions of process effectiveness. A comparison of man-hours expended resulted in a reported 56% savings attributable to Group Support System use. The overwhelmingly positive results of this field study contradict some laboratory experiment findings and support others. Directions for future field and experimental research to resolve apparent differences and provide further clarification are identified.

Keywords: Group Support Systems, GDSS, Productivity, Effectiveness, Efficiency, Field Study

Jay F. Nunamaker, Jr., is Head of the Department of Management Information Systems and is a Professor of Management Information Systems (MIS) and Computer Science at the University of Arizona. He received a PhD from Case Institute of Technology in systems engineering and operations research. He was an Associate Professor of Computer Science and Industrial Administration at Purdue University. Dr. Nunamaker joined the faculty at the University of Arizona in 1974 to develop the MIS program. He has authored numerous papers on group decision support systems, the automation of software construction, performance evaluation of computer systems, decision support systems for systems analysis and design, and has lectured throughout Europe, Russia, Asia, and South America. Dr. Nunamaker is Chairman of the Association for Computing Machinery (ACM) Curriculum Committee on Information Systems.

North-Holland
Decision Support Systems 5 (1989) 183–196

Introduction

Research literature attention to Group Support Systems is increasing. Framework papers [e.g., Huber (1984), DeSanctis and Gallupe (1987)] have been followed by reports of experimental studies [e.g., Lewis (1982), Gallupe (1985), Watson (1987), Beauclair (1987), Zigurs (1987), A. Easton (1988), G. Easton (1988)]. Unfortunately, only minor at-

Douglas R. Vogel is an Assistant Professor of MIS. He has been involved with computers and computer systems in various capacities for over 20 years. He received his M.S. in Computer Science from U.C.L.A. in 1972 and his Ph.D. in MIS from the University of Minnesota in 1986 where he was also research coordinator for the MIS Research Center. His current research interests bridge the business and academic communities in addressing questions of the impact of management information systems on aspects of interpersonal communication, group decision making, and organizational productivity.

Alan Heminger is currently Assistant Professor at Indiana University School of Business in the Department of Operation and Systems Management. He received an MS in Counseling from California State University, Hayward, School of Educational Psychology, in 1978. In 1988 he completed his PhD in MIS at the University of Arizona. His current research interests are in the area of Group Decision Support Systems (GDSS), with particular interest in the assessment of their implementation in operational environments, and the problem of hindsight bias as it affects group work. Heminger was selected to attend the 1987 ICIS Doctoral Consortium.

William Benjamin Martz, Jr. graduated from the College of William and Mary in 1981 with a B.B.A. In 1985, he received his M.S. from the University of Arizona and entered the Ph.D. program seeking a concentration in Management Information Systems. His expected date of completion is Spring, 1989. His experiences cover the design and coding of software for work groups, the facilitation of work groups at Arizona's facilities, and the coordination of the implementation of the work group software at a manufacturing site. His current interests include Group Decision Support Systems; Electronic Business Planning Tools; Small Group Theory in an Electronic Environment.

tention has been given to field experiences with Group Support Systems (e.g., Applegate (1986), Martz (1989), Heminger (1989)] and the literature that does exist tends to contradict the results of many experimental studies. This is indeed a problem if results of academic research are to be applied effectively in business settings. The challenge is to reflect upon field observations and integrate aspects of field and experimental research to achieve a more comprehensive understanding of the implications of real world application of Group Support Systems.

This paper presents the results of a Group Support System field study conducted at an IBM manufacturing site having 6,000 employees. Data collected included pre- and post-session questionnaires and facilitator observations plus followup interviews with managers and participants on issues of process and outcome effectiveness, efficiency, and user satisfaction. A comparison of the actual number of man-hours expended with the number that had been anticipated also was made. Results of the study are compared with those of experimental studies addressing similar issues. Limitations are discussed and directions for future field and experimental research to resolve difference are identified.

Research Model

The research model used in conjunction with this research is illustrated in fig. 1. The model was based on extensive experience coupled with a review of relevant literature. The variables in the model are representative of those variables studied most often in past Group Decision Support System and computer-mediated communication research. Readers are directed to Nunamaker, Applegate, and Konsynski (1988) and Dennis et al. (1988) for additional background on the research model.

As shown in fig. 1, the model addresses issues related to individual, group, project, and organizational levels of analysis that we feel are particularly relevant to Group Support System design and implementation. At the center of the model, the characteristics of the group, task, context, and technology are represented as influencing process and, together with that process, establishing the group work environment. The environment, in turn, drives group outcomes that then provide feedback to the organization's decision-making environment. A group's characteristics include its size and the composite of experience, cohesiveness, motivation, and history that constitutes group member attitudes and involvement. Task characteristics include task type, complexity, degree of

Ronald Grohowski is the Director of Management Information Systems and Telecommunications at the IBM Systems Integration Division in Bethesda, Maryland. Mr. Grohowski has a BS in Mathematics from Wilkes College and an MS in Operations Research from Union College in New York. Ronald Grohowski is responsible for tactical and strategic planning, business control guidance, DP equipment planning and acquisition and telecommunications/networking activities. He is also responsible for the direction of over 1,000 I/S professionals and over 1,000 MIPS for 16,000 employees.

Christopher McGoff is an IBM Program Manager at the IBM Systems Integration Division in Bethesda, Maryland. He received a BS degree in 1980 from the University of Scranton and has done postgraduate studies in Ergonomics/Human Factors at Texas Tech University. As a program manager he is involved in decision center information systems strategy and computer supported cooperative work. The systems integration division supports a population of 19,300 professionals with 10 3090s, 26 308xs, 19 4381s, that provide 14 MVS systems and 19 VM systems.

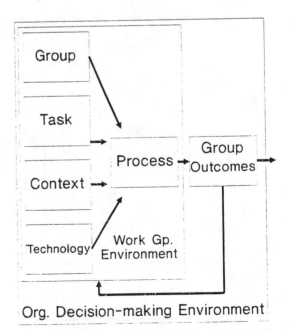

Fig. 1. The Research Model.

rationality, and clarity. Context characteristics include aspects of the organizational environment such as incentives, reward system, and organizational culture. Technology characteristics include hardware, software, and setting configuration. Process includes aspects of the procedures, anonymity, level of participation, facilitation, and interaction of group members that influence group outcomes such as satisfaction, quality of outcomes, time required to reach resolution, consensus, and decision confidence. This model provided the framework for Group Support System implementation and evaluation at an IBM installation. The study addressed the research question of how well an operational Group Support System functions in a real-world, organizational setting?

Implementation Chronology

The purpose of this section is to outline the chronology of events and experiences that took place in conjunction with implementation of University of Arizona Group Support System software at an IBM site. Facility use overviews are provided. Data collection procedures are reviewed.

Grant Support: Phase 0

The University of Arizona was one of 13 schools awarded $2 million grants through IBM's Management of Information Systems (MOIS) program. A portion of this grant and other grants were used to develop software and facilities extending prior University of Arizona Group Support System activities. Experience with the software and facilities established a foundation from which the University of Arizona proceeded in encouraging Group Support System installation and evaluation in a corporate setting.

Site: Phase 1

Following visits by IBM corporate personnel to University of Arizona facilities that included "hands-on" use of the work group support tools to address a major corporate planning problem, company representatives expressed satisfaction with the process and decided to install similar facilities within the corporation for operational use on a daily basis. The site selected for this installation is an IBM manufacturing plant with approximately 6,000 employees, located in a rural setting in upstate New York. A room to house the Group Support System was remodelled according to the design of an operational facility at the

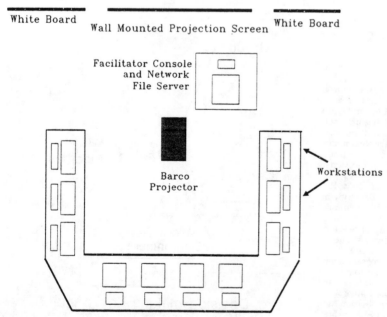

Fig. 2. Corporate Site Facility.

Table 1
Chronology of Phase 1 Implementation Activities.

Date	Activity
4/87	Initial site visit
5/87	Facility construction consultation
5/87	Prototype installation in temporary facility
9/87	Formal Group Support System installation
9/87	Facilitation training
12/87	Operational evaluation

University of Arizona. The corporate site facility is illustrated in fig. 2. In the room, a U-shaped table is equipped with 10 networked microcomputers. An additional microcomputer attached to a large screen projection system is also on the network to permit display of work done at individual workstations or of aggregated information from the total group. An adjacent small room is designated for "backroom" functions such as printing out session results. The Phase 1 software implementation process, initiated in the Spring of 1987 with a site visit, was concluded in December of 1987 with a corporate evaluative report. Data collection using Phase 1 software commenced in January 1988. A Phase 2 system implementation process was initiated in September 1988. Table 1 presents a summary of Phase 1 implementation activities. Close communication and cooperation between IBM and the University of Arizona ensured that the implementation proceeded smoothly and established a strong foundation for extended facility use and evaluative efforts. The transfer of technology from an academic research environment to a corporate mainstream application was a new experience for both the University of Arizona and IBM groups involved in this implementation. Prior University of Arizona experience had been based on six academic implementations. The cooperation led to success in implementing the software at the initial site that has subsequently resulted in Group Support System implementation at six other sites. Further site expansion is envisioned in the near future.

Facility Use

Problem solving groups from throughout the site were encouraged to use the facility. Groups most often heard of the facility through word-of-mouth from other groups. Group participants ranged from the plant manager and high level executives to shop floor personnel. Representa-

tives of several management levels were often included in the same group. Some groups were on-going entities while others were newly established. Group size ranged from 4 to 10 members with an average size of 8. Larger groups tended to be new ones having been assigned a particular task and representing a wide variety of functional areas. Group members typically had detailed knowledge of one aspect of the problem area and general knowledge of the problem domain. As such, the knowledge domains of group members were distinct yet overlapping relative to the question at hand.

Tasks addressed by the groups were for the most part of a planning and problem solving nature, e.g., strategic planning process problems, factors contributing to cost overruns, and functional area data processing needs. Some were cross organizational involving many functional areas; others represented many management/employee layers within a particular functional area. The groups participating in sessions brought with them myriad problem domains, e.g., requirements analysis, strategic planning, and resource allocation. The majority of tasks were complex to the extent that they required creativity and had no known "right" answer, particularly for the larger groups of size 8 to 10. Groups also tended to address tasks that were oriented towards evaluating a set of issues. A pre-planning meeting was typically held before each group session to align the best use of the tools with the task to be undertaken. The technology provided consists of three linked software tools. An *Electronic Brainstorming* tool supports idea generation, allowing group members to simultaneously and anonymously share comments on a specific question. An *Issue Analyzer* tool helps group members identify and consolidate key focus items resulting from idea generation. Support is also provided for integrating external information to support identified focus items. A *Voting* tool provides a variety of prioritizing methods including Likert scales, rank ordering, and multiple choice. All group members cast private ballots. Accumulated results are displayed, at which time action items and an agenda for a future session, if appropriate, are identified. A scenario demonstrating use of the tools is as follows:

A manager responsible for improving shop floor control was having difficulties identifying problem areas that were hindering the process. Those persons knowledgeable about each of the subfunctions seemed unable to isolate primary causes and identify potential solutions that could result in improved productivity. In fact, a two hour meeting of half a dozen of the key participants had resulted in a number of arguments and no solutions. The manager had previously elicited IS support but, without defined requirements, no progress had been made.

The manager elected to try the Group Support System in an attempt to resolve issues and develop a plan of action including information system requirements to improve the shop floor control process. The manager met with the facilitator to express the objective she sought and to understand how the Group Support System might be used. It was mutually decided to use the Electronic Brainstorming tool with the question "What are the key issues in improving shop floor control?" followed by Issue Analysis and Voting. A session agenda and time was established for 10 of the key participants including the manager and two junior analysts assigned to investigate possibilities of information systems support.

The Brainstorming session lasted for 35 minutes during which time the participants generated 645 lines of comments. Comments included issues, ideas, and clarifications as group members shared information. At the end of the brainstorming session, the manager reflected that for the first time she was able to get meaningful answers to questions associated with shop floor control issues. The analysts noted that they were beginning to better understand the interrelated nature of the overall shop floor control process.

A 30 minute period of focus item identification followed by 45 minutes of issue consolidation and face-to-face discussion resulted in a generalized list of requirements for effective shop floor control improvement. Each group member prioritized the list in terms of importance to improved shop floor control and cast a private ballot using the Voting tool. The accumulated results were displayed to the group. After 10 minutes of discussion, the session was concluded with comments from the manager thanking the participants and directing the analysts to proceed towards the development of information systems support for the shop floor control process. The manager was given hardcopy of all of the session input.

Data Collection

A particularly important aspect of the installation and use of the Group Support System at the IBM site was collection of evaluative data from a broad range of end users addressing a variety of tasks. Data collection was accomplished by combining information contained in system log files with that collected from on-line pre- and post-session questionnaires filled out by group members, facilitator observations, and followup interviews with managers and participants on aspects of process and three key objectives: outcome effectiveness, efficiency, and user satisfaction. Session log file, questionnaire, and interview details are provided in the following section. Additional evaluative measures included the time required for completing the project, number of meetings required, the length of individual meetings, and the number of people in the group meetings as well as cost measures that were separated as administrative and man-hour costs. Actual man-hour data were aligned with anticipated time estimates based on leader experience and historical precedents. Initial test data were collected in December 1987. Data collection commenced in January 1988 in conjunction with the pilot testing of the data collection process, the focus of this paper, representing the beginning of a multi-year study.

To facilitate cross-site comparison, data continue to be collected at the IBM sites that are now beginning to use Group Support System software. Each site has a major focus (e.g., customer partnerships, product development cycle) to further investigate the domain of Group Support System applicability as well as provide opportunities for replication and independent confirmation of findings at the initial site. Each site has its own group of facilitators and support staff.

Study Results

The major thrust of this research was to assess the use of an operational Group Support System in an organizational setting. An important facet of this study was to go beyond user acceptance to ascertain reaction to the Group Support System process and outcome in terms of effectiveness, efficiency, and user satisfaction. This section will report the summarized results from sessions using the Group Support System.

Effectiveness

For purposes of this study, Group Support System effectiveness was comprised of two components: quality of session process and quality of outcome. One measure of the quality of session process is the degree to which the participants took part in the process and contributed to its outcome. The quality of outcome is a measure of the degree to which the system provided the product that the session initiator desired. Further indication of outcome quality comes from followup on how the results from the system actually were used.

The quality of session process was measured through the use of log files, through which it is possible to learn the evenness of participation among the participants, and of information gathered from the participant post-session questionnaires, and follow-up interview forms. Analysis of log file data revealed that, compared with traditional group dynamics, Group Support System use tends to equalize participation. Results were independent of participant typing skills and familiarity with micro-computer technology. As an additional indication of Group Support System process effectiveness, participants were asked to express their agreement with a number of statements about the system, using a five-point Likert scale. Table 2 presents participant responses.

These responses indicate a strong agreement among the participants that the system did provide process effectiveness. Further, those who had used the automated system before consistently had a higher mean score on questions of process effectiveness ($p < 0.0001$). These responses indicate a significant increase in belief in the effectiveness of the Group Support System process for those who had used the system before over those who had not. In addition, the question "How would you rate the effectiveness of the automated process?" was asked in the followup interviews with participants. Comments included:

> "It was very effective. Some of the reasons for this assessment are the ability to get all participants together, to capture their thoughts anonymously, the ability to use data for action, and the ability to step strong managers through the process without personalities getting in the way."

> "It was very effective for dynamic problem solving, for generating ideas and for working with group dynamics."

> "We don't have another vehicle which could do what we did for the way we used the system. The brainstorming capability and the anonymity feature were particularly important."

Effectiveness of the output of the Group Support System was addressed in the followup interviews with managers who were also participants. Comments made in response to the question: "What has happened as a result of the automated session(s)? (In general terms, without discussing data.)" included:

> "All sessions have led to follow-up meetings. We definitely have used the data that was generated."

> "Our department and two others put our ideas together and established a mission. We have since implemented that mission."

> "It resulted in moving to the next phase of the project."

Table 2
Levels of Agreement about System Effectiveness.

Post-session questionnaire statement	% of responses ($n = 441$)					
	strongly disagle ←--			strongly agree --→		
	1	2	3	4	5	Mean
The computer-aided process is better than the manual process.	5.5	3.9	11.4	27.4	51.8	4.162
The computer-aided process helps the group generate ideas.	5.0	3.6	6.8	24.8	59.8	4.307
The computer-aided process helps the group identify key ideas.	4.8	5.2	9.8	31.4	48.9	4.143
The computer-aided process helps the group achieve its goals.	4.8	5.2	9.8	31.4	48.9	4.143
The group's problem-solving process was fair.	5.5	2.5	15.8	36.3	40.0	4.027

"The session was input to many different plans. The plans were then developed."

"We got enough information to make a decision."

Comments in response to the question: "What has been done with the data that were generated during the session(s)?" included

"It was fed back to the participants for further work in all cases. It was kept as a book and select people worked with it to provide feedback to the group."

"The data were presented to management. The rank-order charts and histograms were used in later meetings. The raw data were given to management for their review."

"The data were distributed to all members of the department. Open items were displayed at all bi-monthly meetings until closed."

Efficiency

The efficiency of the system as used in this study is an indication of the relative costs and benefits to the organization compared with doing the same function manually. It was not possible to run parallel sessions with control groups to measure efficiency directly. However, prior to use of the facility and without knowledge of automated support capabilities, each group leader was required to recommend and document a feasible project schedule for the accomplishment of his or her group's objectives, based on previous experience with similar projects. These schedules defined historical parameters for the projects and a baseline for comparison with the efficiency of the automated support. The plan provided by the group leader was then translated into an outline for use of the automated support tools.

After completion of the project, expectations before use of the tools was compared with what actually occurred. Further, the output from the sessions was independently evaluated by a knowledgeable third party to gain a measure of what it would take to arrive at the same level of accomplishment using traditional manual processes. Overall, there is reason to believe that the results

Table 3

Comparison of Projected Manual and Automation Supported Man-hour Requirements.

People in session	Man-hours projected	Man-hours actual	Percent man-hours saved
7	204.50	97.50	52.32
10	47.50	20.50	56.84
10	240.00	40.00	83.33
10	132.00	36.00	72.73
10	94.00	46.00	51.06
10	220.00	89.50	59.32
10	400.00	98.50	75.38
9	88.00	43.00	51.14
8	88.00	43.50	50.57
6	20.00	4.50	77.50
9	42.00	29.00	30.95
10	88.00	43.00	51.14
5	30.00	17.70	41.00
7	41.00	30.00	26.83
9	264.00	116.00	56.06
6	36.00	16.00	55.56
9	60.00	31.50	47.50
8	42.00	29.00	30.95
7	72.00	40.50	43.75
4	110.00	18.00	83.64
6	38.00	24.00	36.84
9	153.00	31.00	79.74
10	296.00	128.00	56.76
10	192.00	62.00	67.71
5	72.00	40.50	43.75
9	62.00	35.00	43.55
7	136.00	39.50	70.96
10	100.00	44.50	55.50
9	41.00	22.50	45.12
8	192.00	62.00	67.71

tot.	247	3601.00	1378.70	1665.19
avg.	8	120.03	45.96	55.51

Number of sessions: 29

gave at least a reasonable approximation of the estimated parameters, based on the years of experience of the various group initiators. As illustrated in table 3, man-hours were saved in every case recorded, with an average per session saving of 55.51%. Percentages have been used to compensate for varying project lengths. A matched-pairs *t*-test was significant at a level $p = 0.0001$.

The data align with that recorded in the pilot test that preceded formal data collection. In the pilot test of 11 groups, an average man-hour savings of 61% was reported in conjunction with a 92% average calendar reduction in time required to complete a project. Results from data subsequently collected from nine groups at a second IBM corporate site in a metropolitan setting reflected average man-hour savings of 55.6%. These results strongly confirm the robust nature of man-hour savings because the second site is primarily administratively oriented, as opposed to the manufacturing orientation of the initial site. The time savings reported are independent of particular site characteristics on a group level of analysis.

High levels of performance in terms of man-hour savings were strongly correlated with the degree to which the group's task was stated clearly and concisely ($p = 0.004$). Larger groups (i.e., size 8 to 10) tended slightly to outperform smaller groups relative to expectations. Man-hour savings were independent of the individual knowledge completeness of group members, ongoing nature of the group, degree to which cooperation was required, and composition relative to number of management levels or different departments represented. However, more formal, more recently established, and less cohesive groups tended to achieve higher levels of man-hour savings relative to expectations from similar groups that met without benefit of automated support. These groups also tended to be larger.

Participants were also asked, first in post-session questionnaires and later in follow-up interviews, to provide data on system efficiency. In the post-session questionnaire, one of the questions asked the participants to indicate their levels of agreement with a statement about system efficiency. Results are indicated in table 4. Seventy-two percent of the participants regarded the process to be efficient.

Followup interviews with managers who were also participants provided additional evidence of the efficiency of the Group Support System. In response to the question: "How would you compare the automated process with similar manual processes?" comments from these managers included:

> "The manual process takes approximately 3 to 4 times longer."

> "We could not have done the process we did manually within a similar time frame."

Additional responses to the question: "Looking back on the automated group work session(s), what stands out most in your mind?" included:

> "A lot of ideas were generated. A lot was accomplished in a short period of time. It provided a very organized way to do things."

> "The speed of the process. The way that ideas got flowing and how those ideas triggered other ideas."

> "The volume of information generated in the short amount of time."

User Satisfaction

User satisfaction was evaluated in three ways. First, utilization rates of the Group Support System were maintained as an indication of general user acceptance and satisfaction. Second, the post-session questionnaire provided self reports of user satisfaction. Finally, interviews with 17 users of the automated system were conducted to obtain a broader range of personal impressions. Each of these measures will be reviewed in turn.

One of the strongest measures of this criterion is the utilization rate of the system. Since it was opened in October 1987, the room has been fully utilized, according to the records of those responsible for facilitating sessions. Currently, there is a three week waiting period for use of the room. In fact, the inability to get into the room as soon as desired has been mentioned by some users as a problem with using the system. A further measure of the acceptance of the system by the organization has been the decision to install automated group rooms at additional company sites. Thus, user acceptance, which can be considered a measure of satisfaction, has been demonstrated.

The post-session questionnaire provided self reports of user satisfaction. Two questions were

Table 4
Levels of Agreement about System Efficiency.

Post-session questionnaire statement	% of responses ($n = 387$)					
	strongly disagree ←--			strongly agree --→		
	1	2	3	4	5	Mean
The groups problem solving process was efficient	4.8	5.0	18.6	34.2	37.4	3.946

Table 5

Post-session questionnaire statements	% of responses ($n = 387$)					
	strongly disagree ←--			strongly agree --→		
	1	2	3	4	5	Mean
I am satisfied with the computer-aided process.	5.7	3.6	12.1	31.2	47.4	4.109
The groups problem solving process was satisfying.	5.3	3.7	15.8	34.1	41.2	4.023

specifically directed at this area of interest. The questions and some response data follow. (see Table 5.)

Some of the followup interview comments to the question: "Looking back on the automated group work session(s), what stands out most in your mind?" provide insight into the reported levels of satisfaction. Comments included:

"The synergism of the group. The ability to record data. And the preciseness of the process procedures."

"The way that the room knocked down barriers. It is a good vehicle for communicating, and good for brainstorming. As a result, the decision room assisted in developing a rational outcome."

"Its advantages are that it makes people freer to give ideas and discuss them openly. The participants were less apprehensive than in manual meetings."

"The best thing for me about the automated session was the way that it allowed people from many areas to mesh a plan."

"The openness of the process and its lack of intimidation. This was because of the anonymity of the process."

Referring again to the research model illustrated in fig. 1, it has been shown that we gathered data on Group Support System process and outcome effectiveness, efficiency, and user satisfaction under varying group, task, and context characteristics. The most striking conclusion is the overall positive nature of the results independent of these characteristics. Technological characteristics were maintained constant throughout the evaluation. These results contradict some laboratory experiment findings and support others, as we shall see in the following section.

Comparison with Laboratory Experiments

Key points in this study are related to process and outcome effectiveness, efficiency, and user satisfaction. This section will compare field study results with results from laboratory experiments selected to have been conducted under conditions as similar as possible to the field conditions described. Although comparisons are adversely affected by wide variations in group, task, and technology characteristics as well as measures employed and degree of control, some issues that should influence future research seem to be emerging.

Effectiveness

Experimental studies of Group Support System effectiveness have had mixed results. In terms of participation, Lewis (1982), Zigurs (1987), and G. Easton (1988) found that participation was positively influenced through use of a Group Support System. Beauclair (1987) and Gallupe (1985) found no effect. Ruble (1984), Beauclair (1987), and G. Easton (1988) found no difference in decision quality comparing automated support to control groups. Steeb and Johnston (1981) and Easton (1988), however, found that decision quality was improved through use of a Group Support System. Gallupe (1985) may have found the key to some of these differences, noting that quality was particularly improved for more complex problems. This suggests that sacrificing task complexity in order to speed task solution or enhance quantitative capability in experimental settings may destroy the distinctive competence of automated support, particularly in situations where the group size is small and participant knowledge domains are similar.

Like some experimental studies, ours found participation to be much more evenly distributed than normally occurs in manual sessions. Unlike the experimental studies, the group tasks in our study were by nature complex and required the coordinated input of many people for solution.

Time required to sufficiently address all issues averaged 3.83 hours. System effectiveness was measured in terms of perceived quality of the process and output. Post-session questionnaire responses were consistently in strong agreement that the computer-aided process was better than manual processes, thereby confirming, in part, Gallupe's (1988) conclusion that, in particular, quality was improved for more complex problems.

Comments in response to the question: "What do you consider to be advantages of using the automated system?" included:

> "I see four main advantages to the automated system. These are (1) the structuring that the system imposes on the process, (2) the anonymity which allows so much open participation, (3) the way that personalities are taken out of the process so that the process becomes more rational and (4) the amount of data which is automatically captured."

> "The documentation of the session is very useful. This allows immediate access to the data. It is also an advantage to be able to bring data from outside the session. In one session, we brought in the data from two other meetings and this moved the meeting right along."

Efficiency

Experimental studies have consistently noted that use of automated support either makes no difference in terms of time [e.g., Gallupe (1985), Beauclair (1987)] or tends to take longer than manual processes [e.g., Steeb and Johnston (1981), G. Easton (1988)]. Reasons for these results may have been the difficulty of comparing manual and automated processes as well as a focus on smaller group sizes. Automated support by nature is structured. Control groups may or may not follow structured techniques. Unstructured control groups have been reported to work faster than groups receiving manual support [e.g., Watson (1987), Easton (1988)] in small group settings (i.e., size 3 or 4), albeit often with poorer quality output. Easton, however, in a comparison of groups that were unstructured, groups that received manually structured support, and groups that received technologically structured support reported that the groups that had automated structure completed the task more quickly than manually structured groups.

In our field study, efficiency is documented through a combination of time savings based on experience, post-session questionnaire data, and comments from the followup interviews. In no case did an automated session take longer than a comparable manual session. An average man-hour savings of over 55 percent was reported, independent of site. Questionnaire data expressed strong agreement that the process was efficient. Followup interviews consistently commended the ability of the system to focus thoughts and save time. For example:

> "Time saving is absolutely the biggest advantage of the system. The confidence in the inputs is twice as high with the automated system. The comments increased in intensity as the situation went on. It was a good learning experience for the employees."

Thus, there is partial agreement between experimental and field results when differences resulting from the introduction of structure are equalized. Group size, though, may be an overriding consideration in time savings. The efficiency of automated support becomes increasingly apparent as group size rises. Based on observation [e.g., Vogel et al. (1987)], groups of size 8 or more tend to benefit more than groups of size 3 or 4, consistent with our field study findings.

User Satisfaction

Experimental studies have expressed mixed results regarding user satisfaction. Some studies have reported high levels of satisfaction [e.g., Steeb and Johnston (1981), Applegate (1985), Easton (1988)] with Group Support Systems. Others have found no difference in satisfaction levels that were attributed to the presence or absence of automated support [e.g., Beauclair (1987), G. Easton (1988)]. Yet others have reported dissatisfaction with automated support processes [e.g., Gallupe (1985), Watson (1987)]. Several explanations are possible. First, it is extremely difficult to measure differences in satisfaction unless groups have experienced both manual and automated support for equivalent tasks. In many controlled studies, subjects experiencing the automated support have no direct basis for comparison with an unsupported process. Second, dissatisfaction with the technology in general may be a contributing factor. Many Group Support Systems have been technologically unsophisticated relative to contemporary systems. Finally, experimental subjects rarely have a vested interest in the outcome of comparison studies and therefore are likely to be less enthusiastic than field study groups.

In our study, user satisfaction with the system continues to be confirmed as ongoing use of the room is accompanied by positive user responses on both exit questionnaires and followup interviews. As noted earlier, since use of the system began in October 1987, The room has been fully utilized and there currently is a three-week waiting period for scheduling sessions. Additional sites are being implemented. User questionnaire data reflected strong satisfaction with the computer-aided process and the group problem solving process in general. These findings are especially relevant, given the maturity of the session participants and their familiarity with an equivalent manual process. Finally, followup interview comments on advantages of use of the automated system included:

> "I am less apprehensive about commenting when using the decision room. It is an advantage to have all input captured. I like the quick response of the system."

> "The system brings out more honest ideas without the emotional content. It removes the emotional side of the process."

> "Also the anonymity of the input allows participants to change positions on an issue without embarrassment."

Overall, this field study addressed usefulness and acceptance of the University of Arizona Group Support System software. Interestingly, results were independent of typing and micro-computer skills as well as of the number of sessions (both manual and automated) that users had participated in. Thus the findings seem reasonably robust within the site studied. User acceptance of the system at an organizational level has also been demonstrated by the corporate decision to install this system at additional sites. Thus, at both site and organizational levels there has developed an acceptance of the automated system for group

collaborative work. No study or system, however, is without limitations and opportunities for improvement.

Limitations and Future Research

The limitations pointed out and suggestions made in this section will be focused on opportunities for additional clarification of the impact of Group Support System technology based on the model illustrated in fig. 1. An important aspect of the use of the tools across multiple sites will be evaluation of the impact and implications of extended Group Support System functionality across a wider variety of groups and tasks.

Group

Although several hundred groups have used University of Arizona and IBM facilities, we have only scratched the surface in terms of understanding the implications of varying group characteristics on the process and outcome effectiveness, efficiency, and satisfaction resulting from use of Group Support Systems. Pre-planning data relevant to evaluation of Group Support System impact includes project record keeping detail, e.g., group name, leader, and number of participants. Background information includes prior use of the facilities and corresponding tasks as well as history of the group in terms of activities and meeting history. Data captured at the time of the session should include participant name, title, and other information necessary to generate a session participant roster and coordinate formation of a session database. Yet to be addressed are many broader questions of the effect of group and individual characteristics on Group Support System process and outcome. These can only be answered after longitudinal analysis of data.

Task

Many issues relating to the impact of the nature of the task on Group Support System process and outcome remain to be addressed. Task dimensions explored to date do not even approach the boundaries of the application domain – indicating that the successful application of Group Support Systems seems limited only by the imagination of the users. Accumulation of pre-planning information assists in capturing task variety since task information includes the goal or objective of the project and type of task(s) envisioned as well as estimated number of sessions. Yet to be explored, however, are numerous corporate task environments extending vertically within a functional areas well as horizontally across functional areas that require particularly heavy integration of information between sessions and across groups. Furthermore, data to be stored in Issue Analysis "side files" and extrapolated on-line should be identified to facilitate participant access during the session. The overall purpose of this information is to help the facilitator develop an appropriate agenda of tool use for the group and to track system use at the project level and organizational levels, extending the record beyond a single session or small number of related sessions.

Context

Use at multiple sites presents the opportunity to evaluate Group Support System impact under widely varying site characteristics that can be identified positively as influencing successful use of Group Support Systems. Such characteristics of the site as number of employees, location, overall mission) should be recorded. Site tasks, processes, and use of manual tools or techniques should be documented. Kinds of groups and related site experience that might influence Group Support System acceptance should be captured. Decision making processes as well as control functions should be noted. Aspects of decision room management (e.g., executive sponsor, operating sponsor, facilitator background) should be recorded. Failure to record site data prior to Group Support System installation has the potential to create data analysis confusion and confounding effects.

Technology Limitations

Followup interviews with managers who were also participants included the question: "What do you consider to be disadvantages of using the automated system?" Comments included:

> "The lack of an agreement to follow up and put the system in place. The action plan needed other organizational involvement. That hasn't been pursued yet. Getting the right representatives into the room is crucial. More stations would have helped. We could have used 20 stations."

In the follow-up interviews, each of the interviewed participants was also asked for recommendations for improving the Group Support System. Their responses to the question: "What changes would you like to see made in the automated system? Why?" included:

> "I would like to see Issue Analysis made easier to use. It is clumsy. Also, I didn't like that in EBS I sometimes did not see all the files that were in the system. It would be very helpful to be able to link comments to comments."

> "I would like to see the system on line (in my office) as well as in the decision room environment."

> "I would like to see the system handle more participants. Often, ten people are not enough to do what needs to be done. I would also like to have the underlying comments made available during the ranking process."

IBM and the University of Arizona have taken actions to address these suggestions. Additional facilities are being developed to increase the number of workstations. System functionality has been extended to permit group members to work on group questions in their own offices with less need to meet face-to-face. This means that better use can be made of decision room time. Brainstorming comments have been numbered for reference purposes. A search feature has been added to the Issue Analyzer to assist in organizing information. Capability to review comments during the ranking process has been added. Additional tools support more in-depth exploration of issues and provide more support for multi-criteria decision making situations. Extended capacity for integrating information across sessions and between groups has been developed, including support for generation of action items to drive future session agendas.

These extended capabilities provide opportunities to further our understanding of the implications of the impact of technology on various aspects of Group Support System process and outcome. Extended tool functionality will allow us automatically to record tool usage statistics as well as to examine the benefits of integrating information across sessions and between groups. Data provided through this capability complement those gathered from the on-line questionnaires currently filled out by participants at the conclusion of each session to capture individual reactions and those gleaned from facilitator and follow-up interviews with randomly selected managers and participants. Data collection is currently underway from similar groups established to perform equivalent tasks, with the use or non-use of the Group Support System the variable used as a means for comparison. The overall goal is to collect necessary and sufficient data while minimizing the impact on expenditure of corporate personnel time.

Process

Numerous opportunities exist to capture and make use of session process information. Log-in information recorded by participants and the facilitator provides a link between the pre-planning session and future sessions. Additional information captured by the system during the session includes type and duration of tool use as well as summary participation statistics. Pop-up screens are available to the facilitator to record observations and key events during the group session that might provide Group Support System evaluation insights as well as action items and task assignments for future sessions. At the completion of the session, the facilitator is prompted to record his/her reactions and observations, including impressions of group dynamics (e.g., how well the group worked together) and ease of facilitation. Additional questions address task complexity and accomplishment of objectives. Reflections on the suitability of the technology to the task and the group are also recorded. These are very rich sources of data to assist both in the evaluation process and in consideration of suggestions for system modification and/or procedural improvement to better meet end user and organizational needs. Additional requested data on session "key words" and "wrap-up" information are particularly relevant to integrating information across sessions and between groups involved in larger projects. Follow-up interviews are particularly important in evaluating the longer term impacts of the system and associated output. Feedback from managers and session participants can provide insight into salient determinants of success as well as the ultimate usefulness and disposition of session output.

Conclusion

This field study has documented Group Support System process and outcome effectiveness, efficiency, and user satisfaction at an IBM site. The corporate decision to develop additional sites underscores user and corporate acceptance and satisfaction with the use of Group Support Systems. The overwhelmingly positive results of this field study contradict some laboratory experiment findings and support others. Additional research is warranted to expand field observations and integrate aspects of field and experimental research in order observations and integrate aspects of field and experimental research in order to achieve a more comprehensive understanding of the implications for organizations of the adoption of Group Support Systems. This paper is directed towards that end.

References

Applegate, L., "Idea Management in Organization Planning," Unpublished Doctoral Dissertation, University of Arizona, 1986.

Beauclair, R., "An Experimental Study of the Effects of Group Decision Support System Process Support Applications on Small Group Decision Making," Unpublished Doctoral Dissertation, Indiana University, 1987.

Dennis, A., George, J., Jessup, L., Nunamaker, J., and Vogel, D., "Information Technology to Support Electronic Meetings," MIS Quarterly, December 1988.

Dennis, A., Heminger, A., Nunamaker, J., and vogel, D., "Bringing GDSS to Corporate Planning: the Burr-Brown Experience," University of Arizona Working Paper, 1988.

DeSanctis, G. and Gallupe, B., "A Foundation for the Study of Group Decision Support Systems," Management Science, 33 (5), May, 1987, pp. 589–609.

Easton, A., "An Experimental Investigation of Automated versus Manual Support for Stakeholder Identification and Assumption Surfacing in Small Groups," Unpublished Doctoral Dissertation, University of Arizona, 1988.

Easton, G., "Group Decision Support System versus Face-to-Face Communication for Collaborative Group Work: An Experimental Investigation," Unpublished Doctoral Dissertation, University of Arizona, 1988.

Gallupe, B., "The Impact of Task Difficulty on the Use of a Group Decision Support System". Unpublished Doctoral Dissertation, University of Minnesota, 1985.

Heminger, A., "Assessment of a Group Decision Support System in a Field Setting," Unpublished Doctoral Dissertation, University of Arizona, 1989.

Huber, G., "Issues in the Design of Group Decision Support Systems," MIS Quarterly, September, 1984.

Lewis, F., "Facilitator: A Microcomputer Decision Support Systems for Small Groups," Unpublished Doctoral Dissertation, University of Louisville, 1982.

Martz, B., "Information Systems Infrastructure for Manufacturing Planning Systems," University of Arizona, Unpublished doctoral dissertation, 1989.

Nunamaker, J., Applegate, L., and Konsynski, B., "Computer-Aided Deliberation: Model Management and Group Decision Support," Journal of Operations Research, Nov.-Dec., 1988.

Nunamaker, J., Vogel, D., and Konsynski, B., "Interaction of Task and Technology to Support Large Groups," Decision Support Systems, forthcoming.

Steeb, R. and Johnston, S.C., "A Computer-Based Interactive System for Group Decision Making," IEEE Transactions on Systems, Man, and Cybernetics, August, 1981, pp. 544-552.

Vogel, D. and Nunamaker , J., "Health Service Group Use of Automated Planning Support" Administrative Radiology, September, 1988.

Vogel, D., Nunamaker, J., Applegate, L. and Konsynski, B., "Group Decision Support Systems: Determinants of Success," Proceedings of the 7th International Conference on Decision Support Systems, June 8-11, 1987.

Zigurs, I., "The Effect of Computer Based Support on Influence Attempts and Patterns in Small Group Decision-Making," Unpublished Doctoral Dissertation, University of Minnesota, 1987.

The Impact of Technological Support on Groups: An Assessment of the Empirical Research

Alain PINSONNEAULT
and Kenneth L. KRAEMER

Graduate School of Management and Public Policy Research Organization, University of California, Irvine, CA 92717, USA

In this paper we analyze the empirical findings on the impacts of technological support on groups. We define and differentiate two broad technological support systems for group processes: Group Decision Support Systems (GDSS), and Group Communication Support Systems (GCSS). We then present a framework and method for analyzing the impacts of such information systems on groups. We develop the framework from the literature of organization behavior and group psychology and apply it to literature of MIS. We then review the empirical research and findings concerned with the impacts of GDSS and GCSS on groups, and we compare and contrast these findings. Finally, we conclude by discussing the implications of our analysis on the focus of attention and design of future research. Five Major implications stem from our analysis: (1) there is lack of research on some important "formal" factors of groups, (2) there is a paucity of research on the impacts of GDSS and GCSS on the informal dimension of groups, (3) there is a need to move away from laboratory settings to field study in organization settings, with "real" managers, (4) more research is needed on stages of group development and on how they affect the impacts of GDSS and GCSS on groups, and (5) more research is needed to understand how the structure imposed by the technological supports affect group processes.

Keywords: Literature Review, Group Decision Process, Group Decision Support Systems, Electronic Meetings, Group Decision Making.

Introduction

Historically, the study of group meetings has proven to possess both scientific and practical relevance. Scientifically, the study of meetings provides insight into group processes, and the relationship between group cohesion and task performance. Conceptualized as the essence of modern organizations, groups constitute a key basis for acquisition of knowledge on organizations. The practical relevance of these studies stems from the sheer amount of time managers spend in group meetings. Hymowits (1988) reports that managers spend from 25–50% of their total work time in group meetings. With recent advances in com-

Alain Pinsonneault is a research associate at the Public Policy Research Organization at the University of California, Irvine and a lecturer at the Ecole des Hautes Etudes Commerciales, Montreal. He holds a B. Comm. from Concordia University and a M.Sc. in management from the Ecole des Hautes Etudes Commerciales, Montreal. His current research interests include the organizational implications of computing, especially with regard to the centralization/decentralization of decision making authority and middle managers; the strategic and political uses of computing; the use of information technology to support individual and group decision processes; and the implementation of information systems.

Kenneth L. Kraemer is the director of the Public Policy Research Organization and a professor in the Graduate School of Management and the Department of Information and Computer Science at the University of California, Irvine. Dr. Kraemer received his B. Arch from the University of Notre Dame in 1959, his M.S.C. and R.P. from the University of Southern California in 1964, and his M.P.A. and Ph.D. from the University of Southern California in 1965 and 1967 respectively. His research interests include the management of information systems in organizations; the organizational, social and public policy implications of computing; and the strategic and political uses of computing. His most recent books are *Datawars* (Columbia University Press, 1987), *Wired Cities* (G.K. Hall, 1987), and *Change and Control in Organizational Computing* (Jossey-Bass, forthcoming).

North-Holland
Decision Support Systems 5 (1989) 197–216

puters, telecommunication and management science techniques, serious efforts have been made to use technology to enhance group performance. This paper reviews and assesses the empirical research on the impacts of information technology used to support group processes.

This paper has six sections. First we define and differentiate two broad types of technological support systems for group processes: Group Decision Support Systems (GDSS) and Group Communication Support Systems (GCSS). Second we present a framework and method for analyzing the impacts of technological support systems on group processes and outcomes. We develop this framework from systematic review of relevant literature in group psychology and organization behavior. We use this framework to review the empirical research and findings in MIS. Third, we analyze the studies concerned with the impacts of GDSS on groups. Fourth, we analyze the research concerned with the impacts of GCSS on groups. Fifth, we compare and contrast the empirical findings on the impact of GDSS and GCSS on groups. Sixth, we conclude by discussing the implications of our analysis for future research.

Technological Support of Group Processes

Most of the literature concerned with technological support of group processes goes under the label of GDSS. Yet, there is no consensus in the literature on what exactly constitutes a GDSS. Qualitatively different information systems have been included in GDSS. Based on a previous review of existing aids for group decision making (Kraemer and King, 1988), and on other reviews of literature (Benbasat and Nault, 1988; Dennis, George, Jessup, Nunamaker, and Vogel, 1988, DeSanctis and Gallupe, 1987), it seems that there are basically two types of technological supports for groups: Group Communication Support Systems (GCSS) and Group Decision Support Systems (GDSS).

GCSS are information aids. They are systems that primarily support the communication process between group members, even though they might do other things as well. The main purpose of GCSS is to reduce communication barriers in groups. These systems basically provide informa-

tion control (storage and retrieval of data), representational capabilities (plotting and graph capabilities, large video displays) such as those discussed by Zachary (1986), and group "collaboration support" facilities for idea generation, collection, and compilation such as those discussed by Benbasat and Nault (1988). GCSS also include "Level 1" and "Level 3" supports of DeSanctis and Gallupe (1987) [1]. Examples of GCSS are teleconferencing, electronic mail, electronic boardroom, and local group networks (Kraemer and King, 1988).

GDSS on the other hand are those systems that attempt to structure the group decision process in some way. GDSS can support members' individual decision processes through decision models. This basically corresponds to applying Decision Support Systems (DSS) to groups without supporting the group process per se. Here the technology supports decision processes of individuals working in a group. Examples of such systems are "What if" analyses, PERT, budget allocation models, choice models, analysis and reasoning methods, and judgement refinements such as those discussed by Zachary (1986). GDSS might also be in form of group decision process techniques that support the group decision process itself. Examples of this support are automated Delphi technique, Nominal group technique, information center, decision conference, and collaboration laboratory described by Kraemer and King (1988). This corresponds to "Group 7: Structured Group Decision Techniques" of Benbasat and Nault (1988), and to "Level 2" support of DeSanctis and Gallupe (1987). [2]

---

[1] Level 1 of the typology of DeSanctis and Gallupe (1987) are technological supports that improve the decision process by facilitating information exchange among members. Examples of Level 1 support are anonymous input of ideas and preferences, and electronic message exchange. Level 3 support its characterized by machine-induced group communication patterns.

[2] DeSanctis and Gallupe (1987) describe Level 2 support of their typology as technological supports that provide decision modeling and group techniques aimed at reducing uncertainty and "noise" that occur in the group's decision process. Examples of Level 2 support are modeling tools, risk analysis, and multiattribute utility methods.

A Framework and Method for the Analysis of Impacts

Framework For Analysis

We develop our framework for analysis from systematic review of research in organization behavior and in group psychology (Mitchell, 1978; Schwartzman, 1986, Steers, 1981; Zander, 1979). Based upon that review, we conceptualize the relationship between technological support and group outcomes as involving four broad sets of factors concerned with: (1) the context, (2) the process, (3) the task-related outcomes, and (4) the group-related outcomes of group interaction. Technological support, which is the focus of this analysis, is a contextual factor along with personal factors, situational factors, structure of the group, and task characteristics.

The broad theoretical notion is that technological support facilitates group process through enhancing group capabilities, removing barriers to group interaction, improving the group in its task, and building or reinforcing the social values of the group to its members through successful task performance. Thus, our framework and much of the MIS research, focuses on identifying the impacts of technological support on group processes while controlling for the effect of the other contextual variables. Group processes in turn influence task related outcomes wich conjointly with group processes, affect group related outcomes. Each of these sets of variables is discussed next.

Contextual Variables

Contextual variables refer to factors in the immediate environment of the group rather than in the broader organizational environment. Five con-

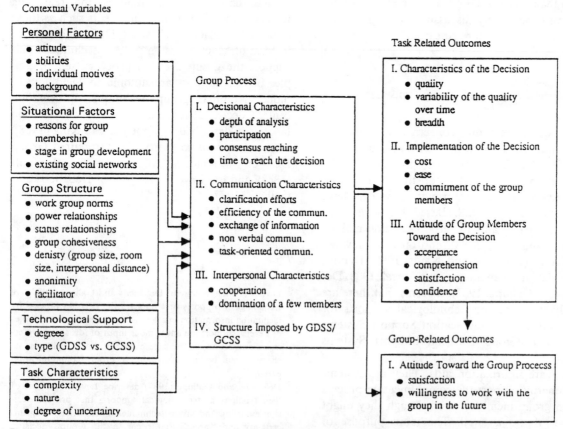

Fig. 1. A Framework for Analyzing the Impacts of GDSS and GCSS on Group Processes and Outcomes. (The framework does not include relationships between independent variables. The framework includes only the most important and relevant variables for GDSS and GCSS studies.)

textual variables appear to be important in the behavioral research on groups: personal factors, situational factors, group structure, technological support, and task characteristics.

Personal factors refer to the attitudes, behaviors, and motives of individual group members. Four personal factors have been found to affect group processes in organization behavior. First is the attitude that group members have toward working in groups and working with the other members of the group. Second is the ability of the members to work in a group. Third is the individual motives, or hidden agendas of group members, and fourth is the background of the group members which includes previous experience in working with groups and other factors like education or specific knowledge.

Situational factors refer to the extent of existing social networks and relationships among members of the group and to the characteristics of the development of the group. There are three main situational factors found to be important in previous research. First are the reasons for group membership,which can be categorized as voluntary reasons (social needs, self-esteem) or involuntary reasons (e.g. superior's request) (Kemp, 1970). Second is the existing social networks between group members, which have a direct impact on the communication and the interpersonal dimensions of group processes (Blau and Scott, 1962; Caudill, 1958). Third is the stage of development of the group. Tuckman (1965) has proposed a model in which groups evolve through four stages: (1) testing and dependence, where group members attempt to understand acceptable and unacceptable behaviors and the norms of the group, (2) intragroup conflict, where members try to establish and solidify their position and also acquire influence over decisions made, (3) development of group cohesion, where members come to accept fellow members and the norms developed, and (4) functional performing, where the efforts of group members become mostly oriented toward task and goal accomplishment.

Group structure refers to patterned relations among members of the group. Five aspects of group structure have been found to influence group process in organization behavior and group psychology research (Cummings and Berger, 1976; Porter and Lawler, 1965): (1) work group norms (Festinger, 1950; Flowers, 1977, Hackman, 1976; Janis, 1972; McGrath, 1964), (2) power relationships (French and Raven, 1968; Mitchell, 1978), (3) status relationships between members (differentiation between the status of members) (Mitchell, 1978; Parson, 1949; Scott, 1967), (4) group cohesiveness (sense of oneness, group spirit) (Cartwright and Zander, 1968; Shaw, 1976), and (5) density of the group, which is a composite factor made of the size of the group, the size of the room, and the interpersonal distance between group members (Cummings and Berger, 1976; Paulus, Annis, Setta, Schkade, and Matthews, 1976; Porter and Lawler, 1965).

Technological support refers to what activities the GDSS and GCSS support and the extent of support they provide. Technological support includes four basic sub-factors. First is the type of support provided, whether it is a GCSS or GDSS, and if it is a GDSS, whether it is a Decision Model or a Group Decision Process Technique. Second, is the degree of support. As stressed by DeSanctis and Gallupe (1987) and Benbasat and Nault (1988), this refers to how through it's structure, capabilities, or technical characteristics the technological support facilitates the generation of alternatives, the choice of alternatives or the negotiation over alternative generation or choice. A third factor is the degree of anonymity the support permits, and a fourth factor is whether a facilitator is part of the support.

Task characteristics refer to attributes of the group's substantive work. Three main factors we found to be important in organization behavior and group psychology. First is the degree of complexity of the task. Second is the nature of the task, e.g. whether it is a financial task or a personnel task (Hofstede, 1968; Janis and Mann, 1977; Mintzberg, Raisinghani, and Theoret, 1976; Pettigrew, 1973). Third is the degree of uncertainty associated with the particular task. For example, in decision making the uncertainty might relate to the consequences of the decision, or to the information provided to make the decision, or both (Bowman, 1958).

Group Process

Group process variables refer to characteristics of the group's interaction, and generally attempt to capture the dynamics of that interaction. We segment group process into three categories: decisional characteristics, communication characteristics, and interpersonal characteristics.

Decisional characteristics basically refer to how decisions are made (Bailey, 1965, Davis, Strasser, Spitzer, and Holt, 1976; Olsen, 1972). This includes the depth of analysis (number of alternatives generated, and number and complexity of criteria used to evaluate these alternatives), the degree of participation of the group members, the degree of consensus reached in making a decision, and the time it takes to reach a decision.

Communication characteristics include the clarification efforts made by group members in trying to understand better the alternatives, the problem or the solution; the exchange of information between members (is there a tendency to withhold information?); non-verbal communication; and the degree of task-oriented communication between members (Argyris, 1975; Delbeq, Van de Ven, and Gustafson, 1975; Van de Ven and Delbeq, 1974).

Interpersonal characteristics include the degree of cooperation in the group (Frenno, 1962; Goldman, Stockbauer, and McAuliffe, 1977; Levit and Benjamin, 1976; Okun and DiVesta, 1975), and the degree to which one or a few members dominate the group processes (Caudill, 1958; Hollander and Julian, 1969; Michener and Burt, 1975; Vroom and Yetton, 1973).

The structure of these group processes (decisional, communication, and interpersonal) is also likely to affect the outcomes of groups. The structure of group processes has two dimensions. First is the degree of structure, or how standardized and stable are the decision, communication, and interpersonal processes. Second is the type of structure, or the extent to which the processes are hierarchically structured, and formal or informal. The structure of group processes is important in MIS research because it is directly affected by technological supports.

Task-Related Outcomes

Task-related outcomes consist of three variables, each of which might be affected by technological support. The first variable is the characteristics of the decision. This includes the decision quality, the variability of the quality of the decision over time (or the consistency of group performance), and the breadth of the decision.

The second task-related outcome variable is the characteristics of decision implementation. This includes the cost of implementation, the ease of implementation, and the commitment of group members to implementation of the decision.

The third task-related outcome is the attitude of the group members toward the decision. This includes the acceptance of the decision by the members, the comprehension of the decision, the satisfaction with the decision, and the confidence in the decision by the group members.

Group Related Outcomes

Group related outcomes include two main variables that might be affected by the technological support. First is the satisfaction of the group members with regard to the process. Second is the willingness of the group members to work in groups in the future, whether in this particular group, or in other groups.

Method Of Analysis

In order to examine what the research says about these foregoing sets of factors, we group the studies by whether they focus on technological supports primarily aimed at reducing noise in *decision* processes (GDSS, table 1) or at reducing communication barriers between members of a group (GCSS, table 2). We characterize further the technological support by specifying whether it is a decision model (support individual decision process) or a group decision process technique (support groups decision process), and whether it supports the generation of alternatives, the choice of alternatives and/or the negotiation over alternative generation or choice. We also characterize the technological supports by the degree of anonimity it permits and by whether a facilitator is part of the support. For each study, we then assess, based on information available in published articles and/or research reports, how each study address the different variables in our framework. We determine what are dependent and independent variables studied, and also what are the contextual variables controlled and not controlled. We do not include all the independent, dependent, and contextual variables addressed in MIS, but only those focused on by several studies and those found to

TABLE 1 EMPIRICAL RESEARCH ON GDSS

The page consists of a large two-part landscape table ("Empirical Research on GDSS", Table 1 and Table 1 continued) listing studies against an extensive set of coded variables grouped under **CONTEXTUAL VARIABLES**, **INDEPENDENT VARIABLES** (Personal Factors, Situational Factors, Task Characteristics, Group Structure, Technological Support — GDSS/GDP with IDP sub-columns: Generate, Choose, Negotiate, Anonymity, Facilitator, Structure Imposed on the Process), **INTERVENING VARIABLES** (Decision Characteristics, Communication Characteristics, Interpersonal Characteristics), and **DEPENDENT VARIABLES** (Task Outcomes, Group Outcomes).

Left table — AUTHORS (YEAR) (by school of 1st Author at the time of Publication):

Authors (Year)	Experimental	Control	Size of Group	Type of Decisions	Goal of Research	Research Strategy
PERCEPTRONICS — Steeb & Johnson (81)	5	5	3	complex political crisis	impact of gdss on decision quality	LAB EXP
SOUTHERN METHODIST UNIVERSITY — Gray (83)	4	0	?	4 different decisions		LAB EXP impression
UNIVERSITY OF ARIZONA — George et al. (87)	7	0	6	sales territories assignment	impact of leadership anonymity and gdss	LAB EXP
Nunamaker et al. (87)			6-22	different strategic planning		Field Study
Nunamaker (87)			5			Case study

Right table — AUTHORS (YEAR):

Authors (Year)	Experimental	Control	Size of Group	Type of Decisions	Goal of Research	Research Strategy
Jessup et al. (88)	5	5	4	university parking problem	impact of anonymity and proximity	LAB EXP
Nunamaker et al. (88), Vogel & Nunamaker (88)	multiple	0	3-22	varied	varied	Field Study / Multiple
OKLAHOMA STATE UNIVERSITY — Sharda et al. (88)	16	16	3	upper mgmt	multi product dec	LAB EXP
NEW YORK UNIVERSITY — Bui & Sivasankaran (87), Bui & Al (87)	6	6	3	selecting a regional director		LAB EXP

TABLE 2

EMPIRICAL RESEARCH ON GCSS

Column header groups (read vertically):

CONTEXTUAL VARIABLES — Number of Groups (Experimental, Control), Size of Group, Type of Decisions, Goal of Research, Research Strategy

INDEPENDENT VARIABLES — Personal Factors (Attitude, Abilities, Motives, Background), Situational Factors (Group Membership, Stage in Group Development, Social Network), Task Characteristics (Complexity, Nature, Uncertainty), Group Structure (Group Norms, Power Relations, Status Relations, Cohesiveness, Group Size, Room Size, Physical Distance), Technological Support GCSS (Generate, Choose, Negotiate), Anonymity, Facilitator, Structure Imposed on the Process

INTERVENING VARIABLES — DECISION: Decisional Characteristics (Depth of Analysis, Participation, Consensus, Time to Decide); PROCESS: Communication Characteristics (Clarification Efforts, Efficiency of Comm, Exchange of Info, Non-Verbal Comm, Task Comm, Cooperation, Domination by Few) Interpersonal Charact.

DEPENDENT VARIABLES — TASK OUTCOMES: Charact. of the Decision (Quality, Quality Variability, Breadth, Cost, Implementation of the Decision, Ease); GROUP OUTCOMES (Commitment, Acceptance, Attitude Toward the Decision, Comprehension, Satisfaction, Confidence, Attitude Toward Grp Proc, Satisfaction, Future Membership)

AUTHORS (YEAR) (by school of 1st Author at the time of Publication)

UNIVERSITY OF MINNESOTA
- Gallupe et al (88)
- Zigurs et al (87)
- Watson et al (88)
- Poole et al (88)

IOWA UNIVERSITY
- LeBlanc & Kozar (87)

TABLE 2

EMPIRICAL RESEARCH ON GCSS (Continued)

AUTHORS (YEAR) (by school of 1st Author at the time of Publication)

CARNEGIE-MELLON UNIVERSITY
- Siegel et al (86) #1
- #2
- #3

(Table consists of a large matrix of symbol entries — o, +, x, ?, NC, etc. — under the column headings listed above.)

TABLE 2 — EMPIRICAL RESEARCH ON GCSS (Continued)

AUTHORS (YEAR) (by school of 1st Author at the time of Publication)	Experimental	Control	Size of Group	Type of Decisions	Goal of Research	Research Strategy	Attitude	Abilities	Motives	Background	Group Membership	Stage in Group Development	Social Network	Complexity	Nature	Uncertainty	Group Norms	Power Relations	Status Relations	Cohesiveness	Group Size	Room Size	Physical Distance	Generate	Choose	Negotiate	Anonymity	Facilitator	Structure Imposed on the Process	Depth of Analysis	Participation	Consensus	Time to Decide
NEW JERSEY INSTITUTE OF TECHNOLOGY Turoff & Hiltz (82) #1	8	8	5	artic survival	impact of gcss on decision quality	LAB EXP	Cr	Cr	Cr	Cr	Cr	1st	L	M	M	H	?	?	?		C	?	NC	X	X	X	?	?	C	+	+	-	+
#2	6	6	5	artic survival	impact of gcss on quality	Field Exp	?	?	?	?	?	1st	L	M	M	H		x	x		C	?	NC	X	X	X	?	?	C				
	6	6	5		decision	Field Exp	?	?	?	?	?	1st	L	M	M	H		x	c	c	C	?	NC	X	X	X	?	?	C			o	+

Legend

H:	High	+:	Variable Increased
M:	Medium	-:	Variable Decreased
L:	Low	o:	Variable Static
C:	Controlled		
Cr:	Controlled (Random Assignment)	IDP:	Individual Decision Process
NC:	Not Controlled and Possibly Important	GDP:	Group Decision Process
Blank:	Not Relevant		
		GDSS:	Group Decision Support System
X:	Variable Manipulated	GCSS:	Group Communication Support System
?:	Insufficient Data, May be Important		

Stage in Group Development:
1 = Testing and dependent
2 = Intragroup conflict
3 = Development of group cohesion
4 = Functional role related efforts

DEPENDENT VARIABLES

Clarification Efforts	Efficiency of Comm	Exchange of Info	Non-Verbal Comm	Task Comm	Cooperation	Domination by Few	Quality	Quality Variability	Breadth	Cost	Ease	Commitment	Acceptance	Comprehension	Satisfaction	Confidence	Satisfaction	Future Membership
	-			+			o					.			+			
							+											
							+											

(Process: Communication Characteristics; Inter-personal Charact. Task Outcomes: Charact. of the Decision; Implementation of the Decision. Group Outcomes: Attitude Toward the Decision; Attitude Toward Grp Proc.)

be important in the organization behavior or group psychology literature.

Even with these limitations on the scope, our assessment provides a powerful and systematic approach to establish the knowledge cumulated to date. What is known, what is not known, where research efforts should be oriented, and what major threats to validity should be addressed stem clearly from such an analysis. For example, for any dependent variable, like decision quality, we can clearly and rapidly determine: (1) which studies found positive (+), negative (−) and no (0) relationship between technological support and decision quality; (2) whether there is a consensus among the findings of different studies; and (3) whether there are any contextual variables that are not controlled across studies that could offer alternative explanations to the findings.

In a literature review such as this one, the validity of a finding depends less on the quality of any one particular study, than on the diversity of contextual variables controlled and not controlled in the set of studies (Averch, Carroll, Donaldson, Kiesleng, and Pincus, 1972; Salipante, Notz and Bigelow, 1982). Consequently, the more heterogeneous the distribution of uncontrolled contextual variables in a set of studies, the more valid the finding common to the set of studies. Our approach to review the literature then is not as much to discuss each study in detail, but to focus on findings across a set of studies and to discuss the similar and differential impacts of GDSS and GCSS on groups. [3]

Impacts of GDSS on Groups

As shown in fig. 2, the research findings on the impacts of GDSS on groups are consistent both internally (i.e. within a set of variables like group processes, task related outcomes, group related outcomes), and externally (i.e. between sets of variables, such as between group processes findings and task-related findings).

Overall, GDSS affect group processes in three major ways. First, GDSS focus the efforts of

group members toward the task, or problem to be solved by the group. GDSS increase the depth of analysis, increase the task-oriented communication, and increase the clarification efforts.

Second, GDSS increase the overall quantity of effort put in the decision process by the group, either by allowing more members to participate and/or the same number of members apply more effort. GDSS were found to increase participation and decrease the domination of the group by one or a few members. This is also consistent with greater clarification efforts caused by GDSS.

Third, GDSS increase consensus reaching. While this appears inconsistent with the previous finding of increased participation, actually it is not. GDSS focus the efforts of the group members on the task to be solved (first finding), and, therefore, greater participation combined with a heightened focus of attention leads to higher consensus reaching.

How these impacts affect decision time is inconsistent. Research shows GDSS to both increase and decrease the time needed to reach a decision. This inconsistency might reflect the fact that GDSS increase participation thereby increasing the needed decision time; however, GDSS focus efforts on the task thereby reducing the need decision time. Depending which variable is more affected, GDSS might increase or decrease the needed decision time.

GDSS were also found to affect task-related outcomes and group related outcomes. GDSS increase the quality of the decision, and the confidence and satisfaction of the group members with the decision. GDSS also increase the group members' satisfaction with the decision process.

By focusing more efforts directly toward the task to be accomplished, GDSS increase the quality of decisions and the confidence and satisfaction of the members with the decision. These effects in turn lead to greater satisfaction of group members with the group processes. Each of these findings are elaborated next in relation to major studies in the field.

Group Process

Depth of Analysis. Five studies focus on the impact of GDSS on the depth of analysis. Steeb and Johnson (1981), Gray (1983), Nunamaker, Applegate and Konsynski (1988), and Vogel and Nunamaker (1988) found a positive impact, while

---

[3] Readers who want to analyze further each study are encouraged to refer to table 1 and table 2 of this article, and to read Benbasat and Nault (1988) and Dennis, George, Jessup, Nunamaker, & Vogel (1988)

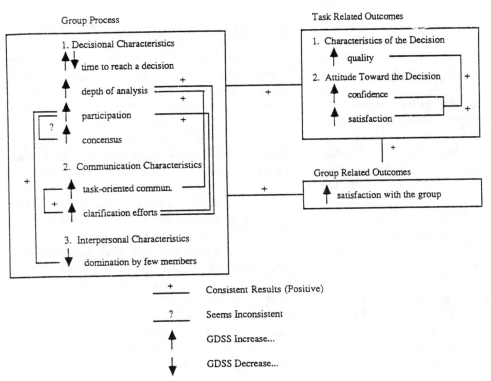

Fig. 2. The Impact of GDSS on Groups.

Sharda, Barr, and McDonnell (1988) found no significant relationship between GDSS and depth of analysis.

Significantly, the type of decision does not appear to affect the positive relationship between GDSS and depth of analysis. This positive impact occurs with decisions ranging from complex political crisis (Steeb and Johnson, 1981) to strategic planning activities (Nunamaker et al. 1988; Vogel and Numamaker, 1988). Moreover, this impact was observed with decision process under varying degrees of uncertainty ranging from very high uncertainty (Steeb and Johnson, 1981) to low uncertainty (Gray, 1983). The validity of this finding is reinforced by its generalized occurrence. The relationship was observed in studies with students (Gray, 1983; Steeb and Johnson, 1981) and with managers performing "real" managerial tasks (Nunamaker et al., 1988). However, it is important to note that the findings with managers are highly impressionistic and not based on controlled experiments.

Sharda et al. (1988) is the only study that did not find a positive relationship between GDSS and the depth of analysis. Unlike the other stud-ies, this study was conducted using a decision model approach, supporting the decision process of individuals working in a group, not the group decision process per se. There seems to exist a synergy which is an important part of the group process; this synergy can be enhanced by supporting the whole group process rather than each individual's decision process.

Task-oriented Communication and Clarification Efforts. Along with an increase in the depth of analysis, research shows that GDSS increase task-oriented communication (Gray, 1983; Sharda et al., 1988) and clarification efforts of group members (Jessup, Tansik, and Laase, 1988; Nunamaker et al., 1988). There are two bases for this conclusion. First, all our studies found a positive relationship; no study obtained counter-findings. Additionally, these findings are consistent with the greater depth of analysis.

Second, these findings seem generalized across multiple studies. The same results were observed with both students (Gray, 1983; Jessup et al., 1988; Sharda et al., 1988) and managers (Nunamaker et al., 1988). Also, groups of varying sizes support the same conclusion [Jessup et al. (1988)

and Sharda et al. (1988) with groups of three or four members, and Nunamaker et al. (1988) with groups ranging from three to twenty-two members. Gray (1983) did not provide this information].

While there is strong support for these findings, there are also notable limitations. Both findings were observed with managerial-planning decisions of medium complexity. Secondly, all four studies focus on the early stages of group development, when members try to establish group norms and typically focus their attention away from the task itself. The benefits of GDSS increasing task-oriented communication and clarification efforts might be minimal at the more advanced stages of group development, when members have already focused on the task. Thirdly, the structure imposed by GDSS on the group processes is not controlled in any study. Consequently, these results might be more indicative of greater structure rather than of technological support itself.

Degree of Participation and Domination by a Few Members. There seems to be an inverse relationship between participation and domination. All studies that found a decrease in the domination structure of groups also found an increase in participation. However, it is unclear which one "causes" the other. It is undetermined whether a decrease in domination incites members to participate more, or by participating more, group members reduce the need and the opportunity for domination.

All four GDSS studies (George, Northcraft, and Nunamaker, 1987; Nunamaker et al., 1987; Nunamaker, Applegate and Konsynski, 1988; Vogel and Nunamaker, 1988) found a positive relationship between GDSS and the degree of participation of group members. Two of these studies also found a negative relationship between GDSS and domination (Nunamaker et al., 1987, 1988).

These findings have three supports. First, all studies found the same relationship between GDSS and participation and domination. These findings are also consistent with an increase in clarification efforts (Jessup et al., 1988; Nunamaker et al., 1988). Second, these findings are valid for groups of varying size. The results were obtained in groups ranging from 3 to 22 members. Third these findings were obtained from both students (George et

al., 1987) and managers (Nunamaker et al., 1987, 1988; Vogel and Nunamaker, 1988).

However, there is one serious threat to the validity of these findings, particularly to the increased participation. Most results are impressionistic in nature and were obtained in case studies with no control group (Nunamaker et al., 1987, 1988; Vogel and Nunamaker, 1988). Moreover, the selection of participants of most of these studies might have been biased. The managers who go to a university setting to use its computerized systems are likely to be very motivated, those who are not motivated, do not go. Therefore, it is normal that participation in the group increases. The selection of participants was also often done on a voluntary basis. Therefore, here again it might well be that the study attracted a very specific group of participants (those who enjoy using computer aids). This might positively bias the participation level of the subjects when they are assigned to computer supported groups, and negatively affect their participation when they are not. Therefore, it is plausible that the control group and the experimental group of this study were not really comparable. In other words, participants might be predisposed toward using a computerized system by the mere fact of participating voluntarily in the experiment.

Decision Time. The findings on the impacts of GDSS on decision time are inconsistent. Bui, Sivasankaran, Fijol, and Woodbury (1987), Nunamaker (1987), Nunamaker et al. (1988), and Vogel and Nunamaker (1988) found a negative relationship; Steeb and Johnson (1981) found a positive relationship; and George et al., (1987) and Sharda et al. (1988) found no relationship.

The finding of a negative relationship between GDSS and decision time is highly impressionistic, and is based on uncontrolled case studies (except Bui et al., 1987). One would expect that because GDSS increase participation, depth of analysis, and clarification efforts, GDSS would also increase the time needed to reach decision. More research is clearly needed in this area.

Consensus Reaching. GDSS were also found to increase consensus reaching. Steeb and Johnson (1981), and Vogel and Nunamaker (1988) found a positive relationship; and George et al. (1987) found no relationship. This finding might seem inconsistent with increased participation and decreased domination; one would expect the consensus to decrease as more people voice their opinion and try to have their agenda supported by others. However, the relationship between GDSS and consensus might be explained by the fact that GDSS focus the attention and efforts of group members on task related activities (increase depth of analysis, task-oriented communication, and clarification efforts) and therefore permit greater consensus even with increased participation.

Task Related Outcomes

Decision Quality. Four studies that focus on the quality variable showed GDSS increased the quality of group decision (Bui et al., 1987; George et al., 1987; Sharda et al., 1988; Steeb and Johnson, 1981).

This finding is consistent with the impacts of GDSS on group processes. Also, there is consistency in that all four studies found a positive relationship between GDSS and decision quality. Moreover, an increased quality of decision was obtained in tasks of different complexity and uncertainty [Sharda et al. (1988) focus on task of medium complexity and uncertainty and Steeb and Johnson (1981) focus on tasks of high complexity and uncertainty].

However, the potential weakness of this finding is the lack of control of the structure imposed on the group process by the GDSS. Also, most studies are done on groups of three members, which limits the generality of this finding. Finally, the studies [4] used groups in their early stages of development, when members typically do not focus on the task. The gain from GDSS might be important for such groups, but not for groups in advanced stages, who are already "functional" and task-oriented.

Confidence in Decisions and Satisfaction with Decisions. Consistent with the previously enumerated findings, Steeb and Johnson (1981), and Nunamaker (1987) also found that GDSS increase the confidence of group members in decisions (Sharda et al., 1988 found no effect). Furthermore, Steeb and Johnson (1981), Nunamaker et al., (1987), and Vogel and Nunamaker (1988) found

---

[4] George et al. (1987) and Sharda et al. (1988) did not provide information on this; however, from the description of their research, they, like Steeb and Johnson (1981) seem to focus on the very early stages of group development.

that GDSS increase the satisfaction of group members with the decision. Bui et al. (1987), and George et al. (1987) found no effect.

However, the validity of these positive relationships is questionable. Most results were obtained in case studies and are impressionistic by nature (Nunamaker, 1987, Vogel and Nunamaker, 1988 did not have control groups and did not carefully control variables). Secondly, the results of these studies might be biased by the fact that managers went to a university setting for their meetings. It is very possible that the "mystique" of the university setting made managers "feel better" with their decision. Finally, the sample of participants might be biased favorably toward using computers to make decisions by the mere fact of their coming to such a laboratory (the studies had no way of controlling such effects).

Steeb and Johnson's study was conducted in a controlled laboratory setting. However, they did not control the effect of GDSS on the structure of group processes, which might well be the case of greater confidence and satisfaction with the decision. The selection process itself might also have biased the results in this study.

Group Related Outcomes

Satisfaction with the Group Process. Steeb and Johnson (1981), Nunamaker (1987), Nunamaker et al. (1987, 1988), Jessup et al. (1988), and Vogel and Nunamaker (1988) found that GDSS increase satisfaction with the group process. The increased satisfaction with the group process is consistent with the findings of higher consensus, better decision quality, higher confidence in the decision, higher satisfaction with the decision, and increased participation.

Discussion

Overall, it seems that GDSS research provides relatively consistent findings both within groups of variables (group process, task related outcomes and group related outcomes) and across groups of variables. The research shows that GDSS (1) increase the depth of analysis; (2) increase the task-oriented communication and the clarification efforts; (3) increase the degree of participation and decrease the domination by a few members; (4) increase consensus among members of the group. These impacts seem to increase the quality of decisions which in turn, increase the confidence and satisfaction of group members towards the decision. Furthermore, the changes in group process and in the task related outcomes increase the satisfaction of group members with the group processes.

However, four points need to be made. First, there is a lack of control for the effect of greater structure on group processes resulting from the technological support in most GDSS studies. This is particularly important because greater structure of the processes might cause changes in the group process variables and in the task- and group-related outcomes, rather than the GDSS. For example, Steeb and Johnson compared groups with no aid other than paper and pencil, with groups using GDSS support that provided computer-aided decision tree analysis. The positive relationship between GDSS and several outcome variables might not be an effect of the technological support, but rather of the greater structure imposed on the group processes by the GDSS. Moreover, different types of GDSS might impose a very different form and degree of structure.

Second, several GDSS studies do not monitor the potential effects of a facilitator (or do not provide enough information to determine if they do). A facilitator might affect group processes and outcomes in two ways: (1) intentionally, by playing an active role in planning, conducting, and facilitating the processes, or (2) unintentionally, by (a) mere presence, which changes the atmosphere or the relationships between group members, or (b) being a good versus bad facilitator (i.e., being able or not being able to provide the information required by the group members). The unintentional effect may be particularly important with student participants. Students may perceive the facilitator as a processor evaluating them, which might influence their behavior.

Thirdly, and as discussed earlier, the selection process of many studies favor "computer prone participants". These participants expect and want to use computer aids, but they also might be favorably biased in their estimate of the capabilities and of the impacts of computer aids on the group processes.

Finally, many GDSS studies focus on the very early stages of group development where group members try to establish and understand the norms of the group, try to define and defend their position, and try to obtain a basis of influence over the decision process. GDSS might have significant effects on groups at the early stages of development because it permits the members to focus more rapidly and intensely on the task itself. In a sense GDSS might decrease the time needed to arrive at the "functional" stage of group processes and therefore permit technologically supported groups to outperform nonsupported groups. However, the vast majority of business meetings are composed of people who know each other very well and are used to working together in groups. Therefore most groups are at the later stages of group development, for which the current findings cannot be extended. Research is clearly needed on the relationship between technological support and the stages of group development.

Impacts of GCSS on Groups

We now turn to examine the research on Communication Support Systems in relation to groups. As discussed earlier, GCSS focus on information aids rather than decision models per se. They primarily support the communication process between group members. As shown in fig. 3, GCSS were found to have numerous impacts on group processes and outcomes, most of which are consistent with one another. However, as we will discuss later, several impacts are different from the impacts of GDSS.

Research shows that GCSS affect group processes in four major ways. GCSS increase the depth of analysis; GCSS increase the total effort put in by the group members. GCSS increase participation of group members and decrease domination of the group by a few members. Consistent with greater participation, GCSS also decrease overall cooperation and consensus reaching. It appears that the increase in participation is not all channeled toward the task but also toward political behaviors. Finally, consistent with the previously listed impacts, research shows that GCSS supported groups take longer to reach a decision.

Research also shows that GCSS increase the quality of decisions. While GCSS increase the quality of the decision, they were surprisingly found to decrease the confidence of group members in the decision, and to decrease their satisfaction with the process. This might be related to

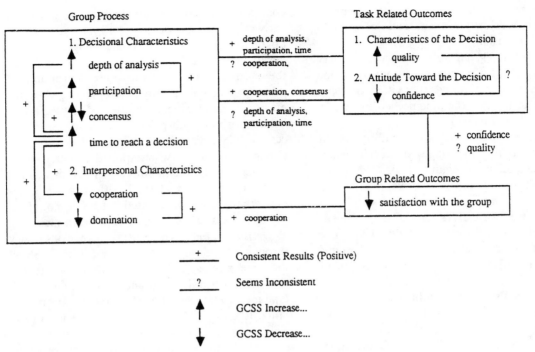

Fig. 3. The impact of GCSS on Groups.

decreased cooperation among group members. GCSS may be efficient in terms of increasing performance of the groups (formal aspect) but not in terms of the interpersonal characteristics of groups (informal aspect). Each of these findings are elaborated next in relation to major studies in the field.

Group Process

Depth of Analysis. Turoff and Hiltz (1982), Siegel, Dubrovsky, Kiesler, and McGuire (1986), and Gallupe, Dickson and DeSanctis (1988) found a positive relationship between GCSS and depth of analysis. Interestingly, this finding was obtained in diverse types of decisions (arctic survival problem and career choice problem), and therefore, it does not seem to be dependent on the type of problem. Although all studies focused on problems of medium complexity, Gallupe et al. (1988) found no difference between high and low complexity problems; therefore, this should not affect the generality of this finding. Alternative explanations were well controlled in this set of studies. At least three studies (Gallupe et al., 1988; and Turoff and Hiltz, 1982) controlled the degree of structure

imposed by the GCSS, and the potential impacts of a facilitator was controlled in one study (Siegel et al., 1986). However, results were identical in all these studies; apparently the facilitator did not have a critical impact on the relationship between GCSS and the depth of analysis.

It is important to note that the positive relationship between GCSS and the depth of analysis was obtained with groups in the very early stages of group development. GCSS might permit groups at this stage to increase their focus on the task, or, in other words, to arrive at a functional stage faster than those not supported. However, the impact might be different in groups of more advanced stages of development. Consequently, the finding is not generalized across groups of varying levels of development.

Participation and Domination. Turoff and Hiltz (1982), Siegel et al. (1986), and Zigurs, Poole, and DeSanctis (1987) found that GCSS increase participation. Gallupe et al. (1988), and Poole, Holmes, and DeSanctis (1988) found that GCSS have no effect on the degree of participation of group members. Consistent with the positive finding, Turoff and Hiltz (1982), and Siegel et al. (1986) also found that GCSS decrease the domination by one or a few members of groups. Zigurs et al. (1987) and Watson, DeSanctis, and Poole (1988) found no relationship.

These two findings are valid for a wide variety of decisions. Also, they are consistent with one another, and with the findings that GCSS decrease consensus and increase the time needed to reach a decision (discussed below).

However, it appears that these findings might also be limited to early stages of development. With the exception of Zigurs et al. (1987), the three studies that found a positive relationship between GCSS and participation focused on groups that were in early stages of development (Siegel et al., 1986, Turoff and Hiltz, 1982. The studies that found no change, focused on groups that were in advanced stages of development (Poole et al., 1988, Gallupe et al. 1988).

This pattern also fits the findings on the dominance in groups. The studies that found negative relationship between GCSS and domination by a few members (Siegel et al., 1986; Turoff and Hiltz, 1982) focused on groups in early stages of development; the studies that found no relationship (Watson et al., 1988; Zigurs et al., 1987) focused on groups in later stages of development. This difference might reflect the fact that the change in the participation pattern and in the structure of dominance is possible only at the beginning of group formation, but not later, when the pattern of participation and the structure dominance is already established. GCSS do not make dominant groups or individuals "powerless", but seem able to prevent their emergence at later stages of group development, if they did not already emerge in the early stages.

Consensus and Cooperation. Gallupe et al. (1988) and Turoff and Hiltz (1982) found that GCSS decrease consensus, while Poole et al. (1988), and Watson et al. (1988) found no impact. Turoff and Hiltz (1982), when incorporating a feedback capability to the GCSS, found a positive relationship between GCSS and the consensus of group members. Two studies (Gallupe et al., 1988; Siegel et al., 1986) found GCSS to decrease cooperation. Poole et al. (1988) found no significant effect.

The research findings appear inconsistent with regard to the impact of GCSS on consensus and on cooperation. However, this inconsistency may be explained by the development factor. The studies that found a negative impact of GCSS on consensus and cooperation focused on groups in early stages of development, and those that found no relationship focused at later stages of group development. This suggests that GCSS reinforce the existing structure of the group. When applied in early stages of group development, when the efforts of the members are oriented toward establishing position, and power over the decision process, GCSS decrease consensus and cooperation. On the other hand, when applied in latter stages of group development, where there is an existing group structure and where the efforts of the members are mainly task-oriented, GCSS do not affect the consensus and cooperation between members.

Decision Time. There is a high consistency throughout the studies on the impact of GCSS on the time groups take to reach decisions. It was found by all studies (Bui and Sivasankaran, 1987; Gallupe, 1988; Siegel et al., 1986; Turoff and Hiltz, 1982) that GCSS increase the decision time. This is consistent with the other findings (increased depth of analysis, decreased consensus and cooperation).

Overall, the finding of the different GCSS studies concerning group processes are quite consistent with one another. The research shows that GCSS increase the depth of analysis, increase participation, decrease the domination by a few members, and decrease cooperation. These changes in the group process apparently cause supported groups to require more decision time.

Task Related Outcomes

Two findings were obtained that seem contradictory to one another. It was found that GCSS increase the quality of decision, but decrease the group members' confidence in their decision.

Decision Confidence. Zigurs et al. (1987), Gallupe et al. (1988), and Watson et al. (1988) found that GCSS decrease the confidence of group members in the decision, and Turoff and Hiltz (1982) found that GCSS increase it. While decreased confidence is consistent with decreased cooperation, it is inconsistent with increased participation, increased depth of analysis, and increased decision quality.

Here again, the studies that found a negative relationship between GCSS and confidence in the decision focused on groups in advanced stages of development; the studies that found a positive relationship focused on groups earlier stages of development. This suggests that GCSS decrease confidence when groups feel they can handle communication through already existing communication structures. In early stages, GCSS facilitate the focus of efforts on problems and seems to provide a support to the process that is needed. This explanation is supported by the negative relationship found in groups (Gallupe et al., 1988; Watson et al., 1988; Zigurs et al., 1987) with high existing social networks, and a positive relationship (Turoff and Hiltz, 1982), found in groups with low social networks.

Also, the studies that found a negative relationship between GCSS and confidence used problems of medium to low uncertainty whereas Turoff and Hiltz (1982) used problems of high uncertainty. It seems that GCSS help groups that deal with decisions that might have high impacts on the group. As members of the group perceive their decision to have critical impacts on themselves, there is a tendency for the group members to attribute greater responsibility to the computer support.

Quality of the Decision. Turoff and Hiltz (1982) Bui and Sivasankaran, 1987), Leblanc and Kozar (1987), and Gallupe et al. (1988) found that GCSS increase the quality of decision; however, Siegel et al. (1986), and Zigurs et al. (1987) found no relationship.

It is significant to note that even if this finding seems inconsistent with some findings about group processes (like decreased cooperation), it is consistent with most other findings (increased depth of analysis, increased participation, increased time to reach a decision). Also, the positive relationship between GCSS and decision quality seems robust. It was found in very diverse types of decisions, at different stages of group development, and at different levels of task uncertainty and complexity.

Group Related Outcomes

Satisfaction with the Group Process. Bui and Sivasankaran (1987) and Gallupe et al. (1988) found that GCSS decrease satisfaction with the process, while Poole et al. (1988) found GCSS to have no effect.

This negative finding seems to be highly correlated with the degree of cooperation found in groups. Members of groups in which there was a low cooperation, were also found to have a low satisfaction with the process, notwithstanding the quality of the decision. Also, the studies that found a negative relationship between GCSS and satisfaction with the process used groups in early stages of development; studies that found no relationship used groups in later stages of development.

Discussion

Overall, the research on GCSS is consistent. The findings show that GCSS (1) increase the depth of analysis; (2) increase participation and decrease domination by a few members; (3) decrease cooperation; and (4) increase the time groups take to reach a decision. The greater depth of analysis, participation, and the increased decision time seem to increase the quality of decisions. The decrease in cooperation seems to decrease confidence in the decision and satisfaction with the process.

However, five qualifying points need to be made. First, as in the GDSS studies, the selection of participants might bias the results obtained, particularly concerning increased participation. Second, all the GCSS studies (except Turoff and Hiltz, 1982) used students which highly limits the generality of the findings. Third, all studies were conducted with small groups (typically three of four members). There are good reasons to expect that the findings would be different in larger groups. Fourth, Bui and Sivasankaran (1987) and Gallupe et al. (1988) showed that the degree of complexity of the task affects the impact of GCSS on groups. However, most studies on GCSS focused on tasks of medium complexity, and are therefore limited in their generality. Significantly, most studies do not account for the effect of the group's stage of development. This deficiency, although it might not be the only factor, seems to explain numerous apparent inconsistencies in the findings, and also limits the generality of the findings.

The Impacts of GDSS and GCSS: Comparison and Contrast

Our review of empirical research suggests that GDSS and GCSS have similar impacts on some aspects of group processes and outcomes, but opposite impacts on other aspects. GDSS and

GCSS both increase the depth of analysis of groups, increase participation, decrease domination by a few members, and increase decision quality.

On the other hand, GDSS are found to increase consensus reaching, increase confidence in the decision by the group members, increase the satisfaction of group members with the process, and increase the satisfaction of the group members with the decision. GCSS are found to decrease cooperation, increase the time to reach decision, decrease the confidence in decisions, and decrease the satisfaction of the members with the group process.

Our differentiation between GDSS and GCSS clarifies the findings of empirical research that otherwise seem inconsistent (Pinsonneault and Kraemer, 1989). When one analyzes the research without differentiating technological supports, one finds very inconsistent results. There is evidence of increased and decreased confidence in decisions, of satisfaction in decisions, and in the group processes. However, by grouping technological supports as either communication related (GCSS) or decision related (GDSS), the empirical evidences become consistent for each type of technological support. This suggests that GCSS and GDSS provide quite different support to groups and, consequently, have different impacts on them. The common impacts of GDSS and GCSS might be due to the similar support they provide facilitating communication between group members. The differential impacts might be due to the difference in support, GDSS supporting the decision process of groups.

Hence, it seems that GDSS and GCSS, by decreasing the communication barrier between group members, permit groups to channel the efforts of the members towards task-oriented activities and therefore increase the depth of analysis and the decision quality. On the other hand, GDSS, by providing additional support to the group, increase the confidence members have in the decision, and increase their satisfaction with the decision and their satisfaction with the group process, while GCSS decrease these aspects. There are three potential explanations for this difference in impacts.

First, GCSS might not meet the expectations of the participants relative to their view of technological supported group process. This might make

them dissatisfied with the process and with the decision, and also decrease their confidence in the decision.

Second, our review of the research shows that when GCSS are applied to groups in early stages of development (when there is no established communication network yet), GCSS increase the confidence of group members in the decision. However, when GCSS are applied to groups at more advanced stages of development (when communication networks are already established), GCSS do not seem to provide any perceived benefits, and consequently the confidence in the decision and the satisfaction with the group process decrease. GDSS on the other hand is perceived by the members as providing additional benefits at all stages of group development. This increases the confidence of the members in the decision, and their satisfaction with the decision and with the group processes.

It is important to note however that both GDSS and GCSS were found to increase the quality of the decision, and therefore the differential impact is in perceived measures. This difference in perception in nonetheless important because, if group members feel that GCSS are not efficient, even harmful, the future of GCSS is threatened.

The third explanation for the difference in impacts is that GDSS focus group processes on the task and facilitate consensus. GCSS, although focussing efforts on the task, increase personally oriented communications. This decreases cooperation and decreases the confidence of group members in the process. It also decreases their satisfaction with the process and with the decision.

Implications for Future Research

This review of empirical findings on the impacts of technological supports on groups has significant implications for both the focus of attention and the design of future research.

Four points concerning the focus of attention of future research stem from our review. First most research effort is focused on a few factors of the formal dimension of group process, like decision quality, decision time, and depth of analysis. There is a lack of research on other important "formal" factors of groups, such as how technological supports affects communication and interpersonal processes of groups and the impacts of technological support on decision implementation and on group related outcomes.

Second, there is a paucity of research on the impacts of technological support on the informal dimension of the group, like power struggles, status establishment, and hidden agendas. Yet, is argued by Schwartzman (1986) and other behavioral scholars, and as reported in the *The Wall Street Journal* (June 21, 1988), the informal dimension of groups might well be the most important function of meetings.

Third, the level of group development significantly affects how the technological supports affect group processes, yet it is not taken into account in current research. This review shows that GDSS and GCSS have different impacts on groups, depending upon whether they are applied to groups that are early or advanced in their developmental process. This factor, however, is not taken into account in present research, and its effect might have biased findings cumulated to date. More research is needed to better understand the impacts of the development factor on the success of GDSS and GCSS. Research in group psychology shows that important differences in group processes can be expected between groups with and without meaningful history and future.

Fourth, the structure imposed on group processes by the technological supports seems to have important effects on groups, but has not been investigated. This review shows that findings on how GDSS and GCSS affect groups are different whether the structure imposed by the technological support is controlled or not. This suggests that some impacts associated with the technological support are in fact due to greater structure in group processes. More research is needed to clarify the importance of this effect.

One important point on the design of future research stems from our review. Most GCSS studies were conducted with students in university settings. The GDSS studies were conducted with both students (George et al., 1987; Gray, 1983; Jessup et al., 1988; Sharda et al., 1988; Steeb and Johnson, 1981) and managers (Nunamaker, 1987; Nunamaker et al., 1987, 1988; Vogel, 1987; Vogel and Nunamaker, 1988; Vogel et al., 1987) which provides greater external validity to the findings. However the GDSS studies typically lack control over contextual variables and leave open many alternative explanations that the GCSS studies control. Also, all studies, except Leblanc and Kozar (1987) were conducted in laboratory settings. Now that more group technological supports become more widespread and that we have a basic understanding of how GDSS and GCSS affect groups, field studies in real organization settings are needed.

Such field studies mean that researchers will have less control over contextual and independent variables than in laboratory settings. Therefore, they need to carefully identify and report the context in which the study is conducted. For this, table 1 and table 2 can be used as guidelines to the factors to be taken into account. The most important factors that stem from our review are: size of the group, type of the decision, complexity of the decision, group's development stage, reasons of members for joining the group, power and status relationships between group members, group's density, degree of anonymity, structure of group processes, and presence and quality of a facilitator.

References

Argyris, C. (1975), Interpersonal barriers to decision-making. In Harvard Business Review, On Management (pp. 425–445). New York: Harper and Row.

Averch, H.A., Carroll, S.J. Donaldson, T.S., Kiesleng, H.J., and Pincus, J. (1972). How Effective is Schooling? A Critical Review and Synthesis of Research Findings. Santa Monica: CA.: The Rand Corporation.

Bailey, F.G. (1965). Decisions by consensus in council and committees. In M. Banton (Ed.), Political Systems and the Distribution of Power. (pp. 1–20). London: Tavistock.

Benbasat, I., & Nault, B.R. (1988). An evaluation of empirical research in managerial support technologies: Decision support systems, group decision support systems, and expert systems.

Blau, P.M., & Scott, W.R. (1962). Formal Organizations, San Francisco: Chandler.

Bowman, M.J. (1958). Expectations, Uncertainty, and Business Behavior, New York: Social Science Research Council.

Bui, T., & Sivasankaran, T.R., (1987). GDSS use under conditions of group task complexity. Monterey, CA: The US Naval Postgraduate School.

Bui, T., Sivasankaran, T.R., Fijol, Y., & Woodbury, M.A. (1987). Identifying organizational opportunities for GDSS use: Some experimental evidence. DSS-87, 68–75.

Campbell, D.T., & Stanley, J.C., (1963), Experimental and Quasi-Experimental Designs for Research Boston: Houghton Mifflin.

Cartwright, D.P., & Zander, A.F. (Eds.). (1968). Group Dynamic, Research and Theory, New York: Harper and Row.

Caudill, W. (1958). The Psychiatric Hospital as a Small Society, Cambridge, MA: Harvard University Press.

Cummings, T.G. & Berger, C.J. (1976). Organization structure: How does it influence attitudes and performance? Organization Dynamics, 5 (2), 34–49.

Davis, J.H., Strasser, G., Spitzer, C.E., & Holt, R.W. (1976). Changes in group members' decision preferences during discussion: an illustration with mock juries. Journal of Personality and Social Psychology, 34, 1177–1187.

Delbeq, A., Van de Ven, A., & Gustafson, D. (1975). Group Techniques: A Guide to Nominal and Delphi Processes, Glenview, IL: Scott Foresman.

Dennis, A.R., George, J.F., Jessup, L.M., Nunamaker, J.F. jr., & Vogel, D. (1988). Group decision support systems: The story thus far. MIS Quarterly, 12, 591–619.

DeSanctis, G., & Gallupe, R.B. (1987). A foundation for the study of group decision support systems. Management Science,33, 589–609.

Festinger, L. (1950). Informal social communication. Psychological Review, 57, 271–282.

Flowers, M.L. (1977). A laboratory test of some implications of Janis' group-think hypothesis. Journal of Personality and Social Psychology, 35, 888–896.

French, J., & Raven, B. (1968). The basis of social power. In D. Cartwright and A. Zander (Eds.), Group Dynamics. New York: Harper and Row.

Frenno, R.F., Jr. (1962). The house appropriations committee as a political system.: The problem of integration. American Political Science Review, 56, 310–324.

Gallupe, R.B., DeSanctis, G. and Dickson, G. (1988). Computer-based support for group problem finding: An experimental investigation, MIS Quarterly, 12 (2), 277–296.

George, J.F., Northcraft, G.B., & Nunamaker, J.F. (1987). Implications of Group Decision Support System Use for Management: Report of a Pilot Study. Tucson, AZ: College of Business and Public Administration, University of Arizona.

Goldman, M., Stockbauer, J.W., & McAuliffe, T.G. (1977). Intergroup and intragroup competition and cooperation. Journal of Experimental Social Psychology, 13, 81–88.

Gray, P. (1983). Initial Observation from the decision room project. In G.P. Huber (Ed.), DSS-83 Transaction. Third International Conference on Decision Support Systems, June 27–29, Boston, MA, Transactions, 135–138.

Hackman, J.R. (1976). Group influence on individuals. In M.D. Dunnette (Ed.), Handbook of Industrial and Organization Psychology, Chicago: Rand McNally.

Hofstede, G.H. (1968). The Game of Budget Control. London: Tavistock.

Hollander, E.P., & Julian, J.W. (1969). Leadership. In E.F. Borgatta (Ed.), Social Psychology: Readings and Perspectives (pp. 275–184), Chicago: Rand McNally.

Hymowits, C. (1988, June 21). A survival guide to the office meeting: Executives face hidden agendas and late bosses. The Wall Street Journal, pp. 35–36.

Janis, I. (1972). Victims of Groupthink. Boston: Houghton Mifflin.

Janis, I.L., & Mann, L. (1977). Decision Making. New York: The Free Press.

Jessup, L.M., Tansik, D.A., & Laase, T.D. (1988). Group problem solving in an automated environment: The effects of anonymity and proximity on group process and outcome with a group decision support system. Manuscript submitted for publication.

Kemp, C. (1970). Perspective on Group Process. Boston: Houghton Mifflin.

Kraemer, K.L., & King, J. (1988). Computer-based systems for cooperation work and group decision making. Computing Surveys, 20, 115–146.

Leblanc, L.A., & Kozar, K.A. (1987). The impact of group decision support system technology on vessel safety. Bloomington, IN: School of Management, Indiana University.

Levit, A.M., & Benjamin, A.(1976). Jews and Arabs rehearse Geneva: a model of conflict resolution. Human Relations, 29, 1035–1044.

McGrath, J.E. (1964). Social Psychology: A Brief Introduction. New York: Holt, Rinehart, and Winston.

Michener, H.A. & Burt, M.R. (1975). Components of "authority" as determinants of compliance. Journal of Personnel Psychology, 31, 606–614.

Mintzberg, H., Raisinghani, D., & Theoret, A. (1976). The structure of "unstructured" decision processes. Administrative Science Quarterly, 21, 246–275.

Mitchell, T.R. (1978). People in Organization. New York: McGraw-Hill.

Nunamaker, J.F. (1987). Collaborate Management Work, Management of Information Systems Conference, 1987.

Nunamaker, J.F., Applegate, L.M., & Konsynski, B.R. (1987). Facilitating group creativity: Experience with a group decision support system. Journal of Management Information Systems, 3 (4), 6–19.

Nunamaker, J.F., Applegate, L.M., & Konsynski, B.R. (Nov.-Dec. 1988). Computer-aided deliberation: Model management and group decision support. Journal of Operations Research.

Okun, M., & DiVesta, F. (1975). Cooperation and competition in coacting groups. Journal of Personality and Social Psychology, 31, 615–620.

Olsen, J.P. (1972). Voting, "sounding out" and the governance of modern organizations. Acta Sociologica, 15, 267–283.

Parson, T. (1949). Essays in Sociological Theory: Pure and Applied. New York: The Free Press of Glencoe.

Paulus, P.B., Annis, A.B., Setta, J.J., Schkade, J.K., & Matthews, R.W. (1976). Density does affect task performance. Journal of Personality and Social Psychology, 34, 248–253.

Pettigrew, A.M. (1973). The Politics of Organizational Decision-Making. London: Tavistock.

Pinsonneault, A. and Kraemer, K.L. (1989). The Effects of Electronic Meetings on Group Processes and Outcomes: An Assessment of Empirical Research. European Journal of Operational Research, forthcoming.

Poole, M.S., Holmes, & DeSanctis, G. (1988). Conflict management and group decision support systems. Proceedings of the Second Conference on Computer Supported Cooperative Work, Portland, Oregon.

Porter, L.W., & Lawler, E.E. (1965). Properties of organization structure in relation to job attitudes and job behavior. Psychological Bulletin, 64, 23–51.

Salipante, P., Notz, W., & Bigelow, J. (1982). A matrix approach to literature review. In B.M. Staw and L.L. Cummings (Eds.), Research in Organizational Behavior (pp. 321–348). Greenwich, Connecticut: JAI Press.

Schwartzman. H.B. (1986). The meetings as a neglected social form in organizational studies in B.M. Staw and L.L. Cummings (Eds.), Research in Organizational Behavior (pp. 233–258). Greenwich, Connecticut: JAI Press.

Scott. W.G. (1967). Organization Theory, Homewood, Ill.: Irwin.

Sharda. R., Bar, S.H., & McDonnell, J.C., Decision support system effectiveness: A review and an empirical test. Management Science, 34, 139–159.

Shaw. M.E. (1976). Group Dynamics: The Psychology of Small Group Behavior. New York: McGraw-Hill.

Siegel. J., Dubrovsky, V. Kiesler, S., & McGuire, T. (1986). Group processes in computer-mediated communication. Organizational Behavior and Human Decision Processes, 37, 157–187.

Steeb. R., & Johnson, S.C. (1981). A computer-based interactive system for group decision-making IEEE Trans., 11, 544–552.

Steers. R.M. (1981). Introduction to Organizational Behavior. Santa Monica, CA: Goodyear Publishing Company.

Tuckman, B.W. (1965). Development sequence in small groups. Psychological Buletin, 64, 384–399.

Turoff, M., & Hiltz, S.R. (1982). Computer support for group versus individual decisions. IEEE Transactions on Communications, COM-30 (1), 82–90.

Van de Ven, A., & Delbeq, A. (1974). The effectiveness of nominal, delphi and interacting group decision-making processes. Academy of Management Journal, 17, 605–621.

Vogel, D., Nunamaker, J., Applegate, L., & Konsynski, B. (1987). Group Decision Support Systems: Determinants of Success, DSS-1987, pp. 118–128.

Vogel, D., & Nunamaker, J.F. (1988). Group Decision support impact: Multi-methodological exploration. In J. Galegher, R.E. Kraut, & C. Egido (Eds.), Conference on technology and Cooperative Work, Tucson, AZ, February 25–28.

Vroom, V.H., & Yetton, P.W. (1973). Leadership and Decision Making. Pittsburgh: University of Pittsburgh Press.

Watson, R.T. (1988). Group decision support systems (GDSS): Improving group decision making with information technology. Proceedings of the IFIP TC-8 Conference: Information Technology Management for productivity and Competitive Advantage, March 7–8, Singapore, pp. 2-56 to 2-71.

Watson, DeSanctis, & Poole, M.S. (1988). Using a GDSS to facilitate group consensus: Some intended and unintended consequences. Forthcoming, MIS Quaterly.

Zachary, W. (1986). A cognitively based functional taxonomy of decision support techniques. Human-Computer Interaction, 2 (1), 25–63.

Zander, A. (1979). The psychology of group processes. Annual Review of Psychology, 30, 417–451.

Zigurs, I., Poole, M.S., & DeSanctis, G. (1987). A study of influence in computer-mediated decision making. Minneapolis. MN: MIS Department, Curtis L. Carlson School of Management, University of Minnesota.

If meeting participants, or, more generally, co-workers or collaborators, are not located in the same physical space, we can use a *media space* to link them together. A media space is a computer-controlled teleconferencing or videoconferencing system in which audio and video communications are used to overcome the barriers of physical separation. Myron Krueger began his pioneering work on media spaces in the late 60s; we include an excerpt from his retrospective book, *Artificial Reality II* (Krueger, 1991, pp. 34–41), that sketches his Videoplace and Videotouch concepts. In Videoplace, for example, he links the body movements of one individual with the hand movements of another in a collaborative video screen dance, thereby demonstrating the compelling possibilities of *computer-supported cooperative play (CSCP)* across a media space.

Krueger used special-purpose computer hardware to combine and transform video images. For most of the 70s and into the 80s, he *was* the media space field. Finally, others joined him in the mid-80s. At first the new efforts used the computer only to switch and control the video; now, in the 90s, we are beginning to compute on video again in more powerful and imaginative ways.

Media spaces as design tools were investigated at Xerox PARC in the mid-80s. The work is described in excerpts from "The Media Space: A Research Project into the Use of Video as a Design Medium" by Harrison and Minneman (1990, pp. 43, 48,

51–58). The authors (in sections of the paper not included in this volume) characterize design as "the creation of experiences," "fundamentally a social activity," and assert that it is characterized by ambiguous communications, continual negotiations, and the enrollment of participants into a group process. They argue that video can help designers connect across space, through transmission over a network, and across time, through recording and later review. They then define the concept of a "media space" and review a number of case studies of early PARC media spaces. Their experiences show that designers can learn quickly to make effective use of video both as a viable alternative to face-to-face interaction and as a means of sharing a workspace.

The first geographically distributed media space designed for cooperative work applications was created by Xerox PARC when it established a remote laboratory in Portland, Oregon in the mid-80s and linked the two sites together with audio and video communications carried over a 56 kbps leased line. "Experiences in an Exploratory Distributed Organization" by Mark Abel (1990) describes what was learned in this remarkable three year experiment. The central feature of the connection was a *video window* between the commons areas at the two sites (see also the paper by Kraut et al., 1990, included in Chapter 5 of this volume). This was later supplemented with a computer-controllable video network which connected most locations in both sites. The body of the paper summarizes lab members' experiences and impressions regarding organizational issues, social issues, and cognitive and physical issues. Despite the crudeness of the media space, it was able to produce enough cohesion that the two labs functioned and felt like one group, and to convey a sense of "presence" of remote individuals. On the other hand, certain verbal and non-verbal cues were not transmitted as well as they would be in a face-to-face situation. This resulted in the need to alter social protocols, to supplement video meetings with occasional face-to-face meetings, and to be sensitive to issues of privacy.

A more recent attempt at building and using media spaces is the Computer Audio Video Enhanced Collaboration and Telepresence (CAVECAT) Project at the University of Toronto. "Experiences in the Use of a Media Space" by Mantei, Baecker, Sellen, Buxton, Milligan, and Wellman (1991) is an early report on the observations of the Toronto group. They begin by noting some of the unexpected affordances of the technology, such as the use of a system intended for desktop videoconferencing to support meetings of groups of individuals, each clustered around a workstation in an office. They review major technological obstacles such as the achievement of appropriate audio signal levels, since they, as did Abel (1990), soon discovered how critical audio is for effective videoconferencing. They also discuss a number of issues of psychological and social impact, such as gaze and eye contact, image size, meeting coordination, and privacy and surveillance.

Research on media spaces typically assumes that full bandwidth video is desirable or necessary. "Portholes: Supporting Awareness in a Distributed Work Group" by Dourish and Bly (1992) challenges this assumption. The Portholes project collects and distributes video snapshots taken every few minutes throughout two laboratory environments separated by thousands of miles. Initial reports suggest that the technology fosters a shared awareness across the two sites and helps build a "sense of community."

Buxton (1992) further advances the CAVECAT work in "Telepresence: Integrating Shared Task and Person Spaces." He defines *telepresence* as "the use of technology to establish a sense of shared *presence* or a shared *space* among geographically separated members of a group." He then distinguishes between a shared *person space* (we prefer the term *interpersonal space*), "the collective sense of co-presence between/among group participants" which mediates collaborator communication, and a shared *task space*, "a co-presence in the domain of the task being undertaken" achieved through a shared workspace. (Chapter 10 dealt primarily with software for shared task spaces, whereas this chapter mainly discusses shared interpersonal space.) The paper presents a number of examples of both kinds of spaces, and stresses the role of body language, gaze, and mutual gaze (eye contact) in shared interpersonal space.

"Design of TeamWorkStation: A Realtime Shared Workspace Fusing Desktops and Computer Screens," by Ishii and Ohkubo (1990), demonstrates the potential payoff from special-purpose hardware for visually combining the displays of shared digital workspaces with the displays of physical work surfaces and materials. Following Stefik's suggestion (Xerox PARC, 1988v) of the importance of developing *seamlessness* between individual and group work, Ishii suggests that it is of equal importance to eliminate the seam between work without a computer, using paper, pens, and pencils on a desktop, and work with a computer. TeamWorkStation achieves this goal through the use of the translucent overlay of individual workspace images, which are live-video analog images of computer screens or physical desktop surfaces. The computer screen which is overlaid is itself a shared screen digital combination of windows from individual collaborators. There is also space on the shared screen for live video windows of the faces of the collaborators. The paper describes the system architecture and the networks required to achieve these results. The approach achieves a strong sense of sharing a task space, but there are problems, such as the fact that the results of collaboration cannot be totally shared, since they exist only in the combination of other "layers," and the fact that the quality of the overlaid video images is neither sharp enough nor stable enough to support the sharing of detailed documents.

One seam that still exists in TeamWorkStation is that between the shared interpersonal space and the shared task space. In "ClearBoard: A Seamless Medium for Shared Drawing and Conversation with Eye Contact," Ishii and Kobayashi (1992) demonstrate one method of removing that seam, of achieving "a smooth transition between face-to-face conversations and shared drawing activities." The authors begin by comparing a number of shared drawing tools and media spaces in terms of their support of shared drawing, their ability to transmit facial expressions and eye contact, and the extent to which the drawing and user images are contiguous. They propose as a metaphor for ClearBoard "talking *through* and drawing *on a transparent glass window*." They then describe how they can achieve an effect of translucent face windows superimposed over the drawing window through the use of polarizing film and half-silvered mirrors. The paper concludes with the assertion of the power of *gaze awareness* supported by ClearBoard, and an enumeration of some problems with ClearBoard-1, including inadequate image clarity and double hand images.

What is it like to work in these media spaces? One possible goal is to achieve Buxton's goal of *telepresence*. Heath and Luff (1991b), on the other hand, argue in "Disembodied Conduct: Communication through Video in a Multi-Media Office Environment" that media spaces may provide a foundation for new forms of sociality in the workplace that have very different characteristics than occur in shared physical space. This is likely to happen, they assert, because gesture and other forms of visual conduct are less effective in a media space than in face-to-face communication. Yet there is an advantage, in

that we may be able to achieve a new sense of co-presence which is not as obtrusive as sharing a physical office, a co-presence that Li and Mantei (1992) call the "virtual open office."

Hollan and Stornetta (1992) go even further in "Beyond Being There." They argue that we need to challenge the "unquestioned presupposition of most current work on supporting communication in electronic media" that we should be imitating face-to-face communication. Their analysis begins from the conjecture that electronic communication can never achieve the *social presence* (Short, Williams, and Christie, 1976) and *media richness* (Daft and Lengel, 1986) of face-to-face communication. The authors suggest that we recognize that there are problems with (physically proximate) reality, that by framing human communication in terms of *needs, media,* and *mechanisms* and by recognizing that new media can support asynchronous communication, anonymous communication, and automatically archived communication, we can go "beyond being there." (So, in a sense, we have come full circle, back to some of the themes of earlier chapters.) They illustrate the argument with some examples—ephemeral interest groups (Brothers et al., 1992), electronic meeting services, anonymous communications, semisynchronous discussions, and "auditory paper."

Notes and Guide to Further Reading

Myron Krueger is one of the founders of what is now commonly known as *virtual reality* (S.R. Ellis, 1991). His book *Artificial Reality II* (1991), from which we included an excerpt in this volume, also describes a number of imaginative and delightful uses of teleconferences for exploration and for play. When we think of the prevalence of the competitive video war games of the 70s and 80s, we can only hope that Krueger's work foreshadows a new collaborative paradigm for adoption by the video games and virtual reality industries of the 90s. Video tapes demonstrating collaborative virtual realities are NTT (1990v) and Koved (1992v).

Doug Engelbart's Augmented Knowledge Workshop demonstrated in the mid-60s (Engelbart, 1963, 1982, 1984; Engelbart and English, 1968) the use of audio and video links for discussing structured documents in shared workspaces.

There are several kinds of teleconferencing—video teleconferencing, computer conferencing, audio teleconferencing, and audiographic teleconferencing. Despite the great promise of videoconferencing, it has not yet achieved the success that early enthusiasts had predicted. Egido (1990) argues that the discrepancy between videoconferencing market forecasts in the 70s and 80s and actual markets achieved to date are due in part to the inadequacy of needs assessment methodologies and in part to the questionable portrayal of videoconferencing as a direct replacement for face-to-face meetings. Yet early work did succeed in demonstrating the potential of the technology (Olgren and Parker, 1983; Parker and Olgren, 1984) and in laying the groundwork for expanded use in the 90s. The term "teleconferencing" represents a spectrum of capabilities depending upon whether or not video is present and upon the bandwidth of the video, and, as is suggested by the work of Dourish and Bly (see their paper included in this chapter), higher bandwidth is not necessarily always cost-effective, necessary, or better. For example, freeze frame (slow scan) can be used in telemedicine and in professional education with dramatic success (Conrath, Dunn, Bloor, and Tranquada, 1977; Dunn, Acton, Conrath, Higgins, and Bain, 1980; Higgins, Dunn, and Conrath, 1984; Dunn and Fisher, 1985).

A video tape demonstrating an early cross-continent video conferencing media space is Galloway and Rabinowitz (1980v). The early Xerox PARC media space work is further described in Stults (1986, 1988), Xerox PARC (1989v), and Bly (1990v). The Portland-Palo Alto experiment is also documented in Olson and Bly (1991). For more information on the University of Toronto CAVECAT Project, see Mantei (1991), Mantei, Buxton, Baecker, and Wellman (1990v), and Louie, Mantei, and Sellen (1992, submitted for publication).

Most of the current work on groupware videoconferencing is directed at bringing these capabilities to the desktop. Yet traditional meetings make very effective use of work at a whiteboard, with all of its rich and communicative body language. We are starting to see some progress toward the development of electronic whiteboards, as demonstrated, for example, by the paper by Elrod et al. (1992, included in Chapter 12 of this volume). Tang and Minneman (1991) extend their earlier VideoDraw prototype (Tang and Minneman, 1990) to achieve VideoWhiteboard, in which wall-mounted rear projection screens image the shadows of collaborators. A commercially available electronic whiteboard with screen sharing software is provided by Smart Technologies (1992). One particularly ingenious aspect of their design is the use of several

magic markers. One of these is sensed automatically by the system to simulate a mouse operating within the context of the application; the others are used for colored annotations, sketching, and telepointing "on top of" the application. Wolf, Rhyne, and Briggs (1992; see also IBM Watson Research, 1989v) discuss the use of a pen-based meeting support tool.

Much imaginative work on media spaces has been carried out at Xerox EuroPARC, and is reviewed in Gaver, Moran, MacLean, Lövstrand, Dourish, Carter, and Buxton (1992). More detailed descriptions of EuroPARC media space projects include Buxton and Moran (1990) for a description of the technical infrastructure, Moran and Anderson (1990) on the workaday world paradigm, MacLean, Carter, Moran, and Lövstrand (1990) on user-tailorable buttons, Gaver, Smith, and O'Shea (1991) on the Arkola experiment, Borning and Travers (1991) on a predecessor to the Portholes system, and Lövstrand (1991) on the Khronika system. Gaver (1992) discusses the affordances of media spaces for collaboration.

Of particular interest is the EuroPARC SharedARK experiment described in Smith, O'Shea, O'Malley, Scanlon, and Taylor (1991). This experiment involved collaborative problem solving with both shared task and interpersonal spaces. The shared interpersonal space was achieved by enabling eye contact through a *video tunnel*. The authors observed that meta-level discourse (e.g., generating hypotheses, discussing problem solving strategies) related to the task were accompanied by much greater levels of eye contact and use of the video channel than was specific talk about the task or meta-level talk about the interface. In other words, when subjects were focused on the task, they hardly used the video channel at all; when they talked about the task, they did look at one another. The authors also noticed, both with the video tunnel and the simulated video tunnel a tendency for "chaotic glance patterns" from both parties to "lock on" eventually in mutual gaze and then result in conversation.

Another pioneer in media space work has been Bellcore. Their Cruiser system is documented in Root (1988), Bell Communications Research (1989v), and Fish, Kraut, and Root (1992). Fish, Kraut, and Chalfonte (1990) is a report on their VideoWindow invention. The initial design of both systems is discussed in Kraut, Fish, Root, and Chalfonte (1990, included in Chapter 5 of this volume).

Cool, Fish, Kraut, and Lowery (1992) review experiences with these designs and postulate four dilemmas for iterative design that result from the inherently social nature of systems for communication and collaboration.

Hiroshi Ishii has with great technical virtuosity for the past three years produced a dazzling sequence of media space innovations. These are documented in Ishii (1990a); Ishii (1990v); Ishii and Ohkubo (1990, included in this chapter of this volume); Ishii and Miyake (1991), which includes an evaluation of the use of TeamWorkStation for the remote teaching of machine operations; Ishii and Arita (1991); Ishii and Kobayashi (1992, included in this chapter of this volume); Ishii, Kobayashi, and Grudin (1992); and Ishii, Arita, and Kobayashi (1992v).

Other exciting media space work is now occurring in Japan (see, for example, Watabe, Sakata, Maeno, Fukuoka, and Ohmori, 1990; Kuzuoka, 1992, which describes collaboration in three-dimensional space using head-mounted displays; and Takemura and Kishino, 1992, which discusses teleconferencing in virtual reality). Media space work from Sweden is presented in Ropa and Ahlstrom (1992v).

A number of investigators have attempted scientific comparisons of communication through various media space configurations. An early example of such work is Chapanis (1975), who investigated problem solving under ten different modes of communication: typewriting only, handwriting only, handwriting and typewriting, typewriting and video, handwriting and video, voice only, voice and typewriting, voice and handwriting, voice and video, and "communication rich." His striking results emphasize the critical importance of the voice channel for speeding up the problem solving process.

Examples of more modern work include Gale (1991), who studies cooperative work with data sharing, data sharing plus audio, and data sharing plus audio and video; Whittaker, Brennan, and Clark (1991), who apply conversation analysis to the study of communication using a shared electronic whiteboard with and without the addition of a speech channel; and McCarthy, Miles, and Monk (1991), who apply conversation analysis to compare communication with and without a shared workspace. Sellen (1992) compares speech patterns in face-to-face multi-party meetings with those in two different desktop videoconferencing media spaces, one of which supports directional gaze cues and selective listening. The Hydra units used in this latter media space are demonstrated in Sellen, Buxton, and Arnott (1992v).

VIDEOPLACE
(Excerpt)
From Artificial Reality II   Myron W. Krueger

VIDEOPLACE had its origin in an incident that occurred during METAPLAY. Digital signals from the computer in the gallery were being transmitted to the graphics display in the computer center. Since both machines had a graphics capability, one displayed the waveform being sent, and the other displayed the information being received.

At first, I talked over the telephone with a colleague in the gallery about the displays we each had in front of us. However, after a few minutes of frustrating discussion, I realized that we had a far more powerful means of communication available. Using the two-way video link, we turned the gallery camera on the computer screen there. The computer-center camera was already aimed at the graphics machine. Both of us could now see a composite image juxtaposing the information being sent with that being received (Fig. 3.1). We discussed the two signals and speculated about the source of our transmission errors. As we did this, it was natural to use our hands to point to various features on the composite display. The resulting conversation was exactly the same as it would have been had we been sitting together at a table with a piece of paper between us.

After a while, I realized that I was seeing more than an illusion. As I moved my finger to point to the data my colleague had just sent, the image of my hand briefly overlapped the image of his. He moved his hand. Although I noticed this phenomenon, its significance did not register immediately. When it happened again, however, I was struck with the thought that he was uncomfortable about our images touching. Without saying anything, I subtely tested my hypothesis. Sure enough, as I moved the image of my hand toward his, he repeatedly, but unconsciously, moved his hand to avoid contact. I even felt a phantom sensation when we touched. Although his reactions were exaggerated and even bizarre, he never noticed my actions or his. The inescapable conclusion was that the etiquette of maintaining personal distance and avoiding touching that exists in the real world was operating at that moment in this purely visual experience.

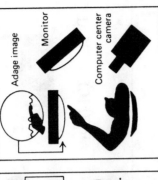
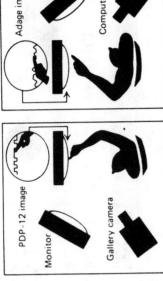

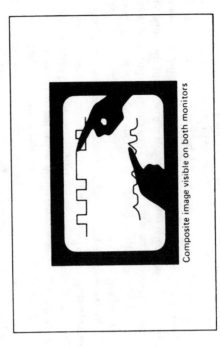

Figure 3.1
Video Communications Link.

VIDEOTOUCH

We experimented after exhibit hours with what I dubbed VIDEOTOUCH, and confirmed that indeed there was a powerful effect operating. In 1972, I submitted a proposal for a two-way installation titled "VIDEOTOUCH" to the National Endowment for the Arts. The piece was to consist of two environments, each containing a rear-screen video projection of a composite image of two participants. A single participant would

the same self-consciousness about their images that they feel about their bodies. Later experimentation convinced me that people have a proprietary feeling about their image. What happens to it, happens to them. What touches it, they feel. When another person's image encounters theirs, a new kind of social situation is created.

Over the next two years, the concept of VIDEOTOUCH matured as I realized its broader implications. Whereas we usually think of telecommunication as being between two points, a new premise evolved: Two-way telecommunication between two places creates a third place consisting of the information that is available to both communicating parties simultaneously (Fig. 3.3). When two-way video is used, a shared visual environment that we call VIDEOPLACE is created.

The idea of a video "place" led me to consider the characteristics of a real place and how they could be reproduced or replaced by alternatives in a video environment. If two people are together, they can see, hear, and touch each other. They can move about the same visual environment, seeing the same objects. They can manipulate objects and hand them to each other. Finally, they can share an activity, such as dining together.

We can embellish the sense of place by providing a graphic setting furnished with graphic objects and inhabited by graphic creatures (PLATE B). The ultimate consequence is an artificial reality experienced through the participation of one's video image in the portrayed world. Although it was conceived in the context of two-way communication, VIDEOPLACE can also be used to stage interactions involving a single participant. By suggesting, but not duplicating, familiar reality, this new graphic

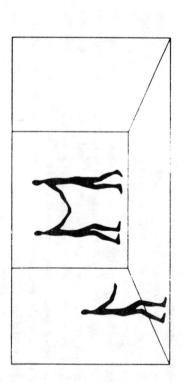
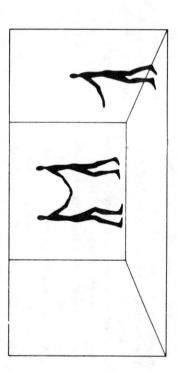

Figure 3.2
The Computer Detects Contact Between the Video Images of Two Participants.

enter each of the separate environments, and each screen would display both of the people's video images (Fig. 3.2). If their images chanced to touch, sound would be generated. The nature of the sounds was to depend on where the images touched. Thus, two strangers would be placed in a situation where their normal embarrassment about touching would be in conflict with their desire to explore this unexpected way of interacting.

VIDEOPLACE: The Concept

The experience during METAPLAY had demonstrated that two people who saw their images juxtaposed would interact as though they were actually together. We also observed that people feel at least some of

TELECOMMUNICATION   ARTIFICIAL REALITY

VIDEOPLACE

Figure 3.3
The VIDEOPLACE Concept.

experience can highlight assumptions and expectations of which we are never aware, because it does not occur to us that our world could be other than it is.

The computer has complete control over the relationship between the participant's image and the objects in the graphic scene (Fig. 3.4). It can also tell when images and objects make contact, and can coordinate the movement of a graphic object with a participant's actions (Fig 3.5). Thus, the participant's video alter ego is able to lift, push, or throw an

Figure 3.5
The Computer Detects Contact Between the Participant's Image and a Generated Object.

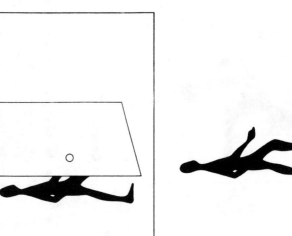

Figure 3.4
Occlusion by a Graphic Object.

object or creature across the screen (Fig. 3.6). One person can lift another's image. He can press down on the image of another person's head and make that person's image shrink under the pressure. A participant in New York could toss a ball to a Californian (Fig. 3.7). The moment an object responds to a participant's touch, both the object and the experience become real.

The world VIDEOPLACE simulates need not be a real one. Unlike the real world, VIDEOPLACE is not governed by immutable physical laws. Gravity may control your physical body, but it need not confine your image, which can float freely about the screen (PLATE A). You can use special gestures simulating flying, swimming, or climbing to maneuver your image around the displayed world (Fig. 3.8). The consequence of any action is programmable. When you push against a graphic object, the

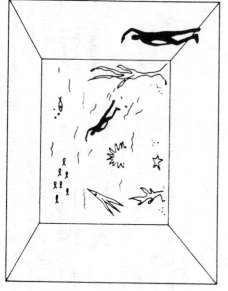

**Figure 3.8
Swimming in VIDEOPLACE.**

that are equally compelling. Thus, although some aspects of reality are abridged in VIDEOPLACE, others are enhanced, since many of the constraints and limitations of reality can be overcome. Interactions within the environment are based on a quest to understand the rules that govern this new universe. A person's expectations can be teased, leading to a startled awareness of previously unquestioned assumptions, much like the experience one has when viewing a Magritte painting.

**Figure 3.6
Picking Up a Graphic Object.**

computer can choose to move the object or to move you. Stamping your feet can cause flowers to grow or volcanoes to erupt.

Although VIDEOPLACE cannot literally duplicate the fullness of the real world, it invents a new model of reality with methods of interacting

**Figure 3.7
Three-Way Catch in VIDEOPLACE.**

The Media Space:
a research project into the use of video as a design medium
(Excerpts)

by Steve Harrison and Scott Minneman
a technical report of the Xerox Palo Alto Research Center

We seek to improve design processes by enabling better communications within the design process.

The communication needs of designers are increasing as their projects become more complex and design teams become distributed; the communications solutions available to designers may have profound changes on the way design is practiced.

We believe that design is a social activity—the interactions of individuals within groups and the relation of groups to one another. Another way we express this point of view is to say design is the social construction of a technical reality.

Video—unlike text, drawings, and computing—delivers the experience of being and working together. It can take you *somewhere* else and *somewhen* else.

We have developed a collection of prototype electronic environments to enhance communications between designers. These workplaces are called "Media Spaces"—environments that support both real-time connection and the creation and management of video documents. Media

Spaces are made of audio, video, and computing systems that connect designers across time and space.

We use these environments as the settings for case studies of existing practice in a variety of design domains. The analysis of these studies yields some insights into the nature of communications and documentation in design, in particular about the relation of public and private behavior in design.

The Promise of Video

One answer to the first question, "How can we do design at a distance?" is video. It can change the nature of work by:

- connecting across space. People and places can be brought into the design studio enlarging it to the limits of the electronic network.

- connecting across time. People who must be in two places at once can be brought into the design studio through recording. Events can be re-experienced.

Reprinted from *Proceedings of the Conference on Participatory Design*, Seattle, WA, March 31–April 1, 1990, pp. 43; 48; 51-58. This paper was presented at the PDC '90 Conference of Computer Professionals for Social Responsibility, P.O. Box 717, Palo Alto, CA 94302.

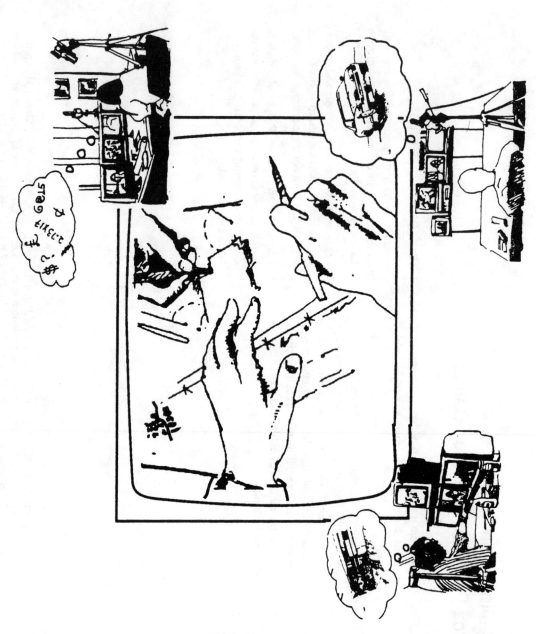

The Media Space

So, what will practice be like when there is a ubiquitous video environment? To explore that question, we built a demonstration design environment which we call "Media Space". We use it everyday as part of our work space and as the test bed for our studies of design communications.

What is a Media Space?

It is a system that integrates video, audio, and computer technologies, allowing individuals and groups to create environments that span physically and temporally disjoint places, events, and realities. It is also a way of working—of being "media aware"—that brings the illusionary power of media into everyday work.

No, Really, What is a Media Space?

In a physical sense, cameras and monitors are placed near drafting tables, desks, conference tables, CAD stations, diazo printers, and coffee pots—wherever people gather at work. The cameras and monitors are linked to each other and to recorders and videodisc players that provide a library of interactions that can be retrieved as an integral part of routine work. These local area audio and video networks can be connected together in remote point-to-point configurations. Subsets of the larger group can then connect themselves together to form project teams that are in the same virtual room or out to a remote location like a job site.

The Office Design Project

Using the Media Space to simulate regionally distributed offices, we had three architects collaborate on a design project. Using video, the architects worked on the design to completion without meeting face-to-face. [4]

Careful consideration was given to simulate a real design project. The designers were given a program by a client. Developing the design in a two-day charrette, the project, a conceptual design for a new kind of office, was then presented to the client.

The program, the introductions of participants to each other, and the presentation by the designers to their client were delivered through videotapes and videodiscs. The Media Space provided live video connection during the charrette so they could talk and draw together from their separate offices. Besides simulating a high-bandwidth connection between the architects' offices, it provided a shared videodisc library of their reference material, paper prints of the real-time and video disc images, and recordings of all their interactions. The recordings of the deliberations in the charrette were edited to form the core of their presentation to their client.

The three designers were able to design effectively in this electronic workplace and they felt the artifact that they designed was constructively influenced by working in a video-based environment. A few phenomena of note were:

- when the designers started the charrette, they behaved as though they knew one another,

Case Studies

What happens when designers actually work in a Media Space? We study actual design projects set in the Media Space, openly intervening in their communications. The methodology is a kind of participatory observation. The means of communication are visible to the participants and under their control. For example, wherever possible, the participants are responsible for pointing their own cameras. Recordings of the actual communications form the basis of the research data. The case studies and technological explorations are closely coupled, each informing the direction and scope of the other.

These case studies, along with other ones of designers in different disciplines, have been reported in more detail elsewhere.

House Addition Design Project

A small architectural design project was tracked from conception through building occupancy using video to record the project. The recordings depict aspects of a design process that are nearly invisible in compuation-based records and demonstrate the possibility for using video to provide connection within a design group. Designers and client used video recordings to track design decisions made in their absence. [7]

The video can be used as an open window from one space to another and, by using recordings (both videotape and videodisc), from one time to another. Instead of physically relocating, virtual groups can be formed by reconfiguring the electronic connections between offices. Video images keep the participants in touch with others who are absent—temporally, physically, or both. Media Space defies walls and clocks.

Coordination of the connections is accomplished using the networks of computers that are already in the workplace for word processing, accounting, project management, and CAD. In addition to controlling access to devices, they are used to organize the video records of the design activity, index and access the recorded material being collected and viewed, collect data about how the material is accessed, and provide groups with the ability to mark their activity (flagging places in their process they or others might want to revisit).

Combining recording and real-time connection has a great systemic synergy: adding a recording capability to real-time connection is cheap and provides a useful journalling service to users, and having retrievable recording makes real-time connection much more than a "picturephone". For example, we frequently use this facility in our everyday work to record meetings that someone else might have a peripheral interest in. By watching snippets of the recordings, the absent individual can stay appraised of an activity without a big time investment. [6]

- having become acquainted with each other only through videotaped interviews;

- the designers learned to operate in Media Space without much training;

- the designers were focused on the design task while working in the Media Space;

- design history became design rationale—the design was described to the client in terms of the process of its creation by showing videotapes from the charrette in their presentation;

- the client became engaged with the experience of the design process through videotape replay; and

- the designers expressed some preference for electronically mediated relations over face-to-face relations since it permitted them to draw together from the privacy and convenience of their own drafting table and to be visible and active in the group while working privately.

Three particular qualities of a Media Space were observed that create and sustain social relationships in a design group: extended awareness of other members of the group, image-based familiarity, and the representation of process. [5]

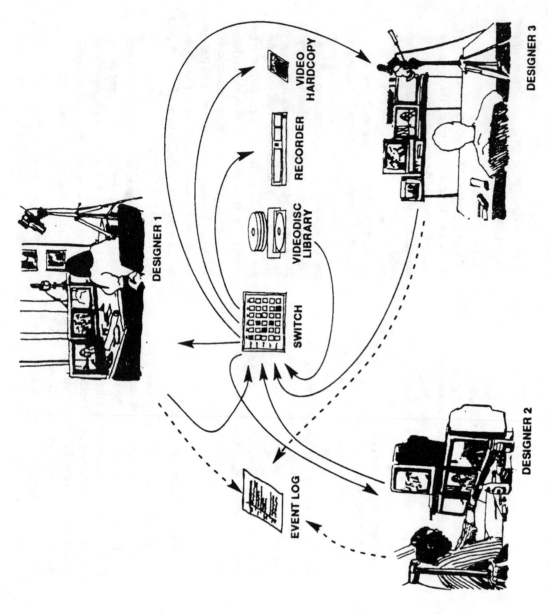

In this charrette, three architects work together in separate locations, meeting only through video. The Media Space also provides a shared library of video scenes, a log of events to aid in retrieving recordings, and hardcopy images. The recordings of the work are both a journal that they use in their design work and one that we use in our design research.

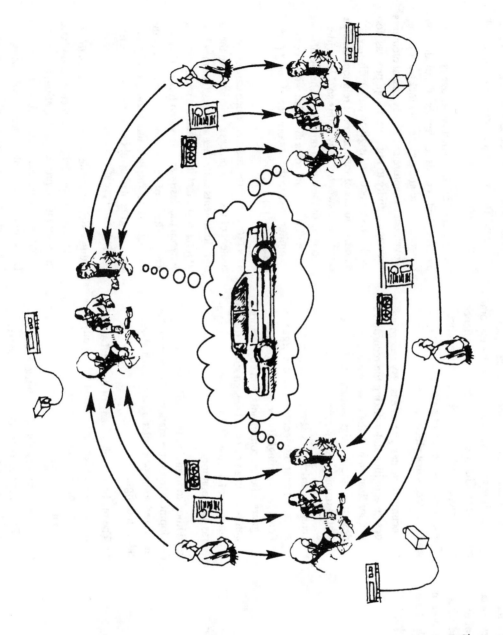

Groups of designers play the roles of Marketing, Manufacturing, and Engineering in a small manufacturing business. Over the course of an afternoon, the groups must interact in order to complete their assigned tasks. They communicate by sending an emissary, written or drawn messages, or videotape recordings to each other. Each group also prepares and circulates a videotape status report at hourly intervals.

Design Communications Workshops

A series of workshops with industrial engineering and designers explored issues surrounding training of designers to make effective use of media in complex work group settings. The workshop simulated the product planning process within a manufacturing company with the participants playing roles in the company's marketing, engineering, and manufacturing divisions. Each division had to communicate with the other two, resolving ambiguous project roles and goals, and negotiating design decisions.

The workshop focused on the use of video to support the interactions within and among the company's divisions. As with the Office Design Video Project, the communications between the designers were carefully structured and the effects identified. The study investigated the way small groups of designers behaved when working together, and the suitability of video to substitute for the physical setting for that behavior.

The groups sent video "memos" to each other. They were quickly made using camcorders and vcr's. The memos conveyed some sense of the degree of agreement on various points and overall intention within a group. Groups began to get a sense of all the members of the project and understand how they "fit" within the development of it. Video memos also allowed distant designers to "get inside" and point at specific problems they were having; they could show what was wrong and how they proposed to solve it by pointing and talking, just as if they had brought the machinery into the design studio.

Control of the communications technology was vital to the functioning of the groups and to individual effectiveness within a group. Some participants preferred to remain "off-camera", but found that they could positively change their relations within the group if they could control the "story" that emerged by being responsible for pointing the camera and selecting images. In addition, some participants became aware of the effect of their own appearance, speech, and other forms of personal presence on the interactions in design development. The workshops helped train them in skills of effective presence and distribution of their working image. [8]

Observations About Video as a Medium for Design

The Media Space is more than the technology. It is a way of working using electronic technology to warp time and space, to bring the illusions of film, radio, and television into everyday work settings. It is believing that an emphasis on communications will extend the common experience of the group, thereby improving both the process of design and the design of buildings. The research suggests that video can:

- document the design process. By recording design activities and indexing the recordings in coordination with the development of the design, a usable design history can be kept that maintains design rationale.

- connect participants. Project teams can be sustained over distances and across organizational lines through live video images. Designers, clients, consultants, and contractors can work in an extended design studio for the duration of a project through the use of cameras and monitors.

In addition to formulating specific technology development recommendations, the research has uncovered some particular observations about video in design:

- The medium retains many of the vital qualities of face-to-face interaction (ambiguity, negotiation, visual communication) that are lacking in computers.

- The necessary facility to both use and act effectively in video can be acquired quickly by designers and integrated into work practice.

- The use of real-time video connection can result in an intense task focus.

- Some people resist being recorded on video and do not cooperate in its use; of these, some lose their resistance if they see that video is under their control and can serve them. This may require development of additional skills.

The effect of all this is that backstage is brought onstage. Video tends to diminish the distinction between public and private. By making it more convenient to capture and replay casual elements of design activity to improve design process, formerly private activity is given public display. Standard forms of interpersonal relations change when the answer to "Why is this so?" is a video recording of the design process. The significance of individual roles diminish with a concommitant rise in the importance of being part of the action. [9]

As a process representation, video carries the content of the work process, references to the design documents and other artifacts (at times becoming an artifact itself), and the social process between the designers. In video form, all these separate kinds of actions are represented together without distinction, in marked contrast with the highly regimented symbolic representations of computerized project management systems.

If this vision of the design practice comes to be, then the nature of design documents, manufcturing observation, project participation, and the relations with other designers will be changed. The settings and rituals of design will change. The issue is message of the medium—the medium's effect on individuals and the way they work together. [10,11]

Ideally, the preceding should have been presented in video form, but the submission requirements dictated printed text. The experience of the video itself would have conveyed the force of the arguments we're making in a direct visceral way that the process of reading ultimately cannot.

References

[1] Stults, R. "SHOPTALK 1 - Representing the Process of Design" (a videotape). Xerox Corporation, Palo Alto. 1985.

[2] Stults, R. & Harrison, S. "SHOPTALK 2 - Two Views of a Conversation" (a videotape). Xerox Corporation, Palo Alto. 1986.

[3] Cuff, Dana. *Negotiating Architecture: A Study of Architects and Clients in Design Practice.* Dissertation, University of California, Berkeley. 1982. (Publication by MIT Press, pending.)

[4] Weber, K. & Minneman, S. "The Office Design Video Project" (a videotape). Xerox Corporation, Palo Alto. 1987.

[5] Stults, R. "Experimental Uses of Video to Support Design". Xerox Corporation, Palo Alto. 1988.

[6] Stults, R. *Media Spaces.* Xerox Corporation, Palo Alto. 1986.

[7] Harrison, S. "SHOPTALK 3 - Design and Media Space" (a videotape). Xerox Corporation, Palo Alto. 1987.

[8] Stults, R., Harrison, S. & Minneman, S. "The Media Space—Experience with Video to Support Design". *Proceedings of the International Workshop on Engineering Design and Manufacturing Management.* University of Melbourne, Melbourne. 1988.

[9] Meyrowitz, J. *No Sense of Place.* Oxford University Press. New York. 1986.

[10] McLuhan, M. & Fiore, Q. *The Medium is the Massage: an Inventory of Effects.* Bantam. New York. 1967.

[11] McLuhan, M. *Understanding Media.* McGraw-Hill. New York. 1964.

Reprinted from *Intellectual Teamwork: Social and Technological Foundations of Cooperative Work* (pp. 489-510), edited by J. Galegher, R. Kraut, C. Egido, 1990, Hillsdale, NJ: Lawrence Erlbaum. © 1990 by Lawrence Erlbaum Associates. Reprinted by permission.

Experiences in an Exploratory Distributed Organization

Mark J. Abel*

U S WEST Advanced Technologies*

Abstract

Between 1985 and early 1988, a research project was conducted within the Xerox Palo Alto Research Center (PARC) to understand the needs of geographically distributed organizations and to build technology that would help distributed organizations function. To provide a testbed, one computer research organization at Xerox PARC was intentionally split between existing facilities in Palo Alto, California and new facilities in Portland, Oregon. A major goal of this exploratory effort was to force the twenty to twenty-five computer researchers in this organization to build and integrate technology to support collaboration over the distance between Palo Alto and Portland. The resulting technology was a combination of computer technology with always-available cross-site video and audio.

This chapter discusses the lab's cross-site experience. To provide a backdrop for this discussion, the paper first describes the motivations, setting and technological support for this distributed organization experiment. The chapter then presents a discussion of the author's and other lab members' cross-site experiences.

MOTIVATIONS

In late 1984, Adele Goldberg and others in the System Concepts Lab (SCL) at Xerox PARC decided to pursue an exploratory effort to build and integrate technology for the support of distributed organizations. They felt that technical and organizational trends would be coming together in the 1990s to provide both the capability and the marketplace for systems that support geographically distributed work groups.

In the technical arena, the lab saw that the merging of computing and communications technology would eventually allow the emergence of interpersonal computing systems. In other words, by combining the capabilities of high bandwidth telecommunications and computer networks with faster, more intelligent, and cheaper computing systems, systems that greatly enhanced human-to-human interaction would eventually be feasible and affordable. Such interpersonal computing/communications systems have since come to be known as "Groupware" (Johansen, 1988) or "Computer-Supported Cooperative Work", (CSCW, 1986).

In the organizational arena, it became clear to SCL leadership that organizations of all sorts were becoming more geographically distributed. For example, the emergence of a competitive global marketplace is causing corporations to disperse sales offices, research and development capabilities, manufacturing, and marketing. A company might have their headquarters in New York City, their research and development facilities in Silicon Valley, Boston, and Munich, their manufacturing capability in Mexico and Taiwan, and their sales and marketing force all over the world. SCL's leadership (and other leaders in the business and research communities) felt that economically viable systems to support such distributed problems could be made available in the 1990s.

Finally, in SCL's pioneering work in personal computing (e.g., Smalltalk), lab members' need for new computing tools and capabilities had helped foster the creation of prototype systems. In other words, lab members' needs had provided a "forcing function" for the creation of new personal computing technology. Lab leadership decided to try to create such a forcing function for technology to support distributed organizations. They created a geographically distributed organization by establishing a second SCL facility in Portland, Oregon about 600 miles from the lab's existing facilities in the Palo Alto, California research center. It was hoped that this separation would provide a forcing function and a laboratory testbed for the prototyping of support systems for distributed organizations.

THE SETTING

The Organizational Environment

The System Concepts Laboratory, the birthplace of Smalltalk, was one of three computer research labs at the Xerox Palo Alto Research Center. Historically, SCL did research in object-oriented systems, user interface design, and personal computing environments.

The lab established the remote Portland facility in May 1985. A research group was established, primarily in Portland, to focus on collaborative sys-

*Formerly with Xerox PARC-Northwest.

tems to support geographically distributed work (see Goodman & Abel, 1986, 1987 for more details). In addition to the collaborative systems project, other continuing projects investigated shared object-oriented databases and programming environments, and the support of group design work over time. Geographic and personnel boundaries between these projects were somewhat fluid. Researchers in both sites sometimes worked on multiple projects and projects often cooperated on particular pieces of technology.

The lab maintained a permanent staff of between twenty and twenty-five, including researchers, managers, and support staff. The lab staff also usually included some visiting scientists, students, and consultants. In general, about a third of the lab members worked in Portland and about two thirds of the lab members worked in Palo Alto. With one exception, the Portland-based lab members were all hired form outside of Xerox PARC.

There were two levels of formal management in the lab. A lab manager who worked primarily in Palo Alto ran the entire lab. During the period of this exploratory effort, either three or four area managers reported to the lab manager. Each area manager had between one and seven researchers and support staff reporting to them. In general, an area manager was responsible for a project area. One area manager resided in Portland and also acted as the Portland site manager. The other area managers resided in Palo Alto. Over the course of this exploratory effort, all the area managers and the lab manager supervised at least one staff member at the other site.

The Physical Setting

The physical layout of SCL's "pod" in the Palo Alto Research Center was important to the way SCL functioned over the years. The main feature of the Palo Alto SCL pod at PARC was a large comfortable commons area. The Palo Alto commons area was a large carpeted area (33 by 40 feet) containing couches, lunch tables and chairs, book shelves, some technical information, some technical toys, and a few computers. One of its main features was a floor to ceiling whiteboard at the front of the room. The commons area provided a comfortable environment for lab get-togethers and informal interactions.

A number of researchers' private offices were arrayed around this rectangular commons area and opened into it. If researchers left their doors open, they could hear a great deal of what happened in the commons. In addition to the doors, most offices had floor to ceiling glass walls/windows facing the commons area. This allowed researchers to see much of what happened in the commons. It also allowed those in the commons to see into researchers' offices.

The physical layout of the Portland site was designed to mirror the already established Palo Alto site. The Portland commons area, offices, and furniture were all carefully chosen to resemble their Palo Alto counterparts. Many people who visited the Portland site after being in the Palo Alto site first, remarked that "the Portland site feels a lot like Palo Alto."

SUPPORT FOR THE DISTRIBUTED ORGANIZATION

Basic Facilities: Telephone and Internetworking

For many years, computer researchers at Xerox PARC have employed individual workstations connected via Ethernet † as a basic research platform. In addition to providing advanced programming environments, networked workstations provided access to internet features like electronic mail and file servers. Electronic mail was in common usage throughout Xerox PARC (and throughout Xerox Corporation). By the end of summer 1985, all of the Portland-based researchers also had workstations running an advanced programming environment, Smalltalk-80 ††, with the availability of electronic mail and other internet features. To provide these features, the Portland workstations were connected to a local 10 Mbps Ethernet, which was gatewayed to Palo Alto initially via a 9.6 kbps data line and later via a 56 kbps data line.

This arrangement allowed a regular electronic mail (e-mail) flow within the distributed laboratory. The difference in geographic location was absolutely transparent in the e-mail world. For example, to send mail to Palo Alto lab member Dave Robson one sent to 'Robson.pa,' whereas to send to Portland lab member Mark Abel one sent to 'Abel.pa' regardless of the sender's location. To send to the entire lab, one simply used a distribution list name. In the author's opinion, this shared e-mail space and the equality of the e-mail world helped enhance the feeling of lab unity despite the lab's geographic distribution.

Initially, the only other electronic connection between Palo Alto and Portland was via telephone lines. For cross-site group meetings in offices and conference rooms, we used normal telephone lines with half duplex (i.e., only one way at a time) speakerphone endpoints. For cross-site meetings in the commons areas, we generally used speakerphones with handheld mikes because the acoustics of the large open rooms rendered the speakerphones' built-in mikes almost useless. To allow document sharing, the lab used fax machines or computer network tools.

Shared Cross-site Space: "Video Walls"

Research by Allen (1977) at MIT, and Kraut and associates (chap. 6 in this volume) at Bellcore, pointed out the importance of physical proximity in research and development organizations. Proximity allows frequent com-

---

† registered trademark of Xerox Corp.

†† registered trademark of ParcPlace Systems, Inc.

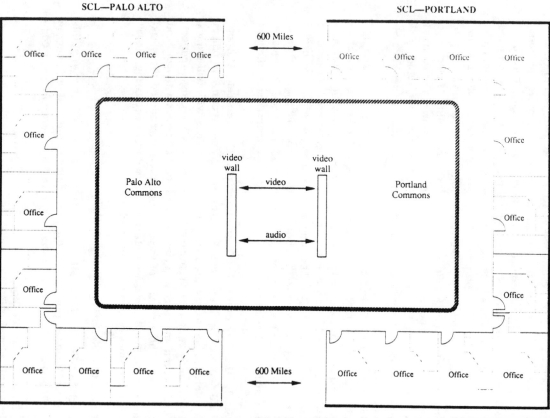

FIG. 18.1.   Shared Cross-Site Commons Space

munication and low-cost unplanned interaction, both of which facilitate the emergence and maintenance of personal/working relationships.

In an attempt to simulate physical proximity across the 600 miles between the Portland and Palo Alto sites, the lab established a "shared cross-site audio/video space." This shared space was established by providing a two-way audio/video connection between the Palo Alto commons area and Portland commons area that was always on. This technology was sometimes characterized as looking through a "video wall" or "video window" to the other site. Figure 18.1 shows a conceptual drawing of the shared cross-site commons space. Fig. 18.2 shows a photograph of the shared cross-site commons space as seen from Portland.

This shared audio/video space provided a constantly available, cross-site facility for drop-in interactions. The shared cross-site commons area also allowed researchers working around the commons to keep in touch with the other site. For example, from many offices around the Portland commons one could see and hear the activities in the Palo Alto commons and vice versa. The shared audio/video space also supported scheduled cross-site meetings like weekly lab meetings, project meetings, and managerial staff meetings.

Audio and Video Facilities
for the Cross-site Sbared Space

To control transmission costs, the always-on cross-site audio and video connections were of limited quality, for example, rapid motion in the video was blurred, details of facial expression were sometimes difficult to discern via the video, and the audio was "telephone quality." The cross-site video was transmitted via a 56 kbps channel using a technique called video compression. Standard full motion NTSC video (i.e., U.S. standard broadcast video) would have required over 1,000 times as much bandwidth (i.e., information-carrying capacity) as the video compression technology that we used. The compressed video signal had lower resolution, less color information, and significantly less ability to follow motion than a standard video signal. The video endpoints were consumer quality NTSC video cameras for input and consumer quality 19-inch monitors for video output. Initially the audio was provided by a pair of centrally located standard speakerphones connected by a standard phone line. The audio and the video were not synchronized with each other.

Later the system was improved by adding 40-inch rear projection monitors for video output in both commons areas and AT&T Quorum †††
linear array microphones as the endpoints for cross-site audio. The Quorum microphone did an outstanding job of covering the large commons areas. However, the Quorum system was still a half-duplex system based on speakerphone technology with a limited frequency range, and lack of audio directionality.

†††registered trademark of AT&T

our environment. Eventually, we had a cross-site video network including ten video sources and destinations in Portland, and twenty video sources and destinations in Palo Alto.

Travel

Although the majority of cross-site interaction took place through the cross-site electronic infrastructure, there was some travel between the two sites. On the average, SCL researchers travelled to the other site one to two times per year for a visit duration of about four days. SCL managers travelled to the other site about five times per year for an average visit duration of about two days.

EXPERIENCES

This section describes the cross-site experiences of the author and other members of the lab. The intent is to provide a set of experiences and impressions that capture, even if informally, the essence of the practical daily use of this technology. Observations of this sort can be useful in the improvement of the technology itself, in the understanding of how to apply the technology, and in providing insights into the likely consequences of using such technology.

Many lab members contributed cross-site experiences and impressions to our collection, primarily by sending electronic mail to a repository established for this purpose. In addition, the author kept a personal journal of cross-site experiences. Key excerpts from these experiences and impressions are used to support the general discussion in this section (note: to protect individual privacy, all names have been removed from these excerpts). These excerpts are delineated by indentation and use of a different font, for example,

Excerpts and quotes from our collection of experiences appear in this manner.

In the following subsections we summarize the lab members' cross-site experiences and impressions regarding (a) organizational issues, (b) social issues, and (c) cognitive and physical issues. In general, the author has tried to relate the lab's consensus opinion on these issues. However, different people often had different impressions of working in our distributed environment. In cases where lab members' opinions differed significantly, the author has tried to present the range of opinion on the issue.

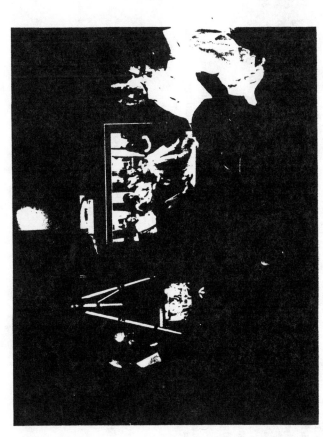

FIG. 18.2. Meeting in Shared Commons Space (As Seen from Portland)

Computer Controllable Video Network

As we experienced the cross-site video in the commons areas, we began to want to use it and control it from offices and other locations. To fill this need, we installed and built a computer controllable video switching network that spanned most locations in both SCL sites. From any network station in the cross-site environment, users were able to control video connection. Control of the cross-site video network from offices allowed lab members to simulate several standard same-site activities remotely, for example, looking around for a particular colleague, meeting and giving tours to visitors, stopping by someone's office to initiate an impromptu meeting, or looking out into the commons or down hallways over the course of the day.

This video network was constructed by outfitting offices, conference rooms, and other areas with cameras, monitors, audio equipment, and wiring. The video cameras and monitors at each site were connected to the site's computer-controllable video switch. The Portland and Palo Alto video switches were connected to each other via the compressed cross-site video. Networking software was built to allow transparent, distributed, and coordinated control of the video switching equipment from any workstation in

Organizational Issues

The operation of our distributed organization was affected in a number of ways by its distributed nature and the cross-site technology used to support it.

Short, Williams, and Christie (1976) talked about group cohesion in individual teleconferencing meetings. One of the goals of our exploratory effort was to see if, over time, a two-site distributed organization supported by technology could function as if it were a single-site organization. The lab tried to function as if it were a single-site organization. We held weekly cross-site lab meetings. Most of the projects in the lab involved researchers at both sites. All managers in the lab had at least one direct report at the other site. Occasionally lab members at the two sites even had lunch together via the cross-site technology.

Many of our experiences support the notion that we were one group. For example, other site visitors were often treated as "locals":

(Four Portland-based lab members) were having a technical discussion and brainstorming session in a Portland common area. (A Palo Alto based lab member) arrived on a (physical) visit from Palo Alto. He had not visited Portland in person for over six months. He happened to arrive during this technical discussion. Almost without missing a beat and without almost any "introduction protocol," the Palo Alto based lab member joined this brainstorming session. As the discussion wound down after about fifteen minutes, the Portland folks realized that (the Palo Alto based lab member) had arrived in person, and welcomed him.

The five lab members felt enough like part of the same group that there was no need for extensive social protocol (e.g., hi, welcome to Portland) and the Palo Alto person could just join right in. In addition, this Palo Alto lab member had enough shared knowledge about the project to join in effectively. Again, although these people interacted over the link frequently, they had not been together physically for over 6 months and had never worked together on a regular basis in the same physical location.

People even became so accustomed to the shared cross-site space that they even found themselves occasionally looking for a local person at the other site:

"I'm going office to office looking for (another Palo Alto person) because he's wanted on the phone. A dozen people have seen him 'over there' or going 'that way' in the past three minutes, but none of the pointers lead to (him). His briefcase is still in his office, there are no feet in either stall in the restroom. I'm doing one more loop around the atrium and heading back toward my office, thinking "now is there anywhere I haven't looked", when I pass the open door of the conference room. I slow my pace slightly to scan the empty

room, turn my head back forward to continue down the hall, then my motor system snaps my head back around in a double-take just a moment before the verbalization gets to consciousness: 'I didn't check Portland.'"[1]

Lab members also noticed that our environment both inhibited and supported cross-site information flow. (Organizational information flow is considered to be a critical factor in organizational success by some organizational theorists; see Galbraith, 1973.) For example, the video link allowed one of the Palo Alto-based managers to develop a feeling of who was working with whom in Portland:

(A Palo Alto based manager) has a good feeling of who's working with whom in Portland by watching the Portland video. For example he mentioned that Portland researcher A and Portland researcher B were working closely together and Portland researcher C was no longer working as much with them. This was exactly correct.

Unfortunately the information flow between the sites was not as good as within a site. People in Portland often did not know things that were almost common knowledge amongst Palo Alto lab members—PARC political gossip. The sites also sometimes did not communicate in other ways. The following comments from a Palo Alto-based manager describe a short impromptu research exploration ("the color activity") that collected enthusiastic contributors in Palo Alto but none in Portland.

"This week's color activity pointed out to me that we lack a sufficient mechanism for communicating enthusiasm. The color work involved the color machine in the Palo Alto commons, with at least six programmers (most of whom joined some time into the project), and with at least 3/4 of the PA people dropping in for demos and other kibbitzing. If our communication channel were more like the hallway, we would have also enrolled some number of programmers and some numbers of drop-ins from Portland. As far as I know, all we accomplished was sending the code to Portland, and getting it demoed there, but none of it was together with PA people. . . . I am not sure what we can or should do to enable packet gusto."

In summary, the lab members felt that this distributed lab functioned as if it were part of the same entity despite the 600-mile gap between the sites. Our experience also showed that although some information flowed between the sites, some types of cross-site information flow were limited.

---

[1] Excerpts in "double quotes" are direct quotes from lab members or visitors. Unquoted excerpts are the author's descriptions as derived from observation or other's descriptions.

Social Issues

In cross-site social interaction we noticed that (a) many social protocols governing interaction had to be altered in cross-site situations, (b) while it was difficult to initiate relationships via the cross-site link, once established via face-to-face interaction, cross-site relationships sometimes grew and developed, (c) making certain types of decisions sometimes required face-to-face interaction (i.e., the link was inadequate), and (d) the presence of face cameras and microphones that acted as remote "eyes and ears" sometimes impacted privacy.

Social interactions are governed by the standard social protocols of the culture in which the interaction takes place (Hall, 1959; 1966). Knowledge of the context provides participants with a set of rules or protocols to follow in an interaction (e.g., this is a formal business meeting at Xerox corporation in the United States, so I'm supposed to act in a certain way). Verbal and nonverbal cues exchanged between meeting participants control the progression through various scenarios (e.g., everyone has quizzical looks on their faces, so I better go back and explain that again). These cues help control turn-taking behavior, conversational repair mechanisms, meeting entry, meeting exit, consensus mechanisms, and so forth (Krauss, Garlock, Bricker, & McMahon, 1977).

In communicating via any medium, even face-to-face, these cues can be lost, misunderstood, and so forth. In communicating via the cross-site media infrastructure, required cues were often lost or altered. For example, visual cues might have been lost because the person in question was out of camera view. Due to the quality and size of the video display, subtle gestural cues or changes in posture might have been less noticeable over the video than they would have been face-to-face. Verbal cues were sometimes lost due to the half-duplex audio or because the quality of the audio prevented their detection.

Standard social rules and protocols were therefore sometimes rendered inoperable in cross-site situations because of this loss of information. In many cases, we were able to compensate for these altered or missing conversational cues by altering or adapting social protocols and procedures to this new environment. For example, we learned quite early that conversational turn-taking in our large cross-site meetings was not as easy as it was in single-site meetings. We adapted to this by occasionally asking people at the other site if they had anything to add, or watching the other site's video very carefully for gestural and postural indications that someone wanted to speak. Over time the group learned to handle many cross-site situations:

"We have become sensitized to the different social protocols of the link. For example, we have adapted to the technology in giving cross-site demos in the following ways: 1. wearing bright colors to give more cross-site presence, 2.

preparing ahead of time because glitches are much more difficult to deal with over the link (the communication mechanism and demo are using the same channel), 3. trying not to move too much so that the video compression doesn't dominate the conversation, 4. doing things "on cue," 5. speaking loudly, and choosing carefully when to speak, etc."

When social protocols were not yet established/adapted for certain cross-site situations, confusion, awkwardness or what we called "video rudeness," sometimes resulted:

A Xerox Corporate VIP came to PARC and visited each lab. SCI's visit included a short presentation by each area manager. The Portland-based area manager's presentation via the link was first. After the end of his presentation and as the next presentation was beginning, most of the Portland contingent left to go to an off-site meeting without saying anything (i.e., without valid exit protocol). At the same time, the first Palo Alto manager began his presentation with a video tape that wasn't transmitted to Portland. The remaining Portlander saw a blank screen and could hear almost nothing. Thinking that the Portland folks were being intentionally excluded, and not wanting to interrupt, the remaining Portlander went to his office, leaving an empty couch in video view. When the videotape was completed in Palo Alto, the Portland image returned to the Palo Alto monitor showing an empty couch. To Palo Alto, it appeared that Portland had given their presentation and then just left, showing no interest in the Palo Alto presentations. In other words, it appeared to Palo Alto that Portland was being extremely rude. It affected the rest of the meeting because the empty Portland couch was constantly in view. From Portland's perspective, it appeared that Palo Alto had intentionally excluded them by turning off Portland's "eyes and ears." So it appeared to Portland that Palo Alto had been rude.

A particularly important social cue that was affected by our video environment was eye-contact. Eye contact provides a number of the nonverbal cues that control interaction (Hall, 1959, 1966; Krauss et al., 1977). Our experience indicates that eye contact was important in interaction over video as well. (The major television networks also feel that video eye contact is important. Television announcers and newspeople usually read things using teleprompter technology, which allows a speaker to read something while looking directly into a camera.)

In our experimental video environment, we occasionally had cameras and monitors positioned such that "video eye contact" was not maintained (e.g., when person A looks at the person B's video image, the camera looking at person A and providing B's view of A may be looking at the side or back of person A). Almost universally when this occurred, people felt uncomfortable:

met for 3 days of intense design discussions in Portland and settled their critical design questions. One Palo Alto-based team member's description was as follows:

"Halfway through the process (the other Palo Alto team member) and I journeyed up to Portland for three days of intensive discussions. I think these played a valuable role both on the technical end (the state of the discussion was such that it really felt like certain issues were ready to "crystallize" or at least "gel") and also for building our personal feelings for each other (bonding is a pretty overused term these days, but there was definitely some kind of bonding going on during these intensive all-in-the-same-room sessions). . . . To me it seems there is something indispensable about face to face contact in those situations where you want someone to 'disconnect' from their position on a solution or from their view of a problem just long enough to really get in touch with your view or position. Somehow, it seems harder to get this kind of temporary disconnection to happen in the more formal setting of a (video) meeting, or via e-mail. . . . Somehow when we were all in the same room together it seemed easier to get this back and forth (discussion) to happen than over the (video)."

This team accomplished some important tasks by meeting face-to-face that they had bee unable to accomplish via the cross-site technology.

Another interesting social issue in our environment was privacy. Whenever the author has described the SCL media environment, someone invariably asks, "Wasn't lack of privacy a problem?" Within a trusted group like SCL, video privacy was not a major problem. Social protocols developed for use of the video mirrored those for face-to-face interaction. For example, when wandering around via video, people generally didn't look in on someone for extended periods without their knowledge, just as people would not generally enter someone's office surreptitiously and watch them without their knowledge. Furthermore, people had several mechanisms to prevent others from looking in on them when they desired privacy. Actually, for the author, audio privacy was more important than video privacy. In other words, the author kept his camera on to allow people to enter his video space, but kept his microphone off so that he had explicit control over who entered his audio space. (Note that standard telephone protocol works this way too.)

From a system design and human interface perspective, we talked about potential privacy designs a great deal. Often privacy traded off with accessibility in system design. In other words, one person's access impinged on another's privacy. Two human interface features were added to our system to try to cope with the privacy issue. One was George Goodman's "Big Brother Detector." This was a set of eyes on the computer interface that opened when someone looked at you and closed when you were

"I attended a meeting in the Palo Alto conference room this morning by Video. The camera was placed at one end of the room and the monitor at the other. This had an interesting effect. Whenever I said anything all the heads I could see turning away from me. Of course they were turning to see me on the monitor so rationally there was nothing rude about it. But I felt much more comfortable when (a Palo Alto lab member) moved the camera near the monitor."

After a few of these incidents, we tried to provide video eye contact whenever possible by placing cameras and monitors very close to each other. This allowed users to look approximately into the camera while they were looking at the monitor.

Another important cross-site social issue involved the development of working relationships between geographically distributed lab members. In team environments the ability to do productive work is affected by the working relationships between work group participants. Our experience indicates that relationships were difficult to initiate via the link. People didn't feel that they had really met one another until they came together in person:

(A visitor) met (two of the Portland researchers) over the video from Palo Alto. The next day she was in Portland physically. Someone said "Well at least you met (the two Portland researchers) via the video before you came up." The visitor emphatically said, "I hadn't really met them until I met them in person in Portland!"

Our experience supports Short, Williams and Christie's (1976) findings that getting to know someone over electronic media can be problematic.

Once cross-site relationships had been established via face-to-face interaction, people were able to work together cross-site and enhance their cross-site personal and working relationships. For example, the author, who was based in Portland, worked closely at times with Palo Alto lab members Steve Harrison, Kim McCall, and Sara Bly. The author eventually became friendly with each of them. Other lab members developed similar cross-site relationships. Geographically distributed lab members rarely visited each other in person, interacting primarily via the cross-site technology.

Just as our cross-site link seemed inadequate for initiating relationships, our experience showed inadequacies in the support of certain other types of cross-site interaction. For example, settling particularly divisive issues sometimes required face-to-face interaction. One five-person project team (three in Portland, two in Palo Alto) was unable to resolve some critical design issues after working together for several months via the cross-site technology. They decided that they had to come together face-to-face. They

unobserved. Another privacy feature was "peek." In the interface "peek" allowed only a 5-second glance into someone's office. This was to simulate "sticking your head in someone's door to see if they're available." People also had the option of turning off their cameras or putting the lens cap on their office cameras to keep people out of their video space.

We also proposed a number of other privacy designs. Many people liked the idea of using the "door metaphor" to represent whether or not someone thing was private. In our environment a closed door normally symbolized "I'm busy or in a private conversation right now and I prefer not to be disturbed." By building software into our system we could have created a "virtual door" that represented one's desired level of privacy. We also considered putting detectors in doorways so that a closed physical door would cause one's virtual door to be closed too.

In any event, although we realized privacy would be a major concern in applying such technology in most settings, our prototype system did not include much privacy protection. As soon as one considers applying this technology across organizational boundaries or in less trusting groups, mechanisms for providing control over the privacy of one's space will probably be required.

In summary, we noticed a number of significant social issues in our distributed environment, including issues involving social protocols, the initiation and development of personal and working relationships, the inadequacies of the link for certain types of interaction, and privacy.

Cognitive and Physical Issues

Our experience highlighted a number of cognitive and physical issues in our distributed environment: (a) people often felt the "presence" of remote individuals, (b) some aspects of our system were felt to be limiting or distracting, and people were able to adapt to many of these limitations, and (c) people tended to orient to audio output rather than video output.

Short, Williams and Christie (1976) discussed the "social presence" of remote individuals in teleconferencing meetings. In our cross-site media environment, lab members often felt the presence of people at the other site. This manifests itself in many ways. Sometimes an action visible to the other site was enough to provide a feeling of remote presence. Sometimes it was the sound of someone's cough at the other end that reminded one that there were other-site participants in a meeting:

The lab manager in Palo Alto was speaking at the beginning of the meeting explaining the meeting's purpose. He was speaking in a normal conversational tone. Then a cough was heard from Portland. The lab manager immediately began speaking in a louder more "public" speaking voice (the "I'm talking over the audio to Portland voice").

Over time, certain lab members were able to establish a strong presence at the other site. For example, one Palo Alto lab member had such a strong and continual presence in Portland via the link that Portland lab members thought he had visited Portland in person before he actually visited:

"(Another Portland-based lab member and I) were talking about which Palo Alto lab members had been to Portland site (physically) and which people had not yet been here. At first, we were certain that (a particular Palo Alto lab member) had been here, but as we carefully checked the travel records and thought about it, we realized that he had actually never been physically present in the Portland site."

These Portland lab members and the Palo Alto lab member had worked closely together for several months via the link. The frequent interaction over the link actually gave the Palo Alto lab member a significant "Portland presence" in the minds of the two Portland-based researchers.

On the down side, a number of equipment limitations in our system were recognized. The limitations imposed by video compression, the half-duplex audio arrangement, and the lack of synchronization of the audio and video signals were all noted as distracting and limiting by system users. Lab members and other regular system users adapted to most of these limitations and rarely commented on them (after an initial novelty period). The major continuing problem was the half-duplex audio that limited interactive discourse. First-time users were especially sensitive to system limitations and almost always commented on them. Our experience showed that within the first half hour of system usage, users generally adapted to most of these limitations.

Our experience also indicated that the video sometimes didn't provide an accurate picture of other-site people and places. In general, this was noted by people who had first seen the person or place in question via video:

A (new Palo Alto-based researcher) joined the lab. She worked with the Portland people over the link for a few months and had not yet met (a particular Portland-based researcher) in-person. When she finally did meet (this Portland researcher) she was surprised at how short he was in person. She thought he was much taller from the "video impression" she had of him.

Another example is described in these comments from a consultant who worked at the Portland site for about 6 months before his first in-person visit to Palo Alto. Until this visit, his impressions of the Palo Alto physical layout and many Palo Alto lab members were obtained via the cross-site video:

"The SCI. (Palo Alto) commons and office space viewable on (video) looked completely different in person: the commons were much larger than I had thought, yet the couch seemed smaller. (Video) gave me no clear perception of where the computers were located in the room. Even the shape of the commons area and the presence of pillars was not clear to me before the trip. The (Palo Alto lab members) that I had met only on (video) seemed different in person. My pre-trip perception of their faces and individual traits did not match reality that well. I had problems matching faces to names. On the other hand, I found talking to (the Portland people) via (video while in Palo Alto) to be easy and very natural."

During the course of experimenting with our environment, we noticed another audio/video artifact that was (at least to me) surprising. When we separated audio and video output, we found that people oriented to the audio:

A Portland researcher and his two year old son were in the Portland commons talking to a Palo Alto researcher in the Palo Alto commons. The video output (large screen display) and audio output (Quorum microphone/speaker system) were about ten feet apart. The Portland researcher was introducing his son to the Palo Alto researcher. The Portland researcher pointed his son toward the Palo Alto researchers' picture on the monitor and explained that "there's (the Palo Alto researcher)." As soon as the Palo Alto researcher spoke, the little boy went over to the Quorum box, turning his back on the monitor where the Palo Alto researcher's picture was, and spoke directly to the speaker where the Palo Alto researcher's voice was coming from. Again the Portland researcher pointed out to the little boy that the Palo Alto researcher's picture was on the monitor and again, as soon as the Palo Alto researcher spoke, the little boy turned his back on the picture and dealt only with the audio box. The two year old clearly believed that someone's presence is "where their voice comes from."

Such reactions were by no means limited to small children:

"A Palo Alto researcher and I were chatting via office-to-office video. The audio was via a speakerphone in my office. The audio box and video box are physically far apart in my office. I found myself talking to the audio box, where (the Palo Alto researcher's) voice was, rather than to his image on the monitor."

Our experience supports Johansen's (1984) conclusions that audio is much more important to videoconferencing users than video.

In summary, our experiences pointed out a number of interesting cognitive and physical issues: the remote presence phenomena, particular lim-

itations of our environment, and people's ability to adapt to many of them, the video not providing an accurate picture of other-site people and places, and people's orientation to audio rather than video.

SPECULATIONS ON OUR EXPERIENCES

In the previous section, we presented a number of cross-site issues derived from the lab's experiences. This section presents some additional information based on the author's informed intuition regarding our cross-site experiences. Although most of these opinions are unsubstantiated in any formal sense, this additional information may be useful to others involved in constructing or studying collaborative systems. This additional section is presented in the spirit of Fred Brooks' (1988) plenary address at CHI'88 where he said that "any data is better than no data."

Our experience showed that there was a sense of group cohesion in our distributed lab despite the 600-mile gap between the sites. Personal and working relationships were able to grow between distributed lab members. How were these things possible? We might speculate that they were possible primarily because we were able to simulate physical proximity to some extent via technology. In particular, the cross-site shared audio/video space and the ability to wander the other site via video allowed us to simulate many informal same-site interactions. For example, it was quite common for conversations to spring up in the shared commons space discussing the weather, someone's family, or a technical issue. As Allen's (1977) work would predict, this frequent informal interaction over time allowed cross-site personal and working relationships to grow. It allowed the lab to become a more cohesive unit. One of our experiences indicated that the simulated physical proximity provided by the shared space was a major reason that the lab felt this organization oneness. This quote came from a Palo Alto lab member after we lost our video link for several days due to an equipment problem:

"I ... have missed the link, and have already started to think of Portland as one might expect a remote lab to be thought of—a group of people who are intellectually known to exist, but that's it. At least with the (video), I felt like we had a kind of common back fence over which to chat."

As discussed earlier, the link seemed to support the growth of relationships over time but not their initiation. Why not? The author believes that this may have been due in part to the limited resolution of the compressed cross-site video. When meeting someone for the first time, people focus very carefully on facial features and other small details of a person (e.g., how tall a person is, how heavy a person is, etc.) to help fix that person in their minds (Krauss et al., 1977). This was difficult to accomplish between our two sites. For example, we documented cases in our environment where cross-site counterparts who had only met over the link had trouble recognizing each other's faces when they later met face-to-face. The limited resolution of the compressed video must have contributed to this problem. One could test this hypothesis by repeating some of our explorations using a higher quality video connection. As discussed previously, the video sometimes also didn't provide an accurate picture of other-site people (i.e., their height or weight) and this may have contributed to the recognition problem as well.

Another problem of perception that the author feels influenced many cross-site interactions involved how people perceived distances over the link. Short, Williams and Christie (1976) discussed the possibility that interacting over telecommunications facilities may distort an interaction by imposing a particular inter-site distance level. Hall (1959; 1966) pointed out that in a given culture, there are normal comfortable distances for particular types of interactions. The author feels that the cross-site link sometimes imposed distances that simply did not match the norm for an interaction. For example, for a small group meeting held in one physical location, Hall claimed that the normal distance between meeting participants would be about 4 to 12 feet. For such a meeting our technology might have imposed a distance level between the two ends of the link which was awkward to meeting participants. One could understand if this meeting split into two separate camps that could not come to a joint consensus. We encountered these situations in our environment at one time or another. The author believes that in designing a video system for distributed work, an attempt should be made to constantly match distance level to the cultural norms for a particular type of interaction (see Hall, 1959; 1966 for more discussion of normal distances).

CONCLUSIONS AND DIRECTIONS FOR FUTURE WORK

The author is in the process of establishing another distributed organization experiment (at U S WEST Advanced Technologies). We plan to base this work on the lessons learned from this exploratory project in distributed organization support at Xerox PARC. We learned a great deal from this effort.

The author believes that the application of shared spaces and the general focus on informal interaction were key aspects of the PARC effort. The

geographically distributed System Concepts Lab, supported by the shared space technology and the ability to wander the other site via video, was able to function to a large extent as if it were a single-site organization. The lab was able to develop a sense of group cohesion. Lab members were able to develop cross-site relationships. The author believes that this was due in large part to the shared cross-site audio/video space (i.e., the always-on audio/video connection between the two commons spaces), the computer-controllable video network, and a strong internetworking (e.g, electronic mail) environment.

We will work to extend the shared spaces concepts of the PARC experiments. We hope to extend the simulated proximity provided by audio and video to include entire information spaces. For example, people should be able to electronically share and browse books and journals, records of previous meetings, electronic mail, videos of their children, the evening news broadcast, and so forth. Artificial intelligence technology might be applied to help navigate through this communications and information environment.

The exploratory effort at PARC also pointed out a number of problems and areas for improvement in the cross-site technology. For example, the author believes that the low quality of the compressed cross-site video contributed to our inability to initiate cross-site relationships. The half duplex audio clearly inhibited interactive discourse across the link. We plan to use better quality cross-site video and full duplex audio in the new environment.

Looking at Portland–Palo Alto social interaction also points out areas for future work. We plan to build the next system to allow a variety of privacy schemes. Our next environment will take into account the social protocols of interaction and the verbal and nonverbal cues that control these protocols. Providing video eye contact will be a priority. It is also the author's belief that an attempt should be made to constantly match the system's imposed distance level to the cultural norms for a particular type of interaction.

We also plan to pursue a number of new experiments in both the behavioral and technical domains. On the technical side, we will also be investigating how the telephone network of the future might best support collaboration over space and time. We plan to investigate various collaborative tools (e.g., shared cross-site drawing, shared computing contexts, remote device control) and new input/output metaphors (e.g., helmet displays).

In the behavioral domain, we see a number of interesting new experiments to try. We would like to understand the needs of distributed organizations. Therefore we plan to compare a distributed organization with a non-distributed one (in our case, this will probably be a before and after comparison). We plan to eventually extend collaboration technologies to support non-research and development organizations (e.g., marketing organizations, upper management). This will allow us to evaluate the (possibly) different needs of such organizations. We want to investigate using these technologies between different types of organizations (e.g., between engineering and manufacturing or between engineering and marketing). We eventually plan to focus these technologies on other domains besides distributed organizations. We may try to prototype a next-generation distance education environment. One could also easily imagine applying such technologies to remote sales, remote consulting, or even the home of the future. Each domain will provide new behavioral issues to investigate.

We also will focus some energy on comparing the environment that we construct with the PARC environment. This may help us determine if the results from the PARC effort are extensible to other organizations. In other words, it may help us determine which behavioral impacts are related to particular aspects of the PARC system design, and which impacts are simply inherent in any system used to support a geographically distributed organization.

ACKNOWLEDGMENTS

The author would like to thank Stu Card and Dave Robson of Xerox PARC, Steve Reder of the Northwest Regional Education Lab, and Bob Johansen of the Institute for the Future, for their significant contributions to this work. Margi Olson of NYU, Sara Bly of Xerox PARC, George Goodman, formerly of Xerox PARC, Steve Bulick of U S WEST Advanced Technologies, and many other colleagues at Xerox PARC and U S WEST Advanced Technologies also provided helpful input. Finally the author would like to thank Paul Bauer at U S WEST Advanced Technologies for allowing the author to complete this work on U S WEST time.

REFERENCES

Allen, T. J. (1977). *Managing the flow of technology: Technology transfer & the dissemination of technical information within the R & D organization*. Cambridge, MA: MIT Press.

Brooks, F. (1988). Plenary address: Grasping reality through illusion. *Proceedings of CHI '88*, May 1988, Washington, D.C.

Galbraith, J. (1973). *Designing complex organizations*. Reading, MA: Addison-Wesley.

Goodman, G. O., & Abel, M. J. (1986). Collaboration research in SCL. *Proceedings of the Conference on Computer Supported Cooperative Work*, December 1986, Austin, TX.

Goodman, G. O., & Abel, M. J. (1987). Communication and collaboration: Facilitating cooperative work through communication. *Office: Technology and People, 3*, 129–145.

Hall, E. T. (1959). *The silent language*. Garden City, NY: Doubleday.

Hall, E. T. (1966). *The hidden dimension*. Garden City, NY: Doubleday.

Johansen, R. (1984). *Teleconferencing and beyond: Communications in the office of the future*. New York: McGraw Hill.

Johansen, R. (1988). *Groupware: Computer support for business teams*. New York: Free Press.

Krauss, R. M., Garlock, C. M., Bricker, P. D., & McMahon, L. E. (1977). The role of audible and visible back-channel responses in interpersonal communication. *Journal of Personality and Social Psychology, 35*, 523–529.

CSCW '86. *Proceedings of the Conference on Computer Supported Cooperative Work*, December 1986, Austin, TX.

Short, J., Williams, E., & Christie, B. (1976). *The social psychology of telecommunications*. New York: Wiley.

Experiences in the Use of a Media Space

Marilyn M. Mantei, Ronald M. Baecker, Abigail J. Sellen,
William A.S.Buxton, and Thomas Milligan

Department of Computer Science

Barry Wellman

Department of Sociology
University of Toronto
Toronto, Ontario M5S 1A4

ABSTRACT

A media space is a system that uses integrated video, audio, and computers to allow individuals and groups to work together despite being distributed spatially and temporally. Our media space, CAVECAT (Computer Audio Video Enhanced Collaboration And Telepresence), enables a small number of individuals or groups located in separate offices to engage in collaborative work without leaving their offices. This paper presents and summarizes our experiences during initial use of CAVECAT, including unsolved technological obstacles we have encountered, and the psychological and social impact of the technology. Where possible we discuss relevant findings from the psychological literature, and implications for design of the next-generation media space.

KEYWORDS

Computer-supported cooperative work, groupware, media spaces, desktop videoconferencing.

INTRODUCTION

Although Engelbart and English (1968) provided the first demonstration of a media space, the current wave of activity began with the Xerox PARC Portland Experiments (Goodman & Abel, 1986; Abel, 1990) and continued with recent developments including those at Xerox PARC (Stults, 1986, 1988; Bly & Minneman, 1990; Tang & Minneman, 1990), Bolt, Beranek and Newman (Thomas, Forsdick, Crowley, Schaaf, Tomlinson & Travers, 1988), Olivetti (Lantz, 1988), Bellcore (Root, 1988), and Rank Xerox EuroPARC (Buxton & Moran, 1990).

Despite marked differences in technology and approach, these experiments suggest common themes:

- Media spaces define new methods of communication, with novel and unforseen uses and potentialities. Communication through a media space is more than

an approximation of face-to-face communication — it has a richness and complexity all its own.

- The effective realization of media spaces requires one to solve serious architectural and implementation problems in distributed computing.

- Group working environments contain an enormously rich collection of communication protocols. The subset of communication metaphors built into existing media spaces only begin to reflect the possibilities.

- Media spaces raise serious ethical issues such as those of surveillance and privacy.

We have constructed a media space that enables a small number of individuals and groups located in separate offices to meet and collaborate without leaving their offices. This paper presents initial observations based on several months use of the system. Our goal is to contribute to the emerging dialogue on the potential, appropriate design, impact, and implications of media spaces. After a brief introduction to our system, we present our observations organized in terms of unexpected affordances, technological obstacles, and social and psychological impact. Each of our observations is discussed in terms of applicable underlying theories and suggested design recommendations.

THE CAVECAT SYSTEM

The CAVECAT (Computer Audio Video Enhanced Collaboration And Telepresence) system consists of a number of enhanced workstations connected by a digital+audio+video network. Each workstation consists of a personal computer, a TV monitor, a TV camera, a pair of speakers, and a microphone. A 4 x 1 video board allows the display of composite images of up to 4 sites (Figure 1). In some locations, video boards can place a lower resolution video image directly on the workstation's screen so that a separate monitor is not necessary.

The heart of the system is the switching network (Figure 2), patterned after the IIIF Server developed at Rank Xerox EuroPARC (Buxton & Moran , 1990; Milligan, 1989). Audio and video transmission is analog, but is switched digitally by the IIIF Server software residing on a workstation. Personal workstations in each office send messages via Ethernet to the IIIF server requesting connections. The IIIF Server also examines privacy settings for each office to determine if requested access by another office is permissible.

Figure 1. Video image of a CAVECAT meeting.

A server agent resides on each personal workstation. The user interface to this agent permits each office occupant to select a variety of communication metaphors: task oriented, (e.g., calling a meeting); spatially oriented, (e.g., walking into someone's office); or object oriented, (e.g., turning off the microphone in your office) (Louie, Mantei & Buxton, 1990).

We are developing shared software to support the computer communication aspect of the media space. These packages include a shared drawing tool and a shared text editor. Until this software is in place, we are using commercial software such as Timbuktu (Farallon, 1989), and ShrEdit, an experimental shared editor (Olson, Olson, Mack & Wellner, 1990).

UNEXPECTED AFFORDANCES

In order to understand the impact of the media space on its users, we applied it to ourselves by setting up CAVECAT nodes linking two faculty offices, the system programmer's office, and a graduate student work area. For the communication interface, we used a spatial metaphor consisting of a layout of the offices involved. We digitized video images of the CAVECAT users and placed these miniaturized images inside their owners respective onscreen offices Moving one or more of these images from one virtual office into another establishes a visual and acoustic link with the office or offices of choice.

Meetings of groups of groups

We had intended our setup to work primarily as a communicating device for one person located in each office. Our camera setups and camera angles were not designed for video conference meetings. However, in reality there was a natural demand for such a facility and it was used in this way. Individual members of the group used CAVECAT to introduce their visitors to others without going through the effort of physically walking the visitor over to the other individual's office for a more time-consuming interruption.

Mirror function

Although the system was designed for displaying other meeting participants, unexpected benefits came from displaying oneself. We used this "mirror" facility to make sure we were properly framed in the camera. The mirror function was included automatically in the split-screen display of 4-way conversations (Figure 1).

Monitoring function

Another surprising use was for the purpose of being virtually in one's own office. Instead of using the media links to place oneself virtually in another's office, we could also use the links as windows into our own offices when we were not there. We could monitor who was looking for us and when the phone rang. We could also use the system for security.

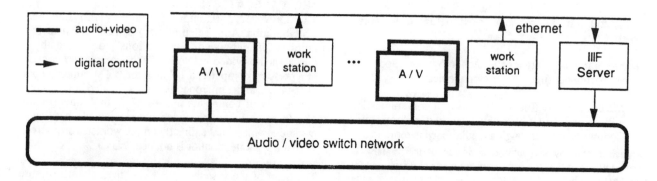

Figure 2 . Schematic diagram of the layout of the CAVECAT network.

TECHNOLOGICAL OBSTACLES

In our experience, a number of technological obstacles presented usability problems:

System response time delays

We initially built a prototype software package to run our virtual office connections. The time to establish a connection or to enter or leave an ongoing meeting was nearly two seconds. This delay quickly became intolerableAlthough system response times improved with a new version of the software, we must note that the two second wait time corresponds well with network switching and satellite delays for very long distance communications. This poses serious problems for the design of virtual offices spanning long distances.

Audio levels and noise

Ambient noise in the speakers' offices presented a major problem for sound quality. Different furniture arrangements, different numbers of people in the office, whether the office door was open or not, and where the office owner chose to sit in relation to speakers and microphones all had the potential to further degrade the quality of the sound. As a result, sound levels had to be continuously adjusted. When CAVECAT participants could not hear another participant, they tended to raise their voices, disturbing the audio levels more.

Obviously, it is inappropriate for us to tamper with the flexibility of individuals to decorate and move around their offices, nor do we have an intelligent device to automatically adjust levels. We are modifying the system by providing each participant with the ability to control their own audio, but we need to determine ways to make such adjustments easy and to guarantee that individual adjustments do not cause deterioration of the overall sound quality through feedback.

Sound localization

Participants of CAVECAT commented on how the sound in the shared communication seemed to come from "out of the air" rather than from the direction of the person speaking. When we had multiple participants communicating, the inability for participants to localize the sound sometimes made it difficult to determine who was speaking. Often, it was also difficult to know if one's phone was ringing, because of confusions with rings in other offices transmitted over the network.

Lighting and camera angles

The automatic light adjustments in our camera were intelligent but not intelligent enough. For example, some cameras were pointing at whiteboards located behind the occupants. The camera automatically adjusted for these white backgrounds, leaving the individuals in the foreground bathed in shadow. Some cameras were perched on bookshelves, while others sat on the side of their personal workstation. The location of the cameras, the lighting and color of the room's background, and the distance the individual chose to sit from the camera all affected the size and quality of the image transferred to the other offices.

Bad camera angles could distort impressions of speakers, which was particularly serious when one was not very familiar with a participant and when one was negotiating. Cameras with automatic focus continually zoomed in and out on the people moving about their offices, tending to make viewers in other offices slightly motion sick. It is clear that we need to consider carefully the placement of both camera and human, and to provide appropriate controls for presenting desirable video images.

PSYCHOLOGICAL AND SOCIAL IMPACT

Meetings between and within offices

Meetings of groups of groups of people were difficult to manage because people within an office were more "present" with each other than they were in the virtual office across the media. The physical closeness of people in the same office made them much more aware of their physical neighbors than of their video neighbors. This fact, combined with the poor acoustic quality across the network, encouraged people to address those in the same room rather than those in the other offices.

Two types of conversations often took place simultaneously. One conversation was public where people spoke to the camera. Private conversations were also being held among individuals in each office. Coordinating these two kinds of conversations and establishing the dominance of the public discussion when appropriate presented a challenge.

Another problem with such large meetings was that the displayed size of many individuals was so reduced that fine points of the interaction were often not visible. Facial expressions and nonverbal gestures were not as salient; interactions seemed less "real" than the ones taking place in the same room. When we switched from a meeting of multiple offices (a 2 x 2 video configuration of all participants) to a two-way communication (a single screen presentation of other participant), conversations again took place between offices rather than within offices.

Gaze and eye contact

Because participants were engaged in looking at the video image of their counterpart, they did not look directly into the TV camera. We did not use teleprompters or half-silvered mirrors to facilitate looking at the screen and the camera simultaneously. Thus eye contact was not established.

Gaze and mutual gaze are an important part of normal face-to-face communication. It is estimated that 61 percent of conversation involves gaze and 31 percent involves mutual gaze (Argyle, Ingham, Alkena & McCallin, 1973). Gaze serves at least five functions (Argyle et al., 1973; Exline, 1971): to regulate the flow of conversation; to provide feedback on how the communication is being perceived by the listener; to communicate emotions; to communicate the nature of the interpersonal relationship; and to reflect status relationships.

Rank Xerox EuroPARC (Buxton & Moran, 1990) used *video tunnels* — boxes containing cameras which pick up the video image of an individual via a half silvered mirror in front of their TV monitor. This solution makes it necessary for people to sit directly in front of big black boxes rather than in normal communicating positions within their office. EuroPARC has removed these video tunnels, but alternate solutions to achieving eye contact have not been devised. Hewlett-Packard embeds a miniature camera in the top of the workstation and uses on-screen video, but even this angle does not permit complete eye contact.

The best solution we have been able to achieve is produced by placing a camera with a wide-angle lens in front of and above the person and just above the monitor. The camera should not be very close to the person; zooming is used to make the person appear closer.

Status of meeting participants

Another interesting observation was that CAVECAT changed social status relationships due to the loss of the usual spatial and nonverbal cues which convey status information.

In face-to-face meetings, the seating of people in a room is usually indicative of a hierarchy with higher status people occupying more central positions or "head of the table" locations.

The design of CAVECAT unintentionally introduced its own social status cues. In meetings of four individuals, CAVECAT arbitrarily positioned participants' images in a 2 x 2 grid. CAVECAT also configured the video images for a meeting based on who requested the meeting. This meant that if meetings were reconvened after a short break by a different person, the result was a different image configuration. This was highly disconcerting to the participants. It was as if everyone had left the room and returned to take new positions around the table.

Meeting coordination

Our observed problems with loss of traditional status cues and generation of new cues speaks to the more general issue of control in discussions. When important cues are missing or degraded, there is a greater need for a moderator to control turn-taking and group decision processes. For example, people wanting to take control in conversations will often lean in to indicate their desire to speak. This cue is difficult to detect on video.

Our observation is that a moderator's success may depend on having "media presence" — a factor which does not necessarily come into play in face-to-face meetings.

Image size and personal impact

A participant's effectiveness within a conversation and the way each participant was perceived by others seemed to be, in part, determined by video image size. Participants with large images appeared to have more impact in the discussion. Participants with small images seemed distant and less effective in the conversation.

The size of the video image was determined by four factors: the screen size of the monitor, the distance of the viewer from the TV monitor, the distance of the person from the camera, and the zoom setting of the camera. Participants often had different sized images because these variables were rarely adjusted.

Video image and social distance

Image size and angle also interacted with people's perception of their social relationship to other participants. Inappropriate image size sometimes gave the sense of people being too personal or too impersonal in the conversation.

These observations are consistent with the social psychology literature which finds that interpersonal physical distance is predictive of relationships between people (Argyle & Dean, 1965). People who are only casually acquainted tend to maintain a distance of about 4 to 12 feet between them while interacting. Distances from 1 1/2 to 4 feet tend to be maintained for friends, while distances of less than 1 1/2 feet are reserved for intimate relationships. It is well established that people quickly become uncomfortable if the distance between them is perceived to be inappropriate for the relationship. Too close, and people feel their space is being violated. Too far, and people are also uncomfortable.

In the media space, what is relevant is the "perceived" interpersonal distance, a virtual distance rather than a physical one. Observation suggests that video images may be viewed as less personal and intrusive in general. In one hot summer's day usage, the participants talked freely with each other over the media space, but one individual immediately donned a lab coat to cover her shorts and tank top when meeting face-to-face with the same individual. One the other hand, occasionally a meeting participant reached for a book from a shelf or stood up, creating views several inches from the participant's neck or stomach, making an onlooker uncomfortable.

What is also unusual about a media space is that the interpersonal distance may be simultaneously different for any member of the group communicating. This is not the case for physical distance where distances between people are, in a sense, negotiated and shared. In CAVECAT, a participant's personal space can be invaded without the invader being aware of this.

Privacy and surveillance

When we first put the system in place, any node on the network could immediately connect with any other node via video and audio. The system was kept running semi-continuously because of the need to troubleshoot startup problems. This lack of privacy led to very strong protection behaviors on the part of two participants — one who was negotiating the secret sale of a company, and another who was negotiating problems in a personal relationship. The first individual unplugged or shut off all CAVECAT connections while the second worked shorter hours.

It became clear very early that "knowing" when you were connected to another office and being able to inhibit the connection were critical and necessary features. The media space, as it was, did not provide enough feedback to indicate that others were suddenly present in your office. In addition, although available, the privacy setting features in the IIIF Server were too complicated for easy use. One good approach to the provision of adequate feedback is through the use of non-speech audio cues (Buxton & Moran, 1990; Gaver & Smith, 1990).

IMPLICATIONS FOR FUTURE DESIGN

Our experiences begin to illustrate how technology can significantly alter the nature of human communication patterns. One important conclusion is that many of the cues implicit in face-to-face communication situations need to be taken into account and provided for in the design of the interface.

There are many communication variables that we had not considered in our original design. It is easy to take for granted aspects implicit in face-to-face communication such as the physical presence of someone in an office implying a desire to communicate, or nonverbal gestures of individuals in a meeting.

Another implication of our observations is that it is important to provide easy-to-use features that place some of the system variables under user control. For example, because there are many aspects of the visual image which affect the way participants perceive each other and interact, it is important that users are able to adjust for viewing and being viewed.

We have a number of specific plans based on our experiences to date:

- We are developing metaphors for communication and privacy protection that follow accepted communication practice. These metaphors consist of interface selections that allow the user to: (1) wait to see someone who is busy talking to someone else; (2) drop by to ask a quick question; (3) shut one's door partially or wholly; or (4) whisper something to a co-worker at a meeting. We are working with variables such as video image size, blurriness of the video image, duration of the video/audio connection and verbal and non-speech audio cues to create these communication protocols.

- We are building an underlying visual language for manipulating the parameters of the system so that its users can build their own protocols for adjusting the media space parameters.

- We are putting in new basic functionalities such as individual control of audio and comparative viewing of video images. We are also trying out automatic audio switching so that the person speaking in a meeting becomes the single image presented to all participants. This avoids our image size problems but may create new problems associated with not being able to view everyone in the meeting.

Despite our current problems, our media space has proved to be a successful tool for collaborative communication. We find that it is used extensively for communicating about software development. The system not only allows an approximation to face-to-face communication, but also confers many new advantages upon its users. We can have virtual open offices with the bad effects of continuous noise and disturbance removed and the good effects of proximity enhanced. Meantime we are continuing the process of iterative design in order to minimize the problems and capitalize on the advantages discussed in this paper.

ACKNOWLEDGEMENTS

For research support, the authors are indebted to the Natural Sciences and Engineering Research Council of Canada, the Information Technology Research Centre of Ontario, Apple Computer, Digital Equipment Corporation, IBM Canada and particularly to Rank Xerox EuroPARC, which contributed the code for the IIIF Server. In addition, we are grateful to the University of Michigan, which loaned us the object code for their shared editor. We also wish to thank the many students who have worked long hours on CAVECAT: Beverly Harrison, Jeffrey Lee, Gifford Louie, Iva Lu, Kelly Mawby, Tracy Narine, Ilona Posner, Michael Sheasby, and Ian Small.

REFERENCES

Abel, M.J,. Experiences in an exploratory distributed organization. In Galegher, Kraut & Egido (Eds), *Intellectual Teamwork: Social and Technological Foundations of Cooperative Work*, Lawrence Erlbaum Associates, 489-510.

Argyle, M. and Dean, J. (1965) Eye contact, distance, and affiliation. *Sociometry*, 28, 289-304.

Argyle, M., Ingham, R., Alkena, F. and McCallin, M. (1973). The different functions of gaze. *Semiotica*, 7, 10-32.

Bly, S.A. and Minneman, S.L. (1990). Commune: a shared drawing surface. In *Proceedings of the Conference of Office Information Systems*, Cambridge, MA, April 1990. 184-192.

Engelbart, D. and English, W.K. (1968). A research center for augmenting human intellect. In Greif, I. (Ed.) . *Computer-Supported Cooperative Work: A Book of Readings*, Morgan Kaufmann Publishers, San Mateo, Calif., 81-105.

Exline, R.V. (1971). Visual interaction: The glances of power and preference. In J. K. Cole (Ed.) *Nebraska Symposium on Motivation* Vol. 19, 163-206, University of Nebraska Press.

Farallon Computing, Inc. (1989). *Timbuktu*. 2201 Dwight Way, Berkeley, CA, 94704 USA.

Gaver, W.W. and Smith, R.B. (1990). Auditory icons in large-scale collaborative environments. In Diaper, D., Gilmore, D. Cockton, G. and Shackel, B. (Eds), *Proceedings of Human-Compuer Interaction, INTERACT'90*, Cambridge, England, August 27-31, 1990, 735-740.

Goodman, G. and Abel, M. (1986). Collaboration research in SCL. In *Proceedings of the First Conference on Computer Supported Cooperative Work*, Austin, TX, December 86.

Lantz, K.A. (1988). An experiment in integrated multimedia conferencing. In Greif, I. (Ed.) . *Computer-Supported Cooperative Work: A Book of Readings*, Morgan Kaufmann Publishers, San Mateo, Calif., 533-552.

Louie, G., Mantei, M. and Buxton, W.A.S.(1990) Making contact in a multi-media environment. HCI Consortium on CSCW, Ann Arbor, MI., February 1991.

Milligan, T. (1989). IIIF: The Integrated Interactive Intermedia Facility design report - Revision 3 January 1989. Rank Xerox EuroPARC working paper.

Buxton, W.A.S. and Moran, T (1990). EuroPARC's Integrated Interactive Intermedia facility (IIIF): Early Experiences. *Proceedings of the IFIP WG8.4 Conference on Multi-user Interfaces and Applications*, Heraklion, Crete, September 1990. 24pp.

Olson, J.R., Olson, G.M., Mack, L.A. and Wellner, P. (1990). Concurrent editing: the group's interface. In Diaper, D., Gilmore, D. Cockton, G. and Shackel, B. (Eds), *Proceedings of Human-Compuer Interaction, INTERACT'90*, Cambridge, England, August 27-31, 1990, 835-840.

Root, R.W. (1988). Design of a multi-media vehicle for social browsing. In *Proceedings of the Second Conference on Computer-Supported Cooperative Work*, Portland, OR, September 1989, 25-38.

Stults, R. (1986). Media space. Xerox PARC technical report. 20 pp.

Stults, R. (1988). Experimental uses of video to support design activities. Xerox PARC technical report SSL-89-19.

Tang, J.C. and Minneman, S.L. (1990). VideoDraw: a video interface for collaborative drawing. *Proceedings of CHI '90*, 313-320.

Thomas, R.H., Forsdick, H.C., Crowley, T.R., Schaaf, R.W., Tomlinson, R.S., and Travers, V.M. (1988). Diamond: a multimedia message system built on a distributed architecture. In Greif, I. (Ed.) *Computer-Supported Cooperative Work: A Book of Readings*, Morgan Kaufmann Publishers, San Mateo, Calif., 509-532.

Portholes: Supporting Awareness in a Distributed Work Group

Paul Dourish

Rank Xerox EuroPARC
61 Regent St
Cambridge CB2 1AB UK
(0223) 341512
dourish@europarc.xerox.com

Sara Bly

Xerox PARC
3333 Coyote Hill Road
Palo Alto, CA 94304
(415) 812 4360
bly@parc.xerox.com

ABSTRACT

We are investigating ways in which media space technologies can support distributed work groups through access to information that supports general awareness. Awareness involves knowing who is "around", what activities are occurring, who is talking with whom; it provides a view of one another in the daily work environments. Awareness may lead to informal interactions, spontaneous connections, and the development of shared cultures—all important aspects of maintaining working relationships which are denied to groups distributed across multiple sites.

The Portholes project, at Rank Xerox EuroPARC in Cambridge, England, and Xerox PARC in Palo Alto, California, demonstrates that awareness can be supported across distance. A data network provides a shared database of image information that is regularly updated and available at all sites. Initial experiences of the system in use at EuroPARC and PARC suggest that Portholes both supports shared awareness and helps to build a "sense of community".

KEYWORDS: group work, collaboration, CSCW, media spaces, distributed workgroups, informal interaction, awareness.

INTRODUCTION AND MOTIVATIONS

Reports on the use of media space technology (e.g. [3], [5], [6], [8], [10], [11]) typically focus on the use of direct audio and video connections as an aid to collaboration among remotely located individuals. The emphasis on real-time connections is not surprising; such uses are highly visible and identifiable mechanisms through which remote

collaboration can be enhanced. However, our experiences of using media space technology at Rank Xerox EuroPARC [4] and at Xerox PARC [9] have also pointed to the importance of a different style of connection. We find that, when their video equipment is otherwise unused, many of our media space users like to observe activities in public areas; they report that they find these connections useful in order to see "what's going on" as members of the group gather for meetings, check their mail, collect coffee, etc. These background connections are used very differently from those of direct connections; in particular, they tend to be long-term and non-engaged. Unlike information which might be gleaned from a direct connection with a colleague, here it is being gathered passively, while other workplace activities progress.

This use of video technology is very similar to the typical awareness activities which occur in a shared physical environment. While sitting at a desk, we are aware of activities going on around us—we hear the sounds of conversations in corridors, see people as they pass by, notice people in offices as we walk down a hallway, and so forth. The *Polyscope* system at EuroPARC [2] and the *Imager* system at PARC were attempts to capture some of this information in the respective media spaces. The basic approach that each took was to present regularly-updated digitised video images from locations around the media space on the workstation screen. These images show activities in public areas and offices. Our media space infrastructures provide the technological base for these applications—users of the awareness services are "inhabitants" of our media spaces.

Following on from positive experiences with Polyscope and Imager, we wished to extend the notion of "awareness" outside a single physical location, and thus support awareness for *distributed* work groups. Such groups, by their nature, are denied the informal information gathered from a physically shared workspace and the proximity which is an important factor in collaboration between colleagues ([1], [7]). We expect that a shared awareness space can be a basis for providing similar information. In addition, awareness services can be achieved with less bandwidth than the usual "live video" connections of existing media spaces. Thus, we

FIGURE 1. A window dump of the "pvc" client to Portholes. The first eight images show EuroPARC nodes; the last seven show PARC nodes. All images were taken at approximately the same time.

could explore the utility of awareness for truly distributed groups without large investment in a technological infrastructure[1].

Our system for distributed awareness is called "Portholes". A multi-site awareness service tackles a number of new issues, including data distribution techniques and the interface problems of dealing with shared information. Portholes consists of a cooperating group of servers which jointly manage a distributed data space. In addition, Portholes includes clients which present the Portholes information in a variety of ways giving users the ability to process and use the information. Figure 1 shows a typical interface to Portholes with images of colleagues who share research interests and projects in both Cambridge and Palo Alto.

This paper focuses on Portholes as an example of the kind of system we think might support our notion of distributed awareness. We will describe Portholes and its existing clients, offer some initial observations of its use, and discuss issues that we consider central to developing an understanding of the role of awareness in everyday work activities and in using technologies to enable that awareness in distributed groups.

---

1. Our infrastructure, of course, is based on an existing media space. In the absence of such a facility, individual Portholes nodes can be set up with separate video cameras and frame-grabbers. Adequate quality can be achieved with relatively inexpensive equipment.

DESIGN CONSTRAINTS AND ARCHITECTURE

Portholes is basically a system for maintaining image information which is both generated and consumed at a number of sites connected via an internet. Essentially, the technical problem is timely distribution of information so that it can be usefully presented to a user, while keeping within the constraints of available network bandwidth. Since we wish to support multiple interfaces and interface styles, we make a strong distinction between the two major system components—a *server* component, which is responsible for maintaining the database, and one or more *client* components, which present the information to users.

Interface Requirements

Interface requirements drive a great deal of the server design, and so it is worth considering what sorts of facilities they might provide, and hence the requirements they impose. An interface client of the Portholes information base will generally be an interactive program running on a user's workstation. It might display not only images, but also information about the image itself (for example, when it was taken). The interface might well provide other information about the source of the image (generally a person), such as office number and e-mail address. In designing the system, we also wanted to allow the image information to be used to access other, externally-provided services (e-mail is an obvious example), and these might well involve some kind of manipulation of the image itself or its associated information. All these needs must be catered for by the server.

Again, the primary problem to be overcome is *latency* in transmitted information. A single interface will typically

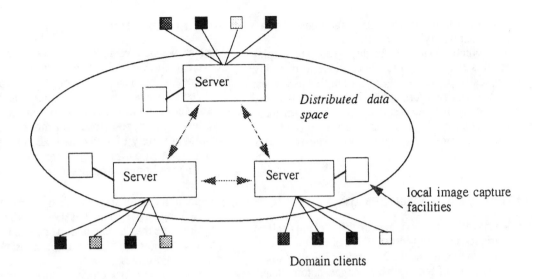

FIGURE 2. The structure of the Portholes system. Portholes consists of a number of cooperating information servers linked by a network. Client programs communicate only with their local servers, although they may display remote information. Servers use local image-processing facilities.

show information from multiple sites, and network access to remote sites will be many orders of magnitude slower than access to local information. We can tolerate a certain amount of latency; image updates may only occur every ten minutes, and so the user will not expect up-to-the-second information. However, latency must not be reflected in the *manipulation* of information in the interface, which must have good interactive response. Thus, all manipulations of image information must result in, at most, an interaction with a *local* information server, rather than with a server at the generating site, possibly thousands of miles away. The image information must be *replicated*, so that a local copy can always be made available when needed.

The Portholes Architecture

Components

The basic architecture of Portholes comprises a set of cooperating information servers, each of which has particular responsibility for a *domain*, typically a media space at one site. A domain contains a number of *sources* of regularly updated awareness information, as well as client programs which *consume* that information. Each server is responsible for distributing information generated by sources in its domain, and for ensuring that information required by client programs within that domain is at-hand. Clients access the shared information base through their closest server. Information flows between the domain servers as required by the various client programs. Client programs access the information space as if it were all located centrally; they need not even be aware that the information is not generated locally. The server, for its part, deals purely with the information distribution, and has no knowledge of the way in which information is presented by

the clients. Thus multiple, very different, client interfaces can present the same information from a single server. The relationship between clients and servers is illustrated in Figure 2.

As well as image information, a source also has a set of *properties*, which hold other information associated with that source. In effect, the image is only a single source property. These other properties then allow clients to perform more useful manipulations based on the awareness data. For instance, most of our clients take advantage of an "e-mail address" property which can be used to provide a user with a mechanism for sending an e-mail message to someone directly from their image in a Portholes window. We can also be more creative, for example by adding audio snippets via the property mechanism.

Data Flow

There are two data sets within Portholes—domain data (e.g. what domains are available, and how they can be reached) and source data (images and property information). The distribution strategy for these two sets is different, because of the way in which they are used.

Although a user will typically only look at a subset of the available source information, browsing all of the domain information is a common activity (e.g. when selecting which of the available sources to display). Therefore, while source information is transmitted only on an as-needed basis, domain data is actively propagated to all sites. This means that domain data is always immediately accessible to the user for browsing and manipulation. Delays in source data, however, can be tolerated, which helps us achieve our goal of keeping network throughput low.

Our clients make use of all these server facilities. Domain information is continually available to the user, so that it is easy to select which images will be displayed. The display space, though, is flat, with no reference made to domains; interfaces typically present images in a single "awareness space". Properties carry information which may be intended for the user directly, for processing by a client, or for inter-server communication. Thus our architecture provides an efficient way of providing multiple interfaces to the awareness information.

PRESENTING PORTHOLES INFORMATION

To date, we have been working with three clients, all of which are variations of one another. The basic client, *pvc*, is an application running under the X Window System, which displays one or more of the available images, automatically updating the images every few minutes. The user can select which images are displayed using an initialisation file or with a menu when the application is running. Another client, *edison,* has the capabilities of pvc and also associates digital audio messages (or "snippets") with images. It allows users to record their audio snippets and listen to those recorded by other Portholes users. Finally, a client *viewmaster* is provided for public use. It is like pvc but with the constraint that the only images available are public spaces; no office nodes are included.

Referring back to Figure 1, note that there are images from both EuroPARC and PARC all taken at approximately the same moment in real-time (all times are presented in the local user's timezone—the times in the figure are British Summer Time). Clicking on an image brings up a dialog box with the properties available for that image (name, phone number, etc.) and a set of action buttons. In pvc, these actions are E-MAIL and GLANCE; edison has an additional action LISTEN for those images with associated audio messages. Clicking on E-MAIL causes a mail system window to open with the *To:* field appropriately completed with the name of the person associated with the selected image. Clicking on GLANCE will invoke a media space glance action[2] at EuroPARC (this feature is not implemented at PARC). Clicking on LISTEN will play the associated audio snippet.

All of the existing clients operate primarily in a broadcast mode. By *broadcast,* we mean that all users of the system have access to all information within the system. Thus, if a user records a voice message in edison, that message may be played by all edison users. Ultimately we believe that Portholes clients will integrate both broadcast and directed information. By *directed,* we mean specifying particular users to be recipients of the information. Note that directed information may come from Portholes (for example, an audio snippet sent only to one recipient) or it may come as an interface to an existing directed system (such as e-mail).

---

2. Glance provides a one-way video connection of a few seconds' duration to a specific media space node.

PORTHOLES IN USE

Just as we believe in an iterative process of design and development, we practice an iterative process of use as well. We begin by using our prototypes ourselves; as we understand ways in which the system can be used and as we stabilise the system itself, we expand our user base. When we feel a prototype is ready for more in-depth analysis, we employ a variety of study methods. Our goal is to reach a point at which our prototypes can be a part of an everyday working environment outside our own research labs.

We are in the early stages of using Portholes. At the time of this writing, the system has been under development for slightly more than a year, and the clients have been available on and off for the last 8-10 months. When clients are available, Portholes has seen regular use at our two sites, and we have grown to include 10 users at PARC and 12 at EuroPARC. All are members of our respective media spaces, and have office nodes comprising video cameras, monitors, microphones and speakers. In addition to the images of the offices of the users, Portholes also has images available from several public areas: the commons area at EuroPARC, a view out to the green behind EuroPARC (called Parker's Piece), a common area at PARC used by many of the Media Space participants, a view of the construction site for another Xerox facility near PARC, and the PARC media lab.

The Portholes users form a distributed work group. Most have met face-to-face and share research interests, and a few subgroups have on-going collaborations across the two sites. Nevertheless, despite knowing each other and having shared research interests, colleagues typically have relatively few interactions across sites. In addition, a summer student working on Portholes at PARC (who wrote the edison interface) has never met any of the EuroPARC users except through Portholes.

During the earlier development phase, we had a core user group of around 10; since then, others have asked to join, and so our user base has expanded to the 22 people mentioned above. We have noted our own observations regarding the use of Portholes over the past few months, and we have asked our users for feedback. The results indicate that Portholes appears to be playing an active role in providing a basis for distributed awareness.

Initial Observations

Our first informal and anecdotal observations have generally fallen into two categories. The first includes user-suggested modifications or enhancements to the Portholes service; for instance, colour is a frequently-requested feature. The second is user references to people and/or events that have occurred "in Portholes". It is not at all uncommon to hear a user refer to some person that he or she "saw" today, when in fact that person was at the remote site, and only available through Portholes. Such "sightings" are especially common when some unusual activity occurs at the other site. Some examples give a flavour of these:

- Recently a participant at PARC was spending many late nights working in his office; his presence was not only noted by EuroPARC participants but also led them to be quite aware of his dissertation progress!

- Another late night worker at PARC was pleased to tell his local colleagues that he had watched the sun rise in England (over Parker's Piece). Similarly, a EuroPARCer says she likes to "watch the day begin" at PARC.

- Recently a EuroPARCer came in late on a Saturday, prompting a PARC Saturday worker to press E-MAIL in edison and say "I see you". The response back from EuroPARC was "It's nice to know I'm not completely alone!"

- Cross-site visits are a particular source of sightings. For instance, a PARC visitor to EuroPARC was amused to notice a EuroPARC visitor to PARC using her "home" workstation to demonstrate software.

- Our summer student at PARC, not having met his colleagues at the other site, nevertheless feels as though he "knows" some of the Portholes users there, and recognises personal characteristics (snippets of favourite music being one form of the edison audio messages).

User Feedback

In order to get more detailed feedback on the use of, and reactions to, our prototype Portholes system, we asked a group of fifteen users to note their usage of Portholes over a three-day period and to fill out an electronic questionnaire. The questionnaire also asked open-ended questions regarding features they liked and disliked.

We received eleven responses by electronic mail. While we do not believe we're ready to "quantify" the effects of awareness, we can observe some patterns in the typical use of Portholes.

Basic Usage

All but one of our questionnaire respondents reported using pvc and/or edison[3] at least a few times a day through the questionnaire period; e-mail and audio snippets were used only occasionally. As we would expect, there are some problems at this stage with the dependability, accessibility, and amount of information. Particular troubles included:

the eratic performance and unreliable images (eg. when were these really taken?)

[that the pvc window] *takes up too much space on my screen to be up continually so it's overhead to see it*

that not much happens; the turn around for new information is so slow that I'm not too motivated to use it; I'm never guaranteed of seeing much

---

3. Differences in hardware platforms meant that the audio facilities were not available to all users. These users had to use pvc instead of edison.

Despite problems our group was (and is) quite positive about having the system. We've found two main modes of use—using the system as a lightweight information tool and using it as a shared space or community.

Portholes as an Information Tool

As an information tool, Portholes offers a lightweight means of finding out the availability of a colleague and in offering quick reports that are not time-urgent:

I remember seeing [a colleague] *in his office and going down to ask him something—checking for* [that colleague] *over pvc is a common event.*

The sense of general awareness which helps save time on wasted visits or phone calls to empty offices. The information it provides also allows you to predict when people will be free, or certain implications for yourself, such as "[A colleague is] *talking to a visitor this morning so I won't get to see him until after lunch."*

...I notice that [a remote colleagues's] *message is an informal bug report.*

Portholes as a Community

In providing a shared space for a community of users, Portholes offers the opportunity to see colleagues who are remote as well as those who are local. Portholes also provides a place for sharing the serious and the whimsical:

I remember seeing people arrive, and leave, people passing through others' offices...

[I remember seeing a few people at the remote site]— *like* [a colleague] *whom I've never met.*

I also liked [a colleague's] *message where he sang happy birthday to himself...*

the sense of whether people were around and seeing my friends; knowing who's around; feeling some connection to folks at [the remote site] *(sharing a "community" with them)*

[I like the fact that pvc/edison] *Brings everybody together, both within* [my local site] *as well as between the labs.*

DISCUSSION: CURRENT RESULTS AND ISSUES

Portholes is meant to provide an awareness of remote colleagues. The image information is intended to be available without necessary actions from the users; other information is intended to be available in a lightweight (without much user involvement) manner. Thus, evaluations are difficult; people are not likely to remember specific experiences, and asking them to think about them too much changes their experiences. In order to understand the system and to plan for future work, we want to consider three different issues:

1. the effect of awareness information in supporting a work group generally;

2. the ability of Portholes to provide meaningful awareness information; and

3. the design of interfaces to present this information usefully.

Although there is considerable attention paid to the value of work group familiarity and proximity in a shared physical space, there has been little research into support of these in a media space environment. Furthermore, there is little research on what role passive awareness itself plays in group work activity and cohesion. We have observed participants in media spaces and in Portholes routinely using these systems for background information. Developing an understanding of how this awareness information is being used in Portholes and what effect it has on the work group interactions will lead to a better understanding of its role in maintaining work group relations generally.

Secondly, the form of the Portholes awareness information should be considered in light of our evolving understanding of awareness itself. As our user observations suggested, the notion of awareness as exemplified in Portholes currently seems to provide a basis for an information tool (community access) and for a shared space (community building). We are exploring the value of other media in providing information in support of both awareness and community building. For instance, audio snippets do not provide *awareness* in the same sense as the automatic images; both sender and receiver must initiate explicit actions to effect the information exchange, making it neither passive nor "background". However, audio snippets do appear to contribute to the sense of community through the awareness they provide of a colleague's personality and nature, and we are interested in exploring this form of information.

Thirdly, the interfaces to systems such as Portholes will have a significant impact on how the information is used. If awareness is a passive and background notion, then the interfaces must be particularly lightweight. At the same time, if the awareness is a basis for more interactive exchanges, then the interface must provide those capabilities. We have already observed with Portholes some of the interface difficulties. Displaying more than a few images takes considerable screen real-estate making it difficult to have Portholes available for peripheral viewing while focusing on other workstation tasks[4]. In addition, many of the actions are still not as flexible for user control as we would like nor as natural for prompting interactions as we would hope.

The "awareness" often seems inconsequential—late night sightings, a voice message that is part of a song, dinosaurs fighting in a commons area. However, the enthusiasm with which our users take up the system suggests to us that they sense the same potential in "awareness information" as we do, and are eager to access and exploit it. Certainly, we have observed that communications among colleagues across sites has increased, especially informal, unprompted communications of a type which would not have occurred before. Four months after our initial questionnaire, some simple statistics collection in the server tells us that participants continue to be regular users of Portholes. Making information available to colleagues in a way that does not distract from the task at hand but rather adds to the sense of work group community is the use of Portholes we hope to achieve.

CONCLUSIONS

Based on our experiences with the notion of awareness, we have designed, implemented, and brought into a use a prototype system to support lightweight awareness-gathering in distributed work groups. We have extended several of the notions from earlier awareness interfaces (Polyscope and Imager) to support a distributed work group, to expand the underlying system architecture, and to begin studying the use of the system in daily work activities. In looking at the feedback from our users and their patterns of usage of this system, we're pleased by the number of people who frequently use pvc and/or edison and by the ways in which they are using it.

Our user observations suggest that awareness may be a useful basis for community access (an information tool, especially for locating colleagues) and for community building (a shared space for "sightings" and personal snippets). In particular, this second usage helps maintain working relationships in a group which would otherwise have few direct interactions.

Our experiences with Portholes suggest that awareness across distance has meaning, that it can lead positively toward communications and interactions, and perhaps most importantly, that it can contribute to a shared sense of community. Furthermore, systems like Portholes show the potential for media spaces and electronic networks as environments for collaboration in low bandwidth situations. We expect the continued use, development, and evaluation of the Portholes system to contribute to a greater understanding of the nature of awareness and the support of distributed work groups.

ACKNOWLEDGEMENTS

We particularly thank Amin Vahdat for implementing edison and Tom Moran, Alan Borning, and Mike Travers for helping us get started. Scott Elrod, Enrique Godreau, Scott Minneman, and Pierre Wellner contributed to making it run,

---

4. A full display of all available images takes almost all of a 17-inch screen, although other windows can be placed on top of it.

particularly the frame-grabbing processes. We also very much appreciate the comments from Victoria Bellotti, Francoise Brun-Cottan, Bill Gaver, Steve Harrison, Susan Irwin, Lennart Lövstrand, Allan MacLean, and Wendy Mackay on this paper. Most importantly, we thank the Portholes-Users for their willingness to explore new ideas and new technologies with enthusiasm.

REFERENCES

1. Allen, T. (1977), *Managing the Flow of Technology*, MIT Press, Cambridge, Massachusetts.

2. Borning, A. and Travers, M. (1991), Two Approaches to Casual Interaction over Computer and Video Networks, Proc. CHI '91 Human Factors in Computer Systems, New Orleans, Louisiana.

3. Bulick, S., Abel, M., Corey, D., Schmidt, J. & Coffin, S. (1989). The US WEST Advanced Technologies Prototype Multi-media Communications System, Proc. GLOBECOM '89 Global Telecommunications Conference, Dallas, Texas.

4. Gaver, W., Moran, T., MacLean, A., Dourish, P., Carter, K. and Buxton, W. (1991), Working Together in Media Space: Collaboration Research at EuroPARC, Proc. UNICOM Symposium on CSCW—The Multimedia and Networking Paradigm, London.

5. Heath, C. & Luff, P. (1991), Disembodied conduct: Communication through video in a multi-media environment, Proc. CHI '91 Human Factors in Computing Systems, New Orleans, Louisiana.

6. Irwin, S. (1990), *Technology, Talk and the Social World: A Study of Video-Mediated Interaction*. Dissertation. Michigan State University.

7. Kraut, R., Egido, C., and Galegher, J. (1988) Patterns of Contact and Communication in Scientific Research Collaboration, Proc. CSCW '88 Computer-Supported Cooperative Work, Portland, Oregon.

8. Mantei, M., Baeker, R., Sellen, A., Buxton, W., Milligan, T. and Wellman, B. (1991), Experiences in the Use of a Media Space, Proc. CHI '91 Human Factors in Computer Systems, New Orleans, Louisiana.

9. Olson, M., and Bly, S. (1991) The Portland Experience: A Report On A Distributed Research Group, Intl. Journal of Man-Machine Studies, 34.

10. Root, R. (1988). Design of a Multi-Media Vehicle for Social Browsing, Proc. CSCW '88 Computer Support for Cooperative Work, Portland, Oregon.

11. Stults, R. (1988) Experimental Use of Video to Support Design Activity, Technical Report SSL-89-19, Xerox Palo Alto Research Centre, Palo Alto, California.

Telepresence: Integrating Shared Task and Person Spaces

William A. S. Buxton

Computer Systems research Institute
University of Toronto
Toronto, Ontario, Canada M5S 1A4

Abstract

From a technological and human perspective, shared space in remote collaboration has tended to focus on shared space of either the people or the task. The former would be characterized by traditional video/teleconferencing or videophones. The latter could be characterized by synchronous computer conferencing or *groupware*.

The focus of this presentation is the area where these two spaces meet and are integrated into what could be characterized as video-enhanced computer conferencing or computer-enhanced video conferencing.

From the behavioural perspective, the interest lies in how - in collaborative work - we make transitions between these two spaces. For example, in negotiating, the activity is mainly in the shared space of the participants themselves, where we are "reading" each other for information about trust and confidence. On the other hand, in preparing a budget using a shared electronic spreadsheet, for example, the visual channel is dominated by the task space.

How well systems affords natural transitions between these spaces will have a large impact on their usability, usefulness, and acceptance. Consequently, we investigate the design space and some of the issues affecting it.

Keywords: Human-computer interaction, CSCW, Videoconferencing, Groupware.

Introduction

Groups play an important role in our work-a-day life. Physical proximity facilitates interaction among group members. Even splitting groups across two floors of the same building can have a negative effect on group dynamics (Kraut & Egido, 1988), yet in many organizations groups are distributed across campuses, cities, countries, or even the globe. The health of these organizations is tightly coupled to the ability to maintain a sense of "group," despite such distances. Our interest lies in developing *telepresence* technologies appropriate for fostering such maintenance.

As we use the term, telepresence is the use of technology to establish a sense of shared *presence* or shared *space* among geographically separated members of a group. The topic is of particular interest now due to the ongoing convergence and affordability of the requisite computer,

telecommunications and audio/video technologies; however, if these technologies are going to be deployed in anything other than a tail-wagging-the-dog technology-driven manner, we must first develop a better understanding of what we mean by "shared space" or "shared presence" in the context of group interactions.

In what follows, we begin to investigate what is shared in various types of group interactions, and some of the technological implications of supporting such sharing. Our purpose is "consciousness raising" rather than the presentation of formal theories or models. Our case is made primarily through the use of examples. Our hope is to provide some foundation for making better design decisions and better exploiting the potential of existing and evolving resources.

Starting from the Known

The terms "meeting" or "group interaction" are almost devoid of information since they encompass such a broad range of activities. Each has its own set of properties and purposes. Only by understanding these properties can we hope to design the appropriate affordances into supporting technologies.

This is nothing new. Take architecture as an example. Because it is a mature discipline, we think of it as part of the general ecology of work, rather than as a technology. Yet a technology it is, and very much a technology to support group activities. Consider, then, the different types of group activities that are a part of our everyday work, and how the affordances of this technology have been designed to support them. We clearly understand differences of purpose, and choose the space (office, lounge, laboratory, board room, gym, lunch room, etc.) accordingly.

Because the technology is mature, we have a good sense of how to match the activity to the space. In order to be considered mature, the electronic meeting spaces of telepresence must meet the same dual criteria of supporting a comparably rich range of group activities and doing so in such a way that users have the same transparent sense of appropriateness of space-to-activity.

To speak of "videoconferencing" or "telepresence" is analogous to speaking about "buildings." While having some value, the grain of analysis is too course to foster an understanding of what goes on "inside." While we would never do so with rooms in a building, our current level of (im)maturity with electronic spaces has a tendency towards "one size fits all." This is something that we must break out of. The range of electronic meeting spaces, like the range of spaces in a well-designed building, must match the richness and range of meeting types. As a start to achieving this, we can move from the level of "buildings" to that of "rooms" and try to gain some insight into the nature of some of the different spaces that we want to share.

Person and Task Spaces

In what follows, we are going to consider presence in terms of two spaces: that of the person and that of the task. From even such a simple cut, several interesting insights emerge.

What we call shared *person space* in telepresence is the collective sense of copresence between/among group participants.[1] This includes things like their facial expressions, voice, gaze and body language.

By shared *task space* we mean a copresence in the domain of the task being undertaken. If we were doing a budget, for example, this might mean that each of us has the budget in front of us in the form of a shared speadsheet. Despite the distance, each of us can act upon it to make changes, annotations, or just to indicate cells that are the subject of discussion.

Sometimes the person and the task spaces are the same. One example would be in negotiations or counseling. Here a major part of the task involves "reading" the other person, such as to evaluate confidence or trust[2]. In other cases, such as our budget example, person and task spaces are more distinct. In what follows we shall see that different technologies lend themselves to differing degrees in supporting these two spaces. The point that we are leading to is that one of the most important attributes of a system is the *seamlessness* of their integration (Ishii & Miyake, 1991), and how well they match the needs of the activity to be supported.

Video Conferencing and Person Space: Some Examples

Traditional videoconferencing is a fairly good example of attempting to establish shared person space. While nobody would ever be fooled into thinking that the remote parties were actually in the same room, one can at least maintain an awareness of who is present and get a general reading of their body language, for example. The absence of checks like, "Are you still there Marilyn?" that are characteristic of telephone conferences is an example of what video contributes to maintaining a sense of personal presence.

---

[1] This is in contrast to 'personal space" which carries the connotation of privacy, not sharing. Thanks to Hiroshii Ishii for making this point and prompting me to change my terminology.

[2] This is sufficiently important that we might well refer to these as *trustification*, rather than *communication* technologies.

Fig. 1, illustrates one example of how video can be used to maintain a sense of personal presence in a four-way meeting.

Figure 1: *A videoconference involving four participants.*

The quality of the shared person space can be improved through design, however. Below, we give some examples that illustrate the breadth of the available design space. While many of these techniques are well known, few have found their way into mainstream videoconferencing. If establishing a strong sense of person space is important, then perhaps current practice needs to be reexamined.

For example, traditional videoconferencing is typically afflicted by an inability to establish eye contact among participants. This is because of the discrepancy of the position of the image of your eyes on my monitor and the position of your effective (surrogate) eyes, the camera, which is typically located on top of the monitor.

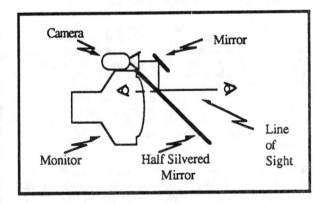

Figure 2: *The Reciprocal Video Tunnel. Through the combination of a mirror and half silvered mirror, there appears to be direct eye-to-eye contact. The mirrors effectively place the camera right in the line of sight. A close approximation to reciprocal eye contact can be obtained if both parties are using such an arrangement (from Buxton & Moran, 1990).*

By adopting teleprompter technology from the broadcast industry, this problem of eye contact can be largely overcome. The technique is shown in Fig. 2, as it was implemented by William Newman at Rank Xerox EuroPARC. Two mirrors, one of which is half silvered, are used to reflect what is in front of the screen up to the camera, which is mounted on top of the monitor.

The use of such teleprompter-like technology to obtain eye contact is not new. It was patented in 1947 (Rosenthal, 1947), has been studied by Acker & Levitt (1987) and used by Newman (as mentioned above), and more recently in a novel form in the *Clearboard* system (Ishii & Kobayashi, 1992). While it's use is not widespread in videoconferencing, users report greater comfort and naturalness in face-to-face meetings carried out using the technique.

Portrait painting provides the lead for another approach to augmenting the nature of personal presence using video. Video monitors have what is called a landscape *aspect ratio* (the ratio of the width to the height of a video monitor), because of their horizontal orientation. A very simple trick is to turn the camera and monitor at both ends of a conference onto their sides. The result, illustrated graphically in Fig. 3, is a *portrait style* aspect ratio.

Landscape   Portrait

Figure 3: *The effect of switching from Landscape to Portrait aspect rations in person-to-person video conferences. Note that, all other things being equal, in the portrait orientation, the hands and desk-top are visible, thereby adding to the ability to use a richer vocabulary of body language in the dialogue.*

When the image of a single person is to be transmitted, more of that person's body is visible without changing the size or resolution of the face. Consequently, in the example, the hands of the participant are visible in the portrait version, as would be the desk-top. The design affords access to a richer vocabulary of body language. As a prototype unit built by colleagues from the University of Ottawa has shown, this approach can be particularly effective where screen size is constrained, such as with small desk-top units, since a larger screen surface is available for a given width of package.

Next, let us consider the case of where we want to have a meeting involving the participation of more than two sites. At the University of Toronto, we have developed a system called *Hydra*, in which each remote participant is represented by a *video surrogate* (Sellen, Buxton & Arnott, 1992; Buxton & Sellen, 1991)[3]. The technique involves having a separate camera, monitor and speaker for each remote participant. As we have implemented it, these com-

---

[3] After the fact, we have become aware that this approach was first developed by Fields (1983).

ponents are housed in very compact desk-top units, as shown in Fig. 4.

Figure 4: *A user is seated in front of three Hydra units. In the photo, the Hydra units sit on the table in the positions that would otherwise be occupied by three remote participants. Each Hydra unit contains a video monitor, camera, and loudspeaker. A single microphone conveys audio to the remote participants (From Buxton & Sellen, 1991).*

Using this arrangement, the notion of person space is preserved. Because of this it is potentially much easier to maintain awareness of who is visually attending to whom, and to take advantage of conversational acts such as head turning. The idea behind the design is to take advantage of existing skills used in the work-a-day world. For example, in comparing this technique to other approaches to supporting multiparty conferences (Sellen, 1992), the *Hydra* units were unique in their ability to support parallel conversations, which naturally occurred in the face-to-face base-line condition.

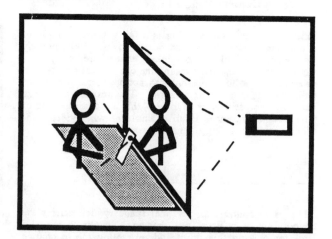

Figure 5: *Using a projected image to obtain a life-sized cross-table presence. Participants are captured using a miniature camera on the desk-top, so as to minimize obstruction of the projectted image. In our installation, we use one of the Hydra units (camera only), illustrated in Fig. 4.*

Finally, the effect of scale has been little explored as a factor that influences a sense of presence. There is a strong possibility that if the video images are life size, that social relationships, such as power, may be more balanced and natural. We have observed this informally where, with head-and-shoulder shots, a projected image is presented at human scale.

Recently, we have been experimenting with projection techniques to achieve the effect of cross-table conversations. In this case, a video projection screen is placed directly against the desk, as illustrated in Fig. 5. The remote participant is then rear projected life-size. The result is powerful. The sense of presence is so strong that there is a compulsion to refer to things on the desk, despite the fact it is not really visible to the remote participant. This leads us to the topic of shared task space: what might be on the desk to discuss in the first place?

Shared Task Space

It takes very limited power of observation to note that we are sharing more than ourselves in face-to-face group interactions. I may be showing you my new sneakers, video or latest budget. Alternatively, we may both be scribbling madly on the whiteboard trying to brainstorm about the design of a new piece of software.

As there is a range of shared "accessories" and how they are used, so must there be a range of technologies in our repertoire to support similar sharing in telepresence. Like shared person space, the design space is rich and largely unexplored. The examples which follow touch the surface to give a feel for some of the issues and alternatives.

The (technically) simplest way to share some things that form part of the task space is to use the same channels as the person space. In videoconferencing, for example, we might just make sure that the subject of interest is visible to the camera. This is illustrated in the video frame shown in Fig. 6, where the participants are discussing the design of a PC board.

Figure 6: *Using videoconferencing as a forum for discussing the design of a PC board. Both participants are shown one on either side of the frame.(from Shomi Corp., San Diego, CA.)*

In many cases, this approach is effective and appropriate - but not always. Consider the difficulty if both participants didn't have the circuit board. Without the physical object, how would the person on the left in Fig. 6 point to problem areas, or indicate where changes should be made? While there is a *telawareness*, for the task at hand, there is clearly is not a *telepresence*.

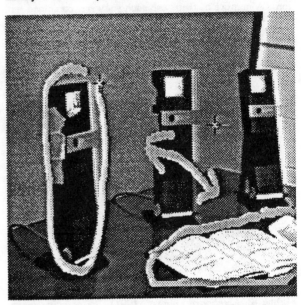

Figure 7: *Distributed shared drawing on video to enhance communications in a videoconference. Here the marking have to do with the space occupied by the Hydra units (seen in Fig. 4) and other articles on the desk.*

There are techniques that can be applied to this situation. One is a variation on a technique frequently used by television sportscasters: using a computer paint program to draw on, or *annotate* a video clip. The variation is to permit each participant in the conference to do so. This is illustrated in Fig. 7 which shows a frame from a conference where two participants are discussing the usage of the Hydra units (seen previously in Fig. 4)[4].

This technique is extended even further by Millgram and Drascic (1990). They use two video cameras mounted side-by-side (like a pair of binoculars) to capture the object under discussion. By alternating between the frames from each camera, they transmit a stereo image of the view. This is overlaid with computer-generated stereo-pair graphics (such as pointers and markers) which permits participants to work in 3D.

At a certain point, or in certain cases, however, the video channel is inappropriate for supporting shared task space. If, for example, the task was to debug some code, then it may well be more appropriate to have the software in ques-

---

[4] Note that the technique described differs from that found in many videoconferencing systems. In such systems, a still video image is transmitted, and one frequently cannot point at or mark-up the image. The technique described makes use of full-motion video, and may well (perhaps temporarily) use the same channel as the face-to-face communication.

tion available, rather than some video image. Here is a situation appropriate for complimenting video conferencing with shared synchronous computation.

Using dial-up telecommunications links, or computer networks, there are a number of ways that multiple users in remote sites can work together on a single computer application. A number of firms use such software, combined with teleconferencing, to provide remote product support.

Figure 8: *Liveboard (Weiser, 1991): by combining large-screen interactive displays with advanced networks and distributed software, shared "whiteboards" can be provided to support brainstorming sessions and other collaborative work from remote sites.*

Environments such as the X window system, coupled with large interactive displays, such as Xerox PARC's *Liveboard* (Weiser, 1991) are leading towards technologies to support distributed brainstorming sessions that preserve many of the properties of same-room sessions based around a whiteboard.

What we see from the examples is that we can use a range of techniques to support both shared and person spaces, and that being able to do so is important to supporting group activity across distances. What we haven't seen - to this point - is very much on how these two types of spaces work together, or relate.

Integrating Shared Task and Person Spaces: Two Examples

Shared ARK (Smith, O'Shea, O'Malley, Scanlon & Taylor, 1990) was one of the first studies to be undertaken at Rank Xerox's Cambridge EuroPARC (Buxton & Moran, 1990). It was an investigation of joint problem solving: subjects had to determine - through the use of a computer simulation - whether one stayed dryer by running or walking in the rain. Subjects were in separate rooms. They had a high fidelity voice link and a video link, implemented using the reciprocal video tunnel shown diagrammatically in Fig. 2.

The simulation was a distributed application presented to each user on a networked workstation, and took two people to operate. Within the task space, each user was "visible" by way of an identifiable cursor in the form of a hand. The

relationship of the workstation and video tunnel is shown in Fig. 9. Note that the position of the video tunnel is akin to having the remote participant sitting right beside you. Eye contact can be established by a simple turn of the head, and voice contact can be maintained throughout.

Figure 9: *Shared ARK (Smith, O'Shea, O'Malley, Scanlon & Taylor, 1990): The shared task space is on the computer display on the left. The shared person space is via the video tunnel on the left which is an implementation by William Newman of the design shown in Fig.2.*

As with working on a paper on your desk with someone by your side, you couldn't look at your collaborator's face and the computer screen at the same time. So one aspect of interest was determining when subjects visually attended to the computer display, and when they established eye contact through the video tunnel. A pattern did emerge in which eye contact was established especially when they were initially negotiating how to proceed and at the end when checking results. When actually running the simulation - which was a visually vigilant task - the video tunnel was seldom used except for short glances.

Remember, however, that the video tunnel was not the only vehicle for establishing shared person space. While attending to the computer display, each user's surrogate "hand" provided a (limited) visual personal presence through its pointing and gesturing capability. This was supplemented by the voice channel (and in a later study, Gaver, Smith & O'Shea, 1991, nonspeech audio). When visual attention was directed at the computer screen, the speech and nonspeech audio established a shared space which was more effective than the highest fidelity video display.

While what we have described is an over simplification of the experiment, it is adequate to establish that subjects moved between task and person spaces as they moved through different components of the overall task. What we take from this is the observation that some (many or most?) complex tasks require a range of channels and modalities of communication in order to be effectively supported. The reason that Shared ARK was so effective was because the methods and overhead in switching contexts (such as from computer screen to eye contact) had the same *overhead* and *action* as is used in analogous work-a-day tasks. That is, they were built on existing everyday skills that subjects already possessed, resulting in a natural behaviour. This is evident to anyone watching the experimental tapes.

Videodraw (Tang & Minneman, 1990) and its successor *Videowhiteboard* (Tang & Minneman, 1991), are excellent examples of a smooth integration of shared personal presence in a distributed task space. The systems were concerned with providing tools to support design and brainstorming activities, such as one would encounter around a drawing pad or whiteboard, respectively.

Videowhiteboard's main power came from its sensitivity to the need to support both drawing and the body language and gestures that typically accompany design and brainstorming at a whiteboard. Consequently, the system cleverly enables participants to be visible one another on the drawing surface, much like in the face-to-face situation. This is illustrated in Fig. 10, which is a frame from a video of a work session with the system.

Summary and Conclusions

Through the use of examples, we have argued that effective telepresence depends on quality sharing of both person and task space. Through this, the interaction breaks out of being like watching TV, into a direct engagement of the participants. They meet each other, not the system.

The integration of these two types of space are important. The smoothness of transitions between them is critical. Without this, the natural flow of interaction is disrupted. If the flow is to be natural, then the overhead and styles of interaction used in everyday face-to-face meetings should set the standards and design basis for telepresence technologies.

Figure 10: *Videowhiteboard (Tang & Minneman, 1991): an excellent example of effectively blending shared person and task space. The remote participant appears as a shadow on the far side of the drawing surface. The approach supports a rich vocabulary of physical gesture, including the ability to anticipate intended actions.*

What we hope the examples have illustrated is that, just as in traditional meeting spaces, one size doesn't fit all. There are a range of reasons that people meet and bonds that hold groups together. Our technologies must reflect these reasons and bonds, and their richness. Current technologies do not excel in this regard. What we hope to have shown is that this need not be so.

The design space, as afforded by available and emerging technologies, is far richer than is evident by popular practice. Hopefully the examples help show the potential and provide some keys to how it can be untapped.

Acknowledgements

This paper reflects the results of countless discussions with colleagues at Rank Xerox EuroPARC, the University of Toronto, and at Xerox PARC. This contribution is gratefully acknowledged.

Our work in this area has been supported by the Ontario Information Technology Research Centre (ITRC), the Natural Sciences and Engineering Research Council of Canada (NSERC), Xerox Palo Alto Research Center (PARC), Rank Xerox EuroPARC, Cambridge, England, The Arnott Design Group, Toronto, Apple Computer's Human-Interface Group, Object Technology International, Ottawa, Digital Equipment Corp., Maynard, MA., and IBM Canada"s Laboratory Centre for Advanced Studies, Toronto. This support is gratefully acknowledged.

References

Acker, S. & Levitt, S. (1987). Designing videoconference facilities for improved eye contact. *Journal of Broadcasting & Electronic Media,* 31(2), 181-191.

Buxton, W. & Moran, T. (1990). EuroPARC's Integrated Interactive Intermedia Facility (iiif): early experience, In S. Gibbs & A.A. Verrijn-Stuart (Eds.). *Multi-user interfaces and applications,* Proceedings of the IFIP WG 8.4 Conference on Multi-user Interfaces and Applications, Heraklion, Crete. Amsterdam: Elsevier Science Publishers B.V. (North-Holland), 11-34.

Buxton, W. & Sellen, A. (1991). Interfaces for multiparty video conferences. University of Toronto. Submitted for publication.

Fields, C.I. (1983). Virtual space teleconference system. *United States Patent 4,400,724,* August 23, 1983.

Gaver, W., Smith, R. & O'Shea, T. (1991). Effective sounds in complex systems: the ARKola simulation. *Proceedings of the 1991 Conference on Human Factors in Computer Systems, CHI '91,* 85-90.

Ishii, H. & Miyake, N. (1991). Toward an open shared workspace: computer and video fusion approach of TeamWorkStation. *Communications of the ACM,* 34(12), 37-50.

Ishii, H. & Kobayashi,M. (1992). Clearboard: a seamless medium for shared drawing and conversation with eye contact. To appear in the Proceedings *of CHI '92,* May 1992.

Kraut, R. & Egido, C. (1988). Patterns in contact and communication in scientific collaboration. *Proceedings of CSCW '88,* 1-12.

Millgram, P. & Drascic, D. (1990). A virtual stereographic pointer for a real three dimensional video world. In D. Diaper et al. (Eds), *Human-Computer Interaction - INTERACT '90.* Amsterdam: Elsevier Science Publishers B.V. (North-Holland), 695-700.

Rosenthal, A.H. (1947). Two-way television communication unit. *United States Patent 2,420,198,* May 6, 1947.

Sellen, A. (1992). Speech patterns in video-mediated conversations. To appear in *The Proceedings of CHI '92, May 1992*.

Sellen, A., Buxton, W. & Arnott, J. (1992). *Using spatial cues to improve desktop video conferencing*. 8 minute videotape. To appear in the *CHI '92 Video Proceedings*.

Smith, R., O'Shea, T., O''Malley, C., Scanlon, E. & Taylor, J. (1990). Preliminary experiments with a distributed multi-media, problem solving environment. Unpublished manuscript. Cambridge: Rank Xerox EuroPARC.

Tang, J. & Minneman, S. (1990). Videodraw: a video interface for collaborative drawing. *Proceedings of the 1990 Conference on Human Factors in Computer Systems, CHI '90*, 313-320.

Tang, J. & Minneman, S. (1991). Videowhiteboard: video shadows to support remote collaboration. *Proceedings of the 1991 Conference on Human Factors in Computer Systems, CHI '91*, 315-322.

Weiser, M. (1991). The computer for the 21st century. *Scientific American*, 265(3), 94-104.

Design of TeamWorkStation: A Realtime Shared Workspace fusing Desktops and Computer Screens

Hiroshi ISHII *   and Masaaki OHKUBO

NTT Human Interface Laboratories

"TeamWorkStation" (TWS) is a realtime groupware which provides "shareable desktop workspaces" for small groups. The design goal of TWS is to effectively eliminate the discontinuities normally present between individual and shared workspaces. TWS utilizes a video overlay technique which permits the fusion of computer screens and actual desktop images. This paper describes the new technique of realtime shared workspace design, prototype system architecture, and a typical applications.

1 Introduction

Groupware, computer and communication schemes designed to support work groups, is now receiving considerable attention because of the spread of LAN, ISDN and E-mail [Ishii 89]. Continuity with existing individual work environments is the key design issue for efficient groupware because users work in either individual or collaborative modes and frequently move back and forth. Therefore, for the design of realtime shared workspaces, the two existing individual workspaces, *computer* and *desktop*, must be integrated so that users can shuttle smoothly between their desktops, computers, and the virtual shared workspace.

There have been two types of approaches proposed to realize realtime shared workspaces for distributed groups:

(1) Shared-window-based groupware running on workstations, such as Cognoter [Foster 86], Dialogo [Lantz 86, 89]. They are often used with voice communication links such as the telephone to augment interactions.

(2) Video and voice communication-based virtual shared work spaces, such as Media Space [Stults 88], CRUISER [Root 88], VideoDraw [Tang 90].

The first is a computer-based approach to handle information stored in computers accessed by groups. The second is a tele-communication-based approach (like video-conferences) that can handle information outside of computers (faces, drawing surfaces, etc.). Both approaches suffer from a lack of flexibility in that information stored in the computer or information from the desktop are

dealt with separately and can never be fused. Users are still stuck with a rather large discontinuity between the computer and the desktop.

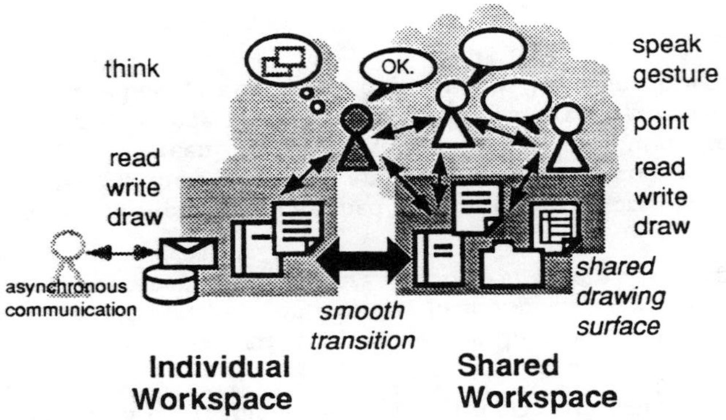

This paper introduces "TeamWorkStation" (TWS) which overcomes this problem of discontinuity by a video overlay technique that fuses computer screens and actual desktop images. TWS is one approach to the utilization of computer-mediated communication technology to provide "shareable desktop workspaces" for small groups. This paper introduces the new technique of realtime shared workspace design, prototype system architecture, and a typical applications.

Figure 1 Key Design Issues: Shared Drawing Surface and Smooth Transition

2 Key Design Concepts of TeamWorkStation

One important feature of face-to-face collaboration is the role of the "shared drawing surface" such as a white board. Stults, Bly and Tang pointed out that the shared drawing surface plays a very crucial role not only to store information and convey ideas, but also to develop ideas and mediate interaction, especially in design sessions [Stults 88, Bly 88, Tang 88, 90]. Therefore, the focus of TWS design is on the shared workspace that every member can see, point to and draw on simultaneously.

At the same time, users must be able to shuttle easily between the shared workspace and their individual workspace (i.e. computer and desktop) with only slight mental stress. Stefik has pointed out that "seamlessness" between these two spaces is a crucial requirement for the next generation collaboration technology [Foster 88]. Figure 1 illustrates these two design requirements: a shared drawing surface and a smooth transition between individual and shared workspaces.

We devised a key TWS design idea, *"overlay of individual workspace images"* in order to satisfy these two requirements. The "overlay" function created with a live-video image synthesis technique allows users to combine individual workspaces, and to point to and draw on the overlaid images "simultaneously".

TWS also allows users to keep using their favorite tools and environment even in the shared workspace and enables smooth transitions. The term "individual workspace" includes not only the virtual work environment realized in a

---

* 1-2356 Take Yokosuka-Shi 238-03 Japan
  E-mail: ishii%ntthif.ntt.jp@relay.cs.net

Multi-User Interfaces and Applications
S. Gibbs and A.A. Verrijn-Stuart (Editors)
Elsevier Science Publishers B.V. (North-Holland)
© IFIP, 1990

Fig. 3   CCD camera mounted on a desk lamp

personal computer, but also the physical work environment such as the desktop. TWS does not restrict the targets to be overlaid. The "overlay" function is flexible in that it can also be applied to the desktop images captured by a CCD camera mounted on a desk lamp. Therefore, collaborators can keep using their favorite tools such as papers, pens, pencils as well as word processors.

"Overlay" is a very simple and intuitive concept but powerful because it has much more flexibility than the existing task-specific groupware approaches. Section 4 compares the TWS approach with other existing realtime shared workspace design approaches.

3 Implementation of TeamWorkStation

TWS provides users with the following major components integrated on a desktop workstation that supports multiple displays:
(1) a shareable computer screen for concurrent pointing, writing and drawing (shared workspace), and
(2) live-video and audio communication links for face-to-face conversation.

Figure 2 shows an example of the standard appearance of a TWS.

The present prototype is based on Macintosh® computers. The workspace displays, individual and shared, are contiguous in video memory. Therefore, by just moving the window of any application program from the individual to the shared display, users can display the application's window for remote collaboration. Face-to-face conversations use an auto-focus video camera to capture face images, wireless microphone and headphone, and a small (4") liquid crystal display with speaker. Face images can also be displayed also in windows on the shared screen as shown in Fig. 2.

A CCD camera is provided to capture the actual desktop image and hand actions. Because the camera is cylindrical, correct orientation was difficult to achieve and images were often skewed. We solved this problem by mounting the camera on a cantilevered desk lamp that had a rectangular head and a flexible arm as shown in Fig. 3. The camera is mounted so that when the head parallels the paper, the image is accurately aligned.

The prototype system architecture is illustrated in Fig. 4. In order to connect distributed workstations, the current prototype system uses five different communication networks:
(1) RGB video network,
(2) NTSC video network,
(3) Voice network,
(4) Input device network, and
(5) Data network (LAN).
Networks (1), (2), (3) and (4) were newly developed and added to an existing Macintosh Local Area Network (5).

The RGB (1) and NTSC (2) video networks gather and distribute the computer screen images, desk images, and face images. These networks are based on a computer-controllable video switching system.

Overlay of video images is done by the "video composite equipment" attached to the NTSC video network and the "desktop video card" installed in each workstation. Overlaid images are redistributed to the shared screens or liquid crystal displays via the video networks. Tiling of images is also possible by using the video composite equipment. Tiling is used mainly for displaying more than two faces on one liquid crystal display. Face and desk images are captured by auto-focus video cameras and CCD cameras respectively. Face images can be displayed on either shareable screens or liquid crystal displays via the video networks.

Hands free voice communication is realized by the voice network (3) and the use of wireless microphones and wireless headphones. We use stereo sound because voice orientation can help users to identify speakers. Existing telephones can be used as an alternative.

The input device network (4) is designed to allow collaborators to share one computer by connecting their keyboards and mice to the computer whose screen is shared in the "tele-screen" mode. We call this mode "computer-sharing". The "computer-sharing" mode is a variation of the "shared hardware approach" taken by "Capture Lab" [Mantei 1988, Halonen 89]. The same function has been

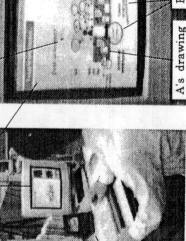

Individual Screen   Shareable Screen   A's mouse cursor   B's mouse cursor

A's drawing   B's comment

Liquid Crystal Display

(1) Appearance of TWS   (2) Shared Screen of TWS

Fig. 2   Standard Appearance of TeamWorkStation

implemented in software such as Timbuktu® [Farallon 88]. However, in the software solution, the computer response delay is intolerable.

In this "computer-sharing" mode, simple floor control is needed to pass the input control among collaborators. The TWS design policy provides no special software or hardware embedded protocol for floor control, but relies on the face-to-face communication links among collaborators. Floor control in TWS depends on informal social protocol among collaborators.

The data network (5) is used for remote control of video and voice switches, in addition to ordinary file and printer sharing. The switch control program was written in HyperCard®. Figure 5 shows an example of the user interface for NTSC video network switching.

TWS currently utilizes five different networks as shown in Fig. 4. In the future, we will integrate these into a multimedia LAN and B-ISDN that are being developed by NTT.

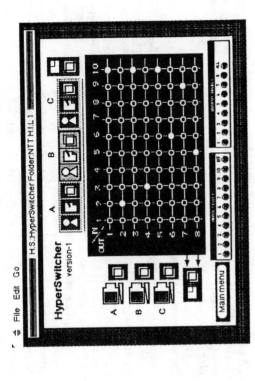

Fig. 5 An Example of Video Switch Control Program User Interface

Figure 6 shows three levels of collaboration and six modes of TWS usage. "Tele-screen" and "tele-desk" modes allow users to share non-overlaid remote work-space images. In "tele-desk", "desk-overlay" and "screen and desk-overlay" modes, the images of member's documents and pointing/drawing activity on desktop can be shared. Since users can use pencil and paper for writing, drawing and pointing, it is very close to the actual "shared drawing surface" common in face-to-face meetings.

An important feature of TWS is that users can choose the most suitable mode from these six modes and move from one mode to another according to task contents and roles played by the coworkers.

For example, suppose user A starts to explain his plan by showing a diagram to user B using the "tele-screen" mode. (If his diagram was written or printed on paper, the "tele-desk" mode would be used instead of "tele-screen" mode.) If B wants to "point" to a part of the diagram to ask a question, they can move to the "screen-overlay" or "screen and desk-overlay" mode and user B can point to the part of A's diagram by B's own pointer (mouse or pencil). If B felt it was necessary to directly change the part of the diagram and if A agreed, they could move to the "computer sharing" mode.

Use of Heterogeneous Computers

Although the TWS prototype uses Macintosh workstations, heterogeneous computers can be also used since overlaying is done at a standard video signal level (NTSC or RGB). Moreover, "screen-overlay" and "tele-screen" functions have been successfully implemented between an NEC PC-9800 series computer running MS-DOS and Macintosh computers. However, "computer-sharing" was not possible because of inconsistency of keyboard and mouse signals.

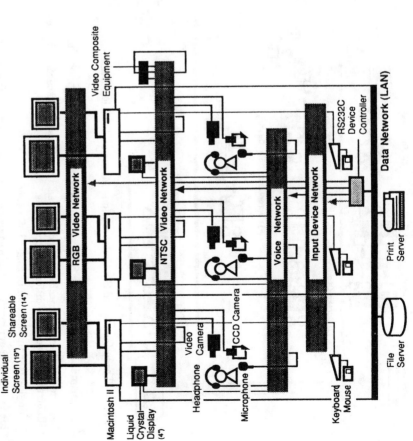

Fig. 4 TWS Prototype System Architecture

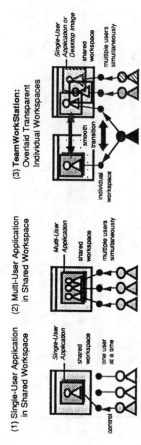

(1) Single-User Application in Shared Workspace

(2) Multi-User Application in Shared Workspace

(3) TeamWorkStation: Overlaid Transparent Individual Workspaces

Figure 7　Three Approaches for Realtime Shared Workspace Design

applications and response delays created to keep the consistency of collaborators' shared windows can be also problems.

(3) Overlay of Individual Workspace Images

We take a different design approach, that is, the "overlay" of transparent individual workspace images. Instead of designing task and window-system specific groupware, we have designed and implemented a more general environment for remote collaboration based on the "overlay" concept. This approach allows multiple users to use the pointing cursors and different (or identical) existing single-user applications simultaneously in a shared workspace.

The "overlay" idea was originally demonstrated by Tang and Minneman in VideoDraw [Tang90]. VideoDraw showed a new way to create shared workspaces by overlaying video images of individual drawing surfaces (desktops). However, VideoDraw restricted the targets to be overlaid to the images of transparent sheet on TV monitor. TWS overcomes this restriction by integrating the images of desktops (printed materials, handwriting on paper, etc.) and computer screens.

The drawback of this overlay approach is that it imposes a "strict WYSIWIG" principle [Stefik 86] on the shared screen. Another drawback is the quality of overlaid video images is not as sharp as is normally expected from a computer display.

5　Experimental Use of TeamWorkStation

We started the design and implementation of TWS in May 1989. Since July 1989, TWS has been experimentally used by the authors for daily work including refining the design of TWS itself, writing papers, and daily communication.

The major TWS usage has been discussion about the system configuration and the outline of issues to be investigated. These tasks are the so-called "upstream" tasks for idea development. The regular tools in our discussion were a draw-editor, an outline editor, and pencil and paper for handwriting. Comments were exchanged mainly by voice with pointing gestures in the overlay mode. Counter ideas were presented with the same type of editors (by screen-overlay mode) or papers (by "screen and desk-overlay" mode).

However, in goal (output) oriented collaborations, we mainly used the "computer sharing" mode to complete the goal such as producing a camera-ready

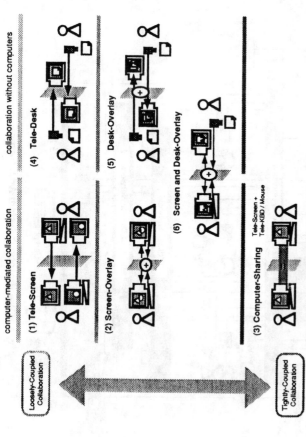

computer-mediated collaboration

collaboration without computers

Loosely-Coupled Collaboration

Tightly-Coupled Collaboration

(1) Tele-Screen

(2) Screen-Overlay

(3) Computer-Sharing

(4) Tele-Desk

(5) Desk-Overlay

(6) Screen and Desk-Overlay

Tele-Screen + Tele-KBD / Mouse

Fig. 6　Three Levels and Six Collaborations Modes in TWS Environment

4　Comparison with Other Shared Workspace Design Approaches

There are three basic approaches to building a realtime shared workspace. Figure 7 illustrates these three different approaches.

(1) Single-User Application in Shared Window

This is a simple approach that allows users to execute single-user applications in a shared window or screen (e.g. DPE [Suzuki 86], Dialogo [Lantz 86, 89]). The advantage of this approach is that there is no need to modify existing single-user application programs for group-use. Therefore, it is not necessary to learn the usage of a new multi-user application. However, usually only one user can have a control of the application program at a time, and a floor control mechanism is needed.

(2) Multi-User Application in Shared Window

Another approach is to implement new multi-user application programs (groupware) for particular tasks (e.g. co-authoring) using a shared window function (e.g. Cognoter [Foster 86]). In this type of system, multiple users can control the editing cursors independently, and an access control mechanism for smaller grain size objects (e.g. words on a screen) is provided. Each user can also have a personalized view if the program supports this function.

The drawback of this approach is the significant programming effort needed to write the new multi-user application. Discontinuities with existing single user

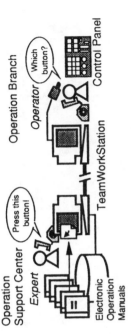

(1) System configuration for remote consultation

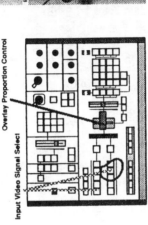

(2) A diagram in an operation manual

(3) Overlaid diagram on actual control panel image

Fig. 8 Remote Consultation Application in Network Operation

paper, or view graphs for presentation.

Through the experimental use of TWS, we realized that the flexibility of selection and movement among the various collaboration modes is very important. Since the pattern of collaboration changes dynamically according to the work content and roles played by group members, TWS's flexibility in shuttling between the six modes and between various application programs is very effective in supporting the dynamic collaboration process.

At the moment, however, switching among six modes is done through a relatively primitive software switch (e.g. Fig. 5) designed for each network. These switches should be integrated and abstracted to make them easy-to-use and enable smoother transitions among the various modes.

While using TWS, we noted that many common work practices such as printing, copying, and distributing documents are unnecessary and time-wasting. In particular, the demand that all information be "hard-copied" and "distributed" is extremely inefficient. Information from either printed materials, handwritten memos, or computer files can be effectively shared with co-workers through TWS.

We also found that the face-to-face conversation link increases system flexibility. The voice channel played an important role in the informal control of group interaction, especially for mouse and keyboard usage in the "computer-sharing" mode. This implies software/hardware embedded protocols are not a necessity if group members share and follow common informal rules.

Overlay problems found in the current implementation of TWS are as follows.

- The quality of overlaid video images is not sharp or stable enough to support long term viewing.
- Identifying the owners of objects (such as cursor, draw object, window, icon, actual paper) on a overlaid screen is difficult especially when more than three screens are overlaid.
- Since overlaid screen images are completely independent from each other, scrolling of a document in one screen breaks the spatial relationships with the marks made on other screens.

Remote Consultation Application

Among the six modes, the most interesting and unique usage of TWS is the "screen and desk-overlay" mode. We often overlaid the actual paper on the word processor or draw editor window for pointing and commenting by the pencil or finger. However, it is not necessary to restrict the images to just the papers on the desktop.

We used this mode in "remote consultation for complex equipment operation" to demonstrate the power gained by fusing the computer world to the rest of the world. Figure 8 shows an example of system configuration and shared screen image in a remote consulting demonstration.

The scenario runs like this:
After receiving a request for support from an operator at a remote operation branch, an expert checks the status of the control panel by looking at the video image sent from the branch. Then, after retrieving the necessary information to fix the problem from an operation manual database, the expert advises the

remote operator with the retrieved diagram . At this stage, to explain what the operator should do, the expert can overlay the diagram on the video image of the control panel as shown in Fig. 8 (3).

We expect that this kind of video-based communication can significantly augment the collaboration and sharing of knowledge between experts and operators. It is far superior to ordinary telephone communication. The fusion of computer screens and actual live video images in combination with tele-communication is expected to enhance the quality and efficiency of remote consulting and training.

6 Conclusion

TWS is a new networking technique that creates a flexible shared workspace by integrating two kinds of individual workspaces: *computers* and *desktop*. Its key concept is the "overlay" of individual shared workspace images. Because each coworker can continue to use his/her favorite application programs or tools on the desktop, there is only minor cognitive discontinuity between the individual and shared workspaces.

The addition of a simple CCD camera at each desktop significantly enhances the effectiveness of cooperative working. Realtime information such as sketches and hand-written comments can be shared between coworkers as well as information contained in printed materials. The fusion of individual workspace in computers with actual desktops leads to many synergistic effects.

Although TWS has some drawbacks such as the complexity of shared displays, the advantages outweigh them because of its simplicity, generality, and a variety of possible applications such as remote consulting or education. We expect that progress in video and HDTV technology will extend the usefulness of the TWS design approach.

TWS is going to be tested with a larger variety of tasks and users to investigate the nature of collaboration and to enhance computer support based on overlay concepts. An expanded TWS system will be implemented on multimedia LAN and B-ISDN.

The current TWS uses the video overlay technique to support remote collaboration. However, the overlay concept can be also applied to support face-to-face collaboration using mutiple projectors. We are now designing this face-to-face version of TWS using "optical overlays" on a wall instead of distributed screens.

Acknowledgements

We would like to thank Dr. John C. Tang, Dr. Scott L. Minneman and Dr. Sara A. Bly at Xerox PARC, their research into "drawing surface" was a stimulus for this work. We would also like to thank Dr. Mark Stefik at Xerox PARC, who pointed out the importance of "seamlessness" in groupware design. Thanks are also due to Prof. Mantei at University of Toronto, whose study on Capture Lab yielded many valuable insights on group interaction and computer support.

We would also like to thank Mr. Takaya Endo, Mr. Isao Kawashima, and Dr. Yukio Tokunaga of NTT Human Interface Laboratories for their encouragement.

References

[Bly 88]   Sara A. Bly, "A Use of Drawing Surfaces in Different Collaborative Settings," Conference on Computer-Supported Cooperative Work (CSCW 88), Portland, Oregon, 1988, pp.250-256.

[Farallon 88]   Farallon Computing Inc., "Timbuktu User's Guide," 1988

[Foster 86]   Gregg Foster and Mark Stefik, "Cognoter, Theory and Practice of a Colab-orative Tool," Conference on Computer-Supported Cooperative Work '86, Austin, Texas, 1986, pp.7-15.

[Foster 88]   Gregg Foster and Deborah Tatar, "Experiments in Computer Support for Teamwork --- Colab (Video)," Xerox PARC, 1988

[Halonen 89]   David Halonen, Marjorie Horton, Robert Kass and Paul Scott, "Shared Hardware: A Novel Technology for Computer Support of Face to Face Meetings," Groupware Technology Workshop, Palo Alto, California, 1989

[Ishii 89]   Hiroshi Ishii, "Cooperative Work Models and Groupware," FRIEND 21 International Symposium on Next Generation Human Interface Technologies, Tokyo, 1989

[Lantz 86]   Keith A. Lantz, "An Experiment in Integrated Multimedia Conferencing," Conference on Computer-Supported Cooperative Work '86, Austin, 1986, pp.267-275

[Lantz 89]   Keith A. Lantz, Chris Lauwers, Barry Arons, Carl Binding, Pehong Chen, Jim Donahue, Thomas A. Joseph, Richard Koo, Allyn Romanow, Chris Schmandt and Wayne Yamamoto, "Collaboration Technology Research at Olivetti Research Center," Gropware Technology Workshop, Palo Alto, 1989

[Mantei 88]   Marilyn Mantei, "Capturing the Capture Concepts: A Case Study in the Design of Computer-Supported Meeting Environments," Conference on Computer-Supported Cooperative Work '88, Portland, Oregon, 1988, pp.257-270

[Root 88]   Robert W. Root, "Design of a Multi-Media Vehicle for Social Browsing," Conference on Computer-Supported Cooperative Work '88, Portland, 1988, pp.25-38

[Stefik 86]   M. Stefik, D. G. Bobrow, S. Lanning, D. Tatar, and G. Foster, "WYSIWIS Revised: Early Experiences with Multi-user Interfaces," Conference on Computer-Supported Cooperative Work '86, Austin, Texas 1986, pp.276-290.

[Stults 88]   R. Stults, "Experimental Uses of Video to Support Design Activities," Xerox Palo Alto Research Center, 1988.

[Suzuki 86]   Tatsuo Suzuki, Hideo Taniguchi and Hisayasu Takada, "A Realtimr Electronic Conferencing System based on Distributed UNIX," USENIX Conference, 1986, pp.189-199

[Tang 88]   John C. Tang and Larry J. Leifer, "A Framework for Understanding the Workspace Activity of Design Teams," Conference on Computer-Supported Cooperative Work '88, Portland, 1988, pp.244-249

[Tang 90]   John C. Tang and Scott L. Minneman, "VideoDraw: A Video Interface for Collaborative Drawing," CHI '90, Seattle, 1990, pp.313-320

ClearBoard: A Seamless Medium for Shared Drawing and Conversation with Eye Contact

Hiroshi Ishii and *Minoru Kobayashi*

NTT Human Interface Laboratories
1-2356 Take, Yokosuka-Shi, Kanagawa, 238-03 Japan
Tel: +81-468-59-3522, Fax: +81-468-59-2332
E-mail: ishii@ntthif.ntt.jp, minoru@ntthcs.ntt.jp

ABSTRACT

This paper introduces a novel shared drawing medium called ClearBoard. It realizes (1) a seamless shared drawing space and (2) eye contact to support realtime and remote collaboration by two users. We devised the key metaphor: "talking *through* and drawing *on* a transparent glass window" to design ClearBoard. A prototype of ClearBoard is implemented based on the "Drafter-Mirror" architecture. This paper first reviews previous work on shared drawing support to clarify the design goals. We then examine three metaphors that fulfill these goals. The design requirements and the two possible system architectures of ClearBoard are described. Finally, some findings gained through the experimental use of the prototype, including the feature of "gaze awareness", are discussed.

INTRODUCTION

A whiteboard (or blackboard) is probably the most typical shared workspace in an ordinary face-to-face meeting. Fig. 1 shows a snapshot of a whiteboard being used in a design session. Participants are concurrently drawing on and pointing to the whiteboard, while speaking and gesturing.

In a design session, the participants' focus can change dynamically. When we discuss concrete system architectures, we intensively use a whiteboard as a shared drawing space by drawing diagrams, marks, and pointing to them. The whiteboard serves as an explicit group memory that each participant can see, point to, and draw on simultaneously [9]. On the other hand, when we discuss abstract concepts or design philosophy, we often concentrate on the partner's face while talking. In face-to-face conversations, mutual gaze (eye-contact), facial expressions and gestures provide a variety of non-verbal cues that are essential in human-human communication [2]. Through the use of TeamWorkStation in design sessions [6], we

Fig. 1 A Whiteboard used in a Design Session

realized that a smooth transition between face-to-face conversations and shared drawing activities is essential in supporting a dynamic collaborative process.

When we design a medium to support these activities, it is not sufficient to simulate the whiteboard function only, the simple video phone function only, or even both functions. It is necessary to integrate a virtual whiteboard with face-to-face communication channels *seamlessly* so that users can switch their focus smoothly from one to another according to the task contents [3].

In a face-to-face meeting, the room is perceived as a *contiguous* space: there are no physical *seams* between the whiteboard and the participants. By simply moving their eyes or heads, participants can look at both other participants and the whiteboard. However, in existing desktop tele-conference systems with shared drawing functions, the participants' images and shared drawing images are usually dealt with separately. These images are displayed in different windows on a screen, or in different screens. Therefore, there are *seams* between the images of participants and the shared drawing images. The virtual meeting space was segregated into several spatially separated windows or displays.

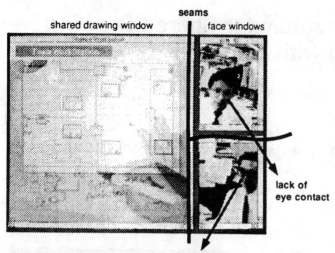

shared drawing window   seams   face windows

lack of
eye contact

Fig. 2   Seam and Eye-Contact Problems in
TeamWorkStation

Lack of *eye contact* has been another problem of existing
desktop video conference systems. People feel it difficult to
communicate when they cannot tell if the partner is looking at
him or her. Eye contact plays an important role in face-to-face
conversations because "eyes are as eloquent as the tongue."
Fig. 2 illustrates these two problems: seams between windows
and the lack of eye-contact in a shared screen of TeamWork-
Station [8].

In order to solve these problems, this paper presents a novel
shared drawing medium, ClearBoard. ClearBoard realizes
both (1) seamless shared workspace and (2) eye contact.
ClearBoard is designed to support realtime and remote collaboration by two users. Therefore, it can be called a
"pairware" instead of "groupware" [11].

This paper first reviews previous work on shared drawing
support and clarifies the goals of this research. We then
examine three metaphors that fulfill these goals. The design
requirements and system architecture of ClearBoard prototype are described. Finally, some findings gained through the
experimental use of the prototype are discussed.

PREVIOUS WORK

As shown in Fig. 3, there have been several systems proposed
to support face-to-face conversations and shared drawing
activities. However, there has been no system that fulfills both
of the following two requirements: (1) a contiguous space that
includes both shared drawings and user image, and (2) eye
contact.

Video Tunnel

Video Tunnel [2] is a kind of video phone developed in
EuroPARC for a computer-controlled video network. It
supports eye-contact between two speakers using the well-
known half mirror technique.

seamlessness: contiguity of drawing and user images
eye-contact
facial expression
shared drawing

	shared drawing	facial expression	eye-contact	seamlessness		
Video Tunnel		O	O		EuroPARC [2]	only for face-to-face conversation
VideoWindow		O			Bellcore [4]	
VideoDraw	O*1	O		*5	Xerox PARC [13]	for shared drawing and face-to-face conversation
Commune	O*2	O		*5	Xerox PARC [1, 10]	
VideoWhiteboard	O*1	*4		△*6	Xerox PARC [14]	
TeamWorkStation	O*3	O		*7	NTT HI Labs [6, 8]	
ClearFace on TWS	O*3	O		*8	NTT HI Labs [7]	
ClearBoard-1	O*1	O	O	O	NTT HI Labs	

*1 direct drawing with whiteboard marker
*2 direct drawing with digitizer
*3 indirect drawing with pen and computer tools
*4 shadow image of user
*5 different screens
*6 shadow and drawing are contiguous.
*7 different windows
*8 translucent face windows over drawing window

Fig. 3 Previous Work and ClearBoard-1

(a) in front of white board (b) over a table (c) through a glass window

Fig. 4 Three Metaphors of Seamless Space for Shared Drawing and Face-to-Face Conversation

VideoWindow

VideoWindow, developed in Bellcore, is a wall-size screen that connects remote rooms to support informal face-to-face communications [4].
Neither Video Tunnel nor VideoWindow support shared drawing activities.

VideoDraw

VideoDraw [13], developed in Xerox PARC, is a pioneering work that supports shared drawing activity using video. It allows a user to draw with a whiteboard marker directly on a transparent sheet attached to the video screen that shows the drawing surface image of the partner. For face-to-face conversations, VideoDraw provides users with another screen.

Commune

Commune [1, 10] is a shared drawing tool based on a digitizer and multi-user paint editor developed in Xerox PARC. It is used with another screen for face-to-face conversation as VideoDraw.

VideoWhiteboard

VideoWhiteboard [14] developed in Xerox PARC, utilizes the shadow of users to convey the gestures of collaborators. Since the marks on the wall-size screen and the shadow of the user are captured by a single camera, it provides remote collaborators with a virtual space in which the marks and the shadow of drawing gestures are contiguous. However, because only shadow images are sent, no facial expression is conveyed.

TeamWorkStation

TeamWorkStation [6, 8] developed by the authors at NTT enables the simultaneous use of heterogeneous tools such as computer tools, printed materials, handwriting and hand gestures in a shared drawing space. Facial images are displayed in different windows on the same display.

ClearFace on TeamWorkStation

ClearFace [7] developed by the authors lays translucent facial images over shared drawing images to utilize the limited screen space more effectively. However, as with TeamWorkStation, the facial images are not contiguous with the drawing space.

THREE METAPHORS FOR SEAMLESS SPACE

In order to design groupware that achieves the two goals of (1) contiguous (seamless) space, and (2) eye contact, we first investigated the following familiar metaphors, and clarified their problems.

(a) talking in front of a whiteboard, and

(b) talking over a table.

(a) is an exact whiteboard metaphor. The advantage of this metaphor is that all the participants can share the common board orientation. However, because two participants share the same space in front of the whiteboard, it is hard to implement a mechanism that can coordinate the use of this shared space. The only way we found of realizing this metaphor is to employ "virtual reality" technology. However, we do not think it is a good idea to force users to wear awkward head-mount displays and special gloves and a suit just to share some drawings. This solution lets users dive into a computer-generated virtual world which definitely increases cognitive loads.

(b) is another quite familiar metaphor, sitting on opposite sides of a table and talking over the table. This metaphor is quite suitable for face-to-face communication because two participants can easily see each other's face. However, the orientation of a drawing becomes upside-down for one of the parties[1]. If we could develop an "L-shaped display", this metaphor could be realized to some extent. However, it is hard to give users a natural sense of sharing the same space over the table.

In order to overcome the problems in metaphors (a) and (b) while utilizing their advantages, we devised the new metaphor (c) as the foundation of our groupware design in September 1990.

(c) talking *through* and drawing *on a transparent glass window*[2].

---

1 VideoDraw [11] and Commune [1, 8] took the human interface close to this metaphor letting users share a common orientation. However, physical seams existed between the separate screens, one for the partner's facial image and the other for shared drawings.

2 VideoWindow [3] and VideoWhiteboard [12] are close to this metaphor. However, as described in Fig. 3, both fail to achieve the two goals of seamless integration and eye contact.

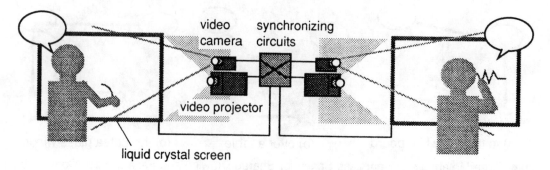

Fig. 5   Liquid Crystal Screen Architecture

Metaphor (c) does not produce any confusion or conflict about shared space use, since each participant's space is isolated from the other partner's space by a transparent glass window. This metaphor has the following advantages. First, as with the table metaphor (b), participants can see the partner's face easily. Second, since the partner's face and drawings are closely located on the board, switching the focus between the drawing and the partner's face requires less eye movements than (a) or (b).

One problem of this metaphor is that participants can not share the common orientation of "right" and "left" of the drawing space. However, this problem can be easily solved in implementing the prototype by mirror-reversing the video image.

We chose this metaphor (c) as the base for pairware design because of its simplicity and the advantages described above.

We coined the name "ClearBoard" for the pairware based on this metaphor (c). There can be several technical approaches to implement this ClearBoard concept. In the following section, we discuss two possible implementations of Clear-Board.

PROTOTYPE IMPLEMENTATION

Design Requirements

In order to implement a ClearBoard prototype which supports remote collaboration, we identified the following three design requirements.

(1) direct drawing on the display screen surface must be supported[3],

(2) the video image of a user must be taken through (behind) the screen surface (to achieve eye contact), and

(3) common orientation of the drawing space, not only "top" and "bottom" but also "right" and "left", must be shared at both sites.

The video tunnel architecture based on half-mirrors satisfies requirement (2). However, the combination of a half-silvered

---

3 Although we had taken the indirect drawing approach in TeamWorkStation [6, 8] to incorporate variety media such as printed materials into shared drawing space, in the design of ClearBoard, we took the direct drawing method to realize the metaphor of glass window illustrated in Fig. 4 (c).

mirror and a CRT display produces the problem of parallax, and does not satisfy requirement (1).

Requirement (3) is important to provide both users with a common orientation of the drawing space. Especially for words, the partner must be able to read the text in its correct orientation. The strict implementation of the transparent glass metaphor does not allow this.

In order to realize a ClearBoard prototype that satisfies all these requirements, we investigated two alternative system architectures based on different techniques.

Liquid Crystal Screen Architecture

In order to take a frontal image of a user who is drawing on a screen, it is necessary to take his or her image through the screen by a video camera placed behind the screen. A liquid crystal screen, which can be rapidly switched between the transparent and light scattering state by the application of a suitable control voltage, can be a key device to fulfill this requirement. Fig. 5 illustrates the system architecture of ClearBoard based on this technique.

Fig. 6 illustrates how this architecture works; the liquid crystal screen is switched between the two states, (1) light scattering

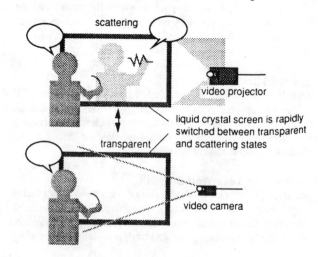

Fig. 6 Light scattering and Transparent States of
Liquid Crystal Screen

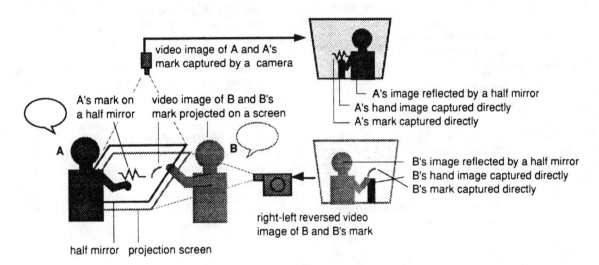

directly drawing on the mirror with a whiteboard marker

half mirror
polarizing film
projection screen

video network

projector

projector

Fig. 7 "Drafter-Mirror" Architecture of ClearBoard Prototype

video image of A and A's mark captured by a camera

A's mark on a half mirror

video image of B and B's mark projected on a screen

A's image reflected by a half mirror
A's hand image captured directly
A's mark captured directly

A

B

B's image reflected by a half mirror
B's hand image captured directly
B's mark captured directly

half mirror   projection screen

right-left reversed video image of B and B's mark

Fig. 8 How Drafter-Mirror Architecture Works

and (2) transparent. In state (1), the screen works as a rear projection screen on which the image of the partner and his or her drawing is displayed. In state (2), the user's image is captured by a video camera located behind the transparent screen. The timing of image capture and image display is synchronized to the switching of liquid crystal display states.

This technique was demonstrated by Shinichi Shiwa [12] at NTT in order to enable eye contact without any shared drawing support consideration. This architecture can be utilized to implement the ClearBoard concept if users are allowed to draw directly on the screen.

The transition frequency of the liquid crystal screen depends on its size. High frequencies, which decrease the physical load on user's eyes, are hard to achieve with large screens. Flickering images can be a serious disadvantage. The high cost of the liquid crystal screen is another drawback. Because of these shortcomings, we devised the next solution, which we refer to as "Drafter-Mirror architecture".

"Drafter-Mirror" Architecture

In order to implement the ClearBoard concept with a *flickerless* and simpler technology, we devised the new system architecture illustrated in Fig. 7. We call it "Drafter-Mirror" because it looks like a drafter (a desk for architectural drawing) and it uses a half-mirror technique to enable eye-contact.

Each Drafter-Mirror terminal is equipped with a tilted screen, a video projector and a video camera. The screen is angled back at about 45 degrees and is composed of a projection screen, a polarizing film and a half-silvered mirror. Video feedback between the two cameras and screen pairs is prevented by a polarizing filter on each camera lens and a nearly orthogonal polarized filter that covers the surface of each screen. Users can write and draw on the surface of the screen using color paint markers. Water-based fluorescent (luminous) paint markers were used in our experiment because these colors are easy to distinguish from the background images including the user and the user's background. Markers can be erased with a cloth.

Fig. 8 illustrates how this Drafter-Mirror architecture works.

The video camera located above the screen captures the drawings and the image of the user reflected by the half-mirror as a continuous video image. This image is sent to the other terminal through a video network, and projected onto the partner's screen from the rear. The partner can draw directly on this transmitted video image. Because of this architecture, the video camera captures double hand images, one being the direct image, and the other being the image reflected by the half-mirror. The image of the user and his or her drawings is projected on the partner's screen so that both users can shared common orientation of the drawing space.

The drawing image captured by the camera is trapezoidally distorted due to perspective because the screen is at an angle. In order to support shared drawing on the screen, the drawing image must be recreated with the original shape and size on the partner's screen. In the current implementation, the distortion is offset by the opposite distortion caused by projecting the image onto the tilted screen. In order to give a suitable distortion rate, the camera and the projector should be symmetrically arranged with respect to the screen.

EXPERIMENTAL USE OF CLEARBOARD-1

We implemented the prototype of a Drafter-Mirror system in November 1990. (We call this prototype "ClearBoard-1".) Since then we have used this prototype in experimental sessions such as icon design, direction of the routes in a map, and discussions about diagrams for this paper. We informally observed the use of ClearBoard-1 by ourselves and our colleagues.
Fig. 9 shows the appearance of the Drafter-Mirror prototype in one of the experimental sessions.

We realized that users can easily achieve eye-contact when needed. This is because the partner's face and drawings are closely located on the board. Easy eye contact even in drawing-intensive activities increased the feeling of intimacy.

We observed that users often worked collaboratively to coordinate the limited shared drawing space. For example, when a user started drawing over some part of the partner's drawing, the partner often voluntarily erased his or her drawing from the screen.

Unlike ClearFace [7], users do not hesitate to draw over the image of the partner's face. In ClearFace, the partner's image was mixed with the drawing image behind it, and users found it difficult to draw over the facial image. In ClearBoard, we assume that users recognize the partner *behind* the drawing on the glass board, and thus feel no difficulty drawing on the board *in front of* the partner. The transparent glass window metaphor seems to make users sensitive to the distance between the drawing and the partner. Even with this overlapped image, users did not report having trouble distinguishing drawing marks from the video background.

Gaze Awareness

The most novel feature of ClearBoard, and the most important, is that it provides precise "gaze awareness" or "gaze tracking." A ClearBoard user can easily recognize what the partner is gazing at on the screen during a conversation. Precise *gaze awareness* can not be easily achieved in an ordinary meeting environment using a whiteboard because both users stand on the same side of the board. We conducted collaborative problem solving experiment on ClearBoard

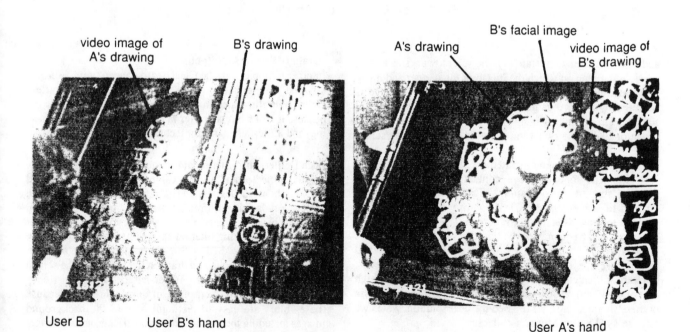

Fig. 9 ClearBoard-1 Prototype in Use
(See also Ishii and Kobayashi, Plate 1 and 2)

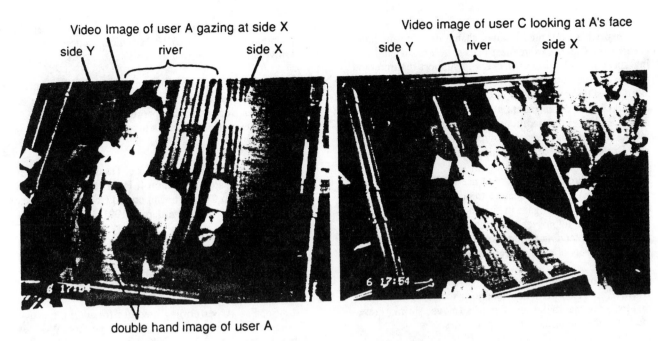

Video Image of user A gazing at side X

side Y   river   side X

Video image of user C looking at A's face

side Y   river   side X

double hand image of user A

Fig. 10 ClearBoard-1 used for solving the "River crossing" problem
(See also Ishii and Kobayashi, Plate 3 and 4)

using the "river crossing problem[4]."

A separate psychological experiment has determined that the success of this game depends heavily on the *points-of-view* of the players [5]. It is thus advantageous for the collaborative players to know what the partner is gazing at.

Through this experiment we confirmed that it is easy for the players to say which side of the river the partner is gazing at and this information was quite useful in advising each other. Fig. 10 shows a snapshot of one such experiment. User A is gazing at side X of the river, and user C is looking at the face of user A to read his *gaze*.

The importance of *eye-contact* is often discussed in the design of face-to-face communication tools. However, we believe the concept of *gaze awareness* is more generalized and is a more important notion. *Gaze awareness* lets a user know what the partner is looking at, the user's face or anything else on the shared workspace. If the partner is looking at you, you can know it. If the partner is gazing at an object in the shared workspace, you can know what the object is. Eye contact can be seen as just a special case of *gaze awareness*.

We think the notion of *gaze awareness* will be an important goal of the next generation of shared drawing tools. It can not

be easily obtained in conventional meeting environments, and only CSCW technology can provide it. ClearBoard-1 is the first system that provides distributed users with the capability of *gaze awareness*.

Problems of ClearBoard-1

Through the experimental sessions using this prototype, we found the following problems.

(1) clarity of images on the screen
It is hard to achieve sharp focus on all the marks on the screen and on the user's face. Since the screen is tilted, the bottom edge is about 40 cm further from the camera than the top edge. In the current prototype, the camera focuses at the center of the screen, so that the user's face and the edges of the screen are slightly out of focus. The quality of the projected video image is not as sharp nor bright as an ordinary computer screen. Because half-mirrors and polarizing films are used, the screen image of Drafter-Mirror architecture is inevitably darkened.

(2) erasing partner's marks
Since the marks drawn by each user exist on their respective screen surfaces, a user can not erase the partner's drawing.

(3) double hand images
As illustrated in Fig. 8 and Fig. 10, each user "sees" two hands for each actual hand with this arrangement. At first glance, a few users said they were disturbed by this. However, they got used to it soon and had no further complaints.

(4) recording of work results
We mainly used a Polaroid™ camera to make a record of work results. However, if we use the appropriate computer input technologies, it will be easier to record and print the work results.

---

4 The "river crossing problem" is a puzzle to get group A members and group B members across a river using a boat. (In the most traditional case, the groups were missionaries and cannibals.) The boat can hold only two members at a time, and must have at least one member in it to cross the river. The number of group A members must be larger than that of group B members on both banks. We played the puzzle on ClearBoard drawing the river on it and using some pieces of sticky paper (Post-it™) to represent the members of each group.

CONCLUSION

This paper has presented a novel shared drawing medium, ClearBoard. ClearBoard realizes (1) a seamless shared drawing space and (2) *gaze awareness* to support realtime and remote collaboration by two users.

We devised the key metaphor of ClearBoard: "talking *through* and drawing *on* a transparent glass window." We compared this metaphor to the traditional concepts of *whiteboard* and *table*. We implemented a prototype of ClearBoard based on the "Drafter-Mirror" approach and confirmed that the prototype fulfills the two goals.

In addition, through the informal use of ClearBoard-1, we found its most important feature to be *gaze awareness*. By referring to the role of gaze in human communication, ClearBoard is shown to provide a new environment for collaboration. We are planning to conduct empirical studies to understand the effects of gaze awareness in collaborative problem solving.

We are also designing a computer-drawing version "ClearBoard-2" to offer several new functions: recording of working results, easy manipulation of marks (move, shrink, erase, etc.), and the use of data in computer files.

ACKNOWLEDGEMENTS

We thank Naomi Miyake at Chukyo University and Isamu Yoroizawa at NTT for their insightful comments on the ClearBoard concept and experiments. Thanks are also due to William Buxton at the University of Toronto, Jonathan Grudin at the University of California, Irvine, and John Tang at Sun Microsystems for their thoughtful comments on this paper. We thank Kazuho Arita for his technical advice. We express our appreciation to Shinichi Shiwa for introducing his work on eye contact using the liquid crystal technique. We also thank Takaya Endo and Gen Suzuki for their encouragement and support for this research project.

REFERENCES

1. Bly, S. A., and Minneman, S. L. Commune: A shared drawing surface. In Proceedings of Conference on Office Information Systems (COIS'90, Boston, Massachusetts), ACM, New York, 1990, pp. 184-192.

2. Buxton, B., and Moran, T. EuroPARC's Integrated Interactive Intermedia Facility (IIIF): Early Experiences. In Proceedings of IFIP WG8.4 Conference on Multi-User Interfaces and Applications (Heraklion, Crete, Greece, September 24-26), North Holland, Amsterdam, 1990, pp. 11-34.

3. Buxton, B. Telepresence: Integrating Shared Task Space and Personal Spaces. In Proceedings of The Potential of Team and Organizational Computing (Groupware '91, Amsterdam, Netherlands, October 29), Software Engineering Research Center, Utrecht, 1991, pp. 27-36.

4. Fish, R. S., Kraut, R. E., and Chalfonte, B. L. The VideoWindow System in Informal Communications. In Proceedings of Conference on Computer Supported Cooperative Work (CSCW '90, Los Angeles, California, October 7-10), ACM, New York, 1990, pp. 1-11.

5. Hutchins, E. L., and Levin, J. A. Point of view in problem solving. In CHIP Technical Report No. 105, University of California at San Diego, 1981.

6. Ishii, H. TeamWorkStation: Towards a Seamless Shared Workspace. In Proceedings of Conference on Computer Supported Cooperative Work (CSCW '90, Los Angeles, California, October 7-10), ACM, New York, 1990, pp. 13-26.

7. Ishii, H., and Arita, K. ClearFace: Translucent multiuser interface for TeamWorkStation. In Proceedings of European Conference on Computer-Supported Cooperative Work 1991(ECSCW'91, Amsterdam), 1991, pp. 163-174.

8. Ishii, H., and Miyake, N. Toward an Open Shared Workspace: Computer and Video Fusion Approach of TeamWorkStation. Communications of the ACM, December 1991, pp. 37-50.

9. Lakin, F. A performing medium for working group graphics. In Computer-Supported Cooperative Work: A book of readings. Morgan Kaufmann Publishers, San Mateo, California, 1988, pp. 367-396.

10. Minneman, S. L., and Bly, S. A. Managing a trois: A study of a multi-user drawing tool in distributed design work. In Proceedings of ACM SIGCHI Conference on Human Factors in Computing Systems (CHI'91, New Orleans, Louisiana, April 27 - May 2), ACM, New York, 1991, pp. 217-224.

11. Schrage, M. Shared Minds. Random House, New York, 1990.

12. Shiwa, S., and Ishibashi, M. A Large-Screen Visual Telecommunication Device Enabling Eye Contact. In Digest of technical papers of Society for Information Display International Symposium 1991(SID 91), 1991, pp. 327-328.

13. Tang, J. C., and Minneman, S. L. VideoDraw: A video interface for collaborative drawing. In Proceedings of ACM SIGCHI Conference on Human Factors in Computing Systems (CHI'90, Seattle, Washington, April 1-5), ACM, New York, 1990, pp. 313-320.

14. Tang, J. C., and Minneman, S. L. VideoWhiteboard: Video shadows to support remote collaboration. In Proceedings of ACM SIGCHI Conference on Human Factors in Computing Systems (CHI'91, New Orleans, Louisiana, April 27 - May 2), ACM, New York, 1991, pp. 315-322.

DISEMBODIED CONDUCT: COMMUNICATION THROUGH VIDEO IN A MULTI-MEDIA OFFICE ENVIRONMENT

Christian Heath[*†] *and Paul Luff*[*†]

*Department of Sociology
University of Surrey
Guildford GU2 5XH
United Kingdom

[†]*Cambridge EuroPARC*
61, Regent Street
Cambridge CB2 1AB
United Kingdom

ABSTRACT

In the following paper we discuss some findings of recent research concerning the organisation of video mediated communication in collaborative work in a dispersed, multi-media office environment. Based on the detailed, naturalistic analysis of video-recordings of individuals collaborating on various tasks through audio-visual links, we describe the ways in which the technology transforms nonverbal and verbal conduct, introducing certain asymmetries into the social interaction between users. It is argued that such communicative asymmetries may facilitate, rather than hinder, certain forms of collaborative work and provide a foundation for the emergence of new forms of sociability in the work place.

> What of the hands? We require, promise, call, dismiss, threaten, pray, supplicate, deny, refuse, interrogate, admire, number, confess, repent, confound, blush, doubt, instruct, admire, number, confess, repent, confound, blush, doubt, instruct, command, incite, encourage, swear, testify, accuse, condemn, absolve, abuse, despise, defy, flatter, applaud, bless, humiliate, mock, reconcile, recommend, exalt, entertain, congratulate, complain, grieve, despair, wonder, exclaim,....There is not a motion that does not speak and in an intelligible language without discipline, and a public language that everyone understands.
>
> Montaigne 1952 pp. 215-216

KEYWORDS: multi-media, video communication, interaction analysis

INTRODUCTION

With the renewed interest in computer systems that support groups of people working together when physically separated has come a recognition of the importance of 'informal communication' to the workplace. Several researchers have tried to develop computer systems that assist with this type of communication (e.g. Kraut and Streeter [12]) while others have suggested that video could offer a solution. Research communities themselves appear to be good places in which to investigate this and several research laboratories, including Bellcore, Olivetti and Hewlett Packard have undertaken initiatives to establish audio-visual connections between their researchers. Abel [1] reports on one such exercise between two Xerox laboratories in Palo Alto and Portland where video connections were used between the two sites to enable cross-site meetings and 'peaking' into other people's offices. Gale [6] describes an experiment that compares users performing several tasks in three conditions; using a common workspace, using a common workspace with audio and using a common workspace with audio and video. In common with Chapanis [3] he finds that video does not significantly enhance the performance of the task. However he suggests that traditional HCI methodologies may have difficulty in assessing the real impact of videos on aspects of social process of group working, especially on informal communication. Similarly, Smith, O'Shea, O'Malley and Taylor [15] observed students using SharedARK, a distributed problem system, and video. They hypothesize by enabling eye-contact and gesture video provides support for users in dividing tasks between them.

In this paper we will report on a detailed naturalistic analysis of the use of, and interaction through audio-visual technologies at Cambridge EuroPARC for informal communication and group work. At EuroPARC a multi-media infrastructure has been created which provides personnel with the possibility of using their workstation to establish audio-visual connections with any member or domain within the laboratory. In particular we will discuss some findings of this research and describe how the technology affects both nonverbal and verbal communication. The analysis reveals the way in which video introduces certain asymmetries into social interaction which can serve to facilitate or undermine certain collaborative tasks between users. We consider why audio-visual technologies introduce such distortions into interpersonal communication and whether these and related problems might be solved in the development of a more 'natural' and versatile multi-media environment.

The data upon which the analysis is based consists of more than a hundred hours of video-recordings of individuals interacting and accomplishing various tasks through video. Our interest is in the day to day use of the system and in generating observations inductively from naturalistic materials. So we undertook a blanket recording of the use of audio-visual connections within EuroPARC over a period of weeks. We also gathered materials in other environments in which audio-visual technologies provided for the possibility of real time interaction across distinct physical locations, such as the Xerox Television link between England and the United States. Various experiments have also been undertaken at EuroPARC which have provided still further data.

METHODOLOGICAL BACKGROUND

The approach used in our research draws from ethnomethodology and conversation analysis and focuses on the interactional and sequential organisation of verbal and nonverbal behaviour in communication mediated through video. As a heuristic device we have drawn on the substantial corpus of findings concerning the organisation of face to face communication and compared and contrasted it with interaction through video. Recent studies concerned with the organisation of visual conduct and its relationship to talk (cf. Kendon [11], Goodwin [8], Heath [9]) have proved particularly useful in exploring communication mediated through video allowing us to focus on the ways in which users produce, interpret and coordinate their ordinary, everyday actions and tasks and collaborate in a real world, work environment.

Naturalistic studies of face to face communication have increasingly found that visual conduct such as gesture plays a critical role in shaping the way in which individuals participate in interaction and accomplish particular activities and tasks. It has been cogently demonstrated that speakers systematically coordinate the delivery of an utterance with the visual conduct of the recipient(s) and rely upon various vocal and visual devices to gain particular forms of co-participation. The very nature of the talk and the activity at hand, emerge in and through this interaction between 'speaker and hearer'. For example, a speaker may stall the gist of an utterance by producing hesitations or inserting a prefatory sentence until he has successfully secured the gaze of the recipient, or transform the description of an object because he has failed to encourage the co-participant to take notice. Gesture plays a particularly important part in this process providing

resources to speakers for securing the relevant forms of participation and attention for the activity or task in which they are are engaged. It has been found that the impact of gesture relies upon its subtle design with respect to the immediate context and even that a single gesture can perform simultaneously, more than a single duty, encouraging different responses from a co-participant at different points within the development of an activity. Visual conduct, like talk, is sequentially and interactionally significant serving to systematically engender specific actions from a co-participant at certain moments in the accomplishment of an activity.

Building on these foundations\ the analysis of video mediated communication has paid particular attention to the ways individuals use gestures and other forms of visual conduct to establish and preserve mutual involvement and coordinate work tasks and activities. Ordinarily we would present a collection of instances drawn from the data and explicate their organisation in detail, however, given the limitations of space it is only possible to briefly summarise some of our findings. In Conference video fragments will be presented and discussed.

VIDEO MEDIATED GESTURE

There are various ways in which members of EuroPARC can establish an audio-visual connection. In certain circumstances where for example, they are collaborating on a particular project such as writing a paper or providing advice to a new member of staff, individuals maintain an open video connection. To speak, they establish an audio connection. We began to notice however, that users will often attempt to interact visually, if only simply to acknowledge the presence of their colleague. Indeed it is not unusual for individuals to attempt to establish visual contact prior to engaging in conversation; where they are co-present persons progress into mutual involvement (cf. Kendon [11]). For example an individual will momentarily glance at a colleague attempt to initiate contact through a look or a wave. Curiously however, in contrast to situations in which individuals are co-present but disengaged such glances, looks and gestures appear to pass unnoticed by their potential recipient. Indeed we find users progressively upgrading and even exaggerating their movements and gestures in an attempt to attract the other's attention. In some cases of course, they simply establish an audio connection and thereby 'formally' summons a response from the other, on other occasions they abandon the attempt to initiate contact altogether.

With an open video connection the data suggest that users treat the situation as if its akin to being co-present with a colleague. They presuppose the effectiveness of their visual conduct and, at least initially, attempt to use the system to support various forms of informal or casual interaction. However certain actions appear to lose their communicative impact when performed through video.

Once users have established mutual engagement and have begun to speak to each other we do find that certain aspects of visual conduct regain their interactional significance. The medium provides the user with the possibility of witnessing their colleagues nonverbal behaviours and thereby coordinating their own conduct. So for example, users may 'mirror' gross shifts in bodily orientation, respond to changes of facial expression or coordinate speaker turns via visual cues. They are also able to assess when they are receiving another's gaze and to subtly differentiate related activities in which the other is engaged. Despite having the facility to witness a co-participants visual conduct however, it is interesting to note that many actions which are performed nonverbally do not achieve sequential performative significance in the interaction. In particular, gestures and other forms of body movement including gaze, which are systematically employed in face to face communication by speakers to organise how the 'recipient' participates prove in large part ineffectual. For example, a speaker will attempt to produce a description and during the course of its production use gesture to gain a visually attentive recipient. The gesture becomes increasingly exaggerated and meets with no response, the description reveals various linguistic difficulties and it may even be abandoned. Even gestures which are not solely concerned with organising co-participation lose their sequential significance. For example, gestures which illustrate or 'iconise' objects or events referred to in the accompanying talk (cf. Ekman and Friessen [5], Birdwhistell [2]), appear to achieve little communicative significance when performed through video. For some reason whilst providing visual access between users the technology transforms the ability of certain forms of conduct to engender action from another.

The relative ineffectiveness of gesture in organising co-participation in video mediated communication is consequential to the delivery of talk and verbal activities. For example, we find speakers systematically delaying even abandoning utterances or parts of an utterance in the light of failing to establish the 'relevant' behaviour from a recipient. Moreover, speakers inevitably have to rely upon vocal attempts to structure co-participation; for example various forms of speech perturbation such as restarts, pauses and sound stretches (cf. Goodwin [8], Heath [9]). However, such devices which appear to operate independently of visual action are less effectual when mediated through video. Indeed, we suspect that the relative inability of gaze to engender a response from a co-participant in video mediated interaction undermines the ability of speakers to secure mutual orientation through perturbations in talk (cf. Heath [10]). Moreover, talk which relies upon iconic or illustrative gestures to communicate certain meanings may also be undermined, since the technology can distort the movement's shape and simultaneously fail to extract the relevant forms of co-participation.

The relative ineffectiveness of certain forms of visual conduct when mediated through video is consequential to the accomplishment of a whole range of activities and tasks whether they are performed through nonverbal or verbal behaviours.

THE DESIGN OF GESTURE

As yet it is unclear whether the relative ineffectiveness of gesture and other forms of visual conduct is a necessary feature of communication mediated through video. In the light of television we may perhaps have become insensitive to screen based images, learning to suspend 'communicative' commitment. More probably, the technology as it is currently designed, fails to provide a suitable environment for the design and receipt of gesture and other forms of visual conduct.

Much of the work performed by gesture in face to face communication is accomplished on the periphery of the participants' visual field. Indeed it is relatively unusual, even in the case of iconic or illustrative gestures, for the movement to be performed in the direct line of regard of the recipient(s). Movements used to organise appropriate forms of co-participation including gestures whose tasks are solely concerned with eliciting a recipient's gaze are designed to engender action from the other whilst masking their own operation; to be 'seen but unnoticed', to 'gloss' their own operation (cf. Garfinkel [7]). In the case of video mediated communication the recipient's access to gesture is the movement's appearance on the screen, a screen which constitutes a small element within the local horizon. The gesture is viewed either directly with the totality of the screen's contents, or, whilst remaining part of the overall image, it features simply as one image within the office environment. Even when the screen is close to the line of regard of the user it is typically only gross changes within the configuration of the screen which serve to attract notice. The screen does feature within the peripheral vision of the user but its contents become one, the gesture simply forms part of an overall, undifferentiated image. The emergence of a gesture, its progressive movement and graduated appearance within the local environment, its complex operation on the periphery of the visual field, is distorted by the technology. It renders the recipient insensitive to the interactional tasks of the movement.

The speaker faces related difficulties. His access to his co-participant and the environment of the other is severely delimited; constrained by the angle of the camera and size and orientation of the screen. He is able to see the head and shoulders of the co-participant and catch a little of the background but unable to gain access to the surrounding environment of the other. In consequence, it can be difficult for the user to discern the focus of orientation of the other and in particular his focus of attention within his immediate horizon of objects and events. Relatively small but potentially significant changes in the other's orientation, such as scanning the contents of the computer screen or even apparently gross events with the other's local environment, such as someone entering the room are unavailable through the medium. With such limited access to the field of action of the other, users are unable to design their visual conduct to successfully achieve performative impact within the interaction, they cannot rely upon the resources they have available. The organisation which underlies the production of gesture and related forms of visual action in face to face interaction, its subtle operation on the periphery of the visual field is inappropriate to a virtual environment supported through video.

In video mediated communication, a gesture is not produced directly for the other, but for the other's appearance on the screen. With limited access to a mutual environment the user is unable to discern how the action appears to the other and in consequence has limited resources with which to achieve gestural effectiveness. Whereas in face to face interaction a speaker can systematically reshape a gesture within the course of its production so as to achieve interactional significance, in mediated communication there is little chance of success-fully redesigning a gesture to render it more appropriate to the circumstances. Perhaps unknown to the speaker, the camera and monitor distort the gesture so that more subtle movements simply pass unnoticed and the more dramatic become larger than life as they fill the recipient's screen. The technology inevitably transforms an individual's gesture, changing its size, shape and pace and placing it within an environment for which it is only partially designed.

The inability of gesture, or more generally visual conduct to achieve interactional significance in video mediated communication derives in part from the relative absence, or rather distortion of a 'common scheme of reference'. Schutz [14] (see also Cicourel [4]) cogently argues that the presupposition of interchangeable standpoints and reciprocity of perspectives is a necessary foundation for socially organised interaction. It is interesting to note that in video mediated communication, individuals assume and attempt to preserve the presupposition of a common frame of reference and the interchangeability of standpoints. Indeed their visual conduct is systematically designed with respect to a common mutual environment. Speakers for example, shape their gestures as if the potential recipient will view it in the way in which it is designed. Yet by providing limited access to the other and 'transforming' the appearance of a gesture, the technology introduces an incongruous mutual environment and a curious subsidence into the foundations of socially organised interaction.

ASYMMETRY AND COLLABORATION

Video mediated communication reveals certain asymmetries which as far as we are aware, are neither found within face to face interaction or other technologically mediated forms, such as telephone based communication. On the one hand the participants are able to monitor each other's behaviour and remain sensitive to their visual conduct. So for example we find speakers systematically coordinating the production of an utterance with the visual conduct of the person to whom they are speaking, as one might in conventional face to face environments. On the other hand the resources that speakers ordinarily use to structure the co-participation of a potential recipient, such as gesture are rendered ineffectual by the technology. Thus in articulating a range of actions and activities speakers remain sensitive to the visual conduct of the recipient and yet the performative impact of their nonverbal behaviour becomes problematic. Participants are aware of each other's presence and appearance but insensitive to aspects of the visual conduct of the other.

The evidence suggests therefore that video technology at least in the way it is currently configured, provides the possibility of building an electronic environment which is akin to or simulates, physical co-presence. Moreover the technology introduces certain asymmetries which render video mediated communication a curious hybrid of face to face interaction and talk on the telephone. It is likely as the technology becomes more available that we will witness the emergence of particular forms of interactional organisation which are sensitive to and deal with the sorts of asymmetries identified within this research.

However the interactional asymmetries found within video mediated communication do not necessarily undermine the usefulness of the technology within a multimedia, physically dispersed, office environment. Indeed the very difficulties that individuals may encounter in first communicating through video, may systematically support the accomplishment of certain collaborative tasks and activities. For example one problem that frequently arises within an open office environment in which personnel work in the same physical space, is the inability to remain insensitive to the surrounding environment of activity when necessary. The individual is continually subject not simply to the demands of others but a range of irrelevant action. Consequently despite the need for cooperation and collaboration in many work environments and informal contact between colleagues, the accomplishment of individual and distinct tasks can be difficult.

Video connectivity between potentially cooperating personnel in a work environment, especially a multimedia setting provides a solution to some of these difficulties. As in co-presence it provides individuals with a way of sensitively timing when it is appropriate to initiate contact and make an assessment of the tasks and activities in which the other might be engaged. Whilst simultaneously the user can work independently, insensitive to the 'surrounding' domain of activity. Despite the relative ineffectiveness of nonverbal behaviour in video mediated communication, once in interaction mutual visual access however delimited does provide users with the ability to coordinate a range of collaborative tasks. In particular in a multimedia environment where interactants may simultaneously converse and use equipment, such as computers, video allows the participants to infer if only grossly what the other is doing and gear there own conduct appropriately. Connectivity through video rather than co-presence also provides the user when in interaction, to avoid having the other's demands continually interrupt a concurrent often screen based activity. Video provides personnel in a dispersed office environment with the ability to coordinate both visual and vocal tasks and activities essential to real time collaboration whilst not being overwhelmed by the demands and actions of colleagues.

Inevitably the form of access that you need with colleagues depends on the nature of tasks involved and the forms of sociality that you wish to support. As part of a various initiatives concerned with developing tools to support connectivity and interaction between physically dispersed locations we have been exploring the possibilities of reinvigorating aspects of visual conduct through video. Large monitors, projected images and the like certainly increase the users sensitivity to the conduct of the other, though not necessarily reinvigorating gestural conduct. But as we hypothesised,. a stronger sense of co-presence is achieved at the cost of obtrusiveness; users becoming increasingly subject to demand and actions of others. Given the wide diversity of tasks in which individuals engage and collaborate in the office environment one key to begin to unlock the usefulness of video is to consider ways in which the user can control the extent of his visual availability and his access to the 'local' office environment.

ACKNOWLEDGEMENTS
We wish to thank Robert Anderson, William Gaver, Thomas Moran, Gary Olson, Judy Olson and Thomas Sebeok for their help in developing some of the issues discussed here, and Marina Jirotka for her careful comments on an earlier draft of the paper.

REFERENCES

1. Abel, M.J. Experiences in an Exploratory Distributed Organization. In *Intellectual Teamwork: The Social and Technological Foundations of Cooperative Work* (Edited by J. Gallagher, R.E. Kraut, and C. Egido), 1990.

2. Birdwhistell, R.L. *Kinesics and Context: Essay in Body-Motion Research.* University of Pennsylvania Press, Phil., 1970.

3. Chapanis, A. Interactive Human Communication. *Scientific American, 232, 3,* (1975), 36-42.

4. Cicourel, A. *Cognitive Sociology: Language and Meaning in Social Interaction.* Penguin, Harmondsworth, 1973.

5. Ekman, P. and Friessen, W.V. The Repertoires of Nonverbal Behaviour: Categories, Origins, Usage and Coding. *Semiotica 1,* (1969), 49-98.

6. Gale, S. Adding audio and video to an office environment. In *Proceedings of the First European Conference on Computer Supported Cooperative Work* (London, Sept. 13-15). 1989, pp. 121-133.

7. Garfinkel, H. *Studies in Ethnomethodology.* Prentice Hall, Englewood Cliffs, 1967.

8. Goodwin, C. *Conversational Organisation: The Interaction between Speaker and Hearer.* Academic Press, New York, 1981.

9. Heath, C.C. *Body Movement and Speech in Medical Interaction.* Cambridge University Press, Cambridge, 1986.

10. Heath, C.C. Communication through video technology: the transformation of actual space within the office environment. Paper presented at *Colloque de l'Association Internationale de Semiotique de l'Espace,* (Universite de Geneve July 27-28) 1990.

11. Kendon, A. *Studies in the Behaviour of Social Interaction.* Peter de Rider Press, Holland (second edition forthcoming with Cambridge University Press), 1977.

12. Kraut, R.E. and Streeter, L.A. Satisfying the Need to Know: Interpersonal Information Access. In *Proceedings of Interact '90 - Third IFIP Conference on Human-Computer Interaction,* (Cambridge, Aug. 27-30). 1990, pp. 909-915.

13. Montaigne, M. Eyquem de Essays, *Book II, no. 12* (Trans. C. Cotton). Encyclopedia Britannica, Chicago, 1952.

14. Schutz, A. *Collected Papers II: Studies in Social Theory* (Edited by A. Broderson). Martinus Nijhoff, The Hague, 1964.

15. Smith, R.B., O' Shea, T., O' Malley, C., and Taylor, J.S. Preliminary experiments with a distributed, multi-media problem solving environment. In *Proceedings of the First European Conference on Computer Supported Cooperative Work* (London, Sept. 13-15). 1989, pp. 19-35.

BEYOND BEING THERE

Jim Hollan and Scott Stornetta

Computer Graphics and Cognitive Science Research Groups
Bellcore, 445 South Street, Morristown, NJ 07962-1910

Email: hollan@bellcore.com, stornetta@bellcore.com

ABSTRACT

A belief in the efficacy of imitating face-to-face communication is an unquestioned presupposition of most current
work on supporting communications in electronic media. In
this paper we highlight problems with this presupposition
and present an alternative proposal for grounding and motivating research and development that frames the issue in
terms of needs, media, and mechanisms. To help elaborate
the proposal we sketch a series of example projects and
respond to potential criticisms.

Keywords: Telecommunications, CSCW.

INTRODUCTION

Face-to-face conversation provides a richness of interaction
seemingly unmatched by any other means of communication. It is also apparent that living and working near others,
whether that be in the same house, adjacent offices, or the
same city, affords certain opportunities for interaction that
are unavailable to those not co-located.

Research has clarified and substantiated both of these com-
monsense intuitions. It has been shown, for example, that
there is a predictable fall-off in likelihood of collaboration
between two researchers as a function of separation distance, even after correcting for factors such as organizational distance and similarity of research interest [5, see also
8]. This is understood to occur because of the large number
of informal interactions necessary to create and maintain
working relationships. There are also well-developed theories of interaction that predict why some interactions seem

to only work when face-to-face, while others can work over
the phone, and still others through written correspondence
[12,3,14].

This research supports the idea that we as humans have
developed a broad range of mechanisms for social interaction, which seem to meet well our needs for initiating and
maintaining friendships and working relationships, for discussing, negotiating, planning, and all other types of social
interactions. These are known to be complex processes, and
ones which physical proximity facilitates.

Many of us in the telecommunications field would like to
create systems that allows the same richness and variety of
interaction, but with distance no longer an issue. Ideally,
these systems should work so well that those at a distance
should be at no disadvantage to those who are physical
present. This in large measure is the telecommunication
problem. But how best to accomplish it?

BEING THERE

*If, as it is said to be not unlikely in the near future, the
principle of sight is applied to the telephone as well as
that of sound, earth will be in truth a paradise, and distance will lose its enchantment by being abolished altogether.* Arthur Strand, 1898 [7].

Roughly speaking, the response of telecommunication
researchers has been to follow the path that Strand implicitly outlined nearly 100 years ago: solve the telecommunication problem by creating a sense of *being there*, by
establishing some form of audio and video connections
between two distant locations (A notable exception to this is
email, about which we will have more to say later). Hence
the introduction of the telephone itself, and its enhancement
through the addition of video, for teleconferencing, shared
informal spaces [1,5], and one-on-one conversation. It is not
too far from the mark to characterize the goal of the
research by quoting from one of the stated goals of a recent
informal telecommunication experiment: *"the total effect is*

to produce an environment at each end... which is as close as possible to being there [10]."

How successful have the many efforts directed at this goal been? To measure progress towards the direct face-to-face part of this goal, social psychologists have evolved measures of *social presence* [12] and *information richness* [3] to estimate how closely telecommunication tools capture the essence of face-to-face communication. To simplify matters slightly, it is generally agreed that various communication options can be ranked on an axis, in order of decreasing social presence, as face-to-face, audio/video communication, audio only, and written correspondence/email. While it is encouraging that the addition of the video channel seems to increase the social presence, it is often (though not always) the conclusion of studies that the audio/video medium is much closer to the audio only medium than it is to the face-to-face condition.

It is tempting to think that with perhaps a little more screen resolution, a little more fidelity in the audio channel, a little more tweaking to bring the machinery in conformance with subtle and long-established social mechanisms such as eye contact, telecommunications systems will achieve a level of information richness so close to face-to-face that for most needs it will be indistinguishable.

But will they ever be close enough? It is clear they can, for example provide a cost-effective and efficient alternative to business travel to a distant location, and may be superior to audio only telephone for some communicative needs. We have no argument with that. But is this general approach going to be adequate for the long term? Is it powerful enough to see us through to achieving the goal that those at a distance will be at no real disadvantage to those co-located?

A recent study of the Cruiser video system suggests that in one important respect, systems designed using this approach may *never* be "close enough." In a recent trial aimed at seeing whether a video/audio system provided enough information richness, it was found that subjects used the mechanism to set up face-to-face conversation with friends down the hall, but not in lieu of them[6]. The result is not surprising. Perhaps we are demanding too much. After all, its purpose is to enable communication between two distant locations, where going into the next office to talk to the person is not an option. When you have the choice between face-to-face and an imitation, no matter how good, it is natural to choose the real thing. This is a problem inherent with imitation, but we think it is particularly telling for communication. When we make a choice between two channels to use for informal interaction, discrepancies between the two channels are decisive. Thus, if one channel is half as good as another, we don't use it half as often, we probably don't use it at all, so long as the other is readily available. And that fundamental edge of real face-to-face and physical proximity over its imitation, accumulated over the hundreds of interactions it takes to form friendships or successful collaborations means, we believe, that organizations will continue to decouple into geographical groups (See, for

example, the discussion of group cohesion in chapter 8 of [12]).

It seems to us that there is no real solution to this situation so long as people use one medium to communicate with those at a distance and another for those for whom distance is not an issue. Those distant will always remain at a disadvantage to those present. It is not really even a question of the quality of the device. It is what it is trying to achieve. It could be 3-D holographic with surround-sound, but if people use an imitation to talk to some people but the "real thing" to those physically proximate, a fundamental difference will always remain.

A logical extension to this line of thinking is that the people at a distance will never stop being at a disadvantage until we use the same mechanisms to interact with each other when we are physically close as when we are physically distant. And that means that to make real progress on the telecommunication problem, we must develop tools that people prefer to use even when they have the option of interacting as they have heretofore in physical proximity. We must develop tools that go beyond being there. But what would it mean for something to be better than being there? And how could we design such a device?

Perhaps a brief analogy could get us moving in the right direction. It is customary for a person with a broken leg to use crutches, but how odd it would be if they continued to use the crutches after their leg was restored to its natural condition. In contrast, one wears shoes because they provide certain advantages over our natural barefoot condition. Special purpose shoes, such as running shoes, are designed to enhance our best performance. Now crutches and shoes are both tools of a sort, but there is a difference. The crutch is designed specifically to make the best of a bad situation -- to let someone hobble around until they are back in shape. On the other hand, shoes are to correct some of the problems of our natural condition, and, in the case of athletic shoes, to enhance our performance.

In telecommunications research perhaps we have been building crutches rather shoes. What we are getting at is this: telecommunications research seems to work under the implicit assumption that there is a natural and perfect state -- *being there* -- and that our state is in some sense *broken* when we are not physically proximate. The goal then is to attempt to restore us, as best as possible, to the state of *being there*. In our view there are a number of problems with this approach. Not only does it orient us towards the construction of crutch-like telecommunication tools but it also implicitly commits us to a general research direction of attempting to imitate one medium of communication with another. A research direction which, as we indicated above and will discuss more fully below, has serious limitations.

BEYOND BEING THERE

No man putteth a piece of new cloth unto an old garment, for that which is put in to fill it up taketh from the garment, and the rent is made worse. Neither do men put new wine into old bottles: else the bottles break, and the wine run-

neth out, and the bottles perish: but they put new wine into new bottles, and both are preserved. Matthew 9:16-17.

To start to elaborate an alternative approach to the telecommunication problem, let's take a step back. For the purpose of discussion, let's frame human communication in terms of needs, media, and mechanisms.

We'll say that communication needs are those human requirements which, when met, encourage and facilitate interaction. They span the whole range of human needs and are the underlying human requirements that get served by communication. They are independent of the medium with which we communicate. For example, we would characterize Daft and Lengel's [4] suggestions of characteristics of information rich channels, *cue variety, feedback, and message personalization*, as candidate needs. Other researchers [6] suggest *simultaneously being reminded of a need to talk to someone* and *having a communication channel* as key aspects of informal communication. Schegloff [15] and others have discussed *turn taking*, *repair*, and *stylized openings* as seemingly essential to conversation. It is such underlying needs that we are referring to in the framework we are proposing.

Media are simply what mediates communication. For face-to-face interactions the medium is physically proximate reality. Viewing physical proximity as a medium might at first seem odd but it is of central importance to our argument since the way it has come to mediate face-to-face interactions serves as *the model* for communication. This in turn we will argue has led to a focus on and imitation of the basic characteristics of face-to-face interactions such as their 3-dimensional high-resolution visual and auditory character.

Finally, mechanisms are ways to meet informal communication needs that are enabled by a medium. While needs are media independent, mechanisms are closely, perhaps inextricably, connected to specific media. Examples of mechanisms that seem to work well for physically-proximate interactions might include eye contact, body posture, stereotypical openings and closings in spoken language, or even the strategy of going down to the lounge to see who's taking a break from work.

In an important sense, computationally-mediated communication is a new medium, potentially as good or better than the physically proximate medium we are used to. Here we mean to include not just email, as if sometimes intended by the term, but all communication that is mediated by any type of electronic or computational device, whether it be an audio amplifier, television camera, or email system. As the quote beginning this section suggests, new mechanisms are required for new media. It is thus crucial to consider what mechanisms of communication the new computational medium enables and to realize that mechanisms that may be effective in face-to-face interactions might be awkward or ineffective if we try to replicate them in an electronic medium. This is one of the inherent limitations in imitating one medium with another. As we discussed above, the imitation will never be as good as the real thing. This is true by definition if one is strict in using the old medium as the stan-

dard of measurement. However, even with a more relaxed standard, the new medium will seldom measure up because of discrepancies in the strengths and weaknesses of the two media. Requiring one medium to imitate the other inevitably pits strengths of the old medium against weaknesses of the new. At the same time, to the extent that the goal is imitation, one will not be led to exploit the distinctive strengths of the new medium.

The assumption that the *media* and *mechanisms* of face-to-face interaction are actually the *requirements* for ideal communication is so pervasive that it is implied in the very name of the industry currently most concerned with supporting informal communication in the new medium -- *tele*-communication. The implication is that we are trying to find ways to communicate at a distance as if we weren't at a distance. But it is our contention that such an approach will always limit our thinking to replicating or imitating the mechanisms of one medium with another.*

In contrast, we argue that a better way to solve the telecommunication is to not focus on the *tele-* part, but the *communication* part. That is, to make the new medium satisfy the needs of communication so well that people, whether physically proximate or not, prefer to use it.

The framework of needs, media, and mechanisms also suggests a way to achieve a level of performance for communication tools that goes beyond being there. First, it frees us to ask "what's right with the new medium?" For example, three significant features of the new medium are its ability to support asynchronous communication, anonymous communication, and to automatically archive communication. Yet all of these potentially important features are ignored when the medium is used just to recreate synchronous face-to-face interactions between distant sites.

It also creates a framework in which it becomes meaningful to ask the question: what's wrong with (physically proximate) reality? That is, when we view physically proximate reality as simply *a* medium, we can ask what requirements it meets well, and also what ones it meets poorly, inefficiently, or not at all. We can then explore new mechanisms to meet those needs, mechanisms which leverage the strengths of the new medium.

EXAMPLES

To further illustrate the approach we are proposing, we offer a sampling of projects which are in various stages of devel-

---

* We are reminded of a colleague's description of his reaction to a demonstration of the clarity of a fiber communications link. He responded that often when one was calling a friend or relative far away what one wanted to communicate was the message that "I am far away and thinking of you." He suggested that the new fiber medium made that harder to say. With the old medium one could *hear the distance* and thus the medium itself helped to convey the message.}

opment in our group. We conclude each example with a set of hypotheses that we expect the project will help us evaluate.

Email communication is surely the paramount success of computationally-mediated informal communication. It's design fits well with the framework we propose since it satisfies a number of communicative requirements primarily by exploiting the asynchronous nature of the electronic medium rather than by attempting to imitate synchronous physical interactions. It meets our critical litmus test of being used by groups even when in close physical proximity. In fact, in our own experience, it is not uncommon to send email to someone in the next adjacent office, or even someone sharing an office. In this light, it is not surprising that email was viewed as one of the most (if not the most) successful communication tools in an extensive study that explored the ability of a research group to function when located at two sites, separated by several hundred miles [1].

Yet the sense that we must imitate face-to-face is strong. In a recent popular article on email communication it was noted almost apologetically: "Electronic mail that includes graphics, pictures, sound and video will eventually become widely available. These advances will make it possible to reintroduce some of the social context cues absent in current electronic communications. Even so, electronic interactions will never duplicate those conducted face-to-face [9]."

One direction that our approach leads one to consider is other elaborations of email that are not at all imitative, but move in complementary or even opposite directions. Four of our examples can roughly be considered as such. The fifth example looks directly at those tasks for which the very rich, synchronous interaction and immediate feedback that face-to-face communication provides seems essential.

Ephemeral Interest Groups

Successful informal discussions often take place when there is both an opportunity to communicate and a natural topic of discussion. For example, suppose you have a colleague you would like to know better. It is easier to start up a conversation when both are sitting in a lounge reading a newspaper, or both are waiting for a meeting to start, than interrupting his work by knocking on his office door. In both of these desirable situations, ones' presence in the lounge or in the meeting room indicates that one is available for conversation, and the approaching meeting or newspaper provides an natural topic of conversation.

A problem with these mechanisms, however, is that both parties need to be free at the same time. Thus, without being too precise, the likelihood of these opportunities goes roughly as the *product* of the fraction of the time that each person is available in these circumstances.

The potentially asynchronous nature of computationally-mediated interactions increases the potentially available time for informal interaction to approximate something proportional to the fraction of time available to each person considered separately. This is a much larger value, and implies the makings of a more effective way of having informal interactions, either to get to know a colleague better, or to maintain contact with a close associate. But how to create natural topics of conversation?

The idea of an ephemeral interest group is to create a mechanism that allows a (typically) short-lived discussion to be attached to any object in a community's electronic "space." Thus, items on an electronic calendar listing research talks, apnews stories in electronic form, and even postings to a company-wide bulletin board can provide a seed for an ephemeral interest group.

The word ephemeral helps to emphasize that these discussions differ from those handled by specialized bulletin boards, netnews groups, or special interest mailing lists. In those cases, interests of a more long-standing nature are well served. The intent is to provide a mechanism that allows a group to be created at virtually zero cost to a potential user, and that these groups can be thought of as disposable, intended only to last a few hours or at most a few days.

We have been operating a first version of such a service for over four months at Bellcore. It has been reasonably successful. Users report that it creates a greater sense of informality than postings to the general bulletin board, while allowing them to potentially reach all the readers of the bulletin board, without bothering those that are not interested in that discussion. And, true to its email heritage, allows those not located at the site to keep up on what's going on with a system that puts them at no apparent to disadvantage to those co-located.

As a result of formal interviews and more general user feedback, we have recently begun limited use of a redesigned system, emphasizing increased visibility, and lower user cost of access and interaction. With these changes, there are preliminary indications of increased participation, and the ability to handle topics that are more ephemeral. We plan to report on this work in more detail elsewhere [2]. These ephemeral interest groups provide a means of initiating friendships electronically which we discuss in the next section.

Hypotheses: People using this system that aren't present rate themselves as more a part of the community than those who don't use it and are present.

Meeting Others

While there is currently much discussion of electronic access to information resources and new kinds of information services that may soon be offered, one might conjecture that many people are more concerned with meeting interesting people and having richer fuller relationships than with access to most forms of electronic information. Let's briefly consider what kinds of systems we might be led to propose based on our framework.

First, we are exploring providing users in our lab with a sort of electronic persona that provides people with access to information about others. This includes their publications, picture, state information that is automatically recorded about activity on their workstation, as well as the opportunity to include the kinds of information that many people now attach to the doors of their offices (cartoons, quotes, etc.). The goal is not to replicate in the electronic media what is available in other media but to provide low-cost access to the information so that when reading about a topic, such as an ephemeral interest group posting, one has ready access to other information about them and an opportunity to initiate a conversation. More importantly we think that these pieces of information can provide opportunities for initiation of informal communication.

A second project is a more ambitious variant of the first. It's goal is to provide a form of what one might call *computing personals* in which people would have the opportunity to compose structured profiles describing themselves and allow those profiles to enter into negotiation with other profiles on the net to attempt to locate other people that they might be interested in meeting. The issues of how to construct initial profiles and tailor them as well as the design of the process of negotiation is challenging. Yet one can project that such a form of interaction might provide an interesting alternative way of meeting others.

Hypotheses: Allowing low cost electronic access to information about others will provide an effective way of learning about people for the first time, decrease the cost of initiating contact, and support the maintenance of interactions over time.

Anonymity

One characteristic of an electronic medium that is not shared with face-to-face interactions is an ability to be anonymous. Sproull and Kiesler [9] note that people are in some cases more truthful in email than in face to face, in part because the interaction is more anonymous. Could one not exploit this property to create a new type of email in which exchanges could happen anonymously? This has the potential of satisfying a set of requirements that are not readily satisfied in face-to-face communications. Anonymity could permit exchanges without some of the costs associated with nonanonymous encounters.

Our point is not primarily that such anonymous exchanges will necessarily be valuable (there are certainly many problems that they might generate) but rather that looking at mechanisms enabled by characteristics of a medium and how they might satisfy needs of individuals and groups leads one to posit systems and services that differ from those that follow from an imitative approach.

Hypotheses: Anonymous exchanges will encourage people to discuss issues that they are reluctant to discuss in face to face encounters and lead to discussion of those issues much earlier in a relationship. There is some evidence already available on this issue. One sees anonymous posting services arising on the internet to allow people to interact about very personal topics that it is clear they would be reluctant to discuss in initial fact-to-face encounters.

Semisynchronous Discussions

The perspective we are proposing also encourages one to explore needs, media, and mechanisms independently as well as the linkages between them. As mentioned earlier the asynchronous nature of email is quite effective in supporting certain communicative requirements but focusing on the medium also leads one to ask how the mechanism might be varied. It is clear that the plasticity of the electronic medium allows us quite a bit of flexibility. One does not need to view things as either synchronous or asynchronous. One can imagine semisynchronous mechanisms that might be useful in meeting certain requirements.

Consider for example the following problem of communicating via an electronic bulletin board system. The problem is that the tone and direction of a discussion can be set from the first few responses to a message and people who might well have responded to the original message are reluctant now to enter the discussion. A variant of this problem is not uncommon in meetings or in the classroom in which the first response to a topic can lead the discussion away from what many people might have thought would have been a more productive direction.

The synchronous nature of face-to-face communication does not afford one many options here but in the electronic medium we can explore a variety of semisynchronous mechanisms. Suppose for example that people sending messages intended for discussion could avail themselves of such a mechanism. One variant would permit people to respond to a message at any time but all responses would get batched up and come out at fixed times.

Hypotheses: Use of semisynchronous mechanisms will encourage a greater range of responses than the normal asynchronous or synchronous mechanisms.

Beyond Face-To-Face

The previous examples have emphasized the idea that many things which currently occur in face-to-face, synchronous interactions might actually benefit from being handled in a way that is not, at least superficially, very imitative of face-to-face encounters. However, we certainly feel that some interactions require very rapid, synchronous feedback, and as much information richness or social presence as can be brought to bear.

There is a great deal of enthusiasm, both among telecommunications researchers and the general public, for the possibilities that widespread use of cellular/PCS phone systems, and pen-based wireless computers will allow. How will they change our world? Certainly we can imagine simple extrapolations of current phone and computer use, making computers easier to work with, and phones more readily available. Does the beyond being there approach suggest more imaginative possibilities for these new technologies?

We'll start by asking a question that's easy to ask in our framework. Much telecommunication research has aimed at achieving the level of information richness that we currently have in face-to-face interactions. But no one seems to be asking the question, "what would happen if we were to develop communication tools with a higher information richness than face-to-face?" In the framework proposed in this paper, such tools are actually not all that hard to imagine. We begin by thinking of needs that are not well met in unassisted face-to-face interaction. While we are just beginning to investigate this area, the following examples illustrate the style of approach we are advocating.

Clarity: Could things be clearer in spoken natural language than they are today? American Sign Language provides an intriguing possibility. In ASL, pronoun reference is handled by indicating spatial locations for objects of discussion, and then referring to the various objects by pointing. Thus, while there may be a reference ambiguity in an English sentence using the word "he," there need be no such confusion in ASL.

Feedback: Facial expressions, head nodding, and verbal cues all are used to indicate back to the speaker that one understands and is following the conversation. We would argue that all these mechanisms are rather imprecise. The speaker may wonder: what aspects of what I am saying does the listener understanding? What does the listener think my key point is? But with the spatial location of key pieces of the discussion in a shared visual space, the listener may be able to use tablet gestures to provide a rich range of feedback that simultaneously indicates what aspect of the speaker's comments he is responding to.

Archive: One problem with spoken words in unenhanced physical proximity is that they leave no easily-searchable archive or trace. Recording and making transcriptions, or annotating records after the fact seems a cumbersome process at best. We are pursuing a way to make a system tightly integrated into the spoken interaction, in such a way that the combination of audio and visual record is created without additional effort beyond that needed to converse, and is easily searchable.

What we are suggesting here is a kind of auditory paper, a real-time visual extension to natural language itself.

Hypotheses: Face-to-face conversations using auditory paper will be rated as having higher social presence than unassisted face-to-face interactions. We conjecture that auditory paper will some day, even without the face-to-face component, be viewed as having greater social presence than unassisted face-to-face conversations.

RESPONSES TO POTENTIAL CRITIQUES

We admittedly are trying to present an extreme position as our use of the phrase *beyond being there* might suggest. Our purpose in taking such a position is to highlight our argument and make crisp an alternative approach to support of informal communication in the electronic medium that we feel isn't currently being adequately pursued. Here we respond to a collection of potential critiques.

Advantages of Imitation

There surely are advantages that arise from the imitation of physically proximate reality. An obvious one is that people are used to it and so they will know how to act in the new situation. We would like to suggest though that there can be subtle problems, even when the imitation is successful, because of slight differences in what the media can support. An example is the eye contact problem associated with

video conferencing systems. More importantly though our concern is that in trying to build things that are easy to get use to because they are familiar we will never get beyond the level that the familiar solutions have taken us. In addition, all of the novel representational and communicative uses of the electronic medium almost by definition fall outside of what people are used to now.

Culture

A more difficult criticism is that in advocating our beyond being there position we do not adequately address the issues of culture that surround the use of any media. This criticism would take us to task for failing to give adequate due to culture. That culture provides an important backdrop for our informal communication with others can not be minimized. Our position is that as we explore the new characteristics of media and how they might better meet our requirements we may well see culture change to incorporate and support mechanisms enabled by the new medium because they provide better ways of meeting underlying requirements.

Intersubjectivity

One of the factors that makes face-to-face communication so compelling is how it supports intersubjectivity. Intersubjectivity is a topic that a number of modern philosophers of communication have discussed. Simply put it refers to the creation of a context in which I know that you know that I know what we are talking about. In face-to-face interactions it is constructed via mechanisms of facial expressions, tone of voice, and body language. Much of the richness of face-to-face conversation has to do with exploiting mechanisms of intersubjectivity. Careful examination of almost any encounter will demonstrate their pervasiveness. One will see how a glance can be used to convey a question or to elaborate or even change the underlying context of a discussion.

No matter how powerful and important such mechanisms are there is no reason in principle that the underlying requirements might not be better serviced via mechanisms of other media or via a combination of mechanisms of multiple media. While current techniques, such as embedding little pictures of smiles in email text, to afford the electronic media some of the mechanisms of face-to-face pale in comparison to the richness of direct interactions, one must remember that the electronic medium is still very young. More importantly, looking at nonimitative approaches that focus on underlying requirements and the distinctive characteristics of the electronic media rather than on imitation of the mechanisms of face-to-face might lead to even better solutions.

For example, the ability to remove or selectively enable intersubjectivity might itself have distinct advantages. This is something that is certainly easier to accomplish in electronic forms of communication. A number of people have commented that they can operate more efficiently when viewing a lecture via video or using multiple authoring software precisely because others are not provided with information about them that would be communicated in face-to-face interactions. They can, for example, timeshare their attention with other activities without making the kinds of statements that doing that would do if they were attending the lecture. Thus, they are able to meet other requirements that might have higher value to them precisely because they don't have the kinds of intersubjectivity afforded so readily in face-to-face interactions.

Thus, it is instructive to realize that since there are certainly costs associated with the maintenance of intersubjectivity there may well be occasions when being able to decide not to bear those costs is advantageous.

SUMMARY AND CONCLUSION

Let us summarize our argument:

1. The general telecommunication problem seems to be to create a system that affords us the same richness and variety of interaction that we have when we are physically proximate, even when we are physically distant.

2. Many current efforts to accomplish this attempt to create a sense of "being there," chiefly by establishing audio and video channels between distant locations.

3. Any system which attempts to bring those that are physically distant into a physically proximate community by imitating physical proximity will always keep the former at a disadvantage. This is not because of the quality of the systems, but because of what they attempt to achieve.

4. If we ever hope to solve the telecommunication problem, we must develop tools that people prefer to use even when they have the option of interacting in physical proximity as they have heretofore. To do that requires tools that go *beyond being there*.

5. To create such tools, we suggest framing the problem in terms of needs, media, and mechanisms. The goal then becomes identifying needs which are not ideally met in the medium of physical proximity, and evolving mechanisms which leverage the strengths of the new medium to meet those needs.

In conclusion, we return to the quote at the beginning of this paper. At least since 1898, people have had a vision of a future where new technologies would allow us to interact with others that are far away just as we do with those that are near. We share that vision, but differ from Strand's quote in how best to accomplish it. In our view of the future, it is not so much distance that will be abolished, but rather our current concept of *being there*.

ACKNOWLEDGMENTS

We want to acknowledge the efforts of Steve Abney and Laurence Brothers as well as the other members of the *Beyond Being There* working group. We also thank Will Hill, Jakob Nielsen, Ed Hutchins and Jonathan Grudin for comments on earlier versions of this paper.

REFERENCES

1. Abel, M. J. Experiences in an Exploratory Distributed Organization. In Galegher, Kraut, & Egido (Eds.), *Intellectual Teamwork: Social and Technological Foundations of Cooperative Work*, Lawrence Erlbaum Associates, 489-51., 1990.

2. Abney, S., Hollan, J., & Stornetta, S. The j-key and Ephemeral Interest Groups, in preparation.

3. Daft, R.L. and Lengel, R.H. Organizational Information requirements, media richness, and structural design. Management Science, 32, 554-571, 1991.

4. Emmory, Karen et al., The Activation of Spatial Antecedents from Overt Pronouns in American Sign Language, *Language and Cognitive Processes*, p. 207, vol. 6, no. 3 1991.

5. Fish, R. S., Kraut, R. E. Chalfonte, B. The VideoWindow System In Informal Communications. Proceedings of the Conference on Computer Supported Cooperative Work (CSCW '90), 1-11, 199, 1990.

6. Fish, R. S., Kraut, R. E., Root, R. W., & Rice, R Evaluating Video as a Technology for Informal Communication. Bellcore Technical Memorandum, TM-ARH017505, 1991.

7. Mee, Arthur, The Pleasure Telephone, the *Strand Magazine*, pp. 339-369, 1898.

8. Monge, P.R. et al. . The dynamics of organizational proximity. *Management Science* 31, 1129-1141., 1985.

9. Sproul, Lee, and Kiesler, Sara, Computers, Networks and Work, *Scientific American*, p. 116, September, 1991.

10. Posting at one location of Videowindow informal communication experiment, Morristown, NJ.

11. Root, R. W. Design Of A Multi-Media Vehicle For Social Browsing. Proceedings ACM CSCW'88 Computer-Supported Cooperative Work, 25-38, 1988.

12. Short, J., Williams, E., and Christie, B., *The Social Psychology of Telecommunications*, London: John WIley and Sons, 1976.

13. Williams, E. . Experimental comparisons of face-to-face and mediated communication: A review. *Psychological Bulletin*, 84, 963-976, 1977.

14. Zmud, R.W., Lind, M.R., and Young, F.W. An attribute space for organizational communication channels. *Information System Research*, 1, 440-457, 1990.

15. Schegloff, E. A. Identification and Recognition In INteractional Openings, In The Social Impact of the Telephone, (Ed.) I. de Sola Pool, MIT Press, 1977.

PART V
Summary and Conclusions

Let us review what we have covered in this book. We defined groupware (using Malone's words, cited in Coleman and Shapiro, 1992) as "information technology used to help people work together" and computer supported cooperative work as "computer-assisted coordinated activity such as communication and problem solving carried out by a group of collaborating individuals." We began in Chapter 1 by sketching the incredible scope and breadth of these fields, and in Chapter 2 we emphasized that even excellent groupware technology must be adopted and deployed with great sensitivity to the work context if it is to be successful.

In Part II we tried to bridge the gaps among the diverse backgrounds of people working in CSCW. We introduced key concepts and theories of group and organizational process in Chapter 3, and reviewed methodologies for groupware design and evaluation in Chapter 4. We tried to ground and illustrate collaborative behavior in groups with some case studies of cooperative work in Chapter 5. Chapter 6 presented a brief introduction to some of the enabling technologies and theories being employed in groupware development.

Part III dealt with asynchronous groupware, software designed to help people work together even though they work at different times (and in many cases, in different places). The most successful groupware applications to date are electronic mail and computer conferencing, which were reviewed in Chapter 7. Extensions of electronic mail that exploit message structure, employ "intelligent" agents, and transact in workflows were covered in Chapter 8. Chapter 9 shifted the point of view from process to structured data and dealt with cooperative hypertext and organizational memory.

The synchronous groupware paradigm, the topic of Part IV, includes both the concept of a shared task space and a shared interpersonal space. Software for the shared task space was covered in Chapter 10; system and language support to enable such applications was the topic of Chapter 11. Chapter 12 examined the environments and software to support electronic meetings within one physical space such as a decision room; Chapter 13 presented technologies and theories of media spaces, environments which create shared interpersonal space across a distance.

We shall now conclude this book with a brief essay suggesting some of the key problems that need to be solved in order that groupware can truly enable and empower computer-supported cooperative work.

CHAPTER 14
The Future of Groupware for CSCW

Following a suggestion by Stefik (Xerox PARC, 1988v) and its elaboration by Ishii (1990a) that identified some *seams, interfaces,* or *gaps* between different kinds of work, and expanding upon a discussion of this idea in Baecker (1991), we assert that, in order to be maximally effective, groupware needs to bridge a number of gaps. Each gap is listed below and is illustrated in terms of collaborative writing as a prototypical kind of cooperative work.

- *The gap between individual and group work and individual process and group process.*

If groupware is to succeed, its users need to be able to move smoothly and gracefully between individual and group work, between working in their own individual manner and working collaboratively in harmony with the styles and practices of the workgroup. For example, documents which are being designed or created will pass through numerous transitions between individual and group effort. These transitions should be as unobtrusive as handing a document to a co-worker and receiving back a marked-up copy. This suggests two more specific gaps that need to be bridged.

- *The gap between work with conventional software and work with groupware.*

The most elegant collaborative writing tool will be only a toy if there is no clean interface between it and the single-user editors used for most work. At a minimum, there must be a way to export documents back and forth between the two environments. Far better is for the single-user software to be a subset of the groupware system, with the same metaphors, conceptual models, and user interface, or for the groupware gracefully to supplant the old technology. One way in which this can be done is through the group-enabling of existing applications (Greif, 1992, included in Chapter 10 of this volume).

- *The gap between work in one's individual office and work in a common meeting space.*

One should also be able to use in a common meeting space the tools and resources available in one's office. If the computer environments in electronic meeting rooms are compatible with and linked to personal office computers, part of the problem is solved. One trades access to the non-computational resources available in his or her own office for the benefits of meeting face-to-face in the common space. Desktop videoconferencing allows one to pick a different point in the cost-benefit space: one remains in his or her own office but accepts the limitations (as well as the strengths) of communicating through a media space in place of working in a traditional face-to-face meeting (Abel, 1990; Mantei, Baecker, Sellen, Buxton, Milligan, and Wellman, 1991; and Heath and Luff, 1991b; all included in Chapter 13 of this volume).

- *The gap between work in a localized meeting and work in a distributed meeting.*

This and the next gap deal with the pragmatics of using synchronous groupware. There is an enormous difference between using collaborative drawing or decision support tools in an electronic meeting room (see Chapter 12 of this volume) and using them in a distributed environment across several rooms (see Chapter 13 of this volume). Yet the discontinuity should not be as great—one should be able to move "into another room" and rejoin the group without missing a beat. One useful technology may be that of video overlays of task and interpersonal space (Ishii and Kobayashi, 1992, included in Chapter 13 of this volume), but much remains to be done (Mantei, Baecker, Sellen, Buxton, Milligan, and Wellman, 1991, included in Chapter 13 of this volume).

- *The gap between work across local area networks and work across wide area networks.*

Furthermore, even if technology is successful in use across several rooms connected by a local area network, it may fail when used through a wide area network. Here the developers of asynchronous groupware have an advantage—there is no presumption of working in close and highly interactive coordination, so delays of a few seconds or minutes are tolerable. There are substantial technical and behavioral challenges in developing synchronous groupware that is effective across wide area networks and effective across wide variations in network bandwidth. This must be done in such a way that those connected locally do not have too great an advantage over those connected at a great distance.

- *The gap between synchronous work and asynchronous work.*

Real collaborative work moves smoothly back and forth between synchronous, real-time interaction and asynchronous, offline activity. For example, co-authors may work together in outlining a document, then work independently on drafting the text of individual sections, then review it in a joint meeting, then trade sections for editing, and then pass the entire document to one individual in order to ensure consistency in style (Posner and Baecker, submitted for review). Yet most CSCW technology and most collaborative writing systems have been developed for one class of work or the other, but not both. (Baecker, Nastos, Posner, and Mawby, submitted for review, describes a system that is an exception to this statement.) To be successful, groupware must allow users fluid motion between working together concurrently and working independently at different times.

- *The gap between work without computers and work with computers.*

The final technological gap affects all computer use, not just CSCW. For instance, although a few young computer scientists eschew paper totally, most computer users do some work in the computer and some on paper. Transforming work products from within the computer to paper is straightforward; going the other way is typically quite difficult. This is changing through advances in optical character recognition and video input (Ishii and Ohkubo, 1990, included in Chapter 13 of this volume), but the graceful introduction of these technologies into common work practice is yet to be achieved. Finally, this gap deals with more than the differences between that of paper and electronic documents—there is also the relationship of work at a desk to work at a terminal, and work at a whiteboard to work at an electronic whiteboard (Elrod et al., 1992, included in Chapter 12 of this volume).

Yet the gaps we face are not entirely technological. There are social, organizational, and cultural issues which are even deeper and more important.

- *The gap between work as computer scientists presume it to be, and work as it really is.*

Many systems built for collaborative writing (Ellis, Gibbs, and Rein, 1991, included in Chapter 1 of this volume; Leland, Fish, and Kraut, 1988) make strong explicit and implicit assumptions about how people write together. In our own work we postponed system design until we could develop a fairly deep understanding of the realities of collaborative writing. This was based on a literature survey, a series of interviews, and an experiment (Posner and Baecker, 1992, this volume; Baecker, Nastos, Posner, and Mawby, submitted for review; Posner and Baecker, submitted for review). In other words, builders of CSCW technology need to take seriously the principles of *user-centered system design* (Norman and Draper, 1986).

- *The gap between the use of CSCW technology in vitro and its use in vivo.*

Effective user-centered system design requires *iterative design* incorporating repeated cycles of design, implementation, and evaluation of new technology. Grudin (1989; 1990, included in Chapter 2 of this volume) asserts that another reason why groupware applications fail is that they are extremely difficult to evaluate. Traditional human-computer interaction (HCI) work has relied both on laboratory usability testing (*in vitro*) and field studies (*in vivo*) to evaluate the suitability and effectiveness of new applications and their interfaces. Because groupware requires the coordinated work of a number of individuals (and effective collaboration requires sustained use over a period of time), both laboratory experiments and field studies are difficult to run, and we must be extremely cautious in assuming that results from the laboratory will necessarily apply in the field (Hollingshead and McGrath, 1991; Kiesler and Sproull, 1992). (Also see Baecker and Buxton, 1987, Case Study A, for a good example of this.)

- *The gap between management benefit and acceptance of CSCW technology and worker benefit and acceptance of the technology.*

Grudin (1989; 1990, included in Chapter 2 of this volume) has argued, for example, that electronic calendaring systems have failed in great part because management gets the primary benefit while workers assume the primary costs of the time and effort of data entry. Lange (1992a, included in Chapter 8 of this volume) reports on a counterexample to this hypothesis. One methodology for avoiding this kind of problem is *participatory design* (Bjerknes, Ehn, and Kyng, 1987; Schuler and Namioko, 1992).

Yet even when there is perceived benefit, there may not be acceptance. Consider the serious issues of surveillance and invasion of privacy raised by one of the most chilling technologies developed to date in the name of enhancing collaborative work—the active badge (Want, 1992, forthcoming). The active badge allows a central computer to track the movements of all employees wherever they move throughout a building! Advocates of active badges paint an idyllic picture in which one never misses a phone call and one can better remember activities, conversations, and ideas through records that link episodes and activities to movements (Newman, Eldridge, and Lamming, 1991). A discussion of attitudes towards active badges in two research laborato-ries may be found in Harper (1992). I believe that the perceived dangers (not to mention the real dangers) from the potential misuse of this technology are so great that no list of modest productivity gains will succeed in making this an acceptable technology.

Issues of video surveillance and invasion of privacy also arise in the use of media spaces. Yet we should not end on too sour a note. All technology can be used for good and for evil. I believe that most collaboration technologies will be generally beneficial to humankind. The gaps listed above can be bridged. If our technological innovation is sensitive to how people work, who they are, and what they feel about their tools, and to the social and organizational culture in which they work, we can develop a new generation of groupware that will empower, enhance, and enliven collaborative work. May this volume contribute to that goal.

References

Abel, M. (1990). Experiences in an Exploratory Distributed Organization. In [Galegher et al. 1990], pp. 489-510.

Ahuja, S.R., Ensor, J.R., and Horn, D.N. (1988). The Rapport Multimedia Conferencing System. *Proceedings of the Conference on Office Information Systems*, ACM, pp. 1-8.

Ahuja, S.R., Ensor, J.R., and Lucco, S.E. (1990). A Comparison of Application Sharing Mechanisms in Real-time Desktop Conferencing Systems. *Proceedings of the Conference on Office Information Systems, SIGOIS Bulletin* 11(2-3), ACM, pp. 238-248.

Aizu, I. (1991). The Japanese Economy as a Community: Cooperating to Compete. *Promethee*, March 1991.

Ancona, D.G. and Caldwell, D.F. (1990). Information Technology and Work Groups: The Case of New Product Teams. In [Galegher et al. 1990], pp. 173-190.

Apple Computer (1988*v*). *Knowledge Navigator.* Video tape.

Applegate, L.M. (1991). Technology Support for Cooperative Work: A Framework for Studying Introduction and Assimilation in Organizations. *Journal of Organizational Computing* 1(1), pp. 11-39.

Applegate, L.M., Ellis, C., Holsapple, C.W., Radermacher, F.J., and Whinston, A.B. (1991). Organizational Computing: Definitions and Issues. *Journal of Organizational Computing* 1(1), pp. 1-10.

Atkinson, J.M. and Heritage, J. (Eds.) (1984). *Structures of Social Action: Studies in Conversation Analysis.* Cambridge University Press.

AT&T Bell Labs (1989*v*). Rapport. *ACM SIGGRAPH Video Review 45,* CHI '89 Technical Video Program.

Austin, L.C., Liker, J.K., and McLeod, P.L. (1990). Determinants and Patterns of Control over Technology in a Computerized Meeting Room. In [Halasz 1990], pp. 39-51.

Baecker, R.M. (1991). New Paradigms for Computing in the 90s. *Proceedings of Graphics Interface '91*, Morgan Kaufmann, pp. 224-229.

Baecker, R.M. and Buxton, W.A.S. (1987). *Readings in Human Computer Interaction: A Multidisciplinary Approach.* Morgan Kaufmann.

Baecker, R.M., Buxton, W.A.S., and Grudin, J. (1993, in preparation). *Readings in Human Computer Interaction and Interface Design for the 1990s.* Morgan Kaufmann.

Baecker, R.M., Nastos, D., Posner, I.R., and Mawby, K. (1992, submitted for publication). The User-Centred Iterative Design of Collaborative Writing Software.

Bales, R.F. (1950). *Interaction Process Analysis: A Method for the Study of Small Groups.* Addison-Wesley.

Bales, R.F. and Cohen, S.P. (1979). *SYMLOG: A System for the Multiple Level Observation of Groups.* Free Press.

Bannon, L. (1991). From Human Factors to Human Actors: The Role of Psychology and Human-Computer Interaction Studies in System Design. In [Greenbaum and Kyng, 1991], pp. 25-44.

Bannon, L., Robinson, M., and Schmidt, K. (Eds.) (1991). *ECSCW '91.* Proceedings of the Second European Conference on Computer Supported Cooperative Work. Kluwer Academic Publishers.

Bannon, L. and Schmidt, K. (1991). CSCW: Four Characters in Search of a Context. In [Bowers and Benford 1991], pp. 3-16.

Bartee, T.C. (Ed.) (1986). *Digital Communications.* Howard W. Sams & Co.

Bartee, T.C. (Ed.) (1989). *ISDN, DECnet, and SNA Communications.* Howard W. Sams & Co.

Beaudouin-Lafon, M. (1991). User Interface Management Systems: Present and Future. In Coquillart, S. (Ed.) (1991). *State of the Art Reports*, Eurographics '91 Technical Report Series, Vienna, Austria, 2-6 September 1991, pp. 209-233.

Beck, E.E. (in press). A Survey of Collaborative Writing. In [Sharples, in press].

Bell Communications Research (1989*v*). Cruiser: A Multimedia System for Social Browsing. *ACM SIGGRAPH Video Review 45,* CHI '89 Technical Video Program.

Bentley, R., Rodden, T., Sawyer, P., Sommerville, I., Hughes, J., Randall, D., and Shapiro, D. (1992). Ethnographically-informed Systems Design for Air Traffic Control. In [Turner and Kraut 1992], pp. 123-129.

Berlin, L., Jeffries, R. M. (1992). Consultants and Apprentices: Observations about Learning and Collaborative Problem Solving. In [Turner and Kraut 1992], pp. 130-137.

Note: Dates followed by *v* indicate video tape material.

Berne, E. (1963). *The Structure and Dynamics of Organizations and Groups.* J.P. Lippincott.

Bier, E.A. and Freeman, S. (1991). MMM: A User Interface Architecture for Shared Editors on a Single Screen. *Proceedings of UIST '91*, ACM, pp. 79-86.

Bier, E., Freeman, S., and Pier, K. (1992v). MMM: The Multi-Device, Multi-User Multi-Editor. *ACM SIGGRAPH Video Review 76* , CHI '92 Technical Video Program.

Bignoli, C. and Simone, C. (1991). AI Techniques for Supporting Human to Human Communication in CHAOS. In [Bowers and Benford 1991], pp. 103-118.

Bikson, T.K. and Eveland, J.D. (1986). *New Office Technology: Planning for People.* Pergamon Press.

Bjerknes, G., Ehn, P., and Kyng, M. (Eds.) (1987). *Computers and Democracy: A Scandinavian Challenge.* Avebury, Gower Publishing Company.

Bly, S. (1990v). Media Spaces. Xerox PARC, Palo Alto, California.

Bly, S. and Minneman , S.L. (1990). Commune: A Shared Drawing Surface. *Proceedings of the COIS '90 Conference on Office Information Systems*, ACM, pp. 184-192.

Böcker, P. (1988). *ISDN — The Integrated Services Digital Network: Concepts, Methods, Systems.* Springer-Verlag.

Bødker, S. and Grønbaek, K. (1991a). Cooperative Prototyping Studies — Users and Designers Envision a Dental Case Record System. In [Bowers and Benford 1991], pp. 315-332.

Bødker, S. and Grønbaek, K. (1991b). Cooperative Prototyping: Users and Designers in Mutual Activity. *International Journal of Man-Machine Studies* 34(3), pp. 453-478. Also appears in [Greenberg 1991], pp. 331-356.

Bonfiglio, A., Malatesta, G., and Tisato F. (1991). Conference Toolkit: A Framework for Real-time Conferencing. In [Bowers and Benford 1991], pp. 63-77.

Borenstein, N.S. (1990). *Multimedia Applications Development with the Andrew Toolkit.* Prentice-Hall.

Borenstein, N.S. (1991). Multimedia Electronic Mail: Will the Dream Become Reality? *Communications of the ACM* 34(4), pp. 117-119.

Borenstein, N.S. (1992). Computational Mail As Network Infrastructure for Computer-Supported Cooperative Work. In [Turner and Kraut 1992], pp. 67-74.

Borenstein, N.S. and Thyberg, C.A. (1991). Power, Ease of Use and Cooperative Work in a Practical Multimedia Message System. *International Journal of Man-Machine Studies* 34(2), pp. 229-259. Also appears in [Greenberg 1991], pp. 99-129.

Borning, A. and Travers, M. (1991). Two Approaches to Casual Interaction Over Computer and Video Networks. *Proceedings of CHI '91*, ACM, pp. 13-19.

Bostrom, R.P., Watson, R., and Kinney, S.T. (Eds.) (1992). *Computer Augmented Teamwork: A Guided Tour.* Van Nostrand Reinhold.

Bowers, J.M. and Benford, S.D. (Eds.) (1991). *Studies in Computer Supported Cooperative Work: Theory, Practice, and Design.* Proceedings of the First European Conference on Computer Supported Cooperative Work. Held in 1989. North-Holland.

Bowers, J. and Churcher, J. (1988). Local and Global Structuring of Computer Mediated Communication: Developing Linguistic Perspectives on CSCW in COSMOS. In [Suchman 1988], pp. 125-139.

Brinck, T. (1992v). The Conversation Board. *ACM SIGGRAPH Video Review*, CSCW '92 Technical Video Program.

Brinck, T. and Gomez, L. M. (1992). A Collaborative Medium for the Support of Conversational Props. In [Turner and Kraut 1992], pp. 171-178.

Brittan, D. (1992). Being There: The Promise of Multimedia Communications. *MIT Technology Review* 95(4), May/June 1992, pp. 42-50.

Brothers, L., Hollan, J., Stornetta, S., Abney, S., Furnas, G., Littman, M., and Nielson, J. (1992). Supporting Informal Communication Via Ephemeral Interest Groups. In [Turner and Kraut 1992], pp. 84-90.

Brown, J.S. (1985). Process Versus Product: A Perspective on Tools for Communal and Informal Electronic Learning. *Journal of Educational Computing Research* 1(2), pp. 179-201.

Brown, J.S. and Newman, S.E. (1985). Issues in Cognitive and Social Ergonomics: From Our House to Bauhaus. *Human-Computer Interaction* 1, pp. 359-391.

Bullen, C.V. and Bennett, J.L. (1990). Learning from User Experience with Groupware. In [Halasz 1990], pp. 291-302.

Bullen, C.V. and Bennett, J.L. (1991). Groupware in Practice: An Interpretation of Work Experiences. In [Dunlop and Kling 1991], pp. 257-287.

Burger, A.M., Meyer, B.D., Jung, C.J., and Long, K.B. (1991). The Virtual Notebook System. *Proceedings of Hypertext '91*, ACM, pp. 395-401.

Burgess Yakemovic, K.C. and Conklin, E.J. (1990). Report on a Development Project Use of an Issue-Based Information System. In [Halasz 1990], pp. 105-118.

Bush, V. (1945). As We May Think. *Atlantic Monthly* 76(1), July 1945, pp. 101-108.

Buxton, W. (1986). There's More to Interaction Than Meets the Eye. In [Norman and Draper 1986], pp. 319-337.

Buxton, W. (1989). Introduction to this Special Issue on Non-Speech Audio. *Human Computer Interaction* 4(1), pp. 1-9.

Buxton, W. (1992). Telepresence: Integrating Shared Task and Person Spaces. *Proceedings of Graphics Interface '92*, Morgan Kaufmann, pp. 123-129.

Buxton, W. and Moran, R. (1990). EuroPARC's Integrated Interactive Intermedia Facility (IIIF): Early Experiences. In [Gibbs and Verrijn-Stuart 1990], pp. 11-34.

Carnegie Mellon University (1989v). An Overview of the Andrew System. *ACM SIGGRAPH Video Review 46*, CHI '89 Technical Video Program.

Carroll, J.M. and Moran, T.P. (Eds.) (1992). Special Issue on Design Rationale. *Human-Computer Interaction* 6(3-4).

Cashman, P.M. and Stroll, D. (1989). Developing the Management Systems of the 1990s: The Role of Collaborative Work. In [Olson 1989], pp. 129-146.

Cavalier, T., Chandhok, R., Kaufer, D., Morris, J., and Neuwirth, C. (1991). A Visual Design for Collaborative Work: Columns for Commenting and Annotation. *Proceedings of the Twenty-fourth Annual Hawaii International Conference on the System Sciences*, Vol. III, IEEE Computer Society Press, pp. 729-738.

Centre for Machine Intelligence (1988v). The Capture Lab. Electronic Data Systems, Ann Arbor, Michigan.

Cerf, V.G. (1991). Networks. *Scientific American* 265(3), September 1991, pp. 72-81.

Chalfonte, B.L., Fish, R.S., and Kraut, R.E. (1991). Expressive Richness: A Comparison of Speech and Text as Media for Revision. *Proceedings of CHI '91*, ACM, pp. 21-26.

Chapanis, A. (1975). Interactive Human Communication. *Scientific American* 232(3), pp. 36-42. Also appears in [Greif 1988], pp. 127-140.

Cicourel, A.V. (1990). The Integration of Distributed Knowledge in Collaborative Medical Diagnosis. In [Galegher et al. 1990], pp. 221-242.

Clark, H.H. and Brennan, S.E. (1991). Grounding in Communication. In [Resnick et al. 1991], pp. 127-149.

Clark, H.H. and Wilkes-Gibbs, D. (1986). Referring as a Collaborative Process. *Cognition* 22, pp. 1-39.

Clement, A. (1990). Cooperative Support for Computer Work: A Social Perspective on the Empowering of End Users. In [Halasz 1990], pp. 223-236.

Clement, A. and Parsons, D. (1990). Work Group Knowledge Requirements for Desktop Computing. *Proceedings of the Twenty-third Annual Hawaii International Conference on the System Sciences*, IEEE Computer Society Press, pp. 84-93.

Cole, P. and Nast-Cole, J. (1992). A Primer on Group Dynamics for Groupware Developers. In [Marca and Bock 1992], pp. 44-57.

Coleman, D. (1992a). *Proceedings of Groupware '92*, Morgan Kaufmann.

Coleman, D. (1992b). Welcome to Groupware '92. In [Coleman 1992a], pp. xiii-xv.

Coleman, D. (1992c). How Do I Sell Groupware and Still Make Money? In [Coleman 1992a], pp. 364-365.

Coleman, D. and Shapiro, R. (1992). Defining Groupware. Special Advertising Section to *Network World*, June 22, 1992.

Collins, A. and Smith, E.E. (Eds.) (1988). *Readings in Cognitive Science: A Perspective from Psychology and Artificial Intelligence*. Morgan Kaufmann.

Conklin, J. (1987). Hypertext: An Introduction and Survey. *IEEE Computer* 20(9), pp. 17-41.

Conklin, E.J. (1992). Capturing Organizational Memory. In [Coleman 1992a], pp. 133-137.

Conklin, J. and Begeman, M. (1988). gIBIS: A Hypertext Tool for Exploratory Policy Discussion. *ACM Transactions on Office Information Systems* 6(4), pp. 303-331.

Conklin, J. and Burgess Yakemovic, K.C. (1992). A Process-Oriented Approach to Design Rationale. *Human-Computer Interaction* 6(3-4), pp. 357-391.

Connolly, T., Jessup, L.M., and Valacich, J.S. (1990). Effects of Anonymity and Evaluative Tone on Idea Generation in Computer-Mediated Groups. *Management Science* 36(6), pp. 689-703.

Connor, D.L. (1992). Making the Most of Information. In [Coleman 1992a], pp. 63-68.

Conrath, D.W., Dunn, E.V., Bloor, W.G., and Tranquada, B. (1977). A Clinical Evaluation of Four Alternative Telemedicine Systems. *Behavioral Science* 22, pp. 12-21.

Cool, C., Fish, R.S., Kraut, R.E., and Lowery, C.M. (1992). Iterative Design of Video Communication Systems. In [Turner and Kraut 1992], pp. 25-32.

Couloris, G.F. and Dollimore, J. (1988). *Distributed Systems: Concepts and Design*. Addison-Wesley.

Cross, T.C. (1992). Meanwhile Back at the Ranch. In [Coleman 1992a], pp. 142-151.

Crowley, T. (1992). Commercial Multimedia Groupware. In [Coleman 1992a], pp. 421-422.

Crowley, T., Milazzo, P., Baker, E., Forsdick, H., and Tomlinson, R. (1990). MMConf: An Infrastructure for Building Shared Multimedia Applications. In [Halasz 1990], pp. 329-342.

Cruse, D. (1992). Workflow Process Automation: Beyond Traditional Workflow. In [Coleman 1992a], pp. 301-311.

Curtis, P. (1992). Mudding: Social Phenomena in Text-based Virtual Realities. In Schuler, D. (Ed.), *Proceedings of the DIAC-92 Conference on Directions and Implications of Advanced Computing*, Computer Professionals for Social Responsibility, May 2-3, 1992, Berkeley, CA, pp. 48-68.

Daft, R.L. and Lengel, R.H. (1986). Organizational Information Requirements, Media Richness, and Structural Design. *Management Science* 32(5), pp. 554-571.

Dallavalle, T., Esposito, A., and Lang, S. (1992). Groupware—One Experience. In [Coleman 1992a], pp. 470-477.

DeCindio, F., DeMichelis, G., Simone, C., Vassallo, R., and Zanaboni, A. (1986). CHAOS as a Coordination Technology. In [Greif 1986].

Dennis, A.R., George, J.F., Jessup, L.M., Nunamaker, J.F., and Vogel, D.R. (1988). Information Technology to Support Electronic Meetings. *MIS Quarterly* 12(4), pp. 591-624.

DeSanctis, G. (1991). Shifting Foundations in GDSS Research. To appear in [Jessup and Valacich 1993].

DeSantis, G. and Gallupe, B. (1987). A Foundation for the Study of Group Decision Support Systems. *Management Science* 33(5), May 1987, pp. 589-609.

Dewan, P. (1992v). Coupling the User Interfaces of a Multi-user Program. *ACM SIGGRAPH Video Review*, CSCW '92 Technical Video Program.

Dewan, P. and Choudhary, R. (1991a). Primitives for Programming Multi-User Interfaces. *Proceedings of UIST '91*, ACM, pp. 41-48.

Dewan, P. and Choudhary, R. (1991b). Flexible User Interface Coupling in a Collaborative System. *Proceedings of CHI '91*, ACM, pp. 41-48.

Di Pietro, C. (1992). Groupware Meetings That Work. In [Coleman 1992a], pp. 50-57.

Dordick, H.S. (1986). *Understanding Modern Telecommunications*. McGraw-Hill.

Dourish, P. and Bellotti, V. (1992). Awareness and Coordination in Shared Workspaces. In [Turner and Kraut 1992], pp. 107-114.

Dourish, P. and Bly, S. (1992). Portholes: Supporting Awareness in a Distributed Work Group. *Proceedings of CHI '92*, ACM, pp. 541-547.

Dubs, S. and Hayne, S. (1992). Distributed Facilitation: A Concept Whose Time Has Come? In [Turner and Kraut 1992], pp. 314-321.

Duff, B. and Florentine, G. (1992). Collaboration and Document Databases. In [Coleman 1992a], pp. 244-248.

Dunlop, C. and Kling, R. (Eds.) (1991). *Computerization and Controversy: Value Conflicts and Social Choices*. Academic Press.

Dunn, E.V., Acton, H., Conrath, D., Higgins, C., and Bain, H. (1980). The Use of Slow-Scan Video for CME in a Remote Area. *Journal of Medical Education* 55, pp. 493-495.

Dunn, E.V. and Fisher, M. (1985). The Use of Freeze Frame (Slow Scan) Video for Health Professional Education. *Medical Education* 19, pp. 148-154.

Dyson, E. (1992). A Framework for Groupware. In [Coleman 1992a], pp. 10-20.

Ede, L. and Lunsford, A. (1990). *Singular Texts / Plural Authors: Perspectives on Collaborative Writing*. Southern Illinois University Press.

Eddy, W.B. (1985). *The Manager and the Working Group*. Praeger Publishers.

Egger, E. and Wagner, I. (1992). Time-Management: A Case for CSCW. In [Turner and Kraut 1992], pp. 249-256.

Egido, C. (1990). Teleconferencing as a Technology to Support Cooperative Work: Its Possibilities and Limitations. In [Galegher et al. 1990], pp. 351-371.

Egido, C., et al. (1987v). Multimedia Technology for Collaborative Writing. Bellcore. *ACM SIGGRAPH Video Review 27*. CHI+GI'87 Technical Video Program.

Ehn, P. (1989). *Work-Oriented Design of Computer Artifacts*. Arbetslivscentrum. Stockholm.

Ehrlich, S.F. (1987a). Social and Psychological Factors Influencing the Design of Office Communication Systems. *Proceedings of CHI+GI 1987*, ACM, pp. 323-329.

Ehrlich, S.F. (1987b). Strategies for Encouraging Successful Adoption of Office Communication Systems. *ACM Transactions on Office Information Systems* 5(4), pp. 340-357.

Ellis, C.A. and Gibbs, S.J. (1989). Concurrency Control in Groupware Systems. *ACM SIGMOD Record* 18(2), June 1989, pp. 399-407.

Ellis, C.A., Gibbs, S.J., and Rein, G.L. (1991). Groupware: Some Issues and Experiences. *Communications of the ACM* 34(1), pp. 39-58.

Ellis, C.A. and Nutt, G.J. (1980). Office Information Systems and Computer Science. *ACM Computing Surveys* 12(1), pp. 27-60. Also appears in [Greif 1988], pp. 199-247.

Ellis, S.R. (1991). Nature and Origins of Virtual Environments: A Bibliographic Essay. *Computing Systems in Engineering* 2(4), pp. 321-347.

Elrod, S., Bruce, R., Gold, R., Goldberg, D., Halasz, F., Janssen, W., Lee, D., McCall, K., Pederson, E., Pier, K., Tang, J., and Welch B. (1992). Liveboard: A Large Interactive Display Supporting Group Meetings, Presentations and Remote Collaboration. *Proceedings of CHI '92*, ACM, pp. 599-607.

Elwart-Keys, M., Halonen, D., Horton, M., Kass, R., and Scott, P. (1990). User Interface Requirements for Face to Face Groupware. *Proceedings of CHI '90*, ACM, pp. 295-301.

Engelbart, D. (1963). A Conceptual Framework for the Augmentation of Man's Intellect. In Howerton, P. (Ed.), *Vistas in Information Handling*, Vol. 1, Spartan Books, pp. 1-29. Reprinted in [Greif 1986].

Engelbart, D. (1982). Towards High-Performance Knowledge Workers. Office Automation Conference. AFIPS Press. Reprinted in [Greif 1986].

Engelbart, D. (1984). Authorship Provisions in Augment. IEEE Compcon Conference. Reprinted in [Greif 1986].

Engelbart, D. and English, W. (1968). A Research Center for Augmenting Human Intellect. *Proceedings of the FJCC* 33(1), pp. 395-410. Reprinted in [Greif 1986].

Ensor, J.R., Ahuja, S.R., Connaghan, R., Horn, D., Pack, M., and Seligmann, D.D. (1991). Control Issues in Multimedia Conferencing. *Proceedings of the IEEE Conference on Communications Software: Communications for Distributed Applications & Systems*, Chapel Hill, N.C., 18-19 April 1991, pp. 133-143.

Ensor, J.R., Ahuja, S.R., Horn, D.N., and Lucco, S.E. (1988). The Rapport Multimedia Conferencing System — A Software Overview. *Proceedings of the Second International Conference on Computer Workstations*, IEEE Computer Society, pp. 52-58.

Ericsson, K.A. and Simon, H.A. (1980). Verbal Reports as Data. *Psychological Review* 87(1), pp. 215-251.

Eveland, J.D. and Bikson, T.K. (1987). Evolving Electronic Communication Networks: An Empirical Assessment. *Office: Technology and People*, November 1987, Elsevier, pp. 103-128.

Eveland, J.D. and Bikson, T.K. (1988). Work Group Structures and Computer Support: A Field Experiment. *ACM Transactions on Office Information Systems* 6(4), pp. 344-379.

Fafchamps, D. (1991). Ethnographic Workflow Analysis: Specifications for Design. In Bullinger, H.-J. (Ed.) (1991). *Human Aspects in Computing: Design and Use of Interactive Systems and Work with Terminals*, Elsevier, pp. 709-715.

Fafchamps, D., Reynolds, D., and Kuchinsky, A. (1991). The Dynamics of Small Group Decision-making Using Electronic Mail. In [Bowers and Benford 1991], pp. 211-224.

Fanning, T. and Raphael, B. (1986). Computer Teleconferencing: Experience at Hewlett Packard. In [Greif 1986], pp. 291-306.

Ferwanger, T., Wang, Y., Lewe, H., and Krcmar, H.

(1991). Experiences in Designing the Hohenheim CATeam Room. In [Bowers and Benford 1991], pp. 251-265.

Finholt, T. and Sproull, L.S. (1990). Electronic Groups at Work. *Organization Science* 1(1), pp. 41-64.

Finholt, T., Sproull, L., and Kiesler, S. (1990). Communication and Performance in Ad Hoc Task Groups. In [Galegher et al. 1990], pp. 291-325.

Fish, R.S., Kraut, R.E., and Chalfonte, B.L. (1990). The VideoWindow System in Informal Communications. In [Halasz 1990], pp. 1-11.

Fish, R.S., Kraut, R.E., Leland, M.D., and Cohen, M. (1988). Quilt: A Collaborative Tool for Cooperative Writing. *Proceedings of COIS '88 Conference on Office Information Systems*, ACM, pp. 30-37.

Fish, R.S., Kraut, R.E., and Root, R.W. (1992). Evaluating Video as a Technology for Informal Communication. *Proceedings of CHI '92*, ACM, pp. 37-48.

Flor, N.V. and Hutchins, E.L. (1991). Analyzing Distributed Cognition in Software Teams: A Case Study of Team Programming During Perfective Software Maintenance. In Koenemann-Belliveau, J., Moher, T.G., and Robertson, S.P. (Eds.). *Proceedings of the Fourth Workshop on Empirical Studies of Programmers*, Ablex, pp. 36-64.

Flores, F., Graves, M., Hartfield, B., and Winograd, T. (1988). Computer Systems and the Design of Organizational Interaction. *ACM Transactions on Office Information Systems* 6(2), pp. 153-172.

Forsdick, H.C. (1985). Explorations in Real-Time Multimedia Conferencing. *Proceedings of the 2nd International Symposium on Computer Message Systems*, IFIP, Sept. 1985, pp. 299-315.

Foroughi, A. and Jelassi, M.T. (1990). NSS Solutions to Major Negotiation Stumbling Blocks. *Proceedings of the Twenty-third Annual Hawaii International Conference on the System Sciences*, Vol. IV, IEEE Computer Society Press, pp. 2-11.

Fox, E.A. (Ed.) (1989). Special Issue on Interactive Technology. *Communications of the ACM* 32(7), July 1989.

Fox, E.A. (Ed.) (1991a). Special Issue on Digital Multimedia Systems. *Communications of the ACM* 34(4), April 1991.

Fox, E.A. (1991b). Special Issue on Multimedia Information Systems. *IEEE Computer* 24(10), October 1991.

Fox, E.A. (1991c). Advances in Interactive Digital Multimedia Systems. *IEEE Computer* 24(10), pp. 9-21.

Francik, E. (1989v). Freestyle. Wang Laboratories. *ACM SIGGRAPH Video Review 45*. CHI '89 Technical Video Program.

Francik, E., Rudman, S.E., Cooper, D., and Levine, S. (1991). Putting Innovation to Work: Adopting Strategies for Multimedia Communication Systems. *Communications of the ACM* 34(12), pp. 52-63.

Gale, S. (1991). Adding Audio and Video to an Office Environment. In [Bowers and Benford 1991], pp. 49-62.

Galegher, J., Kraut, R., and Egido, C. (Eds.) (1990). *Intellectual Teamwork: Social and Technological Foundations of Cooperative Work*. Lawrence Erlbaum Associates.

Galloway and Rabinowitz (1980v). Hole in Space: A Public Communication Sculpture. Mobile Image.

Gardner, H. (1985). *The Mind's New Science: A History of the Cognitive Revolution*. Basic Books.

Garfinkel, H. (1967). *Studies in Ethnomethodology*. Prentice-Hall.

Garfinkel, H. (1986). *Ethnomethodological Studies of Work*. Routledge.

Garfinkel, D., Gust, P., Lemon, M., and Lowder, S. (1989). The SharedX Multi-user Interface User's Guide, Version 2.0, Hewlett-Packard Laboratories Research Report STL-TM-89-07, Palo Alto, CA, March 1989.

Gaver, W.W. (1986). Auditory Icons: Using Sound in Computer Interfaces. *Human-Computer Interaction* 2, pp. 167-177.

Gaver, W.W. (1989). The SonicFinder: An Interface That Uses Auditory Icons. *Human-Computer Interaction* 4, pp. 67-94.

Gaver, W.W. (1991). Sound Support for Collaboration. In [Bannon, Robinson, and Schmidt 1991], pp. 293-308.

Gaver, W.W. (1992). The Affordances of Media Spaces for Collaboration. In [Turner and Kraut 1992], pp. 17-24.

Gaver, W.W., Moran, T., MacLean, A., Lövstrand, L., Dourish, P., Carter, K., and Buxton, W. (1992). Realizing a Video Environment: EuroPARC's RAVE System. *Proceedings of CHI '92*, pp. 27-35.

Gaver, W.W., Smith, R.B., and O'Shea, T. (1991). Effective Sounds in Complex Systems: The ARKola Simulation. *Proceedings of CHI '91*, ACM, pp. 85-90.

George, J.F., Valacich, J.S., and Nunamaker, J.F. (1990). The Organizational Implementation of an Electronic Meeting System: An Analysis of the Innovation Process. *Proceedings of CHI '90*, ACM, pp. 361-367.

Gerrissen, J.F. and Daamen, J. (1990). Inclusion of a "Sharing" Feature in Telecommunication Services. *Proceedings of the Thirteenth International Symposium Human Factors in Telecommunications HFT '90*, Torino, Italy, 10-14 September 1990.

Gerson, E.M. and Star, S.L. (1986). Analyzing Due Process in the Workplace. *ACM Transactions on Office Information Systems* 4(3), pp. 257-270.

Gibbs, S. and Verrijn-Stuart, A.A. (Eds.) (1990). *Multi-User Interfaces and Applications*. North-Holland.

Goldberg, V., Safran, M., and Shapiro, E. (1992). Active Mail: A Framework for Implementing Groupware. In [Turner and Kraut 1992], pp. 75-83.

Goldberg, Y., Safran, M., Silverman, W., and Shapiro, E. (1992). Active Mail: A Framework for Integrated Group Applications. In [Coleman 1992a], pp. 222-224.

Gosling, J., Rosenthal, D.S.H., and Arden, M.J. (1989). *The NeWS Book*. Springer-Verlag.

Gorry, G.A., Long, K.B., Burger, A.M., Jung, C.P., and Meyer, B.D. (1991). The Virtual Notebook System: An Architecture for Collaborative Work. *Journal of Organizational Computing* 1(3), pp. 233-250.

Gould, J.D. (1988). How to Design Usable Systems. In Helander, M. (Ed.) *Handbook of Human-Computer Interaction*, North-Holland, pp. 757-789.

Gould, J.D. and Lewis, C. (1985). Designing for Usability: Key Principles and What Designers Think. *Communications of the ACM* 28(3), pp. 300-311.

Goulde, M.A. (1992). Notes on Information Technology. In [Coleman 1992a], pp. 325-326.

Graham, T. C. N. and Urnes, T. (1992). Relational Views as a Model for Automatic Distributed Implementation of Multi-User Applications. In [Turner and Kraut 1992], pp. 59-66.

Greenbaum, J. and Kyng, M. (Eds.) (1991). *Design at Work: Cooperative Design of Computer Systems*. Lawrence Erlbaum Associates.

Greenberg, S. (1990). Sharing Views and Interactions with Single-User Applications. *Proceedings of the Conference on Office Information Systems*, Cambridge, MA, April 1990, ACM, pp. 227-237.

Greenberg, S. (Ed.) (1991a). *Computer-Supported Cooperative Work and Groupware*. Academic Press.

Greenberg, S. (1991b). Personalizable Groupware: Accommodating Individual Roles and Group Differences. In [Bannon et al. 1991], pp. 17-31.

Greenberg, S. and Bohnet, R. (1991). GroupSketch: A Multi-user Sketchpad for Geographically-distributed Small Groups. *Proceedings of Graphics Interface '91*, Morgan Kaufmann, pp. 207-215.

Greenberg, S. and Bohnet, R. (1992v). Groupsketch. *ACM SIGGRAPH Video Review*, CSCW '92 Technical Video Program.

Greenberg, S., Roseman, M., Webster, D., and Bohnet, R. (1992). Issues and Experiences Designing and Implementing Two Group Drawing Tools *Proceedings of the Twenty-fifth Annual Hawaii International Conference on the System Sciences*, Vol. IV, IEEE Computer Society Press, pp. 139-150.

Greif, I. (Ed.) (1986). *CSCW 86: Proceedings of the Conference on Computer-Supported Cooperative Work*. Austin, Texas, Dec. 3-5, 1986. Microelectronics Computer Corporation.

Greif, I. (Ed.) (1988). *Computer-Supported Cooperative Work: A Book of Readings*. Morgan Kaufmann.

Greif, I. (1992). Designing Group-enabled Applications: A Spreadsheet Example. In [Coleman 1992a], pp. 515-525.

Grimes, J. and Potel, M. (Ed.) (1991). Special Issue on Multimedia. *IEEE Computer Graphics and Applications* 11(4), July 1991.

Grønbaek, K., Kyng, M., and Mogensen, P. (1992). CSCW Challenges in Large-Scale Technical Projects — A Case Study. In [Turner and Kraut 1992], pp. 338-345.

Grohowski, R.B., McGoff, C., Vogel, D.R., Martz, W.B., and Nunamaker, J.F. (1990). Implementation of Electronic Meeting Systems at IBM. *MIS Quarterly* 14(4), pp. 369-383.

Group Technologies (1991*v*). Aspects Demonstration Video Tape. Group Technologies.

Grudin, J. (1989). Why Groupware Applications Fail: Problems in Design and Evaluation. *Office: Technology and People* 4(3), pp. 245-264.

Grudin, J. (1990). Groupware and Cooperative Work: Problems and Prospects. In [Laurel 1990], pp. 171-185.

Grudin, J. (1991a). CSCW: The Convergence of Two Development Paradigms. *Proceedings of CHI '91*, ACM, pp. 91-97.

Grudin, J. (1991b). Obstacles to User Involvement in Software Product Development, with Implications for CSCW. *International Journal of Man-Machine Studies* 34(3), pp. 435-452. Also in [Greenberg 1991a], pp. 313-330.

Grudin, J. (Ed.) (1991c). Special Issue on Collaborative Computing. *Communications of the ACM* 34(12).

Grudin, J. (1991, submitted for publication). Groupware and Social Dynamics: Eight Challenges for Developers.

Grudin, J. (1992). Personal communication. 25 August 1992.

Haake, J. M. and Wilson, B. (1992). Supporting Collaborative Writing of Hyperdocuments in SEPIA. In [Turner and Kraut 1992], pp. 138-146.

Hackman, J.R. (Ed.) (1990). *Groups That Work (and Those That Don't)*. Jossey-Bass.

Halasz, F. (1988). Reflections on Notecards: Seven Issues for the Next Generation of Hypermedia Systems. *Communications of the ACM* 31(7), pp. 836-852.

Halasz, F. (Ed.) (1990). *CSCW 90: Proceedings of the Conference on Computer-Supported Cooperative Work*. Los Angeles, Oct. 7-10, 1990. Association for Computing Machinery.

Hammersley, M. and Atkinson, P. (1989). *Ethnography: Principles in Practice*. Routledge.

Harper, R. H. R. (1992). Looking at Ourselves: An Examination of the Social Organization of Two Research Laboratories. In [Turner and Kraut 1992], pp. 330-337.

Harrison, B.L. and Baecker, R.M. (1992). Designing Video Annotation and Analysis Systems. *Proceedings of Graphics Interface '92*, Morgan Kaufmann, pp. 157-166.

Harrison, S. and Minneman, S. (1990). The Media Space: A Research Project into the Use of Video as a Design Medium. *Proceedings of the Conference on Participatory Design*, Computer Professionals for Social Responsibility, Seattle, WA., March 31-April 1 1990, pp. 43-58.

Heath, C. and Luff, P. (1991a). Collaborative Activity and Technological Design: Task Coordination in London Underground Control Rooms. In [Bannon et al. 1991], pp. 65-80.

Heath, C. and Luff, P. (1991b). Disembodied Conduct: Communication through Video in a Multi-Media Office Environment. *Proceedings of CHI '91*, ACM, pp. 99-103.

Helms, R. (1991). Distributed Knowledge Worker (DKW): A Personal Conferencing System. IBM Canada Laboratory Technical Report TR-74.067.

Hendriks, P.R.H. (Ed.) (1991). *Groupware 1991: The Potential of Team and Organisational Computing*. Software Engineering Research Centre (SERC), P.O. Box 424, 3500 AK Utrecht, The Netherlands.

Heritage, J.C. (1984). *Garfinkel and Ethnomethodology*. Polity Press.

Hewitt, C. (1986). Offices are Open Systems. *ACM Transactions on Office Information Systems* 4(3), pp. 271-287.

Higgins, C., Dunn, E., and Conrath, D. (1984). Telemedicine: An Historical Perspective. *Telecommunications Policy*, December 1984, pp. 307-313.

Higgs, W. (1992). Presentation at Groupware '92 Conference, San Jose, CA., 4 August 1992.

Hill, R.D. (1992). Languages for the Construction of Multi-User Multi-Media Synchronous (MUMMS) Applications. In Myers, B.A. (Ed.), *Languages for Developing User Interfaces*, Jones and Bartlett, pp. 125-143.

Hiltz, S.R. (1984). *Online Communities: A Case Study of the Office of the Future*. Ablex.

Hiltz, S.R. (1986). The Virtual Classroom: Using Computer-Mediated Communication for University Teaching. *Journal of Communication* 36(2), pp. 95-104.

Hiltz, S.R. (1988). Collaborative Learning in a Virtual Classroom: Highlights of Findings. In [Suchman 1988], pp. 282-290.

Hiltz, S.R., Shapiro, H., and Ringsted, M. (1990). Collaborative Teaching in a Virtual Classroom. *Proceedings of the Third Symposium on Computer Mediated Communication.* University of Guelph, Guelph, Ontario, pp. 37-55.

Hiltz, S.R. and Turoff, M. (1978). *The Network Nation: Human Communication via Computer.* Addison-Wesley.

Hiltz, S.R. and Turoff, M. (1981). The Evolution of User Behaviour in a Computerized Conferencing System. *Communications of the ACM* 24(11), pp. 739-751.

Hiltz, S.R. and Turoff, M. (1985). Structuring Computer-Mediated Communication Systems to Avoid Information Overload. *Communications of the ACM* 28(7), pp. 680-689.

Hindus, D. and Schmandt, C. (1992). Ubiquitous Audio: Capturing Spontaneous Collaboration. In [Turner and Kraut 1992], pp. 210-217.

Hirst, G. (1991). Does Conversation Analysis Have a Role in Computational Linguistics? *Computational Linguistics* 17(2), pp. 211-227.

Hollan, J. and Stornetta, S. (1992). Beyond Being There. *Proceedings of CHI '92*, ACM, pp. 119-125.

Hollingshead, A.B. and McGrath, J.E. (1991). The Whole Is Less Than the Sum of its Parts: A Critical Review of Research on Computer-Assisted Groups. To appear in Guzzo, R. (Ed.). *Team Decision Making in Organizations* (tentative title).

Holt, A.W. (1988). Diplans: A New Language for the Study and Implementation of Coordination. *ACM Transactions on Office Information Systems* 6(2), pp. 109-125.

Hopgood, F.R.A. (Ed.) (1986). *Methodology of Window Management.* Springer-Verlag.

Hopper, A. (1992v). The Pandora Multimedia System. *ACM SIGGRAPH Video Review*, CSCW '92 Technical Video Program.

Hughes, J.A., Randall, D., and Shapiro, D. (1992). Faltering From Ethnography to Design. In [Turner and Kraut 1992], pp. 115-122.

Hutchins, E. (1990). The Technology of Team Navigation. In [Galegher et al. 1990], pp. 191-220.

Hymes, C.M. and Olson, G.M. (1992). Unblocking Brainstorming Through the Use of a Simple Group Editor. In [Turner and Kraut 1992], pp. 99-106.

IBM Watson Research (1989v). The Paper-Like Interface. T.J. Watson Research Center. *ACM SIGGRAPH Video Review 47*, CHI '89 Technical Video Program.

Ishii, H. (1990a). TeamWorkStation: Towards a Seamless Shared Workspace. In [Halasz 1990], pp. 13-26.

Ishii, H. (1990b). Cross-Cultural Communication and Computer-Supported Cooperative Work. *Whole Earth Review*, Winter 1990, pp. 48-53.

Ishii, H. (1990v). TeamWorkStation. NTT Human Interface Laboratories.

Ishii, H. and Arita, K. (1991). ClearFace: Translucent Multiuser Interface for TeamWorkStation. In [Bannon et al. 1991], pp. 163-174.

Ishii, H. and Kobayashi, M. (1992). ClearBoard: A Seamless Medium for Shared Drawing and Conversation with Eye Contact. *Proceedings of CHI '92*, ACM, pp. 525-532.

Ishii, H., Arita, K., and Kobayashi, M. (1992v). Towards Seamless Collaboration Media: From TeamWorkStation to ClearBoard. *ACM SIGGRAPH Video Review*, CSCW '92 Technical Video Program.

Ishii, H., Kobayashi, M., and Grudin, J. (1992). Integration of Inter-Personal Space and Shared Workspace: ClearBoard Design and Experiments. In [Turner and Kraut 1992], pp. 33-42.

Ishii, H. and Miyake, N. (1991). Toward an Open Shared Workspace: Computer and Video Fusion Approach of TeamWorkStation. *Communications of the ACM* 34(12), pp. 37-50.

Ishii, H. and Ohkubo, M. (1990). Design of TeamWorkStation: A Realtime Shared Workspace Fusing Desktops and Computer Screens. In [Gibbs and Verrijn-Stuart], pp. 131-142.

Jay, A. (1976). How to Run a Meeting. *Harvard Business Review* 54(2), March-April 1976, pp. 43-57.

Jeffay, K., Lin, J.K., Menges, F.D., Smith, F.D., and Smith, J.B. (1992). Architecture of the Artifact-Based Collaboration System Matrix. In [Turner and Kraut 1992], pp. 195-202.

Jessup, L.M., Connolly, T., and Galegher, J. (1990). The Effects of Anonymity on Group Process in Automated Group Problem Solving. *MIS Quarterly* 14(3), pp. 313-321.

Jessup, L.M. and Valacich, J.S. (Eds.) (1993, expected). *Group Support Systems: A New Perspective.* Macmillan.

Johansen, R. (1984). *Teleconferencing and Beyond: Communications in the Office of the Future.* McGraw-Hill.

Johansen, R. (1988). *Computer Support for Business Teams.* The Free Press.

Johansen, R. (1991a). Teams for Tomorrow. Plenary Speech. *Proceedings of the Twenty-fourth Annual Hawaii International Conference on the System Sciences*, IEEE Computer Society Press, pp. 521-534.

Johansen, R. (1991b). Groupware: Future Directions and Wild Cards. *Journal of Organizational Computing* 1(2), pp. 219-227.

Johansen, R., Vallee, J., and Spangler, K. (1979). *Electronic Meetings: Technical Alternatives and Social Choices*. Addison-Wesley.

Johnson, J., Roberts, T.L. Verplank, W., Smith, D.C., Irby, C.H., Beard, M., and Mackey, K. (1989). The Xerox Star: A Retrospective. *IEEE Computer* 22(9), pp. 11-29.

Johnson-Lenz, P. and Johnson-Lenz, T. (1980). Groupware: The Emerging Art of Orchestrating Collective Intelligence. Presented at the First Global Conference on the Future, Toronto, Canada.

Johnson-Lenz, P. and Johnson-Lenz, T. (1981). Consider the Groupware: Design and Group Process Impacts on Communication in the Electronic Medium. In Hiltz, S.R. and Kerr, E.B. (1981). Studies of Computer-Mediated Communication Systems: A Synthesis of the Findings. Final Report of a Workshop, Computerized Conferencing and Communications Center, New Jersey Institute of Technology.

Johnson-Lenz, P. and Johnson-Lenz, T. (1982). Groupware: The Process and Impacts of Design Choices. In [Kerr and Hiltz 1982], pp. 45-55.

Johnson-Lenz, P. and Johnson-Lenz, T. (1992). Groupware is Computer-Mediated Culture: Some Keys to Using It Wisely. In [Coleman 1992a], pp. 130-132.

Jones, B.H. and Sanford, C. (1990). Negotiation Support Systems: Mini-Track Introduction. *Proceedings of the Twenty-third Annual Hawaii International Conference on the System Sciences*, Vol. IV, IEEE Computer Society Press, p. 1.

Jones, O. (1989). *Introduction to the X Window System*. Prentice Hall.

Kaplan, S.M. (1990). ConversationBuilder: An Open Architecture for Collaborative Work. *Proceedings of Interact '90*, Elsevier (North-Holland), pp. 917-922.

Kaplan, S.M., Carroll, A.M., and MacGregor, K.J. (1991). Supporting Collaborative Processes with Conversation-Builder. *Proceedings of the Conference on Organizational Computing Systems*, 5-8 November 1991, Atlanta, Georgia. In *SIGOIS Bulletin* 12(2-3), ACM, pp. 69-79.

Kaplan, S.M., Tolone, W.J., Bogia, D., and Bignoli, C. (1992). Flexible, Active Support for Collaborative Work with Conversation Builder. In [Turner and Kraut 1992], pp. 378-385.

Karmouch, A., Orozco-Barbosa, L., Georganas, N.D., and Goldberg, M. (1990). A Multimedia Medical Communications System. *IEEE Journal on Selected Areas in Communications* 8(3), April 1990, pp. 325-339.

Karon, P. (1991). Seybold Consultants Aim to Form Close Electronic Links with Clients. *PC Week*, October 14, 1991.

Kawell, L., Beckhardt, S., Halvorsen, T., Ozzie, R., and Greif, I. (1988). Replicated Document Management in a Group Communication System. Presented at CSCW '88. In [Marca and Bock 1992], pp. 226-235.

Kelleher, K. and Cross, T.B. (1985). *Teleconferencing: Linking People Together Electronically*. Prentice-Hall.

Kerr, E.B. and Hiltz, S.R. (1982). *Computer-Mediated Communication Systems: Status and Evaluation*. Academic Press.

Kiesler, S. (1986). The Hidden Messages in Computer Networks. *Harvard Business Review*, Jan.-Feb. 1986, pp. 46-48, 52, 54, 58, 60.

Kiesler, S., Siegel, J., and McGuire, T.W. (1984). Social Psychological Aspects of Computer-Mediated Communication. *American Psychologist* 39(10), pp. 1123-1134. Also appears in [Greif 1988], pp. 657-682.

Kiesler, S. and Sproull, L. (1992). Group Decision Making and Communication Technology. *Organization Behaviour and Human Decision Processes* 52(1), pp. 96-123.

Kim, S. (1990). Interdisciplinary Cooperation. In [Laurel 1990], pp. 31-44.

King, J.L. and Star, S.L. (1990). Conceptual Foundations for the Development of Organizational Decision Support Systems. *Proceedings of the Twenty-third Annual Hawaii International Conference on the System Sciences*, Vol. III, IEEE Computer Society Press, p. 143-151.

Kirkpatrick, D. (1992). Here Comes the Payoff from PCs. *Fortune*, 23 March 1992, pp. 93-102.

Klein, H.K. (1986). Organizational Implications of Office Systems: Toward a Critical Social Action Perspective. In Verrijn-Stuart, A.A. and Hirschheim, R.A. (Eds.), *Office Systems*, North-Holland, pp. 143-159.

Kling, R. (1980). Social Analyses of Computing: Theoretical Perspectives in Recent Empirical Research. *Computing Surveys* 12(1), ACM, pp. 61-110.

Kling, R. and Iacono, S. (1984). Computing as an Occasion for Social Control. *Journal of Social Issues* 40(3), pp. 77-96.

Kling, R. and Iacono, S. (1989). Desktop Computerization and the Organization of Work. In Forester, T. (Ed.), *Computers in the Human Context*, MIT Press.

Kling, R. and Scacchi, W. (1982). The Web of Computing: Computer Technology as Social Organization. *Advances in Computers* 21, Academic Press, pp. 1-90.

Koschmann, T. (Ed.) (1992). Computer Supported Cooperative Learning. Special Issue of the *Bulletin of the Special Interest Group for Computer Uses in Education* 21(3), ACM.

Koved, L. (1992v). Rubber Rocks. *ACM SIGGRAPH Video Review*, CSCW '92 Technical Video Program.

Kraemer, J.L. & King, J.L. (1988). Computer-Based Systems for Cooperative Work and Group Decision Making. *ACM Computing Surveys* 20(2), June 1988, pp. 115-146.

Kraut, R.E. (Ed.) (1987). *Technology and the Transformation of White-Collar Work*. Lawrence Erlbaum Associates.

Kraut, R., Egido, C., and Galegher, J. (1988). Patterns of Contact and Communication in Scientific Collaboration. In [Greif 1986], pp. 1-12.

Kraut, R., Egido, C., and Galegher, J. (1990). Patterns of Contact and Communication in Scientific Research Collaboration. In [Galegher et al. 1990], pp. 149-172.

Kraut, R.E., Fish, R.S., Root, R.W., and Chalfonte, B.L. (1990). Informal Communication in Organizations: Form, Function, and Technology. In Oskamp, S. and Spacapan, S. (Eds.), *People's Reactions to Technology in Factories, Offices, and Aerospace*, The Claremont Symposium on Applied Social Psychology, Sage Publications, pp. 145-199.

Kraut, R., Galegher, J., and Egido, C. (1988). Relationships and Tasks in Scientific Research Collaboration. *Human-Computer Interaction* 3(1), pp. 31-58. Also in [Greif 1988], pp. 741-769.

Kreifelts, T. (1991). Coordination of Distributed Work: From Office Procedures to Customizable Activities. *Verteilte Künstliche Intelligenz and Kooperatives Arbeiten, Proceedings of the 4. International GI-Kongress Wissenbasierte Systeme*, München, 23-24 October 1991, Springer-Verlag, pp. 148-159.

Kreifelts, T., Hinrichs, E., Klein, K.-H., Seuffert, P., and Woetzel, G. (1991). Experiences with the DOMINO Office Procedure System. In [Bannon et al. 1991], pp. 117-130.

Kreifelts, T., Victor, F., Woetzel, G., and Woitass, M. (1991). A Design Tool for Autonomous Group Agents. In [Bowers and Benford 1991], pp. 131-144.

Krueger, M. (1991). *Artificial Reality II*. Addison-Wesley.

Kupperman, R.H. and Wilcox, R.H. (1972). EMISARI—An On-line Management System in a Dynamic Environment. In Winkler, S. (Ed.), *Computer Communications: Impacts and Implications*, Proceedings of the First International Conference on Computer Communication, Washington, D.C., October 1972, pp. 117-120.

Kupperman, R.H., Wilcox, R.H., and Smith, H. A. (1975). Crisis Management: Some Opportunities. *Science* 187(4175), 7 February 1975, pp. 404-410.

Kuutti, K. and Arvonen, T. (1992). Identifying Potential CSCW Applications By Means of Activity Theory Concepts: A Case Example. In [Turner and Kraut 1992], pp. 233-240.

Kuzuoka, H. (1992). Spatial Workspace Collaboration: A Shared Video Support System for Remote Collaboration Capability. *Proceedings of CHI '92*, pp. 533-540.

Kyng, M. (1991). Designing for Cooperation — Cooperating in Design. *Communications of the ACM* 34(12), pp. 65-73.

Lai, K.-Y., Malone, T.W., and Yu, K.-C. (1988). Object Lens: A "Spreadsheet" for Cooperative Work. *ACM Transactions on Office Information Systems* 6(4), pp. 332-353.

Lakin, F. (1988). A Performing Medium for Working Group Graphics. In [Greif 1988], pp. 367-396.

Lakin, F. (1990). Visual Languages for Cooperation: A Performing Medium Approach to Systems for Cooperative Work. In [Galegher et al. 1990], pp. 453-488.

Landow, G. (1990). Hypertext and Collaborative Work: The Example of Intermedia. In [Galegher et al. 1990], pp. 407-428.

Lange, B.M. (1992a). Electronic Group Calendaring: Experiences and Expectations. In [Coleman 1992a], pp. 428-432.

Lange, B.M. (1992b). Personal communication.

Laube, S. (1992). Talk at Groupware '92 Conference, San Jose, 3 August 1992.

Laurel, B. (Ed.) (1990). *The Art of Human-Computer Interface Design*. Addison-Wesley.

Lauwers, J.C. and Lantz, K.A. (1990). Collaboration Awareness in Support of Collaboration Transparency: Requirements for the Next Generation of Shared Window Systems. *Proceedings of CHI '90*, ACM, pp. 303-311.

Lauwers, J.C., Joseph, T.A., Lantz, K.A., and Romanow, A.L. (1990). Replicated Architectures for Shared Window Systems: A Critique. *Proceedings of the Conference on Office Information Systems*, Cambridge, MA, April 1990, ACM, pp. 249-260.

Lederberg, J. and Uncapher, K. (1989). Towards a National Collaboratory. The Rockefeller University, March 17-18, 1989.

Lee, J. and Lai, K.-Y. (1991). What's in Design Rationale. *Human-Computer Interaction* 6(3-4), pp. 251-280.

Leland, M.D., Fish, R.S., and Kraut R.E. (1988). Collaborative Document Production Using Quilt. In [Suchman 1988], pp. 206-215.

Levine, S. and Ehrlich, S.F. (1991). The Freestyle System: A Design Perspective. In Klinger, A. (Ed.), *Human-Machine Interactive Systems*, Plenum, pp. 3-21.

Lewe, H. and Krcmar, H. (1990). The CATeam Meeting Room Environment as a Human-Computer Interfaces. In [Gibbs and Verrijn-Stuart 1990], pp. 143-158.

Li, J. and Mantei, M.M. (1992). Working Together, Virtually. *Proceedings of Graphics Interface '92*, Morgan Kaufmann, pp. 115-122.

Licklider, J.C.R. and Vezza, A. (1978). Applications of Information Networks. *Proceedings of the IEEE* 66(11), November 1978, pp. 1330-1346. Also appears in [Greif 1988], pp. 143-183.

Linde, C. (1988). Who's in Charge Here? Cooperative Work and Authority Negotiation in Police Helicopter Missions. In [Suchman 1988], pp. 52-64.

Long, K. (1991v). The Virtual Notebook System. The Forefront Group, Baylor College of Medicine.

Losada, M. and Markovitch, S. (1990). GroupAnalyzer: A System for Dynamic Analysis of Group Interaction. *Proceedings of the Twenty-third Annual Hawaii International Conference on the System Sciences*, IEEE Computer Society Press, pp. 101-110.

Losada, M., Sanchez, P., and Noble, E.E. (1990). Collaborative Technology and Group Process Feedback: Their Impact on Interactive Sequences in Meetings. In [Halasz 1990], pp. 53-64.

Lottor, M. (1992). Internet Growth. Network Working Group Request for Comments 1296, Network Information Systems Center, SRI International, January 1992.

Louie, G., Mantei, M.M., and Sellen, A. (1992, submitted for publication). Making Contact in a Multi-Media Environment.

Lövstrand, L. (1991) Being Selectively Aware with the Khronika System. In [Bannon et al. 1991], pp. 265-277.

Lu, I.M. and Mantei, M.M. (1991). Idea Management in a Shared Drawing Tool. In [Bannon et al. 1991], pp. 97-112.

Lu, I.M. and Mantei, M.M. (1992, in press). Managing Design Ideas with a Shared Drawing Tool. Accepted for publication in *Interacting with Computers*.

Luff, P., Gilbert, N., and Frohlich, D. (Eds.) (1990). *Computers and Conversation*. Academic Press.

Luff, P., Heath, C., and Greatbatch, D. (1992). Tasks-in-Interaction: Paper and Screen Based Documentation in Collaborative Activity. In [Turner and Kraut 1992], pp. 163-170.

Lynch, K.J., Snyder, J.M., and Vogel, D.R. (1990). The Arizona Analyst Information System: Supporting Collaborative Research on International Technology Trends. In [Gibbs and Verrijn-Stuart 1990], pp. 159-174.

MacIntosh, D. and Yalcinalp, U. (1992). Utilizing Groupware: BP's Knowledge Networks Project. In [Coleman 1992a], pp. 456-460.

Mackay, W. (1989). Diversity in the Uses of Electronic Mail. *ACM Transactions on Office Information Systems* 6(4), pp. 380-397.

Mackay, W. (1990). Patterns of Sharing Customizable Software. In [Halasz 1990], pp. 209-221.

MacLean, A., Carter, K., Moran, T., and Lövstrand, L. (1990). User-tailorable Systems: Pressing the Issue with Buttons. *Proceedings of CHI '90*, ACM, pp. 175-182.

Magee, B. and Cox, G. (1992v). Enhanced Factory Communication. *ACM SIGGRAPH Video Review*, CSCW '92 Technical Video Program.

Malone, T.W. (1985). Designing Organizational Interfaces. *Proceedings of CHI '85*, ACM, pp. 66-71.

Malone, T.W. (1987v). The Information Lens. *ACM SIGGRAPH Video Review 34*, CHI '87 Technical Video Program.

Malone, T.W. and Crowston, K. (1990). What is Coordination Theory and How Can It Help Design Cooperative Work Systems. In [Halasz 1990], pp. 357-370.

Malone, T.W. and Crowston, K. (1991). Toward an Interdisciplinary Theory of Coordination. MIT Center for Coordination Science Technical Report CCS TR #120, April 1991.

Malone, T.W., Grant, K.R., Turbak, F.A., Brobst, S.A., and Cohen, M.D. (1987). Intelligent Information Sharing Systems. *Communications of the ACM* 30(5), pp. 390-402.

Malone, T.W., Grant, K.R., Lai, K.-Y., Rao, R., and Rosenblitt, D.A. (1987). Semistructured Messages are Surprisingly Useful for Computer-Supported Coordination. *ACM Transactions on Office Information Systems* 5(2), pp. 115-131.

Malone, T.W., Grant, K.R., Lai, K.-Y., Rao, R., and Rosenblitt, D.A. (1989). The Information Lens: An Intelligent System for Information Sharing and Coordination. In [Olson 1989], pp. 65-88.

Malone, T.W. and Lai, K.-Y. (1992). Experiments with Oval: A Radically Tailorable Tool for Cooperative Work. In [Turner and Kraut 1992], pp. 289-297.

Malone, T.W. and Rockart, J.F. (1991). Computers, Networks and the Corporation. *Scientific American* 265(3), September 1991, pp. 92-99.

Mantei, M.M. (1989). Observation of Executives Using a Computerized Supported Meeting Environment. *International Journal of Decision Support Systems* 5, June 1989, pp. 153-166.

Mantei, M.M. (1991). Adoption Patterns for Media Space Technology in a University Research Environment. Presented at Friend '21 Conference, Tokyo, Japan, November 25-27, 1991.

Mantei, M.M. (1992). CSCW: Computer-Supported Cooperative Work — What Changes for the Science of Computing. *Proceedings of Graphics Interface '92*, Morgan Kaufmann, pp. 130-139.

Mantei, M.M. (1992v). CaveDraw Demonstration Tape. Dynamic Graphics Project, CSRI, University of Toronto.

Mantei, M.M., Baecker, R.M., Sellen, A., Buxton, W.A.S., Milligan, T., and Wellman, B. (1991). Experiences in the Use of a Media Space. *Proceedings of CHI '91*, ACM, pp. 203-208.

Mantei, M.M., Buxton, W.A.S., Baecker, R.M., and Wellman, B. (1990*v*). CAVECAT Demonstration Tape. Dynamic Graphics Project, CSRI, University of Toronto.

Marca, D. and Bock, G. (Eds.) (1992). *Groupware: Software for Computer-Supported Cooperative Work*. IEEE Computer Society Press.

March, J.G. (1988). *Decisions and Organizations*. Basil Blackwell, Oxford.

March, J.G. (1991). How Decisions Happen in Organizations. *Human-Computer Interaction* 6(2), pp. 95-117.

Marcus, A. (1992). *Graphic Design for Electronic Documents and User Interfaces*. ACM Press. Addison-Wesley.

Markus, M.L. (1990). Towards a "Critical Mass" Theory of Interactive Media. In Fulk, J. and Steinfield, C.W. (Eds.), *Organizations and Communication Technology*, Sage Publications, pp. 194-218.

Markus, M.L. and Connolly, T. (1990). Why CSCW Applications Fail: Problems in the Adoption of Interdependent Work Tools. In [Halasz 1990], pp. 371-380.

Marshak, D.S. (1990). Lotus Notes: A Platform for Developing Workgroup Applications. *Patricia Seybold's Office Computing Report* 13(7), July 1990.

Marshak, R.T. (1992). Requirements for Workflow Products. In [Coleman 1992a], pp. 281-285.

Martens, C. and Lochovsky, F.H. (1991). A Programming Environment for Implementing Distributed Organizational Support Systems. *Proceedings of the Conference on Office Information Systems*, ACM, pp. 29-42.

Martial, F. V. (1991). Activity Coordination via Multiagent and Distributed Planning. *Verteilte Künstliche Intelligenz and Kooperatives Arbeiten, Proceedings of the 4. International GI-Kongress Wissenbasierte Systeme*, München, 23-24 October 1991, Springer-Verlag, pp. 90-101.

Mason, R. and Kaye, A. (Eds.) (1989). *Mindweave: Communication, Computers, and Distance Education*. Pergamon, Oxford.

Mawby, K. (1991). Designing Collaborative Writing Tools. M.Sc. Thesis, Department of Computer Science, University of Toronto.

McCarthy, J.C., Miles, V.C., and Monk, A.F. (1991) An Experimental Study of Common Ground in Text-based Communication. *Proceedings of CHI '91*, pp. 209-215.

McGrath, J.E. (1984). *Groups: Interaction and Performance*. Prentice-Hall.

McGrath, J.E. (1990). Time Matters in Groups. In [Galegher et al. 1990], pp. 23-61.

McGrath, J.E. (1991). Time, Interaction, and Performance. *Small Group Research* 22(2), May 1991, pp. 147-174.

McGrath, J.E. and Hollingshead, A.B. (1991). Putting the "G" Back in GSS: Some Theoretical Issues about Dynamic Processes in Groups with Technological Enhancements. To appear in [Jessup and Valacich 1993].

McGregor, S.L. (1992). Prescient Agents. In [Coleman 1992a], pp. 228-230.

McLuhan, M. (1964). *Understanding Media: The Extensions of Man*. McGraw-Hill.

McLuhan, M. (1988). *Laws of Media*. McLuhan Associates, Ltd.

Medina-Mora, R. (1992). Action Workflow Technology and Applications for Groupware. In [Coleman 1992a], pp. 165-167.

Medina-Mora, R., Winograd, T., Flores, R., and Flores, F. (1992). The Action Workflow Approach to Workflow Management Technology. In [Turner and Kraut 1992], pp. 281-288.

Minneman, S.L. and Bly, S.A. (1990). Experiences in the Development of a Multi-user Drawing Tool. *Proceedings of the 3rd Guelph Symposium on Computer Mediated Communication*, University of Guelph, pp. 154-167.

Minneman, S.L. and Bly, S.A. (1991). Managing a Trois: A Study of a Multi-User Drawing Tool in Distributed Design Work. *Proceedings of CHI '91*, ACM, pp. 217-224.

Mintzberg, H. (1984). A Typology of Organizational Structure. In Miller, D. and Friesen, P.H. (Eds.), *Organizations: A Quantum View*, Prentice-Hall, pp. 68-86.

Mintzberg, H. (1989). *Mintzberg on Management: Inside Our Strange World of Organizations*. The Free Press.

Moran. T.P. and Anderson, R.J. (1990). The Workaday World as a Paradigm for CSCW Design. In [Halasz 1990], pp. 381-393.

Morris, J., Satyanarayanan, M., Conner, M., Howard, M., Rosenthal, D., and Smith, F. (1986). Andrew: A Distributed Personal Computing Environment. *Communications of the ACM* 29(3).

Mullender, S. (Ed.) (1989). *Distributed Systems*. ACM Press. Addison-Wesley.

Muller, M.J. (1991) PICTIVE — An Exploration in Participatory Design. *Proceedings of CHI '91*, pp. 225-231.

Muller, M.J. (1992). Retrospective on a Year of Participatory Design Using the PICTIVE Technique. *Proceedings of CHI '92*, ACM, pp. 455-462.

Muller, M.J., Kuhn, S., and Meskill, J.A. (Eds.) (1992). *Proceedings of the 1992 Conference on Participatory Design*. Computer Professionals for Social Responsibility.

Musliner, D. J., Dolter, J. W., and Shin, K. G. (1992). A Bibliographic Database for Collaboration. In [Turner and Kraut 1992], pp. 386-393.

Myers, B.A. (1992). State of the Art in User Interface Software Tools. In Hartson, H.R. and Hix, D. (Eds.) (1992). *Advances in Human-Computer Interaction*, Volume 4, Ablex, pp. 20-40.

Narayanaswamy, K. and Goldman, N. (1992). Lazy Consistency: A Basis for Cooperative Software Development. In [Turner and Kraut 1992], pp. 257-264.

Nardi, B.A. and Miller, J.R. (1990). The Spreadsheet Interface: A Basis for End User Programming. *Proceedings of Interact '90*, Elsevier (North-Holland), pp. 977-983.

Nardi, B.A. and Miller, J.R. (1991). Twinkling Lights and Nested Loops: Distributed Problem Solving and Spreadsheet Development. *International Journal of Man-Machine Studies* 34(2), pp. 161-184. Also appears in [Greenberg 1991], pp. 29-52.

Nastos, D. (1992). A Structured Environment for Collaborative Writing. M.Sc. Thesis, Department of Computer Science, University of Toronto.

Neilsen, J. (1990). *Hypertext and Hypermedia*. Academic Press.

Neuwirth, C.M. and Kaufer, D.S. (1989). The Role of External Representations in the Writing Process: Implications for the Design of Hypertext-based Writing Tools. *Proceedings of Hypertext '89*, ACM, pp. 319-341.

Neuwirth, C.M., Kaufer, D.S., Chandhok, R., and Morris, J.H. (1990). Issues in the Design of Computer Support for Co-authoring and Commenting. In [Halasz 1990], pp. 183-195.

Neuwirth, C. M., Kaufer, D. S., Morris, J., Chandhok, R., Erion, P., and Miller, D. (1992). Flexible Diff-Ing in a Collaborative Writing System. In [Turner and Kraut 1992], pp. 147-154.

Newman, W.M., Eldridge, M.A. and Lamming, M.G. (1991). PEPYS: Generating Autobiographies by Automatic Tracking. In [Bannon, Robinson, and Schmidt 1991], pp. 175-188.

Newman-Wolfe, R.E. and Montes, M. (1992). Conference Access Control in DCS. In [Coleman 1992a], pp. 433-437.

Newman-Wolfe, R. E., Webb. M. L., and Montes, M. (1992). Implicit Locking in the Ensemble Concurrent Object-Oriented Graphics Editor. In [Turner and Kraut 1992], pp. 265-272.

Norman, D.A. and Draper, S.W. (1986). *User Centered System Design*. Lawrence Erlbaum Associates.

NTT (1990*v*). 3D VideoPlace. NTT Human Interface Laboratories.

Nunamaker, J.F., Dennis, A.R., Valacich, J.S., Vogel, D.R., and George, J.F. (1991). Electronic Meeting Systems to Support Group Work. *Communications of the ACM* 34(7), July 1991, pp. 40-61.

Nunamaker, J.F., Vogel, D.R., Heminger, A., Martz, B., Grohowski, R., and McGoff, C. (1989). Experiences at IBM with Group Support Systems: A Field Study. *Decision Support Systems* 5(2), June 1989, North-Holland, pp. 183-196.

Olgren, C.H. and Parker, L.A. (1983). *Teleconferencing Technology and Applications*. Artech House Inc.

Olson, G.M. and Atkins, D.E. (1990). Supporting Collaboration with Advanced Multimedia Electronic Mail: The NSF EXPRES Project. In [Galegher et al. 1990], pp. 429-451.

Olson, G.M. and Olson, J.S. (1991). User-Centred Design of Collaboration Technology. *Journal of Organizational Computing* 1, pp. 61-83.

Olson, G.M., Olson, J.S., Killey, L.J., Mack, L.A., Cornell, P., and Luchetti, R. (1990, in press). Designing Flexible Facilities for the Support of Collaboration. In [Bostrom, Watson, and Kinney 1992], to appear.

Olson, J.S., Olson, G.M., Mack, L.A., and Wellner, P. (1990). Concurrent Editing: The Group's Interface. *Proceedings of Interact '90*, Elsevier (North-Holland), pp. 835-840.

Olson, J.S., Olson, G.M., Storrøsten, M., and Carter, M. (1992). How a Group Editor Changes the Character of a Design Meeting As Well As Its Outcome. In [Turner and Kraut 1992], pp. 91-98.

Olson, M.H. (Ed.) (1989). *Technological Support for Work Group Collaboration*. Lawrence Erlbaum Associates.

Olson, M.H. and Bly, S.A. (1991). The Portland Experience: A Report on a Distributed Research Group. *International Journal of Man-Machine Studies* 34(2), pp. 211-228. Also appears in [Greenberg 1991], pp. 81-98.

Opper, S. and Fersko-Weiss, H. (1990). *Technology for Teams: Enhancing Productivity in Networked Organizations*. Van Nostrand Reinhold.

Orlikowski, W. (1992). Learning From Notes: Organizational Issues in Groupware Implementation. In [Turner and Kraut 1992], pp. 362-369.

Palaniappan, M. and Fitzmaurice, G. (1991). Internet Express: An Inter-Desktop Multimedia Data-Transfer Service. *IEEE Computer* 24(10), pp. 58-67.

Palermo, A.M. and McCready, S.C. (1992). Workflow Software: A Primer. In [Coleman 1992a], pp. 155-159.

Panko, R.R. (1990). Embedded, Humble, Intimate, and Multicultural Groupware for Real Groups. *Proceedings of the Twenty-third Annual Hawaii International Conference on the System Sciences*, Vol. IV, IEEE Computer Society Press, pp. 52-61.

Pankoke-Babatz, U. (Ed.) (1989). *Computer-Based Group Communication: The AMIGO Activity Model.* Ellis Horwood, Halsted Press (John Wiley & Sons). (Eng.)

Papadimitiriou, C. (1986). *The Theory of Database Concurrency Control.* Computer Science Press.

Parker, L.A. and Olgren, C.H. (1984). *The Teleconferencing Resource Book: A Guide to Applications and Planning.* North-Holland.

Patel, D. and Kalter, S.D. (1992). A Toolkit for Synchronous Distributed Groupware Applications. In [Coleman 1992a], pp. 225-227.

Patterson, J.F. (1990). The Good, the Bad, and the Ugly of Window Sharing in X. *Proceedings of the Fourth Annual X Technical Conference,* Boston, 15-17 January 1990.

Patterson, J.F. (1991). Comparing the Programming Demands of Single-User and Multi-User Applications. *Proceedings of the Fourth Conference on User Interface Software and Technology,* ACM, Nov. 1991, pp. 87-94.

Patterson, J.F., Hill, R.D., Rohall, S.L. and Meeks, W.S. (1990). Rendezvous: An Architecture for Synchronous Multi-User Applications. In [Halasz 1990], pp. 317-328.

Perin, C. (1991). Electronic Social Fields in Bureaucracies. *Communications of the ACM* 34(12), pp. 75-82.

Peterson, J.L. (1977). Petri Nets. *ACM Computing Surveys* 9(3), pp. 223-252.

Petre, D. (1992). Groupware: Evolution Not Revolution. In [Coleman 1992a], pp. 101-105.

Pinsonneault, A. and Kraemer, K.L. (1989). The Impact of Technological Support on Groups: An Assessment of the Empirical Research. *Decision Support Systems* 5(2), June 1989, North-Holland, pp. 197-216.

Poole, M.S. and DeSanctis, G. (1990). Understanding the Use of Group Decision Support Systems: The Theory of Adaptive Structuration. In Fulk, J. and Steinfield, C. (Eds.), *Organizations and Communications Technology,* Sage Publications.

Poole, M.S., Holmes, M., and DeSanctis, G. (1988). Conflict Management and Group Decision Support Systems. In [Suchman 1988], pp. 227-243.

Posner, I.R. (1991). A Study of Collaborative Writing. M.Sc. Thesis, Department of Computer Science, University of Toronto.

Posner, I.R. and Baecker, R.M. (1992). How People Write Together. *Proceedings of the Twenty-fifth Annual Hawaii International Conference on the System Sciences,* Vol. IV, pp. 127-38.

Posner, I.R. and Baecker, R.M. (1992, submitted for publication). A Study of Collaborative Writing.

Posner, M.I. (Ed.) (1989). *Foundations of Cognitive Science.* The MIT Press.

Post, B.Q. (1992). Building the Business Case for Group Support Technology. *Proceedings of the Twenty-fifth Annual Hawaii International Conference on the System Sciences,* Vol. IV, IEEE Computer Society Press, pp. 34-45.

Prakash, A. and Knister. M. J. (1992). Undoing Actions in Collaborative Work. In [Turner and Kraut 1992], pp. 273-280.

Press, L. (1992). Collective Dynabases. *Communications of the ACM* 35(6), pp. 26-32.

Prinz, W. and Pennelli, P. (1991). Relevance of the X.500 Directory to CSCW Applications. In [Bowers and Benford 1989], pp. 289-302. Also appears in [Marca and Bock], pp. 209-225.

Pugh, D.S. and Hickson, D.J. (Eds.) (1989). *Writers on Organizations.* Fourth Edition. Penguin.

Pugh, D.S. (Ed.) (1990). *Organization Theory.* Third Edition. Penguin.

Ramer, J. (1992). Intelligent Agents in Groupware. In [Coleman 1992a], pp. 526-530.

Reder, S. and Schwab, R.G. (1988). The Communicative Economy of the Workgroup: Multi-Channel Genres of Communication. In [Suchman 1988], pp. 354-368.

Reder, S. and Schwab, R.G. (1990). The Temporal Structure of Cooperative Activity. In [Halasz 1990], pp. 303-316.

Reisig, W. (1985). *Petri Nets.* Springer-Verlag.

Resnick, L.B., Levine, J.M., and Teasley, S.D. (Eds.) (1991). *Perspectives on Socially Shared Cognition.* American Psychological Association, Washington, D.C.

Resnick, P. (1992). HyperVoice: A Phone-Based CSCW Platform. In [Turner and Kraut 1992], pp. 218-225.

Rice, R.E. and Associates (1984). *The New Media: Communication, Research, and Technology.* Sage Publications.

Rice, R.E. and Shook, D.E. (1990). Voice Messaging, Coordination, and Communication. In [Galegher et al. 1990], pp. 327-350.

Rice, R.E. and Steinfield, C. (1991, in press). Experiences with New Forms of Organizational Communication via Electronic Mail and Voice Messaging. To appear in Andriessen, J.H. and Roe, R. (Eds.), *Telematics and Work,* Lawrence Erlbaum Associates.

Richman, L. (1987). Software Catches the Team Spirit. *Fortune,* June 8, 1987, pp. 125-136.

Robinson, M. (1991a). Computer Supported Cooperative Work: Cases and Concepts. In [Hendriks 1991], pp. 59-75.

Robinson, M. (1991b). Pay Bargaining in a Shared Information Space. In [Bowers and Benford 1991], pp. 235-248.

Robinson, M. (1991c). Double-Level Languages and Cooperative Working. *AI & Society* 5, Springer-Verlag, pp. 34-60.

Rodden, T., Bentley, R., Sawyer, P., and Sommerville, I. (1992). An Architecture for Tailoring Cooperative Multi-User Displays. In [Turner and Kraut 1992], pp. 187-194.

Rodden, T. and Blair, G. (1991). CSCW and Distributed Systems: The Problem of Control. In [Bannon, Robinson, and Schmidt 1991], pp. 49-64.

Roger, D. and Bull, P. (Eds.) (1989). *Conversation: An Interdisciplinary Perspective*. Multilingual Matters Ltd.

Rogers, Y. (1992). Ghosts in the Network: Distributed Troubleshooting in a Shared Working Environment. In [Turner and Kraut 1992], pp. 346-355.

Rohall, S., Patterson, J., and Hill, R. (1992v). Go Fish! A Multi-User Game in the Rendezvous System. *ACM SIGGRAPH Video Review 76*, CHI '92 Technical Video Program.

Root, R.W. (1988). Design of a Multi-media System for Social Browsing. In [Suchman 1988], pp. 25-38.

Ropa, A., Ahlstrom, B. (1992v). A Case Study of a Multi-media Co-Working Task and the Resulting Interface Design of a Collaborative Communication Tool. *ACM SIGGRAPH Video Review 76*, CHI '92 Technical Video Program.

Rosall, J. (1992). End-User Multimedia and Integrated Messaging Trends: Shifting Priorities. In [Coleman 1992a], pp. 485-495.

Roseman, M. and Greenberg, S. (1992). Groupkit: A Groupware Toolkit for Building Real-Time Conferencing Applications. In [Turner and Kraut 1992], pp. 43-50.

Rosenberg, L.C. (1991). Update on National Science Foundation Funding of the "Collaboratory." *Communications of the ACM* 34(12), p. 83.

Ryan, C. (1992). Group Scheduling—The Next Big Workgroup Application? In [Coleman 1992a], pp. 381-384.

Saffo, P. (1992). Presentation at Groupware '92 Conference, San Jose, CA, 4 August 1992.

Sanderson, D. (1992). The CSCW Implementation Process: An Interpretative Model and Case Study of the Implementation of a Videoconference System. In [Turner and Kraut 1992], pp. 370-377.

Sarin, S.K., Abbott, K.R., and McCarthy, D.R. (1991). A Process Model and System for Supporting Cooperative Work. *Proceedings of the Conference on Office Information Systems*, ACM, pp. 213-224.

Sarin, S. and Greif, I. (1985). Computer-based Real-time Conferencing Systems. *IEEE Computer* 18(10), pp. 33-45. Also appears in [Greif 1988], pp. 397-420.

Sawchuk, W., Bown, H., O'Brien, D., and Thorgeirson, W. (1978). An Interactive Image Communication System Using Narrowband Lines. *Computers and Graphics* 3(4), pp. 129-134.

Scardamalia, M. and Bereiter, C. (1991). High Levels of Agency for Children in Knowledge Building: A Challenge for the Design of New Knowledge Media. *The Journal of the Learning Sciences* 1(1), pp. 37-68.

Scardamalia, M., Bereiter, C., McLean, R.S., Swallow, J., and Woodruff, E. (1989). Computer-Supported Intentional Learning Environments. *Journal of Educational Computing Research* 5(1), pp. 51-68.

Schatz, B.R. (1991). Building an Electronic Scientific Community. *Proceedings of the Twenty-fourth Annual Hawaii International Conference on the System Sciences*, January 1991, pp. 739-748.

Schatz, B.R. (1991-92). Building an Electronic Community System. *Journal of Management Information Systems* 8(3), Winter 1991-92, pp. 87-107.

Schatz, B.R. and Caplinger, M.A. (1989). Searching in a Hyperlibrary. *Proceedings of the Fifth International Conference on Data Engineering*, IEEE, Los Angeles, 6-10 February 1989, pp. 188-197.

Scheifler, R.W. and Gettys, J. (1986). The X Window System. *ACM Transactions on Graphics* 5(2), April 1986, pp. 79-109.

Scheifler, R.W., Gettys, J. and Newman, R. (1988). *X Window System*. DEC Press.

Schein, E. (1985). *Organizational Culture and Leadership*. Jossey-Bass.

Schrage, M. (1990). *Shared Minds: The New Technologies of Collaboration*. Random House.

Schuler, D. and Namioka, A. (Eds.) (1990). *Proceedings of the 1990 Conference on Participatory Design*. Computer Professionals for Social Responsibility.

Schuler, D. and Namioka, A. (Eds.) (1992). Participatory Design: Principles and Practices. Erlbaum.

Schwab, R. G., Hart-Landsberg, S., Reder, S., and Abel, M. (1992). Collaboration and Constraint: Middle School Teaching Teams. In [Turner and Kraut 1992], pp. 241-248.

Scott, W.R. (1987). *Organizations: Rational, Natural, and Open Systems*. 2nd Edition. Prentice-Hall.

Searle, J.R. (1975). A Taxonomy of Illocutionary Acts. In Gunderson, K. (Ed.), *Language, Mind, and Knowledge*. Minnesota Studies in the Philosophy of Science, Volume 11, University of Minnesota Press.

Sellen, A. (1992). Speech Patterns in Video-Mediated Conversations. *Proceedings of CHI '92*, ACM, pp. 49-59.

Sellen, A., Buxton, W.A.S., and Arnott, J. (1992*v*). Using Spatial Cues to Improve Desktop Videoconferencing. *ACM SIGGRAPH Video Review 76*, CHI '92 Technical Video Program.

Sharples, M. (Ed.) (in press). *Computer Supported Collaborative Writing*. Springer-Verlag.

Shen, H. and Dewan, P. (1992). Access Control for Collaborative Environments. In [Turner and Kraut 1992], pp. 51-58.

Shipman, F.M., Chaney, R.J., and Gorry, G.A. (1989). Distributed Hypertext for Collaborative Research: The Virtual Notebook System. *Proceedings of Hypertext '89*, ACM, pp. 129-135.

Shneiderman, B. (1992). *Designing the User Interface: Strategies for Effective Human-Computer Interaction*. Second Edition. Addison-Wesley.

Shneiderman, B. and Kearsley, G. (1989). *Hypertext Hands-On! An Introduction to a New Way of Organizing Information*. Addison-Wesley.

Short, J., Williams, E., and Christie, B. (1976). *The Social Psychology of Telecommunications*. John Wiley & Sons.

Shu, L. and Flowers, W. (1992). Groupware Experiences in Three-Dimensional Computer-Aided Design. In [Turner and Kraut 1992], pp. 179-186.

Sluizer, S. and Cashman, P.M. (1985). XCP: An Experimental Tool for Managing Cooperative Activity. *Proceedings of the 1985 ACM Computer Science Conference*, pp. 251-258.

Smart Technologies (1992). Smart 2000 Conferencing System. Product Literature. Smart Technologies, Suite 599, 240-11 Avenue S.W., Calgary Alberta T2R 0C3 Canada.

Smith, J.B., Weiss, S.F., and Ferguson, G.J. (1987). A Hypertext Writing Environment and its Cognitive Basis. *Proceedings of Hypertext '87*, ACM, pp. 345-365.

Smith, M.B. (1992). Messaging and Mail Enabled Applications for the Workgroup. In [Coleman 1992a], pp. 394-399.

Smith, R.B., O'Shea, T., O'Malley, C., Scanlon, E., and Taylor, J. (1991). Preliminary Experiments with a Distributed, Multi-Media, Problem Solving Environment. In [Bowers and Benford 1991], pp. 31-48.

Sproull, L. and Kiesler, S. (1986). Reducing Social Context Cues: Electronic Mail in Organizational Communication. *Management Science* 32(11), pp. 1492-1512. Also appears in [Greif 1988], pp. 683-712.

Sproull, L. and Kiesler, S. (1991a). *Connections: New Ways of Working in the Networked Organization*. The MIT Press.

Sproull, L. and Kiesler, S. (1991b). Computers, Networks, and Work. *Scientific American* 265(3), September 1991, pp. 116-123.

Sproull, Robert (1991). A Lesson in Electronic Mail. In [Sproull and Kiesler 1991], pp, 177-184.

Stallings, W. (Ed.) (1990). *Local Network Technology*. Third Edition. IEEE Computer Society Press.

Stallings, W. (Ed.) (1992a). *Computer Communication*. Third Edition. IEEE Computer Society Press.

Stallings, W. (Ed.) (1992b). *Advances in ISDN and Broadband ISDN*. IEEE Computer Society Press.

Stefik, M., Bobrow, D.G., Foster, G., Lanning, S., and Tatar, D. (1987). WYSIWIS Revised: Early Experiences with Multiuser Interfaces. *ACM Transactions on Office Information Systems* 5(2), pp. 147-167.

Stefik, M., Foster, G., Bobrow, D.G., Kahn, K., Lanning, S., and Suchman, L. (1987). Beyond the Chalkboard: Computer Support for Collaboration and Problem Solving in Meetings. *Communications of the ACM* 30(1), pp. 32-47. Also appears in [Greif 1988], pp. 335-366.

Steinhart, J., Callow, M., LaVallee, D.S., and Greco, R. (1989). *Introduction to Window Management*. ACM Siggraph '89 Course Notes 11.

Stillings, N.A., Feinstein, M.H., Garfield, J.L., Rissland, E.L., Rosenbaum, D.A., Weisler, S.E., and Baker-Ward, L. (1987). *Cognitive Science: An Introduction*. The MIT Press.

Stults, R. (1986). Media Space. Xerox Palo Alto Research Centre Technical Report.

Stults, R. (1988). Experimental Uses of Video to Support Design Activities. Xerox Palo Alto Research Centre Technical Report SSL-89-19.

Suchman, L. (1983). Office Procedures as Practical Action: Models of Work and System Design. *ACM Transactions on Office Information Systems* 1(4), October 1983, pp. 320-328.

Suchman, L. (1987). *Plans and Situated Action: The Problem of Human-Machine Communication*. Cambridge University Press.

Suchman, L. (Ed.) (1988). *CSCW 88: Proceedings of the Conference on Computer-Supported Cooperative Work*. Portland, Oregon, Sept. 26-29, 1988. Association for Computing Machinery.

Suchman, L. (1991). Constituting Shared Workspaces. To appear in Engestrom, Y. and Middleton, D. (Eds.), *Cognition and Communication at Work*, Sage, in preparation.

Suchman, L. and Trigg, R. (1991). Understanding Practice: Video as a Medium for Reflection and Design. In [Greenbaum and Kyng 1991], pp. 65-89.

Takemura, H. and Kishino, F. (1992). Cooperative Work Environment Using Virtual Workspace. In [Turner and Kraut 1992], pp. 226-232.

Tanenbaum, A.S. (1988). *Computer Networks.* Second Edition. Prentice Hall.

Tang, J.C. (1989). Listing, Drawing, and Gesturing in Design: A Study of the Use of Shared Workspaces by Design Teams. Ph.D. Thesis, Department of Mechanical Engineering, Stanford University. Also available as Xerox Palo Alto Research Center Report SSL-89-3.

Tang, J.C. (1990*v*). Observations on the Use of Shared Drawing Spaces. Xerox PARC, Palo Alto, California.

Tang, J.C. (1991). Findings from Observational Studies of Collaborative Work. *International Journal of Man-Machine Studies* 34(2), pp. 143-160. Also appears in [Greenberg 1991], pp. 11-28.

Tang, J.C. and Minneman, S.L. (1990). Videodraw: A Video Interface for Collaborative Drawing. *Proceedings of CHI '90*, pp. 313-320.

Tang, J.C. and Minneman, S.L. (1991). VideoWhiteboard: Video Shadows to Support Remote Collaboration. *Proceedings of CHI '91*, pp. 315-322.

Tatar, D.G., Foster, G., and Bobrow, D.G. (1991). Design for Conversation: Lessons from Cognoter. *International Journal of Man-Machine Studies* 34(2), pp. 185-209. Also appears in [Greenberg 1991], pp. 55-79.

Thompson, G. (1975). Technical and Research Aspects of Communication. Appears in *Communications Canada 2000*, University of Toronto Press, pp. 25-49.

Trigg, R.H. (1988). Guided Tours and Tabletops: Tools for Communicating in a Hypertext Environment. In [Suchman 1988], pp. 216-226.

Trigg, R.H., Suchman, L.A., and Halasz, F.G. (1986). Supporting Collaboration in NoteCards. In [Greif 1966].

Turner, J. and Kraut, R. (Eds.) (1992). *CSCW 92: Proceedings of the Conference on Computer-Supported Cooperative Work*, Toronto, Canada, Oct. 31-Nov. 4, 1992, ACM.

Turoff, M. (1971). Delphi and Its Potential Impact on Information Systems. *Proceedings of the Fall Joint Computer Conference*, AFIPS Press, November 1971, pp. 317-326.

Turoff, M. (1991). Computer-Mediated Communication Requirements for Group Support. *Journal of Organizational Computing* 1, pp. 85-113.

University of Arizona. (1988*v*). Collaborative Management Room, Management and Information Systems Department, University of Arizona.

University of Minnesota. (1988*v*). SAMM - Software Aided Meeting Management. Information and Decision Sciences, Department, University of Minnesota.

Valacich, J.S., Dennis, A.R., and Nunamaker, J.F. (1991). Electronic Meeting Support: The GroupSystems Concept. *International Journal of Man-Machine Studies* 34(2), pp. 262-282. Also appears in [Greenberg 1991], pp. 133-154.

van der Velden, J. (1992*v*). Delft-Wit: Research Issues and Methods for Behavioral Analysis. *ACM SIGGRAPH Video Review*, CSCW '92 Technical Video Program.

Vaske, J.J. & Grantham, C.E. (1990). *Socializing the Human-Computer Environment.* Ablex.

Viller, S. (1991). The Group Facilitator: A CSCW Perspective. In [Bannon, Robinson, and Schmidt 1991], pp. 81-95.

Vin, H. M., Rangan, P. V., and Chen, M. (1992). System Support for Computer Mediated Multimedia Collaborations. In [Turner and Kraut 1992], pp. 203-209.

Vin, H.M., Zellweger, P.T., Swinehart, D.C., and Rangan, P.V. (1991). Multimedia Conferencing in the Etherphone Environment. *IEEE Computer* 24 (10), pp. 69-79.

Waggoner, M. (Ed.) (1992). *Empowering Networks: Using Computer Conferencing in Education*, Educational Technology Publications.

Want, R. (1992, forthcoming). The Active Badge Locator System. *ACM Transactions on Office Information Systems.*

Watabe, K., Sakata, S., Maeno, K., Fukuoka, H., and Ohmori, T. (1990). Distributed Multiparty Desktop Conferencing System: MERMAID. In [Halasz 1990], pp. 27-38.

Watson, R.G., DeSanctis, G., and Poole M.S. (1988). Using a GDSS to Facilitate Group Consensus: Some Intended and Unintended Consequences. *MIS Quarterly* 12(3).

Weisband, S. and Galegher, J. (1990). Four Goals for the Design of Organizational Information Support Systems. *Proceedings of the Twenty-third Annual Hawaii International Conference on the System Sciences*, Vol. III, IEEE Computer Society Press, pp. 137-142.

Whittaker, S., Brennan, S.E., and Clark, H.H. (1991). Coordinating Activity: An Analysis of Interaction in Computer-Supported Cooperative Work. *Proceedings of CHI '91*, ACM, pp. 361-367.

Wilke, J.R. (1992). Getting Together. *The Wall Street Journal,* 6 April 1992.

Williams, E. (1977). Experimental Comparisons of Face-to-face and Mediated Communications: A Review. *Psychological Bulletin* 84, pp. 963-976.

Winograd, T. (1986). A Language/Action Perspective on the Design of Cooperative Work. In [Greif 1986].

Winograd, T. (1987-88). A Language/Action Perspective on the Design of Cooperative Work. *Human-Computer Interaction* 3(1), pp. 3-30. Also appears in [Greif 1988], pp. 623-653.

Winograd, T. (1988). Where the Action Is. *Byte*, December 1988, pp. 256A-258.

Winograd, T. (1992). Groupware and the Emergence of Business Technology. In [Coleman 1992a], pp. 69-72.

Winograd, T. and Flores, F. (1986). *Understanding Computers and Cognition*. Addison-Wesley.

Wolf, C. G., Rhyne, J. R., and Briggs, L. (1992). Communication and Information Retrieval with a Pen-based Meeting Support Tool. In [Turner and Kraut 1992], pp. 322-329.

Wolfe, A.D., Jr. (1992). Apple's Macintosh: Can It Become the "Cadillac of Collaboration"? *Patricia Seybold's Office Computing Report* 15(6), June 1992.

Wozny, M.C. (1992). Compaq Computer Corporation's World-wide Use of Lotus Notes. In [Coleman 1992a], pp. 511-514.

Xerox PARC. (1988v). Experiments in Computer Support for Teamwork. *ACM SIGGRAPH Video Review 58*, CHI '88 Technical Video Program.

Xerox PARC (1989v). The Office Design Project. *SIGGRAPH Video Review 45*, CHI '89 Technical Video Program.

Yankelovich, N., Haam, B., Meyrowitz, N., and Drucker (1988). Intermedia: The Concept and the Construction of a Seamless Information Environment. *IEEE Computer* 21(1), pp. 81-96.

Yankelovich, N., Meyrowitz, N., and van Dam, A. (1985). Reading and Writing the Electronic Book. *IEEE Computer* 18(10), pp. 15-30.

Yates, J. and Orlikowski, W.J. (1991). Genres of Organizational Communication: An Approach to Studying Communication and Media. MIT Sloan School of Management Center for Coordination Science Technical Report #122.

Zellweger, P.T., Terry, D.B., and Swinehart, D.C. (1988). An Overview of the Etherphone System and its Applications. *Proceedings of the Second IEEE Conference on Computer Workstations*, pp. 160-168.

Zuboff, S. (1988). *In the Age of the Smart Machine: The Future of Work and Power*. Basic Books.

Index

Author Index